About the Cover

The cover photograph shows the George Washington Bridge, which spans the Hudson River between New York City and Fort Lee, N.J. The bridge is 36 meters wide and over 1 kilometer long. The main deck of the bridge, completed in 1931, contains eight traffic lanes. A lower deck with six traffic lanes was opened in 1962. The bridge has two towers, each 180 meters high, which support four huge suspension cables. Each cable is about 90 centimeters in diameter and consists of over 26,000 tightly woven steel wires.

-03000-5
by
. MERRILL PUBLISHING CO.
well Company
hio 43216

l by Bell & Howell. All rights reserved. No part of this book may be
y form, electronic or mechanical, including photocopy, recording,
storage or retrieval system, without permission in writing from the

l States of America

W9-CHH-252

Merrill
ADVANCED MATHEMATICAL CONCEPTS

YUNKER • VANNATTA • CROSSWHITE

Charles E. Merrill Publishing Co.
A Bell & Howell Company
Columbus, Ohio

Toronto • London • Sydney

ISBN 0-67
Published
CHARLES
A Bell & Ho
Columbus, O

Copyright © 19
reproduced in an
or any information
publisher.

Printed in the Unite

AUTHORS

Lee E. Yunker is head of the Mathematics Department at West Chicago Community High School, West Chicago, Illinois. He has taught mathematics courses at every level of the high school curriculum. Mr. Yunker obtained his B.S. from Elmhurst College and his M.Ed. in mathematics from the University of Illinois, with additional graduate work at the University of Illinois, Northwestern University, University of Montana, Northern Illinois University, and National College of Education. Mr. Yunker is very active in professional mathematics organizations at the local, state, and national levels frequently speaking or conducting workshops on a variety of topics. Mr. Yunker has had articles published in *The Illinois Mathematics Teacher* and the *New Mexico Council of Teachers of Mathematics Journal*. For the past two years Mr. Yunker has served as a referee for articles submitted for publication in *The Mathematics Teacher*.

Glen D. Vannatta is Supervisor of Mathematics for the Indianapolis Public Schools in Indianapolis, Indiana. He has taught mathematics at the high school and university levels and served as a high school mathematics department head for eight years. Dr. Vannatta received his B.S., M.S., and Ed. D. from Indiana University. He is a member of several state and national professional organizations and a past president of the Indiana Council of Teachers of Mathematics. He has authored numerous mathematics textbooks, mathematics programs, and articles for *The Mathematics Teacher*. Dr. Vannatta has been a speaker at many programs of the National Council of Teachers of Mathematics.

F. Joe Crosswhite is Professor of Mathematics Education at the Ohio State University. He has taught mathematics at every level of the high school curriculum, at the two-year college level, and at the university level. Dr. Crosswhite obtained his B.S. in Education and M. Ed. from Missouri University and his Ph.D. in mathematics education from the Ohio State University. He took additional graduate work in mathematics at Purdue University and post-doctoral work in educational research at Stanford University. Dr. Crosswhite is active in professional associations and has served on the Board of Directors of the National Council of Teachers of Mathematics. Dr. Crosswhite has published widely in professional journals and has contributed to a number of professional books.

REVIEWERS

Dorothy Barrett
Chairman, Mathematics Department
Classical High School
Lynn, Massachusetts

Robert E. DeVaux
Mathematics Curriculum Specialist
Board of Education of Frederick County
Frederick, Maryland

Frank S. Rogers
Consultant in Mathematics
Lansing School District
Lansing, Michigan

Joan S. Care
Mathematics Teacher
Madison High School
Madison, Tennessee

Russell J. Gustafson
Chairman, Department of Mathematics
Pacific High School
San Leandro, California

Avo L. Sims
Teacher - Math Department Chairman
San Leandro High School
San Leandro, California

STAFF

Editorial
Project Editors: Darlene Lewis,
Evangeline Seltzer
Managing Editor: Donald W. Collins
Assistant Editor: Jack Witherspoon
Photo Editor: Susan Marquart

Art
Project Artist: Lewis H. Bolen
Art Director: Lester Shumaker
Book Designer: Lester Shumaker

PHOTO CREDITS

Cover	Shostal Associates
1	U.S. Air Force
13	Martin Pardo
22	Courtesy U.S. Steel
27	U.S. Bureau of Reclamation
89	Eric Hoffhines
101	Courtesy of Bell Laboratories
115	Rick Norton/Kings Island
147	Linda Young
173	Courtesy New Jersey State Highway Dept.
203	Rich Brommer
235	Ruth Dixon
263	Roger K. Burnard
297	Shostal Associates
321	NASA
329	Battelle's Columbus Laboratories
363	Courtesy of General Motors
383	Monsanto
393	Bruce Kliewe for Jeroboam, Inc.
418	Hickson-Bender Photography
425	M. I. T. Historical Collection

PREFACE

Merrill Advanced Mathematical Concepts both encompasses and extends topics and concepts of intermediate algebra. The goals of the text are to develop proficiency with mathematical skills, to expand understanding of mathematical concepts, to improve logical thinking, and to promote success. To achieve these goals the following strategies are used.

Build upon a Solid Foundation. Review is provided for those topics generally presented in first and second year algebra. Thus, student's understanding is strengthened before the introduction of more difficult concepts.

Utilize Sound Pedagogy. *Merrill Advanced Mathematical Concepts* covers all topics generally presented at this level in logical sequence. Concepts are introduced when they are needed. Each concept presented is then used within that lesson and in later lessons.

Facilitate Learning. A clear, concise format aids the student in understanding the mathematical concepts. Furthermore, many photographs, illustrations, graphs, and tables provide help for the student in visualizing the ideas presented. As a result, the student is able to read with increased understanding.

Use Relevant Real-Life Applications. Applications provide motivation and help in understanding how concepts are used.

The text offers a variety of useful aids for the student studying advanced mathematics.

Student Annotations	Help students to identify important concepts as they study.
Selected Answers	Allow students to check their progress as they work. These answers are provided at the back of the text.
Chapter Summary	Provides students a compact listing of major concepts presented within each chapter.
Chapter Review	Permits students to review each chapter by working sample problems from each section.
Chapter Test	Enables students to check their own progress.

The following special features, which appear periodically throughout the text, provide interesting and useful extra topics.

Careers	Depict a variety of people in different careers using mathematics. These careers are typical of careers that students may pursue.
Using Mathematics	Illustrate how mathematics can be and is used in everyday life.
Excursions in Mathematics	Enliven and help maintain student interest by providing interesting side trips. Topics are varied and include glimpses into the development and uses of mathematics.

Students will find the practical, straightforward approach of *Merrill Advanced Mathematical Concepts* both interesting and easy to understand. Teachers will find that the careful sequencing of topics and thorough treatment of essential ideas provide an effective course in high school advanced mathematics.

CONTENTS

The Circular Functions 89

The Trigonometric Functions 115

Graphs and Inverses of the Trigonometric Functions 147

Applications of Trigonometry 173

Sequences and Series 203

Polar Coordinates and Complex Numbers 235

Exponential and Logarithmic Functions 263

10

The Straight Line 297

11

Conics 321

12

Probability — 363

Descriptive Statistics — 393

Limits, Derivatives, and Integrals — 425

Chapter

1

Linear Relations and Functions

One of the most frequently occurring relationships is the linear relation. The contrail is a graphic illustration of a linear relation. Many interrelationships between two variables can be represented graphically by a line. Thus, they are called linear relations.

1-1 Relations and Functions

A pairing of elements of a set with elements of the same or a second set is called a mathematical **relation.** The following set is a relation.

$$\{(1, 3), (2, 4), (3, 5), (2, 7)\}$$

The set of abscissas $\{1, 2, 3\}$ of the ordered pairs is called the **domain** of the relation. The set of ordinates $\{3, 4, 5, 7\}$ is called the **range.** Notice that an element of the domain is paired with more than one element of the range in this relation.

The first coordinate of an ordered pair is the abscissa. The second coordinate is the ordinate.

A relation is a set of ordered pairs. The domain is the set of all abscissas of the ordered pairs. The range is the set of all ordinates of the ordered pairs.

Definition of Relation, Domain, and Range

example

1 State the relation represented by the equation $y = 5x$, if x is a positive integer less than 6. Then state the domain and range of the relation.

The relation is $\{(1, 5), (2, 10), (3, 15), (4, 20), (5, 25)\}$.

The domain is $\{1, 2, 3, 4, 5\}$.

The range is $\{5, 10, 15, 20, 25\}$.

The ordered pairs are written in the form (x, y).

The relation in the preceding example is a special type of relation, called a **function.** *All functions are relations, but not all relations are functions.*

A function is a relation in which each element of the domain is paired with exactly one element of the range.

Definition of Function

A relation or function can be represented as a graph, a table of values, a list of ordered pairs, or by any rule in words or symbols which determines pairs of values.

examples

2 Is $\left\{\left(2, \frac{1}{2}\right), \left(\frac{1}{4}, 3\right), \left(4, 0\right), \left(1, 5\right)\right\}$ a function?

This relation is a function since each element of the domain is paired with exactly one element of the range.

3 Does $y > 2x$ represent a function?

For each value of x, several values could be chosen for y. Therefore $y > 2x$ does *not* represent a function. *$y > 2x$ is a relation.*

example

4 Does the graph at the right represent a function?

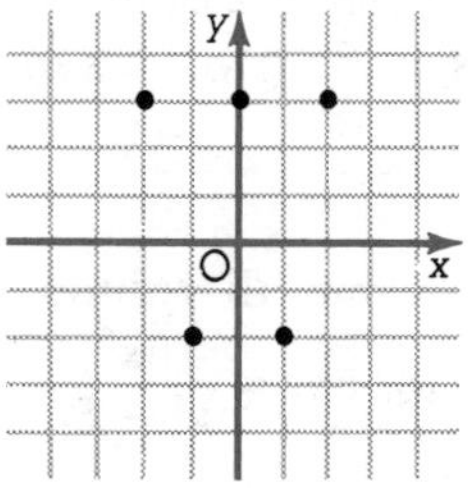

The graph represents the relation
$\{(^-2, 3), (^-1, ^-2), (0, 3), (1, ^-2), (2, 3)\}$.

This relation is a function since each element of the domain is paired with exactly one element of the range.

A function can also be defined as a set of ordered pairs in which no two pairs have the same first element. This definition can be applied when a relation is represented by a graph. If any vertical line drawn on the graph of a relation passes through no more than one point of the graph, then the relation is a function.

This is called the vertical line test.

example

5 Use the vertical line test to determine if the relation graphed is a function.

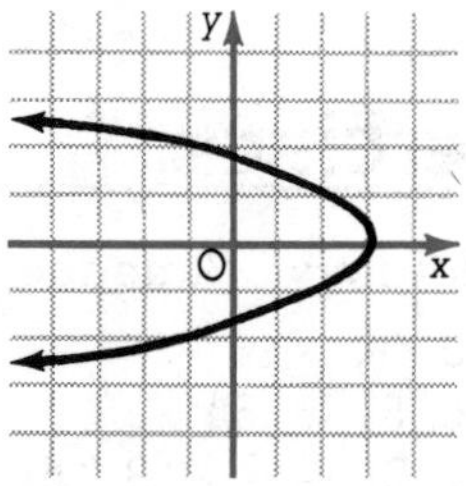

A vertical line will pass through two points of the graph. Therefore the graph does not represent a function.

The letter f is commonly used to denote a function. The expression $y = f(x)$ indicates that for each element which replaces x, the function assigns one and only one replacement for y. The symbol $f(x)$ is read "f of x" and should be interpreted as the value of function f at x. The ordered pairs of the function are written in the form (x, y) or $(x, f(x))$.

x is called the independent variable. y is called the dependent variable.

examples

6 Find $f(3)$ if $f(x) = 2x^2 - 2x + 8$.

$$f(3) = 2(3)^2 - 2(3) + 8$$
$$= 20$$

7 Find $f(^-1)$ if $f(x) = |3x - 2|$. *The two vertical lines represent absolute value.*

$$f(^-1) = |3(^-1) - 2|$$
$$= |^-5|$$
$$= 5$$

Often the equation for a function is given and the domain is not specified. Then, the domain includes all the real numbers for which the corresponding values in the range are also real numbers.

example 8 **Name all values of x which are not in the domain of f, for $f(x) = \frac{3x}{x^2 - 5}$.**

Since $\frac{3x}{0}$ is undefined, any value of x which makes the denominator equal zero must be excluded from the domain of f. By solving the equation $x^2 - 5 = 0$, these values can be obtained. Therefore $x \neq \pm\sqrt{5}$.
The values $+\sqrt{5}$ and $-\sqrt{5}$ are not in the domain of f.

exercises

Exploratory State the domain and range of each relation.

1. $\{(0, 0)\}$
2. $\{(16, ^-4), (16, 4)\}$
3. $\{(5, 5), (6, 6)\}$
4. $\{(^-3, 0), (4, ^-2), (2, ^-6)\}$
5. $\{(1, 2), (2, 4), (^-3, ^-6), (0, 0)\}$
6. $\{(0, 3), (5, 3), (6, 3), (2, 3)\}$
7. $\{(^-2, 9), (^-2, 8), (^-2, 7)\}$
8. $\{(1, 5), (2, 6), (3, 7), (4, 8)\}$
9. $\{(4, ^-2), (4, 2), (9, ^-3), (9, 3)\}$
10. $\{(8, ^-3), (7, 3), (6, ^-3)\}$

11-20. State whether each relation in problems 1-10 is a function. Write *yes* or *no*.

Written State the relation represented by each of the following, given that x is an integer.

1. $y = 3x - 3$ and $0 < x < 6$
2. $y = 11 - x$ and $^-3 \le x \le 0$
3. $y = x^2$ and $^-4 < x \le {}^-2$
4. $y = 5$ and $1 \le x \le 9$
5. $|2y| = x$ and $x = 4$
6. $y = |x| - 1.5$ and $^-2 \le x < 4$

7-12. State the domain and range of each relation in problems 1-6.

13-18. State whether each relation in problems 1-6 is a function. Write *yes* or *no*.

State whether each graph represents a function. Write *yes* or *no*.

19. 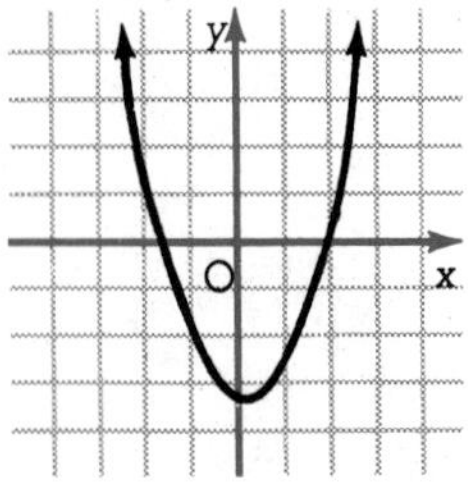

20. 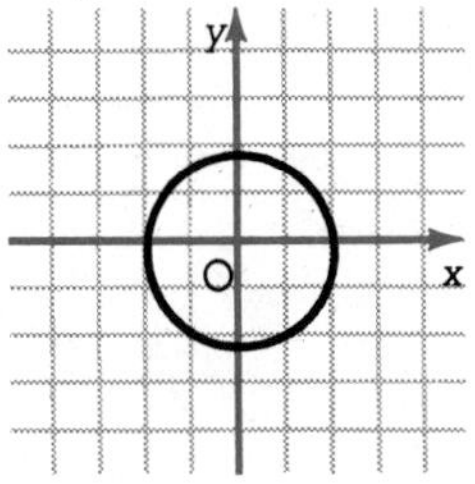

21. 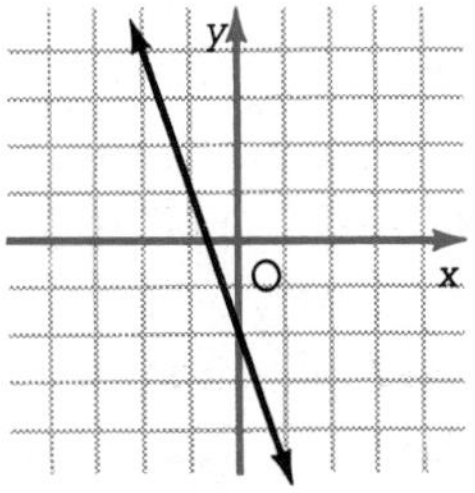

22. 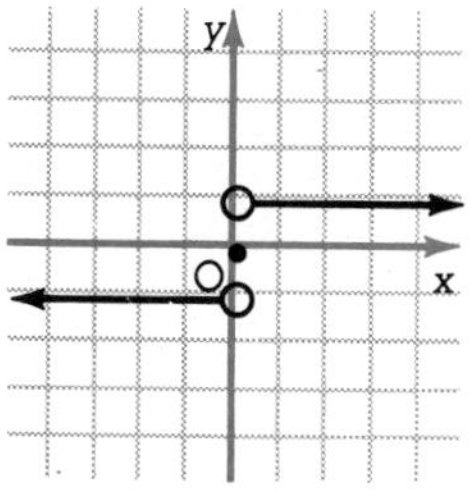

23. 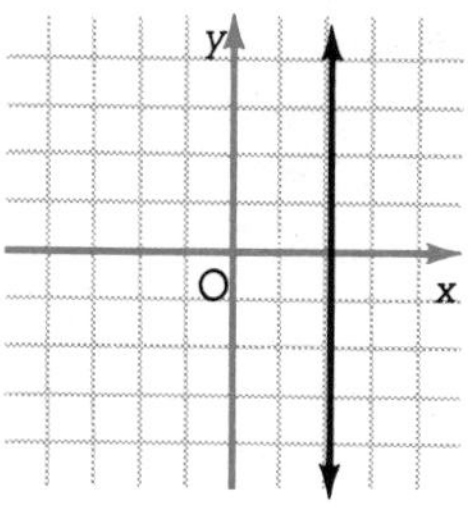

24. 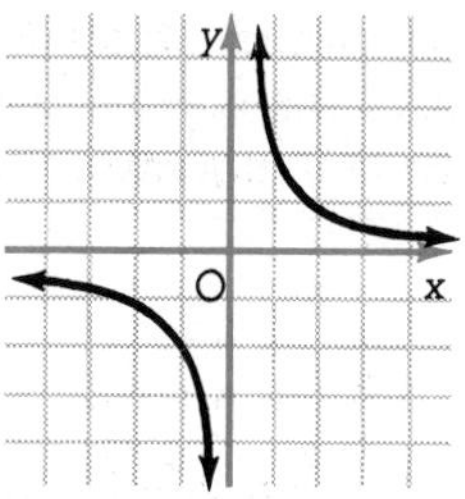

Given $f(x) = 7 - x^2$, find each value.

25. $f(0)$
26. $f(4)$
27. $f(^-3)$
28. $f(11)$
29. $f\left(\frac{1}{2}\right)$
30. $f(3.7)$
31. $f(2a)$
32. $f(6 + n)$

Given $f(x) = 4 + 6x - x^3$, find each value.

33. $f(0)$
34. $f(-1)$
35. $f(3)$
36. $f(14)$
37. $f(9)$
38. $f\left(\frac{1}{2}\right)$
39. $f(2 + a)$
40. $f(3k)$

Given $f(x) = [x] + 4$, find each value. (Hint: $[x]$ means the greatest integer not greater than x.)

41. $f(^-4)$
42. $f(2.5)$
43. $f(^-6.3)$
44. $f(\sqrt{2})$
45. $f(-\sqrt{3})$
46. $f(\pi)$
47. $f(^-4 + t)$
48. $f(q + 1)$

Given $f(x) = |x^2 - 13|$, find each value.

49. $f(0)$
50. $f(^-4)$
51. $f(-\sqrt{13})$
52. $f(2)$
53. $f(4.8)$
54. $f\left(1\frac{1}{2}\right)$
55. $f(n + 4)$
56. $f(5m)$

Name all values of x which are not in the domain of the given function.

57. $f(x) = \dfrac{3}{x - 1}$
58. $f(x) = \dfrac{3 - x}{5 + x}$
59. $f(x) = \dfrac{x^3 + 5x}{4x}$
60. $f(x) = \dfrac{x^2 - 18}{32 - x^2}$
61. $f(x) = \dfrac{15}{|2x| - 9}$
62. $f(x) = \dfrac{x}{x^2 - 6}$

1-2 Linear Functions

A **linear equation** in two variables, such as $3x - 2y = 6$, is an equation whose graph is a straight line. Each term in a linear equation is a constant or the product of a constant and a variable. Any linear equation can be written in **standard form.**

Standard Form of a Linear Equation

> The standard form of a linear equation is
> $$Ax + By + C = 0$$
> where A, B, and C are real numbers, and A and B are not both zero.

Each solution to a linear equation is an ordered pair. Each ordered pair corresponds to a point in the coordinate plane. Since two points determine a line, you need to find only two points to graph a linear equation.

In checking your work it is helpful to graph a third point.

examples

1 **Graph 3x − 2y = 6.**

Isolate one variable.

$$^{-}2y = {}^{-}3x + 6$$

$$y = \frac{3}{2}x - 3$$

Next find three ordered pairs that satisfy the equation.

x	y	(x, y)
0	$^{-}3$	$(0, {}^{-}3)$
1	$-\frac{3}{2}$	$\left(1, -\frac{3}{2}\right)$
2	0	$(2, 0)$

Any real number can be substituted for x.

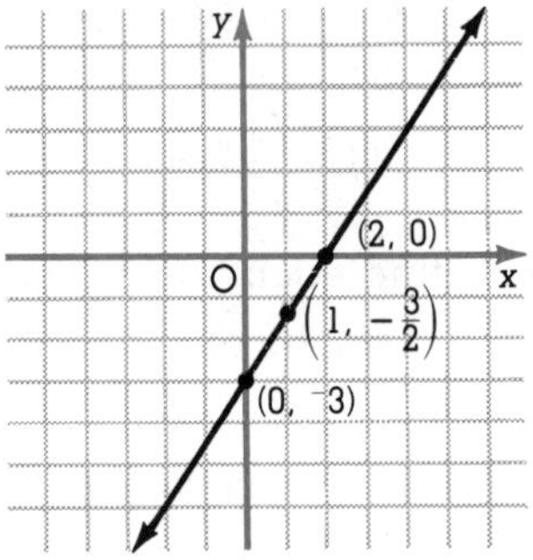

Then, graph the ordered pairs and connect them with a line.

This linear equation represents a function.

2 **Graph 2x = 7.**

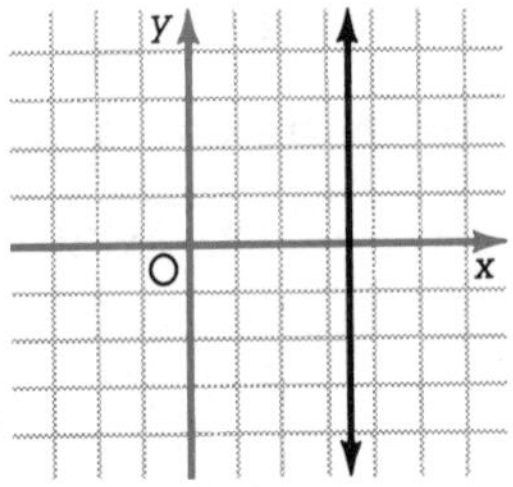

Since $x = \frac{7}{2}$ for all values of y, the graph is a vertical line.

Does this linear equation represent a function?

Not all linear equations represent functions, as shown by the above example. A **linear function** is defined as follows.

A linear function is defined by $f(x) = mx + b$ where m and b are real numbers.

Linear Function

Values of x for which $f(x) = 0$ are called **zeros** of the function. For a linear function, these values are found by solving the equation $mx + b = 0$. If $m \neq 0$, then $-\frac{b}{m}$ is the only zero of the function. The graph of the function crosses the x-axis at the point $\left(-\frac{b}{m}, 0\right)$.

$-\frac{b}{m}$ is called the x-intercept.

example

3 **Find the zero of $f(x) = 3x - 1$. Then graph the function.**

$3x - 1 = 0$

$x = \frac{1}{3}$ Thus, $\frac{1}{3}$ is a zero of the function.

When $x = 1$, $y = 3(1) - 1$, or 2.

Graph $\left(\frac{1}{3}, 0\right)$ and (1, 2) and connect the points with a line.

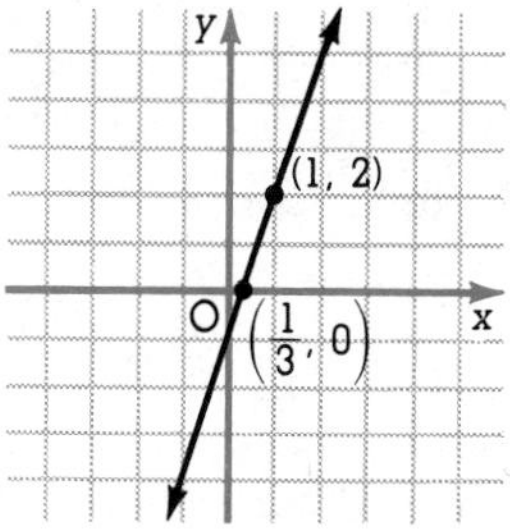

If $m = 0$, then $f(x) = b$. The graph is a horizontal line. This function is also called a **constant function.** A constant function either has *no* zeros ($b \neq 0$), or every value of x is a zero ($b = 0$).

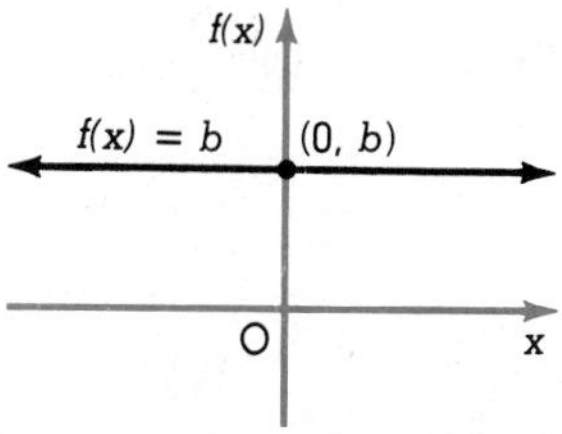

More than one linear equation can be graphed on the same coordinate system. If the graphs intersect, the ordered pair for the point of intersection is the common solution to the equations.

example

4 **Solve the system of equations.**

$y = 5x - 2$
$y = {}^{-}2x + 5$

The solution of the system is (1, 3).

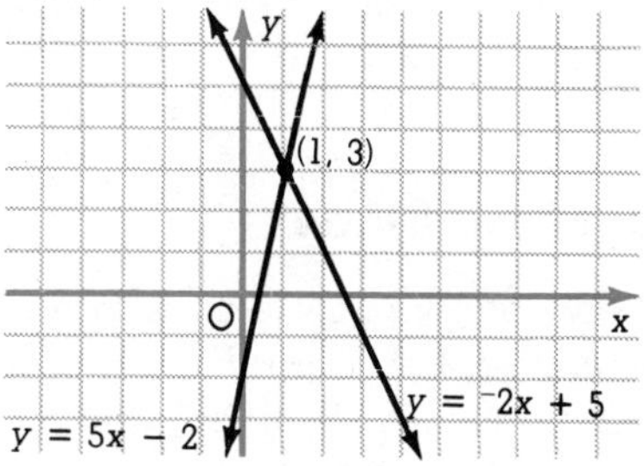

exercises

Exploratory **Write each equation in standard form.**

1. $y = 3x + 2$
2. $2x - 4y = 6$
3. $x = 3$
4. $5 = 9x - 7 + y$
5. $y = {}^{-}4$
6. $x - 6 = 2y$

Name the zero of each function whose graph is shown.

7. 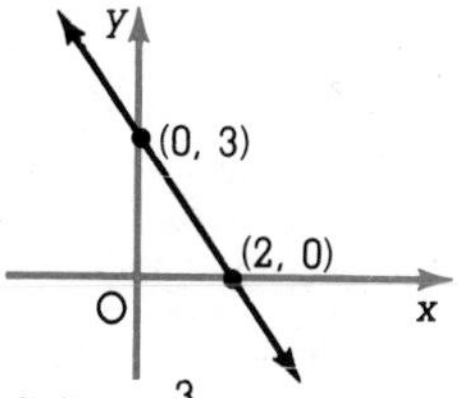

$f(x) = -\frac{3}{2}x + 3$

8. 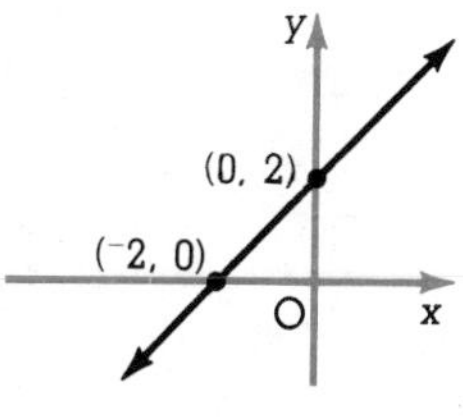

$f(x) = x + 2$

9. 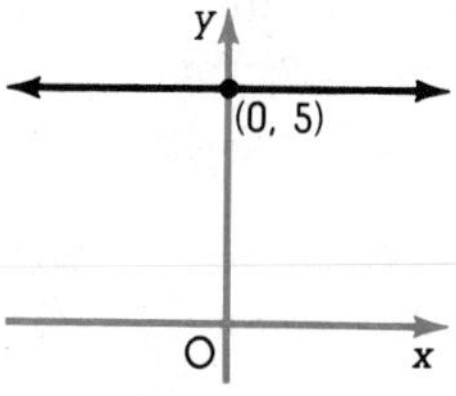

$f(x) = 5$

State whether each ordered pair is a solution to $y = 3x - 7$. Write *yes* or *no*.

10. (0, 7)
11. (0, $^-7$)
12. (15, 38)
13. (2, 1)
14. $(k, 3k - 7)$
15. $(2d, 6d - 14)$
16. $(2r, 6r - 7)$
17. $(m - 1, 3m - 10)$

Written Graph each equation.

1. $y = 3x - 2$
2. $3x = 2y$
3. $y - 7 = x$
4. $x + 2y = 5$
5. $x = -\frac{1}{2}y$
6. $7 - x = y$
7. $4y = 2 + 3x$
8. $y = \frac{1}{2}x - 1.5$

Find the zero of each function.

9. $f(x) = 0.5x + 6$
10. $f(x) = 14x$
11. $f(x) = 9x + 5$
12. $f(x) = 5x - 8$
13. $f(x) = 19$
14. $f(x) = 3x + 1$

Solve each system of equations by graphing.

15. $x = 0$, $y = 1$
16. $x = 0$, $4x + 5y = 20$
17. $x + 4y = 12$, $3x - 2y = {}^-6$
18. $3x - 2y = {}^-6$, $x + y = {}^-2$
19. $x + y = {}^-2$, $3x - y = 10$
20. $3x - y = 10$, $x + 4y = 12$

Challenge Find the vertices of the triangle with sides determined by the following equations: $4x + 3y + 1 = 0$, $4x - 3y - 17 = 0$, and $4x - 9y + 13 = 0$.

1-3 Distance and Slope

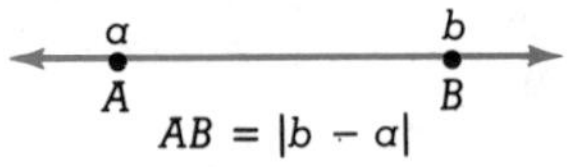

AB denotes the length of $\overline{AB}$, the segment with endpoints A and B.

The distance between two points on a number line can be found by using absolute value. Let A and B be two points on the line with coordinates a and b, respectively. The distance between A and B is $|a - b|$ or $|b - a|$.

You can find the distance between points in the coordinate plane. Consider points $R(^-3, 2)$ and $S(4, 12)$. To find RS, first choose a point T such that $\overline{RT}$ is parallel to the x-axis and $\overline{ST}$ is parallel to the y-axis, as shown at the right. T has coordinates (4, 2). Since S has the same abscissa as T, ST is equal to the absolute value of the difference in the ordinates of S and T, $|12 - 2|$. Similarly, RT is equal to the absolute value of the difference in the abscissas of R and T, $|4 - {}^-3|$.

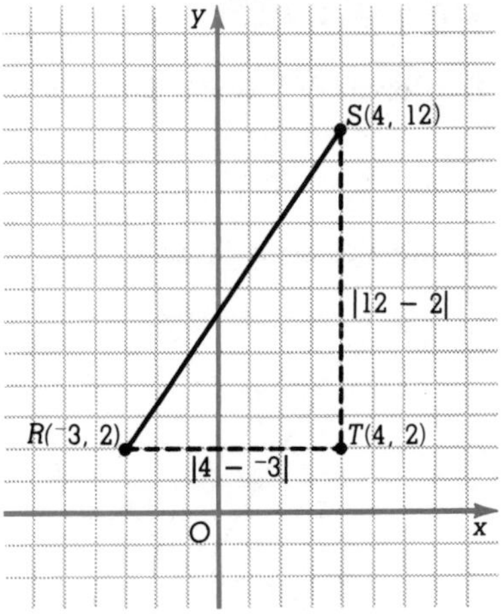

Since $\triangle RST$ is a right triangle, RS can be found by using the Pythagorean theorem.

$$\begin{aligned}(RS)^2 &= (RT)^2 + (ST)^2 \\ RS &= \sqrt{(RT)^2 + (ST)^2} \\ &= \sqrt{|4 - {}^-3|^2 + |12 - 2|^2} \\ &= \sqrt{7^2 + 10^2} \\ &= \sqrt{149} \text{ or } 12.2 \text{ units}\end{aligned}$$

Assume (x_1, y_1) and (x_2, y_2) represent the coordinates of any two points in the plane. The figure at the right illustrates how the formula for finding the distance between (x_1, y_1) and (x_2, y_2) is derived.

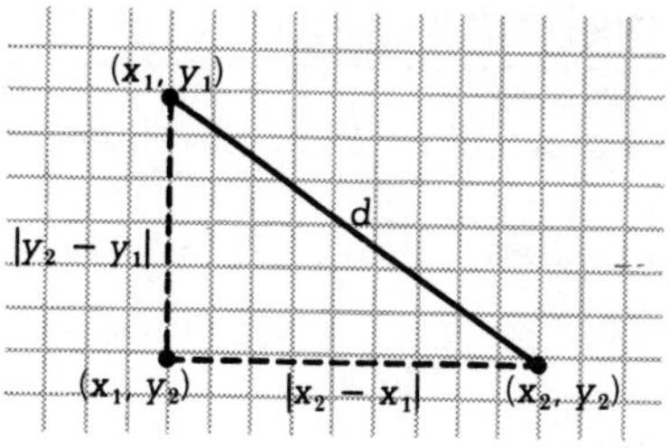

$$d = \sqrt{|x_2 - x_1|^2 + |y_2 - y_1|^2}$$

Why does $|x_2 - x_1|^2 = (x_2 - x_1)^2$?

Distance Formula for Two Points in the Plane

The distance, d, between two points (x_1, y_1) and (x_2, y_2) is given by the following formula.

$$d = \sqrt{(x_2 - x_1)^2 + (y_2 - y_1)^2}$$

example

1 **Find the distance between $(3, {}^-5)$ and $({}^-1, 2)$.**

$$d = \sqrt{(x_2 - x_1)^2 + (y_2 - y_1)^2}$$
$$= \sqrt{({}^-1 - 3)^2 + (2 - ({}^-5))^2}$$
$$= \sqrt{({}^-4)^2 + 7^2}$$
$$= \sqrt{65}$$

The distance is about 8.1 units.

Any two points determine a line. The **slope** of the line is the ratio of the change in the ordinates of the points to the corresponding change in the abscissas. The slope of a line is constant.

Slope is often defined as $\frac{rise}{run}$.

Definition of Slope

The slope of a line through (x_1, y_1) and (x_2, y_2) is given by the following equation, if $x_2 \neq x_1$.

$$\text{slope} = \frac{y_2 - y_1}{x_2 - x_1}$$

examples

2 **Find the slope of the line through $({}^-3, 2)$ and $(5, 7)$.**

$$\text{slope} = \frac{y_2 - y_1}{x_2 - x_1} = \frac{7 - 2}{5 - ({}^-3)} = \frac{5}{8}$$

Either point can be (x_1, y_1).

3 **Graph the line through $(4, 5)$ and $(4, {}^-3)$. Then find the slope of the line.**

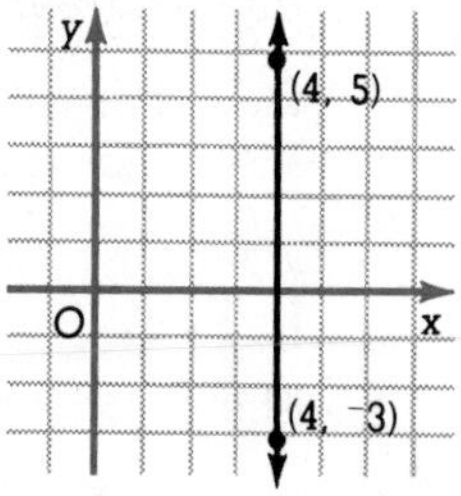

Because the abscissas of the two points are the same, the slope is undefined. Any line parallel to the y-axis has undefined slope.

exercises

Exploratory Find the distance between the given points.

1. $(4, 1), (7, 1)$
2. $(5, 1), (5, 11)$
3. $(^-1, 3), (^-1, ^-3)$
4. $(0, 0), (^-4, ^-3)$
5. $(^-1, 1), (4, 13)$
6. $(^-2, 2), (0, 4)$

7-12. Find the slope of the line passing through each pair of points in problems **1-6**.

Written Find the distance between the given points.

1. $(5, ^-3), (^-1, ^-6)$
2. $(6, 0), (0, 6)$
3. $(5, 7), (0, 0)$
4. $(1, ^-5), (^-7, 11)$
5. $(3, a), (8, a)$
6. $(b, 6 + a), (b, a + 3)$
7. $(2t, t), (5t, 5t)$
8. $(r, s), (r + 2, s - 1)$
9. $(n, 4n), (n + 1, n)$

10-18. Find the slope of the line passing through each pair of points in problems **1-9**.

Find the perimeter of the triangle with the given points as vertices.

19. $(2, 3), (14, 3), (14, 8)$
20. $(2, 2), (5, 2), (2, 6)$
21. $(1, ^-1), (1, 3), (^-2, ^-1)$
22. $(3, 3), (3, ^-9), (^-2, 3)$

Challenge **Collinear points lie on the same line. Find the value of k for which each set of points is collinear.** *Remember, the slope of a line is constant.*

1. $(4, 0), (k, 3), (4, ^-3)$
2. $(2, ^-5), (^-4, ^-11), (k, 1)$
3. $(7, ^-2), (0, 5), (3, k)$
4. $(15, 1), (^-3, ^-8), (3, k)$
5. $(9, 2), (k, 3), (^-1, 4)$
6. $(3, 7), (4, k), (2, 7)$

1-4 Forms of Linear Equations

The graph of $y = 3x + 7$ has slope 3 and y-intercept 7. When the equation is written in this form the slope and y-intercept are easy to find. The equation is said to be in **slope-intercept form.**

Since the y-intercept is 7, (0, 7) is a point on the graph.

Slope-Intercept Form

> **The slope-intercept form of the equation of a line is $y = mx + b$. The slope is m and the y-intercept is b.**

example

1 **Write the equation $2x + 5y - 10 = 0$ in slope-intercept form. Then name the slope and y-intercept.**

$2x + 5y - 10 = 0$ *This equation is in standard form.*

$$5y = ^-2x + 10$$

$$y = -\frac{2}{5}x + 2$$

The slope is $-\frac{2}{5}$ and the y-intercept is 2.

If one point and the slope of a line are known, you can use the slope-intercept form to find the equation of the line.

example

2 **Write the equation for the line through (1, 5) which has a slope of $^{-}2$.**

Substitute the slope and coordinates of the point in the general slope-intercept form of a linear equation and solve for b.

$y = mx + b$
$5 = {}^{-}2(1) + b$
$7 = b$

The slope-intercept form of the equation of the line is $y = {}^{-}2x + 7$.

The slope formula can also be used to find the equation of a line when a point and the slope are known.

example

3 **Find an equation for the line through (1, 6) which has a slope of 2. Then write the equation in slope-intercept form.**

Suppose a second point on the line is (x, y). Substitute the values into the slope formula.

$$m = \frac{y_2 - y_1}{x_2 - x_1}$$

$$2 = \frac{y - 6}{x - 1}$$

$2(x - 1) = y - 6$ *This equation is in point-slope form.*
$2x - 2 = y - 6$
$2x + 4 = y$

The slope intercept form of the equation is $y = 2x + 4$.

The form of a linear equation derived from the slope formula is called the **point-slope form** of the equation.

If the point (x_1, y_1) lies on a line having slope m, the point-slope form of the equation of the line can be written as follows.

$$y - y_1 = m(x - x_1)$$

Point-Slope Form

If two points on a line are known, the slope can be found. Then the equation for the line can be written using slope-intercept form or point-slope form.

examples

4 **Find the slope-intercept form of the equation of the line through (1, 4) and (5, 7).**

First, find the slope. $m = \frac{7-4}{5-1} = \frac{3}{4}$

Then, substitute values into the general slope-intercept form and solve for b.

$y = mx + b$

$4 = \frac{3}{4}(1) + b$ *The coordinates of either point can be used.*

$3\frac{1}{4} = b$

The slope-intercept form of the equation is $y = \frac{3}{4}x + 3\frac{1}{4}$.

5 **Find the point-slope form of the equation of the line through (2, 5) and (6, 3). Then write the equation in slope-intercept form.**

First, find the slope. $m = \frac{3-5}{6-2}$ or $-\frac{1}{2}$

Then, substitute values into the general point-slope form.

$y - y_1 = m(x - x_1)$ *The ordered pair for either point can be (x_1, y_1).*

$y - 5 = -\frac{1}{2}(x - 2)$ *This equation is in point-slope form.*

$y = -\frac{1}{2}x + 6$

The slope-intercept form of the equation is $y = -\frac{1}{2}x + 6$.

exercises

Exploratory Write each equation in slope-intercept form. Then name the slope and y-intercept.

1. $3x - 2y = 7$
2. $^-3x + 4y = 0$
3. $5x + 11y = 2$
4. $15y - x = 1$
5. $x - 2y - 4 = 0$
6. $3x + y = 2$
7. $8x = 2y - 1$
8. $2x - 5y - 10 = 0$
9. $4x + 3y = 0$

Written Write the slope-intercept form of the line through the given point with the given slope.

1. (3, 2), 4
2. (5, 7), 0
3. ($^-$3, $^-$4), $^-$6
4. ($^-$6, 2), 8
5. ($^-$5, $^-$12), $^-$5
6. (3, 5), $^-$3
7. ($^-$10, 4), $\frac{3}{4}$
8. ($^-$7, 3), $-\frac{1}{4}$
9. (9, 11), $\frac{2}{3}$

Write the slope-intercept form of the line through the given points.

10. (6, 6), ($^-$6, $^-$6)
11. ($^-$2, 0), (1, $^-$3)
12. (4, 2), (7, 2)
13. ($^-$1, 4), ($^-$1, 7)
14. (3, $^-$5), (2, $^-$1)
15. (5, 2), (7, 9)
16. (2, 5), (7, 8)
17. (3, 1), ($^-$2, 4)
18. ($^-$7, $^-$1), (4, $^-$2)

Challenge Write equations for the sides of the triangle which has vertices $A(2, {}^-7)$, $B(5, 1)$, and $C({}^-3, 2)$.

All measurements are approximations. The **significant digits** of an approximate number are those digits which indicate the results of a measurement.

The mass of the coins shown at the right, measured to the nearest 100 g, is 200 grams. The measurement 200 g has one significant digit. The mass of the coins, to the nearest gram, is 210 grams. The measurement $21\underline{0}$ g has 3 significant digits, 2, 1, and 0.

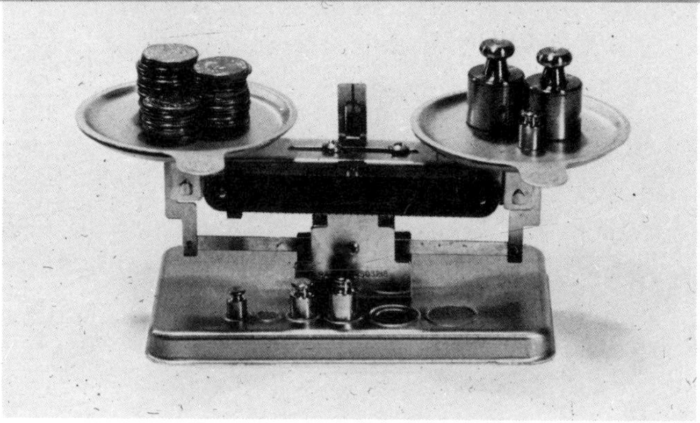

Several identifying characteristics of significant digits are listed below, with examples.

1. Non-zero digits and zeros between significant digits are significant. *For example, the measurement 9.071 m has 4 significant digits, 9, 0, 7, and 1.*
2. Zeros at the end of a decimal fraction are significant. *The measurement 0.050 mm has 2 significant digits, 5 and 0.*
3. Under lined zeros in whole numbers are significant. *The measurement $104{,}0\underline{0}0$ km has 5 significant digits, 1, 0, 4, 0, and 0.*

In general, a computation involving multiplication or division of measurements *cannot* be more accurate than the least accurate measurement in the computation. Thus, the result of computation involving multiplication or division of measurements should be rounded to the number of significant digits in the least accurate measurement.

Example The mass of 37 quarters is $21\underline{0}$ g. Find the mass of one quarter.

mass of 1 quarter $= 21\underline{0}\text{ g} \div 37$ *$21\underline{0}$ has 3 significant digits.*
37 does not represent a measurement.

$= 5.68$ g *Round the result to 3 significant digits. Why?*

Exercises Write the number of significant digits for each measurement.

1. 8314.20 m **2.** 30.70 cm **3.** 0.01 mm **4.** 0.0605 mg
5. $37\underline{0}{,}000$ km **6.** $370{,}0\underline{0}0$ km **7.** 9.7×10^4 g **8.** 3.20×10^{-2} g

Solve each problem. Round each result to the correct number of significant digits.

9. 23 m × 1.54 m **10.** $12{,}0\underline{0}0$ ft ÷ $52\underline{0}$ ft **11.** 2.5 cm × 25
12. 11.01 mm × 11 **13.** 908 yd ÷ 0.5 **14.** 38.6 m × 4.0 m

1-5 Linear Inequalities in Two Variables

The graph of $y = -\frac{1}{2}x + 2$ is a line which separates the coordinate plane into two regions. The graph of $y > -\frac{1}{2}x + 2$ is the region above the line. The graph of $y < -\frac{1}{2}x + 2$ is the region below the line.

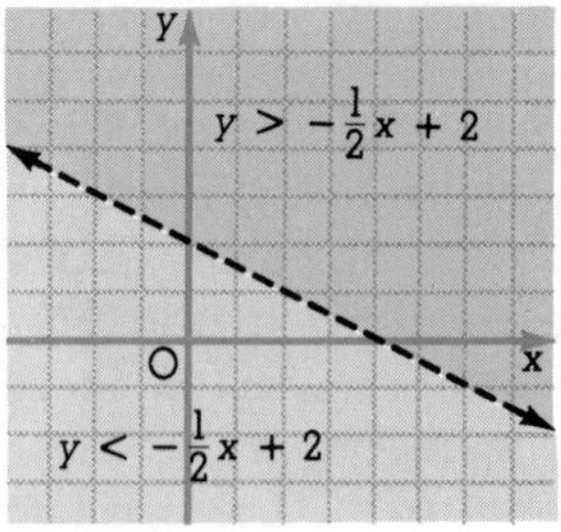

The line described by $y = -\frac{1}{2}x + 2$ is called the **boundary** of each region. If the boundary is part of a graph it is drawn as a solid line. If the boundary is not part of a graph it is drawn as a broken line.

examples

1 **Graph $5y + 2x \leq {}^-10$.**

$$5y + 2x \leq {}^-10$$
$$5y \leq {}^-2x + {}^-10$$
$$y \leq -\frac{2}{5}x - 2$$

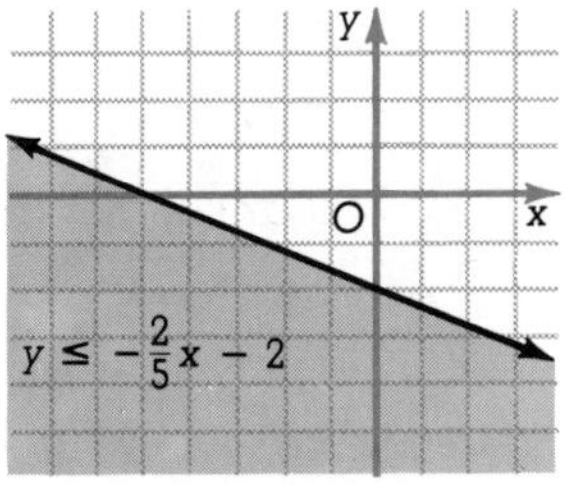

2 **Graph $8 - y > 3x$**

$$8 - y > 3x$$
$$-y > 3x - 8$$
$$y < {}^-3x + 8$$

Remember to reverse the direction of an inequality when you multiply by a negative number.

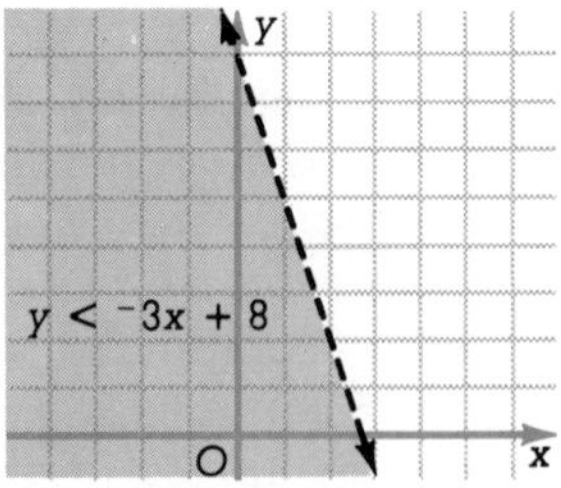

Relations such as $2 < x + y \leq 5$ also can be graphed. The graph of this relation is the intersection of the graph of $2 < x + y$ and the graph of $x + y \leq 5$, as shown at the right. Notice that the boundary $x + y = 5$ is part of the graph.

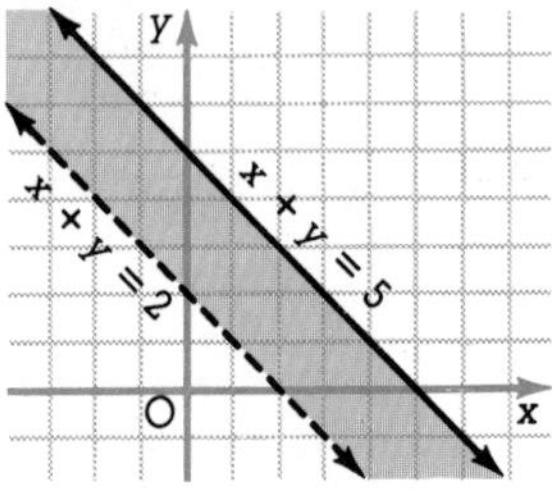

example

3 **Graph $3 \leq 2x - y \leq 8$**

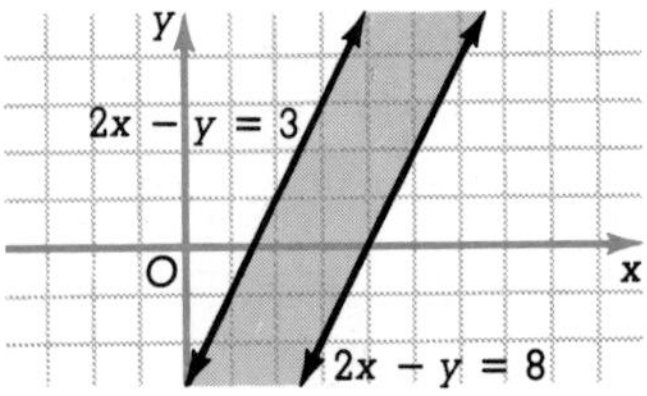

A system of two or more inequalities may be graphed on the same coordinate plane. The intersection of the graphs represents common solutions to the inequalities.

examples

4 **Solve the following system by graphing.**

$x + 2y \geq 4$
$x - y \leq 3$

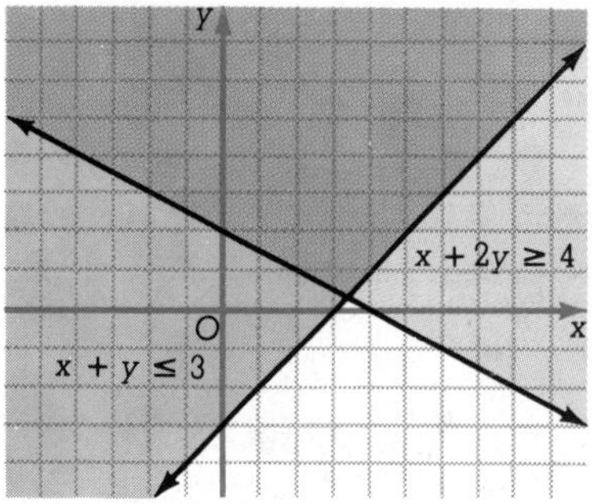

Points in the darkest region satisfy both inequalities.

5 **Solve the following system by graphing.**

$y > x + 5$
$y < x - 2$

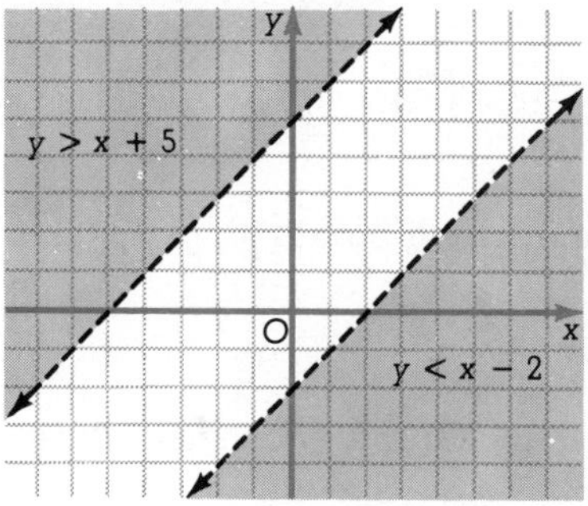

Because the graphs have no points in common, no ordered pairs satisfy both inequalities.

If a system of linear inequalities is graphed so that the intersection set is a convex polygon and its interior, the region is called a **polygonal convex set.**

example

6 **Solve the following system by graphing. Then name the vertices of the polygonal convex set.**

$x \geq 0,\ y \geq 0,\ x + y \leq 5$

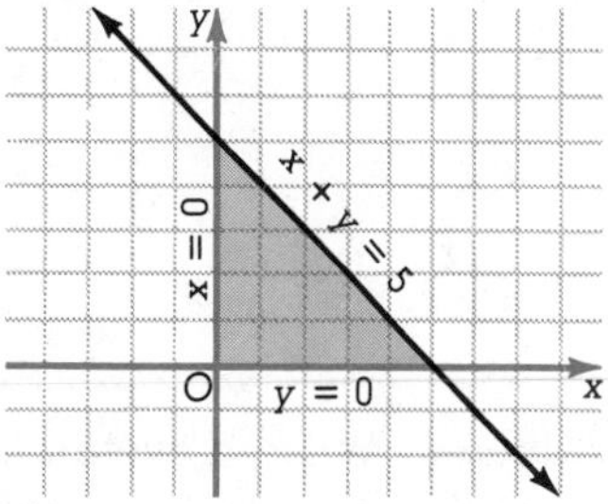

The vertices of the region are (0, 0), (5, 0), and (0, 5).

exercises

Exploratory Describe the shaded region with an inequality.

1. 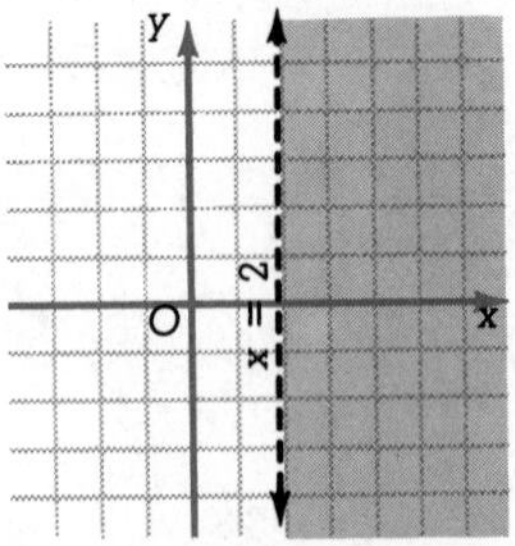

2. 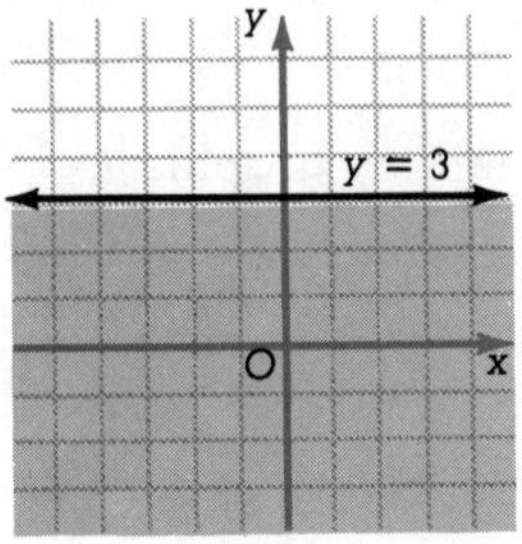

3. 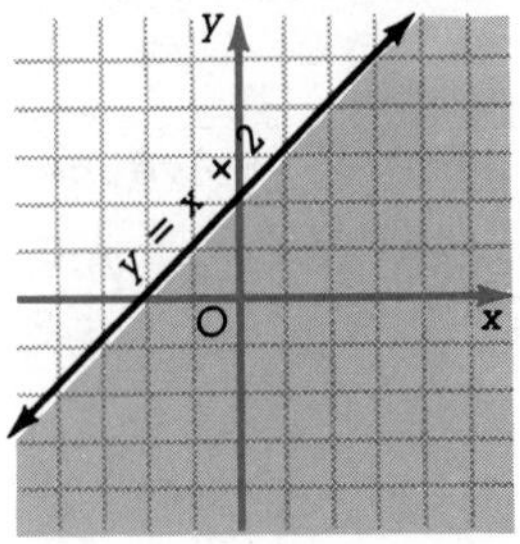

4. 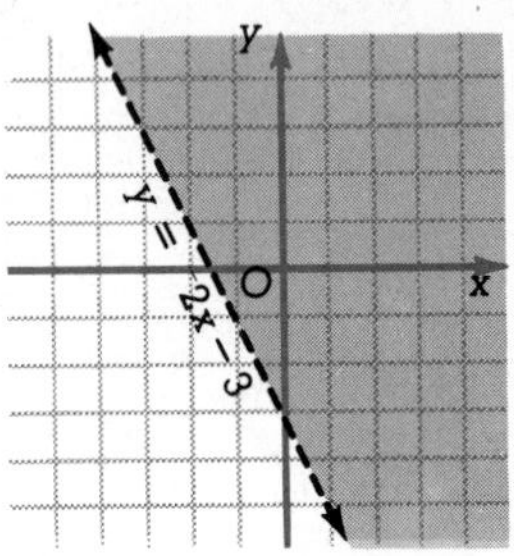

5. 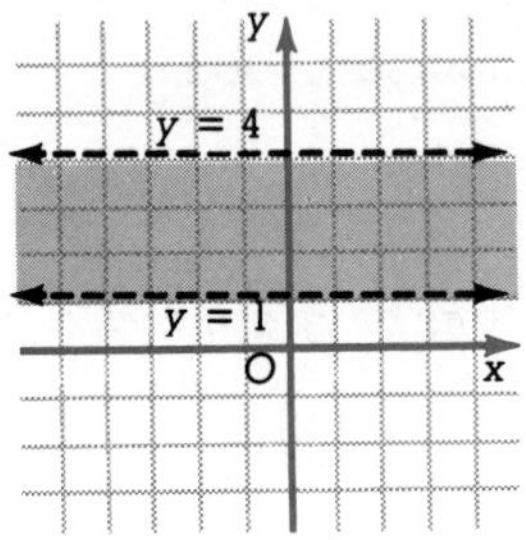

6. 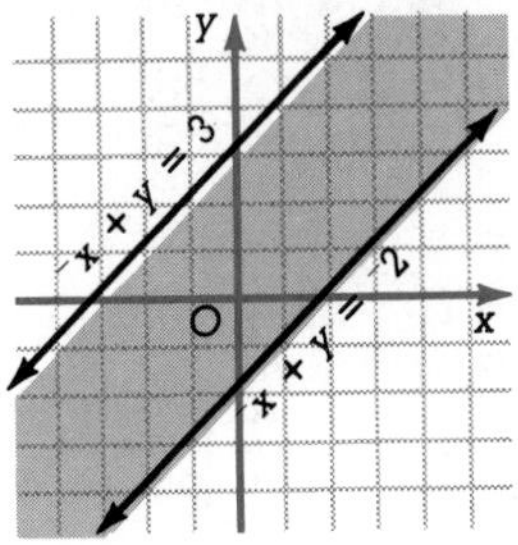

Name which points (0, 0), (3, 2), ($^-4$, 2), or ($^-2$, 4) satisfy each inequality.

7. $x + y \geq 3$
8. $x > 4y + 3$
9. $y < x + 2$
10. $x + y \leq 4$
11. $y \neq x - 5$
12. $3x - 4y \geq {}^-5$

Written Graph each inequality.

1. $x < 5$
2. $y \geq {}^-2$
3. $y > {}^-x$
4. $x - y < 5$
5. $y < {}^-2x + 8$
6. $2y \leq x - 5$
7. ${}^-y < 2x + 1$
8. $y \leq -\frac{1}{3}x + 2$
9. $y > \frac{2}{5}x + \frac{19}{5}$
10. $0 < x - y < 2$
11. $2 < 2x + y < 8$
12. ${}^-6 \leq 3x - y \leq 12$
13. ${}^-2 \leq x + 2y \leq 4$
14. $y > |x|$
15. $|x + 3| < y - 1$

Solve the following systems by graphing. Then name the vertices of each polygonal convex set.

16. $x \geq 0$
    $y \geq 0$
    $2x + y \leq 4$
17. $x \leq 0$
    $y + 3 \geq 0$
    $y \leq x$
18. $x + y \leq 5$
    $y - x \leq 5$
    $y \geq {}^-10$
19. $y \geq 0$
    $0 \leq x \leq 5$
    ${}^-x + y \leq 2$
    $x + y \leq 6$
20. $x \geq 1$
    $y \geq 2$
    $y \leq 8$
    $x + y \leq 10$
    $2x + y \leq 14$
21. $x \leq 3$
    $y \leq 5$
    $x + y \geq 1$
    $x \geq 0$
    $y \geq 0$

Challenge Write a system of inequalities which determines the polygonal convex set with vertices (0, 0), (5, 1), (1, 6), and (6, 4).

1-6 Maximum or Minimum of a Polygonal Convex Set

Linear programming is a procedure for finding the maximum or the minimum value of a function in two variables, subject to given conditions, called **constraints,** on the variables. The constraints are often expressed as linear inequalities.

Suppose you want to find the maximum or minimum value for the function $f(x, y) = 5x - 3y$. The values of x and y have the following constraints.

$$y \geq 0 \qquad 0 \leq x \leq 5$$
$$^{-}x + y \leq 2 \qquad x + y \leq 6$$

By graphing each inequality and finding the intersection of the graphs, you can determine a polygonal convex set of points for which the function can be evaluated. The region shown at the right is the polygonal convex set determined by the above inequalities.

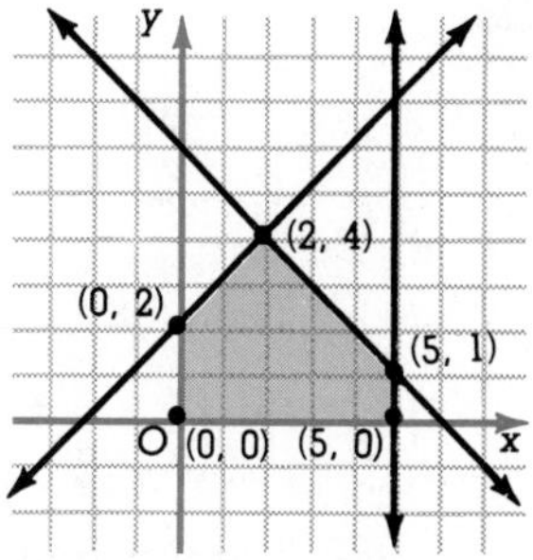

The polygonal convex set has an infinite number of points. It would be impossible to evaluate the function for all points within the region. According to the theorem below, the function needs to be evaluated *only* for the vertices of the polygon.

Vertex Theorem

The maximum or minimum value of $f(x, y) = ax + by + c$, defined for a polygonal convex set, occurs at a vertex of the polygon.

The value of $5x - 3y$ at each vertex can be found as follows.

$$f(x, y) = 5x - 3y \qquad f(2, 4) = 5(2) - 3(4) = {}^{-}2$$
$$f(0, 0) = 5(0) - 3(0) = 0 \qquad f(5, 1) = 5(5) - 3(1) = 22$$
$$f(0, 2) = 5(0) - 3(2) = {}^{-}6 \qquad f(5, 0) = 5(5) - 3(0) = 25$$

Thus, the maximum value is 25 and the minimum value is $^{-}6$.

The following intuitive argument supports the results obtained by the vertex theorem.

When $5x - 3y$ is equal to some constant k, a line is determined by the equation. The figure at the right shows lines determined by $5x - 3y = k$, where each value of k is the value of $5x - 3y$ at a vertex. Notice that the distance from a line to the origin varies according to the value of k. Any value of k greater than 25 or less than $^{-}6$ will determine a line which passes outside the polygon. Therefore the maximum value of $f(x, y) = 5x - 3y$ for the polygonal convex set is 25 and the minimum is $^{-}6$.

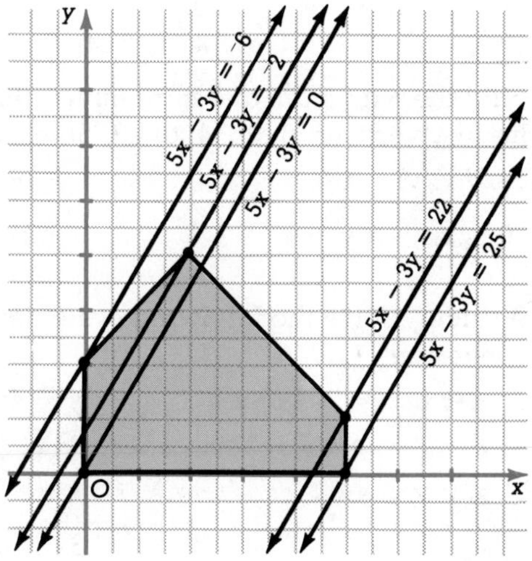

If the value of a function is the same for two consecutive vertices of a polygon, any point on that side of the polygon represents a maximum or minimum as the case may be. *Why?*

example

1 Find the maximum and minimum values of $f(x, y) = x + 2y + 1$ for the polygonal convex set determined by the following inequalities.

$$x \geq 0,\ y \geq 0,\ 2x + y \leq 4,\ x + y \leq 3$$

First, graph the inequalities and find the coordinates of the vertices of the resulting polygon.

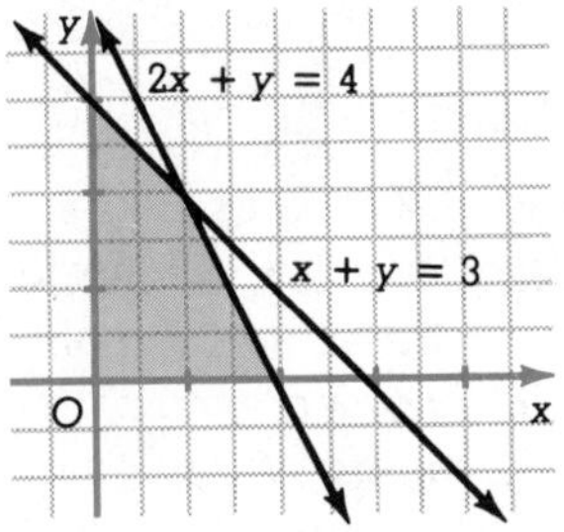

The coordinates of the vertices are (0, 0), (2, 0), (1, 2), and (0, 3).

Then evaluate the function $f(x, y) = x + 2y + 1$ at each vertex.

$f(0, 0) = 0 + 2(0) + 1 = 1$ $\quad$ $f(1, 2) = 1 + 2(2) + 1 = 6$
$f(2, 0) = 2 + 2(0) + 1 = 3$ $\quad$ $f(0, 3) = 0 + 2(3) + 1 = 7$

The maximum value of the function is 7 and the minimum value is 1.

exercises

Exploratory Given $f(x, y) = 3x + 2y + 1$, find each value.

1. $f(3, 2)$
2. $f(^-2, 1)$
3. $f(2, 4)$
4. $f(^-3, ^-4)$
5. $f(0, 0)$
6. $f\left(\frac{1}{3}, \frac{1}{2}\right)$
7. $f(0, 4)$
8. $f\left(-\frac{3}{2}, 4\right)$

Given $f(x, y) = 5x - 2y + 1$, find each value.

9. $f(0, 0)$
10. $f(^-3, 2)$
11. $f(^-3, ^-5)$
12. $f(7, ^-3)$
13. $f(4, 2)$
14. $f(^-7, 4)$
15. $f(^-7, ^-1)$
16. $f(4, ^-4)$

Find the maximum and minimum values of each function defined for the polygonal convex set having vertices (0, 0), (4, 0), (3, 5), and (0, 5).

17. $f(x, y) = x + y$
18. $f(x, y) = 8x + y$
19. $f(x, y) = 4y - 3x$
20. $f(x, y) = y - x$
21. $f(x, y) = x + 2y$
22. $f(x, y) = \frac{1}{2}x - \frac{1}{3}y$

Written Solve the following systems by graphing. Then name the vertices of each polygonal convex set.

1. $x \geq 0$
   $y \geq 1$
   $x + y \leq 4$
2. $x + 4y \leq 12$
   $3x - 2y \geq {}^-6$
   $x + y \geq {}^-2$
   $3x - y \leq 10$
3. $y \geq x - 4$
   $y \geq {}^-3x$
   $y \leq \frac{1}{2}x + \frac{7}{2}$
   $x \leq 5$

4-6. Find the maximum and minimum values of $f(x, y) = 4x + 2y + 7$ for each polygonal convex set in problems **1-3**.
7-9. Find the maximum and minimum values of $f(x, y) = x - y + 2$ for each polygonal convex set in problems **1-3**.
10-12. Find the maximum and minimum values of $f(x, y) = y + 2x + 7$ for each polygonal convex set in problems **1-3**.
13-15. Find the maximum and minimum values of $f(x, y) = 2x + 8y + 10$ for each polygonal convex set in problems **1-3**.

Challenge Graph the following system of inequalities to form a polygonal convex set. Determine which lines intersect at each vertex, and solve pairs of equations simultaneously to determine the exact coordinates of each vertex. Then find the maximum and minimum values of $f(x, y) = 5x + 6y$ for the region defined by the inequalities.

$$0 \le 2y \le 17 \qquad y \le 3x + 1$$
$$y \ge 7 - 2x \qquad y \ge 2x - 13$$
$$3y \ge {}^{-}2x + 11 \qquad y \le 16 - x$$

1-7 Linear Programming

Many practical problems can be solved by linear programming. These problems are of such a nature that certain constraints exist or are placed upon the variables, and some function of these variables must be maximized or minimized. Use the following method to solve linear programming problems.

Linear Programming Procedure

1. **Define variables.**
2. **Write the constraints as a system of inequalities.**
3. **Graph the system. Find vertices of the polygon formed.**
4. **Write an expression to be maximized or minimized.**
5. **Substitute values from vertices into the expression.**
6. **Select the greatest or least result.**

example

1 **A farmer has a choice of planting a combination of two different crops on 20 acres of land. For crop *A* seed costs \$120 per acre, and for crop *B* seed costs \$200 per acre. Government restrictions limit acreage of crop *A* to 15 acres but do not limit crop *B*. Crop *A* will take 15 hours of labor per acre at a cost of \$5.60 per hour, and crop *B* will require 10 hours of labor per acre at \$5.00 per hour. If the expected income from crop *A* is \$600 per acre, and from crop *B* is \$520 per acre, how should the 20 acres be apportioned between the two crops to get maximum profit?**

Define variables.	Let x equal the number of acres of crop A. Let y equal the number of acres of crop B.
Write inequalities.	$x \geq 0$, $y \geq 0$ *The number of acres of crops cannot be less than 0.* $x \leq 15$ *No more than 15 acres of crop A are permitted.* $x + y \leq 20$ *No more than 20 acres can be planted in all.*
Graph the system.	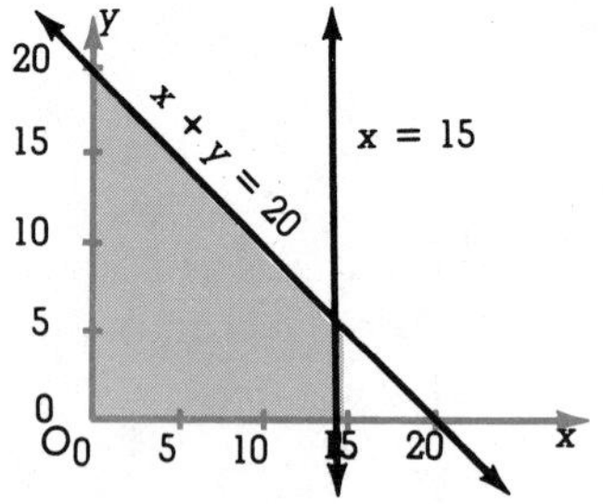 *The vertices are (0, 0), (15, 0), (15, 5), and (0, 20).*
Write an expression to be maximized.	The profit from any crop equals the income less the costs. The profit from crop A equals $600x - 120x - 15(5.60)x$, or $396x$. The profit from crop B equals $520y - 200y - 10(5.00)y$, or $270y$. Thus, the profit function is $P(x, y) = 396x + 270y$.
Substitute values into the expression.	$P(0, 0) = 396(0) + 270(0) = 0$ $P(15, 0) = 396(15) + 270(0) = 5940$ $P(15, 5) = 396(15) + 270(5) = 7290$ $P(0, 20) = 396(0) + 270(20) = 5400$
Answer the problem.	The farmer should plant 15 acres of crop A and 5 acres of crop B to obtain the maximum profit of $7290.

exercises

Exploratory The Champion Lumber Company converts logs into lumber or plywood. In a given week, the total production cannot exceed 800 units, of which 200 units of lumber and 300 units of plywood are required by regular customers. The profit on a unit of lumber is $20 and the profit on a unit of plywood is $30. Let x represent the units of lumber and y represent the units of plywood.

1. Write an inequality to represent the total production.
2. Write an inequality to represent the production of lumber.
3. Write an inequality to represent the production of plywood.
4. Write an equation to represent the total profit.
5. Graph the polygonal convex set determined by the inequalities.
6. Name the vertices of the polygon.
7. Find the number of units each of lumber and plywood which should be produced to maximize profit.
8. What is the maximum profit?

Written Solve each problem.

1. A manufacturer makes widgets and gadgets. At least 500 widgets and 700 gadgets are needed to meet minimum daily demands. The machinery can produce no more than 1200 widgets and 1400 gadgets per day. The combined number of widgets and gadgets that the packaging department can handle is 2300 per day. If the company sells widgets for 40 cents each and gadgets for 50 cents each, how many of each item should be produced for maximum daily income? What is the maximum daily income?

2. A company makes two models of light fixtures, *A* and *B*, each of which must be assembled and packed. The time required to assemble model *A* is 12 minutes, and model *B* takes 18 minutes. It takes 2 minutes to package model *A* and 1 minute to package model *B*. Each week there are available 240 hours of assembly time and 20 hours for packing. If model *A* sells for \$1.50 and model *B* sells for \$1.70, how many of each model should be made to obtain the maximum weekly income? What is the maximum weekly income?

3. For problem **1**, suppose the cost of producing a widget is 7 cents and the cost of a gadget is 16 cents. How many of each item should be produced for maximum daily profit? What is the maximum daily profit?

4. For problem **2**, suppose the cost of producing model *A* is 65¢ and the cost of producing model *B* is 90¢. How many of each model should be produced for maximum weekly profit? What is the maximum weekly profit?

5. For problem **1**, suppose the cost of producing a widget is 7 cents and the cost of a gadget is 18 cents. How many of each item should be produced for maximum daily profit? What is the maximum daily profit?

6. For problem **2** above, suppose the cost of producing model A is 75¢ and model B is 85¢. How many of each model should be produced for maximum weekly profit? What is the maximum weekly profit?

7. A meat packer makes a kind of wurst using beef, pork, cereal, fat, water, and spices. The minimum cereal content is 12%, the minimum fat content is 15%, the minimum water content is 6.5%, and the spices are 0.5%. The remaining ingredients are beef and pork. There must be at least 30% beef for good flavor and at least 20% pork for texture. The beef content must equal or exceed the pork content. The cost of all the content except beef and pork is \$32 per 100 lb. Beef can be purchased for \$140 per 100 lb and pork for \$90 per 100 lb. Find the combination of beef and pork for the minimum cost. What is the minimum cost per 100 lb?

8. A company is planning to buy new fork hoists for material handling. There are two models that will serve their needs. The warehouse supervisor feels that a minimum of 3 Model M hoists and 5 Model R hoists will be needed. The supplier has 8 Model M hoists and 10 Model R hoists on hand for delivery. The company purchasing agent has decided that no more than 14 hoists can be purchased. Model M can handle 12,000 kg per hour and Model R can handle 10,000 kg per hour. What number of hoists of each model should be purchased for maximum weight handling capacity?

9. For problem **7**, suppose that the cost of beef is \$180 per 100 lb and pork is \$160 per 100 lb. Find the combination of beef and pork for minimum cost. What is the minimum cost per 100 lb?

10. For problem **8**, suppose that Model R has an attachment that will enable it to handle 12,500 kg per hour. What number of hoists of each model should be purchased for maximum weight-handling capacity if the attachment is used?

Nick Perrini is a metallurgist for a steel refinery. He deals with the nature, structure, and physical properties of metals and their alloys, and with methods of converting refined metals into final products.

Many problems about alloys can be solved using systems of linear equations.

Example Suppose an alloy contains 11% chromium and no nickel. How much chromium and nickel must be added to 50 tons of the alloy to produce an alloy of 18% chromium and 8% nickel.

First, define the variables.

x = tons of chromium added y = tons of nickel added

Then write a system of equations.

$$0.11(50) + x = 0.18(50 + x + y)$$
$$y = 0.08(50 + x + y)$$

For both chromium and nickel, the initial amount plus the added amount is equal to the final amount.

Simplify the equations.

$$18y = 82x - 350$$
$$92y = 8x + 400$$

$$828y = 3772x - 16{,}100$$
$$-(828y = 72x + 3\,600)$$
$$0 = 3700x - 19{,}700$$

Multiply the first equation by 46 and the second by 9. Then subtract to eliminate y.

Determine values for x and y.

$$x = \frac{19{,}700}{3700} \text{ or about } 5.3$$

$$y = \frac{82x - 350}{18} \text{ or about } 4.8$$

Do you see how this was obtained?

About 5.3 tons of chromium and 4.8 tons of nickel must be added.

Exercises Solve each problem.

1. A certain alloy of steel contains 5% nickel and no chromium. How much chromium and nickel must be added to 50 tons of the alloy to produce an alloy of 18% chromium and 8% nickel?
2. A certain alloy of steel contains 1.5% nickel and no chromium. How much chromium and nickel must be added to 40 tons of the alloy to produce an alloy of 3.5% nickel and 1.5% chromium?

Chapter Summary

1. Definition of Relation, Domain, and Range: A relation is a set of ordered pairs. The domain is the set of all abscissas of the ordered pairs. The range is the set of all ordinates of the ordered pairs. (2)
2. Definition of Function: A function is a relation in which each element of the domain is paired with exactly one element of the range. (2)
3. Standard Form of a Linear Equation: The standard form of a linear equation is $Ax + By + C = 0$, where A, B, and C are real numbers, and A and B are not both zero. (5)
4. Linear Function: A linear function can be defined by $f(x) = mx + b$ where m and b are real numbers. (6)
5. Distance Formula for Two Points in the Plane: The distance, d, between two points (x_1, y_1) and (x_2, y_2) is given by the formula $d = \sqrt{(x_2 - x_1)^2 + (y_2 - y_1)^2}$. (9)
6. Slope: The slope of a line through (x_1, y_1) and (x_2, y_2) is given by the following equation, if $x_2 \neq x_1$, then

$$\text{slope} = \frac{y_2 - y_1}{x_2 - x_1} \qquad (9)$$

7. Slope-Intercept Form: The slope-intercept form of the equation of a line is $y = mx + b$. The slope is m and the y-intercept is b. (10)
8. Point-Slope Form: If the point (x_1, y_1) lies on a line having slope m, the point-slope form of the equation of the line can be written as follows.

$$y - y_1 = m(x - x_1) \qquad (11)$$

9. A system of two or more inequalities may be graphed on the same coordinate plane. The intersection of the graphs represents the common solutions to the inequalities. (15)
10. If a system of linear inequalities is graphed so that the intersection set is a convex polygon and its interior, the region is called a polygonal convex set. (15)
11. Vertex Theorem: The maximum or minimum value of $f(x, y) = ax + by + c$, defined for a polygonal convex set occurs at a vertex of the polygon. (17)
12. Linear Programming Procedure:
    1. Define variables.
    2. Write the constraints as a system of inequalities.
    3. Graph the system. Find vertices of the polygon formed.
    4. Write an expression to be maximized or minimized.
    5. Substitute values from the vertices into the expression.
    6. Select the greatest or least result. (19)

Chapter Review

1-1 **State the domain and range of the each relation.**

1. $\{(3, 5), (4, 5), (5, 5)\}$
2. $\{(0, 4), (0, 5)\}$
3. $\{(8, 4), (8, ^-4), (10, 5), (10, ^-5)\}$
4. $\{(^-2, 1), (^-1, 2), (0, 3)\}$
5. $\{(9, 81), (8, 64), (7, 49)\}$
6. $\{(5, 11), (11, 5), (6, 11), (11, 6)\}$

State the relation represented by each of the following, given that x is an integer.

7. $y = 5x - 7$ and $0 \le x \le 3$
8. $y = 3x^3$ and $^-2 < x < 3$
9. $|y| = x - 4$ and $5 \le x < 7$
10. $y = |4 + x|$ and $^-8 \le x < ^-2$

11-20. State whether each relation in problems **1-10** is a function. Write *yes* or *no*.

Given $f(x) = |x - 6| + x^2$, find each value.

21. $f(0)$
22. $f(3)$
23. $f(11)$
24. $f(5.9)$

Name all values of x which are not in the domain of the given function.

25. $f(x) = \dfrac{5}{x}$
26. $f(x) = \dfrac{x^2}{x^2 - 3}$
27. $f(x) = \dfrac{2(x^2 - 9)}{x + 3}$
28. $f(x) = \dfrac{2x^3 - 5}{2|x| - 5}$

1-2 **Write each equation in standard form.**

29. $y = \frac{1}{3}x + \frac{5}{3}$
30. $y = \frac{1}{2}x - 3$
31. $3x = 2y + x$
32. $y + 9 = 4x + 7$
33. $y = ^-8$
34. $7 = x$

35-40. Graph each equation in problems **29-34**.

Find the zero of each function.

41. $f(x) = 3x - 8$
42. $f(x) = 19$
43. $f(x) = 0.25x - 5$

Solve each system of equations by graphing.

44. $y = ^-2x$, $x + y = ^-2$
45. $x - y = 5$, $x = 6y$
46. $5y - 2x = 0$, $3y + x = ^-1$

1-3 **Find the distance between the given points.**

47. $(0, 0), (5, 12)$
48. $(3, 8), (5, 11)$
49. $(a, b), (a + 3, b + 4)$
50. $(2k, 4k), (3k, 6k)$

51-54. Find the slope of the line passing through each pair of points in problems **47-50**.

1-4 **Write the slope-intercept form of the line through the given point with the given slope.**

55. $(5, 5), 2$
56. $(^-2, 3), ^-1$
57. $(0, 0), \frac{3}{5}$
58. $(1, 4), -\frac{4}{3}$

Write the slope-intercept form of the line through the given points.

59. (3, 7), (6, 10)
60. (5, $^-2$), (3, $^-8$)
61. (9, 6), ($^-3$, 3)
62. ($^-1$, 0), (5, 9)
63. (4, 4), (2, $^-3$)
64. (11, $^-6$), (10, $^-9$)

1-5 **Graph each inequality.**

65. $x + y < 8$
66. $y < x - 5$
67. $3y \geq 2x + 6$
68. $^-2 \leq x - 3y \leq 4$
69. $0 < y + x < 10$
70. $|x - 2| \leq 3y$

Solve the following systems by graphing. Then name the vertices of each polygonal convex set.

71. $x \geq 0$
$y \geq 0$
$4y + x \leq 10$

72. $x \geq 1$
$y \geq {}^-2$
$y \leq 6 - x$
$y + 2x \leq 10$

73. $x \geq 0$
$y \geq 4$
$2y \leq 18 - x$
$x \leq 6$
$y \leq 11 - x$

1-6 **Given $f(x, y) = 7x + 3y$, find each value.**

74. $f(0, 3)$
75. $f(4, 7)$
76. $f(6, 2)$
77. $f(^-3, ^-2)$
78. $f(2, 1.5)$
79. $f(2.3, 5)$
80. $f(^-4, 9)$
81. $f(0.5, 3.5)$

Find the maximum and minimum values of the given function, defined for the polygonal convex set having vertices (1, 4), (11, 4), (9, 6), (6, 8), and (1, 8).

82. $f(x, y) = 4y + 3x$
83. $f(x, y) = 6x + y$

84-86. Find the maximum and minimum values of $f(x, y) = 3y + 2x - 4$ for each polygonal convex set in problems **71-73**.

1-7 **Solve each problem.**

87. Joe has a small carpentry shop in his basement to make bookcases. He makes two sizes, large and small. His profit on a large bookcase is \$50 and his profit on a small bookcase is \$20. It takes Joe 6 hours to make a large bookcase and 2 hours to make a small one. He can spend only 24 hours each week on his carpentry work. He must make at least two of each size each week. How many of each size should Joe make each week to obtain the maximum weekly profit? What is the maximum weekly profit?

88. A company manufactures two types of clocks, Model 82 and Model 47. There are three stations, *A*, *B*, and *C*, on the assembly line. The assembly of one Model 82 requires 30 minutes at station *A*, 20 minutes at station *B*, and 12 minutes at station *C*. Model 47 requires 15 minutes at station *A*, 30 minutes at station *B*, and 10 minutes at station *C*. Station *A* can be operated for no more than 4 hours a day, station *B* can be operated for no more than 6 hours, and station *C* can be operated for no more than 8 hours. If the profit on each Model 82 is \$10 and on Model 47 is \$6, how many of each model should be assembled each day to provide maximum profit? What is the maximum daily profit?

Chapter Test

State the relation represented by each of the following, given that x is an integer.

1. $y = 3x - 1$ and $^-3 < x \leq 2$
2. $|y| = 2x + 5$ and $0 \leq x \leq 4$

3-4. State whether each relation in problems **1-2** is a function. Write *yes* or *no*.

Given $f(x) = x - 3x^2$, find each value.

5. $f(0)$
6. $f(4)$
7. $f(13)$
8. $f(7.1)$

Write each equation in standard form.

9. $2x = 5$
10. $y = 0.2x + 0.4$
11. $3x = x - 2y$

Find the zero of each function.

12. $f(x) = 5x + 8$
13. $f(x) = 25$
14. $f(x) = 0.3 + 2x$

Solve each system of equations by graphing.

15. $x - 4 = y$; $y = 2x - 8$
16. $x + 5 = y$; $3x = y - 1$
17. $y - 3x = 8$; $x + y = 4$

Find the distance between the given points.

18. $(^-1, 2), (3, 1)$
19. $(5, 11), (12, 12)$
20. $(3k, k + 1), (2k, k - 1)$

21-23. Find the slope of the line passing through each pair of points in problems **18-20**.

Write the slope-intercept form of the line through the given point with the given slope.

24. $(0, 0), \frac{3}{8}$
25. $(2, 7), -\frac{1}{2}$
26. $(^-1, 3), \frac{5}{3}$

Write the slope-intercept form of the line through the given points.

27. $(5, 1), (8, 10)$
28. $(6, ^-4), (1, 2)$
29. $(0, 4), (8, ^-2)$

Solve the following systems by graphing. Then name the vertices of each polygonal convex set.

30. $y \geq 0$, $x \geq 1$, $x + y \leq 6$, $y + 3x \leq 12$
31. $y \leq 5$, $y + 2x \geq 0$, $x \leq 3$, $y \geq x - 2$

Given $f(x, y) = 5x - 2y$, find each value.

32. $f(3, 0)$
33. $f(4, 2)$
34. $f(1.5, 4)$
35. $f(5, 3.2)$

36-37. Find the maximum and minimum values of $f(x, y) = 5y + 3x$ for each polygonal convex set in problems **30-31**.

Solve the following problem.

38. A toy manufacturer produces two types of models space ships, the Voyager and the Explorer. Each of the toys requires the same three operations, plastic molding, machining, and bench assembly. Each Voyager requires 5 minutes for molding, 3 minutes for machining, and 5 minutes for assembly. Each Explorer requires 6 minutes for molding, 2 minutes for machining, and 18 minutes for assembly. The manufacturer can afford a daily schedule of not more than 4 hours for molding, 2 hours for machining, and 9 hours for assembly. If the profit is \$2.40 on each Voyager and \$5.00 on each Explorer, how many of each toy should be produced for maximum profit? What is the maximum daily profit?

Chapter 2

Theory of Equations

The graph of a polynomial equation is a smooth curve. The design of this curved bridge is based upon many complicated polynomial equations. In this chapter you will learn more about polynomial equations and their graphs.

2-1 Polynomial Equations

A **polynomial** in one variable, x, is an expression of the form $a_0x^n + a_1x^{n-1} + \cdots + a_{n-1}x + a_n$. The coefficients $a_0, a_1, \cdots, a_n$ are real numbers, and n is a nonnegative integer. The **degree** of a polynomial in one variable is n, the greatest exponent of its variable.

The terms of a polynomial are usually written in order of decreasing degree.

A **linear expression** such as $4x - 7$ is a first degree polynomial. A second degree polynomial, such as $5x^2 + 6x - 3$ is called a **quadratic expression.**

Third, fourth, and fifth degree expressions are called cubic, quartic, and quintic, respectively.

example

1 **Which of the following expressions are polynomials in one variable?**

a. $b^2 + 2a^2 + 2b$
b. $y^3 - y + 4y^4 - 3y^3$
c. $x^2 + \frac{3}{x} + 7$

a. $b^2 + 2a^2 + 2b$ is not a polynomial in one variable. *There are two variables.*
b. $y^3 - y + 4y^4 - 3y^3$ is a polynomial in one variable.
c. $x^2 + \frac{3}{x} + 7$ is not a polynomial in one variable. *$\frac{3}{x}$ cannot be written in the form x^n, where n is a nonnegative integer.*

If a polynomial is equal to zero, the equation is called a polynomial equation. Thus, if $P(x)$ represents a polynomial, $P(x) = 0$ is a **polynomial equation.** A **root** of the equation is a value of x for which the value of $P(x)$ is zero. Thus, 5 is a root of the equation $x^2 - 6x + 5 = 0$, since $(5)^2 - 6(5) + 5 = 0$. A root is also called a solution.

A root of $P(x) = 0$ is a zero of $P(x)$.

examples

2 **Is 6 a root of $x^3 - 5x^2 - 3x - 18 = 0$?**

$$\begin{aligned} P(6) &= 6^3 - 5(6)^2 - 3(6) - 18 \\ &= 216 - 180 - 18 - 18 \\ &= 0 \end{aligned}$$

Thus, 6 is a root of the equation.

3 **Is $^-2$ a root of $x^4 - 3x^2 - 2x + 4 = 0$?**

$$\begin{aligned} P(^-2) &= (^-2)^4 - 3(^-2)^2 - 2(^-2) + 4 \\ &= 16 - 12 + 4 + 4 \\ &= 12 \end{aligned}$$

$$P(^-2) \neq 0$$

Thus, $^-2$ is not a root of the equation.

To solve an equation means to find the roots of the equation. Some polynomial equations can be solved by factoring. If the product of two or more factors is zero, at least one of the factors must be zero. Study the following examples.

examples

4 **Solve $x^2 - 4x - 21 = 0$.**

$x^2 - 4x - 21 = 0$

$(x - 7)(x + 3) = 0$ *If $ab = 0$, either $a = 0$ or $b = 0$.*

$x - 7 = 0$ or $x + 3 = 0$

$x = 7$ or $x = {}^-3$

The roots are 7 and $^-3$.

5 **Solve $(x - 4)(x + 9)(2x + 7) = 0$**

$(x - 4)(x + 9)(2x + 7) = 0$

$x - 4 = 0$, $x + 9 = 0$, or $2x + 7 = 0$

$x = 4$, $x = {}^-9$, or $x = -\frac{7}{2}$

The roots are 4, $^-9$, and $-\frac{7}{2}$.

exercises

Exploratory Which of the following expressions are polynomials in one variable?

1. $5x + xy + y$
2. $a^3 + 2a + \sqrt{3}$
3. $\frac{1}{c} + c^2$
4. $\frac{1}{x} = \frac{1}{2x}$
5. $2m^3 + 5m^2 + 9$
6. $5a + 4b + 2c$
7. $x^4 - 3x^3 + x - \sqrt{7}$
8. $y\sqrt{2} + y$

Which of the following are roots of $x^4 - 4x^3 - x^2 + 4x = 0$?

9. 2
10. 0
11. $^-1$
12. $^-2$
13. 4
14. $^-4$
15. 3
16. 1

Written Solve each equation.

1. $x - 2 = 0$
2. $2a + 4 = 0$
3. $x^2 - 4 = 0$
4. $t^2 - t = 0$
5. $z^2 - z - 2 = 0$
6. $(s - 2)(s - 5) = 0$
7. $(u + 2)(u^2 - 4) = 0$
8. $(2q - 3)(3q - 2) = 0$
9. $(x - 1)(x - 2)(x - 3)(x - 4) = 0$
10. $x^2 - x - 6 = 0$
11. $r^2 - 18r + 81 = 0$
12. $6c^2 - 3c - 45 = 0$
13. $y^2 - 9 = 0$
14. $6m^2 - 39m + 45 = 0$
15. $14y^2 + 19y - 3 = 0$
16. $6y^2 + y - 2 = 0$
17. $20x^2 - 73x + 63 = 0$
18. $2x^2 + x - 6 = 0$
19. $18x^2 + 3x - 1 = 0$
20. $n^3 - 9n = 0$
21. $12x^2 + 8x - 15 = 0$
22. $6m^2 + 7m - 3 = 0$
23. $16b^2 - 121 = 0$
24. $18x^3 - 34x^2 + 16x = 0$

2-2 Quadratic Equations and Imaginary Roots

Any **quadratic equation** can be written in the form $ax^2 + bx + c = 0$, when a, b, and c are real numbers and $a \neq 0$. Many quadratic equations can be solved by factoring. If the factors of a quadratic equation are difficult to determine, other methods can be used to solve the equation.

If an equation can be written as a perfect square equal to a constant, it can be solved by using square roots. For example, the equation $(x + 3)^2 = 5$ can be solved as follows.

$(x + 3)^2 = 5$ — *The quadratic form of this equation is* $x^2 + 6x + 4 = 0$.

$x + 3 = \pm\sqrt{5}$ — *Why is the symbol ± necessary?*

$x = {}^-3 \pm \sqrt{5}$ — *The roots are* ${}^-3 + \sqrt{5}$ *and* ${}^-3 - \sqrt{5}$.

A method called **completing the square** is based on this concept. For any real number b, the perfect square of a binomial $(x + b)$ has the form $x^2 + 2bx + b^2$. Notice that the constant term is equal to the square of half the coefficient of the middle term. The following example shows how to solve a quadratic equation by completing the square.

example

1 **Solve $3x^2 - 14x + 8 = 0$**

Divide each side by 3 so that the leading coefficient is 1.

$$x^2 - \frac{14}{3}x + \frac{8}{3} = 0$$

$$x^2 - \frac{14}{3}x = -\frac{8}{3}$$ *Subtract $\frac{8}{3}$ from each side.*

$$x^2 - \frac{14}{3}x + \frac{49}{9} = -\frac{8}{3} + \frac{49}{9}$$ *Add $\left(-\frac{14}{3} \div 2\right)^2$ or $\frac{49}{9}$ to each side.*

$$\left(x - \frac{7}{3}\right)^2 = \frac{25}{9}$$ *Factor.*

$$x - \frac{7}{3} = \pm\frac{5}{3}$$ *Take the square root of each side.*

$$x = 4 \text{ or } \frac{2}{3}$$ *Solve for x.*

The roots are 4 and $\frac{2}{3}$.

Completing the square can be used to develop a general formula for solving equations of the form $ax^2 + bx + c = 0$. The formula is called the **quadratic formula** and can be used to find the roots of any quadratic equation.

The roots of a quadratic equation of the form $ax^2 + bx + c = 0$ are given by the following formula.

$$x = \frac{{}^-b \pm \sqrt{b^2 - 4ac}}{2a}$$

Quadratic Formula

example

2 **Solve $6x^2 + 7x + 2 = 0$ using the quadratic formula.**

$$x = \frac{^-b \pm \sqrt{b^2 - 4ac}}{2a} \qquad a = 6, b = 7, c = 2$$

$$x = \frac{^-7 \pm \sqrt{7^2 - 4(6)(2)}}{2(6)}$$

$$x = \frac{^-7 \pm \sqrt{1}}{12}$$

$$x = \frac{^-7 \pm 1}{12} \qquad \frac{^-7 + 1}{12} = -\frac{1}{2} \text{ and } \frac{^-7 - 1}{12} = -\frac{2}{3}$$

The roots are $-\frac{1}{2}$ and $-\frac{2}{3}$.

Many equations have roots which are not real numbers. Consider the following example.

example

3 **Solve $x^2 - 6x + 13 = 0$**

$$x = \frac{^-b \pm \sqrt{b^2 - 4ac}}{2a} \qquad a = 1, b = {^-6}, c = 13$$

$$x = \frac{6 \pm \sqrt{36 - 52}}{2}$$

$$x = \frac{6 \pm \sqrt{^-16}}{2}$$

$$x = 3 \pm 2\sqrt{^-1} \qquad \textit{There is no real number whose square is } {^-1}.$$

The square root of a negative number is an **imaginary number.** Imaginary numbers can be represented by using the number i, which is called the **imaginary unit.** The imaginary unit i is defined by $i^2 = {^-1}$. For example, the imaginary numbers $\sqrt{^-11}$ and $\sqrt{^-36}$ can be represented as $i\sqrt{11}$ and $6i$, respectively.

Numbers such as $3 + 2i$ and $4 - i\sqrt{3}$ are complex numbers. A **complex number** is any number that can be written in the form $a + bi$, where a and b are real numbers and i is the imaginary unit. A complex number is real when $b = 0$ and imaginary when $b \neq 0$.

The roots of the equation in the above example are complex numbers, $3 + 2i$ and $3 - 2i$. Complex numbers of the form $a + bi$ and $a - bi$ are called **conjugates** of each other.

In general, the roots of a quadratic equation are imaginary if the value of the **discriminant,** $b^2 - 4ac$, is negative. Such roots always occur as conjugate pairs as an inspection of the formula $x = \frac{^-b \pm \sqrt{b^2 - 4ac}}{2a}$ will show, providing a, b, and c are real numbers. Imaginary roots also occur in pairs for higher degree polynomial equations.

> Suppose a and b are real numbers with $b \neq 0$. Then, if $a + bi$ is a root of a polynomial equation, $a - bi$ is also a root of the equation.

Complex Conjugates Theorem

exercises

Exploratory Name the conjugate of each complex number.

1. i
2. $3 + i$
3. $5 - 2i$
4. ^-2i
5. $-\frac{1}{2} + \frac{1}{2}i$
6. $^-4 + 2i$
7. $5 - i\sqrt{2}$
8. $^-7 - i\sqrt{5}$

Find the value of c that makes each trinomial a perfect square.

9. $x^2 + 4x + c$
10. $x^2 - 8x + c$
11. $p^2 - p + c$
12. $y^2 + \frac{3}{2}y + c$
13. $z^2 + \frac{4}{3}z + c$
14. $y^2 - 25y + c$
15. $n^2 - 30n + c$
16. $r^2 + 50r + c$
17. $x^2 - \frac{1}{4}x + c$
18. $a^2 + 11a + c$
19. $x^2 - \frac{4}{7}x + c$
20. $m^2 - 3m + c$

Written Solve each equation by completing the square.

1. $y^2 - 3y - 88 = 0$
2. $z^2 - 2z = 24$
3. $x^2 + 8x - 20 = 0$
4. $x^2 + 2x - 48 = 0$
5. $x^2 - \frac{3}{4}x + \frac{1}{8} = 0$
6. $6m^2 + 7m - 3 = 0$
7. $2y^2 + 11y - 21 = 0$
8. $4x^2 + 19x - 5 = 0$
9. $x^2 - 3x - 7 = 0$
10. $r^2 + 5r - 8 = 0$
11. $3x^2 - 12x + 4 = 0$
12. $6s^2 + 2s - 3 = 0$

Solve each equation using the quadratic formula. The roots may be real or complex.

13. $3x^2 - 7x - 20 = 0$
14. $r^2 + 13r + 42 = 0$
15. $4x^2 - 9x + 5 = 0$
16. $12x^2 - 7x - 12 = 0$
17. $7n^2 + 20n - 32 = 0$
18. $5m^2 + 7m + 3 = 0$
19. $6y^2 - 5y - 6 = 0$
20. $2z^2 + 2z + 3 = 0$
21. $2x^2 + 3x + 3 = 0$
22. $8r^2 + 6r + 1 = 0$
23. $6y^2 + 8y + 5 = 0$
24. $x^2 - 7x + 5 = 0$
25. $3x^2 + 7x + 4 = 0$
26. $15a^2 - 10a + 1 = 0$
27. $4b^2 + b - 6 = 0$
28. $r^2 - 4r + 10 = 0$
29. $5x^2 - 2x + 8 = 0$
30. $3k^2 + 3k + 2 = 0$

Challenge Derive the quadratic formula. (Hint: Solve the equation $ax^2 + bx + c = 0$ by completing the square.)

2-3 Synthetic Division

Synthetic division is a shortcut for dividing a polynomial by a binomial of the form $x - r$. This procedure is helpful when factoring polynomials. To divide $x^3 + 3x^2 - 2x - 8$ by $x + 2$, follow the steps below.

Step 1 Arrange the terms of the polynomial in descending order. Then write the coefficients as shown.

$$\begin{array}{cccc} x^3 & + 3x^2 & - 2x & - 8 \\ 1 & 3 & ^{-}2 & ^{-}8 \end{array}$$

The coefficient of x^3 is 1.

Step 2 Write the constant r of the divisor $x - r$ to the left. For the divisor $x + 2$, r is $^{-}2$.

$$\begin{array}{r|rrrr} ^{-}2 & 1 & 3 & ^{-}2 & ^{-}8 \end{array}$$

Step 3 Bring down the first coefficient.

$$\begin{array}{r|rrrr} ^{-}2 & 1 & 3 & ^{-}2 & ^{-}8 \\ & & & & \\ \hline & 1 & & & \end{array}$$

Step 4 Multiply the first coefficient by r. Then write the product under the second coefficient. Add.

$$\begin{array}{r|rrrr} ^{-}2 & 1 & 3 & ^{-}2 & ^{-}8 \\ & & ^{-}2 & & \\ \hline & 1 & 1 & & \end{array}$$

Step 5 Multiply the sum by r. Then write the product under the next coefficient. Add.

$$\begin{array}{r|rrr|r} ^{-}2 & 1 & 3 & ^{-}2 & ^{-}8 \\ & & ^{-}2 & ^{-}2 & \\ \hline & 1 & 1 & ^{-}4 & \end{array}$$

Step 6 Repeat step 5 until all coefficients in the dividend have been used.

$$\begin{array}{r|rrr|r} ^{-}2 & 1 & 3 & ^{-}2 & ^{-}8 \\ & & ^{-}2 & ^{-}2 & 8 \\ \hline & 1 & 1 & ^{-}4 & 0 \end{array}$$

Step 7 Write the quotient and remainder. The last sum represents the remainder. The other sums are the coefficients of the quotient.

$$x^2 + x - 4$$

The remainder is zero.

Compare the long division process to the synthetic division process.

$$\begin{array}{r} x^2 + x - 4 \\ x + 2 \overline{) x^3 + 3x^2 - 2x - 8} \\ \underline{x^3 + 2x^2} \qquad\qquad \\ x^2 - 2x \qquad \\ \underline{x^2 + 2x} \qquad \\ ^{-}4x - 8 \\ \underline{^{-}4x - 8} \\ 0 \end{array}$$

$$\begin{array}{r|rrr|r} ^{-}2 & 1 & 3 & ^{-}2 & ^{-}8 \\ & & ^{-}2 & ^{-}2 & 8 \\ \hline & 1 & 1 & ^{-}4 & 0 \end{array}$$

A vertical bar separates the quotient from the remainder.

Because the remainder is zero, $x + 2$ is a factor of $x^3 + 3x^2 - 2x - 8$.

examples

1 **Use synthetic division to divide $x^3 - 2x - 18$ by $x - 3$.**

$$\begin{array}{r|rrrr} 3 & 1 & 0 & ^-2 & ^-18 \\ & & 3 & 9 & 21 \\ \hline & 1 & 3 & 7 & 3 \end{array}$$

Notice that there is no x^2 term. Therefore a zero is placed in the x^2 position.

The quotient is $x^2 + 3x + 7$ and the remainder is 3.

2 **Use synthetic division to divide $x^5 - 3x^2 - 20$ by $x - 2$.**

$$\begin{array}{r|rrrrrr} 2 & 1 & 0 & 0 & ^-3 & 0 & ^-20 \\ & & 2 & 4 & 8 & 10 & 20 \\ \hline & 1 & 2 & 4 & 5 & 10 & 0 \end{array}$$

What does each zero represent?

The quotient is $x^4 + 2x^3 + 4x^2 + 5x + 10$.

A combined and shortened form of synthetic division is shown below for binomial divisors of $x^3 - 4x^2 - 7x + 10$. The value of r in $x - r$ is shown at the left, and beside it is the last line of the synthetic division procedure. The last numeral in each row is the remainder. Notice how this procedure can be used to determine factors of a polynomial.

r	1	⁻4	⁻7	10	
1	1	⁻3	⁻10	0	*$x - 1$ is a factor*
2	1	⁻2	⁻11	⁻12	
3	1	⁻1	⁻10	⁻20	
4	1	0	⁻7	⁻18	
5	1	1	⁻2	0	*$x - 5$ is a factor*
⁻1	1	⁻5	⁻2	12	
⁻2	1	⁻6	5	0	*$x - {}^-2$, or $x + 2$ is a factor*

example

3 **Use synthetic division to determine the binomial factors of $x^3 + 2x^2 - 16x - 32$. Test all integral values of r from ⁻4 to 4.**

r	1	2	⁻16	⁻32	
⁻4	1	⁻2	⁻8	0	*$x + 4$ is a factor*
⁻3	1	⁻1	⁻13	7	
⁻2	1	0	⁻16	0	*$x + 2$ is a factor*
⁻1	1	1	⁻17	⁻15	
0	1	2	⁻16	⁻32	
1	1	3	⁻13	⁻45	
2	1	4	⁻8	⁻48	
3	1	5	⁻1	⁻35	
4	1	6	8	0	*$x - 4$ is a factor*

Thus, $x + 4$, $x + 2$, and $x - 4$ are binomial factors of $x^3 + 2x^2 - 16x - 32$.

exercises

Exploratory For each synthetic division shown, state the divisor, dividend, quotient, and remainder.

1. $$\begin{array}{r|rrrr} 2 & 3 & 0 & ^{-}5 & 10 \\ & & 6 & 12 & 14 \\ \hline & 3 & 6 & 7 & \vert\, 24 \end{array}$$

2. $$\begin{array}{r|rrrr} ^{-}3 & 1 & 3 & ^{-}4 & 1 \\ & & ^{-}3 & 0 & 12 \\ \hline & 1 & 0 & ^{-}4 & \vert\, 13 \end{array}$$

3. $$\begin{array}{r|rrrr} ^{-}3 & 1 & 0 & ^{-}11 & 10 \\ & & ^{-}3 & 9 & 6 \\ \hline & 1 & ^{-}3 & 2 & \vert\, 16 \end{array}$$

4. $$\begin{array}{r|rrrr} 2 & 1 & 6 & 3 & ^{-}38 \\ & & 2 & 16 & 38 \\ \hline & 1 & 8 & 19 & \vert\, 0 \end{array}$$

5. $$\begin{array}{r|rrrr} ^{-}1 & 2 & 0 & ^{-}5 & 1 \\ & & ^{-}2 & 2 & 3 \\ \hline & 2 & ^{-}2 & ^{-}3 & \vert\, 4 \end{array}$$

6. $$\begin{array}{r|rrrr} 5 & 1 & 2 & ^{-}35 & 4 \\ & & 5 & 35 & 0 \\ \hline & 1 & 7 & 0 & \vert\, 4 \end{array}$$

7. $$\begin{array}{r|rrrr} \frac{1}{2} & 1 & \frac{3}{2} & 3 & ^{-}2 \\ & & \frac{1}{2} & 1 & 2 \\ \hline & 1 & 2 & 4 & \vert\, 0 \end{array}$$

8. $$\begin{array}{r|rrrr} -\frac{3}{4} & 2 & \frac{1}{2} & \frac{1}{4} & -\frac{1}{4} \\ & & -\frac{3}{2} & \frac{3}{4} & -\frac{3}{4} \\ \hline & 2 & ^{-}1 & 1 & \vert\, ^{-}1 \end{array}$$

Written Divide using synthetic division.

1. $(x^2 + 8x + 12) \div (x + 2)$
2. $(x^2 - x - 56) \div (x + 7)$
3. $(x^3 + 2x + 3) \div (x - 2)$
4. $(x^2 - x + 4) \div (x - 2)$
5. $(x^4 - 8x^2 + 16) \div (x + 2)$
6. $(x^3 + x^2 - 17x + 15) \div (x + 5)$
7. $(x^3 - x^2 + 2) \div (x + 1)$
8. $(x^4 + x^3 - 1) \div (x - 2)$
9. $(x^3 + 6x^2 + 12x + 12) \div (x + 2)$
10. $(x^3 - 9x^2 + 27x - 28) \div (x - 3)$
11. $(2x^3 - 2x - 3) \div (x - 1)$
12. $(x^2 + 20x + 91) \div (x + 7)$
13. $(8x^2 - 4x + 11) \div (x + 5)$
14. $(3x^4 - 2x^3 + 5x^2 - 4x - 2) \div (x + 1)$

Find the remainder for each of the following. Is the divisor a factor of the polynomial?

15. $(x^3 - 3x + 2) \div (x + 1)$
16. $(x^3 - 30x) \div (x + 5)$
17. $(x^4 - 2x^2 - 8) \div (x - 3)$
18. $(x^4 - 6x^2 + 8) \div (x - \sqrt{2})$
19. $(x^4 - 36) \div (x - \sqrt{6})$
20. $(5x^2 - 2x + 6) \div \left(x - \frac{2}{5}\right)$
21. $(12x^2 + 19x + 4) \div \left(x + \frac{4}{3}\right)$
22. $(x^5 + 32) \div (x + 2)$
23. $(x^5 - 6x^3 + 4x^2 - 3) \div (x - 2)$
24. $(3x^2 - 7x + 5) \div \left(x - \frac{7}{3}\right)$

Challenge Divide using synthetic division. (Hint: First transform the problem so that the divisor has the form $x - r$.)

1. $(4y^4 - 5y^2 - 8y + 3) \div (2y - 3)$
2. $(6x^3 - 28x^2 + 19x + 3) \div (3x - 2)$
3. $(2b^3 - 3b^2 - 8b + 4) \div (2b + 1)$
4. $(3a^4 - 2a^3 + 5a^2 - 4a - 2) \div (3a + 1)$
5. $(4x^3 - 4x^2 - 17x - 3) \div (4x + 6)$
6. $(10x^3 + x^2 - 7x + 2) \div (5x - 2)$

The length of the nail shown at the right, to the nearest centimeter, is 3 cm. This measurement has a **maximum possible error** of 0.5 cm. The length of the nail, to the nearest millimeter, is 32 mm or 3.2 cm, and the maximum possible error is 0.5 mm or 0.05 cm.

Since the maximum possible error for the second measurement is less, the second measurement is more precise. **Precision** is the degree of exactness with which a quantity is measured.

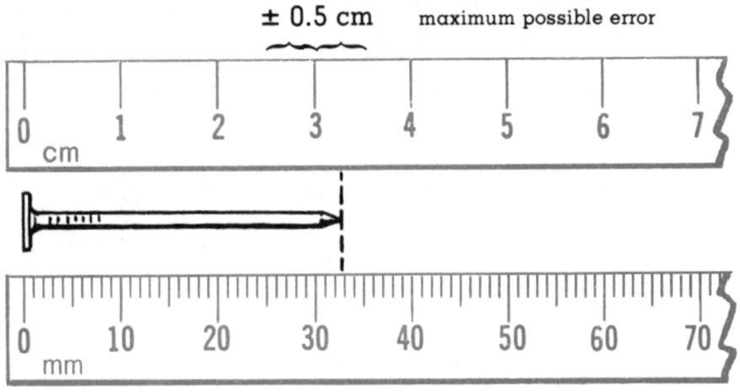

Smaller units of measure produce more precise measurements.

The **error** of a measurement is the difference between the accepted length and the measured length. Suppose the accepted length of the nail is 3.24 cm. The first measurement has an error of 0.24 cm and the second measurement has an error of 0.04 cm.

The **accuracy,** or correctness, of a measurement can be defined by a percent of error. The percent of error is equal to the ratio of the error to the accepted length, expressed as a percent.

The ratio of the error to the accepted length is the relative error.

Example Find the percent of error for a measurement of 7.4 cm if the accepted length is 7.43 cm. Round to the nearest tenth.

$$\frac{\textit{accepted length} - \textit{measured length}}{\textit{accepted length}} = \frac{7.43 - 7.4}{7.43}$$
$$= \frac{0.03}{7.43}$$
$$= 0.4\%$$

The percent of error is 0.4%.

Exercises Find the maximum possible error for each measurement. Then name the measurement that is more precise.

1. 8.3 m 8.34 m
2. 0.261 cm 0.3 cm
3. 206,000 mi 210,000 mi
4. 5280 mi 5300 mi
5. 204 m 204.1 m
6. 4 yd 13 ft

Find the percent of error, to the nearest tenth, for each measurement. The accepted length is given in parentheses.

7. 8 cm (8.5 cm)
8. 2 mm (2.4 mm)
9. 4.1 m (4.06 m)
10. 5.3 m (525 cm)
11. $5\frac{1}{2}$ yd (202 in.)
12. $6\frac{1}{4}$ in. $\left(6\frac{1}{3}\text{ in.}\right)$

2-4 The Remainder and Factor Theorems

Assume $P(x)$ is any polynomial of degree n in x, and let $(x - r)$ be a divisor. The quotient, $Q(x)$, will be of degree $n - 1$, and the remainder, R, will be a real number since the divisor is of the first degree. The relationship between the dividend, divisor, quotient, and remainder can be expressed as follows.

$$P(x) = (x - r) \cdot Q(x) + R$$

Notice the result when r is substituted for x in the equation.

$$P(r) = (r - r) \cdot Q(x) + R$$
$$P(r) = R$$

This result is called the **Remainder Theorem.**

If a polynomial $P(x)$ is divided by $x - r$, the remainder is a constant, $P(r)$, and

$$P(x) = (x - r) \cdot Q(x) + P(r)$$

where $Q(x)$ is a polynomial with degree one less than the degree of $P(x)$.

The Remainder Theorem

examples

1 **Let $P(x) = x^3 - 7x - 4$. Show that $P(^-1)$ is the remainder when $P(x)$ is divided by $x + 1$.**

Divide using synthetic division.

$^-1$	1	0	$^-7$	$^-4$
		$^-1$	1	6
	1	$^-1$	$^-6$	2

The remainder is 2.

Evaluate $P(^-1)$.

$P(^-1) = (^-1)^3 - 7(^-1) - 4$

$= 2$ *The result is the same as the remainder.*

2 **Use the Remainder Theorem to find the remainder when $x^3 + 8x + 1$ is divided by $x - 2$.**

Let $f(x) = x^3 + 8x + 1$.

$f(2) = 2^3 + (8)2 + 1$

$= 25$

The remainder is 25. *You can check this by synthetic division.*

If the remainder is zero when $P(x)$ is divided by $x - r$, then $x - r$ is a factor of $P(x)$. A corollary to the Remainder Theorem, called the **Factor Theorem,** can be used to identify factors of a polynomial.

The binomial $x - r$ is a factor of the polynomial $P(x)$ if and only if $P(r) = 0$.

The Factor Theorem

examples

3 Is $x - 5$ a factor of $x^3 - 4x^2 - 7x + 10$?

$P(x) = x^3 - 4x^2 - 7x + 10$
$P(5) = 5^3 - 4(5)^2 - 7(5) + 10$
$P(5) = 0$

Since $P(5) = 0$, $x - 5$ is a factor.

4 Is $x + 1$ a factor of $x^3 - 4x^2 - 3x + 12$?

$P(^-1) = (^-1)^3 - 4(^-1)^2 - 3(^-1) + 12$
$P(^-1) = 10$

Since $P(^-1) = 10$, $x + 1$ is not a factor.

For some polynomials, factors can be tested more quickly by using synthetic division instead of substitution.

A calculator can be used to evaluate polynomials quickly.

exercises

Exploratory Find the value of $P(3)$ for each of the following polynomials.

1. $P(x) = x^2 - 6x + 9$
2. $P(x) = x^2 + 2x - 15$
3. $P(x) = x^2 - 5x + 6$
4. $P(x) = x^4 + x^2 - 2$

5-8. State whether $(x - 3)$ is a factor of each polynomial in problems 1-4. Write *yes* or *no*.

Written Use the Remainder Theorem to find the remainder when the given polynomial is divided by the given binomial.

1. $(x^2 - 2) \div (x - 1)$
2. $(x^2 + 1) \div (x + 1)$
3. $(x^2 + x - 1) \div (x - 3)$
4. $(x^2 + 5x - 2) \div (x + 5)$
5. $(x^2 - 2x - 63) \div (x + 7)$
6. $(2x^2 - x + 3) \div (x - 3)$
7. $(x^3 - x + 6) \div (x - 2)$
8. $(2x^3 - 3x^2 + x) \div (x - 1)$
9. $(x^4 + x^2 + 2) \div (x - 3)$
10. $(2x^4 - x^3 + 1) \div (x + 3)$

11-20. State whether the given binomial is a factor of the polynomial for problems 1-10.

Find values of k so that each remainder is zero.

21. $(x^2 + 8x + k) \div (x - 2)$
22. $(x^3 + 8x^2 + kx + 4) \div (x + 2)$
23. $(x^2 + kx + 3) \div (x - 1)$
24. $(x^3 + 4x^2 - kx + 1) \div (x + 1)$

Challenge Solve each problem.

1. Find $P(x)$ of the form $P(x) = ax^2 + bx + c$ if $P(3 + 4i) = 0$ and $P(3 - 4i) = 0$.
2. Find $P(x)$ of the form $P(x) = ax^3 + bx^2 + cx + d$ if $P(3) = 0$, $P(^-2) = 0$, and $P(2) = 0$.

2-5 The Fundamental Theorem of Algebra

An important theorem concerning roots of polynomial equations is the **Fundamental Theorem of Algebra.**

> Every polynomial equation with degree greater than zero has at least one root in the set of complex numbers.

The Fundamental Theorem of Algebra

Karl Friedrich Gauss (1777-1855) is credited with the first proof of the Fundamental Theorem.

The Fundamental Theorem of Algebra has an important corollary which can be derived using the Factor Theorem.

> Every polynomial $P(x)$ of degree n can be transformed into the product of n linear factors. That is, $P(x)$ of degree n equals $k(x - r_1)(x - r_2)(x - r_3) \cdots (x - r_n)$. Thus a polynomial equation of the form $P(x) = 0$ of degree n has exactly n roots, namely, $r_1, r_2, r_3, \cdots r_n$.

Corollary

For example, the equation $x^3 - 2x^2 - 8x - 3 = 0$ has three roots. Since it can be written as $(x - 4)(x + 1)(x + 1) = 0$, the roots are $^-1$, $^-1$, and 4. Notice that r is a root of $P(x) = 0$ if and only if $x - r$ is a factor of $P(x)$.

examples

1 Find the roots of $x^3 - 2x^2 - 5x + 6 = 0$.

First, write the polynomial as a product of linear factors.

Synthetic division can be used to find one or more factors.

r	1	$^-2$	$^-5$	6
1	1	$^-1$	$^-6$	0

$x - 1$ is a factor

$x^2 - x - 6$

The product of the remaining factors is $x^2 - x - 6$, which is equal to $(x + 2)(x - 3)$. Thus, $x^3 - 2x^2 - 5x + 6 = (x - 1)(x + 2)(x - 3)$.

Since $(x - 1)(x + 2)(x - 3) = 0$, the roots are 1, $^-2$, and 3.

2 Find the roots of $2x^3 + 2x^2 + 8x + 8 = 0$. (Hint: $x + 1$ is one factor of the polynomial.)

$2x^3 + 2x^2 + 8x + 8 = 0$

$2(x^3 + x^2 + 4x + 4) = 0$ — *Each term has a factor of 2.*

$2(x + 1)(x^2 + 4) = 0$ — *Factor $x + 1$ from the polynomial.*

$2(x + 1)(x - 2i)(x + 2i) = 0$ — *The quadratic formula can be used to factor $x^2 + 4$.*

The roots of $2x^3 + 2x^2 + 8x + 8 = 0$ are $^-1$, $2i$, and ^-2i.

The roots of an equation $P(x) = 0$ are not necessarily unique. If $x - r$ occurs as a factor of $P(x)$ more than once, r is a **multiple root** of $P(x) = 0$.

A root which is not a multiple root is called a simple root.

example

3 **The equation $x^5 - 15x^3 - 10x^2 + 60x + 72 = 0$ has multiple roots $^{-}2$ and 3. Determine how many times each root occurs.**

Use synthetic division to write the equation as a product of linear factors.

r	1	0	$^{-}15$	$^{-}10$	60	72
3	1	3	$^{-}6$	$^{-}28$	$^{-}24$	0
3	1	6	12	8	0	
$^{-}2$	1	4	4	0		
$^{-}2$	1	2	0			
$^{-}2$	1	0				

Notice the arrangement of successive synthetic divisions.

The equation $x^5 - 15x^3 - 10x^2 + 60x + 72 = 0$ can be written as follows.
$(x - 3)(x - 3)(x + 2)(x + 2)(x + 2) = 0$

Thus, 3 is a double root and $^{-}2$ is a triple root.

If all the roots of a polynomial equation are known, the equation can be written, as shown in the example below.

examples

4 **Write the simplest equation with 2 as a simple root and $3i$ as another root. Express the answer as a polynomial equation with integral coefficients.**

Since imaginary roots occur in pairs, $^{-}3i$ is also a root. Therefore $x - 2$, $x - 3i$, and $x + 3i$ are the linear factors of the polynomial. Find the product of the linear factors.

$$\begin{aligned}(x - 3i)(x + 3i)(x - 2) &= (x^2 - 9i^2)(x - 2)\\ &= (x^2 + 9)(x - 2)\\ &= x^3 - 2x^2 + 9x - 18\end{aligned}$$

Remember that $i^2 = {}^{-}1$.

Thus, the simplest equation with roots 2, $3i$, and $^{-}3i$ is $x^3 - 2x^2 + 9x - 18 = 0$.

5 **Write the simplest equation with roots $^{-}4$, 2, and i.**

The linear factors are $x + 4$, $x - 2$, $x - i$, and $x + i$.
$(x + 4)(x - 2)(x - i)(x + i) = 0$
$(x^2 + 2x - 8)(x^2 + 1) = 0$
$(x^4 + 2x^3 - 7x^2 + 2x - 8) = 0$

The simplest equation with roots $^{-}4$, 2, and i is $x^4 + 2x^3 - 7x^2 + 2x - 8 = 0$.

exercises

Exploratory State the number of roots of each equation.

1. $2x^2 - x = 0$
2. $x^2 + 3x + 2 = 0$
3. $2x^2 + 3x - 20 = 0$
4. $5x^2 - 14x + 8 = 0$
5. $6x^2 + 7x - 3 = 0$
6. $x^3 - 3x^2 + x + 1 = 0$
7. $2x^3 - 3x^2 - 11x + 6 = 0$
8. $x^4 - 10x^2 + 9 = 0$
9. $6x^3 + 37x^2 + 32x - 15 = 0$
10. $x^3 - 6x^2 + 11x - 6 = 0$
11. $x^3 + x^2 - 4x - 4 = 0$
12. $x^3 + 2x^2 - x - 2 = 0$
13. $2x^3 - 11x^2 + 12x + 9 = 0$
14. $x^3 - 3x^2 - 53x - 9 = 0$

Written

1-14. Find the roots of each equation in the exploratory exercises.

Determine how many times 2 is a root of each equation.

15. $x^4 - 5x^2 + 4 = 0$
16. $x^2 + 8x - 20 = 0$
17. $x^4 - 8x^2 + 16 = 0$
18. $x^6 - 9x^4 + 24x^2 - 16 = 0$

Determine how many times $^-1$ is a root of each equation.

19. $x^4 + 8x^3 + 22x^2 + 24x + 9 = 0$
20. $x^4 - 5x^3 + 9x^2 - 7x + 2 = 0$
21. $x^3 - x^2 - 5x - 3 = 0$
22. $x^3 + 2x^2 - x - 2 = 0$

23-30. Find all other roots of each equation in problems **15-22.**

Write the simplest equation which has the given roots. Express the answer as a polynomial equation with integral coefficients.

31. $2, 1 + i, 1 - i$
32. $1, ^-1, 1 + i, 1 - i$
33. $1, \frac{^-1 \pm i\sqrt{3}}{2}$
34. $^-2 + i, 1 - 3i$
35. $3, 3, 2i$
36. $2, 2 + 3i, ^-1 + i$

2-6 The Rational Root Theorem

The **Rational Root Theorem** can be used to identify possible roots of polynomial equations which have integral coefficients.

Rational Root Theorem

> Let $a_0x^n + a_1x^{n-1} + \cdots + a_{n-1}x + a_n = 0$ represent a polynomial equation of degree n with integral coefficients. If a rational number $\frac{p}{q}$, where p and q have no common factors, is a root of the equation, then p is a factor of a_n and q is a factor of a_0.

example

1 **Find all rational roots of $2x^5 + 3x^4 - 6x^3 + 6x^2 - 8x + 3 = 0$.**

According to the Rational Root Theorem, if $\frac{p}{q}$ is a root of the equation, then p is a factor of 3 and q is a factor of 2.

p is $^{\pm}1$ or $^{\pm}3$
q is $^{\pm}1$ or $^{\pm}2$

The possible rational roots are $^{\pm}1$, $^{\pm}3$, $\pm\frac{1}{2}$, and $\pm\frac{3}{2}$. You can test each possible root using substitution or synthetic division.

r	2	3	$^{-}6$	6	$^{-}8$	3	
1	2	5	$^{-}1$	5	$^{-}3$	0	*1 is a root*
$^{-}1$	2	1	$^{-}7$	13	$^{-}21$	24	
3	2	9	21	69	199	600	
$^{-}3$	2	$^{-}3$	3	$^{-}3$	1	0	*$^{-}3$ is a root*
$\frac{1}{2}$	2	4	$^{-}4$	4	$^{-}6$	0	*$\frac{1}{2}$ is a root*
$-\frac{1}{2}$	2	2	$^{-}7$	$9\frac{1}{2}$	$^{-}12\frac{3}{4}$	$9\frac{3}{8}$	
$\frac{3}{2}$	2	6	3	$10\frac{1}{2}$	$7\frac{3}{4}$	$14\frac{1}{8}$	
$-\frac{3}{2}$	2	0	3	$1\frac{1}{2}$	$^{-}10\frac{1}{4}$	$18\frac{3}{8}$	

The rational roots of $2x^5 + 3x^4 - 6x^3 + 6x^2 - 8x + 3 = 0$ are 1, $^{-}3$, and $\frac{1}{2}$.

The Rational Root Theorem can be proven as follows.

First, replace x by the known root $\frac{p}{q}$.

$$a_0\frac{p^n}{q^n} + a_1\frac{p^{n-1}}{q^{n-1}} + \cdots + a_{n-1}\frac{p}{q} + a_n = 0$$

Then multiply both sides by q^n.

$$a_0p^n + a_1p^{n-1}q + \cdots + a_{n-1}pq^{n-1} + a_nq^n = 0$$

Next factor p from the first n terms and subtract a_nq^n from both sides.

$$p(a_0p^{n-1} + a_1p^{n-2}q + \cdots + a_{n-1}q^{n-1}) = {}^{-}a_nq^n$$

Since p is a factor of the left side, it is also a factor of the right side. But p and q have no common factors, so p is a factor of a_n rather than q^n. Using a similar approach but factoring q from the last n terms, you can prove that q is a factor of a_0. Therefore p is a factor of a_n and q is a factor of a_0.

The Rational Root Theorem has an important corollary that pertains to integral roots of polynomial equations.

Integral Root Theorem

Let $x^n + a_1x^{n-1} + \cdots + a_{n-1}x + a_n = 0$ represent a polynomial equation which has leading coefficient 1, integral coefficients, and $a_n \neq 0$. Then any rational roots of the equation must be integral factors of a_n.

example

2 Find all rational roots of $x^3 - x^2 - x - 2 = 0$.

The possible rational roots are $^{\pm}1$ and $^{\pm}2$.
Test each possible root by substitution or synthetic division.

r	1	$^-1$	$^-1$	$^-2$
1	1	0	$^-1$	$^-3$
$^-1$	1	$^-2$	1	$^-3$
2	1	1	1	0
$^-2$	1	$^-3$	5	$^-12$

The only rational root is 2.

It may *not* always be necessary to test all possible roots. Once a root is found, the polynomial can be factored. In the example above, 2 was found to be a root of $x^3 - x^2 - x - 2 = 0$. Therefore $x - 2$ is a factor of $x^3 - x^2 - x - 2$ and the quotient is $x^2 + x + 1$, as shown by synthetic division. All other roots of $x^3 - x^2 - x - 2 = 0$ must also be roots of $x^2 + x + 1 = 0$. Thus, possible rational roots of $x^2 + x + 1 = 0$ are 1 and $^-1$, which were already tested. Thus, $^-2$ does not need to be tested, and 2 is the only rational root of $x^3 - x^2 - x - 2 = 0$.

exercises

Exploratory Find all possible rational roots of each equation.

1. $x^3 - 4x^2 + x + 2 = 0$
2. $x^3 + 2x^2 - 5x - 6 = 0$
3. $x^4 + 5x^3 + 5x^2 - 5x - 6 = 0$
4. $x^3 - 5x^2 - 4x + 20 = 0$
5. $x^3 + 2x^2 + x + 18 = 0$
6. $x^4 - 5x^3 + 9x^2 - 7x + 2 = 0$
7. $2x^3 + 3x^2 - 8x + 3 = 0$
8. $6x^3 - 11x^2 - 24x + 9 = 0$
9. $4x^3 + 5x^2 + 2x - 6 = 0$
10. $2x^4 - x^3 - 6x + 3 = 0$
11. $x^3 - x^2 - 40x + 12 = 0$
12. $6x^3 + 4x^2 - 14x + 4 = 0$

Written

1-12. Find all rational roots of the equations in problems **1-12** in the exploratory exercises.

Find all rational roots of each equation.

13. $x^4 + x^2 - 2 = 0$
14. $3x^4 - 5x^2 + 4 = 0$
15. $x^3 + 5x^2 - 3 = 0$
16. $3x^4 - 2x^2 + 18 = 0$
17. $2x^3 + x^2 + 5x - 3 = 0$
18. $2x^3 - 5x^2 - 28x + 15 = 0$
19. $6x^4 + 35x^3 - x^2 - 7x - 1 = 0$
20. $x^3 - 3x^2 + x - 3 = 0$

2-7 Locating Zeros of Functions

A **zero** of a function is a value of x for which $f(x) = 0$. A theorem first proved by the French mathematician René Descartes provides information about the existence of zeros of a polynomial function.

A zero of a function $y = f(x)$ is a root of the equation $f(x) = 0$.

Suppose $P(x)$ is a polynomial whose terms are arranged in descending powers of the variable. The number of positive real zeros of $y = P(x)$ is the same as the number of changes in sign of the coefficients of the terms, or is less than this by an even number. The number of negative real zeros is the same as the number of changes in sign of $P(^-x)$, or is less than this by an even number.

Descartes' Rule of Signs

Zero coefficients are ignored.

example

1 **State the number of positive and negative real zeros for $P(x) = x^4 - 3x^3 - 2x^2 + 3x + 8$.**

There is a sign change from the first to the second term and another from the third to the fourth term. Thus, there must be 2 or 0 positive real zeros.

To determine the number of negative zeros, write an expression for $P(^-x)$.

$P(^-x) = x^4 + 3x^3 - 2x^2 - 3x + 8$ *Notice that the terms with odd powers change signs.*

There are two sign changes so there must be 2 or 0 negative real zeros.

The graph of a polynomial function $y = f(x)$ is a continuous curve. Thus, if $f(x)$ is positive for some values of x and negative for other values of x, the graph of $y = f(x)$ must cross the x-axis. The point at which the graph crosses the x-axis represents a zero of the function. The figure at the right illustrates the **location principle.**

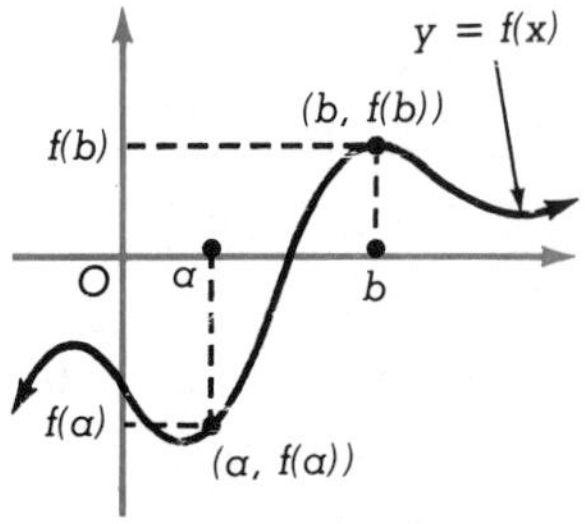

Suppose $y = f(x)$ represents a polynomial function. If a and b are two numbers with $f(a)$ negative and $f(b)$ positive, the function has at least one real zero between a and b.

The Location Principle

examples

2 **Locate between successive integers the real zeros of $f(x) = x^3 + 2x^2 - 3x - 5$.**

Use synthetic division or substitution to evaluate the function for successive integral values of x.

r	1	2	$^-3$	$^-5$
$^-4$	1	$^-2$	5	$^-25$
$^-3$	1	$^-1$	0	$^-5$
$^-2$	1	0	$^-3$	1
$^-1$	1	1	$^-4$	$^-1$
0	1	2	$^-3$	$^-5$
1	1	3	0	$^-5$
2	1	4	5	5

← *Since $^-5$ and 1 have opposite signs, a zero is located between $^-3$ and $^-2$.*

← *What does this indicate?*

← *What does this indicate?*

The changes in sign indicate that zeros are located between $^-3$ and $^-2$, between $^-2$ and $^-1$, and between 1 and 2.

3 **Approximate to the nearest tenth the positive real zeros of the function $f(x) = x^4 - 3x^3 - 2x^2 + 3x + 8$.** *Use a calculator for easier evaluation.*

By Descartes Rule of Signs, there must be 2 or 0 positive real zeros. Use synthetic division or substitution to evaluate the function for several positive values of x.

r	1	$^-3$	$^-2$	3	8
1	1	$^-2$	$^-4$	$^-1$	7
2	1	$^-1$	$^-4$	$^-5$	$^-2$
3	1	0	$^-2$	$^-3$	$^-1$
4	1	1	2	11	52

By the Location Principle, there is a zero between 1 and 2, and a zero between 3 and 4.

Locate the zero between 1 and 2.

x	$f(x)$
2.0	$^-2$
1.9	$^-1.06$
1.8	$^-0.08$
1.7	0.93

The zero is "closer" to 1.8.

← $f(1.75) \approx 0.43$

Locate the zero between 3 and 4.

x	$f(x)$
3.0	$^-1$
3.1	1.06
3.2	3.67

← $f(3.05) \approx 0.04$

The zero is "closer" to 3.0.

The positive real zeros are approximately 1.8 and 3.0.

The function $f(x) = x^3 - 2x^2 + x - 3$ has 3 or 1 positive real zero. Synthetic division can be used to find several values of $f(x)$, as shown in the table at the right. Notice that the table indicates that a zero exists between 2 and 3.

r	1	$^-2$	1	$^-3$
1	1	$^-1$	0	$^-3$
2	1	0	1	$^-1$
3	1	1	4	9
4	1	2	9	33

Instead of testing higher values of x to determine if more positive zeros exist, you can apply the theorem below to the results shown in the table. The theorem can be used to determine an **upper bound** of the zeros of a function.

Upper Bound Theorem

Suppose c is a positive number and $P(x)$ is divided by $x - c$ (using synthetic division). If the resulting quotient and remainder have no changes in sign, then $P(x)$ has no real zeros greater than c. Thus, c is an upper bound of the zeros of $P(x)$.

The synthetic divisions shown above indicate that 3 and 4 are upper bounds of the zeros of $f(x) = x^3 - 2x^2 + x - 3$. Notice that there can be more than one upper bound. Therefore, it is helpful to find the least integral upper bound of the zeros of a function. The least positive integral upper bound of the zeros of $f(x) = x^3 - 2x^2 + x - 3$ is 3.

example

4 **Find the least positive integral upper bound of the zeros of the function $f(x) = x^4 - 3x^3 - 2x^2 + 3x - 5$.**

r	1	$^-3$	$^-2$	3	$^-5$
1	1	$^-2$	$^-4$	$^-1$	$^-6$
2	1	$^-1$	$^-4$	$^-5$	$^-15$
3	1	0	$^-2$	$^-3$	$^-14$
4	1	1	2	11	39

This row has no changes in sign.

Any value greater than 4 is also an upper bound.

Thus, 4 is the least positive integral upper bound.

A **lower bound** of the zeros of $P(x)$ can be found by determining an upper bound for the zeros of $P(^-x)$. Therefore, if c is an upper bound of $P(^-x)$, then ^-c is a lower bound of $P(x)$.

example

5 **Find the greatest negative integer which is a lower bound of the function $f(x) = x^4 - 3x^3 - 2x^2 + 3x - 5$.**

$f(^-x) = x^4 + 3x^3 - 2x^2 - 3x - 5$

r	1	3	⁻2	⁻3	⁻5
1	1	4	2	⁻1	⁻6
2	1	5	8	13	21

Since this row has no changes in sign, 2 is the least positive integral upper bound of $f(^-x)$.

Since 2 is an upper bound of $f(^-x)$, ⁻2 is the greatest negative integral lower bound of $f(x)$.

exercises

Exploratory State the number of positive real zeros of each function.

1. $f(x) = x^3 - 4x^2 + x + 2$
2. $f(x) = x^3 + 2x^2 - 5x - 6$
3. $f(x) = x^4 + 5x^3 + 5x^2 - 5x - 6$
4. $f(x) = 2x^3 + 3x^2 - 8x + 3$
5. $f(x) = x^3 - 5x^2 - 4x - 20$
6. $f(x) = 6x^3 - 11x^2 - 24x + 9$
7. $f(x) = x^3 + 2x^2 + x + 18 = 0$
8. $f(x) = 4x^3 + 5x^2 + 2x - 6$
9. $f(x) = x^4 - 5x^3 + 9x^2 - 7x + 2$
10. $f(x) = 2x^4 - x^3 - 6x + 3$

11-20. For each function in problems **1-10**, state the number of negative real zeros.

Written Locate between successive integers the real zeros of each function.

1. $f(x) = x^2 + 3x + 1$
2. $f(x) = x^2 - x - 1$
3. $f(x) = x^2 - 4x - 2$
4. $f(x) = 2x^2 - 5x + 1$
5. $f(x) = x^3 - 2$
6. $f(x) = x^3 - 3x + 1$
7. $f(x) = x^4 - 2x^3 + x - 2$
8. $f(x) = 2x^4 + x^2 - 3x + 5$

Approximate to the nearest tenth the real zeros of each function.

9. $f(x) = x^2 - x - 5$
10. $f(x) = 2x^2 + x - 1$
11. $f(x) = x^2 + 3x + 2$
12. $f(x) = 2x^3 - 4x^2 - 3$
13. $f(x) = x^3 - 4x + 6$
14. $f(x) = 3x^4 + x^2 - 1$
15. $f(x) = 2x^4 - x^3 + x - 2$
16. $f(x) = {}^-x^3 + x^2 - x + 1$

Find the least positive integral upper bound of the zeros of each function.

17. $f(x) = x^3 + 3x^2 - 5x - 10$
18. $f(x) = x^4 - 8x + 2$
19. $f(x) = 3x^3 - 2x^2 + 5x - 1$
20. $f(x) = x^5 + 5x^4 - 3x^3 + 20x^2 - 15$

21-24. Find the greatest negative integral lower bound of the zeros of each function in problems **17-20**.

Diminished Roots

Excursions in Mathematics

Suppose you would like to write an equation with roots which are 2 less than those of $x^2 - 8x + 15 = 0$. One method is to find the roots of the given equation, subtract 2 from each root, and then form the new equation by multiplying the appropriate linear factors together. For example, the roots of $x^2 - 8x + 15 = 0$ are 3 and 5. The roots of the desired equation are 1 and 3. By multiplying $x - 1$ by $x - 3$, you obtain the desired equation, $x^2 - 4x + 3 = 0$.

Another method is sometimes used, especially when the roots of an equation are difficult to identify. Suppose each root of $P(x) = 0$ is to be decreased by a constant, h. By successively dividing $P(x)$ and the resulting quotients by $x - h$, you can obtain the coefficients of the desired equation. Study the following example.

Example Write the equation which has roots that are 2 less than those of $2x^3 - x^2 - 13x - 6 = 0$.

Divide $2x^3 - x^2 - 13x - 6$ by $x - 2$.
Then divide the quotient by $x - 2$.
Divide until the quotient is a constant.

	2	$^{-}1$	$^{-}13$	$^{-}6$
2	2	3	$^{-}7$	($^{-}20$)
2	2	7	(7)	
2	2	(11)		

$2x^3 + 11x^2 + 7x - 20$

The final quotient and the remainders in parentheses are the coefficients of the desired equation.

The equation is $2x^3 + 11x^2 + 7x - 20 = 0$.

Verify that the roots of the given equation are 3, $^{-}2$, and $-\frac{1}{2}$, and the roots of the derived equation are 1, $^{-}4$, and $^{-}2\frac{1}{2}$.

Exercises Solve each problem.

1. Write an equation with real roots that are one less than the roots of
$$x^3 - 4x^2 + x - 2 = 0.$$

2. Write an equation with real roots that are two less than the roots of
$$x^3 + 2x^2 - 5x - 6 = 0.$$

3. Write an equation with real roots that are one more than the roots of
$$x^4 - 5x^3 + 9x^2 - 7x + 2 = 0.$$

4. Write an equation with real roots that are two more than the roots of
$$3x^4 - 7x^3 - 23x^2 + 7x + 20 = 0.$$

5. Write an equation with real roots that are two less than the roots of
$$x^4 + 5x^3 - 25x^2 - 5x + 24 = 0.$$

6. Write an equation with real roots that are one more than the roots of
$$14x^3 + 5x^2 - 71x + 10 = 0.$$

2-8 Tangent to a Curve

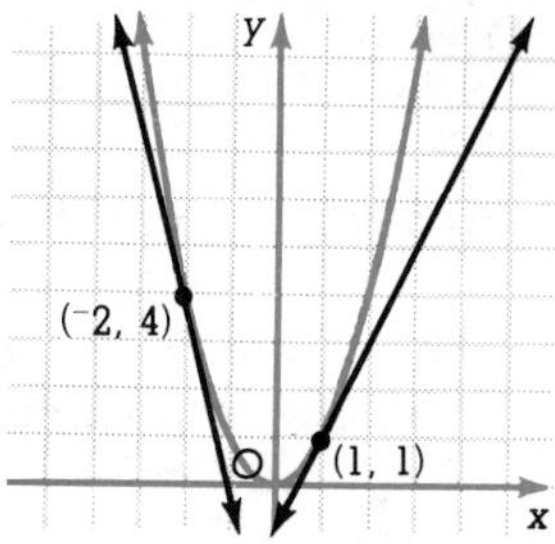

A **tangent** is a straight line which touches a curve at a point on the curve. The drawing at the right shows two tangents to the graph of $f(x) = x^2$. The slope of a tangent to a curve at a point on the curve can be found.

Suppose the graph of an equation $y = f(x)$ has been drawn in the coordinate plane. Let A and B be two points near each other on the continuous curve, and let the coordinates of A be $(x, f(x))$. Suppose the abscissa of B differs from the abscissa of A by a small amount, h. Then the coordinates of B are $(x + h, f(x + h))$, as shown at the right.

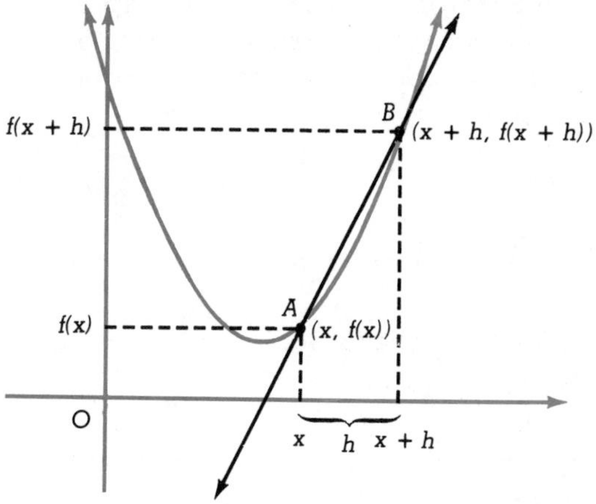

A straight line that passes through A and B is called a **secant line** to the curve. Its slope is $\frac{f(x+h) - f(x)}{h}$. *Why?*

Now suppose that A remains fixed while B moves along the curve toward A. Then the value of h will become smaller, approaching zero. Thus, h can be considered as a variable which approaches zero as B approaches A. If B is made to coincide with A, then the secant line becomes a tangent to the curve at point A.

Notice that $\frac{f(x+h) - f(x)}{h}$ is undefined for $h = 0$. Therefore, in order to evaluate the slope of the tangent, the slope must be defined in a special way. The slope can be defined by examining a function to which it is equal.

Consider the slope of the tangent to the graph of $y = 2x^2 - 3x + 1$ at the point (2, 3) on the curve. The slope of the secant through two general points $A(x, f(x))$ and $B(x + h, f(x + h))$ is equal to $\frac{f(x+h) - f(x)}{h}$. An expression for the slope of the secant to the graph of $y = 2x^2 - 3x + 1$ can be found as follows.

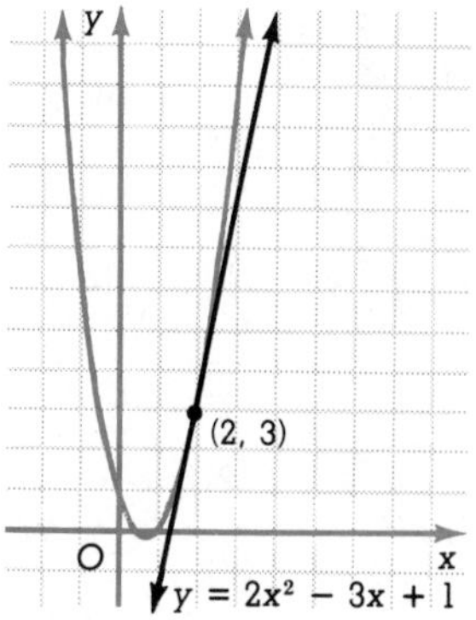

$$f(x + h) = 2(x + h)^2 - 3(x + h) + 1$$

or

$$\begin{array}{rl} f(x+h) &= 2x^2 + 4xh + 2h^2 - 3x - 3h + 1 \\ f(x) &= 2x^2 \qquad\qquad\qquad\;\; - 3x \qquad\;\; + 1 \\ \hline f(x+h) - f(x) &= \qquad\quad 4xh + 2h^2 \qquad\;\; - 3h \end{array}$$

$$\frac{f(x+h) - f(x)}{h} = \frac{4xh + 2h^2 - 3h}{h} = 4x + 2h - 3$$

An expression for the slope of the secant is $4x + 2h - 3$. The slope of the secant through specific points can be found by substituting values for x and h.

When $x = 2$ and $h = 1$, the slope of the secant is $4(2) + 2(1) - 3 = 7$.

When $x = 2$ and $h = \frac{1}{2}$, the slope of the secant is $4(2) + 2\left(\frac{1}{2}\right) - 3 = 6$.

When $x = 2$ and $h = \frac{1}{4}$, the slope of the secant is $4(2) + 2\left(\frac{1}{4}\right) - 3 = 5\frac{1}{2}$.

As h approaches zero, the slope of the secant becomes very close to the slope of the tangent. The middle term of $4x + 2h - 3$ vanishes as h approaches zero. Thus, an expression for the slope of the tangent is $4x - 3$.

The slope of the tangent to $y = 2x^2 - 3x + 1$ at point (2, 3) can be found by replacing x by 2 in the expression $4x - 3$. Thus, the slope of the tangent at the point (2, 3) is equal to $4(2) - 3$, or 5.

The symbol $f'(x)$ is often used to denote the slope of the tangent. It is defined as follows.

$$f'(x) = \lim_{h \to 0} \frac{f(x + h) - f(x)}{h}$$

f′(x) is read "f prime of x."

The symbol $\lim\limits_{h \to 0}$ means the limiting value of the function as the value of h approaches zero. The function $f'(x)$ is called the **derivative** of $f(x)$.

example

1 Find the slope of the tangent to the graph of $y = 5x^3 - 2x^2 + x - 1$ at the point on the curve where the abscissa is $^-1$.

Let $(x, f(x))$ and $(x + h, f(x + h))$ be two points on the curve.

First, write an expression for $f(x + h) - f(x)$.

$$f(x + h) = 5(x + h)^3 - 2(x + h)^2 + (x + h) - 1$$

or

$$\begin{array}{rl} f(x + h) = & 5x^3 + 15x^2h + 15xh^2 + 5h^3 - 2x^2 - 4xh - 2h^2 + x + h - 1 \\ f(x) = & 5x^3 \qquad\qquad\qquad\qquad\qquad\quad - 2x^2 \qquad\qquad\qquad + x \quad - 1 \\ \hline f(x + h) - f(x) = & \qquad 15x^2h + 15xh^2 + 5h^3 \qquad -4xh - 2h^2 \qquad + h \end{array}$$

Next, divide the expression by h to obtain an expression for the slope of the secant.

$$\frac{f(x + h) - f(x)}{h} = 15x^2 + 15xh + 5h^2 - 4x - 2h + 1$$

Then, write an expression for the slope when $h = 0$.

$$\lim_{h \to 0} \frac{f(x + h) - f(x)}{h} = 15x^2 - 4x + 1$$

$$f'(x) = 15x^2 - 4x + 1$$

Finally, substitute $^-1$ for x in the equation for $f'(x)$.

$$f'(^-1) = 15(^-1)^2 - 4(^-1) + 1 = 20$$

The slope of the tangent at the point $(^-1, {}^-9)$ is 20. *$f(^-1) = {}^-9$*

If coordinates of one point on a curve are known, and the slope of the tangent to the curve at the point is known, the equation for the tangent can be written in point-slope form.

example

2 **Find the equation of the tangent to the graph of $y = 2x^3 - x^2 + 3x - 1$ at the point $(^-2, ^-27)$.**

First, write an expression for the slope of the tangent.

$$f(x+h) = 2(x+h)^3 - (x+h)^2 + 3(x+h) - 1$$

or

$$\begin{array}{rl} f(x+h) = & 2x^3 + 6x^2h + 6xh^2 + 2h^3 - x^2 - 2xh - h^2 + 3x + 3h - 1 \\ ^-f(x) = & 2x^3 \qquad\qquad\qquad\qquad\quad - x^2 \qquad\qquad\quad + 3x \qquad - 1 \\ \hline f(x+h) - f(x) = & 6x^2h + 6xh^2 + 2h^3 - 2xh - h^2 + 3h \end{array}$$

$$\frac{f(x+h) - f(x)}{h} = 6x^2 + 6xh + 2h^2 - 2x - h + 3$$

$$f'(x) = \lim_{h \to 0} \frac{f(x+h) - f(x)}{h} = 6x^2 - 2x + 3$$

Next, evaluate $f'(^-2)$.

$f'(^-2) = 6(^-2)^2 - 2(^-2) + 3 = 31$

Then, write an equation in point-slope form for the line through $(^-2, ^-27)$ which has slope 31.

$y - {^-27} = 31(x - {^-2})$ *The point-slope form is $y - y_1 = m(x - x_1)$.*

In slope-intercept form the equation is $y = 31x + 35$.

exercises

Exploratory For each given function, write an expression for $\dfrac{f(x+h) - f(x)}{h}$.

1. $f(x) = x^2$
2. $f(x) = x^2 + 1$
3. $f(x) = 2x^2$
4. $f(x) = \frac{1}{2}x^2$
5. $f(x) = {^-2}x^2 + 3x + 1$
6. $f(x) = 0.5x^2 - 0.4x - 0.3$

7-12. For each function in problems **1-6**, write an expression for $f'(x)$.

Written Find the slope of the tangent to the graph of the given function at the indicated point.

1. $y = x^2, (1, 1)$
2. $y = x^2, (0, 0)$
3. $y = x^2 + 1, (2, 5)$
4. $y = x^2 + 1, (0, 1)$
5. $y = 2x^2, (2, 8)$
6. $y = 2x^2, (^-1, 2)$
7. $y = \frac{1}{2}x^2, (2, 2)$
8. $y = \frac{1}{2}x^2, \left(^-3, 4\frac{1}{2}\right)$
9. $y = {^-2}x^2 + 3x + 1, (0, 1)$
10. $y = {^-2}x^2 + 3x + 1, (1, 2)$

11. $y = 0.5x^2 - 0.4x - 0.3$, $(1, ^-0.2)$

12. $y = 0.5x^2 - 0.4x - 0.3$, $(^-1, 0.6)$

13. $y = x^2 + \frac{1}{6}x - \frac{1}{3}$, $\left(\frac{1}{2}, 0\right)$

14. $y = \frac{x^3 - 1}{8}$, $\left(2, \frac{7}{8}\right)$

15. $y = 2x^2 - 3x - 4$ at the point with abscissa $^-2$.

16. $y = \frac{1}{2}x^2 + \frac{1}{4}x + \frac{1}{8}$ at the point with abscissa $\frac{1}{2}$.

Find the equation of the tangent to the graph of the given function at the indicated point.

17. $y = x^2$, $(2, 4)$

18. $y = x^2 - 3$, $(3, 6)$

19. $y = 2x^2 - 3x$, $(^-1, 5)$

20. $y = x^2 - 3x + 2$, $(1, 0)$

21. $y = x^2 - 5x + 6$, $\left(2\frac{1}{2}, -\frac{1}{4}\right)$

22. $y = {^-x^2} - x + 2$, $\left(\frac{1}{2}, 1\frac{1}{4}\right)$

23. $y = {^-3x^2} + 5$, $(^-2, ^-7)$

24. $y = \frac{1}{2}x^2 + x - 1$, $(^-4, 3)$

2-9 Critical Points

When $f'(x) = 0$, the tangent to the curve at (x, y) is parallel to the x-axis. There are three possible forms a curve may have around a point for which $f'(x) = 0$. Points for which the derivative equals zero are called **critical points.** In the figure below, P represents a **maximum point.** Q represents a **minimum point**, and R represents a **point of inflection.**

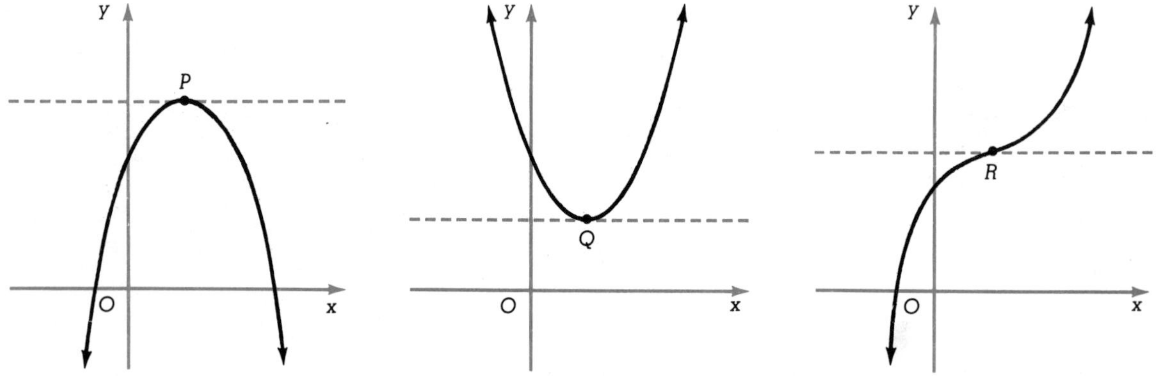

Sometimes a function has a **relative maximum** or a **relative minimum.** Point A shown at the right represents a relative maximum. The ordinate of A is *not* the greatest value of the function, although it represents a maximum for a small interval. Likewise, point B shown at the right represents a relative minimum.

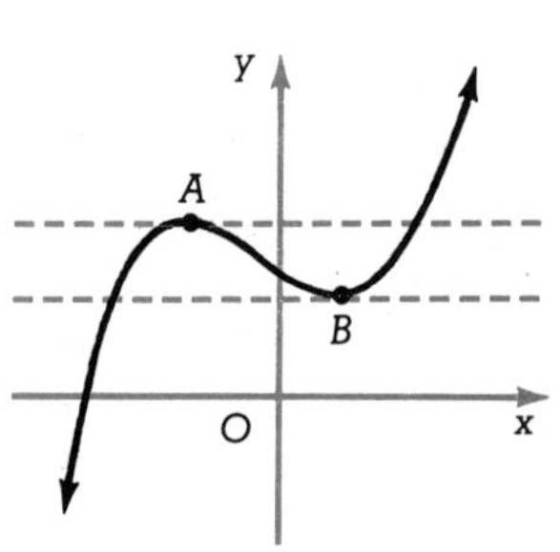

example

1 **The derivative of the function $f(x) = 3x^3 - 9x + 5$ is given by $f'(x) = 9x^2 - 9$. Find the critical points of the graph of $f(x)$.**

First, set $f'(x) = 0$ and solve for x.

$9x^2 - 9 = 0$
$9(x^2 - 1) = 0$
$9(x - 1)(x + 1) = 0$
$x = 1$ or $^-1$

Next, evaluate $f(x)$ for $x = 1$ or $^-1$.
$f(1) = 3(1)^3 - 9(1) + 5 = {}^-1$
$f(^-1) = 3(^-1)^3 - 9(^-1) + 5 = 11$

The critical points are $(1, {}^-1)$ and $(^-1, 11)$.

Suppose $(a, f(a))$ is a critical point. You can determine if the critical point represents a maximum, a minimum, or a point of inflection by evaluating $f(a + h)$ and $f(a - h)$ for small values of h. The critical point represents a maximum if $f(a + h)$ and $f(a - h)$ are both less than $f(a)$, for small values of h. The critical point represents a minimum if $f(a + h)$ and $f(a - h)$ are both greater than $f(a)$. If one is greater than $f(a)$ and the other is less than $f(a)$, the critical point represents a point of inflection.

For a maximum or minimum, the slope of the tangent is positive on one side of the critical point and negative on the other side.

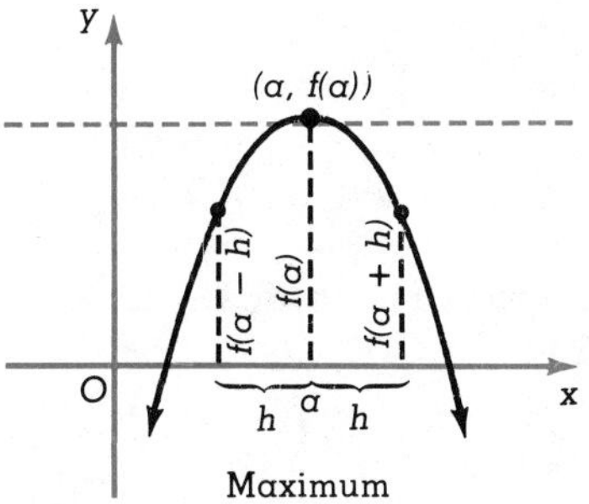

Maximum

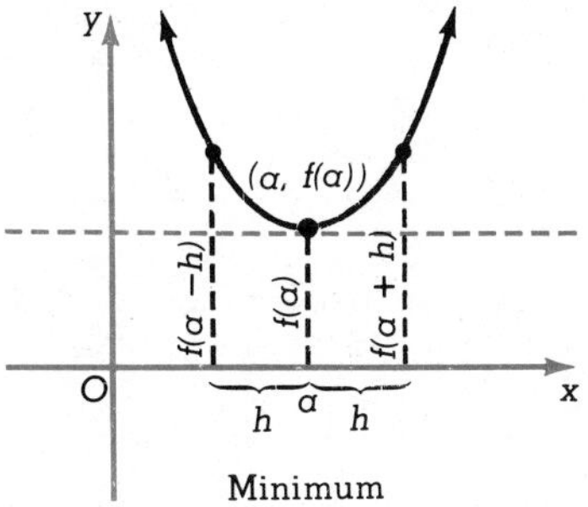

Minimum

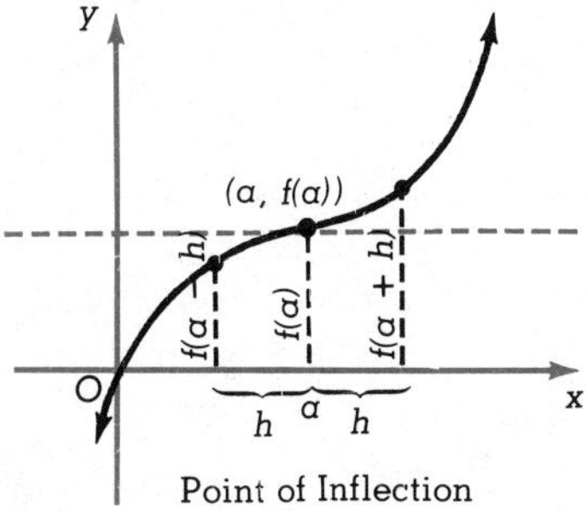

Point of Inflection

example

2 **The point (0, 1) is a critical point of the function $f(x) = x^3 - x^2 + 1$. Determine whether the point (0, 1) represents a maximum, a minimum, or a point of inflection.**

$f(0) = 1$
$f(0.1) = (0.1)^3 - (0.1)^2 + 1 = 0.991$ *Use a calculator for easier evaluation.*
$f(^-0.1) = (^-0.1)^3 - (^-0.1)^2 + 1 = 0.989$

Since $f(0.1)$ and $f(^-0.1)$ are both less than $f(0)$, the point (0, 1) represents a maximum value for the function. *This is a relative maximum.*

example

3 **Find the critical points of the graph of $f(x) = x^2 + 4x - 12$. Then determine whether each point represents a maximum, a minimum, or a point of inflection.**

First, find $f'(x)$.

$$f(x + h) - f(x) = (x + h)^2 + 4(x + h) - 12 - (x^2 + 4x - 12)$$
$$= 2xh + h^2 + 4h$$
$$\frac{f(x + h) - f(x)}{h} = 2x + h + 4$$
$$f'(x) = 2x + 4$$

Then set $f'(x) = 0$ to find the abscissas of the critical points.

$$2x + 4 = 0$$
$$x = {}^-2$$

Find values of $f(x)$ at and near the critical point.

$f(^-1.9) = {}^-15.99$
$f(^-2) = {}^-16$ *The point $(^-2, {}^-16)$ is a critical point.*
$f(^-2.1) = {}^-15.99$

Since $f(^-1.9)$ and $f(^-2.1)$ are both greater than $f(^-2)$, the point $(^-2, {}^-16)$ represents a minimum for the function.

Critical points can be used when graphing equations. If the zeros and the critical points of a polynomial function are graphed, the general shape of the graph can usually be determined.

example

4 **The zeros of the function $f(x) = x^3 + x^2 - 6x$ occur at 2, $^-3$, and 0. The critical points are approximately $(^-1.8, 8.2)$ and $(1.1, {}^-4.1)$. Graph the function.**

Graph the zeros on the x-axis.
Then graph the critical points.
Connect the points with a smooth curve.

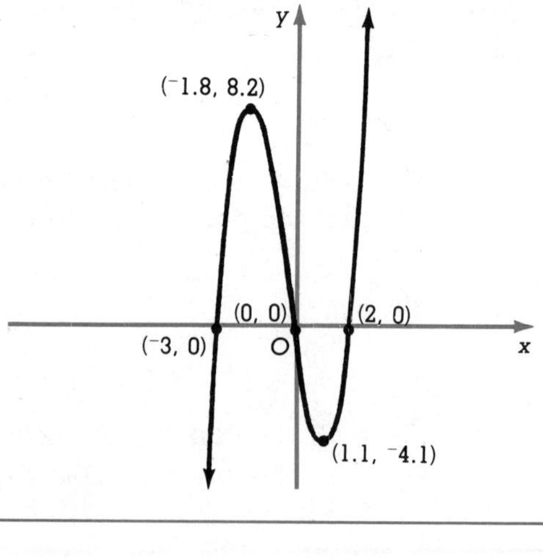

exercises

Exploratory **Find the critical points of each function. The derivative of each function is given.**

1. $f(x) = 3x^2 - 6x - 1$, $f'(x) = 6x - 6$
2. $f(x) = x^2 - 8x + 10$, $f'(x) = 2x - 8$
3. $f(x) = 2x^2 + 6x - 5$, $f'(x) = 4x + 6$
4. $f(x) = x - x^2$, $f'(x) = 1 - 2x$
5. $f(x) = \frac{1}{3}x^3 - 9x - 1$, $f'(x) = x^2 - 9$
6. $f(x) = 3x^3 - \frac{9}{2}x^2 - 4$, $f'(x) = 9x^2 - 9x$

Written **Find the critical points of the graph of each function. Then determine whether each point represents a maximum, a minimum, or a point of inflection.**

1. $y = x^2 - x - 6$
2. $y = 8 - 2x - x^2$
3. $y = x^2 + 2x - 15$
4. $y = 2x^2 - 3x + 1$
5. $y = x^3 - x^2 + 3$
6. $y = x^4 - 8x^2 + 16$

7-12. Locate the zeros of each function in problems **1-6.** Then graph each function.

Graph each function.

13. $y = x^3 - 2x^2 - 5x + 6$
14. $y = x^3 + x$
15. $y = x^4 - 2x^2 - 8$
16. $y = x^3 - 7x - 6$
17. $y = x^4 + x^2$
18. $y = \sqrt{2}\,x^2 - 1$

Chapter Summary

1. The degree of a polynomial in one variable is the greatest exponent of its variable. (28)
2. If $P(x)$ represents a polynomial, then $P(x) = 0$ is a polynomial equation. A root of the equation is a value of x for which the value of $P(x)$ is zero. (28)
3. To solve an equation means to find the roots of the equation. (29)
4. Any quadratic equation can be written in the form $ax^2 + bx + c = 0$, where a, b, and c are real numbers and $a \neq 0$. (30)
5. Quadratic Formula: The roots of a quadratic equation of the form $ax^2 + bx + c = 0$ are given by the following formula.

$$x = \frac{^-b \pm \sqrt{b^2 - 4ac}}{2a} \qquad (30)$$

6. Complex Conjugates Theorem: Suppose a and b are real numbers with $b \neq 0$. Then, if $a + bi$ is a root of a polynomial equation, $a - bi$ is also a root of the equation. (32)
7. The Remainder Theorem: If a polynomial $P(x)$ is divided by $x - r$, the remainder is a constant, $P(r)$, and $P(x) = (x - r) \cdot Q(x) + P(r)$, where $Q(x)$ is a polynomial with degree one less than the degree of $P(x)$. (37)
8. The Factor Theorem: The binomial $x - r$ is a factor of the polynomial $P(x)$ if and only if $P(r) = 0$. (38)

9. The Fundamental Theorem of Algebra: Every polynomial with degree greater than zero has at least one root in the set of complex numbers. (39)
10. Corollary: Every polynomial $P(x)$ of degree n can be transformed into the product of n linear factors. That is, $P(x)$ of degree n equals $k(x - r_1)(x - r_2)(x - r_3) \ldots (x - r_n)$. Thus a polynomial equation of the form $P(x) = 0$ of degree n has exactly n roots, namely, $r_1, r_2, r_3, \ldots r_n$. (39)
11. Rational Root Theorem: Let $a_0x^n + a_1x^{n-1} + \ldots + a_{n-1}x + a_n = 0$ represent a polynomial equation of degree n with integral coefficients. If a rational number $\frac{p}{q}$, where p and q have no common factors, is a root of the equation, then p is a factor of a_n and q is a factor of a_0. (41)
12. Integral Root Theorem: Let $x^n + a_1x^{n-1} + \ldots a_{n-1}x + a_n = 0$ represent a polynomial equation which has leading coefficient 1, integral coefficients, and $a_n \neq 0$. Then any rational roots of the equation must be integral factors of a_n. (43)
13. Descartes Rule of Signs: Suppose $P(x)$ is a polynomial whose terms are arranged in descending powers of the variable. The number of positive real zeros of $y = P(x)$ is the same as the number of changes in sign of the coefficients of the terms, or is less than this by an even number. The number of negative real zeros is the same as the number of changes in sign of $P(^-x)$, or is less than this by an even number. (44)
14. The Location Principle: Suppose $y = f(x)$ represents a polynomial function. If a and b are two numbers with $f(a)$ negative and $f(b)$ positive, the function has at least one real zero between a and b. (45)
15. Upper Bound Theorem: Suppose c is a positive number and $P(x)$ is divided by $x - c$ (using synthetic division). If the resulting quotient and remainder have no changes in sign, then $P(x)$ has no real zeros greater than c. Thus, c is an upper bound of the zeros of $P(x)$. (46)
16. The derivative of $f(x)$ is defined as follows.

$$f'(x) = \lim_{h \to 0} \frac{f(x + h) - f(x)}{h} \qquad (50)$$

17. Points for which the derivative equals zero are called critical points. A critical point $(a, f(a))$ represents a maximum if $f(a + h)$ and $f(a - h)$ are both less than $f(a)$, for small values of h. The critical point is a minimum if $f(a + h)$ and $f(a - h)$ are both greater than $f(a)$. If one is greater and the other is less, the critical point is a point of inflection. (53)

Chapter Review

2-1 **Solve each equation.**

1. $(3x - 2)(x - 4)(x - 6) = 0$
2. $x^2 - 40x + 400 = 0$

2-2 **Solve each equation by completing the square.**

3. $2x^2 + 7x - 4 = 0$
4. $x^2 - 7x - 1 = 0$

Solve each equation by using the quadratic formula.

5. $3x^2 + 5x - 3 = 0$
6. $4x^2 + 5x - 6 = 0$

2-3 **Divide using synthetic division. Write the quotient and remainder.**

7. $(5x^3 - 4x^2 - 8x + 2) \div (x - 2)$
8. $(x^4 + 5x^3 - 18x - 8) \div (x + 4)$

2-4 **Use the remainder theorem to find the remainder when the given polynomial is divided by the given binomial.**

9. $(x^3 - 5x + 8) \div (x + 3)$
10. $(3x^3 - 5x^2 + 4) \div (x - 1)$

2-5 **Find all roots of the following equations.**

11. $x^3 + 4x^2 - 3x - 18 = 0$
12. $x^4 - 2x^3 + 13x^2 - 32x - 48 = 0$

2-6 **Find all rational roots of each equation.**

13. $8x^2 - 6x + 1 = 0$
14. $x^4 + x^3 - 11x^2 + x - 12 = 0$

2-7 **State the number of positive real zeros of each function.**

15. $y = 4x^2 - 3x + 2$
16. $y = x^5 + 3x^4 - x^3 - 2x - 5$

17-18. For each function in problems **15-16**, state the number of negative real zeros.

Find the least positive integral upper bound of the zeros of each function.

19. $f(x) = x^4 + x^2 - 6$
20. $f(x) = x^4 - x^3 - 4x^2 + 8x - 4$

21-22. Find the greatest negative integral lower bound of the zeros of each function in problems **19-20**.

23-24. Approximate to the nearest tenth the real zeros of each function in problems **19-20**.

2-8 **Find the slope of the tangent to the graph of the given function at the indicated point.**

25. $y = 3x^2 + 4x - 2$, $(1, 5)$
26. $y = 2x^2 - 9x + 5$, $(2, {}^-3)$

27-28. For each function and point given in problems **25-26**, find the equation of the tangent to the graph of the given function at the indicated point.

2-9 **Find the critical points of each function. Then determine whether each point represents a maximum, a minimum, or a point of inflection.**

29. $f(x) = 4 + x - x^2$
30. $f(x) = x^3 - 6x^2 + 9x$

31-32. Find the zeros of each function in problems **29-30**. Round values to the nearest tenth. Then graph each function.

Chapter Test

Solve each equation.

1. $x^2 - 5x + 4 = 0$
2. $(3x - 5)(x - 3)(2x + 5) = 0$
3. $3x^2 + 4x - 15 = 0$
4. $6x^2 + 7x - 3 = 0$
5. $6m^2 - 2m + 1 = 0$
6. $2x^2 - 5x + 4 = 0$

Divide using synthetic division. Write the quotient and remainder.

7. $(2x^3 - x^2 - 10x + 8) \div (x - 2)$
8. $(x^4 + x^2 - 5) \div (x + 3)$

Use the remainder theorem to find the remainder when the given polynomial is divided by the given binomial.

9. $(x^3 - 5x + 1) \div (x + 1)$
10. $(2x^3 - 3x^2 - 8x + 4) \div (x + 2)$

Find all roots of each equation.

11. $x^3 - 2x^2 - 2x - 3 = 0$
12. $x^3 + 2x^2 - 1 = 0$

Find all rational roots of each equation.

13. $x^3 - 2x^2 - 13x - 10 = 0$
14. $x^4 - 13x^2 + 36 = 0$
15. $2x^2 - 7x + 3 = 0$
16. $x^4 - 6x^2 + 8 = 0$

State the number of positive real zeros of each function.

17. $y = x^7 - x^3 + 2x - 1$
18. $y = 4x^4 - 3x^3 + 2x^2 - x + 1$

19-20. For each function in problems **17-18**, state the number of negative real zeros.

Approximate to the nearest tenth the real zeros of each function.

21. $y = x^2 - 3x - 3$
22. $y = x^3 - x + 1$

For each given function, write an expression for $f'(x)$.

23. $f(x) = 3x - 4$
24. $f(x) = 2x^2 + 3x - 1$
25. $f(x) = 2x^3 - x$
26. $f(x) = x^4 + 7$

Find the slope of the tangent to the graph of the given function at the indicated point.

27. $y = x^2 - 4x + 1$, $(1, {}^-2)$
28. $y = 3x^2 - 2x + 1$, $(2, 9)$

29-30. For each function and point given in problems **27-28**, find the equation of the tangent to the graph of the given function at the indicated point.

Find the critical points of each function. Then determine whether each point represents a maximum, a minimum, or a point of inflection.

31. $y = x^2 - 8x + 4$
32. $y = 3 - 2x - x^2$

33-34. Find the zeros of each function in problems **31-32**. Round values to the nearest tenth. Then graph each function.

Chapter 3

Matrices and Vectors

Matrices and vectors have many scientific and business applications, including applications related to the shipping industry. Matrices are used by computers to organize, store, and use the vast amounts of shipping data available. Vectors can be used to determine the velocity or the displacement of a ship.

3-1 Matrices and Determinants

A **matrix** is any rectangular array of terms called **elements.** The elements of a matrix are arranged in rows and columns and are usually enclosed by brackets. A matrix with m rows and n columns is an $\boldsymbol{m \times n}$ **matrix** (read "m by n"). The **dimensions** of the matrix are m and n.

Large parentheses are sometimes used instead of brackets.

$$\begin{bmatrix} 5 & -7 \\ 10 & 2 \end{bmatrix} \qquad \begin{bmatrix} 3 & \frac{1}{2} & 5 & 25 \\ -8 & 2 & 14 & -4 \end{bmatrix} \qquad \begin{bmatrix} 1 & -4 \\ 0 & 8 \\ 9 & 6 \end{bmatrix}$$

2 × 2 Matrix — 2 × 4 Matrix — 3 × 2 Matrix

A **square matrix** has the same number of rows as columns. A matrix of **nth order** has n rows and n columns.

Each square matrix has a **determinant.** The determinant of $\begin{bmatrix} 8 & 7 \\ 4 & 5 \end{bmatrix}$ is denoted by det$\begin{bmatrix} 8 & 7 \\ 4 & 5 \end{bmatrix}$ or $\begin{vmatrix} 8 & 7 \\ 4 & 5 \end{vmatrix}$. The value of a second order determinant is defined as follows.

The term determinant is often used to mean the value of the determinant.

The value of det$\begin{bmatrix} a_1 & b_1 \\ a_2 & b_2 \end{bmatrix}$ or $\begin{vmatrix} a_1 & b_1 \\ a_2 & b_2 \end{vmatrix} = a_1b_2 - a_2b_1$.

The Value of a Second Order Determinant

example

1 Find the value of $\begin{vmatrix} 7 & 9 \\ 3 & 6 \end{vmatrix}$.

$$\begin{vmatrix} 7 & 9 \\ 3 & 6 \end{vmatrix} = 7(6) - 3(9)$$
$$= 42 - 27$$
$$= 15$$

To evaluate a determinant of the nth order, expand the determinant by minors, using the elements in the first row. The **minor** of an element is a determinant of $(n - 1)$th order. This minor can be found by deleting the row and column containing the element. The expansion of a third order determinant is shown below. Notice that the signs of the terms alternate, with the first term being positive.

$$\begin{vmatrix} a_1 & b_1 & c_1 \\ a_2 & b_2 & c_2 \\ a_3 & b_3 & c_3 \end{vmatrix}$$

The minor of a_1 is $\begin{vmatrix} b_2 & c_2 \\ b_3 & c_3 \end{vmatrix}$.

$$\begin{vmatrix} a_1 & b_1 & c_1 \\ a_2 & b_2 & c_2 \\ a_3 & b_3 & c_3 \end{vmatrix} = a_1 \begin{vmatrix} b_2 & c_2 \\ b_3 & c_3 \end{vmatrix} - b_1 \begin{vmatrix} a_2 & c_2 \\ a_3 & c_3 \end{vmatrix} + c_1 \begin{vmatrix} a_2 & b_2 \\ a_3 & b_3 \end{vmatrix}$$

Expansion of a Third Order Determinant

example

2 Find the value of $\begin{vmatrix} 8 & 9 & 3 \\ 3 & 5 & 7 \\ ^-1 & 2 & 4 \end{vmatrix}$.

$$\begin{vmatrix} 8 & 9 & 3 \\ 3 & 5 & 7 \\ ^-1 & 2 & 4 \end{vmatrix} = 8\begin{vmatrix} 5 & 7 \\ 2 & 4 \end{vmatrix} - 9\begin{vmatrix} 3 & 7 \\ ^-1 & 4 \end{vmatrix} + 3\begin{vmatrix} 3 & 5 \\ ^-1 & 2 \end{vmatrix}$$

$$= 8(6) - 9(19) + 3(11)$$

$$= {}^-90$$

Determinants can be used to solve systems of linear equations. If a system of two equations in two variables is given, the solution set, if it exists as a single ordered pair, can be found by using Cramer's rule.

Cramer's Rule

Notice the positions of the constants, c_1 and c_2, in the top determinants.

The solution to $\begin{matrix} a_1x + b_1y = c_1 \\ a_2x + b_2y = c_2 \end{matrix}$ is (x, y) where

$$x = \frac{\begin{vmatrix} c_1 & b_1 \\ c_2 & b_2 \end{vmatrix}}{\begin{vmatrix} a_1 & b_1 \\ a_2 & b_2 \end{vmatrix}} \text{ and } y = \frac{\begin{vmatrix} a_1 & c_1 \\ a_2 & c_2 \end{vmatrix}}{\begin{vmatrix} a_1 & b_1 \\ a_2 & b_2 \end{vmatrix}} \text{ and } \begin{vmatrix} a_1 & b_1 \\ a_2 & b_2 \end{vmatrix} \neq 0.$$

example

3 Use Cramer's rule to solve the following system of equations.

$$2x - 3y = 12$$
$$5x + 9y = 63$$

$$x = \frac{\begin{vmatrix} 12 & ^-3 \\ 63 & 9 \end{vmatrix}}{\begin{vmatrix} 2 & ^-3 \\ 5 & 9 \end{vmatrix}} = \frac{297}{33} = 9 \qquad y = \frac{\begin{vmatrix} 2 & 12 \\ 5 & 63 \end{vmatrix}}{\begin{vmatrix} 2 & ^-3 \\ 5 & 9 \end{vmatrix}} = \frac{66}{33} = 2$$

The solution is (9, 2).

This method can be extended to solve a system of n linear equations in n variables. The determinant in each denominator contains the coefficients of the variables arranged in order and is called the **determinant of the system.** If the determinant of the system is equal to zero, there is no unique common solution. *Why?*

A matrix which has a non-zero determinant is called a non-singular matrix.

exercises

Exploratory Find the value of each determinant.

1. $\begin{vmatrix} 3 & -5 \\ 7 & 9 \end{vmatrix}$
2. $\begin{vmatrix} 7 & 16 \\ 3 & 8 \end{vmatrix}$
3. $\begin{vmatrix} -4 & 8 \\ 0 & 2 \end{vmatrix}$
4. $\begin{vmatrix} 10 & 50 \\ -5 & 25 \end{vmatrix}$
5. $\begin{vmatrix} 14 & 21 \\ 26 & 39 \end{vmatrix}$
6. $\begin{vmatrix} 16 & 17 \\ 15 & 16 \end{vmatrix}$

Name the determinants you would use to solve each system by Cramer's rule.

7. $3x + 2y = 5$
   $4x - 3y = 1$
8. $2x - 3y = 7$
   $3x + y = 16$
9. $2x + y = 6$
   $6x - y = 2$
10. $5x - 3y = 7$
    $2x + y = 27$
11. $4x + y = 6$
    $x - 2y = -12$
12. $8x + 12y = 6$
    $4x - 3y = 0$

Written Find the value of each determinant using expansion by minors.

1. $\begin{vmatrix} 7 & 1 & 6 \\ 3 & -1 & 4 \\ -2 & 3 & 0 \end{vmatrix}$
2. $\begin{vmatrix} 2 & 3 & 4 \\ 5 & 6 & 7 \\ 8 & 9 & 10 \end{vmatrix}$
3. $\begin{vmatrix} 6 & 7 & 4 \\ -2 & -4 & 3 \\ 1 & 1 & 1 \end{vmatrix}$
4. $\begin{vmatrix} 2 & 4 & 6 \\ 1 & 2 & 3 \\ 3 & -1 & 4 \end{vmatrix}$
5. $\begin{vmatrix} 3 & 0 & 2 \\ 0 & -1 & 5 \\ 6 & 7 & 0 \end{vmatrix}$
6. $\begin{vmatrix} 4 & 2 & -3 \\ 5 & 1 & 0 \\ -2 & 1 & 11 \end{vmatrix}$

7-12. Solve each system of equations in problems **7-12** of the exploratory exercises using Cramer's rule.

Solve each system of equations using Cramer's rule.

13. $5x - y = 16$
    $2x + 3y = 3$
14. $-7x + y = 19$
    $2x - y = -9$
15. $2x + 5y = 23$
    $3x - 2y = 6$
16. $2x + y = 13$
    $x - 5y = 1$
17. $x - y = 8$
    $3x + 2y = 4$
18. $7x + 8y = -5$
    $4x + 9y = 6$
19. $x + 6y = 6$
    $3x - 2y = 8$
20. $3x - y = 3$
    $6x + 5y = -1$
21. $5x + y = 0$
    $10x - 3y = -15$

Challenge Find the value of each determinant using expansion by minors.

1. $\begin{vmatrix} 1 & 2 & 3 & 1 \\ 4 & 3 & -1 & 0 \\ 2 & -5 & 4 & 4 \\ 1 & -2 & 0 & 2 \end{vmatrix}$
2. $\begin{vmatrix} 7 & 0 & 9 & 5 \\ 8 & 2 & -1 & 2 \\ -5 & 3 & 7 & 9 \\ 0 & -1 & -4 & -6 \end{vmatrix}$
3. $\begin{vmatrix} 3 & 0 & 0 & 4 & 0 \\ 6 & -3 & 2 & 0 & 7 \\ 0 & 4 & 3 & 0 & 5 \\ 0 & 2 & 1 & 3 & -4 \\ 6 & 0 & -2 & -3 & 0 \end{vmatrix}$

Solve each system of equations using Cramer's rule.

4. $4x + 3y + z = -10$
   $x - 12y + 2z = -5$
   $x + 18y + z = 4$
5. $x + y + z = -1$
   $2x + 4y + z = 1$
   $3x - y - z = -15$

3-2 Addition of Matrices

Many of the properties and operations of real numbers also apply to matrices. For example, two matrices are equal if and only if they have the same dimensions and are identical, element by element.

example

1 **Find the values of x and y for which the following equation is true.**

$$\begin{bmatrix} y - 3 \\ y \end{bmatrix} = \begin{bmatrix} x \\ 2x \end{bmatrix}$$

Since corresponding elements are equal, the following equations are true.

$$y - 3 = x$$
$$y = 2x$$

Solve the system of equations.

$2x - 3 = x$ *Substitute 2x for y.*

$x = 3$ *Solve for x.*

$y = 2(3)$ or 6 *Substitute 3 for x to find y.*

The matrices are equal if $x = 3$ and $y = 6$.

The elements of an $m \times n$ matrix can be represented using double subscript notation.

$$\begin{bmatrix} a_{11} & a_{12} & a_{13} & \cdots & a_{1n} \\ a_{21} & a_{22} & a_{23} & \cdots & a_{2n} \\ \cdots & \cdots & \cdots & \cdots & \cdots \\ a_{m1} & a_{m2} & a_{m3} & \cdots & a_{mn} \end{bmatrix}$$

a_{ij} would be the element in the ith row and the jth column.

Matrices with the same dimensions can be added. The ijth element of the sum of A and B is $a_{ij} + b_{ij}$.

Addition is not defined for matrices with different dimensions.

Definition of Addition of Matrices

The sum of two $m \times n$ matrices is an $m \times n$ matrix in which the elements are the sum of the corresponding elements of the given matrices.

example

2 **Find the sum of A and B if** $A = \begin{bmatrix} 3 & 4 & ^-7 \\ ^-2 & 0 & 4 \end{bmatrix}$ **and** $B = \begin{bmatrix} ^-2 & 7 & 3 \\ 5 & ^-9 & 1 \end{bmatrix}$.

$$A + B = \begin{bmatrix} 3 + {}^-2 & 4 + 7 & ^-7 + 3 \\ ^-2 + 5 & 0 + {}^-9 & 4 + 1 \end{bmatrix}$$

$$A + B = \begin{bmatrix} 1 & 11 & ^-4 \\ 3 & ^-9 & 5 \end{bmatrix}$$

Matrices, like real numbers, have identity elements. For every matrix A you can find another matrix such that their sum is A. For example, if $A = \begin{bmatrix} a_{11} & a_{12} \\ a_{21} & a_{22} \end{bmatrix}$, then $\begin{bmatrix} a_{11} & a_{12} \\ a_{21} & a_{22} \end{bmatrix} + \begin{bmatrix} 0 & 0 \\ 0 & 0 \end{bmatrix} = \begin{bmatrix} a_{11} & a_{12} \\ a_{21} & a_{22} \end{bmatrix}$.

Zero is the additive identity element for the real numbers.

The matrix $\begin{bmatrix} 0 & 0 \\ 0 & 0 \end{bmatrix}$ is called a **zero matrix.** Thus, the **identity matrix under addition** for any $m \times n$ matrix is an $m \times n$ zero matrix.

A zero matrix is often denoted by 0.

Matrices also have additive inverses. If $A = \begin{bmatrix} a_{11} & a_{12} \\ a_{21} & a_{22} \end{bmatrix}$, the matrix which must be added to A to obtain a zero matrix is $\begin{bmatrix} ^-a_{11} & ^-a_{12} \\ ^-a_{21} & ^-a_{22} \end{bmatrix}$ or ^-A. Therefore ^-A is the additive inverse of A.

$A + {}^-A = 0$

The additive inverse of any real number a is ^-a.

example

3 **Write the additive inverse of each matrix.**

a. $\begin{bmatrix} 4 & ^-7 \\ ^-9 & 3 \end{bmatrix}$ b. $\begin{bmatrix} c^2 & ^-t \\ 3x & ^-r^3 \end{bmatrix}$

You must write the additive inverse of each element.

a. $\begin{bmatrix} ^-4 & 7 \\ 9 & ^-3 \end{bmatrix}$ b. $\begin{bmatrix} ^-c^2 & t \\ ^-3x & r^3 \end{bmatrix}$

The additive inverse is used when subtracting matrices.

The difference $A - B$ of two $m \times n$ matrices is equal to the sum $A + {}^-B$, where ^-B represents the additive inverse of B.

Definition of Subtraction of Matrices

example

4 **Find $A - B$ if $A = \begin{bmatrix} 3 & 8 \\ ^-2 & 4 \end{bmatrix}$ and $B = \begin{bmatrix} 1 & 5 \\ ^-2 & 8 \end{bmatrix}$.**

$$\begin{aligned} A - B &= A + {}^-B \\ &= \begin{bmatrix} 3 & 8 \\ ^-2 & 4 \end{bmatrix} + \begin{bmatrix} ^-1 & ^-5 \\ 2 & ^-8 \end{bmatrix} \\ &= \begin{bmatrix} 3 + {}^-1 & 8 + {}^-5 \\ ^-2 + 2 & 4 + {}^-8 \end{bmatrix} \\ &= \begin{bmatrix} 2 & 3 \\ 0 & ^-4 \end{bmatrix} \end{aligned}$$

exercises

Exploratory Using double subscript notation, write the general matrix which has the given dimensions.

1. 3×3
2. 2×5
3. 6×4
4. 1×6

Find the additive inverse of each matrix.

5. $\begin{bmatrix} 6 & 5 \\ 8 & 4 \end{bmatrix}$
6. $\begin{bmatrix} ^-3 & ^-2 \\ ^-5 & ^-9 \end{bmatrix}$
7. $\begin{bmatrix} ^-2 & 1 \\ 0 & ^-3 \end{bmatrix}$
8. $\begin{bmatrix} 8 & ^-3 \\ 4 & ^-5 \end{bmatrix}$

Written Use matrices A, B, and C to find each sum or difference.

$$A = \begin{bmatrix} 1 & 5 & 7 \\ 5 & 2 & ^-6 \\ 3 & 0 & ^-2 \end{bmatrix} \quad B = \begin{bmatrix} ^-3 & 6 & ^-9 \\ 4 & ^-3 & 0 \\ 8 & ^-2 & 3 \end{bmatrix} \quad C = \begin{bmatrix} 6 & 9 & ^-4 \\ ^-11 & 13 & ^-8 \\ 20 & 4 & ^-2 \end{bmatrix}$$

1. $A + B$
2. $A + C$
3. $B + C$
4. $(A + B) + C$
5. $B + {^-A}$
6. $C - B$
7. $B - C$
8. $C - A$

Find the values of x and y for which each matrix equation is true.

9. $[x \quad 2y] = [y + 5 \quad x - 3]$
10. $[5 \quad 4x] = [2x \quad 5y]$
11. $\begin{bmatrix} 2x \\ 0 \\ 16 \end{bmatrix} = \begin{bmatrix} 8 - y \\ y \\ 4x \end{bmatrix}$
12. $\begin{bmatrix} y \\ 8x \end{bmatrix} = \begin{bmatrix} 15 + x \\ 2y \end{bmatrix}$

Prove each statement.

13. Addition of second order matrices is commutative.
14. Addition of second order matrices is associative.

3-3 Multiplication of Matrices

A matrix can be multiplied by a constant called a **scalar**. The product of a scalar k and a matrix A is defined as follows.

> The product of an $m \times n$ matrix A and a scalar k is an $m \times n$ matrix kA. Each element of kA is equal to k times the corresponding element of A.

Scalar Product

$k[a_{ij}] = [ka_{ij}]$

example

1 Multiply the matrix $\begin{bmatrix} 4 & 3 & ^-2 \\ ^-2 & 7 & ^-9 \end{bmatrix}$ by 6.

$$6\begin{bmatrix} 4 & 3 & ^-2 \\ ^-2 & 7 & ^-9 \end{bmatrix} = \begin{bmatrix} 6(4) & 6(3) & 6(^-2) \\ 6(^-2) & 6(7) & 6(^-9) \end{bmatrix} = \begin{bmatrix} 24 & 18 & ^-12 \\ ^-12 & 42 & ^-54 \end{bmatrix}$$

A matrix can also be multiplied by another matrix, provided that the first matrix has the same number of columns as the second matrix has rows. The product of the two matrices is found by multiplying rows and columns. The product of a row $[a\ b\ c]$ and a column $\begin{bmatrix} x \\ y \\ z \end{bmatrix}$ is the real number $ax + by + cz$. The row and column must have the same number of elements.

Suppose $A = \begin{bmatrix} a_1 & b_1 \\ a_2 & b_2 \end{bmatrix}$ and $X = \begin{bmatrix} x_1 & y_1 \\ x_2 & y_2 \end{bmatrix}$. Each element of matrix AX is the product of one row of matrix A and one column of matrix X, as shown below.

$$AX = \begin{bmatrix} a_1 & b_1 \\ a_2 & b_2 \end{bmatrix} \begin{bmatrix} x_1 & y_1 \\ x_2 & y_2 \end{bmatrix} = \begin{bmatrix} a_1x_1 + b_1x_2 & a_1y_1 + b_1y_2 \\ a_2x_1 + b_2x_2 & a_2y_1 + b_2y_2 \end{bmatrix}$$

In general, the product of two matrices is defined as follows.

The product of an $m \times n$ matrix A and an $n \times r$ matrix B is an $m \times r$ matrix AB. The ijth element of AB is the product of the ith row of A and the jth column of B.

Product of Two Matrices

examples

2 Find the product of A and B if $A = \begin{bmatrix} 4 & 3 \\ 7 & 2 \end{bmatrix}$ and $B = \begin{bmatrix} 8 & 5 \\ 9 & 6 \end{bmatrix}$.

$$AB = \begin{bmatrix} 4(8) + 3(9) & 4(5) + 3(6) \\ 7(8) + 2(9) & 7(5) + 2(6) \end{bmatrix}$$

$$AB = \begin{bmatrix} 59 & 38 \\ 74 & 47 \end{bmatrix}$$

3 Find the product of C and D if $C = \begin{bmatrix} 3 & 0 & {}^-4 & {}^-1 \\ {}^-6 & 9 & 8 & {}^-2 \end{bmatrix}$ and $D = \begin{bmatrix} 3 \\ 7 \\ {}^-1 \\ 5 \end{bmatrix}$.

$$CD = \begin{bmatrix} 3(3) + 0(7) + {}^-4({}^-1) + {}^-1(5) \\ {}^-6(3) + 9(7) + 8({}^-1) + {}^-2(5) \end{bmatrix}$$

$$CD = \begin{bmatrix} 9 + 0 + 4 + {}^-5 \\ {}^-18 + 63 + {}^-8 + {}^-10 \end{bmatrix}$$

$$CD = \begin{bmatrix} 8 \\ 27 \end{bmatrix}$$

The product has as many rows as the first matrix and as many columns as the second matrix.

exercises

Exploratory Find each product.

1. $3\begin{bmatrix}6 & 10\end{bmatrix}$
2. $^-5\begin{bmatrix}7 & 8 & ^-\sqrt{2}\end{bmatrix}$
3. $6\begin{bmatrix}\sqrt{5} & ^-1 & 4\end{bmatrix}$
4. $8\begin{bmatrix}^-3\\ 5\end{bmatrix}$
5. $\frac{1}{2}\begin{bmatrix}9 & ^-3\\ ^-6 & 6\end{bmatrix}$
6. $\frac{3}{4}\begin{bmatrix}8 & ^-7\\ ^-4 & 0\end{bmatrix}$

Name the dimensions of matrix C for each of the following. The dimensions of A and B are written as subscripts.

7. $A_{2\times3} \cdot B_{3\times6} = C$
8. $A_{5\times2} \cdot B_{2\times1} = C$
9. $A_{6\times4} \cdot C = B_{6\times3}$
10. $A_{4\times5} \cdot C = B_{4\times3}$
11. $C \cdot B_{1\times3} = A_{3\times3}$
12. $C \cdot B_{2\times4} = A_{4\times4}$

Written Use matrices A, B, and C to find each product.

$$A = \begin{bmatrix}7 & 0\\ 5 & 3\end{bmatrix} \qquad B = \begin{bmatrix}2 & 4\\ 8 & ^-4\\ ^-2 & 6\end{bmatrix} \qquad C = \begin{bmatrix}3 & ^-3 & 6\\ 5 & 4 & ^-2\end{bmatrix}$$

1. $3A$
2. $4B$
3. $2C$
4. ^-5A
5. BA
6. BC
7. CB
8. AC
9. AA
10. $(CB)A$
11. $B(AC)$
12. ^-4BC
13. Find $2A - 3B$ if $A = \begin{bmatrix}1 & ^-7\\ 3 & 2\end{bmatrix}$ and $B = \begin{bmatrix}^-4 & 5\\ 1 & ^-1\end{bmatrix}$.
14. Write the following equation as a system of 3 equations in 3 variables.

$$\begin{bmatrix}a_1 & b_1 & c_1\\ a_2 & b_2 & c_2\\ a_3 & b_3 & c_3\end{bmatrix}\begin{bmatrix}x\\ y\\ z\end{bmatrix} = \begin{bmatrix}d_1\\ d_2\\ d_3\end{bmatrix}$$

15. Let $A = \begin{bmatrix}a_{11} & a_{12}\\ a_{21} & a_{22}\end{bmatrix}$, $X = \begin{bmatrix}x\\ y\end{bmatrix}$, $Z = \begin{bmatrix}0\\ 0\end{bmatrix}$, and $B = \begin{bmatrix}b_1\\ b_2\end{bmatrix}$. Write $AX + B = Z$ as a system of linear equations.
16. Prove that the product of two general second order matrices is not commutative.
17. Prove that the product of three general second order matrices is associative.
18. Find two square matrices A and B for which $(A + B)^2$ does not equal $A^2 + 2AB + B^2$.

3-4 Inverses of Matrices

The identity matrix under multiplication for any matrix A is the matrix I, such that $IA = A$ and $AI = A$. A second order matrix can be represented by $\begin{bmatrix}a_1 & b_1\\ a_2 & b_2\end{bmatrix}$. Since $\begin{bmatrix}a_1 & b_1\\ a_2 & b_2\end{bmatrix}\begin{bmatrix}1 & 0\\ 0 & 1\end{bmatrix} = \begin{bmatrix}a_1 & b_1\\ a_2 & b_2\end{bmatrix}$, the

The multiplicative identity element for the real numbers is 1.

matrix $\begin{bmatrix} 1 & 0 \\ 0 & 1 \end{bmatrix}$ is the identity matrix under multiplication for any second order matrix.

The identity matrix of nth order, I_n, is the square matrix whose elements in the main diagonal, from upper left to lower right, are 1's, while all other elements are 0's.

Identity Matrix under Multiplication

example

1 Write the identity matrix under multiplication for a fifth order matrix.

$$I_5 = \begin{bmatrix} 1 & 0 & 0 & 0 & 0 \\ 0 & 1 & 0 & 0 & 0 \\ 0 & 0 & 1 & 0 & 0 \\ 0 & 0 & 0 & 1 & 0 \\ 0 & 0 & 0 & 0 & 1 \end{bmatrix}$$

Multiplicative inverses exist for some matrices. Suppose A is equal to $\begin{bmatrix} a_1 & b_1 \\ a_2 & b_2 \end{bmatrix}$, a non-zero matrix of second order. You can designate the inverse matrix, A^{-1}, as $\begin{bmatrix} x_1 & y_1 \\ x_2 & y_2 \end{bmatrix}$. The product of a matrix A and its inverse matrix A^{-1} must equal the identity matrix for multiplication, I, as shown below.

The multiplicative inverse of a non-zero real number x is $\frac{1}{x}$.

$$\begin{bmatrix} a_1 & b_1 \\ a_2 & b_2 \end{bmatrix} \begin{bmatrix} x_1 & y_1 \\ x_2 & y_2 \end{bmatrix} = \begin{bmatrix} 1 & 0 \\ 0 & 1 \end{bmatrix}$$

$$\begin{bmatrix} a_1x_1 + b_1x_2 & a_1y_1 + b_1y_2 \\ a_2x_1 + b_2x_2 & a_2y_1 + b_2y_2 \end{bmatrix} = \begin{bmatrix} 1 & 0 \\ 0 & 1 \end{bmatrix}$$

From the previous matrix equation, you can write two systems of linear equations.

$$a_1x_1 + b_1x_2 = 1 \qquad a_1y_1 + b_1y_2 = 0$$
$$a_2x_1 + b_2x_2 = 0 \qquad a_2y_1 + b_2y_2 = 1$$

By solving each pair of equations simultaneously, you can obtain values for x_1, x_2, y_1, and y_2.

$$x_1 = \frac{b_2}{a_1b_2 - a_2b_1} \qquad y_1 = \frac{^-b_1}{a_1b_2 - a_2b_1}$$

$$x_2 = \frac{^-a_2}{a_1b_2 - a_2b_1} \qquad y_2 = \frac{a_1}{a_1b_2 - a_2b_1}$$

The denominator $a_1b_2 - a_2b_1$ is equal to the determinant of A. If the determinant of $A \neq 0$, the inverse exists and can be defined as follows.

$$\text{If } A = \begin{bmatrix} a_1 & b_1 \\ a_2 & b_2 \end{bmatrix} \text{ and } \begin{vmatrix} a_1 & b_1 \\ a_2 & b_2 \end{vmatrix} \neq 0, \text{ then}$$

$$A^{-1} = \frac{1}{\begin{vmatrix} a_1 & b_1 \\ a_2 & b_2 \end{vmatrix}} \begin{bmatrix} b_2 & {}^-b_1 \\ {}^-a_2 & a_1 \end{bmatrix}$$

Inverse of a Second Order Matrix

example

2 **Find the inverse under multiplication of the matrix** $\begin{bmatrix} 3 & {}^-1 \\ 4 & 2 \end{bmatrix}$

$$\begin{vmatrix} 3 & {}^-1 \\ 4 & 2 \end{vmatrix} = 3(2) - 4({}^-1) = 10$$

The inverse is $\frac{1}{10}\begin{bmatrix} 2 & 1 \\ {}^-4 & 3 \end{bmatrix}$ or $\begin{bmatrix} \frac{1}{5} & \frac{1}{10} \\ -\frac{2}{5} & \frac{3}{10} \end{bmatrix}$

The inverse exists only when the determinant is not zero. Why?

Matrix equations can be solved using inverse matrices.

example

3 **Find matrix** M **if** $\begin{bmatrix} 2 & 1 \\ {}^-3 & 2 \end{bmatrix} M = \begin{bmatrix} 8 & {}^-9 \\ 5 & {}^-3 \end{bmatrix}$

$$\frac{1}{\begin{vmatrix} 2 & 1 \\ {}^-3 & 2 \end{vmatrix}} \begin{bmatrix} 2 & {}^-1 \\ 3 & 2 \end{bmatrix} \begin{bmatrix} 2 & 1 \\ {}^-3 & 2 \end{bmatrix} M = \frac{1}{\begin{vmatrix} 2 & 1 \\ {}^-3 & 2 \end{vmatrix}} \begin{bmatrix} 2 & {}^-1 \\ 3 & 2 \end{bmatrix} \begin{bmatrix} 8 & {}^-9 \\ 5 & {}^-3 \end{bmatrix}$$

$$\frac{1}{7}\begin{bmatrix} 7 & 0 \\ 0 & 7 \end{bmatrix} M = \frac{1}{7}\begin{bmatrix} 11 & {}^-15 \\ 34 & {}^-33 \end{bmatrix}$$

$$\begin{bmatrix} 1 & 0 \\ 0 & 1 \end{bmatrix} M = \begin{bmatrix} \frac{11}{7} & \frac{{}^-15}{7} \\ \frac{34}{7} & \frac{{}^-33}{7} \end{bmatrix}$$

$$M = \begin{bmatrix} \frac{11}{7} & \frac{{}^-15}{7} \\ \frac{34}{7} & \frac{{}^-33}{7} \end{bmatrix}$$

Notice that the inverse is written at the left of both sides of the equation. This is necessary since multiplication of matrices is not commutative.

exercises

Exploratory Find the determinant of each matrix.

1. $\begin{bmatrix} 1 & 3 \\ 2 & 5 \end{bmatrix}$
2. $\begin{bmatrix} ^-1 & ^-2 \\ 3 & ^-6 \end{bmatrix}$
3. $\begin{bmatrix} 4 & 3 \\ 8 & 6 \end{bmatrix}$
4. $\begin{bmatrix} 7 & 40 \\ 2 & 12 \end{bmatrix}$
5. $\begin{bmatrix} 5 & 9 \\ 7 & ^-3 \end{bmatrix}$
6. $\begin{bmatrix} 4 & 1 \\ ^-6 & 2 \end{bmatrix}$
7. $\begin{bmatrix} ^-9 & 3 \\ 14 & ^-3 \end{bmatrix}$
8. $\begin{bmatrix} 29 & ^-32 \\ 16 & ^-12 \end{bmatrix}$

9-16. State whether an inverse exists for each matrix in problems **1-8**.

Written

1-8. Find the inverse of each matrix in the exploratory exercises, if it exists.

Find matrix X for each of the following.

9. $\begin{bmatrix} 2 & ^-1 \\ 3 & 5 \end{bmatrix} X = \begin{bmatrix} 4 & 3 \\ 1 & ^-2 \end{bmatrix}$
10. $\begin{bmatrix} 5 & 1 \\ ^-2 & 2 \end{bmatrix} X + \begin{bmatrix} 3 & ^-2 \\ 4 & 6 \end{bmatrix} = \begin{bmatrix} 4 & 3 \\ 10 & 2 \end{bmatrix}$
11. $\begin{bmatrix} 1 & 2 \\ 3 & 6 \end{bmatrix} \begin{bmatrix} 2 & 2 \\ ^-1 & ^-1 \end{bmatrix} = X$
12. $\begin{bmatrix} 1 & 1 \\ 1 & 1 \end{bmatrix} \begin{bmatrix} 3 & 5 \\ ^-3 & ^-5 \end{bmatrix} = X$
13. $\begin{bmatrix} 3 & 7 \\ 8 & 9 \end{bmatrix} X - \begin{bmatrix} 2 & 7 \\ 6 & 9 \end{bmatrix} = \begin{bmatrix} 3 & 6 \\ 9 & 6 \end{bmatrix}$
14. $\begin{bmatrix} 3 & 1 \\ ^-2 & 0 \end{bmatrix} - \begin{bmatrix} 3 & 7 \\ 5 & ^-8 \end{bmatrix} X = \begin{bmatrix} ^-2 & 8 \\ 7 & 4 \end{bmatrix}$

Prove each statement.

15. $AI = IA = A$ for second order matrices.
16. $AA^{-1} = A^{-1}A = I$ for second order matrices.
17. If $AB = C$, where A, B, and C are second order matrices, prove that the product of the determinants of A and B is the determinant of C.

3-5 Augmented Matrix Solutions

Matrices can be used to solve systems of linear equations. The coefficients and constants of the system of equations shown below can be written in the form of a 3 × 4 **augmented matrix.**

An augmented matrix is an array of the coefficients and constants of a system of equations.

System of Equations	Augmented Matrix
$x - 2y + z = 7$ $3x + y - z = 2$ $2x + 3y + 2z = 7$	$\begin{bmatrix} 1 & ^-2 & 1 & 7 \\ 3 & 1 & ^-1 & 2 \\ 2 & 3 & 2 & 7 \end{bmatrix}$

This matrix can be modified by transforming rows since each row represents an equation. Each change of the matrix represents a corresponding change of the system. Any operation which results in an equivalent system of equations is permitted for the matrix. In general, you may use any of the following row operations to transform an augmented matrix.

1. Interchange any two rows.
2. Replace any row with a non-zero multiple of that row.
3. Replace any row with the sum of that row and another row.

Row Operations on Matrices

Why are these operations permitted?

example

1 **Solve the system of equations by using row operations.**

$$x - 2y + z = 7$$
$$3x + y - z = 2$$
$$2x + 3y + 2z = 7$$

First, write the augmented matrix.

$$\begin{bmatrix} 1 & -2 & 1 & 7 \\ 3 & 1 & -1 & 2 \\ 2 & 3 & 2 & 7 \end{bmatrix}$$

The objective is to get as many zeros in the matrix as possible.

Multiply row one by $^-3$ and add the result to row two.

$$\begin{bmatrix} 1 & -2 & 1 & 7 \\ 0 & 7 & -4 & -19 \\ 2 & 3 & 2 & 7 \end{bmatrix}$$

A zero is obtained in the a_{21} position.

Multiply row one by $^-2$ and add the result to row three.

$$\begin{bmatrix} 1 & -2 & 1 & 7 \\ 0 & 7 & -4 & -19 \\ 0 & 7 & 0 & -7 \end{bmatrix}$$

A zero is obtained in the a_{31} position.

Multiply row two by $^-1$ and add the result to row three.

$$\begin{bmatrix} 1 & -2 & 1 & 7 \\ 0 & 7 & -4 & -19 \\ 0 & 0 & 4 & 12 \end{bmatrix}$$

Add row three to row two.

$$\begin{bmatrix} 1 & -2 & 1 & 7 \\ 0 & 7 & 0 & -7 \\ 0 & 0 & 4 & 12 \end{bmatrix}$$

Multiply row three by $\frac{1}{4}$.

$$\begin{bmatrix} 1 & -2 & 1 & 7 \\ 0 & 7 & 0 & -7 \\ 0 & 0 & 1 & 3 \end{bmatrix}$$

The system of equations which this matrix represents could be easily solved by substitution.

$$x - 2y + z = 7$$
$$7y = {}^-7$$
$$z = 3$$

Multiply row three by $^-1$ and add the result to row one.

$$\begin{bmatrix} 1 & -2 & 0 & 4 \\ 0 & 7 & 0 & -7 \\ 0 & 0 & 1 & 3 \end{bmatrix}$$

Multiply row two by $\frac{1}{7}$.

$$\begin{bmatrix} 1 & -2 & 0 & 4 \\ 0 & 1 & 0 & -1 \\ 0 & 0 & 1 & 3 \end{bmatrix}$$

Multiply row two by 2 and add the result to row one.

$$\begin{bmatrix} 1 & 0 & 0 & 2 \\ 0 & 1 & 0 & -1 \\ 0 & 0 & 1 & 3 \end{bmatrix}$$

Notice the positions of the 1's and 0's.

Thus, $x = 2$, $y = {}^-1$, and $z = 3$.

exercises

Exploratory State the row operations you would use to locate a zero in the second column of row one.

1. $\begin{bmatrix} 3 & 5 & 7 \\ 6 & ^{-}1 & ^{-}8 \end{bmatrix}$
2. $\begin{bmatrix} 4 & ^{-}7 & ^{-}2 \\ 1 & 2 & 7 \end{bmatrix}$
3. $\begin{bmatrix} 3 & 3 & ^{-}9 \\ ^{-}2 & 1 & ^{-}4 \end{bmatrix}$
4. $\begin{bmatrix} 2 & 4 & 3 \\ ^{-}2 & ^{-}3 & 1 \end{bmatrix}$
5. $\begin{bmatrix} ^{-}6 & ^{-}2 & ^{-}3 \\ 4 & 3 & 1 \end{bmatrix}$
6. $\begin{bmatrix} 5 & ^{-}3 & 0 \\ 3 & 6 & ^{-}6 \end{bmatrix}$

7-12. State the row operations you would use to locate a zero in the first column of row two for the matrices in problems **1-6**.

Written Solve each system of equations using augmented matrices.

1. $3x + 5y = 7$
   $6x - y = ^{-}8$
2. $4x - 7y = ^{-}2$
   $x + 2y = 7$
3. $3x + 3y = ^{-}9$
   $^{-}2x + y = ^{-}4$
4. $x - y + z = 3$
   $2y - z = 1$
   $2y - x + 1 = 0$
5. $x + y + z = ^{-}2$
   $2x - 3y + z = ^{-}11$
   $^{-}x + 2y - z = 8$
6. $2x + 6y + 8z = 5$
   $^{-}2x + 9y - 12z = ^{-}1$
   $4x + 6y - 4z = 3$

Write each equation in standard form. Then solve each system of equations using matrices.

7. $5x = 3y - 50$
   $2y = 1 - 3x$
8. $2x + y - 2z - 7 = 0$
   $x - 2y - 5z + 1 = 0$
   $4x + y + z + 1 = 0$
9. $x + y + z - 6 = 0$
   $2x - 3y + 4z - 3 = 0$
   $4x - 8y + 4z - 12 = 0$
10. $x + 2y = 5$
    $3x + 4z = 2$
    $2y + 3w = ^{-}2$
    $3z - 2w = 1$
11. $w + x + y + z = 0$
    $2w + x - y - z = ^{-}4$
    $^{-}w - x + y + z = 2$
    $2x + y = 1$
12. $4x + 2y + 3z = 6$
    $2x + 7y = 3z$
    $^{-}3x - 9y + 13 = ^{-}2z$

3-6 Geometrical Vectors

A **vector** is a quantity which possesses both magnitude and direction. For example, velocity and voltage may be represented as vectors. Geometrically, a vector is represented as a directed line segment.

A scalar possesses only magnitude. Real numbers are scalars.

A directed line segment with an initial point at O and terminal point at P is shown at the right. It can be designated $\vec{v}$ or $\overrightarrow{OP}$. The direction of the arrowhead indicates the direction of the vector, and the length of the line segment indicates its **magnitude.** The magnitude of $\vec{v}$ is denoted by $|\vec{v}|$.

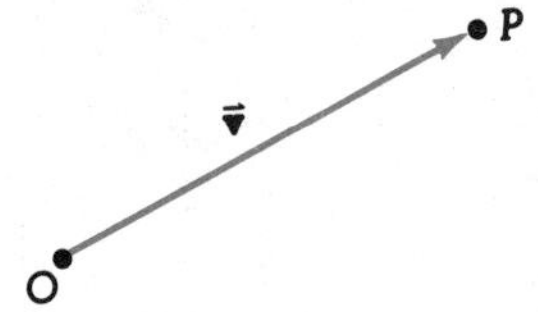

A vector in **standard position** has its initial point at the origin. The **amplitude** of the vector is the directed angle between the positive x-axis and the vector. The amplitude of $\vec{u}$ is 65°.

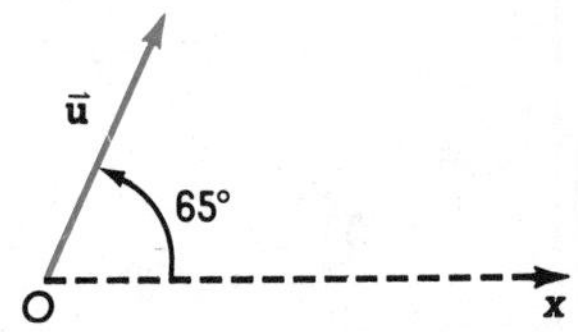

example

1 Measure the magnitude (in centimeters) and amplitude of $\vec{a}$.

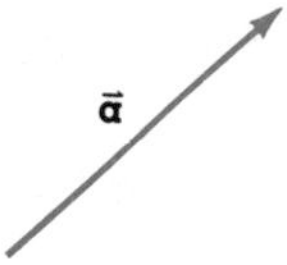

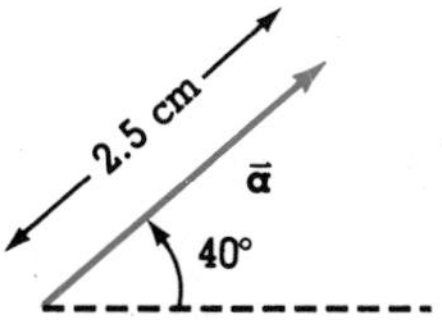

The magnitude is 2.5 cm.
The amplitude is 40°.

Two vectors are equal if and only if they have the same direction and the same magnitude. Five vectors are shown at the right. Vectors $\vec{a}$ and $\vec{b}$ are equal, since $|\vec{a}| = |\vec{b}|$ and they have the same direction. Since $|\vec{c}| \neq |\vec{d}|$, $\vec{c} \neq \vec{d}$. Since $\vec{c}$ and $\vec{e}$ have different directions, $\vec{c} \neq \vec{e}$, although $|\vec{c}| = |\vec{e}|$.

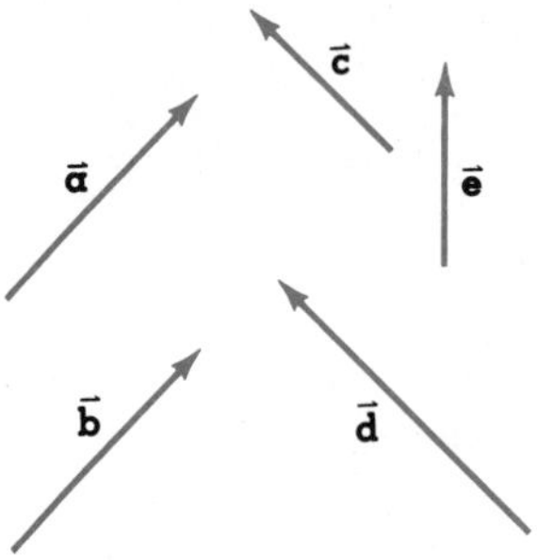

Addition of vectors involves both direction and magnitude. The sum of two or more vectors is called the **resultant** of the vectors. You can find the resultant of vectors by using the **triangle method** or the **parallelogram method.** These methods are illustrated by the following examples.

example

2 Find the sum of $\vec{p}$ and $\vec{q}$.

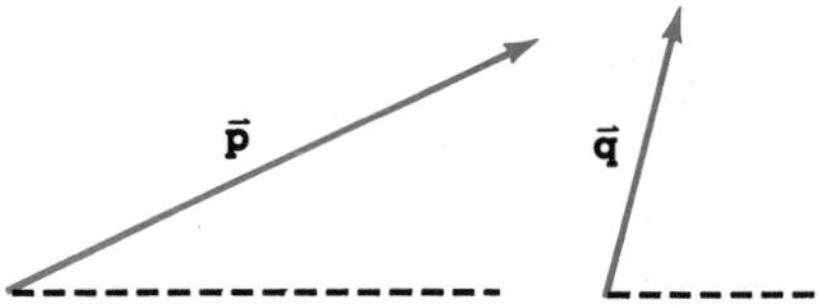

Copy $\vec{p}$. Then copy $\vec{q}$, placing the initial point of $\vec{q}$ at the initial point of $\vec{p}$.
Form a parallelogram which has $\vec{p}$ and $\vec{q}$ as two of its sides. Draw broken lines to represent the other two sides.

This is called the parallelogram method.

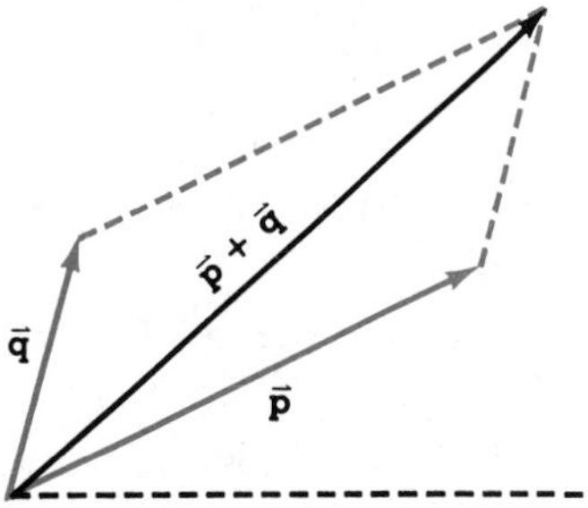

The resultant is the vector from the initial point of $\vec{p}$ and $\vec{q}$ to the opposite corner of the parallelogram.

example

3 **Find the sum of $\vec{r}$ and $\vec{s}$.**

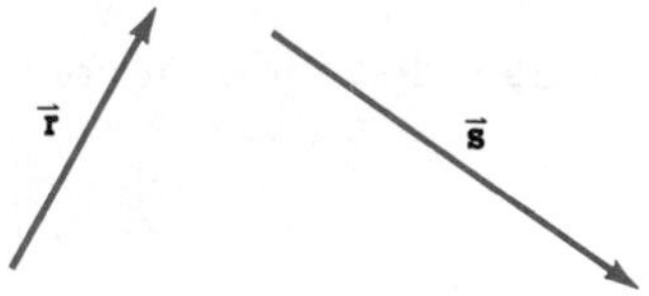

Copy $\vec{r}$. Then copy $\vec{s}$, placing the initial point of $\vec{s}$ at the terminal point of $\vec{r}$.

This is called the <u>triangle method</u>.

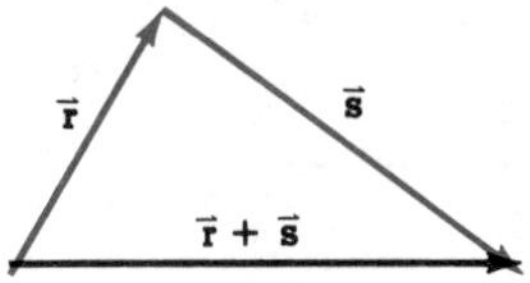

The resultant is the vector from the initial point of $\vec{r}$ to the terminal point of $\vec{s}$.

The product of a scalar k and a vector $\vec{a}$ is a vector with the same direction as $\vec{a}$. The magnitude of $k\vec{a}$ is equal to $k|\vec{a}|$. In the figure at the right, $\vec{d}$ is equal to $3\vec{c}$.

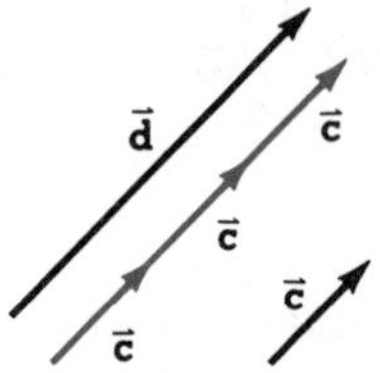

A vector having direction opposite to that of a vector $\vec{v}$ and having the same magnitude is represented by $^-\vec{v}$. Vectors can be subtracted, since $\vec{u} - \vec{v} = \vec{u} + {}^-\vec{v}$.

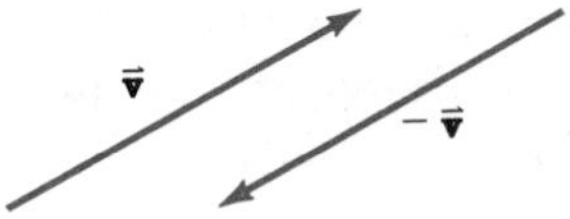

example

4 **Subtract $\vec{s}$ from $2\vec{r}$.**

$2\vec{r} - \vec{s} = 2\vec{r} + {}^-\vec{s}$

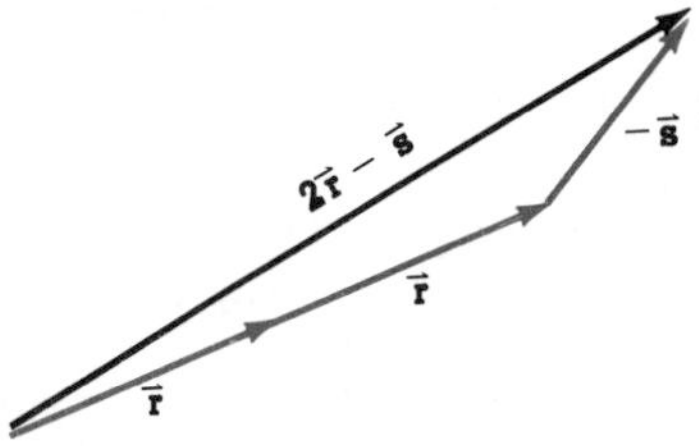

Two or more vectors whose sum is a given vector are called components of this vector. Components of a vector can be found in any direction. In the figure at the right, $\vec{x}$ and $\vec{y}$ are the vertical and horizontal components of $\vec{a}$.

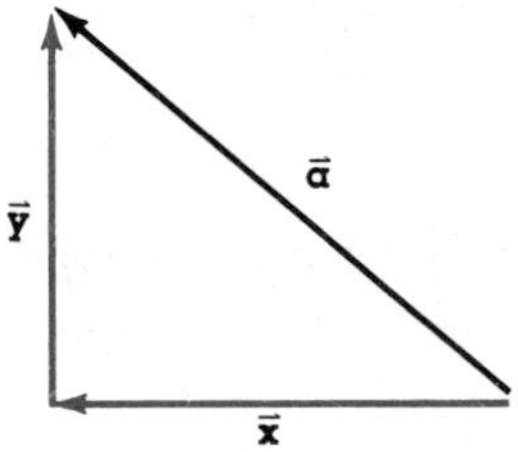

example

5 **Graph a vector which has a magnitude of 3 cm and an amplitude of 53°. Then graph its vertical and horizontal components. Find the magnitude of each component.**

Graph the vector. Then draw a horizontal line through the initial point of the vector, and a vertical line through the terminal point of the vector. The lines will form a triangle. Measure the sides of the triangle to determine their magnitudes.

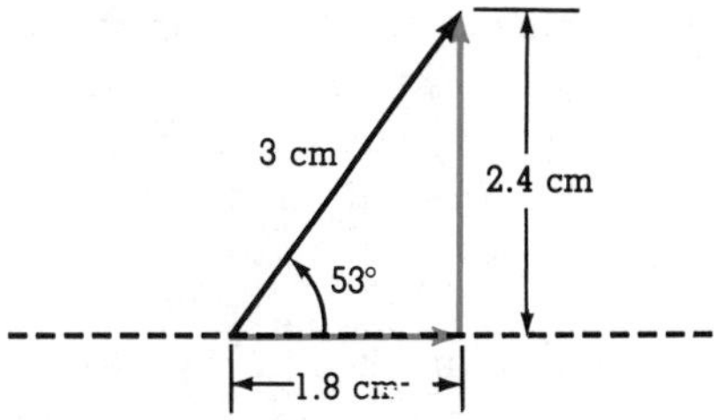

The magnitude of the vertical component is 2.4 cm. The magnitude of the horizontal component is 1.8 cm.

exercises

Exploratory Draw a vector with the given magnitude and amplitude. Use a metric ruler and a protractor.

1. 5 cm; 40°
2. 10 cm; 50°
3. 4 cm; 180°
4. 3 cm; 120°
5. 7.5 cm; 270°
6. 6 cm; 65°

Answer each question.

7. Is vector addition commutative?
8. Is vector addition associative?

Written Use vectors $\vec{a}$, $\vec{b}$, $\vec{c}$, and $\vec{d}$, a metric ruler, and a protractor to find each vector sum or difference.

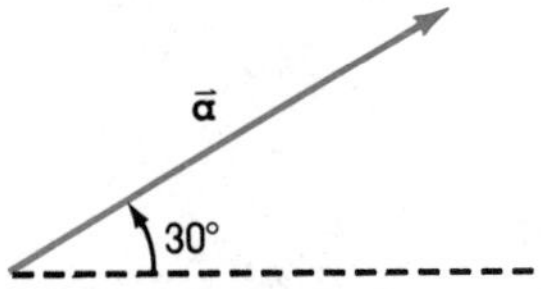

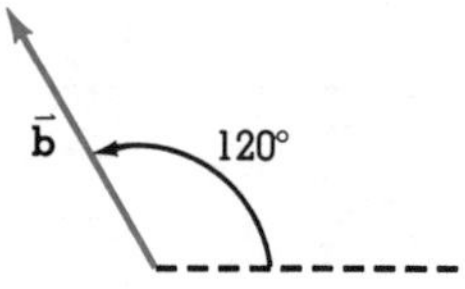

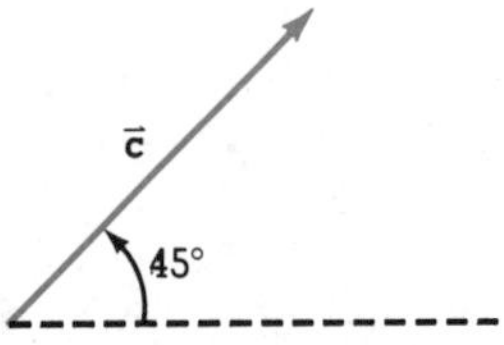

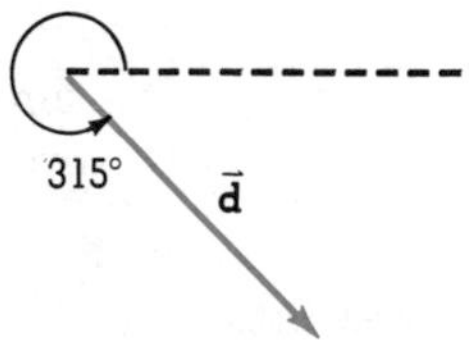

1. $\vec{a} + \vec{b}$
2. $\vec{a} + \vec{c}$
3. $\vec{c} + \vec{d}$
4. $\vec{b} + \vec{d}$
5. $\vec{a} + \vec{d}$
6. $\vec{b} + \vec{c}$
7. $\vec{a} + \vec{b} + \vec{c}$
8. $2\vec{a} + \vec{b}$
9. $3\vec{c} + 2\vec{d}$
10. $\vec{a} + (^-\vec{b})$
11. $\vec{b} - \vec{c}$
12. $2\vec{b} - \vec{d}$

13-24. Measure to find the magnitude and amplitude of each resultant in problems 1-12.

Find the magnitude of the vertical and horizontal components of each vector.

25. $\vec{a}$
26. $\vec{b}$
27. $\vec{c}$
28. $\vec{d}$

Vector Diagrams

Using Mathematics

You can solve problems involving forces, velocity, and displacements by drawing vector diagrams. You will need a sharp pencil, a metric ruler, and a protractor.

Example A plane flying due east at 100 m/sec is blown due south at 40 m/sec by a strong wind. Find the plane's resultant velocity (speed and direction).

First, choose an appropriate scale. Let 1 cm = 20 m/sec.

Next, draw the two component vectors to scale. Place the initial point of the second vector at the terminal point of the first vector.

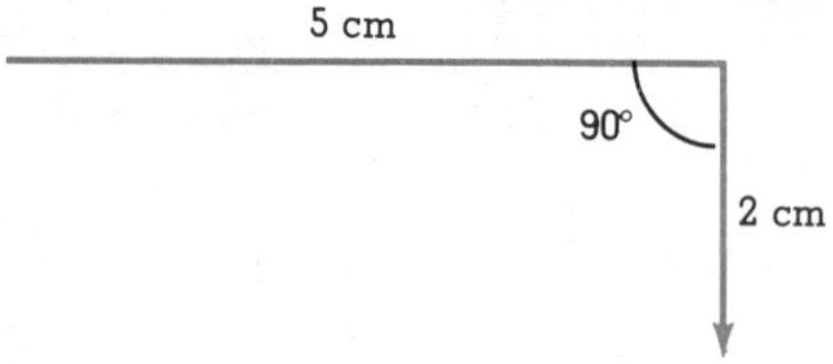

Finally, draw the resultant and measure its direction and length. Multiply the length of the resultant by the scale to find the magnitude.

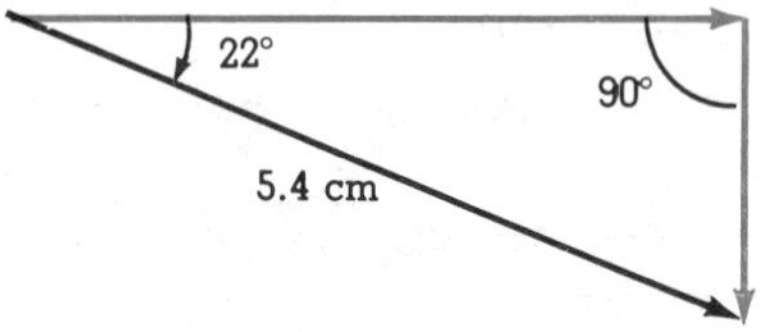

The direction is 22° south of east.
The speed of the plane is 5.4 × 20 m/sec, or 108 m/sec.

Exercises Use vector diagrams to solve each problem.

1. An airplane flies due west at 240 km/hr. At the same time, the wind blows it due south at 70 km/hr. What is the plane's resultant velocity?
2. A hiker leaves camp and walks 15 km due north. The hiker then walks 15 km due east. What is the hiker's direction and displacement from the starting point?
3. Two soccer players kick the ball at the same time. One player's foot exerts a force of 70 newtons west. The other's foot exerts a force of 50 newtons north. What is the magnitude and direction of the resultant force on the ball?
4. An airplane flies at 150 km/hr and heads 30° south of east. A 40 km/hr wind blows it in the direction 30° west of south. What is the plane's resultant velocity?

3-7 Algebraic Vectors

Vectors can be represented algebraically, using ordered pairs of real numbers. The ordered pair (x, y) represents the vector $\overrightarrow{OP}$ from the origin O to the point P with coordinates (x, y). For example, the ordered pair (1, 2) represents the vector from the origin to the point (1, 2).

Since vectors having the same magnitude and direction are equal, many vectors can be represented by the same ordered pair. Each vector at the right can be represented by the ordered pair (1, 2). *The initial point of a vector can be anywhere in the plane.*

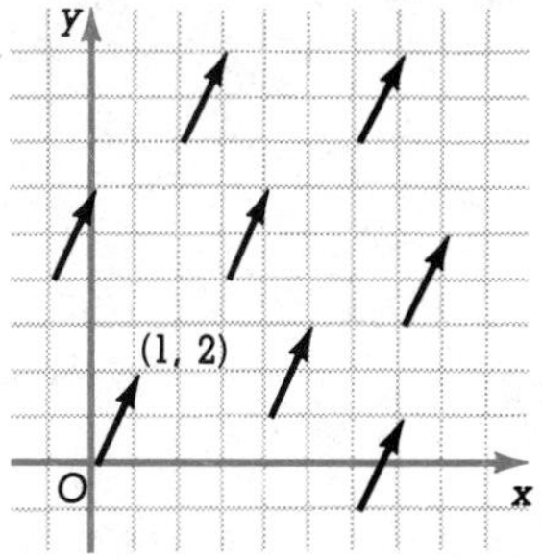

Suppose P_1 and P_2 are any two points in the plane. The diagram at the right shows a right triangle with $\overrightarrow{P_1P_2}$ as its hypotenuse. A single ordered pair can be found to represent $\overrightarrow{P_1P_2}$.

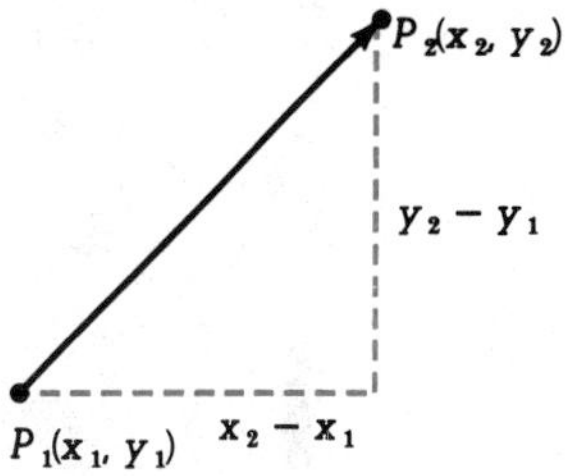

Representation of a Vector as an Ordered Pair

> **Suppose $P_1(x_1, y_1)$ is the initial point of a vector, and $P_2(x_2, y_2)$ is the terminal point. The ordered pair of numbers which represents $\overrightarrow{P_1P_2}$ is $(x_2 - x_1, y_2 - y_1)$.**
>
> **Its magnitude $|\overrightarrow{P_1P_2}| = \sqrt{(x_2 - x_1)^2 + (y_2 - y_1)^2}$.**

The order of the coordinates of P_1 and P_2 is important. For example, $\overrightarrow{P_2P_1}$ is represented by $(x_1 - x_2, y_1 - y_2)$.

examples

1 Find the ordered pair which represents the vector from $A(4, 9)$ to $B(8, 3)$.

$\overrightarrow{AB} = (8 - 4, 3 - 9) = (4, {}^{-}6)$

2 Find the magnitude of the vector from $C(5, 7)$ to $D({}^{-}3, 8)$.

$$|\overrightarrow{CD}| = \sqrt{({}^{-}3 - 5)^2 + (8 - 7)^2}$$
$$= \sqrt{({}^{-}8)^2 + 1^2}$$
$$= \sqrt{65}$$

Vectors, when represented as ordered pairs, can be added or subtracted algebraically. A vector can also be multiplied by a scalar. The rules for operations on vectors are similar to those for matrices.

The following operations are true for $\vec{a} = (a_1, a_2)$, $\vec{b} = (b_1, b_2)$, and any real number k.

Addition $\vec{a} + \vec{b} = (a_1, a_2) + (b_1, b_2) = (a_1 + b_1, a_2 + b_2)$

Subtraction $\vec{a} - \vec{b} = (a_1, a_2) + (^-b_1, {}^-b_2)$
$= (a_1 - b_1, a_2 - b_2)$

Scalar Multiplication $k\vec{a} = k(a_1, a_2) = (ka_1, ka_2)$

Vector Operations

example

3 If $\vec{r} = (4, 5)$, and $\vec{s} = (^-2, 7)$, find each of the following.
a. $\vec{r} + \vec{s}$ b. $\vec{r} - \vec{s}$ c. $6\vec{s}$

a. $\vec{r} + \vec{s} = (4, 5) + (^-2, 7)$
$= (2, 12)$

b. $\vec{r} - \vec{s} = (4, 5) - (^-2, 7)$
$= (6, {}^-2)$

c. $6\vec{s} = 6(^-2, 7)$
$= (^-12, 42)$

A vector of unit length in the direction of the positive x-axis is represented by the symbol $\vec{i}$ (not to be confused with the imaginary unit i). Also $\vec{j}$ is a vector of unit length in the positive direction of the y-axis. Therefore, $\vec{i} = (1, 0)$ and $\vec{j} = (0, 1)$. These vectors are called **unit vectors.**

A vector of unit length has a magnitude of 1.

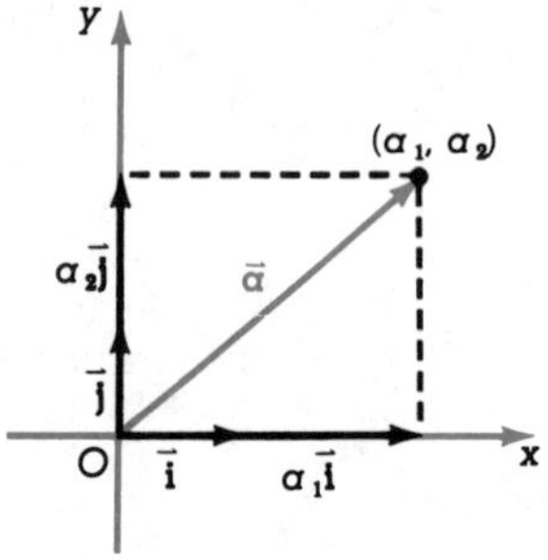

Vector $\vec{a}$, (a_1, a_2) can be expressed as $a_1\vec{i} + a_2\vec{j}$. The proof is shown below.

$a_1\vec{i} + a_2\vec{j} = a_1(1, 0) + a_2(0, 1)$
$= (a_1, 0) + (0, a_2)$ *Scalar Product*
$= (a_1 + 0, 0 + a_2)$ *Addition of Vectors*
$= (a_1, a_2)$ *Zero is the additive identity element.*

But $(a_1, a_2) = \vec{a}$, so $\vec{a} = a_1\vec{i} + a_2\vec{j}$.

Thus, any vector which is represented by an ordered pair can also be written as the sum of unit vectors.

examples

4 **Write $\vec{r}$, $(^-4, 6)$, as the sum of unit vectors.**

$\vec{r} = {}^-4\vec{i} + 6\vec{j}$

5 **Write $\overrightarrow{ST}$ as the sum of unit vectors, for points $S(^-1, 3)$ and $T(3, 8)$.**

First, write $\overrightarrow{ST}$ as an ordered pair.

$\overrightarrow{ST} = (3 - {}^-1, 8 - 3) = (4, 5)$

Then, write $\overrightarrow{ST}$ as the sum of unit vectors.

$\overrightarrow{ST} = 4\vec{i} + 5\vec{j}$

exercises

Exploratory Find the magnitude of each vector.

1. (4, 3)
2. (6, 7)
3. (5, 8)
4. ($^-2$, $^-3$)
5. (5, $^-9$)
6. (24, 7)
7. ($^-16$, 11)
8. ($^-5$, 15)

9-16. Write each vector in problems 1-8 as the sum of unit vectors.

Find the sum of the given vectors algebraically.

17. (3, 5) + ($^-1$, 2)
18. ($^-5$, 2) + (1, $^-8$)
19. ($^-1$, 6) + ($^-8$, $^-5$)
20. ($^-2$, $^-3$) + (2, 4)
21. $\vec{i} + \vec{j}$
22. $2\vec{i} + {}^-\vec{j}$
23. $3\vec{i} + 4\vec{j}$
24. $5\vec{i} + {}^-3\vec{j}$
25. ${}^-7\vec{i} + 5\vec{j}$

Answer each question.

26. If two vectors have the same magnitude, is it true that the ordered pairs representing them are necessarily identical?
27. If two vectors have the same amplitude, is it true that the ordered pairs representing them are necessarily identical?

Written Find an ordered pair which represents $\overrightarrow{AB}$, for points A and B with the given coordinates.

1. $A(1, 3)$; $B(^-2, 5)$
2. $A(7, 7)$; $B(^-2, ^-2)$
3. $A(5, 0)$; $B(7, 6)$
4. $A(0, 5)$; $B(^-5, 0)$
5. $A(5, ^-6)$; $B(6, ^-5)$
6. $A(^-4, ^-3)$; $B(^-9, 2)$

7-12. Find the magnitude of $\overrightarrow{AB}$ for problems 1-6.

Find an ordered pair to represent $\vec{u}$ in each equation below, if $\vec{v}$ = (3, $^-5$) and $\vec{w}$ = ($^-4$, 2).

13. $\vec{u} = \vec{v} + \vec{w}$
14. $\vec{u} = \vec{v} - \vec{w}$
15. $\vec{u} = 5\vec{w}$
16. $\vec{u} = 3\vec{v}$
17. $\vec{u} = \vec{w} - 2\vec{v}$
18. $\vec{u} = \vec{v} - 3\vec{w}$
19. $\vec{u} = 4\vec{v} + 3\vec{w}$
20. $\vec{u} = 5\vec{w} - 3\vec{v}$
21. $\vec{u} = 6\vec{w} - 2\vec{v}$
22. Prove that $\vec{a} + \vec{b} = \vec{b} + \vec{a}$.
23. Find the zero vector in two dimensions. By definition this is the vector which does not alter any vector upon addition.

3-8 Vectors in Space

Imagine three real number lines intersecting at the zero point of each in a manner such that each line is perpendicular to the plane determined by the other two. To show this arrangement on paper, a figure is used which conveys the feeling of depth. The axes are named the *x*-axis, *y*-axis, and z-axis.

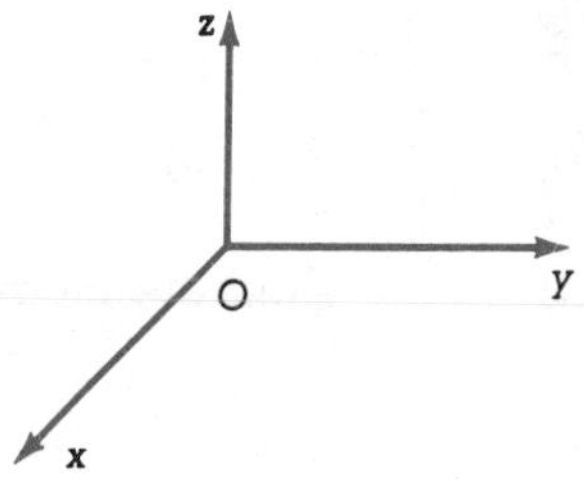

Each point in space corresponds to an ordered triple of real numbers. To locate a point P which has the coordinates (x_1, y_1, z_1), first find x_1 on the x-axis, y_1 on the y-axis, and z_1 on the z-axis. Then construct (in your imagination) a plane perpendicular to the x-axis at x_1, and construct planes in a similar manner to the y-axis and z-axis at y_1 and z_1, respectively. The three planes intersect at the point P, the only point in space with the coordinates (x_1, y_1, z_1).

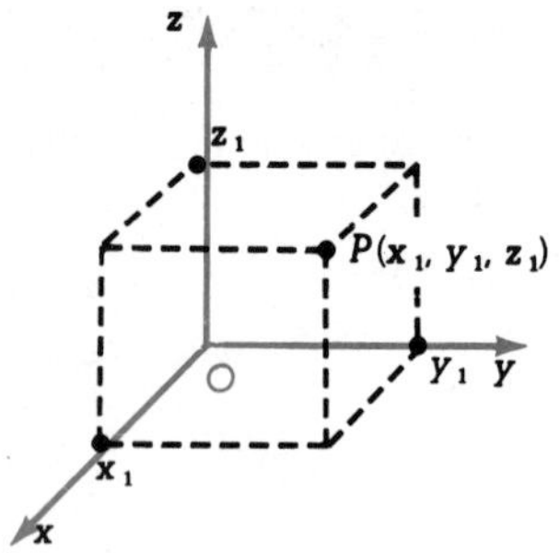

example

1 **Locate the point (3, 5, 4).**

First, locate 3 on the x-axis, 5 on the y-axis, and 4 on the z-axis.

Then, draw broken lines, forming parallelograms to represent planes.

The planes intersect at the point (3, 5, 4).

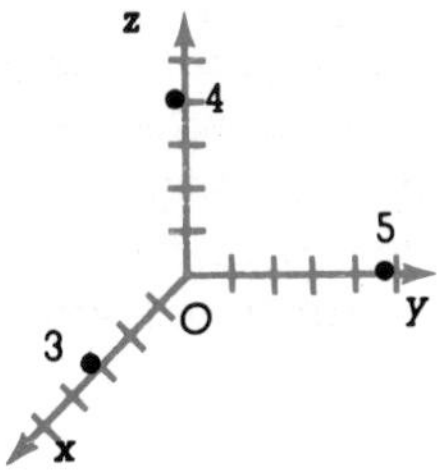

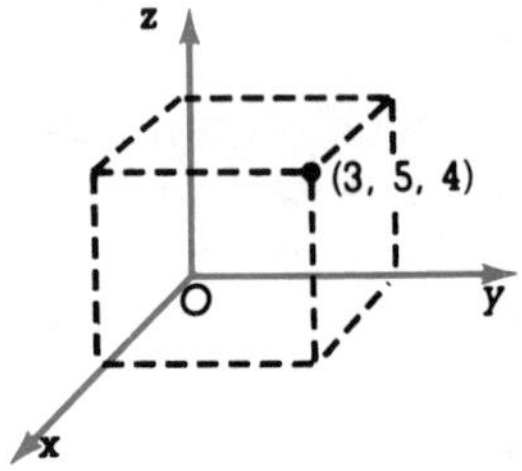

A vector in space can be represented as an ordered triple. The geometric interpretation is basically the same as that for a vector in the plane. A directed line segment from the origin O to $P(x, y, z)$ is called the vector $\overrightarrow{OP}$ corresponding to vector (x, y, z).

All vectors have both magnitude and direction, except the zero vector.

The distance between two points in space is found by a formula which is an extension of that used in the plane. The distance from the origin to point (x, y, z) is $\sqrt{x^2 + y^2 + z^2}$. Therefore, the magnitude of a vector (x, y, z) is $\sqrt{x^2 + y^2 + z^2}$.

A vector from $P_1(x_1, y_1, z_1)$ to $P_2(x_2, y_2, z_2)$ in space can be represented by an ordered triple as follows.

$$\overrightarrow{P_1P_2} = (x_2 - x_1, y_2 - y_1, z_2 - z_1)$$

Its magnitude $|\overrightarrow{P_1P_2}| = \sqrt{(x_2 - x_1)^2 + (y_2 - y_1)^2 + (z_2 - z_1)^2}$

Representation of a Vector as an Ordered Triple

examples

2 **Find the ordered triple which represents the vector from Q (9, 8, 7) to R (10, 6, 4).**

$$\overrightarrow{QR} = (10 - 9, 6 - 8, 4 - 7) = (1, ^-2, ^-3)$$

3 **Find the magnitude of $\overrightarrow{QR}$.**

$$|\overrightarrow{QR}| = \sqrt{1^2 + (^-2)^2 + (^-3)^2} = \sqrt{14}$$

You can add or subtract vectors in space which are represented by ordered triples. They can also be multiplied by scalars.

example

4 **Find an ordered triple which represents $2\vec{u} - \vec{w}$, if $\vec{u} = (3, ^-2, 7)$ and $\vec{w} = (4, 7, ^-5)$.**

$$2\vec{u} - \vec{w} = 2(3, ^-2, 7) - (4, 7, ^-5)$$
$$= (6, ^-4, 14) - (4, 7, ^-5)$$
$$= (2, ^-11, 19)$$

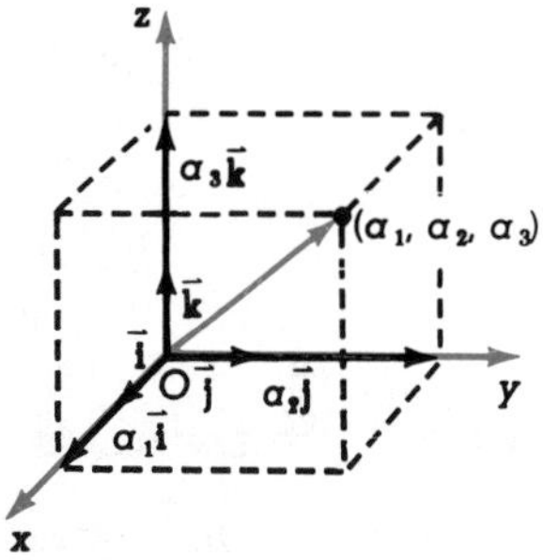

Three unit vectors, called $\vec{\mathbf{i}}$, $\vec{\mathbf{j}}$, and $\vec{\mathbf{k}}$ are required for a three-dimensional coordinate system. The unit vector on the x-axis is $\vec{\mathbf{i}}$, $\vec{\mathbf{j}}$ is the unit vector on the y-axis, and $\vec{\mathbf{k}}$ is the unit vector on the z-axis. Therefore $\vec{\mathbf{i}} = (1, 0, 0)$, $\vec{\mathbf{j}} = (0, 1, 0)$, and $\vec{\mathbf{k}} = (0, 0, 1)$. These unit vectors are shown at the right with a representation of vector $\vec{a}(a_1, a_2, a_3)$. The component vectors of $\vec{a}$ along the three axes are $a_1\vec{\mathbf{i}}$, $a_2\vec{\mathbf{j}}$, and $a_3\vec{\mathbf{k}}$. Vector $\vec{a}$ can be written in the form $\vec{a} = a_1\vec{\mathbf{i}} + a_2\vec{\mathbf{j}} + a_3\vec{\mathbf{k}}$.

examples

5 **Write $\vec{v}$, (4, $^-8$, 1), as the sum of unit vectors.**

$$\vec{v} = 4\vec{i} + {}^-8\vec{j} + \vec{k}$$

6 **Write $\overrightarrow{PQ}$ as the sum of unit vectors, for points $P(2, 5, 5)$ and $Q(3, ^-1, 4)$.**

$$\overrightarrow{PQ} = (3 - 2, ^-1 - 5, 4 - 5)$$
$$\overrightarrow{PQ} = (1, ^-6, ^-1)$$
$$\overrightarrow{PQ} = \vec{i} + {}^-6\vec{j} + {}^-\vec{k} \text{ or } \vec{i} - 6\vec{j} - \vec{k}$$

exercises

Exploratory Locate points having the given coordinates.

1. (2, 1, 3)
2. (3, 4, 9)
3. (1, 0, 3)
4. (5, 2, 6)
5. (4, 1, $^-3$)
6. (6, $^-2$, 4)

7-12. Find the magnitude of a vector from the origin to the given point for problems 1-6.

13-18. Write each vector in problems 1-6 as the sum of unit vectors.

Written Find an ordered triple which represents $\overrightarrow{AB}$, for points A and B with the given coordinates.

1. $A(3, 3, ^-1)$; $B(5, 3, 2)$
2. $A(8, 1, 1)$; $B(4, 0, 1)$
3. $A(^-2, 5, 8)$; $B(3, 9, ^-3)$
4. $A(^-2, 4, 7)$; $B(^-3, 5, 2)$
5. $A(32, 6, 9)$; $B(20, 11, 10)$
6. $A(23, 17, 56)$; $B(20, 21, 44)$

7-12. Find the magnitude of $\overrightarrow{AB}$ for problems 1-6.

13-18. Write $\overrightarrow{AB}$ as the sum of unit vectors for problems 1-6.

Find an ordered triple to represent $\vec{u}$ in each equation below, if $\vec{v} = (2, ^-5, ^-3)$ and $\vec{w} = (^-3, 4, ^-7)$.

19. $\vec{u} = \vec{v} + \vec{w}$
20. $\vec{u} = \vec{w} - \vec{v}$
21. $\vec{u} = 3\vec{v} - \vec{w}$
22. $\vec{u} = \vec{v} - 3\vec{w}$
23. $\vec{u} = 5\vec{v} - 3\vec{w}$
24. $\vec{u} = 2\vec{w} - 4\vec{v}$

25-30. Write $\vec{u}$ as the sum of unit vectors for problems 19-24.

31. Show that $|\overrightarrow{P_1P_2}| = |\overrightarrow{P_2P_1}|$.

32. If $\vec{a} = (a_1, a_2, a_3)$, then $^-\vec{a}$ is defined to be $(^-a_1, ^-a_2, ^-a_3)$. Show that $|^-\vec{a}| = |\vec{a}|$.

3-9 Perpendicular Vectors

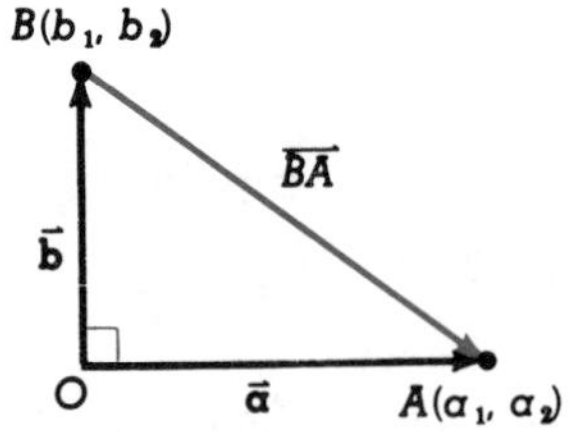

The vectors $\vec{a}$, $\vec{b}$, and $\overrightarrow{BA}$ are shown in the figure at the right. If $\vec{a}$ is perpendicular to $\vec{b}$, their magnitudes satisfy the Pythagorean theorem, as shown below.

$$|\overrightarrow{BA}|^2 = |\vec{a}|^2 + |\vec{b}|^2$$

The equation can be rewritten as follows.

$$\begin{aligned}
|\overrightarrow{BA}|^2 &= \left(\sqrt{(a_1 - b_1)^2 + (a_2 - b_2)^2}\right)^2 \\
&= (a_1 - b_1)^2 + (a_2 - b_2)^2 \\
&= a_1^2 - 2a_1b_1 + b_1^2 + a_2^2 - 2a_2b_2 + b_2^2 \\
&= (a_1^2 + a_2^2) + (b_1^2 + b_2^2) - 2(a_1b_1 + a_2b_2) \\
|\overrightarrow{BA}|^2 &= |\vec{a}|^2 + |\vec{b}|^2 - 2(a_1b_1 + a_2b_2)
\end{aligned}$$

Compare this equation with the original one.

Thus, $|\overrightarrow{BA}|^2 = |\vec{a}|^2 + |\vec{b}|^2$ if and only if $a_1b_1 + a_2b_2 = 0$.

The expression $a_1b_1 + a_2b_2$ is often used in studying vectors. It has a special name, the **inner product** of $\vec{a}$ and $\vec{b}$.

If $\vec{a}$ and $\vec{b}$ are two vectors, (a_1, a_2) and (b_1, b_2), the inner product of $\vec{a}$ and $\vec{b}$ is defined as follows.

$$\vec{a} \cdot \vec{b} = a_1b_1 + a_2b_2$$

$\vec{a} \cdot \vec{b}$ is read "$\vec{a}$ dot $\vec{b}$" and is often called the dot product.

Inner Product of Vectors in the Plane

Two vectors are perpendicular if and only if their inner product is zero.

The inner product of two vectors is a scalar.

examples

1 Find the inner product of $\vec{a}$ and $\vec{b}$ if $\vec{a} = (3, 5)$ and $\vec{b} = (8, {}^-3)$.

$\vec{a} \cdot \vec{b} = 3(8) + 5({}^-3)$
$= 9$ *The vectors are not perpendicular.*

2 Find the inner product of $\vec{p}$ and $\vec{q}$, if $\vec{p} = (7, {}^-2)$ and $\vec{q} = (4, 14)$.

$\vec{p} \cdot \vec{q} = 7(4) + {}^-2(14)$
$= 0$ *The vectors are perpendicular.*

You can also find the inner product of vectors in space.

Inner Product of Vectors in Space

If $\vec{a} = (a_1, a_2, a_3)$ and $\vec{b} = (b_1, b_2, b_3)$, then $\vec{a} \cdot \vec{b} = a_1b_1 + a_2b_2 + a_3b_3$.

example

3 Find the inner product of $\vec{u}$ and $\vec{v}$ if $\vec{u} = (2, {}^-1, 3)$ and $\vec{v} = (5, 3, 0)$.

$\vec{u} \cdot \vec{v} = 2(5) + {}^-1(3) + 3(0)$
$= 10 + {}^-3 + 0$
$= 7$ *The vectors are not perpendicular.*

Another important product of vectors in space is called the **cross product.** The cross product of two vectors is a vector which does not lie in the plane of the given vectors but is perpendicular to each. Thus, it is perpendicular to the plane containing the two vectors.

Cross Product

The cross product of $\vec{a}$ and $\vec{b}$ if $\vec{a} = (a_1, a_2, a_3)$ and $\vec{b} = (b_1, b_2, b_3)$ is defined as follows.

$$\vec{a} \times \vec{b} = \begin{vmatrix} a_2 & a_3 \\ b_2 & b_3 \end{vmatrix} \vec{i} - \begin{vmatrix} a_1 & a_3 \\ b_1 & b_3 \end{vmatrix} \vec{j} + \begin{vmatrix} a_1 & a_2 \\ b_1 & b_2 \end{vmatrix} \vec{k}$$

An easy way to remember the coefficients of $\vec{i}$, $\vec{j}$, and $\vec{k}$ is to set up a determinant as shown at the right and expand by minors using the first row.

$$\begin{vmatrix} \vec{i} & \vec{j} & \vec{k} \\ a_1 & a_2 & a_3 \\ b_1 & b_2 & b_3 \end{vmatrix}$$

example

4 Find the cross product of $\vec{a}$ and $\vec{b}$ if $\vec{a} = (2, 4, ^-3)$ and $\vec{b} = (^-1, 5, 2)$. Then verify that the resulting vector is perpendicular to $\vec{a}$ and $\vec{b}$.

$$\vec{a} \times \vec{b} = \begin{vmatrix} \vec{i} & \vec{j} & \vec{k} \\ 2 & 4 & ^-3 \\ ^-1 & 5 & 2 \end{vmatrix}$$

$$= \begin{vmatrix} 4 & ^-3 \\ 5 & 2 \end{vmatrix}\vec{i} - \begin{vmatrix} 2 & ^-3 \\ ^-1 & 2 \end{vmatrix}\vec{j} + \begin{vmatrix} 2 & 4 \\ ^-1 & 5 \end{vmatrix}\vec{k}$$

$$= 23\vec{i} - 1\vec{j} + 14\vec{k}$$

$$= (23, ^-1, 14)$$

Check the inner product of $(23, ^-1, 14)$ and $(2, 4, ^-3)$.
$23(2) + ^-1(4) + 14(^-3) = 0$ *The vectors are perpendicular.*

Check the inner product of $(23, ^-1, 14)$ and $(^-1, 5, 2)$.
$23(^-1) + ^-1(5) + 14(2) = 0$ *The vectors are perpendicular.*

exercises

Exploratory Find each inner product.

1. $(4, ^-2) \cdot (3, 5)$
2. $(^-3, 6) \cdot (4, 2)$
3. $(2, 4) \cdot (8, 4)$
4. $\vec{i} \cdot \vec{j}$
5. $\vec{j} \cdot \vec{j}$
6. $\vec{j} \cdot \vec{i}$

7-12. State whether the vectors in problems **1-6** are perpendicular.

Set up the cross product of the following vectors using determinants. Do not evaluate.

13. $(2, 3, ^-4), (^-2, ^-3, 1)$
14. $(5, 2, 3), (^-2, 5, 0)$
15. $(7, ^-2, 4), (3, 8, 1)$
16. $(1, ^-3, 2), (5, 1, ^-2)$
17. $(^-6, 2, 10), (4, 1, 9)$
18. $(^-4, 9, ^-8), (3, 2, ^-2)$

Written

1-6. Find the inner product of each pair of vectors in problems **13-18** in the exploratory exercises.

7-12. State whether the vectors given in problems **13-18** in the exploratory exercises are perpendicular.

13-18. Find the cross product of each pair of vectors in problems **13-18** in the exploratory exercises.

19-24. Verify that the cross products obtained in problems **13-18** are perpendicular to each vector used in finding the cross products.

25. Prove $\vec{a} \cdot \vec{b} = \vec{b} \cdot \vec{a}$ for two-dimensional vectors.
26. Prove $\vec{a} \cdot \vec{b} = \vec{b} \cdot \vec{a}$ for three-dimensional vectors.
27. Show that $\vec{a} \times \vec{b} = {}^-(\vec{b} \times \vec{a})$ for three-dimensional vectors.
28. Prove that $\vec{i} \cdot \vec{i} = 1$, $\vec{j} \cdot \vec{j} = 1$, and $\vec{k} \cdot \vec{k} = 1$.

Chapter Summary

1. The Value of a Second Order Determinant: The value of $\det\begin{bmatrix} a_1 & b_1 \\ a_2 & b_2 \end{bmatrix}$ or $\begin{vmatrix} a_1 & b_1 \\ a_2 & b_2 \end{vmatrix} = a_1b_2 - a_2b_1$. (60)
2. Expansion of a Third Order Determinant:
$$\begin{vmatrix} a_1 & b_1 & c_1 \\ a_2 & b_2 & c_2 \\ a_3 & b_3 & c_3 \end{vmatrix} = a_1\begin{vmatrix} b_2 & c_2 \\ b_3 & c_3 \end{vmatrix} - b_1\begin{vmatrix} a_2 & c_2 \\ a_3 & c_3 \end{vmatrix} + c_1\begin{vmatrix} a_2 & b_2 \\ a_3 & b_3 \end{vmatrix} \quad (60)$$
3. Cramer's Rule: The solution to the system $\begin{matrix} a_1x + b_1y = c_1 \\ a_2x + b_2y = c_2 \end{matrix}$ is (x, y) where $x = \dfrac{\begin{vmatrix} c_1 & b_1 \\ c_2 & b_2 \end{vmatrix}}{\begin{vmatrix} a_1 & b_1 \\ a_2 & b_2 \end{vmatrix}}$ and $y = \dfrac{\begin{vmatrix} a_1 & c_1 \\ a_2 & c_2 \end{vmatrix}}{\begin{vmatrix} a_1 & b_1 \\ a_2 & b_2 \end{vmatrix}}$ and $\begin{vmatrix} a_1 & b_1 \\ a_2 & b_2 \end{vmatrix} \neq 0$. (61)
4. Addition of Matrices: The sum of two $m \times n$ matrices is an $m \times n$ matrix in which the elements are the sum of the corresponding elements of the given matrices. (63)
5. Subtraction of Matrices: The difference $A - B$ of two $m \times n$ matrices is equal to the sum $A + {}^-B$, where ${}^-B$ is the additive inverse of B. (64)
6. Scalar Product: The product of an $m \times n$ matrix A and a scalar k is an $m \times n$ matrix kA. Each element of kA is equal to k times the corresponding element of A. (65)
7. Product of Two Matrices: The product of an $m \times n$ matrix A and an $n \times r$ matrix B is an $m \times r$ matrix AB. The ijth element of AB is the product of the ith row of A and the jth column of B. (66)
8. Identity Matrix under Multiplication: The identity matrix of nth order, I_n, is the square matrix whose elements in the main diagonal, from upper left to lower right, are 1's, while all other elements are 0's. (68)
9. Inverse of a Second Order Matrix: If $A = \begin{bmatrix} a_1 & b_1 \\ a_2 & b_2 \end{bmatrix}$ and $\begin{vmatrix} a_1 & b_1 \\ a_2 & b_2 \end{vmatrix} \neq 0$, then $A^{-1} = \dfrac{1}{\begin{vmatrix} a_1 & b_1 \\ a_2 & b_2 \end{vmatrix}}\begin{bmatrix} b_2 & {}^-b_1 \\ {}^-a_2 & a_1 \end{bmatrix}$. (69)
10. Row Operations on Matrices:
    1. Interchange any two rows.
    2. Replace any row with a non-zero multiple of that row.
    3. Replace any row with the sum of that row and another row. (71)
11. A vector is a quantity which possesses both magnitude and direction. (72)

12. Representation of a Vector as an Ordered Pair: Suppose P_1 is the initial point of a vector, and P_2 is the terminal point. The ordered pair of numbers which represents $\overrightarrow{P_1P_2}$ is $(x_2 - x_1, y_2 - y_1)$. Its magnitude $|\overrightarrow{P_1P_2}| = \sqrt{(x_2 - x_1)^2 + (y_2 - y_1)^2}$. (73)
13. The following operations are true for $\vec{a} = (a_1, a_2)$, $\vec{b} = (b_1, b_2)$, and any real number k.
Addition: $\vec{a} + \vec{b} = (a_1, a_2) + (b_1, b_2) = (a_1 + b_1, a_2 + b_2)$
Subtraction: $\vec{a} - \vec{b} = (a_1, a_2) + (^-b_1, ^-b_2) = (a_1 - b_1, a_2 - b_2)$
Scalar Multiplication: $k\vec{a} = k(a_1, a_2) = (ka_1, ka_2)$ (78)
14. Representation of a Vector as an Ordered Triple: A vector from $P_1(x_1, y_1, z_1)$ to $P_2(x_2, y_2, z_2)$ in space can be represented by an ordered triple as follows; $\overrightarrow{P_1P_2} = (x_2 - x_1, y_2 - y_1, z_2 - z_1)$. Its magnitude $|\overrightarrow{P_1P_2}| = \sqrt{(x_2 - x_1)^2 + (y_2 - y_1)^2 + (z_2 - z_1)^2}$ (80)
15. Inner Product of Vectors in the Plane: If $\vec{a}$ and $\vec{b}$ are two vectors, (a_1, a_2) and (b_1, b_2), the inner product of $\vec{a}$ and $\vec{b}$ is defined as $\vec{a} \cdot \vec{b} = a_1b_1 + a_2b_2$ (82)
16. Inner Product of Vectors in Space: If $\vec{a} = (a_1, a_2, a_3)$ and $\vec{b} = (b_1, b_2, b_3)$, then $\vec{a} \cdot \vec{b} = a_1b_1 + a_2b_2 + a_3b_3$. (83)
17. Cross Product: The cross product of $\vec{a}$ and $\vec{b}$ for $\vec{a} = (a_1, a_2, a_3)$ and $\vec{b} = (b_1, b_2, b_3)$ is defined as follows.

$$\vec{a} \times \vec{b} = \begin{vmatrix} a_2 & a_3 \\ b_2 & b_3 \end{vmatrix} \vec{i} - \begin{vmatrix} a_1 & a_3 \\ b_1 & b_3 \end{vmatrix} \vec{j} + \begin{vmatrix} a_1 & a_2 \\ b_1 & b_2 \end{vmatrix} \vec{k} \quad (83)$$

Chapter Review

3-1 Find the value of each determinant.

1. $\begin{vmatrix} 7 & ^-4 \\ 5 & ^-3 \end{vmatrix}$
2. $\begin{vmatrix} 8 & ^-4 \\ ^-6 & 3 \end{vmatrix}$
3. $\begin{vmatrix} 5 & 0 & 4 \\ 7 & 3 & ^-1 \\ 2 & ^-2 & 6 \end{vmatrix}$
4. $\begin{vmatrix} 3 & ^-1 & 4 \\ 5 & ^-2 & 6 \\ 7 & 3 & ^-4 \end{vmatrix}$

Solve each system of equations using Cramer's rule.

5. $3x + 2y = {}^-2$
$6x - y = 6$
6. $x + 4y = {}^-9$
$3x - 2y = 8$

3-2 Use matrices A, B, and C to find each matrix sum or difference.

$$A = \begin{bmatrix} 3 & 0 & 4 \\ 1 & 2 & ^-3 \\ 2 & ^-5 & 1 \end{bmatrix} \quad B = \begin{bmatrix} 6 & ^-1 & 5 \\ 2 & 1 & 3 \\ ^-4 & ^-3 & 3 \end{bmatrix} \quad C = \begin{bmatrix} 3 & 0 & ^-1 \\ ^-4 & 5 & 2 \\ 9 & ^-3 & 1 \end{bmatrix}$$

7. $A + B$
8. $A + C$
9. $B - C$
10. $C - B$

3-3 Use matrices R, S, and T to find each product.

$$R = \begin{bmatrix} 2 & 1 \\ ^-3 & 4 \end{bmatrix} \quad S = \begin{bmatrix} 5 & ^-1 & ^-3 \\ 7 & 2 & 5 \end{bmatrix} \quad T = [5 \quad ^-7]$$

11. $3R$
12. $4S$
13. TR
14. RS

3-4 Find the inverse of each matrix.

15. $\begin{bmatrix} 3 & 2 \\ 1 & {}^-5 \end{bmatrix}$ 16. $\begin{bmatrix} {}^-3 & 5 \\ {}^-2 & 4 \end{bmatrix}$ 17. $\begin{bmatrix} 5 & {}^-4 \\ {}^-4 & 3 \end{bmatrix}$ 18. $\begin{bmatrix} 7 & 5 \\ 9 & 8 \end{bmatrix}$

Find matrix X for each of the following.

19. $X\begin{bmatrix} 2 & 5 \\ {}^-1 & {}^-3 \end{bmatrix} = \begin{bmatrix} 1 & {}^-3 \\ 2 & {}^-1 \end{bmatrix}$ 20. $\begin{bmatrix} 3 & 2 \\ {}^-6 & 4 \end{bmatrix} X = \begin{bmatrix} {}^-3 & 5 \\ 6 & 10 \end{bmatrix}$

3-5 Solve each system of equations using augmented matrices.

21. $x - 2y - 3z = 2$
$x - 4y + 3z = 14$
${}^-3x + 5y + 4z = 0$

22. $2x + 3y - 4z = 5$
$x + y + 2z = 3$
${}^-x + 2y - 6z = 4$

3-6 Given vectors $\vec{a}$, $\vec{b}$, $\vec{c}$, and $\vec{d}$, find each vector sum or difference.

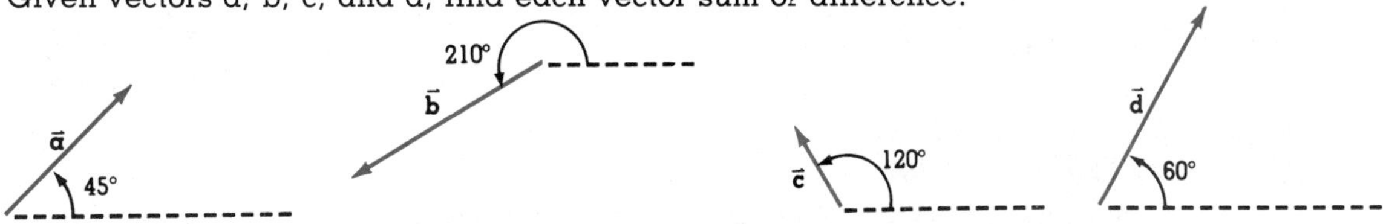

23. $\vec{a} + \vec{b} + \vec{c}$ 24. $2\vec{c} - \vec{d}$ 25. $2\vec{a} - 3\vec{b}$ 26. $4\vec{d} - \vec{c}$

27-30. Find the magnitude and amplitude of each resultant in exercises **23-26**.

Find the magnitude of the vertical and horizontal components of each vector shown above.

31. $\vec{a}$ 32. $\vec{b}$ 33. $\vec{c}$ 34. $\vec{d}$

3-7 Find an ordered pair which represents $\overrightarrow{AB}$ for points A and B with the given coordinates.

35. $A(2, 3)$; $B(7, 15)$ 36. $A({}^-2, 8)$; $B(4, 12)$

37-38. Find the magnitude of $\overrightarrow{AB}$ for problems **35-36**.

Find an ordered pair to represent $\vec{u}$ in each equation below, if $\vec{v} = (2, {}^-5)$ and $\vec{w} = (3, {}^-1)$.

39. $\vec{u} = \vec{v} + \vec{w}$ 40. $\vec{u} = \vec{w} - \vec{v}$ 41. $\vec{u} = 3\vec{v} + 2\vec{w}$ 42. $\vec{u} = 3\vec{v} - 2\vec{w}$

3-8 Find an ordered triple which represents $\overrightarrow{AB}$ for points A and B with the given coordinates.

43. $A(2, {}^-1, 4)$; $B(6, {}^-2, 1)$ 44. $A(9, 8, 5)$; $B({}^-1, 5, 11)$

45-46. Find the magnitude of $\overrightarrow{AB}$ for problems **43-44**.

Find an ordered triple to represent $\vec{u}$ in each equation below, if $\vec{v} = (4, 1, {}^-2)$ and $\vec{w} = ({}^-7, 3, 6)$.

47. $\vec{u} = 2\vec{v} + \vec{w}$ 48. $\vec{u} = \vec{v} - 3\vec{w}$ 49. $\vec{u} = 3\vec{v} + 2\vec{w}$ 50. $\vec{u} = 5\vec{w} - 3\vec{v}$

51-54. Write $\vec{u}$ as the sum of unit vectors for problems **47-50**.

3-9 Find each inner product or cross product.

55. $(5, {}^-1) \cdot ({}^-2, 6)$ 56. $(6, {}^-5) \cdot (5, 6)$ 57. $(4, 1, {}^-2) \cdot (3, {}^-4, 4)$
58. $(3, 8, 2) \cdot (7, {}^-3, 1)$ 59. $(2, {}^-1, 4) \times (6, {}^-2, 1)$ 60. $(5, 2, {}^-1) \times (2, {}^-4, {}^-4)$

Chapter Test

Find the value of each determinant.

1. $\begin{vmatrix} 8 & 5 \\ ^{-}3 & ^{-}2 \end{vmatrix}$

2. $\begin{vmatrix} 2 & 1 & ^{-}1 \\ 6 & 4 & ^{-}3 \\ 0 & 2 & ^{-}2 \end{vmatrix}$

Solve each system of equations using Cramer's rule.

3. $2x - y = 5$
   $5x - 4y = {}^{-}1$

4. $3x + y = 2$
   $6x + 3y = 11$

Use matrices A, B, C, and D to find each sum, difference, or product.

$$A = \begin{bmatrix} 5 & 4 \\ ^{-}1 & ^{-}2 \end{bmatrix} \quad B = \begin{bmatrix} ^{-}1 & ^{-}2 \\ 5 & 4 \end{bmatrix} \quad C = \begin{bmatrix} ^{-}2 & 4 & 6 \\ 5 & ^{-}7 & ^{-}1 \end{bmatrix} \quad D = \begin{bmatrix} 1 & ^{-}2 \\ 0 & 4 \\ ^{-}3 & 4 \end{bmatrix}$$

5. $2A + B$
6. $2B - A$
7. CD
8. $AB + CD$
9. Find matrix X if $AX = B$.
10. **Solve the following system of equations using augmented matrices.**
    $x + 2y + z = 3$
    $2x - 3y + 2z = {}^{-}1$
    $x - 3y + 2z = 1$

Use vectors $\vec{a}$ and $\vec{b}$ to solve each problem.

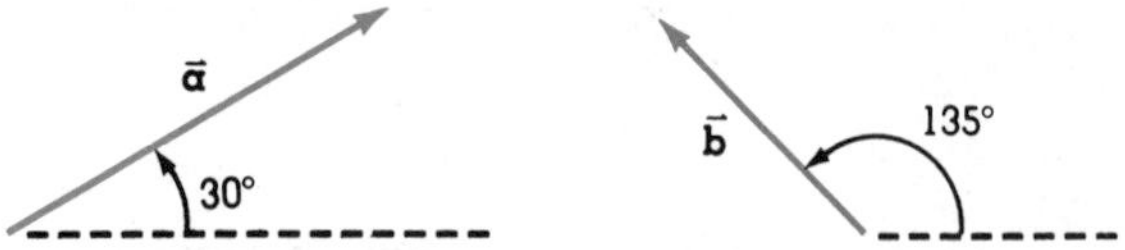

11. Find the magnitude and amplitude of $\vec{a} + \vec{b}$.
12. Find the magnitude and amplitude of $2\vec{a} - 3\vec{b}$.
13. Find the vertical and horizontal components of $\vec{a}$.
14. Find the vertical and horizontal components of $\vec{b}$.

Find an ordered pair or ordered triple which represents $\overrightarrow{AB}$, for points A and B with the given coordinates.

15. $A(3, 6)$; $B({}^{-}1, 9)$
16. $A({}^{-}2, 7)$; $B(3, 10)$
17. $A(2, {}^{-}4, 5)$; $B(9, {}^{-}3, 7)$
18. $A({}^{-}4, {}^{-}8, {}^{-}2)$; $B({}^{-}8, {}^{-}10, 2)$

Solve each of the following, for $\vec{u} = ({}^{-}3, 7)$ and $\vec{v} = (4, 2)$.

19. Find $\vec{u} + \vec{v}$.
20. Find $4\vec{u} - 3\vec{v}$.
21. Find $|\vec{u}|$.
22. Find $|\vec{v}|$.
23. Write $\vec{u}$ as the sum of unit vectors.
24. Write $\vec{v}$ as the sum of unit vectors.
25. Find $\vec{u} \cdot \vec{v}$.
26. Is $\vec{u}$ perpendicular to $\vec{v}$?

Solve each of the following, for $\vec{r} = ({}^{-}1, 3, 4)$ and $\vec{s} = (4, 3, {}^{-}6)$.

27. Find $\vec{r} - \vec{s}$
28. Find $3\vec{s} - 2\vec{r}$.
29. Find $|\vec{r}|$.
30. Find $|\vec{s}|$.
31. Write $\vec{r}$ as the sum of unit vectors.
32. Write $\vec{s}$ as the sum of unit vectors.
33. Find $\vec{r} \cdot \vec{s}$.
34. Find $\vec{r} \times \vec{s}$.

Chapter

4

The Circular Functions

An electrocardiogram (EKG) shows that the heartbeat has a repetitive pattern. The circular functions also have the special property of repetitiveness.

4-1 The Wrapping Function

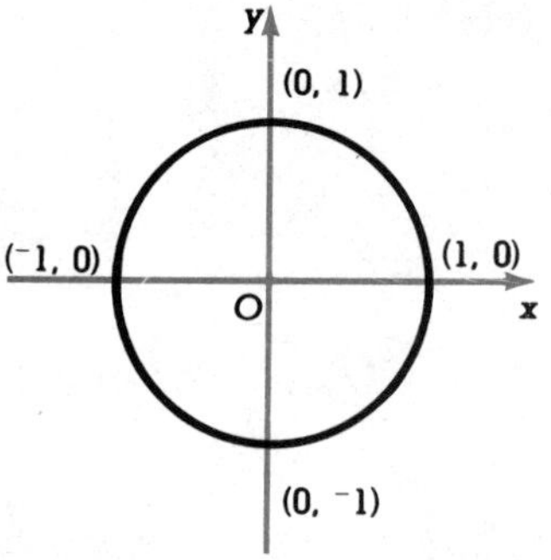

The set of real numbers is sometimes associated with points on a circle to form a function. Under this function each real number corresponds to *exactly one* point on the **unit circle.** A unit circle is a circle on the coordinate plane with its center at the origin and with radius 1 unit.

The set of real numbers has a one-to-one correspondence with the points of a number line as shown below. Let the measure of one unit of the number line be equal to the measure of the radius of the unit circle.

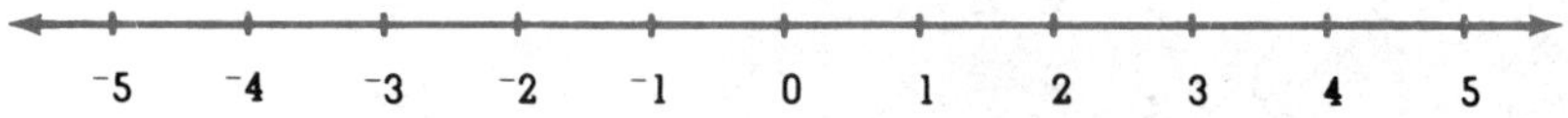

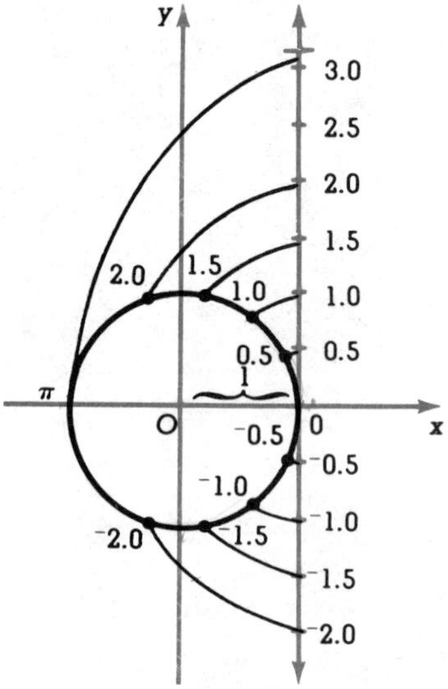

Next, orient the number line so that it is tangent to the unit circle at the point (1, 0) as shown at the right. The zero point on the number line is the point of tangency.

Imagine that the number line is a string which is *wrapped* around the unit circle in both directions from the point of tangency. Each point on the number line would coincide with a point on the circle. For example, the point π on the number line would lie on the point on the unit circle which has coordinates $(^-1, 0)$ since the circumference of the unit circle is 2π. This wrapping procedure describes a function whose domain is the set of real numbers and whose range is the set of points on the unit circle. The inverse relation is *not* a function since each point on the circle can be associated with many real numbers.

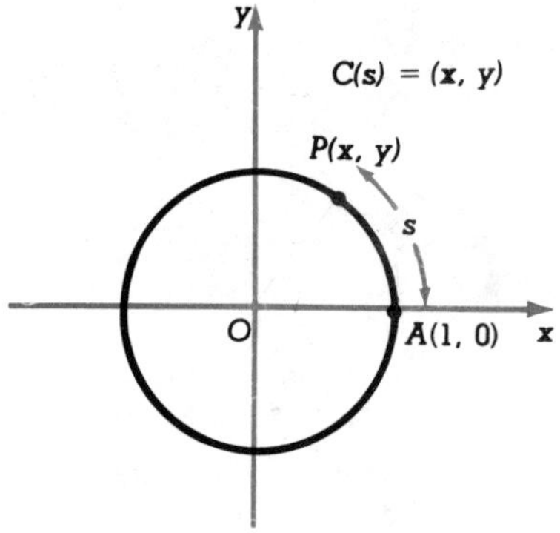

Consider an arc from the point $A(1, 0)$ to the point $P(x, y)$ on the unit circle. The real number $|s|$ represents the measure of the arc length in the same units as the number line. We shall define **function C** such that for each real number s, there corresponds exactly one ordered pair of real numbers, $C(s) = (x, y)$, which are coordinates of a point on the unit circle. If $s > 0$, the arc is measured counterclockwise along the circle from the point (1, 0). If $s < 0$, the arc is measured clockwise along the circle from the point (1, 0).

example

1 Complete the following table by using geometric relationships.

Function C

s	0	$\frac{\pi}{2}$	π	$\frac{-\pi}{2}$	$\frac{\pi}{4}$
C(s)	a.	b.	c.	d.	e.

a. $C(0) = (1, 0)$

b. $C\left(\frac{\pi}{2}\right) = (0, 1)$

c. $C(\pi) = (^-1, 0)$

d. $C\left(-\frac{\pi}{2}\right) = (0, ^-1)$

Use the fact that the circumference of a unit circle is 2π.

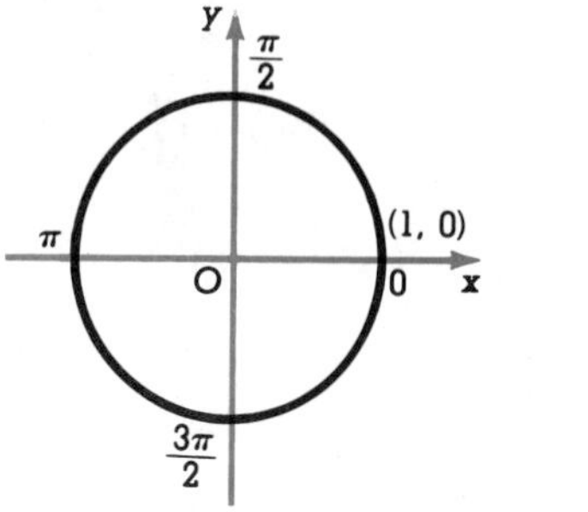

e. Let $P(x, y)$ represent $C\left(\frac{\pi}{4}\right)$. The length of the arc from (x, y) to $(0, 1)$ is equal to the length of the arc from (x, y) to $(1, 0)$. Thus, (x, y) is equidistant from $(0, 1)$ and $(1, 0)$.

Use the distance formula.

$$\sqrt{(x-0)^2 + (y-1)^2} = \sqrt{(x-1)^2 + (y-0)^2}$$

$y = x$ *Solve for x.*

$x^2 + y^2 = 1$ *Why?*

$x^2 + x^2 = 1$ *Substitute x for y.*

$x = \frac{\sqrt{2}}{2}$ and $y = \frac{\sqrt{2}}{2}$

Thus $C\left(\frac{\pi}{4}\right) = \left(\frac{\sqrt{2}}{2}, \frac{\sqrt{2}}{2}\right)$.

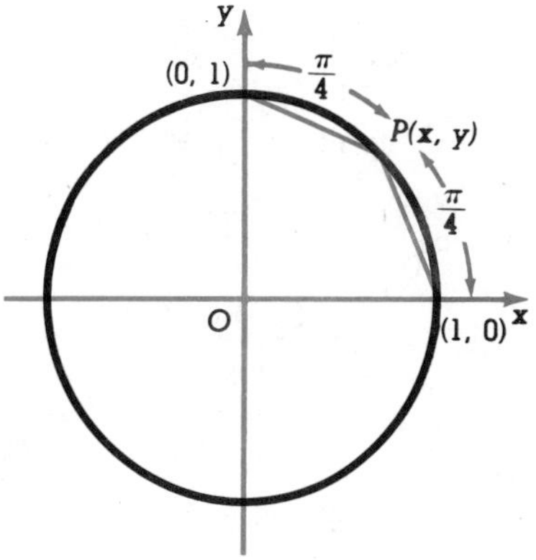

A closer look at $C(s) = (x, y)$ will show the nature of function C. Suppose that s assumes a sequence of values increasing from 0 to $\frac{\pi}{2}$. Intuitively you can see that the value of x decreases from 1 to 0 and the value of y increases from 0 to 1. Similarly, as s varies from $\frac{\pi}{2}$ to π, the value of x decreases from 0 to $^-1$ and the value of y decreases from 1 to 0. When s is greater than 2π, x and y assume values that repeat those for $0 \leq s \leq 2\pi$.

How do x and y change as s increases from π to 2π?

Since the values of function C are the same for $C(s)$ and $C(s + 2\pi)$, function C is called a **periodic function** with a **period** of 2π.

Periodic Function and Period

A function is periodic if, for some real number α, $f(x + \alpha) = f(x)$ for each x in the domain of f. The least positive value of α for which $f(x) = f(x + \alpha)$ is the period of the function.

example

2 For each value of s, find the quadrant in which C(s) is located.

a. $\frac{7\pi}{4}$ b. $-\frac{3\pi}{4}$ c. $\frac{14\pi}{3}$ d. 10

a. $s = \frac{7\pi}{4}$

$\frac{3\pi}{2} < \frac{7\pi}{4} < 2\pi$

Thus, $C\left(\frac{7\pi}{4}\right)$ is in Quadrant IV.

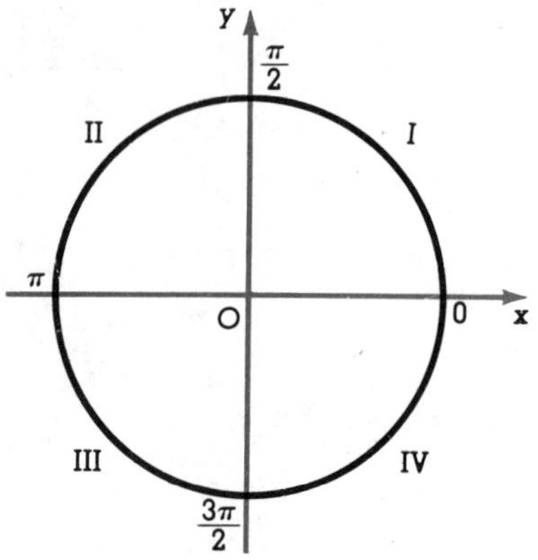

b. $s = -\frac{3\pi}{4}$

$^{-}\pi < -\frac{3\pi}{4} < -\frac{\pi}{2}$

Thus, $C\left(-\frac{3\pi}{4}\right)$ is in Quadrant III.

c. $s = \frac{14\pi}{3}$ or $4\pi + \frac{2\pi}{3}$

$C\left(\frac{14\pi}{3}\right) = C\left(2(2\pi) + \frac{2\pi}{3}\right)$ or $C\left(\frac{2\pi}{3}\right)$ *Why?*

$\frac{\pi}{2} < \frac{2\pi}{3} < \pi$

Thus, $C\left(\frac{14\pi}{3}\right)$ is in Quadrant II.

d. $s = 10 = 6.28 + 3.72$ or $2\pi + 3.72$

$C(10) = C(2\pi + 3.72)$ or $C(3.72)$

$\pi < 3.72 < \frac{3\pi}{2}$

Thus, C(10) is in Quadrant III.

exercises

Exploratory **For each value of s, find the quadrant in which C(s) is located.**

1. $\frac{6\pi}{5}$
2. $\frac{16\pi}{3}$
3. 2
4. $-\frac{8\pi}{5}$
5. $^{-}5$
6. $-\frac{\pi}{4}$
7. $\frac{5\pi}{6}$
8. $-\frac{48\pi}{7}$
9. 7.5

Suppose $C\left(\frac{7\pi}{8}\right) = (p, q)$. Solve each problem.

10. Find a positive real number, a, other than $\frac{7\pi}{8}$, such that $C(a) = (p, q)$.
11. Find a negative real number, b, such that $C(b) = (p, q)$.

Suppose $C(4) = (s, t)$. Solve each problem.

12. Write an expression that names all the other positive real numbers with coordinates (s, t) under function C.

13. Write an expression that names all the negative real numbers with coordinates (s, t) under function C.

Written For each real number s, find the coordinates (x, y) determined by $C(s) = (x, y)$. Make a sketch of the unit circle if necessary.

1. $s = -\pi$
2. $s = \frac{5\pi}{4}$
3. $s = 4\pi$
4. $s = -\frac{19\pi}{4}$
5. $s = \frac{3\pi}{4}$
6. $s = 15\pi$
7. $s = -\frac{13\pi}{2}$
8. $s = -\frac{23\pi}{2}$

Make a sketch of the unit circle, dividing it into 6 congruent arcs starting at (1, 0).

9-14. Find the smallest positive arc lengths in terms of π from (1, 0) to each point of division.

15-20. Use geometric relationships to find the coordinates (x, y) of each point of division.

For each real number s, find the coordinates (x, y) determined by $C(s) = (x, y)$. Use the results of problems 9-20.

21. $-\frac{\pi}{3}$
22. $6\pi - \frac{5\pi}{3}$
23. $\frac{79\pi}{3}$
24. $-\frac{5\pi}{3} + \pi$

Suppose $C(s) = \left(\frac{5}{13}, \frac{12}{13}\right)$. Find each of the following.

25. $C(^-s)$
26. $C(s + 2\pi)$
27. $C(s + \pi)$
28. $C(\pi - s)$

Estimate the least positive value of s if $C(s) = (x, y)$. Use $\pi = 3.14$.

29. $(x, y) = (0, 1)$
30. $(x, y) = (^-1, 0)$
31. $(x, y) = (0.97, 0.25)$
32. $(x, y) = (0.45, ^-0.89)$

33-36. Estimate the negative value of s which has the least absolute value for problems 29-32.

37-40. Estimate a positive value of s such that $s > 2\pi$ for problems 29-32.

Challenge If $C(s) = (x, y)$, show that $C(^-s) = (x, ^-y)$.

4-2 The Circular Functions

Using function C, each real number s now can be associated with a certain point on the unit circle having coordinates (x, y).

Two new functions may be formed from function C. The **cosine function** maps each real number s onto the value of the x-coordinate of $C(s)$. The **sine** function maps each real number s onto the value of the y-coordinate of $C(s)$.

Cosine and Sine Functions

For any real number s, where $C(s) = (x, y)$ such that $x^2 + y^2 = 1$, the cosine of $s = x$ and the sine of $s = y$. In abbreviated form, $\cos s = x$ and $\sin s = y$.

The cosine function assigns a real number x to each real number s such that $^-1 \le x \le 1$. The sine function assigns a real number y to each real number s such that $^-1 \le y \le 1$. The domain of each of these circular functions is the set of all real numbers, and the range of each consists of the set of real numbers between $^-1$ and $^+1$, inclusive.

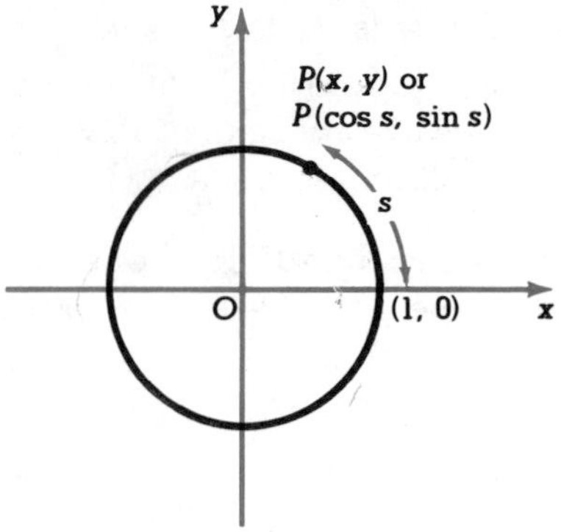

If (x, y) are the coordinates of any point $C(s)$ on the unit circle, then $x^2 + y^2 = 1$. But since $x = \cos s$ and $y = \sin s$ for any real number s, we have the following equation.

$$\cos^2 s + \sin^2 s = 1$$ *$\cos^2 s$ means $(\cos s)^2$.*

example

1 **Find $\sin s$ when $\cos s = \frac{3}{4}$ and $C(s)$ is in Quadrant I.**

$$\sin^2 s + \cos^2 s = 1$$

$$\sin^2 s + \left(\frac{3}{4}\right)^2 = 1$$ *Substitute $\frac{3}{4}$ for $\cos s$.*

$$\sin^2 s = 1 - \frac{9}{16}$$

$$\sin s = \pm\sqrt{\frac{7}{16}}$$

Since $C(s)$ is in Quadrant I, $\sin s = +\sqrt{\frac{7}{16}}$ or $\frac{\sqrt{7}}{4}$.

The ratios $\frac{\sin s}{\cos s}$ and $\frac{\cos s}{\sin s}$ and the reciprocals of the sine and cosine functions also determine circular functions. They are the **tangent** (tan), **cotangent** (cot), **cosecant** (csc), and **secant** (sec) functions.

Tangent, Cotangent, Secant, and Cosecant Functions

Let s represent any real number. The tangent, cotangent, secant, and cosecant functions are defined as follows.

$$\tan s = \frac{\sin s}{\cos s} \qquad (\cos s \ne 0)$$

$$\cot s = \frac{\cos s}{\sin s} \qquad (\sin s \ne 0)$$

$$\sec s = \frac{1}{\cos s} \qquad (\cos s \ne 0)$$

$$\csc s = \frac{1}{\sin s} \qquad (\sin s \ne 0)$$

example

2 Find the values of the six circular functions of s if $s = \frac{3\pi}{4}$.

Using the definitions of the circular functions, each value can be found from $C\left(\frac{3\pi}{4}\right)$.

Recall that $C\left(\frac{3\pi}{4}\right) = \left(-\frac{\sqrt{2}}{2}, \frac{\sqrt{2}}{2}\right)$.

$$\cos\frac{3\pi}{4} = -\frac{\sqrt{2}}{2}$$

$$\sin\frac{3\pi}{4} = \frac{\sqrt{2}}{2}$$

$$\tan\frac{3\pi}{4} = \frac{\frac{\sqrt{2}}{2}}{-\frac{\sqrt{2}}{2}} \text{ or } -1$$

$$\cot\frac{3\pi}{4} = \frac{-\frac{\sqrt{2}}{2}}{\frac{\sqrt{2}}{2}} \text{ or } -1$$

$$\sec\frac{3\pi}{4} = \frac{1}{-\frac{\sqrt{2}}{2}} \text{ or } -\sqrt{2}$$

$$\csc\frac{3\pi}{4} = \frac{1}{\frac{\sqrt{2}}{2}} \text{ or } \sqrt{2}$$

exercises

Exploratory State whether the value of each of the following is *positive* or *negative*.

1. $\sin\frac{\pi}{3}$
2. $\cos\frac{7\pi}{3}$
3. $\sec\frac{6\pi}{5}$
4. $\tan\frac{12\pi}{7}$
5. $\csc\frac{5\pi}{6}$
6. $\sin\left(-\frac{3\pi}{4}\right)$
7. $\cot\frac{9\pi}{4}$
8. $\cos\left(-\frac{5\pi}{4}\right)$

Determine the quadrant of the point C(s) on the unit circle for each of the following conditions. Let n be some whole number.

9. $0 < (s \pm 2\pi n) < \frac{\pi}{2}$
10. $\frac{3\pi}{2} < (s \pm 2\pi n) < 2\pi$
11. $\pi < (s \pm 2\pi n) < \frac{3\pi}{2}$
12. $\frac{\pi}{2} < (s \pm 2\pi n) < \pi$

Suppose $C(s) = (0.6, 0.8)$. Find each of the following.

13. $\cos s$
14. $\csc s$
15. $\sin s$
16. $\cot s$

Suppose $C(s) = \left(\frac{\sqrt{2}}{2}, \frac{\sqrt{2}}{2}\right)$. Find each of the following.

17. $\tan s$
18. $\sec s$
19. $\cot s$
20. $\cos s$

Written Copy and complete the following table using geometric relationships and the definitions of the six circular functions.

1.

s	cos s	sin s	tan s	sec s	csc s	cot s
0						
$\frac{\pi}{6}$						
$\frac{\pi}{4}$						
$\frac{\pi}{3}$						
$\frac{\pi}{2}$						

Find the value of each of the following.

2. $\sin \pi$
3. $\cos (^{-}4\pi)$
4. $\sin 15\pi$
5. $\cos \frac{3\pi}{4}$
6. $\tan 2\pi$
7. $\sin \frac{15\pi}{2}$
8. $\cos \left(-\frac{5\pi}{6}\right)$
9. $\cot \frac{11\pi}{3}$
10. $\cos \frac{7\pi}{4}$
11. $\csc \frac{3\pi}{2}$
12. $\sec \frac{5\pi}{2}$
13. $\sin \left(-\frac{5\pi}{3}\right)$

Suppose $\cos r = \frac{3}{4}$ and $C(r)$ is in the first quadrant. Find the value of each of the following.

14. $\sec r$
15. $\tan r$
16. $\cot r$
17. $\csc r$

Suppose $\sin r = \frac{1}{2}$ and $C(r)$ is in the second quadrant. Find the value of each of the following.

18. $\cos r$
19. $\tan r$
20. $\csc r$
21. $\sec r$

Suppose $\cos r = \frac{8}{17}$ and $C(r)$ is in the fourth quadrant. Find the value of each of the following.

22. $\tan r$
23. $\sec r$
24. $\cot r$
25. $\csc r$

Copy and complete the following table which gives the signs of the circular functions in each quadrant.

26.

Function	I	II	III	IV
Cosine	+			+
Sine		−		−
Tangent	+		+	
Secant			−	
Cosecant		−		−
Cotangent	+			

Consider $\cos (s + \alpha)$ and $\sin (s + \alpha)$ where α is any real number.

27. Find three different values of α such that $\cos (s + \alpha) = \cos s$.
28. Find three different values of α such that $\sin (s + \alpha) = \sin s$.
29. What is the period of the cosine function?
30. What is the period of the sine function?

4-3 Finding Values of Circular Functions

Tables of values of circular functions usually are given only for s when $0 \leq s \leq \frac{\pi}{2}$. Therefore relationships must be developed that permit use of the tables when s is either a negative number or a positive number greater than $\frac{\pi}{2}$.

It is possible to find an arc measured by s', where $0 < s' < \frac{\pi}{2}$, which is related to values of s outside the interval from 0 to $\frac{\pi}{2}$.

Multiples of $\frac{\pi}{2}$ are excluded in this development.

Values of the Circular Functions in Quadrant I

When the arc measured by s terminates in Quadrant I, every circular function $f(s)$ is equal to $f(s')$ where $s' = s - 2\pi n$, n is an integer, and $0 < s' < \frac{\pi}{2}$.

When the arc measured by s terminates in Quadrant II, the terminal point of the related arc with measure s' has the same ordinate of $C(s)$, y, and the additive inverse of the abscissa of $C(s)$, ^-x. This is equivalent to finding the image of $P(x, y)$ reflected on the y-axis.

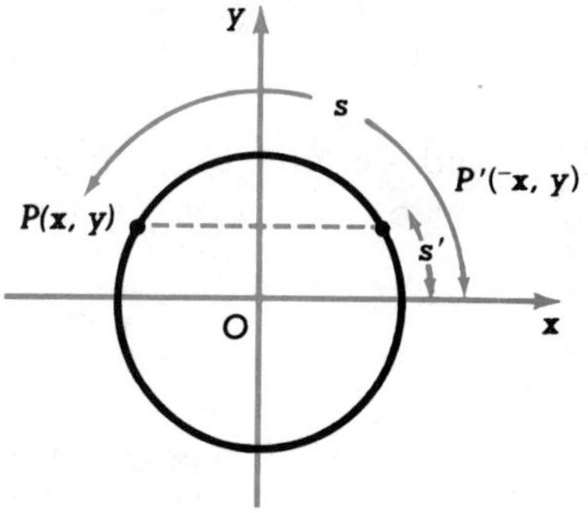

$s' = (2n - 1)\pi - s$

Values of Circular Functions in Quadrant II

The following equations hold for any real number s when $C(s)$ is in Quadrant II where $s' = (2n - 1)\pi - s$, n is an integer, and $0 < s' < \frac{\pi}{2}$.

$\sin s = \sin s'$	$\cot s = {}^-\cot s'$
$\cos s = {}^-\cos s'$	$\sec s = {}^-\sec s'$
$\tan s = {}^-\tan s'$	$\csc s = \csc s'$

Suppose $\pi < s < \frac{3\pi}{2}$. A double reflection, one on the x-axis and one on the y-axis, produces point $P'(^-x, {}^-y)$ which is the image of $P(x, y)$. Thus, when the arc measured by s terminates in Quadrant III, $P'(^-x, {}^-y)$ determines s', the measure of the related arc of s.

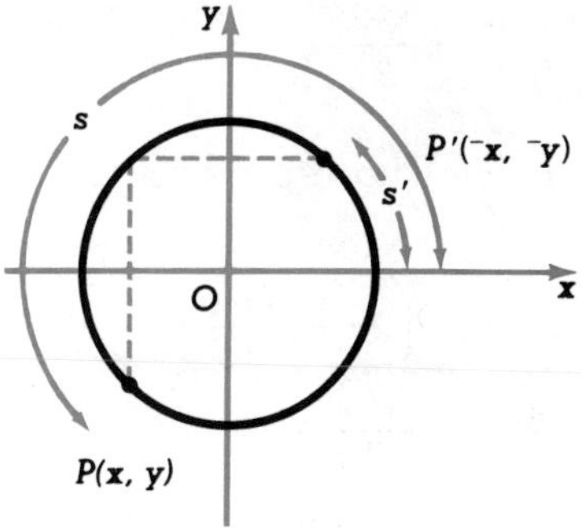

$s' = s - (2n - 1)\pi$

The following equations hold for any real number s when $C(s)$ is in Quadrant III where $s' = s - (2n - 1)\pi$, n is an integer, and $0 < s' < \frac{\pi}{2}$.

Values of Circular Functions in Quadrant III

$\sin s = {}^-\sin s'$	$\csc s = {}^-\csc s'$
$\cos s = {}^-\cos s'$	$\sec s = {}^-\sec s'$
$\tan s = \tan s'$	$\cot s = \cot s'$

For $\frac{3\pi}{2} < s < 2\pi$, the image of $P(x, y)$ under a reflection on the x-axis is $P'(x, {}^-y)$. Thus, when the arc measured by s terminates in Quadrant IV, the terminal point of the related arc with measure s' has the same abscissa, x, and an ordinate which is the additive inverse of y.

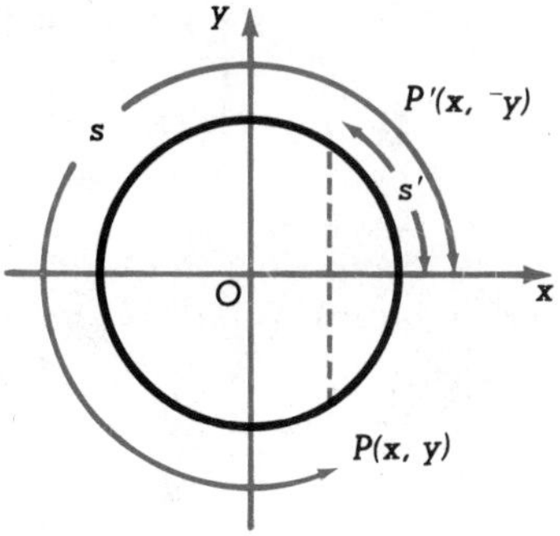

$s' = 2\pi n - s$

The following equations hold for any real number s when $C(s)$ is in Quadrant IV where $s' = 2\pi n - s$, n is an integer, and $0 < s' < \frac{\pi}{2}$.

Values of Circular Functions in Quadrant IV

$\sin s = {}^-\sin s'$	$\csc s = {}^-\csc s'$
$\cos s = \cos s'$	$\sec s = \sec s'$
$\tan s = {}^-\tan s'$	$\cot s = {}^-\cot s'$

example

1 Find the value of each of the following circular functions.

a. $\cos \frac{7\pi}{6}$ b. $\sin \frac{29\pi}{3}$

a. $s = \frac{7\pi}{6}$. The arc measured by s terminates in Quadrant III and $s' = \frac{7\pi}{6} - \pi$.

$$\cos \frac{7\pi}{6} = {}^-\cos\left(\frac{7\pi}{6} - \pi\right)$$
$$= {}^-\cos \frac{\pi}{6} \text{ or } -\frac{\sqrt{3}}{2}$$

b. $s = \frac{29\pi}{3}$ or $9\pi + \frac{2\pi}{3}$. The arc measured by s terminates in Quadrant IV and $s' = 10\pi - s$.

$$\sin \frac{29\pi}{3} = {}^-\sin\left(10\pi - \left(9\pi + \frac{2\pi}{3}\right)\right)$$
$$= {}^-\sin \frac{\pi}{3} \text{ or } -\frac{\sqrt{3}}{2}$$

The values of the circular functions of any real number s may be found in the table on page 503. A portion of the table of values is shown below.

The real number s is represented by **radians** in the table. On a unit circle, an arc 1 unit in length is intercepted by the sides of a central angle whose measurement is one radian. Therefore, the measure of an intercepted arc on a unit circle, or s, is equal to the measure in radians of its central angle.

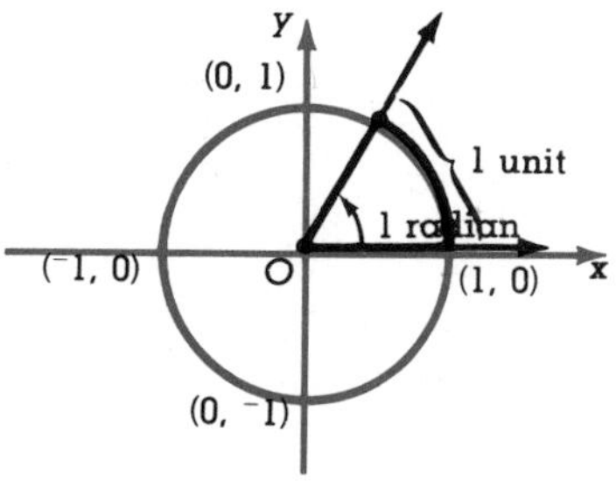

Values of Trigonometric Functions

Angle	Radians	Sin	Cos	Tan	Cot	Sec	Csc		
18°00′	0.3142	0.3090	0.9511	0.3249	3.078	1.051	3.236	1.2566	72°00′
10′	0.3171	0.3118	0.9502	0.3281	3.047	1.052	3.207	1.2537	50′
20′	0.3200	0.3145	0.9492	0.3314	3.018	1.053	3.179	1.2508	40′
30′	0.3229	0.3173	0.9483	0.3346	2.989	1.054	3.152	1.2479	30′
40′	0.3258	0.3201	0.9474	0.3378	2.960	1.056	3.124	1.2450	20′
50′	0.3287	0.3228	0.9465	0.3411	2.932	1.057	3.098	1.2421	10′
19°00′	0.3316	0.3256	0.9455	0.3443	2.904	1.058	3.072	1.2392	71°00′
10′	0.3345	0.3283	0.9446	0.3476	2.877	1.059	3.046	1.2363	50′
30′	0.4625	0.4462	0.8949	0.4986	2.006	1.117	2.241	1.1083	30′
40′	0.4654	0.4488	0.8936	0.5022	1.991	1.119	2.228	1.1054	20′
50′	0.4683	0.4514	0.8923	0.5059	1.977	1.121	2.215	1.1025	10′
27°00′	0.4712	0.4540	0.8910	0.5095	1.963	1.122	2.203	1.0996	63°00′
		Cos	Sin	Cot	Tan	Csc	Sec	Radians	Angle

Angle and radian measures are listed on both sides of the table. Use the radian column heading at the top and read down the left-hand side to find the circular functions of s for $0 \le s \le 0.7854$. For example, tan 0.3229 = 0.3346. Use the radian column heading at the bottom and read up the right-hand side to find the circular functions of s for $0.7854 \le s \le 1.5708$. For example, cot 1.2479 = 0.3346.

$0.7854 \approx \frac{\pi}{4}$ and $1.5708 \approx \frac{\pi}{2}$.

example

2 **Find the approximate value of each circular function using the table on page 503.**
a. cot (⁻1.86) **b. csc 12.04**

a. $s = {}^{-}1.86$. The arc terminates in Quadrant III and $s' = s - (0 - 1)\pi$.

cot (⁻1.86) = cot (⁻1.86 + 3.14) *$\pi \approx 3.14$*
= cot (1.28) or 0.2994

b. $s = 12.04$. The arc terminates in Quadrant IV and $s' = 2\pi \cdot 2 - s$.

csc 12.04 = csc(4(3.14) − 12.04)
= csc 0.52 or 2.010

example

3 Find the approximate value of each s using the table on page 503.
a. $\sin s = 0.9869$ b. $\cot s = 2.494$

a. $\sin s = 0.9869$
The nearest sine value to 0.9869 is 0.9868. The value of s when $\sin s = 0.9868$ is 1.4079. Thus, $s \approx 1.4079$.

b. $\cot s = 2.494$
The nearest cotangent value to 2.494 is 2.496. The value of s when $\cot s = 2.496$ is 0.3811. Thus, $s \approx 0.3811$.

exercises

Exploratory Name the quadrant(s) which is described by each set of conditions.

1. $\sin s < 0$, $\tan s < 0$
2. $\sin s > 0$, $\cot s < 0$
3. $\cos s > 0$, $\csc s < 0$
4. $\cos s < 0$, $\sin s < 0$
5. $\tan s < 0$, $\cos s < 0$
6. $\sec s > 0$, $\cos s > 0$
7. $\cos s < 0$, $\csc s < 0$
8. $\sin s > 0$, $\cot s > 0$
9. $\sec s < 0$, $\csc s > 0$
10. $\sec s > 0$, $\tan s < 0$

Written Find the approximate value of each of the following using the table on page 503 and $\pi = 3.14$.

1. $\sin 0.175$
2. $\cos \frac{1}{3}$
3. $\tan (\pi + 1)$
4. $\cos \frac{2\pi}{5}$
5. $\tan \left(-\frac{\pi}{10}\right)$
6. $\csc 4$
7. $\sec 32$
8. $\cot 6$
9. $\sin (^-13.25)$
10. $\sec (3\pi - 2)$
11. $\cot (^-3\pi)$
12. $\csc \left(\frac{5\pi}{12} + 1.46\right)$
13. $\cos (4\pi + 2)$
14. $\tan \frac{\pi}{7}$
15. $\sin 100$
16. $\sec (5\pi - 1)$

Find the approximate value of s using the table on page 503.

17. $\sin s = 0.1451$
18. $\csc s = 1.053$
19. $\tan s = 0.9000$
20. $\csc s = 4.396$
21. $\cos s = 0.9908$
22. $\sec s = 1.305$
23. $\cot s = 1.799$
24. $\sin s = 0.8708$
25. $\cot s = 0.2517$
26. $\cos s = 0.5449$
27. $\sec s = 6.291$
28. $\tan s = 2.460$

Challenge Solve each problem.

1. Make a table of ordered pairs for $(x, \sin x)$ where x is an element of $\{0, 0.2, 0.4, 0.6, \ldots 6.4\}$.
2. Make a table of ordered pairs for $(x, \cos x)$ where x is an element of $\{0, 0.2, 0.4, 0.6, \ldots 6.4\}$.
3. Plot the points whose coordinates are given in the table in problem **1**.
4. Plot the points whose coordinates are given in the table in problem **2**.

Gary Herr is an acoustical scientist. He develops acoustical systems. He also does research in the control of sound.

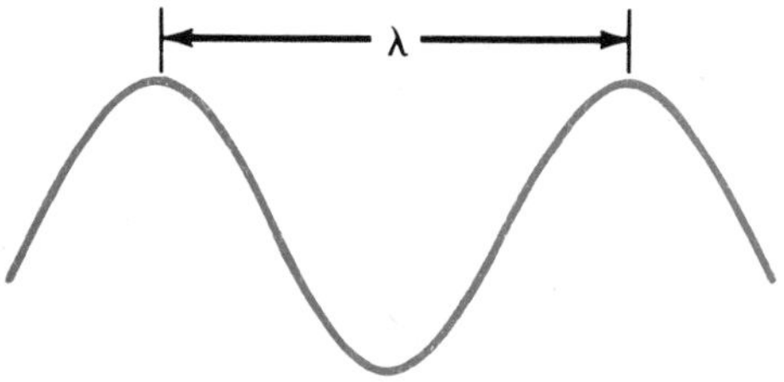

Sound waves are produced by vibrations. The wavelength, λ, of a sound wave is the distance between successive crests of the wave. The frequency, f, of a sound wave is the number of wavelengths that pass a given point per second. Frequency is measured in a unit called a hertz (1 hertz = 1 wave/sec).

If the wavelength and the frequency of a wave are both known, the velocity, v, or speed, of a sound wave can be found.

$$v = f\lambda$$

Example Sound waves traveling through air have a frequency of 250 hertz. The sound waves are 1.3 m in length. Find the speed of sound in air.

$$\begin{aligned} v &= f\lambda \\ &= (250 \text{ hertz})(1.3 \text{ m}) \\ &= 325 \text{ m/sec} \end{aligned}$$

Exercises Solve each problem.

1. The speed of sound waves in air is 330 m/sec. A sound wave has a frequency of 500 hertz. Find its wavelength as it travels through air.
2. The speed of sound waves through water is 1450 m/sec. A sound wave is 5 m long. Find the frequency of the sound wave.
3. A radio wave has a frequency of 3×10^7 hertz. It is 10 m long. Find the speed of the radio wave.

4-4 Graphs of the Circular Functions

The sine function generates ordered pairs of numbers of the form (s, sin s). If s is any real number, then sin s is a number such that $^-1 \le \sin s \le 1$. The ordered pairs for values of s between 0 and $\frac{\pi}{2}$ can be read directly from the table on page 503. For values of s outside the interval from 0 to $\frac{\pi}{2}$, ordered pairs can be determined by finding s' such that $0 \le s' \le \frac{\pi}{2}$ and then using the table.

To graph the sine function, use the horizontal axis for values of s. Use the vertical axis for sin s. The following charts provide the information necessary for plotting points.

s		0	$\frac{\pi}{6}$	$\frac{\pi}{4}$	$\frac{\pi}{3}$	$\frac{\pi}{2}$	$\frac{2\pi}{3}$	$\frac{3\pi}{4}$	$\frac{5\pi}{6}$	π	$\frac{7\pi}{6}$	$\frac{5\pi}{4}$	$\frac{4\pi}{3}$	$\frac{3\pi}{2}$	$\frac{5\pi}{3}$	$\frac{7\pi}{4}$	$\frac{11\pi}{6}$	2π
sin s	exact	0	$\frac{1}{2}$	$\frac{\sqrt{2}}{2}$	$\frac{\sqrt{3}}{2}$	1	$\frac{\sqrt{3}}{2}$	$\frac{\sqrt{2}}{2}$	$\frac{1}{2}$	0	$-\frac{1}{2}$	$-\frac{\sqrt{2}}{2}$	$-\frac{\sqrt{3}}{2}$	$^-1$	$-\frac{\sqrt{3}}{2}$	$-\frac{\sqrt{2}}{2}$	$-\frac{1}{2}$	0
	nearest tenth	0.0	0.5	0.7	0.9	1.0	0.9	0.7	0.5	0.0	$^-0.5$	$^-0.7$	$^-0.9$	$^-1.0$	$^-0.9$	$^-0.7$	$^-0.5$	0.0

After plotting points, complete the graph by connecting the plotted points with a smooth continuous curve.

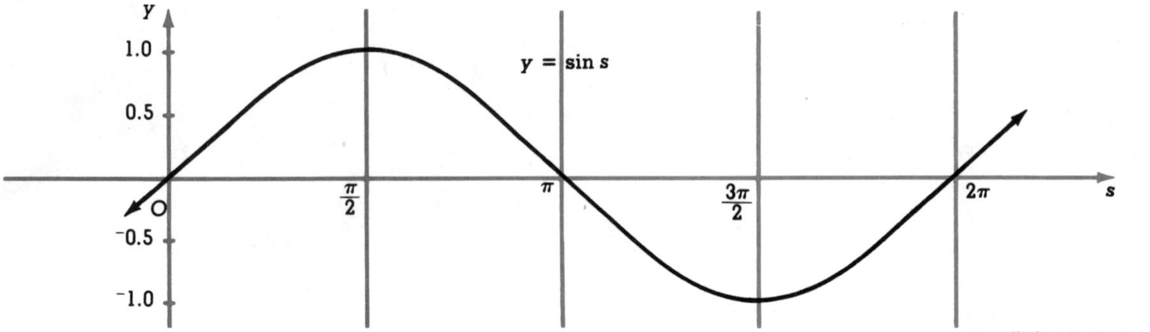

Recall that both the sine and cosine function have a period of 2π.

The graph of the cosine function is done in a similar manner.

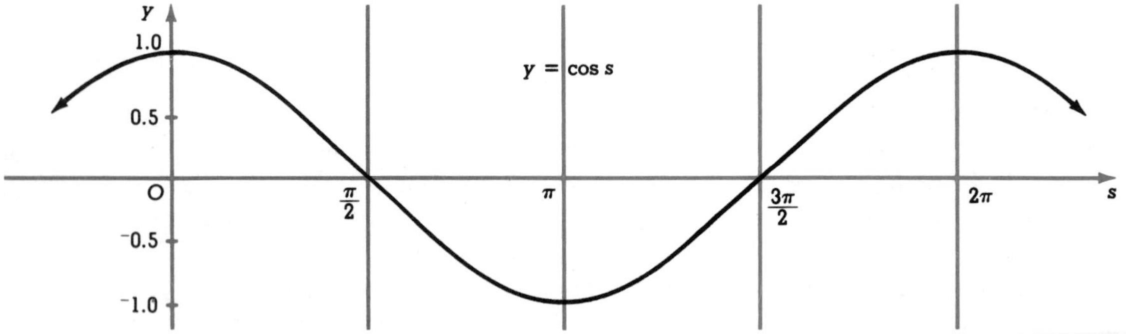

example

1 **Find the quadrants in which both the sine and cosine functions are increasing.**

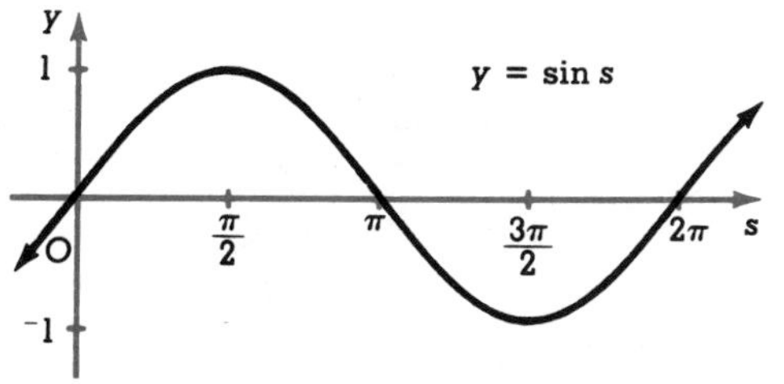

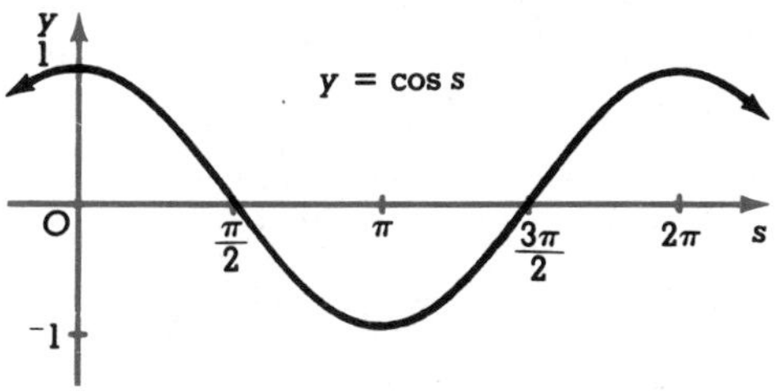

Look at the graphs of each function to find where each function is increasing. The sine function is increasing from 0 to $\frac{\pi}{2}$ and from $\frac{3\pi}{2}$ to 0. The cosine function is increasing from π to $\frac{3\pi}{2}$ and from $\frac{3\pi}{2}$ to 0. Thus, both functions are increasing from $\frac{3\pi}{2}$ to 0 or in the fourth quadrant.

The graph of the ordered pairs (s, tan s) is shown below. The tangent function is not defined for $\frac{\pi}{2}$ or $\frac{3\pi}{2}$. The graph is separated at these points by vertical asymptotes, indicated by broken lines. The graph of tan s approaches the asymptotes as s approaches $\frac{\pi}{2}$ and $\frac{3\pi}{2}$ from either side. The period of the tangent function is π.

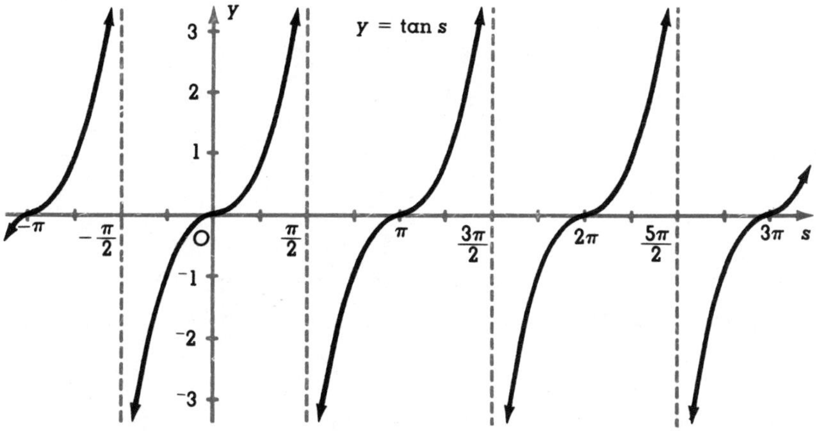

The graphs of the secant, cosecant, and cotangent functions are shown on the next page. Notice how they compare to the graphs of the cosine, sine, and tangent functions, indicated by the broken curves.

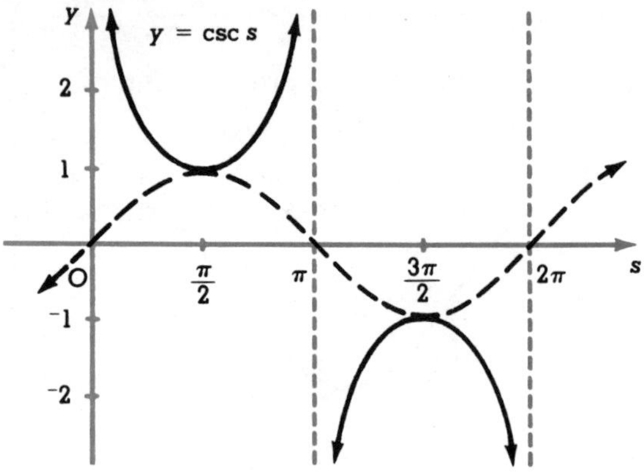

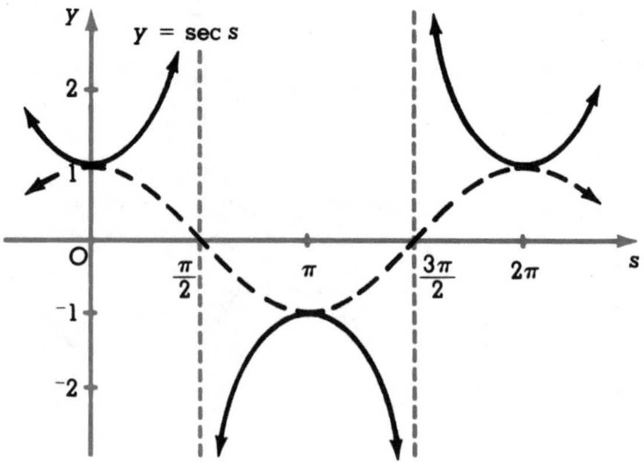

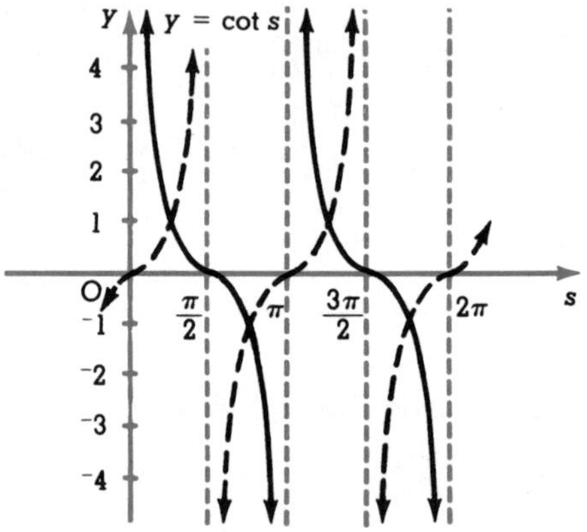

example

2 **State which circular functions of s are decreasing as values of s are increasing from 0 to $\frac{\pi}{2}$.**

This information can be taken directly from the graphs of the circular functions. The cosine, cosecant, and cotangent functions are decreasing in the interval 0 to $\frac{\pi}{2}$.

exercises

Exploratory **State whether values of the following functions are increasing or decreasing as values of s increase from $\frac{\pi}{2}$ to π.**

1. $y = \sin s$
2. $y = \cos s$
3. $y = \tan s$
4. $y = \cot s$
5. $y = \sec s$
6. $y = \csc s$

7-12. State whether values of the functions in problems **1-6** are increasing or decreasing as values of s increase from π to $\frac{3\pi}{2}$.

Written State the values of s between and including 0 and 2π for which each expression is *not* defined.

1. $\sin s$
2. $\cos s$
3. $\tan s$
4. $\cot s$
5. $\sec s$
6. $\csc s$

Make a table of values for each of the following functions consisting of at least ten points for $0 \leq s \leq 2\pi$.

7. $y = \cos s$
8. $y = \tan s$
9. $y = \sec s$
10. $y = \cot s$

11-14. Graph each function in problems **7-10** using the tables from problems **7-10**.

Graph each of the following for values of s from $^-2\pi$ to 2π.

15. $y = \sin s$
16. $y = \cos s$

17-18. Find the negative value of s at which the functions in problems **15-16** are at a minimum.

19-20. Find the negative value of s at which the functions in problems **15-16** are at a maximum.

Find the quadrant(s) in which each pair of functions is decreasing.

21. $y = \sin s$, $y = \sec s$
22. $y = \cot s$, $y = \cos s$
23. $y = \sec s$, $y = \csc s$
24. $y = \csc s$, $y = \cot s$

Graph the sine and cosine functions on the same coordinate axes for $0 \leq s \leq 2\pi$. Use the graph to find values for s for which the equation or inequality is true.

25. $\sin s = \cos s$
26. $\sin s > \cos s$
27. $\sin s + \cos s = 2$
28. $|\sin s + \cos s| = 1$
29. $\cos s - \sin s = 1$
30. $\sin s \cdot \cos s = 0$

Challenge Graph the six circular functions on the same coordinate axes for values of s from 0 to 2π. Use a different color for each function to distinguish curves.

4-5 Addition Formulas

It is sometimes necessary to find the circular function of the sum or difference of two real numbers. A formula can be developed to find the cosine of the sum or difference of two real numbers.

Consider the unit circle on the right. The points P_1, P_2, and P_3 have coordinates as indicated. The measure of $\widehat{AP_1}$ is s_1. The measure of $\widehat{P_1P_2}$ and $\widehat{AP_3}$ is s_2. Thus $\widehat{AP_2}$ is congruent to $\widehat{P_1P_3}$ since each is measured by the sum, $s_1 + s_2$. From geometry, congruent arcs in the same circle have congruent chords. Therefore, $AP_2 = P_1P_3$.

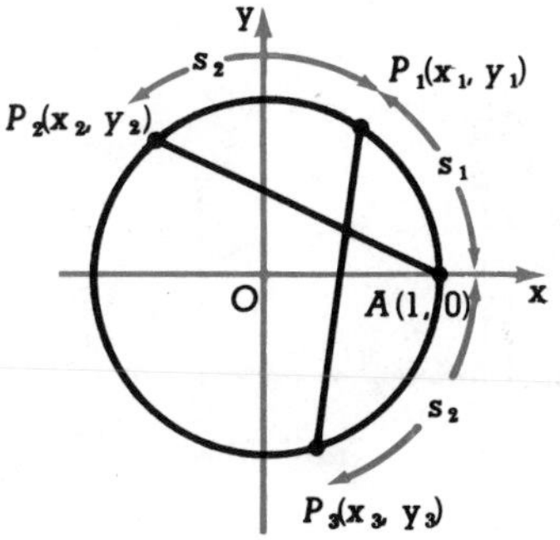

$$AP_2 = P_1P_3$$

$$\sqrt{(x_2 - 1)^2 + (y_2 - 0)^2} = \sqrt{(x_1 - x_3)^2 + (y_1 - y_3)^2}$$ *Use the distance formula*

$$x_2^2 - 2x_2 + 1 + y_2^2 = x_1^2 - 2x_1x_3 + x_3^2 + y_1^2 - 2y_1y_3 + y_3^2$$

$$(x_2^2 + y_2^2) - 2x_2 + 1 = (x_1^2 + y_1^2) + (x_3^2 + y_3^2) - 2x_1x_3 - 2y_1y_3$$

$$1 - 2x_2 + 1 = 1 + 1 - 2x_1x_3 - 2y_1y_3$$ *Substitute, using the fact $x^2 + y^2 = 1$.*

$$x_2 = x_1x_3 + y_1y_3$$

The following formula is obtained by substituting the appropriate function of s in the above equation. For example, $x_3 = \cos(^-s_2)$.

Recall that $\cos(^-s) = \cos s$ and $\sin(^-s) = {^-\sin s}$.

$$\cos(s_1 + s_2) = \cos s_1 \cos(^-s_2) + \sin s_1 \sin(^-s_2)$$

$$\mathbf{\cos(s_1 + s_2) = \cos s_1 \cos s_2 - \sin s_1 \sin s_2}$$

To find a formula for $\cos(s_1 - s_2)$, write $\cos(s_1 - s_2)$ as $\cos[s_1 + (^-s_2)]$ and use the formula above.

$$\cos[s_1 + (^-s_2)] = \cos s_1 \cos(^-s_2) - \sin s_1 \sin(^-s_2)$$

$$\mathbf{\cos(s_1 - s_2) = \cos s_1 \cos s_2 + \sin s_1 \sin s_2}$$

The development of several other equations will lead to the formula for the sine of the sum or difference of two real numbers.

If s_1 is replaced with $\frac{\pi}{2}$ and s_2 with s in the formulas for $\cos(s_1 \pm s_2)$, the following equations are the result.

$$\cos\left(\frac{\pi}{2} + s\right) = {^-\sin s}$$

$$\cos\left(\frac{\pi}{2} - s\right) = \sin s$$

Replace s with $\frac{\pi}{2} + s$ in the previous equation to obtain the following equation.

$$\cos s = \sin\left(\frac{\pi}{2} + s\right)$$

Replace s with $\frac{\pi}{2} - s$ in the equation for $\cos\left(\frac{\pi}{2} - s\right)$ to obtain the following equation.

$$\cos s = \sin\left(\frac{\pi}{2} - s\right)$$

In the equation for $\cos\left(\frac{\pi}{2} - s\right)$ replace s with $s_1 + s_2$.

$$\cos\left[\frac{\pi}{2} - (s_1 + s_2)\right] = \sin(s_1 + s_2)$$

$$\cos\left[\left(\frac{\pi}{2} - s_1\right) - s_2\right] = \sin(s_1 + s_2)$$

$$\cos\left(\frac{\pi}{2} - s_1\right)\cos s_2 + \sin\left(\frac{\pi}{2} - s_1\right)\sin s_2 = \sin(s_1 + s_2)$$ *Use formula for $\cos(s_1 - s_2)$.*

$$\mathbf{\sin(s_1 + s_2) = \sin s_1 \cos s_2 + \cos s_1 \sin s_2}$$ *Substitute using previous equations.*

To obtain $\sin(s_1 - s_2)$ replace s_2 with $(^{-}s_2)$ in the above formula.

$$\sin[s_1 + (^{-}s_2)] = \sin s_1 \cos(^{-}s_2) + \cos s_1 \sin(^{-}s_2)$$

$$\mathbf{\sin(s_1 - s_2) = \sin s_1 \cos s_2 - \cos s_1 \sin s_2}$$

The following formulas hold for any real numbers s_1 and s_2.

$$\cos(s_1 \pm s_2) = \cos s_1 \cos s_2 \mp \sin s_1 \sin s_2$$

$$\sin(s_1 \pm s_2) = \sin s_1 \cos s_2 \pm \cos s_1 \sin s_2$$

Notice how the operation symbols in each equation are related.

Addition Formulas of Sine and Cosine Functions

example

1 Find the cosine and sine of $\frac{7\pi}{12}$.

$$\frac{7\pi}{12} = \frac{\pi}{4} + \frac{\pi}{3}$$

$$\cos\frac{7\pi}{12} = \cos\left(\frac{\pi}{4} + \frac{\pi}{3}\right)$$

$$= \cos\frac{\pi}{4}\cos\frac{\pi}{3} - \sin\frac{\pi}{4}\sin\frac{\pi}{3}$$ *Use formula for $\cos(s_1 + s_2)$.*

$$= \frac{\sqrt{2}}{2}\cdot\frac{1}{2} - \frac{\sqrt{2}}{2}\cdot\frac{\sqrt{3}}{2}$$

$$= \frac{\sqrt{2} - \sqrt{6}}{4}$$

$$\sin\frac{7\pi}{12} = \sin\left(\frac{\pi}{4} + \frac{\pi}{3}\right)$$

$$= \sin\frac{\pi}{4}\cos\frac{\pi}{3} + \cos\frac{\pi}{4}\sin\frac{\pi}{3}$$ *Use formula for $\sin(s_1 + s_2)$.*

$$= \frac{\sqrt{2}}{2}\cdot\frac{1}{2} + \frac{\sqrt{2}}{2}\cdot\frac{\sqrt{3}}{2}$$

$$= \frac{\sqrt{2} + \sqrt{6}}{4}$$

The cosine and sine of $\frac{7\pi}{12}$ are $\frac{\sqrt{2} - \sqrt{6}}{4}$ and $\frac{\sqrt{2} + \sqrt{6}}{4}$, respectively.

exercises

Exploratory Write each value in terms of sums or differences of $\frac{\pi}{6}$, $\frac{\pi}{4}$, $\frac{\pi}{3}$, and $\frac{\pi}{2}$ or their multiples.

1. $\frac{5\pi}{6}$
2. $-\frac{\pi}{12}$
3. $-\frac{11\pi}{12}$
4. $\frac{11\pi}{12}$
5. $\frac{5\pi}{12}$
6. $-\frac{5\pi}{12}$
7. $\frac{19\pi}{12}$
8. $\frac{17\pi}{12}$

Written Let $s_1 = \frac{\pi}{2}$ and $s_2 = \frac{\pi}{2}$. Verify the formulas for each of the following.

1. $\cos(s_1 + s_2)$
2. $\cos(s_1 - s_2)$
3. $\sin(s_1 + s_2)$

Let $s_1 = 0$ and $s_2 = \frac{\pi}{3}$. Verify the formulas for each of the following.

4. $\sin(s_1 - s_2)$
5. $\cos(s_1 - s_2)$
6. $\sin(s_1 + s_2)$

Evaluate each expression using the addition formulas.

7. $\sin \frac{5\pi}{12}$
8. $\sin \frac{11\pi}{12}$
9. $\sin\left(-\frac{19\pi}{12}\right)$
10. $\cos \frac{5\pi}{12}$
11. $\cos \frac{13\pi}{12}$
12. $\cos \frac{17\pi}{12}$
13. $\cos\left(-\frac{\pi}{12}\right)$
14. $\sin \frac{5\pi}{6}$
15. $\cos\left(-\frac{11\pi}{12}\right)$

Develop a formula for each of the following sums or differences.

16. $\sin(\pi + s)$
17. $\sin(\pi - s)$
18. $\cos(\pi - s)$
19. $\cos(\pi + s)$
20. $\sin(2\pi + s)$
21. $\sin(2\pi - s)$
22. $\cos(2\pi - s)$
23. $\cos(2\pi + s)$
24. $\tan(s_1 + s_2)$
25. $\tan(s_1 - s_2)$
26. $\cot(s_1 + s_2)$
27. $\cot(s_1 - s_2)$

Verify each of the following equations.

28. $\cos\left(\frac{\pi}{6} + s\right) + \sin\left(\frac{\pi}{3} + s\right) = \sqrt{3}\cos s$
29. $\sin\left(\frac{3\pi}{2} + s\right) - \cos\left(\frac{\pi}{2} - s\right) = -(\cos s + \sin s)$
30. $\tan(\pi + s)\cos s = -\cos\left(\frac{3\pi}{2} - s\right)$
31. $\cos\left(\frac{\pi}{3} - s_1\right)\cos\left(\frac{5\pi}{3} + s_2\right) - \sin\left(\frac{\pi}{3} - s_1\right)\sin\left(\frac{5\pi}{3} + s_2\right) = \cos(s_2 - s_1)$

4-6 Double and Half Number Formulas

The formula for $\sin(s_1 + s_2)$ can be used to find $\sin 2s$.

$$\begin{aligned}\sin 2s &= \sin(s + s)\\ &= \sin s\cos s + \cos s\sin s\\ &= 2\sin s\cos s\end{aligned}$$

Likewise, a formula for $\cos 2s$ can be developed.

$$\begin{aligned}\cos 2s &= \cos(s + s)\\ &= \cos s\cos s - \sin s\sin s\\ &= \cos^2 s - \sin^2 s\end{aligned}$$

Substituting $1 - \cos^2 s$ for $\sin^2 s$ and $1 - \sin^2 s$ for $\cos^2 s$ respectively in the formula above yields alternate forms of $\cos 2s$.

Since $\sin^2 s + \cos^2 s = 1$, $\sin^2 s = 1 - \cos^2 s$ and $\cos^2 s = 1 - \sin^2 s$.

$$\cos 2s = 2\cos^2 s - 1$$
$$\cos 2s = 1 - 2\sin^2 s$$

Double Number Formulas

The following formulas hold for any real number s.

$$\sin 2s = 2 \sin s \cos s \qquad \cos 2s = \cos^2 s - \sin^2 s$$
$$= 2\cos^2 s - 1$$
$$= 1 - 2\sin^2 s$$

example

1 Suppose C(s) is in Quadrant I and $\sin s = \frac{4}{5}$. Find sin 2s.

Since $\sin 2s = 2 \sin s \cos s$, find $\cos s$ first. Use $\cos^2 s + \sin^2 s = 1$.

$$\cos^2 s + \left(\frac{4}{5}\right)^2 = 1$$

Substitute $\frac{4}{5}$ for sin s.

$$\cos^2 s = 1 - \left(\frac{4}{5}\right)^2$$

$$\cos s = \pm\sqrt{\frac{9}{25}} \text{ or } \pm\frac{3}{5}$$

Since C(s) is in Quadrant I, cos s must be positive.

$$\sin 2s = 2 \sin s \cos s$$
$$= 2\left(\frac{4}{5}\right)\left(\frac{3}{5}\right) \text{ or } \frac{24}{25}$$

The two alternate forms of the formula for cos 2s may be solved for cos s and sin s, respectively.

$$\cos s = \pm\sqrt{\frac{1 + \cos 2s}{2}}$$

$$\sin s = \pm\sqrt{\frac{1 - \cos 2s}{2}}$$

The sign is chosen according to the quadrant in which the point determined by C(s) is located.

Since s is a real number, 2s may be replaced with r and thus s with $\frac{r}{2}$ to derive the formulas for half of any real number r.

Half Number Formulas

The following formulas hold for any real number r.

$$\cos\frac{r}{2} = \pm\sqrt{\frac{1 + \cos r}{2}} \qquad \sin\frac{r}{2} = \pm\sqrt{\frac{1 - \cos r}{2}}$$

example

2 Find $\sin \frac{\pi}{8}$.

$$\sin \frac{\pi}{8} = \sin \frac{\frac{\pi}{4}}{2}$$

$$= \pm\sqrt{\frac{1 - \cos \frac{\pi}{4}}{2}} \qquad \textit{Use the formula for } \sin \frac{r}{2}.$$

$$= \pm\sqrt{\frac{1 - \frac{\sqrt{2}}{2}}{2}} \text{ or } \pm\sqrt{\frac{2 - \sqrt{2}}{4}} \qquad \cos \frac{\pi}{4} = \frac{\sqrt{2}}{2}$$

Since $C\left(\frac{\pi}{8}\right)$ is in Quadrant I, the value of $\sin \frac{\pi}{8}$ is positive.

The solution is $\frac{\sqrt{2 - \sqrt{2}}}{2}$.

exercises

Exploratory Find the value of each of the following using the half number formulas.

1. $\sin \frac{\pi}{12}$
2. $\sin \frac{3\pi}{8}$
3. $\sin \frac{3\pi}{16}$
4. $\cos \frac{7\pi}{12}$
5. $\cos \frac{3\pi}{8}$
6. $\sin \frac{11\pi}{12}$
7. $\cos \frac{3\pi}{16}$
8. $\cos \frac{11\pi}{12}$

Written Find sin 2*s* for each of the following.

1. $\sin s = \frac{1}{2}$, $C(s)$ is in Quadrant I
2. $\cos s = \frac{3}{5}$, $C(s)$ is in Quadrant I
3. $\cos s = -\frac{2}{3}$, $C(s)$ is in Quadrant III
4. $\sin s = \frac{4}{5}$, $C(s)$ is in Quadrant II
5. $\sin s = \frac{5}{13}$, $C(s)$ is in Quadrant II
6. $\cos s = \frac{1}{5}$, $C(s)$ is in Quadrant IV
7. $\sin s = -\frac{3}{4}$, $C(s)$ is in Quadrant IV
8. $\cos s = -\frac{1}{3}$, $C(s)$ is in Quadrant III

9-16. Find $\cos \frac{s}{2}$ for problems **1-8**.

17-24. Find $\sin \frac{s}{2}$ for problems **1-8**.

25-32. Find cos 2*s* for problems **1-8**.

Solve each problem.

33. Develop a formula for tan 2*s* in terms of tan *s*.
34. Develop a formula for $\tan \frac{r}{2}$ in terms of cos *r*.
35. Develop a formula for sin 3*s* in terms of sin *s*.
36. Develop a formula for cos 3*s* in terms of cos *s*.

Using Mathematics

The figure at the right represents an alternating current generator. A rectangular coil of wire is suspended between the poles of a magnet. As the coil of wire is rotated, it passes through the magnetic field and generates current.

As point X on the coil passes through the points A and C, its *motion* is along the direction of the magnetic field between the poles. Therefore, no current is generated. However, through points B and D, the motion of X is perpendicular to the magnetic field. This induces maximum current in the coil. Between A and B, B and C, C and D, and D and A, the current in the coil will have an intermediate value. Thus, the graph of the current of an alternating current generator is closely related to the sine curve.

The actual current, i, in a household current is given by $i = I_M \sin(120\pi t + \alpha)$ where I_M is the maximum value of the current, t is the elapsed time in seconds, and α is the angle determined by the position of the coil at time t_0.

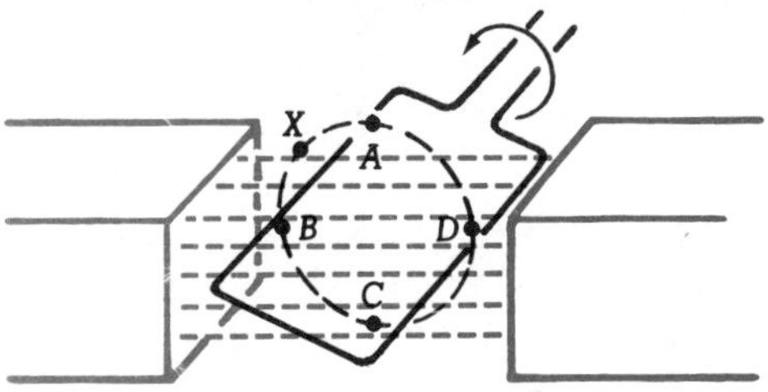

The maximum current may have a positive or negative value.

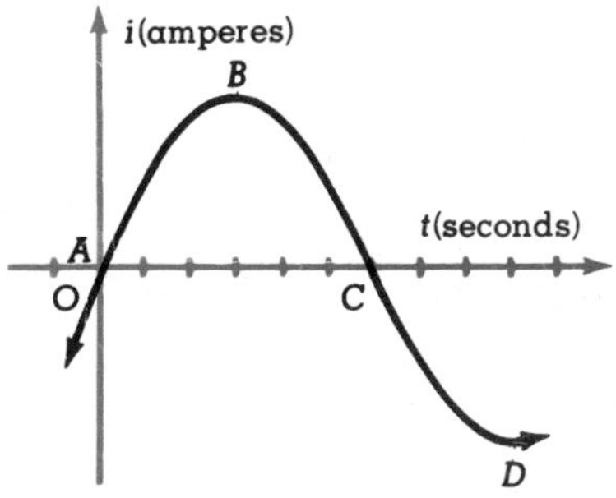

Example If $\alpha = \frac{\pi}{2}$, find a value of t for which $i = 0$.

If $i = 0$, then $I_M\sin(120\pi t + \alpha) = 0$. *$i = I_M \sin(120\pi t + \alpha)$*

Since $I_M \neq 0$, $\sin(120\pi t + \alpha) = 0$. *If $ab = 0$ and $a \neq 0$, then $b = 0$.*

Let $120\pi t + \alpha = s$. Thus, $\sin s = 0$.

$s = \pi$ because $\sin \pi = 0$.

$120\pi t + \alpha = \pi$ *Substitute $120\pi t + \alpha$ for s.*

$120\pi t + \frac{\pi}{2} = \pi$ *Substitute $\frac{\pi}{2}$ for α.*

$t = \frac{1}{240}$ *Solve for t.*

Exercises Using the equation for the actual current in a household circuit, $i = I_M\sin(120\pi t + \alpha)$, solve each problem.

1. If $\alpha = 0$, find a value of t for which $i = 0$.
2. If $\alpha = 0$, find a value of t for which $i = +I_M$.
3. If $\alpha = \frac{\pi}{2}$, find a value of t for which $i = {}^-I_M$.
4. If $\alpha = \frac{\pi}{4}$, find a value of t for which $i = 0$.

Chapter Summary

1. Function C is defined such that for each real number s, there corresponds exactly one ordered pair of real numbers (x, y) which are coordinates of a point on the unit circle. (90)
2. Periodic Function and Period: A function is periodic if, for some real number α, $f(x + \alpha) = f(x)$ for each x in the domain of f. The least positive value of α for which $f(x) = f(x + \alpha)$ is the period of the function. (91)
3. Cosine and Sine Functions: For any real number s, where $C(s) = (x, y)$ such that $x^2 + y^2 = 1$, the cosine of $s = x$ and the sine of $s = y$. In abbreviated form, $\cos s = x$ and $\sin s = y$. (93)
4. Tangent, Cotangent, Secant, and Cosecant Functions: Let s represent any real number. The tangent, cotangent, secant, and cosecant functions are defined as follows. (94)

$$\tan s = \frac{\sin s}{\cos s} \qquad (\cos s \neq 0)$$

$$\cot s = \frac{\cos s}{\sin s} \qquad (\sin s \neq 0)$$

$$\sec s = \frac{1}{\cos s} \qquad (\cos s \neq 0)$$

$$\csc s = \frac{1}{\sin s} \qquad (\sin s \neq 0)$$

5. Values of the Circular Functions in Quadrants: (97, 98)

Quadrant s' Function	I $s' = s - 2\pi n$	II $s' = (2n - 1)\pi - s$	III $s' = s - (2n - 1)\pi$	IV $s' = 2\pi n - s$
$\sin s$	$\sin s'$	$\sin s'$	$^-\sin s'$	$^-\sin s'$
$\cos s$	$\cos s'$	$^-\cos s'$	$^-\cos s'$	$\cos s'$
$\tan s$	$\tan s'$	$^-\tan s'$	$\tan s'$	$^-\tan s'$
$\csc s$	$\csc s'$	$\csc s'$	$^-\csc s'$	$^-\csc s'$
$\sec s$	$\sec s'$	$^-\sec s'$	$^-\sec s'$	$\sec s'$
$\cot s$	$\cot s'$	$^-\cot s'$	$\cot s'$	$^-\cot s'$

6. Addition Formulas of Sine and Cosine Functions: The following formulas hold for any real numbers s_1 and s_2. (107)

$$\cos(s_1 \pm s_2) = \cos s_1 \cos s_2 \mp \sin s_1 \sin s_2$$
$$\sin(s_1 \pm s_2) = \sin s_1 \cos s_2 \pm \cos s_1 \sin s_2$$

7. Double Number Formulas: The following formulas hold for any real number s. (109)

$$\sin 2s = 2 \sin s \cos s \qquad \cos 2s = \cos^2 s - \sin^2 s = 2\cos^2 s - 1 = 1 - 2\sin^2 s$$

8. Half Number Formulas: The following formulas hold for any real number r. (109)

$$\cos \frac{r}{2} = \pm\sqrt{\frac{1 + \cos r}{2}} \qquad \sin \frac{r}{2} = \pm\sqrt{\frac{1 - \cos r}{2}}$$

Chapter Review

4-1 For each real number s, find the coordinates (x, y) determined by $C(s) = (x, y)$.

1. $\frac{5\pi}{4}$
2. $-\frac{13\pi}{2}$
3. 15π
4. $-\frac{\pi}{4}$
5. $^{-}4\pi$
6. $6\pi - \frac{5\pi}{3}$
7. $-\frac{4\pi}{3} + \pi$
8. $-\frac{41\pi}{3}$

4-2 Suppose $C(s) = \left(\frac{3}{5}, \frac{4}{5}\right)$. Find each of the following.

9. $\sin s$
10. $\cos s$
11. $\tan s$
12. $\csc s$

Find the value of each of the following.

13. $\cos 0$
14. $\sin \frac{\pi}{6}$
15. $\cot \frac{\pi}{6}$
16. $\sec \frac{\pi}{4}$
17. $\csc \frac{\pi}{3}$
18. $\tan \frac{\pi}{2}$
19. $\cos (^{-}3\pi)$
20. $\cot \frac{11\pi}{4}$
21. $\sin \left(-\frac{5\pi}{3}\right)$
22. $\sec \frac{3\pi}{2}$
23. $\tan \pi$
24. $\csc \left(-\frac{5\pi}{6}\right)$

4-3 Find the approximate value of each of the following using the table on page 503 and $\pi = 3.14$.

25. $\sin \frac{1}{3}$
26. $\tan \frac{3\pi}{8}$
27. $\cos (^{-}6)$
28. $\csc \frac{2\pi}{7}$
29. $\sec (^{-}12.35)$
30. $\sin 15$
31. $\sec 1.776$
32. $\cot \pi + 0.5$

Find the approximate value of s using the table on page 503.

33. $\sin s = 0.9939$
34. $\tan s = 0.6164$
35. $\cos s = 0.3121$
36. $\cot s = 3.275$
37. $\sec s = 1.427$
38. $\csc s = 48.79$

4-4 Graph each of the following for values of s from 0 to 4π.

39. $y = \cos s$
40. $y = \sin s$
41. $y = \tan s$

4-5 Evaluate each expression using the sum or difference formulas.

42. $\sin \frac{\pi}{12}$
43. $\cos \left(-\frac{5\pi}{12}\right)$
44. $\cos \frac{5\pi}{6}$
45. $\sin \left(-\frac{19\pi}{12}\right)$

4-6

46. If $\sin s = -\frac{3}{5}$ and $C(s)$ is in the third quadrant, find $\sin 2s$.
47. If $\sin s = \frac{1}{4}$ and $C(s)$ is in the first quadrant, find $\cos 2s$.
48. If $\cos s = \frac{17}{25}$ and $C(s)$ is in the fourth quadrant, find $\cos \frac{s}{2}$.

Chapter Test

For each real number s, find the coordinates (x, y) determined by C(s) = (x, y).

1. $\frac{3\pi}{2}$
2. $-\frac{5\pi}{4}$
3. $\frac{16\pi}{3}$
4. 32π
5. $-7\pi + \frac{4\pi}{3}$
6. $\frac{7\pi}{4}$
7. $^{-}5\pi$
8. $\frac{5\pi}{3} - 9\pi$

Find the value of each of the following.

9. $\sin \frac{11\pi}{3}$
10. $\tan 0$
11. $\cos\left(-\frac{4\pi}{3}\right)$
12. $\sec \frac{3\pi}{4}$
13. $\cot \frac{\pi}{3}$
14. $\csc \frac{\pi}{2}$
15. $\sin\left(-\frac{\pi}{6}\right)$
16. $\cos 7\pi$

Suppose $\sin r = \frac{\sqrt{2}}{2}$ and r is in the second quadrant. Evaluate each of the following.

17. $\cos r$
18. $\tan r$
19. $\cot r$
20. $\sec r$

Find the approximate value of each of the following using the table on page 503 and $\pi = 3.14$.

21. $\sin 4$
22. $\cos \frac{4\pi}{5}$
23. $\tan (^{-}6.1)$
24. $\csc \frac{15\pi}{8}$

Find the approximate value of s using the table on page 503.

25. $\cos s = 0.3805$
26. $\tan s = 0.0260$
27. $\sec s = 4.400$
28. $\sin s = 0.5830$

Graph each of the following for values of s from 0 to 2π.

29. $y = \sin s$
30. $y = \tan s$

Evaluate each expression using the sum or difference formulas.

31. $\sin \frac{17\pi}{12}$
32. $\cos \frac{5\pi}{12}$
33. $\sin\left(-\frac{\pi}{12}\right)$

34. If C(s) is in the first quadrant and $\cos s = \frac{3}{4}$, find $\sin \frac{s}{2}$.

35. If C(s) is in the third quadrant and $\sin s = \frac{4}{5}$, find $\cos 2s$.

Chapter

5

The Trigonometric Functions

The angles and triangles in the structure of a roller coaster are crucial to its construction. An area of mathematics which deals with the functions of angles is called trigonometry.

5-1 Trigonometric Functions of an Angle

In the circular functions, the coordinates of the points on a unit circle are the basis for the definitions of the sine and cosine functions with the real numbers as the domain. An area of mathematics called **trigonometry** also involves the sine and cosine functions. In trigonometry the domain of each function is also the set of real numbers. However, each real number is the measure of an angle rather than the measure of an arc.

An **angle** is the union of two rays that have a common endpoint. An angle may be generated by the rotation of a ray with a fixed endpoint. The starting position of the ray is called the **initial side** and the final position is called the **terminal side.** If the rotation is counterclockwise, the measure of the angle is positive. If the rotation is clockwise, the measure of the angle is negative.

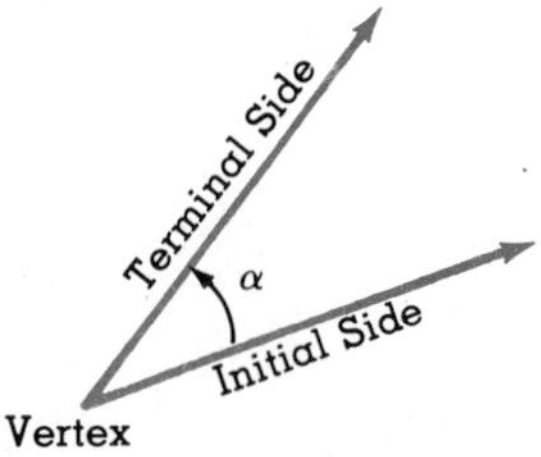

An angle with its vertex at the origin and its initial side along the positive x-axis is in *standard position.*

Let the positive x-axis of the coordinate system be the initial side of an angle with measure α, and let $P(x, y)$ be a point on the terminal side of an angle with measure α. The distance from the origin is given by r and is defined to be positive. By the Pythagorean Theorem, $r = \sqrt{x^2 + y^2}$.

The three numbers represented by x, y, and r can be arranged into six ratios. The values of these ratios depend upon the measure α of $\angle POM$. These ratios are called the **trigonometric functions** of α.

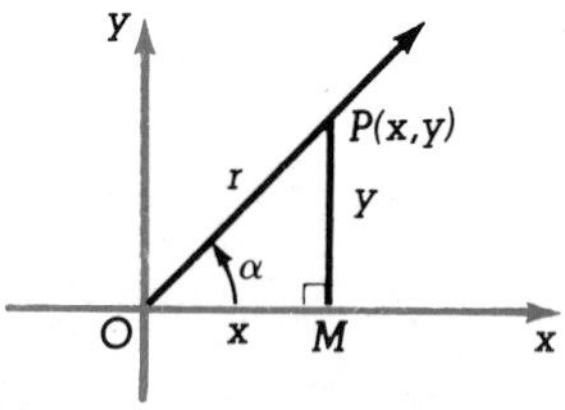

Trigonometric Functions of an Angle in Standard Position

For any angle with measure α, point $P(x, y)$ on its terminal side, and $r = \sqrt{x^2 + y^2}$, the trigonometric functions of α are as follows.

$$\sin \alpha = \frac{y}{r} \qquad \cos \alpha = \frac{x}{r} \qquad \tan \alpha = \frac{y}{x}$$

$$\csc \alpha = \frac{r}{y} \qquad \sec \alpha = \frac{r}{x} \qquad \cot \alpha = \frac{x}{y}$$

example

1 **Find the values of the six trigonometric functions of an angle in standard position with measure α if the point (4, 3) lies on its terminal side.**

First find the value of r.

$$\begin{aligned} r &= \sqrt{x^2 + y^2} \\ &= \sqrt{16 + 9} \\ &= 5 \end{aligned}$$

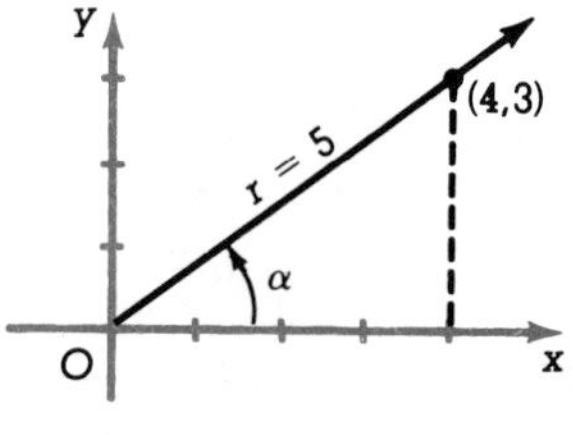

$$\sin \alpha = \frac{y}{r} \text{ or } \frac{3}{5} \qquad \cos \alpha = \frac{x}{r} \text{ or } \frac{4}{5} \qquad \tan \alpha = \frac{y}{x} \text{ or } \frac{3}{4}$$

$$\csc \alpha = \frac{r}{y} \text{ or } \frac{5}{3} \qquad \sec \alpha = \frac{r}{x} \text{ or } \frac{5}{4} \qquad \cot \alpha = \frac{x}{y} \text{ or } \frac{4}{3}$$

Right triangles are also used to define trigonometric functions. Let A, B, and C designate the vertices of a right triangle and the angles at those vertices. The lengths of the opposite sides are designated by a, b, and c, respectively. Possible ratios of the sides are $\dfrac{b}{a}$, $\dfrac{a}{b}$, $\dfrac{a}{c}$, $\dfrac{c}{a}$, $\dfrac{b}{c}$, and $\dfrac{c}{b}$.

All right triangles having acute angles congruent to angles A and B are similar. Thus, the ratios of corresponding sides are equal. These ratios are determined by the measures of the acute angles. Therefore, any two congruent angles of different right triangles will have the same ratios associated with them.

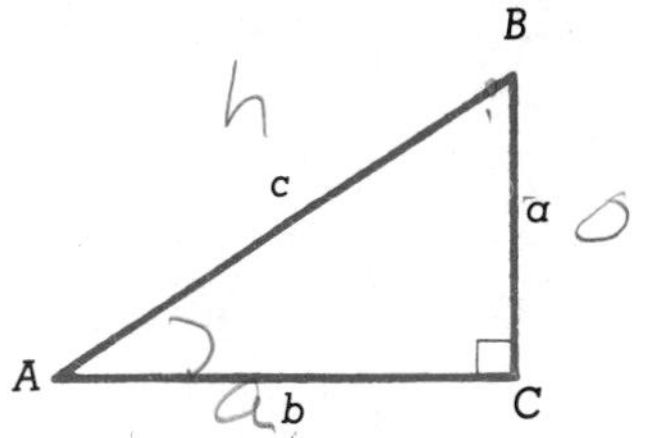

A and B may represent either the angle itself or its measure as determined by the context.

For an acute angle A in right triangle ABC, the trigonometric functions are as follows.

$$\sin A = \frac{\text{side opposite}}{\text{hypotenuse}} = \frac{a}{c} \qquad \cos A = \frac{\text{side adjacent}}{\text{hypotenuse}} = \frac{b}{c}$$

$$\tan A = \frac{\text{side opposite}}{\text{side adjacent}} = \frac{a}{b} \qquad \cot A = \frac{\text{side adjacent}}{\text{side opposite}} = \frac{b}{a}$$

$$\sec A = \frac{\text{hypotenuse}}{\text{side adjacent}} = \frac{c}{b} \qquad \csc A = \frac{\text{hypotenuse}}{\text{side opposite}} = \frac{c}{a}$$

Old hands (sin)
Always Help (cos)
Old Aviators (tan)

Trigonometric Functions in A Right Triangle

What are the trigonometric functions of angle B in right triangle ABC?

example 2   A right triangle has sides whose lengths are 7 cm, 24 cm, and 25 cm. Find the values of the six trigonometric functions of the angle opposite the shorter leg.

$$\sin \alpha = \frac{\text{side opposite}}{\text{hypotenuse}} = \frac{7}{25}$$

$$\tan \alpha = \frac{\text{side opposite}}{\text{side adjacent}} = \frac{7}{24}$$

$$\sec \alpha = \frac{\text{hypotenuse}}{\text{side adjacent}} = \frac{25}{24}$$

$$\cos \alpha = \frac{\text{side adjacent}}{\text{hypotenuse}} = \frac{24}{25}$$

$$\cot \alpha = \frac{\text{side adjacent}}{\text{side opposite}} = \frac{24}{7} \qquad \csc \alpha = \frac{\text{hypotenuse}}{\text{side opposite}} = \frac{25}{7}$$

Sin 30 = ½   Cos 30 = √3/2
Sin 60 = √3/2   Cos 60 = ½

The trigonometric functions of certain angles may be derived from geometric relationships.

Recall that the hypotenuse of a 30°-60° right triangle is twice the length of the shorter leg. If A is 30° and C is the right angle, let the measurement of c be 2 units and the measurement of a be 1 unit. The measurement of b is $\sqrt{3}$ units found by using the Pythagorean Theorem. Now the values of the trigonometric functions can be written directly from the values of a, b, and c.

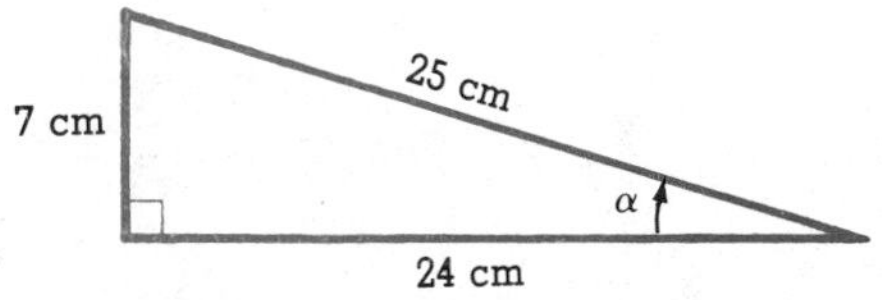

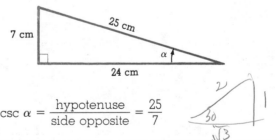

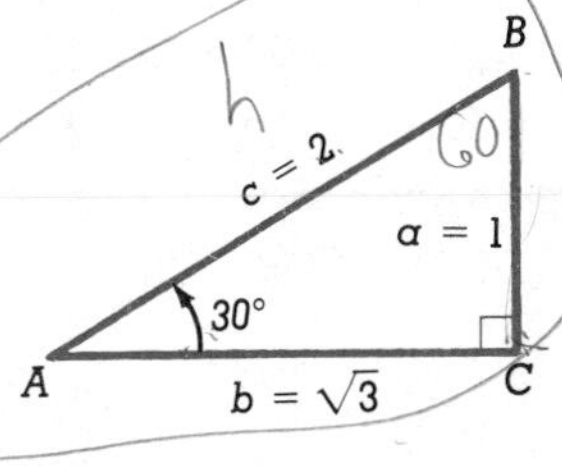

example

3 **Find the trigonometric functions of a 45° angle of a right triangle.**

Recall that the legs of a 45°–45° right triangle are equal. If A and B are the 45° angles, let the measure of a and b equal 1. Thus, $c = \sqrt{(1)^2 + (1)^2}$ or $\sqrt{2}$.

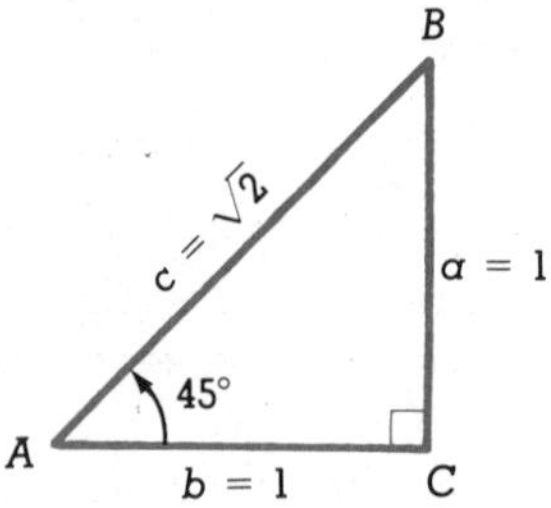

$\sin A = \dfrac{1}{\sqrt{2}}$ or $\dfrac{\sqrt{2}}{2}$ $\qquad$ $\cos A = \dfrac{1}{\sqrt{2}}$ or $\dfrac{\sqrt{2}}{2}$

$\tan A = \dfrac{1}{1}$ or 1 $\qquad$ $\cot A = \dfrac{1}{1}$ or 1

$\sec A = \dfrac{\sqrt{2}}{1}$ or $\sqrt{2}$ $\qquad$ $\csc A = \dfrac{\sqrt{2}}{1}$ or $\sqrt{2}$

The coordinate graph is used to verify the trigonometric functions of 0° and 90°. An angle of 0° in standard position has point $P(1, 0)$ on its terminal side. Since $r = \sqrt{x^2 + y^2}$, $r = 1$. By referring to the definitions in terms of the graph, values of the six trigonometric functions may be found directly.

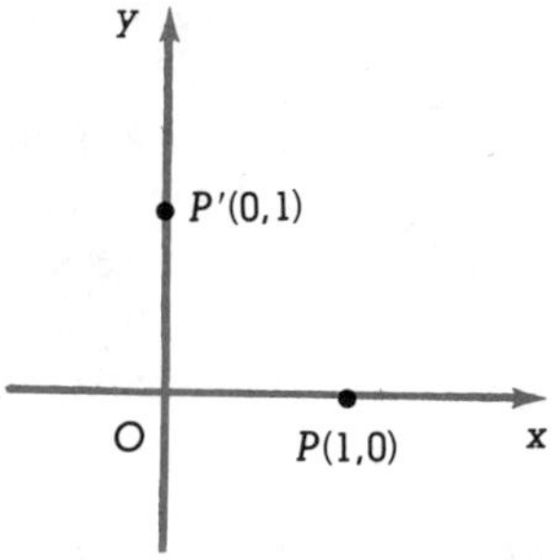

The values of the functions of 90° may be determined in a similar manner using the fact the point $P'(0, 1)$ lies on the terminal side of a 90° angle in standard position.

The following table summarizes the values of the trigonometric functions of 0°, 30°, 45°, 60°, and 90°. These values are used often and you should be able to state any value either from memory or by making a quick sketch.

A	$\sin A$	$\cos A$	$\tan A$	$\cot A$	$\sec A$	$\csc A$
0°	0	1	0	—	1	—
30°	$\frac{1}{2}$	$\frac{\sqrt{3}}{2}$	$\frac{\sqrt{3}}{3}$	$\sqrt{3}$	$\frac{2\sqrt{3}}{3}$	2
45°	$\frac{\sqrt{2}}{2}$	$\frac{\sqrt{2}}{2}$	1	1	$\sqrt{2}$	$\sqrt{2}$
60°	$\frac{\sqrt{3}}{2}$	$\frac{1}{2}$	$\sqrt{3}$	$\frac{\sqrt{3}}{3}$	2	$\frac{2\sqrt{3}}{3}$
90°	1	0	—	0	—	1

A dash "—" means that the function is undefined for this angle.

exercises

Exploratory Write an expression for each value in terms of a, b, c, h, x, and y.

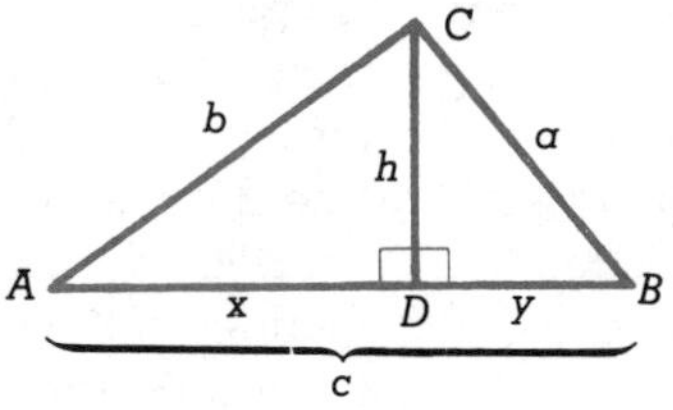

1. $\cos B$
2. $\cot \angle DCB$
3. $\sin A$
4. $\sec \angle ACD$
5. $\sin B$
6. $\tan B$
7. $\tan A$
8. $\sec \angle DCB$
9. $\cos A$
10. $\csc \angle DCB$
11. $\cot \angle CDA$
12. $\csc \angle ACD$

Find the value of each expression.

13. sin 30°
14. cos 45°
15. sec 30°
16. cot 45°
17. tan 60°
18. sin 90°
19. csc 90°
20. cos 60°

Written Find the values of the six trigonometric functions of an angle in standard position if each of the following points lies on its terminal side.

1. (5, 12)
2. (15, 8)
3. (3, 4)
4. (1, ⁻8)
5. (⁻3, 0)
6. $(^-\sqrt{2}, \sqrt{2})$
7. (5, ⁻3)
8. (0, 2)

Find the value of each expression.

9. sin 30° + cos 30°
10. sin 45° + cos 45°
11. sin 45° + cos 60°
12. sin 60° − cos 60°
13. sin 45° − sin 90°
14. 2 sin 45° − cos 30°
15. sin 60° + cos 30° − tan 45°
16. sin 45° cos 60° − tan 30° sin 90°
17. 2 cos 30°
18. ⁻sin 60°
19. 2 sin 60° cos 60°
20. $\cos^2 30° - \sin^2 30°$
21. sec 60° + cot 30°
22. csc 45° − sec 30°

Find each value to four decimal places.

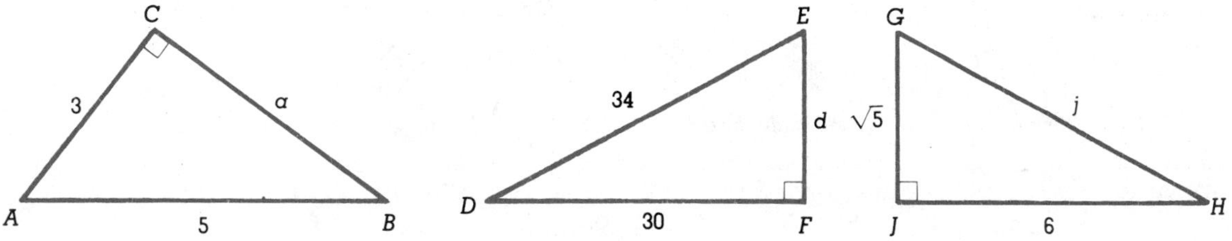

23. cos *A*
24. sin *B*
25. tan *B*
26. sin *E*
27. cos *D*
28. tan *E*
29. cos *G*
30. tan *G*
31. sin *G*
32. tan *H*
33. cot *B*
34. sec *D*
35. csc *H*
36. csc *A*
37. sec *E*
38. cot *A*

Show that each of the following statements is true.

39. $1 - 2\sin^2 30° = \cos 60°$
40. $1 = \cos^2 90° + \sin^2 90°$
41. 2 sin 90° cos 60° = 1
42. $1 - \sin^2 45° = \cos^2 45°$
43. $\sec^2 30° - \cot^2 60° = 1$
44. $\sin^2 30° + \cos^2 30° = 1$
45. $\csc^2 45° - 1 = \cot^2 45°$
46. $\cos 60° = \cos^2 30° - \sin^2 30°$

Solve each problem.

47. The altitude to the hypotenuse of a right triangle is 6 inches long. If the hypotenuse is divided into segments 4 inches and 9 inches long by the altitude, find the values of the six trigonometric functions of the acute angles of the right triangle.

48. The longer base of an isosceles trapezoid is 10 m long. The legs of the trapezoid are 5 m long each. The base angles of the trapezoid are 60° each. Find the length of the shorter base of the trapezoid.

Angle of Inclination of the Sun

Using Mathematics

The angle of inclination of the sun affects the heating and cooling of buildings. The angle is greater in the summer than in the winter. Thus, the overhang of the roof can be designed to shade the windows for cooling in the summer and also permit the sun's rays to enter for heating in the winter.

The sun's angle of inclination also varies according to the latitude. For example, the angle of inclination of the sun at noon January 1 is greater at Miami, Florida than at Rochester, Minnesota.

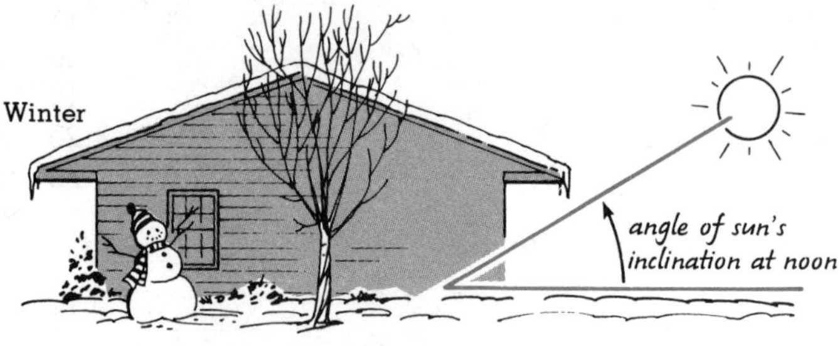

If the latitude is known, the following formula can be used to determine the sun's angle of inclination at noon on any given date. The formula is accurate to $\pm \frac{1}{2}°$.

$$\text{Angle of Sun} = 90° - L + {}^{-}23.5° \times \cos\left[(N + 10)\tfrac{360}{365}\right]$$

L is the latitude of the building site. N is the number of days elapsed in the year.

Example Find the measurement of the sun's angle of inclination for Anderson, Indiana, latitude 40°, March 10, the 69th day of the year.

$$\begin{aligned}\text{Angle of Sun} &= 90° - 40° + {}^{-}23.5° \times \cos\left[(69 + 10)\tfrac{360}{365}\right]\\ &= 50° + {}^{-}23.5° \times 0.2093\\ &= 45° \qquad \textit{Round to the nearest degree.}\end{aligned}$$

The measurement of the sun's angle of inclination is 45°.

Exercises Find the measurement of the angle of inclination of the sun for each of the following cities and dates. Round answers to the nearest degree.

City	Latitude	*Day 80* Mar. 21	*Day 172* June 21	*Day 264* Sept. 21	*Day 355* Dec. 21
Albany, NY	42°	1.	2.	3.	4.
Charleston, SC	32°	5.	6.	7.	8.
Helena, MT	46°	9.	10.	11.	12.
Honolulu, HI	21°	13.	14.	15.	16.

Solve each problem.

17. On what date is the angle of inclination of the sun the greatest in Charleston?

18. On what date is the angle of inclination of the sun the least in Honolulu?

5-2 Using Trigonometric Tables

Decimal approximations for values of trigonometric functions are given in the table on page 503. Values of all six functions of angle measurements from 0° to 90° in intervals of 10 minutes are given, accurate to four decimal places.

This table was also used to find values of circular functions.

The table is arranged so that angle measurements from 0° to 45° are read *down*, in the left-hand column. The headings at the top of the table are used for these measurements. The angle measurements from 45° to 90° are read *up* in the right-hand column. The headings at the bottom of the table are used for these measurements.

Degrees are separated into minutes. Sixty minutes are equivalent to one degree.

examples

1 Find the value of cos 19°30′.

In the left-hand column of the table find 19°30′. Under the heading **cos**, find the value which corresponds to 19°30′.

cos 19°30′ = 0.9426

2 Find the value of tan 72°12′.

Since the values in the table are given for the nearest ten minutes, interpolation must be used. Use the table to find tan 72°10′ and tan 72°20′.

$$10'\left[\begin{array}{l} \tan 72°20' = 3.1397 \\ 2'\left[\begin{array}{l}\tan 72°12' = \text{unknown} \\ \tan 72°10' = 3.1084\end{array}\right]d \end{array}\right] 0.0313$$

d represents the difference between 3.1084 and the unknown value.

Set up a proportion and solve for *d*.

$$\frac{2}{10} = \frac{d}{0.0313}$$

$$10\,d = 2(0.0313)$$

$$d = 0.0063$$

Round the value of d to four decimal places.

Add 0.0063 to the value of tan 72°10′.

tan 72°12′ ≈ 3.1084 + 0.0063 or 3.1147

3 If cos x = 0.8151, find the value of x to the nearest minute.

$$10'\left[\begin{array}{l} d\left[\begin{array}{l}\cos 35°20' = 0.8158 \\ \cos x \quad\;\; = 0.8151\end{array}\right] 0.0007 \\ \cos 35°30' = 0.8141 \end{array}\right] 0.0017$$

The value of x must be between 35°20′ and 35°30′.

$$\frac{d}{10} = \frac{0.0007}{0.0017}$$

$$0.0017d = 0.0070$$

$$d \approx 4$$

Round to the nearest whole number.

$x \approx 35°20' + 4'$ or $35°24'$

exercises

Exploratory Use the table to find each trigonometric value.

1. $\sin 16°10'$
2. $\cos 38°$
3. $\tan 66°20'$
4. $\sin 55°40'$
5. $\cot 41°$
6. $\csc 5°20'$
7. $\cos 83°50'$
8. $\sec 29°30'$

Find the value of x.

9. $\tan x = 0.9217$
10. $\sec x = 5.487$
11. $\sin x = 0.5373$
12. $\csc x = 1.058$
13. $\cos x = 0.9899$
14. $\cot x = 0.3939$

Written Approximate each trigonometric value. Use interpolation when necessary.

1. $\sin 26°$
2. $\csc 33°33'$
3. $\sec 47°10'$
4. $\cos 17°30'$
5. $\sin 86°27'$
6. $\cot 68°13'$
7. $\tan 39°$
8. $\csc 11°14'$
9. $\cos 74°14'$
10. $\cot 11°40'$
11. $\sec 77°19'$
12. $\tan 85°16'$
13. $\sin 56°25'$
14. $\tan 88°39'$
15. $\sin 4°1'$
16. $\cos 72°53'$

Find x to the nearest minute.

17. $\sin x = 0.0872$
18. $\csc x = 1.4129$
19. $\tan x = 0.3153$
20. $\sec x = 1.319$
21. $\cos x = 0.8601$
22. $\tan x = 0.2222$
23. $\cot x = 2.300$
24. $\csc x = 1.319$
25. $\sin x = 0.9219$
26. $\sin x = 0.5132$
27. $\cos x = 0.0562$
28. $\cos x = 0.7193$
29. $\cot x = 1.2555$
30. $\tan x = 0.9493$
31. $\sin x = 0.7224$

5-3 Basic Trigonometric Identities

Equations which are true for all values of the variables for which they are defined are called **identities.** Various relationships exist between the trigonometric functions which are identities. Such relationships are often called **trigonometric identities.**

The six trigonometric functions can be paired so that a function is associated with a **cofunction.** The sine and cosine are cofunctions, as are the tangent and cotangent, and the secant and cosecant.

The right triangle at the right shows the following.

$$\sin A = \cos B = \frac{a}{c}$$

$$\tan A = \cot B = \frac{a}{b}$$

$$\sec A = \csc B = \frac{c}{b}$$

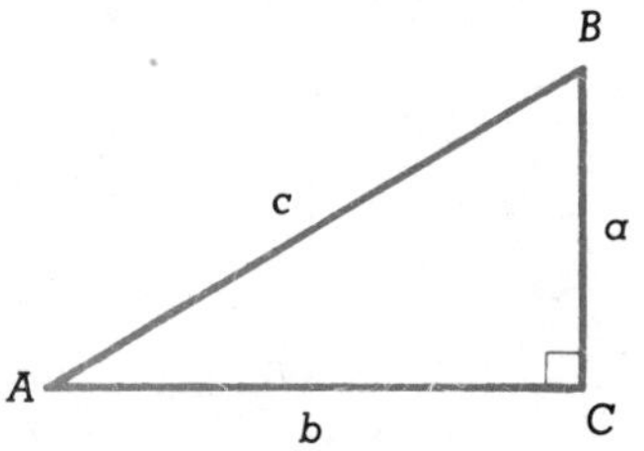

But angle A is the complement of angle B. Thus the trigonometric function of an acute angle is equal to the cofunction of the complement of the angle.

The following trigonometric identities hold for all values of A when $0° \leq A \leq 90°$.

$\sin A = \cos (90°-A)$	$\cos A = \sin (90°-A)$
$\tan A = \cot (90°-A)$	$\cot A = \tan (90°-A)$
$\sec A = \csc (90°-A)$	$\csc A = \sec (90°-A)$

Cofunction Identities

example

1 **If $\cos 11° = 0.9816$, find $\sin 79°$.**

Use a cofunction identity.

$$\begin{aligned} \sin A &= \cos (90°-A) \\ \sin 79° &= \cos (90°-79°) \\ &= \cos 11° \\ &= 0.9816 \end{aligned}$$

The definitions of the trigonometric functions are used to derive the following reciprocal relations.

The following trigonometric identities hold for all values of A except those for which any function is undefined.

$\sin A = \dfrac{1}{\csc A}$	$\csc A = \dfrac{1}{\sin A}$
$\cos A = \dfrac{1}{\sec A}$	$\sec A = \dfrac{1}{\cos A}$
$\tan A = \dfrac{1}{\cot A}$	$\cot A = \dfrac{1}{\tan A}$

Reciprocal Identities

example

2 **If $\cos B = 1.7$, find $\sec B$.**

Use a reciprocal identity.

$$\begin{aligned} \sec B &= \frac{1}{\cos B} \\ &= \frac{1}{1.7} \\ &\approx 0.5882 \end{aligned}$$

By definition, $\sin A = \frac{a}{c}$ and $\cos A = \frac{b}{c}$. Thus, the quotient $\frac{\sin A}{\cos A}$ is equal to $\frac{\frac{a}{c}}{\frac{b}{c}}$ or $\frac{a}{b}$. But $\tan A = \frac{a}{b}$. Thus, $\frac{\sin A}{\cos A} = \tan A$.

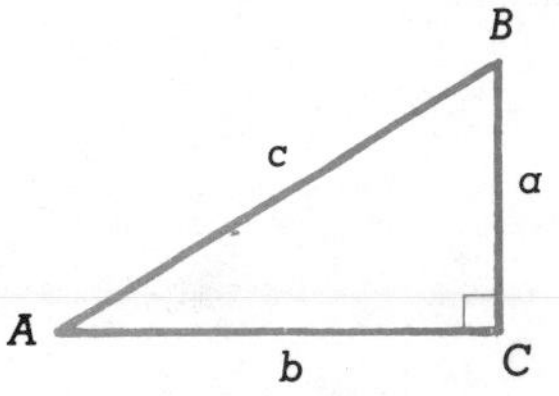

The identity, $\frac{\cos A}{\sin A} = \cot A$, is derived in the same manner.

The following trigonometric identities hold for all values of A, except those for which any function is undefined.

$$\frac{\sin A}{\cos A} = \tan A \qquad \sin A = \cos A \tan A$$

$$\frac{\cos A}{\sin A} = \cot A \qquad \cos A = \sin A \cot A$$

Quotient Identities

The Pythagorean Theorem states that $a^2 + b^2 = c^2$ in the right triangle shown on the previous page. If each member is divided by c^2, the following equation results.

$$\frac{a^2}{c^2} + \frac{b^2}{c^2} = 1 \text{ or } \left(\frac{a}{c}\right)^2 + \left(\frac{b}{c}\right)^2 = 1$$

If the ratios are replaced with the proper trigonometric functions, the following identity results.

$$\sin^2 A + \cos^2 A = 1$$

Similarly, the following identities result when each member of $a^2 + b^2 = c^2$ is divided by b^2 and a^2, respectively.

$$\tan^2 A + 1 = \sec^2 A$$
$$1 + \cot^2 A = \csc^2 A$$

The following trigonometric identities hold for all values of A, except those for which any function is undefined.

$$\sin^2 A + \cos^2 A = 1$$
$$\tan^2 A + 1 = \sec^2 A$$
$$1 + \cot^2 A = \csc^2 A$$

Pythagorean Identities

example

3 If $\sin A = 0.5$, find $\tan A$.

To find $\tan A$, first find $\cos A$.

Use a Pythagorean identity.

$$\sin^2 A + \cos^2 A = 1$$
$$(0.5)^2 + \cos^2 A = 1$$
$$\cos A = \sqrt{1 - 0.25}$$
$$\cos A \approx \pm 0.87$$

Use a quotient identity.

$$\tan A = \frac{\sin A}{\cos A}$$
$$\approx \pm \frac{0.5}{0.87}$$
$$\approx \pm 0.57$$

exercises

Exploratory Solve each problem by referring to the figure at the right.

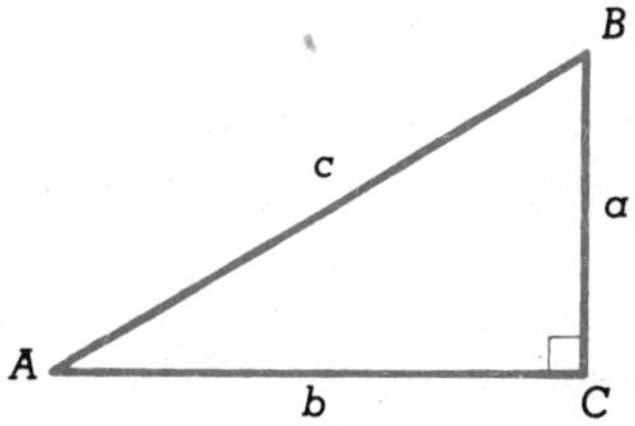

1. If $\sin A = \frac{\sqrt{3}}{3}$, find $\cos B$.
2. If $\tan B = 1.7$, find $\cot A$.
3. If $\cos A = 0.109$, find $\sin (90° - A)$.
4. If $\csc A = 2.736$, find $\sec B$.

Solve each problem.

5. If $\tan 30° = \frac{\sqrt{3}}{3}$, find $\cot 60°$.
6. If $\sin 45° = \frac{\sqrt{2}}{2}$, find $\cos 45°$.
7. If $\cos 4° = 0.9976$, find $\sin 86°$.
8. If $\tan 69° = 2.605$, find $\cot 21°$.
9. If $\tan 84° = 9.514$, find $\cot 6°$.
10. If $\sec 12° = 1.022$, find $\csc 78°$.

Written Solve each of the following for values of θ between 0° and 90°.

1. If $\sin \theta = \frac{3}{4}$, find $\sec \theta$.
2. If $\cos \theta = \frac{3}{5}$, find $\sin \theta$.
3. If $\csc \theta = 3$, find $\sin \theta$.
4. If $\cot \theta = 2$, find $\tan \theta$.
5. If $\cos \theta = \frac{\sqrt{2}}{3}$, find $\sin \theta$.
6. If $\tan \theta = \frac{\sqrt{11}}{2}$, find $\sec \theta$.
7. If $\cos \theta = \frac{2}{3}$, find $\csc \theta$.
8. If $\tan \theta = \frac{\sqrt{3}}{2}$, find $\sec \theta$.
9. If $\sec \theta = 1.3$, find $\cos \theta$.
10. If $\cos \theta = 0.032$, find $\sec \theta$.
11. If $\sin \theta = \frac{4}{5}$, find $\cos \theta$.
12. If $\tan \theta = \frac{\sqrt{2}}{5}$, find $\cot \theta$.
13. If $\sec \theta = \frac{5}{3}$, find $\tan \theta$.
14. If $\cos \theta = \frac{2}{3}$, find $\sin \theta$.
15. If $\sec \theta = 1.7$, find $\cos \theta$.
16. If $\cos \theta = 0.32$, find $\sin \theta$.
17. If $\tan \theta = 4$, find $\sin \theta$.
18. If $\cot \theta = 0.8$, find $\csc \theta$.
19. If $\tan \theta = 1$, find $\cot \theta$.
20. If $\cos \theta = 0.32$, find $\tan \theta$.
21. If $\sin \theta = \frac{1}{2}$, find $\cos \theta$.
22. If $\sin \theta = \frac{1}{2}$, find $\csc \theta$.
23. If $\cos \theta = \frac{4}{5}$, find $\tan \theta$.
24. If $\tan \theta = \frac{7}{2}$, find $\sec \theta$.

Simplify each of the following.

25. $\tan \theta \cot \theta$
26. $\sec^2 \theta - 1$
27. $\sin x + \cos x \tan x$
28. $\csc \theta \cos \theta \tan \theta$
29. $2(\csc^2 \theta - \cot^2 \theta)$
30. $\frac{\tan^2 \theta - \sin^2 \theta}{\tan^2 \theta \sin^2 \theta}$

Solve each problem.

31. Write a formula for $\tan \theta$ in terms of $\sin \theta$.
32. Write a formula for $\sec \theta$ in terms of $\cot \theta$.
33. Write a formula for $\sin \theta$ in terms of $\sec \theta$.
34. Write a formula for $\cos \theta$ in terms of $\tan \theta$.
35. Write a formula for $\cot \theta$ in terms of $\csc \theta$.
36. Write a formula for $\csc \theta$ in terms of $\cos \theta$.

5-4 Verifying Trigonometric Identities

Verifying trigonometric identities involves transforming one side of the equation into the same form as the other side by using the basic trigonometric identities and the principles of algebra. Either side may be transformed into the form of the other side, or both sides may be transformed separately into two other forms which are the same.

The following suggestions are helpful in verifying trigonometric identities. Study the examples to see how these suggestions can be used.

Suggestions for Verifying Identities

1. **Transform the more complicated side of the equation into the form of the simpler side.**
2. **Substitute one or more basic trigonometric identities to simplify the expression.**
3. **Factor or multiply to simplify the expression.**
4. **Multiply both numerator and denominator by the same trigonometric expression.**

examples

1 **Verify that $\frac{\cos A}{\cot^2 A} = \sin A \tan A$ is an identity.**

$$\frac{\cos A}{\cot^2 A} \stackrel{?}{=} \sin A \tan A$$

Arrange the work so that there is a vertical sequence of steps in the transformation of a side.

$$\frac{\cos A}{\frac{\cos^2 A}{\sin^2 A}} \stackrel{?}{=} \sin A \tan A$$

$\cot^2 A = \frac{\cos^2 A}{\sin^2 A}$

$$\frac{\sin^2 A}{\cos A} \stackrel{?}{=} \sin A \tan A$$

Simplify.

$$\sin A \left(\frac{\sin A}{\cos A}\right) \stackrel{?}{=} \sin A \tan A$$

Factor.

$$\sin A \tan A = \sin A \tan A$$

$\frac{\sin A}{\cos A} = \tan A$

The transformation of the left side has produced an expression which is the same as the right side. Thus, $\frac{\cos A}{\cot^2 A} = \sin A \tan A$ is an identity.

2 **Verify that $\frac{\tan A - \sin A}{\tan A + \sin A} = \frac{\sec A - 1}{\sec A + 1}$ is an identity.**

$$\frac{\tan A - \sin A}{\tan A + \sin A} = \frac{\sec A - 1}{\sec A + 1}$$

$$\frac{\frac{\sin A}{\cos A} - \sin A}{\frac{\sin A}{\cos A} + \sin A} =$$

$\tan A = \frac{\sin A}{\cos A}$

$$\frac{\sin A\left(\frac{1}{\cos A} - 1\right)}{\sin A\left(\frac{1}{\cos A} + 1\right)} =$$ *Factor.*

$$\frac{\frac{1}{\cos A} - 1}{\frac{1}{\cos A} + 1} =$$ *Simplify.*

$$\frac{\sec A - 1}{\sec A + 1} = \frac{\sec A - 1}{\sec A + 1}$$ $\frac{1}{\cos A} = \sec A$

Thus the identity has been verified.

3 **Find a numerical value of one trigonometric function of S if $\tan S \cos S = \frac{1}{2}$.**

$$\tan S \cos S = \frac{1}{2}$$

$$\frac{\sin S}{\cos S} \cdot \cos S = \frac{1}{2}$$

$$\sin S = \frac{1}{2}$$

A numerical value of one trigonometric function of S is given by $\sin S = \frac{1}{2}$.

exercises

Exploratory **State an identity which could be used to verify each of the following.**

1. $\csc^2 \alpha - \cot^2 \alpha = 1$
2. $\tan \theta \cot \theta = 1$
3. $\tan x \csc x = \sec x$
4. $\cos \alpha \csc \alpha = \cot \alpha$
5. $\sin \theta \cot \theta = \cos \theta$
6. $\cos^2 \theta = 1 - \sin^2 \theta$
7. $\frac{\tan x}{\sin x} = \sec x$
8. $\frac{\sin^2 \theta + \cos^2 \theta}{\sin^2 \theta} = \csc^2 \theta$
9. $\sec^2 \theta - 1 = \tan^2 \theta$
10. $\csc \theta \cos \theta \tan \theta = 1$

11-20. Verify each identity in problems 1-10.

Written **Verify each identity.**

1. $\sin^2 A \cot^2 A = (1 - \sin A)(1 + \sin A)$
2. $\cos^2 x + \tan^2 x \cos^2 x = 1$
3. $\tan B = \frac{\cos B}{\sin B \cot^2 B}$
4. $\frac{\tan \theta \cos \theta}{\sin \theta} = 1$
5. $\frac{1}{\sec^2 x} + \frac{1}{\csc^2 x} - 1 = 0$
6. $\frac{\sec x - 1}{\sec x + 1} + \frac{\cos x - 1}{\cos x + 1} = 0$
7. $\sin \theta (1 + \cot^2 \theta) = \csc \theta$
8. $\sin^4 A + \cos^2 A = \cos^4 A + \sin^2 A$
9. $\frac{\sin (90° - w)}{\cos (90° - w)} = \cot w$
10. $\sec (90° - z) = \frac{1}{\sin z}$

11. $1 + \tan^2 (90° - x) = \dfrac{1}{\cos^2 (90°-x)}$

12. $\dfrac{\sin A}{\csc A} + \dfrac{\cos A}{\sec A} = 1$

13. $\dfrac{\sec B}{\cos B} - \dfrac{\tan B}{\cot B} = 1$

14. $\dfrac{1}{\csc^2 \theta} + \sec^2 \theta + \dfrac{1}{\sec^2 \theta} = 2 + \dfrac{\sec^2 \theta}{\csc^2 \theta}$

15. $\sec^4 \alpha - \sec^2 \alpha = \dfrac{1}{\cot^4 \alpha} + \dfrac{1}{\cot^2 \alpha}$

16. $\dfrac{\cos x}{1 + \sin x} + \dfrac{\cos x}{1 - \sin x} = 2 \sec x$

17. $\dfrac{1 + \tan^2 A}{\csc^2 A} = \tan^2 A$

18. $\dfrac{1 - 2 \cos^2 \theta}{\sin \theta \cos \theta} = \tan \theta - \cot \theta$

Find a numerical value of one trigonometric function of each x.

19. $\sin x \sec x = 1$

20. $\sin x = \tan x$

21. $\sin x = 2 \cos x$

22. $2 \tan x = \cot x$

23. $2 \sin^2 x = 3 \cos^2 x$

24. $1 - \sin^2 x = \dfrac{1}{9}$

25. $\dfrac{\tan x}{\sin x} = \sqrt{2}$

26. $1 + \tan^2 x = \sin^2 x + \dfrac{1}{\sec^2 x}$

Solve each problem.

27. If $\sin \alpha = \dfrac{1}{3}$, find $\dfrac{\cos \alpha \tan \alpha}{\csc \alpha}$.

28. If $\tan \beta = \dfrac{3}{4}$, find $\dfrac{\sin \beta \sec \beta}{\cot \beta}$.

29. Show that $\sin x + \cos x \geq 1$ if $0° \leq x \leq 90°$.

30. Show that $\tan x + \cot x \geq 2$ if $0° \leq x \leq 90°$.

5-5 Radians and Arc Length

A **radian** is the measure of a central angle whose sides intercept an arc which is the same length as the radius of the circle. If a central angle is measured in radians, the number of linear units in the intercepted arc on a unit circle is equal to the number of radians. Circular functions are functions of the measure of the intercepted arc while trigonometric functions are functions of the measure of the central angle.

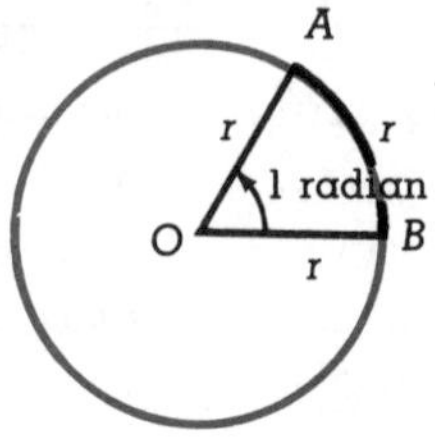

Since the circumference of a unit circle is 2π, an angle representing one complete revolution of the circle is 2π radians or 360°. Thus the proportion relating radians to degrees is as follows.

The Degree/Radian Proportion

Let R represent a number of radians. Let D represent a number of degrees.

$$\frac{R}{\pi} = \frac{D}{180°}$$

If either R or D is known, the proportion can be solved for the other. Frequently, angles expressed in radians are given in terms of π. *1 radian ≈ 57° 18′*

examples

1 **Change 60° to radian measure in terms of π.**

$$\frac{R}{\pi} = \frac{60°}{180°}$$

$$R = \frac{\pi}{3}$$

2 **Change $\frac{5\pi}{6}$ radians to degrees.**

$$\frac{\frac{5\pi}{6}}{\pi} = \frac{D}{180°}$$

$$D = 180°\left(\frac{5}{6}\right) \text{ or } 150°$$

If two central angles in different circles are congruent, the ratio of the lengths of their intercepted arcs is equal to the ratio of their radii. For example, in the figure below left, if $\angle O \cong \angle Q$, then $\frac{m\widehat{AB}}{m\widehat{CD}} = \frac{OA}{QC}$.

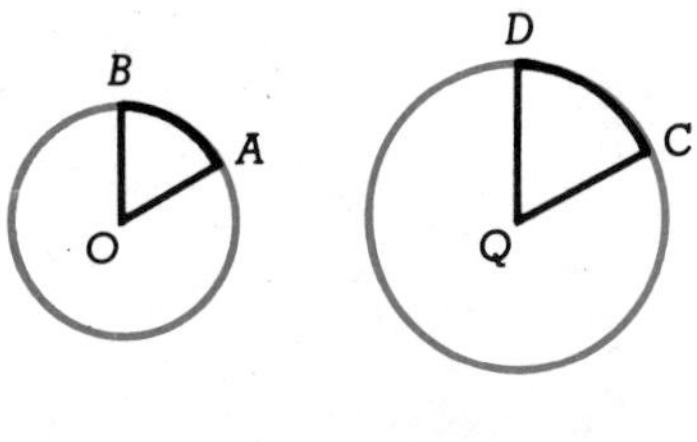

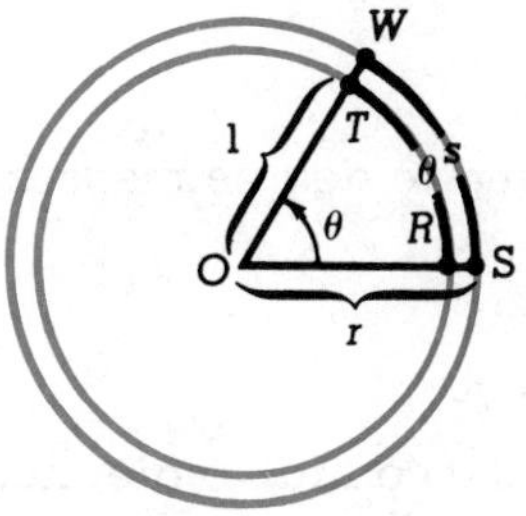

Now let O be the center of two concentric circles. Let r be the radius of the larger circle, and let the smaller circle be a unit circle. If a central angle of θ radians is drawn in the two circles it will intercept $\widehat{RT}$ on the unit circle and $\widehat{SW}$ on the other circle. Suppose $\widehat{SW}$ is s units long. $\widehat{RT}$ is θ units since it is an arc of a unit circle intercepted by a central angle of θ radians. The following proportion can be written.

$$\frac{s}{\theta} = \frac{r}{1} \text{ or } s = r\,\theta$$

The length of any circular arc, s, is equal to the product of the radius of the circle, r, and the radian measure of the central angle it subtends, θ.

$$s = r\,\theta$$

Length of an Arc

example

3 Find the length of an arc that subtends a central angle of 32° in a circle of radius 11 cm.

$\frac{R}{\pi} = \frac{32}{180}$ *Find the radian measure of the central angle.*

$R = \frac{8\pi}{45}$

$s = (11)\left(\frac{8\pi}{45}\right)$ $s = r\theta$

≈ 6.14 cm

exercises

Exploratory Change each of the following to radian measure.

1. 18°
2. 30°
3. 240°
4. 1°

Change each of the following to degree measure.

5. π
6. $\frac{\pi}{4}$
7. $\frac{3\pi}{4}$
8. $\frac{\pi}{6}$

Written Change each of the following to radian measure.

1. 270°
2. 135°
3. 210°
4. 300°
5. 75°
6. 15°
7. 225°
8. 360°

Change each of the following to degree measure.

9. $\frac{5\pi}{4}$
10. $\frac{7\pi}{8}$
11. $\frac{11\pi}{6}$
12. $\frac{3\pi}{5}$
13. 4π
14. 2
15. 0.75
16. 3.14

Given the radian measure of a central angle, find the measure of its intercepted arc in a circle of radius 10 cm.

17. $\frac{\pi}{4}$
18. $\frac{2\pi}{3}$
19. $\frac{5\pi}{6}$
20. $\frac{2\pi}{5}$

Given the degree measure of a central angle, find the measure of its intercepted arc in a circle of diameter 30 in.

21. 30°
22. 5°
23. 77°
24. 57°18′

Given the measurement of an arc, find the degree measure of the central angle it subtends in a circle of radius 8 cm.

25. 5 cm
26. 14 cm
27. 24 cm
28. 12.5 cm

Solve each problem.

29. An arc is 6.5 cm long and it subtends a central angle of 45°. Find the radius of the circle.
30. An arc is 70.7 m long and it subtends a central angle of $\frac{2\pi}{7}$. Find the diameter of the circle.

5-6 Functions of Angles

The definitions of trigonometric functions provide a basis for finding functions of angles in any quadrant, positive or negative. Let $P_1(x_1, y_1)$ be a point in the first quadrant on the terminal side of angle A_1; let $P_2(x_2, y_2)$ be a point in the second quadrant on the terminal side of angle A_2; let $P_3(x_3, y_3)$ be a point in the third quadrant on the terminal side of angle A_3; and let $P_4(x_4, y_4)$ be a point in the fourth quadrant on the terminal side of angle A_4.

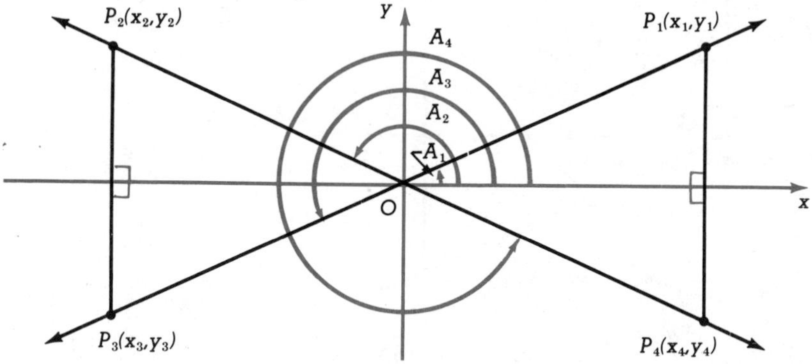

With each angle in standard position, recall the following ratios.

$$\sin A = \frac{y}{r} \qquad \csc A = \frac{r}{y} \qquad r = \sqrt{x^2 + y^2}$$

$$\cos A = \frac{x}{r} \qquad \sec A = \frac{r}{x}$$

$$\tan A = \frac{y}{x} \qquad \cot A = \frac{x}{y}$$

These definitions apply regardless of the quadrant in which the terminal side lies, or if it lies on either of the axes. Since r is defined to be positive, the signs of the functions in each quadrant will be determined by the signs of the coordinates x and y. The following table shows the signs of the six functions in each quadrant. You should verify each sign by considering the signs of the coordinates of a point in each quadrant.

	Quadrant			
Function	First	Second	Third	Fourth
sin A	+	+	−	−
cos A	+	−	−	+
tan A	+	−	+	−
csc A	+	+	−	−
sec A	+	−	−	+
cot A	+	−	+	−

You should memorize the functions which are positive in each quadrant.

Note that the signs of reciprocally related functions are the same.

If a line is drawn from each of the points P_1, P_2, P_3, and P_4 perpendicular to the x-axis, right triangles are formed. For each right triangle the acute angle with its vertex at the origin is called the **reference angle** α. For each angle A, there is an angle α. In the first quadrant, $\alpha_1 = A_1$. In the second quadrant, $\alpha_2 = 180° - A_2$ or $\pi - A_2$. In the third quadrant, $\alpha_3 = A_3 - 180°$ or $A_3 - \pi$. In the fourth quadrant, $\alpha_4 = 360° - A_4$ or $2\pi - A_4$.

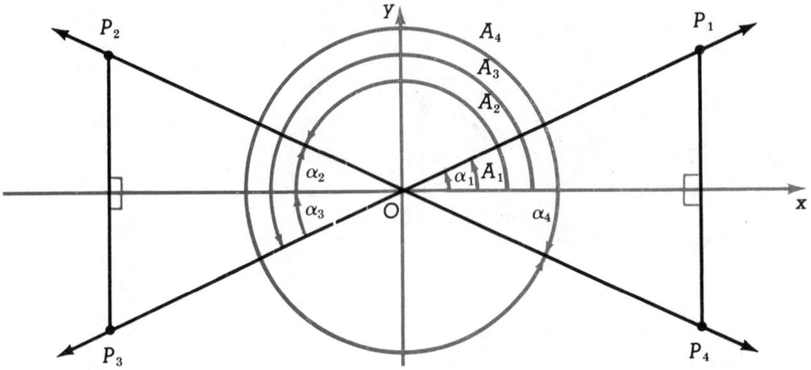

Since α is a positive angle less than 90°, the function of an angle of any size may be reduced to a function of an acute angle and the value found in the table on page 503. The proper sign for the given function can be selected from the table on page 131 or can be determined by the signs of the coordinates in the quadrant in which the terminal side lies.

examples

1 **Find sin 120° in terms of the sine of an acute angle.**

The terminal side of 120° is in the second quadrant.

Find the reference angle.

$\alpha = 180° - 120°$
$= 60°$

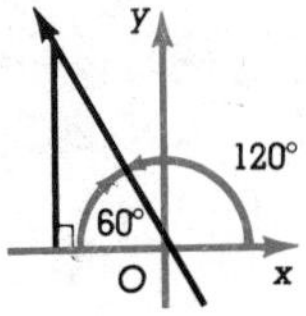

Thus, sin 120° = sin 60°. *The sine function is positive in the second quadrant.*

2 **Find tan 307°.**

The terminal side of 307° is in the fourth quadrant.

Find the reference angle.

$\alpha = 360° - 307°$
$= 53°$

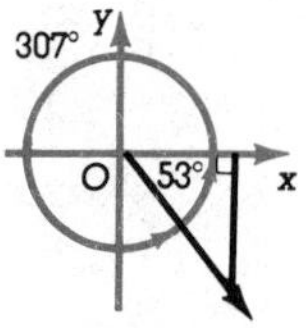

$\tan 307° = {}^{-}\tan 53°$
$= {}^{-}1.327$

The tangent function is negative in the fourth quadrant.

Thus, tan 307° = ⁻1.327.

example

3 Find cos 575°.

An angle with measurement 575° is equivalent to an angle with measurement 215° since 575° = 360° + 215°. The terminal side of 215° is in the third quadrant.

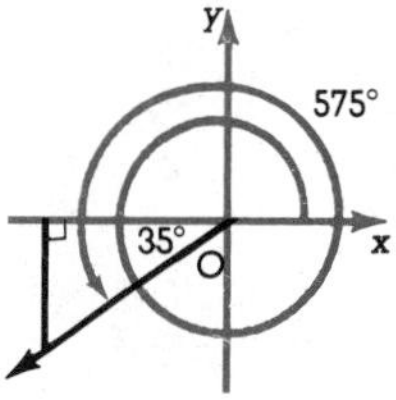

Find the reference angle.

$$\alpha = 215° - 180°$$
$$= 35°$$

$$\cos 575° = \cos 215°$$
$$= {}^{-}\cos 35°$$
$$= {}^{-}0.8192$$

The cosine function is negative in the third quadrant.

Thus, $\cos 575° = {}^{-}0.8192$

The cosine function has the property such that $\cos({}^{-}x) = \cos x$. A function with this property is called an **even function.** The sine function has the property such that $\sin({}^{-}x) = {}^{-}\sin x$. A function with this property is called an **odd function.**

exercises

Exploratory Find the reference angle for each of the following angles.

1. 206°
2. 111°
3. $^{-}16°$
4. 424°
5. $^{-}127°$
6. 248°
7. 358°
8. $^{-}102°$

Express each of the following in terms of the same function of a positive acute angle.

9. sin 135°
10. cos 210°
11. tan 320°
12. cot 260°
13. sin 340°
14. cos 175°
15. tan 204°
16. sec 142°

Written **Express each of the following in terms of the same function of a positive acute angle.**

1. sin ($^{-}30°$)
2. sin ($^{-}50°$)
3. cot ($^{-}80°$)
4. sin ($^{-}100°$)
5. cos ($^{-}150°$)
6. tan ($^{-}200°$)
7. sec ($^{-}135°$)
8. sin ($^{-}300°$)

Express each of the following in terms of a function of a positive angle less than 45°.
(Hint: Use cofunctions when necessary.)

9. cot 310°
10. cos 100°
11. tan 210°
12. sec ($^{-}125°$)
13. sin 305°
14. cos 355°
15. tan ($^{-}262°$)
16. csc 73°
17. sec ($^{-}213°$)
18. sin ($^{-}128°$)
19. csc 287°
20. cot 96°

21-28. Find the value of each expression in problems **9-16** of the Exploratory Exercises.

29-48. Find the value of each expression in problems **1-20** of the Written Exercises.

State whether each function is odd or even.

49. $y = \tan x$
50. $y = \cot x$
51. $y = \csc x$
52. $y = \sec x$

5-7 Functions of Quadrantal Angles

An angle whose terminal side coincides with one of the coordinate axes is called a **quadrantal angle.** A quadrantal angle can be written as $n \cdot 90°$ where n is an integer. The values of the functions of 0° and 90° were determined previously using the coordinate graph. The values of functions of other quadrantal angles can be found in the same manner.

For the point $(^-1, 0)$ on the terminal side of a 180° angle, $x = {}^-1$, $y = 0$, $r = 1$.

$$\sin 180° = \frac{y}{r} = \frac{0}{1} \text{ or } 0$$

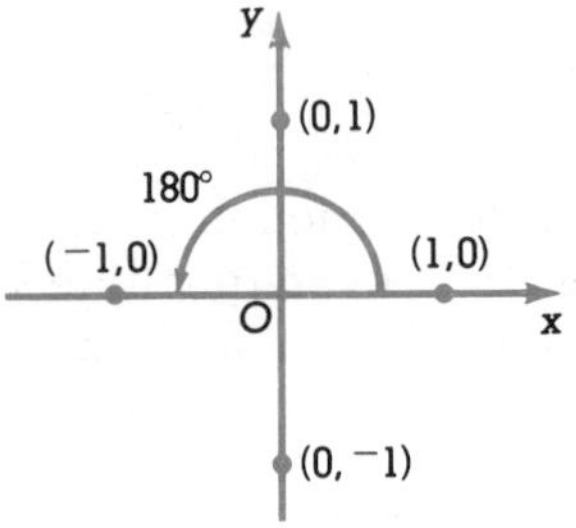

$$\cos 180° = \frac{x}{r} = \frac{^-1}{1} \text{ or } {}^-1$$

$$\tan 180° = \frac{y}{x} = \frac{0}{^-1} \text{ or } 0$$

$$\sec 180° = \frac{r}{x} = \frac{1}{^-1} \text{ or } {}^-1$$

The values of cot 180° and csc 180° are undefined because division by zero is undefined.

example

1 Find the trigonometric functions of a 270° angle.

$x = 0$, $y = {}^-1$, and $r = 1$

$$\sin 270° = \frac{y}{r} = \frac{^-1}{1} \text{ or } {}^-1 \qquad \csc 270° = \frac{r}{y} = \frac{1}{^-1} \text{ or } {}^-1$$

$$\cos 270° = \frac{x}{r} = \frac{0}{1} \text{ or } 0 \qquad \sec 270° = \frac{r}{x} = \frac{1}{0} \text{ or undefined}$$

$$\tan 270° = \frac{y}{x} = \frac{^-1}{0} \text{ or undefined} \qquad \cot 270° = \frac{x}{y} = \frac{0}{^-1} \text{ or } 0$$

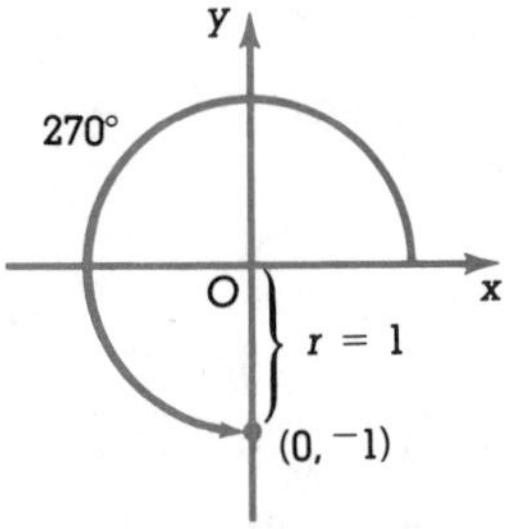

The following table gives the values of the trigonometric functions of common quadrantal angles.

Angle	Function					
	sin	cos	tan	csc	sec	cot
0	0	1	0	—	1	—
90° or $\frac{\pi}{2}$	1	0	—	1	—	0
180° or π	0	$^-1$	0	—	$^-1$	—
270° or $\frac{3\pi}{2}$	$^-1$	0	—	$^-1$	—	0
360° or 2π	0	1	0	—	1	—

exercises

Exploratory   Copy and complete the following table of quadrantal values of sin x and cos x.

1.

x	radians	0	$\frac{\pi}{2}$	π	$\frac{3\pi}{2}$	2π	$-\frac{\pi}{2}$	$^-\pi$	$\frac{^-3\pi}{2}$	$^-2\pi$
	degrees	0°	90°	180°	270°	360°	$^-90°$	$^-180°$	$^-270°$	$^-360°$
sin x		0								
cos x		1								

Find two values of x which make each statement true.

2. cos x = 1
3. sin x = 1
4. cos x = 0
5. sin x = 0
6. cos x = $^-1$
7. sin x = $^-1$

Written   Find the value of each of the following without using tables.

1. cos π
2. sin 360°
3. cos 450°
4. tan 2π
5. csc $\frac{3\pi}{2}$
6. sin 450°
7. sec 270°
8. cos 90°
9. csc 180°
10. sin $\left(-\frac{\pi}{2}\right)$
11. tan 90°
12. sec ($^-90°$)

Solve each problem.

13. Find the values of k for which tan ($k90°$) = 0.
14. Find the values of k for which tan ($k90°$) is undefined.
15. Find the values of k for which sin ($k90°$) = 1.
16. Find the values of k for which cos ($k90°$) = 1.
17. Find the values of k for which sin ($k90°$) = csc ($k90°$).
18. Find the values of k for which tan ($k90°$) = cot ($k90°$).

Challenge   Solve each problem.

1. Show that sin ($k90°$) = 0 if k is any even integer.
2. Show that cos ($k90°$) = 0 if k is any odd integer.

5-8 Functions of $(\alpha + \beta)$

Circular functions and trigonometric functions are related by the radian and degree measures of an angle. Thus, every formula or identity that was proved for circular functions is also true for trigonometric functions whether the variable represents degree or radian measure of an angle.

The sine and cosine of the sum or difference of the measurement of two angles are given by the following identities.

Sum and Difference Identities for Sine and Cosine Function

If α and β represent the measures of two angles, then the following identities hold for all values of α and β.

$$\sin(\alpha \pm \beta) = \sin\alpha\cos\beta \pm \cos\alpha\sin\beta$$
$$\cos(\alpha \pm \beta) = \cos\alpha\cos\beta \mp \sin\alpha\sin\beta$$

example

1 Find sin 75° and cos 75° from the functions of 30° and 45°.

$$\begin{aligned}\sin 75^\circ &= \sin(45^\circ + 30^\circ)\\ &= \sin 45^\circ \cos 30^\circ + \cos 45^\circ \sin 30^\circ\\ &= \frac{\sqrt{2}}{2}\cdot\frac{\sqrt{3}}{2} + \frac{\sqrt{2}}{2}\cdot\frac{1}{2}\\ &= \frac{\sqrt{6}+\sqrt{2}}{4} \text{ or } 0.966\end{aligned}$$

$$\begin{aligned}\cos 75^\circ &= \cos(45^\circ + 30^\circ)\\ &= \cos 45^\circ \cos 30^\circ - \sin 45^\circ \sin 30^\circ\\ &= \frac{\sqrt{2}}{2}\cdot\frac{\sqrt{3}}{2} - \frac{\sqrt{2}}{2}\cdot\frac{1}{2}\\ &= \frac{\sqrt{6}-\sqrt{2}}{4} \text{ or } 0.259\end{aligned}$$

The sin 75° is 0.966 and the cos 75° is 0.259.

Since $\tan x = \dfrac{\sin x}{\cos x}$, identities for $\tan(\alpha \pm \beta)$ can be developed.

$$\tan(\alpha + \beta) = \frac{\sin(\alpha + \beta)}{\cos(\alpha + \beta)}$$

$$\tan(\alpha + \beta) = \frac{\sin\alpha\cos\beta + \cos\alpha\sin\beta}{\cos\alpha\cos\beta - \sin\alpha\sin\beta}$$

$$= \frac{\dfrac{\sin\alpha\cos\beta}{\cos\alpha\cos\beta} + \dfrac{\cos\alpha\sin\beta}{\cos\alpha\cos\beta}}{\dfrac{\cos\alpha\cos\beta}{\cos\alpha\cos\beta} - \dfrac{\sin\alpha\sin\beta}{\cos\alpha\cos\beta}}$$

Divide both numerator and denominator by $\cos\alpha\cos\beta$. Assume $\cos\alpha \neq 0$ and $\cos\beta \neq 0$.

$$\tan(\alpha + \beta) = \frac{\tan\alpha + \tan\beta}{1 - \tan\alpha\tan\beta}$$

Replace β by $^-\beta$ to find $\tan(\alpha - \beta)$.

$$\tan(\alpha - \beta) = \frac{\tan\alpha - \tan\beta}{1 + \tan\alpha\tan\beta}$$

If α and β represent the measures of two angles, then the following identities hold for all values of α and β.

$$\tan(\alpha \pm \beta) = \frac{\tan\alpha \pm \tan\beta}{1 \mp \tan\alpha\tan\beta}$$

Sum and Difference Identities for the Tangent Functions

example

2 **Find tan 105° from functions of 60° and 45°.**

$$\begin{aligned}\tan 105° &= \tan(60° + 45°)\\ &= \frac{\tan 60° + \tan 45°}{1 - \tan 60° \tan 45°}\\ &= \frac{\sqrt{3} + 1}{1 - \sqrt{3}\cdot 1}\\ &= {}^-2 - \sqrt{3}\end{aligned}$$

Multiply by $\frac{1+\sqrt{3}}{1+\sqrt{3}}$ to simplify.

$\tan 105° \approx {}^-3.732$

The sum and difference identities may be used to verify other identities.

example

3 **Verify that $\sin\left(x + \frac{\pi}{4}\right) = \frac{\sqrt{2}}{2}(\sin x + \cos x)$ is an identity.**

$$\sin\left(x + \frac{\pi}{4}\right) = \frac{\sqrt{2}}{2}(\sin x + \cos x)$$

$$\sin x \cos\frac{\pi}{4} + \cos x \sin\frac{\pi}{4} =$$ *Use $\sin(\alpha + \beta)$.*

$$\sin x\left(\frac{\sqrt{2}}{2}\right) + \cos x\left(\frac{\sqrt{2}}{2}\right) =$$ *$\cos\frac{\pi}{4} = \frac{\sqrt{2}}{2}$ and $\sin\frac{\pi}{4} = \frac{\sqrt{2}}{2}$*

$$\frac{\sqrt{2}}{2}(\sin x + \cos x) = \frac{\sqrt{2}}{2}(\sin x + \cos x)$$

exercises

Exploratory **Use the sum and difference identities to solve each problem.**

1. Find sin 105° from functions of 60° and 45°.
2. Find cos 105° from functions of 60° and 45°.
3. Find tan 75° from functions of 45° and 30°.
4. Find sin 15° from functions of 45° and 30°.
5. Find cos 15° from functions of 45° and 30°.
6. Find cos 15° from functions of 45° and 60°.

7. Find tan 15° from functions of 45° and 60°.

8. Find sin 150° from functions of 120° and 30°.

9. Find cos 150° from functions of 180° and 30°.

10. Find tan 150° from functions of 180° and 30°.

Write each of the following as a function of x.

11. $\sin\left(\frac{\pi}{2} - x\right)$

12. $\cos\left(\frac{3\pi}{2} + x\right)$

13. $\tan(2\pi - x)$

Find the value of each function for $0 < x < 90°$, $0 < y < 90°$, $\sin x = \frac{4}{5}$, and $\cos y = \frac{3}{5}$.

14. $\sin(x + y)$

15. $\cos(x - y)$

16. $\tan(x + y)$

Written **Use the sum and difference identities to evaluate each of the following.**

1. sin 75°
2. tan (⁻105°)
3. sin 195°
4. cos 255°
5. cos 195°
6. tan 30°
7. tan (⁻195°)
8. tan 255°
9. sin 255°
10. cos (⁻15°)
11. sin 30°
12. tan (⁻75°)

If α and β are the measures of two first quadrant angles, find $\cos(\alpha + \beta)$.

13. $\sin\alpha = \frac{5}{13}$, $\cos\beta = \frac{4}{5}$

14. $\tan\alpha = \frac{4}{3}$, $\cot\beta = \frac{5}{12}$

15. $\cos\alpha = \frac{5}{13}$, $\cos\beta = \frac{35}{37}$

16. $\sin\alpha = \frac{8}{17}$, $\tan\beta = \frac{7}{24}$

17-20. If α and β are the measures of two first quadrant angles, find $\sin(\alpha - \beta)$ for problems **13-16.**

21-24. If α and β are the measures of two first quadrant angles, find $\tan(\alpha + \beta)$ for problems **13-16.**

Verify each identity.

25. $\sin(180° - \theta) = \sin\theta$

26. $\tan(270° - x) = \cot x$

27. $\cos\left(\frac{3\pi}{2} + \theta\right) = \sin\theta$

28. $\sin(270° + x) = {}^-\cos x$

29. $\tan(90° + \theta) = {}^-\cot\theta$

30. $\cos(360° - \theta) = \cos\theta$

31. $\tan(\pi - \theta) = {}^-\tan\theta$

32. $\sin\left(\frac{\pi}{2} + x\right) = \cos x$

33. $\cos\left(\frac{\pi}{2} + \theta\right) = {}^-\sin\theta$

34. $\tan\left(\frac{\pi}{2} - x\right) = \cot x$

35. $\cos(\pi + \theta) = {}^-\cos\theta$

36. $\cos(180° - \theta) = {}^-\cos\theta$

37. $\cos(30° - x) + \cos(30° + x) = \sqrt{3}\cos x$

38. $\sin(\alpha + \beta)\sin(\alpha - \beta) = \sin^2\alpha - \sin^2\beta$

39. $\cos(\alpha + \beta) + \cos(\alpha - \beta) = 2\cos\alpha\cos\beta$

40. $\cot\alpha - \cot\beta = \frac{\sin(\beta - \alpha)}{\sin\alpha\sin\beta}$

Challenge **Solve each problem.**

1. Derive a formula for $\cot(\alpha + \beta)$ in terms of $\cot\alpha$ and $\cot\beta$.

2. Derive a formula for $\sin(\alpha + \beta + \gamma)$ in terms of the functions of α, β, and γ.

5-9 Functions of Double Angles and Half Angles

The formulas which were used to find the sine or cosine of a double number may also be used to find the sine or cosine of a double angle. The variable may represent either the radian or degree measure of an angle.

The tangent of a double angle may be found by substituting θ for both α and β in $\tan(\alpha + \beta)$.

$$\tan(\alpha + \beta) = \frac{\tan\alpha + \tan\beta}{1 - \tan\alpha\tan\beta}$$

$$\tan(\theta + \theta) = \frac{\tan\theta + \tan\theta}{1 - \tan\alpha\tan\theta}$$

$$= \frac{2\tan\theta}{1 - \tan^2\theta}$$

If θ represents the measure of an angle, then the following identities hold for all values of θ.

$$\sin 2\theta = 2\sin\theta\cos\theta$$

$$\cos 2\theta = \cos^2\theta - \sin^2\theta$$

$$= 1 - 2\sin^2\theta$$

$$= 2\cos^2\theta - 1$$

$$\tan 2\theta = \frac{2\tan\theta}{1 - \tan^2\theta} \qquad (\tan^2\theta \neq 1)$$

Double Angle Identities

example

1 If $\sin\theta = \frac{2}{\sqrt{5}}$ and θ terminates in the first quadrant, find each of the following.

a. $\cos 2\theta$ b. $\sin 2\theta$ c. $\tan 2\theta$

$$\sin^2\theta + \cos^2\theta = 1$$

$$\frac{4}{5} + \cos^2\theta = 1$$

$$\cos\theta = \frac{1}{\sqrt{5}}$$

$$\tan\theta = 2 \qquad \textit{Why?}$$

a. $$\cos 2\theta = \cos^2\theta - \sin^2\theta$$

$$= \left(\frac{1}{\sqrt{5}}\right)^2 - \left(\frac{2}{\sqrt{5}}\right)^2$$

$$= -\frac{3}{5}$$

b. $$\sin 2\theta = 2\sin\theta\cos\theta$$

$$= 2\left(\frac{2}{\sqrt{5}}\right)\left(\frac{1}{\sqrt{5}}\right)$$

$$= \frac{4}{5}$$

c. $$\tan 2\theta = \frac{2\tan\theta}{1 - \tan^2\theta}$$

$$= \frac{2(2)}{1 - (2)^2}$$

$$= -\frac{4}{3}$$

The formulas which were used to find the sine or cosine of half of a number may also be used to find the sine or cosine of half of an angle.

The formula for the tangent of half of an angle is found by dividing $\sin\frac{\alpha}{2}$ by $\cos\frac{\alpha}{2}$.

$$\tan\frac{\alpha}{2} = \frac{\pm\sqrt{\frac{1-\cos\alpha}{2}}}{\pm\sqrt{\frac{1+\cos\alpha}{2}}}$$

$$= \pm\sqrt{\frac{1-\cos\alpha}{1+\cos\alpha}}$$

If α represents the measure of an angle, then the following identities hold for all values of α.

$$\sin\frac{\alpha}{2} = \pm\sqrt{\frac{1-\cos\alpha}{2}} \qquad \cos\frac{\alpha}{2} = \pm\sqrt{\frac{1+\cos\alpha}{2}}$$

$$\tan\frac{\alpha}{2} = \pm\sqrt{\frac{1-\cos\alpha}{1+\cos\alpha}}$$

Half Angle Identities

The sign of the radical is chosen according to the quadrant in which the terminal side of $\frac{\alpha}{2}$ lies.

example

2 **Find the value of each of the following.**

a. cos 15° **b. sin 15°**

a. $\cos 15° = \cos\frac{30°}{2}$

$$= +\sqrt{\frac{1+\cos 30°}{2}}$$

$$= +\sqrt{\frac{1+\frac{\sqrt{3}}{2}}{2}}$$

$$= \frac{\sqrt{2+\sqrt{3}}}{2}$$

b. $\sin 15° = \sin\frac{30°}{2}$

$$= +\sqrt{\frac{1-\cos 30°}{2}}$$

$$= +\sqrt{\frac{1-\frac{\sqrt{3}}{2}}{2}}$$

$$= \frac{\sqrt{2-\sqrt{3}}}{2}$$

The double angle and half angle identities may also be used to verify other identities.

example

3 **Verify that $\cot A = \dfrac{\sin 2A}{1 - \cos 2A}$ is an identity.**

$$\cot A = \frac{\sin 2A}{1 - \cos 2A}$$

$$= \frac{2 \sin A \cos A}{1 - (2 \cos^2 A - 1)} \qquad \textit{$\sin 2A = 2 \sin A \cos A$, $\cos 2A = 2 \cos^2 A - 1$}$$

$$= \frac{2 \sin A \cos A}{2 - 2 \cos^2 A} \qquad \textit{Simplify.}$$

$$= \frac{2 \sin A \cos A}{2(1 - \cos^2 A)} \qquad \textit{Factor.}$$

$$= \frac{\sin A \cos A}{\sin^2 A} \qquad \textit{$1 - \cos^2 A = \sin^2 A$}$$

$$= \frac{\cos A}{\sin A} \qquad \textit{Simplify.}$$

$$\cot A = \cot A \qquad \textit{$\frac{\cos A}{\sin A} = \cot A$}$$

exercises

Exploratory **Solve each problem.**

1. x is a first quadrant angle. In which quadrant does the terminal side for $2x$ lie?
2. x is a second quadrant angle. In which quadrant does the terminal side for $2x$ lie?
3. $2x$ is a third quadrant angle. In which quadrant does the terminal side for x lie?
4. $2x$ is a fourth quadrant angle. In which quadrant does the terminal side for x lie?
5. $\frac{x}{2}$ is a first quadrant angle. In which quadrant does the terminal side for x lie?
6. $\frac{x}{2}$ is a second quadrant angle. In which quadrant does the terminal side for x lie?
7. x is a third quadrant angle. In which quadrant does the terminal side for $\frac{x}{2}$ lie?
8. x is a fourth quadrant angle. In which quadrant does the terminal side for $\frac{x}{2}$ lie?
9. $\frac{x}{2}$ is a first quadrant angle. In which quadrant does the terminal side for $2x$ lie?
10. $2x$ is a second quadrant angle. In which quadrant does the terminal side for $\frac{x}{2}$ lie?

Simplify each expression.

11. $1 - 2 \sin^2 10°$
12. $2 \cos^2 15° - 1$
13. $2 \sin 35° \cos 35°$
14. $\cos^2 25° - \sin^2 25°$
15. $\dfrac{2 \tan 50°}{1 - \tan^2 50°}$
16. $\sqrt{\dfrac{1 - \cos 40°}{2}}$
17. $\sqrt{\dfrac{1 + \cos 62°}{2}}$
18. $\sqrt{\dfrac{1 - \cos 16°}{1 + \cos 16°}}$
19. $\cos^2 3x - \sin^2 3x$

Written If $\sin r = \frac{3}{5}$ and r is in the first quadrant, find each of the following.

1. $\sin 2r$
2. $\cos 2r$
3. $\tan 2r$
4. $\sin \frac{r}{2}$
5. $\cos \frac{r}{2}$
6. $\tan \frac{r}{2}$

If $\tan y = \frac{5}{12}$ and y is in the third quadrant, find each of the following.

7. $\sin 2y$
8. $\cos 2y$
9. $\tan 2y$
10. $\sin \frac{y}{2}$
11. $\cos \frac{y}{2}$
12. $\tan \frac{y}{2}$

Use the half-angle identities to find each of the following.

13. $\sin 22°30'$
14. $\cos 22°30'$
15. $\tan 22°30'$
16. $\sin 7°30'$
17. $\cos 7°30'$
18. $\tan 7°30'$

If $P(^-3, ^-4)$ is on the terminal side of an angle in standard position with measure θ, find each of the following.

19. $\sin \theta$
20. $\cos \theta$
21. $\tan \theta$
22. $\sin 2\theta$
23. $\cos 2\theta$
24. $\tan 2\theta$
25. $\sin \frac{\theta}{2}$
26. $\cos \frac{\theta}{2}$
27. $\tan \frac{\theta}{2}$

Verify each identity.

28. $\frac{1}{2} \sin 2A = \frac{\tan A}{1 + \tan^2 A}$
29. $1 + \cos 2A = \frac{2}{1 + \tan^2 A}$
30. $\cot \frac{x}{2} = \frac{1 + \cos x}{\sin x}$
31. $\tan 2x \tan x + 2 = \frac{\tan 2x}{\tan x}$
32. $\sin 2B (\cot B + \tan B) = 2$
33. $\csc A \sec A = 2 \csc 2A$
34. $\frac{1 - \tan^2 \theta}{1 + \tan^2 \theta} = \cos 2\theta$
35. $\cot X = \frac{\sin 2X}{1 - \cos 2X}$
36. $1 - \sin A = \left(\sin \frac{A}{2} - \cos \frac{A}{2}\right)^2$
37. $\cos^4 A = \frac{2 \cos 2A + \cos^2 2A + 1}{4}$
38. $\frac{\sin \alpha + \sin 3\alpha}{\cos \alpha + \cos 3\alpha} = \tan 2\alpha$
39. $\frac{\cos 2A}{1 + \sin 2A} = \frac{\cot A - 1}{\cot A + 1}$
40. $\frac{\cos A + \sin A}{\cos A - \sin A} = \frac{1 + \sin 2A}{\cos 2A}$
41. $\tan \frac{x}{2} = \frac{1 - \cos x}{\sin x}$
42. $\tan \frac{x}{2} = \frac{\sin x}{1 + \cos x}$
43. $\cot \frac{\alpha}{2} = \frac{\sin \alpha}{1 - \cos \alpha}$
44. $\frac{\sin A + \sin B}{\sin A - \sin B} = \frac{\tan \frac{A + B}{2}}{\tan \frac{A - B}{2}}$

Challenge Solve each problem.

1. Derive a formula for $\sin 3\alpha$ in terms of $\sin \alpha$.
2. Derive a formula for $\cos 3\alpha$ in terms of $\cos \alpha$.
3. Derive a formula for $\tan 3\alpha$ in terms of $\tan \alpha$.

Chapter Summary

1. Trigonometric Functions of an Angle in Standard Position: For any angle with measure α, point $P(x, y)$ on its terminal side, and $r = \sqrt{x^2 + y^2}$, the trigonometric functions of α are as follows. (116)

$$\sin \alpha = \frac{y}{r} \qquad \cos \alpha = \frac{x}{r} \qquad \tan \alpha = \frac{y}{x}$$

$$\csc \alpha = \frac{r}{y} \qquad \sec \alpha = \frac{r}{x} \qquad \cot \alpha = \frac{x}{y}$$

2. Trigonometric Functions in a Right Triangle: For an acute angle A in right triangle ABC, the trigonometric functions are as follows. (117)

$$\sin A = \frac{\text{side opposite}}{\text{hypotenuse}} = \frac{a}{c} \qquad \cos A = \frac{\text{side adjacent}}{\text{hypotenuse}} = \frac{b}{c}$$

$$\tan A = \frac{\text{side opposite}}{\text{side adjacent}} = \frac{a}{b} \qquad \cot A = \frac{\text{side adjacent}}{\text{side opposite}} = \frac{b}{a}$$

$$\sec A = \frac{\text{hypotenuse}}{\text{side adjacent}} = \frac{c}{b} \qquad \csc A = \frac{\text{hypotenuse}}{\text{side opposite}} = \frac{c}{a}$$

3. Cofunction Identities: The following trigonometric identities hold for all values of A when $0° \leq A \leq 90°$. (123)

$$\sin A = \cos (90° - A) \qquad \cos A = \sin (90° - A)$$
$$\tan A = \cot (90° - A) \qquad \cot A = \tan (90° - A)$$
$$\sec A = \csc (90° - A) \qquad \csc A = \sec (90° - A)$$

4. Reciprocal Identities: The following trigonometric identities hold for all values of A, except those for which any function is undefined. (123)

$$\sin A = \frac{1}{\csc A} \qquad \cos A = \frac{1}{\sec A}$$

$$\tan A = \frac{1}{\cot A} \qquad \cot A = \frac{1}{\tan A}$$

$$\sec A = \frac{1}{\cos A} \qquad \csc A = \frac{1}{\sin A}$$

5. Quotient Identities: The following trigonometric identities hold for all values of A, except those for which any function is undefined. (124)

$$\frac{\sin A}{\cos A} = \tan A \qquad \sin A = \cos A \tan A$$

$$\frac{\cos A}{\sin A} = \cot A \qquad \cos A = \sin A \cot A$$

6. Pythagorean Identities: The following trigonometric identities hold for all values of A, except those for which any function is undefined. (124)

$$\sin^2 A + \cos^2 A = 1$$
$$\tan^2 A + 1 = \sec^2 A$$
$$1 + \cot^2 A = \csc^2 A$$

7. Suggestions for Verifying Identities: (126)
   1. Transform the more complicated side of the equation into the form of the simpler side.
   2. Substitute one or more basic trigonometric identities to simplify the expression.
   3. Factor or multiply to simplify the expression.
   4. Multiply both numerator and denominator by the same trigonometric expression.
8. The Degree/Radian Proportion: Let R represent a number of radians. Let D represent a number of degrees. (128)
$$\frac{R}{\pi} = \frac{D}{180°}$$
9. Length of an Arc: The length of any circular arc, s, is equal to the product of the radius of the circle, r, and the radian measure of the central angle it subtends. (129)
$$s = r\,\theta$$
10. The trigonometric function of an angle of any size may be reduced to function of an acute angle. This acute angle is called the reference angle.
11. Sum and Difference Identities for Sine and Cosine Functions: If α and β represent the measures of two angles, then the following identities hold for all values of α and β. (136)
$$\sin(\alpha \pm \beta) = \sin\alpha\cos\beta \pm \cos\alpha\sin\beta$$
$$\cos(\alpha \pm \beta) = \cos\alpha\cos\beta \mp \sin\alpha\sin\beta$$
12. Sum and Difference Identities for the Tangent Function: If α and β represent the measures of two angles, then the following identities hold for all values of α and β. (137)
$$\tan(\alpha \pm \beta) = \frac{\tan\alpha \pm \tan\beta}{1 \mp \tan\alpha\tan\beta}$$
13. Double Angle Identities: If θ represents the measure of an angle, then the following identities hold for all values of θ. (139)
$$\sin 2\theta = 2\sin\theta\cos\theta$$
$$\begin{aligned}\cos 2\theta &= \cos^2\theta - \sin^2\theta \\ &= 1 - 2\sin^2\theta \\ &= 2\cos^2\theta - 1\end{aligned}$$
$$\tan 2\theta = \frac{2\tan\theta}{1 - \tan^2\theta} \qquad (\tan^2\theta \neq 1)$$
14. Half Angle Identities: If α represents the measure of an angle, then the following identities hold for all values of α. (140)
$$\sin\frac{\alpha}{2} = \pm\sqrt{\frac{1-\cos\alpha}{2}} \qquad \cos\frac{\alpha}{2} = \pm\sqrt{\frac{1+\cos\alpha}{2}}$$
$$\tan\frac{\alpha}{2} = \pm\sqrt{\frac{1-\cos\alpha}{1+\cos\alpha}}$$

Chapter Review

5-1 Find the values of the six trigonometric functions of an angle in standard position if each of the following points lies on its terminal side.

1. (5, 3) 2. (12, 5) 3. ($^-6$, 8) 4. (2, 0)

Find the value of each expression without using tables.

5. $\sin 30° - \cos 60°$ 6. $2 \sin 90° \cos 90°$ 7. $\sin^2 30° + \cos 60°$

5-2 Use the table on page 503 to find each trigonometric value. Use interpolation when necessary.

8. $\cos 38°$ 9. $\csc 32°18'$ 10. $\sin 79°42'$ 11. $\tan 42°51'$

Find x to the nearest minute.

12. $\cot x = 0.1234$ 13. $\sin x = 0.1115$ 14. $\cos x = 0.5132$

5-3 Solve each of the following for values of θ between 0° and 90°.

15. If $\cos \theta = \frac{2}{3}$, find $\sin \theta$.
16. If $\sin \theta = \frac{1}{2}$, find $\csc \theta$.
17. If $\tan \theta = 4$, find $\sec \theta$.
18. If $\csc \theta = \frac{5}{3}$, find $\cos \theta$.

5-4 Verify each identity.

19. $\frac{\sin \theta}{\sec \theta} = \frac{1}{\tan \theta + \cot \theta}$
20. $\frac{1}{\sec^2 \theta} + \frac{1}{\csc^2 \theta} = 1$
21. $\csc x \sec x = \cot x + \tan x$
22. $\cos^2 x + \tan^2 x \cos^2 x = 1$
23. $\frac{1 - \cos \theta}{1 + \cos \theta} = (\csc \theta - \cot \theta)^2$
24. $\frac{\sec \theta + 1}{\tan \theta} = \frac{\tan \theta}{\sec \theta - 1}$

5-5 Change each of the following to degree measure.

25. $\frac{\pi}{3}$ 26. $-\frac{5\pi}{12}$ 27. $\frac{4\pi}{3}$ 28. $\frac{7\pi}{4}$

Given the degree measure of a central angle, find the measure of its intercepted arc in a circle of radius 8 cm.

29. 120° 30. 40° 31. 28° 32. 64°

5-6 Express each of the following in terms of a function of a positive angle less than 45°.

33. $\cos 210°$ 34. $\sin 355°$ 35. $\sec (^-128°)$ 36. $\tan 96°$

37-40. Find the value of each expression in problems 33-36.

5-7 Find the value of each of the following without using tables.

41. $\cos 360°$ 42. $\sin (^-\pi)$ 43. $\cos 90°$ 44. $\tan (^-90°)$

5-8 Use the sum and difference identities to evaluate each of the following.

45. $\sin 105°$ 46. $\cos 240°$ 47. $\cos 15°$ 48. $\sin (^-255°)$

5-9 If $P(^-4, 3)$ is on the terminal side of an angle in standard position with measure α, find each of the following.

49. $\cos \frac{\alpha}{2}$ 50. $\tan 2\alpha$ 51. $\sin \frac{\alpha}{2}$ 52. $\cos 2\alpha$

Chapter Test

Find the value of each of the following to four decimal places.

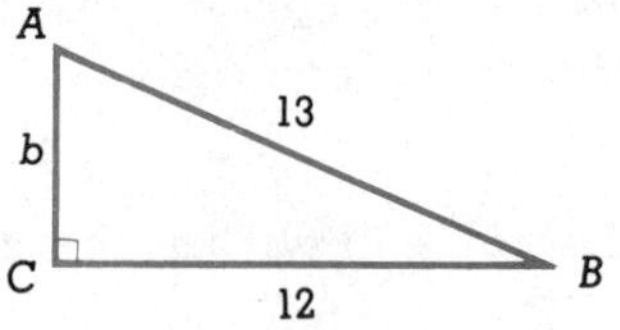

1. $\sin A$
2. $\cos A$
3. $\tan B$
4. $\csc B$
5. $\sec B$
6. $\cot A$

Show that each of the following statements is true.

7. $\cos 90° = 2\cos^2 45° - 1$
8. $\cos^2 90° - \sin^2 90° = \cos 180°$
9. $1 + \tan^2 60° = \sec^2 60°$
10. $\tan^2 45° + \cot^2 45° = 2$

Use the table on page 503 to find each trigonometric value. Use interpolation when necessary.

11. $\sin 32°10'$
12. $\tan 79°16'$
13. $\sec 38°22'$

Find x to the nearest minute.

14. $\sin x = 0.9165$
15. $\csc x = 1.0175$
16. $\cot x = 0.2137$

Solve each of the following for values of θ between 0° and 90°.

17. If $\sin \theta = \frac{1}{2}$, find $\cos \theta$.
18. If $\csc \theta = \frac{5}{3}$, find $\cos \theta$.
19. If $\sec \theta = 3$, find $\tan \theta$.
20. If $\sin \theta = \frac{4}{5}$, find $\sec \theta$.

Verify each identity.

21. $\tan \beta(\cot \beta + \tan \beta) = \sec^2 \beta$
22. $\sin^2 A \cot^2 A = (1 - \sin A)(1 + \sin A)$
23. $\frac{\sec x}{\sin x} - \frac{\sin x}{\cos x} = \cot x$
24. $\frac{\cos x}{1 + \sin x} + \frac{\cos x}{1 - \sin x} = 2 \sec x$

Change each of the following to radian measure.

25. 135°
26. 275°
27. $^-150°$

Given the radian measure of a central angle, find the measure of its intercepted arc in a circle of radius 12 in.

28. $\frac{4\pi}{5}$
29. $\frac{5\pi}{12}$
30. 1.5

Find the value of each of the following.

31. $\cos(^-50°)$
32. $\cot 240°$
33. $\sin 142°$

Find the value of each of the following without using tables.

34. $\csc 180°$
35. $\sin\left(-\frac{\pi}{2}\right)$
36. $\sec 90°$

Use the sum and difference formulas to evaluate each of the following.

37. $\sin 255°$
38. $\cos 165°$
39. $\sin(^-195°)$

If $\cos x = \frac{3}{4}$ and x is in the fourth quadrant, find each of the following.

40. $\sin 2x$
41. $\cos \frac{x}{2}$
42. $\tan 2x$

Chapter

6

Graphs and Inverses of the Trigonometric Functions

When the sound waves from a harp are made visible by an oscilloscope, they have a regular pattern which repeats itself many times per second. Joseph Fourier (1768–1830) showed that every sound wave that repeats itself is related to a trigonometric curve called the sine curve.

6-1 Graphs of the Trigonometric Functions

The graphs of the trigonometric functions are identical to the graphs of the circular functions. The table of values for $0° \le \theta \le 90°$ determines the set of ordered pairs $(\theta, f(\theta))$ for an angle θ and any trigonometric function f. Ordered pairs can be found for any value of θ by using the concept of the reference angle. The measure of angle θ is plotted using the x-axis. Each trigonometric function of angle θ, that is, $f(\theta)$, is plotted using the y-axis.

The graphs of the six trigonometric functions for $^-360° \le \theta \le 360°$ are shown.

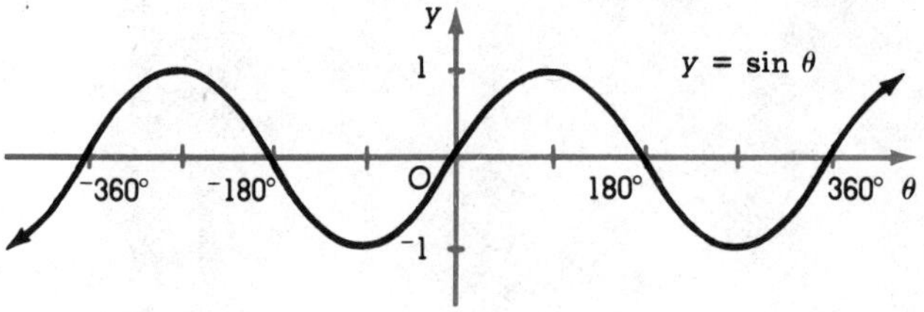

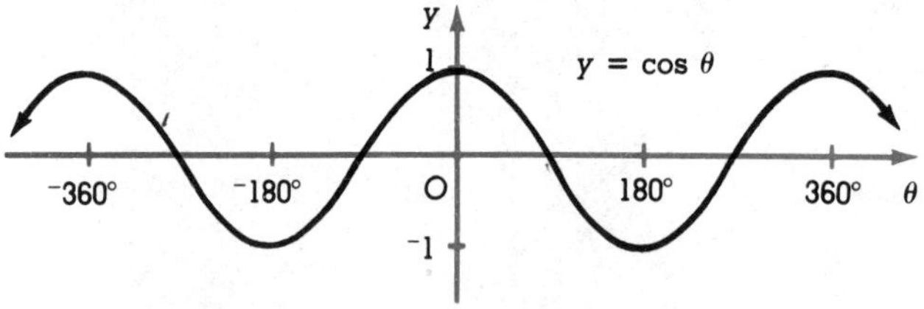

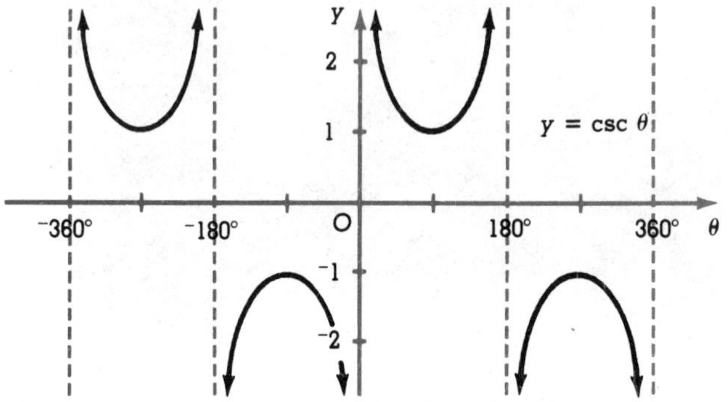

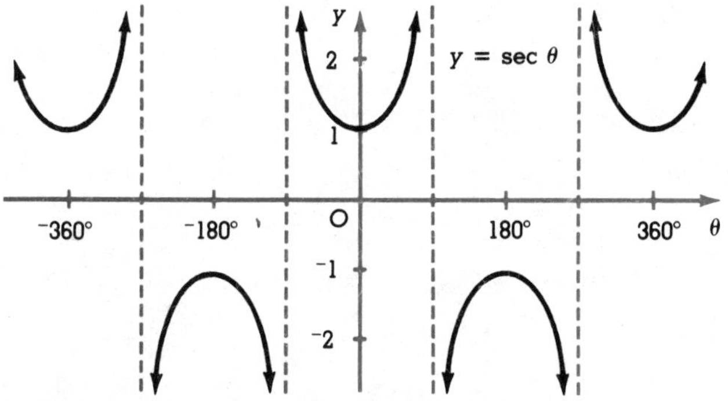

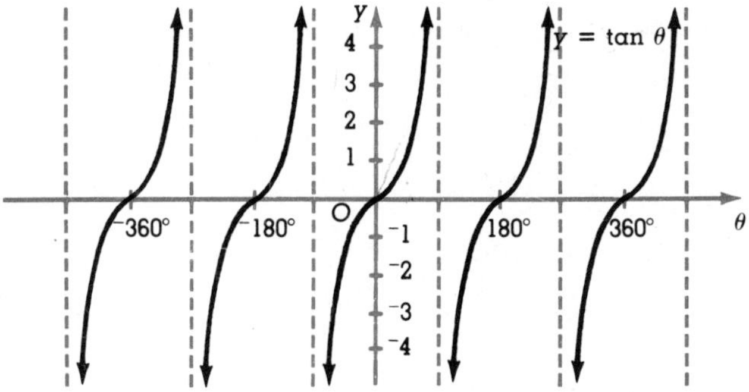

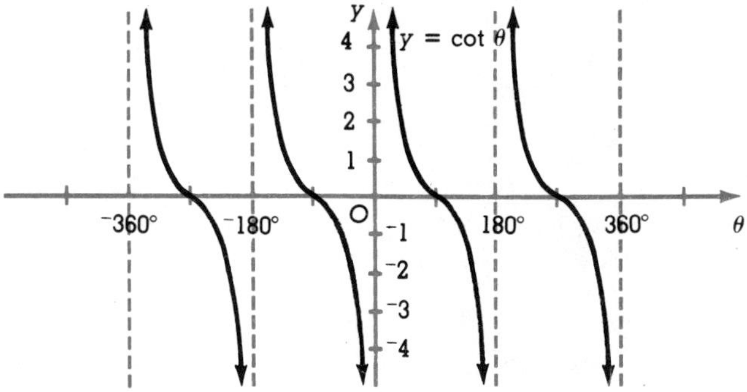

Note the resemblance of the cosine curve to the sine curve. Actually, since the sin x = cos (90° − x), the cosine curve is 90° out of phase with the sine curve. In other words, the cosine curve is a sine curve displaced 90° to the left along the x-axis.

Knowledge of the characteristics of the graphs of the functions can be used to quickly determine the quadrantal values of the functions. At a glance it is obvious that the sine function is 0 at −360°, −180°, 0°, 180°, 360°, and at every integral multiple of 180°. The maximum value of the sine function is 1 at x = 90° or −270°, and the minimum is −1 at x = 270° or −90°. Since the graph is periodic and repeats itself every 360°, other zero, maximum, and minimum points can be readily found. Similar special values of the other functions may be determined by an inspection of their graphs.

example

1 Use the graph of the cosine function to find the values of θ for which cos θ = 0.

When cos θ = 0, the value of θ is −270°, −90°, 90°, or 270°. Since the cosine function has a period of 360°, the values of θ for which cos θ = 0 are given by 90° + $n \cdot$ 360° where n is any integer.

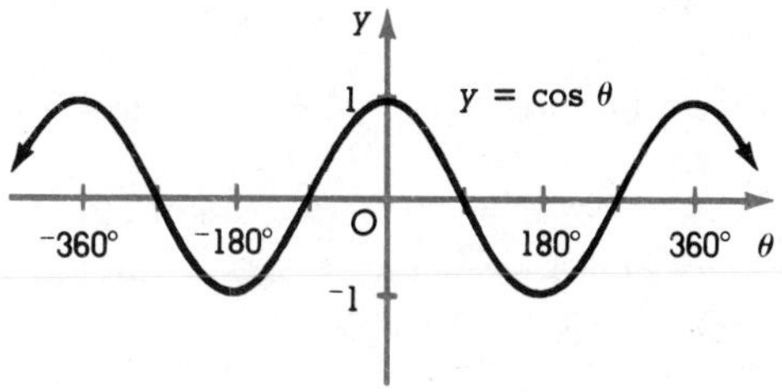

The graph of a trigonometric function may be drawn from the knowledge of its shape and the values of the function at integral multiples of 90°.

example

2 **Graph the sine curve in the interval $^-540° \leq \theta \leq 0°$.**

Find the value of $\sin \theta$ for $\theta = {}^-540°, {}^-450°, {}^-360°, {}^-270°, {}^-180°, {}^-90°$, and $0°$.

$$\sin(^-540°) = 0 \qquad \sin(^-450°) = {}^-1$$
$$\sin(^-360°) = 0 \qquad \sin(^-270°) = 1$$
$$\sin(^-180°) = 0 \qquad \sin(^-90°) = {}^-1$$
$$\sin 0° = 0$$

Plot the points from these ordered pairs.

$(^-540°, 0)$ $(^-450°, {}^-1)$
$(^-360°, 0)$ $(^-270°, 1)$
$(^-180°, 0)$ $(^-90°, {}^-1)$
$(0°, 0)$

Connect these points with a smooth continuous curve.

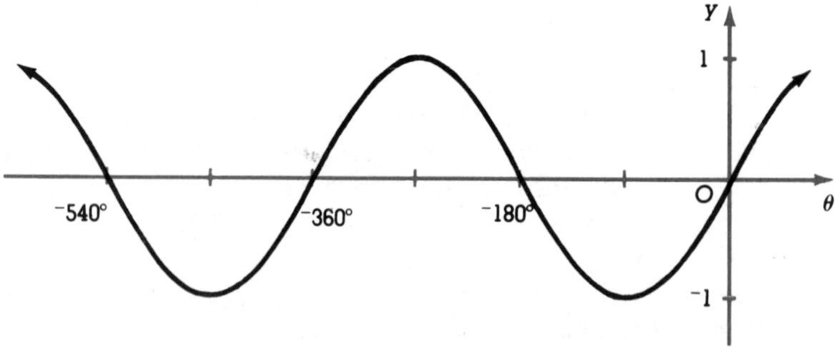

exercises

Exploratory Evaluate each of the following by referring to the graphs of the sine and cosine functions.

1. sin 90°
2. cos 270°
3. sin 360°
4. cos 450°
5. cos 90°
6. cos (⁻90°)
7. sin 180°
8. sin 450°

State whether the value of each of the following is positive or negative.

9. sin 50°
10. cos 140°
11. tan 280°
12. csc 440°
13. sec 150°
14. cot 250°
15. sin 350°
16. cos (⁻500°)

State which value is greater.

17. cos 20° or cos 80°
18. sin 10° or sin 100°
19. sin 40° or sin 50°
20. cos 70° or cos 170°

Written Find the values of θ for which each of the following is true.

1. $\cos \theta = 1$
2. $\sin \theta = 1$
3. $\tan \theta = 1$
4. $\cos \theta = {}^{-}1$
5. $\sin \theta = 0$
6. $\sin \theta = {}^{-}1$

State the domain for each of the following.

7. $y = \sin \theta$
8. $y = \cos \theta$
9. $y = \cot \theta$
10. $y = \sec \theta$
11. $y = \tan \theta$
12. $y = \csc \theta$

13-18. State the range of each function in problems **7-12.**

Graph each function in the indicated interval.

19. $y = \sin x;\ {}^{-}180° \leq x \leq 180°$
20. $y = \cos x;\ 270° \leq x \leq 630°$
21. $y = \tan x;\ 90° \leq x \leq 450°$
22. $y = \csc x;\ {}^{-}540° \leq x \leq 0°$
23. $y = \sec x;\ {}^{-}180° \leq x \leq 360°$
24. $y = \cot x;\ {}^{-}90° \leq x \leq 360°$

Graph the sine and cosine functions on the same coordinate axes for $0° \leq x \leq 360°$. Use the graph to find values of x, if any, for which each of the following is true.

25. $\sin x = {}^{-}\cos x$
26. $\sin x \leq \cos x$
27. $\sin x \cdot \cos x > 1$
28. $\sin x \cdot \cos x \leq 0$
29. $\sin x + \cos x = 1$
30. $\sin x - \cos x = 0$

6-2 Amplitude, Period, and Phase Shift

The graphs of the trigonometric functions can be modified by constants. Consider an equation of the form $y = A \sin \theta$. The maximum absolute value of $\sin \theta$ is 1. If every value of $\sin \theta$ is multiplied by A, the maximum value of $A \sin \theta$ is $|A|$. Similarly, the maximum value of $A \cos \theta$ is $|A|$. The absolute value of A, or $|A|$, is called the **amplitude** of the functions $y = A \sin \theta$ and $y = A \cos \theta$.

If $A < 0$, the curve is a reflection of the graph of the function on the x-axis for the coefficient having the same absolute value but opposite sign.

The amplitude of the functions, $y = A \sin \theta$ and $y = A \cos \theta$, is the absolute value of A, or $|A|$.

Amplitude of a Sine or Cosine Function

The tangent function does *not* have an amplitude because $y = \tan \theta$ increases without limit as θ approaches values such as 90°.

example

1 Graph $y = 2 \sin \theta$. State the amplitude.

Complete a table of values.

θ	0°	45°	90°	135°	180°	225°	270°	315°	360°
$\sin \theta$	0	$\frac{\sqrt{2}}{2}$	1	$\frac{\sqrt{2}}{2}$	0	$-\frac{\sqrt{2}}{2}$	$^{-}1$	$-\frac{\sqrt{2}}{2}$	0
$2 \sin \theta$	0	$\sqrt{2}$	2	$\sqrt{2}$	0	$^{-}\sqrt{2}$	$^{-}2$	$^{-}\sqrt{2}$	0

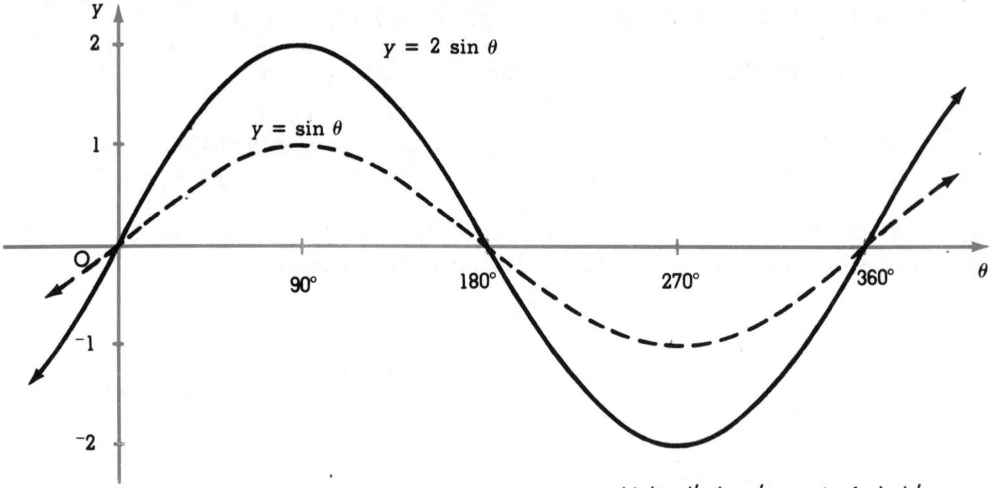

The amplitude of $y = 2 \sin \theta$ is 2.

Notice that a change in A stretches or shrinks the curve vertically.

Consider an equation of the form $y = \sin k\theta$, where k is a constant. Since the period of the sine function is 360°, the following identity can be written.

$$y = \sin k\theta = \sin (k\theta + 360°)$$

or

$$y = \sin k\left(\theta + \frac{360°}{k}\right)$$

Thus, the period of $y = \sin k\theta$ is $\frac{360°}{k}$. Similarly, the period of $y = \cos k\theta$ is $\frac{360°}{k}$. The period of $y = \tan k\theta$ is $\frac{180°}{k}$ since the period of the tangent function is 180°.

If the measure of angle θ is expressed in radians, the period of the sine and cosine functions is $\frac{2\pi}{k}$. The period of the tangent function is $\frac{\pi}{k}$.

The period of the functions, $y = \sin k\theta$ and $y = \cos k\theta$ is $\frac{360°}{k}$. The period of the function, $y = \tan k\theta$ is $\frac{180°}{k}$.

Periods of a Sine, Cosine, or Tangent Function

example

2 Graph $y = \cos 2\theta$. State the period.

θ	0	30°	45°	60°	90°	120°	135°	150°	180°
2θ	0	60°	90°	120°	180°	240°	270°	300°	360°
$\cos 2\theta$	1	$\frac{1}{2}$	0	$-\frac{1}{2}$	$^-1$	$-\frac{1}{2}$	0	$\frac{1}{2}$	1

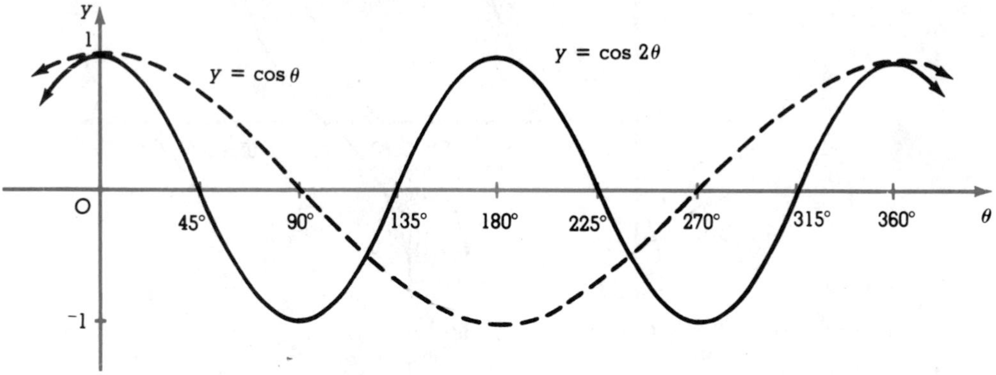

The period of $y = \cos 2\theta$ is $\frac{360°}{2}$ or 180°.

Notice that a change in k stretches or shrinks the curve horizontally.

Consider an equation of the form $y = A \sin (k\theta + c)$ where $A \neq 0$, $k \neq 0$, and $c \neq 0$. To find a zero of the function find the value of θ such that $0 = A \sin (k\theta + c)$. The value of θ is found by solving $k\theta + c = 0$ for θ. *Why?*

$$k\theta + c = 0$$
$$\theta = -\frac{c}{k}$$

Thus, if $y = 0$, then $\theta = -\frac{c}{k}$. The value of $-\frac{c}{k}$ is called the **phase shift.** When $c > 0$, the graph of $y = A \sin (k\theta + c)$ is similar to the graph of $y = A \sin k\theta$, but is shifted $\left|\frac{c}{k}\right|$ units to the *left*. When $c < 0$, the graph of $y = A \sin (k\theta + c)$ is similar to the graph of $y = A \sin k\theta$, but is shifted $\left|\frac{c}{k}\right|$ units to the *right*.

The phase shift of the function, $y = A \sin (k\theta + c)$, is $-\frac{c}{k}$. If $c > 0$, the shift is to the left and if $c < 0$ the shift is to the right. This definition applies to all trigonometric functions.

Phase Shift of All Trigonometric Functions

examples

3 Graph $y = \tan(\theta - 45°)$. State the phase shift.

θ	0°	45°	90°	135°	180°	225°	270°	315°	360°
$\theta - 45°$	$^-45°$	0°	45°	90°	135°	180°	225°	270°	315°
$\tan(\theta - 45°)$	$^-1$	0	1	undefined	$^-1$	0	1	undefined	$^-1$

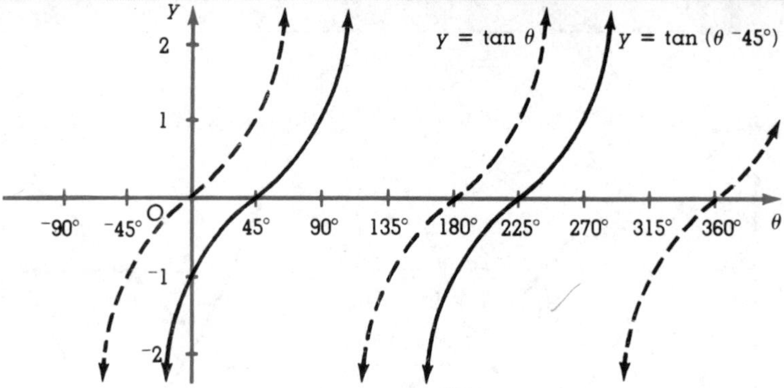

The phase shift of $y = \tan(\theta - 45°)$ is $-\frac{^-45°}{1}$ or 45°.

4 Find the possible equations of a sine function with amplitude 2, period 180°, and phase shift 45°.

Find the possible values of the amplitude.

$$|A| = 2$$
$$A = 2 \text{ or } A = {}^-2$$

Find the period.

$$\frac{360°}{k} = 180°$$
$$k = 2$$

Find the phase shift.

$$-\frac{c}{k} \text{ or } -\frac{c}{2} = 45°$$
$$c = {}^-90°$$

The possible equations are $y = 2\sin(2x - 90°)$ and $y = {}^-2\sin(2x - 90°)$.

exercises

Exploratory State the amplitude, period, and phase shift for each of the following.

1. $y = 2\sin 5\theta$
2. $y = 4\sin\theta$
3. $y = 3\cos(\theta - 90°)$
4. $y = 2\cos 2\theta$
5. $y = \tan(2\theta - 180°)$
6. $y = 10\tan 4\theta$
7. $y = 110\sin 20\theta$
8. $y = \tan 2(\theta - 180°)$
9. $y = 2\sin\theta$
10. $y = 243\sin(15\theta - 40°)$
11. $y = {}^-7\sin 6\theta$
12. $y = {}^-6\cos(180° - \theta)$
13. $y = \frac{1}{4}\cos\frac{\theta}{2}$
14. $y = 12\cos 3(\theta - 90°)$
15. $y = 10\sin\left(\frac{1}{3}\theta - 300°\right)$

Written Write an equation of the sine function for each amplitude, period, and phase shift.

1. amplitude = 3, period = 720°, phase shift = 60°
2. amplitude = 5, period = 360°, phase shift = 60°
3. amplitude = $\frac{2}{3}$, period = 180°, phase shift = 45°
4. amplitude = 17, period = 45°, phase shift = $^{-}60°$
5. amplitude = $\frac{1}{2}$, period = $\frac{3\pi}{2}$, phase shift = $-\frac{\pi}{4}$
6. amplitude = 7, period = 225°, phase shift = $^{-}90°$

Write an equation of the cosine function for each amplitude, period, and phase shift.

7. amplitude = $\frac{1}{3}$, period = 180°, phase shift = 0°
8. amplitude = 3, period = 180°, phase shift = 120°
9. amplitude = 4, period = 720°, phase shift = 90°
10. amplitude = 100, period = 630°, phase shift = $^{-}90°$
11. amplitude = $\frac{7}{3}$, period = 150°, phase shift = 270°
12. amplitude = 1, period = $\frac{3\pi}{4}$, phase shift = $-\frac{\pi}{3}$

Identify the amplitude, period, and phase shift of each sine curve.

13.
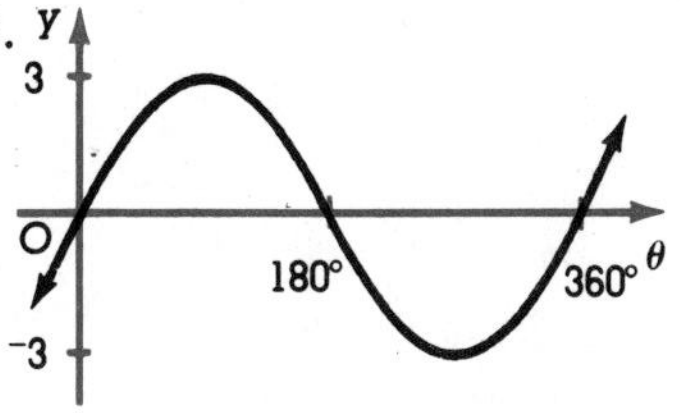

14.
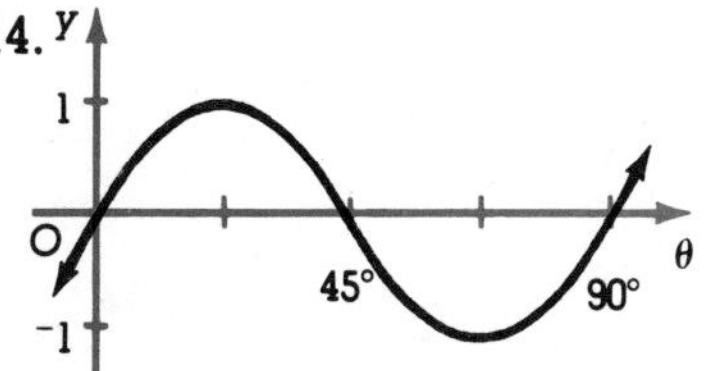

15.
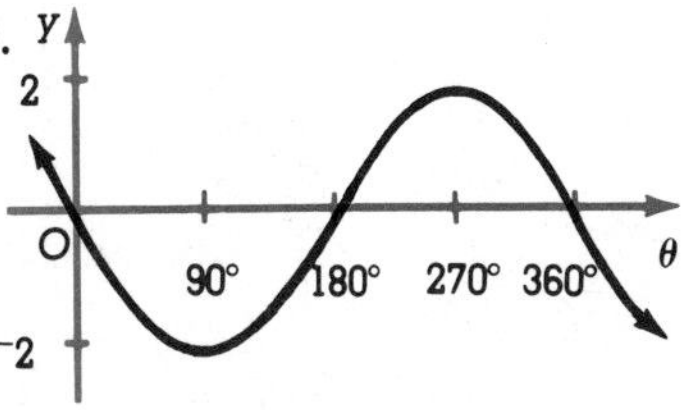

16.
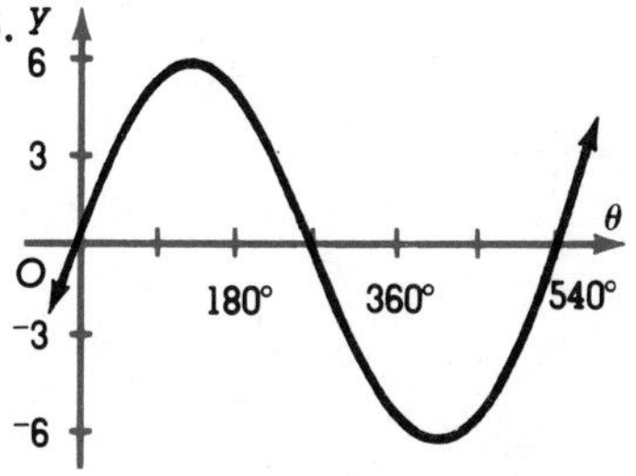

17.
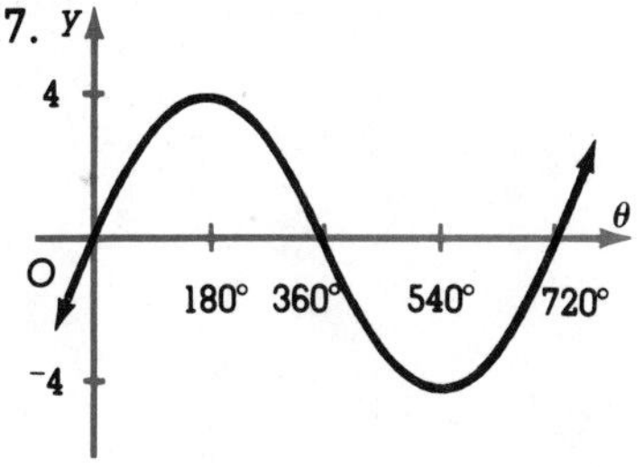

18.
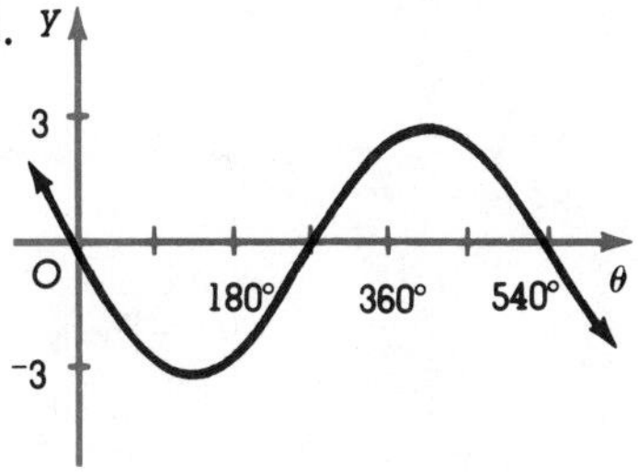

Graph each of the following.

19. $y = \frac{1}{2}\cos\theta$
20. $y = \frac{2}{3}\cos\theta$
21. $y = \sin\left(x + \frac{\pi}{3}\right)$
22. $y = \sin 4\theta$
23. $y = \cos 3\theta$
24. $y = 3\sin\theta$
25. $y = 3\sec\theta$
26. $y = \cos(\theta - 30°)$
27. $y = 2\tan\theta$
28. $y = \cos(\theta + 30°)$
29. $y = {}^{-}\cot\theta$
30. $y = \sin(\theta - 45°)$
31. $y = 4\sin\frac{1}{2}\theta$
32. $y = -\frac{1}{2}\cos\frac{3}{4}\theta$
33. $y = {}^{-}6\sin\left(2x + \frac{\pi}{4}\right)$

Miriam Crowe is a cabinet maker and quality control supervisor at Quality Cabinet Company. A type of joint known as the dovetail joint provides a firm interlocking fit between two cabinet components. The dovetail joint is carefully crafted, fitted, and tested to assure that it is a quality piece. Miriam tests the dimensions of a dovetail joint by using a pair of plugs.

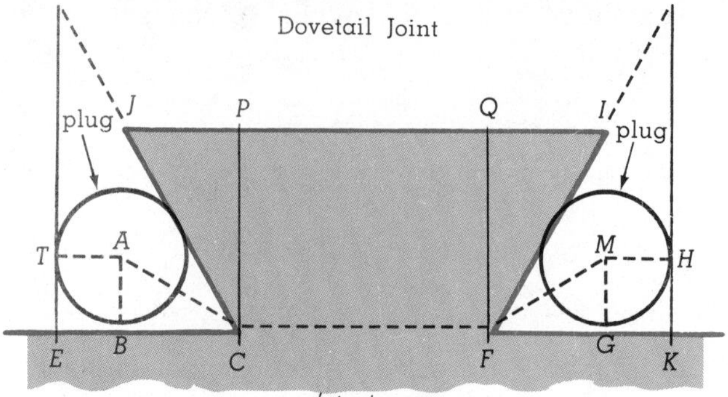

Example Find the measures for $\angle MFG$, $\overline{EK}$, and $\overline{JI}$ if $AB = 56$ mm, $CF = 140$ mm, $\angle IFG = 60°$ and $FQ = 125$ mm. Round answers to nearest tenth.

$2 \cdot \angle MFG = \angle IFG$ *Tangents drawn from an external point to a circle form congruent angles.*
$2 \cdot \angle MFG = 60°$
$\angle MFG = 30°$

Use the tangent ratio to find FG and thus BC.

$$\frac{MG}{FG} = \tan \angle MFG$$

$$\frac{56 \text{ mm}}{FG} = 0.5774$$

$FG = 96$ mm *Thus, $BC = 96$ mm*

$EK = EB + BC + CF + FG + GK$ *$EB = GK =$ radius of plugs or AB*

$EK = 56 \text{ mm} + 96 \text{ mm} + 140 \text{ mm} + 96 \text{ mm} + 56 \text{ mm}$ or 444 mm *$BC = FG$*

Use the tangent ratio to find JP and thus QI.

$$\frac{CP}{JP} = \tan \angle CJP$$ *$\angle CJP = 60°$, an alternate interior angle with $\angle JCB$*

$$\frac{125 \text{ mm}}{JP} = 1.732$$ *$CP = QF = 125$ mm*

$JP = 72.2$ mm

$JI = JP + PQ + QI$ *$PQ = CF$*

$JI = 72.2 \text{ mm} + 140 \text{ mm} + 72.2 \text{ mm}$ or 284.4 mm

Thus $\angle MFG = 60°$, $EK = 444$ mm, and $JI = 284.4$ mm.

Exercises Find the measures for $\angle MFG$, $\overline{EK}$, and $\overline{JI}$ using the figure at the top of the page. Round answers to the nearest tenth.

1. $AB = 43$ mm, $\angle IFG = 50°$, $CF = 130$ mm, $FQ = 146$ mm
2. $MG = 5.1$ cm, $\angle ECJ = 55°$, $PQ = 13.6$ cm, $PC = 14.8$ cm
3. $TA = 35$ mm, $\angle ACE = 24°$, $CF = 127$ mm, $FQ = 132$ mm

6-3 Graphing the Trigonometric Functions

A function of the form $y = A \sin (k\theta + c)$ can be graphed after finding the amplitude, period, and phase shift of the function. Once these values are known, a rough curve can be sketched using the general knowledge of the shape of the sine curve.

example

1 Graph $y = 4 \sin 2\theta$.

Find the amplitude. $|A| = 4$ *The values of the function vary from 4 to $^-4$.*

Find the period. $\frac{360°}{k} = \frac{360°}{2}$ or $180°$ *The curve repeats at each 180° interval.*

Find the phase shift. $-\frac{c}{k} = \frac{0}{2}$ or 0 *There is no phase shift.*

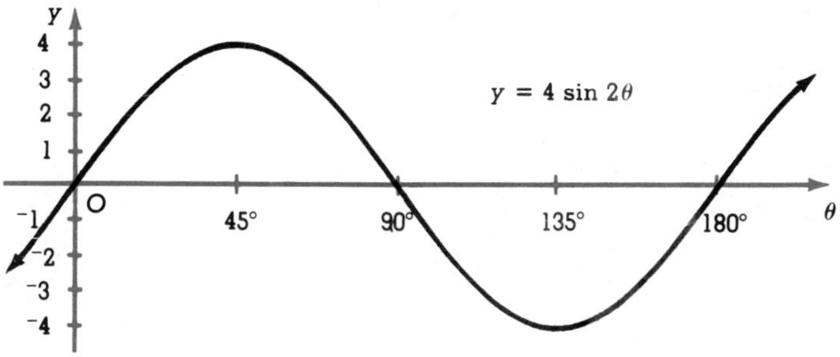

The functions $y = A \cos (k\theta + c)$ and $y = A \tan (k\theta + c)$ can be graphed in a similar manner.

example

2 Graph $y = 3 \cos (2\theta + 180°)$.

Find the amplitude. $|A| = 3$

Find the period. $\frac{360°}{k} = \frac{360°}{2}$ or $180°$

Find the phase shift. $-\frac{c}{k} = -\frac{180°}{2}$ or $^-90°$ *Since $c > 0$, the graph is shifted 90° to the left.*

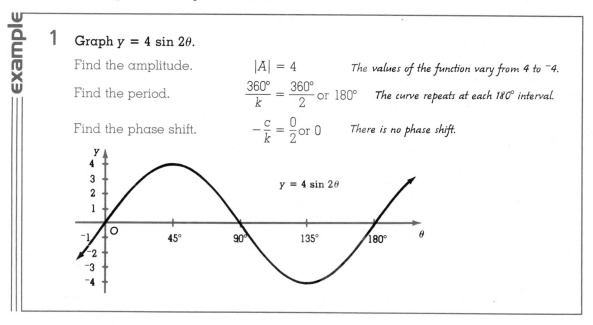

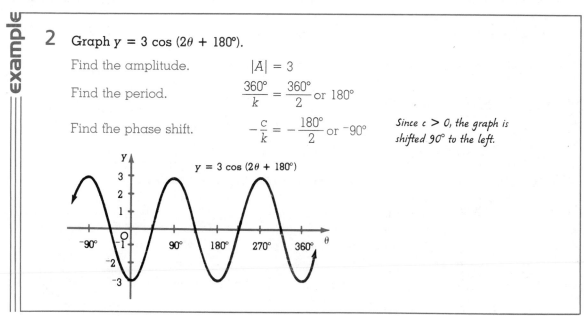

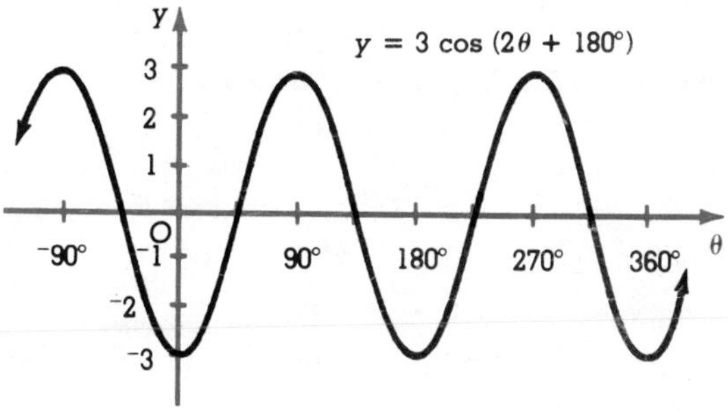

example

3 Graph $y = \tan\left(\frac{x}{2} - \frac{\pi}{6}\right)$.

Find the period. $\frac{\pi}{k} = \frac{\pi}{\frac{1}{2}}$ or 2π

Find the phase shift. $-\frac{c}{k} = -\left(\frac{-\frac{\pi}{6}}{\frac{1}{2}}\right)$ or $\frac{\pi}{3}$

Since c < 0, the graph is shifted $\frac{\pi}{3}$ to the right.

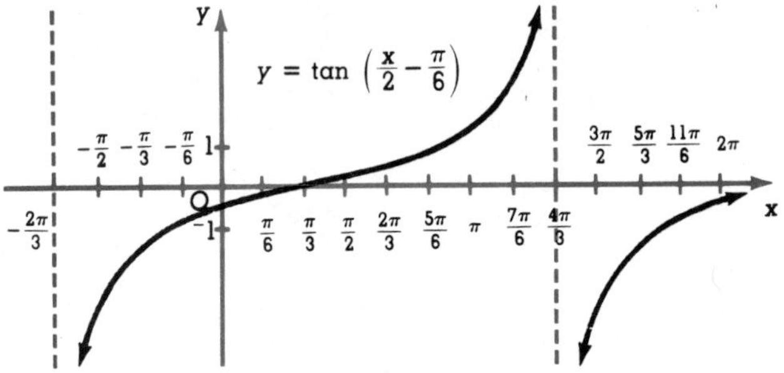

exercises

Exploratory State the amplitude, period, and phase shift for each of the following.

1. $y = \sin(\theta + 90°)$
2. $y = \sin(\theta - 180°)$
3. $y = 3\cos(\theta - 90°)$
4. $y = 2\cos\left(\frac{x}{2} + \pi\right)$
5. $y = {}^-3\sin(6\theta - 180°)$
6. $y = -\frac{1}{3}\sin(2\theta + 45°)$
7. $y = \frac{1}{2}\cos\left(\frac{\theta}{2} - 180°\right)$
8. $y = \frac{1}{2}\sin 2(\theta - 180°)$
9. $y = \frac{1}{10}\sin\left(\frac{2}{3}x - \frac{\pi}{3}\right)$
10. $y = 6\sin\left(6x + \frac{3\pi}{2}\right)$
11. $\frac{1}{2}y = \sin(3\theta + 180°)$
12. $2y = 10\sin\left(\frac{\theta}{2} + 90°\right)$

Written Graph each of the following.

1. $y = \frac{1}{2}\cos 2\theta$
2. $y = \tan\left(\frac{x}{2} + \frac{\pi}{2}\right)$
3. $y = 6\sin 4\theta$
4. $y = 5\cos(2\theta + 180°)$
5. $y = {}^-\sin(\theta - 45°)$
6. $y = {}^-3\sin(\theta - 45°)$

7-18. Graph each equation in problems **1-12** of the Exploratory Exercises.

Graph each of the following.

19. $y = \sec 3\theta$
20. $y = \tan(\theta + 90°)$
21. $y = \cot(\theta - 90°)$
22. $y = \csc(\theta + 60°)$
23. $y = \tan(2\theta - 90°)$
24. $y = \csc(3\theta + 180°)$

Challenge Sketch the graph of $y = \sin\frac{1}{x}$. (Hint: Start with values of x greater than $\frac{1}{180}^{\circ}$ and decrease the values.)

6-4 Graphing Compound Functions

Compound functions may consist of sums or products of trigonometric functions. They may also consist of sums or products of the trigonometric functions and other functions. For example, $y = x + \sin x$ is a compound function which is the sum of a linear function and a trigonometric function.

Some compound functions may be graphed by graphing each function separately on the same coordinate axes and adding the ordinates geometrically. After a few critical points are determined, the remainder of the curve of the compound function can be sketched.

A compass may be used to find the sum of the ordinates.

examples

1 **Graph $y = x + \sin x$.**

First graph each function, $y = x$ and $y = \sin x$, separately on the same axes. Next add the ordinates of special values, such as zeros, for one of the functions or the points of intersection. Then sketch the graph with a smooth curve.

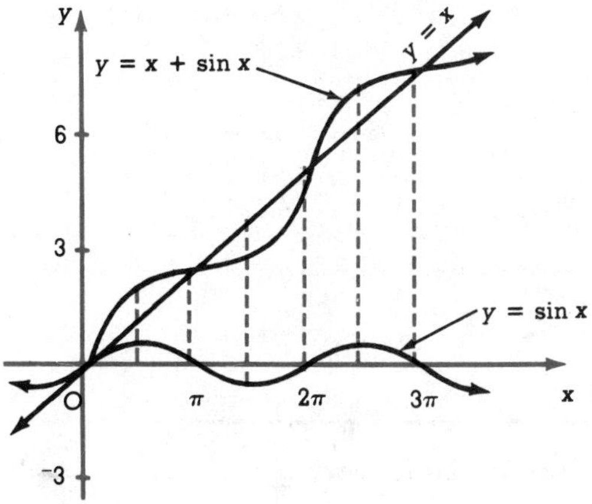

2 **Graph $y = \sin x + \cos x$.**

First graph each function, $y = \sin x$ and $y = \cos x$, separately on the same axes. Next add the ordinates of special values. Then sketch the graph with a smooth curve.

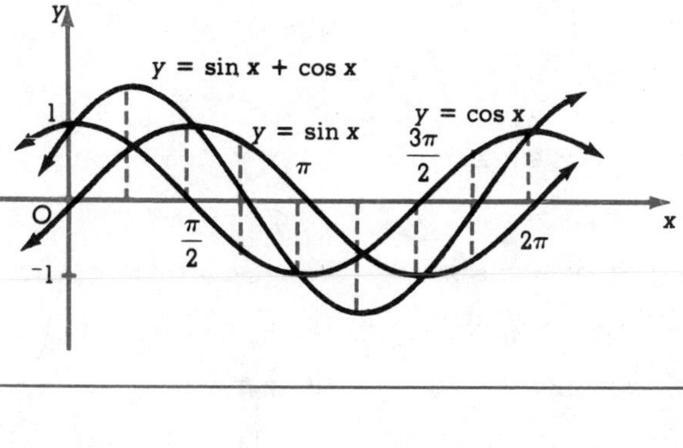

The table on page 503 may be used to find ordered pairs of the compound function as a check on geometric methods.

The following example shows the graph of a compound function which is the *product* of a linear function and a trigonometric function.

example

3 **Graph $y = x \sin x$.**

First graph each function, $y = x$ and $y = \sin x$, separately on the same axes. Then find key points. Since the maximum or minimum points of $y = \sin x$ are ± 1, the values of $x \sin x$ are $\pm x$ at these points. At the points where $\sin x = 0$, $x \sin x = 0$. After these points are plotted, sketch the graph with a smooth curve.

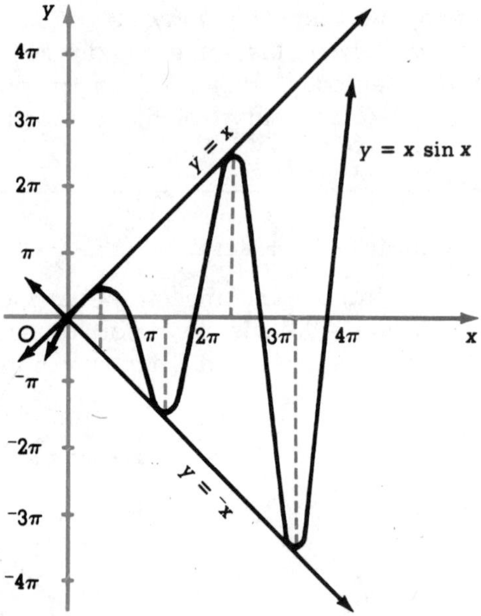

exercises

Exploratory Find $f\left(\frac{\pi}{2}\right)$ for each of the following.

1. $f(x) = \sin x + \cos x$
2. $f(x) = \sin x - \cos x$
3. $f(x) = x + \cos x$
4. $f(x) = x + \sin x$
5. $f(x) = 3 \sin x$
6. $f(x) = \sin x + \sin 2x$
7. $f(x) = x \sin x$
8. $f(x) = x \cos x$
9. $f(x) = \cos x - \sin 2x$

10-18. Find $f\left(\frac{\pi}{4}\right)$ for problems 1-9.

Written Graph each of the following.

1. $y = x + \cos x$
2. $y = \sin \frac{x}{3} + \frac{x}{3}$
3. $y = \cos x - 2$
4. $y = \sin x - \cos x$
5. $y = \sin x + \sin 2x$
6. $y = 2x + 2 \sin x$
7. $y = x - \sin x$
8. $y = 2 \sin x - \frac{1}{2}x$
9. $y = \cos x - \sin x$
10. $y = 2 \sin x - 3 \cos x$
11. $y = \cos 2x - \cos 3x$
12. $y = 2 \sin x + 3 \cos x$
13. $y = \frac{1}{2} \sin x - \cos 3x$
14. $y = 2 \sin x - \frac{1}{2} \cos x$
15. $y = \sin x + \sin\left(x + \frac{\pi}{2}\right)$
16. $y = x \cos x$
17. $y = 2x \sin 2x$
18. $y = \sin^2 x$

Excursions in Mathematics

The design of underwater diving equipment uses information about human breathing patterns. One complete cycle of a breathing pattern, inhaling and exhaling, can be represented by the sine curve.

The **vital capacity** is the maximum volume of air inhaled and exhaled at each breath for a given size lung. Note that the amplitude of the breathing cycle of a resting body is much smaller than that of the vital capacity. The lung capacity of a body at a resting state is approximately 20% of its vital capacity.

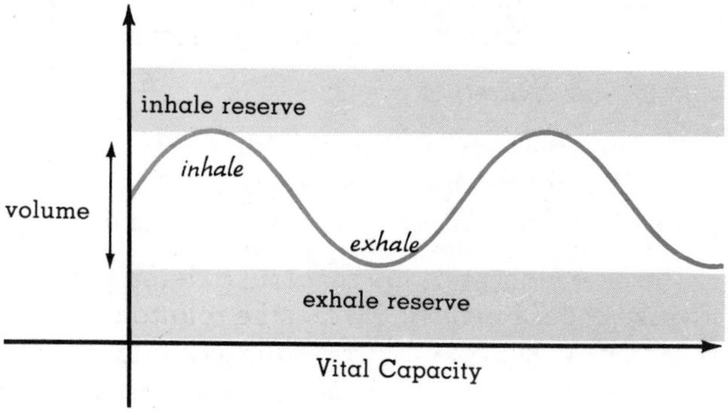

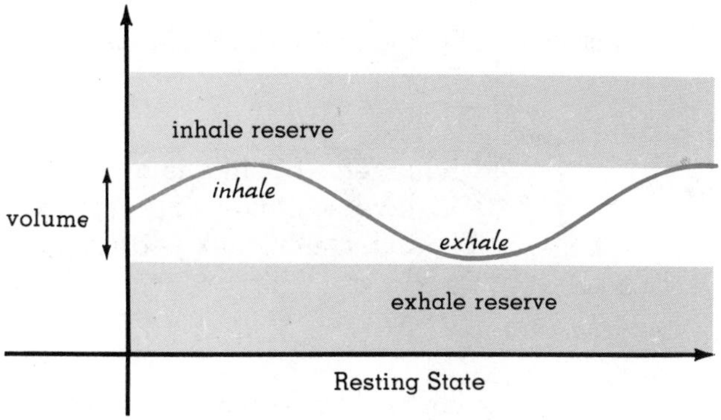

As a gaseous body, such as an aqualung tank, is submerged to various depths of water, the volume of the gas is affected by the pressure of the water. The volume can be found by using the following formula.

$$V_d = \frac{33V_s}{d + 33}$$

V_s is the volume of gas at sea level.
V_d is the volume of gas at depth d.

This information is used to solve problems about underwater diving.

Example An aqualung tank contains 70 ft^3 of air. The diver who is breathing 12 breaths per minute in a resting state has a 0.21 ft^3 vital capacity. Find the present lung capacity of the diver, the volume of air in the tank at a 66 ft depth, and the length of time the diver can remain at a depth of 66 ft.

lung capacity $= 20\%$ of $0.21\ ft^3$
$= 0.042\ ft^3$/breath

volume of air needed/minute $= 0.042\ ft^3/\text{breath} \cdot 12$ breaths/minute
$= 0.504\ ft^3$/minute

volume of gas at 66 ft $= \dfrac{33 \cdot 70}{66 + 33}$
$= 23.3\ ft^3$

time at 66 ft $= \dfrac{23.3\ ft^3}{0.504\ ft^3/\text{minute}}$
$= 46$ minutes

Exercises Find the resting state lung capacity of the diver, the volume of air in the tank at the given depth, and the possible length of time the diver can remain at the given depth. Assume 12 breaths per minute in the resting state.

1. $V_s = 60\ ft^3$; $d = 45$ ft
   vital capacity $= 0.158\ ft^3$
2. $V_s = 65\ ft^3$; $d = 70$ ft
   vital capacity $= 0.105\ ft^3$
3. $V_s = 56\ ft^3$; $d = 60$ ft
   vital capacity $= 0.21\ ft^3$

6-5 Inverse Trigonometric Functions

The **inverse** of a function may be found by interchanging the elements of the ordered pairs of the function. In other words, the domain of a function becomes the range of its inverse and the range of the function becomes the domain of its inverse. For example, the inverse of $y = 2x + 5$ is $y = \frac{x - 5}{2}$.

To find the inverse of $y = 2x + 5$, solve for x and switch the variables.

The inverse may *not* be a function. For example, if $f(x) = x^2$, the ordered pairs of f are of the form (x, x^2). The inverse of f has ordered pairs of the form (x^2, x) or $(x, \pm\sqrt{x})$ and is *not* a function.

Why?

The sine function is the set of all ordered pairs $(x, \sin x)$. Thus the inverse of this function, the **arcsine relation,** is the set of all ordered pairs $(\sin x, x)$. Note that $y = \arcsin x$ and $x = \sin y$ generate the same set of ordered pairs and therefore, describe the same relation. The domain of $y = \arcsin x$ is $^{-}1 \leq x \leq 1$ or $|x| \leq 1$, and the range of the relation is the set of real numbers.

The inverses of the trigonometric functions are named as follows.

The inverse of sin x is arcsin x.
The inverse of cos x is arccos x.
The inverse of tan x is arctan x.

Names of the Inverses of the Trigonometric Functions

An equation such as $\sin x = 0.3393$ can be written in the form $x = \arcsin 0.3393$. The last equation is read "x is an angle whose sine is 0.3393," or "x equals the arcsine of 0.3393." The solutions for x consist of all angles that have as their sine the number 0.3393. An infinite number of such angles exist.

An alternate notation for arcsin x is $\sin^{-1} x$. The $^{-}1$ is not an exponent. The inverses of the other trigonometric functions may be written in a similar manner.

examples

1 **Find x if sin x = 0.5.**

If $\sin x = 0.5$, then x is an angle whose sine is 0.5.
Thus, $x = 30°, 150°, 390°, 510° \ldots$

2 **Find all positive values of x less than 360° which satisfy the equation tan x = ⁻1.**

$\tan x = {}^{-}1$
$x = \arctan({}^{-}1)$
$x = 135°, 315°$

examples

3 **Evaluate sin (arcsin 0.8660).**

Let $A = \arcsin 0.8660$.
Then $\sin A = 0.8660$ and $\sin(\arcsin 0.8660) = 0.8660$.

4 **Evaluate** $\tan\left(\cos^{-1}\frac{3}{5}\right)$.

Let $A = \cos^{-1}\frac{3}{5}$.

Then $\cos A = \frac{3}{5}$.

Draw a right triangle and call one acute angle A. Since $\cos A = \frac{3}{5}$, the adjacent side of angle A can be set equal to 3 and the hypotenuse equal to 5. Next find the length of the opposite side.

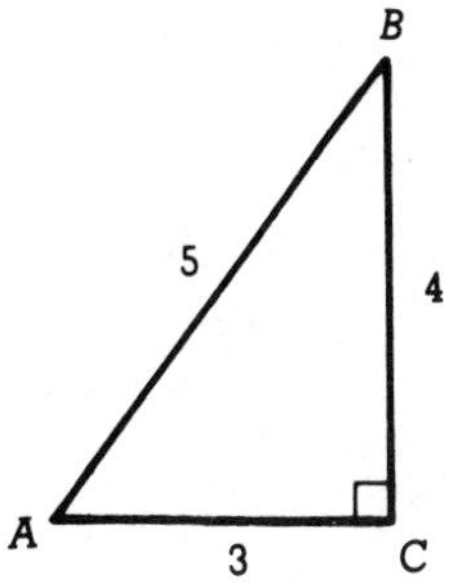

$3^2 + x^2 = 5^2$ *Use the Pythagorean Theorem.*

$x = 4$

$\tan\left(\cos^{-1}\frac{3}{5}\right) = \tan A$ $A = \cos\frac{3}{5}$

$= \frac{\text{side opposite}}{\text{side adjacent}}$

$= \frac{4}{3}$

Thus, $\tan\left(\cos^{-1}\frac{3}{5}\right) = \frac{4}{3}$.

exercises

Exploratory Write the inverse of each function.

1. $f = \{(3, 1), (2, 4), (1, 5)\}$
2. $f = \{(3, 8), (4, ^-2), (5, ^-3)\}$
3. $g = \{(3, 2), (4, 2)\}$
4. $g = \{(^-3, 1), (2, 4), (7, 8)\}$
5. $h = \{(^-1, ^-2), (^-3, ^-2), (^-1, ^-4), (0, 6)\}$
6. $h = \{(4, ^-2), (3, 7), (5, 7), (3, 8)\}$

Write each of the following in the form of an inverse relation.

7. $x = \sin\theta$
8. $\cos\alpha = \frac{1}{3}$
9. $\tan y = {}^-3$
10. $y = \cos x$
11. $\frac{4}{3} = \tan\theta$
12. $\sin x = 2$
13. $n = \sin\theta$
14. $\sin\beta = 1$
15. $\cos\theta = y$

Written Find values of x in the interval $0° \leq x \leq 360°$ that satisfy each equation.

1. $x = \arcsin 0$
2. $x = \cos^{-1} 0$
3. $x = \arctan 1$
4. $x = \arcsin \frac{\sqrt{3}}{2}$
5. $x = \arctan \frac{\sqrt{3}}{3}$
6. $x = \sin^{-1} \frac{1}{\sqrt{2}}$
7. $x = \sec^{-1} 2$
8. $x = \text{arccot } 2.1445$
9. $x = \arcsin (^{-}0.5)$

Evaluate each of the following. Assume that angles are acute.

10. $\sin \left(\sin^{-1} \frac{1}{2}\right)$
11. $\cot \left(\arctan \frac{4}{5}\right)$
12. $\cos \left(\arcsin \frac{\sqrt{3}}{2}\right)$
13. $\tan \left(\arcsin \frac{5}{13}\right)$
14. $\sec \left(\cos^{-1} \frac{1}{2}\right)$
15. $\cos \left(\text{arccot } \frac{4}{3}\right)$
16. $\sin (\tan^{-1} 1) + \cos (\cos^{-1} 0.5)$
17. $\sin (\arctan \sqrt{3} + \text{arccot } \sqrt{3})$
18. $\tan \left(\arcsin \frac{\sqrt{2}}{2}\right) - \cot \left(\arccos \frac{\sqrt{2}}{2}\right)$
19. $\tan \left(\sin^{-1} \frac{\sqrt{3}}{2} - \cos^{-1} \frac{\sqrt{3}}{2}\right)$

Verify each expression. Assume that angles are acute.

20. $\sin^{-1} \frac{\sqrt{2}}{2} + \cos^{-1} \frac{\sqrt{2}}{2} = 90°$
21. $\arccos \frac{\sqrt{3}}{2} + \arcsin \frac{\sqrt{3}}{2} = \frac{\pi}{2}$
22. $\arcsin \frac{2}{5} + \arccos \frac{2}{5} = \frac{\pi}{2}$
23. $\tan^{-1} 1 + \cos^{-1} \frac{\sqrt{3}}{2} = \sin^{-1} \frac{1}{2} + \sec^{-1} \sqrt{2}$
24. $\tan^{-1} \frac{3}{4} + \tan^{-1} \frac{5}{12} = \tan^{-1} \frac{56}{33}$
25. $\arcsin \frac{3}{5} + \arccos \frac{15}{17} = \arctan \frac{77}{36}$

6-6 Principal Values of the Inverse Trigonometric Functions

The inverse of any trigonometric function is *not* a function since one value in the domain corresponds to more than one value in the range. The domains of the trigonometric functions may be limited so that their inverse relations are functions.

Consider only a part of the domain of the sine function, namely any x so that $^{-}90° \leq x \leq 90°$. It is possible to define a new function, called Sine, whose inverse is a function.

Capital letters are used to distinguish the function with restricted domains from the usual trigonometric functions.

$$y = \text{Sin } x \text{ if and only if } y = \sin x \text{ and } {}^{-}90° \leq x \leq 90°$$

The values in the domain of Sine are called **principal values.** Other new functions that have inverses can be defined as follows.

$$y = \text{Cos } x \text{ if and only if } y = \cos x \text{ and } 0 \leq x \leq 180°$$
$$y = \text{Tan } x \text{ if and only if } y = \tan x \text{ and } {}^{-}90° < x < 90°$$

The inverses of the Sine, Cosine, and Tangent functions are called the Arcsine, Arccosine, and Arctangent functions, respectively. They are defined as follows.

Note the capital "A" in the name of each inverse function.

Given $y = \text{Sin } x$, the inverse sine function is defined by the following equation.

$$y = \text{Sin}^{-1}x \quad \text{or} \quad y = \text{Arcsin } x$$

Arcsine Function

Given $y = \text{Cos } x$, the inverse cosine function is defined by the following equation.

$$y = \text{Cos}^{-1}x \quad \text{or} \quad y = \text{Arccos } x$$

Arccosine Function

Given $y = \text{Tan } x$, the inverse tangent function is defined by the following equation.

$$y = \text{Tan}^{-1}x \quad \text{or} \quad y = \text{Arctan } x$$

Arctangent Function

examples

1 Find Arcsin $\left(-\frac{1}{2}\right)$.

$$\theta = \text{Arcsin}\left(-\frac{1}{2}\right)$$

$$\text{Sin } \theta = -\frac{1}{2}$$

$$\theta = {}^{-}30^\circ$$

Why is θ not 210°?

2 Find cos $(\text{Tan}^{-1} 1)$.

Let $\theta = \text{Tan}^{-1} 1$

$\text{Tan } \theta = 1$ *$^{-}90^\circ < \theta < 90^\circ$*

$\theta = 45^\circ$

$$\cos(\text{Tan}^{-1} 1) = \cos 45^\circ = \frac{\sqrt{2}}{2}$$

3 Find cos $\left(\text{Tan}^{-1}\sqrt{3} - \text{Sin}^{-1}\frac{1}{2}\right)$

Let $\alpha = \text{Tan}^{-1}\sqrt{3}$ and let $\beta = \text{Sin}^{-1}\frac{1}{2}$

$\text{Tan } \alpha = \sqrt{3}$ $\quad$ $\text{Sin } \beta = \frac{1}{2}$

$\alpha = 60^\circ$ $\quad$ $\beta = 30^\circ$

$$\cos\left(\text{Tan}^{-1}\sqrt{3} - \text{Sin}^{-1}\frac{1}{2}\right) = \cos(\alpha - \beta)$$
$$= \cos(60^\circ - 30^\circ)$$
$$= \cos 30^\circ$$
$$= \frac{\sqrt{3}}{2}$$

example

4 Find x if $x = \arcsin \frac{1}{2}$.

Since $\arcsin \frac{1}{2}$ is *not* capitalized, *general* values of x must be given.

$\sin x = \frac{1}{2}$

$x = 30°$ and $x = 150°$ for $0° \leq x \leq 360°$

General values are given by $x = 30° + n \cdot 360°$ and $x = 150° + n \cdot 360°$ where n is any integer.

exercises

Exploratory Evaluate each of the following.

1. $\text{Cos}^{-1} \frac{1}{2}$
2. $\text{Sin}^{-1} \left(-\frac{\sqrt{3}}{2}\right)$
3. Arctan 1
4. $\text{Sin}^{-1} \left(-\frac{1}{2}\right)$
5. Arctan 0.8693
6. Arccos 0.8910
7. $\text{Sin}^{-1}\, 0$
8. $\text{Tan}^{-1}\, 1$
9. $\text{Cos}^{-1} \left(-\frac{\sqrt{3}}{2}\right)$
10. $\text{Arcsin}\, \frac{\sqrt{3}}{2}$
11. $\text{Arcsin} - \left(\frac{\sqrt{2}}{2}\right)$
12. $\text{Arctan}\, \frac{3}{4}$
13. $\text{Sin}^{-1} \frac{\sqrt{3}}{2}$
14. $\text{Tan}^{-1} \left(\frac{\sqrt{3}}{3}\right)$
15. $\text{Sin}^{-1}\, 1$
16. $\text{Sin}^{-1}\, (^-1)$
17. Arctan ($^-$0.3443)
18. $\text{Arccos} \left(-\frac{\sqrt{2}}{2}\right)$
19. $\text{Cos}^{-1}\, 0$
20. Arccos ($^-$0.5746)

Written Evaluate each of the following.

1. $\text{Tan}^{-1}\, (^-1)$
2. $\text{Arccos}\, \frac{\sqrt{3}}{2}$
3. $\arcsin \frac{\sqrt{3}}{2}$
4. $\text{Cos}^{-1} \left(-\frac{1}{2}\right)$
5. $\arctan\, (^-1)$
6. $\text{Arctan}\, \sqrt{3}$
7. $\arccos \frac{\sqrt{2}}{2}$
8. $\sin \left(\text{Sin}^{-1} \frac{1}{2}\right)$
9. $\text{Sin}^{-1} \left(\cos \frac{\pi}{2}\right)$
10. $\text{Sin}^{-1} \left(\tan \frac{\pi}{4}\right)$
11. $\arcsin \frac{3}{4}$
12. $\cos \left(\text{Cos}^{-1} \frac{1}{2}\right)$
13. $\cos \left(\text{Cos}^{-1} \frac{4}{5}\right)$
14. $\sin \left(\text{Sin}^{-1} \frac{\sqrt{3}}{2}\right)$
15. arctan 5
16. $\tan \left(\text{Sin}^{-1} \frac{5}{13}\right)$
17. $\tan \left[\text{Cos}^{-1} \left(-\frac{3}{5}\right)\right]$
18. $\sin \left[\text{Arctan}\, (^-\sqrt{3})\right]$
19. $\arccos \left(-\frac{1}{2}\right)$
20. $\sin \left(2\, \text{Cos}^{-1} \frac{3}{5}\right)$
21. $\cos (\text{Tan}^{-1} \sqrt{3})$
22. $\cos \left[\text{Arcsin} \left(-\frac{1}{2}\right)\right]$
23. $\arctan \frac{1}{2}$
24. $\sin \left(2\, \text{Sin}^{-1} \frac{1}{2}\right)$
25. $\cos (\text{Tan}^{-1}\, 1)$
26. $\sin \left(2\, \text{Sin}^{-1} \frac{\sqrt{3}}{2}\right)$
27. $\arcsin\, (^-1)$
28. $\tan \left(\frac{1}{2}\, \text{Sin}^{-1} \frac{15}{17}\right)$
29. $\sin \left(\frac{1}{2}\, \text{Arctan}\, \frac{3}{5}\right)$
30. $\cos (2\, \text{Tan}^{-1} \sqrt{3})$

31. $\sin\left(\text{Sin}^{-1} 1 - \text{Cos}^{-1} \frac{1}{2}\right)$

32. $\cos\left(\text{Cos}^{-1} 0 + \text{Sin}^{-1} \frac{1}{2}\right)$

33. $\cos\left(\text{Tan}^{-1} \sqrt{3} - \text{Sin}^{-1} \frac{1}{2}\right)$

34. $\sin\left[\text{Arctan}\left(-\frac{3}{4}\right) + \text{Arccot}\left(-\frac{4}{3}\right)\right]$

35. $\sin\left(\text{Tan}^{-1} 1 - \text{Sin}^{-1} 1\right)$

36. $\cos\left[\text{Cos}^{-1}\left(-\frac{1}{2}\right) - \text{Sin}^{-1} 1\right]$

37. $\cos\left[\text{Cos}^{-1}\left(-\frac{\sqrt{2}}{2}\right) - \frac{\pi}{2}\right]$

38. $\cos\left[\frac{4}{3}\pi - \text{Cos}^{-1}\left(-\frac{1}{2}\right)\right]$

39. $\tan\left(\text{Cos}^{-1} \frac{3}{5} - \text{Sin}^{-1} \frac{5}{13}\right)$

40. $\sin\left[\frac{\pi}{2} - \text{Cos}^{-1}\left(\frac{1}{2}\right)\right]$

Challenge **Express each of the following in terms of u and v.**

1. $\sin(\text{Arcsin } u - \text{Arccos } v)$

2. $\cos(\text{Arcsin } u + \text{Arccos } v)$

6-7 Graphing Inverses of Functions

The inverse of a function can be found by reversing the elements of each ordered pair in the given function. For example, if a function consists of the ordered pairs $(5, 3)$, $(6, {}^-2)$, $(4, 3)$, $\left(3, -\frac{1}{2}\right)$, its inverse consists of $(3, 5)$, $({}^-2, 6)$, $(3, 4)$, $\left(-\frac{1}{2}, 3\right)$.

In this case, is the inverse a function?

The graph of the inverse of a function may be drawn by reflecting the graph of the given function over the line $x = y$.

example

1 **Draw the graph of the inverse of $y = 2x - 2$.**

First draw the graph of $y = 2x - 2$. Then reflect this graph over the line $x = y$ to get the graph of its inverse.

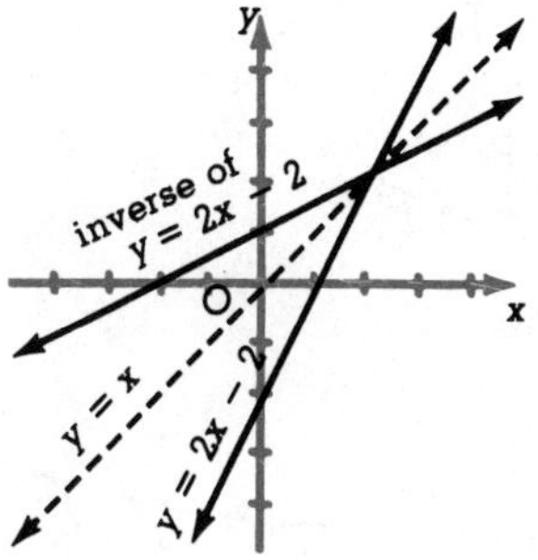

The inverse trigonometric relations can be illustrated by means of the graphs of the relations.

Let x assume all permissable values in the relation $y = \arcsin x$. Thus, $^{-}1 \leq x \leq 1$. If general values are plotted for y, the graph of $y = \arcsin x$ is obtained, as shown at the right. Notice that the graph of $y = \arcsin x$ has the same relation to the y-axis that the graph of $y = \sin x$ has to the x-axis.

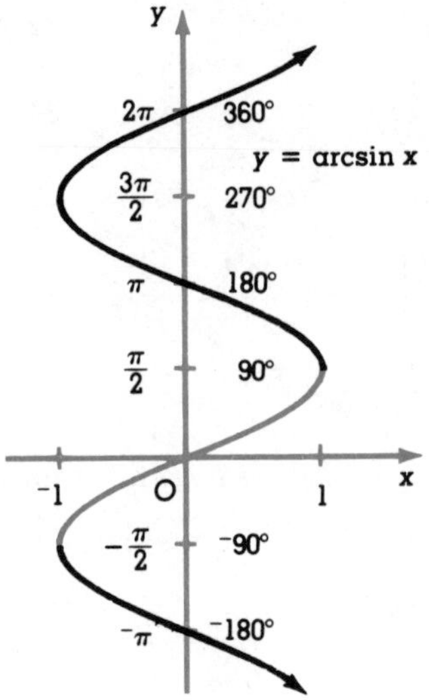

Values of Arcsin x are shown as a color portion of the curve. Note that $y = \text{Arcsin } x$ is a function because each value of x determines only one value of y. The range is $^{-}90° \leq \text{Arcsin } x \leq 90°$.

But $y = \arcsin x$ is *not* a function. A vertical line drawn on the graph would pass through more than one point.

The inverse of the cosine function may be graphed in a similar way. The graph of the principal values is shown as a color portion of the curve at the right. Although there are an unlimited number of values of the $\arccos x$ for a given value of x, there is only one value of Arccos x for each x. The range of Arccos x is $0° \leq \text{Arccos } x \leq 180°$.

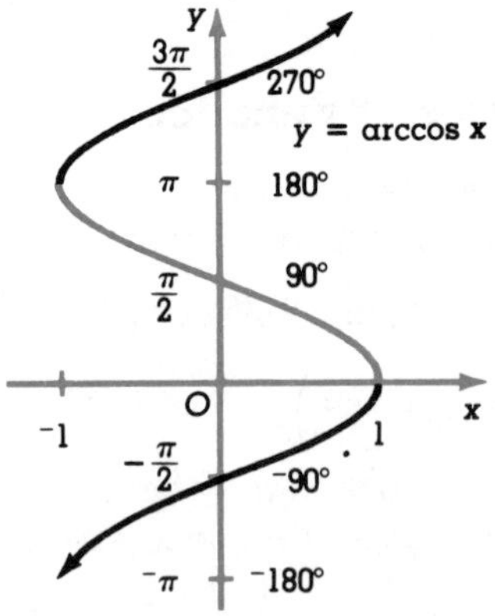

The graph of the inverse of the tangent function is shown below. Notice its similarity to the graph of $y = \tan x$ with the axes interchanged. Values of Arctan x are shown as a color portion of the curve. For each value of x, there is only one value of Arctan x, but an unlimited number of values for $\arctan x$. The range of Arctan x is $^{-}90° < \arctan x < 90°$.

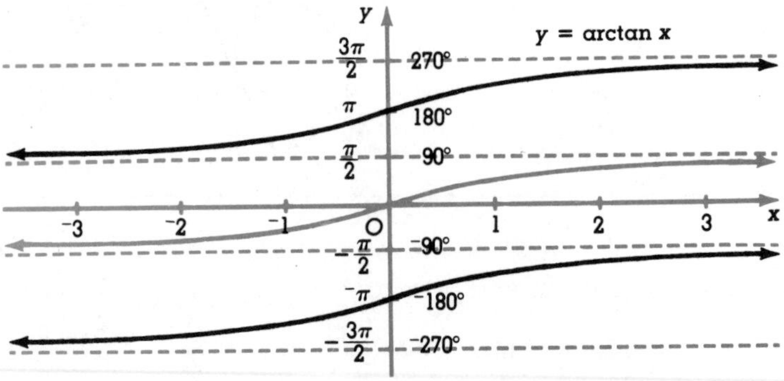

exercises

Exploratory **State the domain of each function or relation.**

1. $y = \sin x$
2. $y = \cos x$
3. $y = \tan x$
4. $y = \text{Sin } x$
5. $y = \text{Cos } x$
6. $y = \text{Tan } x$
7. $y = \arcsin x$
8. $y = \arccos x$
9. $y = \arctan x$
10. $y = \text{Arcsin } x$
11. $y = \text{Arccos } x$
12. $y = \text{Arctan } x$

13-24. State the range of each function or relation in problems **1-12.**

Written **Write the equation for the inverse of each function.**

1. $y = x + 2$
2. $y = \cos x$
3. $y = 3$
4. $y = \text{Arctan } x$
5. $y = \text{Arcsin } x$
6. $y = \frac{1}{2}x + 4$
7. $y = x$
8. $y = \frac{x - 3}{5}$
9. $y = {}^{-}3x - 1$
10. $y = x^2$
11. $y = \text{Sin } x$
12. $y = (x - 4)^2$

13-24. Graph each function and its inverse in problems **1-12.**

Determine if the inverse of each relation graphed below is a function.

25.

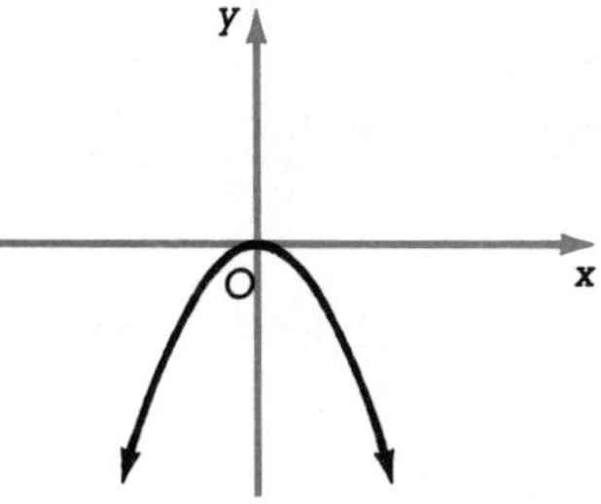

26.

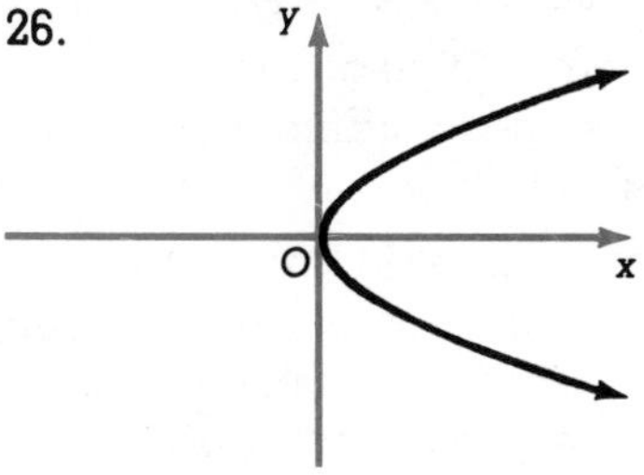

27.

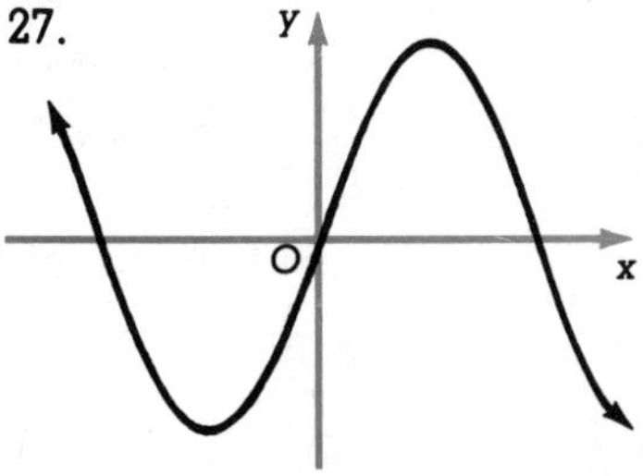

28.

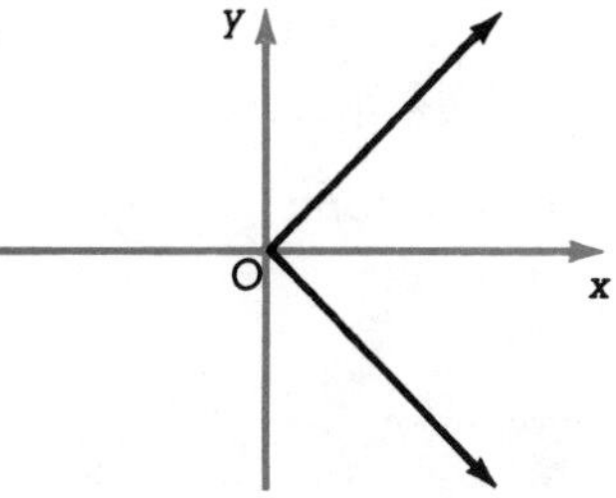

29.

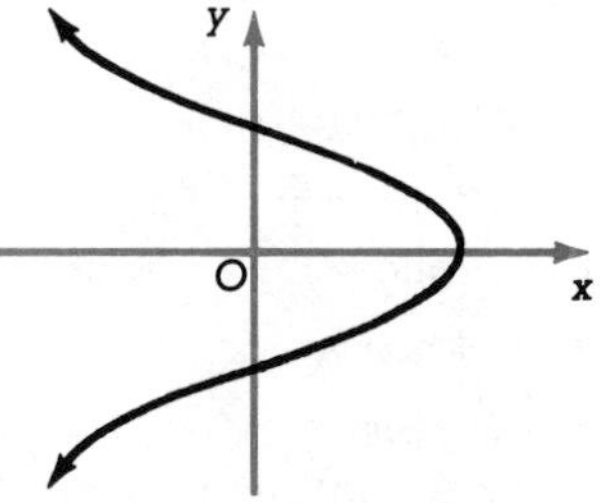

30.

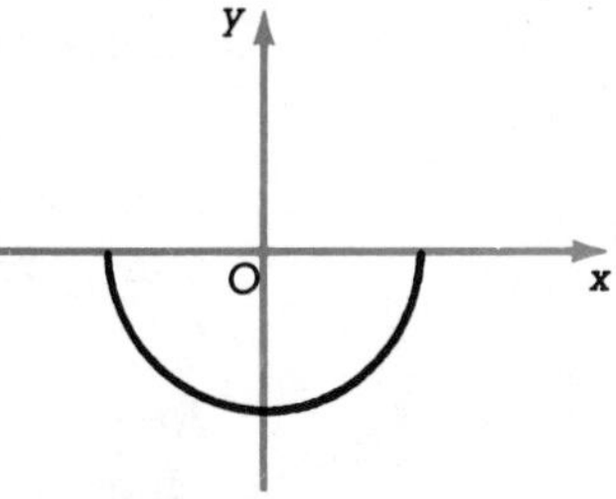

Determine if each of the following is true or false. If false, give a counterexample.

31. $\tan(\text{Tan}^{-1} x) = x$ for all x
32. $\text{Sin}^{-1} x = {}^{-}\text{Sin}^{-1}({}^{-}x), {}^{-}1 \le x \le 1$
33. $\text{Tan}^{-1}(\tan x) = x$ for all x
34. $\text{Cos}^{-1}({}^{-}x) = {}^{-}\text{Cos}^{-1} x, {}^{-}1 \le x \le 1$
35. $\text{Sin}^{-1} x + \text{Cos}^{-1} x = \frac{\pi}{2}, {}^{-}1 \le x \le 1$
36. $\text{Arccos } x = \text{Arccos}({}^{-}x), {}^{-}1 \le x \le 1$
37. $\text{Cos}^{-1} x = \frac{1}{\text{Cos } x}$
38. $\text{Tan}^{-1} x = \frac{1}{\text{Tan } x}$

Sketch the graph of each of the following.

39. $y = \tan(\text{Tan}^{-1} x)$
40. $y = \sin(\text{Tan}^{-1} x)$

Challenge **Sketch $y = \arcsin x$ and $y = \arccos x$ on the same coordinate axes.**

1. Give four values of y corresponding to points of intersection of the graphs.

Chapter Summary

1. The curve of a trigonometric function can be drawn from the knowledge of its shape and the values of the function at integral multiples of 90°. (150)
2. Amplitude of a Sine or Cosine Function: The amplitude of the functions, $y = A \sin \theta$ and $y = A \cos \theta$ is the absolute value of A, or $|A|$. (151)
3. Periods of a Sine, Cosine, or Tangent Function: The period of the functions, $y = \sin k\theta$ and $y = \cos k\theta$ is $\frac{360°}{k}$. The period of the function, $y = \tan k\theta$ is $\frac{180°}{k}$. (152)
4. Phase Shift of All Trigonometric Functions: The phase shift of the function, $y = A \sin (k\theta + c)$, is $-\frac{c}{k}$. If $c > 0$, the shift is to the left and if $c < 0$, the shift is to the right. This definition applies to all trigonometric functions. (153)
5. Compound functions can be graphed by graphing each function separately on the same coordinate axes and adding or multiplying the ordinates. (158)
6. Inverses of the Trigonometric Functions:

   The inverse of $\sin x$ is $\arcsin x$.
   The inverse of $\cos x$ is $\arccos x$.
   The inverse of $\tan x$ is $\arctan x$. (162)
7. Arcsine Function: Given $y = \text{Sin } x$, the inverse sine function is defined by the following equation.

   $$y = \text{Sin}^{-1} x \quad \text{or} \quad y = \text{Arcsin } x$$

   Arccosine Function: Given $y = \text{Cos } x$, the inverse cosine function is defined by the following equation.

   $$y = \text{Cos}^{-1} x \quad \text{or} \quad y = \text{Arccos } x$$

   Arctangent Function: Given $y = \text{Tan } x$, the inverse tangent function is defined by the following equation.

   $$y = \text{Tan}^{-1} x \quad \text{or} \quad y = \text{Arctan } x \qquad (165)$$
8. The graph of the inverse of a function can be drawn by reflecting the graph of the given function over the line $x = y$. (167)

Chapter Review

6-1 **State which value is greater.**

1. sin 20° or sin 50°
2. cos 90° or cos 190°
3. cos 28° or cos 29°
4. sin 120° or sin 240°

Graph each function in the indicated interval.

5. $y = \sin x;\ 90° \le x \le 450°$
6. $y = \cos x;\ {}^-90° \le x \le 360°$
7. $y = \tan x;\ {}^-180° \le x \le 180°$
8. $y = \cot x;\ {}^-180° < x < 360°$

6-2 **State the amplitude, period, and phase shift for each of the following.**

9. $y = 4 \cos 2x$
10. $y = 15 \sin \left(\frac{3}{2}x + 90°\right)$
11. $y = 5 \cot \left(\frac{x}{2} - 45°\right)$
12. $y = {}^-\sqrt{3} \cos (x - 180°)$
13. $y = 2 \tan 5x$
14. $y = {}^-7 \sin 5x$

Write an equation of a sine function for each amplitude, period, and phase shift.

15. amplitude = 3, period = 360°, phase shift = 45°
16. amplitude = 17, period = 270°, phase shift = $^-90°$
17. amplitude = $\frac{1}{3}$, period = 180°, phase shift = 90°

Graph each of the following.

18. $y = \frac{1}{2} \sin 2\theta$
19. $y = 3 \cos \frac{\theta}{2}$

6-3

20. $y = 2 \tan (3\theta + 90°)$
21. $y = \sin (4\theta + 60°)$
22. $y = 4 \cos (\theta + 180°)$
23. $y = {}^-3 \sin (\theta - 45°)$

6-4

24. $y = 2 \sin x - \cos x$
25. $y = x + 2 \sin 2x$

6-5 **Write each of the following in the form of an inverse trigonometric relation.**

26. $y = \sin \alpha$
27. $\tan y = x$
28. $n = \cos \theta$

Evaluate each of the following. Assume that angles are acute.

29. $\cos \left(\operatorname{arccos} \frac{1}{2}\right)$
30. $\tan \left(\operatorname{arccot} \frac{4}{5}\right)$
31. $\cot \left(\cos^{-1} \frac{3}{5}\right)$
32. $\sin (\tan^{-1} 1) + \cos (\sin^{-1} 1)$
33. $\tan \left(\arcsin \frac{\sqrt{3}}{2} + \arccos \frac{\sqrt{3}}{2}\right)$

6-6 **Evaluate each of the following.**

34. $\sin \left(\operatorname{Arcsin} \frac{1}{2}\right)$
35. $\cos (\operatorname{Tan}^{-1} 1)$
36. $\sin 2 \left(\operatorname{Arcsin} \frac{1}{2}\right)$
37. $\cos \left(\frac{\pi}{2} - \operatorname{Cos}^{-1} \frac{\sqrt{2}}{2}\right)$
38. $\cos \left(\operatorname{Sin}^{-1} \frac{1}{2}\right)$
39. $\sin \left(3 \operatorname{Sin}^{-1} \frac{\sqrt{3}}{2}\right)$
40. $\sin \left[\operatorname{Cos}^{-1} \left(-\frac{1}{2}\right) + \operatorname{Tan}^{-1} 1\right]$
41. $\cos \left(\operatorname{Arctan} \sqrt{3} + \operatorname{Arcsin} \frac{1}{2}\right)$

6-7 **Write the equation for the inverse of each function or relation.**

42. $y = \arcsin x$
43. $y = x^2 + 1$
44. $y = \operatorname{Cos} x$

45-47. Graph each function and its inverse in problems **42-44**.

48-50. Determine if each inverse in problems **42-44** is a function.

Chapter Test

Find the values of x in degrees for which each of the following is true.

1. $\cos x = 1$
2. $\tan x = 0$
3. $\sin x = {}^{-}1$
4. $\cos x = \frac{\sqrt{2}}{2}$

Graph each function in the indicated interval.

5. $y = \sin x;\ {}^{-}180° \leq x \leq 180°$
6. $y = \tan x;\ 0° \leq x \leq 360°$

State the amplitude, period, and phase shift for each of the following.

7. $y = 2 \sin 2\theta$
8. $y = 3 \cos 4\theta$
9. $y = 110 \sin (15\theta - 40°)$
10. $y = 10 \sin (180° - \alpha)$

Graph each of the following.

11. $y = 3 \cos \frac{\theta}{2}$
12. $y = 2 \sin (4\theta + 90°)$
13. $y = \tan (2\theta - 45°)$
14. $y = 2 \cos x - x$

Evaluate each of the following. Assume that angles are acute.

15. $\sin \left(\arccos \frac{\sqrt{3}}{2}\right)$
16. $\tan \left(\cos^{-1} \frac{5}{13}\right)$
17. $\sec \left(\sin^{-1} \frac{1}{2}\right)$
18. $\cos (\arctan \sqrt{3} + \operatorname{arccot} \sqrt{3})$

Evaluate each of the following.

19. $\sin \left(\text{Arccos} \frac{1}{2}\right)$
20. $\tan \left[\text{Sin}^{-1} \left(-\frac{\sqrt{2}}{2}\right)\right]$
21. $\cos \left(\frac{1}{2} \text{Tan}^{-1} \frac{3}{4}\right)$
22. $\tan \left(\pi + \text{Arcsin} \frac{2}{3}\right)$

Write the equation for the inverse of each function.

23. $y = 3x - 7$
24. $y = \tan x$

25-26. Graph each function and its inverse in problems **23-24**.

27-28. Determine if each inverse in problems **23-24** is a function.

Chapter

7

Applications of Trigonometry

When a cloverleaf intersection is designed many items must be considered. For example, the radii of the interchange loops, the transition curves to the highways, and the bank of the curves all must be designed so that a certain speed will be safe. The applications of trigonometric functions play a prominent part in the layout of a cloverleaf intersection.

7-1 Solving Trigonometric Equations

A **trigonometric equation** is an equation involving a trigonometric function. If the equation is true for all values of the variable, it is an **identity**.

Trigonometric equations may be solved by the same methods used to solve other equations. For example, the use of algebraic techniques such as factoring and substitution may be helpful in solving trigonometric equations.

example

1 Solve $2\sin^2 x - 3\sin x + 1 = 0$ for principal values of x.

$$2\sin^2 x - 3\sin x + 1 = 0$$
$$(2\sin x - 1)(\sin x - 1) = 0 \quad \textit{Factor.}$$

$2\sin x - 1 = 0$ or $\sin x - 1 = 0$

$\sin x = \frac{1}{2}$ $\qquad \sin x = 1$

$x = \text{Arcsin}\,\frac{1}{2}$ $\qquad x = \text{Arcsin}\,1$

$x = 30°$ $\qquad x = 90°$

The solutions are 30° and 90°.

Usually trigonometric equations are solved for principal values of the variable. However, there are other solutions which differ by integral multiples of the period of the function.

example

2 Solve $2\tan x \sin x + 2\sin x = \tan x + 1$ for all values of x.

$$2\tan x \sin x + 2\sin x = \tan x + 1$$
$$2\tan x \sin x + 2\sin x - \tan x - 1 = 0$$
$$(\tan x + 1)(2\sin x - 1) = 0$$

$\tan x + 1 = 0$ or $2\sin x - 1 = 0$

$\tan x = {}^-1$ $\qquad \sin x = \frac{1}{2}$

$x = \arctan({}^-1)$ $\qquad x = \arcsin\frac{1}{2}$

$x = {}^-45° + n \cdot 180°$ $\qquad x = 30° + n \cdot 360°$

The solutions are $^-45° + n \cdot 180°$ and $30° + n \cdot 360°$ where n is any integer.

example

3 **Solve $\sin(x + 30°) = \cos 2x$ if $0 \le x \le 90°$.**

$\sin(x + 30°) = \cos 2x$

$(x + 30°) + 2x = 90°$

$3x = 60°$ or $x = 20°$

If $\sin A = \cos B$, then $A + B = 90°$ since the sine and cosine are cofunctions.

The solution is 20°.

If an equation cannot be easily solved by factoring, try writing the expressions in terms of only one trigonometric function.

example

4 **Solve $2\sin^2 x - \cos x - 1 = 0$ for all values of x.**

$2\sin^2 x - \cos x - 1 = 0$

$2(1 - \cos^2 x) - \cos x - 1 = 0$ *$\sin^2 x = 1 - \cos^2 x$*

$2\cos^2 x + \cos x - 1 = 0$

$(2\cos x - 1)(\cos x + 1) = 0$

$2\cos x - 1 = 0$ or $\cos x + 1 = 0$

$\cos x = \frac{1}{2}$ $\qquad$ $\cos x = {}^-1$

$x = \arccos \frac{1}{2}$ $\qquad$ $x = \arccos({}^-1)$

$x = 60° + n \cdot 360°$ and $300° + n \cdot 360°$ $\qquad$ $x = 180° + n \cdot 360°$

The solutions are $60° + n \cdot 360°$, $300° + n \cdot 360°$, and $180° + n \cdot 360°$ for any integer n.

Some trigonometric equations have no solutions. In other words, there is no replacement for the variable that will result in a true sentence. For example, the equation $\sin x = 2$ has no solution. *Why?*

example

5 **Solve $2\sin^2 x + 3\sin x - 2 = 0$ for principal values of x.**

$2\sin^2 x + 3\sin x - 2 = 0$

$(2\sin x - 1)(\sin x + 2) = 0$

$2\sin x - 1 = 0$ or $\sin x + 2 = 0$

$\sin x = \frac{1}{2}$ $\qquad$ $\sin x = {}^-2$

$x = \text{Arcsin}\, \frac{1}{2}$ $\qquad$ $x = \text{Arcsin}\,({}^-2)$ *There is no solution since $\sin x$ is in the interval ${}^-1 \le \sin x \le 1$.*

$x = 30°$

The solution is 30°.

It is important to check your solutions. Some algebraic operations may introduce answers that are *not* solutions to the original equation.

exercises

Exploratory Solve each equation for principal values of x.

1. $2 \cos x - 1 = 0$
2. $2 \sin x + 1 = 0$
3. $\sqrt{2} \sin x - 1 = 0$
4. $2 \cos x - \sqrt{3} = 0$
5. $2 \cos x + 1 = 0$
6. $\sqrt{3} \tan x + 1 = 0$
7. $\sin 2x - 1 = 0$
8. $\cos 3x - 0.5 = 0$
9. $\tan 2x - \sqrt{3} = 0$

Each equation has how many solutions if $0° \leq \theta \leq 360°$?

10. $\sin \theta = 1$
11. $\cos \theta = -\frac{\sqrt{3}}{2}$
12. $\tan \theta = {}^{-}3$
13. $\sin 2\theta = \frac{1}{2}$
14. $\sin 2\theta = -\frac{\sqrt{3}}{2}$
15. $\sin 3\theta = {}^{-}2$
16. $\sin^2 2\theta = \frac{1}{2}$
17. $\tan^2 2\theta = 3$
18. $\sin \frac{1}{2}\theta = -\frac{\sqrt{3}}{2}$

Written Solve each equation for general values of x.

1. $2 \sin^2 x - \sin x - 1 = 0$
2. $\sin x + \sin x \cos x = 0$
3. $2 \sin^2 x - 1 = 0$
4. $2 \sin x + \sqrt{3} = 0$
5. $\tan^2 x - 1 = 0$
6. $\cos x - 2 \cos x \sin x = 0$
7. $4 \cos^2 x = 1$
8. $\sqrt{3} \cot x + 1 = 0$
9. $2 \cos^2 x - 5 \cos x + 2 = 0$
10. $\sin (x + 10°) = \cos 3x$

Solve each equation for principal values of x.

11. $2 \sin^2 x + \sin x = 0$
12. $\sqrt{2} \cos x - 1 = 0$
13. $4 \sin^2 x - 3 = 0$
14. $\tan 2x = \cot x$
15. $2 \cos^2 x = \sin x + 1$
16. $2 \tan x - 4 = 0$
17. $\sin^2 x - 3 \sin x + 2 = 0$
18. $\sin x + \cos x = 0$
19. $\sin 2x = \cos x$
20. $\cos^2 x - \frac{7}{2} \cos x - 2 = 0$
21. $\tan x + \cot x = 2$
22. $\sin 2x = 2 \cos x$
23. $\sin^2 x - \sin x = 0$
24. $\cos x \tan x - \sin^2 x = 0$
25. $\sin^2 x - 2 \sin x - 3 = 0$
26. $\sin^2 x - 2 \sin x - 1 = 0$
27. $\sqrt{3} \cot x \sin x + 2 \cos^2 x = 0$
28. $3 \cos 2x - 5 \cos x = 1$
29. $\sin^2 x = \cos x - 1$
30. $\tan x + \sec x = \sqrt{3}$
31. $\tan^2 x = 3 \tan x$
32. $3 \tan^2 x + 4 \sec x + 4 = 0$
33. $3 \sin^2 x - \cos^2 x = 0$
34. $4 \tan x + \sin 2x = 0$
35. $\sin 2x \sin x + \cos 2x \cos x = 1$
36. $\cos 2x + 3 \cos x - 1 = 0$
37. $\sin 2x = \cos 3x$
38. $\cos 2x + \sin x = 1$
39. $\sin 2x = 2 \sin x$
40. $2 \sin x \cos x + 4 \sin x = \cos x + 2$

Using Mathematics

Interpreting blueprints requires the ability to select and use trigonometric functions and geometric properties. The figure below represents a plan for an improvement to a roof. The metal fitting shown makes a 30° angle with the horizontal. The vertices of the geometric shapes are not labeled in these plans. Relevant information must be selected and the appropriate function used to find the unknown measures.

Example Find the unknown measures in the figure at the right.

Roofing Improvement

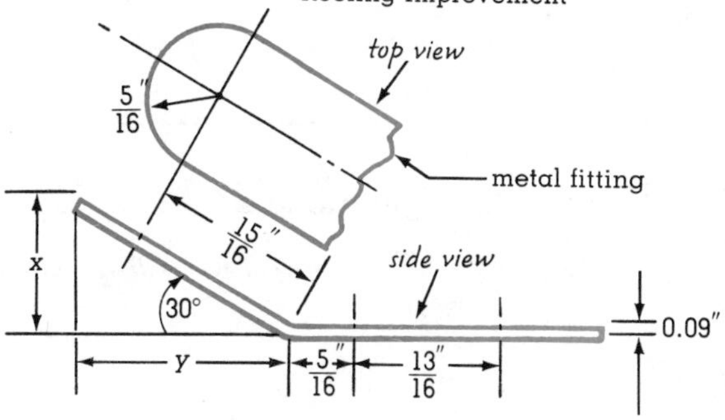

The measures x and y are the legs of a right triangle.

The measure of the hypotenuse is $\frac{15''}{16} + \frac{5''}{16}$ or $\frac{20''}{16}$.

$$\frac{y}{\frac{20}{16}} = \cos 30°$$

$$\frac{x}{\frac{20}{16}} = \sin 30°$$

$y = 1.08''$ $\quad$ $x = 0.63''$

Exercises Find the unknown measures of each of the following.

1. Chimney on Roof

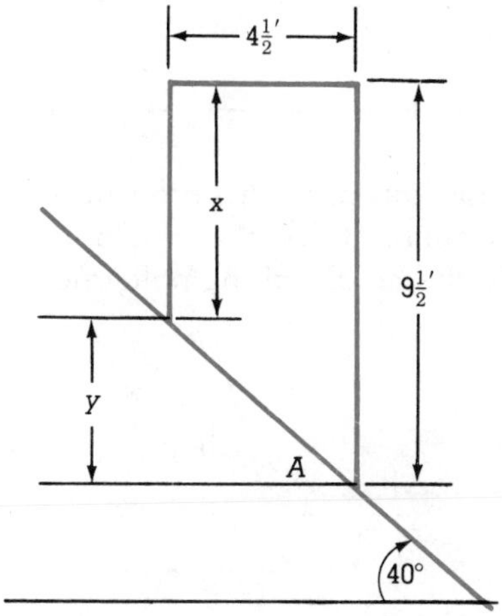

2. Air Vent

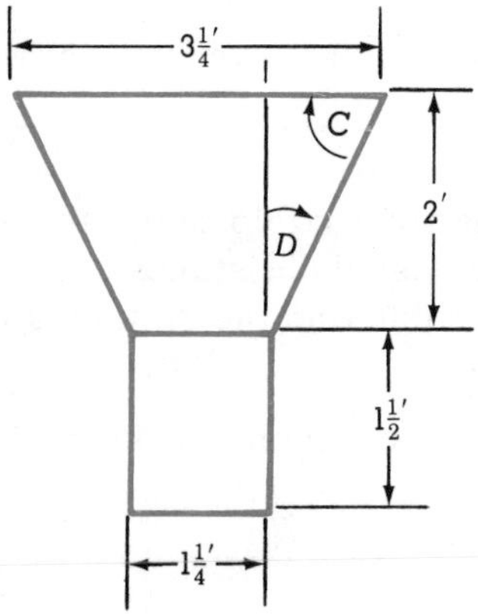

3. Elbow Joint

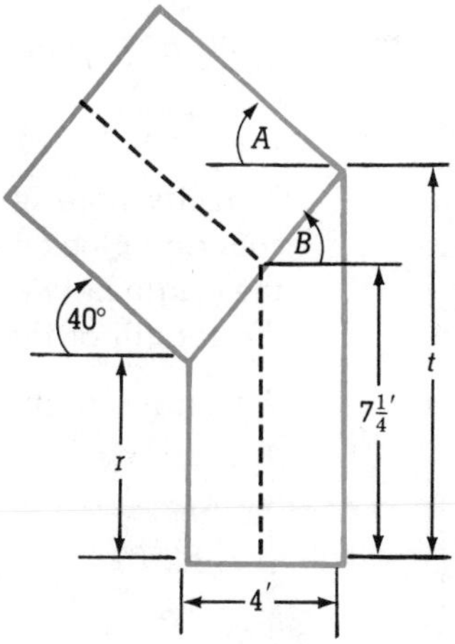

7-2 Right Triangles

Trigonometric functions can be used to solve problems involving right triangles. Usually, two measures such as a side and an angle or two sides are known and the measure of a side or an angle is to be found.

Recall the definitions of the trigonometric functions using right triangle ABC.

SOH-CAH-TOA is a helpful mnemonic device for remembering the first three equations.

$$\text{sin} = \frac{\text{opposite}}{\text{hypotenuse}} \qquad \text{cos} = \frac{\text{adjacent}}{\text{hypotenuse}} \qquad \text{tan} = \frac{\text{opposite}}{\text{adjacent}}$$

$$\sin A = \frac{a}{c} \qquad \csc A = \frac{c}{a}$$

$$\cos A = \frac{b}{c} \qquad \sec A = \frac{c}{b}$$

$$\tan A = \frac{a}{b} \qquad \cot A = \frac{b}{a}$$

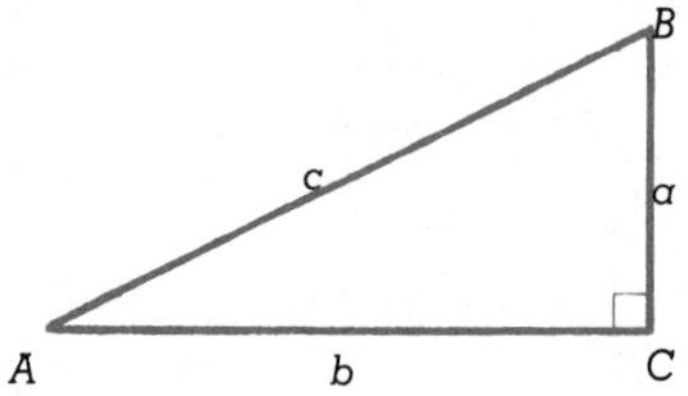

example

1 **Solve the right triangle.**

To solve a right triangle means to find all the measures of the sides and angles.

$49° + B = 90°$ *Angles A and B are complementary.*

$B = 41°$

$\frac{7}{c} = \sin 49°$

$\frac{7}{c} = 0.7547$

$c = 9.3$ *Round to the nearest tenth.*

$\frac{7}{b} = \tan 49°$

$\frac{7}{b} = 1.150$

$b = 6.1$ *Round to the nearest tenth.*

Therefore, $B = 41°$, $c = 9.3$, and $b = 6.1$.

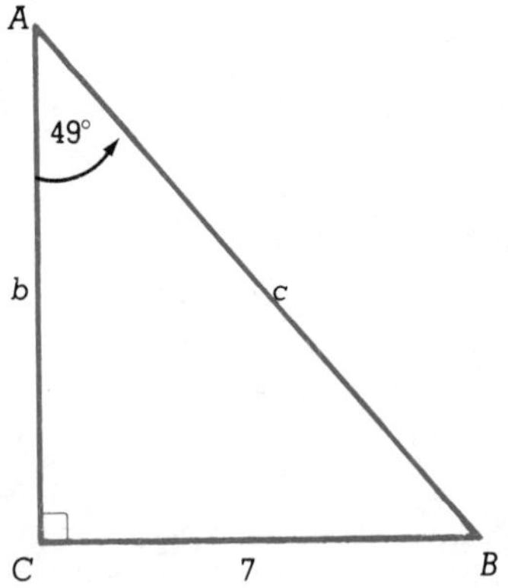

The following examples illustrate applications of trigonometry.

examples

2 **A utility pole is braced by a cable attached to it at the top and anchored in a concrete block at ground level a distance of 4 meters from the base of the pole. If the angle between the cable and the ground is 73° find the height of the pole and the length of the cable.**

Write an equation using a trigonometric function.

$\frac{h}{4} = \tan 73°$

$\frac{h}{4} = 3.2709$ *Solve for h.*

$h = 13.1$

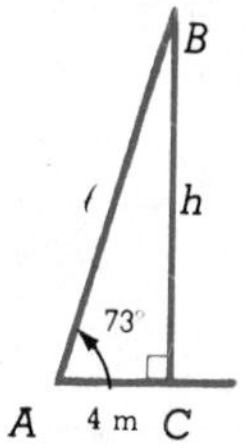

Find the length of the cable in a similar manner.

$\frac{4}{\ell} = \cos 73°$

$\frac{4}{\ell} = 0.2924$

$\ell = 13.8$

The height of the pole is about 13.1 meters and the length of the cable is about 13.8 meters.

3 **A 7 meter ladder leans against a building. It forms an angle with the building measuring 16°. How far is the foot of the ladder from the base of the building?**

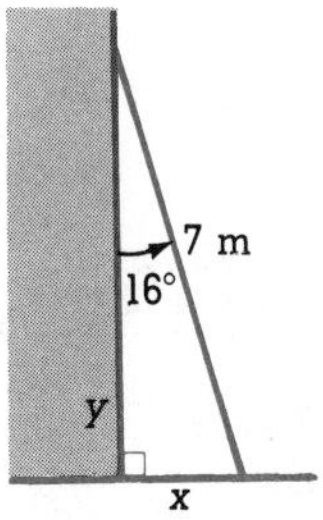

$\frac{x}{7} = \sin 16°$

$\frac{x}{7} = 0.2756$

$x = 1.9$

The foot of the ladder is about 1.9 meters from the building.

In problems where an observer is involved, an angle of elevation or an angle of depression is frequently given. An **angle of elevation** is the angle between a horizontal line and the line of sight from the observer to an object at a higher level. An **angle of depression** is the angle between a horizontal line and the line of sight from the observer to an object at a lower level.

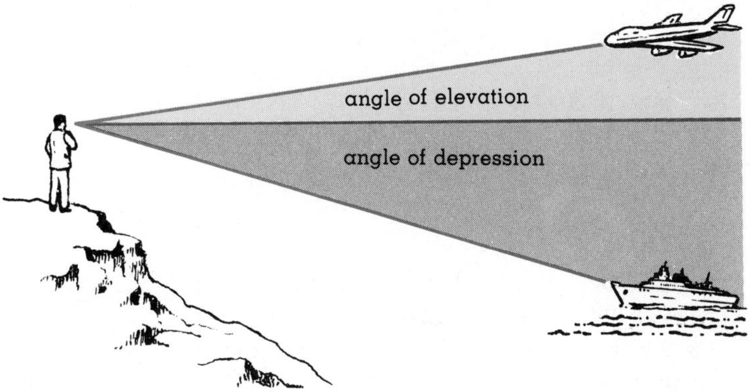

example

4 **When the angle of elevation of the sun is 27°, the shadow of a tree is 25 meters long. How tall is the tree?**

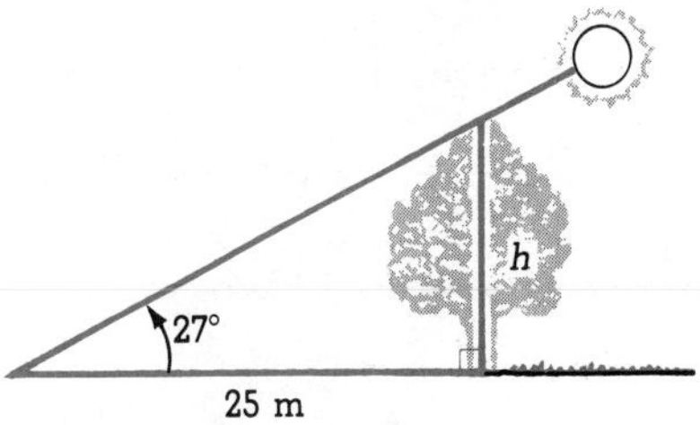

$\frac{h}{25} = \tan 27°$

$\frac{h}{25} = 0.5095$

$h = 12.7$

The tree is about 12.7 meters tall.

example

5 **Felipe is standing on top of a 200-foot cliff above a lake. The measurement of the angle of depression to a boat on the lake is 21°. How far is the boat from the base of the cliff?**

$$\frac{200}{x} = \tan 21°$$
$$= 0.3839$$
$$x = 521$$

The angle of elevation from the boat to the top of the cliff is also 21°. Why?

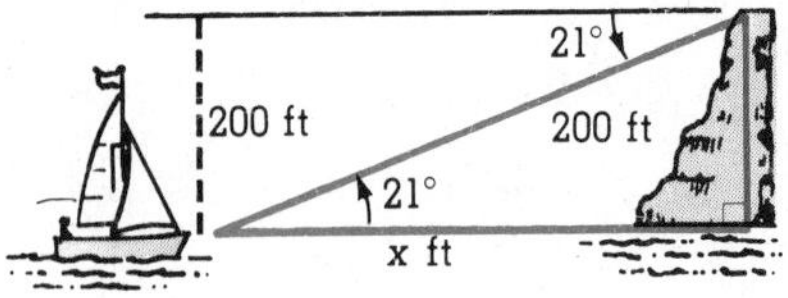

The boat is about 521 feet from the base of the cliff.

exercises

Exploratory **State equations that would enable you to solve each problem. Use the triangle at the right.**

1. If $A = 20°$ and $c = 35$, find a.
2. If $b = 13$ and $A = 76°$, find a.
3. If $a = 6$ and $c = 12$, find B.
4. If $a = 21.2$ and $b = 9$, find A.
5. If $B = 16°$ and $c = 13$, find a.
6. If $A = 49°13'$ and $a = 10$, find b.
7. If $c = 16$ and $a = 7$, find b.
8. If $a = 7$ and $b = 12$, find A.
9. If $a = 5$ and $b = 6$, find c.
10. If $B = 78°8'$ and $a = 4.1$, find c.

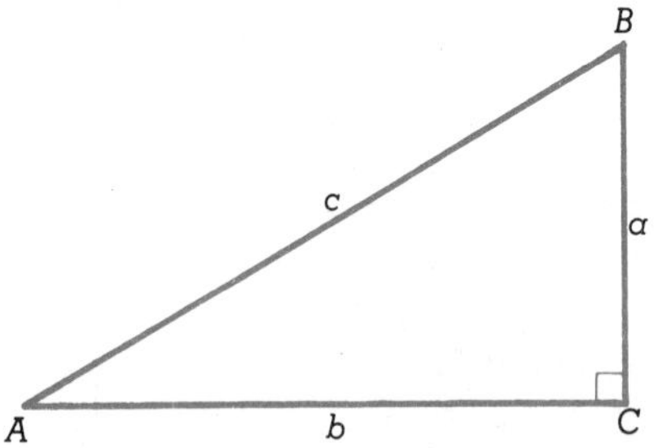

11. The base angles of an isosceles triangle are 57°30′, and the base is 7.5 cm long. Find the equal sides and the altitude to the base.

12. A TV tower is 250 meters high and casts a shadow 176 meters long. Find the angle of elevation of the sun to the nearest minute.

Written **Suppose ΔABC is a right triangle. Let A and B be the acute angles, and a and b be the measures of the sides opposite these angles. The measure of the hypotenuse is c. Solve each triangle.**

1. $A = 41°$, $b = 7.44$
2. $B = 42°10'$, $a = 9$
3. $b = 22$, $A = 22°22'$
4. $a = 21$, $c = 30$
5. $A = 45°$, $c = 7\sqrt{2}$
6. $a = 31.2$, $c = 42.4$
7. $A = 37°15'$, $b = 11$
8. $a = 11$, $b = 21$
9. $A = 55°55'$, $c = 16$

Solve each problem. Round all answers to two decimal places or the nearest minute.

10. A ladder is 6 meters long, stands on level ground, and rests against a wall at a point 4 meters from the ground. How far from the wall is the foot of the ladder?

11. A regular hexagon is inscribed in a circle whose diameter is 7.52 cm. Find the length of its apothem (the distance from the center to the midpoint of a side).

12. A regular pentagon has an apothem of 7.43 centimeters. Find the length of a side of the pentagon and the radius of the circumscribed circle.

13. A monument is 112.5 meters high and casts a shadow 201.2 meters long. Find the angle of elevation of the sun.

14. Find the bearing of a road that runs directly from A to B, with B being 3 miles north and 1.7 miles east of A. (The bearing of B from A is the positive angle with vertex at A measured clockwise from north to B.)

15. A flagpole 40 feet high stands on top of a building. From a point P on the street, the angle of elevation of the top of the pole is 54°54′ and the angle of elevation of the bottom of the pole is 47°30′. How high is the building?

16. A rectangle is 17.5 cm by 26.2 cm. Find the angle made by the longer side and a diagonal.

17. A 7.4 cm chord subtends a central angle of 41° in a circle. Find the radius of the circle.

18. The diameter of a circle is 13.4 cm. Find the length of a chord that subtends a central angle of 26°20′.

19. Find the area of a regular pentagon that is inscribed in a circle whose diameter is 7.3 cm.

20. To find the height of a mountain peak two points, A and B, were located on a plain in line with the peak and the angles of elevation were measured from each point. The angle at A was 36°40′ and the angle at B was 21°10′. The distance from A to B was 570 feet. How high is the peak above the level of the plain?

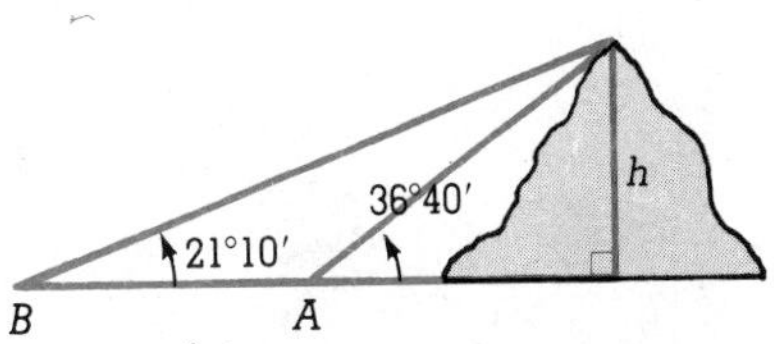

21. A mountain peak stands near a level plain on which are two farm houses C and D that are in a straight line from the peak. The angle of depression from the peak to C is 49°42′, and the angle of depression to D is 26°27′. The peak is known to be 1004 feet above the level of the plain. Find the distance from C to D.

22. Mr. Riegle observes that the angle of elevation of the top of a building is 41°30′. After moving back a distance of 265 feet and in the same vertical plane with the building, Mr. Riegle finds that the angle of elevation of the top of the building is now 28°10′. Find the height of the building.

23. In order to find the height of a chimney CT, the angle of elevation of the top T is measured by means of a transit from point A, whose distance from the chimney is not known. Then the transit is turned through a horizontal angle of 90° and point B is located. At B the angle of elevation of the top of the chimney is measured again. Find the height of the chimney if $\angle CAT$ is 37°17′, $\angle CBT$ is 24°42′, and AB is 73 meters.

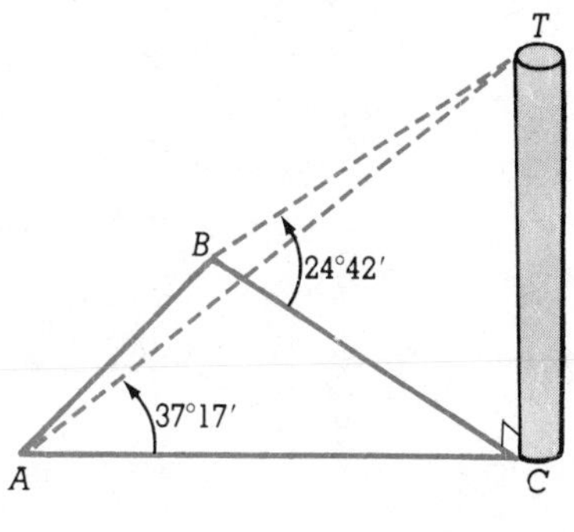

7-3 The Law of Sines

The trigonometric functions also can be used to solve problems involving triangles that are not right triangles.

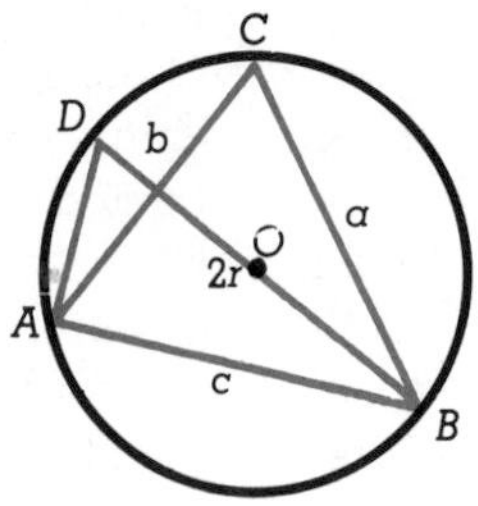

Consider $\triangle ABC$ which is inscribed in a circle with a diameter through vertex B. Let $2r$ be the length of the diameter. Draw $\overline{AD}$. Then $\angle D \cong \angle C$ and $\sin C = \sin D$. But $\angle BAD$ is a right angle, so $\sin D = \frac{c}{2r}$. Thus, $\sin C = \frac{c}{2r}$ or $\frac{c}{\sin C} = 2r$. Similarly, by drawing diameters through A and C, $\frac{b}{\sin B} = 2r$ and $\frac{a}{\sin A} = 2r$. The following equations can be written.

$$\frac{a}{\sin A} = \frac{b}{\sin B} = \frac{c}{\sin C}$$

These equations are known as the Law of Sines. It states that the ratio of any side of a triangle to the sine of the angle opposite that side is a constant for a given triangle. For example, in a 30°-60° right triangle with sides 1, $\sqrt{3}$, and 2, the ratios are $\frac{1}{\sin 30°} = \frac{\sqrt{3}}{\sin 60°} = \frac{2}{\sin 90°}$. *The ratio is 2 to 1 in this case.*

> Let $\triangle ABC$ be any triangle with a, b, and c representing the measures of sides opposite angles with measurements A, B, and C respectively. Then, the following equations are true.
>
> $$\frac{a}{\sin A} = \frac{b}{\sin B} = \frac{c}{\sin C}$$

Law of Sines

example

1 Solve the triangle on the right.

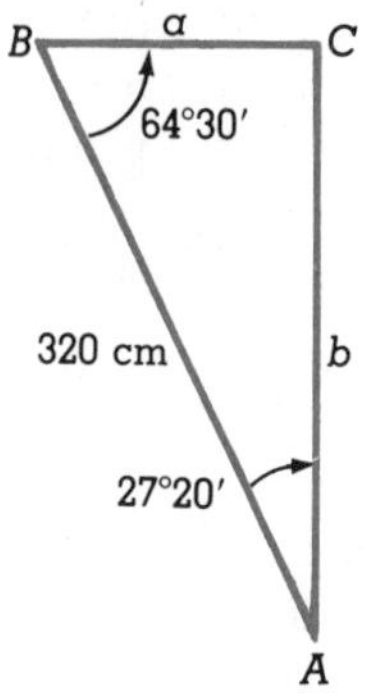

Find the measurement of $\angle C$.

$27°20' + 64°30' + C = 180°$

$C = 180° - 27°20' - 64°30'$ or $88°10'$

Use the Law of Sines to find a and b.

$$\frac{c}{\sin C} = \frac{a}{\sin A}$$
$$\frac{320}{\sin 88°10'} = \frac{a}{\sin 27°20'}$$
$$a = \frac{320 \sin 27°20'}{\sin 88°10'}$$
$$= \frac{320(0.4592)}{0.9995}$$
$$= 147$$

$$\frac{c}{\sin C} = \frac{b}{\sin B}$$
$$\frac{320}{\sin 88°10'} = \frac{b}{\sin 64°30'}$$
$$b = \frac{320 \sin 64°30'}{\sin 88°10'}$$
$$= \frac{320(0.9026)}{0.9995}$$
$$= 289$$

Therefore, $C = 88°10'$, a is 147 cm and b is 289 cm.

When the lengths of two sides of a triangle and the measurement of the angle opposite one of them is given, one solution does not always exist. In such a case, one of the following will be true.

1. No triangle exists.
2. Exactly one triangle exists.
3. Two triangles exist.

In other words, there may be no solution, one solution, or two solutions.

Suppose you are given a, b, and A. Consider the case where $A < 90°$.

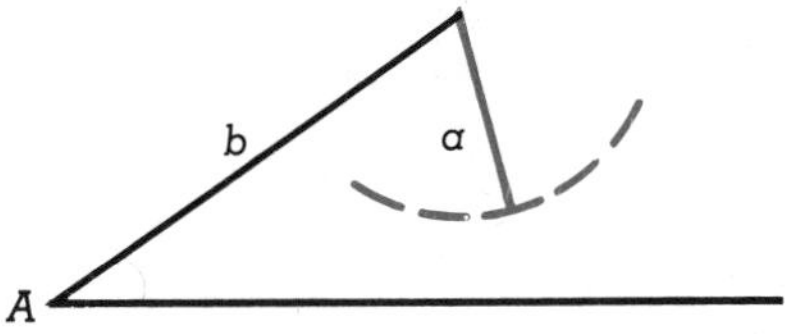

If $a < b \sin A$, no solution exists.

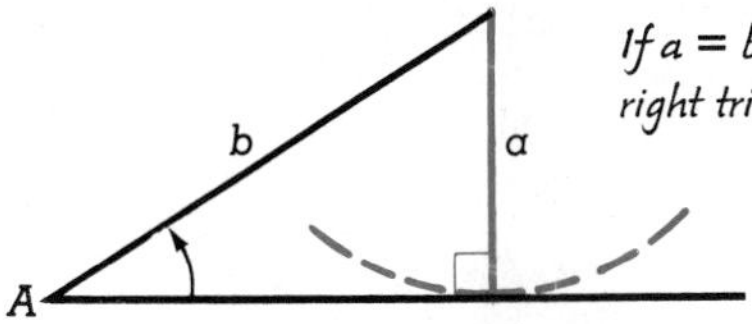

If $a = b \sin A$, the solution is a right triangle.

If $a = b \sin A$, one solution exists.

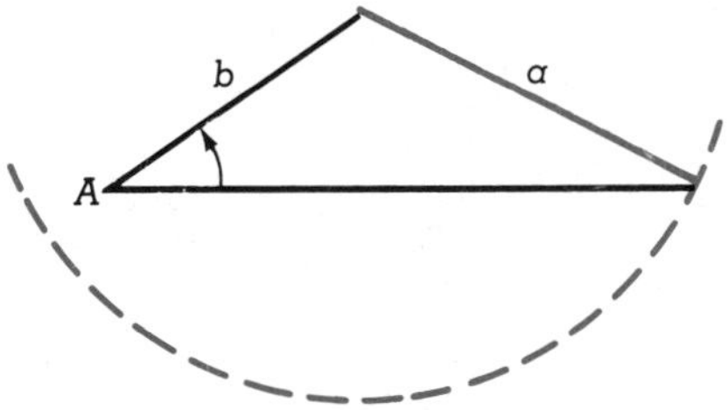

If $a > b \sin A$ and $a > b$, one solution exists.

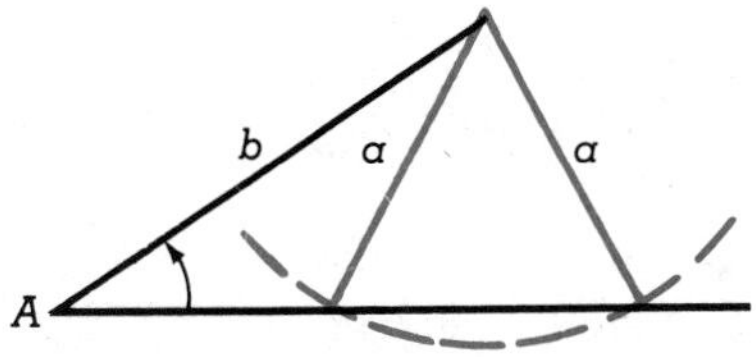

If $b \sin A < a < b$, two solutions exist.

Consider the case where $A \geq 90°$.

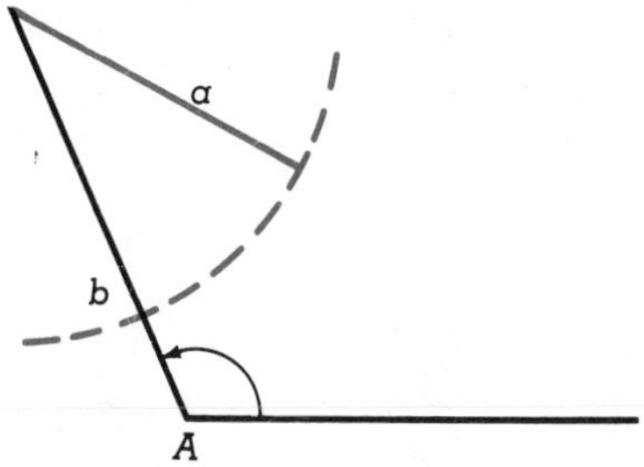

If $a \leq b$, no solution exists.

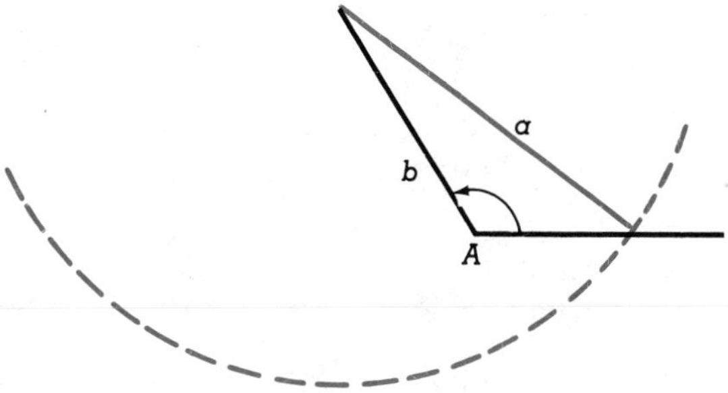

If $a > b$, one solution exists.

examples

2 **Solve the triangle where $A = 63°10'$, $b = 18$, and $a = 17$.**

$$\begin{aligned} b \sin A &= 18 \sin 63°10' \\ &= 18(0.8923) \\ &= 16.1 \end{aligned}$$

Since $63°10' < 90°$ and $16.1 < 17 < 18$, two solutions exist.

$$\frac{17}{\sin 63°10'} = \frac{18}{\sin B}$$

$$\begin{aligned} \sin B &= \frac{18 \sin 63°10'}{17} \\ &= \frac{18(0.8923)}{17} \\ &= 0.9448 \end{aligned}$$

$B = 70°50'$ or $B = 109°10'$ *Round to the nearest 10 minutes.*

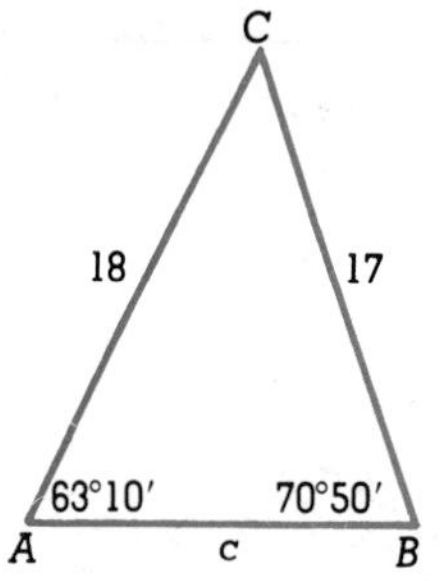

$$63°10' + 70°50' + C = 180°$$
$$\begin{aligned} C &= 180° - (63°10' + 70°50') \\ &= 46° \end{aligned}$$

$$\frac{17}{\sin 63°10'} = \frac{c}{\sin 46°}$$
$$\begin{aligned} c &= \frac{17 \sin 46°}{\sin 63°10'} \\ &= \frac{17(0.7193)}{0.8923} \\ &= 13.7 \end{aligned}$$

One solution is $B = 70°50'$ $C = 46°$, and $c = 13.7$.

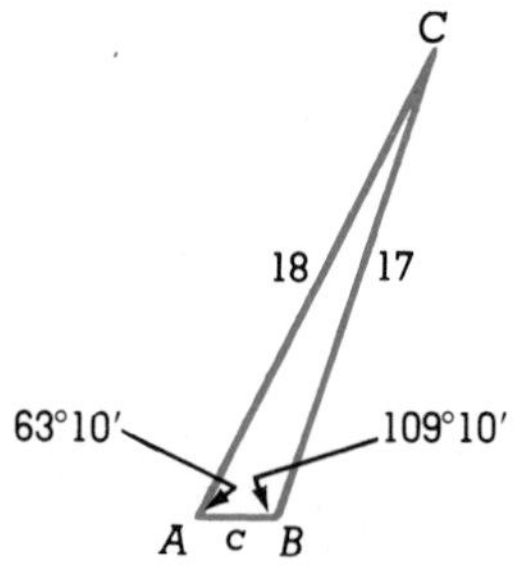

$$63°10' + 109°10' + C = 180°$$
$$\begin{aligned} C &= 180° - (63°10' + 109°10') \\ &= 7°40' \end{aligned}$$

$$\frac{17}{\sin 63°10'} = \frac{c}{\sin 7°40'}$$
$$\begin{aligned} c &= \frac{17 \sin 7°40'}{\sin 63°10'} \\ &= \frac{17(0.1334)}{0.8923} \\ &= 2.5 \end{aligned}$$

Another solution is $B = 109°10'$ $C = 7°40'$, and $c = 2.5$.

3 **Solve the triangle where $A = 40°$, $b = 16$, and $a = 9$.**

$$\begin{aligned} b \sin A &= 16 \sin 40° \\ &= 16(0.6428) \\ &= 10.28 \end{aligned}$$

Since $40° < 90°$ and $9 < 10.28$, no solution exists.

exercises

Exploratory State if the given information determines one triangle, two triangles, or no triangle.

1. $A = 140°, b = 10, a = 3$
2. $C = 17°, a = 10, c = 11$
3. $B = 160°, a = 10, A = 41°$
4. $A = 30°, a = 4, b = 8$
5. $A = 43°, b = 20, a = 11$
6. $A = 60°, b = 2, a = \sqrt{3}$
7. $a = 20, b = 19, A = 90°$
8. $A = 38°, b = 10, a = 8$
9. $A = 118°, b = 11, a = 17$
10. $A = 58°, a = 17, b = 13$
11. $c = 4, C = 30°, b = 10$
12. $b = 2, B = 140°, a = 3$

State an equation which would enable you to solve each triangle described below. Do *not* solve.

13. If $A = 40°$, $B = 60°$, and $a = 20$, find b.
14. If $b = 2.8$, $A = 53°$, and $B = 61°$, find a.
15. If $b = 10$, $a = 14$, and $A = 50°$, find B.

Written Determine the number of possible solutions. If a solution exists, solve the triangle.

1. $a = 8, A = 49°, B = 57°$
2. $a = 6, b = 8, A = 150°$
3. $A = 37°20', B = 51°30', c = 125$
4. $a = 26, b = 29, A = 58°$
5. $A = 40°, B = 60°, c = 20$
6. $A = 29°10', B = 62°20', c = 11.5$
7. $b = 40, a = 32, A = 125°20'$
8. $B = 70°, C = 58°, a = 84$
9. $a = 12, b = 14, A = 90°$
10. $A = 107°13', a = 17.2, c = 12.2$
11. $A = 25°, a = 125, b = 150$
12. $A = 76°, a = 5, b = 20$

Solve each problem. Round all answers to two decimal places or the nearest minute.

13. A triangular lot faces two streets which meet at an angle measuring 85°. The sides of the lot facing the street are each 160 feet in length. Find the perimeter of the lot.
14. A flower bed is in the shape of an obtuse triangle. One angle is 45°, the side opposite is 28 feet, and another side is 36 feet. Find the remaining angles and side.
15. A building 60 feet tall is on top of a hill. A surveyor is at a point on the hill and observes the angle of elevation to the top of the building has measurement 42° and to the bottom of the building has measurement 18°. How far is the surveyor from the bottom of the building?
16. A 35 foot pole stands vertically on a uniformly sloped hillside. At a time when the angle of elevation of the sun is 37°12′ the shadow of the pole extends directly down the slope. If the hillside has an angle of inclination of 6°40′, find the length of the shadow.

Use the Law of Sines to show that each statement is true.

17. $\frac{a - c}{c} = \frac{\sin A - \sin C}{\sin C}$
18. $\frac{b + c}{b - c} = \frac{\sin B + \sin C}{\sin B - \sin C}$
19. $\frac{a}{b} = \frac{\sin A}{\sin B}$
20. $\frac{b}{a + b} = \frac{\sin B}{\sin A + \sin B}$
21. Use the Law of Sines to show that the bisector of an interior angle of a triangle divides the opposite side into parts that have the same ratio as the sides adjacent to the angle bisected.

7-4 The Law of Cosines

If two sides and the included angle or three sides of a triangle are given, the Law of Sines *cannot* be used to solve the triangle. Another formula is needed.

Consider $\triangle ABC$ with height measuring h units and sides measuring a units, b units, and c units. Suppose segment DC is x units long. Then segment BD is $(a - x)$ units long.

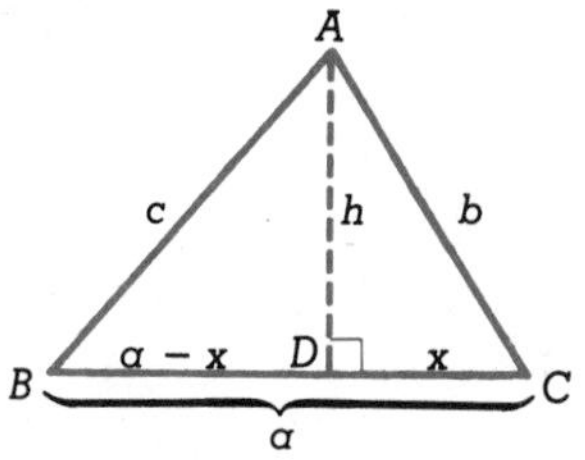

The Pythagorean Theorem and the definition of the cosine function can be used to show how $\angle C$, a, b, c, are related.

$c^2 = (a - x)^2 + h^2$	*Use the Pythagorean Theorem.*
$= a^2 - 2ax + x^2 + h^2$	*Expand* $(a - x)^2$
$= a^2 - 2ax + b^2$	$b^2 = x^2 + h^2$
$= a^2 - 2a(b \cos C) + b^2$	$\cos C = \frac{x}{b}$ *so* $x = b \cos C$
$= a^2 + b^2 - 2ab \cos C$	

By drawing altitudes from B and C, similar formulas for a^2 and b^2 can be found. All three formulas, the Law of Cosines, can be summarized as follows.

Let $\triangle ABC$ be any triangle with a, b, and c representing the measures of sides opposite angles with measurements A, B, and C respectively. Then, the following equations are true.

$$a^2 = b^2 + c^2 - 2bc \cos A$$
$$b^2 = a^2 + c^2 - 2ac \cos B$$
$$c^2 = a^2 + b^2 - 2ab \cos C$$

Law of Cosines

examples

1 Solve the triangle where $S = 48°40'$, $r = 32.4$, and $t = 26.7$.

$s^2 = r^2 + t^2 - 2rt \cos S$ *Use the Law of Cosines.*

$= (32.4)^2 + (26.7)^2 - 2(32.4)(26.7) \cos 48°40'$

$= (32.4)^2 + (26.7)^2 - 2(32.4)(26.7)(0.6604)$

$= 620$

$s = 24.9$

$$\frac{24.9}{\sin 48°40'} = \frac{32.4}{\sin R}$$ *Use the Law of Sines.*

$$\sin R = \frac{32.4 \sin 48°40'}{24.9}$$

$$= \frac{32.4(0.7509)}{24.9}$$

$$= 0.9771$$

$$R = 77°40'$$ *Round to the nearest 10 minutes.*

$$48°40' + 77°40' + T = 180°$$

$$T = 180° - 48°40' - 77°40'$$

$$= 53°40'$$

Therefore, $s = 24.9$, $R = 77°40'$, and $T = 53°40'$.

2 **Solve the triangle where $a = 7.23$, $b = 5.81$, and $c = 4.93$.**

$$(7.23)^2 = (5.81)^2 + (4.93)^2 - 2(5.81)(4.93) \cos A$$ *Use the Law of Cosines.*

$$\cos A = \frac{(5.81)^2 + (4.93)^2 - (7.23)^2}{2(5.81)(4.93)}$$

$$= 0.1011$$

$$A = 84°10'$$

$$\frac{\sin 84°10'}{7.23} = \frac{\sin B}{5.81}$$ *Use the Law of Sines.*

$$\sin B = \frac{5.81 \sin 84°10'}{7.23}$$

$$\sin B = \frac{5.81(0.9948)}{7.23}$$

$$= 0.7994$$

$$B = 53°$$

$$84°10' + 53° + C = 180°$$

$$C = 180° - 84°10' - 53°$$

$$= 42°50'$$

Therefore, $A = 84°10'$, $B = 53°$, and $C = 42°50'$.

exercises

Exploratory In each of the following, three parts of a triangle are given. Determine whether the Law of Sines or the Law of Cosines would be used first to solve the triangle.

1. $a = 14$, $b = 15$, $c = 16$
2. $C = 35°$, $a = 11$, $b = 10.5$
3. $a = 10$, $A = 40°$, $c = 8$
4. $A = 40°$, $b = 6$, $c = 7$
5. $c = 21$, $a = 14$, $B = 60°$
6. $A = 40°$, $C = 70°$, $c = 14$
7. $c = 10.3$, $a = 21$, $b = 16.7$
8. $c = 14.1$, $A = 29°$, $b = 7.8$
9. $b = 17$, $B = 45°28'$, $a = 12$
10. $A = 28°50'$, $b = 4$, $c = 2.9$

Written Solve each triangle.

1. $A = 52°10'$, $b = 6$, $c = 8$
2. $a = 4$, $b = 5$, $c = 7$
3. $b = 7$, $c = 10$, $A = 51°$
4. $A = 52°40'$, $b = 540$, $c = 490$
5. $a = 5$, $b = 6$, $c = 7$
6. $C = 105°18'$, $a = 6.11$, $b = 5.84$
7. $A = 61°25'$, $b = 191$, $c = 205$
8. $a = 3$, $b = 7$, $c = 5$
9. $b = 13$, $a = 21.5$, $C = 39°20'$
10. $a = 11.4$, $b = 13.7$, $c = 12.2$
11. $A = 40°$, $B = 59°$, $c = 14$
12. $a = 9$, $c = 5$, $B = 120°$

Solve each problem.

13. The sides of a triangle are 6.8 cm, 8.4 cm, and 4.9 cm. Find the measure of the smallest angle.
14. The sides of a parallelogram are 55 cm and 71 cm. Find the length of each diagonal if the larger angle is 106°.
15. Nathan is flying from Chicago to Columbus, a distance of 300 miles. He starts his flight 15° off course and flies on this course for 75 miles. How far is he from Columbus?
16. Two ships leave San Francisco at the same time. One travels 40° west of north at a speed of 20 knots. The other travels 10° west of south at a speed of 15 knots. How far apart are they after 11 hours?
17. A 40 foot television antenna stands on top of a building. From a point on the ground, the angles of elevation of the top and bottom of the antenna, respectively have measurements of 56° and 42°. How tall is the building?
18. From a point of observation on a level plain the distance to one of two houses is 253 meters and to the other house is 319 meters. What is the distance between the houses if the angle subtended by them at the point of observation is 42°12'?

7-5 Area of a Triangle

The area of a triangle can be expressed in terms of two sides of the triangle and the measure of the included angle.

Suppose lengths b and c and the measure of the included angle A in $\triangle ABC$ are given. Let K represent the area of $\triangle ABC$ and let h represent the length of the altitude from B. Then $K = \frac{1}{2}bh$.

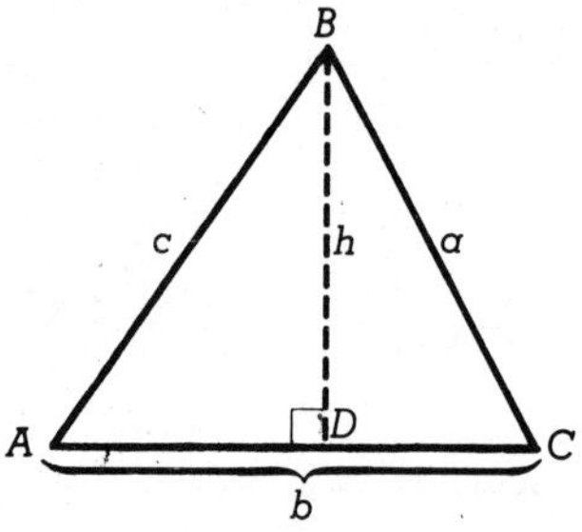

But, $\frac{h}{c} = \sin A$ or $h = c \sin A$.

By substituting $c \sin A$ for h, you obtain the following formula.

$$K = \frac{1}{2}bc \sin A$$

Similarly, if altitudes are drawn from A and C, the formulas, $K = \frac{1}{2}ab \sin C$ and $K = \frac{1}{2}ac \sin B$, can be developed.

example 1 **Find the area of $\triangle ABC$ if $a = 17.7$, $b = 21.0$, and $C = 78°10'$.**

$$K = \frac{1}{2}ab \sin C$$
$$= \frac{1}{2}(17.7)(21.0) \sin 78°10'$$
$$= \frac{1}{2}(17.7)(21.0)(0.9787)$$
$$= 181.9$$

To the nearest whole unit, the area is 182 square units.

The area of a triangle also can be expressed in terms of one side of the triangle and two angles.

By the Law of Sines, $\frac{b}{\sin B} = \frac{c}{\sin C}$ or $b = \frac{c \sin B}{\sin C}$. Substituting this expression for b in $K = \frac{1}{2}bc \sin A$ gives the following formula.

$$K = \frac{1}{2}c^2 \frac{\sin A \sin B}{\sin C}$$

Similarly, $K = \frac{1}{2}a^2 \frac{\sin B \sin C}{\sin A}$ and $K = \frac{1}{2}b^2 \frac{\sin A \sin C}{\sin B}$.

example 2 **Find the area of $\triangle ABC$ if $a = 10$, $A = 75°20'$, and $B = 49°40'$.**

Find the measurement of angle C.

$$180° = 75°20' + 49°40' + C$$
$$C = 180° - 75°20' - 49°40'$$
$$= 55°$$

Use $K = \frac{1}{2}a^2 \frac{\sin B \sin C}{\sin A}$.

$$K = \frac{1}{2}(10)^2 \frac{\sin 49°40' \sin 55°}{\sin 75°20'}$$
$$= \frac{1}{2}(100) \frac{(0.7623)(0.8192)}{(0.9674)}$$
$$= 32.3$$

To the nearest whole unit, the area is 32 square units.

If the lengths of three sides of a triangle are given, the area can be found by using the Law of Cosines and the formula $K = \frac{1}{2}ab \sin C$.

example

3 **Find the area of $\triangle ABC$ if $a = 17$, $b = 13$, and $c = 19$.**

Solve for A using the Law of Cosines.

$$(17)^2 = (13)^2 + (19)^2 - 2(13)(19)\cos A$$

$$\cos A = \frac{(17)^2 - (13)^2 - (19)^2}{^{-}2(13)(19)}$$

$$= \frac{^{-}241}{^{-}494}$$

$$= 0.4879$$

$$A = 60°50'$$

Use $K = \frac{1}{2}bc \sin A$.

$$K = \frac{1}{2}(13)(19)\sin 60°50'$$

$$= \frac{1}{2}(13)(19)(0.8732)$$

$$= 107.8$$

To the nearest whole unit, the area is 108 square units.

Hero's formula also can be used when finding the area of a triangle given the lengths of three sides.

$$K = \sqrt{s(s-a)(s-b)(s-c)} \text{ where } s = \frac{1}{2}(a+b+c)$$

example

4 **Use Hero's formula to find the area of $\triangle ABC$ if $a = 17$, $b = 13$, and $c = 19$.**

$$s = \frac{1}{2}(17 + 13 + 19)$$

$$= 24.5$$

$$K = \sqrt{(24.5)(24.5 - 17)(24.5 - 13)(24.5 - 19)}$$

$$= \sqrt{11{,}622.18}$$

$$= 107.8$$

To the nearest whole unit, the area is 108 square units.

exercises

Exploratory **State an equation that would enable you to find the area of each triangle described below.**

1. $a = 3$, $b = 4$, $C = 120°$
2. $c = 20$, $A = 45°$, $B = 30°$
3. $a = 4$, $b = 6$, $c = 8$
4. $A = 43°$, $b = 16$, $c = 12$
5. $A = 19°20'$, $a = 18.6$, $C = 63°50'$
6. $a = 20$, $b = 30$, $c = 40$
7. $a = 6$, $B = 52°$, $c = 4$
8. $b = 12$, $B = 135°$, $C = 30°$

Written Find the area of each triangle described below.

1. $a = 7.5$, $b = 9$, $C = 100°$
2. $c = 3.2$, $A = 16°$, $B = 31°45'$
3. $a = 2$, $b = 7$, $c = 8$
4. $b = 146.2$, $c = 209.3$, $A = 61°12'$
5. $A = 60°$, $a = 2$, $B = 75°$
6. $a = \sqrt{2}$, $b = 2$, $c = 3$
7. $a = 19.42$, $c = 19.42$, $B = 31°16'$
8. $a = 174$, $b = 138$, $c = 188$
9. $a = 8$, $B = 60°$, $C = 75°$
10. $a = 11$, $B = 50°6'$, $c = 5$

Solve each problem.

11. A triangular plot of land has two sides which have lengths of 400 feet and 600 feet. The measurement of the angle between those sides is 46°20'. Find its perimeter and area.
12. The adjacent sides of a parallelogram are 8 cm and 12 cm and one angle is 60°. Find the area of the parallelogram.
13. The sides of a rhombus are 5 cm each and one diagonal is 6 cm. Find the area of the rhombus.
14. A regular pentagon is inscribed in a circle whose radius is 7 cm. Find the area of the pentagon.
15. A regular octagon is inscribed in a circle whose radius is 5 cm. Find the area of the octagon.
16. The area of $\triangle ABC$ is 24 cm², $a = 6$ cm, and $b = 10$ cm. Find the measure of angle C.
17. The diagonals of the quadrilateral at the right are x and y units long. Their intersection forms angle A. Show that the area of the quadrilateral is $\frac{1}{2}xy \sin A$.

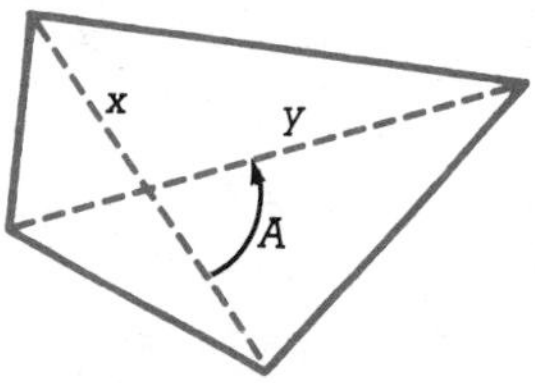

18. Find a formula for the area enclosed by a circle of radius r and a regular inscribed hexagon.

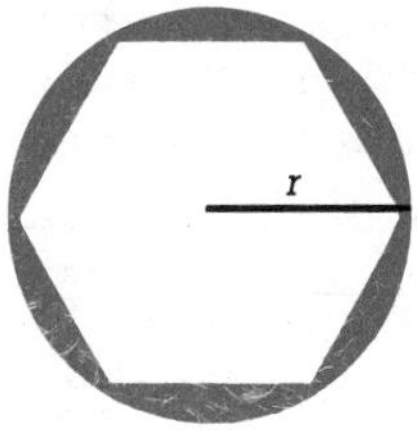

7-6 Vector Triangles

Vectors can be used to represent quantities having magnitude and direction. Common quantities which can be represented by vectors are velocity, acceleration, wind, force, and electric voltage.

Graphically, vectors can be added by forming a triangle or parallelogram with the given vectors as sides. Trigonometric solutions of vector triangles usually provide more accurate results than graphical solutions. Study the following examples.

The vector sum of two or more vectors is called the resultant.

examples

1 **A plane is flying due east at 245 km/h. A 22 km/h wind is blowing from the northeast. Find the ground speed and the direction of the plane.**

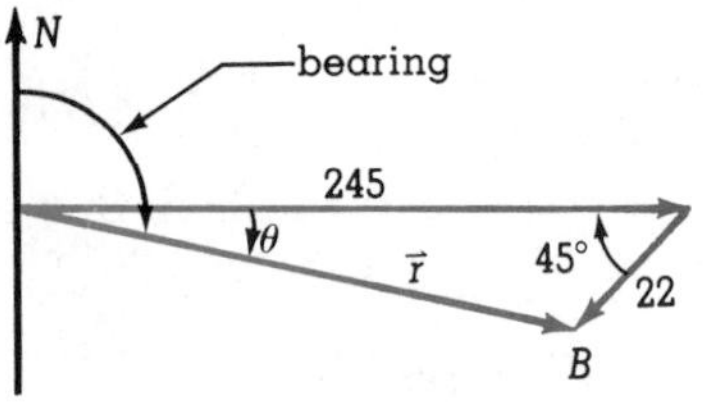

Make a sketch showing the given vector quantities and the resultant. Let $\vec{r}$ be the resultant velocity and let the bearing of the plane be $90° + \theta$.

Use the Law of Cosines to find the magnitude of $\vec{r}$.

$$|\vec{r}|^2 = 245^2 + 22^2 - 2(245)(22)\cos 45°$$
$$= 245^2 + 22^2 - 2(245)(22)(0.7071) \text{ or } 52{,}886$$
$$|\vec{r}| = 230 \text{ km/h}$$

Use the Law of Sines to find θ.

$$\frac{230}{\sin 45°} = \frac{22}{\sin\theta}$$
$$\sin\theta = \frac{22\sin 45°}{230}$$
$$= \frac{22(0.7071)}{230} \text{ or } 0.0676$$
$$\theta = 3°50'$$ *Round to the nearest 10 minutes.*

The bearing of the plane is $90° + 3°50'$ or $93°50'$.

Thus, the plane is actually flying 230 km/h $3°50'$ south of east or at a bearing of $93°50'$.

2 **Two forces, one of 30 kg and the other of 50 kg act on an object. If the angle between the forces is 40°, find the magnitude and the direction of the resultant force.** *The familiar unit kilogram is used with force rather than the actual metric unit newton.*

Make a sketch showing the given vector quantities and the resultant. Let the resultant be force $\vec{r}$ and let the angle it makes with the 50 kg vector be θ.

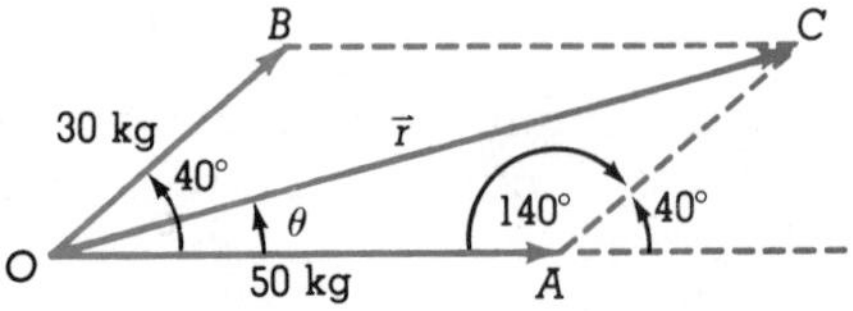

Angle OAC is the supplement of 40°. So you know two sides and the included angle in $\triangle OAC$.

Use the Law of Cosines to find the magnitude of $\vec{r}$.

$$|\vec{r}|^2 = 50^2 + 30^2 - 2(50)(30)\cos 140°$$
$$= 2500 + 900 - 3000(^-0.7660) \text{ or } 5698$$
$$|\vec{r}| = 75.5 \text{ kg}$$

Use the Law of Sines to find the direction of $\vec{r}$.

$$\frac{75.5}{\sin 140°} = \frac{30}{\sin\theta}$$
$$\sin\theta = \frac{30\sin 140°}{75.5}$$
$$= \frac{30(0.6428)}{75.5} \text{ or } 0.2554$$
$$\theta = 14°50'$$ *Round to the nearest 10 minutes.*

Thus, $\vec{r}$ has a magnitude of 75.5 kg and makes a $14°50'$ angle with the 50 kg vector.

example

3 **An object which weighs 30 grams is attached to a length of string and whirled around in a circle. If the magnitude of the centrifugal force is 50 grams, find the angle which the string makes with a vertical line and the resultant force pulling the string outward.**

The figure at the right shows the given vector quantities and the resultant. $|\vec{r}|$ is the force outward on the string and θ is the angle that the string makes with a vertical line.

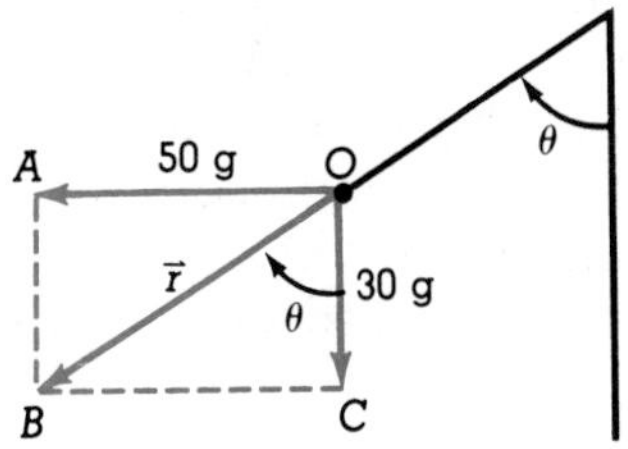

Find θ.

$$\tan\theta = \frac{50}{30}$$
$$= 1.6667$$
$$\theta = 59°$$

Find $|\vec{r}|$.

$$\cos 59° = \frac{30}{|\vec{r}|}$$
$$|\vec{r}| = \frac{30}{\cos 59°}$$
$$|\vec{r}| = 58$$

Thus, the string makes a 59° angle from the vertical line. The force pulling the string outward is 58 grams.

exercises

Exploratory **Make a sketch to show the given vectors.**

1. A plane headed due west at a velocity of 320 mph.
2. A force of 35 kg acting on an object at an angle of 30° with the level ground.
3. A boat traveling at 16 knots at an angle of 25° with the current.
4. A force of 18 kg acting on an object while another force of 51 kg acts on the same object at an angle of 45° from the first.

Find the magnitude and direction of the resultant of the vectors shown in each diagram.

5.

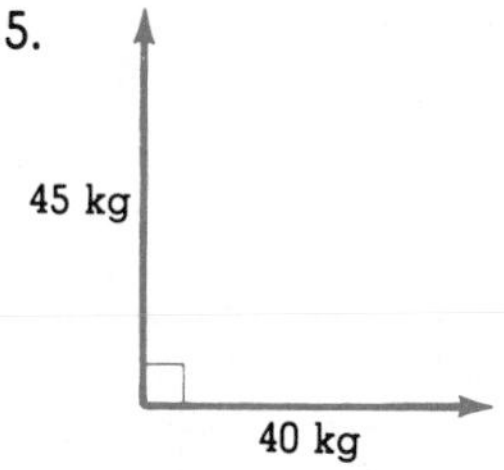

6.

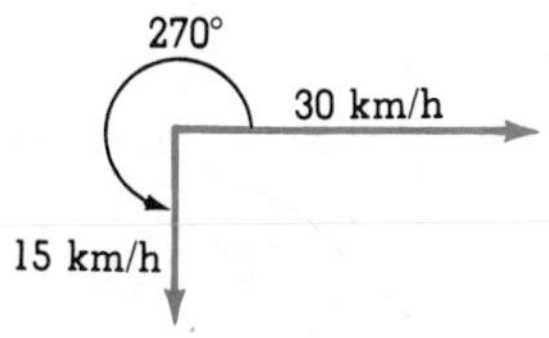

7.

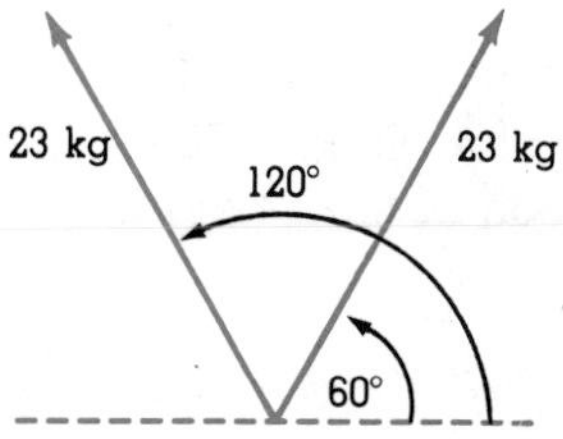

8.

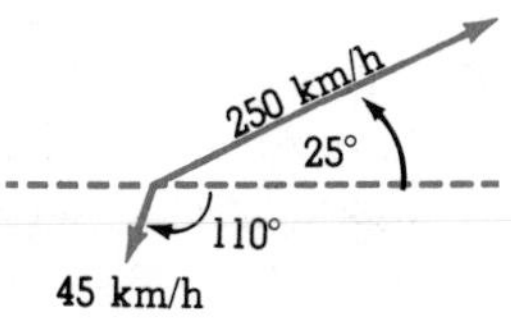

Written Two 10-lb forces act on the same object at the same time. Find the magnitude of their resultant if each of the following is the measurement of the angle between them.

1. 30°
2. 90°
3. 120°
4. 180°

Solve each problem.

5. A 100-kg force and a 50-kg force act on the same object. The angle between the forces measures 90°. Find the magnitude and direction of the resultant force.
6. An airplane flies at 150 km/h and heads 30° south of east. A 50 km/h wind blows in the direction 25° west of south. Find the ground speed and direction of the plane.
7. An airplane is heading due north at 260 mph. A wind from the east is 16 mph. Find the ground speed and direction of the plane.
8. An airplane is heading due north at 260 mph. A 16-mph wind blows from the northwest at an angle of 110° clockwise from north. Find the ground speed and direction of the plane.
9. One force of 125 kg acts on an object. Another force of 85 kg acts on the same object at an angle of 72° from the first. Find the magnitude and direction of the resultant force.
10. A wagon is pulled along level ground by a force of 18 kg in the handle at an angle of 30° to the horizontal. Find the horizontal and vertical components of this vector.
11. Points C and D are directly across from each other on the opposite banks of a river. A boat traveling at a speed of 12 mph crosses the river from C to D. If the current of the river has a speed of 4 mph, at what angle must the skipper head to to travel directly from C to D?
12. A force F_1 of 36 kg acts at an angle of 20° above the horizontal. Pulling in the opposing direction is a force F_2 of 48 kg acting at an angle of 42° below horizontal. Find the magnitude and direction of the resultant force.
13. Three forces in a horizontal plane act on an object. The forces are 7 kg, 11 kg, and 15 kg. The angle between the 7 kg and 11 kg forces is 105°, between the 11 kg and the 15 kg forces is 147°, and between the 15 kg and the 7 kg forces is 108°. Find the magnitude and direction of the resultant force.

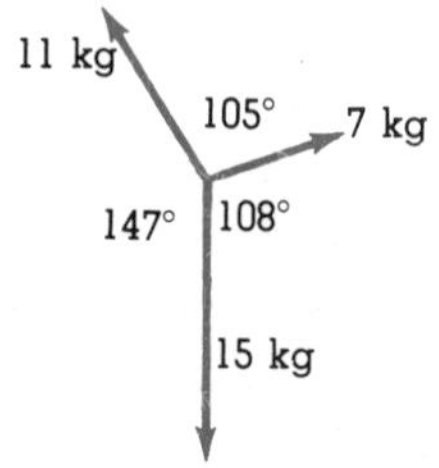

A boat heads directly across a river 320 m wide at 40 m/sec. The current is flowing at 8 m/sec.

14. Find the resultant velocity of the boat.
15. How long does it take the boat to reach the opposite shore?

A boat heads directly across a river 40 m wide at 8 m/sec. The current flowing at 3.8 m/sec.

16. Find the resultant velocity of the boat.
17. How far downstream is the boat when it reaches the other side?
18. An airplane flies east for 210 km. It then flies 70° south of east for 100 km. Find the distance and direction of the plane from its starting place.

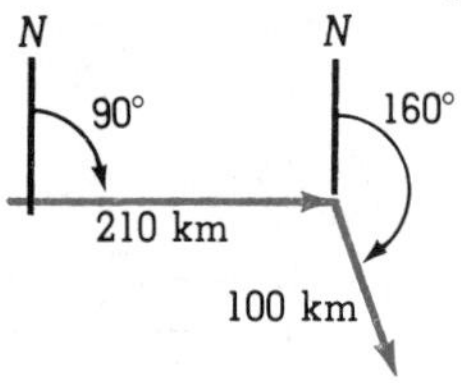

Machinist

Careers

James Soldano operates a lathe to produce a variety of nuts, bolts, and screws. As the lathe turns, the cutting tool moves parallel to the centerline of the metal and cuts a groove in the piece. This groove (thread) is called a **helix** or **helical curve.**

Jim sets the tool bits at different angles for different type threads. These angles are called **helix angles.** The **lead** as shown in the figure at the right is the vertical distance advanced by the helix in one revolution of the bolt or screw. The circumference of the cross section of the metal cylinder and the lead of the bolt or screw are used to find the helix angle. The tangent of the helix angle is found as follows.

$$\text{tangent of helix angle} = \frac{\text{lead}}{\text{circumference}}$$

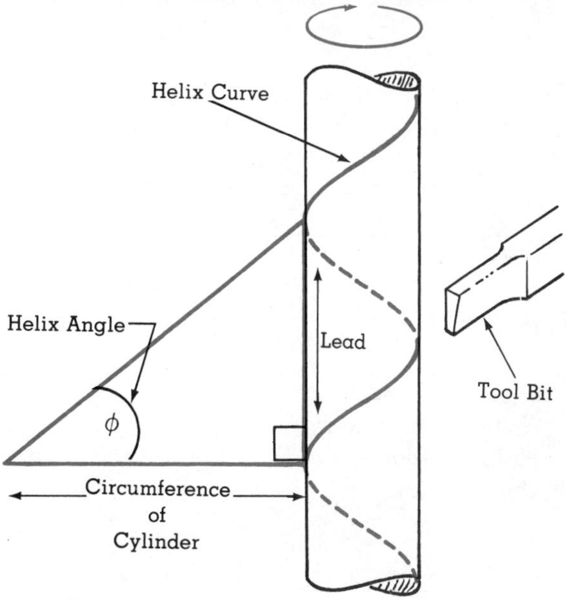

Example Find the helix angle for a screw thread with a diameter of $2\frac{1}{4}$ in. and 5 threads per inch. Use $\pi = 3.14$. Round to the nearest ten minutes.

The lead, for one revolution, is $\frac{1}{5}$ or 0.2. *This is derived from 5 threads to 1 inch.*

$$\tan \phi = \frac{0.2}{3.14 \cdot 2.25}$$
$$= 0.0283$$
$$\phi = \text{Arctan } 0.0283$$

The helix angle, ϕ, is 1° 40.

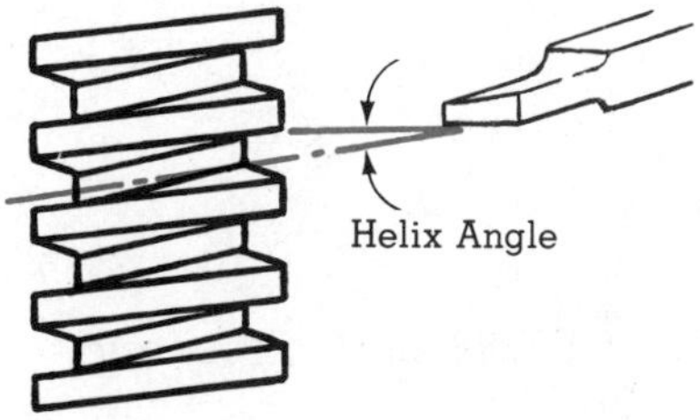

Exercises Find the helix angle for each of the following. Use $\pi = 3.14$. Round to the nearest ten minutes.

	1.	2.	3.	4.	5.	6.	7.
diameter	2 in.	$1\frac{1}{2}$ in.	3 in.	5 mm	$3\frac{1}{8}$ in.	$\frac{3}{8}$ cm	$\frac{1}{4}$ in.
lead	$\frac{1}{8}$ in.	$\frac{2}{9}$ in.	$\frac{2}{5}$ in.	$\frac{2}{7}$ mm	$\frac{1}{10}$ in.	$\frac{1}{16}$ cm	$\frac{1}{20}$ in.

7-7 Area of a Circular Sector and Segment

A **sector** of a circle is the region bounded by an arc of a circle and the radii drawn to its endpoints. For example, figure $ORTS$ is a sector of the circle on the right.

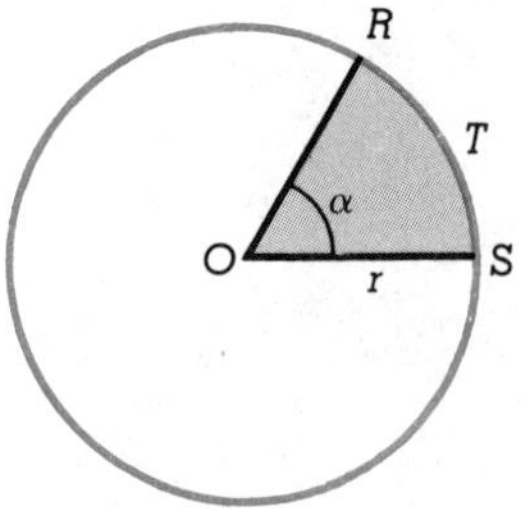

The ratio of the area of a sector to the area of the circle is equal to the ratio of its arc to the circumference. Let A represent the area of the sector. Then, $\frac{A}{\pi r^2} = \frac{\text{length of } \widehat{RTS}}{2\pi r}$. But, the length of $\widehat{RTS}$ is $r \cdot \alpha$. Thus, the following formula is true.

If α is the measure of the central angle expressed in radians and r is the radius of the circle, then the area of the sector, A, is as follows.

$$A = \frac{1}{2}r^2\alpha$$

Area of a Circular Sector

example

1 **A sector has arclength 6 cm and central angle 0.8 radians. Find the radius of the circle and the area of the sector.**

Find the radius of the circle.

$$\text{arclength} = r \cdot \alpha$$
$$6 \text{ cm} = r \cdot 0.8$$
$$r = 7.5$$

Find the area of the sector.

$$A = \frac{1}{2}r^2\alpha$$
$$= \frac{1}{2}(7.5)^2(0.8)$$
$$= 22.5$$

Thus, the radius is 7.5 cm and the area is 22.5 cm^2.

A **segment** of a circle is the region bounded by an arc and its chord. If the arc is a minor arc, then the area of the segment can be found by subtracting the area of $\triangle OAB$ from the area of sector $OACB$. Let S represent the area of the segment.

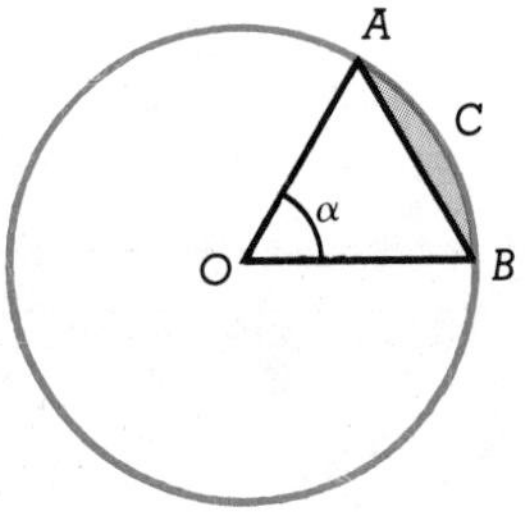

$$S = (\text{area of sector } OACB) - (\text{area of } \triangle OAB)$$
$$= \frac{1}{2}r^2\alpha - \frac{1}{2}ab \sin C$$
$$= \frac{1}{2}r^2\alpha - \frac{1}{2}r \cdot r \sin \alpha \qquad a = r, b = r, \text{ and } C = \alpha$$
$$S = \frac{1}{2}r^2(\alpha - \sin \alpha)$$

If α is the measure of the central angle expressed in radians and r is the radius of the circle, then the area of the segment, S, is as follows.

$$S = \frac{1}{2}r^2(\alpha - \sin \alpha)$$

Area of a Circular Segment

example

2 **A sector has a central angle of 100° in a circle of radius 3 cm. Find the area of the circular sector and the area of the corresponding circular segment.**

Convert 100° to radian measure.

$$\frac{R}{\pi} = \frac{D}{180°}$$
$$\frac{R}{\pi} = \frac{100°}{180°}$$
$$R = \frac{5}{9}\pi \text{ or } 1.745 \text{ radians}$$

Find the area of the sector.

$$A = \frac{1}{2}r^2\alpha$$
$$= \frac{1}{2}(3)^2(1.745)$$
$$= 7.9$$

Find the area of the segment.

$$S = \frac{1}{2}r^2(\alpha - \sin \alpha)$$
$$= \frac{1}{2}(3)^2(1.745 - \sin 1.745)$$
$$= \frac{1}{2}(3)^2(1.745 - 0.985)$$
$$= 3.4$$

Thus, the area of the circular sector is 7.9 cm^2 and the area of the corresponding circular segment is 3.4 cm^2.

exercises

Exploratory Change the following degree measures to radian measures.

1. 225°
2. 60°
3. 90°
4. 330°
5. 62°
6. 28°
7. 171°
8. 143°

Find the arclength of each of the following.

9.

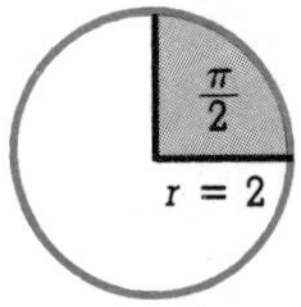

10.

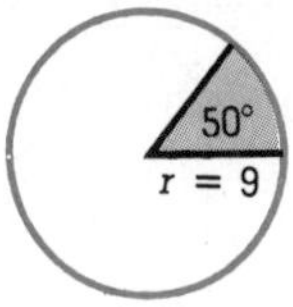

11.

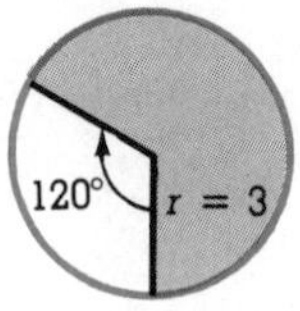

12.

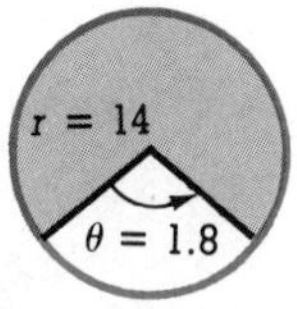

Written Find the area of each sector, given its central angle, θ, and the radius of the circle.

1. $\theta = \frac{\pi}{8}$, $r = 7$
2. $\theta = \frac{5\pi}{12}$, $r = 10$
3. $\theta = 48°$, $r = 22$
4. $\theta = 54°$, $r = 6$
5. $\theta = \frac{2\pi}{3}$, $r = 1.36$
6. $\theta = 82°$, $r = 7.3$

Find the area of each circular segment, given its central angle, θ, and the radius of the circle.

7. $\theta = \frac{5\pi}{6}$, $r = 15$
8. $\theta = \frac{3\pi}{4}$, $r = 24$
9. $\theta = 120°$, $r = 8$
10. $\theta = 81°$, $r = 16$
11. $\theta = \frac{5\pi}{8}$, $r = 6$
12. $\theta = 85°$, $r = 2.1$

Solve each problem.

13. A sector has arclength 6 cm and central angle 1.2 radians. Find the radius and area of the circle.
14. A sector has area of 15 cm² and central angle of 0.2 radians. Find the radius of the circle and arclength of the sector.
15. A sector has a central angle of 20° and arclength of 3.5 cm. Find the radius and area of the circle.
16. A sector has a central angle of 24° and arclength of 8.3 cm. Find the radius and area of the circle.
17. Find the area swept over by the spoke of a wheel of radius 15 cm as the wheel rotates through an angle of 270°.
18. Find the area of the circular segment between a 4.8 cm chord and its arc if the diameter of the circle is 7.2 cm.

The change of the direction in a highway is given by the central angle, θ, subtended by the arc of the curve.

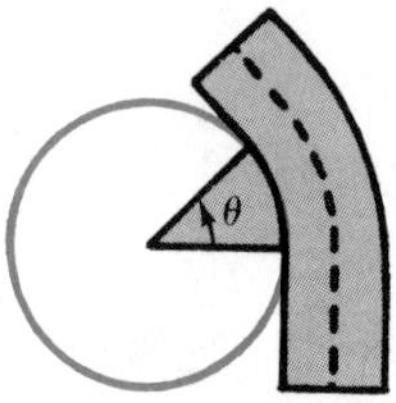

19. A highway curve, in the shape of an arc of a circle, is 0.25 miles. The direction of the highway changes 45° from one end of the curve to the other. Find the radius of the circle in feet which the curve follows.
20. A highway curve, in the shape of an arc of a circle, is 500 ft. The radius of the circle which the curve follows is 2500 ft. Find the change in direction of the highway in degrees formed by the curve.

Challenge Solve this problem.

1. The radius of a circle is 20.4 cm. In the circle is inscribed a polygon of five sides. Four of the central angles subtended by the sides are $\frac{\pi}{6}$, $\frac{\pi}{4}$, $\frac{2\pi}{3}$, and $\frac{2\pi}{5}$. Find the area of the polygon.

Chapter Summary

1. A trigonometric equation is an equation involving a trigonometric function. It is solved by the same methods used to solve other equations. (174)
2. Trigonometric functions can be used to solve problems involving right triangles. (178)
3. Law of Sines: Let $\triangle ABC$ be any triangle with a, b, and c representing the measures of sides opposite angles with measurements A, B, and C respectively. Then, the following equations are true.

$$\frac{a}{\sin A} = \frac{b}{\sin B} = \frac{c}{\sin C} \qquad (182)$$

4. When the measures of two sides of a triangle and the measurement of the angle opposite one of them is given, one solution does not always exist. No triangle may exist, one triangle may exist, or two triangles may exist. (183)
5. Law of Cosines: Let $\triangle ABC$ be any triangle with a, b, and c representing the measures of sides opposite angles with measurements A, B, and C respectively. Then, the following equations are true.

$$a^2 = b^2 + c^2 - 2bc \cos A$$
$$b^2 = a^2 + c^2 - 2ac \cos B$$
$$c^2 = a^2 + b^2 - 2ab \cos C \qquad (186)$$

6. If the measures of two sides of a triangle and the measurement of the included angle are given, the area of the triangle, K, is found as follows.

$$K = \frac{1}{2}bc \sin A \qquad K = \frac{1}{2}ab \sin C \qquad K = \frac{1}{2} ac \sin B \qquad (188)$$

7. If the measure of one side of a triangle and the measurements of two angles are given, the area of the triangle, K, is found as follows.

$$K = \frac{1}{2}c^2\frac{\sin A \sin B}{\sin C}$$
$$K = \frac{1}{2}a^2\frac{\sin B \sin C}{\sin A}$$
$$K = \frac{1}{2}b^2\frac{\sin A \sin C}{\sin B} \qquad (189)$$

8. If the measures of three sides of a triangle are given, the area of the triangle, K, is found as follows. (Hero's Formula)

$$K = \sqrt{s(s-a)(s-b)(s-c)} \text{ where } s = \frac{1}{2}(a+b+c) \qquad (190)$$

9. Vector triangles can be solved by using the trigonometric functions. (191)

10. Area of a Circular Sector: If α is the measure of the central angle expressed in radians and r is the radius of the circle, then the area of the sector, A, is as follows.

$$A = \frac{1}{2}r^2\alpha \qquad (196)$$

11. Area of a Circular Segment: If α is the measure of the central angle expressed in radians and r is the radius of the circle, then the area of the segment, S, is as follows.

$$S = \frac{1}{2}r^2(\alpha - \sin \alpha) \qquad (197)$$

Chapter Review

7-1 **Solve each equation for general values of x.**

1. $2 \cos^2 x - 1 = 0$
2. $\tan x + 1 = \sec x$
3. $\sin^2 x + \cos 2x - \cos x = 0$
4. $\sin x \tan x - \tan x = 0$

Solve each equation for principal values of x.

5. $\tan^2 x - 2 \tan x = 3$
6. $\cos x = 3 \cos x - 2$
7. $\cos 2x + \sin x = 1$
8. $4 \sin^2 x - 4 \sin x + 1 = 0$

7-2 **Solve each right triangle. Angle C is the right angle.**

9. $A = 63°$, $a = 9.7$
10. $a = 2$, $b = 7$
11. $B = 83°$, $b = \sqrt{31}$
12. $a = 44$, $B = 44°44'$

Solve each problem. Round answers to two decimal places or the nearest minute.

13. A flagpole casts a shadow 40 feet long when the measurement of the angle of the sun is 31°20′. How tall is the flagpole?
14. In a parking garage, the floors are 20 feet apart. The ramp to each floor is 120 feet long. Find the measurement of the angle of elevation of the ramp.
15. A 24 foot ladder leans against a building. It forms an angle with the building measuring 18°. How far is the foot of the ladder from the base of the building?
16. A train travels 5000 meters along a track whose angle of elevation has a measurement of 6°. How much did it rise during this distance?

7-3 **Determine the number of possible solutions. If a solution exists, solve the triangle.**

17. $A = 38°42'$, $a = 172$, $c = 203$
18. $a = 12$, $b = 19$, $A = 57°$
19. $A = 29°$, $a = 12$, $b = 15$
20. $A = 45°$, $a = 83$, $b = 79$

Solve each problem. Round answers to two decimal places.

21. A triangular piece of sheet metal has sides 23.4 cm and 29.6 cm long with the angle opposite the shorter side 47°15′. Find the length of the third side.
22. Two planes leave an airport at the same time. Each flies at a speed of 110 miles per hour. One flies in the direction 60° east of north. The other flies in the direction 40° east of south. How far apart are the planes after 3 hours?

7-4 Solve each triangle.

23. $A = 51°$, $b = 40$, $c = 45$
24. $a = 5$, $b = 12$, $c = 13$
25. $B = 19°$, $a = 51$, $c = 61$
26. $A = 25°26'$, $a = 13.7$, $B = 78°$
27. $a = 11$, $b = 13$, $c = 20$
28. $B = 24°$, $a = 42$, $c = 6.5$

Solve each problem. Round answers to two decimal places or the nearest minute.

29. The sides of a triangular city lot have lengths of 50 meters, 70 meters, and 85 meters. Find the measurement of the angle opposite the shortest side.
30. The sides of a parallelogram are 3 cm and 5 cm. If the parallelogram has a 120° angle, how long are its diagonals?

7-5 Find the area of each triangle described below.

31. $a = 6$, $B = 54°$, $c = 4$
32. $A = 20°$, $a = 19$, $C = 64°$
33. $a = 5$, $b = 7$, $c = 9$
34. $a = 11.7$, $b = 13.5$, $C = 81°20'$
35. $a = 2$, $b = 3$, $C = 70°$
36. $A = 42°$, $B = 65°$, $a = 63$

Solve each problem.

37. The diagonals of a parallelogram are 60 cm and 40 cm. They intersect at an angle of 60°. Find the area of the parallelogram.
38. The area of $\triangle ABC$ is 90 cm², $b = 12$ cm, and $c = 15$ cm. Find the measure of angle A.

7-6 Solve each problem.

39. An airplane flies due south at 265 km/h. It flies against a headwind of 60 km/h from a direction 30° east of south. Find the ground speed and direction of the airplane.
40. Steve and Rachel are moving a stove. They are applying forces of 70 kg and 90 kg at an angle of 30° to each other. Find the resultant force and the angle it makes with the larger force.

A metal ball weighing 115 grams is attached to the end of a string and whirled in a circle. The centrifugal force at a given velocity is 290 grams.

41. Find the angle which the string makes with a vertical line.
42. Find the force on the string.

7-7 Find the area of each sector, given its central angle, θ, and the radius of the circle.

43. $\theta = \frac{3\pi}{5}$, $r = 13$
44. $\theta = \frac{\pi}{6}$, $r = 4$
45. $\theta = 45°$, $r = 8$
46. $\theta = 19°$, $r = 19$

Find the area of each circular segment, given its central angle, θ, and the radius of the circle.

47. $\theta = \frac{4\pi}{7}$, $r = 17$
48. $\theta = \frac{2\pi}{5}$, $r = 51$
49. $\theta = 73°$, $r = 7$
50. $\theta = 41°$, $r = 0.5$

Chapter Test

Solve each equation for principal values of x.

1. $\sin x - \cos x = 0$
2. $\sin^2 x - \cos^2 x = 0$
3. $2 \cos^2 x + 3 \sin x - 3 = 0$
4. $\sin 3x = \sin x$
5. $\tan^2 x - \sqrt{3} \tan x = 0$
6. $\tan 2x \cot x - 3 = 0$

Solve each right triangle. Angle C is the right angle.

7. $b = 42$, $A = 77°$
8. $c = 13$, $a = 12$

Solve each problem. Round answers to two decimal places.

9. At ground level, the measurement of the angle of elevation of a kite is 70°. It is held by a string 65 meters long. How far is the kite above the ground?
10. A ship sails due north from port for 90 kilometers, then 40 kilometers east, and then 70 kilometers north. How far is the ship from port?

Determine the number of possible solutions. If a solution exists, solve the triangle.

11. $a = 64$, $c = 90$, $C = 98°$
12. $a = 9$, $b = 20$, $A = 31°$
13. $a = 13$, $b = 7$, $c = 15$
14. $a = 20$, $c = 24$, $B = 47°$

Solve each problem. Round answers to two decimal places.

15. An isosceles triangle has a base of 22 centimeters and a vertex angle measuring 36°. Find its perimeter.
16. A ship at sea is 70 miles from one radio transmitter and 130 miles from another. The measurement of the angle between signals is 130°. How far apart are the transmitters?

Find the area of each triangle described below.

17. $A = 70°11'$, $B = 43°55'$, $b = 16.7$
18. $b = 11.5$, $c = 14$, $A = 20°$

A boat that travels at 16 knots in calm water is moving across a current of 3 knots in a river 250 m wide. The boat makes an angle of 35° with the current (heading into the current).

19. Find the resultant velocity of the boat.
20. How far upstream is the boat when it reaches the other shore?

Find the area of each sector given its central angle, θ, and the radius of the circle.

21. $\theta = \frac{\pi}{3}$, $r = 21$
22. $\theta = 27°$, $r = 5$

23-24. Find the area of the corresponding circular segment for problems 21-22.

Chapter

8

Sequences and Series

The numbers in the following sequence are often found in nature.

$$1, 1, 2, 3, 5, 8, 13, 21, 34, \ldots$$

For example, the number of spirals on a sunflower is usually a number of the sequence. Can you tell what the next number of the sequence will be?

8-1 Arithmetic Sequences and Series

A **sequence** is a set of numbers in a specific order. The **terms** of a sequence are the numbers in it. The first term of a sequence is denoted a_1 or a, the second term a_2, and so on up to the nth term, a_n.

A sequence is sometimes called a progression.

symbol	a_1	a_2	a_3	a_4	a_5	a_6
term	14.2	20.4	26.6	32.8	39.0	45.2

Can you see how to find a_7?

The sequence above is an arithmetic sequence. The difference between successive terms is a constant, which is called the **common difference.**

Arithmetic Sequence

An arithmetic sequence is a sequence in which each term after the first, a, is equal to the sum of the preceding term and the common difference, d. The general form of the sequence, either finite or infinite, is represented as follows.

$$a, a + d, a + 2d, \ldots$$

example

1 **Find the next three terms of the arithmetic sequence $^-2, 3, 8, \ldots$.**

Find the common difference.

$3 - (^-2) = 5$ $\quad$ $8 - 3 = 5$ $\quad$ $d = 5$

Add 5 to the third term to get the fourth, and so on.

$8 + 5 = 13$ $\quad$ $13 + 5 = 18$ $\quad$ $18 + 5 = 23$

The next three terms are 13, 18, and 23.

The nth term of an arithmetic sequence can be found if the first term and the common difference are known. Consider the sequence having $a = 3$ and $d = 2$. Notice the pattern in the way the terms are formed.

first term	a	3
second term	$a + d$	$3 + 2 = 5$
third term	$a + 2d$	$3 + 2(2) = 7$
fourth term	$a + 3d$	$3 + 3(2) = 9$
fifth term	$a + 4d$	$3 + 4(2) = 11$
nth term	$a + (n - 1)d$	$3 + (n - 1)2 = a_n$

The nth Term of an Arithmetic Sequence

The nth term of an arithmetic sequence with the first term a and the common difference d is given by the following formula.

$$a_n = a + (n - 1)d$$

Notice that the preceding formula has four variables, a_n, a, n, and d. If any three of these are known, the fourth can be found.

examples

2 Find the 79th term of the sequence $^-7, ^-4, ^-1, \ldots$.

$a = {}^-7 \qquad d = {}^-4 - ({}^-7) = 3 \qquad n = 79$

$a_n = {}^-7 + (79 - 1)3 = 227$

3 Find the first term of the sequence for which $a_{15} = 38$ and $d = {}^-3$.

$$\begin{aligned} a_{15} &= a + (15 - 1)d \\ 38 &= a + 14({}^-3) \\ 38 &= a - 42 \\ a &= 80 \end{aligned}$$

The terms between any two nonconsecutive terms of an arithmetic sequence are called **arithmetic means.** In the following sequence, 76 and 85 are the arithmetic means between 67 and 94.

49, 58, 67, 76, 85, 94

example

4 Form an arithmetic sequence which has seven arithmetic means between 7 and $^-2$.

$a = 7 \qquad a_9 = {}^-2$

${}^-2 = 7 + (9 - 1)d$ *Why does $n = 9$?*

$d = -\frac{9}{8}$

One such sequence is $7, 5\frac{7}{8}, 4\frac{3}{4}, 3\frac{5}{8}, 2\frac{1}{2}, 1\frac{3}{8}, \frac{1}{4}, -\frac{7}{8}, {}^-2.$ *This sequence can be extended in either direction.*

An **arithmetic series** is the indicated sum of the terms of an arithmetic sequence. The symbol S_n is used to represent the sum of n terms. To find an expression for S_n, a series can be written in two ways and simplified by adding term by term, as shown below. The second equation is obtained by reversing the order of the terms in the series.

$$\begin{aligned} S_n &= a + (a + d) + (a + 2d) + \ldots + (a_n - 2d) + (a_n - d) + a_n \\ +(S_n &= a_n + (a_n - d) + (a_n - 2d) + \ldots + (a + 2d) + (a + d) + a) \\ \hline 2S_n &= (a + a_n) + (a + a_n) + (a + a_n) + \ldots + (a + a_n) + (a + a_n) + (a + a_n) \\ 2S_n &= n(a + a_n) \end{aligned}$$

There are n terms in the series.

The sum of the first n terms of an arithmetic series is given by the following formula.

$$S_n = \frac{n}{2}(a + a_n)$$

Sum of an Arithmetic Series

example

5 Find the sum of the first 63 terms of the series $^-19 - 13 - 7 - \ldots$.

$a = {}^-19 \quad d = 6 \quad n = 63$

$$S_{63} = \frac{63}{2}[^-19 + a_{63}]$$

$$= \frac{63}{2}[^-19 + (^-19 + 62(6))] \qquad a_{63} = {}^-19 + 62(6)$$

$$= \frac{63}{2}(^-19 - 19 + 372)$$

$$= 10{,}521$$

exercises

Exploratory Find the next five terms of each arithmetic sequence.

1. 5, 9, 13, . . .
2. 17, 29, 41, . . .
3. 19, 25, 31, . . .
4. 0, 7, 14, . . .
5. $^-9, {}^-2, 5, \ldots$
6. 27, 23, 19, . . .
7. 1.5, 3, 4.5, . . .
8. $5, {}^-1, {}^-7, \ldots$
9. $a, a + 3, a + 6, \ldots$
10. $^-n, 0, n, \ldots$
11. $x, 2x, 3x, \ldots$
12. $n + 5, n + 11, \ldots$
13. $b, {}^-b, {}^-3b, \ldots$
14. $5k, {}^-k, \ldots$
15. $r + 15, r + 8, \ldots$

Written Solve each problem.

1. Find the 19th term of the sequence for which $a = 11$ and $d = {}^-2$.
2. Find the 16th term of the sequence for which $a = 1.5$ and $d = 0.5$.
3. Find n for the sequence for which $a_n = 37$, $a = {}^-13$ and $d = 5$.
4. Find n for the sequence for which $a_n = 633$, $a = 9$, and $d = 24$.
5. Find the first term of the sequence for which $d = {}^-2$ and $a_7 = 3$.
6. Find the first term of the sequence for which $d = \frac{2}{3}$ and $a_8 = 15$.
7. Find d for the sequence for which $a = 4$ and $a_{11} = 64$.
8. Find d for the sequence for which $a = {}^-6$ and $a_{29} = 50$.
9. Find the sixth term in the sequence $^-2 + \sqrt{3}, {}^-1, {}^-\sqrt{3}, \ldots$.
10. Find the seventh term in the sequence $1 + i, 2 - i, 3 - 3i, \ldots$.
11. Find the 43rd term of the sequence $^-19, {}^-15, {}^-11, \ldots$.
12. Find the 58th term of the sequence $10, 4, {}^-2, \ldots$.
13. Form a sequence which has one arithmetic mean between 12 and 21.
14. Form a sequence which has one arithmetic mean between 36 and 48.
15. Form a sequence which has two arithmetic means between $^-4$ and 5.
16. Form a sequence which has two arithmetic means between $\sqrt{2}$ and 10.

17. Form a sequence which has three arithmetic means between 1 and 4.
18. Form a sequence which has seven arithmetic means between 5 and 17.
19. Find S_{14} for the series for which $a = 3.2$ and $d = 1.5$.
20. Find S_{23} for the series for which $a = {}^{-}3$ and $d = 6$.
21. Find the sum of the first 11 terms of the series $^{-}3 - 1 + 1 + 3 + \ldots$.
22. Find the sum of the first 32 terms of the series $0.5 + 0.75 + 1 + \ldots$.
23. Find n for a sequence for which $a = {}^{-}7$, $d = 1.5$, and $S_n = -14$.
24. Find n for a sequence for which $a = 5$, $d = 3$, and $S_n = 440$.
25. Cylindrical tiles of uniform size are stacked in the form of a triangle. There are 21 tiles on the bottom row. Find the total number of tiles in the stack.

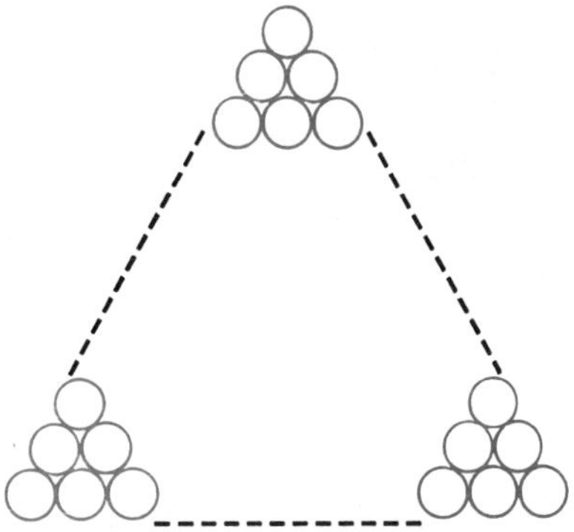

26. A person has \$650 in a bank and is closing out the account by writing one check a week against it. The first check is \$20, the second is \$25, and so on. Each check exceeds the previous one by \$5. In how many weeks will the account be closed if there is no service charge?

8-2 Geometric Sequences and Series

The following sequence is an example of a **geometric sequence.**

Can you find the next term?

1, 0.2, 0.04, 0.008, . . .

The ratio of successive terms is a constant, called the **common ratio.** *The common ratio is considered to be unequal to 1. ($r \neq 1$)*

Geometric Sequence

> **A geometric sequence is a sequence in which each term after the first, a, is the product of the preceding term and the common ratio, r. The general form of the sequence is**
> **$a, ar, ar^2, \ldots$.**

The common ratio of a geometric sequence can be found by dividing any term by the preceding term.

example

1 **Find the common ratio and the next two terms of the geometric sequence 13, 91, 637, ...**

$91 \div 13 = 7 \quad 637 \div 91 = 7 \quad r = 7$
$637 \cdot 7 = 4459 \quad 4459 \cdot 7 = 31{,}213$

The common ratio is 7 and the next two terms are 4459 and 31,213.

The terms of a geometric sequence for which $a = 3$ and $r = 2$ can be represented as follows.

first term	a	$3 = 3$
second term	ar	$3 \cdot 2 = 6$
third term	ar^2	$3 \cdot 2^2 = 12$
fourth term	ar^3	$3 \cdot 2^3 = 24$
nth term	ar^{n-1}	$3 \cdot 2^{n-1} = a_n$

The nth term of a geometric sequence with the first term a and the common ratio r is given by the following formula.

$$a_n = ar^{n-1}$$

The nth Term of a Geometric Sequence

By definition, the nth term is also equal to $a_{n-1}r$, where a_{n-1} is the $(n - 1)$th term.

example 2

Find the 17th term of the sequence $1, \frac{1}{2}, \frac{1}{4}, \ldots$.

$\frac{1}{2} \div 1 = \frac{1}{2} \qquad \frac{1}{4} \div \frac{1}{2} = \frac{1}{2} \qquad r = \frac{1}{2}$

$$a_n = ar^{n-1}$$

$$a_{17} = 1\left(\frac{1}{2}\right)^{17-1}$$

$$a_{17} = \left(\frac{1}{2}\right)^{16}$$

$$= \frac{1}{2^{16}} \text{ or } \frac{1}{65{,}536}$$

The terms between any two nonconsecutive terms of a geometric sequence are called **geometric means.**

example 3

Form a sequence which has two geometric means between 125 and 216.

$a = 125 \qquad a_4 = 216$

$$a_4 = ar^3$$

$$216 = 125r^3$$

$r^3 = \frac{216}{125} \qquad r = \frac{6}{5}$

Assume that 125 is the first term of a geometric sequence.

$125 \cdot \frac{6}{5} = 150 \qquad 150 \cdot \frac{6}{5} = 180$

One such sequence is 125, 150, 180, 216.

The sum of the terms of a geometric sequence is called a **geometric series.** A formula for the sum of a series, S_n, can be found by writing an expression for $S_n - rS_n$, then solving for S_n.

$$\begin{aligned} S_n &= a + ar + ar^2 + \ldots + ar^{n-2} + ar^{n-1} \\ -(rS_n &= \quad\;\; ar + ar^2 + \ldots + ar^{n-2} + ar^{n-1} + ar^n) \\ \hline S_n - rS_n &= a \qquad\qquad\qquad\qquad\qquad\qquad - ar^n \\ S_n(1 - r) &= a - ar^n \\ S_n &= \frac{a - ar^n}{1 - r} \end{aligned}$$

The sum of the first n terms of a geometric series is given by the following formula.

$$S_n = \frac{a - ar^n}{1 - r} \qquad (r \neq 1)$$

Sum of a Geometric Series

example

4 Find the sum of the first 9 terms of the series $\frac{2}{3} + \frac{1}{3} + \frac{1}{6} + \cdots$.

$$\frac{1}{3} \div \frac{2}{3} = \frac{1}{2} \qquad \frac{1}{6} \div \frac{1}{3} = \frac{1}{2} \qquad r = \frac{1}{2}$$

$$S_9 = \frac{\frac{2}{3} - \frac{2}{3}\left(\frac{1}{2}\right)^9}{1 - \frac{1}{2}}$$

$$= \frac{511}{384}$$

exercises

Exploratory Find the next four terms of each geometric sequence.

1. 4, 2, 1, . . .
2. 2, 3, . . .
3. $\frac{1}{3}, \frac{2}{3}, \ldots$
4. $\frac{1}{2}, \frac{1}{4}, \ldots$
5. 7, 3.5, . . .
6. 1.2, 3.6, . . .
7. 2, 5, . . .
8. 4, 5.6, . . .

Determine whether the given terms form a geometric sequence. Write *yes* or *no*.

9. $\sqrt{2}, 2, \sqrt{8}, \ldots$
10. $\sqrt[3]{3^2}, 3, 3\sqrt[3]{3}, \ldots$
11. $t^{-2}, t^{-1}, 1, \ldots$
12. $\frac{1}{2}, \frac{1}{6}, \frac{1}{10}, \ldots$
13. $\frac{\sqrt{3}}{2}, \frac{\sqrt{3}}{4}, \frac{\sqrt{3}}{8}, \ldots$
14. $\frac{3}{4}, \frac{9}{8}, \frac{27}{12}, \ldots$

Written Solve each problem.

1. The first term of a geometric sequence is $^{-}3$ and the common ratio is $\frac{2}{3}$. Find the next four terms.
2. The first term of a geometric sequence is 8 and the common ratio is $\frac{3}{2}$. Find the next three terms.
3. The first term of a geometric sequence is $\frac{1}{2}$ and the common ratio is $\frac{2}{3}$. Find the ninth term of the sequence.
4. If $r = 2$ and $a_5 = 24$, find the first term of the geometric sequence.
5. Find the ninth term of the geometric sequence $\sqrt{2}, 2, 2\sqrt{2}, \cdots$
6. Find the sixth term of the geometric sequence 10, 0.1, 0.001, ...
7. Find the first four terms of the geometric sequence for which $a_5 = 32\sqrt{2}$ and $r = {}^{-}\sqrt{2}$.
8. Find the first three terms of the geometric sequence for which $a_4 = 2.5$ and $r = 2$.
9. Form a sequence which has one geometric mean between $\frac{1}{4}$ and 4.
10. Form a sequence which has two geometric means between 1 and 27.
11. Form a sequence which has two geometric means between $^{-}2$ and 54.
12. Form a sequence which has three geometric means between 2 and $\frac{1}{8}$.
13. Find the sum of the first seven terms of the series $\frac{1}{2} + \frac{1}{4} + \frac{1}{8} + \cdots$.
14. Find the sum of the first six terms of the series $2 + 3 + 4.5 + \ldots$.
15. Find the sum of the first five terms of the series $\frac{5}{3} + 5 + 15 + \cdots$.
16. Find the sum of the first eight terms of the series $3 - 6 + 12 + \ldots$.
17. Find the sum of the first nine terms of the series $0.5 + 1 + 2 + \ldots$.
18. Find the sum of the first ten terms of the series $1, \sqrt{2}, 2, 2\sqrt{2}, \ldots$.

8-3 Infinite Sequences

An infinite sequence has an unlimited number of terms. For example, the sequence $1, \frac{1}{2}, \frac{1}{3}, \frac{1}{4}, \frac{1}{5}, \cdots, \frac{1}{n}, \cdots$ is an infinite sequence whose nth term is $\frac{1}{n}$. Several terms of this sequence are graphed below.

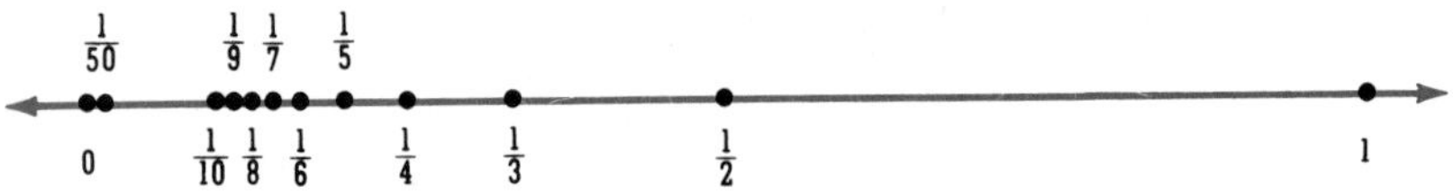

Notice that the terms approach zero as n increases in value. Zero is called the limit of the terms of this sequence. This can be expressed as follows.

$$\lim_{n\to\infty} \frac{1}{n} = 0$$

∞ is the symbol for infinity.

This is read "the limit of 1 over n as n approaches infinity equals zero."

If a general expression for the nth term of a sequence is known, the limit can usually be estimated by substituting large values for n. Consider the following examples.

examples

1 **Find the limit of the sequence $\frac{1}{2}, \frac{1}{4}, \frac{1}{8}, \frac{1}{16}, \ldots$.**

The nth term of this sequence is $\frac{1}{2^n}$.

The 50th term is $\frac{1}{2^{50}}$, or about 1×10^{-15}. The 100th term is $\frac{1}{2^{100}}$, or about 1×10^{-30}. Notice that the values approach zero.

Therefore, $\lim_{n\to\infty} \frac{1}{2^n} = 0$.

Zero is the limit of any geometric sequence for which $|r| < 1$. Why?

2 **Find the limit of the sequence $\frac{1-2}{5}, \frac{1-4}{10}, \frac{1-6}{15}, \ldots, \frac{1-2n}{5n}, \ldots$**

The 50th term is $\frac{1-100}{250}$, or $\frac{-99}{250}$. The 100th term is $\frac{1-200}{500}$, or $\frac{-199}{500}$.

Therefore, $\lim_{n\to\infty} \frac{1-2n}{5n} = -\frac{2}{5}$

The form of the expression for the nth term of a sequence can be altered to make the limit easier to find.

example

3 **Evaluate $\lim_{n\to\infty} \frac{3n+1}{n}$.**

Since $\frac{3n+1}{n} = 3 + \frac{1}{n}$, $\lim_{n\to\infty} \frac{3n+1}{n} = \lim_{n\to\infty} \left(3 + \frac{1}{n}\right)$.

$\lim_{n\to\infty} \frac{1}{n} = 0$ Therefore, $\lim_{n\to\infty} \left(3 + \frac{1}{n}\right) = 3 + 0$ or 3

The limit is 3.

example

4 Evaluate $\lim_{n\to\infty} \frac{4n^2 + n}{2n^2 + 1}$.

Divide the numerator and denominator by the highest power of n which occurs in the denominator.

$$\lim_{n\to\infty} \frac{4n^2 + n}{2n^2 + 1} = \lim_{n\to\infty} \frac{\frac{4n^2}{n^2} + \frac{n}{n^2}}{\frac{2n^2}{n^2} + \frac{1}{n^2}} \text{ or } \lim_{n\to\infty} \frac{4 + \frac{1}{n}}{2 + \frac{1}{n^2}}$$

$$= \frac{4 + 0}{2 + 0} \text{ or } 2$$

The limit is 2.

Limits do not exist for all sequences. If the terms of a sequence become arbitrarily large or approach two different values, the sequence has no limit.

examples

5 Evaluate $\lim_{n\to\infty} \frac{3n^2 + 1}{n}$.

$$\lim_{n\to\infty} \frac{3n^2 + 1}{n} = \lim_{n\to\infty} \left(3n + \frac{1}{n}\right) \text{ or } 3n$$

$\lim_{n\to\infty} \frac{1}{n} = 0$

Since $3n$ becomes infinitely large as n approaches infinity, the sequence has no limit.

6 Evaluate $\lim_{n\to\infty} (^-1)^n\left(\frac{5n + 3}{n}\right)$.

$$\lim_{n\to\infty} (^-1)^n\left(\frac{5n + 3}{n}\right) = \lim_{n\to\infty} (^-1)^n\left(5 + \frac{3}{n}\right)$$
$$= 5(^-1)^n$$

When n is even, $(^-1)^n = 1$. When n is odd, $(^-1)^n = {}^-1$.

Thus, the odd numbered terms approach $^-5$ and the even-numbered terms approach 5. Therefore the sequence has no limit.

exercises

Exploratory Write an expression for the nth term of each given sequence.

1. 1, 2, 4, 8, . . .
2. 1, 3, 9, 27, . . .
3. 5, 7, 9, 11, . . .
4. 4, 7, 10, 13, . . .
5. $3, 2, \frac{4}{3}, \frac{8}{9}, \ldots$
6. $5, 2, \frac{4}{5}, \frac{8}{25}, \ldots$
7. $\frac{4}{2}, \frac{9}{4}, \frac{14}{6}, \frac{19}{8}, \ldots$
8. $3, \frac{5}{2}, \frac{7}{3}, \frac{9}{4}, \ldots$

Written Evaluate each limit, or state that the limit does not exist.

1. $\lim_{n\to\infty} \frac{n+1}{n}$
2. $\lim_{n\to\infty} \frac{n-1}{n}$
3. $\lim_{n\to\infty} \frac{3n-5}{n}$
4. $\lim_{n\to\infty} \frac{4n+2}{n}$
5. $\lim_{n\to\infty} \frac{1}{3^n}$
6. $\lim_{n\to\infty} \frac{2}{5^n}$
7. $\lim_{n\to\infty} \frac{3n^2+4}{2n}$
8. $\lim_{n\to\infty} \frac{n^3+6n}{3n^3}$
9. $\lim_{n\to\infty} \frac{2n^2-6n}{5n^2}$
10. $\lim_{n\to\infty} \frac{n^2-4}{2n}$
11. $\lim_{n\to\infty} \frac{(n+2)(2n-1)}{n^2}$
12. $\lim_{n\to\infty} \frac{n^2+n-3}{n^2}$
13. $\lim_{n\to\infty} \frac{3n+1}{n-3}$
14. $\lim_{n\to\infty} \frac{4n^2+5}{3n^2+2n}$
15. $\lim_{n\to\infty} \frac{5n}{n^2+2}$
16. $\lim_{n\to\infty} \frac{2n^3}{n^2+4n}$
17. $\lim_{n\to\infty} \frac{2n+(^-1)^n}{n^2}$
18. $\lim_{n\to\infty} \frac{(^-1)^n n^3}{3n^3+4n}$

19–26. Find the limit as $n \to \infty$ of each sequence in problems 1–8 in the exploratory exercises, or state that the limit does not exist.

8-4 Sum of an Infinite Series

The indicated sum of the terms of an infinite sequence is an **infinite series.** Consider the geometric series $\frac{1}{2} + \frac{1}{4} + \frac{1}{8} + \frac{1}{16} \cdot \cdot \cdot$ Since this is a geometric series, you can find the sum of the first n terms, S_n, using the formula $\frac{a - ar^n}{1 - r}$.

example

1 **Find the sum of the first 100 terms of the series $\frac{1}{2} + \frac{1}{4} + \frac{1}{8} + \ldots$.**

$$r = \frac{1}{2}$$

$$S_{100} = \frac{\frac{1}{2} - \frac{1}{2}\left(\frac{1}{2}\right)^{100}}{1 - \frac{1}{2}} = \frac{\frac{1}{2} - \left(\frac{1}{2}\right)^{101}}{\frac{1}{2}} = \frac{\frac{1}{2}}{\frac{1}{2}} - \frac{\left(\frac{1}{2}\right)^{101}}{\frac{1}{2}} = 1 - \left(\frac{1}{2}\right)^{100}$$

Since $\left(\frac{1}{2}\right)^{100}$ is very small, S_{100} is nearly equal to 1.

In the preceding example, the sum of the first 100 terms was shown to be very close to 1. No matter how many terms are added, the sum will never exceed 1. Therefore 1 is called the **sum of the infinite series.** The sum of an infinite series is defined as follows.

If S_n is the sum of n terms of a series, and S is a number such that $S > S_n$ for all n, and $S - S_n$ approaches zero as n increases without limit, then the sum of the infinite series is S.

$$\lim_{n \to \infty} S_n = S$$

Sum of an Infinite Series

If an infinite series has a limit, or sum, the nth term of the series, a_n, must approach zero as $n \to \infty$. Thus, if $\lim_{n \to \infty} a_n \neq 0$, the series has no limit. If $\lim_{n \to \infty} a_n = 0$, the series may or may not have a limit.

Since the terms of an arithmetic series do not approach zero as $n \to \infty$, no limit exists for an infinite arithmetic series. However, limits do exist for certain geometric series, such as the one in the preceding example.

The formula for the sum of the first n terms of a geometric sequence can be written as follows.

$$S_n = \frac{a(1 - r^n)}{1 - r} \qquad r \neq 1$$

Suppose $n \to \infty$, that is, the number of terms increases without limit. If $|r| > 1$, r^n increases without limit as $n \to \infty$. However, when $|r| < 1$, $r^n \to 0$ as $n \to \infty$. Then S_n approaches the value $\frac{a}{1 - r}$, called the **sum of an infinite geometric series.**

The sum, S, of an infinite geometric series for which $|r| < 1$ is given by the following formula.

$$S = \frac{a}{1 - r}$$

Sum of an Infinite Geometric Series

example

2 Find a and r for the following series. Then find the sum of the series, if it exists.

$$1 - \frac{1}{3} + \frac{1}{9} - \frac{1}{27} + \cdots$$

$a = 1 \qquad r = -\frac{1}{3}$

$$S = \frac{1}{1 - \left(-\frac{1}{3}\right)}$$

$$= \frac{1}{\frac{4}{3}} \text{ or } \frac{3}{4}$$

example

3 **Write the repeating decimal 0.454545 . . . or $0.\overline{45}$ as a fraction.**

Write $0.\overline{45}$ as an infinite geometric series.

$$0.\overline{45} = \frac{45}{100} + \frac{45}{10{,}000} + \frac{45}{1{,}000{,}000} + \cdots$$

This is an infinite geometric series with a common ratio of $\frac{1}{100}$.

The sum can be found as follows.

$$S = \frac{\frac{45}{100}}{1 - \frac{1}{100}}$$

$$= \frac{45}{99} \text{ or } \frac{5}{11}$$

Thus, $0.454545 \cdots = \frac{5}{11}$.

exercises

Exploratory **Write an expression for the sum of the first 10 terms of each series.**

1. $4 + 1 + \frac{1}{4} + \frac{1}{16} + \cdots$
2. $4 + 3 + \frac{9}{4} + \cdots$
3. $20 + 2 + 0.2 + \cdots$
4. $300 + 30 + 3 + \cdots$
5. $25 + 5 + 1 + \cdots$
6. $36 + 6 + 1 + \cdots$

7–12. For problems 1–6, guess the sum of the infinite series.

Written **Find the sum of each infinite geometric series, if it exists.**

1. $\frac{2}{3} + \frac{1}{3} + \frac{1}{6} + \frac{1}{12} + \cdots$
2. $1 + \frac{2}{5} + \frac{4}{25} + \cdots$
3. $\sqrt{3} + 1 + \frac{\sqrt{3}}{3} + \cdots$
4. $2\sqrt{2} + 8 + 16\sqrt{2} + \ldots.$
5. $\frac{1}{20} + \frac{1}{40} + \frac{1}{80} + \cdots$
6. $\frac{2}{7} + \frac{4}{7} + \frac{8}{7} + \cdots$
7. $0.2 + 0.02 + 0.002 + \cdots$
8. $\frac{1}{25} + \frac{1}{250} + \frac{1}{2500} + \cdots$
9. $2 + 3 + \frac{9}{2} + \cdots$
10. $10 + 5 + 2.5 + \cdots$

Write each repeating decimal as a fraction.

11. 0.555 . . .
12. 0.888 . . .
13. 0.2727 . . .
14. 0.370370370 . . .
15. 0.123123 . . .
16. 0.3636 . . .
17. 2.205205205 . . .
18. 3.242424 . . .
19. 0.3181818 . . .
20. 7.259259 . . .

The ratio of the circumference to the diameter of a circle is a constant, π. The number π is **irrational**. That is, the value is an infinite, non-repeating decimal. It has been proven that π is also **transcendental**. That is, π cannot be the root of a polynomial equation with rational coefficients.

In the history of mathematics, many expressions have been found which represent the value of π.

In 1593 a French mathematician, François Viète, found an infinite irrational product for π.

$$\frac{\pi}{2} = \frac{1}{\sqrt{\frac{1}{2}} \cdot \sqrt{\frac{1}{2} + \frac{1}{2}\sqrt{\frac{1}{2}}} \cdot \sqrt{\frac{1}{2} + \frac{1}{2}\sqrt{\frac{1}{2} + \frac{1}{2}\sqrt{\frac{1}{2}}}} \cdots}$$

In 1655 an English mathematician, John Wallis, found an infinite rational product for π.

$$\frac{\pi}{2} = \frac{2}{1} \cdot \frac{2}{3} \cdot \frac{4}{3} \cdot \frac{4}{5} \cdot \frac{6}{5} \cdot \frac{6}{7} \cdot \frac{8}{7} \cdot \frac{8}{9} \cdots$$

One of the simplest expressions for π was discovered by Wilhelm von Leibniz, a German mathematician and philosopher. In 1674 Leibniz expressed π as the limit of an infinite series.

$$\frac{\pi}{4} = 1 - \frac{1}{3} + \frac{1}{5} - \frac{1}{7} + \frac{1}{9} - \frac{1}{11} + \frac{1}{13} \cdots$$

Each of the expressions given above can be used to approximate π to any given number of decimal places. However, an accurate approximation requires lengthy calculations. More recently, other expressions have been found which can be used to approximate π more quickly.

Computers have been used to calculate over a million decimal places for π. The first 100 decimal places for π are given below.

$$\pi = 3.1415926535\ 8979323846\ 2643383279\ 5028841971\ 6939937510$$
$$5820974944\ 5923078164\ 0628620899\ 8628034825\ 3421170679 \ldots$$

Exercises Use a calculator for each approximation.

1. Use the first 3 products in Viète's expression to approximate π.
2. Use the first 4 products in Viète's expression to approximate π.
3. Use the first 10 products in Wallis's expression to approximate π.
4. Use the first 20 products in Wallis's expression to approximate π.
5. Use the first 5 terms of Leibniz's series to approximate π.
6. Use the first 10 terms of Leibniz's series to approximate π.

8-5 Convergence and Divergence

Convergence and divergence are terms which relate to the existence of a limit, or sum, of an infinite series.

If an infinite series has a sum, or limit, the series is convergent. If an infinite series is not convergent, it is divergent.

Convergent and Divergent Series

example

1 **Determine whether each series is convergent or divergent.**

a. $\frac{2}{3} + \frac{1}{3} + \frac{1}{6} + \cdots$

b. $^-5 - 3 - 1 + 1 + 3 + \cdots$

c. $1 + 4 + 16 + 64 + \cdots$

a. This is a geometric series, $r = \frac{1}{2}$. Since $|r| < 1$, the series has a limit. Therefore the series is convergent.

b. This is an arithmetic series, $d = 2$. Since an arithmetic series has no limit, the series is divergent.

c. This is a geometric series, $r = 4$. Since $|r| > 1$, the series has no limit. Therefore the series is divergent.

When a series is neither arithmetic nor geometric, it is more difficult to determine whether the series is convergent or divergent. Several different techniques can be used.

One test for convergence is the ratio test. The test can be used when all terms of a series are positive. The test depends upon the ratio of consecutive terms of a series, which must be expressed in general form.

Let a_n and a_{n+1} represent two consecutive terms of a series of positive terms. Suppose r is defined as follows.

$$r = \lim_{n \to \infty} \frac{a_{n+1}}{a_n}$$

The series is convergent if $r < 1$ and divergent if $r > 1$. If $r = 1$, the test fails.

Ratio Test for Convergence

example

2 **Use the ratio test to determine whether the following series is convergent or divergent.**

$$10 + \frac{10^2}{1 \cdot 2} + \frac{10^3}{1 \cdot 2 \cdot 3} + \cdots + \frac{10^n}{1 \cdot 2 \cdot 3 \cdots n} + \cdots$$

$$a_n = \frac{10^n}{1 \cdot 2 \cdot 3 \cdots n}, \quad a_{n+1} = \frac{10^{n+1}}{1 \cdot 2 \cdot 3 \cdots (n+1)}$$

$$\lim_{n\to\infty} \frac{\dfrac{10^{n+1}}{1 \cdot 2 \cdot 3 \cdots (n+1)}}{\dfrac{10^n}{1 \cdot 2 \cdot 3 \cdots n}} = \lim_{n\to\infty} \frac{10}{n+1} = 0$$

Thus, the series is convergent.

When the ratio test fails, other methods can be used to determine if a series is convergent or divergent. Study the methods used in the next two examples.

examples

3 **Determine whether the following series is convergent or divergent.**

$$1 + \frac{1}{2} + \frac{1}{3} + \frac{1}{4} + \frac{1}{5} + \cdots$$

Suppose the terms are grouped as follows. Beginning after the second term, the number of terms in each successive group is doubled.

$$(1) + \left(\frac{1}{2}\right) + \left(\frac{1}{3} + \frac{1}{4}\right) + \left(\frac{1}{5} + \frac{1}{6} + \frac{1}{7} + \frac{1}{8}\right) + \left(\frac{1}{9} + \cdots + \frac{1}{16}\right) + \cdots.$$

Notice that the first enclosed expression is greater than $\frac{1}{2}$, and the second is equal to $\frac{1}{2}$. Beginning with the third expression, each sum of enclosed terms is greater than $\frac{1}{2}$. There are an unlimited number of such expressions, so the series is unlimited. Therefore the series is divergent.

4 **Determine whether the following series is convergent or divergent.**

$$1 + \frac{1}{2^p} + \frac{1}{3^p} + \frac{1}{4^p} + \frac{1}{5^p} + \frac{1}{6^p} + \frac{1}{7^p} + \frac{1}{8^p} + \cdots + \frac{1}{n^p} \cdots \quad \textbf{where } (p > 1).$$

The terms can be grouped as shown.

$$1 + \left(\frac{1}{2^p} + \frac{1}{3^p}\right) + \left(\frac{1}{4^p} + \frac{1}{5^p} + \frac{1}{6^p} + \frac{1}{7^p}\right) + \left(\frac{1}{8^p} + \cdots + \frac{1}{15^p}\right) + \cdots$$

Notice that the first term of each group is greater than the successive terms. Therefore the sum of a group of t terms is less than t times the first term.

$$\left(\frac{1}{2^p} + \frac{1}{3^p}\right) < \left(\frac{1}{2^p} + \frac{1}{2^p}\right) = \frac{2}{2^p} = \frac{1}{2^{p-1}} \text{ and}$$

$$\left(\frac{1}{4^p} + \frac{1}{5^p} + \frac{1}{6^p} + \frac{1}{7^p}\right) < \frac{1}{4^{p-1}} = \left(\frac{1}{2^{p-1}}\right)^2, \text{ and so on.}$$

Thus, another series can be formed which is greater than the given series.

$$\left[1 + \frac{1}{2^p} + \frac{1}{3^p} + \cdots\right] < \left[1 + \frac{1}{2^{p-1}} + \frac{1}{(2^{p-1})^2} + \frac{1}{(2^{p-1})^3} + \cdots\right]$$

The second series is geometric and the common ratio is $\frac{1}{2^{p-1}}$. Since $p > 1$, $\left|\frac{1}{2^{p-1}}\right| < 1$. Thus, the second series has a limit. Since the sum of the given series must be less than that limit, the given series must also be convergent.

As shown in example **4**, a series can be compared to a series known to be convergent or divergent. The following list of series can be used for reference.

Summary of Series for Reference

1. Convergent: $a + ar + ar^2 + \cdots + ar^{n-1} + \cdots, |r| < 1$
2. Divergent: $a + ar + ar^2 + \cdots + ar^{n-1} + \cdots, |r| > 1$
3. Divergent: $a + (a + d) + (a + 2d) + (a + 3d) + \cdots$
4. Divergent: $1 + \frac{1}{2} + \frac{1}{3} + \frac{1}{4} + \frac{1}{5} + \cdots + \frac{1}{n} + \cdots$
5. Convergent: $1 + \frac{1}{2^p} + \frac{1}{3^p} + \cdots + \frac{1}{n^p} + \cdots, p > 1$

If a series has all positive terms, the **comparison test** can be used to determine whether the series is convergent or divergent.

Comparison Test

A series of positive terms is convergent if each term of the series is equal to or less than the value of the corresponding term of some convergent series of positive terms. The series is divergent if each term is equal to or greater than the corresponding term of some divergent series of positive terms.

example

5 **Use the comparison test to determine whether the following series is convergent or divergent.**

$$\frac{1}{2 + 1^2} + \frac{1}{2 + 2^2} + \frac{1}{2 + 3^2} + \cdots$$

The general term of this series is $\frac{1}{2 + n^2}$. The general term of the convergent series $1 + \frac{1}{2^2} + \frac{1}{3^2} + \frac{1}{4^2} + \cdots$ is $\frac{1}{n^2}$. Since $\frac{1}{2 + n^2} < \frac{1}{n^2}$ for any n, the series $\frac{1}{2 + 1^2} + \frac{1}{2 + 2^2} + \frac{1}{2 + 3^2} + \cdots$ is also convergent.

example

6 **Use the comparison test to determine whether the following series is convergent or divergent.**

$$\frac{1}{2} + \frac{2}{3} + \frac{3}{4} + \cdots + \frac{n}{n+1} + \cdots$$

The general term of this series is $\frac{n}{n+1}$. The general term of the divergent series $1 + \frac{1}{2} + \frac{1}{3} + \frac{1}{4} + \cdots$ is $\frac{1}{n}$. You can show that $\frac{n}{n+1} > \frac{1}{n}$ for $n > 2$, as follows.

If $n > 2$, then $n - 1 > 1$.

$$n(n-1) > 1 \text{ or } n^2 - n > 1$$
$$n^2 > n + 1$$
$$\frac{n^2}{n+1} > 1$$
$$\frac{n}{n+1} > \frac{1}{n}$$

Thus, the series is divergent.

The series is divergent for $n > 2$. Therefore it is also divergent for $n > 0$. Why?

exercises

Exploratory Determine whether each series is convergent or divergent.

1. $1 + 3 + 5 + \cdots$
2. $\frac{1}{4} + \frac{5}{16} + \frac{3}{8} + \frac{7}{16} + \cdots$
3. $\frac{1}{9} + \frac{1}{27} + \frac{1}{81} + \cdots + \frac{1}{3^{n+1}} + \cdots$
4. $1 + \frac{1}{5} + \frac{1}{25} + \cdots + \frac{1}{5^{n-1}} + \cdots$
5. $\frac{1}{2} + \frac{1}{8} + \frac{1}{32} + \cdots + \frac{1}{2^{2n-1}} + \cdots$
6. $\frac{8}{3} + \frac{32}{9} + \frac{128}{27} + \cdots + \frac{2^{2n+1}}{3^n} + \cdots$

Written Use the ratio test to determine whether each series is convergent or divergent.

1. $\frac{1}{2} + \frac{2}{2^2} + \frac{3}{2^3} + \cdots + \frac{n}{2^n} + \cdots$
2. $1 + \frac{1}{2^2} + \frac{1}{3^3} + \frac{1}{4^4} + \cdots + \frac{1}{n^n} + \cdots$
3. $1 + \frac{1}{1 \cdot 2} + \frac{1}{1 \cdot 2 \cdot 3} + \frac{1}{1 \cdot 2 \cdot 3 \cdot 4} + \cdots$
4. $\frac{1}{1 \cdot 2} + \frac{1}{2 \cdot 2^2} + \frac{1}{3 \cdot 2^3} + \cdots + \frac{1}{n \cdot 2^n} + \cdots$
5. $1 + \frac{2}{1 \cdot 2 \cdot 3} + \frac{3}{1 \cdot 2 \cdot 3 \cdot 4 \cdot 5} + \cdots$
6. $1 + \frac{1}{1 \cdot 2 \cdot 3} + \frac{1}{1 \cdot 2 \cdot 3 \cdot 4 \cdot 5} + \cdots$
7. $\frac{1}{1 \cdot 2} + \frac{1}{3 \cdot 4} + \frac{1}{5 \cdot 6} + \cdots$
8. $\frac{1}{1 \cdot 2} + \frac{1}{1 \cdot 2 \cdot 3 \cdot 4} + \frac{1}{1 \cdot 2 \cdot 3 \cdot 4 \cdot 5 \cdot 6} + \cdots$

Determine whether each series is convergent or divergent.

9. $\frac{1}{1^2} + \frac{1}{3^2} + \frac{1}{5^2} + \cdots + \frac{1}{(2n-1)^2} + \cdots$
10. $\frac{2}{1} + \frac{3}{2} + \frac{4}{3} + \cdots + \frac{n+1}{n} + \cdots$
11. $\frac{1}{2 \cdot 1} + \frac{1}{2 \cdot 2} + \frac{1}{2 \cdot 3} + \cdots + \frac{1}{2n} + \cdots$
12. $\frac{3}{4} + \frac{3}{5} + \frac{3}{6} + \frac{3}{7} + \cdots + \frac{3}{n+3} + \cdots$

Excursions in Mathematics

The following sequence is called the **Fibonacci sequence.**

1, 1, 2, 3, 5, 8, 13, 21, 34, 55, . . .

Each term after the second is the sum of the two previous terms. The numbers in the sequence are called **Fibonacci numbers.**

Fibonacci numbers are often found in nature. For example, the seeds of a sunflower are arranged in spirals, 34 in one direction and 55 in the other direction.

Leonardo Fibonacci first discovered this sequence while studying rabbits. He wanted to know how many pairs of rabbits would be produced in n months, starting with a single pair of newborn rabbits. He made the following assumptions.

1. Newborn rabbits become adults in one month.
2. Each pair of adult rabbits produces one pair each month.
3. No rabbits die.

Let F_n represent the number of pairs of rabbits at the end of n months. If you begin with one pair of newborn rabbits, $F_0 = F_1 = 1$. This pair of rabbits would produce one pair at the end of the second month, so $F_2 = 1 + 1$, or 2. At the end of the third month the first pair of rabbits would produce another pair. Thus, $F_3 = 2 + 1$, or 3.

The chart below shows the number of rabbits each month for several months. Do you see the pattern?

Month	Adult Pairs	Newborn Pairs	Total
F_0	0	1	1
F_1	1	0	1
F_2	1	1	2
F_3	2	1	3
F_4	3	2	5
F_5	5	3	8

In general, at the end of the nth month all pairs of rabbits which were alive at the end of the $(n - 2)$nd month would produce one pair. Thus, there would be F_{n-1} adult pairs and F_{n-2} newborn pairs.

Exercises Solve each problem.

1. Write the first 20 terms of the Fibonacci sequence.
2. Starting with a single pair of newborn rabbits, how many rabbits would there be at the end of 12 months?
3. Write the first 10 terms of the sequence for which $F_0 = 3$, $F_1 = 4$, and $F_n = F_{n-2} + F_{n-1}$.
4. Write the first 10 terms of the sequence for which $F_0 = 1$, $F_1 = 5$, and $F_n = F_{n-2} + F_{n-1}$.

8-6 Sigma Notation and the *n*th Term

In mathematics, the Greek letter sigma, Σ, is used to indicate a sum or series. For example, $\sum_{k=1}^{4} 4k$ represents a series of terms which are obtained by multiplying 4 times k, first for $k = 1$, then for $k = 2$, then for $k = 3$, and finally for $k = 4$.

This is read "the summation from k = 1 to 4 of 4 times k."

$$\sum_{k=1}^{4} 4k = 4(1) + 4(2) + 4(3) + 4(4)$$
$$= 4 + 8 + 12 + 16$$
$$= 40$$

The variable used with the summation symbol, Σ, is called the **index of summation.** In the example shown above, the index of summation is k.

Any variable can be used for the index.

examples

1 **Write $\sum_{S=4}^{9} (2S - 1)$ in expanded form and find the sum.**

$$\sum_{S=4}^{9} (2S - 1) = \underbrace{(2\cdot 4 - 1)} + \underbrace{(2\cdot 5 - 1)} + \underbrace{(2\cdot 6 - 1)} + \underbrace{(2\cdot 7 - 1)} + \underbrace{(2\cdot 8 - 1)} + \underbrace{(2\cdot 9 - 1)}$$
$$= 7 + 9 + 11 + 13 + 15 + 17$$
$$= 72$$

2 **Find the sum of the infinite geometric series $\sum_{r=0}^{\infty} 5(0.2)^r$ if it exists.**

$$\sum_{r=0}^{\infty} 5(0.2)^r = 5 + 1 + 0.2 + 0.04 + \ldots \qquad a = 5 \text{ and } r = 0.2$$

The sum, S, equals $\frac{a}{1 - r}$, for $|r| < 1$. Therefore $S = \frac{5}{1 - 0.2}$ or 6.25.

A series in expanded form can be written using sigma notation if a general formula can be written for the nth term of the series.

example

3 **Write the series 3 + 5 + 7 + . . . + 53 using sigma notation.**

The nth term of the series is $1 + 2n$.
Since $53 = 1 + 2(26)$, the series has 26 terms.

$$3 + 5 + 7 + \ldots + 53 = \sum_{n=1}^{26} (1 + 2n).$$

Notice that $\sum_{n=2}^{27} (2n - 1)$ represents the same series. Why?

exercises

Exploratory Write each expression in expanded form and find the sum.

1. $\sum_{j=1}^{4} (j + 2)$
2. $\sum_{r=1}^{3} (r - 3)$
3. $\sum_{a=4}^{7} 2a$
4. $\sum_{k=5}^{8} 3k$
5. $\sum_{n=0}^{5} (2n - 1)$
6. $\sum_{n=0}^{6} ({}^-n - 1)$
7. $\sum_{p=5}^{7} (3p + 2)$
8. $\sum_{b=4}^{8} (4 - 2b)$

Written Write each expression in expanded form and find the sum.

1. $\sum_{p=3}^{7} (2p - 1)$
2. $\sum_{z=1}^{9} (10 - z)$
3. $\sum_{r=3}^{6} (r + 2)$
4. $\sum_{j={}^-3}^{3} (2j + 2)$
5. $\sum_{r=6}^{10} (r + 4)$
6. $\sum_{k=2}^{7} (5 - 2k)$
7. $\sum_{m=1}^{4} 4^m$
8. $\sum_{n=3}^{6} (3^n + 1)$
9. $\sum_{b=2}^{5} (b^2 + b)$
10. $\sum_{b=3}^{5} (2^b - b)$
11. $\sum_{a=0}^{4} (0.5 + 2^a)$
12. $\sum_{p=1}^{4} \left(3^{p-1} + \frac{1}{2}\right)$
13. $\sum_{k=1}^{\infty} 4\left(\frac{1}{2}\right)^k$
14. $\sum_{n=1}^{\infty} 3\left(\frac{1}{2}\right)^{n+1}$
15. $\sum_{b=0}^{\infty} 6\left(\frac{2}{3}\right)^b$
16. $\sum_{j=0}^{\infty} 5\left(\frac{3}{4}\right)^j$
17. $\sum_{r=2}^{\infty} \left(\frac{9}{10}\right)^r$
18. $\sum_{b=3}^{\infty} 2\left(\frac{3}{8}\right)^b$

Write each series using sigma notation.

19. $3 + 6 + 9 + 12$
20. $10 + 20 + 30 + 40 + 50$
21. $2 + 4 + 8 + \cdots + 64$
22. $3 + 6 + 12 + \cdots + 48$
23. $\frac{1}{2} + \frac{1}{3} + \frac{1}{4} + \cdots + \frac{1}{10}$
24. $\frac{1}{2} + \frac{1}{4} + \frac{1}{6} + \cdots + \frac{1}{14}$
25. $30 + 300 + 3000 + 30,000$
26. $16 + 8 + 4 + 2 + 1$
27. $11 + 9 + 7 + 5$
28. 19, 18, 16, 12, 4
29. ${}^-8 + 4 - 2 + 1$
30. $10 + 17 + 26 + 37$
31. $2 + 4 + 6 + \cdots$
32. $4 + 9 + 14 + \cdots$
33. $\frac{2}{5} + \frac{3}{5} + \frac{4}{5} + \cdots$
34. $\frac{2}{3} + \frac{2}{4} + \frac{2}{5} + \cdots$
35. $3 + 9 + 27 + \cdots$
36. $5 + 25 + 125 + \cdots$

Challenge Determine whether the given equations are *true* or *false*.

1. $\sum_{k=0}^{5} a^k + \sum_{n=6}^{10} a^n = \sum_{b=0}^{10} a^b$
2. $\sum_{r=3}^{7} 3^r + \sum_{a=7}^{9} 3^a = \sum_{j=3}^{9} 3^j$
3. $\sum_{n=1}^{10} (5 + n) = \sum_{m=0}^{9} (4 + m)$
4. $\sum_{r=2}^{8} (2r - 3) = \sum_{s=3}^{9} (2s - 5)$
5. $2 \sum_{k=3}^{7} k^2 = \sum_{k=3}^{7} 2k^2$
6. $3 \sum_{n=1}^{5} (n + 3) = \sum_{n=1}^{15} (n + 3)$
7. $\sum_{a=1}^{12} ({}^-a) + \sum_{a=1}^{12} (2a + 9) = \sum_{a=1}^{12} (a + 9)$
8. $2 \sum_{b=2}^{9} b^3 + \sum_{b=1}^{8} \frac{1}{b} = \sum_{b=1}^{8} \left[2(b + 1)^3 + \frac{1}{b}\right]$

8-7 The Binomial Theorem

The binomial expression $(x + y)$ can be raised to various powers. An important series is generated when $(x + y)^n$ is expanded. Consider the special cases where n is a small positive integer.

$$(x + y)^0 = 1$$
$$(x + y)^1 = x + y$$
$$(x + y)^2 = x^2 + 2xy + y^2$$
$$(x + y)^3 = x^3 + 3x^2y + 3xy^2 + y^3$$
$$(x + y)^4 = x^4 + 4x^3y + 6x^2y^2 + 4xy^3 + y^4$$

The following patterns are seen in the above expansions.

1. The expansion of $(x + y)^n$ has $n + 1$ terms.
2. The first term is x^n and the last term is y^n.
3. In successive terms the exponent of x decreases by 1 and the exponent of y increases by 1.
4. The degree of each term is n.
5. In any term if the coefficient is multiplied by the exponent of x and the product is divided by the number of that term, the result is the coefficient of the following term.
6. The coefficients are symmetric. They increase at the beginning and decrease at the end of the expansion.

example

1 Use the patterns to write $(x + y)^6$ in expanded form.

First, write the series, omitting coefficients. The exponents of x decrease from 6 to 0 while the exponents of y increase from 0 to 6.

$$x^6 + x^5y + x^4y^2 + x^3y^3 + x^2y^4 + xy^5 + y^6 \qquad y^0 = 1,\ x^0 = 1$$

Then, find the coefficients of each term. The first coefficient is 1. Pattern **5** listed above can be used to find successive coefficients.

Second Coefficient	Third Coefficient	Fourth Coefficient
$\frac{6 \cdot 1}{1} = 6$	$\frac{5 \cdot 6}{2} = 15$	$\frac{4 \cdot 15}{3} = 20$

Since the coefficients are symmetric, the coefficients of the last three terms are 15, 6, and 1.

Thus, $(x + y)^6 = x^6 + 6x^5y + 15x^4y^2 + 20x^3y^3 + 15x^2y^4 + 6xy^5 + y^6$

The general form of the expansion of $(x + y)^n$ is given by the **binomial theorem.**

If n is a positive integer, then the following is true.

$$(x + y)^n = x^n + nx^{n-1}y^1 + \frac{n(n-1)}{1 \cdot 2}x^{n-2}y^2 + \frac{n(n-1)(n-2)}{1 \cdot 2 \cdot 3}x^{n-3}y^3 + \cdots + y^n$$

The Binomial Theorem

example

2 **Use the binomial theorem to expand $(3a^2 - 2b)^4$.**

$$(3a^2 - 2b)^4 = (3a^2)^4 + 4(3a^2)^3(^-2b) + \frac{4 \cdot 3(3a^2)^2(^-2b)^2}{1 \cdot 2} + \frac{4 \cdot 3 \cdot 2(3a^2)(^-2b)^3}{1 \cdot 2 \cdot 3} + \frac{4 \cdot 3 \cdot 2(^-2b)^4}{1 \cdot 2 \cdot 3 \cdot 4}$$
$$= 81a^8 - 216a^6b + 216a^4b^2 - 96a^2b^3 + 16b^4$$

When using the binomial theorem, often it is necessary to find the product of consecutive integers. The product $1 \cdot 2 \cdot 3 \cdot 4 \cdot 5$ is called **5 factorial** and symbolized **5!**

The expression $n!$ (n factorial) is defined as follows if n is an integer greater than zero.

$$n! = n(n - 1)(n - 2) \ldots (1)$$

Definition of n Factorial

By definition, $0! = 1$.

examples

3 **Evaluate 7!.**

$7! = 7 \cdot 6 \cdot 5 \cdot 4 \cdot 3 \cdot 2 \cdot 1 = 5040$

4 **Evaluate $\frac{6!}{4!}$.**

Notice that in the expansion of $n!$, you can stop writing the individual factors with any number d, and write as the final factor $(d - 1)!$.

$$\frac{6!}{4!} = \frac{6 \cdot 5 \cdot 4!}{4!} = 30$$

An equivalent form of the binomial theorem uses both sigma notation and factorial notation. It is written as follows.

$$(x + y)^n = \sum_{r=0}^{n} \frac{n!}{r!(n - r)!} x^{n-r} y^r$$

Here n is a positive integer, and r is a positive integer or zero.

example

5 **Find the fifth term of $(2a - 3b)^8$.**

$$(2a - 3b)^8 = \sum_{r=0}^{8} \frac{8!}{r!(8 - r)!}(2a)^{8-r}(^-3b)^r$$

Since r increases from 0 to n, r is one less than the number of the term.

The fifth term, $\frac{8!}{4!(8 - 4)!}(2a)^{8-4}(^-3b)^4$, is $\frac{8 \cdot 7 \cdot 6 \cdot 5}{4 \cdot 3 \cdot 2 \cdot 1}(2a)^4(^-3b)^4$, or $90{,}720a^4b^4$.

The coefficients of the terms in the expansion of $(x + y)^n$ can be arranged in the form of a number pyramid called **Pascal's triangle,** as shown below. In the first row, $n = 0$.

```
            1
          1   1
        1   2   1
      1   3   3   1
    1   4   6   4   1
  1   5  10  10   5   1
1   6  15  20  15   6   1
```

The triangle may be extended indefinitely.

If two consecutive numbers in any row are added, the sum is a number in the following row. The three numbers form a triangle, as shown above. In any row the second number indicates the power to which the binomial is raised.

example

6 **Use Pascal's triangle to expand $(2a + b)^7$.**

Extend the triangle to the row which has a seven as the second number.

1 7 21 35 35 21 7 1

Then write the expansion and simplify each term.

$$(2a + b)^7 = (2a)^7 + 7(2a)^6b + 21(2a)^5b^2 + 35(2a)^4b^3 + 35(2a)^3b^4 + 21(2a)^2b^5 + 7(2a)b^6 + b^7$$

$$(2a + b)^7 = 128a^7 + 448a^6b + 672a^5b^2 + 560a^4b^3 + 280a^3b^4 + 84a^2b^5 + 14ab^6 + b^7$$

exercises

Exploratory Write each product in factorial notation.

1. $1 \cdot 2 \cdot 3 \cdot 4 \cdot 5 \cdot 6$
2. $5 \cdot 4 \cdot 3 \cdot 2 \cdot 1$
3. $1 \cdot 3 \cdot 5 \cdot 7 \cdot 8 \cdot 6 \cdot 4 \cdot 2$
4. $9 \cdot 4 \cdot 5 \cdot 6 \cdot 8 \cdot 3 \cdot 2 \cdot 7 \cdot 1$
5. $8 \cdot 7 \cdot 6 \cdot 5$
6. $7 \cdot 6 \cdot 5 \cdot 4$
7. $17 \cdot 16 \cdot 15$
8. $12 \cdot 11 \cdot 10 \cdot 9 \cdot 8$

Written Evaluate each expression.

1. $5!$
2. $9!$
3. $7!$
4. $4!$
5. $3(6!)$
6. $2(5!)$
7. $3!4!$
8. $5!3!$
9. $\frac{6!}{4!3!}$
10. $\frac{9!}{5!3!}$
11. $\frac{10!}{8!}$
12. $\frac{12!}{11!}$

Use the binomial theorem to expand each binomial.

13. $(n + 2)^7$
14. $(x + 3)^6$
15. $(2 + d)^4$
16. $(4 - b)^4$
17. $(2x - 3y)^3$
18. $(x - 2y)^4$
19. $(2x + y)^6$
20. $(3x - y)^5$
21. $(2x + \sqrt{3})^4$
22. $\left(\frac{x}{y} + v\right)^5$
23. $\left(3v - \frac{1}{2}w\right)^5$
24. $\left(\frac{1}{2}a + \frac{2}{3}b\right)^5$

Find the designated term of each binomial.

25. 4th term of $(a + b)^7$
26. 5th term of $(2x - y)^9$
27. 3rd term of $(x - 3y)^5$
28. 7th term of $\left(x - \frac{1}{2}y\right)^{10}$
29. 4th term of $(a - \sqrt{2})^8$
30. 6th term of $(3x - 2y)^{11}$

Use Pascal's triangle to expand each binomial.

31. $(x + y)^5$
32. $(a + b)^7$
33. $(r - s)^6$
34. $(x - 2)^7$

Simplify each of the following as far as possible. Assume x and y are positive integers, x > y, x > 2.

35. $\frac{x!}{(x - 2)!}$
36. $\frac{x!}{(x - y)!}$
37. $\frac{(x + 1)!}{(x - 1)!}$
38. $\frac{x!}{(x - y)!y!}$
39. $\frac{(x - y)!}{(x - y - 1)!}$
40. $\frac{x!(x - 3)!}{(x - 2)!(x - 1)!}$

Challenge Assume the binomial theorem is true for all rational values of n. Find an approximate value of $\sqrt{6}$ by applying the binomial theorem to the form of $\sqrt{6}$ derived below.

$$\sqrt{6} = \sqrt{4 + 2} = 2\sqrt{1 + \frac{2}{4}} = 2\left(1 + \frac{1}{2}\right)^{\frac{1}{2}}$$

8-8 Mathematical Induction

A method of proof called mathematical induction can be used when you have a formula or conjecture to prove.

Mathematical induction is a proof which depends on a process that is much like climbing a ladder. First you must get on the first step. Then you must show that you can always advance from one step to the next. Thus, if you can get onto the first step you can certainly climb to the second. If you are on the second step you can climb to the third. If you are on the third step you can climb to the fourth; and so on, indefinitely, for all steps.

Consider the series $1 + 3 + 5 + 7 + \cdots$. What is the sum of the first two terms? The first three terms? The first four terms? Notice that the sum seems to be the square of the number of terms being added. Mathematical induction can be used to prove that the sum of n terms of this sequence is indeed n^2. The proof is based on two essential steps.

1. Verify that $S_n = n^2$ is the correct formula for the sum of n terms when $n = 1$, the first possible case.

Certainly the sum is 1 and $n^2 = 1$, so the formula $S_n = n^2$ is valid for the first case. You are on the first step of the ladder.

2. Show that if the formula is valid for any special case (say $n = k$) then it is necessarily valid for the next case ($n = k + 1$). Notice that the kth term of the series $1 + 3 + 5 + \cdots$ is $2k - 1$. You must prove that if $1 + 3 + 5 + \cdots + (2k - 1) = k^2$, then the formula is also valid for $n = k + 1$, shown below.

$$1 + 3 + 5 + \cdots + (2k - 1) + (2k + 1) = (k + 1)^2$$

The $(k + 1)$th term is $2k + 1$.

This means that the sum S_k is given by $1 + 3 + 5 + \ldots + (2k - 1) = k^2$, and you must prove that $S_{k+1} = (k + 1)^2$. From the assumption that $S_k = k^2$, you can write a formula for S_{k+1} by adding the next term $(2k + 1)$ to both sides.

$$S_{k+1} = 1 + 3 + 5 + \cdots + (2k - 1) + (2k + 1) = k^2 + (2k + 1)$$

When the formula $S_n = n^2$ is applied for $n = k + 1$, the result is $S_{k+1} = (k + 1)^2$. Is the result obtained by direct addition, $k^2 + (2k + 1)$, equal to $(k + 1)^2$? This can be verified as follows.

$$\begin{aligned}(k + 1)^2 &= k^2 + 2k + 1\\ &= k^2 + (2k + 1)\end{aligned}$$

Since the formula for the sum for $n = k + 1$ gives the same result as the direct computation of the sum of the series, the formula is valid for $n = k + 1$ if it is valid for $n = k$. Thus, you can conclude that since the formula is valid for $n = 1$, it is also valid for $n = 2$. Since it is valid for $n = 2$, it is valid for $n = 3$, and so on, indefinitely. Therefore the following formula is valid for any positive integer n.

$$S_n = 1 + 3 + 5 + \cdots + (2n - 1) = n^2$$

In general, the following steps must be included in any proof by mathematical induction.

Proof by Mathematical Induction

1. **First, verify that the formula is valid for the first possible case, usually $n = 1$.**
2. **Then assume that the formula is valid for $n = k$ and prove that it is also valid for $n = k + 1$. Usually the result obtained by some direct method of arriving at the $(k + 1)$ case from the k case is compared with the result obtained by the formula to be verified.**
3. **Since the formula is valid for $n = 1$ (or other first case), it is valid for $n = 2$. Since it is valid for $n = 2$, it is valid for $n = 3$, and so on, indefinitely.**

example

1 **Prove that the formula for the sum of the first n positive integers is $\frac{n(n+1)}{2}$.**

To prove that $1 + 2 + 3 + \ldots + n = \frac{n(n+1)}{2}$, first verify that the formula is valid for $n = 1$. Since $S_1 = 1$ and $\frac{1(1+1)}{2} = 1$, the formula is valid for $n = 1$.

Then, assume that the formula is valid for $n = k$, and show that it must also be valid for $n = k + 1$. Write the formula for $n = k$. Then derive a formula for $n = k + 1$ by adding the $(k + 1)$ term to both sides. Simplify the result.

$$1 + 2 + 3 + \cdots + k = \frac{k(k+1)}{2}$$

$$\begin{aligned} 1 + 2 + 3 + \cdots + k + (k+1) &= \frac{k(k+1)}{2} + (k+1) \\ &= \frac{k^2 + k}{2} + \frac{2k+2}{2} \\ &= \frac{k^2 + 3k + 2}{2} \end{aligned}$$

Apply the formula to be proved for $n = k + 1$.

$$S_{k+1} = \frac{(k+1)(k+2)}{2} \text{ or } \frac{k^2 + 3k + 2}{2}$$

The formula gives the same result as adding the $(k + 1)$ term directly. Thus, if the formula is valid for $n = k$ it is also valid for $n = k + 1$.

Since the formula is valid for $n = 1$, it is also valid for $n = 2$. Since it is valid for $n = 2$, it is valid for $n = 3$, and so on, indefinitely.

Therefore, the formula $S_n = 1 + 2 + 3 + \cdots + n = \frac{n(n+1)}{2}$ is valid for all positive integral values of n.

Mathematical induction can be used to prove that the expansion formula for the binomial $(x + y)^n$ is valid for all positive integral values of n.

example

2 **Prove that the following formula is valid for all positive integral values of n.**

$$(x + y)^n = x^n + nx^{n-1}y^1 + \frac{n(n-1)}{2!}x^{n-2}y^2 + \frac{n(n-1)(n-2)}{3!}x^{n-3}y^3 + \cdots + y^n$$

First, show that the formula is valid for $n = 1$.

Since, $(x + y)^1 = x^1 + 1x^0y^1$, or $x + y$, the formula is valid for $n = 1$.

Next, assume that the formula is valid for $n = k$ and prove that it is also valid for $n = k + 1$. By substituting k for n, the following formula is obtained.

$$(x + y)^k = x^k + kx^{k-1}y + \frac{k(k - 1)}{2!}x^{k-2}y^2 + \cdots + y^k$$

To find the value for $n = k + 1$ directly, you can multiply each side of the above equation by $(x + y)$.

$$(x + y)^k(x + y) = (x + y)\left(x^k + kx^{k-1}y + \frac{k(k - 1)}{2!}x^{k-2}y^2 + \cdots + y^k\right)$$

This can be simplified as shown below.

$$\begin{aligned}(x + y)^{k+1} &= x\left(x^k + kx^{k-1}y + \frac{k(k - 1)}{2!}x^{k-2}y^2 + \cdots + y^k\right) + \\ &\quad y\left(x^k + kx^{k-1}y + \frac{k(k - 1)}{2!}x^{k-2}y^2 + \cdots + y^k\right) \\ &= x^{k+1} + kx^ky + \frac{k(k - 1)}{2!}x^{k-1}y^2 + \cdots + xy^k + \\ &\quad x^ky + kx^{k-1}y^2 + \frac{k(k - 1)}{2!}x^{k-2}y^3 + \cdots + y^{k+1}\end{aligned}$$

The following result is obtained when like terms are combined.

$$(x + y)^{k+1} = x^{k+1} + (k + 1)x^ky + \frac{k(k + 1)}{2!}x^{k-1}y^2 + \cdots + y^{k+1}$$

If $(k + 1)$ is substituted into the original formula, the same result is obtained. Thus, if the formula is valid for $n = k$ it is also valid for $n = k + 1$.

The formula is valid for $n = 1$. Therefore it is also valid for $n = 2$. If it is valid for $n = 2$, it is valid for $n = 3$, and so on. Thus, the formula is valid for all positive integral values of n.

exercises

Written Use mathematical induction to prove that the following formulas are valid for all positive integral values of n.

1. $2 + 4 + 6 + \cdots + 2n = n(n + 1)$
2. $1 + 4 + 7 + \cdots + (3n - 2) = \frac{n(3n - 1)}{2}$
3. $1 + 3 + 6 + \cdots + \frac{n(n + 1)}{2} = \frac{n(n + 1)(n + 2)}{6}$
4. $1^2 + 2^2 + 3^2 + \cdots + n^2 = \frac{n(n + 1)(2n + 1)}{6}$
5. $1^3 + 2^3 + 3^3 + \cdots + n^3 = \frac{n^2(n + 1)^2}{4}$
6. $1^2 + 3^2 + \cdots + (2n - 1)^2 = \frac{n(2n - 1)(2n + 1)}{3}$

7. $1 + 2 + 4 + 8 + \cdots + 2^{n-1} = 2^n - 1$

8. $2 + 2^2 + 2^3 + \cdots + 2^n = 2^{n+1} - 2$

9. $\frac{1}{2} + \frac{1}{2^2} + \frac{1}{2^3} + \cdots + \frac{1}{2^n} = 1 - \frac{1}{2^n}$

10. $-\frac{1}{2} - \frac{1}{4} - \frac{1}{8} - \cdots - \frac{1}{2^n} = \frac{1}{2^n} - 1$

Use the preceding formulas to solve each problem.

11. Find the sum of the series $2 + 4 + 6 + \cdots + 48$.
12. Find the sum of the series $1 + 4 + 7 + \cdots + 148$.
13. Find the sum of the even integers between 19 and 41.
14. Find the sum of the even integers between 29 and 51.
15. Find the sum of the first ten terms of the series $1^3 + 2^3 + \cdots$.
16. Find the sum of the first nine terms of the series $1^2 + 3^2 + 5^2 + \cdots$.
17. Find the sum of the first six terms of the series $2^5 + 2^6 + 2^7 + \cdots$.
18. Find the sum of the first seven terms of the series $3^2 + 4^2 + 5^2 + \cdots$.

Challenge **Use mathematical induction to prove that the following formulas are valid for all positive integral values of *n*.**

1. $1^4 + 2^4 + \cdots + n^4 = \dfrac{6n^5 + 15n^4 + 10n^3 - n}{30}$.
2. $1^5 + 2^5 + \cdots + n^5 = \dfrac{2n^6 + 6n^5 + 5n^4 - n^2}{12}$
3. $a + (a + d) + (a + 2d) + \cdots + (a + (n - 1)d) = \frac{n}{2}(2a + (n - 1)d)$
4. $\dfrac{1}{1 \cdot 2} + \dfrac{1}{2 \cdot 3} + \dfrac{1}{3 \cdot 4} + \cdots + \dfrac{1}{n(n + 1)} = \dfrac{n}{n + 1}$

Chapter Summary

1. An arithmetic sequence is a sequence in which each term after the first, a, is equal to the sum of the preceding term and the common difference, d. The general form of the sequence, either finite or infinite, is $a, a + d, a + 2d, \cdots$. (204)
2. The nth term of an arithmetic sequence with the first term a and the common difference d is given by $a_n = a + (n - 1)d$. (204)
3. The sum of the first n terms of an arithmetic series is given by the formula $S_n = \frac{n}{2}(a + a_n)$. (206)
4. A geometric sequence is a sequence in which each term after the first, a, is the product of the preceding term and the common ratio, r. The general form of the sequence is
$$a, ar, ar^2, ar^3, \ldots . \quad (207)$$
5. The nth term of a geometric sequence is given by the formula $a_n = ar^{n-1}$. (208)
6. The sum of the first n terms of a geometric series is given by the formula $S_n = \dfrac{a - ar^n}{1 - r}$ $(r \neq 1)$. (209)

7. Definition of the Sum of an Infinite Series: If S_n is the sum of n terms of a series, and S is a number such that S is greater than S_n for all n, and $S - S_n$ approaches zero as n increases without limit, then the sum of the infinite series is S. $\lim_{n \to \infty} S_n = S$ (214)
8. The sum, S, of an infinite geometric series for which $|r| < 1$ is given by the formula $S = \frac{a}{1 - r}$. (214)
9. Definition of Convergent and Divergent Series: If an infinite series has a sum, or limit, the series is convergent. If an infinite series is not convergent, it is divergent. (217)
10. Ratio Test for Convergence: Let a_n and a_{n+1} represent two consecutive terms of a series of positive terms. Suppose r is defined as follows.

$$r = \lim_{n \to \infty} \frac{a_{n+1}}{a_n}$$

The series is convergent if $r < 1$ and divergent if $r > 1$. If $r = 1$, the test fails. (217)
11. Comparison Test: A series of positive terms is convergent if each term of the series is equal to or less than the value of the corresponding term of some convergent series of positive terms. The series is divergent if each term is equal to or greater than the corresponding term of some divergent series of positive terms. (219)
12. The Binomial Theorem: If n is a positive integer, then $(x + y)^n = x^n + nx^{n-1}y^1 + \frac{n(n-1)}{1 \cdot 2}x^{n-2}y^2 + \frac{n(n-1)(n-2)}{1 \cdot 2 \cdot 3}x^{n-3}y^3 + \cdots + y^n$. (224)
13. Definition of n Factorial: $n! = n(n - 1)(n - 2) \ldots (1)$ (225)
14. Proof by Mathematical Induction:
    1. Verify that the formula is valid for $n = 1$.
    2. Assume that the formula is valid for $n = k$ and prove that it is also valid for $n = k + 1$.
    3. Since the formula is valid for $n = 1$, it is valid for $n = 2$. Since it is valid for $n = 2$, it is valid for $n = 3$, and so on, indefinitely. (228)

Chapter Review

8-1 **Solve each problem.**

1. Find the next six terms of the sequence 3, 4.3, 5.6, ...
2. Find the 20th term of the arithmetic sequence for which $a = 7$ and $d = -4$.
3. Form a sequence which has three arithmetic means between 6 and -4.
4. Find the sum of the first 23 terms of the the series $-3 + 3 + 9 + \cdots$.

8-2 **Solve each problem.**

5. Find the next four terms of the sequence 343, 49, 7, ...
6. Find the 7th term of the geometric sequence for which $a = 2.2$ and $r = 2$.
7. Form a sequence which has three geometric means between 0.2 and 125.
8. Find the sum of 9 terms of the series $1.5 + 3 + 6 + \cdots$.

8-3 **Evaluate each limit, or state that the limit does not exist.**

9. $\lim_{n\to\infty} \frac{2n}{5n+1}$
10. $\lim_{n\to\infty} \frac{4n+1}{n}$
11. $\lim_{n\to\infty} \frac{n^2+3}{2n}$
12. $\lim_{n\to\infty} \frac{3n^2+n}{n^2-n}$
13. $\lim_{n\to\infty} \frac{(-1)^n n^2}{5n^2}$
14. $\lim_{n\to\infty} \frac{4n^3-3n}{n^4-4n^3}$

8-4 **Find the sum of each infinite geometric series, if it exists.**

15. $3 + 1 + \frac{1}{3} + \frac{1}{9} + \cdots$
16. $\frac{3}{16} + \frac{3}{8} + \frac{3}{4} + \cdots$

Write each repeating decimal as a fraction.

17. 0.727272 . . .
18. 3.454545 . . .

8-5 **Determine whether each series is convergent or divergent.**

19. $\frac{2}{3} + \frac{1}{9} + \frac{1}{54} + \frac{1}{324} + \cdots$
20. $1 + \frac{3}{2} + 2 + \frac{5}{2} + \cdots$
21. $\frac{1}{4} + 1 + 4 + 16 + \cdots$
22. $2 + 1 + \frac{2}{3} + \frac{1}{2} + \frac{2}{5} + \frac{1}{3} + \frac{2}{7} + \cdots$

8-6 **Write each expression in expanded form and find the sum.**

23. $\sum_{a=5}^{11} (2a - 4)$
24. $\sum_{k=1}^{\infty} (0.4)^k$

Write each series using sigma notation.

25. $^{-}1 + 1 + 3 + 5 + \cdots$
26. $2 + 5 + 10 + 17 + \cdots + 82$

8-7 **Evaluate each expression.**

27. 6!
28. 8!
29. $\frac{7!}{4!}$
30. $\frac{12!}{9!3!}$

Expand each binomial.

31. $(a - x)^6$
32. $(2r + 3s)^4$
33. $(2x - y)^7$

Find the designated term of each binomial.

34. 5th term of $(x - 1)^{15}$
35. 10th term of $(x + 1)^{15}$
36. 8th term of $(x + 3y)^{10}$

8-8 37. Use mathematical induction to prove that the following formula is valid for all positive integral values of n.

$$1 \cdot 3 + 2 \cdot 4 + 3 \cdot 5 + \cdots + n(n + 2) = \frac{n(n + 1)(2n + 7)}{6}$$

Chapter Test

Solve each problem.

1. Find the next five terms of the sequence 3, 4.5, 6, ...
2. Find the next four terms of the sequence $\frac{1}{4}, \frac{1}{10}, \frac{1}{25}, \frac{2}{125}, \ldots$.
3. Form a sequence which has 3 arithmetic means between $^-4$ and 8.
4. Form a sequence which has three geometric means between 16 and 1.
5. Find the 24th term of the sequence $^-6$, $^-1$, 4, ...
6. Find the 8th term of the sequence $\frac{1}{2}, \frac{3}{4}, \frac{9}{8}, \frac{27}{16}, \ldots$.
7. Find n for an arithmetic sequence for which $S_n = 345$, $a = 12$, and $d = 5$.
8. Find the sum of the first 10 terms of the geometric series $\frac{5}{2} + 5 + 10 + \cdots$.

Evaluate each limit, or state that the limit does not exist.

9. $\lim\limits_{n\to\infty} \dfrac{n^3 + 3}{3n^2 + 1}$
10. $\lim\limits_{n\to\infty} \dfrac{n^3 + 4}{2n^3 + 3n}$

Find the sum of each infinite geometric series, if it exists.

11. $\frac{1}{4} + \frac{1}{8} + \frac{1}{16} + \cdots$
12. $1 + \frac{4}{3} + \frac{16}{9} + \cdots$

Write each repeating decimal as a fraction.

13. 0.324324324 . . .
14. 1.91919 . . .

Determine whether each series is convergent or divergent.

15. $\frac{1}{6} + \frac{1}{3} + \frac{1}{2} + \frac{2}{3} + \cdots$
16. $1 + \frac{2}{3} + \frac{3}{3^2} + \frac{4}{3^3} + \cdots$

Write each expression in expanded form and find the sum.

17. $\sum\limits_{n=3}^{8} (n^2 + 1)$
18. $\sum\limits_{k=2}^{7} (2^k - k)$

Write each series using sigma notation.

19. $5 + 10 + 15 + \cdots + 95$
20. $7 + 9 + 11 + 13 + \cdots$

Evaluate each expression.

21. $\dfrac{9!}{4!5!}$
22. $\dfrac{11!}{8!2!}$

Find the designated term of each binomial.

23. 6th term of $(a + 2)^{10}$
24. 5th term of $(3x - y)^8$
25. Use mathematical induction to prove that the following formula is valid for all positive integral values of n.

$$2 \cdot 3 + 4 \cdot 5 + 6 \cdot 7 + \cdots + 2n(2n + 1) = \frac{n(n + 1)(4n + 5)}{3}.$$

Chapter 9

Polar Coordinates and Complex Numbers

This nautilus shell is shaped like a spiral. The graph of a spiral can be drawn using polar coordinates.

9-1 Polar Coordinates

Points in a plane can be identified using **polar coordinates** of the form (r, θ). A fixed point O in the plane is called the **pole** or origin. The **polar axis** is a ray whose initial point is the pole. The distance from the pole to a point P with polar coordinates (r, θ) is $|r|$.

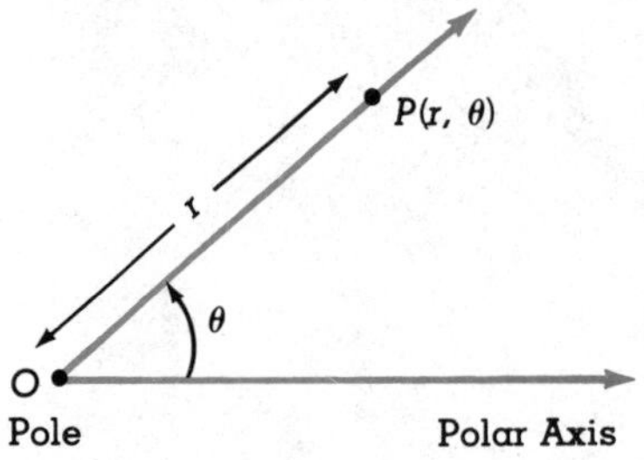

The polar axis is usually a horizontal line directed toward the right from the pole.

If r is positive, θ (theta) is the measure of any angle in standard position having $\overrightarrow{OP}$ as terminal side, as shown below. If r is negative, θ is the measure of any angle having the ray opposite $\overrightarrow{OP}$ as terminal side. The angle can be measured in degrees or radians.

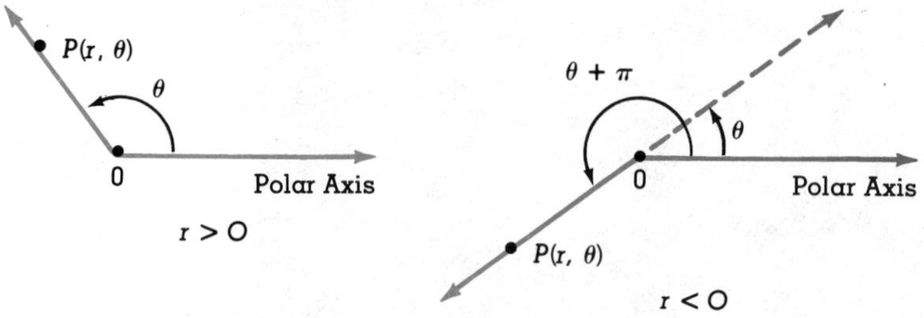

When θ is positive, the angle is measured counterclockwise from the polar axis.

example

1 **Graph the point P which has polar coordinates $\left(2, \frac{\pi}{3}\right)$.**

$\frac{\pi}{3} = 60°$ *Remember,* $\frac{R}{\pi} = \frac{D}{180°}$

Draw the terminal side of a 60° angle which has the polar axis as its initial side. Then find the point on the ray which is 2 units from the pole.

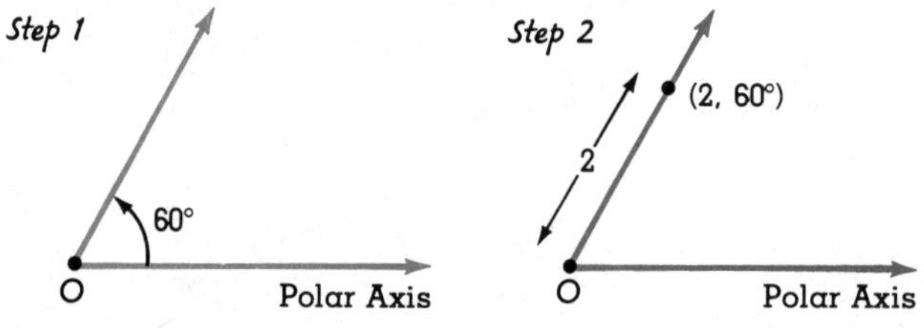

Either r or θ can be negative. If r is negative, the point (r, θ) is $|r|$ units from the pole on the ray opposite the terminal side of the angle with measure θ. If θ is negative, the angle is measured clockwise from the polar axis.

example

2 **Graph the point P which has polar coordinates $(^-2, {}^-60°)$.**

First, draw the terminal side of the angle. Negative angles are measured clockwise.

Since r is negative, the point $(^-2, {}^-60°)$ is 2 units from the pole along the ray opposite the terminal side of the angle.

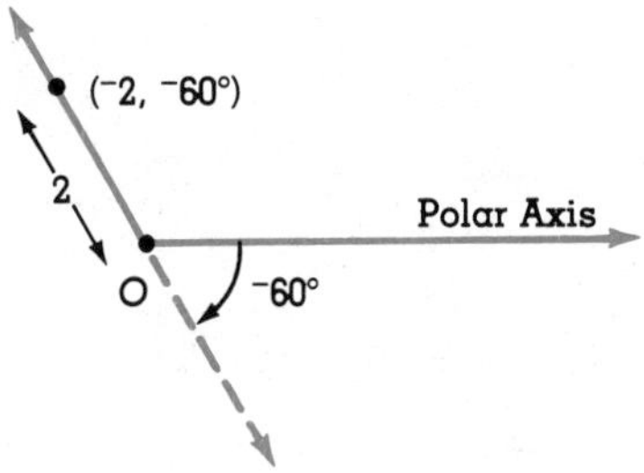

A point can be represented by more than one pair of polar coordinates. For example, the polar coordinates $(3, 150°)$, $(^-3, {}^-30°)$, $(^-3, 330°)$, and $(3, {}^-210°)$ all represent the same point, as shown below. In general, any point (r, θ) can also be represented by $(^-r, \theta \pm 180°)$ or $(r, \theta + n \cdot 360°)$ where n is any integer.

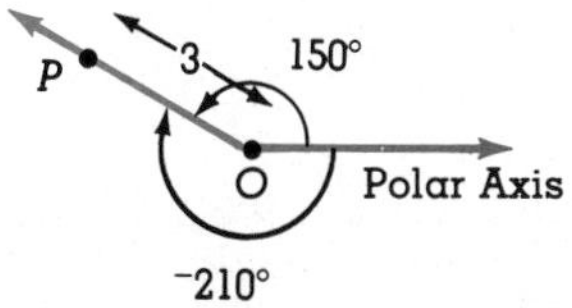

(3, 150°) or (3, ⁻210°)

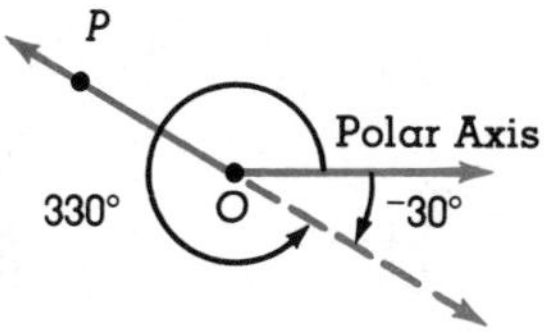

(⁻3, ⁻30°) or (⁻3, 330°)

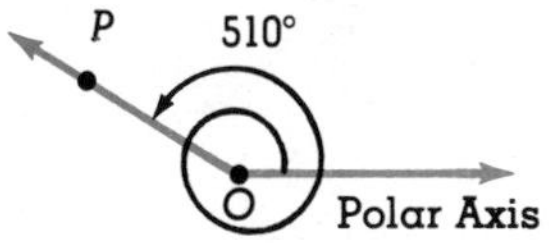

(3, 510°)

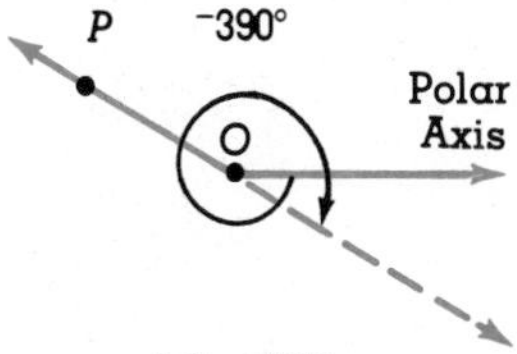

(⁻3, ⁻390°)

example

3 **Name four different pairs of polar coordinates which represent point R shown below. Suppose $^-360° \leq \theta \leq 360°$.**

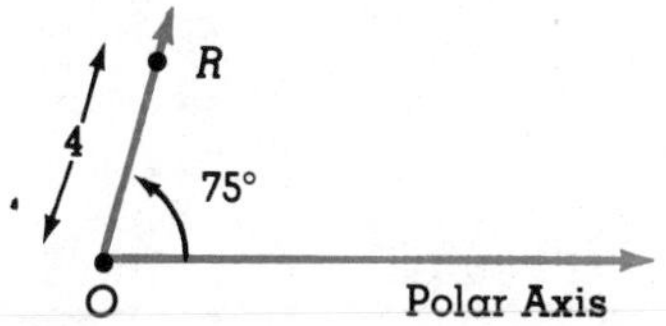

Point R can be represented by $(4, 75°)$, $(^-4, {}^-105°)$, $(^-4, 255°)$, or $(4, {}^-285°)$.

An equation which uses polar coordinates is called a **polar equation.** For example, $r = 2\theta$ is a polar equation. A **polar graph** represents the set of all points (r, θ) which satisfy a given equation.

examples

4 Graph $\theta = 30°$.

In this equation, r can have any value while θ must always be 30°. Thus, the graph is a line through the origin which forms an angle of 30° with the polar axis.

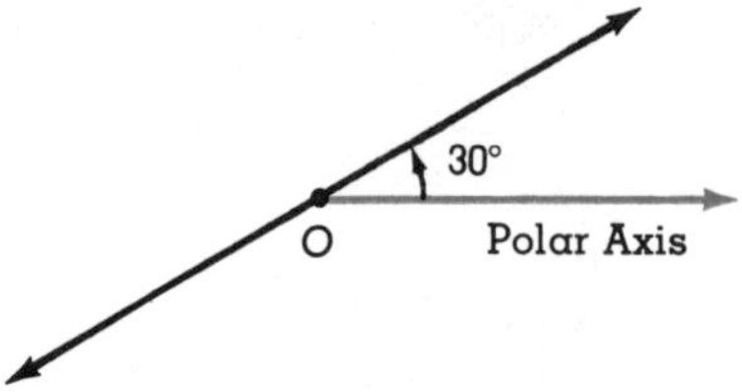

5 Graph $r = 3$.

In this equation θ can have any value while r must always equal 3. Thus, the graph is a circle with radius 3.

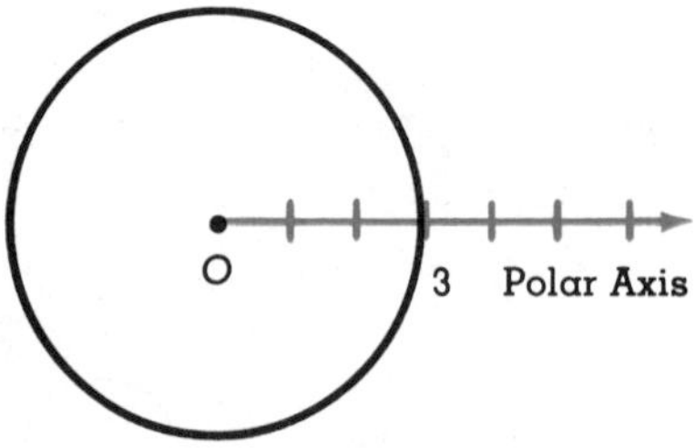

Compare this to the graph of $r = {}^{-}3$.

exercises

Exploratory Change each of the following radian measures to degrees. Round answers to the nearest degree.

1. π
2. $-\frac{\pi}{2}$
3. $-\frac{\pi}{4}$
4. $\frac{5\pi}{4}$
5. $-\frac{8}{3}\pi$
6. $\frac{5}{6}\pi$
7. $\frac{11\pi}{6}$
8. $\frac{7\pi}{4}$
9. 2
10. 5
11. $^{-}3$
12. $^{-}4$

Graph the point represented by the given polar coordinates. Then name three other pairs of polar coordinates which represent the same point. Suppose $^{-}360° \leq \theta \leq 360°$.

13. $\left(3, \frac{\pi}{6}\right)$
14. $\left({}^{-}2, -\frac{\pi}{3}\right)$
15. $({}^{-}2.4, 55°)$
16. $(3.1, {}^{-}100°)$

Written Graph the point which has the given polar coordinates.

1. $(1, 0)$
2. $\left(2, \frac{\pi}{2}\right)$
3. $\left(0.25, \frac{2\pi}{3}\right)$
4. $\left(0.5, -\frac{3\pi}{2}\right)$
5. $\left(^{-}1, \frac{\pi}{3}\right)$
6. $\left(^{-}3, \frac{5\pi}{6}\right)$
7. $\left(\frac{1}{2}, 1\right)$
8. $(4, {}^{-}3)$
9. $(5, {}^{-}45°)$
10. $(6, 225°)$
11. $(3, 315°)$
12. $(1, 330°)$

Graph each polar equation.

13. $r = 2$
14. $r = {}^{-}5$
15. $r = \sqrt{5}$
16. $r = 2^3$
17. $\theta = \frac{\pi}{2}$
18. $\theta = \frac{3\pi}{2}$
19. $\theta = -\frac{5\pi}{6}$
20. $\theta = -\pi$
21. $\theta = 135°$
22. $\theta = 80°$
23. $\theta = {}^{-}95°$
24. $\theta = {}^{-}220°$

9-2 Graphs of Polar Equations

Many interesting curves are obtained when polar equations are graphed. Study the following examples.

example

1 Graph $r = 8 \cos \theta$

First, make a table of values. Round values to the nearest tenth.

θ	$\cos \theta$	$8 \cos \theta$	(r, θ)
0°	1	8	(8, 0°)
30°	0.9	6.9	(6.9, 30°)
60°	0.5	4	(4, 60°)
90°	0	0	(0, 90°)
120°	⁻0.5	⁻4	(⁻4, 120°)
150°	⁻0.9	⁻6.9	(⁻6.9, 150°)
180°	⁻1	⁻8	(⁻8, 180°)
210°	⁻0.9	⁻6.9	(⁻6.9, 210°)
240°	⁻0.5	⁻4	(⁻4, 240°)
270°	0	0	(0, 270°)
300°	0.5	4	(4, 300°)
330°	0.9	6.9	(6.9, 330°)
360°	1	8	(8, 360°)

Then graph each point and connect the points with a smooth curve.

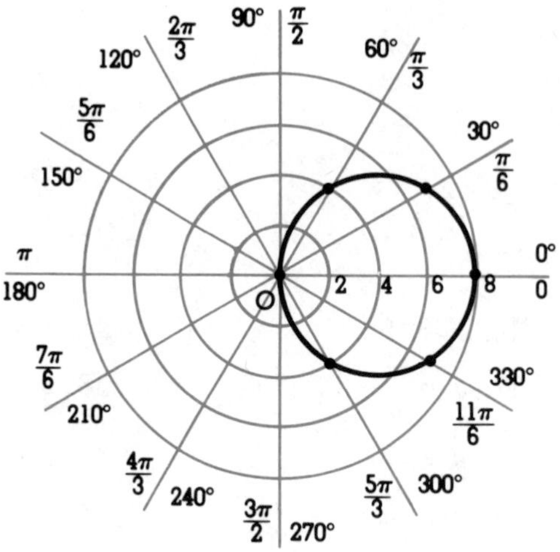

Notice that the entire graph is determined for 0° ≤ θ ≤ 180°

The graph of any polar equation of the form $r = 2a \cos \theta$ forms a circle centered at $(a, 0)$, as in the previous example.

example

2 **Graph $r = 1 + 2 \cos \theta$.**

θ	$1 + 2 \cos \theta$	(r, θ)
0°	3	(3, 0°)
30°	2.7	(2.7, 30°)
60°	2	(2, 60°)
90°	1	(1, 90°)
120°	0	(0, 120°)
150°	$^-0.7$	($^-0.7$, 150°)
180°	$^-1$	($^-1$, 180°)
210°	$^-0.7$	($^-0.7$, 210°)
240°	0	(0, 240°)
270°	1	(1, 270°)
300°	2	(2, 300°)
330°	2.7	(2.7, 330°)
360°	3	(3, 360°)

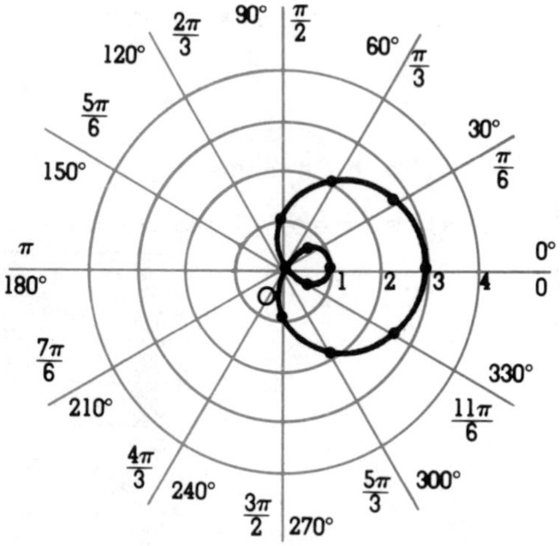

Notice that the graph is symmetric with respect to the polar axis.

The curve which represents the equation $r = 1 + 2 \cos \theta$ is called a **limaçon.** The limaçon is one of several **classical curves**, which can be formed by graphing polar equations. The equations which distinguish other classical curves are listed in the following chart.

Classical Curves				
Rose	**Lemniscate**	**Limaçon**	**Cardioid**	**Spiral of Archimedes**
$r = a \cos n\theta$ $r = a \sin n\theta$ *n is an integer > 0*	$r^2 = a^2 \cos 2\theta$ $r^2 = a^2 \sin 2\theta$	$r = a + b \cos \theta$ $r = a + b \sin \theta$	$r = a + a \cos \theta$ $r = a + a \sin \theta$	$r = a\theta$

Roses

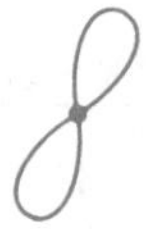

Lemniscate

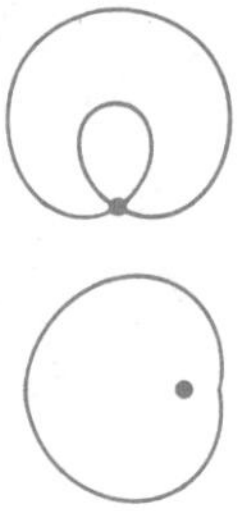

Limaçons

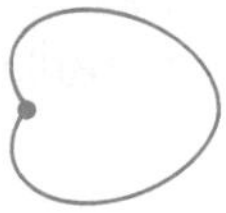

Cardioid

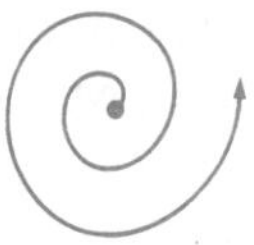

Spiral

To determine the exact shape of a classical curve you may need to graph many polar coordinates.

example

3 Graph $r = 2\theta$.

θ	2θ	r
$\frac{\pi}{6}$	$\frac{\pi}{3}$	1.0
$\frac{\pi}{3}$	$\frac{2\pi}{3}$	2.1
$\frac{\pi}{2}$	π	3.1
$\frac{2\pi}{3}$	$\frac{4\pi}{3}$	4.2
$\frac{5\pi}{6}$	$\frac{5\pi}{3}$	5.2
π	2π	6.3
$\frac{7\pi}{6}$	$\frac{7\pi}{3}$	7.3
$\frac{4\pi}{3}$	$\frac{8\pi}{3}$	8.4
$\frac{3\pi}{2}$	3π	9.4
$\frac{5\pi}{3}$	$\frac{10\pi}{3}$	10.5
$\frac{11\pi}{6}$	$\frac{11\pi}{3}$	11.5
2π	4π	12.6

In this example, θ must be expressed in radians since r is a real number.

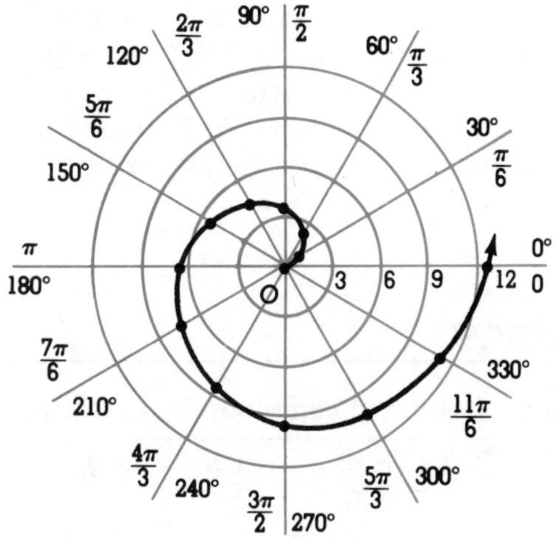

This curve is a spiral of Archimedes.

More than one polar equation can be graphed on the same polar coordinate system. However, the points where the graphs intersect do *not* always represent common solutions to the equations. This is possible since points in the polar coordinate system are *not* uniquely represented. Consider the following example.

example 4

Solve the following system of polar equations. Then compare the common solutions to the points of intersection of the polar graphs shown at the right.

$$r = 3 \cos 2\theta \qquad r = {}^{-}3$$

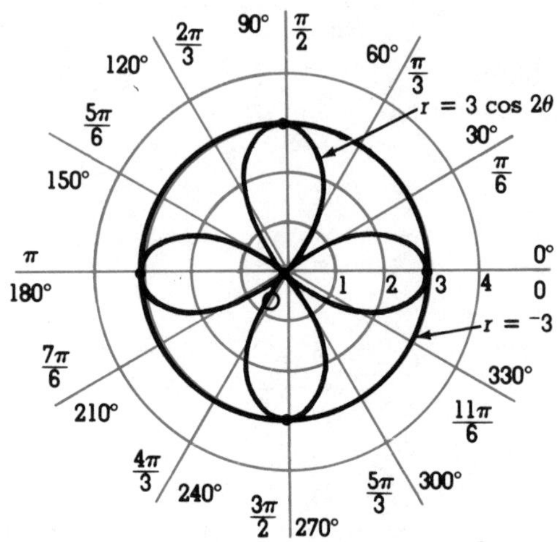

To solve the system of equations, eliminate r and solve for θ.

$$\begin{aligned} 3 \cos 2\theta &= {}^{-}3 \\ \cos 2\theta &= {}^{-}1 \\ 2\theta &= \arccos({}^{-}1) \\ 2\theta &= 180° \text{ or } {}^{-}180° \\ \theta &= 90° \text{ or } {}^{-}90° \end{aligned}$$

Thus, the common solutions are $({}^{-}3, 90°)$ and $({}^{-}3, {}^{-}90°)$.

The graphs of $r = 3 \cos 2\theta$ and $r = {}^{-}3$ intersect at the points (3, 0°), (3, 90°), (3, 180°), and (3, 270°). The point (3, 90°) is the same point as $({}^{-}3, {}^{-}90°)$. The point (3, 270°) is the same point as $({}^{-}3, 90°)$. Thus, two points of intersection, (3, 0°) and (3, 180°), do *not* represent common solutions to the polar equations.

exercises

Exploratory Copy and complete the following chart for the equation $r = 3 + 3 \cos \theta$.

	θ	$\cos \theta$	$3 + 3 \cos \theta$	(r, θ)
1.	0°			
2.	30°			
3.	60°			
4.	90°			
5.	120°			
6.	150°			

	θ	$\cos \theta$	$3 + 3 \cos \theta$	(r, θ)
7.	180°			
8.	210°			
9.	240°			
10.	270°			
11.	300°			
12.	330°			

13. Graph the equation $r = 3 + 3 \cos \theta$.

Written Graph each polar equation. In exercises 11-12 use radian measure for θ.

1. $r = 3 + 2 \sin \theta$ (limaçon)
2. $r = 10 \sin 3\theta$ (rose)
3. $r = 5 + 5 \sin \theta$ (cardioid)
4. $r^2 = 9 \cos 2\theta$ (lemniscate)
5. $r = 5 \cos 2\theta$ (rose)
6. $r = 1 + 4 \cos \theta$ (limaçon)
7. $r^2 = 8 \sin 2\theta$ (lemniscate)
8. $r = 2 + 2 \cos \theta$ (cardioid)
9. $r = 6 \cos 3\theta$ (rose)
10. $r = 4 \cos 4\theta$ (rose)
11. $r = \theta$ (spiral of Archimedes)
12. $r = \frac{1}{2}\theta$ (spiral of Archimedes)

Solve each system of equations. Then graph each system of equations and determine the points of intersection.

13. $r = 6$
    $r = 6 \cos \theta$
14. $r = \sin \theta$
    $r = 1 - \sin \theta$
15. $r = 2 \sin \theta$
    $r = 2\sqrt{3} \cos \theta$
16. $r = 2$
    $r = 4 \cos \theta$

9-3 Polar and Rectangular Coordinates

Suppose a rectangular coordinate system is superimposed on a polar coordinate system. Let the two origins coincide and let the positive x-axis of the rectangular system coincide with the polar axis of the polar system.

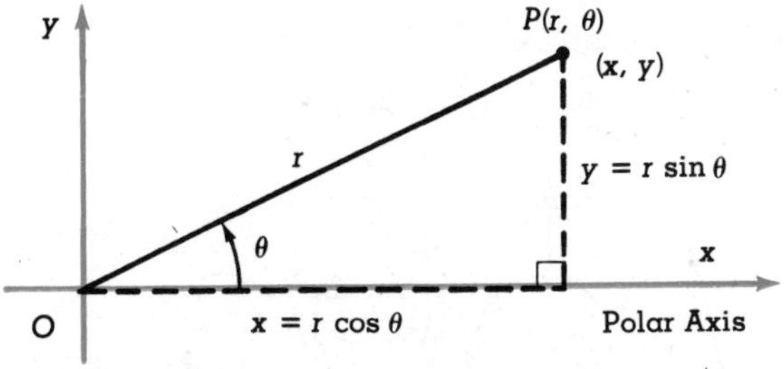

Let P be any point in the plane. In polar coordinates P is identified by the ordered pair (r, θ). In rectangular coordinates P is identified by the ordered pair (x, y). Suppose the polar coordinates of a point are known. The trigonometric functions can be used to find the rectangular coordinates of the point. Assume the unit distances are the same in each coordinate system.

The rectangular coordinates (x, y) of a point named by polar coordinates (r, θ) can be found by the following formulas.

$$x = r \cos \theta \qquad y = r \sin \theta$$

Conversion from Polar to Rectangular Coordinates

examples

1 **Find the rectangular coordinates of $A\left(-3, \frac{2\pi}{3}\right)$.**

Notice that θ is given in radians.

$$x = r\cos\theta \qquad\qquad y = r\sin\theta$$
$$= {}^-3\cos\frac{2\pi}{3} \qquad\qquad = {}^-3\sin\frac{2\pi}{3}$$
$$= {}^-3\left(-\frac{1}{2}\right) \text{ or } \frac{3}{2} \qquad\qquad = {}^-3\left(\frac{\sqrt{3}}{2}\right) \text{ or } -\frac{3\sqrt{3}}{2}$$

The rectangular coordinates of A are $\left(\frac{3}{2}, \frac{{}^-3\sqrt{3}}{2}\right)$ or $(1.5, {}^-2.6)$.

2 **Find the rectangular coordinates of $B(4, {}^-70°)$.**

$$x = r\cos\theta \qquad\qquad y = r\sin\theta$$
$$= 4\cos({}^-70°) \qquad\qquad = 4\sin({}^-70°)$$
$$= 4\cos 70° \qquad\qquad = 4({}^-\sin 70°)$$

Why?

$$= 4(0.3420) \qquad\qquad = 4({}^-0.9397)$$
$$= 1.37 \qquad\qquad = {}^-3.76$$

Round to the nearest hundredth.

The rectangular coordinates of B are $(1.37, {}^-3.76)$.

If a point is identified by rectangular coordinates (x, y), the polar coordinates (r, θ) of the point can be determined using the Pythagorean theorem and the Arctangent function. Recall that the Arctangent function determines angles in the first or fourth quadrants. Therefore, $\theta = \text{Arctan}\,\frac{y}{x}$ when (x, y) is in the first or fourth quadrant, as shown below. However, when (x, y) is in the second or third quadrant it is necessary to add π radians or 180° to $\text{Arctan}\,\frac{y}{x}$.

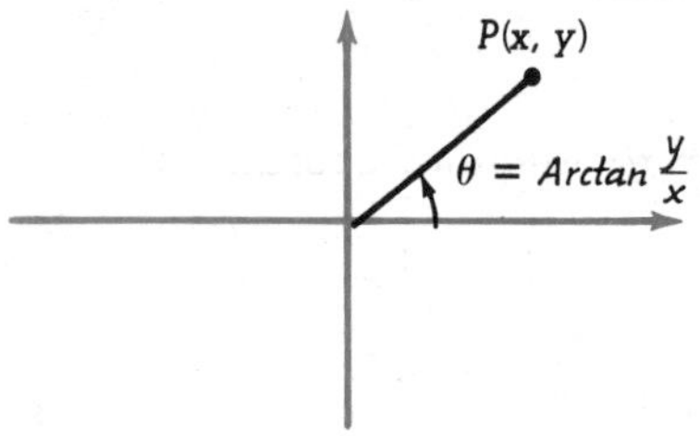

When $x > 0$, $\theta = \text{Arctan}\,\frac{y}{x}$

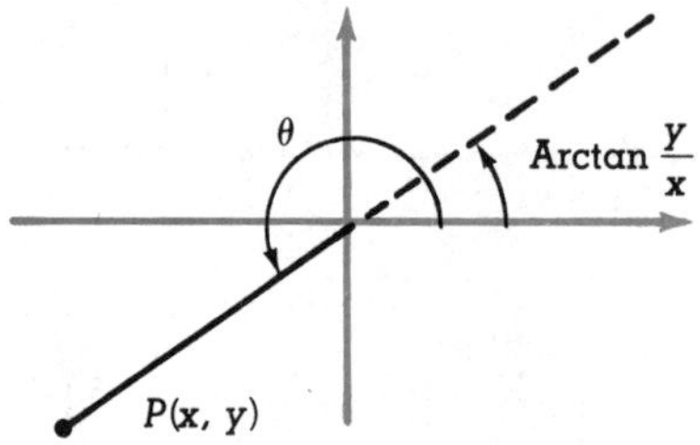

When $x < 0$, $\theta = \text{Arctan}\,\frac{y}{x} + \pi$

When x is zero, $\theta = \pm\frac{\pi}{2}$. Why?

Conversion from Rectangular to Polar Coordinates

The polar coordinates (r, θ) of a point named by the rectangular coordinates (x, y) can be found by the following formulas.

$$r = \sqrt{x^2 + y^2} \qquad \theta = \text{Arctan}\,\frac{y}{x} \text{ when } x > 0$$
$$\theta = \text{Arctan}\,\frac{y}{x} + \pi \text{ when } x < 0$$

example

3 Find the polar coordinates of the point named by the rectangular coordinates $(^-2, 5)$.

$$r = \sqrt{x^2 + y^2} \qquad \theta = \text{Arctan}\,\frac{y}{x} + \pi \quad \textit{Here } \theta \textit{ is expressed in radians.}$$

$$= \sqrt{(^-2)^2 + 5^2} \qquad = \text{Arctan}\,\frac{5}{^-2} + \pi$$

$$= \sqrt{29} \qquad = {}^-1.19 + 3.14$$

$$= 5.39 \qquad = 1.95$$

The polar coordinates are (5.39, 1.95). *Other polar coordinates can name the same point.*

Equations in rectangular coordinates can be written as polar equations and vice versa. Study the following example.

example

4 Change the equation $x^2 + y^2 = 9$ into a polar equation.

$x^2 + y^2 = 9$
$(r \cos \theta)^2 + (r \sin \theta)^2 = 9$
$r^2 (\cos^2 \theta + \sin^2 \theta) = 9$
$r^2 = 9$ or $r = \pm 3$.
The polar equation is $r = 3$ or $r = {}^-3$.

exercises

Exploratory Evaluate each of the following. Express θ in radians.

1. Arctan $\sqrt{3}$
2. Arctan 1
3. Arctan 3.5
4. Arctan 1.4

Written Find the polar coordinates of the point with the given rectangular coordinates.

1. (3, 4)
2. (5, 12)
3. (1, 1)
4. $(^-2, {}^-2)$
5. $(2, {}^-5)$
6. $(^-1, {}^-3)$
7. $(3, {}^-2)$
8. $(^-\sqrt{3}, 3)$

Find the rectangular coordinates of the point with the given polar coordinates.

9. $\left(1, \frac{\pi}{6}\right)$
10. $\left(1.5, \frac{\pi}{2}\right)$
11. $\left({}^-3, -\frac{\pi}{2}\right)$
12. $\left({}^-2, \frac{\pi}{4}\right)$
13. (2, 0)
14. $(0.25, \pi)$
15. (2.5, 2)
16. (3, 3.5)

Change each equation into a polar equation.

17. $x = 5$
18. $y = {}^-2$
19. $x = y$
20. ${}^-y = x$
21. $x^2 + y^2 = 25$
22. $2x^2 + 2y^2 - 5y = 0$

Change each polar equation into an equation in rectangular coordinates.

23. $r = {}^-7$
24. $r = 6$
25. $\theta = 45°$
26. $\theta = \pi$
27. $r \sin \theta = 2$
28. $r = 5 \csc \theta$
29. $r = {}^-2 \sec \theta$
30. $r = \cos \theta + \sin \theta$

Using Mathematics

Polar transformations are sometimes used to simulate growth patterns or to alter the shape of an object. The following transformation formulas were used to alter the shape of a butterfly.

$$\theta' = \theta \qquad\qquad \theta'' = \theta$$
$$r' = r(1 + \tfrac{1}{3}(1 + \sin\theta)) \qquad\qquad r'' = r(1 + \tfrac{1}{2}(1 + \sin\theta))$$

The original outline is shown as a solid black line. The (r', θ') transformation is shown as a colored line. The (r'', θ'') transformation is shown as a broken line.

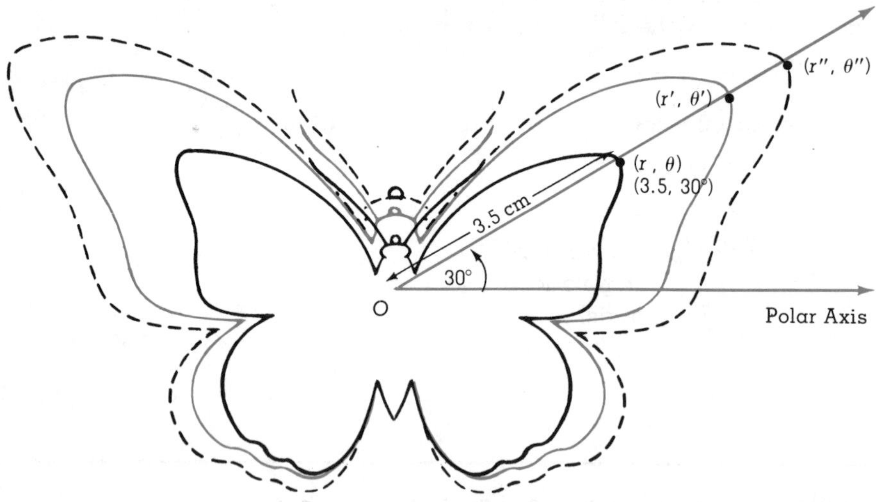

Consider the (r', θ') transformation. The image of any point (r, θ) on the black line is (r', θ') on the colored line. For example, the image, (r', θ'), of (3.5, 30°) was determined as follows.

$$\theta' = \theta \qquad\qquad r' = r(1 + \tfrac{1}{3}(1 + \sin\theta))$$
$$\theta' = 30^\circ \qquad\qquad r' = 3.5(1 + \tfrac{1}{3}(1 + \sin 30^\circ))$$
$$= 5.25$$

The image of (3.5, 30°) is (5.25, 30°). The coordinates of the images of other points were determined in a similar manner.

Exercises Use the formulas $\theta' = \theta + 45^\circ$ and $r' = 2r$ to determine the image of each point whose polar coordinates (r, θ) are given.

1. (3, 20°)
2. (1.3, 50°)
3. (7, 110°)
4. (5.6, 300°)

9-4 Simplifying Complex Numbers

A complex number can be written in the form $a + bi$ where a and b are real numbers and i is defined by $i^2 = {}^-1$. Since $i^1 = i$ and $i^2 = {}^-1$, higher powers of i can be found by multiplication. The first few powers of i are given below.

$$i^3 = {}^-i \qquad i^6 = {}^-1$$
$$i^4 = 1 \qquad i^7 = {}^-i$$
$$i^5 = i \qquad i^8 = 1$$

Notice that the values i, ⁻1, ⁻i, and 1 repeat in cycles of four.

In general, i^n, where n is a whole number, can be simplified to 1, i, ⁻1, or ^-i. Thus, to simplify i^n, divide n by 4 and express the result as 1, i, ⁻1, or ^-i if the remainder is 0, 1, 2, or 3, respectively. For example, i^{35} can be simplified as shown below.

$$\begin{aligned} i^{35} &= i^{4(8)+3} \\ &= (i^4)^8 \cdot i^3 \\ &= 1^8 \cdot i^3 \\ &= 1 \cdot {}^-i \\ &= {}^-i \end{aligned}$$

Complex numbers are called imaginary numbers when $b \neq 0$ and pure imaginary numbers when $a = 0$ and $b \neq 0$.

The real part of the complex number $a + bi$ is a, and the imaginary part is b. Complex numbers can be added by adding their real parts and adding their imaginary parts.

examples

1 **Find $(4 + 5i) + (3 + 2i)$.**

$$\begin{aligned} (4 + 5i) + (3 + 2i) &= (4 + 3) + (5 + 2)i \\ &= 7 + 7i \end{aligned}$$

2 **Find $(8 + 3i) - (1 - 6i)$.**

$$\begin{aligned} (8 + 3i) - (1 - 6i) &= (8 - 1) + (3 - {}^-6)i \\ &= 7 + 9i \end{aligned}$$

Subtract the real parts and the imaginary parts.

The product of two or more complex numbers can also be found.

example

3 **Find $(3 + 7i)(2 - 4i)$.**

$$\begin{aligned} (3 + 7i)(2 - 4i) &= 6 - 12i + 14i - 28i^2 \\ &= 6 + 2i + 28 \\ &= 34 + 2i \end{aligned}$$

Multiply the complex numbers as binomials using the FOIL method (First, Outer, Inner, Last).

Complex numbers of the form $a + bi$ and $a - bi$ are called **conjugates** of each other. The product of complex conjugates is always a real number. Thus, when a fraction has a complex number as the denominator, you can use conjugates to **rationalize the denominator.** This will produce a real number in the denominator.

example

4 Simplify $\frac{1 + i}{3 + 2i}$.

$$\frac{1 + i}{3 + 2i} = \frac{(1 + i)(3 - 2i)}{(3 + 2i)(3 - 2i)}$$
$$= \frac{3 - 2i + 3i - 2i^2}{9 - 6i + 6i - 4i^2}$$
$$\frac{5 + i}{13} \text{ or } \frac{5}{13} + \frac{1}{13}i$$

The following chart summarizes the basic operations with complex numbers.

For any complex numbers $a + bi$ and $c + di$,
$(a + bi) + (c + di) = (a + c) + (b + d)i$
$(a + bi) - (c + di) = (a - c) + (b - d)i$
$(a + bi)(c + di) = (ac - bd) + (ad + bc)i$
$\frac{(a + bi)}{(c + di)} = \frac{(ac + bd) + (bc - ad)i}{c^2 + d^2}$

exercises

Exploratory Simplify.

1. i^{15}
2. i^{46}
3. $(2 + 5i) + (^-8 - i)$
4. $(3 - 7i) + (2 + 5i)$
5. $(9 + 6i) - (i + 5)$
6. $(^-12 + 3i) - (7 - 5i)$
7. $(^-6 - 2i) - (^-8 - 3i)$
8. $(2 + 3i)(4 - i)$
9. $(1 + 3i)(2 + 4i)$
10. $(2 + i)^2$
11. $(i - 5)^2$
12. $(3i + 5)^2$

Find the product of each complex number and its conjugate.

13. $3 - 2i$
14. $12 + i$
15. $7i$
16. ^-5i

Written Simplify.

1. i^{24}
2. i^{61}
3. $i^2(2 + 7i)$
4. $4(1 + i^3)$
5. $(1 - 4i) + (^-3 + 3i)$
6. $(9 + 7i) - (^-1 - 2i)$
7. $(2 + 3i\sqrt{2}) - i\sqrt{2}$
8. $4i + (6 + 3i)$
9. $(3i - 2) - (^-3 + 2i)$
10. $(6 - 3i) - (7 + 3i)$
11. $(\sqrt{2} + i)(4\sqrt{2} + i)$
12. $(4 - 3i)(^-4 + 3i)$

13. $(\sqrt{2} + i)(\sqrt{2} - i)$
14. $2(4 - 3i)(7 - 2i)$
15. $(2 + i)(3 - 4i)(1 + 2i)$
16. $(2 + i\sqrt{3})^2$
17. $(3 - 2i)^3$
18. $(1 - i)^4$
19. $\frac{3 + 7i}{2i}$
20. $\frac{4 - 3i}{2 + i}$
21. $\frac{^-15 + i}{4 + 2i}$
22. $\frac{4}{\sqrt{3} + 2i}$
23. $\frac{2 + i\sqrt{3}}{2 - i\sqrt{3}}$
24. $\frac{2 - i\sqrt{7}}{2 + i\sqrt{7}}$
25. $\frac{7}{\sqrt{2} - 3i}$
26. $\frac{(1 - i)^2}{(1 + i)^2}$
27. $\frac{(4 + 3i)^2}{(3 - i)^2}$

9-5 Polar Form of Complex Numbers

Every complex number can be written in the form $x + yi$ where x is the real part and y is the imaginary part. This form is called the **rectangular form** of a complex number. Sometimes the rectangular form is written as the ordered pair (x, y).

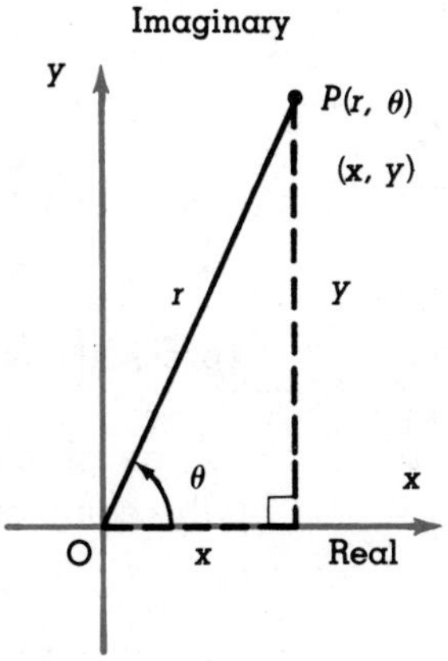

A complex number can be represented graphically as a point in the complex plane. In the complex plane, the horizontal axis is the real axis and the vertical axis is the imaginary axis. The point P graphed at the right corresponds to the complex number $x + yi$.

The angle θ is called the **amplitude** and r is called the **modulus.** Two complex numbers are equal if and only if their moduli are equal and their amplitudes differ by integral multiples of 2π radians. Thus, θ can be replaced by $\theta + 2n\pi$, for any integer n.

In the figure, notice that $y = r \sin \theta$ and $x = r \cos \theta$. These values can be substituted for x and y in the rectangular form to obtain the **polar**, or **trigonometric form** of a complex number.

$$x + yi = r(\cos \theta + i \sin \theta)$$

Polar Form of $x + yi$

$r(\cos \theta + i \sin \theta)$ is often written as r cis θ

Values for r and θ can be obtained by using the formulas shown below.

$$r = \sqrt{x^2 + y^2} \qquad \theta = \text{Arctan}\,\frac{y}{x} \quad \text{when } x > 0$$

$$\theta = \text{Arctan}\,\frac{y}{x} + \pi \quad \text{when } x < 0$$

Thus, if x and y are known, r and θ can be found and a complex number in rectangular form $(x + yi)$ can be written in polar form $r(\cos \theta + i \sin \theta)$, and conversely. The amplitude θ is usually expressed in radian measure and the angle is placed in standard position.

examples

1 **Express $^-1 + i$ in polar form.**

First, graph the complex number on the complex plane.

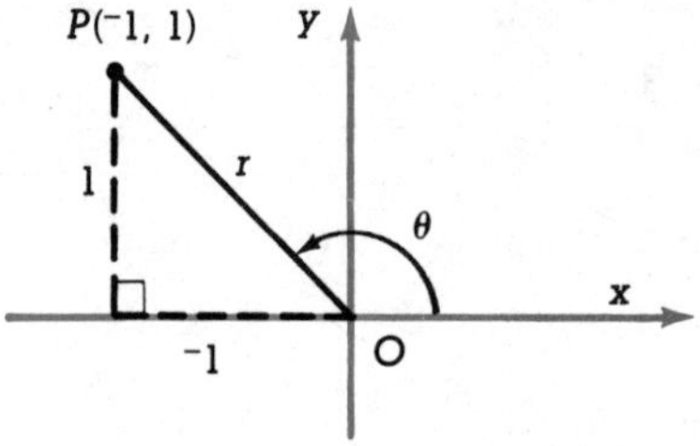

Notice that $x = {}^-1$ and $y = 1$.

Next, find values for r and θ.

$$r = \sqrt{x^2 + y^2} = \sqrt{(^-1)^2 + 1^2} = \sqrt{2}$$

$$\theta = \text{Arctan}\,\frac{y}{x} + \pi = \text{Arctan}\,\frac{1}{^-1} + \pi = \text{Arctan}\,(^-1) + \pi = -\frac{\pi}{4} + \pi \text{ or } \frac{3\pi}{4}$$

Therefore $^-1 + i = \sqrt{2}\left(\cos\frac{3\pi}{4} + i\sin\frac{3\pi}{4}\right)$.

2 **Express $4\left(\cos\frac{7\pi}{6} + i\sin\frac{7\pi}{6}\right)$ in rectangular form.**

First, graph the complex number on the complex plane.

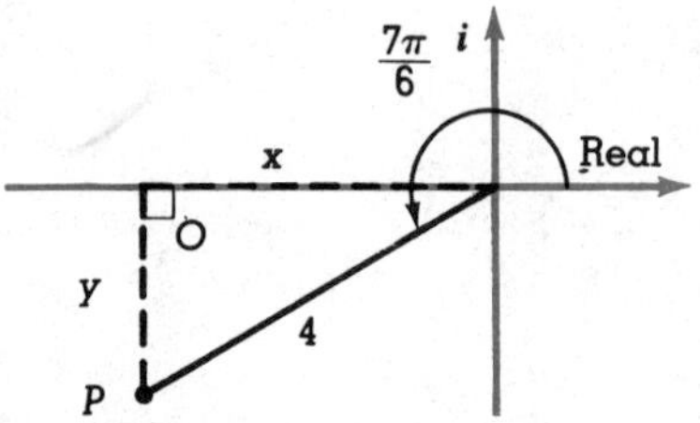

$4\left(\cos\frac{7\pi}{6} + i\sin\frac{7\pi}{6}\right)$

Then find values for x and y.

$$x = r\cos\theta = 4\cos\frac{7\pi}{6} = {}^-4\cos\frac{\pi}{6} = {}^-4\left(\frac{\sqrt{3}}{2}\right) \text{ or } {}^-2\sqrt{3}$$

$$y = r\sin\theta = 4\sin\frac{7\pi}{6} = {}^-4\sin\frac{\pi}{6} = {}^-4\left(\frac{1}{2}\right) \text{ or } {}^-2$$

The reference angle for $\frac{7\pi}{6}$ is $\frac{\pi}{6}$.

Therefore $4\left(\cos\frac{7\pi}{6} + i\sin\frac{7\pi}{6}\right) = {}^-2\sqrt{3} - 2i$.

exercises

Exploratory Graph each complex number. Then express the number in polar form.

1. $1 - i$
2. $^-2 + 2i$
3. $7i$
4. $4i$
5. $^-5$
6. $^-3$
7. $3 - i\sqrt{3}$
8. $2 - 2i\sqrt{3}$

Graph each complex number. Then express the number in rectangular form.

9. $2(\cos 0 + i \sin 0)$
10. $3(\cos \pi + i \sin \pi)$
11. $\cos \frac{\pi}{2} + i \sin \frac{\pi}{2}$
12. $\cos \frac{3\pi}{2} + i \sin \frac{3\pi}{2}$
13. $\frac{1}{2}\left(\cos \frac{5\pi}{6} + i \sin \frac{5\pi}{6}\right)$
14. $2\left(\cos\left(-\frac{3\pi}{4}\right) + i \sin\left(-\frac{3\pi}{4}\right)\right)$

Written Express each complex number in polar form.

1. $1 + i$
2. $^-3 - 3i$
3. $3i$
4. $6i$
5. $^-5 - i$
6. $3 + 4i$
7. $^-2 + 5i$
8. $2\sqrt{3} - 3i$

Express each complex number in rectangular form.

9. $\sqrt{2}\left(\cos \frac{5\pi}{4} + i \sin \frac{5\pi}{4}\right)$
10. $6\left(\cos \frac{3\pi}{2} + i \sin \frac{3\pi}{2}\right)$
11. $12\left(\cos \frac{5\pi}{3} + i \sin \frac{5\pi}{3}\right)$
12. $\sqrt{3}\left(\cos \frac{\pi}{3} + i \sin \frac{\pi}{3}\right)$
13. $2(\cos 3 + i \sin 3)$
14. $3(\cos 2 + i \sin 2)$

9-6 Products and Quotients of Complex Numbers in Polar Form

When two complex numbers are written in polar form, their product and quotient can be easily computed.

Let $r_1(\cos \theta_1 + i \sin \theta_1)$ and $r_2(\cos \theta_2 + i \sin \theta_2)$ represent two complex numbers. A simple formula for the product of the two numbers can be obtained by multiplying the two numbers directly, then simplifying the result.

$$\begin{aligned} & r_1(\cos \theta_1 + i \sin \theta_1) \cdot r_2(\cos \theta_2 + i \sin \theta_2) \\ &\quad = r_1r_2(\cos \theta_1 \cos \theta_2 + \cos \theta_1\, i \sin \theta_2 + i \sin \theta_1 \cos \theta_2 + i^2 \sin \theta_1 \sin \theta_2) \\ &\quad = r_1r_2[(\cos \theta_1 \cos \theta_2 - \sin \theta_1 \sin \theta_2) + i(\sin \theta_1 \cos \theta_2 + \cos \theta_1 \sin \theta_2)] \\ &\quad = r_1r_2[\cos (\theta_1 + \theta_2) + i \sin (\theta_1 + \theta_2)] \end{aligned}$$

The product of two complex numbers $r_1(\cos \theta_1 + i \sin \theta_1)$ and $r_2(\cos \theta_2 + i \sin \theta_2)$ can be found by using the following formula.

$$\mathbf{r_1(\cos \theta_1 + i \sin \theta_1) \cdot r_2(\cos \theta_2 + i \sin \theta_2) = r_1r_2[\cos (\theta_1 + \theta_2) + i \sin (\theta_1 + \theta_2)]}$$

Product of Complex Numbers in Polar Form

Notice that the modulus of the product of two complex numbers is the product of their moduli. The amplitude of the product is the sum of their amplitudes.

example

1 Find the product of $6\left(\cos \frac{\pi}{6} + i \sin \frac{\pi}{6}\right)$ and $2\left(\cos \frac{2\pi}{3} + i \sin \frac{2\pi}{3}\right)$.

Find the modulus and amplitude of the product.

$$r = 6(2) \qquad \theta = \frac{\pi}{6} + \frac{2\pi}{3}$$

$$= 12 \qquad = \frac{5\pi}{6}$$

Therefore $6\left(\cos \frac{\pi}{6} + i \sin \frac{\pi}{6}\right) \cdot 2\left(\cos \frac{2\pi}{3} + i \sin \frac{2\pi}{3}\right) = 12\left(\cos \frac{5\pi}{6} + i \sin \frac{5\pi}{6}\right)$.

A formula for the quotient of two complex numbers $r_1(\cos \theta_1 + i \sin \theta_1)$ and $r_2(\cos \theta_2 + i \sin \theta_2)$ can be found by multiplying the numerator and denominator by $(\cos \theta_2 - i \sin \theta_2)$ as follows.

$$\frac{r_1(\cos \theta_1 + i \sin \theta_1)}{r_2(\cos \theta_2 + i \sin \theta_2)} = \frac{r_1(\cos \theta_1 + i \sin \theta_1)}{r_2(\cos \theta_2 + i \sin \theta_2)} \cdot \frac{(\cos \theta_2 - i \sin \theta_2)}{(\cos \theta_2 - i \sin \theta_2)}$$

$$= \frac{r_1}{r_2} \cdot \frac{(\cos \theta_1 \cos \theta_2 + \sin \theta_1 \sin \theta_2) + i(\sin \theta_1 \cos \theta_2 - \cos \theta_1 \sin \theta_2)}{\cos^2 \theta_2 + \sin^2 \theta_2}$$

$$= \frac{r_1}{r_2}[\cos(\theta_1 - \theta_2) + i \sin(\theta_1 - \theta_2)]$$ *Remember that $\cos^2 \theta + \sin^2 \theta = 1$*

The quotient of two complex numbers $r_1(\cos \theta_1 + i \sin \theta_1)$ and $r_2(\cos \theta_2 + i \sin \theta_2)$ can be found by using the following formula.

$$\frac{r_1(\cos \theta_1 + i \sin \theta_1)}{r_2(\cos \theta_2 + i \sin \theta_2)} = \frac{r_1}{r_2}[\cos(\theta_1 - \theta_2) + i \sin(\theta_1 - \theta_2)]$$

Quotient of Complex Numbers in Polar Form

Notice that the modulus of the quotient of two complex numbers is the quotient of their moduli. The amplitude of the quotient is the difference of their amplitudes.

example

2 Find the quotient of $6\left(\cos \frac{\pi}{6} + i \sin \frac{\pi}{6}\right)$ and $2\left(\cos \frac{2\pi}{3} + i \sin \frac{2\pi}{3}\right)$.

Find the modulus and amplitude of the quotient.

$$r = 6 \div 2 \qquad \theta = \frac{\pi}{6} - \frac{2\pi}{3}$$

$$= 3 \qquad = -\frac{\pi}{2} \text{ or } \frac{3\pi}{2}$$

Therefore $\dfrac{6\left(\cos \frac{\pi}{6} + i \sin \frac{\pi}{6}\right)}{2\left(\cos \frac{2\pi}{3} + i \sin \frac{2\pi}{3}\right)} = 3\left(\cos \frac{3\pi}{2} + i \sin \frac{3\pi}{2}\right)$.

exercises

Exploratory Find each product or quotient.

1. $2(\cos \pi + i \sin \pi) \cdot 5(\cos 2\pi + i \sin 2\pi)$
2. $6(\cos 2\pi + i \sin 2\pi) \div 2(\cos \pi + i \sin \pi)$
3. $2\left(\cos \frac{\pi}{6} + i \sin \frac{\pi}{6}\right) \div \left(\cos \frac{\pi}{3} + i \sin \frac{\pi}{3}\right)$
4. $3\left(\cos \frac{\pi}{2} + i \sin \frac{\pi}{2}\right) \cdot 6\left(\cos \frac{3\pi}{4} + i \sin \frac{3\pi}{4}\right)$

5-8. Express the results of problems 1-4 in rectangular form.

Written Find each product or quotient.

1. $8\left(\cos \frac{3\pi}{4} + i \sin \frac{3\pi}{4}\right) \cdot 2\left(\cos \frac{5\pi}{4} + i \sin \frac{5\pi}{4}\right)$
2. $3\left(\cos \frac{7\pi}{6} + i \sin \frac{7\pi}{6}\right) \cdot 6\left(\cos \frac{\pi}{6} + i \sin \frac{\pi}{6}\right)$
3. $3\sqrt{2}\left(\cos \frac{\pi}{4} + i \sin \frac{\pi}{4}\right) \div \sqrt{2}\left(\cos \frac{\pi}{6} + i \sin \frac{\pi}{6}\right)$
4. $6\left(\cos \frac{5\pi}{8} + i \sin \frac{5\pi}{8}\right) \div 12\left(\cos \frac{\pi}{2} + i \sin \frac{\pi}{2}\right)$
5. $2(\cos 0.8 + i \sin 0.8) \cdot 3.2(\cos 1.5 + i \sin 1.5)$
6. $9.24(\cos 1.8 + i \sin 1.8) \div 3.1(\cos 0.7 + i \sin 0.7)$

Find each product or quotient. Express each result in rectangular form.

7. $(1 + i)(^-1 - i)$
8. $(\sqrt{3} + i)(^-2 + 2i)$
9. $(^-4 - 4\sqrt{3}i) \div 2i$
10. $(3 - 3i) \div (^-2 + 2i)$
11. $(2 - 2i)(1 - i)$
12. $(6 + 6i) \div {}^-3i$

13-18. Express the results of problems 1-6 in rectangular form.

9-7 Powers and Roots of Complex Numbers

The formula for the product of complex numbers can be used to find the square of a complex number.

$$\begin{aligned}[r(\cos \theta + i \sin \theta)]^2 &= [r(\cos \theta + i \sin \theta)] \cdot [r(\cos \theta + i \sin \theta)] \\ &= r^2[\cos(\theta + \theta) + i \sin(\theta + \theta)] \\ &= r^2(\cos 2\theta + i \sin 2\theta)\end{aligned}$$

Other powers of complex numbers can be found by using De Moivre's Theorem.

$$[r(\cos \theta + i \sin \theta)]^n = r^n(\cos n\theta + i \sin n\theta)$$

De Moivre's Theorem

Mathematical induction can be used to prove that De Moivre's Theorem is valid for any positive integer n. The formula has been shown to be valid when $n = 1$ and $n = 2$. Assume the formula is valid for $n = k$.

$$[r(\cos\theta + i\sin\theta)]^k = r^k(\cos k\theta + i\sin k\theta)$$

Then multiply each side of the equation by $r(\cos\theta + i\sin\theta)$.

$$\begin{aligned}[r(\cos\theta + i\sin\theta)]^{k+1} &= [r^k(\cos k\theta + i\sin k\theta)][r(\cos\theta + i\sin\theta)]\\ &= r^{k+1}(\cos k\theta\cos\theta + \cos k\theta\, i\sin\theta + i\sin k\theta\cos\theta + i^2\sin k\theta\sin\theta)\\ &= r^{k+1}[(\cos k\theta\cos\theta - \sin k\theta\sin\theta) + i(\sin k\theta\cos\theta + \cos k\theta\sin\theta)]\\ &= r^{k+1}[\cos(k+1)\theta + i\sin(k+1)\theta]\end{aligned}$$

Since the right side of the last equation gives the same result as can be obtained directly for $n = k + 1$, the formula is valid for all positive integral values of n.

example

1 **Find $(1 + i)^5$.**

First, write $1 + i$ in polar form.

$$1 + i = \sqrt{2}\left(\cos\frac{\pi}{4} + i\sin\frac{\pi}{4}\right)$$

Then use DeMoivre's Theorem to find the 5th power of the complex number in polar form.

$$\begin{aligned}(1+i)^5 &= \left[\sqrt{2}\left(\cos\frac{\pi}{4} + i\sin\frac{\pi}{4}\right)\right]^5\\ &= (\sqrt{2})^5\left(\cos\frac{5\pi}{4} + i\sin\frac{5\pi}{4}\right)\\ &= 4\sqrt{2}\left(\cos\frac{5\pi}{4} + i\sin\frac{5\pi}{4}\right)\end{aligned}$$

Write the result in rectangular form.

$$\begin{aligned}4\sqrt{2}\left(\cos\frac{5\pi}{4} + i\sin\frac{5\pi}{4}\right) &= 4\sqrt{2}\left(-\frac{\sqrt{2}}{2} - i\frac{\sqrt{2}}{2}\right)\\ &= {}^-4 - 4i.\end{aligned}$$

Thus, $(1 + i)^5 = {}^-4 - 4i$.

It can be proven that DeMoivre's Theorem is also valid when n is a rational number. Therefore the roots of complex numbers can be found by letting $n = \frac{1}{2}, \frac{1}{3}, \frac{1}{4}, \ldots$. In general, the pth root of a complex number can be found by the following formula.

$$(x + yi)^{\frac{1}{p}} = [r(\cos\theta + i\sin\theta)]^{\frac{1}{p}} = r^{\frac{1}{p}}\left(\cos\frac{\theta}{p} + i\sin\frac{\theta}{p}\right)$$

This equation identifies the principal root.

example

2 Find $\sqrt{i}$.

$$\begin{aligned}\sqrt{i} &= i^{\frac{1}{2}} \\ &= (0 + i)^{\frac{1}{2}} \\ &= \left[1\left(\cos\frac{\pi}{2} + i\sin\frac{\pi}{2}\right)\right]^{\frac{1}{2}} \\ &= 1^{\frac{1}{2}}\left(\cos\frac{\pi}{4} + i\sin\frac{\pi}{4}\right) \\ &= 1\left(\cos\frac{\pi}{4} + i\sin\frac{\pi}{4}\right)\end{aligned}$$

Thus, $\sqrt{i} = \frac{\sqrt{2}}{2} + \frac{\sqrt{2}}{2}i$. *This is the principal square root of* i.

It can be proven that any complex number has p distinct pth roots. That is, it has two square roots, three cube roots, four fourth roots, and so on. Since $\cos\theta = \cos(\theta + 2n\pi)$ and $\sin\theta = \sin(\theta + 2n\pi)$, where $n = 1, 2, 3, \ldots$, a more general formula for finding pth roots of complex numbers can be written.

The p distinct pth roots of $x + yi$ can be found by replacing n by 0, 1, 2, . . . , $p - 1$, successively, in the following equation.

$$\begin{aligned}(x + yi)^{\frac{1}{p}} &= \left(r[\cos(\theta + 2n\pi) + i\sin(\theta + 2n\pi)]\right)^{\frac{1}{p}} \\ &= r^{\frac{1}{p}}\left(\cos\frac{\theta + 2n\pi}{p} + i\sin\frac{\theta + 2n\pi}{p}\right)\end{aligned}$$

The p Distinct Roots of a Complex Number

example

3 **Find the three cube roots of 1.** *Remember, all real numbers are complex numbers.*

In rectangular form, $1 = 1 + 0i$. Write the polar form of $1 + 0i$.
$1 + 0i = 1[\cos(0 + 2n\pi) + i\sin(0 + 2n\pi)]$.

Then write an expression for the cube roots of $1 + 0i$.

$$\begin{aligned}(1 + 0i)^{\frac{1}{3}} &= (1[\cos(0 + 2n\pi) + i\sin(0 + 2n\pi)])^{\frac{1}{3}} \\ &= 1^{\frac{1}{3}}\left(\cos\frac{0 + 2n\pi}{3} + i\sin\frac{0 + 2n\pi}{3}\right)\end{aligned}$$

Let $n = 0$, 1, and 2 successively to find the 3 cube roots.

$$1(\cos 0 + i\sin 0) = 1$$

$$1\left(\cos\frac{2\pi}{3} + i\sin\frac{2\pi}{3}\right) = -\frac{1}{2} + \frac{\sqrt{3}}{2}i$$

$$1\left(\cos\frac{4\pi}{3} + i\sin\frac{4\pi}{3}\right) = -\frac{1}{2} - \frac{\sqrt{3}}{2}i$$

If you replace n by 4, what root is obtained?

Thus, the three cube roots of 1 are 1, $-\frac{1}{2} + \frac{\sqrt{3}}{2}i$, $-\frac{1}{2} - \frac{\sqrt{3}}{2}i$. *These results can be checked by multiplication.*

example

4 **Solve the equation $x^4 + 1 = 0$.**

$$x^4 + 1 = 0$$
$$x^4 = {}^-1$$
$$= {}^-1 + 0i$$

Write an expression for the fourth roots of $^-1 + 0i$.

$$({}^-1 + 0i)^{\frac{1}{4}} = (1\,[\cos(\pi + 2n\pi) + i\sin(\pi + 2n\pi)])^{\frac{1}{4}}$$
$$= 1^{\frac{1}{4}}\left(\cos\frac{\pi + 2n\pi}{4} + i\sin\frac{\pi + 2n\pi}{4}\right)$$

Let $n = 0, 1, 2,$ and 3 successively to find the 4 fourth roots, x_1, x_2, x_3, and x_4.

$$x_1 = 1\left(\cos\frac{\pi}{4} + i\sin\frac{\pi}{4}\right) = \frac{\sqrt{2}}{2} + \frac{\sqrt{2}}{2}i$$
$$x_2 = 1\left(\cos\frac{3\pi}{4} + i\sin\frac{3\pi}{4}\right) = -\frac{\sqrt{2}}{2} + \frac{\sqrt{2}}{2}i$$
$$x_3 = 1\left(\cos\frac{5\pi}{4} + i\sin\frac{5\pi}{4}\right) = -\frac{\sqrt{2}}{2} - \frac{\sqrt{2}}{2}i$$
$$x_4 = 1\left(\cos\frac{7\pi}{4} + i\sin\frac{7\pi}{4}\right) = \frac{\sqrt{2}}{2} - \frac{\sqrt{2}}{2}i$$

The roots of $x^4 + 1 = 0$ are $\frac{\sqrt{2}}{2} + \frac{\sqrt{2}}{2}i$, $-\frac{\sqrt{2}}{2} + \frac{\sqrt{2}}{2}i$, $-\frac{\sqrt{2}}{2} - \frac{\sqrt{2}}{2}i$, and $\frac{\sqrt{2}}{2} - \frac{\sqrt{2}}{2}i$.

The roots of a complex number are cyclic in nature. Thus, when graphed on the complex plane, the pth roots of a complex number are equally spaced around a circle. The figures below show the three cube roots of 1 and the four fourth roots of $^-1$.

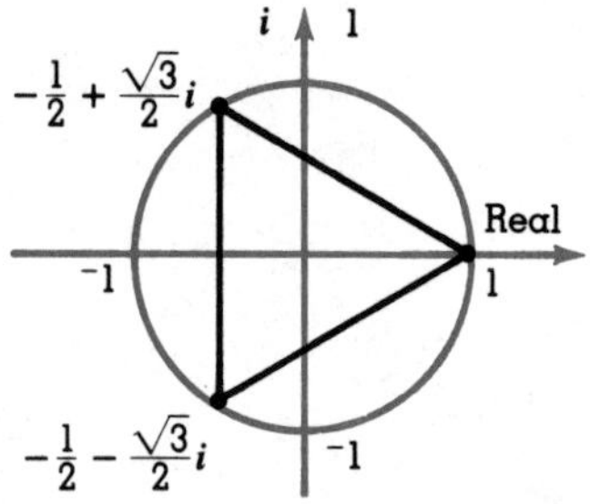

Cube roots of 1

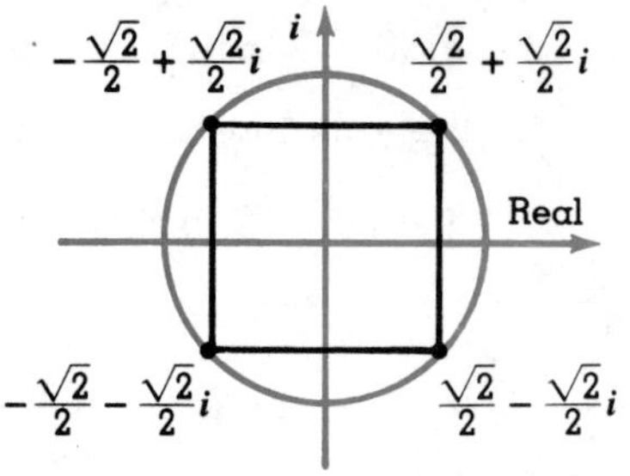

Fourth roots of $^-1$

The cube roots of 1 form the vertices of an equilateral triangle. The fourth roots of $^-1$ form the vertices of a square.

If one pth root of a complex number is known, all the pth roots can be graphed on the complex plane. First, draw a circle of radius $r^{\frac{1}{p}}$ with its center at the origin of the complex plane. Then graph the known root. Finally, separate the circle into p arcs of equal length to locate the other roots.

example

5 **Graph the three cube roots of 8.**

The modulus of $8 + 0i$ is 8, and $8^{\frac{1}{3}} = 2$.

Draw a circle of radius 2 centered at the origin of the complex plane. Since $2^3 = 8$, one cube root of 8 is 2. Graph $2 + 0i$. Then separate the circle into three arcs of equal length to locate the other two cube roots of 8.

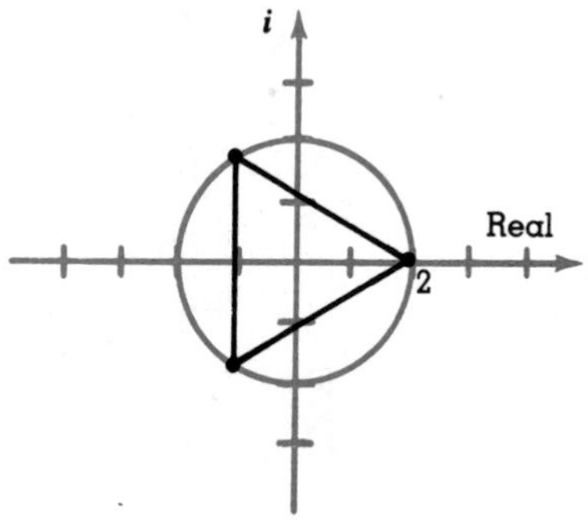

The other roots are $2\left(\cos \frac{2\pi}{3} + i \sin \frac{2\pi}{3}\right)$ *and* $2\left(\cos \frac{4\pi}{3} + i \sin \frac{4\pi}{3}\right)$.

exercises

Exploratory Find each of the following powers. Express each result in rectangular form.

1. $[3(\cos \pi + i \sin \pi)]^3$
2. $\left[2\left(\cos \frac{\pi}{2} + i \sin \frac{\pi}{2}\right)\right]^5$
3. $\left(\cos \frac{\pi}{6} + i \sin \frac{\pi}{6}\right)^4$
4. $\left[3\left(\cos \frac{\pi}{3} + i \sin \frac{\pi}{3}\right)\right]^2$
5. $\left[2\left(\cos \frac{\pi}{4} + i \sin \frac{\pi}{4}\right)\right]^5$
6. $\left(\cos \frac{7\pi}{6} + i \sin \frac{7\pi}{6}\right)^3$

Find one of the indicated roots. Express the result in rectangular form.

7. $\left[4\left(\cos \frac{\pi}{2} + i \sin \frac{\pi}{2}\right)\right]^{\frac{1}{2}}$
8. $\left[4\left(\cos \frac{2\pi}{3} + i \sin \frac{2\pi}{3}\right)\right]^{\frac{1}{4}}$
9. $[^-1(\cos \pi + i \sin \pi)]^{\frac{1}{3}}$

Written Find each of the following powers. Express each result in rectangular form.

1. $(1 - i)^5$
2. $(^-2 + 2i\sqrt{3})^4$
3. $(^-3 + 3i)^3$
4. $(1 + i)^{10}$
5. $(3 + 4i)^4$
6. $(^-5 + 12i)^2$

Find each indicated root.

7. $(1 + i)^{\frac{1}{3}}$
8. $(2\sqrt{3} + 2i)^{\frac{1}{5}}$
9. $(^-2 - 2i)^{\frac{1}{4}}$
10. $(^-4i)^{\frac{1}{10}}$
11. $\sqrt[5]{^-1}$
12. $\sqrt[3]{i}$

Solve the following equations.

13. $x^3 + 1 = 0$
14. $x^3 - 8 = 0$
15. $x^5 - 1 = 0$
16. $x^4 - 1 = 0$
17. $x^6 + 1 = 0$
18. $x^5 + 1 = 0$

19–24. Graph the roots of each equation in problems **13–18**.

Grace Waite is an engineer for the Signal Phone Company. She plans the location of signal towers and antennae for routing relay signals.

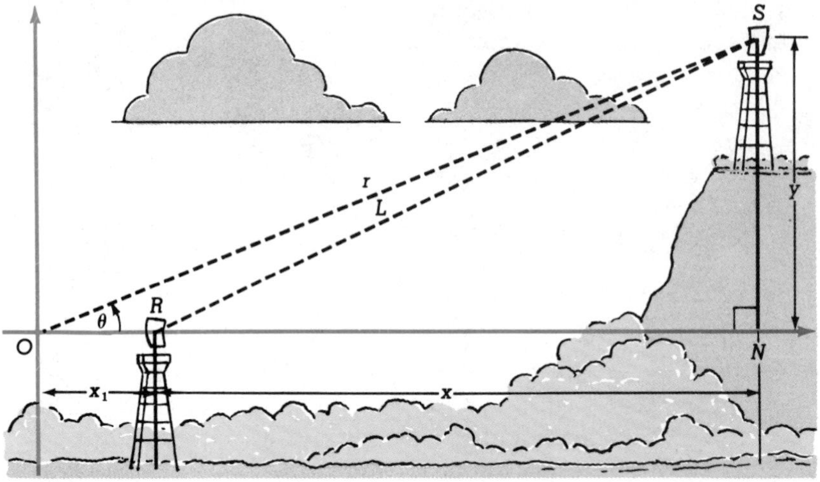

The figure above shows the location of a transmitting tower and a receiving antenna. Point S represents the point from which the signal is emitted. Point R represents a possible location for a receiving antenna. The fixed reference point O is r units from point S, $\angle SON = \theta$, and $OR = x_1$.

Grace finds the measure of L to help determine the strength of the signal between S and R. As L increases, the strength of the signal diminishes. She uses the Pythagorean Theorem and polar coordinates to find L.

$L^2 = y^2 + x^2$ — *Pythagorean Theorem*

$L^2 = (r \sin \theta)^2 + (r \cos \theta - x_1)^2$ — *Substitution using polar coordinates*

$L = \sqrt{(r \sin \theta)^2 + (r \cos \theta - x_1)^2}$ — *Take the square root of both sides.*

Example Find L if $r = 28$ km, $\theta = 60°$, and $x_1 = 7$ km. Round to the nearest tenth.

$$L = \sqrt{(28 \sin 60)^2 + (28 \cos 60° - 7)^2}$$
$$= \sqrt{587.97 + 49}$$
$$= 25.2$$

L is 25.2 km.

Exercises Find L for each of the following. Round to the nearest tenth.

1. $r = 100$, $\theta = 48°$, $x_1 = 25$
2. $r = 400$, $\theta = 20°$, $x_1 = 150$
3. $r = 40$, $\theta = 80°$, $x_1 = {}^-8$
4. $r = 80$, $\theta = 65°$, $x_1 = {}^-10$

Chapter Summary

1. Points in the plane can be identified using polar coordinates of the form (r, θ). The distance from a fixed point, called the **pole**, to a point $P(r, \theta)$ is $|r|$. The **polar axis** is a ray whose initial point is the pole. When r is positive, θ is the measure of any angle having the polar axis as its initial side and $\overrightarrow{OP}$ as its terminal side. (236)
2. Classical Curves

   Rose: $r = a \cos n\theta$ or $r = a \sin n\theta$, where n is a positive integer
   Lemniscate: $r^2 = a^2 \cos 2\theta$ or $r^2 = a^2 \sin 2\theta$
   Limaçon: $r = a + b \cos \theta$ or $r = a + b \sin \theta$
   Cardioid: $r = a + a \cos \theta$ or $r = a + a \sin \theta$
   Spiral of Archimedes: $r = a\theta$ (241)
3. Conversion from Polar to Rectangular Coordinates: The rectangular coordinates (x, y) of a point named by polar coordinates (r, θ) can be found by the following formulas.

   $$x = r \cos \theta \qquad y = r \sin \theta \quad (243)$$
4. Conversion from Rectangular to Polar Coordinates: The polar coordinates (r, θ) of a point named by the rectangular coordinates (x, y) can be found by the following formulas.

   $$r = \sqrt{x^2 + y^2} \qquad \theta = \text{Arctan}\,\frac{y}{x} \text{ when } x > 0$$

   $$\theta = \text{Arctan}\,\frac{y}{x} + \pi \text{ when } x < 0 \quad (244)$$

5.

For any complex numbers $a + bi$ and $c + di$.
$(a + bi) + (c + di) = (a + c) + (b + d)i$
$(a + bi) - (c + di) = (a - c) + (b - d)i$
$(a + bi)(c + di) = (ac - bd) + (ad + bc)i$
$\frac{(a + bi)}{(c + di)} = \frac{(ac + bd) + (bc - ad)i}{c^2 + d^2}$

(248)

6. Polar Form of $x + yi$: $x + yi = r(\cos \theta + i \sin \theta)$ (249)
7. Values for r and θ can be obtained by using the following formulas.

   $$r = \sqrt{x^2 + y^2} \qquad \theta = \text{Arctan}\,\frac{y}{x} \text{ when } x > 0$$

   $$\theta = \text{Arctan}\,\frac{y}{x} + \pi \text{ when } x < 0 \quad (249)$$
8. The product of two complex numbers $r_1(\cos \theta_1 + i \sin \theta_1)$ and $r_2(\cos \theta_2 + i \sin \theta_2)$ can be found by using the following formula.

   $$r_1(\cos \theta_1 + i \sin \theta_1) \cdot r_2(\cos \theta_2 + i \sin \theta_2) =$$
   $$r_1 r_2[\cos (\theta_1 + \theta_2) + i \sin (\theta_1 + \theta_2)] \quad (251)$$

9. The quotient of two complex numbers $r_1(\cos\theta_1 + i\sin\theta_1)$ and $r_2(\cos\theta_2 + i\sin\theta_2)$ can be found by using the following formula. (252)

$$\frac{r_1(\cos\theta_1 + i\sin\theta_1)}{r_2(\cos\theta_2 + i\sin\theta_2)} = \frac{r_1}{r_2}[\cos(\theta_1 - \theta_2) + i\sin(\theta_1 - \theta_2)]$$

10. DeMoivre's Theorem: $[r(\cos\theta + i\sin\theta)]^n = r^n(\cos n\theta + i\sin n\theta)$ (253)

11. The p distinct roots of a complex number $x + yi$ can be found by replacing n by 0, 1, 2, . . . p − 1, successively, in the following formula. (255)

$$(x + yi)^{\frac{1}{p}} = r^{\frac{1}{p}}\left(\cos\frac{\theta + 2n\pi}{p} + i\sin\frac{\theta + 2n\pi}{p}\right)$$

Chapter Review

9-1 **Graph the point which has the given polar coordinates.**

1. $(^-3, 50°)$ 2. $(1.5, ^-110°)$ 3. $\left(2, \frac{\pi}{4}\right)$ 4. $\left(^-3, -\frac{\pi}{2}\right)$

5–8. Name three other pairs of polar coordinates for each point named above.

Graph each polar equation.

9. $r = \sqrt{7}$ 10. $r = {}^-2$ 11. $\theta = 75°$
12. $\theta = {}^-80°$ 13. $\theta = -\frac{5\pi}{6}$ 14. $\theta = \frac{3\pi}{4}$

9-2 **Graph each polar equation.**

15. $r = 7\cos\theta$ 16. $r = 2 + 4\cos\theta$
17. $r = 3 + 3\sin\theta$ 18. $r = 6\sin 2\theta$

9-3 **Find the polar coordinates of the point with the given rectangular coordinates.**

19. $(^-\sqrt{3}, ^-3)$ 20. $(5, 5)$ 21. $(3, ^-2)$ 22. $(^-4, 2)$

Find the rectangular coordinates of the point with the given polar coordinates.

23. $\left(6, \frac{\pi}{4}\right)$ 24. $\left(2, -\frac{\pi}{6}\right)$ 25. $(^-2, 2.3)$ 26. $(^-1, ^-4.5)$

9-4 **Simplify.**

27. i^{55} 28. $i^{10} \cdot i^{25}$
29. $(2 + 3i) + (4 - 4i)$ 30. $(^-3 - i) - (2 + 7i)$
31. $i^3(4 - 3i)$ 32. $(^-i - 7)(i - 7)$
33. $(2 + 9i)(1 - 3i)$ 34. $(5 + 6i)(^-2 - 8i)$

35. $\dfrac{4 + i}{5 - 2i}$

36. $\dfrac{5}{\sqrt{2} - 4i}$

37. $\dfrac{7 + 5i}{7 - 5i}$

38. $\dfrac{8 - i}{2 + 3i}$

9-5 Express each complex number in polar form.

39. $^{-}6i$

40. $2 + 2i$

41. $^{-}2 + 2i\sqrt{3}$

42. $6 - 8i$

43. $5 - 3i$

44. $^{-}3 + i\sqrt{2}$

Express each complex number in rectangular form.

45. $4\left(\cos \dfrac{5\pi}{6} + i \sin \dfrac{5\pi}{6}\right)$

46. $8\left(\cos \dfrac{7\pi}{4} + i \sin \dfrac{7\pi}{4}\right)$

47. $\sqrt{3}\left(\cos \dfrac{3\pi}{2} + i \sin \dfrac{3\pi}{2}\right)$

48. $2\left(\cos \dfrac{2\pi}{3} + i \sin \dfrac{2\pi}{3}\right)$

49. $3(\cos 1 + i \sin 1)$

50. $5(\cos 2 + i \sin 2)$

9-6 Find each product or quotient. Express each result in rectangular form.

51. $2\left(\cos \dfrac{\pi}{3} + i \sin \dfrac{\pi}{3}\right) \cdot 4\left(\cos \dfrac{\pi}{3} + i \sin \dfrac{\pi}{3}\right)$

52. $3\left(\cos \dfrac{\pi}{2} + i \sin \dfrac{\pi}{2}\right) \cdot 2\left(\cos \dfrac{3\pi}{4} + i \sin \dfrac{3\pi}{4}\right)$

53. $1.9(\cos 2.1 + i \sin 2.1) \cdot 3(\cos 0.8 + i \sin 0.8)$

54. $8\left(\cos \dfrac{7\pi}{6} + i \sin \dfrac{7\pi}{6}\right) \div 2\left(\cos \dfrac{5\pi}{3} + i \sin \dfrac{5\pi}{3}\right)$

55. $6\left(\cos \dfrac{\pi}{2} + i \sin \dfrac{\pi}{2}\right) \div 4\left(\cos \dfrac{\pi}{6} + i \sin \dfrac{\pi}{6}\right)$

56. $2.2(\cos 1.5 + i \sin 1.5) \div 4.4(\cos 0.6 + i \sin 0.6)$

Find each product or quotient. Express each result in rectangular form.

57. $(^{-}3 + i\sqrt{3})(2 + 2i\sqrt{3})$

58. $(7 + 7i)(6 - 6i)$

59. $5i \div (1 + i\sqrt{3})$

60. $(2 + 2i) \div (^{-}6 - 6i)$

9-7 Find each of the following powers.

61. $(2 + 2i)^8$

62. $(\sqrt{3} - i)^7$

63. $(^{-}1 + i)^4$

64. $(^{-}2 - 2i\sqrt{3})^3$

Find each indicated root.

65. $\sqrt[4]{i}$

66. $(\sqrt{3} + i)^{\frac{1}{3}}$

Solve the following equations.

67. $x^5 - 32 = 0$

68. $x^6 - 1 = 0$

69–70. Graph the roots of each equation in problems 67–68.

Chapter Test

Graph the point which has the given polar coordinates. Then name three other pairs of polar coordinates which represent the same point.

1. $\left(^-2, \frac{5\pi}{4}\right)$
2. $\left(3, -\frac{\pi}{6}\right)$
3. $(2.5, 140°)$
4. $(^-1.7, 25°)$

Graph each polar equation.

5. $r = {}^-4$
6. $\theta = \frac{3\pi}{2}$
7. $r = 8 \sin \theta$
8. $r = 10 \sin 2\theta$
9. $r = 6 \cos 3\theta$
10. $r = 6 + \sin \theta$

Find the polar coordinates of the point with the given rectangular coordinates.

11. $(2, 2)$
12. $(^-3, 1)$

Find the rectangular coordinates of the point with the given polar coordinates.

13. $\left(3, -\frac{5\pi}{4}\right)$
14. $(^-4, 1.4)$

Simplify.

15. i^{93}
16. $(2 - 5i) + (^-2 + 4i)$
17. $(^-4 + i) - (4 - 2i)$
18. $(3 + 5i)(3 - 2i)$
19. $(7 + i)^2$
20. $\frac{6 - 2i}{2 + i}$

Express each complex number in polar form.

21. $^-4 + 4i$
22. $^-5$
23. $6 - 6i\sqrt{3}$

Express each complex number in rectangular form.

24. $2\left(\cos \frac{\pi}{3} + i \sin \frac{\pi}{3}\right)$
25. $\sqrt{2}\left(\cos\left(-\frac{\pi}{4}\right) + i \sin\left(-\frac{\pi}{4}\right)\right)$

Find each product or quotient. Express each result in rectangular form.

26. $4\left(\cos \frac{3\pi}{2} + i \sin \frac{3\pi}{2}\right) \cdot 3\left(\cos \frac{\pi}{4} + i \sin \frac{\pi}{4}\right)$
27. $2\sqrt{3}\left(\cos \frac{2\pi}{3} + i \sin \frac{2\pi}{3}\right) \div \sqrt{3}\left(\cos \frac{\pi}{6} + i \sin \frac{\pi}{6}\right)$
28. $(\sqrt{3} - 3i)(\sqrt{3} + i)$

Solve each problem.

29. Find $(1 - i)^8$ by DeMoivre's Theorem.
30. Solve the equation $x^8 - 1 = 0$ for all roots.

Chapter

10

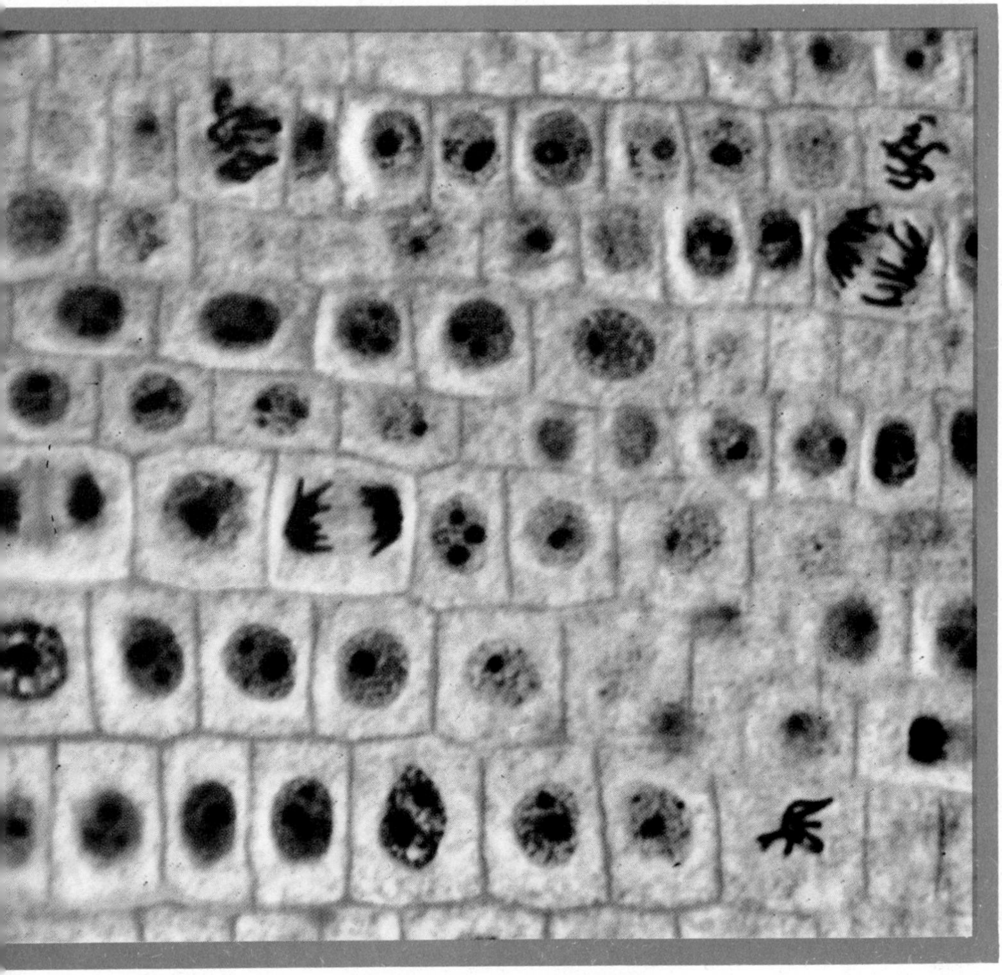

Exponential and Logarithmic Functions

The photograph shows cells of an onion in various stages of cell division. Suppose a cell divides once each week. The number of cells created by one cell in n weeks can be found as follows.

Week	0	1	2	3	4	5	n
Number of Cells	1	2	4	8	16	32	2^n

The function $y = 2^n$ is an exponential function.

10-1 Rational Exponents

The definitions and properties of rational exponents are an extension of those for integral exponents. You should be familiar with the following definitions of x^n for any real number x and positive integer n.

$$\text{If } n = 1,\ x^n = x$$

$$\text{If } n > 1,\ x^n = \overbrace{x \cdot x \cdot x \cdots x}^{n \text{ factors}}$$

$$\text{If } x \neq 0,\ x^0 = 1$$

$$\text{If } x \neq 0,\ x^{-n} = \frac{1}{x^n}$$

These definitions can be used to verify the properties of exponents for positive integers m and n and real numbers a and b.

Properties of Exponents

1. $a^m a^n = a^{m+n}$
2. $(a^m)^n = a^{mn}$
3. $\left(\frac{a}{b}\right)^m = \frac{a^m}{b^m},\ b \neq 0$
4. $(ab)^m = a^m b^m$
5. $\frac{a^m}{a^n} = a^{m-n},\ a \neq 0$

example

1 **Verify that the five properties of exponents given above are valid when $m = 3$, $n = 2$, $a = 2$, and $b = 4$.**

1. $$a^m a^n = a^{m+n}$$
$$2^3 \cdot 2^2 = 2^{3+2}$$
$$8 \cdot 4 = 2^5$$
$$32 = 32$$

2. $$(a^m)^n = a^{mn}$$
$$(2^3)^2 = 2^{3 \cdot 2}$$
$$8^2 = 2^6$$
$$64 = 64$$

3. $$\left(\frac{a}{b}\right)^m = \frac{a^m}{b^m}$$
$$\left(\frac{2}{4}\right)^3 = \frac{2^3}{4^3}$$
$$\frac{8}{64} = \frac{8}{64}$$

4. $$(ab)^m = a^m b^m$$
$$(2 \cdot 4)^3 = 2^3 \cdot 4^3$$
$$8^3 = 8 \cdot 64$$
$$512 = 512$$

5. $$\frac{a^m}{a^n} = a^{m-n}$$
$$\frac{2^3}{2^2} = 2^{3-2}$$
$$\frac{8}{4} = 2^1$$
$$2 = 2$$

Expressions with rational exponents can be defined such that the laws of exponents are still valid. Consider the expressions $7^{\frac{1}{2}}$ and $8^{\frac{1}{3}}$. According to the laws of exponents, the following must be true.

$$7^{\frac{1}{2}} \cdot 7^{\frac{1}{2}} = 7^{\frac{1}{2}+\frac{1}{2}} = 7$$
$$\text{But } \sqrt{7} \cdot \sqrt{7} = 7 \text{ also.}$$

Thus, $7^{\frac{1}{2}}$ and $\sqrt{7}$ must be equal.

$$8^{\frac{1}{3}} \cdot 8^{\frac{1}{3}} \cdot 8^{\frac{1}{3}} = 8^{\frac{1}{3}+\frac{1}{3}+\frac{1}{3}} = 8$$
$$\text{But } \sqrt[3]{8} \cdot \sqrt[3]{8} \cdot \sqrt[3]{8} = 8 \text{ also.}$$

Thus, $8^{\frac{1}{3}}$ and $\sqrt[3]{8}$ must be equal.

In general, let $y = b^{\frac{1}{n}}$ for a real number b and positive integer n. Then $y^n = \left(b^{\frac{1}{n}}\right)^n = b^{\frac{n}{n}}$ or b. But $y^n = b$ if and only if $y = \sqrt[n]{b}$. Therefore $b^{\frac{1}{n}}$ is defined as follows.

For any real number $b \geq 0$ and any integer $n > 1$,

$$b^{\frac{1}{n}} = \sqrt[n]{b}.$$

This also holds when $b < 0$ and n is odd.

Definition of $b^{\frac{1}{n}}$

What difficulties occur if $b < 0$ and n is even?

examples

2 **Evaluate $16^{\frac{1}{4}}$.**

$16^{\frac{1}{4}} = (2^4)^{\frac{1}{4}}$ or 2

Recall that $(a^m)^n = a^{mn}$.

3 **Evaluate $7^{\frac{1}{2}} \cdot 14^{\frac{1}{2}}$.**

$$7^{\frac{1}{2}} \cdot 14^{\frac{1}{2}} = 7^{\frac{1}{2}} \cdot 7^{\frac{1}{2}} \cdot 2^{\frac{1}{2}}$$
$$= 7\sqrt{2}$$

Recall that $(ab)^m = a^m b^m$.

Next consider the expression $8^{\frac{2}{3}}$.

$$8^{\frac{2}{3}} = \left(8^{\frac{1}{3}}\right)^2 \quad \text{or} \quad (8^2)^{\frac{1}{3}}$$
$$\left(8^{\frac{1}{3}}\right)^2 = (\sqrt[3]{8})^2 \qquad (8^2)^{\frac{1}{3}} = \sqrt[3]{8^2}$$

Thus, $(\sqrt[3]{8})^2$ and $\sqrt[3]{8^2}$ must be equal to $8^{\frac{2}{3}}$.

In general, $b^{\frac{m}{n}}$ is equal to $\left(b^{\frac{1}{n}}\right)^m$ or $(b^m)^{\frac{1}{n}}$.

$$\left(b^{\frac{1}{n}}\right)^m = (\sqrt[n]{b})^m \qquad (b^m)^{\frac{1}{n}} = \sqrt[n]{b^m}$$

Thus, $b^{\frac{m}{n}}$ is equal to $(\sqrt[n]{b})^m$ or $\sqrt[n]{b^m}$.

For any nonzero number b, and any integers m and n with $n > 1$,

$$b^{\frac{m}{n}} = \sqrt[n]{b^m} = (\sqrt[n]{b})^m$$

except when $\sqrt[n]{b}$ is not a real number.

Definition of Rational Exponents

examples

4 Evaluate $81^{\frac{3}{4}}$.

$$81^{\frac{3}{4}} = (3^4)^{\frac{3}{4}} = 3^3 = 27$$

5 Use radicals to express $(3m)^{\frac{2}{5}}n^{\frac{3}{5}}$.

$$(3m)^{\frac{2}{5}}n^{\frac{3}{5}} = ((3m)^2n^3)^{\frac{1}{5}} = (3^2m^2n^3)^{\frac{1}{5}} = \sqrt[5]{3^2m^2n^3}$$

6 Use rational exponents to express $\sqrt{r^3s^4}$.

$$\sqrt{r^3s^4} = (r^3s^4)^{\frac{1}{2}} = r^{\frac{3}{2}}s^2$$

exercises

Exploratory Evaluate.

1. $7^{\frac{1}{4}} \cdot 7^{\frac{7}{4}}$
2. $81^{\frac{1}{2}}$
3. $27^{-\frac{2}{3}}$
4. $\sqrt[3]{125}$
5. $\sqrt[4]{16^2}$
6. $(5^{\frac{3}{4}})^4$
7. $3^{-4} \cdot 3^8$
8. $64^{\frac{5}{6}}$
9. $\sqrt[5]{32}$
10. $(121^{\frac{1}{2}})^0$
11. $2^{-8} \cdot 2^5$
12. $(8^{-\frac{1}{2}})^{-\frac{2}{3}}$
13. $81^{\frac{1}{2}} - 81^{-\frac{1}{2}}$
14. $16^{\frac{3}{4}}$
15. $(3^{-1} + 3^{-2})^{-1}$
16. $(\sqrt[3]{216})^2$
17. $(5^{\frac{2}{5}})^{-5}$
18. $(\sqrt[3]{343})^{-2}$
19. $\dfrac{64}{64^{\frac{2}{3}}}$
20. $\dfrac{25^{\frac{3}{4}}}{25^{\frac{1}{4}}}$

Written Express each of the following using rational exponents.

1. $\sqrt{r^6s^3}$
2. $\sqrt[3]{8x^3y^6}$
3. $\sqrt[4]{a}$
4. $\sqrt{xy^3}$
5. $\sqrt[4]{x^{16}y^8}$
6. $\sqrt[6]{b^3}$
7. $\sqrt[3]{125a^2b^3}$
8. $\sqrt{25a^4b^{10}}$
9. $\sqrt[3]{64x^9y^{15}}$
10. $\sqrt[6]{27}$
11. $\sqrt[5]{32x^5y^8}$
12. $\sqrt{121a^5}$
13. $\sqrt[4]{24a^{12}b^{16}}$
14. $\sqrt[3]{ab^6c^4}$
15. $\sqrt{16y^8c}$
16. $\sqrt[3]{343x}$
17. $\sqrt[5]{y^3}$
18. $\sqrt[5]{15x^3y^{15}}$
19. $\sqrt{20x^4y^{12}}$
20. $\sqrt[4]{81x^4ya}$
21. $\sqrt[6]{12a^4b^2c^3}$
22. $\sqrt[4]{8x^2y^8}$
23. $\sqrt[5]{25a^{-5}b^{-10}}$
24. $\sqrt[6]{64a^6b^{-2}}$

Express each of the following using radicals.

25. $64^{\frac{1}{6}}$ 26. $25^{\frac{1}{3}}$ 27. $15^{\frac{1}{5}}$ 28. $a^{\frac{2}{3}}$

29. $a^{\frac{3}{4}}y^{\frac{1}{4}}$ 30. $4^{\frac{1}{3}}a^{\frac{2}{3}}y^{\frac{4}{3}}$ 31. $x^{\frac{4}{7}}y^{\frac{3}{7}}$ 32. $a^{\frac{1}{6}}b^{\frac{4}{6}}c^{\frac{3}{6}}$

33. $r^{\frac{5}{2}}q^{\frac{3}{4}}$ 34. $(c^3b^2)^{\frac{1}{5}}x^{\frac{3}{5}}$ 35. $a^{\frac{1}{5}}b^{\frac{1}{10}}$ 36. $(4x)^{\frac{1}{3}}a^{\frac{1}{2}}$

37. $3^{\frac{5}{3}}x^{\frac{7}{3}}$ 38. $(x^{10}y^2)^{\frac{1}{5}}a^{\frac{2}{5}}$ 39. $(2^5a^4y)^{\frac{1}{3}}$ 40. $ay^{\frac{2}{3}}\left(a^{\frac{1}{2}}y^{\frac{3}{2}}\right)$

41. $(2m)^{\frac{2}{5}}n^{\frac{3}{5}}$ 42. $\dfrac{x^{\frac{2}{3}}}{x^{\frac{1}{3}}}$ 43. $\dfrac{17^{\frac{3}{4}}}{17^{\frac{1}{4}}}$ 44. $15x^{\frac{1}{3}}y^{\frac{1}{5}}$

Simplify each given expression.

45. $x^6 \cdot x^{-3} \cdot x^2$ 46. $4x^2(4x)^{-2}$ 47. $\left(5x^{\frac{1}{3}}\right)^3$

48. $(4y^4)^{\frac{3}{2}}$ 49. $(y^{-2})^4 \cdot y^8$ 50. $((2x)^4)^{-2}$

51. $\left(x^{\frac{1}{2}}y^{-2}a^{\frac{5}{4}}\right)^{-4}$ 52. $\sqrt{a^3b^2} \cdot \sqrt{a^4b^5}$ 53. $(5ac)^{\frac{1}{3}}(a^2c^3)^{\frac{1}{3}}$

10-2 Exponential Functions

The expression a^x has been defined for integral and rational exponents. The next step is to define irrational exponents such that the properties of exponents remain valid.

Consider the graph of $y = 2^x$, where x is an integer. This is a function, since for each value of x there is a unique y-value.

x	2^x
-4	$\frac{1}{16}$
-3	$\frac{1}{8}$
-2	$\frac{1}{4}$
-1	$\frac{1}{2}$
0	1
1	2
2	4
3	8
4	16
5	32

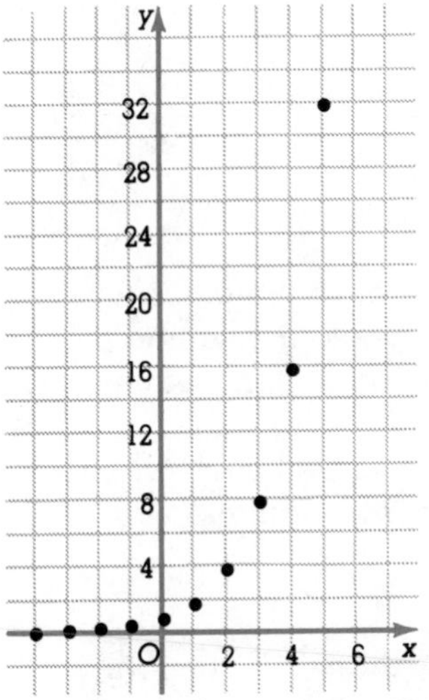

Notice that the vertical scale is condensed.

From the graph, it is clear that the function is increasing. That is, for any values x_1 and x_2, if $x_1 < x_2$ then $2^{x_1} < 2^{x_2}$.

Suppose the domain of $y = 2^x$ is expanded to include rational numbers. Notice that the additional points graphed below seem to "fill in" the graph of $y = 2^x$. That is, if a is between x_1 and x_2, then 2^a is between 2^{x_1} and 2^{x_2}. The graph of $y = 2^x$, when x is a rational number, is indicated by the broken line.

x	2^x
−3.5	0.09
−2.5	0.18
−1.5	0.35
−0.5	0.71
0.5	1.41
1.5	2.83
2.5	5.66
3.5	11.31
4.5	22.63

Values given in the table are approximate.

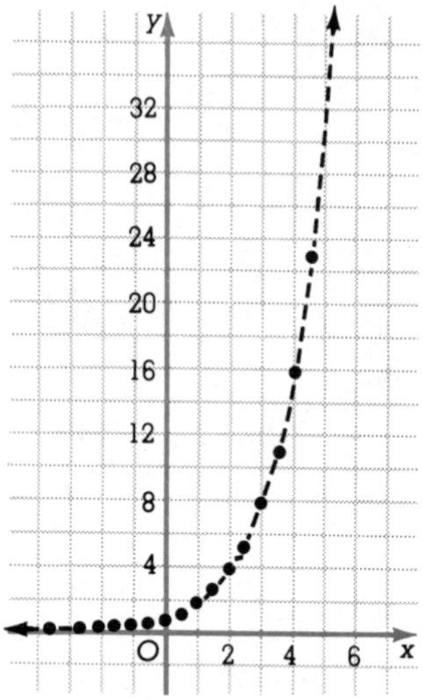

Since a^x has not been defined for irrational numbers, "holes" still remain in the graph of $y = 2^x$. How could you expand the domain of $y = 2^x$ to include both rational and irrational numbers? Consider a possible meaning for an expression such as $2^{\sqrt{3}}$. Since $1.7 < \sqrt{3} < 1.8$, it seems clear that $2^{1.7} < 2^{\sqrt{3}} < 2^{1.8}$. By using closer approximations for $\sqrt{3}$, closer approximations for $2^{\sqrt{3}}$ are possible.

$$2^{1.7} < 2^{\sqrt{3}} < 2^{1.8}$$
$$2^{1.73} < 2^{\sqrt{3}} < 2^{1.74}$$
$$2^{1.732} < 2^{\sqrt{3}} < 2^{1.733}$$
$$2^{1.7320} < 2^{\sqrt{3}} < 2^{1.7321}$$
$$2^{1.73205} < 2^{\sqrt{3}} < 2^{1.73206}$$

The sequence $2^{1.7}$, $2^{1.73}$, $2^{1.732}$, . . . converges to the value $2^{\sqrt{3}}$. The sequence $2^{1.8}$, $2^{1.74}$, $2^{1.733}$, . . . converges to the same value. Thus, $2^{\sqrt{3}}$ is **bounded** by the terms of the convergent sequences.

Therefore it is now possible to determine a value for a^x, when x is an irrational number, by using rational approximations.

> If x is an irrational number and $a > 0$, then a^x is the real number between a^{x_1} and a^{x_2}, for all possible choices of rational numbers x_1 and x_2 such that $x_1 < x < x_2$.

Definition of Irrational Exponents

example

1 Use the graph of $y = 2^x$ and the properties of exponents to evaluate x or y to the nearest tenth.

a. $y = 2^{1.8}$ b. $y = 2^{3.1}$ c. $5.2 = 2^x$ d. $40 = 2^x$

a. $y = 2^{1.8}$
From the graph, $y = 3.5$.

b. $y = 2^{3.1}$
$= 2^1 \cdot 2^{2.1}$
$= 2 \cdot 4.3$
$= 8.6$

c. $5.2 = 2^x$
From the graph, $x = 2.4$.

d. $40 = 2^x$
$8 \cdot 5 = 2^x$
$2^3 \cdot 2^{2.3} = 2^x$
$2^{5.3} = 2^x$
$x = 5.3$

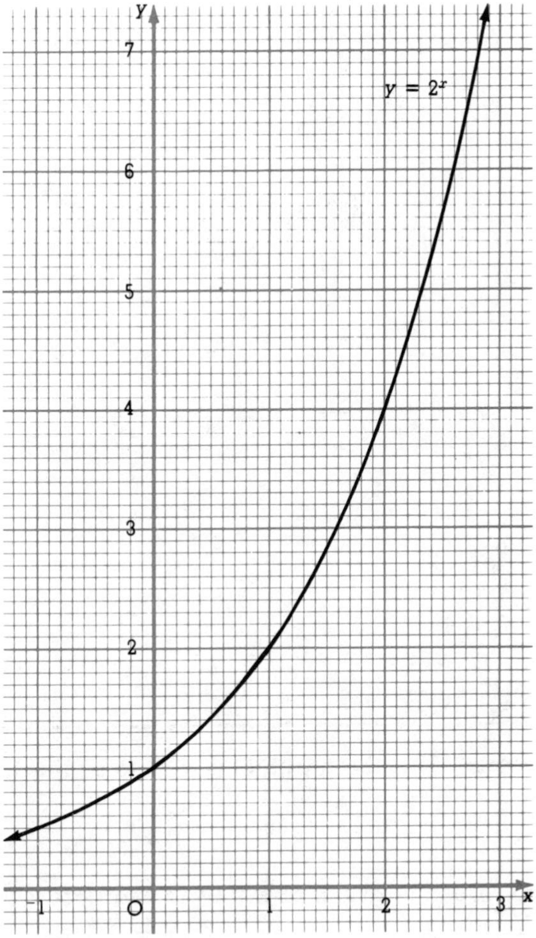

An exponential function has the form $y = a^x$, where a is a positive real number. The figure at the right shows graphs of several exponential functions. Notice that the point (0, 1) is common to each function. Compare the graph of $y = 2^x$ with the graph of $y = \left(\frac{1}{2}\right)^x$. What do you notice? When $a > 1$, is the graph of $y = a^x$ increasing or decreasing? When $a < 1$, is the graph increasing or decreasing?

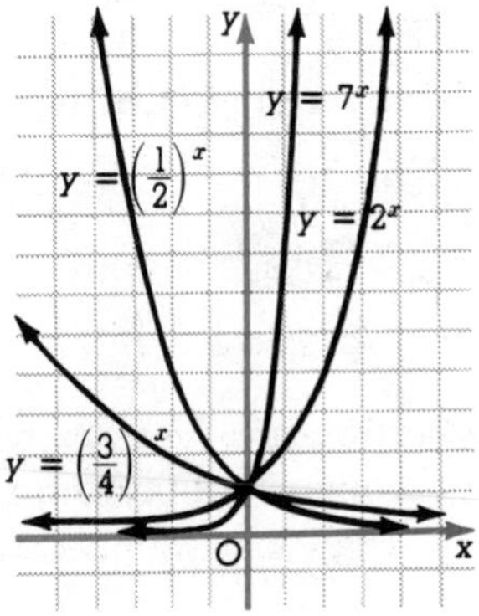

example

2 Graph the function $y = 3^x$.

First, make a table of ordered pairs. Then graph the ordered pairs and connect the points with a smooth curve.

x	3^x
−3	$\frac{1}{27}$
−2	$\frac{1}{9}$
−1	$\frac{1}{3}$
0	1
1	3
2	9
3	27

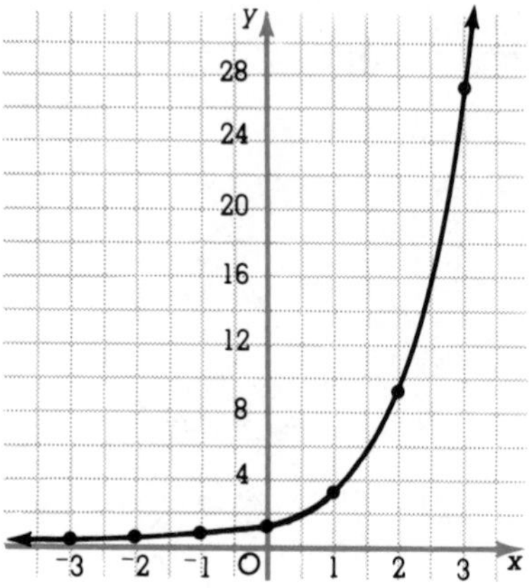

exercises

Exploratory Use the graph of $y = 2^x$ to evaluate each expression to the nearest tenth.

1. $2^{0.5}$
2. $2^{1.4}$
3. $2^{-1.5}$
4. $2^{2.5}$
5. $2^{0.8}$
6. $2^{\sqrt{2}}$
7. $2^{-0.1}$
8. $2^{2.1}$

Written Use the graph of $y = 2^x$ to evaluate x or y to the nearest tenth.

1. $y = 2^{4.5}$
2. $y = 2^{3.8}$
3. $y = 2^{-2.6}$
4. $3.7 = 2^x$
5. $4.1 = 2^x$
6. $\sqrt{7} = 2^x$
7. $12 = 2^x$
8. $y = 2^{2.9}$
9. $48 = 2^x$

Graph each equation.

10. $y = 4^x$
11. $y = 3^x$
12. $y = 5^{-x}$
13. $y = \left(\frac{1}{4}\right)^x$
14. $y = \left(\frac{1}{3}\right)^x$
15. $y = 7^{-x}$
16. Compare the graphs for problems 10 and 13. What do you notice?

Challenge An amoeba divides once every hour. Beginning with a single amoeba, how many amoebae will there be after the given amount of time?

1. 3 hours
2. 7 hours
3. 10 hours
4. 1 day

10-3 The Number e

Perhaps the most well-known and widely used irrational number is π. In 1748 Leonhard Euler, a Swiss mathematician, published a work in which he developed another irrational number which ranks along with π in importance. In his honor the number is called **e**, the **Euler number**. The number is the limit of the sum of the following infinite series.

$$e = 1 + \frac{1}{1!} + \frac{1}{2!} + \frac{1}{3!} + \frac{1}{4!} + \frac{1}{5!} + \cdots + \frac{1}{n!} + \cdots$$

The binomial formula can be used to derive the series for e, as follows. Let v be any variable and apply the binomial formula to $(1 + v)^n$.

$$(1 + v)^n = 1 + nv + \frac{n(n-1)}{2!}v^2 + \frac{n(n-1)(n-2)}{3!}v^3 + \cdots$$

Now let k be a variable such that $v = \frac{1}{k}$ and let x be a variable such that $kx = n$. Then substitute these values for v and n.

$$\left(1 + \frac{1}{k}\right)^{kx} = 1 + kx\left(\frac{1}{k}\right) + \frac{kx(kx-1)}{2!}\left(\frac{1}{k}\right)^2 + \frac{kx(kx-1)(kx-2)}{3!}\left(\frac{1}{k}\right)^3 + \cdots$$

$$= 1 + x + \frac{x\left(x - \frac{1}{k}\right)}{2!} + \frac{x\left(x - \frac{1}{k}\right)\left(x - \frac{2}{k}\right)}{3!} + \cdots$$

Then find the limit as k increases without bound.

$$\lim_{k\to\infty}\left(1 + \frac{1}{k}\right)^{kx} = 1 + x + \frac{x^2}{2!} + \frac{x^3}{3!} + \frac{x^4}{4!} + \frac{x^5}{5!} + \cdots$$

Recall that $\lim_{k\to\infty} \frac{1}{k} = 0.$

Let $x = 1$.

$$\lim_{k\to\infty}\left(1 + \frac{1}{k}\right)^{k} = 1 + 1 + \frac{1}{2!} + \frac{1}{3!} + \frac{1}{4!} + \cdots$$

Thus, e can be defined as follows.

$$e = \lim_{k\to\infty}\left(1 + \frac{1}{k}\right)^{k} = 1 + 1 + \frac{1}{2!} + \frac{1}{3!} + \cdots$$

Definition of e

The following computation for e is correct to three decimal places.

$$e = 1 + 1 + \frac{1}{2!} + \frac{1}{3!} + \frac{1}{4!} + \frac{1}{5!} + \frac{1}{6!} + \frac{1}{7!} + \cdots$$
$$= 1 + 1 + \frac{1}{2} + \frac{1}{6} + \frac{1}{24} + \frac{1}{120} + \frac{1}{720} + \frac{1}{5040} + \cdots$$
$$= 1 + 1 + 0.5 + 0.16667 + 0.04167 + 0.00833 + 0.00138 + 0.000198 + \cdots$$
$$= 2.718$$

If x is a variable, then e^x can be approximated using the following series.

$$e^x = 1 + x + \frac{x^2}{2!} + \frac{x^3}{3!} + \frac{x^4}{4!} + \cdots$$

This series is often called the exponential series.

One of the most important exponential functions is $y = e^x$. It is often referred to as **the exponential function.** A graph of $y = e^x$ is shown below. The graph can be used to find appoximate values.

example

1 Use the graph of $y = e^x$ to evaluate x or y to the nearest tenth.

a. $y = e^{1.3}$ b. $y = e^{3.2}$ c. $8 = e^x$ d. $y = 6^{0.8}$

a. $y = e^{1.3}$
From the graph, $e^{1.3} = 3.7$

b. $y = e^{3.2}$
$= e^{1.6}e^{1.6}$ *From the graph, $e^{1.6} = 4.9$*
$= (4.9)^2$
$= 24.0$

c. $8 = e^x$
From the graph, $x = 2.1$

d. $y = 6^{0.8}$
$= (e^{1.8})^{0.8}$ *$6 = e^{1.8}$*
$= e^{1.4}$
$= 4.1$

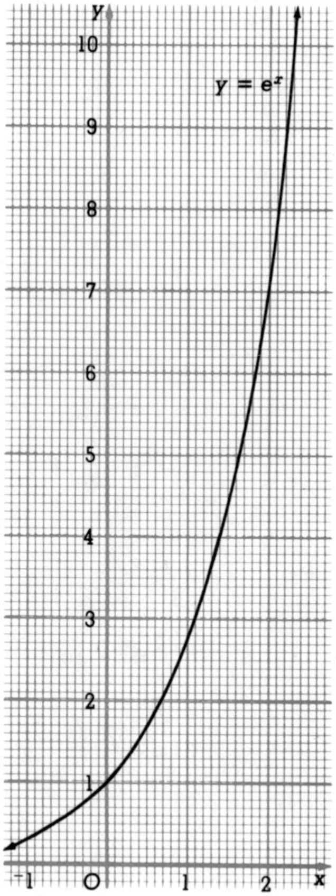

Values for $y = e^x$ and $y = e^{-x}$ are given in the table on page 512. Use this table to check the values found in the previous example. Notice that the graph is much less accurate than the table of values.

example

2 Use the table of values on page 512 to graph $y = e^{-x}$.

x	e^{-x}
−2	7.3891
−1	2.7183
0	1
1	0.3679
2	0.1353
3	0.0498

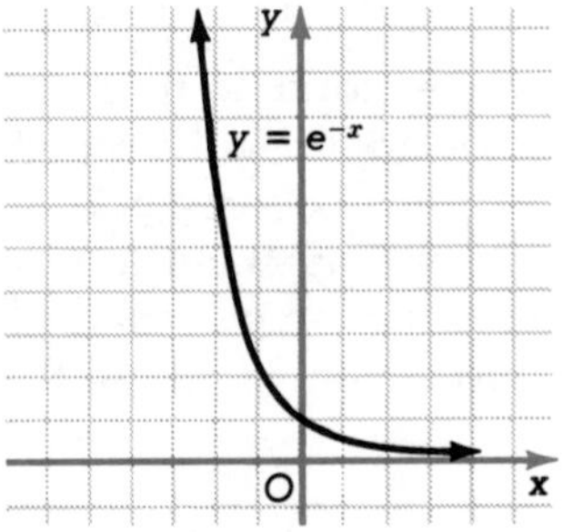

exercises

Exploratory Use the graph of $y = e^x$ on page 272 to evaluate **x** or y to the nearest tenth.

1. $y = e^{1.1}$
2. $y = e^{1.4}$
3. $y = e^{0.5}$
4. $y = e^{0.8}$
5. $7 = e^x$
6. $y = e^{-0.5}$
7. $5.5 = e^x$
8. $y = e^{1.6}$

Written Use the graph of $y = e^x$ on page 272 to evaluate **x** or y to the nearest tenth. Check your answers by using the table of values for e^x on page 512.

1. $y = e^{4.4}$
2. $y = e^{4.2}$
3. $y = e^{3.9}$
4. $y = \sqrt[3]{e}$
5. $y = 2\sqrt{e}$
6. $9 = e^x$
7. $6 = e^x$
8. $y = 5^{0.8}$
9. $y = 4^{0.5}$
10. $y = 2\sqrt[4]{e^3}$
11. $y = e^{6.4}$
12. $y = 4\sqrt[3]{e^2}$

Evaluate **x** to the nearest tenth given that $2 = e^{0.6932}$.

13. $32 = e^x$
14. $x = e^{2.0796}$
15. $x = e^{4.159}$
16. $x = e^0$
17. $16 = e^x$
18. $x = e^{0.346}$
19. Compute, correct to 5 decimal places, the values of $\frac{1}{8!}$ and $\frac{1}{9!}$ to verify that they do not affect the three-place value of **e** given.

Challenge Use the first 5 terms of the exponential series $e^x = 1 + x + \frac{x^2}{2!} + \frac{x^3}{3!} + \frac{x^4}{4!} \cdots$ to approximate the following.

1. $e^{1.5}$
2. $e^{.45}$
3. $e^{4.6}$
4. $e^{2.3}$
5. $e^{.8}$
6. $e^{1.9}$

Solve each problem. Use the table on page 512.

7. Graph $y = e^{-x^2}$. This graph approximates the bell-shaped curve. This curve is often used to represent the distribution of a particular trait in a normal population. It has many applications in statistics.
8. Graph $\frac{e^x + e^{-x}}{2}$. This graph is called the catenary curve. A flexible cable suspended between two points approximates this curve.

Compound Interest

Often money is lent with the understanding that when earnings accumulate they are to be added to the original investment at specified times and thus become part of a new principal. Interest computed on this basis is called **compound interest.** When interest is compounded, the effective annual yield from an investment is higher than the annual interest rate.

Federal Savings

12-month money market certificate

10.75%
Annual Interest Rate

11.35%
Effective Annual Yield

If P dollars are loaned at r percent for one interest period, the amount $A_1 = P + Pr = P(1 + r)$. This amount bears interest for the second period at r percent and the second amount $A_2 = P(1 + r) + rP(1 + r) = P(1 + r)^2$.

The accumulated amount of an investment at the end of a number of periods can be shown by means of a table.

End of Period	1	2	3	4	k
Accumulated Amount A	$P(1 + r)$	$P(1 + r)^2$	$P(1 + r)^3$	$P(1 + r)^4$	$\cdots P(1 + r)^k$

Thus, the compound interest formula is $A = P(1 + r)^k$.

When interest is compounded n times per year at rate r per year, then the rate per period is $\frac{r}{n}$ and the number of periods in t years is nt. The formula is then modified to the following form.

$$A = P\left(1 + \frac{r}{n}\right)^{nt}$$

Compound Interest Formula

Example Find the amount accumulated if \$100 is invested for 1 year at 8% annual interest compounded quarterly.

In 1 year there are 4 quarters. The quarterly rate is 2%. *Why?*

$$A = 100(1 + .02)^4$$
$$= 100(1.08243)$$
$$= \$108.24$$

In this case, the effective annual yield is 8.24%. Why?

Consider the special case where $rt = 1$. This could happen, for example, if money were invested for 20 years at 5%, or 1 year at 100%. Then $r = \frac{1}{t}$.

$$A = P\left(1 + \frac{1}{nt}\right)^{nt}$$

Suppose the interest is compounded continuously. Then n increases without limit. Thus, $nt \to \infty$, since t cannot equal zero. If the principal P is equal to 1, the value of A has the following limit as $nt \to \infty$.

$$A = \lim_{nt \to \infty} \left(1 + \frac{1}{nt}\right)^{nt} = e$$

That is, if \$1 is continuously compounded at rate r for t years where $rt = 1$, the amount accumulated will be \$2.71828 . . . or \$2.72.

Suppose the beginning principal is P, the annual interest rate is r, and the time in years is t. Then the following formula can be used to find the final amount, A, when interest is compounded continuously.

$$A = Pe^{rt}$$

Continuously Compounded Interest Formula

Example If \$500 is invested at 6% continuously compounded for 40 years, what is the final amount?

$A = 500e^{.06(40)}$ *Use the formula* $A = Pe^{rt}$

$= 500e^{2.4}$

$= 500(11.023)$

$= \$5511.50$

Exercises Solve each problem.

1. If interest is compounded annually, find the compound amount of \$1000 invested for 5 years at $9\frac{1}{2}$%.
2. If interest is compound semiannually, find the compound amount of \$2500 invested for 3 years at 10% per year.
3. If interest is compounded semiannually, find the compound amount of \$1200 invested for $4\frac{1}{2}$ years at 12% per year.
4. If \$100 is invested at 7% continuously compounded for 15 years, what is the amount at the end of that time?
5. If \$350 is invested at $14\frac{1}{2}$% continuously compounded for 50 years, what is the amount at the end of that time?
6. If \$500 is invested at 6% continuously compounded for 20 years, how much more is the amount than if it were compounded annually?
7. Suppose you invest \$3.00 at 15% annual interest. Calculate the amount you would have after one year if interest is compounded (a) quarterly (b) monthly (c) continuously.
8. Repeat exercise 7 using an annual rate of 12%.
9. One hundred dollars deposited in a bank which compounds interest quarterly yields \$115.00 at the end of a year. What is the annual rate of interest?
10. Which yields more, an amount invested at 12% compounded annually over a 10-year period, or the same amount invested at 11.5% compounded quarterly over a ten-year period?

10-4 Composition and Inverses of Functions

A function can be described as a mapping of the elements of one set, the domain, onto a second set, the range. Let function f map the elements in set R onto those in set S. Let function g map the elements in S onto those in T.

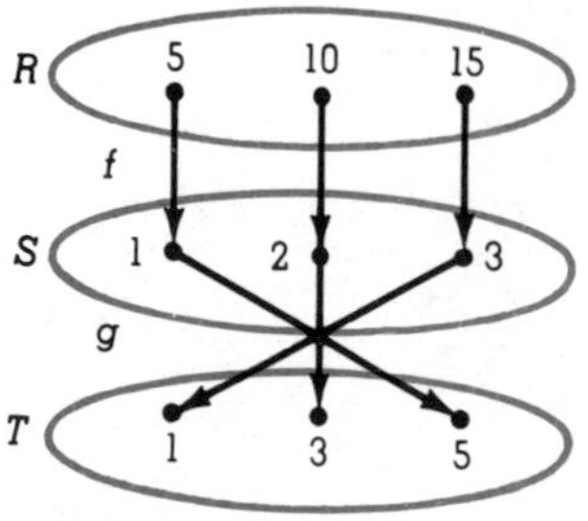

$f(x) = \frac{1}{5}x$

$g(x) = {}^{-}2x + 7$

By combining f and g in this way, a function from R to T is defined, since each element of R is associated with exactly one element of T. For example, $f(15) = 3$ and $g(3) = 1$. This new function that maps R onto T is called the **composite** of f and g. It is denoted by $g \circ f$, as shown at the right. Composition of functions is *not* commutative.

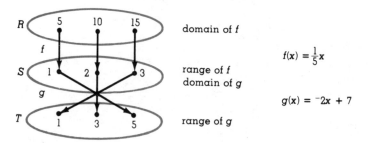

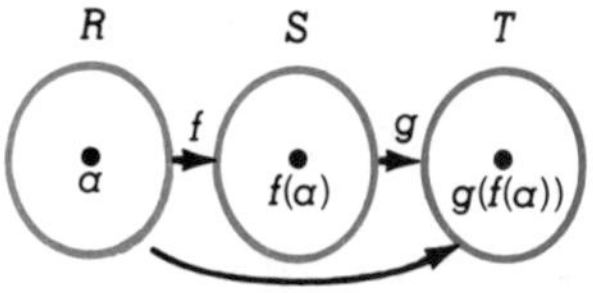

$g \circ f(x) = g(f(x))$

Given functions f and g the composite function $f \circ g$ can be described by the following equation.

$$f \circ g(x) = f(g(x))$$

The domain of $f \circ g$ includes all elements x in the domain of g for which $g(x)$ is in the domain of f.

Composition of Functions

example

1 If $f(x) = \dfrac{1}{x - 1}$ and $g(x) = x + 1$, find $f \circ g(x)$.

$$\begin{aligned} f \circ g(x) &= f(g(x)) \\ &= f(x + 1) \\ &= \frac{1}{(x + 1) - 1} \\ &= \frac{1}{x} \end{aligned}$$

The composite function $f \circ g$ exists only when the range of g is a subset of the domain of f. Otherwise the composition is undefined. For example, $f \circ g(x)$ does not exist for the following functions.

$$g(x) = {}^{-}\sqrt{x}$$
$$f(x) = \sqrt{x} + 1$$
$$f \circ g(x) = f(g(x)) = \sqrt{({}^{-}\sqrt{x})} + 1$$

Does $g \circ f(x)$ exist?

Consider two functions $f(x) = 5x - 3$ and $g(x) = \dfrac{x+3}{5}$. Functions $f \circ g(x)$ and $g \circ f(x)$ can be found as follows.

$$\begin{aligned} f \circ g(x) &= f(g(x)) \\ &= f\left(\frac{x+3}{5}\right) \\ &= 5\left(\frac{x+3}{5}\right) - 3 \\ &= x \end{aligned} \qquad \begin{aligned} g \circ f(x) &= g(f(x)) \\ &= g(5x - 3) \\ &= \frac{(5x-3)+3}{5} \\ &= x \end{aligned}$$

Notice that $f(g(x)) = g(f(x)) = x$. Functions f and g are called **inverse functions.**

Inverse Functions

Two polynomial functions f and g are inverse functions if and only if both their compositions are the identity function. That is, $f \circ g(x) = g \circ f(x) = x$.

The inverse function of f, if it exists, is denoted by f^{-1}. If f and g are inverse functions, then $f = g^{-1}$ and $g = f^{-1}$.

The notation f^{-1} is read "f inverse," or "the inverse of f." The $^{-1}$ is not an exponent.

The inverse of a function can be shown as a mapping.

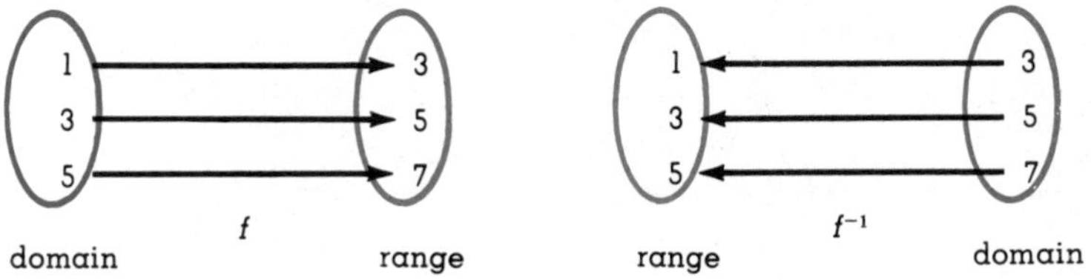

If $f = \{(1, 3), (3, 5), (5, 7)\}$ then $f^{-1} = \{(3, 1), (5, 3), (7, 5)\}$.

Notice that the inverse is found by reversing the order of the coordinates of each ordered pair for the function. The mapping shown above is one-to-one. The mapping shown at the right is *not* one-to-one. The inverse of f is a function only if f represents a one-to-one mapping. *Why?*

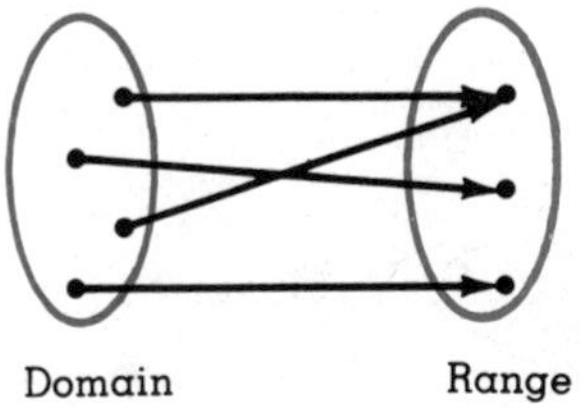

Property of Inverse Functions

Suppose f and f^{-1} are inverse functions. Then $f(a) = b$ if and only if $f^{-1}(b) = a$.

The graphs of $f(x) = 5x - 3$ and $f^{-1}(x) = \dfrac{x+3}{5}$ are shown at the right. Notice that the graph of f^{-1} is the reflection of f about the line $y = x$. Any two points (a, b) and (b, a) are symmetric with respect to the line $y = x$. The inverse of a function can be graphed by reflecting the graph of the function about the line $y = x$.

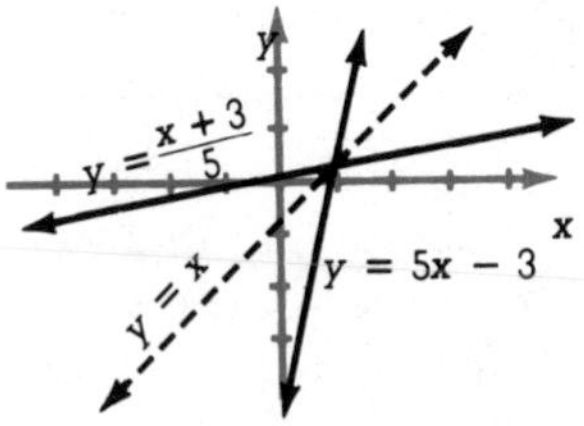

example

2 Suppose $f(x) = 2x + 5$. Find $f^{-1}(x)$, and show that f and f^{-1} are inverse functions.

Recall that $f(a) = b$ if and only if $f^{-1}(b) = a$. Since $f(x) = 2x + 5$, you know that $f(a) = 2a + 5$. Use $2a + 5 = b$ to find $f^{-1}(b)$.

Solve the equation for a.

$$2a = b - 5$$

$$a = \frac{b - 5}{2}$$

$$f^{-1}(b) = \frac{b - 5}{2}$$

$$f^{-1}(x) = \frac{x - 5}{2} \qquad \textit{Replace } b \textit{ by } x.$$

Now show that the compositions of f and f^{-1} are identity functions.

$$f \circ f^{-1}(x) = f(f^{-1}(x)) = f\left(\frac{x - 5}{2}\right) = 2\left(\frac{x - 5}{2}\right) + 5 = x$$

$$f^{-1} \circ f(x) = f^{-1}(f(x)) = f^{-1}(2x + 5) = \frac{(2x + 5) - 5}{2} = x$$

So, $f \circ f^{-1}(x) = f^{-1} \circ f(x) = x$.

Not all functions have inverses which are functions.

example

3 Given $f(x) = x^2$, find $f^{-1}(x)$.

Since $f(x) = x^2$, you know that $f(a) = a^2$. Use $a^2 = b$ to find $f^{-1}(b)$. *Why?*

Solve the equation for a.

$$a^2 = b$$

$$a = \pm\sqrt{b}$$

$$f^{-1}(b) = \pm\sqrt{b} \qquad \textit{Replace } a \textit{ by } f^{-1}(b).$$

$$f^{-1}(x) = \pm\sqrt{x} \qquad \textit{Replace } b \textit{ by } x.$$

The equation does not define a function. Why?

You can determine if a function will have an inverse function by using the **horizontal line test.** If any horizontal line drawn on the graph of a function passes through no more than one point of the graph, then the function has an inverse which is also a function.

exercises

Exploratory Find $f \circ g(4)$ and $g \circ f(4)$.

1. $f(x) = x + 2$
   $g(x) = x - 3$
2. $f(x) = x^2 + 7$
   $g(x) = x - 5$
3. $f(x) = x^2 - 1$
   $g(x) = x + 1$
4. $f(x) = 2x + 5$
   $g(x) = x - 6$
5. $f(x) = x^2$
   $g(x) = x^5$
6. $f(x) = x^2 + 2x + 1$
   $g(x) = x - 1$
7. $f(x) = 3x^2 - 4$
   $g(x) = 5x + 1$
8. $f(x) = x^2 - 4x + 5$
   $g(x) = x - 2$
9. $f(x) = 5x + 9$
   $g(x) = \frac{1}{2}x - 1$

Determine if the inverse of each relation graphed below is a function.

10.

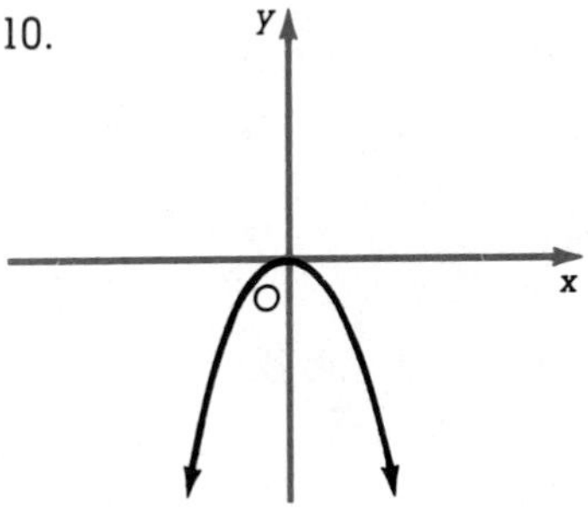

11.

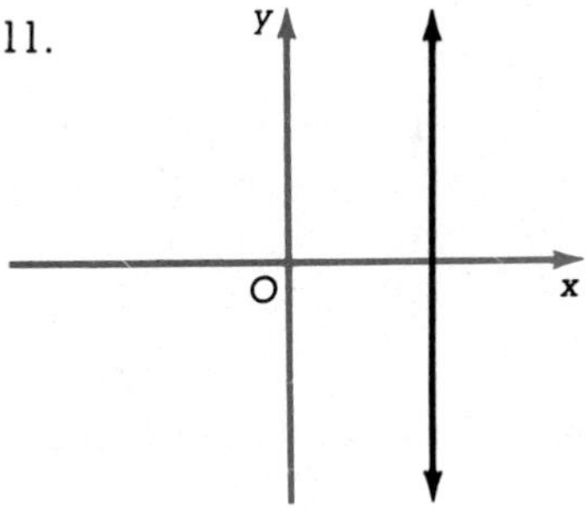

12.

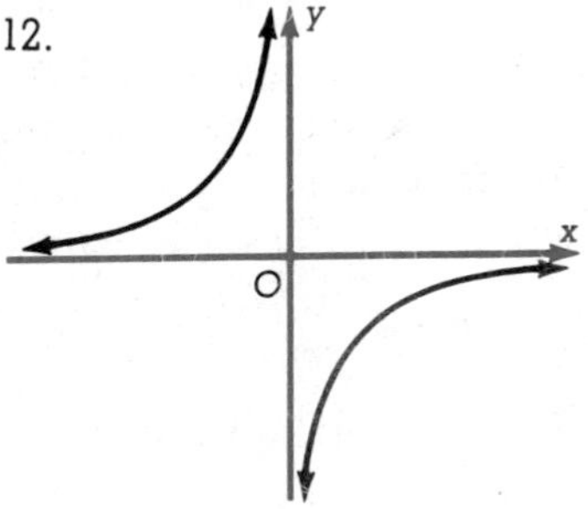

Written Find $f \circ g(x)$ and $g \circ f(x)$.

1. $f(x) = x + 3$
   $g(x) = 2x + 5$
2. $f(x) = x^2 - 9$
   $g(x) = x + 4$
3. $f(x) = \frac{1}{2}x - 7$
   $g(x) = x + 6$
4. $f(x) = x^2 + 3x + 2$
   $g(x) = x - 1$
5. $f(x) = 3x^2$
   $g(x) = x - 4$
6. $f(x) = x$
   $g(x) = 4x^2 - 7$
7. $f(x) = \frac{2}{5}x$
   $g(x) = 40x - 10$
8. $f(x) = x^3 + x^2 + 1$
   $g(x) = 2x$
9. $f(x) = 5x^2$
   $g(x) = x^2 - 1$
10. $f(x) = {}^{-}2x + 11$
    $g(x) = x - 6$
11. $f(x) = x^2 + 5x + 6$
    $g(x) = x + 1$
12. $f(x) = x^3$
    $g(x) = x + 1$

For each of the following, determine whether the given functions are inverses of one another.

13. $y = 3x + 1$
    $y = \frac{x - 1}{3}$
14. $y = 5x - 6$
    $y = \frac{x + 6}{5}$
15. $y = \frac{1}{2}x - 5$
    $y = 2x + 5$
16. $y = x + 5$
    $y = x - 5$
17. $y = {}^{-}x$
    $y = x$
18. $y = {}^{-}3x + 7$
    $y = 3x - 7$

Graph each function and its inverse.

19. $y = x - 5$
20. $f = \{(0, 1), (2, 3), (4, 5)\}$
21. $y = 4x$
22. $f(x) = \frac{x - 3}{2}$
23. $y = {}^{-}3x - 1$
24. $f(x) = (x - 2)^2$

10-5 Logarithmic Functions

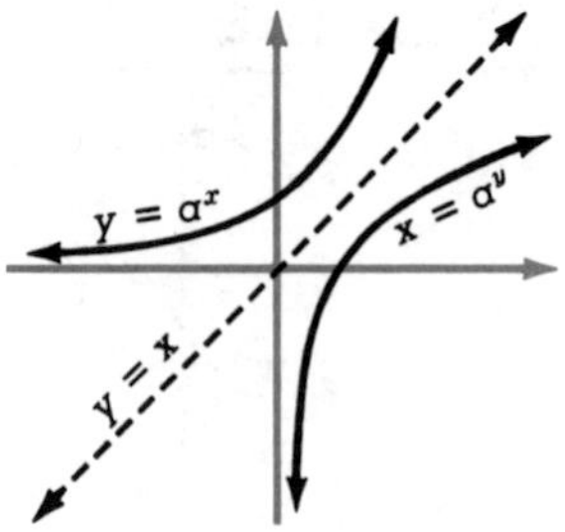

The exponential function $y = a^x$ is increasing for $a > 1$ and decreasing for $0 < a < 1$. Since the function is one-to-one, it has an inverse which is also a function. The inverse of $y = a^x$ is $x = a^y$. In the function $x = a^y$, y is called the **logarithm** of x. It is more conveniently written as $y = \log_a x$ and is read y *equals the log of x to the base a.* The logarithm is the exponent. The function $y = \log_a x$ is called a **logarithmic function**.

> The logarithmic function $y = \log_a x$, $a > 0$ and $a \neq 1$, is the inverse of the exponential function $y = a^x$.

Definition of Logarithmic Function

Thus, $y = \log_a x$ if and only if $x = a^y$.

As a result, each logarithmic equation corresponds to an exponential equation. For example, the equation $y = \log_2 16$ can be written $2^y = 16$. Since $2^4 = 16$, $\log_2 16 = 4$.

example

1 Write the equation $\log_{27} 3 = \dfrac{1}{3}$ in exponential form.

$27^{\frac{1}{3}} = 3$

$\log_a b = c$

$27^{1/3} = 3$

$a^c = b$

2 Solve the equation $\log_b 36 = {}^-2$.

In exponential form the equation is $b^{-2} = 36$.

Thus, $\dfrac{1}{b^2} = 36$, or $b^2 = \dfrac{1}{36}$.

Therefore $b = \dfrac{1}{6}$.   *Why is b not equal to $-\dfrac{1}{6}$?*

Since the logarithmic function and the exponential function are inverses, both of their compositions yield the identity function.

$$a^{\log_a x} = x \qquad \log_a a^x = x$$

To show this, let $f(x) = \log_a x$ and $g(x) = a^x$. Then find $f \circ g$ and $g \circ f$.

Since logarithms are exponents, the properties of logarithms can be derived from the properties of exponents.

> Suppose m and n are positive numbers, b is a positive number other than 1, and p is any number. Then the following properties hold.
>
> Product Property: $\log_b mn = \log_b m + \log_b n$
>
> Quotient Property: $\log_b \dfrac{m}{n} = \log_b m - \log_b n$
>
> Power Property: $\log_b m^p = p \cdot \log_b m$

Properties of Logarithms

example

3 Use the properties of exponents to show that the product property of logarithms is valid.

Let $\log_b m = x$ and $\log_b n = y$.

$b^x = m$ and $b^y = n$ — *Change to exponential form.*

$mn = b^x b^y$ — *Find the product of m and n.*

$= b^{x+y}$

$\log_b mn = \log_b b^{x+y}$ — *Change to logarithmic form.*

$= x + y$

$= \log_b m + \log_b n$ — *Substitute for x and y.*

Thus, $\log_b mn = \log_b m + \log_b n$.

4 **Solve the equation $\log_4(2x - 3) = \log_4(x + 2)$.**

$\log_4 (2x - 3) = \log_4 (x + 2)$

$2x - 3 = x + 2$ — *If $\log_a x = \log_a y$, then $x = y$.*

$x = 5$

The solution is 5.

5 **Solve the equation $4 \log_5 x - \log_5 4 = \log_5 4$.**

$4 \log_5 x - \log_5 4 = \log_5 4$

$4 \log_5 x = 2 \log_5 4$

$2 \log_5 x = \log_5 4$

$\log_5 x^2 = \log_5 4$ — *Power property of logarithms*

$x^2 = 4$

$x = 2$ — *$^-2$ is not a solution since $\log_a x$ has not been defined for negative numbers.*

The solution is 2.

exercises

Exploratory Change each equation to logarithmic form.

1. $2^3 = 8$
2. $5^2 = 25$
3. $10^4 = 10{,}000$
4. $6^{-2} = \frac{1}{36}$
5. $3^{-3} = \frac{1}{27}$
6. $49^{\frac{1}{2}} = 7$

Change each equation to exponential form.

7. $\log_2 16 = 4$
8. $\log_{10} 0.01 = {}^-2$
9. $\log_2 32 = 5$
10. $\log_5 \frac{1}{25} = {}^-2$
11. $\log_{16} 4 = \frac{1}{2}$
12. $\log_9 27 = \frac{3}{2}$

Evaluate each expression.

13. $\log_{10} 1000$
14. $\log_3 81$
15. $\log_{10} 0.001$
16. $\log_7 \frac{1}{343}$
17. $\log_2 \frac{1}{16}$
18. $\log_6 6^5$
19. $\log_a a^5$
20. $\log_8 16$
21. $8^{\log_8 3}$

Written Solve each equation.

1. $\log_x 25 = 2$
2. $\log_x 36 = 2$
3. $\log_5 0.04 = x$
4. $\log_5 (3x) = \log_5 (2x + 7)$
5. $\log_6 (4x + 4) = \log_6 64$
6. $\log_3 (3x) = \log_3 36$
7. $\log_{\frac{1}{3}} x = {}^-4$
8. $\log_3 27 = x$
9. $\log_x 16 = {}^-4$
10. $\log_x \sqrt{3} = \frac{1}{4}$
11. $\log_{10} \sqrt[3]{10} = x$
12. $\log_{\sqrt{5}} 5 = x$
13. $\log_2 4 + \log_2 6 = \log_2 x$
14. $2 \log_6 4 - \frac{1}{4} \log_6 16 = \log_6 x$
15. $\log_3 12 - \log_3 x = \log_3 3$
16. $\log_5 x = 4 \log_5 3$
17. $3 \log_7 4 + 4 \log_7 3 = \log_7 x$
18. $\log_4 (x - 3) + \log_4 (x + 3) = 2$
19. $\log_2 (4x + 10) - \log_2 (x + 1) = 3$
20. $\log_6 x = \frac{1}{2} \log_6 9 + \frac{1}{3} \log_6 27$
21. $\log_{10} x + \log_{10} x + \log_{10} x = \log_{10} 8$
22. $\log_9 5x = \log_9 6 + \log_9 (x - 2)$

10-6 Common Logarithms

Logarithms which use 10 as a base are called **common logarithms.** When the base of a logarithm is not indicated, the base is assumed to be 10. Thus, log 25 means $\log_{10} 25$.

The common logarithms of integral powers of 10 can easily be determined.

$$\begin{aligned}
\log 1000 &= 3 \text{ since } 1000 = 10^3\\
\log 100 &= 2 \text{ since } 100 = 10^2\\
\log 10 &= 1 \text{ since } 10 = 10^1\\
\log 1 &= 0 \text{ since } 1 = 10^0\\
\log 0.1 &= {}^-1 \text{ since } 0.1 = 10^{-1}\\
\log 0.01 &= {}^-2 \text{ since } 0.01 = 10^{-2}
\end{aligned}$$

Notice that log 1 = 0 and log 10 = 1. Thus, the logarithm of any number between 1 and 10 must be greater than zero and less than one. For example, log 5 = 0.6990.

The equals symbol (=) is used with the understanding that the numbers are approximate.

The logarithms of numbers which differ by integral powers of ten are closely related.

example 1

Given that log 5 = 0.6990, evaluate each logarithm.

a. log 5000 **b. log 0.05**

a. $\log 5000 = \log (1000 \cdot 5)$
$= \log 1000 + \log 5$
$= 3 + 0.6990$
$= 3.6990$

b. $\log 0.05 = \log \left(\frac{5}{100}\right)$
$= \log 5 - \log 100$
$= 0.6990 - 2$
$= {}^-2 + 0.6990$

The common logarithm of a number is composed of 2 parts, the **characteristic** and the **mantissa.** The characteristic precedes the decimal point. The mantissa is a positive decimal less than 1. For example, the characteristic of 3.6990 is 3 and the mantissa is .6990. The mantissa always represents the logarithm of a number between 1 and 10.

By using the table of common logarithms on pages 508-509, the logarithm of any number can be determined. First, write the number in scientific notation. The exponent of 10 in this form is always the characteristic of the logarithm of the number. Then, find the mantissa in the table of logarithms. To find log 1.23, read across the row labeled 12 and down the column labeled 3.

Common Logarithms of Numbers

n	0	1	2	3	4
10	0000	0043	0086	0128	0170
11	0414	0453	0492	0531	0569
12	0792	0828	0864	0899	0934

$\log 1.23 = 0.0899$

Remember that the logarithms are, in general, irrational numbers and the values given in the table are mantissas that have been rounded to four decimal places.

example

2 Find the common logarithm of each number. Use the table on pages 508-509.

a. 5280

b. 0.0351

a.
$$\begin{aligned}\log 5280 &= \log (5.28 \times 10^3)\\ &= \log 5.28 + \log 10^3\\ &= 0.7226 + 3\\ &= 3.7226\end{aligned}$$

b.
$$\begin{aligned}\log 0.0351 &= \log (3.51 \times 10^{-2})\\ &= \log 3.51 + \log 10^{-2}\\ &= 0.5453 + (^-2)\\ &= 0.5453 - 2\end{aligned}$$

When the characteristic of a logarithm is negative, the logarithm can be written in many ways. To preserve the positive mantissa, the characteristic and mantissa are usually not added.

$$\begin{aligned}\log 0.0351 &= {}^-2 + 0.5453\\ &= 8.5453 - 10\end{aligned}$$

Two other ways are $\bar{2}.5453$ and 0.5453 − 2.

Most calculators display the sum of the characteristic and the mantissa. Thus, log 0.0351 would be displayed as $^-1.4547$.

If the logarithm of a number is known, then the number which corresponds to it is known as the **antilogarithm.** If $\log x = a$, then $x = \text{antilog } a$.

example

3 **If log x = 4.8825, find x.**

$\log x = 4.8825$
$x = \text{antilog } 4.8825$ — *4 is the characteristic and 0.8825 is the mantissa.*
$= (\text{antilog } 0.8825) \times 10^4$
$= 7.63 \times 10^4$ — *Find antilog 0.8825 in the table of mantissas.*
$= 76{,}300$

Many problems involving powers and roots are much easier to solve if logarithms are used.

examples

4 **Use logarithms to evaluate the following expression.**

$$\frac{37.9\sqrt{488}}{(1.28)^3}$$

Let $A = \dfrac{37.9\sqrt{488}}{(1.28)^3}$

Then, $\log A = \log \left[\dfrac{37.9\sqrt{488}}{(1.28)^3}\right]$
$= \log 37.9 + \frac{1}{2}\log 488 - 3 \log 1.28$ — *Which properties are used here?*
$= 1.5786 + \frac{1}{2}(2.6884) - 3(0.1072)$
$= 2.6012$

Therefore, $A = \text{antilog } 2.6012$
$= 399$

The value of the given expression is approximately 399.

5 **Use logarithms to evaluate $\sqrt[5]{0.0641}$.**

Let $A = \sqrt[5]{0.0641}$

Then, $\log A = \log \sqrt[5]{0.0641}$
$= \frac{1}{5}\log 0.0641$ — 6.41×10^{-2}
$= \frac{1}{5}(0.8069 - 2)$
$= \frac{1}{5}(3.8069 - 5)$ — *$0.8069 - 2 = 3.8069 - 5$*
$= 0.7614 - 1$
$A = \text{antilog } (0.7614 - 1)$
$= (\text{antilog } 0.7614) \times 10^{-1}$
$= 5.77 \times 10^{-1}$
$= 0.577$

Since the multiplying factor is $\frac{1}{5}$, the negative characteristic should be a multiple of 5.

The value of $\sqrt[5]{0.0641}$ is approximately 0.577.

exercises

Exploratory Given that log 375 = 2.5740, find each of the following.

1. characteristic of log 375
2. mantissa of log 375
3. log 3750
4. log 37.5
5. antilog $\overline{1}.5740$
6. log 0.000375
7. antilog 4.5740
8. antilog 8.5740 − 10
9. antilog 0.5740 − 3

Written Use the table on pages 508–509 to find the common logarithm of each number.

1. 64.8
2. 572
3. 8.91
4. 25,600
5. 0.00357
6. 0.654
7. 0.0123
8. 873,000

Use the table on pages 508–509 to find the antilogarithm of each number.

9. 3.8899
10. 1.8082
11. 0.7348 − 2
12. 5.3181
13. 8.9149 − 10
14. 2.5239
15. 0.9265
16. 0.7340 − 3

Evaluate each given expression using logarithms.

17. $24.5 \times 754 \times 0.0128$
18. $\dfrac{7.12 \times 5.43}{2.28}$
19. $(1.12)^3 \times 425$
20. $\sqrt{4.63 \times 54.8}$
21. $\sqrt[3]{(2.03)(612)}$
22. $6.73 \div \sqrt[4]{0.0063}$
23. $\left(\dfrac{1}{0.381}\right)^2$
24. $\sqrt[5]{45.8}$
25. $\dfrac{24.8\sqrt{451}}{(39.6)^3}$

10-7 Exponential Equations

Logarithms can be used to solve equations in which variables appear as exponents. Such equations are called **exponential equations.** Solutions to equations involving exponential expressions are based on the fact that if $a^{x_1} = a^{x_2}$ for some base a and real numbers x_1 and x_2, then $x_1 = x_2$.

example

1 **Solve the equation $5^x = 100$.**

$$\begin{aligned} 5^x &= 100 \\ \log 5^x &= \log 100 \\ x \log 5 &= \log 100 \qquad \textit{Power property} \\ x &= \frac{\log 100}{\log 5} \\ &= \frac{2}{0.6990} \text{ or } 2.8612 \end{aligned}$$

The solution is approximately 2.8612.

example

2 **Express $\log_4 78$ in terms of common logarithms. Then find its value.**

Let $x = \log_4 78$.

$$4^x = 78$$
$$\log 4^x = \log 78$$
$$x \log 4 = \log 78 \quad \textit{Power property}$$
$$x = \frac{\log 78}{\log 4}$$

The logarithm may be expressed as $\frac{\log 78}{\log 4}$.

$\frac{\log 78}{\log 4} = \frac{1.8921}{.6021}$ or 3.1425

The value of $\log_4 78$ is approximately 3.1425.

Any logarithm can be expressed in terms of a different base. Usually the base is changed to base e or base 10, as shown in the preceding example.

Suppose a, b, and n are positive numbers, and neither a nor b is 1. Then the following equation is true.

$$\log_a n = \frac{\log_b n}{\log_b a}$$

Change of Bases

examples

3 **Find the value of $\log_9 27$ using the formula above.**

$$\log_9 27 = \frac{\log_3 27}{\log_3 9} \quad \textit{$\log_3$ was chosen because 27 and 9 are powers of 3.}$$
$$= \frac{3}{2} \quad \textit{Why?}$$

The value of $\log_9 27$ is $\frac{3}{2}$.

4 **Solve the equation $5^{x-1} = 3^x$.**

$$5^{x-1} = 3^x$$
$$\log 5^{x-1} = \log 3^x$$
$$(x - 1) \log 5 = x \log 3$$
$$x \log 5 - \log 5 = x \log 3$$
$$x \log 5 - x \log 3 = \log 5$$
$$x (\log 5 - \log 3) = \log 5$$
$$x = \frac{\log 5}{\log 5 - \log 3}$$
$$= \frac{0.6990}{0.6990 - 0.4771}$$
$$= 3.1501$$

exercises

Exploratory State x in terms of common logarithms.

1. $2^x = 46$
2. $3^x = 72$
3. $6^{2x} = 63$
4. $5^{3x} = 128$
5. $x = \log_5 121$
6. $x = \log_4 75$
7. $x = \log_3 16$
8. $x = \log_4 35$
9. $2^{-x} = 10$
10. $3^{-x} = 18$
11. $2^x = 14$
12. $3^x = 3\sqrt{2}$

Change each expression to an expression in terms of the given base.

13. $\log_4 7$, base 10
14. $\log_5 4.25$, base 10
15. $\log_{10} 5$, base 8
16. $\log_4 0.033$, base 10
17. $\log_a t$, base 10
18. $\log_2 6.7$, base 10

Written 1-12. Evaluate x for problems **1-12** in the exploratory exercises.

Solve each equation using logarithms.

13. $3.6^x = 52.5$
14. $4.3^x = 76.2$
15. $6.7^{x-2} = 42$
16. $2.2^{x-5} = 9.32$
17. $9^{x-4} = 7.13$
18. $5^{x+2} = 14.5$
19. $x = \log_3 52.7$
20. $x = \log_4 19.5$
21. $x^{\frac{2}{3}} = 27.6$
22. $x^{\frac{3}{4}} = 89.8$
23. $5^{x-1} = 2^x$
24. $6^{x-2} = 4^x$
25. $3^{2x} = 7^{x-1}$
26. $12^{x-4} = 3^{x-2}$
27. $\log_2 x = {}^-3$
28. $\log_x 6 = 1$
29. $\log_{27} 3^{\frac{1}{3}} = x$
30. $\log_3 \sqrt[4]{5} = x$

The formula $y = y_0 \cdot c^{\frac{t}{T}}$ can be used to describe growth and decay in nature. The final count is y, the initial count is y_0, c is the constant of proportionality, t is time, and T is time per cycle of c.

31. The population of single-celled organisms in a pond doubles every 5 days. If the initial count of organisms is 5000 and the final count is 25,000 how many days have passed? (Hint: $c = 2$ because the population is doubling and $T = 5$ because the population doubles every 5 days).
32. A certain radioactive substance has a half-life of 5.5 years. If 0.0469 kilograms are remaining from an initial sample of 6 kilograms, how many years have passed? (Hint: $c = \frac{1}{2}$ because the population is halving and $T = 5.5$ because half of the sample remains after 5.5 years).
33. After 13 years there are 2.1 pounds of radioactive material remaining from an original sample of 7 pounds. What is the half-life of this material?
34. A single-celled animal divides every 3 hours. How many hours does it take for 1 organism to increase to 1000?
35. A certain strain of bacteria increases from an initial count of 1000 to a final count of 35,000 in 6 hours. If $c = 3$ how often does the strain triple?
36. A 5 pound sample of a radioactive substance has a half life of 3.5 years. How many years have passed if 0.078 pounds of the substance remains?

10-8 Natural Logarithms

Logarithms to base e are called **natural logarithms** and are usually denoted **ln x**. Natural logarithms often are used to solve scientific and economic problems related to growth and decay.

The table on pages 510–511 gives values for ln x for values of x between 1 and 10, inclusive. For example, ln 5.63 = 1.7281.

Natural Logarithms of Numbers

n	0	1	2	3	4
5.5	1.7048	1.7066	1.7084	1.7102	1.71
5.6	1.7228	1.7246	1.7263	1.7281	1.72
5.7	1.7405	1.7422	1.7440	1.7457	1.74
5.8	1.7579	1.7596	1.761	1.7630	1.7

ln 5.63 = 1.7281

Natural logarithms do not have a characteristic or mantissa. However, ln x can be determined for other values of x by using the properties of logarithms.

example

1 **Find each natural logarithm. Use the table on pages 510–511.**

a. ln 8.37 b. ln 3.965 c. ln 2040

a. ln 8.37 = 2.1247

b. ln 3.965 = 1.3775 (by interpolation)

c. $\ln 2040 = \ln (2.04 \cdot 10^3)$ *Scientific notation*

$= \ln 2.04 + \ln 10^3$ *Product property*

$= \ln 2.04 + 3 \ln 10$ *Power property*

$= 0.7129 + 3(2.3026)$ *ln 10 = 2.3026*

$= 7.6207$

If ln x = a, then x = antiln a. The table of natural logarithms can also be used to find antilogarithms.

example

2 **Find each antilogarithm. Use the table on pages 510–511.**

a. antiln 2.2039 b. antiln 1.3720 c. antiln 3.9824

a. antiln 2.2039 = 9.06

b. antiln 1.3720 = 3.943 (by interpolation)

c. antiln 3.9824 = antiln (2.3026 + 1.6798) *ln 10 = 2.3026*

= 10(5.364) *Product property*

= 53.64

Natural logarithms can be used to solve interest problems. The formula to calculate continuously compounded interest is

$$A = Pe^{rt}.$$

The final amount is A, the initial investment is P, r is the annual interest rate, and the time in years is t.

example

3 **Suppose \$175 is deposited in a savings account. The interest rate is $9\frac{1}{2}\%$ compounded continuously. When will the original deposit be doubled?**

$A = Pe^{rt}$

$350 = 175e^{0.095t}$ *Substitute 350 for A, 175 for P, and 0.095 for r.*

$2 = e^{0.095t}$

$\ln 2 = \ln e^{0.095t}$

$\ln 2 = 0.095t$ *Definition of Natural Logarithms*

$\frac{\ln 2}{0.095} = t$

$t = \frac{0.6932}{0.095}$ or about 7.3

The original amount will double in about 7.3 years.

The general formula for growth and decay is $y = ne^{kt}$. The final amount is y, the initial amount is n, k is a constant, and t is time. For growth $k > 0$ and for decay $k < 0$.

example

4 **For a certain strain of bacteria, $k = 0.584$ when t is measured in hours. In how many hours will 4 bacteria increase to 2500 bacteria?**

$y = ne^{kt}$

$2500 = 4e^{0.584t}$ *Substitute 2500 for y, 4 for n, and 0.584 for k.*

$625 = e^{0.584t}$

$\ln 625 = \ln e^{0.584t}$

$\ln 625 = 0.584t$

$\frac{\ln 625}{0.584} = t$

$$t = \frac{\ln (6.25 \cdot 10^2)}{0.584}$$

$$= \frac{\ln 6.25 + 2 \ln 10}{0.584}$$

$$= \frac{1.8326 + 2(2.3026)}{0.584}$$

$$\approx 11$$

The solution is approximately 11 hours.

exercises

Exploratory Find each of the following. Use the table on pages 510–511.

1. ln 2.58
2. ln 9.45
3. ln 4.28
4. ln 7.21
5. antiln 0.4253
6. antiln 2.0807
7. antiln 1.5707
8. antiln 0.3788
9. antiln 1.7015

Written Use the table on pages 510–511 to find each of the following.

1. ln 56.9
2. ln 0.0543
3. ln 650
4. antiln 3.5674
5. antiln 4.6789
6. antiln 5.2094

Evaluate the variable for each of the following.

7. $2000 = 5e^{0.045t}$
8. $2 = e^{5k}$
9. $\ln 4.5 = \ln e^{0.031t}$
10. $732 = e^{6k}$
11. $45.9 = e^{0.075t}$
12. $\ln 60.3 = \ln e^{0.21t}$

Solve each problem.

13. For a certain strain of bacteria $k = 0.658$ when t is measured in hours. How long will 15 bacteria take to increase to 250 bacteria?
14. Radium 226 decomposes radioactively. Its half-life (the time half the sample takes to decompose) is 1800 years. Find the constant k for the decay formula. Use 300 grams as the original amount.
15. Find k for a radioactive element for which half of a 45 milligram sample remains after 15 years.
16. In a certain solution bacteria can grow from 75 to 210 bacteria in 5 hours. Find the constant k for the growth formula.
17. For certain single-celled organisms, $k = 0.845$ when t is measured in days. How long will it take 14 organisms to increase to 600?
18. Bill has saved \$2000 to buy a car which will cost about \$5,500. If his money is in a savings account paying $8\frac{1}{2}\%$ compounded continuously, when will he have enough money to buy the car?
19. Mr. Hammond invests a sum of money at 8% interest compounded continuously. If he makes his investment on January 1, 1981, and has \$10,000 in his account by January 1, 2000, what was his original investment?
20. Assume \$15 is invested at $10\frac{1}{2}\%$ compounded continuously. When will the investment be worth \$45?
21. How much money must be invested at $11\frac{1}{2}\%$ interest compounded continuously to yield \$3,000 after 2 years?
22. For a radioactive substance $k = {}^{-}0.048$. How much time does it take for a 3 pound sample to decrease to $1\frac{1}{2}$ pounds?
23. At what rate of interest compounded continuously will \$200 triple in 25 years?
24. For a radioactive substance $k = {}^{-}0.0954$. How long will it take for 365 grams of the substance to reduce to 45 grams?
25. In 7 days a sample of a radioactive substance decreases from 200 grams to 40 grams. Calculate k for this substance.
26. Jill invests a sum of money at 9% interest compounded continuously. How much must she invest now to have a total of \$25,000 in 5 years?

10-9 Euler's Formulas

Leonhard Euler was a very prolific writer on mathematics. His name is associated with a number of important mathematical relations. Among these is the relation between the trigonometric series and the exponential series. The **trigonometric series** for cos x and sin x are given below.

$$\cos x = 1 - \frac{x^2}{2!} + \frac{x^4}{4!} - \frac{x^6}{6!} + \frac{x^8}{8!} - \cdots$$
$$\sin x = x - \frac{x^3}{3!} + \frac{x^5}{5!} - \frac{x^7}{7!} + \frac{x^9}{9!} - \cdots$$

The two series are convergent for all values of x. By replacing x in the above relations with any angle in radians and carrying out the computations as far as desired, approximate values of the trigonometric functions can be found to any desired degree of accuracy. The numbers in the tables of values were calculated in this manner.

Recall that the exponential series is the series for e^x.

$$e^x = 1 + x + \frac{x^2}{2!} + \frac{x^3}{3!} + \frac{x^4}{4!} + \cdots$$

Suppose x is replaced by $i\alpha$ in the exponential series.

$$\begin{aligned} e^{i\alpha} &= 1 + i\alpha + \frac{(i\alpha)^2}{2!} + \frac{(i\alpha)^3}{3!} + \frac{(i\alpha)^4}{4!} + \cdots \\ &= 1 + i\alpha - \frac{\alpha^2}{2!} - i\frac{\alpha^3}{3!} + \frac{\alpha^4}{4!} + \cdots \end{aligned}$$

The terms can be grouped according to whether or not they contain the factor i.

$$e^{i\alpha} = \left(1 - \frac{\alpha^2}{2!} + \frac{\alpha^4}{4!} - \frac{\alpha^6}{6!} + \cdots\right) + i\left(\alpha - \frac{\alpha^3}{3!} + \frac{\alpha^5}{5!} - \frac{\alpha^7}{7!} + \cdots\right)$$

Notice that the real part is exactly $\cos \alpha$ and the coefficient of i in the imaginary part is exactly $\sin \alpha$. This important relationship is called **Euler's formula.**

$$e^{i\alpha} = \cos \alpha + i \sin \alpha$$

Euler's Formula

If $^-i\alpha$ had been substituted for x in this development the result would have been $e^{-i\alpha} = \cos \alpha - i \sin \alpha$.

Euler's formula can be used to write the **exponential form** of a complex number, θ in radians.

$$\begin{aligned} x + yi &= r(\cos \theta + i \sin \theta) \\ &= re^{i\theta} \end{aligned}$$

example

1 Write the exponential form of $1 + i\sqrt{3}$.

First, write the polar form of $1 + i\sqrt{3}$.

$r = \sqrt{1^2 + \sqrt{3}^2}$ or 2 and $\theta = \text{Arctan } \frac{\sqrt{3}}{1}$ or $\frac{\pi}{3}$

$$1 + i\sqrt{3} = 2\left(\cos \frac{\pi}{3} + i \sin \frac{\pi}{3}\right) = 2e^{\frac{i\pi}{3}}$$

The exponential form of $1 + i\sqrt{3}$ is $2e^{\frac{i\pi}{3}}$.

The equations for $e^{i\alpha}$ and $e^{-i\alpha}$ can be used to derive the exponential values of $\sin \alpha$ and $\cos \alpha$, as shown below.

$$e^{i\alpha} - e^{-i\alpha} = (\cos \alpha + i \sin \alpha) - (\cos \alpha - i \sin \alpha) \text{ or } 2i \sin \alpha$$

$$e^{i\alpha} + e^{-i\alpha} = (\cos \alpha + i \sin \alpha) + (\cos \alpha - i \sin \alpha) \text{ or } 2 \cos \alpha$$

$$\sin \alpha = \frac{e^{i\alpha} - e^{-i\alpha}}{2i} \qquad \cos \alpha = \frac{e^{i\alpha} + e^{-i\alpha}}{2}$$

You know from your study of logarithms that there is no real number which is the logarithm of a negative number. However, a special case of Euler's formula can be used to find a complex number which is the logarithm of a negative number.

$$e^{i\alpha} = \cos \alpha + i \sin \alpha$$
$$e^{i\pi} = \cos \pi + i \sin \pi \qquad \textit{Let } \alpha = \pi.$$
$$e^{i\pi} = {}^-1 + i(0)$$
$$e^{i\pi} = {}^-1$$

This relation has been described as the most beautiful one in mathematics for it relates three of the most important mathematical numbers, e, π, and i.

If the logarithm to the base e is taken of both sides of $e^{i\pi} = {}^-1$, a value for $\ln({}^-1)$ is obtained.

$$\ln e^{i\pi} = \ln ({}^-1)$$
$$i\pi = \ln ({}^-1)$$

The logarithm of a negative number ^-k can be found since $\ln({}^-k) = \ln ({}^-1)k = \ln ({}^-1) + \ln k$, a complex number.

example

2 Evaluate $\ln({}^-8)$. Use $\ln({}^-1) = i\pi$.

$\ln({}^-8) = \ln({}^-1) + \ln 8$

$\quad = i\pi + 2.079$

Thus, $\ln({}^-8) = i\pi + 2.079$. *The logarithm is a complex number.*

exercises

Exploratory Evaluate the following.

1. $\ln(^-4)$
2. $\ln(^-7)$
3. $\ln(^-9)$
4. $\ln(^-6.2)$
5. $\ln(^-7.85)$
6. $\ln(^-5.23)$
7. $\ln(^-2.01)$
8. $\ln(^-3.49)$

Write the exponential form of the following.

9. $2\left(\cos\frac{\pi}{3} + i\sin\frac{\pi}{3}\right)$
10. $5\left(\cos\frac{5\pi}{3} + i\sin\frac{5\pi}{3}\right)$
11. $\sqrt{2}\left(\cos\frac{5\pi}{4} + i\sin\frac{5\pi}{4}\right)$
12. $12\left(\cos\frac{\pi}{6} + i\sin\frac{\pi}{6}\right)$
13. $1\left(\cos\frac{\pi}{4} + i\sin\frac{\pi}{4}\right)$
14. $3\left(\cos\frac{3\pi}{4} + i\sin\frac{3\pi}{4}\right)$

Written Evaluate the following.

1. $\ln(^-48.2)$
2. $\ln(^-0.036)$
3. $\ln(^-540)$
4. $\ln(^-21.6)$
5. $\ln(^-68.7)$
6. $\ln(^-0.0082)$
7. $\ln(^-4320)$
8. $\ln(^-147)$

Write the exponential form of the following complex numbers.

9. $^-1 + i$
10. $4 - 4i$
11. $6i$
12. i
13. $^-1 + i\sqrt{3}$
14. $3 + 3i\sqrt{3}$
15. $^-2\sqrt{3} - 2i$
16. $\sqrt{3} + i$

Challenge Use the first 5 terms of the appropriate trigonometric series to approximate the value of each of the following. Then compare the approximation to the actual value.

1. $\sin\pi$
2. $\cos\pi$

Chapter Summary

1. Properties of Exponents: For any numbers a, b, m, and n,
   1. $a^m a^n = a^{m+n}$
   2. $(a^m)^n = a^{mn}$
   3. $\left(\frac{a}{b}\right)^m = \frac{a^m}{b^m}$, $b \neq 0$
   4. $(ab)^m = a^m b^m$
   5. $\frac{a^m}{a^n} = a^{m-n}$, $a \neq 0$ (264)
2. Definition of $b^{\frac{1}{n}}$: For any real number $b \geq 0$ and any integer $n > 1$, $b^{\frac{1}{n}} = \sqrt[n]{b}$. This also holds when $b < 0$ and n is odd. (265)

3. Definition of Rational Exponents: For any nonzero number b, and any integers m and n, with $n > 1$,

$$b^{\frac{m}{n}} = \sqrt[n]{b^m} = (\sqrt[n]{b})^m$$

except when $\sqrt[n]{b}$ is not a real number. (265)

4. Definition of Irrational Exponents: If x is an irrational number and $a > 0$, then a^x is the real number between a^{x_1} and a^{x_2}, for all possible choices of rational numbers x_1 and x_2 such that $x_1 < x < x_2$. (268)
5. An exponential function has the form $y = a^x$, where a is a positive real number. (269)
6. Definition of e: $e = \lim_{k \to \infty} \left(1 + \frac{1}{k}\right)^k = 1 + 1 + \frac{1}{2!} + \frac{1}{3!} + \cdots$ (271)
7. An important exponential function is $y = e^x$. (272)
8. Composition of Functions: Given functions g and f, the composite function $g \circ f$ can be described by the following equation.

$$g \circ f(x) = g(f(x))$$

The domain of $g \circ f$ includes all elements x in the domain of f for which $f(x)$ is in the domain of g. (276)

9. Inverse Functions: Two polynomial functions f and g are inverse functions if and only if both their compositions are the identity functions. That is, $f \circ g(x) = g \circ f(x) = x$. (277)
10. Property of Inverse Functions: Suppose f and f^{-1} are inverse functions. Then $f(a) = b$ if and only if $f^{-1}(b) = a$. (277)
11. The logarithmic function $y = \log_a x$, $a > 0$ and $a \neq 1$, is the inverse of the exponential function $y = a^x$. (280)
12. Properties of Logarithms: Suppose m and n are positive numbers, b is a positive number other than 1, and p is any number. Then the following properties hold.

Product Property: $\log_b mn = \log_b m + \log_b n$

Quotient Property: $\log_b \frac{m}{n} = \log_b m - \log_b n$

Power Property: $\log_b m^p = p \cdot \log_b m$ (280)

13. Logarithms to base 10 are called common logarithms. The characteristic of a common logarithm precedes the decimal point. The mantissa is a positive decimal less than 1. (283)
14. Change of Bases: Suppose a, b, and n are positive numbers, and neither a nor b is 1. Then the following equation is true.

$$\log_a n = \frac{\log_b n}{\log_b a} \quad (286)$$

15. Logarithms to base e are called natural logarithms. (288)
16. Euler's Formula: $e^{i\alpha} = \cos \alpha + i \sin \alpha$ (291)
17. The exponential form of a complex number $r(\cos \theta + i \sin \theta)$ is $re^{i\theta}$, where θ is expressed in radians. (291)
18. Since $e^{i\pi} = {}^-1$, $\ln({}^-1) = i\pi$, and $\ln({}^-k) = i\pi + \ln k$. (292)

Chapter Review

10-1 **Express each of the following using rational exponents.**

1. $\sqrt[5]{a^3}$
2. $\sqrt{9x^4y^5}$
3. $\sqrt[4]{16a^4b^3c^8}$
4. $\sqrt[3]{18x^3y^7}$

Express each of the following using radicals.

5. $15^{\frac{1}{5}}$
6. $(2^4a^3b)^{\frac{1}{5}}$
7. $(4x)^{\frac{6}{5}}$
8. $(x^2y^3)^{\frac{1}{4}}$

Simplify the given expressions.

9. $3x^2(3x)^{-2}$
10. $\left(6a^{\frac{1}{3}}\right)^3$
11. $\left(\frac{1}{2}x^4\right)^3$
12. $(2a)^{\frac{1}{3}}(a^2b)^{\frac{1}{3}}$

10-2 **Graph each equation.**

13. $y = 3^{-x}$
14. $y = \left(\frac{1}{2}\right)^x$
15. $y = 2^x$

10-3 **Evaluate x given that $1.5 \approx e^{0.4055}$.**

16. $(1.5)^3 = e^x$
17. $x = e^{0.811}$
18. $x = e^{0.2027}$

10-4 **Find $f \circ g(x)$ and $g \circ f(x)$.**

19. $f(x) = 3x - 5$, $g(x) = x + 2$
20. $f(x) = {}^-3x^2$, $g(x) = 2x^3$
21. $f(x) = x^2 + 2x + 3$, $g(x) = x + 1$

10-5 **Solve each equation for x.**

22. $\log_x 49 = 2$
23. $\log_3 (3x) = \log_3 45$
24. $\log_{\frac{1}{2}} x = {}^-4$

10-6 **Use the table on pages 508–509 to find the common logarithms of the following.**

25. 0.0459
26. 363
27. 42.8

10-7 **Solve each equation using logarithms.**

28. $2.5^x = 65.7$
29. $x = \log_3 8.9$
30. $4^{y+3} = 28.4$

10-8 **Use the table on pages 510–511 to find each of the following.**

31. ln 8.63
32. ln 403
33. antiln 3.7015

Solve each problem.

34. For certain single-celled organisms, $k = 0.732$ when t is measured in days. How long will it take 15 organisms to increase to 1000?
35. Joan has saved \$1500 for a new set of living room furniture that will cost \$3000. If her money is in a savings account paying 9% compounded continuously, when will she have enough money to buy the furniture?

10-9 **Evaluate the following.**

36. ln (⁻8)
37. ln (⁻46.2)
38. ln (⁻234)

Write the exponential form of the following.

39. $3\left(\cos \frac{5\pi}{4} + i \sin \frac{5\pi}{4}\right)$
40. $1 + i$

Chapter Test

Simplify each expression.

1. $((2a)^3)^{-2}$
2. $\left(x^{\frac{3}{2}}y^2a^{\frac{5}{4}}\right)^4$
3. $\sqrt{a^2b} \cdot \sqrt{a^3b^5}$

Evaluate x given that $3 \approx e^{1.0986}$.

4. $27 = e^x$
5. $x = e^{0.5493}$
6. $243 = e^x$

Find $f \circ g(x)$ and $g \circ f(x)$.

7. $f(x) = \sqrt{x}$
   $g(x) = 2x^2 - 5$
8. $f(x) = 2x^2$
   $g(x) = 5x + 6$
9. $f(x) = {}^-x - 7$
   $g(x) = {}^-3x$

Solve each equation.

10. $\log_x \sqrt[3]{8} = \frac{1}{3}$
11. $\log_5 (2x) = \log_5 (3x - 4)$
12. $3.6^x = 72.4$
13. $4^{x+3} = 25.8$

Use the appropriate table to find each of the following.

14. log 542
15. ln 0.248
16. antiln 1.1217
17. log 0.00762
18. antilog (.0899 − 2)
19. ln (⁻5.4)

Write the exponential form of the following.

20. $3\left(\cos \frac{\pi}{6} + i \sin \frac{\pi}{6}\right)$
21. $8i$

Solve each problem.

22. In a certain solution, bacteria can grow from 50 to 250 in 6 hours. Find the constant k for the growth formula $y = ne^{kt}$.
23. How much money must be invested at 12% interest compounded continuously to yield $2500 after 2 years?
24. Graph the equation $y = 5^{-x}$.

Chapter

11

The Straight Line

Bridges, as well as other structures, are often composed of parts which follow straight paths or lines. The interaction of these lines with one another is an integral part of engineering design.

11-1 Parallel and Perpendicular Lines

Lines which are parallel or perpendicular can be studied by means of their equations.

Recall that a linear equation can be written in many forms. The **standard form** of a linear equation is $Ax + By + C = 0$, where A, B, and C represent real numbers and A and B are not both zero. The **slope-intercept form** is $y = mx + b$, where m is the slope and b is the y-intercept. The **point-slope form** is $y - y_1 = m(x - x_1)$ where m is the slope and (x_1, y_1) is a point on the line.

Lines which are **parallel** have the same slope. That is, if m_1 is the slope of ℓ_1 and m_2 is the slope of ℓ_2, then ℓ_1 and ℓ_2 are parallel if and only if $m_1 = m_2$. Vertical lines are also parallel. However, the slope of a vertical line is undefined.

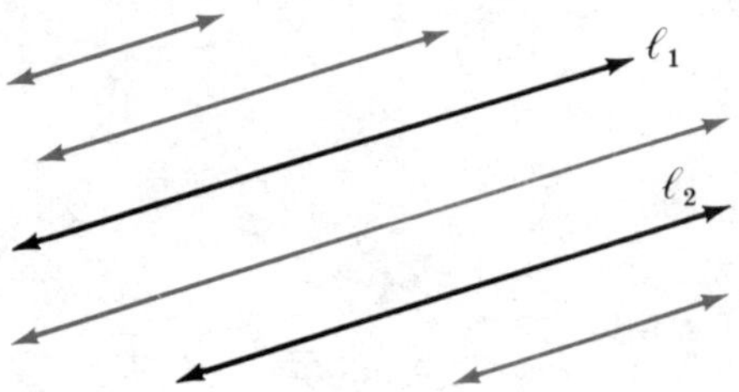

Two non-vertical lines are parallel if and only if their slopes are equal.

Parallel Lines

The slope of a line can be obtained directly from the standard form of the linear equation. By solving $Ax + By + C = 0$ for y, you obtain $y = -\frac{A}{B}x - \frac{C}{B}$. Therefore the slope is $-\frac{A}{B}$. For example, the slope of the line $3x + 6y - 5 = 0$ is $-\frac{3}{6}$ or $-\frac{1}{2}$.

The expression "the line $Ax + By + C = 0$" means "the line which is the graph of $Ax + By + C = 0$."

Since parallel lines have the same slope, the equation of a line parallel to a given line and through a given point can be written using point-slope form.

example

1 **Write the standard form of the equation of the line through $(3, ^-2)$ which is parallel to the line $3x - y + 7 = 0$.**

Since $-\frac{A}{B} = -\left(\frac{3}{-1}\right)$, the slope is 3.

$y - y_1 = m(x - x_1)$
$y + 2 = 3(x - 3)$ *Replace y_1 by $^-2$ and x_1 by 3.*
$y + 2 = 3x - 9$
$3x - y - 11 = 0$

The equation is $3x - y - 11 = 0$.

In the figure at the right, the angle of inclination of $\overleftrightarrow{P_1P_2}$ is α. The slope of the line through points $P_1(x_1, y_1)$ and $P_2(x_2, y_2)$ is $\frac{y_2 - y_1}{x_2 - x_1}$. Notice that the tangent of the angle of inclination is equal to the slope. That is, $\tan \alpha = m$. The range of α is $0° \leq \alpha < 180°$. Tan α is positive if $\alpha < 90°$ and negative if $90° < \alpha < 180°$. Tan α is undefined if $\alpha = 90°$. *Why?*

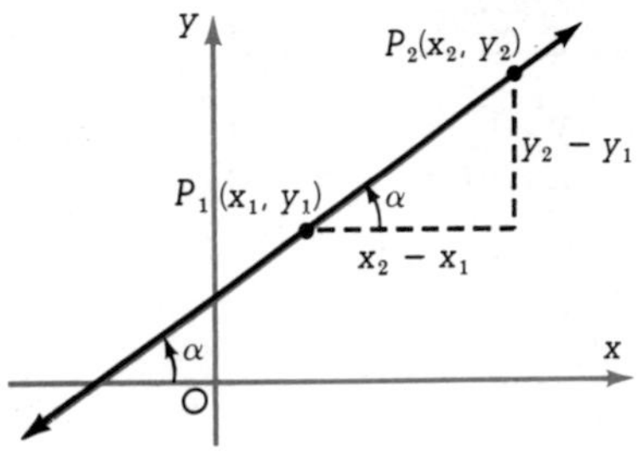

What relation do m_1 and m_2 have if ℓ_1 and ℓ_2 are perpendicular? Let α_1 be the angle of inclination of ℓ_1 and α_2 be the angle of inclination of ℓ_2. It can be seen that $\alpha_1 + (180 - \alpha_2) = 90°$ or $\alpha_2 = \alpha_1 + 90°$. Take the tangent of both sides of the equation.

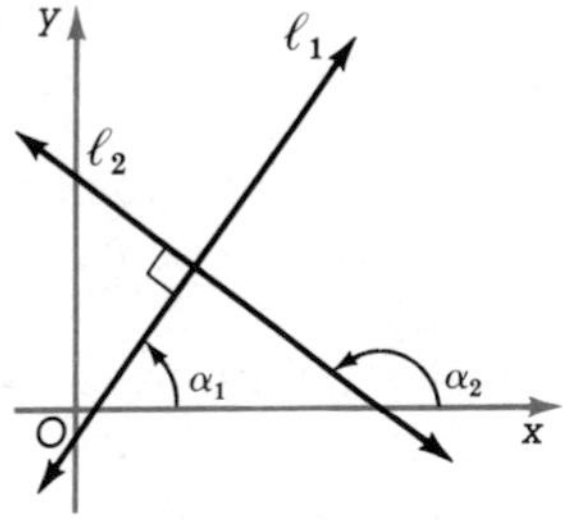

$$\tan \alpha_2 = \tan (\alpha_1 + 90°)$$

$$\tan \alpha_2 = {}^-\cot \alpha_1 \qquad \textit{tan } (\theta + 90°) = {}^-\textit{cot } \theta$$

$$\frac{\tan \alpha_2}{\cot \alpha_1} = \frac{{}^-\cot \alpha_1}{\cot \alpha_1} \qquad \textit{Divide both sides by cot } \alpha_1. \ \textit{cot } \alpha \neq 0$$

$$\tan \alpha_1 \cdot \tan \alpha_2 = {}^-1 \qquad \frac{1}{\cot \alpha_1} = \tan \alpha_1$$

But $m_1 = \tan \alpha_1$ and $m_2 = \tan \alpha_2$. Thus, when ℓ_1 is perpendicular to ℓ_2, the following is true.

$$m_1 m_2 = {}^-1 \text{ or } m_1 = -\frac{1}{m_2}$$

Two non-vertical lines are perpendicular if and only if the slope of one is the negative reciprocal of the slope of the other.

Perpendicular Lines

example

2 Write the standard form of the equation of the line which passes through (1, 4) and is perpendicular to the line $3x - y + 4 = 0$.

Since $m = -\frac{A}{B}$, the line $3x - y + 4 = 0$ has slope 3. Therefore the slope of the perpendicular line is $-\frac{1}{3}$.

$$y - y_1 = m(x - x_1)$$

$$y - 4 = -\frac{1}{3}(x - 1) \qquad x_1 = 1 \textit{ and } y_1 = 4$$

$$3y - 12 = {}^-x + 1$$

$$x + 3y - 13 = 0$$

Th equation is $x + 3y - 13 = 0$.

exercises

Exploratory Find the slope of each line whose equation is given. Then determine whether the lines are parallel, perpendicular, or neither.

1. $y = 3x - 2$; $y = {}^-3x + 2$
2. $y = 6x - 2$; $y = 6x + 7$
3. $y = x - 9$; $x + y + 9 = 0$
4. $y = 2x + 4$; $x + 2y + 10 = 0$
5. $y + 4x - 2 = 0$; $y + 4x + 1 = 0$
6. $y = 8x - 1$; $7x - y - 1 = 0$

Write the standard form of the equation of the line which is parallel to $y = 2x - 3$ and passes through the given point.

7. $(4, 2)$
8. $({}^-3, 6)$
9. $(8, {}^-2)$
10. $({}^-5, {}^-7)$

11–14. For each point given in problems **7–10**, write the standard form of the equation of the line which passes through the point and is perpendicular to $y = 2x - 3$.

Written Write the standard form of the equation of each line described below.

1. Parallel to $y = 3x - 5$, passes through $(0, 6)$
2. Parallel to $y = 2x + 6$, passes through $({}^-1, {}^-2)$
3. Parallel to $y = 6x + 7$, passes through $(0, {}^-3)$
4. Parallel to $y = {}^-4x - 3$, passes through $(5, {}^-7)$
5. Parallel to $2x + 3y - 5 = 0$, passes through $(2, 4)$
6. Parallel to $2x - 7y = 3$, passes through $(8, 0)$
7. Perpendicular to $y = {}^-2x + 5$, passes through $(0, {}^-3)$
8. Perpendicular to $y = 4x - 2$, passes through $(3, {}^-4)$
9. Perpendicular to $5y = 4x - 10$, passes through $({}^-15, 8)$
10. Perpendicular to $3y = {}^-2x + 3$, passes through $({}^-9, {}^-6)$
11. Perpendicular to $6x - 4y + 8 = 0$, passes through $(2, 12)$
12. Perpendicular to $3x - y = 8$, passes through $({}^-1, 5)$

Solve each of the following.

13. Point $(5, 3)$ is joined to $(9, 1)$ and to $(2, {}^-3)$. Show that the two lines formed are perpendicular.
14. Write the standard form of the equation of the line which passes through the intersection of $x - 3y + 2 = 0$ and $2x + y - 2 = 0$ and has slope $\frac{3}{2}$.

11-2 Analytic Proofs

The study of certain functions geometrically, particularly those of first and second degree, by means of their graphs is called **analytic geometry.** Many theorems of plane geometry can be more easily proved by analytic methods. That is, they can be proved by algebraic operations in reference to a coordinate system.

A relation that is frequently needed is the distance formula. Recall that the distance between two points (x_1, y_1) and (x_2, y_2) is

$$\sqrt{(x_2 - x_1)^2 + (y_2 - y_1)^2}.$$

The distance formula can be used to find the coordinates of the midpoint of a line segment, as shown at the right.

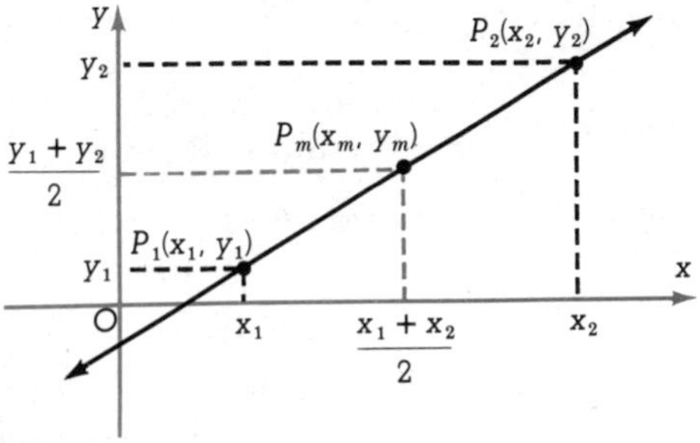

If the coordinates of P_1 and P_2 are (x_1, y_1) and (x_2, y_2), respectively, then the midpoint, P_m, of $\overline{P_1P_2}$ has coordinates

$$\left(\frac{x_1 + x_2}{2}, \frac{y_1 + y_2}{2}\right).$$

Midpoint Formula

example

1 Find the midpoint of the segment which has endpoints (5, 6) and (2, 8). Then show that the midpoint is equidistant from the endpoints.

The midpoint is $\left(\frac{5 + 2}{2}, \frac{6 + 8}{2}\right)$ or (3.5, 7).

Find the distance between the midpoint and each endpoint.

distance between (3.5, 7) and (5, 6)

$$d = \sqrt{(3.5-5)^2+(7-6)^2}$$
$$= \sqrt{(^-1.5)^2+1^2}$$
$$= \sqrt{3.25}$$

distance between (3.5, 7) and (2, 8)

$$d = \sqrt{(3.5-2)^2+(7-8)^2}$$
$$= \sqrt{1.5^2+(^-1)^2}$$
$$= \sqrt{3.25}$$

Thus, the midpoint (3.5, 7) is equidistant from the endpoints (5, 6) and (2, 8).

When using the analytic method to prove theorems from geometry, you may arbitrarily select the position of the figure in the coordinate plane as long as complete generality is preserved. Usually in straight line figures a vertex is located at the origin and one line is made to coincide with the x-axis, as shown below.

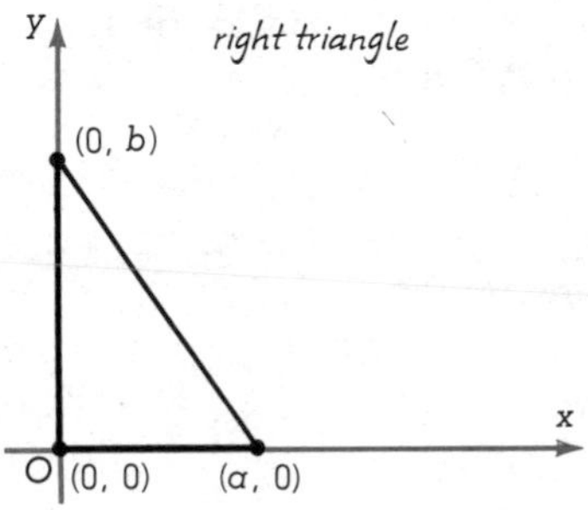

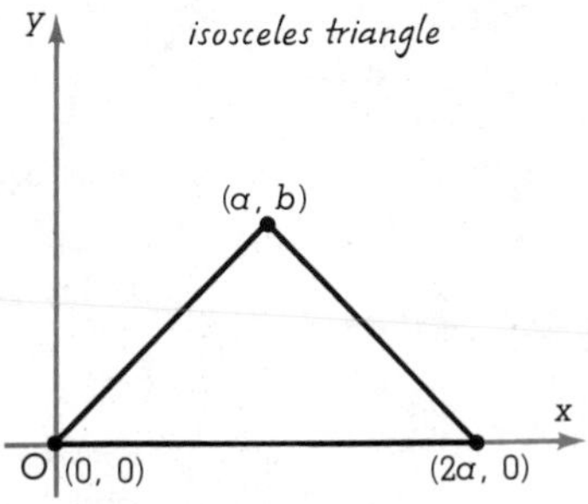

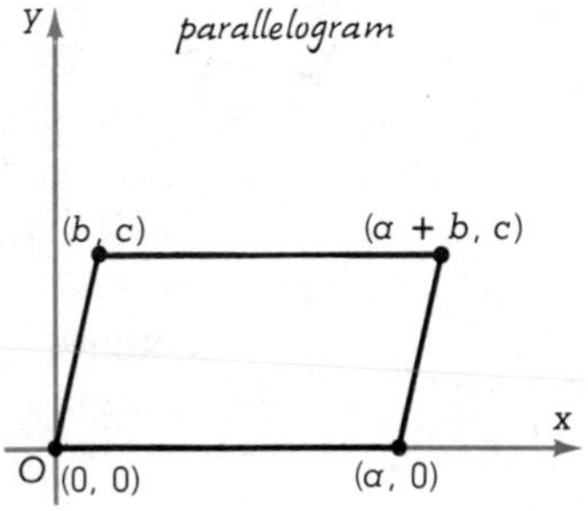

example

2 **Prove that the line segment joining the midpoints of two sides of a triangle is parallel to the third side of the triangle.**

Let vertex A of $\triangle ABC$ be at (0, 0) as shown in the figure at the right. Let vertex B be located on the x-axis at $(a, 0)$ and let vertex C be at (b, c). Then M and N are midpoints of $\overline{AC}$ and $\overline{BC}$, respectively. To prove that $\overline{MN}$ is parallel to $\overline{AB}$, show that their slopes are equal.

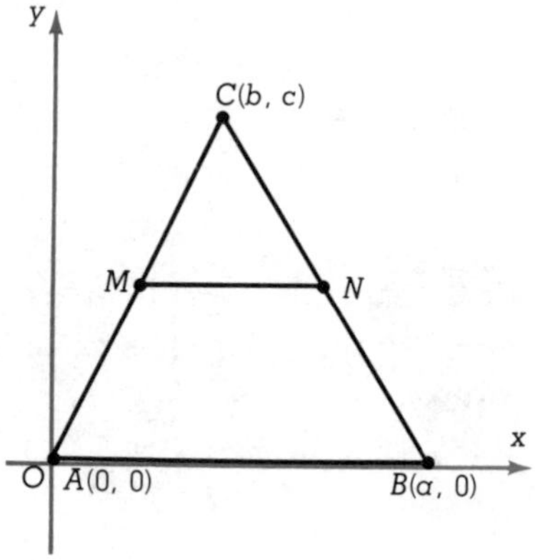

The slope of $\overline{AB}$ is $\frac{0}{a}$ or 0.

The coordinates of M and N are $\left(\frac{b}{2}, \frac{c}{2}\right)$ and $\left(\frac{a+b}{2}, \frac{c+0}{2}\right)$, respectively.

Therefore the slope of $\overline{MN}$ is as follows.

$$\frac{\frac{c+0}{2} - \frac{c}{2}}{\frac{a+b}{2} - \frac{b}{2}} = \frac{\frac{c+0-c}{2}}{\frac{a+b-b}{2}} = \frac{\frac{0}{2}}{\frac{a}{2}} \text{ or } 0$$

Since $\overline{AB}$ and $\overline{MN}$ have the same slope, $\overline{AB}$ is parallel to $\overline{MN}$.

Therefore, the line segment joining the midpoints of two sides of a triangle is parallel to the third side of the triangle.

exercises

Exploratory Name the midpoint of the segment which has the given endpoints.

1. (8, 0), ($^-6$, 0)
2. (24, 0), (0, $^-18$)
3. (11, 7), (5, 11)
4. ($^-3$, $^-2$), (8, 4)
5. (0, 0), (a, b)
6. (a, b), (c, d)

Written Solve each of the following analytically.

1. The vertices of a rectangle are ($^-3$, 1), ($^-1$, 3), (3, $^-1$), (1, $^-3$). Find the area of the rectangle.
2. Show that the points ($^-1$, 3), (3, 6), (6, 2), and (2, $^-1$) are the vertices of a square.
3. The vertices of a parallelogram are (2, 4), (5, 9), (14, 9), and (11, 4). Find the lengths of the diagonals.
4. The vertices of a triangle are (5, 0), ($^-3$, 2), and ($^-1$, $^-4$). Find the coordinates of the midpoints of the sides.
5. Show that the points ($^-3$, 1), (9, $^-4$), (12, 0), and (0, 5) are the vertices of a parallelogram.
6. Three vertices of a parallelogram are ($^-2$, $^-1$), ($^-1$, 4), and (5, 1). Find the coordinates of the fourth vertex. (three possibilities)

Prove each of the following analytically.

7. Given rectangle $ABCD$ as shown at the right, prove that $\overline{AC} \cong \overline{BD}$. That is, prove that the diagonals of a rectangle are congruent.
8. Given rectangle $ABCD$, prove $\overline{AE} \cong \overline{EC}$ and $\overline{BE} \cong \overline{ED}$. What can you conclude about the diagonals of a rectangle?

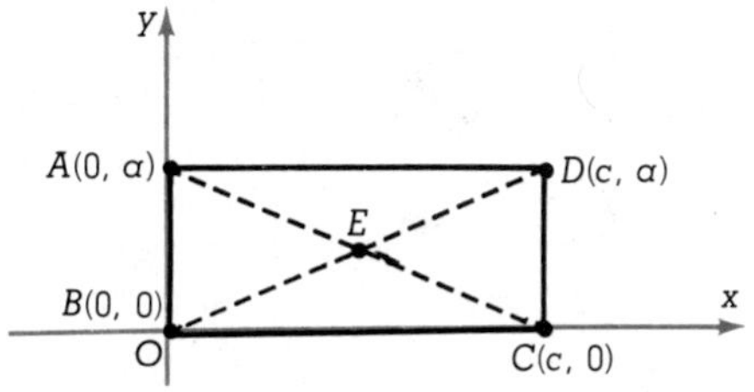

9. The diagonals of a square are perpendicular.
10. The diagonals of a parallelogram bisect each other.
11. The square of the hypotenuse of a right triangle is equal to the sum of the squares of the other sides.
12. The medians to the congruent sides of an isosceles triangle are congruent.
13. The line segment joining the midpoints of two sides of a triangle is equal in length to one-half the third side.
14. The line joining the midpoints of the non-parallel sides of a trapezoid (the median) is parallel to the bases of the trapezoid.
15. The median of a trapezoid is equal in length to one-half the sum of the lengths of the parallel sides.
16. The sum of the squares of the four sides of a parallelogram is equal to the sum of the squares of the diagonals.

Challenge Prove that the lines joining midpoints of successive sides of any quadrilateral form a parallelogram.

11-3 Angles of Intersecting Lines

The angle of inclination of a line is measured from the positive direction of the x-axis counterclockwise to the line. The angle of inclination of a horizontal line is zero.

The slope of a line is equal to the tangent of the angle of inclination. Thus, the formula $\tan \alpha = m$ can be used to find the angle of inclination of a line when the slope is known. Consider the line $4x - y + 3 = 0$. The slope of the line is 4. Why? Therefore $\tan \alpha = 4$ and $\alpha = \arctan 4$ or 76°.

Let ℓ_1 and ℓ_2 be two non-vertical lines that intersect at C, and let the measures of their angles of inclination be α_1 and α_2, respectively. Let θ represent the measure of the angle of intersection of the lines. Then θ can be expressed in terms of α_1 and α_2. Since α_2 is the measure of an exterior angle of $\triangle ABC$, it is equal to the sum of the measures of the non-adjacent opposite interior angles, α_1 and θ.

$$\alpha_2 = \alpha_1 + \theta$$
$$\theta = \alpha_2 - \alpha_1$$

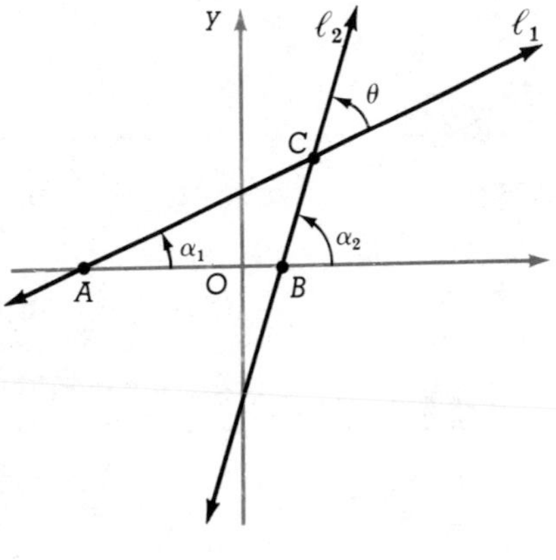

Using this you have the following.

$$\tan \theta = \tan (\alpha_2 - \alpha_1)$$

$$\tan \theta = \frac{\tan \alpha_2 - \tan \alpha_1}{1 + \tan \alpha_2 \tan \alpha_1}$$

But $\tan \alpha_1 = m_1$ and $\tan \alpha_2 = m_2$. Therefore

$$\tan \theta = \frac{m_2 - m_1}{1 + m_1 m_2}.$$

Note that m_2 is the slope of the left side of the angle and m_1 the slope of the right side.

Angle of Intersection

If m_1 is the slope of ℓ_1 and m_2 is the slope of ℓ_2, then the angle of intersection, measured from ℓ_1 to ℓ_2, is θ and

$$\tan \theta = \frac{m_2 - m_1}{1 + m_1 m_2}.$$

If either of the lines is vertical the formula fails. However, in this event the angle θ can be found directly. If the angle of inclination of ℓ_1 is α_1 and ℓ_2 is vertical, then $\theta = 90° - \alpha_1$. *Why?*

example

1 **Find the acute angle formed by the intersection of the lines $y = 2x - 7$ and $y = {}^-x + 1$.**

From the equations you can see that $m_1 = 2$ and $m_2 = {}^-1$.

$$\tan \theta = \frac{m_2 - m_1}{1 + m_1 m_2}$$

$$= \frac{{}^-1 - 2}{1 + 2({}^-1)} \text{ or } 3$$

$$\theta = \text{Arctan } 3 \text{ or } 71° 30'$$

Thus, θ is approximately $71° 30'$.

If $\tan \theta$ is a positive number the acute angle from ℓ_1 to ℓ_2 is measured counterclockwise. If $\tan \theta$ is a negative number, the acute angle from ℓ_1 to ℓ_2 is measured clockwise.

exercises

Exploratory **Find the angle of inclination of each line whose equation is given.**

1. $y = 3x + 6$
2. $y = 2 - 5x$
3. $2x + y = 4$
4. $x - y = 6$
5. $y + 4x = 3$
6. $2x + 3y = 4$
7. $2y - 5x + 7 = 0$
8. $3x - 2y + 6 = 0$
9. ${}^-2x + 3y + 7 = 0$

Find the acute angle formed by the intersection of lines with the given slopes.

10. $m_1 = 5, m_2 = 3$
11. $m_1 = 4, m_2 = 7$
12. $m_1 = {}^-1, m_2 = {}^-3$
13. $m_1 = {}^-6, m_2 = {}^-2$
14. $m_1 = 8, m_2 = {}^-9$
15. $m_1 = {}^-10, m_2 = 5$

Written Find the acute angle formed by the intersection of the graphs of each pair of equations.

1. $y = {}^{-}3x + 2$
   $y = {}^{-}x$
2. $y = {}^{-}10x - 9$
   $y = {}^{-}6x + 4$
3. $y = 4x + 20$
   $y = {}^{-}8x - 15$
4. $2x - 5y = 4$
   $3x - 2y = 0$
5. $y - 3x = 2$
   $x = {}^{-}4$
6. $9x - 2y + 5 = 0$
   $x = 7$
7. $x - y = 2$
   $2x + 3y = 9$
8. $3x - 2y = 10$
   $x + y = 0$
9. $5x - 3y = 12$
   $2x - 3y = 3$
10. $x + 5y - 2 = 0$
    $y + x - 6 = 0$
11. $3x - y - 2 = 0$
    $4x - y - 6 = 0$
12. $9x - 4y - 2 = 0$
    $x + y - 6 = 0$

Solve each of the following.

13. Show that the lines $x - 7y - 2 = 0$ and $4x - 3y - 6 = 0$ intersect at a 45° angle.
14. Show that the lines ${}^{-}4x + 2y - 5 = 0$ and $3x - y + 2 = 0$ intersect at an angle of 8°, to the nearest degree.
15. Find the acute angle between the diagonals of a parallelogram whose vertices are (3, 5), (7, 5), (9, 8), and (5, 8).
16. Find the acute angle between the diagonals of a parallelogram whose vertices are (4, 7), (10, 7), (2, 4), and (8, 4).
17. Find the angle of intersection between the two longer sides of a triangle whose vertices are (0, 0), (5, 0), and (7, 9).
18. Find the angle of intersection between the two longer sides of a triangle whose vertices are (2, 0), (9, 0), and (8, 9).
19. The angle between two lines is 60°. The slope of ℓ_1 is $\frac{2}{3}$. What is the slope of ℓ_2?
20. The angle between two lines is 60°. The slope of ℓ_2 is $\frac{2}{3}$. What is the slope of ℓ_1?
21. Write the equation of the line which passes through the origin and intersects the line $2x - y + 3 = 0$ at an angle of 45°. (two possibilities)
22. Write the equation of the line which passes through (2, 3) and intersects the line $3x + 2y - 1 = 0$ at an angle of 30°. (two possibilities)

11-4 Normal Form of a Linear Equation

A **normal** is a line which is perpendicular to another line or surface. The **normal form** of the equation of a line is written in terms of the length of the normal from the line to the origin.

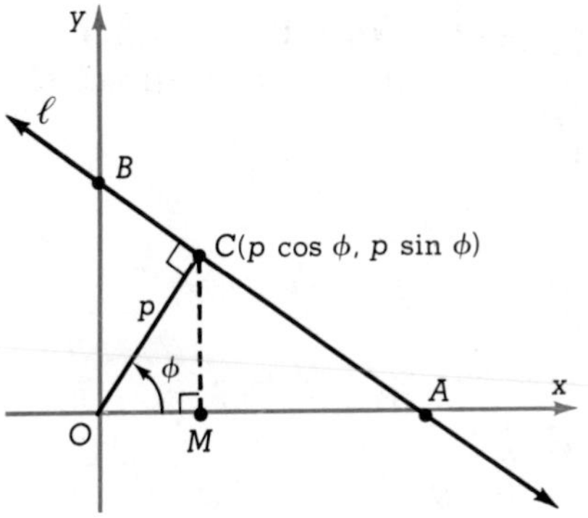

Let ℓ be a line that does not pass through the origin. Let p be the length of its normal to the origin. Let ϕ be the positive angle between the positive x-axis and p. Draw $\overline{MC}$ perpendicular to the x-axis. Then $OM = p \cos \phi$, and $MC = p \sin \phi$.

The equation of a line through the origin is of the form $y = mx$. Hence, the equation of $\overleftrightarrow{OC}$ is

$$y = \frac{MC}{OM} \cdot x = \frac{p \sin \phi}{p \cos \phi} \cdot x$$

$$\text{or} \quad x \sin \phi - y \cos \phi = 0.$$

Since ℓ is perpendicular to $\overleftrightarrow{OC}$, its slope, $-\frac{\cos \phi}{\sin \phi}$, is the negative reciprocal of the slope of $\overleftrightarrow{OC}$. Then the equation of ℓ is of the form

$$y = -\frac{\cos \phi}{\sin \phi} x + b \quad \text{or}$$

$$x \cos \phi + y \sin \phi - b \sin \phi = 0.$$

Since the line passes through C, the equation is satisfied by the coordinates of C. Therefore you can replace x by $p \cos \phi$ and y by $p \sin \phi$.

The point C can be in any quadrant.
$0° \leq \phi < 360°$

$$\begin{aligned} p \cos \phi (\cos \phi) + p \sin \phi (\sin \phi) - b \sin \phi &= 0 \\ p \cos^2 \phi + p \sin^2 \phi - b \sin \phi &= 0 \\ p (\cos^2 \phi + \sin^2 \phi) - b \sin \phi &= 0 \\ p(1) - b \sin \phi &= 0 \\ p &= b \sin \phi \end{aligned}$$

Thus, you can replace $b \sin \phi$ by p in the equation of line ℓ to obtain the normal form of a linear equation.

Normal Form

The normal form of a linear equation is

$$x \cos \phi + y \sin \phi - p = 0$$

where p is the length of the normal from the line to the origin and ϕ is the positive angle between the positive x-axis and the normal.

example

1 **Write the equation of a line in standard form for which the normal p is 5, and makes an angle of 30° with the x-axis.**

$$\begin{aligned} x \cos \phi + y \sin \phi - p &= 0 \\ x \cos 30° + y \sin 30° - 5 &= 0 \\ \frac{\sqrt{3}}{2}x + \frac{1}{2}y - 5 &= 0 \\ \sqrt{3}x + y - 10 &= 0 \end{aligned}$$

Normal form
$\phi = 30°$ and $p = 5$

The equation is $\sqrt{3}x + y - 10 = 0$.

The standard form of a linear equation $Ax + By + C = 0$ can be transformed to normal form $x \cos \phi + y \sin \phi - p = 0$ if the relationship between the coefficients in the two forms is known. The equations will represent the same line if and only if their corresponding coefficients are proportional. That is, if $\frac{A}{\cos \phi} = \frac{B}{\sin \phi} = \frac{C}{^-p}$, then

$$\sin \phi = \frac{^-Bp}{C}, \quad \text{and} \quad \cos \phi = \frac{^-Ap}{C}.$$

The first equation can be divided by the second ($\cos \phi \neq 0$).

$$\frac{\sin \phi}{\cos \phi} = \frac{B}{A} = \tan \phi$$

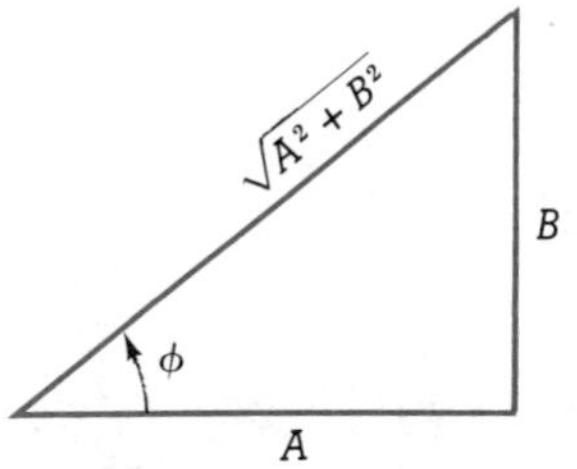

Consider a right triangle with an acute angle ϕ such that $\tan \phi = \frac{B}{A}$. The length of the hypotenuse is $\sqrt{A^2 + B^2}$. Thus,

$$\sin \phi = \frac{B}{\pm\sqrt{A^2 + B^2}}, \cos \phi = \frac{A}{\pm\sqrt{A^2 + B^2}}, \text{ and } p = \frac{C}{\pm\sqrt{A^2 + B^2}}.$$

The double sign, $\pm$, is used since p must be positive in the equation $x \cos \phi + y \sin \phi - p = 0$. Thus, the sign must be chosen opposite the sign of C. That is, if C is positive use $-\sqrt{A^2 + B^2}$, and if C is negative use $\sqrt{A^2 + B^2}$.

If $C = 0$, the sign is chosen so that $\sin \phi$ is positive, that is, the same sign as that of B.

The values for $\sin \phi$, $\cos \phi$, and p can be substituted into the normal form to obtain the following.

$$\frac{Ax}{\pm\sqrt{A^2 + B^2}} + \frac{By}{\pm\sqrt{A^2 + B^2}} + \frac{C}{\pm\sqrt{A^2 + B^2}} = 0$$

Notice that the standard form of an equation is closely related to the normal form.

Changing the Standard Form to Normal Form

The standard form of a linear equation, $Ax + By + C = 0$, can be changed to normal form by dividing each term by $\pm\sqrt{A^2 + B^2}$. The sign is chosen opposite the sign of C.

If the equation of a line is in normal form, the length of the normal, p, can be obtained directly. The angle ϕ can be determined using the relation $\tan \phi = \frac{B}{A}$. The quadrant in which the normal lies must be determined so the correct angle can be found. When the equation of a line is in a normal form, the coefficient of x is equal to $\cos \phi$ and the coefficient of y is equal to $\sin \phi$. Thus, the correct quadrant can be determined by studying the signs of $\cos \phi$ and $\sin \phi$. For example, if $\sin \phi$ is negative and $\cos \phi$ is negative the normal lies in the third quadrant.

example

2 **Change $2x - 5y + 3 = 0$ to normal form. Then find the length of the normal and the angle it makes with the x-axis.**

$2x - 5y + 3 = 0$ *Since C is positive, use $-\sqrt{A^2 + B^2}$, or $-\sqrt{29}$.*

The normal form is $\frac{2x}{-\sqrt{29}} - \frac{5y}{-\sqrt{29}} + \frac{3}{-\sqrt{29}} = 0$ or $-\frac{2x}{\sqrt{29}} + \frac{5y}{\sqrt{29}} - \frac{3}{\sqrt{29}} = 0.$

Thus, $\sin\phi = \frac{5}{\sqrt{29}}$, $\cos\phi = -\frac{2}{\sqrt{29}}$, and $p = \frac{3}{\sqrt{29}}$.

$\tan\phi = -\frac{5}{2}$ *Why?*

$\phi = \arctan(^-2.5)$ *Since $\sin\phi$ is positive and $\cos\phi$ is negative, choose*
$= 112°$ *an angle which terminates in quadrant II.*

Therefore the angle is 112° and the length of the normal is $\frac{3}{\sqrt{29}}$, or about 0.56 units.

exercises

Exploratory Find A, B, C, and $\sqrt{A^2 + B^2}$ for each of the following.

1. $2x + 3y + 4 = 0$
2. $3x + 4y - 6 = 0$
3. $5x + y = 7$
4. $3x - y = 4$
5. $y = 4x + 9$
6. $y = {}^-7x - 6$

7-12. For problems 1-6, write the equation in normal form. Then find the length of the normal and name the quadrant in which the normal lies.

Simplify each of the following.

13. $x \cos 60° + y \sin 60° - 7 = 0$
14. $x \cos 45° + y \sin 45° - 11 = 0$
15. $x \cos 225° + y \sin 225° - 6 = 0$
16. $x \cos 135° + y \sin 135° - 3 = 0$

Written Write the standard form of the equation of each line described below.

1. $p = 3$, $\phi = 60°$
2. $p = 5$, $\phi = 45°$
3. $p = 25$, $\phi = 225°$
4. $p = 8$, $\phi = 240°$
5. $p = 2$, $\phi = 150°$
6. $p = 32$, $\phi = 120°$

Write the normal form of each equation.

7. $x + y - 8 = 0$
8. $y = x + 6$
9. $2x - 3y - 1 = 0$
10. $6x - 8y - 15 = 0$
11. $3x + 4y - 1 = 0$
12. $x - 3y - 2 = 0$

13-16. For problems 9-12, find the length of the normal (p) and the angle which the normal makes with the positive x-axis (ϕ).

Solve each problem.

17. Write the equation of a line if the point on the line nearest the origin is (3, 3).
18. Write the equation of a line if the point on the line nearest the origin is ($^-4$, 4).
19. What is the equation of a line that makes an angle of 150° with the positive x-axis and is 1 unit from the origin? (two solutions)
20. A line makes an angle of 135° with the positive x-axis and is 3 units from the origin. Find its equation in standard form. (two solutions)

Vector and Parametric Equations of Lines

Lines in the coordinate plane can be described by vector equations. Consider the line which passes through $P(1, 4)$ and $Q(4, 6)$. A **direction vector** for the line is $\overrightarrow{PQ}$.

$$\overrightarrow{PQ} = (4 - 1, 6 - 4) \quad \text{or} \quad (3, 2)$$

Let $R(x, y)$ be any other point on the line. Then $\overrightarrow{PR}$ is a scalar multiple of $\overrightarrow{PQ}$. That is, $\overrightarrow{PR} = t\overrightarrow{PQ}$ or $t(3, 2)$. The **vector equation** of the line can be written as follows.

$$\overrightarrow{OR} = \overrightarrow{OP} + \overrightarrow{PR}$$ *Why?*

$$(x, y) = (1, 4) + t(3, 2)$$

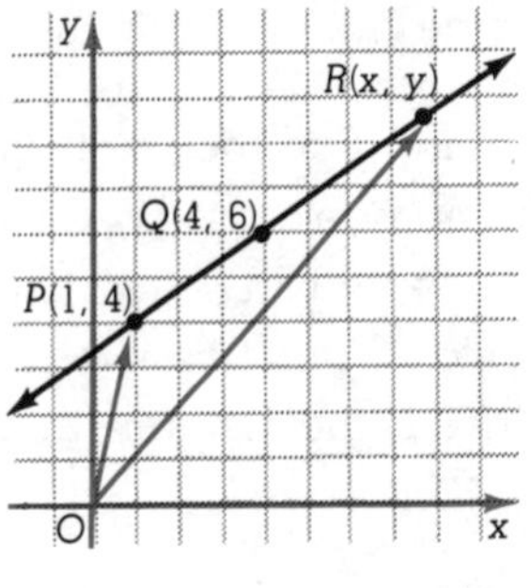

By substituting specific values for t, points on the line can be determined.

$$(1, 4) + t(3, 2) = (x, y)$$
$$(1, 4) + 0(3, 2) = (1, 4)$$
$$(1, 4) + 1(3, 2) = (4, 6)$$
$$(1, 4) + 2(3, 2) = (7, 8)$$
$$(1, 4) + {}^{-}1(3, 2) = ({}^{-}2, 2)$$

$t(x,y) = (tx,ty)$

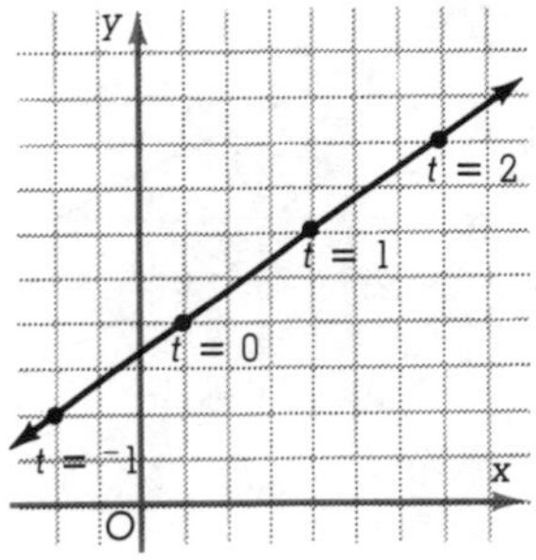

Example Write a vector equation for the line through $P({}^{-}1, 3)$ and $Q(1, 7)$.

$$\overrightarrow{PQ} = (1 - {}^{-}1, 7 - 3) \quad \text{or} \quad (2, 4)$$

Therefore $(x, y) = ({}^{-}1, 3) + t(2, 4)$ is a vector equation of the line.

A vector equation can be expressed as a pair of equations, called **parametric equations.** For example, the equation $(x, y) = ({}^{-}1, 3) + t(2, 4)$ can be expressed as follows.

Vector and parametric equations are not unique.

$$x = {}^{-}1 + 2t \qquad y = 3 + 4t$$

If the **parameter,** t, can be eliminated, then y can be expressed in terms of x. This can be accomplished by solving the first equation for t, then substituting for t in the second equation.

Exercises Write a vector equation of the line which passes through the given points.

1. $P({}^{-}1, 4), Q(0, {}^{-}3)$
2. $P(4, 9), Q(6, 2)$
3. $P({}^{-}3, {}^{-}2), Q(1, 4)$

4-6. Write the parametric equations of each line for problems **1-3**.

Write the slope-intercept form of the equation of the line for each pair of parametric equations.

7. $x = 3 - t$
   $y = 2 + t$
8. $x = 1 + t$
   $y = {}^{-}2 - 3t$
9. $x = 3 - 2t$
   $y = t + 5$

11-5 Distance from a Point to a Line

Often you need to find the distance from a point to a line. For example, finding the length of an altitude of a triangle requires that the distance from a vertex to the opposite side be determined.

Two cases must be considered. In one case, the point lies on the same side of the line as the origin and in the other the point lies on the opposite side of the line from the origin. If the line segment joining P to the origin does not intersect the line, point P is on the same side of the line as the origin. Let $\overleftrightarrow{RS}$ be a line in the coordinate plane and let $P(x_1, y_1)$ be a point not on $\overleftrightarrow{RS}$. Construct line TV parallel to $\overleftrightarrow{RS}$ and passing through P. The distance d between the parallel lines is the distance from $\overleftrightarrow{RS}$ to P.

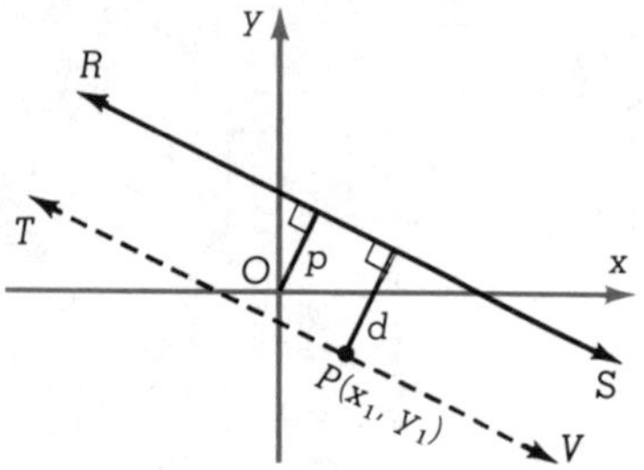

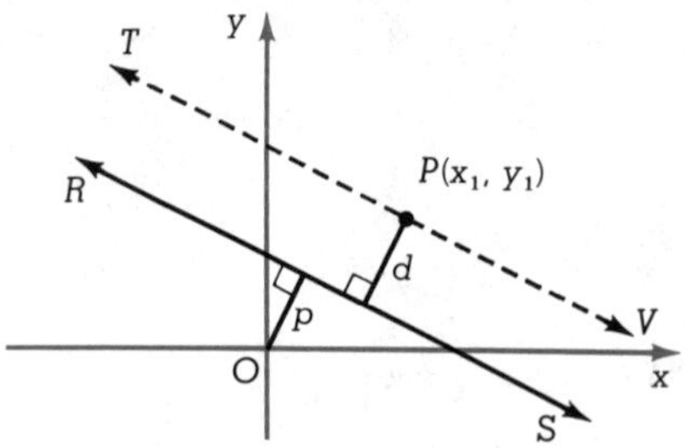

Let $x \cos \phi + y \sin \phi - p = 0$ be the equation of $\overleftrightarrow{RS}$ in normal form. If $\overleftrightarrow{TV}$ is parallel to $\overleftrightarrow{RS}$ then the equation of $\overleftrightarrow{TV}$ is $x \cos \phi + y \sin \phi - (p + d) = 0$. Then, solve for d.

$$d = x \cos \phi + y \sin \phi - p$$

Since $P(x_1, y_1)$ is on $\overleftrightarrow{TV}$ its coordinates satisfy the above equation.

$$d = x_1 \cos \phi + y_1 \sin \phi - p$$

An equivalent form of the expression above is used to find d when the equation of a line is given in standard form.

> **The following formula can be used to find the distance from a point (x_1, y_1) to a line $Ax + By + C = 0$.**
>
> $$d = \frac{Ax_1 + By_1 + C}{\pm\sqrt{A^2 + B^2}}$$
>
> **The sign of the radical is chosen opposite the sign of C.**

Distance from a Point to a Line

The distance will be positive if the point and the origin are on opposite sides of the line. The distance will be negative if the point is on the same side of the line as the origin. In an application of the formula the absolute value of d is usually desired.

example

1 **Find the distance between $P(^-1, 4)$ and the line $3x - 7y - 1 = 0$.**

$$d = \frac{Ax_1 + By_1 + C}{\pm\sqrt{A^2 + B^2}}$$

$$= \frac{3x_1 + {}^-7y_1 + {}^-1}{\sqrt{3^2 + (^-7)^2}} \qquad \textit{A = 3, B = }{}^-7\textit{, and C = }{}^-1$$

$$= \frac{3(^-1) + (^-7)4 + {}^-1}{\sqrt{9 + 49}} \qquad \textit{Since C is negative, use } +\sqrt{A^2 + B^2}.$$

$$= \frac{^-32}{\sqrt{58}}$$

$$= \frac{^-16\sqrt{58}}{29} \text{ or about } {}^-4.2 \qquad |d| = 4.2$$

Thus, the point P is about 4.2 units from the line $3x - 7y - 1 = 0$ and is on the same side of the line as the origin.

You also can use the formula to find the distance between two parallel lines.

example

2 **Find the distance between the lines $3x + 2y = 10$ and $y = -\frac{3}{2}x + 7$.**

The lines are parallel. Why? The distance between the lines can be found by choosing a point on one line, then finding the distance from the point to the other line. Since the second linear equation is in slope-intercept form, the line passes through the point (0, 7). Find the distance from (0, 7) to the line $3x + 2y = 10$. *Another point could have been chosen instead of (0, 7).*

$$3x + 2y = 10$$

$$3x + 2y - 10 = 0 \qquad \textit{Change the other equation to standard form.}$$

$$d = \frac{Ax_1 + By_1 + C}{\pm\sqrt{A^2 + B^2}}$$

$$= \frac{3x_1 + 2y_1 - 10}{\sqrt{3^2 + 2^2}} \qquad \textit{Let A = 3, B = 2, and C = }{}^-10$$

$$= \frac{3(0) + 2(7) - 10}{\sqrt{13}} \qquad \textit{Replace } x_1 \textit{ by 0 and } y_1 \textit{ by 7.}$$

$$= \frac{4}{\sqrt{13}} \text{ or } \frac{4\sqrt{13}}{13}$$

Thus, the parallel lines are $\frac{4\sqrt{13}}{13}$, or about 1.1 units apart.

exercises

Exploratory State whether you would use a positive or negative value of $\pm\sqrt{A^2 + B^2}$ to find the distance from a point to the line which has the given equation.

1. $2x + 5y - 2 = 0$
2. $x - 7y + 4 = 0$
3. $2x - y + 6 = 0$
4. $4x + 3y - 6 = 0$
5. $x - y - 14 = 0$
6. $2x + 4y + 7 = 0$

Name the coordinates of one point which satisfy the first equation given. Then find the distance from the point to the graph of the second equation.

7. $x + 2y + 4 = 0$
   $2x + 4y - 7 = 0$
8. $y = 3x + 9$
   $2y = 6x - 4$
9. $2x - 7y + 9 = 0$
   $2x - 7y - 9 = 0$

Written Solve each of the following. Draw a graph for each problem.

1. Find the distance from the line $2x + 5y - 2 = 0$ to $(3, ^-1)$.
2. Find the distance from the line $x - 7y + 4 = 0$ to $(^-4, 2)$.
3. Find the distance from the line $3x - y + 1 = 0$ to $(0, 0)$.
4. Find and interpret the distance from the line $2x + 3y + 2 = 0$ to $(2, ^-2)$.
5. Find the distance between the lines $3x - 5y + 7 = 0$ and $6x - 10y - 2 = 0$.
6. Find the distance between the lines $2x - 3y + 1 = 0$ and $3y - 2x = 5$.
7. Write equations for the lines which are at a distance of 3 units from the line $x - 5y + 10 = 0$.
8. Write equations for the lines which are at a a distance of 4 units from the line $3x + 3y = 5$.
9. Find the lengths of the three altitudes of a triangle which has vertices at $(5, 3)$, $(1, ^-4)$, and $(^-4, 1)$.
10. Find the lengths of the three altitudes of a triangle which has vertices at $(1, 1)$, $(4, 2)$, and $(3, 6)$.

11-6 Bisector of an Angle

The bisector of an angle is the set of points equidistant from the sides of the angle. Using this definition, the equations of the bisectors of the angles formed by two lines can be found.

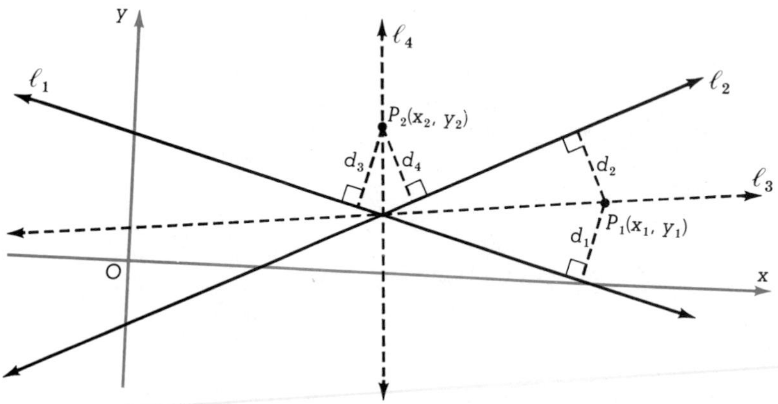

In the figure, ℓ_3 and ℓ_4 are the bisectors of the angles formed by ℓ_1 and ℓ_2. Also, $P_1(x_1, y_1)$ is a point on ℓ_3 and $P_2(x_2, y_2)$ is a point on ℓ_4. Let d_1 be the distance from ℓ_1 to P_1 and let d_2 be the distance from ℓ_2 to P_1.

Notice that P_1 and the origin lie on opposite sides of ℓ_1. Therefore d_1 is positive. Since the origin and P_1 are on opposite sides of ℓ_2, d_2 is also positive. Thus, for any point $P_1(x_1, y_1)$ on ℓ_3, $d_1 = d_2$. However, d_3 is positive and d_4 is negative. Why? Therefore for any point $P_2(x_2, y_2)$ on ℓ_4, $d_3 = {}^-d_4$.

Notice that the origin is in the interior of the angle that is bisected by ℓ_3 but in the exterior of the angle bisected by ℓ_4. Thus, a simple way to determine whether to equate distances or to let one distance equal the opposite of the other is given as follows.

If the origin lies within the angle being bisected, the distances from each line to a point on the bisector have the same sign. If the origin does not lie within the angle being bisected, the distances have opposite signs.

Relative Position of the Origin

To find the equation of a specific angle bisector, first graph the lines. Then determine whether to equate the distances or to let one distance equal the opposite of the other.

example

1 **Find the equation of the line that bisects the acute angle formed by the lines $2x - 3y + 6 = 0$ and $3x + y - 9 = 0$.**

As shown by the graph below, the origin is in the interior of the acute angle. Therefore $d_1 = d_2$.

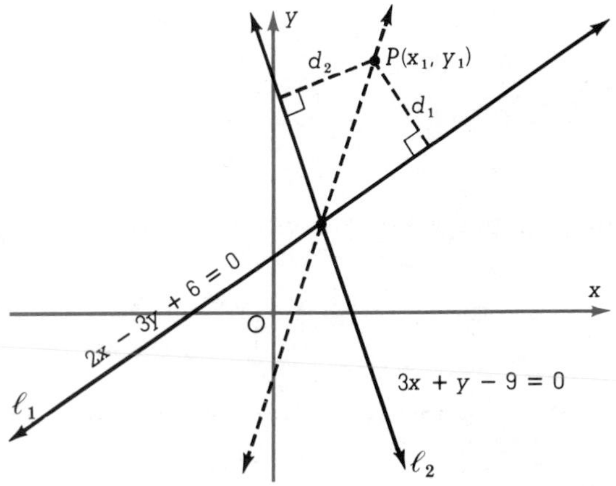

Write expressions for the distances from each line to $P_1(x_1, y_1)$.

$$d_1 = \frac{2x_1 - 3y_1 + 6}{^-\sqrt{13}} \qquad \textit{Use the formula } d = \frac{Ax_1 + By_1 + C}{\pm\sqrt{A^2 + B^2}}.$$

$$d_2 = \frac{3x_1 + y_1 - 9}{\sqrt{10}}$$

Since $d_1 = d_2$, you can equate the previous expressions.

$$\frac{2x_1 - 3y_1 + 6}{^-\sqrt{13}} = \frac{3x_1 + y_1 - 9}{\sqrt{10}}$$

The equation of the bisector can be obtained by simplifying and dropping the subscripts.

The equation is $(2\sqrt{10} + 3\sqrt{13})x + (^-3\sqrt{10} + \sqrt{13})y + 6\sqrt{10} - 9\sqrt{13} = 0$.

exercises

Exploratory Graph each pair of equations. Then state whether you would equate the distances or let one distance be the opposite of the other to find the equation of a line which bisects the acute angle between them.

1. $x + 2y - 7 = 0$; $4x + 5y + 2 = 0$
2. $7x + 4y - 5 = 0$; $x - 2y + 3 = 0$
3. $x = y + 1$; $y = 3x + 4$

Written Find the equation of the line that bisects the acute angle formed by the graphs of each pair of equations.

1. $2x + y - 1 = 0$; $x - y + 3 = 0$
2. $4x + y + 3 = 0$; $x + y + 2 = 0$
3. $3x + 2y - 2 = 0$; $2x + 3y + 2 = 0$
4. $x - y + 4 = 0$; $x + 4y + 6 = 0$

Find the equation of the line that bisects the obtuse angle formed by the graphs of each pair of equations.

5. $2x + 5y + 3 = 0$; $3x + y - 7 = 0$
6. $6x + y - 3 = 0$; $x + 3y + 1 = 0$
7. $x + y + 2 = 0$; $3x - y - 1 = 0$
8. $2x + 5y = 0$; $5x + 2y = 0$

Find the equations of two lines that make a 45° angle with the graph of the given equation and pass through the given point.

9. $x - y + 3 = 0$, $(1, 4)$
10. $x - y = 0$, $(2, 2)$
11. $y = 2x + 4$, $(^-2, 0)$
12. $3x + y - 7 = 0$, $(2, 1)$

Challenge Find the equations of the bisectors of the interior angles of the triangle formed by $x + 2y = 1$, $2x + y = 3$, and $x - y + 5 = 0$. Show that these bisectors are concurrent by showing that their equations have a common solution.

11-7 Polar Form of a Linear Equation

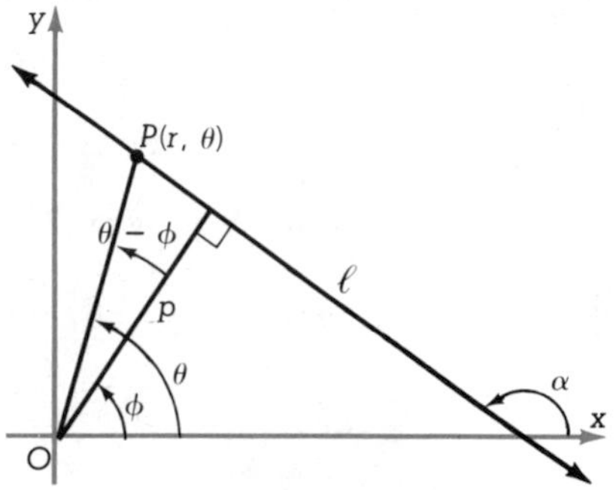

The polar form of a linear equation is closely related to the normal form, which is

$$x \cos \phi + y \sin \phi - p = 0.$$

But $x = r \cos \theta$ and $y = r \sin \theta$. Therefore the polar form of the equation of a line can be obtained by substitution.

$$r \cos \theta \cos \phi + r \sin \theta \sin \phi - p = 0$$
$$\text{or } p = r \cos (\theta - \phi)$$

Recall that $\cos(\theta - \phi) = \cos \theta \cos \phi + \sin \theta \sin \phi$. For reference, see page 136.

Polar Form of a Linear Equation

The polar form of a linear equation is

$$p = r \cos (\theta - \phi)$$

where p is the length of the normal and ϕ is the positive angle between the positive x-axis and the normal.

Notice that θ and r are variables, and p and ϕ are constants for any specific line. Values for p and ϕ can be obtained from the normal form of the equation. Remember to choose the value for ϕ according to the quadrant in which the normal lies.

example

1 **Change $3x - 5y + 5 = 0$ to polar form.**

First change to normal form.

$\pm\sqrt{A^2 + B^2} = \pm\sqrt{3^2 + (^-5)^2} = \pm\sqrt{34}$ *Since C is positive, choose $-\sqrt{A^2 + B^2}$.*

The normal form is $-\frac{3x}{\sqrt{34}} + \frac{5y}{\sqrt{34}} - \frac{5}{\sqrt{34}} = 0$

Therefore $\sin \phi = \frac{5}{\sqrt{34}}$, $\cos \phi = -\frac{3}{\sqrt{34}}$, and $p = \frac{5}{\sqrt{34}}$.

$\phi = \arctan \frac{B}{A}$ *The angle must terminate in the second quadrant. Why?*

$= \arctan \left(-\frac{5}{3}\right)$

$= 121°$

Then substitute the values for p and ϕ into the polar form.

$p = r \cos (\theta - \phi)$

$\frac{5}{\sqrt{34}} = r \cos (\theta - 121°)$

Thus, $\frac{5}{\sqrt{34}} = r \cos (\theta - 121°)$ is the polar form of $3x - 5y + 5 = 0$.

You can graph a polar equation by preparing a table of coordinates as shown below.

example

2 **Graph the equation $2 = r \cos(\theta + 20°)$.**

First change the equation to $r = \dfrac{2}{\cos(\theta + 20°)}$

Then make a table of values and graph the equation on a polar grid.

θ	r
0°	2.1
10°	2.3
25°	2.8
40°	4
100°	−4

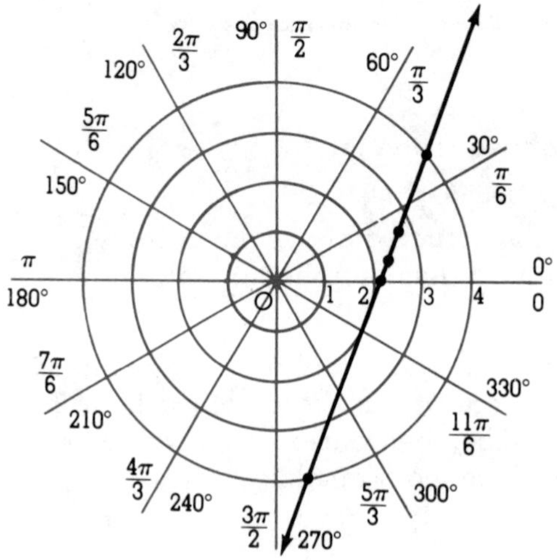

An equation in polar form can be changed to an equation in rectangular coordinates.

example

3 **Change $2 = r \cos\left(\theta - \frac{\pi}{4}\right)$ to an equation in rectangular coordinates.**

$$\begin{aligned}
2 &= r\left(\cos\theta \cos\frac{\pi}{4} + \sin\theta \sin\frac{\pi}{4}\right) \\
&= r\left(\cos\theta \cdot \frac{\sqrt{2}}{2} + \sin\theta \cdot \frac{\sqrt{2}}{2}\right) \\
&= r\cos\theta \cdot \frac{\sqrt{2}}{2} + r\sin\theta \cdot \frac{\sqrt{2}}{2} \\
&= \frac{\sqrt{2}}{2}x + \frac{\sqrt{2}}{2}y \\
2\sqrt{2} &= x + y
\end{aligned}$$

The standard form of the equation in rectangular coordinates is $x + y - 2\sqrt{2} = 0$.

exercises

Exploratory Change each of the following to normal form.

1. $x - y + 4 = 0$
2. $2x + 3y - 5 = 0$
3. $2x - y + 6 = 0$

Evaluate each of the following. Assume the angle terminates in the first or fourth quadrant.

4. $\arctan \frac{3}{5}$
5. $\arctan \frac{5}{12}$
6. $\arctan \left(-\frac{12}{5}\right)$

Find ϕ and p for each of the following.

7. $3x - 2y + 4 = 0$
8. $x + 4y - 7 = 0$
9. $9x + y + 3 = 0$

For each equation complete the table that follows.

10. $r = \dfrac{1}{\cos(\theta + 15°)}$

θ	15°	30°	45°	60°
r				

11. $r = \dfrac{2}{\cos(\theta + 30°)}$

θ	0°	15°	30°	70°
r				

12. $r \cos(\theta + 10°) = 2$

θ	20°	25°	50°	60°
r				

13. $r \cos(\theta + 20°) = 3$

θ	10°	25°	40°	60°
r				

Written Graph each of the following polar equations.

1. $5 = r \cos(\theta + 45°)$
2. $1.5 = r \cos(\theta - 10°)$
3. $3 = r \cos(\theta + 15°)$
4. $1.6 = r \cos(\theta - 15°)$
5. $2.5 = r \cos\left(\theta - \frac{\pi}{2}\right)$
6. $2.4 = r \cos\left(\theta + \frac{\pi}{3}\right)$

Change each of the following to polar form.

7. $x = 10$
8. $x = y$
9. $y = 3x + 4$
10. $y = {}^{-}2x + 5$
11. $2x + 3y - 1 = 0$
12. $3x - 4y + 5 = 0$

Change each of the following to an equation in rectangular coordinates.

13. $0 = r \cos(\theta + 90°)$
14. $1 = r \cos(\theta + 30°)$
15. $1 = r \cos \theta$
16. $3 = r \cos \theta$
17. $4 = r \cos\left(\theta - \frac{\pi}{3}\right)$
18. $2 = r \cos\left(\theta + \frac{\pi}{2}\right)$

Find the polar form of the equation of the line which passes through each pair of points below.

19. (0, 0) and (4, 2)
20. (1, 3) and (2, $^{-}4$)

Find the polar form of the equation of a line for which the slope and a point on the line are given below.

21. $\frac{3}{5}$ and (0, 4)
22. $-\frac{1}{2}$ and (3, $^{-}2$)

Chapter Summary

1. Parallel Lines: Two non-vertical lines are parallel if and only if their slopes are equal. (298)
2. The slope of a line is equal to the tangent of the angle of inclination. (299)
3. Perpendicular Lines: Two non-vertical lines are perpendicular if and only if the slope of one is the negative reciprocal of the slope of the other. (299)
4. Midpoint Formula: If the coordinates of P_1 and P_2 are (x_1, y_1) and (x_2, y_2), respectively, then the midpoint P_m has coordinates
$$\left(\frac{x_1 + x_2}{2}, \frac{y_1 + y_2}{2}\right). \qquad (301)$$
5. Many theorems of plane geometry can be proved by analytic methods. Usually in straight line figures a vertex is placed at the origin and one line is made to coincide with the x-axis. (301)
6. Angle of Intersection: If m_1 is the slope of ℓ_1 and m_2 is the slope of ℓ_2, then the angle of intersection, measured from ℓ_1 to ℓ_2, is θ and $\tan \theta = \dfrac{m_2 - m_1}{1 + m_1 m_2}$. (304)
7. The normal form of a linear equation is
$$x \cos \phi + y \sin \phi - p = 0$$
where p is the length of the normal from the line to the origin and ϕ is the positive angle between the positive x-axis and the normal. (306)
8. The standard form of a linear equation, $Ax + By + C = 0$, can be changed to normal form by dividing each term by $\pm\sqrt{A^2 + B^2}$. The sign is chosen opposite the sign of C. (307)
9. Distance from a Point to a Line: The distance from a point (x_1, y_1) to a line $Ax + By + C = 0$ is $\dfrac{Ax_1 + By_1 + C}{\pm\sqrt{A^2 + B^2}}$. The sign of the radical is chosen opposite to the sign of C. (310)
10. Relative Position of the Origin: If the origin lies within the angle being bisected, the distances from each line to a point on the bisector have the same sign. If the origin does not lie within the angle being bisected, the distances have opposite signs. (313)
11. To find the equation of a specific angle bisector, first graph the lines. Then determine whether to equate the distances or to let one distance equal the opposite of the other. (313)
12. The polar form of a linear equation is $p = r \cos(\theta - \phi)$, where p is the length of the normal and ϕ is the angle between the positive x-axis and the normal. (315)

Chapter Review

11-1 Write the standard form of the equation of each line described below.

1. Parallel to $y = 4x - 7$, passes through $(^-2, 3)$.
2. Parallel to $^-2x + 3y - 5 = 0$, passes through $(2, 4)$.
3. Perpendicular to $6x = 2y - 4$, y intercept 4.
4. Perpendicular to $5y = 4x + 2$, x intercept 5.

11-2 Prove the following analytically.

5. If the diagonals of a parallelogram are perpendicular then the parallelogram is a rhombus.
6. The midpoint of the hypotenuse of a right triangle is equidistant from the vertices.

11-3 Find the acute angle formed by the graphs of each pair of equations.

7. $2x + y - 2 = 0$; $3x + y + 1 = 0$
8. $^-3x - 2y + 3 = 0$; $2x + 5y - 2 = 0$
9. $2x - y = 6$; $3x + y - 1 = 0$
10. $3x + y = 2$; $x - 4y = 5$
11. $^-x = 5y + 2$; $y = 4x - 7$
12. $x = 6y - 5$; $2y - x = 1$

11-4 Change the following linear equations to normal form. Then find the length of the normal and the angle it makes with the positive x-axis.

13. $3x + 2y - 6 = 0$
14. $7x + 3y - 8 = 0$
15. $6x = 4y - 5$
16. $9x = {}^-5y + 3$
17. $^-2x - 9y = {}^-10$
18. $^-x + 2y = 7$

11-5 Find the distance from the given point to the graph of the given equation.

19. $(5, 6)$; $2x - 3y + 2 = 0$
20. $(^-1, 3)$; $^-3x + 4y = {}^-5$
21. $(^-3, ^-4)$; $2y = {}^-3x + 6$
22. $(^-2, 4)$; $4y = 3x - 1$

11-6 Find the equation of the line that bisects the acute angle formed by the graphs of each pair of equations.

23. $3x + y - 2 = 0$; $x + 2y - 3 = 0$
24. $y = \frac{2}{3}x - 6$; $y = \frac{3}{4}x + 2$

11-7 Change each of the following to an equation in rectangular coordinates.

25. $3 = r\cos\left(\theta - \frac{\pi}{3}\right)$
26. $4 = r\cos\left(\theta + \frac{\pi}{2}\right)$

Change each of the following to polar form.

27. $2x + y = {}^-3$
28. $y = {}^-3x - 4$

Chapter Test

Write the standard form of the equation of each line described below.

1. Parallel to $3x + 2y - 3 = 0$, passes through (3, 4).
2. Perpendicular to $^-x + 5y = {}^-3$, passes through the origin.

Find the acute angle formed by the graphs of each pair of equations.

3. $y = {}^-2x + 5$
   $y = {}^-x$
4. $2y = {}^-5x + 6$
   $3x + y - 5 = 0$
5. $y = \frac{2}{3}x - 1$
   $y = -\frac{4}{3}x + 2$

Change the following linear equations to normal form. Then find the length of the normal and the angle it makes with the positive x-axis.

6. $^-x + y - 3 = 0$
7. $^-3x = 6y - 7$
8. $^-10x + 5 = {}^-5y$

Find the distance from the given point to the graph of the given equation.

9. $(^-5, 8)$; $2x + y - 6 = 0$
10. $(^-6, 8)$; $^-3x - 4y = 2$

Find the equation of the line that bisects the acute angle formed by the graphs of each pair of equations.

11. $^-x + 3y - 2 = 0$
    $y = \frac{3}{5}x + 3$
12. $7 = 5x + 2y$
    $y = -\frac{3}{4}x + 1$

Change each of the following to polar form.

13. $5x + 6y = {}^-3$
14. $2x - 4y = 1$
15. $y = -\frac{1}{3}x + 2$

Change each of the following to an equation in rectangular coordinates.

16. $5 = r \cos \theta$
17. $3 = r \cos (\theta + 45°)$
18. $4 = r \cos\left(\theta - \frac{\pi}{2}\right)$

19. Prove analytically that the segment joining the midpoints of two sides of a triangle is parallel to the third side and one-half its length.

Chapter

12

Conics

The Earth's orbit around the sun follows an elliptical path. The ellipse is one of the four conic sections. Equations of conic sections have the form $Ax^2 + Bxy + Cy^2 + Dx + Ey + F = 0$.

12-1 The Circle

A **circle** is a set of points in the plane at a given distance from a fixed point. The fixed point is the **center** of the circle and the given distance is the **radius**.

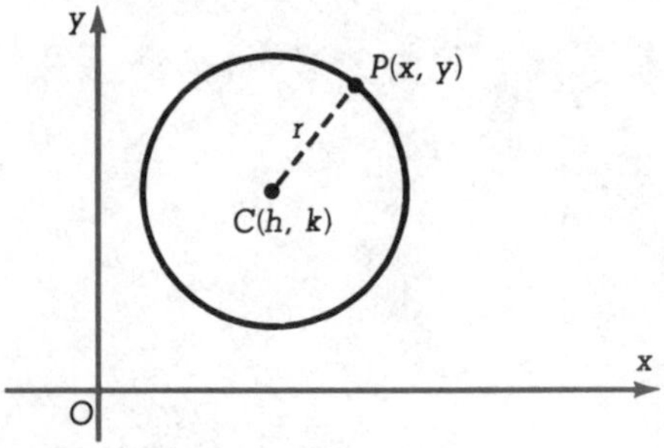

Let $C(h, k)$ be the center of a circle, and let $P(x, y)$ be any point on the circle. Thus, $r = CP$, as shown at the right. The distance formula can be used to write the equation for the circle.

$$r^2 = (x - h)^2 + (y - k)^2$$

This is called the **standard form** of the equation of a circle.

The standard form of the equation of a circle with radius r and center (h, k) is $(x - h)^2 + (y - k)^2 = r^2$.

Standard Form of the Equation of a Circle.

example

1 **Write the equation of a circle that is tangent to the y-axis and has center $(^-6, 7)$. Then draw the graph.**

Since the circle is tangent to the y-axis, the radius is 6. Thus, the equation of the circle can be found by substituting 6 for r, $^-6$ for h, and 7 for k.

The equation is $(x + 6)^2 + (y - 7)^2 = 36$.

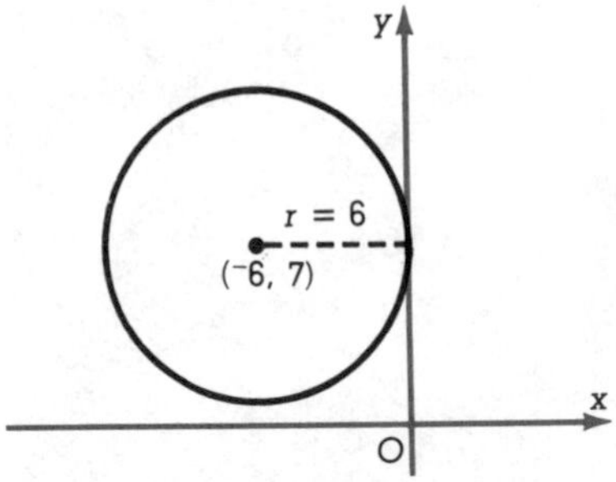

The standard form of the equation of a circle can be expanded to obtain another form of the equation.

$$(x - h)^2 + (y - k)^2 = r^2$$
$$x^2 - 2hx + h^2 + y^2 - 2ky + k^2 = r^2$$

If $r = 0$, the circle becomes a point. If $r < 0$, a real circle does not exist.

Since h, k, and r are constants, the equation can be written as $x^2 + y^2 + Dx + Ey + F = 0$. This equation is called the **general form** of the equation of a circle. Notice that the coefficients of x^2 and y^2 must be equal. Also, there is no term containing xy, the product of the variables.

When the equation of a circle is given in general form, you can transform the equation into standard form by completing the square for the terms in x and the terms in y.

If the coefficients of x^2 and y^2 are not 1, the equation can be transformed by division so that they are 1.

examples

2 **The equation of a circle is $x^2 + y^2 - 4x + 6y - 12 = 0$. Find the center and radius of the circle. Then draw the graph.**

$$x^2 + y^2 - 4x + 6y - 12 = 0$$
$$(x^2 - 4x + \quad) + (y^2 + 6y + \quad) = 12$$
$$x^2 - 4x + \left(\frac{^-4}{2}\right)^2 + y^2 + 6y + \left(\frac{6}{2}\right)^2 = 12 + \left(\frac{^-4}{2}\right)^2 + \left(\frac{6}{2}\right)^2$$
$$(x - 2)^2 + (y + 3)^2 = 25$$

The center is $(2, ^-3)$ and the radius is 5.

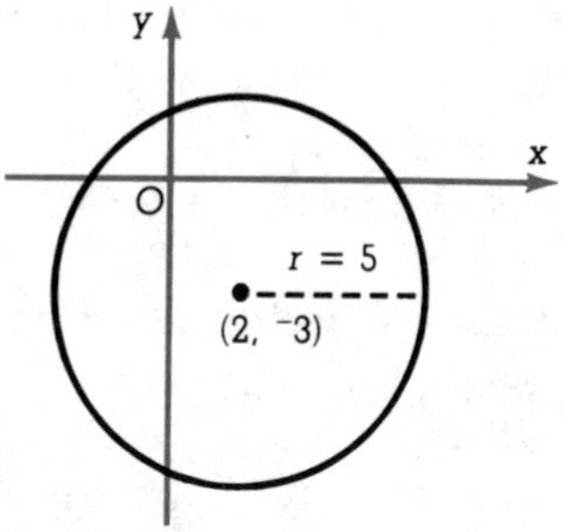

Any three non-collinear points in the plane determine a unique circle. You can find the equation of the circle by substituting the coordinates of each point into the general form of the equation. This will determine a system of three equations in three variables, D, E, and F. By solving the equations you can find the general form of the equation of the circle which passes through the three given points.

The system can be solved by addition, substitution or matrices.

examples

3 **Find the equation of the circle which passes through the points $(2, ^-1)$, $(^-3, 0)$, and $(1, 4)$.**

Substitute the coordinates of each point into the form $x^2 + y^2 + Dx + Ey + F = 0$.

$4 + 1 + 2D - E + F = 0$
$9 + 0 - 3D + F = 0$
$1 + 16 + D + 4E + F = 0$

Simplify the system of equations.

$2D - E + F = ^-5$
$^-3D + F = ^-9$
$D + 4E + F = ^-17$

The solution to the system is $D = \frac{1}{3}$, $E = -\frac{7}{3}$, and $F = ^-8$.

Thus, the general form of the required equation is $x^2 + y^2 + \frac{1}{3}x - \frac{7}{3}y - 8 = 0$, or $3x^2 + 3y^2 + x - 7y - 24 = 0$.

exercises

Exploratory Write the standard form of the equation of a circle with the given center and radius.

1. (0, 0), 8
2. (0, 0), $\sqrt{3}$
3. (2, $^-7$), 9
4. ($^-2$, 3), 5
5. ($^-3$, $^-5$), 1
6. (7, 4), $\sqrt{2}$

Find the center and radius of each circle whose equation is given. Then graph the equation.

7. $(x - 2)^2 + (y - 3)^2 = 7$
8. $(x + 4)^2 + (y - 5)^2 = 9$
9. $(x - 2)^2 + (y - 6)^2 = 10$
10. $(x + 7)^2 + (y + 12)^2 = 36$
11. $4(x + 3)^2 + 4(y + 2)^2 = 7$
12. $9(x - 5)^2 = 4 - 9(y - 3)^2$

Written Write the standard form of each equation. Then graph the equation.

1. $x^2 + y^2 - 18 = 0$
2. $x^2 + y^2 - y = 0.75$
3. $x^2 + y^2 - 6x + 4y - 3 = 0$
4. $3x^2 + 3y^2 - 9 = 0$
5. $x^2 + y^2 + 8x + 2y - 8 = 0$
6. $x^2 + y^2 - 10x + 4y + 17 = 0$
7. $16x^2 + 16y^2 + 8x - 32y - 127 = 0$
8. $4x^2 + 4y^2 + x - 24y + 21 = 0$
9. $2x^2 - 4x + 2y^2 + 12y - 12 = 0$
10. $16x^2 + 16y^2 - 48x + 8y - 75 = 0$

Write the standard form of the equation of the circle which passes through the given points.

11. (0, 0), (3, 0), (5, 2)
12. ($^-2$, 3), (6, $^-5$), (0, 7)
13. (5, 5), (5, 3), (1, 3)
14. (5, 0), (1, $^-2$), (4, $^-3$)
15. (5, 3), ($^-2$, 2), ($^-1$, $^-5$)
16. (0, $^-9$), (7, $^-2$), ($^-5$, $^-10$)
17. (7, 5), (1, $^-1$), (7, $^-1$)
18. ($^-1$, 7), ($^-5$, 11), ($^-5$, 3)

Write the equation of each circle described below.

19. The circle passes through the origin and has center (4, $^-3$).
20. The circle passes through (7, $^-1$) and has center ($^-2$, 4).
21. The circle is tangent to the axes and has center (5, $^-5$).
22. The circle is tangent to the x-axis and has center (2, $^-4$).
23. The endpoints of a diameter are ($^-2$, $^-3$) and (4, 5).
24. The endpoints of a diameter are ($^-3$, 4) and (1, 2).

Challenge Solve each problem.

1. The center of a circle is on the x-axis, the radius is 1, and it passes through $\left(\frac{\sqrt{2}}{2}, \frac{\sqrt{2}}{2}\right)$. Write the equation of the circle.
2. A circle has center (5, 12) and is tangent to the line $2x - y + 3 = 0$. Write the equation of the circle.
3. Write the equation of the family of circles in which $h = k$ and the radius is 7. Let k be any real number. Describe this family of circles.
4. In the equation $(x - h)^2 + (y - k)^2 = r^2$, what is true if $(h^2 + k^2 - r^2)$ is zero?
5. Write the equation of the line which passes through the center of the circle $x^2 + y^2 - 8x - 4y + 11 = 0$ and is parallel to the line $3x - 4y = 7$.
6. Write the equation of the line which passes through the center of the circle $x^2 + y^2 - 14x + 10y + 73 = 0$ and is parallel to the line $x + 2y = 5$.

12-2 The Parabola

A **parabola** is the set of all points which are the same distance from a given point and a given line. The point is called the **focus**. The line is called the **directrix**.

In the figure at the right, F is the focus of the parabola and ℓ is the directrix. The parabola is symmetric with respect to the line $y = k$. This line is called the **axis of symmetry**, or **axis**, of the parabola. The point at which the axis intersects the parabola is called the **vertex**. Let the vertex, V, have the coordinates (h, k) and let $FV = p$. Thus $VT = p$. Why? The coordinates of F are $(h + p, k)$ and the equation of the directrix is $x = h - p$.

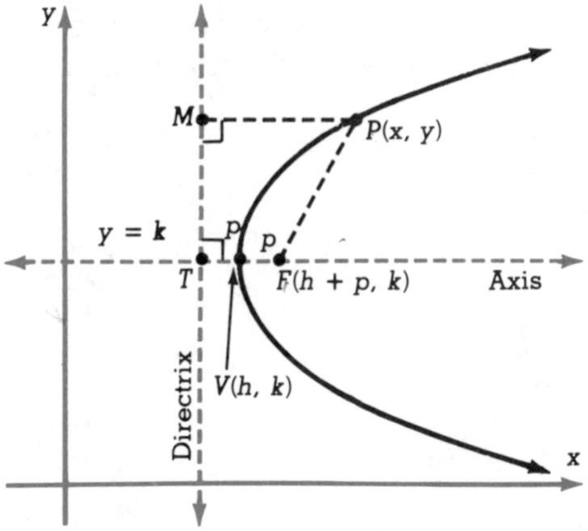

Consider any point $P(x, y)$ on the parabola. From the definition of a parabola, you know that $PF = PM$. The coordinates of M are $(h - p, y)$. Thus, the distance formula can be used to determine an equation for the parabola.

$$PF = PM$$
$$\sqrt{(x - (h + p))^2 + (y - k)^2} = \sqrt{(x - (h - p))^2}$$
$$(x - (h + p))^2 + (y - k)^2 = (x - (h - p))^2$$
$$x^2 - 2x(h + p) + (h + p)^2 + (y - k)^2 = x^2 - 2x(h - p) + (h - p)^2$$

The above equation can be simplified to obtain the following equation.

$$(y - k)^2 = 4p(x - h)$$

When p is positive the parabola opens to the right or upward. When p is negative the parabola opens to the left or downward.

If the directrix of the parabola is parallel to the x-axis, the equation of the parabola is $(x - h)^2 = 4p(y - k)$.

Standard Form of the Equation of a Parabola

The standard form of the equation of a parabola with vertex (h, k) and directrix parallel to the y-axis, is

$$(y - k)^2 = 4p(x - h)$$

where p is the distance from the vertex to the focus.

The standard form of the equation of a parabola with vertex (h, k) and directrix parallel to the x-axis, is

$$(x - h)^2 = 4p(y - k)$$

where p is the distance from the vertex to the focus.

example

1 Find the coordinates of the focus and the equation of the directrix of the parabola $y^2 = 12x$. Then draw the graph.

Since the equation has the form $(y - k)^2 = 4p(x - h)$ with $h = 0$ and $k = 0$, the vertex is (0, 0). Also $4p = 12$, so $p = 3$. Since $p > 0$, the focus is 3 units to the right of the vertex and has coordinates (3, 0). The equation of the directrix is $x = {}^-3$.

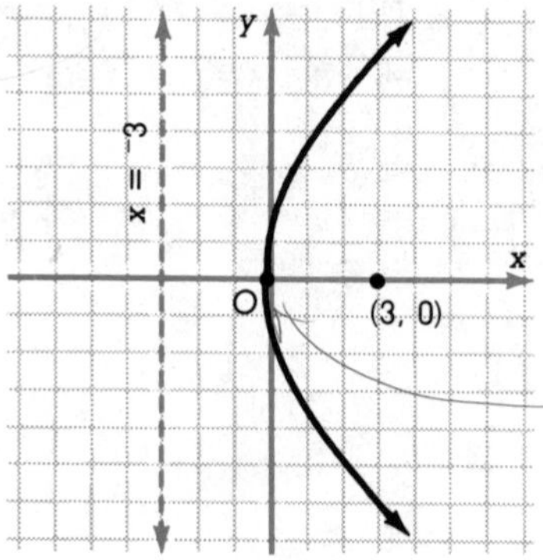

The standard form of the equation of a parabola may be transformed into the general form.

$$\begin{aligned} (y - k)^2 &= 4p(x - h) \\ y^2 - 2ky + k^2 &= 4px - 4ph \\ y^2 - 4px - 2ky + k^2 + 4ph &= 0 \\ \mathbf{y^2 + Dx + Ey + F} &\mathbf{= 0} \end{aligned}$$

h, k, and p are constants.
$D = {}^-4p$, $E = {}^-2k$, $F = k^2 + 4ph$

$$\begin{aligned} (x - h)^2 &= 4p(y - k) \\ x^2 - 2hx + h^2 &= 4py - 4pk \\ x^2 - 2hx - 4py + h^2 + 4pk &= 0 \\ \mathbf{x^2 + Dx + Ey + F} &\mathbf{= 0} \end{aligned}$$

$D = {}^-2h$, $E = {}^-4p$, $F = h^2 + 4pk$

Thus the general form of the equation of a parabola is $y^2 + Dx + Ey + F = 0$ or $x^2 + Dx + Ey + F = 0$.

example

2 The equation of a parabola is $x^2 + 4x + 2y + 10 = 0$. Write the equation in standard form.

$x^2 + 4x + 2y + 10 = 0$
$x^2 + 4x + 4 = {}^-2y - 10 + 4$ *Complete the square.*
$(x + 2)^2 = {}^-2(y + 3)$

The standard form of the equation is $(x + 2)^2 = {}^-2(y + 3)$.

The **latus rectum** of a parabola is the line segment perpendicular to the axis through the focus with endpoints on the parabola. In the figure at the right, the latus rectum is $\overline{RS}$. Since $RU = RF$ and $RU = FT = 2p$, the length of the latus rectum is $4p$.

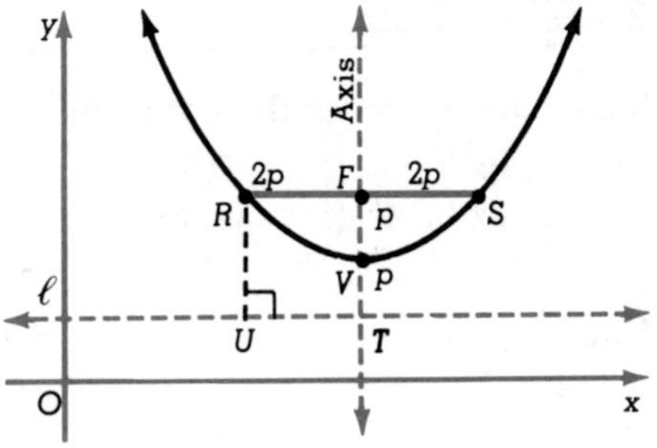

Latus Rectum of a Parabola

> The length of the latus rectum of a parabola is $4p$, where p is the distance from the vertex to the focus.

example

3 Name the coordinates of the vertex and the focus, the equation of the directrix, and the equation of the axis of the parabola $x^2 - 4x - 12y - 32 = 0$. Then find the length of the latus rectum and draw the graph.

Write the equation in standard form.

$$x^2 - 4x + 4 = 12y + 36$$
$$(x - 2)^2 = 12(y + 3)$$

Thus, the vertex is $(2, {}^-3)$. Since $4p = 12$, $p = 3$. Therefore the parabola opens upward and the focus is $(2, 0)$, or 3 units above the vertex. The equation of the directrix is $y = {}^-6$ and the equation of the axis is $x = 2$. The length of the latus rectum is $4p$, or 12 units.

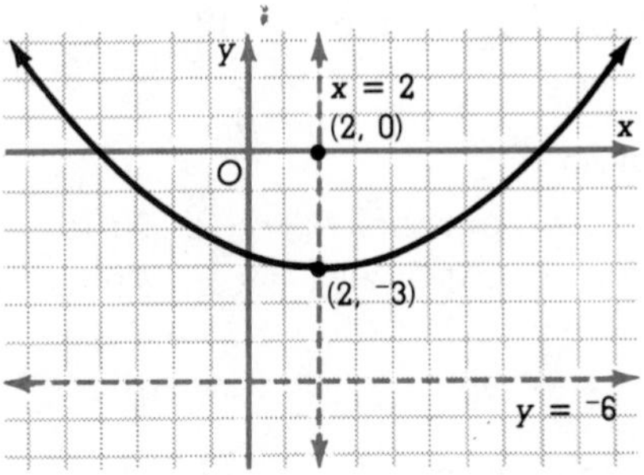

Parabolas have many applications. If a source of light or sound is placed at the focus of a parabolic reflector, the rays will be reflected along parallel paths. In this way, a straight beam of light or sound is formed. Also, the parabola is the path of an object given a velocity in a gravitational field. A thrown ball, or any projectile, will follow a parabolic path unless acted upon by additional forces or thrown directly upward.

exercises

Exploratory Write the equation of each parabola described below.

1. Vertex (0, 0), focus (2, 0)
2. Vertex (0, 3), focus (0, 0)
3. Vertex (2, 4), focus (2, 6)
4. Vertex ($^-2$, 5), focus ($^-2$, $^-8$)
5. Vertex ($^-1$, 4), focus (5, 4)
6. Vertex ($^-3$, 4), focus ($^-3$, 8)

Name the vertex, focus, and directrix of the parabola whose equation is given. Then draw the graph.

7. $y^2 = {}^-2x$
8. $8y = x^2$
9. $(y - 3)^2 = 4x$
10. $(x + 5)^2 = 12y$
11. $(x - 2)^2 = 8(y + 1)$
12. $(y + 2)^2 = {}^-16(x - 3)$

Write the standard form of each equation.

13. $x^2 - 11y = 0$
14. $3y^2 - 19x = 0$
15. $x^2 - 6x - 10y - 1 = 0$
16. $y^2 + 3x - 6y = 0$
17. $y^2 - 4x + 2y + 5 = 0$
18. $x^2 - 8x + 8y + 32 = 0$

Written 1-6. Name the focus, vertex, directrix, and axis of each parabola for problems 13-18 in the exploratory exercises. Then find the length of the latus rectum and draw the graph.

Write the equation of each parabola described below. Then draw the graph.

7. Vertex (0, 0), focus (0, $^-3$)
8. Vertex (6, $^-1$), focus (3, $^-1$)
9. Focus (3, 5), directrix $y = 3$
10. Focus (2, 5), directrix $x = 4$
11. Vertex ($^-2$, 1), axis $y = 1$, length of latus rectum 4, $p > 0$
12. Vertex (3, 2), axis $x = 3$, length of latus rectum 8, $p < 0$
13. Vertex (4, 3), passes through (5, 2), vertical axis
14. Vertex ($^-7$, $^-5$), passes through (2, $^-1$), horizontal axis
15. Focus (2, $^-6$), $p = {}^-2$, axis $x = 2$
16. Focus (3, 0), $p = 2$, vertical axis
17. Endpoints of latus rectum (0, 3) and (0, $^-3$), $p < 0$
18. Endpoints of latus rectum (4, 0) and ($^-4$, 0), $p > 0$

Challenge Solve each problem.

1. Write the equation of the parabola which has a horizontal axis and passes through the points (0, 0), ($^-1$, 2), and (3, $^-2$). (Hint: Determine D, E, and F in the general formula.)
2. Write the equation of the parabola which has a vertical axis and passes through the points (0, 0), ($^-1$, 2), and (3, $^-2$).
3. The latus rectum of the parabola $(x - 4)^2 = 8(y - 1)$ coincides with the diameter of a circle. Write the equation of the circle.
4. The latus rectum of the parabola $(y - 2)^2 = 5(x - 4)$ coincides with the diameter of a circle. Write the equation of the circle.

Suppose an object is thrown vertically upward with an initial velocity v_0. Its distance, s, above the ground after t seconds (neglecting air resistance) is $s = v_0t - 16t^2$ where $v_0 = 64$ ft/sec.

5. Graph the function $s = v_0t - 16t^2$.
6. Name the coordinates of the vertex.
7. What is the significance of s at the vertex?
8. How many seconds will it take the object to hit the ground?

Concentrating Solar Collectors

Using Mathematics

Part of a solar powered irrigation system is shown at the right. Trough shaped parabolic cylinders track the sun's movement to collect solar energy. The focus of each parabolic cylinder is a tube of water. Solar energy heats the water to provide input energy for turbine engines which power irrigation pumps.

The surface of each collector is covered with reflective material. The amount of reflective material needed for a collector like the one shown at the right can be found by multiplying the length of $\overline{ST}$ by the length of the parabolic segment RVS.

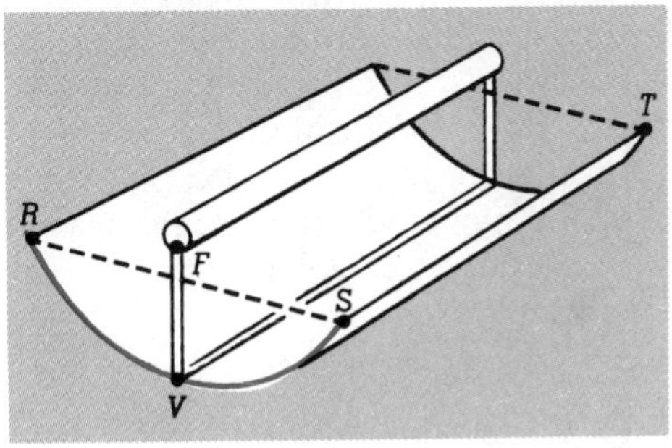

The following formula can be used to find the length of the parabolic segment RVS, if the width of the collector, RS, and the focal length, FV, are known.

$$RVS = FV\left(\frac{x}{2}\sqrt{4 + x^2} + 2\ln\left(\frac{x}{2} + \frac{1}{2}\sqrt{4 + x^2}\right)\right) \quad \text{where } x = \frac{RS}{2FV}$$

Example Find the surface area of the parabolic collector for which $FV = 1$ meter, $RS = 4$ meters, and $ST = 10$ meters.

$x = \frac{4}{2}$ or 2 *Find x, then use the formula to find RVS.*

$$RVS = 1\left(\frac{2}{2}\sqrt{4 + 2^2} + 2\ln\left(\frac{2}{2} + \frac{1}{2}\sqrt{4 + 2^2}\right)\right)$$
$$= 2\sqrt{2} + 2\ln(1 + \sqrt{2})$$
$$\approx 4.59 \text{ meters}$$

Therefore, the surface area is 4.59 m × 10 m, or 45.9 m².

Exercises Find the surface area of each parabolic collector described below.

1. $FV = 0.5$ m, $RS = 2$ m, $ST = 5$ m
2. $FV = 0.5$ m, $RS = 1.5$ m, $ST = 5$ m
3. $FV = 0.4$ m, $RS = 1.2$ m, $ST = 3$ m
4. $FV = 0.7$ m, $RS = 1.4$ m, $ST = 4$ m

12-3 Translation of Axes

The axes with respect to which a graph is drawn can be changed. In a **translation of axes** the new axes are parallel to the given axes.

Consider a point $P(x,y)$ in a coordinate plane with respect to a given x-axis and y-axis. Suppose you want to express P in coordinates with respect to new axes such that the x'-axis is parallel to the x-axis, and the y'-axis is parallel to the y-axis as shown below.

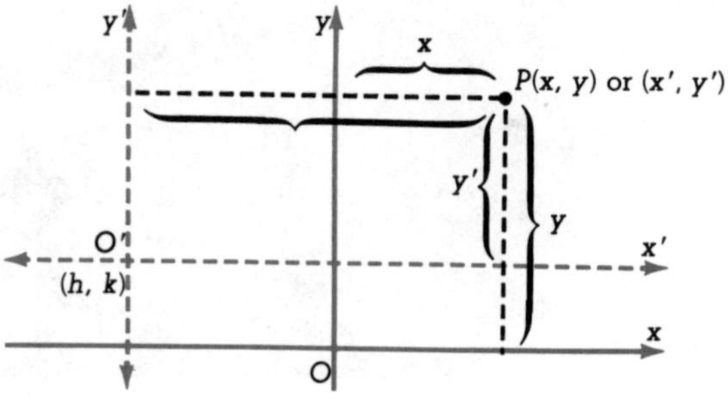

When $x' = y' = 0$, $x = h$ and $y = k$.

Let the intersection of the new axes be the point (h,k). All points given with respect to the x'-axis and y'-axis will be designated by a prime(′) notation. Thus the coordinates of P with respect to the new axes are (x', y'). In order to transform a point (x, y) into (x', y') the relation between the new and old coordinates is required. It can be seen from the figure that $x = x' + h$ and $y = y' + k$. These are called the **translation formulas.**

Translation Formulas

> The translation formulas are
>
> $$x = x' + h \quad \text{and} \quad y = y' + k$$
>
> where (h, k) represents the origin of the coordinate system (x', y').

The shape of a graph is not affected by a translation of axes. Therefore a translation can be used to obtain a simpler form of the equation of a parabola, circle, or other curve.

The new axes may intersect at any point, but a common and very useful translation for parabolas is to translate the origin to the vertex. For circles, it is often useful to translate the origin to the center.

A parabola with vertex (h, k) is of the form $(y - k)^2 = 4p(x - h)$ or $(x - h)^2 = 4p(y - k)$. You can translate the axes so that the y'-axis is the line $x = h$ and the x'-axis is the line $y = k$. The point of intersection of the axes is (h, k), the vertex of the parabola. Thus, in terms of coordinates of the new axes, the equation becomes $(y')^2 = 4px'$ or $(x')^2 = 4py'$.

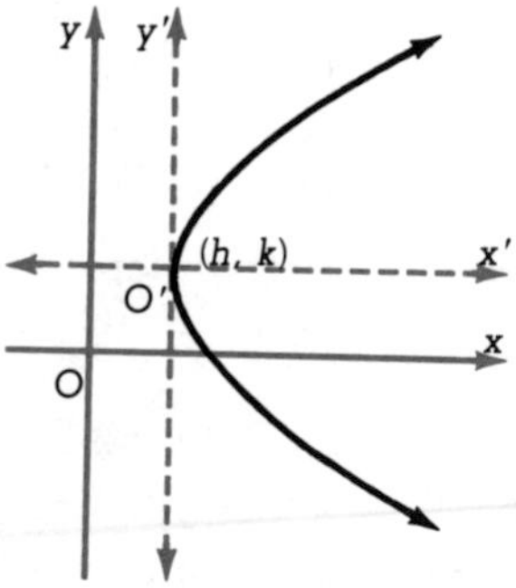

examples

1 Express the equation of the parabola $(y - 1)^2 = 6(x + 4)$ with respect to new axes such that $x = x' - 4$ and $y = y' + 1$.

$$((y' + 1) - 1)^2 = 6((x' - 4) + 4) \quad \textit{Replace } x \textit{ by } x' - 4 \textit{ and } y \textit{ by } y' + 1.$$
$$(y')^2 = 6x'$$

Thus, $(y')^2 = 6x'$ is the equation of the parabola with respect to the x'-axis and the y'-axis. The new origin is at the vertex.

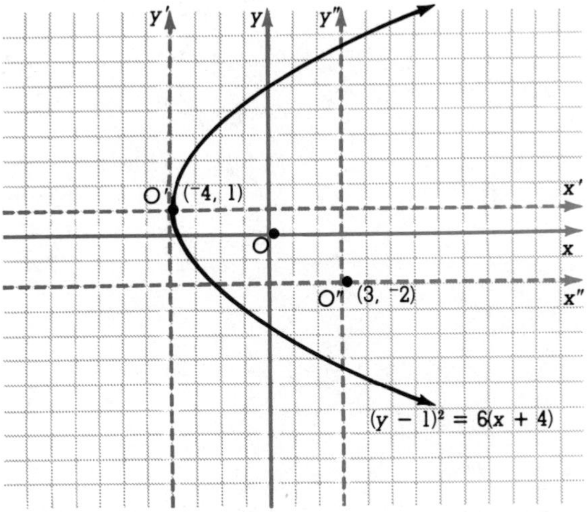

2 Express the equation $(y - 1)^2 = 6(x + 4)$ in terms of a coordinate system (x'', y'') for which the origin is $(3, ^-2)$.

$$((y'' - 2) - 1)^2 = 6((x'' + 3) + 4) \quad \textit{Replace } x \textit{ by } x'' + 3 \textit{ and } y \textit{ by } y'' - 2.$$
$$(y'' - 3)^2 = 6(x'' + 7)$$

Thus, the equation with respect to axes which intersect at $(3, ^-2)$ is $(y'' - 3)^2 = 6(x'' + 7)$.

exercises

Exploratory Find the center of each circle whose equation is given. Then name the translation formulas which will translate the origin to the center of the circle.

1. $(x - 3)^2 + (y - 1)^2 = 4$
2. $(x + 4)^2 + (y - 6)^2 = 16$
3. $x^2 + y^2 + 2x = 0$
4. $x^2 + y^2 + 6x - 4y + 4 = 0$

Find the vertex of each parabola whose equation is given. Then name the translation formulas which will translate the origin to the vertex.

5. $(y - 4)^2 = 2(x - 3)$
6. $(x + 5)^2 = 8(y - 1)$
7. $x^2 + 4x - 6y + 34 = 0$
8. $y^2 - 8x - 2y - 15 = 0$

Written 1-8. Write the equation of each circle or parabola in the exploratory exercises with respect to axes translated so that the new origin is at the center or vertex.

Solve each problem.

9. Write the equation of the circle $(x - 8)^2 + (y + 3)^2 = 25$ with respect to axes translated so that the origin is $(8, ^-3)$.
10. Write the equation of the circle $x^2 + y^2 = 36$ with respect to axes translated so that the origin is $(0, ^-4)$.
11. Write the equation of the circle $x^2 + (y - a)^2 = c^2$ with respect to axes translated so that the origin is $(a, 0)$.
12. Write the equation of the circle $(x - h)^2 + (y - k)^2 = r^2$ with respect to axes translated so that the origin is $(0, k)$.
13. Write the equation of the parabola $(x - 3)^2 = 4(y + 5)$ with respect to axes translated so that the origin is $(3, ^-5)$.
14. Write the equation of the parabola $y^2 = 4px$ with respect to axes translated so that the origin is $(3, 0)$.
15. Write the equation of the parabola $x^2 = 4py$ with respect to axes translated so that the origin is $(0, 4)$.
16. Write the equation of the parabola $y^2 = 4px$ with respect to axes translated so that the origin is $(p, 0)$.

12-4 The Ellipse

An **ellipse** is the set of all points in the plane such that the sum of the distances from two given points, called the **foci**, is constant. Thus, if F and F' are the foci and P and Q are any two points on an ellipse, $PF + PF' = QF + QF'$.

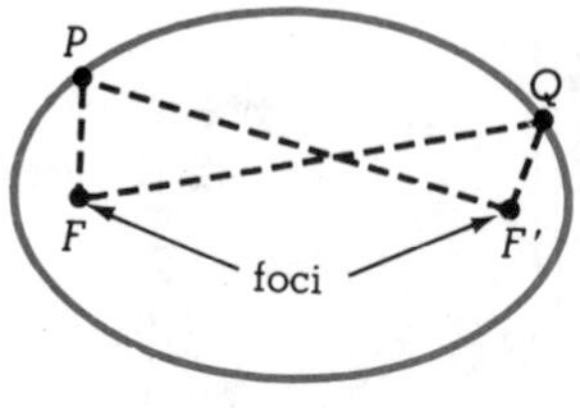

An ellipse has two axes of symmetry. The segments of these axes cut off by the ellipse are called the **major** (longer) and **minor** (shorter) axes. The endpoints of the major axis are called **vertices** and the intersection of the two axes is the **center** of the ellipse. In the figure below, a and b represent the lengths of the **semi-major axis** and **semi-minor axis**, respectively. The distance from the center to a focus is **c**.

What are the lengths of the major axis $\overline{VV'}$ and the minor axis $\overline{BB'}$?

An important relationship exists between the lengths a, b, and c. Since $V'F' = VF$, then $VF + VF' = VV'$, or $2a$. Thus, the sum of the distances from the foci to any point on the ellipse is $2a$. Since $BF + BF' = 2a$ and $BF = BF'$, then $BF = a$. However, by the Pythagorean Theorem, $BF = \sqrt{b^2 + c^2}$. Therefore $a = \sqrt{b^2 + c^2}$, or $a^2 = b^2 + c^2$.

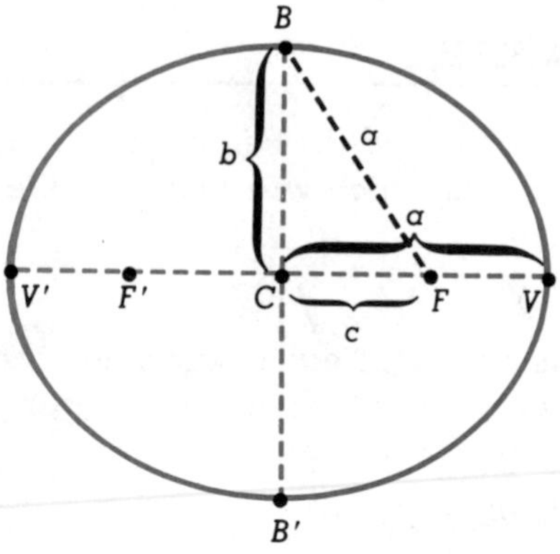

example

1 Name the coordinates of the foci of the ellipse shown below.

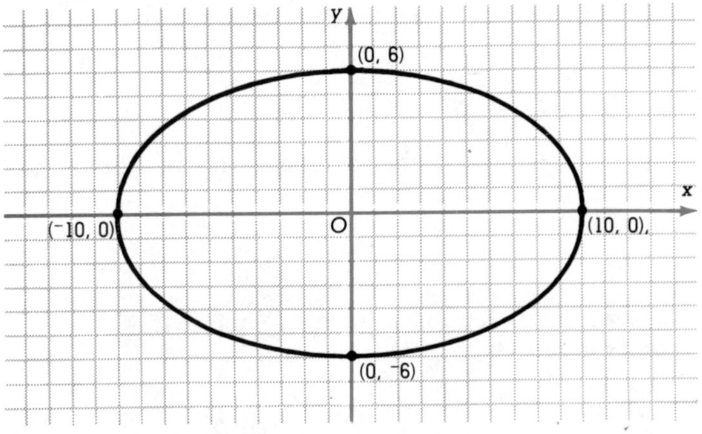

First, find the lengths of the semi-major axis and semi-minor axis.

$a = 10 \qquad b = 6$

Then, find the value of c.

$$a^2 = b^2 + c^2$$
$$100 = 36 + c^2$$
$$64 = c^2$$
$$8 = c$$

Since the center of the ellipse is at the origin the coordinates of the foci are (8, 0) and (⁻8, 0).

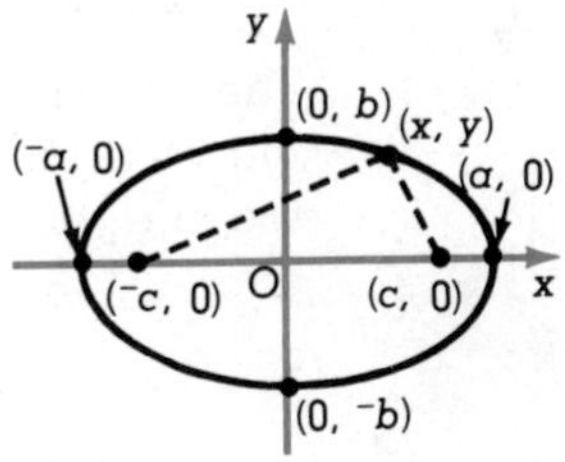

The standard form of the equation of an ellipse can be derived from the definition and the distance formula. Consider the special case when the center is at the origin. Suppose the foci are (c, 0) and (⁻c, 0), and (x, y) is any point on the ellipse. Let $2a$ represent the sum of the distances from (x, y) to the foci.

$\sqrt{(x+c)^2+y^2} + \sqrt{(x-c)^2+y^2} = 2a$	*Apply the distance formula.*
$\sqrt{(x+c)^2+y^2} = 2a - \sqrt{(x-c)^2+y^2}$	*Rearrange terms.*
$(x+c)^2+y^2 = 4a^2 + (x-c)^2 + y^2 - 4a\sqrt{(x-c)^2+y^2}$	*Square each side.*
$a^2 - xc = a\sqrt{(x-c)^2+y^2}$	*Simplify.*
$a^4 - 2a^2xc + x^2c^2 = a^2((x-c)^2+y^2)$	*Square.*
$x^2(a^2-c^2) + a^2y^2 = a^2(a^2-c^2)$	*Simplify.*
$\frac{x^2}{a^2} + \frac{y^2}{a^2-c^2} = 1$	*Divide by $a^2(a^2-c^2)$.*
$\frac{x^2}{a^2} + \frac{y^2}{b^2} = 1$	*Substitute b^2 for $a^2 - c^2$.*

The equation $\frac{x^2}{a^2} + \frac{y^2}{b^2} = 1$ is the equation of an ellipse whose foci are on the x-axis at (c, 0) and (⁻c, 0). Suppose the center of the ellipse is (h, k). The equation of the ellipse in this case is $\frac{(x-h)^2}{a^2} + \frac{(y-k)^2}{b^2} = 1$.

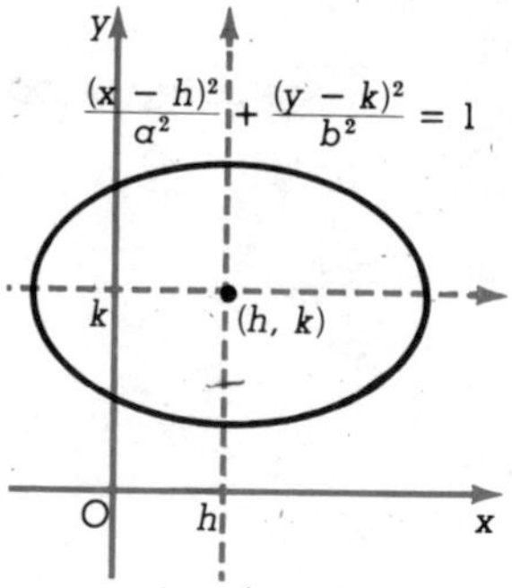

If the foci are on the y-axis at (0, c) and (0, ⁻c), then the equation of the ellipse is $\frac{y^2}{a^2} + \frac{x^2}{b^2} = 1$. If the center is (h, k), then $\frac{(y-k)^2}{a^2} + \frac{(x-h)^2}{b^2} = 1$ is the equation of the ellipse.

Standard Form of the Equation of an Ellipse

The standard form of the equation of an ellipse with center (h, k) and major axis of length 2a, parallel to the x-axis, is

$$\frac{(x-h)^2}{a^2} + \frac{(y-k)^2}{b^2} = 1 \quad \text{where } b^2 = a^2 - c^2.$$

The standard form of the equation of an ellipse with center (h, k) and major axis of length 2a, parallel to the y-axis, is

$$\frac{(y-k)^2}{a^2} + \frac{(x-h)^2}{b^2} = 1 \quad \text{where } b^2 = a^2 - c^2.$$

example

2 Draw the ellipse which is given by the equation $\frac{(x-4)^2}{121} + \frac{(y+5)^2}{64} = 1$.

$a = \sqrt{121}$ or 11 $\qquad b = \sqrt{64}$ or 8

The center of the ellipse is (4, ⁻5). Thus, the vertices are (15, ⁻5) and (⁻7, ⁻5) and the endpoints of the minor axis are (4, 3) and (4, ⁻13).

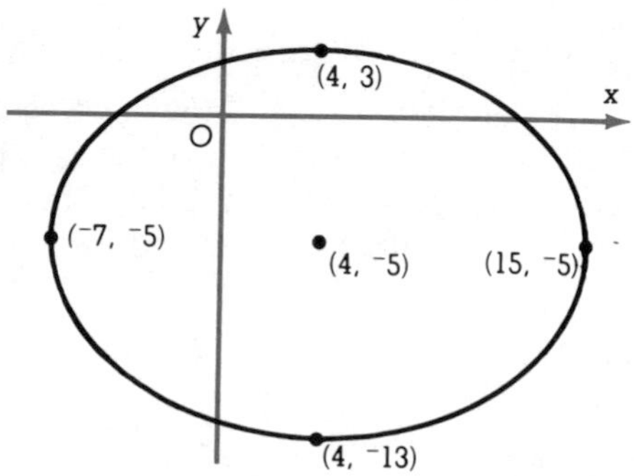

The general form of the equation of an ellipse is a second-degree equation of the form $Ax^2 + Cy^2 + Dx + Ey + F = 0$, where $A \neq 0$, $C \neq 0$, and A and C have the same sign. An equation in general form can be transformed into standard form to determine the center, (h, k), the semi-major axis, a, and the semi-minor axis, b.

If the major axis of the ellipse is not parallel to the x-axis or y-axis, the general equation has an additional term, Bxy.

example

3 **Find the coordinates of the center, the foci, and the vertices of the ellipse $9x^2 + 4y^2 - 18x + 16y - 11 = 0$. Then draw the graph.**

Write the equation in standard form.

$$(9x^2 - 18x + \quad) + (4y^2 + 16y + \quad) = 11 \qquad \textit{Group the terms.}$$

$$9(x^2 - 2x + 1) + 4(y^2 + 4y + 4) = 11 + 9 + 16 \qquad \textit{Complete the square.}$$

$$9(x - 1)^2 + 4(y + 2)^2 = 36$$

$$\frac{(y + 2)^2}{9} + \frac{(x - 1)^2}{4} = 1 \qquad h = 1, k = {}^-2, a = 3, b = 2$$

The coordinates of the center are $(1, {}^-2)$.

To determine coordinates of the foci, first find c.

$$a^2 = b^2 + c^2$$

$$9 = 4 + c^2 \qquad \textit{a is 3 and b is 2}$$

$$5 = c^2$$

$$\pm\sqrt{5} = c$$

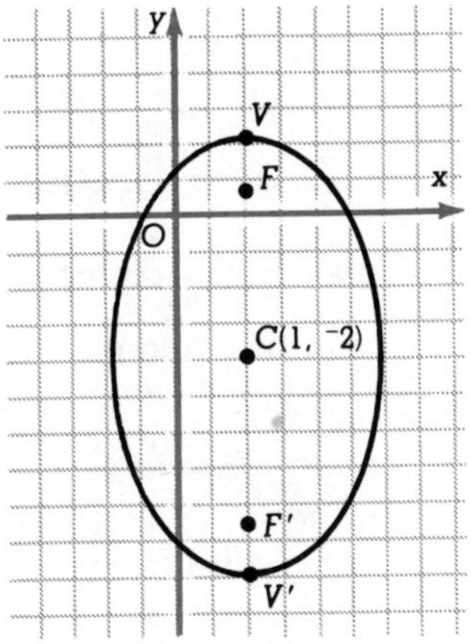

The coordinates of the foci are $(1, {}^-2 + \sqrt{5})$ and $(1, {}^-2 - \sqrt{5})$. The coordinates of the vertices are $(1, 1)$ and $(1, {}^-5)$. *Why?*

exercises

Exploratory Write the equation of each ellipse described below.

1. Center $(0, 0)$, $a = 6$, $b = 4$, horizontal major axis
2. Center $(0, 0)$, $a = 8$, $b = 6$, vertical major axis
3. Center $(3, 5)$, $a = 4$, $b = 2$, vertical major axis
4. Center $({}^-3, {}^-1)$, $a = 7$, $b = 5$, horizontal major axis
5. Foci $({}^-2, 0)$ and $(2, 0)$, $a = 7$
6. Foci $(2, 3)$ and $(2, {}^-3)$, $a = 4$

Written Name the center, the foci, and the vertices of each ellipse whose equation is given. Then draw the graph.

1. $\frac{(x - 5)^2}{25} + \frac{y^2}{4} = 1$
2. $\frac{(y - 3)^2}{16} + \frac{x^2}{9} = 1$
3. $\frac{(x - 3)^2}{25} + \frac{(y - 4)^2}{16} = 1$
4. $\frac{(y + 2)^2}{25} + \frac{(x - 1)^2}{4} = 1$
5. $4y^2 + x^2 - 8y + 6x + 9 = 0$
6. $x^2 - 12x + 3y^2 + 12y + 39 = 0$
7. $4x^2 + 25y^2 + 250y + 525 = 0$
8. $x^2 - 2x + y^2 - 2y - 6 = 0$
9. $y^2 - 8y + 3x^2 + 30x + 85 = 0$
10. $9y^2 + 108y + 4x^2 - 56x = {}^-484$
11. $4y^2 - 4y + 16x^2 + 16x - 11 = 0$
12. $12x^2 + 36x + 16y^2 + 32y - 5 = 0$

12-5 More about the Ellipse

The shape of an ellipse is determined by its **eccentricity.** The eccentricity, e, of an ellipse is defined as $e = \frac{c}{a}$. Since $0 < c < a$, then $0 < e < 1$. If e is close to zero, the two foci are near the center of the ellipse. In this case, the ellipse looks nearly like a circle. If e is close to one, then the foci are near the ends of the major axis. In this case, the ellipse is very elongated.

Sometimes it is necessary to find the length of the semi-minor axis, b, when the length of the semi-major axis, a, and the eccentricity, e, are known. You know that $a^2 = b^2 + c^2$. Since $c = ae$ and $c^2 = a^2e^2$, it can be shown that $b^2 = a^2(1 - e^2)$.

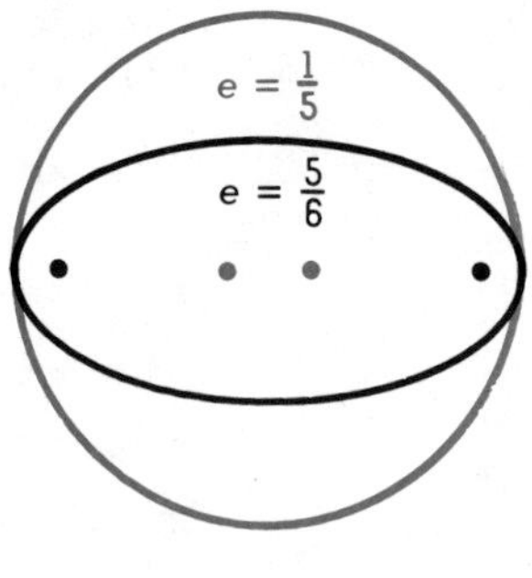

When e = 0, the ellipse is a circle.

example

1 **Write the equation of the ellipse with center (⁻2, 3), semi-major axis of length 7 units, and eccentricity $\frac{1}{2}$. The major axis is parallel to the x-axis.**

First, find b^2.

$$b^2 = a^2(1 - e^2)$$

$$b^2 = 49\left(1 - \frac{1}{4}\right) \qquad \textit{a = 7 and e} = \frac{1}{2}$$

$$= \frac{147}{4}$$

Then, write the equation of the ellipse.

$$\frac{(x-h)^2}{a^2} + \frac{(y-k)^2}{b^2} = 1$$

$$\frac{(x+2)^2}{49} + \frac{(y-3)^2}{\frac{147}{4}} = 1 \qquad h = {}^-2,\ k = 3,\ a = 7, \text{ and } b^2 = \frac{147}{4}$$

The equation of the ellipse is $\frac{(x+2)^2}{49} + \frac{(y-3)^2}{\frac{147}{4}} = 1$ or $\frac{(x+2)^2}{49} + \frac{4(y-3)^2}{147} = 1$.

A more accurate graph of an ellipse can be drawn if the length of the **latus rectum** is known. The latus rectum of an ellipse is a chord perpendicular to the major axis through a focus. In the figure at the right, $\overline{MN}$ is the latus rectum.

If the center of the ellipse is (0, 0) and the ellipse has foci (c, 0) and (⁻c, 0), the equation has the form $\frac{x^2}{a^2} + \frac{y^2}{b^2} = 1$. If $x = c$ the value of y is $\pm\frac{b}{a}\sqrt{a^2 - c^2}$, or $\pm\frac{b^2}{a}$. Thus, the coordinates of point M shown in the figure at the right are $\left(c, \frac{b^2}{a}\right)$ and therefore $MN = \frac{2b^2}{a}$.

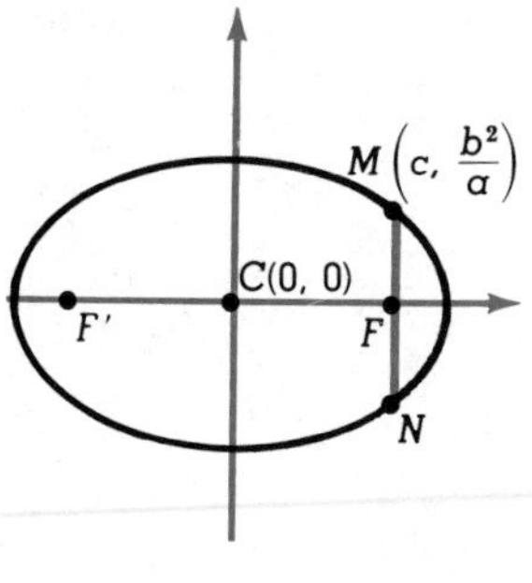

The length of a latus rectum of an ellipse is $\frac{2b^2}{a}$, where a is the length of the semi-major axis and b is the length of the semi-minor axis.

Latus Rectum of an Ellipse

example

2 An ellipse has center (0, 3), major axis of length 12 units parallel to the y-axis, and eccentricity $\frac{1}{2}$. Find the length of the latus rectum and determine a, b, and c. Then draw the graph.

Use the formula $b^2 = a^2(1 - e^2)$ to determine b^2.

$b^2 = 36\left(1 - \frac{1}{4}\right)$ or 27   *$a = 6$ and $e = \frac{1}{2}$.*

$b = \sqrt{27}$ or $3\sqrt{3}$

Then find the length of the latus rectum.

$\frac{2b^2}{a} = \frac{2(27)}{6}$ or 9

Use the formula $a^2 = b^2 + c^2$ to determine c.

$c^2 = a^2 - b^2$

$c^2 = 36 - 27$

$c^2 = 9$ so $c = 3$

The length of the latus rectum is 9, a is 6, b is $3\sqrt{3}$, and c is 3.

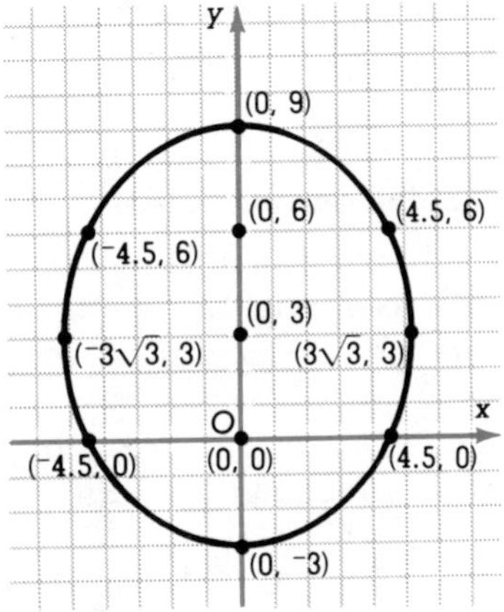

Ellipses have many applications. An ellipse is the path of an object in orbit such as the planets around the sun and satellites around the planets. Elliptic gears have special uses where slow, powerful action is needed. Sometimes bridge arches are elliptic in shape. An ellipse has the property that light rays or other radiated energy emitted from one focus will be reflected to the other focus. This property of an ellipse is utilized in the construction of "whispering galleries" where walls and ceilings are roughly elliptical. Any sound emitted from a position at one focus is reflected from walls and ceiling to the other focus where even a whisper can be heard distinctly although other sounds may be in the room.

exercises

Exploratory Name the coordinates of the foci of each ellipse described below. The major axis of each ellipse is horizontal.

1. Center (0, 0), $a = 6$, $b = 4$
2. Center (0, 0), $a = 5$, $b = 3$
3. Center (3, 5), $a = 4$, $b = 1$
4. Center ($^-3$, 2), $a = 7$, $b = 2$

5-8. Find the eccentricity of each ellipse described in problems 1-4.

9-12. Find the length of the latus rectum for each ellipse described in problems 1-4.

Written Name the center, foci, eccentricity, and the length of the latus rectum for each ellipse whose equation is given. Then draw the graph.

1. $4x^2 + 9y^2 = 36$
2. $5x^2 + 8y^2 = 40$
3. $4y^2 - 8y + 9x^2 - 54x + 49 = 0$
4. $x^2 + 16y^2 - 6x - 64y + 57 = 0$
5. $25x^2 + y^2 - 100x + 6y + 84 = 0$
6. $18x^2 + 12y^2 - 144x - 48y + 120 = 0$

Write the equation of each ellipse described below.

7. Center (0, 0), $a = 2$, $e = 0.75$, vertical major axis
8. Center (0, 0), $a = 10$, $e = 0.5$ horizontal major axis
9. Center (2, $^-2$), $a = 9$, $e = \frac{2}{3}$, horizontal major axis
10. Center (3, 1), $a = 6$, $e = \frac{1}{3}$, vertical major axis
11. Foci (3, 5) and (1, 5), $e = 0.25$
12. Foci (2, 1) and ($^-4$, 1), $e = 0.6$
13. Foci (1, $^-1$) and (1, 5), passes through (4, 2)
14. Center (3, 0), $e = 0.7$, $2a = 20$, vertical major axis

Challenge Solve each problem.

1. Draw the ellipse which is tangent to the coordinate axes and has center ($^-3$, 7). Then write the equation in general form.
2. Find the equation of the circle that passes through the endpoints of the latera recta of the ellipse $\frac{x^2}{16} + \frac{y^2}{12} = 1$.
3. Find the equation of the circle that passes through the endpoints of the latera recta of the ellipse $\frac{y^2}{25} + \frac{x^2}{9} = 1$.
4. Write the equations of the circles which are internally and externally tangent to the ellipse $4x^2 + 9y^2 = 36$ if the three conics have the same center.
5. The orbit of an earth satellite is an ellipse with the center of the earth at one focus. The eccentricity of the orbit is 0.16 and the major axis is 10,440 miles. If the mean diameter of the earth is 7920 miles find the greatest and least distances of the satellite from the surface of the earth.

12-6 The Hyperbola

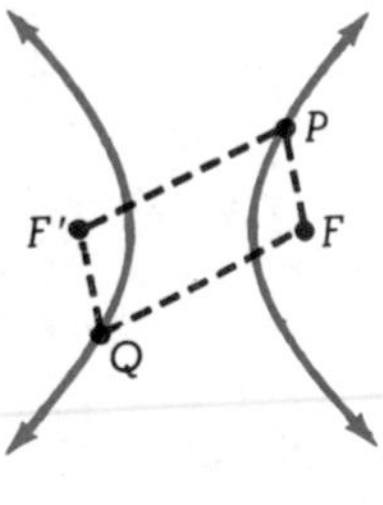

A **hyperbola** is the set of all points in the plane such that the absolute value of the difference of the distances from two given points, called the **foci**, is constant. Thus, if F and F' are the foci of a hyperbola and P and Q are any two points on the hyperbola, $|PF - PF'| = |QF - QF'|$.

The **center** of a hyperbola is the midpoint of the segment connecting the foci. The point on each branch of the hyperbola nearest the center is called a **vertex.** The **asymptotes** of a hyperbola are lines which the branches of the curve approach as the curve recedes from the center. Like the ellipse, the distance from the center to a vertex is a units and the distance from the center to a focus is c units.

A hyperbola has two axes of symmetry, as shown below. The line segment of length $2a$ which has its endpoints at the vertices is called the **transverse axis.** The segment of length $2b$ perpendicular to the transverse axis at its center is called the **conjugate axis.** For a hyperbola, the lengths a, b, and c are related by the formula $a^2 + b^2 = c^2$.

The relationship between a, b, and c is different for ellipses and hyperbolas.

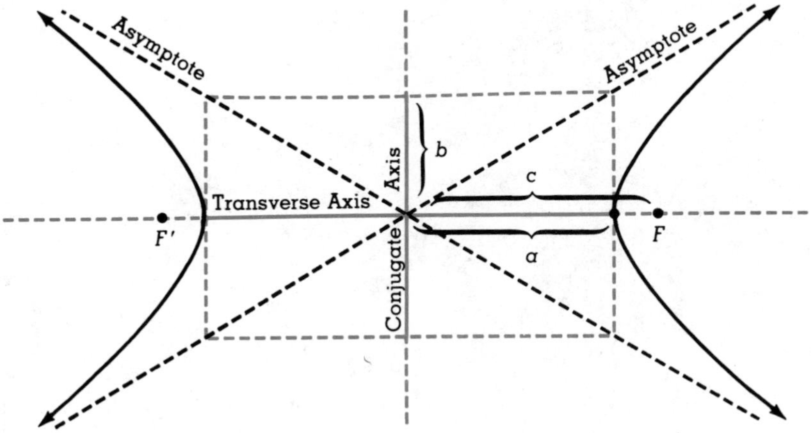

The **standard form** of the equation of a hyperbola can be derived from the definition and the distance formula. Consider the special case when the center is at the origin. Suppose the foci are on the x-axis at $(c, 0)$ and $(^-c, 0)$ and (x, y) is any point on the hyperbola. Let $2a$ represent the constant difference.

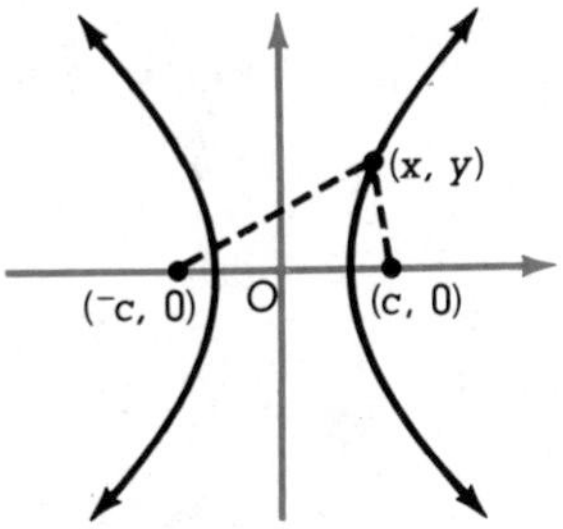

$$\sqrt{(x-c)^2+y^2} - \sqrt{(x+c)^2+y^2} = 2a$$ *Apply the distance formula.*

$$\sqrt{(x-c)^2+y^2} = 2a + \sqrt{(x+c)^2+y^2}$$ *Rearrange terms.*

$$(x-c)^2+y^2 = 4a^2 + 4a\sqrt{(x+c)^2+y^2} + (x+c)^2+y^2$$ *Square each side.*

$$^-4xc - 4a^2 = 4a\sqrt{(x+c)^2+y^2}$$ *Simplify.*

$$xc + a^2 = {}^-a\sqrt{(x+c)^2+y^2}$$

$$x^2c^2 + 2a^2xc + a^4 = a^2x^2 + 2a^2xc + a^2c^2 + a^2y^2$$ *Square.*

$$(c^2-a^2)x^2 - a^2y^2 = a^2(c^2-a^2)$$ *Simplify.*

$$\frac{x^2}{a^2} - \frac{y^2}{c^2-a^2} = 1$$ *Divide by $a^2(c^2 - a^2)$.*

$$\frac{x^2}{a^2} - \frac{y^2}{b^2} = 1$$ $c^2 - a^2 = b^2$

The equation $\frac{x^2}{a^2} - \frac{y^2}{b^2} = 1$ is the equation of a hyperbola whose foci are on the x-axis at $(c, 0)$ and $(^-c, 0)$. Suppose the center of the hyperbola is (h, k). Then the equation of the hyperbola is $\frac{(x-h)^2}{a^2} - \frac{(y-k)^2}{b^2} = 1$.

If the foci are on the y-axis at $(0, c)$ and $(0, ^-c)$, the equation of the hyperbola is $\frac{y^2}{a^2} - \frac{x^2}{b^2} = 1$. If the center is (h, k) the equation of the hyperbola is $\frac{(y-k)^2}{a^2} - \frac{(x-h)^2}{b^2} = 1$.

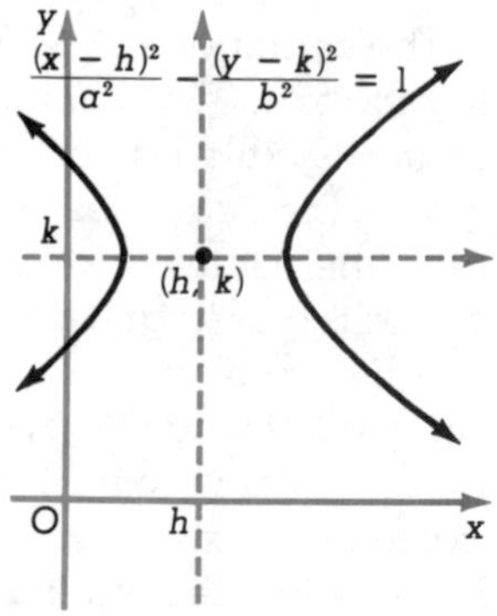

Standard Form of the Equation of a Hyperbola

The standard form of the equation of a hyperbola with center (h, k) and transverse axis of length $2a$, parallel to the x-axis, is

$$\frac{(x-h)^2}{a^2} - \frac{(y-k)^2}{b^2} = 1 \qquad \text{where } b^2 = c^2 - a^2.$$

The standard form of the equation of a hyperbola with center (h, k) and transverse axis of length $2a$, parallel to the y-axis, is

$$\frac{(y-k)^2}{a^2} - \frac{(x-h)^2}{b^2} = 1 \qquad \text{where } b^2 = c^2 - a^2.$$

example

1 **Find the equation of a hyperbola if the foci are $F(2, 5)$ and $F'(^-4, 5)$, and the transverse axis is 4 units long.**

First find the center. *A sketch is helpful.*

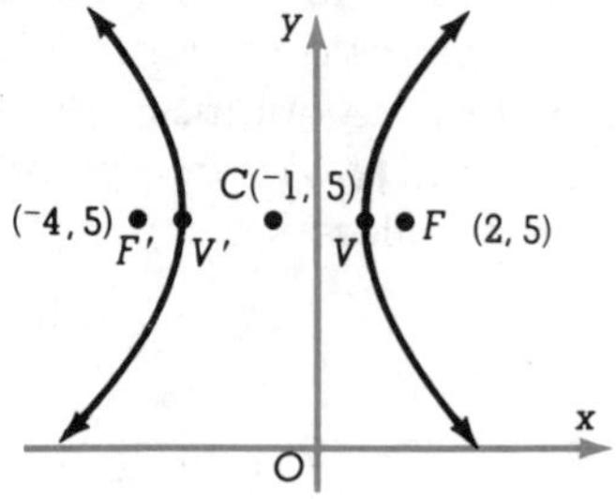

The center is the midpoint of FF'. Thus, the center is $(^-1, 5)$.

Then determine c, a^2, and b^2.

$c = CF$	$2a = VV'$	$c^2 = a^2 + b^2$
$c = 3$	$2a = 4$	$9 = 4 + b^2$
	$a = 2$	$5 = b^2$
	$a^2 = 4$	

Since the transverse axis is parallel to the x-axis, substitute values into the standard form $\frac{(x-h)^2}{a^2} - \frac{(y-k)^2}{b^2} = 1$.

The equation of the hyperbola is $\frac{(x+1)^2}{4} - \frac{(y-5)^2}{5} = 1$.

Before graphing a hyperbola, it is helpful to sketch the asymptotes. Valuable information about asymptotes can be obtained by studying the equation of a hyperbola centered at the origin.

Consider the equation $\frac{x^2}{a^2} - \frac{y^2}{b^2} = 1$. If the equation is solved for y, then $y = \pm\frac{b}{a}\sqrt{x^2 - a^2}$. As x becomes very large, $x^2 - a^2$ comes close to x^2 and y comes close to $\pm\frac{b}{a}x$. Thus, the equations of the asymptotes are $y = \frac{b}{a}x$ and $y = -\frac{b}{a}x$, as shown below. In this case, the asymptotes form the diagonals of the rectangle which has vertices (a, b), $(^-a, b)$, $(^-a, ^-b)$, and $(a, ^-b)$. Notice that the endpoints of the transverse and conjugate axes are the midpoints of the sides of the rectangle.

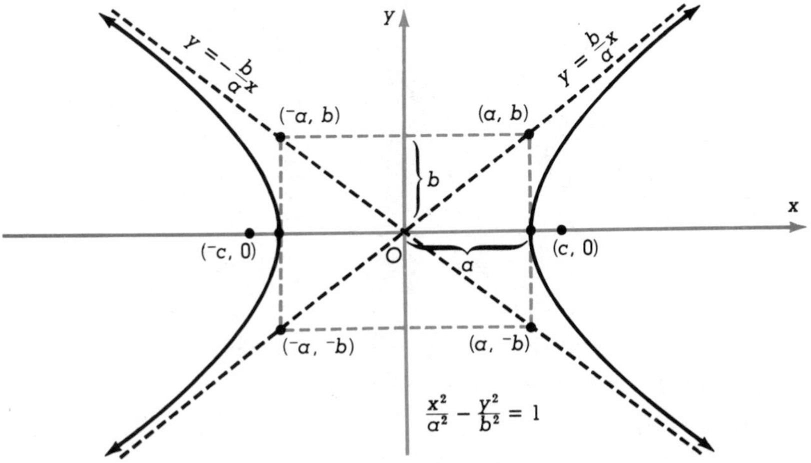

The asymptotes of a hyperbola always intersect at the center (h, k) of the hyperbola. If a hyperbola has a horizontal transverse axis the asymptotes have slope $\pm\frac{b}{a}$. If a hyperbola has a vertical transverse axis the asymptotes have slope $\pm\frac{a}{b}$. Thus, the equations of the asymptotes can be written using point-slope form.

Equations of Asymptotes

The equations of the asymptotes of a hyperbola with a horizontal transverse axis are

$$y - k = \pm\frac{b}{a}(x - h).$$

The equations of the asymptotes of a hyperbola with a vertical transverse axis are

$$y - k = \pm\frac{a}{b}(x - h).$$

example

2 Write equations for the asymptotes of the hyperbola $\frac{(y-4)^2}{16} - \frac{(x+2)^2}{9} = 1$. Then find the foci and vertices and draw the graph.

The hyperbola has a vertical transverse axis and center $(^-2, 4)$. Since $a = 4$ and $b = 3$, the equations of the asymptotes are $y - 4 = \pm\frac{4}{3}(x + 2)$.

The vertices are $(^-2, 8)$ and $(^-2, 0)$. *Why?* Also, $c^2 = a^2 + b^2$, so $c^2 = 25$ and $c = 5$. Therefore the foci are $(^-2, 9)$ and $(^-2, ^-1)$.

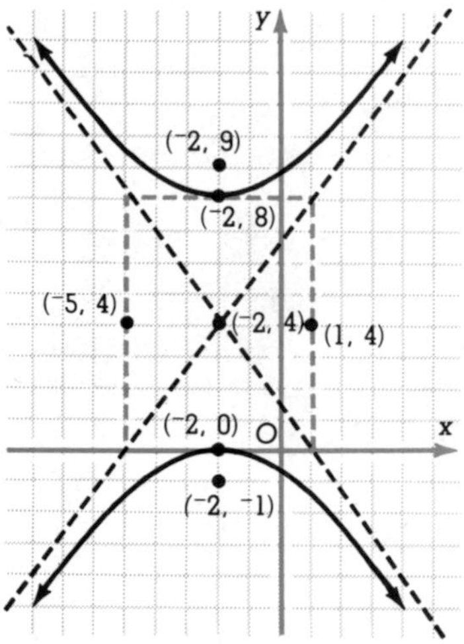

exercises

Exploratory Write the equation of each hyperbola described below.

1. Center (0, 0), $a = 8$, $b = 5$, horizontal transverse axis
2. Center (0, 0), $a = 7$, $b = 4$, vertical transverse axis
3. Center $(6, ^-2)$, $a = 4$, $b = 5$, vertical transverse axis
4. Center $(^-1, 4)$, $a = 2$, $b = 3$, horizontal transverse axis
5. Foci (10, 0) and $(^-10, 0)$, $2a = 16$
6. Foci (0, 5) and $(0, ^-5)$, $2a = 8$
7. Vertices (1, 2) and $(1, ^-2)$, $b = 2$
8. Vertices (3, 4) and (3, 0), $b = 3$

Written Name the center, foci, vertices, and the equations of the asymptotes of each hyperbola whose equation is given. Then draw the graph.

1. $\frac{y^2}{64} - \frac{x^2}{36} = 1$
2. $\frac{x^2}{9} - \frac{y^2}{10} = 1$
3. $\frac{x^2}{36} - \frac{y^2}{81} = 1$
4. $\frac{x^2}{25} - \frac{y^2}{16} = 1$
5. $\frac{(x+6)^2}{36} - \frac{(y+3)^2}{9} = 1$
6. $\frac{(y-3)^2}{25} - \frac{(x-2)^2}{16} = 1$

Write the equation of each hyperbola described below.

7. Center $(4, ^-2)$, focus $(7, ^-2)$, vertex $(6, ^-2)$
8. Center (3, 3), focus (8, 3), vertex (6, 3)
9. Center $(3, ^-1)$, vertex $(6, ^-1)$, equation of one asymptote $2x - 3y = 9$
10. Center (4, 2), vertex (4, 5), equation of one asymptote $4y - 3x = ^-4$

12-7 More about the Hyperbola

The general form of the equation of a hyperbola which has axes parallel to the coordinate axes is $Ax^2 + Cy^2 + Dx + Ey + F = 0$, where $A \neq 0$, $C \neq 0$, and A and C have different signs. An equation in general form can be transformed into standard form by grouping and completing the square.

example

1 **Find the coordinates of the center, the foci, and the vertices of the hyperbola $25x^2 - 9y^2 - 100x - 72y - 269 = 0$. Then draw the graph.**

Write the equation in standard form.

Group the terms.
Complete the square.

$$(25x^2 - 100x + \quad) - (9y^2 + 72y + \quad) = 269$$
$$25(x^2 - 4x + 4) - 9(x^2 + 8y + 16) = 269 + 100 - 144$$
$$25(x - 2)^2 - 9(y + 4)^2 = 225$$
$$\frac{(x - 2)^2}{9} - \frac{(y + 4)^2}{25} = 1$$

Thus, the center is $(2, {}^-4)$, a is 3, b is 5, and c is $\sqrt{a^2 + b^2}$ or $\sqrt{34}$. The foci are $(2 + \sqrt{34}, {}^-4)$ and $(2 - \sqrt{34}, {}^-4)$. The vertices are $(5, {}^-4)$ and $({}^-1, {}^-4)$.

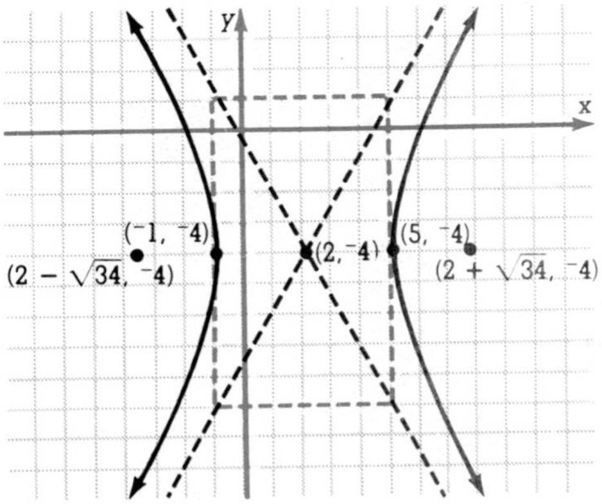

The shape of a hyperbola is determined by its eccentricity. As for the ellipse, the eccentricity, e, is defined as $e = \frac{c}{a}$. Since $c^2 = a^2 + b^2$ for a hyperbola, it can be shown that $b^2 = a^2(e^2 - 1)$.

$e > 1$
for a hyperbola

example

2 **Write the equation of the hyperbola with center $({}^-3, 1)$, a focus $(2, 1)$, and eccentricity $\frac{5}{4}$.**

This hyperbola has a horizontal transverse axis, so the equation has the form $\frac{(x - h)^2}{a^2} - \frac{(y - k)^2}{b^2} = 1$. Since the focus is 5 units to the right of center, c is 5. Also, $e = \frac{c}{a}$ where $e = \frac{5}{4}$. Thus, $\frac{5}{4} = \frac{5}{a}$, so $a = 4$. Then $b^2 = c^2 - a^2$, or 9.

Therefore the equation is $\frac{(x + 3)^2}{16} - \frac{(y - 1)^2}{9} = 1$.

As in the other conics, the **latus rectum** of a hyperbola is a chord through a focus. The length of a latus rectum of a hyperbola is $\frac{2b^2}{a}$. The equation of the hyperbola at the right is $\frac{x^2}{4} - \frac{y^2}{9} = 1$ and the latera recta are $\overline{PQ}$ and $\overline{RS}$. Therefore, $PQ = RS = \frac{2(9)}{2}$ or 9.

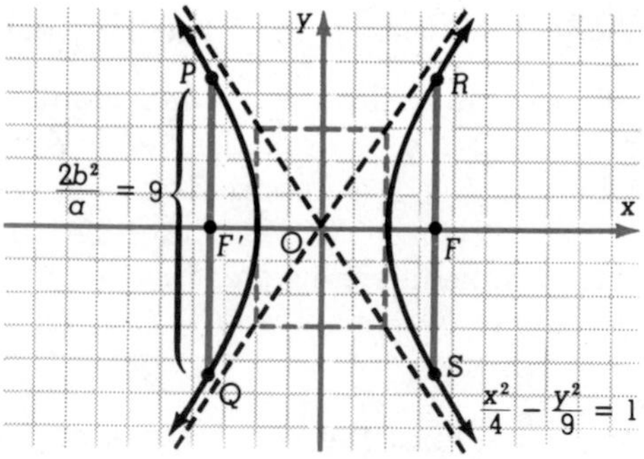

Two hyperbolas such that the transverse axis of one is the conjugate axis of the other, and conversely, are said to be **conjugate hyperbolas**. Conjugate hyperbolas share the same asymptotes. The equations of conjugate hyperbolas are closely related. If the equation of a hyperbola is in standard form, the equation of its conjugate can be written by reversing the x^2 and y^2 terms. For example, the equations $\frac{x^2}{9} - \frac{y^2}{4} = 1$ and $\frac{y^2}{4} - \frac{x^2}{9} = 1$ represent conjugate hyperbolas.

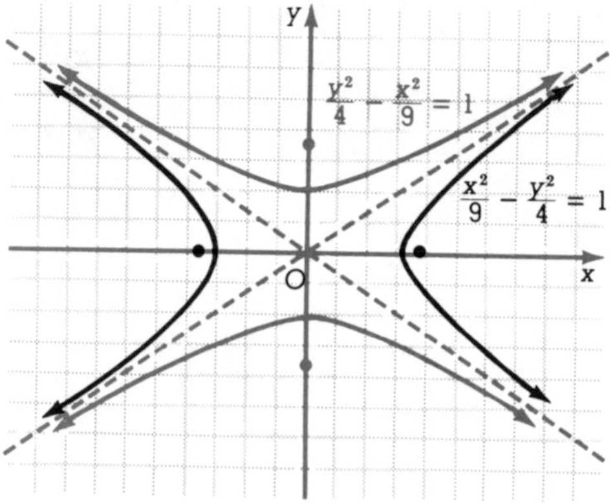

If $a = b$ in the standard form of a hyperbola, it is an **equilateral hyperbola** and the asymptotes are perpendicular. A special case of the equilateral hyperbola is when the coordinate axes are the asymptotes. The equation of such a hyperbola is $xy = k$, where k is a positive or negative constant. The branches of the equilateral hyperbola lie in the first and third quadrants if k is positive and in the second and fourth quadrants if k is negative.

example

3 **Graph the hyperbola $xy = 9$.**

The vertices of the hyperbola must lie along the line $y = x$, since the branches lie in the first and third quadrants. Thus, the vertices are (3, 3) and ($^-3$, $^-3$).

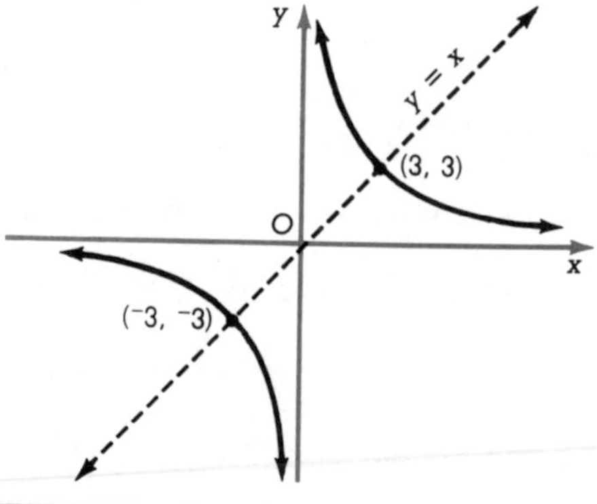

exercises

Exploratory Write the standard form of each equation.

1. $5x^2 - 9y^2 = 45$
2. $25y^2 - 4x^2 - 100 = 0$
3. $4y^2 - x^2 + 4x - 8 = 0$
4. $x^2 - y^2 + 2y - 5 = 0$

5-8. Find the eccentricity of each hyperbola whose equation is given in problems 1-4.

9-12. Find the length of the latus rectum of each hyperbola whose equation is given in problems 1-4.

13-16. Write the equation of the conjugate of each hyperbola whose equation is given in problems 1-4.

17-20. Graph each equation given in problems 1-4.

Written Graph each equation.

1. $xy = 25$
2. $xy = 12$
3. $xy = 8$
4. $xy = {}^-16$
5. $4xy = {}^-9$
6. $9xy = 25$

Name the center, foci, vertices, and the equations of the asymptotes of the hyperbola which has the given equation. Then draw the graph.

7. $y^2 - 5x^2 + 20x = 50$
8. $9x^2 - 4y^2 - 54x - 40y - 55 = 0$
9. $9x^2 - 4y^2 - 90x - 24y = {}^-153$
10. $49x^2 - 25y^2 + 294x + 200y = 1184$

Write the equation of each hyperbola described below.

11. Center $(3, {}^-1)$, focus $(3, {}^-4)$, $e = \frac{3}{2}$
12. Center $(0, 4)$, focus $(0, 9)$, $e = \frac{5}{4}$
13. Foci $({}^-5, 0)$ and $(5, 0)$, $e = \frac{5}{3}$
14. Foci $(0, 8)$ and $(0, {}^-8)$, $e = \frac{4}{3}$
15. Foci $(4, 0)$ and $({}^-2, 0)$, slope of asymptotes $= \pm 4$
16. Foci $(1, 5)$ and $(1, {}^-3)$, slope of asymptotes $= \pm 2$
17. Center $({}^-3, 1)$, $a = 4$, horizontal transverse axis, length of latus rectum $= 8$
18. Center $(0, 5)$, $b = 3$, vertical transverse axis, length of latus rectum $= 9$
19. Vertices $(5, {}^-1)$ and $(5, 7)$, $e = 2$
20. Vertices $({}^-3, 1)$ and $(7, 1)$, $e = \frac{6}{5}$

Solve each problem.

21. Write the equation of an equilateral hyperbola with foci $(0, 5)$ and $(0, {}^-5)$.
22. Write the equation of an equilateral hyperbola with foci $(8, 0)$ and $({}^-8, 0)$.

Challenge Solve each problem.

1. Write the equation of the hyperbola which passes through $(2, 0)$ and has asymptotes with equations $x - 2y = 0$ and $x + 2y = 0$.
2. Write the equation of the hyperbola which passes through $(4, 2)$ and has asymptotes with equations $y = 2x$ and $y = {}^-2x + 4$.
3. Find the eccentricity of the hyperbola which has foci $(1, {}^-4)$ and $(1, 6)$ and passes through $(1, 4)$.
4. Find the eccentricity of the hyperbola which has foci $(0, 3)$ and $(0, {}^-3)$ and passes through $(0, 2)$.

Parabola

Given a point F and a line ℓ, you can determine points of a parabola. Join any point, say M, on line ℓ by a straight line to F, the focus. Then construct the perpendicular bisector of $\overline{FM}$. It will intersect the perpendicular to line ℓ from M at a point P on the parabola. By selecting another point M' and repeating the construction, additional points on the parabola can be found. Find several points, then connect the points with a smooth curve.

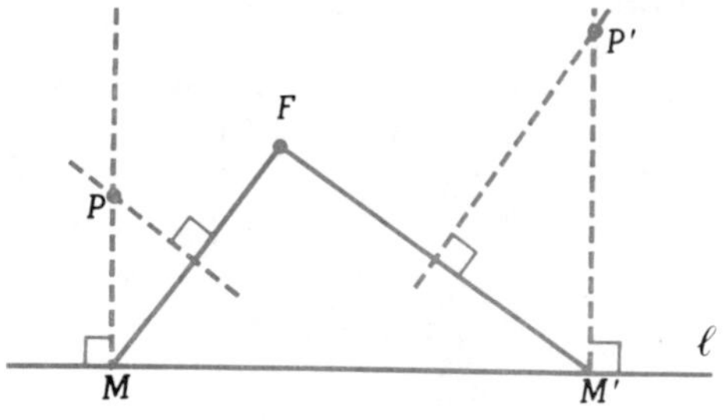

To prove this, draw $\overline{PF}$ and prove that $\overline{PF}$ is congruent to $\overline{PM}$.

Ellipse

An ellipse can be drawn as follows. Place a thumb tack on a drawing board at each of two points, F and F'. Then knot together the ends of a piece of string to form a loop of length greater than $2FF'$. Place the loop over the tacks. Trace the ellipse by moving a pencil around the loop, keeping the string taut, as shown at the right.

By modifying the distance FF' and the length of the loop, various sizes and shapes of ellipses can be drawn.

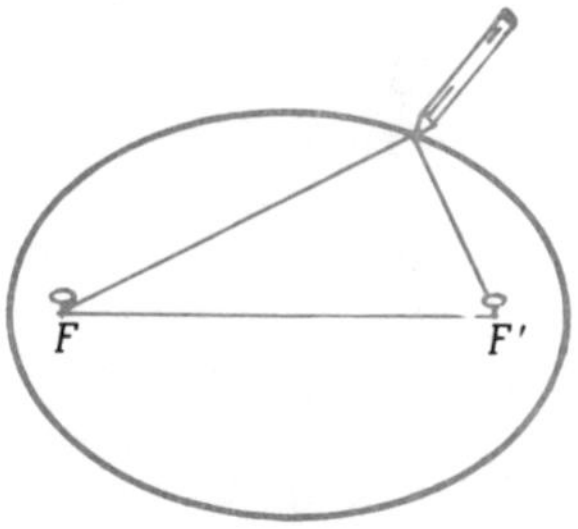

What special case results if F coincides with F'?

Hyperbola

A hyperbola can be drawn as follows. Place thumb tacks at the points to be used as foci. Tie a string to a pencil, allowing two free lengths of string. Knot together the ends of the string so that the lengths from the knot to the pencil differ less than the distance between the thumb tacks. Loop both strands over one tack and run the longer strand around the other tack. Hold the strings below the knot and draw taut by means of the pencil, as shown at the right. Keeping the strings taut, pull on the strings. The pencil will trace part of one branch of a hyperbola. By reversing the position of the knot and pencil another portion of the hyperbola can be drawn.

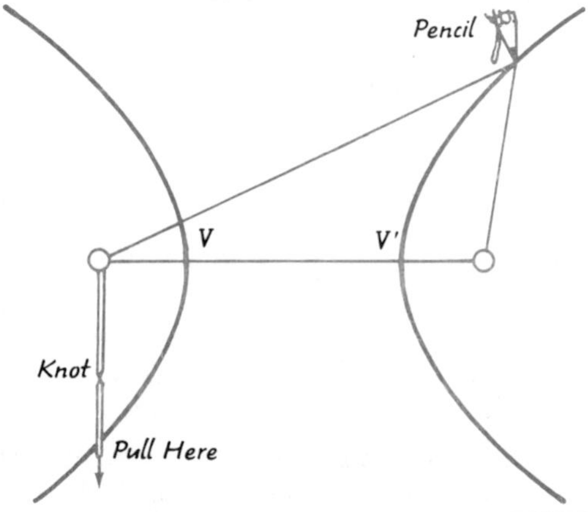

12-8 Conic Sections

Parabolas, circles, ellipses, and hyperbolas can be formed by the intersection of a plane with a conical surface, as shown below. Thus, these curves are called **conic sections.**

Each conical surface has two nappes, separated by a vertex.

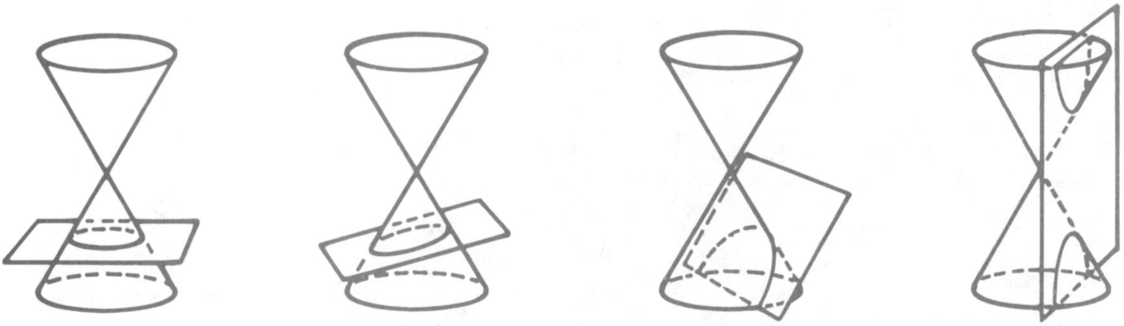

circle | ellipse | parabola | hyperbola

If the plane passes through the vertex of the conical surface, the intersection is a **degenerate case.** The degenerate cases are a point, a line, and two intersecting lines.

How can each degenerate case be formed?

The conic sections can also be defined using eccentricity. A conic section is a set of points in the plane such that for any point of the set the ratio of its distance from a fixed point to its distance from a fixed line is constant. The ratio is the eccentricity of the curve, denoted by e. When $e = 1$, the conic is a parabola. When $e < 1$, the conic is a circle or an ellipse, and when $e > 1$, the conic is a hyperbola.

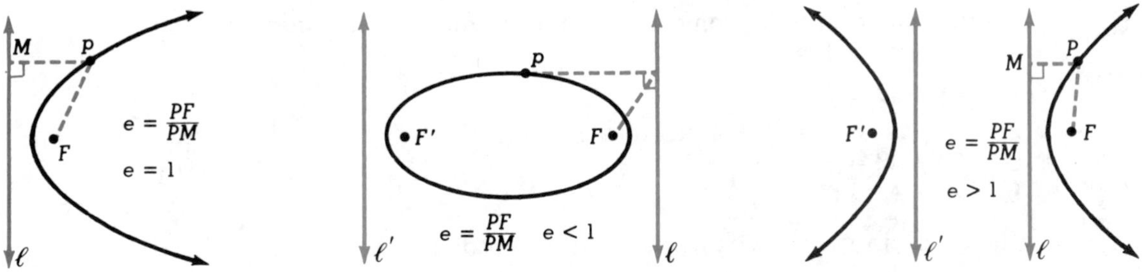

Parabola | Ellipse | Hyperbola

Notice that hyperbolas and ellipses have two directrices.

As you have seen, each conic section can be described by a second-degree equation in two variables.

> The equation of a conic section can be written in the form $Ax^2 + Bxy + Cy^2 + Dx + Ey + F = 0$ where A, B, and C are not all zero.

General Equation for Conic Sections

The graph of a second-degree equation in two variables always represents a conic or a degenerate case, unless the equation has no graph at all in the real number plane.

The equation $x^2 + y^2 = {}^-8$ has no graph in the real number plane.

Most of the conic sections which you have studied have axes parallel to the x-axis and y-axis. The general equations of these conic sections have $B = 0$. To identify the conic section represented by a given equation, write the equation in standard form. The following table summarizes the standard forms of the conic sections.

Conic Section	Standard Form of Equation
circle	$(x - h)^2 + (y - k)^2 = r^2$
parabola	$(y - k)^2 = 4p(x - h)$ or $(x - h)^2 = 4p(y - k)$
ellipse	$\frac{(x - h)^2}{a^2} + \frac{(y - k)^2}{b^2} = 1$ or $\frac{(y - k)^2}{a^2} + \frac{(x - h)^2}{b^2} = 1$
hyperbola	$\frac{(x - h)^2}{a^2} - \frac{(y - k)^2}{b^2} = 1$ $\frac{(y - k)^2}{a^2} - \frac{(x - h)^2}{b^2} = 1$ or $xy = k$

If $A = C$, the equation represents a circle. If A and C have the same sign and $A \neq C$, the equation represents an ellipse. If A and C have opposite signs, the equation represents a hyperbola. If either A or C is zero, the equation represents a parabola.

examples

1 **Identify and graph the conic section represented by the equation $x^2 + y^2 - 4x + 1 = 0$.**

$x^2 + y^2 - 4x + 1 = 0$

$x^2 - 4x + 4 + y^2 = {}^-1 + 4$ *Complete the square.*

$(x - 2)^2 + y^2 = 3$

$(x - 2)^2 + (y - 0)^2 = (\sqrt{3})^2$

The graph is a circle with center (2, 0) and radius $\sqrt{3}$.

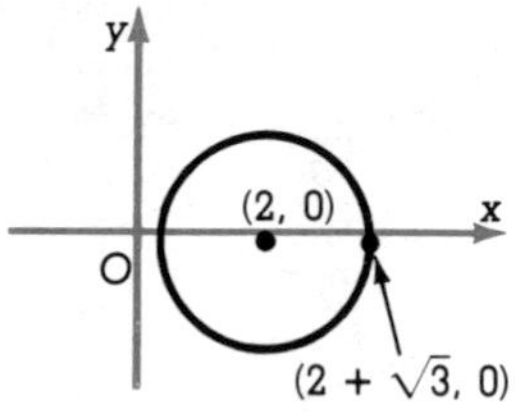

2 **Write the standard form of the equation $x^2 - y^2 + 6y - 18 = 0$. Then identify the conic section.**

$$x^2 - y^2 + 6y - 18 = 0$$
$$x^2 - (y^2 - 6y + 9) = 18 - 9$$
$$x^2 - (y - 3)^2 = 9$$
$$\frac{x^2}{9} - \frac{(y - 3)^2}{9} = 1$$

The equation represents a hyperbola. *The hyperbola is equilateral. Why?*

exercises

Exploratory Write the standard form of each equation.

1. $x^2 - 8x + y^2 = {}^-11$
2. $x^2 - 6x - 4y + 9 = 0$
3. $9x^2 + 25y^2 - 54x - 50y = 119$
4. $x^2 + y^2 + 6y - 8x = {}^-24$
5. $4y^2 + 4y + 8x - 15 = 0$
6. $x^2 - 4y^2 + 10x - 16y = {}^-5$
7. $3y^2 + 24y - x^2 - 2x = {}^-41$
8. $9y^2 + 27x^2 - 6y - 108x + 82 = 0$

9-16. State whether the graph of each equation in problems **1-8** is a circle, parabola, ellipse, or hyperbola. Then draw the graph.

Written Graph each equation. Some equations represent degenerate conics.

1. $x^2 = 5 - y^2$
2. $9xy = 4$
3. $y^2 + 8 = 8x$
4. $x^2 - 4y = 28$
5. $xy = 12$
6. $2x^2 + 5y^2 = 0$
7. $x^2 - 4x - y^2 = 5 + 4y$
8. $x^2 - 6x + y^2 - 12y = {}^-41$
9. $3(x - 1)^2 + 4(y + 4)^2 = 0$
10. $(x + 1)^2 + 9(y - 6)^2 = 9$
11. $y^2 = 8x - 24$
12. $y^2 = 9x^2$
13. $(x - 2)^2 = {}^-(y - 3)^2$
14. $(y + 5)^2 = 36 + 4(x + 1)^2$
15. $2(y - 3)^2 + 25(x + 1)^2 = 50$
16. $x^2 = y + 8x - 16$
17. $\dfrac{(y - 5)^2}{4} - (x + 1)^2 = 4$
18. $\dfrac{(x - 2)^2}{9} + \dfrac{y^2}{9} = 1$

12-9 Systems of Second-Degree Equations and Inequalities

To solve a system of two equations, you must find the ordered pairs which satisfy both equations. One way is to graph each equation and find the coordinates of the points of intersection of the two graphs. Sometimes algebra must be used to find the exact solutions.

example

1 **Graph the following system. Then state the solutions of the system of equations.**

$$x^2 + 4y^2 = 36$$
$$x^2 = {}^-y + 3$$

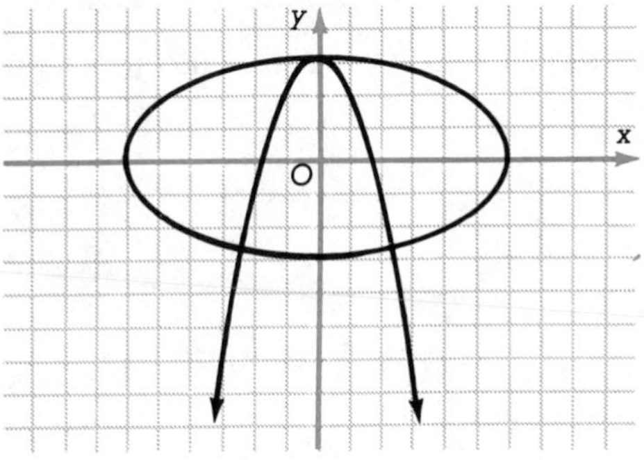

The graph of $x^2 + 4y^2 = 36$ is an ellipse centered at the origin, with $a = 6$ and $b = 3$. The major axis is horizontal. The graph of $x^2 = {}^-y + 3$ is a parabola with $p = -\frac{1}{4}$ and vertex (0, 3). The parabola opens downward.

The graphs show that there are three solutions to the system.

Use the substitution method to find the exact solutions.

$$x^2 + 4y^2 = 36$$
$$(^-y + 3) + 4y^2 = 36$$
$$4y^2 - y - 33 = 0 \quad \textit{Use the quadratic formula.}$$
$$y = 3 \text{ or } -\frac{11}{4}.$$
$$x^2 = {^-y} + 3$$
$$x^2 = {^-3} + 3 \quad \text{or} \quad x^2 = \frac{11}{4} + 3$$
$$x = 0 \qquad x = \pm\frac{\sqrt{23}}{2}$$

The solutions are $(0, 3)$, $\left(\frac{\sqrt{23}}{2}, -\frac{11}{4}\right)$, and $\left(-\frac{\sqrt{23}}{2}, -\frac{11}{4}\right)$.

Graphs also can be used to indicate the solutions of a system of inequalities.

example

2 Graph the solutions for the following system of inequalities.

$$\mathbf{x^2 + y^2 \le 36}$$
$$\mathbf{4x^2 - 9y^2 \ge 36}$$

The graph of $x^2 + y^2 \le 36$ consists of all points on or within the circle $x^2 + y^2 = 36$. The graph of $4x^2 - 9y^2 \ge 36$ consists of all points on or between the branches of the hyperbola $4x^2 - 9y^2 = 36$.

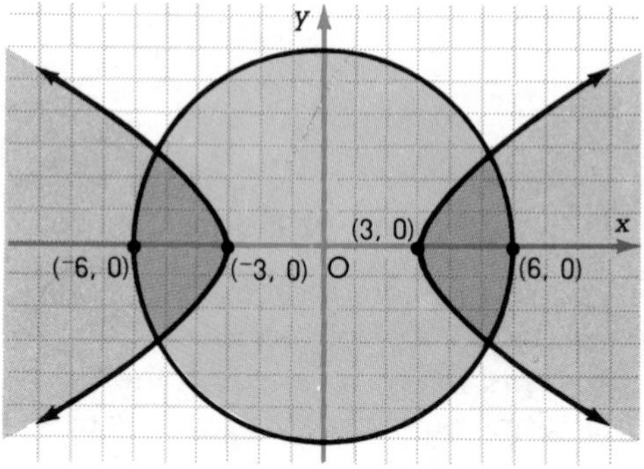

The intersection of these two graphs represents the solutions for the system of inequalities.

exercises

Written Graph the following systems of equations. Then state the solutions of the systems.

1. $x^2 + y^2 = 49$
   $x = {^-1}$
2. $y - 3 = 2x$
   $y = x^2$
3. $x^2 + y^2 = 16$
   $x^2 + y^2 = 9$
4. $y^2 = x^2 + 4$
   $y = 5$
5. $x^2 = y^2 + 9$
   $2y - x = {^-3}$
6. $(x - 1)^2 + 4(y - 1)^2 = 20$
   $x = y$
7. $x^2 - y^2 = 3$
   $xy = 2$
8. $x^2 = {^-y}$
   $y = {^-x} - 2$
9. $(x - 2)^2 - 9(y + 3)^2 = 36$
   $y = x$
10. $x^2 + y^2 = 64$
    $x^2 + 64y^2 = 64$
11. $x^2 - 4y = 0$
    $y = 2x - 3$
12. $(y - 1)^2 = x + 4$
    $y + x = {^-1}$

Graph the solutions for the following systems of inequalities.

13. $x^2 < 9 - y^2$
$y < {}^-x^2$
14. $x^2 \ge 16 + 16y^2$
$x^2 \ge 49 - y^2$
15. $4x^2 - 9(y-1)^2 < 36$
$x^2 + y^2 < 25$
16. $(x+1)^2 + (y+1)^2 > 16$
$9x^2 + y^2 < 81$
17. $y \ge x^2 - 4$
$(y-3)^2 \ge x + 2$
18. $(x+3)^2 + (y+2)^2 \le 36$
$y = {}^-4$
19. $xy < {}^-3$
$(x-1)^2 + (y-2)^2 < 25$
20. $16x^2 - 25y^2 \ge 400$
$xy \ge 2$
21. $4(x-2)^2 + (y-3)^2 \le 16$
$2y = x + 1$
22. $x^2 - 4y^2 < 16$
$x > (y-1)^2$
23. $xy \ge 2$
$x - 3y = 2$
24. $9x^2 + 4y^2 \le 36$
$4x^2 + 9y^2 \ge 36$

12-10 Tangents and Normals to the Conic Sections

The tangent to a circle is perpendicular to the radius at the point of tangency. Since the slope of the radius to (x, y) on a circle with center (0, 0) is $\frac{y_1}{x_1}$, the slope of the tangent is $-\frac{x_1}{y_1}$. Thus if point $P_1(x_1, y_1)$ is on the circle, the point-slope form of the equation can be written.

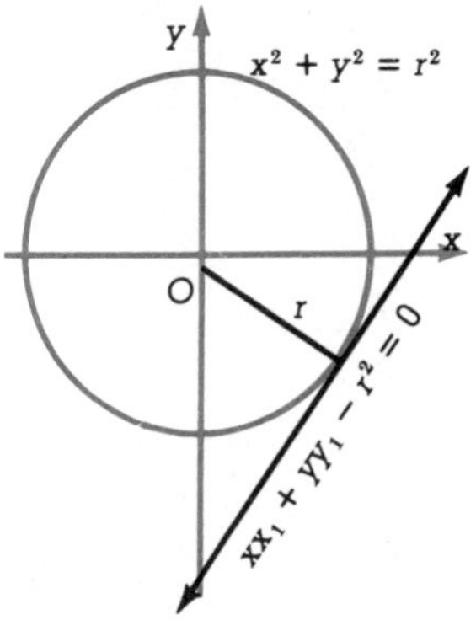

$$-\frac{x_1}{y_1} = \frac{y - y_1}{x - x_1}$$
$$xx_1 - x_1^2 = {}^-yy_1 + y_1^2$$
$$xx_1 + yy_1 = x_1^2 + y_1^2$$
$$xx_1 + yy_1 = r^2$$

Since (x_1, y_1) is on the circle, $x_1^2 + y_1^2 = r^2$.

The equation of the tangent to the circle $x^2 + y^2 = r^2$ at (x_1, y_1) is $xx_1 + yy_1 - r^2 = 0$.

Equation of the Tangent to a Circle

example

1 **Find the equation of the tangent to the circle $x^2 + y^2 = 25$ at the point $({}^-3, 4)$ on the circle.**

$$xx_1 + yy_1 - r^2 = 0$$
$$x({}^-3) + y(4) - 25 = 0 \qquad x_1 = {}^-3 \text{ and } y_1 = 4$$
$$3x - 4y + 25 = 0$$

The equation of the tangent is $3x - 4y + 25 = 0$.

Equations for tangents to the graphs of other conic sections can also be found. The following chart lists formulas for the slope of tangents to the graphs of given equations. After the slope is found, the equation of the tangent can be written by applying the point-slope form of the equation of a line.

Conic Section	Standard Form of Equation	Slope of Tangent at (x, y)
circle	$(x-h)^2 + (y-k)^2 = r^2$	$-\frac{(x-h)}{(y-k)}$
parabola	$(y-k)^2 = 4p(x-h)$	$\frac{2p}{y-k}$
	$(x-h)^2 = 4p(y-k)$	$\frac{x-h}{2p}$
ellipse	$\frac{(x-h)^2}{a^2} + \frac{(y-k)^2}{b^2} = 1$	$-\frac{b^2(x-h)}{a^2(y-k)}$
	$\frac{(y-k)^2}{a^2} + \frac{(x-h)^2}{b^2} = 1$	$-\frac{a^2(x-h)}{b^2(y-k)}$
hyperbola	$\frac{(x-h)^2}{a^2} - \frac{(y-k)^2}{b^2} = 1$	$\frac{b^2(x-h)}{a^2(y-k)}$
	$\frac{(y-k)^2}{a^2} - \frac{(x-h)^2}{b^2} = 1$	$\frac{a^2(x-h)}{b^2(y-k)}$

example

2 **Find the equation of the tangent to the parabola $2x^2 - 3x + 2y - 4 = 0$ at the point $(^-2, ^-5)$.**

First, write the equation in standard form.

$$2x^2 - 3x + 2y - 4 = 0$$

$$x^2 - \frac{3}{2}x + y - 2 = 0$$

$$x^2 - \frac{3}{2}x + \frac{9}{16} = {}^-y + 2 + \frac{9}{16} \qquad \textit{Complete the square.}$$

$$\left(x - \frac{3}{4}\right)^2 = 4\left(-\frac{1}{4}\right)y + 2\frac{9}{16} \qquad h = \frac{3}{4} \text{ and } p = -\frac{1}{4}$$

Then, find the slope of the tangent at the point $(^-2, ^-5)$.

$$\frac{x-h}{2p} = \frac{^-2 - \frac{3}{4}}{2\left(-\frac{1}{4}\right)} = \frac{11}{2}$$

Finally, write the equation for the line through $(^-2, ^-5)$ which has slope $\frac{11}{2}$.

$$\frac{11}{2} = \frac{y+5}{x+2}$$

$$11(x+2) = 2(y+5)$$

$$11x - 2y + 12 = 0$$

The equation of the tangent is $11x - 2y + 12 = 0$.

If $P(x_1, y_1)$ is a point and $(x - h)^2 + (y - k)^2 = r^2$ is the equation of a circle, then P lies outside the circle if $(x_1 - h)^2 + (y_1 - k)^2 > r^2$. In this case there are two tangents from P to the circle. It is sometimes necessary to find the length of a tangent segment, that is, the line segment joining a given point to a point of tangency on a circle.

The formula for the length of the tangent segment from an exterior point can be developed as follows. Let $C(h, k)$ be the center of the circle, $P(x_1, y_1)$ be the exterior point, and $T(x_2, y_2)$ be a point on the circle where a tangent from P touches the circle. Let $CT = r$, $PC = d$, and $PT = t$. The formula for t in terms of d and r is found using the Pythagorean Theorem.

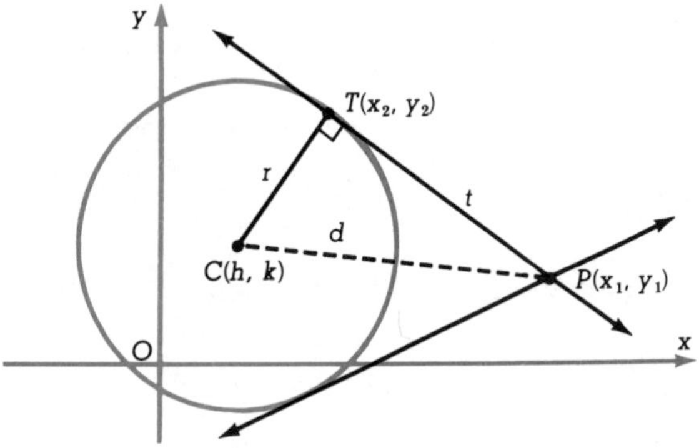

$$t = \sqrt{d^2 - r^2}$$

According to the distance formula, $d^2 = (x_1 - h)^2 + (y_1 - k)^2$. Thus, the formula for the length of the tangent segment can be expressed as follows.

Length of a Tangent Segment to a Circle

The length of a tangent segment, t, from (x_1, y_1) to the circle $(x - h)^2 + (y - k)^2 = r^2$ can be found using the following formula.

$$t = \sqrt{(x_1 - h)^2 + (y_1 - k)^2 - r^2}$$

example

3 Find the length of the tangent segment from $(^-1, 3)$ to the circle $(x - 2)^2 + (y + 5)^2 = 16$.

$$\begin{aligned} t &= \sqrt{(x_1 - h)^2 + (y_1 - k)^2 - r^2} \\ &= \sqrt{(^-1 - 2)^2 + (3 + 5)^2 - 16} \qquad h = 2, k = {}^-5, \text{ and } r = 4 \\ &= \sqrt{9 + 64 - 16} \\ &= \sqrt{57} \end{aligned}$$

The **normal** to a curve at any point on it is the line perpendicular to the tangent at the point. Thus, the slope of the normal is the negative reciprocal of the slope of the tangent at any point.

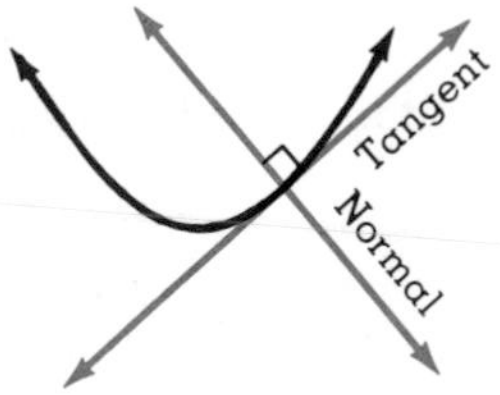

example

4 Find the equations of the tangent and the normal to the hyperbola $\frac{x^2}{9} - \frac{y^2}{4} = 1$ at the point $(6, 2\sqrt{3})$.

Find the slope of the tangent.

$$\frac{b^2(x-h)}{a^2(y-k)} = \frac{4(6)}{9(2\sqrt{3})} \text{ or } \frac{4\sqrt{3}}{9}$$ *h and k are zero.*

Then find the equation of the tangent.

$$\frac{4\sqrt{3}}{9} = \frac{y - 2\sqrt{3}}{x - 6} \text{ or } 4x - 3\sqrt{3}\,y - 6 = 0$$

Since the slope of the tangent is $\frac{4\sqrt{3}}{9}$, the slope of the normal is $-\frac{9}{4\sqrt{3}}$ or $-\frac{3\sqrt{3}}{4}$.

Find the equation of the normal.

$$-\frac{3\sqrt{3}}{4} = \frac{y - 2\sqrt{3}}{x - 6} \text{ or } 9x + 4\sqrt{3}\,y - 78 = 0$$

The equation of the tangent is $4x - 3\sqrt{3}y - 6 = 0$ and the equation of the normal is $9x + 4\sqrt{3}y - 78 = 0$.

exercises

Exploratory Given the slope of the tangent to a curve at a point, name the slope of the normal.

1. $\frac{3\sqrt{5}}{8}$
2. $-\frac{4}{5\sqrt{10}}$
3. $-\frac{25}{16}$
4. $\frac{7}{30}$

Find the equation of the tangent to the given circle at the given point.

5. $x^2 + y^2 = 25, (2, \sqrt{21})$
6. $x^2 + y^2 = 49, (\sqrt{13}, 6)$
7. $x^2 + y^2 = 145, (9, {}^-8)$
8. $x^2 + y^2 = 116, ({}^-10, {}^-4)$

Find the slope of the tangent to the graph of the given equation at the given point.

9. $(x-2)^2 + (y-3)^2 = 10, ({}^-1, 2)$
10. $(x+4)^2 = 8(y+3), (0, {}^-1)$
11. $\frac{(x+2)^2}{36} + \frac{(y-3)^2}{9} = 1, ({}^-2, 6)$
12. $\frac{(x-3)^2}{4} + \frac{(y-1)^2}{25} = 1, (3, {}^-4)$
13. $(y+2)^2 = 8(x-3), (5, 2)$
14. $\frac{x^2}{8} - \frac{y^2}{9} = 1, ({}^-4, {}^-3)$

Written Find the equations of the tangent and the normal to the given circle at the given point.

1. $x^2 + y^2 - 19 = 0, ({}^-2, \sqrt{15})$
2. $3x^2 + 3y^2 - 5 = 0, \left(1, \frac{\sqrt{6}}{3}\right)$
3. $(x-4)^2 + (y-3)^2 - 16 = 0, (8, 3)$
4. $(x+2)^2 + y^2 - 9 = 0, ({}^-4, \sqrt{5})$

Find the equations of the tangent and the normal to the parabola at the given point.

5. $x^2 + 4x - y + 1 = 0$, $(0, 1)$
6. $y^2 - x + y - 5 = 0$, $(1, {}^{-}3)$
7. $2x^2 - 7x + 5y - 11 = 0$, $\left({}^{-}1, \frac{2}{5}\right)$
8. $2y^2 + 4x - 3y - 11 = 0$, $\left(\frac{9}{4}, 2\right)$

Find the equations of the tangent and the normal to the ellipse at the given point.

9. $\frac{y^2}{64} + \frac{x^2}{49} = 1$, $\left(\frac{7\sqrt{3}}{2}, 4\right)$
10. $\frac{x^2}{25} + \frac{y^2}{9} = 1$, $\left(4, \frac{9}{5}\right)$
11. $\frac{(x - 4)^2}{12} + \frac{y^2}{4} = 1$, $(7, 1)$
12. $\frac{(y - 3)^2}{36} + \frac{x^2}{4} = 1$, $(\sqrt{3}, 6)$

Find the equations of the tangent and the normal to the hyperbola at the given point.

13. $\frac{x^2}{16} - \frac{y^2}{4} = 1$, $\left(5, \frac{3}{2}\right)$
14. $\frac{x^2}{4} - y^2 = 1$, $(2, 0)$
15. $\frac{(x - 1)^2}{25} - \frac{(y + 3)^2}{9} = 1$, $({}^{-}4, {}^{-}3)$
16. $\frac{(x - 2)^2}{18} - \frac{(y - 1)^2}{64} = 1$, $({}^{-}4, {}^{-}7)$

Find the length of the tangent segment from the given point to the given circle.

17. $({}^{-}4, 7)$, $x^2 + y^2 = 10$
18. $(9, 9)$, $x^2 + y^2 = 2$
19. $(6, 2)$, $x^2 + y^2 = 37$
20. $(10, 1)$, $x^2 + y^2 - 6x - 8y = 0$
21. $(4, {}^{-}1)$, $(x + 3)^2 + y^2 - 4 = 0$
22. $({}^{-}7, 2)$, $(x + 3)^2 + (y - 2)^2 = 4$

Solve each problem.

23. Find the equations of the horizontal tangents to the circle $x^2 + y^2 = 25$.
24. Find the equations of the vertical tangents to the circle $x^2 + y^2 = 49$.
25. Find the equations of the horizontal tangents to the ellipse $\frac{x^2}{25} + \frac{y^2}{64} = 1$.
26. Find the equations of the vertical tangents to the ellipse $\frac{x^2}{64} + \frac{y^2}{16} = 1$.

Challenge Solve each problem.

1. Find the point on the parabola $x^2 - 6x - 2y + 1 = 0$ at which the tangent makes a 45° angle with the positive x-axis.
2. The line $x + y = 4$ is tangent to an equilateral hyperbola $xy = k$, where $k > 0$. Determine the value of k.
3. Find the slopes of the tangents at the endpoints of the latus rectum of the parabola $y^2 - 4x - 2y + 9 = 0$. How are the tangents related?
4. Find the equations of the tangents at the endpoints of the latera recta of the hyperbola $\frac{x^2}{4} - \frac{y^2}{12} = 1$.

12-11 Polar Equations of Conic Sections

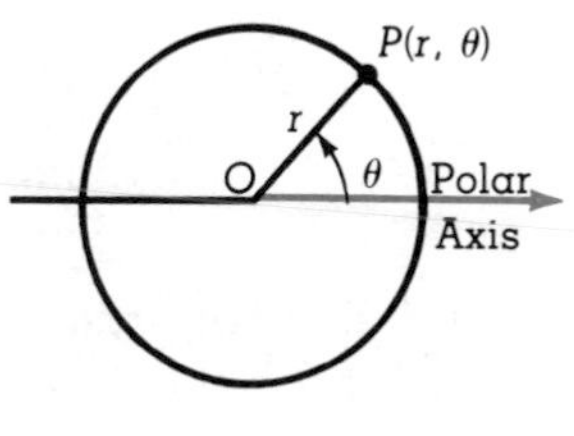

Conic sections can be represented using polar equations. For example, if the center of a circle is at the pole and the radius is 5, then the polar equation of the circle is $r = 5$. In general, if any point $P(r, \theta)$ lies on a circle centered at the origin, the polar distance r is the radius of the circle.

example

1 **If the equation of a circle in rectangular coordinates is $x^2 + y^2 = 12$, find the polar equation. Assume that the pole coincides with the origin and the polar axis coincides with the positive x-axis.**

$$\begin{aligned} r &= \sqrt{x^2 + y^2} \\ &= \sqrt{12} \text{ or } 2\sqrt{3} \end{aligned}$$

The polar equation is $r = 2\sqrt{3}$.

The simplest form of the polar equation of a parabola is obtained if the focus is taken as the pole and a line perpendicular to the directrix is taken as the polar axis. By definition, any point P on a parabola is equidistant from the focus, F, and a point on the directrix, M, as shown at the right.

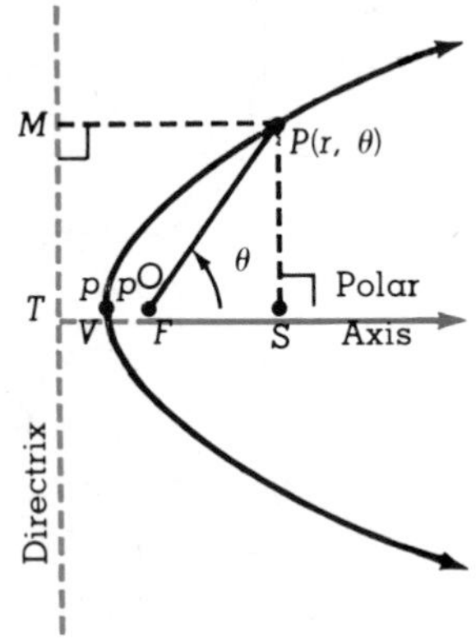

Therefore $PF = PM$. Since $PM = ST$, the formula for PF can be derived as follows.

$$\begin{aligned} PF &= PM \\ &= ST \\ &= SF + FV + VT \\ &= r \cos \theta + p + p \\ &= r \cos \theta + 2p \end{aligned}$$

Replace PF by r and solve for r to obtain the polar equation.

$$r = \frac{2p}{1 - \cos \theta}$$ *The parabola opens toward the polar axis, and its focus is at the pole.*

The polar equation of a parabola which opens in the opposite direction has the form $r = \frac{2p}{1 + \cos \theta}$. Again, the polar axis is perpendicular to the directrix.

example

2 **Change the equation of the parabola $y^2 = 5x$ to the polar equation where the pole is at the focus and the polar axis coincides with the positive x-axis.**

$4p = 5$ *Why?*

$p = \frac{5}{4}$ or 1.25

The polar equation is $r = \frac{2.5}{1 - \cos \theta}$.

The simplest form of the polar equation of an ellipse is determined if a focus is at the pole and both foci are on the polar axis.

Let F be a focus, ℓ the corresponding directrix, and $P(r, \theta)$ a point on the ellipse. By definition, $\frac{PF}{PM} = e$ or $PF = e \cdot PM$ where $e < 1$. Also, $PM = SF + FT$ and $SF = r\cos\theta$. Let $FT = 2p$. Since $PF = r$, then $r = e(SF + FT)$ or $e(r\cos\theta + 2p)$. The following equation is obtained by solving for r.

$$r = \frac{2ep}{1 - e\cos\theta} \quad (e < 1)$$

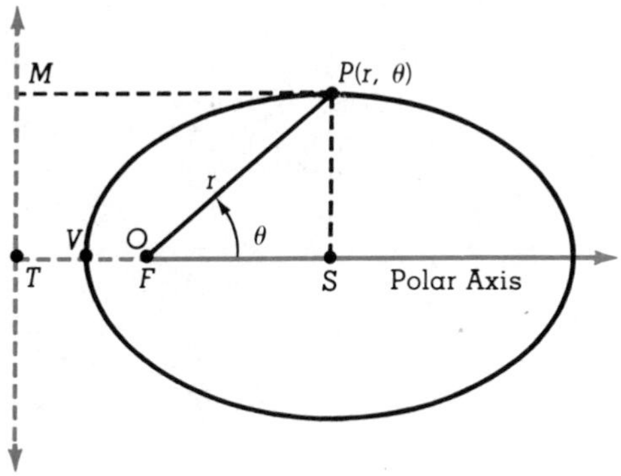

This is the polar equation of an ellipse when the pole coincides with one focus and the polar axis is directed toward the other focus. If the polar axis has the opposite direction the polar equation has the form $r = \frac{2ep}{1 + e\cos\theta}$. In either case the polar axis is perpendicular to each directrix, and $2p = \frac{b^2}{c}$.

example

3 **The equation of an ellipse in rectangular coordinates is $16x^2 + 49y^2 = 784$. Find the equation in polar coordinates if the pole is at the left focus and the polar axis is directed toward the right focus.**

The standard form of the equation is $\frac{x^2}{49} + \frac{y^2}{16} = 1$.

Thus, $a = 7$ and $b = 4$. Since $a^2 = b^2 + c^2$, $c = \sqrt{33}$.

Also, $e = \frac{c}{a}$, or $\frac{\sqrt{33}}{7}$, and $2p = \frac{b^2}{c}$, or $\frac{16}{\sqrt{33}}$.

$$r = \frac{2ep}{1 - e\cos\theta}$$

$$r = \frac{\frac{\sqrt{33}}{7} \cdot \frac{16}{\sqrt{33}}}{1 - \frac{\sqrt{33}}{7}\cos\theta}$$

The origin of the rectangular coordinate system is at the center of the ellipse and the pole is at the left focus with the polar axis directed toward the positive x-axis.

$$r = \frac{16}{7 - \sqrt{33}\cos\theta}$$

The polar equation of the hyperbola can be developed in the same manner as that of the parabola and ellipse. The polar equation is $r = \frac{2ep}{1 \pm e\cos\theta}$ where e is the eccentricity ($e > 1$) and $2p$ is the distance from the focus to the directrix. Again, the polar axis is perpendicular to the directrix and $2p = \frac{b^2}{c}$.

Note that for the parabola $e = 1$ and the equation reduces to $r = \frac{2p}{1 \pm \cos\theta}$.

Notice the similarity among the polar equations for conic sections.

The polar equation of any conic section where the pole is at a focus and the polar axis is perpendicular to the directrix can be written as follows, where e is the eccentricity and $2p$ is the distance from the focus to the directrix.

$$r = \frac{2ep}{1 \pm e \cos \theta}$$

Polar Equation of a Conic Section

If the polar axis is parallel to the directrix it can be shown that the polar equation of a conic section has following form.

$$r = \frac{2ep}{1 \pm e \sin \theta}$$

Thus, if $e = 1$, the equation is a parabola. If $e < 1$, the equation is an ellipse. If $e > 1$, the equation is a hyperbola.

exercises

Exploratory Identify the conic represented by each of the following polar equations.

1. $r = \dfrac{3.2}{1 - 0.6 \cos \theta}$
2. $r = \dfrac{1}{1 - \cos \theta}$
3. $r = 6\sqrt{5}$
4. $r = \dfrac{16}{5 + 3 \cos \theta}$
5. $r = \dfrac{6}{1 + \cos \theta}$
6. $r = 8$
7. $r = \dfrac{3}{1 - 2 \cos \theta}$
8. $r = \dfrac{6}{1 + 0.5 \cos \theta}$

9-16. Graph each equation in problems **1-8.**

Write a polar equation of each circle whose rectangular equation is given.

17. $x^2 + y^2 = 25$
18. $x^2 + y^2 = 49$

Written Find the values of p and e for each of the following equations of conics.

1. $y^2 = 9x$
2. $y^2 = {}^-7x$
3. $9x^2 + 16y^2 = 144$
4. $(y - 2)^2 = 3(x + 5)$
5. $x^2 - \dfrac{y^2}{4} = 1$
6. $\dfrac{x^2}{9} + \dfrac{y^2}{4} = 1$
7. $\dfrac{x^2}{16} + \dfrac{y^2}{36} = 1$
8. $3x^2 + 5y^2 = 15$
9. $9x^2 - 25y^2 = 225$
10. $\dfrac{x^2}{16} - \dfrac{y^2}{9} = 1$

11-20. Write a polar equation of each conic section in problems **1-10.**

Chapter Summary

1. The standard form of the equation of a circle with radius r and center (h, k) is $(x - h)^2 + (y - k)^2 = r^2$. (322)
2. The standard form of the equation of a parabola with vertex (h, k) and directrix parallel to the y-axis, is
$$(y - k)^2 = 4p(x - h)$$
where p is the distance from the vertex to the focus.

   The standard form of the equation of a parabola with vertex (h, k) and directrix parallel to the x-axis, is
$$(x - h)^2 = 4p(y - k)$$
where p is the distance from the vertex to the focus. (325)
3. The length of the latus rectum of a parabola is $4p$. (327)
4. The translation formulas are
$$x = x' + h \text{ and } y = y' + k$$
where (h, k) represents the origin of the coordinate system (x', y'). (330)
5. For an ellipse, $a^2 = b^2 + c^2$, where a is the length of the semi-major axis, b is the length of the semi-minor axis, and c is the distance from the center to a focus. (332)
6. The standard form of the equation of an ellipse with center (h, k) and major axis of length $2a$, parallel to the x-axis, is
$$\frac{(x - h)^2}{a^2} + \frac{(y - k)^2}{b^2} = 1 \quad \text{where } b^2 = a^2 - c^2.$$
The standard form of the equation of an ellipse with center (h, k) and major axis of length $2a$, parallel to the y-axis, is
$$\frac{(y - k)^2}{a^2} + \frac{(x - h)^2}{b^2} = 1 \quad \text{where } b^2 = a^2 - c^2. \quad (334)$$
7. For an ellipse, the eccentricity $e = \dfrac{c}{a}$ and $e < 1$. Also, $b^2 = a^2(1 - e^2)$. (336)
8. The length of a latus rectum of an ellipse is $\dfrac{2b^2}{a}$. (336)
9. For a hyperbola, $a^2 + b^2 = c^2$, where $2a$ is the length of the transverse axis, $2b$ is the length of the conjugate axis, and c is the distance from the center to a focus. (339)
10. The standard form of the equation of a hyperbola with center (h, k) and transverse axis of length $2a$, parallel to the x-axis, is
$$\frac{(x - h)^2}{a^2} - \frac{(y - k)^2}{b^2} = 1 \quad \text{where } b^2 = c^2 - a^2.$$
The standard form of the equation of a hyperbola with center (h, k) and transverse axis of length $2a$, parallel to the y-axis, is
$$\frac{(y - k)^2}{a^2} - \frac{(x - h)^2}{b^2} = 1 \quad \text{where } b^2 = c^2 - a^2. \quad (340)$$

11. The equations of the asymptotes of a hyperbola with a horizontal transverse axis are

$$y - k = \pm \frac{b}{a}(x - h).$$

The equations of the asymptotes of a hyperbola with a vertical transverse axis are

$$y - k = \pm \frac{a}{b}(x - h). \quad (341)$$

12. For a hyperbola, $e = \frac{c}{a}$ and $e > 1$. Also, $b^2 = a^2(e^2 - 1)$. (343)

13. The length of a latus rectum of a hyperbola is $\frac{2b^2}{a}$. (344)

14. Two hyperbolas such that the transverse axis of one is the conjugate axis of the other, and conversely, are called conjugate hyperbolas. Conjugate hyperbolas share the same asymptotes. (344)

15. If $a = b$ in the standard form of a hyperbola, it is an equilateral hyperbola and the asymptotes are perpendicular. The equation of a special case of an equilateral hyperbola has the form $xy = k$. (344)

16. The equation of a conic section can be written in the form $Ax^2 + Bxy + Cy^2 + Dx + Ey + F = 0$ where A, B, and C are not all zero. (347)

17. The equation of the tangent to the circle $x^2 + y^2 = r^2$ at (x_1, y_1) is $xx_1 + yy_1 - r^2 = 0$. (351)

18. The slope of the tangent to the graph of any conic section can be found by using the formulas on page 352.

19. The length of the tangent segment, t, from (x_1, y_1) to the circle $(x - h)^2 + (y - k)^2 = r^2$ can be found using the formula

$$t = \sqrt{(x_1 - h)^2 + (y_1 - k)^2 - r^2}. \quad (353)$$

20. The normal to a curve at any point on it is the line perpendicular to the tangent at the point. The slope of the normal is the negative reciprocal of the slope of the tangent. (353)

21. The polar equation of any conic section where the pole is at a focus and the polar axis is perpendicular to the directrix can be written as follows, where e is the eccentricity and 2p is the distance from the focus to the directrix.

$$r = \frac{2ep}{1 \pm e \cos \theta} \quad (358)$$

Chapter Review

12-1 Write the equation of each circle described below.

1. Center $(3, {}^-7)$, radius 3

2. Passes through $({}^-2, 1)$, $(5, 6)$, and $({}^-3, 6)$

12-2 Name the focus, vertex, directrix, and axis of each parabola whose equation is given. Then draw the graph.

3. $(x - 7)^2 = 8(y - 3)$

4. $y^2 + 6y - 4x + 25 = 0$

12-3 Solve each problem.

5. Write the equation of the circle $x^2 - 6x + 9 + y^2 = 4$ with respect to axes translated so that the origin is (3, 0).

6. Write the equation of the parabola $y^2 = 4x + 4y - 4$ with respect to axes translated so that the origin is at the vertex.

12-4 Name the center, foci, and the vertices of each ellipse whose equation is given. Then draw the graph.

7. $(x - 4)^2 + 4(y - 6)^2 = 36$

8. $3(x + 3)^2 + 2(y - 4)^2 = 12$

12-5 Write the equation of each ellipse described below.

9. Foci $(5, ^-1)$ and $(^-1, ^-1)$, $2a = 10$

10. Foci (3, 0) and (3, 4), $e = 0.5$

12-6 Name the center, foci, vertices, and the equations of the asymptotes of each hyperbola whose equation is given. Then draw the graph.

11. $9x^2 - 16y^2 - 36x + 96y + 36 = 0$

12. $2(x + 5)^2 - (y - 1)^2 = 8$

12-7 Solve each problem.

13. Write the equation of an equilateral hyperbola with foci (0, 7) and $(0, ^-7)$.

14. Find the length of the latera recta of the hyperbola $y^2 - 3x^2 - 8y - 6x + 4 = 0$.

15. Write the equation of a hyperbola which has $e = \frac{3}{2}$ and foci (1, 4) and $(1, ^-2)$.

16. Write the equation of the conjugate of the hyperbola $9(x + 2)^2 - (y - 3)^2 = 9$.

12-8 Graph each equation. Some equations represent degenerate conics.

17. $4x^2 - 8x + y^2 = 12$

18. $xy = 0$

19. $2(x - 4)^2 = {}^-(y - 1)^2$

20. $x^2 - 6y - 8x + 16 = 0$

12-9 Graph each system.

21. $x^2 - 4x - 4y - 4 = 0$
 $(x - 2)^2 = {}^-4y$

22. $x^2 + (y - 2)^2 \geq 0$
 $x^2 + 9(y - 2)^2 \leq 9$

12-10 Solve each problem.

23. Find the length of the tangent segment from the point $(5, ^-1)$ to the circle $x^2 + y^2 + 6x - 10y - 2 = 0$.

24. Write the equations of the tangent and normal to the hyperbola $x^2 - 4y^2 + 2x + 8y - 7 = 0$ at (1, 1).

12-11 Write a polar equation of each conic section whose equation is given.

25. $x^2 - 4x + y^2 = 5$

26. $y^2 = 12x - 12$

Chapter Test

Solve each problem.

1. Write the equation of the circle with center $(^-3, 7)$ that is tangent to the y-axis.
2. Write the equation of the circle with center $(^-8, 3)$ that passes through the point $(^-6, ^-4)$.
3. Name the focus, vertex, directrix, and axis of the parabola $y^2 - 2x + 10y + 27 = 0$. Then draw the graph.
4. Write the equation of the parabola which has a focus at $(3, ^-5)$ and whose directrix is $y = {}^-2$.
5. Write the equation of the parabola $y^2 = 8x - 4$ with respect to axes translated so that the origin is $(1, 0)$.
6. Find the length of the latus rectum of the parabola $x^2 - 8x - 12y - 20 = 0$.
7. Name the center, foci, vertices, and find the length of the latus rectum for the ellipse $x^2 + 2y^2 + 2x - 12y + 11 = 0$. Then draw the graph.
8. Write the equation of an ellipse centered at the origin which has a horizontal major axis, $e = \frac{1}{2}$ and $2c = 1$.
9. Name the center, foci, vertices, and the equations of the asymptotes of the hyperbola $(x - 4)^2 - 9(y - 5)^2 = 36$. Then draw the graph.
10. Write the equation of the hyperbola which has eccentricity $\frac{3}{2}$ and foci $(^-5, ^-2)$ and $(^-5, 4)$.
11. Find the length of the tangent from the point $(5, 5)$ to the circle $x^2 + y^2 = 9$.
12. Graph the following system.
    $x^2 + y^2 - 2x - 4y + 1 \geq 0$
    $x^2 - 4y - 2x + 5 \geq 0$
13. Write the equations of the tangent and normal to the hyperbola $16x^2 - y^2 - 4y - 20 = 0$ at $(\sqrt{2}, 2)$.
14. Write a polar equation of the conic section which has the following rectangular equation. $4(x - 3)^2 + (y - 2)^2 = 4$

Chapter

13

Probability

When a new car is ordered, many choices such as color, type of transmission, and engine size must be considered. The probability of a certain car being ordered is related to the number of possible combinations of these choices.

13-1 Permutations

Suppose there are two tunnels under a river by which one can enter a city from the west and three highways by which one can leave the city going east. After entering the city by the first tunnel, one has the choice of leaving the city by three exits, and so there are three routes by way of the first tunnel. Likewise, there are three routes by way of the second tunnel. Altogether there are $2 \times 3 = 6$ possible routes through the city from west to east.

The choice of tunnels does *not* affect the choice of highways. Thus, these two choices are called **independent events.**

The above illustration of choice of ways is an example of an important principle called the **Basic Counting Principle.**

Suppose an event can be chosen in p different ways. Another independent event can be chosen in q different ways. Then the two events can be chosen successively in $p \cdot q$ ways.

Basic Counting Principle

This principle can be extended to any number of independent events.

examples

1 **On a trip a man took 3 suits, 2 ties, and 2 hats. How many different choices of these items of clothing are possible?**

There are $3 \cdot 2 \cdot 2 = 12$ different choices possible. The possible choices can be shown in a diagram.

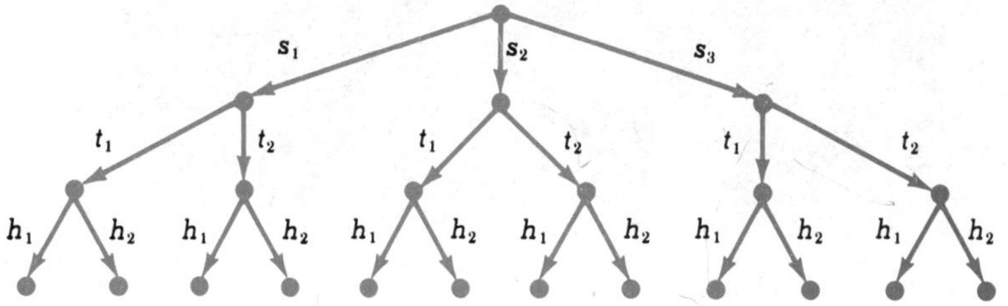

This diagram is called a tree diagram. Notice that there are 12 choices each of which differs from the other in some way.

2 **How many seven-digit phone numbers can begin with the prefix 364?**

Digit in phone number:	1st	2nd	3rd	4th	5th	6th	7th
Ways to choose:	1	1	1	10	10	10	10

There are $1 \cdot 1 \cdot 1 \cdot 10 \cdot 10 \cdot 10 \cdot 10 = 10^4$ or 10,000 numbers.

Suppose that seniors Pat, Corinne, and Wayne have been selected to be speakers at the graduation program. In how many different orders can they speak? If Pat speaks first then either Corinne or Wayne can speak second and so on. The possible arrangement of speakers on the program are listed below.

1. Pat	1. Pat	1. Corinne	1. Corinne	1. Wayne	1. Wayne
2. Corinne	2. Wayne	2. Pat	2. Wayne	2. Pat	2. Corinne
3. Wayne	3. Corinne	3. Wayne	3. Pat	3. Corinne	3. Pat

There are six distinct orders in which the speakers can be scheduled. This can also be confirmed by the Basic Counting Principle.

The arrangement of objects in a certain order is called a **permutation.** In a permutation, the order of the objects is very important.

Suppose that there is time for only two speakers on the program. How many ways can a program be arranged if two of the three persons are to be selected?

1. Pat	1. Pat	1. Corinne	1. Corinne	1. Wayne	1. Wayne
2. Corinne	2. Wayne	2. Pat	2. Wayne	2. Pat	2. Corinne

There are six ways to arrange the three speakers taken two at a time as can be verified by the Basic Counting Principle.

The symbol $P(n, n)$ denotes the number of permutations of n objects taken all at once. The symbol $P(n, r)$ denotes the number of permutations of n objects taken r at a time.

The number of permutations of n objects, taken n at a time, is defined as follows.

$$P(n, n) = n!$$

The number of permutations of n objects, taken r at a time, is defined as follows.

$$P(n, r) = \frac{n!}{(n - r)!}$$

Definition of $P(n, n)$ and $P(n, r)$

example

3 **How many different three-letter patterns can be formed using the letters a, b, c, d, and e without repetition?**

Find the number of permutations of 5 objects, taken 3 at a time.

$$P(n, r) = \frac{n!}{(n - r)!}$$

$$P(5, 3) = \frac{5!}{(5 - 3)!}$$

$$= \frac{5 \cdot 4 \cdot 3 \cdot 2 \cdot 1}{2 \cdot 1} \text{ or } 60$$

There are 60 ways to arrange the letters a, b, c, d, and e three at a time.

example

4 **How many ways can five books be selected from a group of eleven books?**

$$P(11, 5) = \frac{11!}{(11 - 5)!}$$
$$= \frac{11 \cdot 10 \cdot 9 \cdot 8 \cdot 7 \cdot 6 \cdot 5 \cdot 4 \cdot 3 \cdot 2 \cdot 1}{6 \cdot 5 \cdot 4 \cdot 3 \cdot 2 \cdot 1} \text{ or } 55{,}440$$

There are 55,440 ways the books can be selected.

exercises

Exploratory State whether these events are independent or not.

1. choosing color and size when ordering an item of clothing
2. choosing a president, secretary, and treasurer for a club
3. choosing five numbers in a bingo game
4. throwing one die two times
5. tossing three coins at one time
6. each of four people writing down their guess of the total number of runs in a baseball game without telling what it is

State whether each statement below is true or false.

7. $6! - 3! = 3!$
8. $5 \cdot 4! = 5!$
9. $\frac{8!}{4!} = 2!$
10. $(5 - 3)! = 5! - 3!$
11. $\frac{P(9, 9)}{9!} = 1$
12. $\frac{3!}{3} = \frac{2!}{2}$

Written Find the value of each of the following.

1. $P(4, 3)$
2. $P(5, 2)$
3. $P(7, 1)$
4. $P(5, 3)$
5. $P(11, 10)$
6. $P(7, 4)$
7. $P(5, 5)$
8. $\frac{P(6, 4)}{P(5, 3)}$
9. $\frac{P(6, 3) \cdot P(4, 2)}{P(5, 2)}$

Find the value of n in each of the following equations.

10. $n[P(5, 3)] = P(7, 5)$
11. $P(n, 4) = 3[P(n, 3)]$
12. $P(n, 4) = 40[P(n - 1, 2)]$

Solve each problem.

13. Akiko has six dresses, five pairs of shoes, and two coats. How many choices of outfits with these items are possible?
14. A penny, a nickel, and a dime are tossed simultaneously. How many different ways can the coins land?
15. A license plate must have two letters (not I or O) followed by three digits. The last digit cannot be zero. How many possible plates are there?
16. There are five roads from Ada to Bluffton, three from Bluffton to Pandora, and four from Pandora to Lafayette. How many different routes are there from Ada to Lafayette?

17. Using the letters from the word *equation*, how many five-letter patterns can be formed in which *q* is followed immediately by *u*?

18. How many five-digit numbers between and including 56,000 and 59,999 can be made if no digit is repeated?

19. There are 10 students in a class that meets in a room that has 12 chairs. How many ways is it possible for the students to be seated?

20. How many ways can eight different cans of vegetables be placed in a row on a shelf?

Find the number of different ways the letters of the word *pairs* can be arranged given the following.

21. The first letter must be *p*.

22. The first letter must be a vowel.

23. The first letter cannot be a vowel.

24. The letter *r* must be in the middle place.

Find the number of three-letter, three-digit license plates which are possible given the following.

25. There are no restrictions.

26. The letters must be different.

27. The letter O cannot be used.

28. The three digits cannot be 000.

Urn *A* contains two white balls, urn *B* contains one white and one red ball, and urn *C* contains two white balls and one red ball. A die is thrown. If a 1 or 2 shows, a ball is drawn from urn *A*. If a 3 or 4 shows, a ball is drawn from urn *B*. If a 5 or 6 shows, a ball is drawn from urn *C*.

29. How many possible outcomes are there?

30. Make a tree diagram to show all possible outcomes.

31. In how many of the possible outcomes is a red ball drawn?

32. In how many of the possible outcomes is a white ball drawn?

13-2 Permutations with Repetitions and Circular Permutations

Consider the problem of making distinct arrangements of the five letters of the word *teeth*. One of these arrangements is *eteth*, but there are several arrangements with the same appearance since the e's or *t*'s may be reversed. The arrangements are exactly the same unless the e's and *t*'s are "tagged."

In a simpler case, how many permutations of the letters of the word *tee* are there? By tagging the e's as e_1 and e_2 the following arrangèments are possible.

te_1e_2	e_1te_2	e_1e_2t
te_2e_1	e_2te_1	e_2e_1t

There are six arrangements when subscripts are taken into account but only three distinct arrangements without subscripts.

When some objects are alike, use the following rule to find the number of permutations of those objects.

Permutations with Repetitions

> **The number of permutations of n objects of which p are alike and q are alike is found by evaluating the following expression.**
>
> $$\frac{n!}{p!q!}$$

examples

1 **How many five-letter patterns can be formed from the letters of the word *teeth*?**

Find the number of permutations of 5 objects of which 2 are *t*'s and 2 are e's.

$$\frac{5!}{2!2!} = \frac{5 \cdot 4 \cdot 3 \cdot 2 \cdot 1}{2 \cdot 1 \cdot 2 \cdot 1}$$
$$= 30$$

There are 30 five-letter patterns.

2 **How many eleven-letter patterns can be formed from the letters of the word *Mississippi*?**

$$\frac{11!}{4!4!2!} = \frac{11 \cdot 10 \cdot 9 \cdot 8 \cdot 7 \cdot 6 \cdot 5 \cdot 4 \cdot 3 \cdot 2 \cdot 1}{4 \cdot 3 \cdot 2 \cdot 1 \cdot 4 \cdot 3 \cdot 2 \cdot 1 \cdot 2 \cdot 1}$$
$$= 34{,}650$$

There are 34,650 eleven-letter patterns.

Suppose that five people are to be seated at a round table. How many seating arrangements are possible?

Let the letters *A*, *B*, *C*, *D*, and *E* represent the five people. Three possible arrangements are shown below.

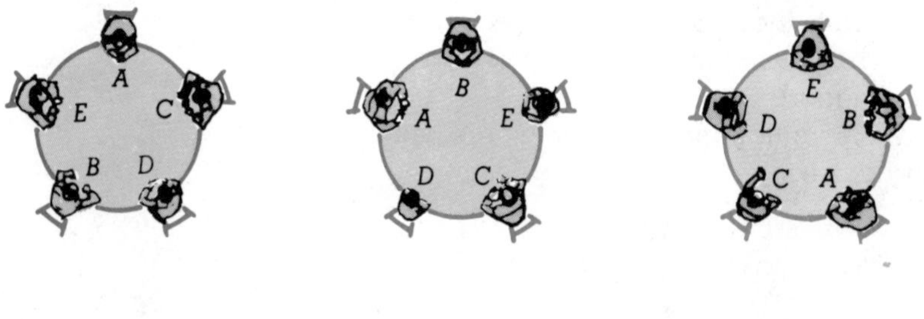

How does the first arrangement change if each person moves two places to his left? Which arrangement is really different from the other two?

When objects are arranged in a circle, some of the arrangements are alike. In the above example, these arrangements fall into groups of five, each of which can be found from one another by turning the circle. Thus, the number of distinct arrangements around the table is $\frac{1}{5}$ of the total number of arrangements in a line.

$$\begin{aligned} \frac{1}{5} \cdot 5! &= \frac{5 \cdot 4 \cdot 3 \cdot 2 \cdot 1}{5} \\ &= 4 \cdot 3 \cdot 2 \cdot 1 \\ &= 4! \text{ or } (5 - 1)! \end{aligned}$$

There are $(5 - 1)!$ arrangements of 5 objects around a circle.

Circular Permutations

> Suppose n objects are arranged in a circle. Then there are $\frac{n!}{n}$ or $(n - 1)!$ permutations of the n objects around the circle.

example

3 **A food vending machine has 6 different items on a revolving tray. How many ways can the items be arranged on the tray?**

$$\begin{aligned} (6 - 1)! &= 5! \\ &= 5 \cdot 4 \cdot 3 \cdot 2 \cdot 1 \text{ or } 120. \end{aligned}$$

There are 120 ways in which the items can be arranged on the tray.

Suppose that five people are to be seated at a round table where one person is seated next to the door as shown.

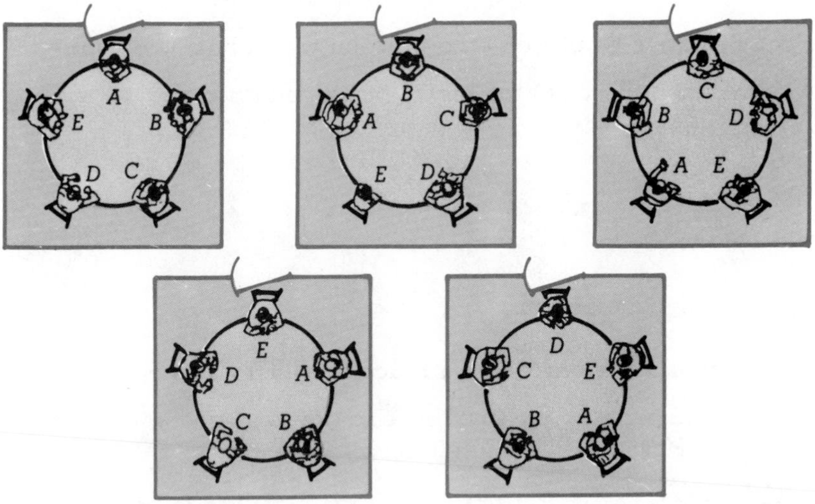

These arrangements are different. In each one, a different person sits closest to the door. Thus, there are $P(5, 5)$ or $5!$ arrangements relative to the door.

If n objects on a circle are arranged in relation to a fixed point, then there are $n!$ permutations.

Suppose three charms are placed on a bracelet which has no clasp. It appears that there are at most $(3 - 1)!$ or 2 different arrangements of charms on the bracelet.

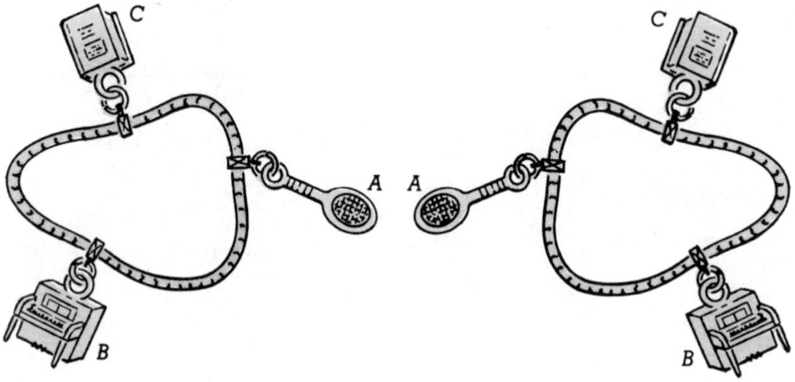

What happens if the bracelet with the first arrangement is turned over? The second arrangement appears. Thus there is really only one arrangement of the three charms. These two arrangements are reflections of one another. There are only half as many arrangements when reflections are possible.

$$\frac{(3-1)!}{2} = \frac{2}{2} \text{ or } 1$$

examples

4 **How many ways can 6 charms be placed on a bracelet which has no clasp?**

This is a circular permutation. Because the bracelet can be turned over, it is also reflective.

$$\frac{(6-1)!}{2} = \frac{5!}{2}$$
$$= \frac{5 \cdot 4 \cdot 3 \cdot 2 \cdot 1}{2} \text{ or } 60$$

There are 60 ways to arrange the charms.

5 **How many ways can 6 charms be placed on a bracelet which has a clasp?**

This is no longer a circular permutation since objects are arranged with respect to a fixed point, the clasp. However it is still reflective.

$$\frac{6!}{2} = \frac{6 \cdot 5 \cdot 4 \cdot 3 \cdot 2 \cdot 1}{2} \text{ or } 360$$

There are 360 ways to arrange the charms.

exercises

Exploratory State whether arrangements of the following objects are reflective or not reflective.

1. a football huddle of 11 players
2. chairs arranged in a circle
3. beads on a necklace with no clasp
4. chairs arranged in a row
5. people seated around a square table relative to each other
6. people seated around a square table relative to one chair
7. a list of students in a given class
8. placing 6 coins in a circle on a table

9-16. State whether the arrangements of the objects in problems **1-8** are circular or not circular.

Written How many ways can the letters of the following words be arranged?

1. FLOWER
2. ALGEBRA
3. PARALLEL
4. CANDIDATE
5. ARREARS
6. MONOPOLY
7. QUADRATIC
8. BASKETBALL
9. CLOCKMAKER

Solve each problem.

10. How many different arrangements can be made with ten pieces of silverware laid in a row if three are spoons, four are forks, and three are knives?
11. How many different six-digit license plates of the same state can have the digits 3, 5, 5, 6, 2, and 6?
12. There are 3 identical red flags and 5 identical white flags that are used to send signals. All 8 flags must be used. How many signals can be given?
13. Five algebra and four geometry books are to be placed on a shelf. How many ways can they be arranged if all the algebra books must be together?
14. How many ways can 6 keys be arranged on a key ring?
15. How many ways can 6 people be seated around a campfire?
16. How many ways can 8 charms be arranged on a charm bracelet which has no clasp?
17. How many ways can 4 men and 4 women be seated alternately at a round table?
18. How many ways can 5 people be seated at a round table relative to each other?
19. How many ways can 5 people be seated at a round table relative to the door in the room?
20. How many ways can 5 people be seated around a circular table if 2 of the people must be seated next to each other?
21. Twenty beads are strung in a circle. Fourteen are natural wood and six are red. How many ways can the red beads be strung in the circle?

Three men and three women are to be seated in a row containing six chairs. Find the number of ways the seating can be arranged given the following.

22. The men and the women are to sit in alternate chairs.
23. The men are to sit in three adjoining chairs.
24. The men are to sit in three adjcining chairs and the women are to sit in three adjoining chairs.

13-3 Combinations

Suppose 3 persons are to be chosen from a group of 5 to work on a certain project. The first person can be selected in 5 ways, the second person in 4 ways, and the third person in 3 ways or a total of $5 \cdot 4 \cdot 3 = 60$ ways. But consider these 60 possible selections. There is no difference between A, B, and C as one selection, A, C, and B as another, and B, C, and A as a third, and so on. For each group of 3 there are 3! ways they can be arranged in order. Thus, if order of selection is disregarded, there are $\frac{60}{3!}$ or 10 different groups of 3 that can be selected from the 5 boys.

$$\frac{60}{3!} = \frac{60}{3 \cdot 2 \cdot 1} \text{ or } 10$$

In this situation the order in which the people are chosen is *not* a consideration. The selection above is called a **combination** of 5 things taken 3 at a time. It is denoted by $C(5, 3)$.

$$C(5, 3) = \frac{5!}{2!3!}$$
$$= \frac{5 \cdot 4 \cdot 3 \cdot 2 \cdot 1}{2 \cdot 1 \cdot 3 \cdot 2 \cdot 1} \text{ or } 10$$

The number of combinations of n objects, taken r at a time, is written $C(n, r)$.

$$C(n, r) = \frac{n!}{(n - r)!r!}$$

Definition of $C(n, r)$

The main difference between a permutation and a combination is whether order is considered (permutation) or not (combination).

example

1 **From a list of 12 books, how many groups of 5 books can be selected?**

This selection is a combination of 12 things taken 5 at a time.

$$C(12, 5) = \frac{12!}{(12 - 5)!5!}$$
$$= \frac{12!}{7!5!}$$
$$= \frac{12 \cdot 11 \cdot 10 \cdot 9 \cdot 8 \cdot 7 \cdot 6 \cdot 5 \cdot 4 \cdot 3 \cdot 2 \cdot 1}{7 \cdot 6 \cdot 5 \cdot 4 \cdot 3 \cdot 2 \cdot 1 \cdot 5 \cdot 4 \cdot 3 \cdot 2 \cdot 1}$$
$$= \frac{12 \cdot 11 \cdot 10 \cdot 9 \cdot 8}{5 \cdot 4 \cdot 3 \cdot 2 \cdot 1} \text{ or } 792$$

There are 792 groups.

examples

2 **From a group of 4 men and 5 women, how many committees of 3 men and 2 women can be formed?**

Order is *not* considered. The questions are: How many ways can 3 men be chosen from 4? How many ways can 2 women be chosen from 5?

$$C(4, 3) \cdot C(5, 2) = \frac{4!}{(4-3)!3!} \cdot \frac{5!}{(5-2)!2!}$$
$$= \frac{4!}{1!3!} \cdot \frac{5!}{3!2!}$$
$$= 4 \cdot 10 \text{ or } 40$$

The combinations are multiplied to use the Basic Counting Principle

There are 40 possible committees.

3 **A bag contains 3 red, 5 white, and 8 blue marbles. How many ways can 2 red, 1 white, and 2 blue marbles be chosen?**

$C(3, 2)$ Two of 3 red ones will be chosen.
$C(5, 1)$ One of 5 white ones will be chosen.
$C(8, 2)$ Two of 8 blue ones will be chosen.

$$C(3, 2) \cdot C(5, 1) \cdot C(8, 2) = \frac{3}{1} \cdot \frac{5}{1} \cdot \frac{8 \cdot 7}{2 \cdot 1} \text{ or } 420$$

There are 420 different ways.

exercises

Exploratory State whether arrangements of the following represent a combination or a permutation.

1. seating students in a row
2. the answers on a true-false test
3. a committee of 4 men and 5 women chosen from 8 men and 7 women
4. the subsets of a given set
5. a team of 5 people chosen from a group of 12 people
6. three-letter patterns chosen from the letters of the word *algebra*
7. a hand of 5 cards
8. a batting order in baseball

Written Find the value of each of the following.

1. $C(4, 2)$
2. $C(12, 7)$
3. $C(6, 6)$
4. $C(20, 15)$

Find the value of n in each of the following.

5. $C(n, 12) = C(30, 18)$
6. $C(14, 3) = C(n, 11)$
7. $C(n, 5) = C(n, 7)$

Solve each problem.

8. From a list of 10 books, how many groups of 4 books can be selected?
9. How many baseball teams of 9 members can be formed from 14 players?
10. How many ways can a club of 13 members choose 4 different officers?
11. How many ways can a club of 13 members choose a 4-person committee?

12. Suppose there are 9 points on a circle. How many different 4-sided closed figures can be formed by joining any 4 of these points?

13. Suppose there are 8 points in a plane, no 3 of which are collinear. How many distinct triangles could be formed with these points as vertices?

14. How many diagonals does a convex polygon that has 24 vertices have?

15. There are 85 telephones at Kennedy High School. How many 2-way connections can be made among the school telephones?

16. From a standard deck of cards, how many different 5-card hands can have 5 cards of the same suit?

17. From a standard deck of cards, how many different 4-card hands can have each card from a different suit?

A bag contains 4 red, 6 white, and 9 blue marbles. How many ways can 5 marbles be selected to meet the following conditions?

18. All the marbles are white.
19. All the marbles are blue.
20. Two must be blue.
21. Two are 1 color and 3 are another color.

From a group of 8 men and 10 women, a committee of 5 is to be formed. How many committees can be formed if the committee is to be comprised as follows?

22. All are men.
23. There are 3 men and 2 women.
24. There is 1 man and 4 women.
25. All are women.

26. The cast of a school play which requires 4 girls and 3 boys is to be selected from 7 eligible girls and 9 eligible boys. How many ways can the cast be selected?

27. Al's Pizza Palace offers pepperoni, mushrooms, sausage, onions, anchovies, and peppers as toppings for their regular plain pizza. How many different pizzas can be made?

13-4 Probability

When a coin is tossed, only two outcomes are possible. Either the coin will show a head or a tail. The desired outcome is called a **success**. Any other outcome is called a **failure**.

The probability of success for heads is $\frac{1}{2}$, as is the probability of success for tails.

Probability of Success and of Failure

If an event can succeed in s ways and fail in f ways, then the probability of success and the probability of failure are as follows.

$$P(s) = \frac{s}{s+f} \qquad P(f) = \frac{f}{s+f}$$

An event that cannot fail has a probability of 1. An event that cannot succeed has a probability of 0. Thus, the probability of success, $P(s)$, is always between 0 and 1 inclusive.

$$0 \leq P(s) \leq 1$$

The sum of the probability of success and the probability of failure for any event is always equal to 1.

$$P(s) + P(f) = \frac{s}{s+f} + \frac{f}{s+f}$$
$$= \frac{s+f}{s+f} \text{ or } 1$$

This property is often used in finding the probability of events. For example, if $P(s) = \frac{1}{4}$, then $P(f)$ is $1 - \frac{1}{4}$ or $\frac{3}{4}$. Because their sum is 1, $P(s)$ and $P(f)$ are called **complements**.

examples

1 **A box contains 3 baseballs, 7 softballs, and 11 tennis balls. What is the probability that a ball selected at random will be a tennis ball?**

$$P(\text{tennis ball}) = \frac{s}{s+f}$$
$$= \frac{11}{11 + (3+7)} \text{ or } \frac{11}{21}$$

The probability of selecting a tennis ball is $\frac{11}{21}$.

2 **Two cards are drawn at random from a standard deck of 52 cards. What is the probability that both are hearts?**

$$P(\text{two hearts}) = \frac{C(13, 2)}{C(52, 2)}$$

There are C(13, 2) ways to select 2 of 13 hearts.
There are C(52, 2) ways to select 2 of 52 cards.

$$= \frac{\frac{13!}{11!2!}}{\frac{52!}{50!2!}}$$
$$= \frac{78}{1326} \text{ or } \frac{1}{17}$$

The probability of selecting two hearts is $\frac{1}{17}$.

3 **A collection of 15 transistors contains 3 that are defective. If 2 transistors are selected at random, what is the probability that at least 1 of them is good?**

The complement of selecting at least 1 good transistor is selecting 2 defective transistors.

$$P(2 \text{ defective}) = \frac{C(3, 2)}{C(15, 2)}$$
$$= \frac{3}{105} \text{ or } \frac{1}{35}$$

Thus, the probability of selecting at least one good transistor is $1 - \frac{1}{35}$ or $\frac{34}{35}$.

The probability of the success of an event and its complement are used in computing the **odds** on an event.

The odds of the successful outcome of an event is the ratio of the probability of its success to the probability of its failure.

$$\text{Odds} = \frac{P(s)}{P(f)}$$

Definition of Odds

example

4 What are the odds of getting 2 ones in a single throw of a pair of dice?

There are 6 · 6 or 36 possible outcomes when throwing two dice.

$P(s) = \frac{1}{36}$ $\qquad P(f) = 1 - \frac{1}{36}$ or $\frac{35}{36}$

$$\text{Odds} = \frac{P(s)}{P(f)}$$

$$= \frac{\frac{1}{36}}{\frac{35}{36}} \text{ or } \frac{1}{35}$$

The odds of getting two ones is $\frac{1}{35}$. *This is read "one to thirty-five."*

exercises

Exploratory State the odds of an event occurring given the probability that it occurs as follows.

1. $\frac{1}{2}$
2. $\frac{3}{4}$
3. $\frac{7}{15}$
4. $\frac{3}{20}$

State the probability of an event occurring given the following odds.

5. $\frac{3}{4}$
6. $\frac{6}{5}$
7. $\frac{4}{9}$
8. $\frac{1}{1}$

Solve each problem.

9. The odds are 6-to-1 *against* an event occurring. What is the probability that it will occur?
10. The probability of an event occurring is $\frac{3}{4}$. What are the odds that it will not occur?

A card is drawn at random from a standard deck of cards. Find the probability of each of the following.

11. heart
12. ace
13. ace of hearts

Written Solve each problem.

1. Two dice are thrown. Find the probability that the same number will show on both dice.
2. Four coins are tossed at the same time. Find the probability that four heads will come up.
3. If the odds are 50 to 1 that it will rain today, find the probability that it will not rain.
4. Find the odds of throwing a sum of 7 on a throw of a pair of dice.
5. A die is thrown twice and a 3 shows on the first throw. Find the probability that a 3 also shows on the second throw.
6. A pair of dice are thrown and their sum is 6. Find the probability that each dice shows a 3.

In a box are 4 black socks, 5 white socks, and 2 red socks. A sock is drawn at random.

7. Find the probability that it will not be red.
8. Find the probability that it will be white or red.

A number is picked at random from the integers 1 through 50. Find the probability of each of the following.

9. Odd integer
10. Multiple of 5
11. Perfect square

In a bag are 5 red, 9 blue, and 6 white marbles. Two are selected at random. Find the probability of each of the following selections.

12. 2 red
13. 2 white
14. 2 blue
15. 1 red and 1 blue
16. 1 red and 1 white

Suppose you select 2 letters from the word *algebra*. What is the probability of selecting 2 letters and having the following occur?

17. 2 consonants
18. 1 vowel and 1 consonant
19. 2 vowels

A die is thrown two times. Find the odds of each of the following.

20. no fives
21. at least one five
22. both fives

The table below gives the status of employment of 500 students at Hawkins College.

Employment	Class				
	Freshman	Sophomore	Junior	Senior	Totals
Unemployed	75	56	35	18	184
Part-time	55	46	45	45	191
Full-time	30	28	30	37	125
Totals	160	130	110	100	500

23. If a student is selected at random, find the probability that the student is unemployed.
24. If a student is selected at random, find the probability that the student is a freshman employed part-time.
25. If a sophomore is selected at random, find the probability that the student is employed full-time.
26. Find the probability that a student selected at random is a junior.
27. Find the probability that a senior selected at random is unemployed.
28. Find the probability that an unemployed student selected at random is a senior.

13-5 Probabilities of Independent and Dependent Events

Suppose a die is thrown twice. The second throw of the die is *not* affected by the first throw of the die. Thus, the events are independent. The probability of getting a 5 on each throw of the die is $\frac{1}{6} \cdot \frac{1}{6}$ or $\frac{1}{36}$.

If two events, A and B, are independent, then the probability of both events occurring is found as follows.

$$P(A \text{ and } B) = P(A) \cdot P(B)$$

Probability of Two Independent Events

examples

1 **Find the probability of getting a sum of 7 on the first throw of two dice and a sum of 4 on the second throw.**

Let A be a sum of 7 on the first throw. Let B be a sum of 4 on the second throw.

$P(A) = \frac{6}{36}$ $\quad$ $P(B) = \frac{3}{36}$ $\quad$ *Why?*

$$P(A \text{ and } B) = P(A) \cdot P(B)$$
$$= \frac{6}{36} \cdot \frac{3}{36} \text{ or } \frac{1}{72}$$

The probability is $\frac{1}{72}$.

2 **A new phone is being installed at the Steiner residence. Find the probability that the final three digits in the telephone number will be even.**

$P(\text{any digit being even}) = \frac{5}{10}$ or $\frac{1}{2}$

$P(\text{final three being even}) = \frac{1}{2} \cdot \frac{1}{2} \cdot \frac{1}{2}$ or $\frac{1}{8}$

The probability that the final three digits will be even is $\frac{1}{8}$.

Suppose two cards are drawn from a standard deck of cards. What is the probability that both cards are clubs? These events are **dependent** because the outcome of the first selection has an effect on the second selection.

$P(\text{1st club}) = \frac{13}{52}$ or $\frac{1}{4}$ $\quad$ *Thirteen of the 52 cards are clubs.*

$P(\text{2nd club}) = \frac{12}{51}$ or $\frac{4}{17}$ $\quad$ *Twelve of the remaining 51 cards are clubs.*

$P(\text{both clubs}) = \frac{1}{4} \cdot \frac{4}{17} = \frac{1}{17}$

If two events, A and B, are dependent, then the probability of both events occurring is found as follows.

$$P(A \text{ and } B) = P(A) \cdot P(B \text{ following } A)$$

Probability of Two Dependent Events

example

3 **There are 5 red, 3 blue, and 7 black marbles in a bag. Three marbles are chosen without replacement. Find the probability of selecting a red one, then a blue one, and then a red one.**

$P(\text{red, blue, and red})$
$= P(\text{red}) \cdot P(\text{blue following red}) \cdot P(\text{red following red and blue})$
$= \frac{5}{15} \cdot \frac{3}{14} \cdot \frac{4}{13} \text{ or } \frac{2}{91}$

The probability is $\frac{2}{91}$.

exercises

Exploratory Identify the events in each of the following problems as *independent* or *dependent*.

1. There are 2 cups of coffee and 4 cups of tea on the counter. Dave drinks two of them. What is the probability that he drank 2 cups of coffee?
2. In a bag are 5 oranges and 4 tangerines. Noelle selects one, replaces it and selects another. What is the probability that both selections were oranges?
3. A green die and a red die are thrown. What is the probability that a 4 shows on the green die and a 5 shows on the red die?
4. When Luis plays Jose in backgammon, the odds are 4 to 3 that Luis will win. What is the probability that Luis will win the next 4 games?
5. In a bag are 4 red, 4 green, and 7 blue marbles. Three are selected in sequence without replacement. What is the probability of selecting a red, green, and blue in that order?
6. Two cards are drawn from a standard deck of cards with replacement. What is the probability of drawing a heart and a spade in that order?

7–12. Solve problems 1–6.

Written Solve each problem.

1. Two dice are thrown. What is the probability that a 3 will show on each die?
2. A die is thrown three times. What is the probability that 6 will show all three times?

A bag contains 5 red, 4 white, and 7 blue marbles. If 3 marbles are selected in succession, what is the probability that they are red, white, and blue in that order given the following conditions?

3. No replacement occurs.
4. Replacement occurs each time.

Fifty tickets, numbered consecutively 1 to 50, are placed in a box. What is the probability that in 4 separate drawings, the following selections occur?

5. 4 odd numbers, if replacement occurs
6. 4 odd numbers, if no replacement occurs
7. 4 consecutive numbers if no replacement occurs
8. 4 consecutive numbers if replacement occurs

A red and a green die are thrown. What is the probability that the following occurs?

9. neither shows a 2
10. both show the same number
11. both show different numbers
12. the red shows a 2 and the green shows any other number

Diane's batting average is .300. That is, she gets an average of 3 hits for every 10 times at bat. What is the probability that the following occurs? Assume that she gets an out if she does not get a hit.

13. 3 hits for the next 3 times at bat
14. 3 outs for the next 3 times at bat
15. In one dresser drawer Kenneth has 6 pairs of black socks and 3 pairs of gray socks. In another drawer he has 11 white handkerchiefs and 6 colored handkerchiefs. In the dark he selects 2 pairs of socks and a handkerchief. What is the probability that he has a pair of black socks and a white handkerchief?
16. There are 100 clocks in a certain overseas shipment. Assume that there are 4 clocks damaged in shipment but the packaging gives no indication of such damage. If a dealer buys 6 clocks without examining the contents, what is the probability that he does not have a damaged clock?

A standard deck of cards contains 4 suits of 13 cards each.

17. What is the probability of drawing 13 diamonds without replacement?
18. What is the probability of drawing 13 cards of one suit without replacement?
19. What is the probability of drawing 13 red cards without replacement?
20. What is the probability of drawing 13 face cards without replacement?

13-6 Probability of Mutually Exclusive Events or Inclusive Events

Suppose a coin purse contains 5 nickels, 6 dimes, and 2 quarters. What is the probability of selecting a nickel or a dime? Since no coin is both a nickel and a dime the events are **mutually exclusive.** That is, if one event occurs, the other *cannot* occur. The probability of selecting a nickel or a dime is $\frac{5}{13} + \frac{6}{13}$ or $\frac{11}{13}$.

If two events, A and B, are mutually exclusive, then the probability of both events occurring is found as follows.

$$P(A \text{ or } B) = P(A) + P(B)$$

Probability of Mutually Exclusive Events

example

1 **Find the probability of a sum of 6 or a sum of 9 on a single throw of two dice.**

$P(\text{sum of } 6) = \frac{5}{36}$ $\quad$ $P(\text{sum of } 9) = \frac{4}{36}$

Since the sum cannot be both 6 and 9, these events are mutually exclusive.

$P(\text{sum of 6 or sum of 9}) = \frac{5}{36} + \frac{4}{36} \text{ or } \frac{9}{36}$

The probability is $\frac{9}{36}$ or $\frac{1}{4}$.

What is the probability of drawing a king or a black card? It is possible to draw both a king and a black card. Therefore, these events are *not* mutually exclusive. They are called **inclusive**. The probability of selecting a king or a black card is as follows.

king		*black*		*black king*				*black or king*
$\frac{4}{52}$	+	$\frac{26}{52}$	−	$\frac{2}{52}$	=	$\frac{28}{52}$	or	$\frac{7}{13}$

If two events, A and B, are inclusive, then the probability of either A or B occurring is found as follows.

$$P(A \text{ or } B) = P(A) + P(B) - P(A \text{ and } B)$$

Probability of Inclusive Events

examples

2 **A letter is picked at random from the alphabet. Find the probability that the letter is contained in the word *house* or in the word *phone*.**

Let event A be a letter from *house*. Let event B be a letter from *phone*.

$P(A) = \frac{5}{26}$ $\quad$ $P(B) = \frac{5}{26}$ $\quad$ $P(A \text{ and } B) = \frac{3}{26}$ $\quad$ *Why?*

$P(A \text{ or } B) = \frac{5}{26} + \frac{5}{26} - \frac{3}{26} \text{ or } \frac{7}{26}$

The probability is $\frac{7}{26}$.

3 **A committee of 5 people is to be selected from a group of 6 men and 7 women. What is the probability that the committee will have at least 3 men?**

These events are mutually exclusive. Why?

$$\begin{aligned} P(\text{at least 3 men}) &= P(\text{3 men}) + P(\text{4 men}) + P(\text{5 men}) \\ &= \frac{C(6, 3) \cdot C(7, 2)}{C(13, 5)} + \frac{C(6, 4) \cdot C(7, 1)}{C(13, 5)} + \frac{C(6, 5) \cdot C(7, 0)}{C(13, 5)} \\ &= \frac{140}{429} + \frac{35}{429} + \frac{2}{429} = \frac{177}{429} = \frac{59}{143} \end{aligned}$$

The probability of at least 3 men on the committee is $\frac{59}{143}$.

EXERCISES

Exploratory Identify each of the following events as mutually exclusive or inclusive.

1. Ten slips of paper numbered from 1 to 10 are in a box. A slip of paper is drawn and a die is thrown. What is the probability of getting a 2 on one of them?
2. Two cards are drawn from a standard deck of cards. What is the probability of having drawn an ace or a red card?
3. The Ranger pitching staff has 5 left handers and 8 right-handers. If 2 are selected what is the probability that at least one of them is a right-hander?
4. Five coins are tossed. What is the probability of getting at least 3 tails?
5. In a certain class, 5 of the 12 girls are blondes and 6 of the 15 boys are blondes. What is the probability of selecting a girl or a blonde?
6. A bag contains 7 red, 4 blue, and 14 black marbles. If 3 marbles are selected, what is the probability that all are red or all are blue?

7-12. Solve problems 1-6.

Written Two faces of a die are red, two are blue, and two are white. If the die is thrown, what is the probability that the following occurs?

1. The die shows either red or blue.
2. The die does not show red.

A bag contains 7 red and 4 white marbles. Three marbles are selected. What is the probability that the following occurs?

3. all 3 red or all 3 white
4. at least 2 red
5. at least 1 white
6. exactly 2 white

Two cards are drawn from a standard deck of cards. What is the probability that the following occurs?

7. both aces or both face cards
8. both aces or both black
9. both black or both face cards
10. both either red or an ace

Six coins are tossed. What is the probability that the following occurs?

11. 3 heads or 2 tails
12. at least 4 tails
13. 4 heads or 1 tail
14. all heads or all tails

A committee of 6 people is to be selected from a group of 7 men and 7 women. What is the probability of the following?

15. all men or all women
16. 5 men or 5 women
17. 3 men and 3 women
18. at least 4 women

Slips of paper numbered from 1 to 25 are in a box. A slip of paper is drawn at random. What is the probability that the following occurs?

19. The number is a multiple of 2 or 5.
20. The number is a multiple of 3 or is an odd number.
21. The number is a multiple of 3 or is a prime number.
22. The number is a multiple of 7 or is an even number.

Truman Reed is a geneticist (juh NET uh suhst). He determines the probable ratios of certain traits occurring in the offspring of plants. He uses this information to develop varieties of plants that are better suited for use than those presently available. For example, the acid-free tomato was developed by this type of work.

Genes are the units which transmit hereditary traits. The possible forms which a gene may take, **dominant** and **recessive,** are called **alleles.** A particular trait is determined by two alleles, one from the female parent and one from the male parent. If an organism has the trait which is dominant, it may have either two dominant alleles or one dominant and one recessive allele. If the organism has the trait which is recessive, it must have two recessive alleles.

Example Consider a plant in which tall stems, T, are dominant to short stems, t. What is the probability of obtaining a long-stemmed plant if two long-stemmed plants both with the genetic formula Tt are crossed?

	T	t
T	TT	Tt
t	Tt	tt

A Punnett square is a chart used to determine the possible combinations of characteristics among offspring.

3 tall-stemmed
1 short-stemmed
4 total

Thus, the probability is $\frac{3}{4}$.

Exercises In a certain plant, red flowers, R, are dominant to white flowers, r. If a white-flowered plant, rr is crossed with a red-flowered plant, Rr, find the probability of each of the following.

1. white-flowered plant
2. red-flowered plant
3. In a certain plant, tall, T, is dominant to short, t. Green pods, G, are dominant to yellow pods, g. Plants with the genetic formulas $TtGg$ and $TTGg$ are crossed. Find the probability of an offspring being tall and having green pods.

13-7 Conditional Probability

Suppose Jack says, "If it rains, I will stay in and do my homework." While you cannot be certain that Jack will not do his homework if it does not rain, the occurrence of rain will have some effect on the completion of the homework.

The probability of an event given the occurrence of another event is called **conditional probability.** The conditional probability of A, given B, is denoted by $P(A/B)$.

Conditional Probability

The conditional probability of event A, given event B, is found as follows.

$$P(A/B) = \frac{P(A \text{ and } B)}{P(B)} \quad \text{where } P(B) \neq 0$$

examples

1 **A pair of dice are thrown. Find the probability that the numbers of the dice match given that their sum is greater than 7.**

Let event A be that the numbers match. Let event B be that their sum is greater than 7.

$P(B) = \frac{15}{36}$ $\quad$ $P(A \text{ and } B) = \frac{3}{36}$ $\quad$ *Why?*

$$P(A/B) = \frac{P(A \text{ and } B)}{P(B)}$$

$$= \frac{\frac{3}{36}}{\frac{15}{36}} \text{ or } \frac{1}{5}$$

The probability is $\frac{1}{5}$.

2 **A pair of dice are thrown. Find the probability that their sum is greater than 7 given that the numbers match.**

Let event A be that the sum of the dice is greater than 7. Let event B be that the numbers match.

$P(B) = \frac{6}{36}$ $\quad$ $P(A \text{ and } B) = \frac{3}{36}$

$$P(A/B) = \frac{P(A \text{ and } B)}{P(B)}$$

$$= \frac{\frac{3}{36}}{\frac{6}{36}} \text{ or } \frac{1}{2}$$

The probability is $\frac{1}{2}$.

Suppose a die is thrown twice. What is the probability of a 3 on the second throw given that a 3 occurred on the first throw?

$$P(A/B) = \frac{\frac{1}{36}}{\frac{6}{36}} \text{ or } \frac{1}{6}$$

But $P(A)$ is also $\frac{1}{6}$. Thus, in this case $P(A) = \frac{P(A \text{ and } B)}{P(B)}$ or $P(A \text{ and } B) = P(A) \cdot P(B)$. Therefore events A and B are independent. The fact that a 3 occurred on the first throw does *not* affect the probability that a 3 will occur on the second throw.

example

3 **One card is drawn from a standard deck of 52 cards. What is the probability that it is a queen if it is known to be a face card?**

$P(B) = \frac{12}{52}$ or $\frac{3}{13}$ $\quad$ $P(A \text{ and } B) = \frac{4}{52}$ or $\frac{1}{13}$ $\quad$ *event A = queen* *event B = face card*

$$P(A/B) = \frac{\frac{1}{13}}{\frac{3}{13}} \text{ or } \frac{1}{3}$$

The probability is $\frac{1}{3}$.

exercises

Exploratory The conditional probability of A given B is represented as $P(A/B)$. Identify events A and B in each of the following problems.

1. A die is thrown three times. What is the probability that 4 shows on the third throw given that a 6 showed on the first two throws?
2. A coin is tossed three times. What is the probability that at the most 2 heads show given that at least one head shows?
3. Two coins are tossed. What is the probability that one coin shows tails if it is known that at least one coin shows heads?
4. Two boys and two girls are lined up at random. What is the probability that the girls are separated if a girl is on an end?
5. One bag contains 4 red marbles and 4 blue marbles. Another bag contains 2 red marbles and 6 blue marbles. A marble has been drawn from one of the bags at random and found to be blue. What is the probability that the marble came from the first bag?
6. A city council consists of six Democrats, two of whom are women, and six Republicans, four of whom are men. A member is chosen at random. If the member is a man, what is the probability that he is a Democrat?

7-12. Solve problems 1-6.

Written Solve each problem.

1. One card is drawn from a standard deck of cards. What is the probability that it is a red king if it is known to be a face card?
2. A coin is tossed three times. What is the probability that the third toss shows heads given that the first two tosses showed heads?

A green die and a red die are thrown.

3. What is the probability that the sum of the dice is greater than 10 if the red die came up 6?
4. What is the probability that the sum of the dice is less than 6 if the red die came up 2?
5. What is the probability that the sum of the dice is 10 or greater if a 5 came up on at least one die?
6. What is the probability that the sum of the dice is 7 if the green die resulted in a number less than 4?

Three coins are tossed. What is the probability that they are all tails if the following events have occurred?

7. The first coin is a tail.
8. One of the coins is a head.
9. At least one of the coins is a tail.
10. At least two of the coins are tails.

Two dice are thrown. If the two numbers showing are different, what is the probability of each of the following?

11. Their sum is 5.
12. One of the dice shows a 1.
13. Their sum is greater than 9.
14. Their sum is 4 or less.
15. Five-digit numbers are formed from the numbers 7, 7, 7, 6, and 6. If a number is even, what is the probability that the 6's are together?
16. Two numbers are selected at random from the numbers 1 through 9. If their sum is even, what is the probability that both numbers are odd?

A committee of 3 is selected from Ron, Becky, Wes, Kay, Jo, and Rich.

17. If Becky is on the committee, what is the probability that Wes is also on it?
18. If Wes and Kay are on the committee, what is the probability that Jo is not on it?
19. If Ron was not selected, what is the probability that Becky and Kay were selected?
20. If neither Ron nor Rich were selected, what is the probability that Becky and Wes were selected?
21. One box contains 3 red balls and 4 white balls. A second box contains 5 red balls and 3 white balls. A box is selected at random and one ball is withdrawn. If the ball is white, what is the probability that it was taken from the second box?
22. A buyer for a department store will accept a carton containing 10 clocks if a sample of 2, chosen at random, are not defective. What is the probability that she will accept a carton of 10 if it contains 4 defective clocks?

In a game played with a standard deck of cards, each face card has a value of 10, each ace a value of 1, and each number card a value equal to the number. Two cards are drawn.

23. If one card is the queen of hearts, what is the probability that the sum of the cards is greater than 18?
24. If one card is an ace, what is the probability that the sum of the cards is 7 or less?

13-8 The Binomial Theorem and Probability

Suppose that 5 coins are tossed at the same time. What is the probability that exactly 2 coins will show heads? The number of ways this can happen is given by C(5, 2) or 10.

The probability may be found by using the binomial expansion. Let p_h represent the probability that heads will show on one coin on one toss. Let p_t represent the probability that tails will show on one coin.

$$(p_h + p_t)^5 = 1p_h^5 + 5p_h^4p_t + 10\,p_h^3p_t^2 + 10p_h^2p_t^3 + 5p_hp_t^4 + 1p_t^5$$

coefficient	term	meaning	probability
C(5, 0)	$1p_h^5$	1 way to get 5 heads	$1\left(\frac{1}{2}\right)^5$ or $\frac{1}{32}$
C(5, 1)	$5p_h^4p_t$	5 ways to get 4 heads and 1 tail	$5\left(\frac{1}{2}\right)^4\left(\frac{1}{2}\right)$ or $\frac{5}{32}$
C(5, 2)	$10p_h^3p_t^2$	10 ways to get 3 heads and 2 tails	$10\left(\frac{1}{2}\right)^3\left(\frac{1}{2}\right)^2$ or $\frac{5}{16}$
C(5, 3)	$10p_h^2p_t^3$	10 ways to get 2 heads and 3 tails	$10\left(\frac{1}{2}\right)^2\left(\frac{1}{2}\right)^3$ or $\frac{5}{16}$
C(5, 4)	$5p_hp_t^4$	5 ways to get 1 head and 4 tails	$5\left(\frac{1}{2}\right)\left(\frac{1}{2}\right)^4$ or $\frac{5}{32}$
C(5, 5)	$1p_t^5$	1 way to get 5 tails	$1\left(\frac{1}{2}\right)^5$ or $\frac{1}{32}$

$p_h = p_t = \frac{1}{2}$

Thus, the probability that exactly two coins will show heads is $\frac{5}{16}$.

Other probabilities can be determined from the above expansion. For example, what is the probability of at least 2 heads showing if 5 coins are tossed simultaneously? The first, second, third, and fourth terms represent the condition that two or more heads show. Thus the probability of this happening is as follows.

$$P(\text{at least 2 heads}) = \frac{1}{32} + \frac{5}{32} + \frac{5}{16} + \frac{5}{16}$$
$$= \frac{26}{32} \text{ or } \frac{13}{16}$$

Problems which can be solved using a binomial expansion are called **binomial experiments.**

Binomial Experiments

A binomial experiment exists if and only if the following conditions occur.

1. **The experiment consists of n identical trials.**
2. **Each trial results in one of two outcomes.**
3. **The trials are independent.**

examples

1 **Suppose that three dice are thrown at the same time. Find the probability that at least one 4 will show.**

Let p_4 represent the probability that 4 shows on one throw of one die. Let q_4 represent the probability of failure of 4 to show on one throw of one die.

$$(p_4 + q_4)^3 = p_4^3 + 3p_4^2q_4 + 3p_4q_4^2 + q_4^3$$

$$P(\text{at least one } 4) = \left(\frac{1}{6}\right)^3 + 3\left(\frac{1}{6}\right)^2\left(\frac{5}{6}\right) + 3\left(\frac{1}{6}\right)\left(\frac{5}{6}\right)^2 \qquad p_4 = \frac{1}{6}, q_4 = \frac{5}{6}$$

$$= \frac{1}{216} + 3\left(\frac{1}{36}\right)\left(\frac{5}{6}\right) + 3\left(\frac{1}{6}\right)\left(\frac{25}{36}\right)$$

$$= \frac{1 + 15 + 75}{216} \text{ or } \frac{91}{216}$$

The probability is $\frac{91}{216}$.

2 **Peggy guesses on all 10 questions on a true-false quiz. What is the probability that exactly half of the answers are correct?**

There are only two outcomes on each question: true (T) or false (F). When $(T + F)^{10}$ is expanded, the term containing T^5F^5 will give the desired probability.

$$C(10, 5)T^5F^5 = \frac{10 \cdot 9 \cdot 8 \cdot 7 \cdot 6}{5 \cdot 4 \cdot 3 \cdot 2 \cdot 1} \cdot \left(\frac{1}{2}\right)^5\left(\frac{1}{2}\right)^5$$

Replace T by P(T) which is $\frac{1}{2}$ and F by P(F) which is $\frac{1}{2}$.

$$= 252\left(\frac{1}{32}\right)\left(\frac{1}{32}\right) \text{ or } \frac{63}{256}$$

The probability is $\frac{63}{256}$.

exercises

Exploratory **State whether each of the following situations represents a binomial experiment or not. Solve those that represent a binomial experiment.**

1. A coin is tossed 4 times. What is the probability of 2 heads and 2 tails?
2. Five coins are tossed. What is the probability of at least 3 tails?
3. Bianca draws 4 cards from a standard deck of cards. What is the probability of drawing 4 kings if she replaces each card?
4. Randy draws 3 cards from a standard deck of cards. What is the probability of drawing 3 aces if he does not replace the cards?
5. On a shelf are 8 cans of vegetables and 4 cans of fruit. If 2 cans are selected and each is replaced, what is the probability that they both contain fruit?
6. A die is thrown 2 times. What is the probability that the die shows a 3 both times?

Written Three coins are tossed. What is the probability of the following?

1. 3 heads
2. 3 tails
3. at least 2 heads
4. exactly 2 tails

A die is thrown 5 times. What is the probability of the following?

5. only one 4
6. at least three 4's
7. no more than two 4's
8. exactly five 4's

Connie has a bent coin. The probability of heads is $\frac{2}{3}$ with this coin. She tosses the coin 4 times. What is the probability of the following?

9. no heads
10. 4 heads
11. at least 3 heads

Maroa guesses on all 10 questions on a true-false test. What is the probability of the following?.

12. 7 correct
13. at least 6 correct
14. all incorrect
15. at least half incorrect

A batter is now batting .200 (meaning 200 hits in 1000 times at bat). In the next 5 at-bats, what is the probability of having the following?

16. exactly 1 hit
17. exactly 3 hits
18. at least 4 hits

If a tack is dropped, the probability that it will land point up is $\frac{2}{5}$. Six tacks are dropped. What is the probability of the following?

19. all point up
20. exactly 3 point up
21. exactly 5 point up
22. at least 6 point up

A "wheel of fortune" at a carnival has the numbers from 1 through 10.

23. What is the probability of 7 never coming up in 5 spins of the wheel?
24. What is the probability of 7 coming up exactly once in 5 spins of the wheel?
25. What is the probability of 7 coming up each time in 5 spins of the wheel?
26. What is the probability of 7 coming up at least once in 5 spins of the wheel?
27. The probability that Jeff wins a game of table tennis with John is $\frac{3}{5}$. Suppose they play 10 games. What is the probability that John will win 5 games?
28. A box contains 3 red and 3 white marbles. An experiment consists of selecting one marble at random, noting the color, and then replacing the ball in the box. What is the probability of selecting 5 white balls in 8 trials?
29. The probability that the Mustang baseball team will win a home game is $\frac{3}{5}$. The team plays 10 homè games before its next road trip. What is the probability that it will win 8 out of the 10 games?
30. The probability that a 55-year-old man will die before his next birthday is .02. What is the probability that no more than three 55-year-old men in a sample of 10 will die within a year?

Chapter Summary

1. Basic Counting Principle: Suppose an event can be chosen in p different ways. Another independent event can be chosen in q different ways. Then the two events can be chosen successively in $p \cdot q$ ways. (364)
2. Definition of $P(n, r)$: The number of permutations of n objects, taken r at a time, is defined as follows. $P(n, r) = \frac{n!}{(n-r)!}$ (365)
3. Permutations with Repetitions: The number of permutations of n objects of which p are alike and q are alike is found by evaluating the following expression. $\frac{n!}{p!q!}$ (368)
4. Circular Permutations: If n objects are arranged in a circle, then there are $\frac{n!}{n}$ or $(n-1)!$ permutations of the n objects. (369)
5. Definition of $C(n, r)$: The number of combinations of n objects, taken r at a time, is written $C(n, r)$. $C(n, r) = \frac{n!}{(n-r)!r!}$ (372)
6. Probability of Success and of Failure: If an event can succeed in s ways and fail in f ways, then the probability of success and the probability of failure are as follows.

   $$P(s) = \frac{s}{s+f} \qquad P(f) = \frac{f}{s+f} \quad (374)$$
7. Definition of Odds: The odds of the successful outcome of an event is the ratio of the probability of its success to the probability of its failure. Odds $= \frac{P(s)}{P(f)}$ (376)
8. Probability of Two Independent Events: If two events, A and B, are independent, then the probability of both events occurring is found as follows. $P(A \text{ and } B) = P(A) \cdot P(B)$ (378)
9. Probability of Two Dependent Events: If two events, A and B, are dependent, then the probability of both events occurring is found as follows. $P(A \text{ and } B) = P(A) \cdot P(B \text{ following } A)$ (379)
10. Probability of Mutually Exclusive Events: If two events, A and B, are mutually exclusive, then the probability of both events occurring is found as follows. $P(A \text{ or } B) = P(A) + P(B)$ (380)
11. Probability of Inclusive Events: If two events, A and B, are inclusive, then the probability of either A or B occurring is found as follows. $P(A \text{ or } B) = P(A) + P(B) - P(A \text{ and } B)$ (381)
12. Conditional Probability: The conditional probability of event A, given event B, is found as follows. $P(A/B) = \frac{P(A \text{ and } B)}{P(B)}$ where $P(B) \neq 0$ (384)
13. Binomial Experiments: A binomial experiment exists if and only if the following conditions occur. The experiment consists of n identical trials. Each trial results in one of two outcomes. The trials are independent. (387)

Chapter Review

13-1 **Find the value of each of the following.**

1. $P(6, 3)$
2. $P(8, 6)$
3. $\dfrac{P(4, 2) - P(6, 3)}{P(5, 3)}$

4. How many different three-digit numbers can be formed using the digits 1, 2, 3, 4, 5, and 6 without repeating digits?
5. How many ways can six books be placed on a shelf if the only dictionary must be on an end?

13-2 **How many ways can the letters of the following words be arranged?**

6. LEVEL
7. CINCINNATI

8. How many ways can 8 people be seated at a round table?
9. How many ways can 5 keys be placed on a key ring?

13-3 **Find the value of each of the following.**

10. $C(5, 3)$
11. $C(11, 8)$
12. $C(5, 5)$

13. From a standard deck of cards, how many different 4-card hands can have 4 cards of the same suit?
14. From a group of 3 men and 7 women, how many committees of 2 men and 2 women can be formed?

13-4 **State the odds of an event occurring given the probability that it occurs as follows.**

15. $\frac{4}{9}$
16. $\frac{3}{5}$
17. $\frac{1}{12}$

A bag contains 7 pennies, 4 nickels, and 5 dimes. Three coins are selected at random with replacement. What is the probability of each of the following selections?

18. all 3 pennies
19. all 3 dimes
20. 2 pennies, 1 nickel

13-5 **A green die and a red die are thrown. What is the probability that the following occurs?**

21. The red die shows a 1 and the green die shows any other number.
22. Neither shows a 1.

13-6 **Slips of paper numbered from 1 to 14 are in a box. A slip of paper is drawn at random. What is the probability that the following occurs?**

23. The number is a prime or is a multiple of 4.
24. The number is a multiple of 2 or a multiple of 3.

13-7 **A green die and a red die are thrown.**

25. What is the probability that the sum of the dice is less than 5 if the green die shows a 1?
26. What is the probability that the sum of the dice is 9 if the two numbers showing are different?

13-8 **A coin is tossed 4 times. What is the probability that the following occurs?**

27. exactly 1 head
28. no heads
29. 2 heads and 2 tails
30. at least 3 tails

Chapter Test

Solve each problem.

1. The letters r, s, t, u, and v are to be used to form five-letter patterns. How many patterns can be formed if repetitions are not allowed?

2. There are 5 persons who are applicants for 3 different positions in a store, each person being qualified for each position. In how many ways is it possible to fill the positions?

3. How many ways can 6 charms be arranged on a charm bracelet which has no clasp?

4. How many ways can 7 people be seated at a round table relative to each other?

5. How many baseball teams can be formed from 15 players if only 3 pitch and the others play the remaining 8 positions?

6. A bag contains 4 red and 6 white marbles. How many ways can 5 marbles be selected if 2 must be red?

7. The probability that the Pirates will win a game against the Hornets is $\frac{4}{7}$. What are the odds that the Pirates will beat the Hornets?

8. Five cards are drawn from a standard deck of cards. What is the probability that they are all from one suit?

9. Find the probability of getting a sum of 8 on the first throw of two dice and a sum of 4 on the second throw.

10. A new phone is being installed at the Collier residence. What is the probability that the final 3 digits in the telephone number will be odd?

11. A bag contains 3 red, 4 white, and 5 blue marbles. If 3 marbles are selected at random what is the probability that all are red or all are blue?

12. Two cards are drawn from a standard deck of cards. What is the probability of having drawn an ace or a black card?

13. Four-digit numbers are formed from the numbers 7, 3, 3, 2, and 2. If a number is odd, what is the probability that the 3's are together?

14. Two numbers are selected at random from the numbers 1 through 9. If their product is even, what is the probability that both numbers are even?

15. Five bent coins are tossed. The probability of heads is $\frac{2}{3}$ for each of them. What is the probability that no more than 2 will show heads?

16. While shooting arrows, Archie can hit the center of the target 4 out of 5 times. What is the probability that he will hit it exactly 4 out of the next 7 times?

Chapter

14

Descriptive Statistics

The advertising industry uses statistics to a great extent in making decisions. For example, an advertiser may collect data on costs, previous sales, consumer preference, and demand of a product. The techniques of collection, organization, analysis, and presentation of data are called descriptive statistics.

14-1 Measures of Central Tendency

A **measure of central tendency** is a number which represents a set of data. Measures of central tendency may be used to summarize a set of data. They also may be used to compare one set of data with another.

The **arithmetic mean** is a measure of central tendency which is found by adding the values in the set and dividing by the number of values in the set. For example, the arithmetic mean of 89, 73, and 92 is $\frac{89 + 73 + 92}{3}$ or $84\frac{2}{3}$. Frequently the arithmetic mean is referred to simply as the mean.

This is commonly called an average.

If X is a variable used to represent any value in a set of data, then the arithmetic mean, $\overline{X}$, of n values is given by the following formula.

$\overline{X}$ is read "X bar."

$$\overline{X} = \frac{X_1 + X_2 + X_3 + \ldots + X_n}{n}$$

The sum of the specified terms can be abbreviated using the summation symbol, Σ.

$$\sum_{i=1}^{n} X_i = X_1 + X_2 + X_3 + \ldots + X_n$$

The left member is read "the summation of X-sub-i from i equals 1 to n." The symbol X_i represents successive values of the set of data as i assumes successive integral values from 1 to n.

If a set of data has n values, given by X_i such that $1 \le i \le n$, then the arithmetic mean, $\overline{X}$, can be found as follows.

$$\overline{X} = \frac{1}{n}\sum_{i=1}^{n} X_i$$

The Arithmetic Mean

example

1 **Find the arithmetic mean of {24, 28, 21, 37, 31, 29, 23, 22, 34, 31}.**

$n = 10$

$$\overline{X} = \frac{1}{10}\sum_{i=1}^{10} X_i$$

$$= \frac{1}{10}(24 + 28 + 21 + 37 + 31 + 29 + 23 + 22 + 34 + 31)$$

$$= 28$$

The **median, M_d,** is another measure of central tendency. It is the mid-value of a set of data.

Before the median can be found, the data must be placed in an **array.** An array is formed by arranging the data into an ordered sequence. The **range** is the difference of the greatest and least values in the array.

The median of an odd number of data is the middle value of their array. The median of an even number of data is the arithmetic mean of the two middle values of their array.

example

2 Find the median and range of each of the following sets of data.

{21, 19, 17, 19, 19}

The array is {17, 19, 19, 19, 21}. There are five values. The middle value is 19. Thus, the median is 19. The range is 21 − 17 or 4.

{4, 10, 1, 61}

The array is {1, 4, 10, 61}. Since there are four values, the median is the mean of the two middle values. Thus, $M_d = \frac{4 + 10}{2}$ or 7. The range is 61 − 1 or 60.

Compare the arithmetic means of these two sets of data.

The **mode** of a set of data is the value which appears more frequently than any other in the set. For example, the mode of {17, 19, 19, 19, 21} is 19. The mode is important in such data as sizes of shoes or clothing. *Why?*

Some sets of data have multiple modes. Data with two modes are said to be bimodal. Some sets have no mode.

example

3 Find the mean, median, and mode of the following set of data.
{64, 87, 62, 87, 63, 98, 76, 54, 87, 58, 70, 76}

$$\overline{X} = \frac{1}{n}\sum_{i=1}^{n} X_i$$

$$= \frac{1}{12}(64 + 87 + 62 + 87 + 63 + 98 + 76 + 54 + 87 + 58 + 70 + 76)$$

$$= 73.5$$

To find the median and mode, place the data in an array.

{54, 58, 62, 63, 64, 70, 76, 76, 87, 87, 87, 98}

There are two middle values, the 6th value, 70 and the 7th value, 76. Thus, $M_d = \frac{70 + 76}{2}$ or 73. The mode, the most frequently occurring value, is 87.

The mean is 73.5, the median is 73, and the mode is 87.

The mode, in this case, is not a representative value.

exercises

Exploratory Find the median for each set of data.

1. {14, 15, 16, 17}
2. {3, 3, 6, 12, 3}
3. {10, 45, 58, 10}
4. {6, 10, 8, 5, 11, 6, 7, 12, 11, 11, 9, 6}

5-8. Find the mode or modes for each set of data in problems **1-4**.

9-12. Find the mean for each set of data in problems **1-4**.

Find a set of numbers which satisfies the conditions in each of the following.

13. The mean, median, and mode are all the same number.
14. The mean is greater than the median.
15. The mode is 10 and the median is greater than the mean.
16. The mean is 6, the median is $5\frac{1}{2}$, and the mode is 9.

Written Solve each problem.

1. Martin's scores on five tests were 84, 72, 91, 64, and 83. Find his mean score.
2. Find the mean of 5′7″, 4′8″, 6′1″, 5′4″, 8′0″, 6′7″, and 5′4″.

The weights in pounds of the members of the wrestling team at Allen East High School are 124, 155, 172, 117, 146, 138, 151, 160, and 142.

3. Find the difference between the arithmetic mean and the median of their weights.
4. If each member gains 5 lb, how are the mean and median affected?

Find the value of x so that the set of data given has the indicated arithmetic mean.

5. $\{2, 4, 6, 8, x\}; \overline{X} = 7\frac{1}{2}$
6. $\{x, 2x - 1, 2x, 3x + 1\}; \overline{X} = 6$
7. The mean height of five boys is 68 inches. If one boy is 5 feet tall and another is 6 feet tall, give possible heights for the other three boys.
8. Find possible values of x if the median of $\{11, 2, 3, 3.2, 13, 14, 8, x\}$ is 8.

The D & R Construction Company is owned by two partners and has eight employees. The partners are each taking salaries of \$50,000 from the company. Of the eight employees, two earn \$12,700 each, two earn \$9600 each, and four earn \$8700 each.

9. Make an array of the ten salaries.
10. Find the mean of the ten salaries.
11. Find the median of the ten salaries.
12. Find the mode of the ten salaries.
13. The D & R Construction Company and the union representing its employees each give statements to the press concerning "the average salaries of D & R employees". Which "average" might each side favor in its press release?
14. Which of the measures of central tendency best describes the salaries of D & R employees?

A math test is given to a large number of students.

15. Assume the test is very easy. Would the mode of the scores likely be higher or lower than the mean?
16. Assume the test is very difficult. Would the mode of the scores likely be higher or lower than the mean?

Statements such as the following are often made. "The average American family owns a car." "The average American woman wears a size 7 shoe."

17. What is meant by the word "average"?
18. Is the use of "average" closest to the mean, median, or mode?

The grade point averages for a random sample of thirty graduating seniors at Valley Green College are listed below.

3.4	2.4	2.6	3.6	3.8	3.4	2.0	3.0	2.8	2.6
3.2	2.4	4.0	2.8	3.6	3.2	2.8	2.2	2.6	3.6
2.0	2.2	2.4	3.2	3.6	2.6	2.2	4.0	2.2	2.6

19. Find the mean of the grade point averages.
20. Find the percentage of seniors in the sample who had a grade point average above the mean.
21. Since this is a random sample, estimate the number of seniors in the class of 472 who had a grade point average above the mean.

Challenge **A light metal rod one meter long is suspended at the middle so that it balances. Suppose that one gram weights are hung on the rod at the following distances from one end: 5 cm, 20 cm, 37 cm, 44 cm, 52 cm, 68 cm, 71 cm, 85 cm. It is observed that the rod does not balance at the 50 cm mark.**

1. Where must one more 1 gram weight be hung so that the rod will balance at the 50 cm mark?
2. Where must a 2 gram weight be hung so that the rod will balance at the 50 cm mark?

14-2 Harmonic and Quadratic Means

Other measures of central tendency of a set of data exist which may better describe the set.

The **harmonic mean,** ***H,*** is useful in special cases for averaging rates. It is given by the following formula.

The Harmonic Mean

If a set of data has n values, given by X_i such that $1 \leq i \leq n$, then the harmonic mean, H, can be found as follows.

$$H = \frac{n}{\frac{1}{X_1} + \frac{1}{X_2} + \cdots + \frac{1}{X_n}} = \frac{n}{\sum_{i=1}^{n} \frac{1}{X_i}}$$

The following example compares the use of the harmonic mean with the arithmetic mean.

example

1 **Jim Taulman travels two hours at a rate of 30 miles per hour and then on a freeway travels the next two hours at a rate of 55 miles per hour. What is his average speed?**
Meiko King travels 100 miles at the rate of 30 miles per hour and then on a freeway travels the next 100 miles at the rate of 55 miles per hour. What is her average speed?

Jim's average speed is the arithmetic mean of 30 mph and 55 mph.

$$\overline{X} = \frac{30 + 55}{2} = 42.5 \text{ mph}$$

Meiko's average speed is the harmonic mean of 30 mph and 55 mph.

$$H = \frac{2}{\frac{1}{30} + \frac{1}{55}} = 38.8 \text{ mph}$$

Check these averages. Jim travels a total distance of 170 miles in 4 hours or at an average speed of 42.5 miles per hour. Meiko travels a total distance of 200 miles in approximately 5.15 hours or at an average speed of 38.8 miles per hour.
Driving 100 miles at 30 mph takes 3.3 hours. Driving 100 miles at 55 mph takes 1.8 hours.

When equal *times* are involved the arithmetic mean of the rates is used. When equal *distances* are involved the harmonic mean is used.

Another measure of central tendency is the **quadratic mean.** It is the square root of the arithmetic mean of the squared values in a set of data.

The Quadratic Mean

If a set of data has n values, given by X_i such that $1 \le i \le n$, then the quadratic mean, Q, can be found by using the following formula.

$$Q = \sqrt{\frac{X_1^2 + X_2^2 + X_3^2 + \cdots + X_n^2}{n}} = \sqrt{\frac{\sum_{i=1}^{n} X_i^2}{n}}$$

example

2 **Find the quadratic mean of {1.3, 1.5, 1.7, 1.0, 1.1}.**

$$Q = \sqrt{\frac{(1.3)^2 + (1.5)^2 + (1.7)^2 + (1.0)^2 + (1.1)^2}{5}}$$

$$= \sqrt{\frac{9.04}{5}}$$

$$\approx \sqrt{1.8} \text{ or } 1.34$$

exercises

Exploratory State whether the arithmetic mean or the harmonic mean is used to find the correct average.

1. A team of three students competed in a 375-mile relay race. Each student drove 125 miles. Assume their driving speeds are known. Find the average driving speed of the three students during the race.
2. A team of three students competed in a 375-mile relay race. Each student drove for 2.5 hours. Assume their driving speeds are known. Find the average driving speed of the team during the race.
3. Kathy Brauen purchased four different cuts of beef. Assume the price per pound of each cut of beef is known. If she purchased the same quantity of each cut, find the average price per pound.
4. Tony Canode purchased three different cuts of pork. Assume the price per pound of each cut of pork is known. If he spent the same amount of money for each cut, find the average price per pound.

Written Find the harmonic mean of each set of data.

1. {3, 4, 5, 6}
2. {5, 10, 15, 20, 25}

Find the quadratic mean of each set of data.

3. {6, 6, 7, 8, 8, 11, 11, 12}
4. {2.5, 2.5, 2.5, 3.5, 3.5, 3.8, 4.0, 4.2}

Find $\overline{X}$, M_d, H, and Q for each set of data.

5. {3, 2, 6, 8, 5}
6. {4, 8, 1, 15}

Solve each problem.

7. A team of three students competed in a 375-mile relay race. The driving speed of each student is as follows. Student A drives 40 mph. Student B drives 50 mph. Student C drives 60 mph. If each student drives 125 miles, find the average driving speed of the three students.
8. A team of three students competed in a 375-mile relay race. The driving speed of each student is as follows. Student A drives 45 mph. Student B drives 50 mph. Student C drives 55 mph. If each student drives for 2.5 hours, find the average driving speed of the three students.
9. At the Round-Up Butcher Shop the prices of each cut of beef are as follows. Chuck roast is $1.80/lb, round steak is $2.60/lb, T-bone steak is $4.10/lb, and rib-eye steak is $3.90/lb. If Ladene purchased 5 lb of each cut, find the average price per pound.
10. At the Sunset Drive Grocery, the prices of each cut of pork are as follows. Pork chops are $2.00/lb, ham is $2.30/lb, and pork roast is $2.00/lb. If Benjamin purchased $10 worth of each cut of pork, find the average price per pound.
11. A salesperson travels from Louisville to Chicago at an average speed of 36 mph and returns by the same route at an average speed of 55 mph. Find the average speed for the round trip.
12. Five employees punch IBM cards for a one hour period. The punching speeds of the five employees are 10, 20, 24, 30, and 40 seconds per card respectively. Find the average speed per card.

14-3 Measures of Variability

The arithmetic mean and median are measures of central tendency and hence are statistics which describe a certain important characteristic of a set of data. However, they do *not* indicate anything about the variability of the data. For example, the mean of 35, 40, and 45 is 40, and the mean of 10, 40, and 70 is also 40. The variability is much greater in the second case than in the first, but this is *not* indicated by the mean.

One measure of variability is the **mean deviation.** If the deviations from the mean, $X_i - \overline{X}$, are found, it is evident that the sum of the deviations from the mean is zero. That is, $\sum_{i=1}^{n} (X_i - \overline{X}) = 0$. Thus, the average of the deviations can be found only if the absolute values of the deviations are considered. The arithmetic mean of the absolute values of the deviations from the mean of a set of data is called the mean deviation, *M.D.*

The Mean Deviation

If a set of data has n values, given by X_i such that $1 \leq i \leq n$, with arithmetic mean, $\overline{X}$, then the mean deviation, *M.D.*, can be found as follows.

$$M.D. = \frac{1}{n} \sum_{i=1}^{n} |X_i - \overline{X}|$$

example

1 **Find the mean deviation for each of the following sets of data.**

{35, 40, 45}

$$M.D. = \frac{1}{3} \sum_{i=1}^{3} |X_i - 40|$$
$$= \frac{1}{3}(|^-5| + |0| + |5|)$$
$$= 3\frac{1}{3}$$

{10, 40, 70}

$$M.D. = \frac{1}{3} \sum_{i=1}^{3} |X_i - 40|$$
$$= \frac{1}{3}(|^-30| + |0| + |30|)$$
$$= 20$$

Another measure of the variability is the **semi-interquartile range.** If the array of a set of data is separated into four parts having an equal number of data, each part is called a *quartile*. The median separates the data into two equal parts and thus is the second quartile point, Q_2. Each half can be separated into two equal parts to find the first and third quartile points. One-fourth of the data lie below the first quartile point, Q_1, and three-fourths of the data lie below the third quartile point, Q_3. The difference between the first quartile point and the third quartile point is called the *interquartile range*. When this difference is divided by 2, the quotient is the semi-interquartile range.

Q_1 and Q_3 are the medians of each half of the data.

If a set of data has first quartile point, Q_1, and third quartile point, Q_3, the semi-interquartile range, Q_R, can be found as follows.

$$Q_R = \frac{Q_3 - Q_1}{2}$$

The Semi-Interquartile Range

example

2 **Find the semi-interquartile range of {38, 47, 18, 26, 41, 30, 27, 21, 35, 31, 29, 32, 25, 22}.**

First make an array. {18, 21, 22, 25, 26, 27, 29, 30, 31, 32, 35, 38, 41, 47}

The midpoint or median is $\frac{29 + 30}{2}$ or 29.5. Q_1 is 25 and Q_3 is 35.

The semi-interquartile range is $\frac{35 - 25}{2}$ or 5.

A measure of variability that is often associated with the arithmetic mean is the **standard deviation.** The standard deviation of a set of data is the quadratic mean of the individual deviations from the arithmetic mean. Each individual deviation can be found by subtracting the arithmetic mean from each individual value, $X_i - \overline{X}$. Some of these differences will be negative, but since they are to be squared in computing their quadratic mean the results will be positive.

The square of the standard deviation, called the variance, often is used as a measure of variability.

If a set of data has n values, given by X_i such that $1 \leq i \leq n$, with arithmetic mean, $\overline{X}$, the standard deviation, σ, can be found by using the following formula.

$$\sigma = \sqrt{\frac{1}{n} \sum_{i=1}^{n} (X_i - \overline{X})^2}$$

The Standard Deviation

σ is the Greek lower case letter sigma.

example

3 **Compute the arithmetic mean and the standard deviation for {54, 57, 59, 59, 60, 61, 61, 62, 62, 62, 63, 64, 65, 65, 66, 66, 66, 66, 67, 67, 68, 68, 68, 68, 68, 69, 69, 69, 70, 71, 71, 72, 72, 73, 75, 75, 77, 79, 81, 83, 90}.**

$$\overline{X} = \frac{1}{41}(54 + 57 + \cdots + 90) = 68.$$

$$\sigma = \sqrt{\frac{1}{41} \sum_{i=1}^{41} (X_i - 68)^2}$$

$$= \sqrt{\frac{1}{41}[(54 - 68)^2 + (57 - 68)^2 + \cdots + (90 - 68)^2]}$$

$$\approx 7.1$$

The arithmetic mean is 68 and the standard deviation is 7.1.

exercises

Exploratory An astronomer made ten measurements of the angular distance between two stars. His measurements were 11.20°, 11.17°, 10.92°, 11.06°, 11.19°, 10.97°, 11.09°, 11.05°, 11.22°, and 11.03°.

1. Find the mean of the measurements of the angular distance between the two stars.
2. Find the individual deviation of each value in the set of data.
3. Find the mean deviation of the measurements.
4. Find the values of Q_1, Q_2, and Q_3 for this set of data.
5. Find the interquartile range for this set of data.
6. Find the semi-interquartile range for this set of data.
7. Find the sum of the squares of the individual deviations for this set of data.
8. Find the standard deviation of the angular distance between the two stars.

Find the mean deviation of each set of data.

9. {2, 4, 3, 5, 2.9, 2.6, 3.0, 1.5}
10. {200, 476, 721, 579, 152, 158}

11-12. Find the semi-interquartile range for each set of data in problems **9-10.**

Written The hourly wages of eight employees of the Ottawa Insurance Company are $3.10, $4.50, $4.50, $5.30, $6.80, $10.00, $11.20, and $16.20.

1. Find the mean of the hourly wages of Ottawa employees.
2. Find the mean deviation of the hourly wages of Ottawa employees.
3. Find the semi-interquartile range of the hourly wages of Ottawa employees.
4. Find the standard deviation of the hourly wages of Ottawa employees.

The number of students in each grade of two school systems is as follows.
Governor Schools: 369, 398, 381, 392, 406, 413, 376, 454, 420, 385, 402, 446
Wolf Local Schools: 360, 399, 413, 370, 431, 446, 427, 352, 493, 410, 363, 447

5. Find the range of grade size in the Governor School system.
6. Find the range of grade size in the Wolf Local School System.
7. Find the mean grade size in the Governor School System.
8. Find the mean grade size in the Wolf Local School System.
9. Find the mean deviation of grade size in the Governor School System.
10. Find the mean deviation of grade size in the Wolf Local School System.
11. Find the semi-interquartile range of the grade size in the Governor School System.
12. Find the semi-interquartile range of the grade size in the Wolf Local School System.
13. Find the standard deviation in grade size in the Governor School System.
14. Find the standard deviation in grade size in the Wolf Local School System.

At Funland Amusement Park, the ages of the riders on a ferris wheel in years are 38, 34, 12, 8, 64, 25, 32, 12, 10, 8, 5, 30, 28, 3, 17, 18, 31, 60, 13, and 12.

15. Find the mean age of the riders.
16. Find the mean deviation from the mean age.
17. Find the semi-interquartile range of ages of the riders.
18. Find the standard deviation of the ages of the riders.
19. Compute the standard deviation and the mean deviation of the numbers 56, 83, 74, 50, 58, 66, 72, 41, 75, 64, 66, 57, 68, 54, and 61. Which measure of variability is greater?

14-4 The Frequency Distribution

The number of values in a set of data is often too large for each value to be considered individually. In this case a **frequency distribution** is a convenient system of organizing the data. A number of classes are determined and all values in a class are tallied and grouped together.

example

1 Prepare a frequency distribution of the weights of 200 boys at a certain high school. Assume the smallest weight is 99 pounds and the largest is 203 pounds.

First, copy the raw data from the school health records onto a data sheet. Next make an array from the raw data and find the range. The range is 203 − 99 = 104. Now group the data into classes. Eleven classes, each having a width of 10 pounds, are suitable. Let the lowest class be from 95 pounds to 105 pounds, the next class from 105 pounds to 115 pounds, and so on. The **class limits** are 95, 105, 115, . . . , 205. If a given weight falls on one of these class limits, the weight is tallied in the higher class. For example, 115 is tallied in the 115-125 class rather than the 105-115 class. The frequency distribution is as follows.

Class Limits	Class Marks (X)	Tally	Frequency f
95 - 105	100	|||	3
105 - 115	110	~~||||~~ ||	7
115 - 125	120	~~||||~~ ~~||||~~ ~~||||~~	15
125 - 135	130	~~||||~~ ~~||||~~ ~~||||~~ ~~||||~~ ~~||||~~ ~~||||~~ ||||	34
135 - 145	140	~~||||~~ ~~||||~~ ~~||||~~ ~~||||~~ ~~||||~~ ~~||||~~ ~~||||~~ ~~||||~~ ||	42
145 - 155	150	~~||||~~ ~~||||~~ ~~||||~~ ~~||||~~ ~~||||~~ ~~||||~~ ~~||||~~ |||	38
155 - 165	160	~~||||~~ ~~||||~~ ~~||||~~ ~~||||~~ ||||	24
165 - 175	170	~~||||~~ ~~||||~~ ~~||||~~	15
175 - 185	180	~~||||~~ ~~||||~~ |	11
185 - 195	190	~~||||~~ ||	7
195 - 205	200	||||	4
		Total	200

The **class interval** is the width of each class. The class interval is 10 in the previous example. For most purposes, all class intervals in a frequency distribution should be equal.

The averages of the class limits are called **class marks** and are represented by X. In the previous example the class marks are 100, 110, 120, . . . , 200.

The **frequency,** f, is the sum of the tallies of a class.

The number of classes in a distribution usually varies from 5 to 20 depending upon various factors such as range, the number of values in the data, and the purpose of grouping. If fewer than 5 classes are recorded, the grouping is coarse. If more than 20 classes are recorded, the distribution is difficult to manage.

example

2 Make a frequency distribution of the following scores made by a class of freshmen students on an algebra test of 20 problems. The scores are 13, 19, 17, 15, 20, 9, 16, 15, 17, 14, 10, 16, 19, 20, 13, 17, 15, 18, 12, 16, 14, 18, 16, 7, 17, 19 and 15.

First make an array.
{7, 9, 10, 12, 13, 13, 14, 14, 15, 15, 15, 15, 16, 16, 16, 16, 17, 17, 17, 17, 18, 18, 19, 19, 19, 20, 20}
The range is 20 − 7 or 13. Form seven classes, each having a class interval of 2. The lowest class limit should be 6.5 so that the lowest score is included.

Class Limits	Class Mark (X)	Tally	Frequency (f)
6.5 - 8.5	7.5	|	1
8.5 - 10.5	9.5	||	2
10.5 - 12.5	11.5	|	1
12.5 - 14.5	13.5	||||	4
14.5 - 16.5	15.5	~~||||~~ |||	8
16.5 - 18.5	17.5	~~||||~~ |	6
18.5 - 20.5	19.5	~~||||~~	5
		Total	27

exercises

Exploratory The following frequency distribution gives the annual salaries of a random sample of 100 U.S. citizens.

Annual Salary	Frequency
Under $6000	9
$6000 to $12,000	21
$12,000 to $18,000	31
$18,000 to $24,000	26
$24,000 to $30,000	13

1. State the class interval of the frequency distribution.
2. State the class limits of the frequency distribution.
3. State the class marks of the frequency distribution.
4. What percent of the 100 people made $18,000 to $24,000?
5. What percent of the 100 people made at least $18,000?

Find suitable class intervals, class limits, and class marks for each set of numbers. Assume that the two numbers given are the least and greatest values in a certain set of data.

6. {1, 7}
7. {2.1, 3.5}
8. {400, 1000}

Find the class interval and the class limits for each set of numbers. Assume that the numbers given are class marks of a frequency distribution.

9. {10, 20, 30, 40, 50}
10. {1.1, 1.2, 1.3, 1.4, 1.5, 1.6, 1.7}
11. {2.5, 5, 7.5, 10, 12.5}
12. {25, 26, 27, 28, 29, 30, 31, 32}

Written The ages in years of a random sample of 60 patients admitted to City Memorial Hospital during October are given below.

45	70	8	68	53	28	95	39	77	21
20	62	38	57	38	31	43	29	61	63
21	63	49	65	89	80	76	49	43	35
57	54	63	57	49	40	31	18	13	28
27	37	1	34	47	16	57	76	79	48
75	46	72	59	32	3	81	41	66	50

1. Make a frequency distribution of the data using a class interval of ten.
2. Make a frequency distribution of the data using a class interval of eight.
3. Make a frequency distribution of the data with fourteen classes.
4. Make a frequency distribution of the data with eleven classes.

The IQ's of a random sample of 100 people in a certain population are given below.

84	120	78	89	107	116	73	88	106	117
144	92	100	124	84	100	115	76	93	112
89	109	110	128	101	109	135	100	112	81
99	119	88	117	110	81	103	127	97	120
93	115	92	116	68	97	66	102	84	108
95	72	104	95	80	85	106	99	87	115
104	100	95	85	121	112	97	106	113	82
104	102	111	103	125	95	102	88	102	97
99	100	103	78	99	99	91	97	99	103
102	110	88	100	90	100	103	92	103	100

5. Make a frequency distribution of the data using a class interval of ten.
6. Make a frequency distribution of the data using a class interval of twelve.
7. Make a frequency distribution of the data with sixteen classes.
8. Make a frequency distribution of the data with ten classes.

The weights in pounds of children in a certain fourth grade class are given below.

64	71	57	67	74	65	59	62	67
72	84	60	68	72	91	55	69	71
69	71	69	75	59	60	70	76	62
88	57	78	63	74	77	62	68	63
60	69	74	90	63	79	66	75	93

9. Make a frequency distribution using an appropriate class interval.

Independent measurements of the length in meters of a college campus taken by twenty-four students in a civil engineering class are given below.

2013.3	2012.8	2013.4	2012.2	2012.0	2012.2	2011.8	2011.7
2012.6	2013.5	2012.4	2012.1	2012.6	2013.9	2013.7	2012.8
2012.3	2011.4	2012.3	2011.6	2012.2	2012.7	2012.4	2012.7

10. Make a frequency distribution of the data using an appropriate class interval.
11. How should the data be handled if the last measurement was reported as 2112.7 m rather than 2012.7 m?
12. Think of a situation from which a frequency distribution could be made. Collect the data and make the frequency distribution.

Francine Blair is an actuary for a life insuance company. She designs insurance plans and rates for her company that are financially sound. She must calculate rates that will be profitable to the company but also competitive with other life insurance companies. Death statistics and life expectancy charts provide most of the data needed to draw up actuarial tables.

Life Expectancy, 1976

Source: Department of Health, Education, and Welfare

Age	Expected Remaining Years of Life	
	Female	Male
0	75.0	66.9
10	66.6	58.7
20	56.8	49.2
30	47.3	40.3
40	38.0	31.6
50	29.0	23.5
60	21.4	16.6
70	14.4	11.1
80	9.7	7.6

Notice that the older a person gets, the shorter the expectation of life, but the greater the age expectancy. Why?

Example Suppose an insurance company sells one type of life insurance for an annual premium of $15.40 for each $1000 of insurance to women at age 20. What is the average return the company can expect to receive?

From the table above, at age 20 the life expectancy of females is 56.8. Therefore the average return will be as follows. *Why "average"?*

$$(56.8)(\$15.40) = \$874.72$$

It appears that the insurance company is losing money. However, the premiums earn interest from the first year and in 56.8 years the total premiums and interest would amount to much more than $1000.

Exercises Solve each problem using the table above.

1. An insurance company sells one type of life insurance for an annual premium of $17.25 per $1000 of insurance to 30 year old men. How much can the company expect to receive in total premiums from a $25,000 policy?
2. Suppose you won a contest at age 20 that promised to pay you $100 a week for the rest of your life. How much money can you expect to receive in your lifetime?

14-5 Graphical Representation of Data

Graphs often are used to represent the data in a frequency distribution. Two ways of representing the data in the following frequency distribution are shown below.

Test Scores on a History Test

Score	6.5-8.5	8.5-10.5	10.5-12.5	12.5-14.5	14.5-16.5	16.5-18.5	18.5-20.5
Frequency	1	2	1	4	8	6	5

The **bar graph** consists of parallel bars, either vertical or horizontal. Each bar represents the frequency, f, of the values in a class.

The graph at the right is a horizontal bar graph.

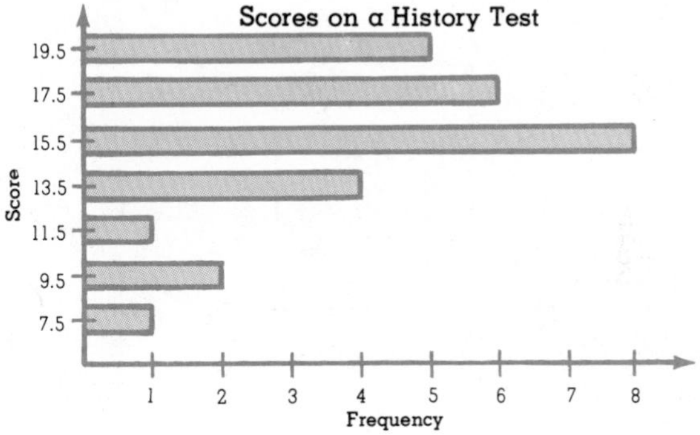

The **histogram** is a vertical bar graph whose bars are next to each other. The class marks, X, are measured on the horizontal axis and the frequency, f, is measured on the vertical axis. Bar graphs and histograms are used to compare frequencies.

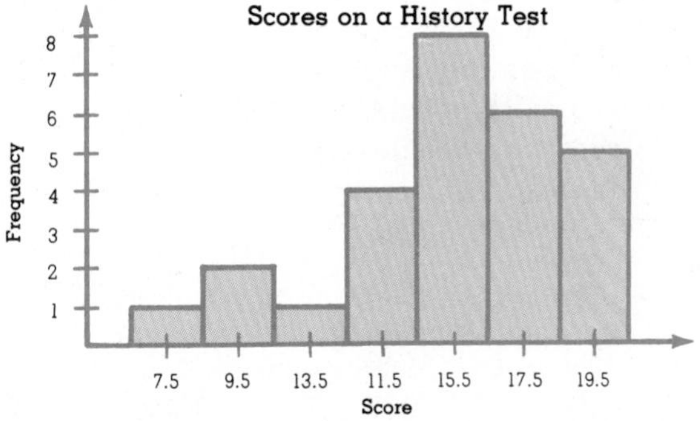

The **broken line graph**, sometimes called a frequency polygon, is useful in showing changing conditions over a period of time. For example, the graph at the right shows the median family income in the United States from 1970 to 1977.

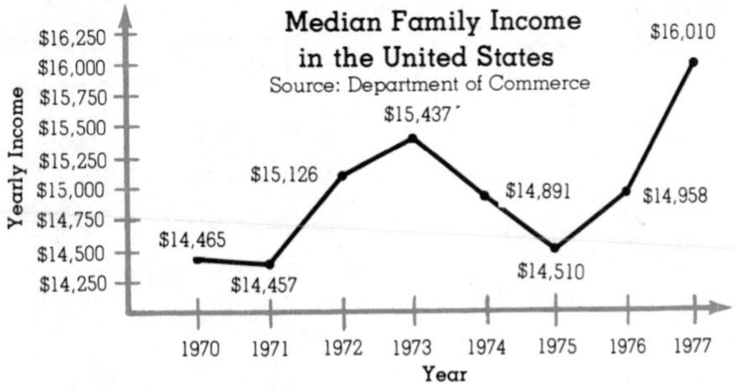

example

1 Draw a histogram and a broken line graph to present the following data.

Number of Immigrants to U.S.

(in thousands of persons)

Source: Department of Justice

Year	1900	1910	1920	1930	1940	1950	1960	1970
Immigrants	449	1042	430	242	71	249	265	373

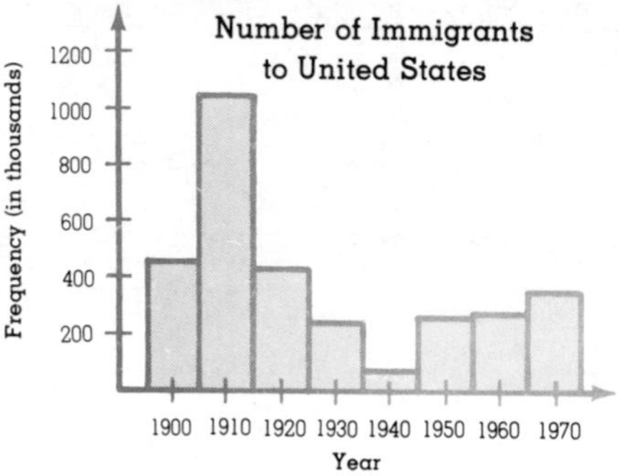

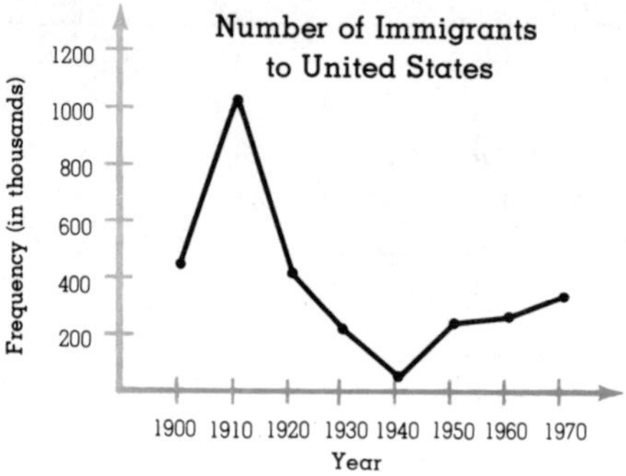

The **circle graph** shows the relationship between the parts and the whole. The circle is separated into proportional parts called sectors. For example, 19% of the U.S. sources of energy in 1978 were coal. Thus, the sector which represents coal has a central angle of 19% of 360° or 68.4°.

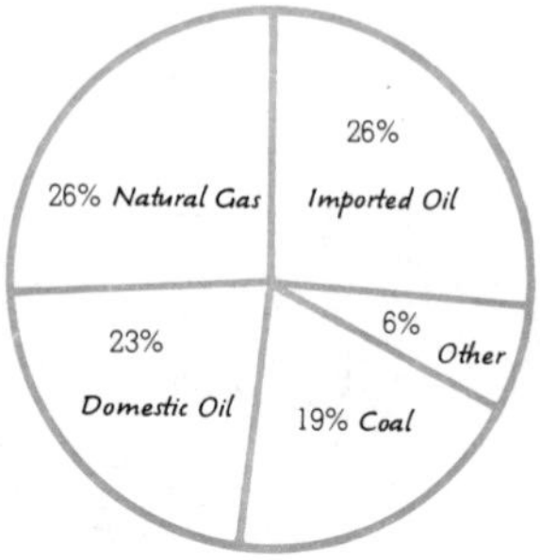

U. S. Sources of Energy, 1978

Source: Department of Energy

example

2 Draw a circle graph for the following data.

Oil Production by States - 1975

(in millions of 42-gallon barrels)

Source: Department of the Interior

State	Oil
Texas	1222
Louisiana	651
California	322
Oklahoma	163
Wyoming	136
Other States	566

First, find the percent of the circle area represented by each state. Then, figure the number of degrees of the central angle to obtain the sector having that percent of the area.

State	Percent of Circle Area	Approximate Degrees of Central Angle
Texas	$\frac{1222}{3060}$ or 40%	360° × 40% or 144°
Louisiana	$\frac{651}{3060}$ or 21%	360° × 21% or 75.6°
California	$\frac{322}{3060}$ or 11%	360° × 11% or 39.6°
Oklahoma	$\frac{163}{3060}$ or 5%	360° × 5% or 18°
Wyoming	$\frac{136}{3060}$ or 4%	360° × 4% or 14.4°
Other States	$\frac{566}{3060}$ or 19%	360° × 19% or 68.4°

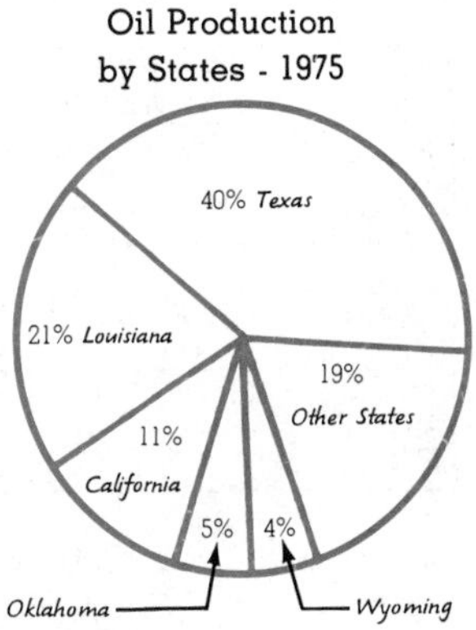

EXERCISES

Exploratory Use the histogram below to solve each of the following.

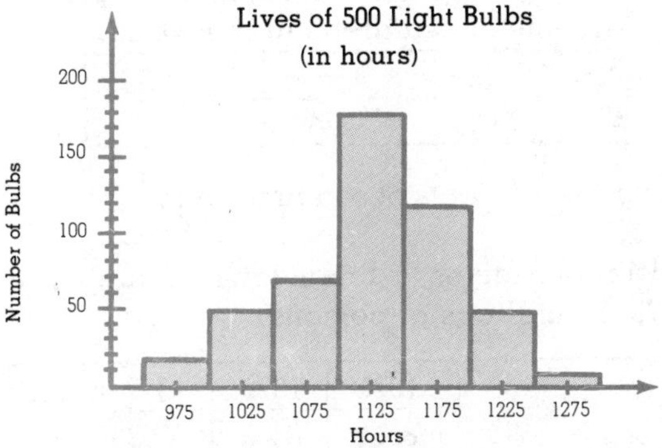

1. Find the class limits.
2. Find the class interval.
3. Find the number of light bulbs that had lives between 1000 and 1050 hours.
4. Find the number of light bulbs that had lives over 1250 hours.
5. Find the number of light bulbs that had lives over 1100 hours.
6. Find the number of light bulbs that had lives less than 1150 hours.
7. Find the percent of light bulbs that had lives less than 1100 hours.
8. Find the percent of light bulbs that had lives less than 1200 hours.
9. Make a horizontal bar graph of the data from the histogram above.
10. Make a broken line graph of the data from the histogram above.

Written Draw bar graphs for the data in each of the following frequency distributions.

1. Number of hours of daily TV viewing

Hours	0-1	1-2	2-3	3-4	4-5	5-6	6-7	7-8
Frequency	8	6	38	72	61	44	20	4

2. U.S. Population by Age, 1977 (in millions of persons)
Source: Department of Commerce

Ages	0-10	10-20	20-30	30-40	40-50	50-60	60-70	70-80	over 80
Population	32	40	38	28	23	23	18	10	5

3. Population of the 150 Largest Metropolitan Areas in the U.S. - 1975 (in thousands)
Source: Department of Commerce

Population	Under 1000	1000-2000	2000-3000	3000-4000	4000-5000	Over 5000
Frequency	113	21	8	3	2	3

4. Birth Rates (per 1000 population)
Source: Department of Commerce

Year	1915	1935	1955	1975
Rate	29.5	25.1	25.0	14.8

5. Institutions of Higher Education
Source: Department of Health, Education, & Welfare

Year	1930	1940	1950	1960	1970
Number	1409	1708	1863	1959	2525

6. College Graduates in U.S. (in thousands)
Source: Department of Health, Education and Welfare

Year	1900	1910	1920	1930	1940	1950	1960	1970
Graduates	27	37	49	122	187	432	392	827

7-12. Draw histograms for the frequency distributions in problems 1-6.

13-15. Draw broken line graphs for the frequency distributions in problems 4-6.

The following table gives the percents of sea areas in the world.

Sea Area	Pacific	Atlantic	Indian	Arctic	Other Seas
Percentage	46%	23%	20%	4%	7%

16. Draw a circle graph to show the percents of sea area in the world.

The following frequency distribution gives a breakdown of the civilian labor force in the United States from 1975 to 1978, in millions of persons.
Source: Department of Labor

Employment Status	1975	1976	1977	1978
Employed in Nonagricultural Industries	81.4	84.2	87.3	91.0
Employed in Agriculture	3.4	3.3	3.2	3.4
Unemployed	7.8	7.3	6.9	6.2

17-20. For each year 1975-1978, draw a circle graph to show the breakdown of the civilian labor force.

Find a statistical graph in a newspaper or magazine.

21. Does the graph accurately represent the data?

22. Could the data have been presented as effectively without the graph?

14-6 Using the Frequency Distribution

In a frequency distribution, each individual value in the data loses its identity. The data in each class are assumed to be uniformly distributed over the class. Thus, the class mark is assumed to be the mean of the data tallied in its class. For example, the mean of the data in a class with limits 22.5-27.5 is assumed to be 25, the class mark.

In a frequency distribution the sum of the values in a class is found by multiplying the class mark, X, by the frequency, f, of that class. The sum of the values in a class can be represented by $f \cdot X$. The sum of all the values in a given set of data is found by adding the sums of the values of each class in the frequency distribution. The sum of all values in the set can be represented by $\sum_{i=1}^{k} (f_i \cdot X_i)$ where k is the number of classes in the frequency distribution. Thus, the arithmetic mean of n values in a frequency distribution is found by dividing the sum of the values in the set by n or $\sum_{i=1}^{k} f_i$.

The Mean of the Data in a Frequency Distribution

If $X_1, X_2, \ldots, X_k$ are the class marks in a frequency distribution with k classes and $f_1, f_2, \ldots, f_k$ are the corresponding frequencies, then the arithmetic mean, $\overline{X}$, is approximated by the following.

$$\overline{X} \approx \frac{\sum_{i=1}^{k} f_i \cdot X_i}{\sum_{i=1}^{k} f_i}$$

example

1 **Find the arithmetic mean of the scores of 90 students on a mathematics test given in the following frequency distribution.**

Class Limits	Class Marks (X)	Frequency (f)	$f \cdot X$
93 - 101	97	12	1164
85 - 93	89	19	1691
77 - 85	81	38	3078
69 - 77	73	11	803
61 - 69	65	7	455
53 - 61	57	3	171
		$\sum_{i=1}^{6} f_i = 90$	$\sum_{i=1}^{6} f_i \cdot X_i = 7362$

$\overline{X} \approx \frac{7362}{90}$ or 81.8

The median, M_d, of the data in a frequency distribution is found from a cumulative frequency distribution. The cumulative frequency of each class is the sum of the frequency of the class and the frequencies of the previous classes. The two columns at the right show the frequency, f, and the cumulative frequency, *cum f*, of the frequency distribution in Example 1. Since the median is the value below which 50% of the data lie, the class in which the median lies can be located. This class is called the **median class.** Now the median can be found by using linear interpolation. This method can also be used to find any percentile value other than 50%.

Frequency f	Cumulative Frequency *cum f*
12	90
19	78
38	59
11	21
7	10
3	3

Notice that you read up this cum f column.

example

2 Find the median of the data in the frequency distribution in Example 1.

Since there are 90 scores in this frequency distribution, 45 scores are below the median. From the cumulative frequency column above, it is apparent that the median class is the class, 77 − 85. The *cum f* column also shows that 21 scores fall below point 77. Thus, by subtracting 21 from 45, it is found that 24 scores above the point 77 are required to reach the median of the frequency distribution. Since there are 38 scores in the median class, $\frac{24}{38}$ of 8, the class interval, must be added to the lower limit of that class to reach the median.

$$M_d = 77 + \left(\frac{24}{38} \times 8\right)$$
$$\approx 82.1$$

In a frequency distribution, deviations from the mean are found for a given class by subtracting the mean from the class mark and multiplying this result by the frequency of the class. Then, the standard deviation can be found by computing the quadratic mean of these deviations.

The Standard Deviation of the Data in a Frequency Distribution

If $X_1, X_2, \ldots, X_k$ are the class marks in a frequency distribution with k classes, and $f_1, f_2, \ldots, f_k$ are the corresponding frequencies, then the standard deviation, σ, of the data in the frequency distribution is approximated by the following.

$$\sigma \approx \sqrt{\frac{\sum_{i=1}^{k} (X_i - \overline{X})^2 f_i}{\sum_{i=1}^{k} f_i}}$$

example

3 **Find the standard deviation of the data in the frequency distribution in Example 1.**

Repeat the X and f columns of the frequency distribution. Then find $(X - \overline{X})$, and $(X - \overline{X})^2 f$. The results are shown below.

X	f	$(X - \overline{X})$	$(X - \overline{X})^2 f$
97	12	15.2	2772.48
89	19	7.2	984.96
81	38	$^-0.8$	24.32
73	11	$^-8.8$	851.84
65	7	$^-16.8$	1975.68
57	3	$^-24.8$	1845.12

$$\sum_{i=1}^{6} f_i = 90 \qquad \sum_{i=1}^{6} f_i(X_i - \overline{X})^2 = 8454.40$$

$$\sigma = \sqrt{\frac{8454.40}{90}} \text{ or } 9.69$$

exercises

Exploratory Solve each problem using the following frequency distribution.

Weekly Wages	Frequency
\$130 – \$140	11
140 – 150	24
150 – 160	30
160 – 170	10
170 – 180	13
180 – 190	8
190 – 200	4

1-7. Find the sum of the values in each class.

8. Find the sum of the values in the frequency distribution.
9. Find the number of values in the frequency distribution.
10. Find the arithmetic mean of the data in the frequency distribution.
11. Make a column showing the cumulative frequency of the classes.
12. Find the median class of the frequency distribution.
13. Find the median of the data in the frequency distribution.

Written Solve each problem using the following frequency distribution.

Class	1 - 5	5 - 9	9 - 13	13 - 17	17 - 21	21 - 25	25 - 29	29 - 33
Frequency	2	8	15	6	38	31	13	7

1. Find the arithmetic mean of the data in the frequency distribution.
2. Find the median class of the frequency distribution.

3. Find the median of the data in the frequency distribution.
4. Find the standard deviation of the data in the frequency distribution.

The sales made by 200 stores in Lafayette during September are given in the following frequency distribution.

Sales	Frequency
Less than $10,000	15
$10,000 – $20,000	30
$20,000 – $30,000	50
$30,000 – $40,000	60
$40,000 – $50,000	30
$50,000 and over	15

5. Is it possible to find the arithmetic mean? Why or why not?
6. Make a column showing the cumulative frequency of the classes.
7. Find the median class of the frequency distribution.
8. Find the median of the data in the frequency distribution.

The following data is a random sample of the amounts in dollars and cents spent on purchases at the Super Saver Market on a certain day.

$24.60	34.56	53.62	24.52	54.28	20.53	13.19	32.54
51.83	8.68	34.23	20.72	32.03	32.35	33.20	43.90
31.97	2.80	14.53	12.00	14.09	14.10	22.75	23.24
41.09	40.70	10.10	44.73	21.60	62.95	53.30	12.98
32.78	14.45	32.43	14.98	23.60	9.90	7.41	30.81
4.36	8.88	24.54	32.85	47.40	21.64	18.18	45.49

9. Make a frequency distribution of the data using $8.00 as the class interval.
10. Find the arithmetic mean of the data in the frequency distribution.
11. Make a column showing the cumulative frequency of the classes.
12. Find the median class of the frequency distribution.
13. Find the median of the data in the frequency distribution.
14. Find the standard deviation of the data in the frequency distribution.

Challenge **Using the frequency distribution from problem 9, find the point below which 70% of values lie.**

14-7 The Normal Distribution Curve

A frequency distribution that often occurs when there is a large number of values in a set of data is called the **normal distribution.** In a normal distribution small deviations are much more frequent than large ones. Negative deviations and positive deviations usually occur with about the same frequency.

When a normal distribution is shown graphically, the curve representing the distribution, called the **normal curve,** is symmetrical or bell-shaped. The points on the x-axis represent values which are a certain number of standard deviations from the mean. The total area under the normal curve and above the x-axis represents the total probability of the distribution which is 1.

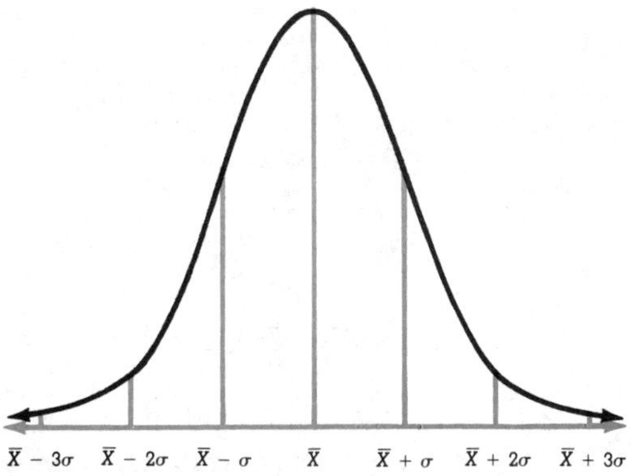

The following table gives the fractional parts of a normally distributed set of data for selected ranges about the mean. The expression, $\overline{X} \pm t\sigma$, indicates the upper and lower limits of the range of numbers in the data for any selected value of t. The fractional part of the data, P, is also the probability that a randomly selected value will lie in the interval $\overline{X} \pm t\sigma$. For example, the fractional part of normally distributed data which is within one standard deviation is 0.683. Thus, if the mean of the data is 60 and the standard deviation is 6, then 68.3% of the data are within the limits 60 ± (1)(6) or 54 and 66.

The percentage of the data which is within these limits is 100 · P.

t	P
0.0	0.000
0.1	0.080
0.2	0.159
0.3	0.236
0.4	0.311
0.5	0.383
0.6	0.451
0.7	0.516
0.8	0.576
0.9	0.632
1.0	0.683
1.1	0.729

t	P
1.2	0.770
1.3	0.807
1.4	0.838
1.5	0.866
1.6	0.891
1.65	0.900
1.7	0.911
1.8	0.928
1.9	0.943
1.96	0.950
2.0	0.955
2.1	0.964

t	P
2.2	0.972
2.3	0.979
2.4	0.984
2.5	0.988
2.58	0.990
2.6	0.991
2.7	0.993
2.8	0.995
2.9	0.996
3.0	0.997
3.5	0.9995
4.0	0.9999

Thus, normal distributions have the following properties.

1. The maximum point of the curve is at the mean.
2. About 68.3% of the data are within one standard deviation from the mean.
3. About 95.5% of the data are within two standard deviations from the mean.
4. About 99.7% of the data are within three standard deviations from the mean.

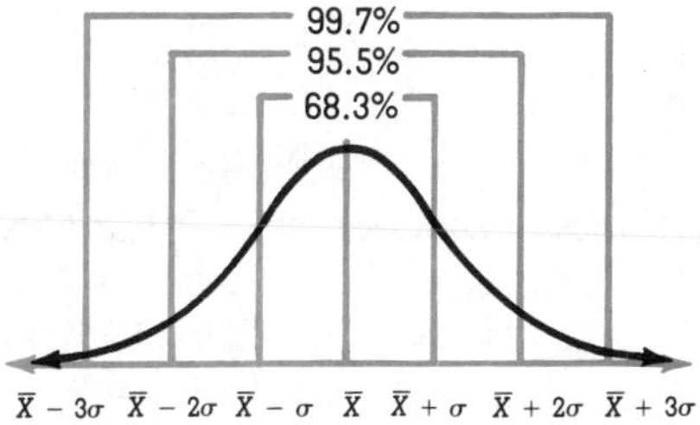

examples

1 **Find the upper and lower limits within which 80% of the values of a set of normally distributed data are found. Suppose the mean, $\overline{X}$, is 65 and the standard deviation, σ, is 6.**

Find t in the table when P = 0.80. $t = 1.3$

Find the limits. $\overline{X} \pm t\sigma = 65 \pm (1.3)(6)$

$= 72.8$ and 57.2

Thus 80% of the values lie between 57.2 and 72.8.

2 **A value is selected at random from a normally distributed set of data. Suppose the mean $\overline{X}$ is 65 and the standard deviation σ is 5. What is the probability that the selected value lies within the limits 61 and 69?**

Express the limits using the mean. $61 = 65 - 4$ and 69 or $65 + 4$

$\overline{X} \pm t\sigma = 65 \pm 4$

Solve for t. $t\sigma = 4$

$t \cdot 5 = 4$

$t = 0.8$

Find P in the table when t = 0.8 $P = 0.576$

Thus the probability is 0.576 that a value selected at random from the data will lie within 4 units of the mean, that is, between 61 and 69.

3 **The grades on a standardized college entrance examination are assumed to form a normal distribution with a mean score of 80 and a standard deviation of 12. What is the probability that an entering student will score between 86 and 100 on the examination?**

First, find the probability that the score is between the mean and the upper limit.

$\overline{X} + t\sigma = 100$

$80 + t \cdot 12 = 100$

Find P in the table when t = 1.7. $t = 1.7$

$P = 0.911$

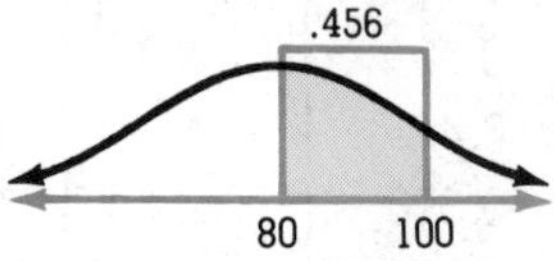

The probability that a student's score is between 80 and 100 is $\frac{1}{2}(0.911)$ or 0.456. One-half of the P value in the table must be taken since only the values above the mean are being considered.

Next, find the probability that the score is between the mean and the lower limit.

$\overline{X} + t\sigma = 86$

$80 + t \cdot 12 = 86$

Find P in the table when t = 0.5. $t = 0.5$

$P = 0.383$

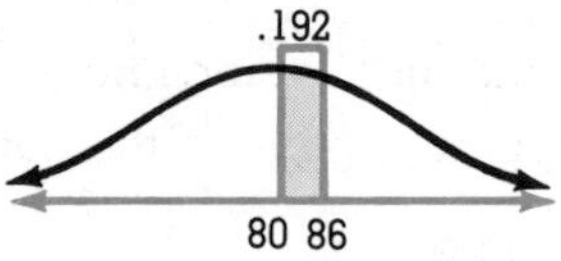

The probability that a student's score is between 80 and 86 is $\frac{1}{2}(0.383)$ or 0.192.

Therefore the probability that an entering student will score between 86 and 100 is $0.456 - 0.192$ or 0.264.

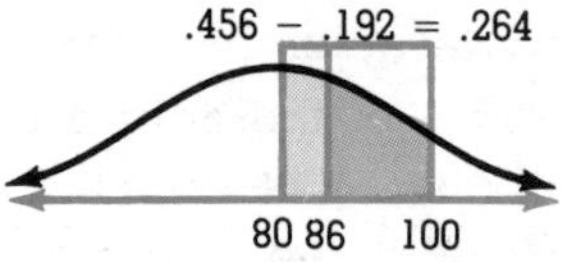

exercises

Exploratory Suppose 200 values in a set of data have a normal distribution.

1. How many values are within one standard deviation from the mean?
2. How many values are within two standard deviations from the mean?
3. How many values are within one standard deviation greater than the mean?
4. How many values are between two and three standard deviations less than the mean?

5-8. Answer problems 1-4 for a normal distribution of 5000 values.

9-12. Answer problems 1-4 for a normal distribution of 100,000 values.

A teacher decides to grade a certain test by marking "on the curve." He determines that the A grades will fall in the range above $\overline{X} + 1.5\sigma$, the B grades from $\overline{X} + 0.5\sigma$ to $\overline{X} + 1.5\sigma$, the C grades from $\overline{X} + 0.5\sigma$ to $\overline{X} - 0.5\sigma$, the D grades from $\overline{X} - 0.5\sigma$ to $\overline{X} - 1.5\sigma$, and the F grades below $\overline{X} - 1.5\sigma$.

13-17. What percent of the class will receive each letter grade?

Written **A set of 500 values has a normal distribution. The mean of the data is 24 and the standard deviation is 2.**

1. What percent of the data is in the range 22 to 26?
2. What percent of the data is in the range 20.5 to 27.5?
3. Find the range about the mean which includes 95% of the data.
4. Find the range about the mean which includes 50% of the data.

The mean of a set of normally distributed data is 140 and the standard deviation is 20.

5. What percent of the data is in the range 120 to 160?
6. What percent of the data is in the range 130 to 150?
7. Find the probability that a value selected at random from the data will be within the limits 110 and 170.
8. Find the probability that a value selected at random from the data will be less than 100.
9. Find the probability that a value selected at random from the data will be greater than 160.
10. Find the probability that a value selected at random from the data will be within the limits 110 and 200.
11. Find the range about the mean which includes 90% of the data.
12. Find the point below which 90% of the data lie.

The lengths of 2400 babies born at Valley Hospital in the past year were normally distributed. The mean length was 50.5 cm and the standard deviation was 3.6 cm.

13. Find the range about the mean which includes 80% of the babies' lengths.
14. Find the range about the mean which includes 50% of the babies' lengths.
15. Find the probability that a baby's length selected at random from this set of data is within the limits 49 cm and 52 cm.
16. Find the probability that a baby's length selected at random from this set of data is within the limits 45 cm and 56 cm.
17. Find the probability that a baby's length selected at random from this set of data is greater than 50.5 cm.
18. Find the probability that a baby's length selected at random from this set of data is less than 45 cm.
19. What percent of babies' lengths were between 48 cm and 50.5 cm?
20. What percent of babies' lengths were between 52 and 55 cm?

Using Mathematics

The picture on the right shows a device often used to illustrate a normal probability distribution. The device is filled with small steel marbles. The marbles roll past a series of hexagonal obstacles, collecting at the bottom in each of nine columns.

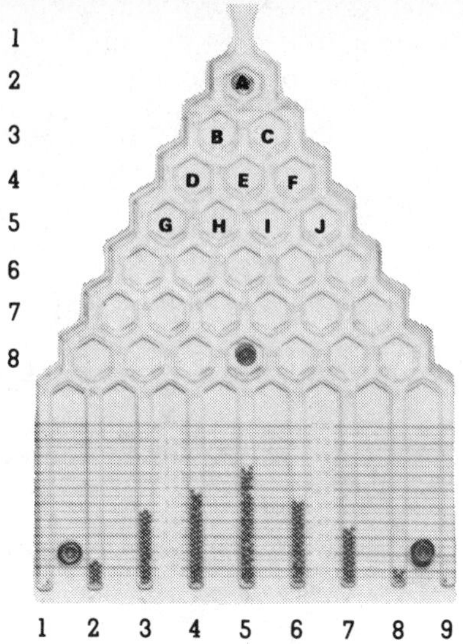

It can be shown that the number of paths from A to G is 1, A to J is 1, A to H is 3, and A to I is 3. For example, H can be reached by the way of D or by way of E. Hence the number of paths to H is the sum of the number of paths to D and the number of paths to E. Likewise the number of paths to any point can be found by adding the number of paths to points diagonally above it. This is precisely the method by which the numbers in Pascal's triangle are obtained.

The numbers in Pascal's triangle are the coefficients in the expansion of $(x + y)^n$ where n is any positive integer. Therefore, the probability of a marble falling in any given column is proportional to the coefficient of the corresponding term in the binomial expansion of a power. The power is a whole number equal to the row being considered. For example, in the illustration above the columns are in the *eighth* row. Thus the probability of a marble falling in the *third* column is proportional to the coefficient of the *third* term in the binomial expansion of $(x + y)^8$.

The figure at the right has equally-spaced vertical segments whose lengths are proportional to the numbers in a row of Pascal's triangle. A smooth curve connecting the tops of these segments suggests the probable distribution of marbles in the column. Notice the similarity of this curve to the normal distribution curve.

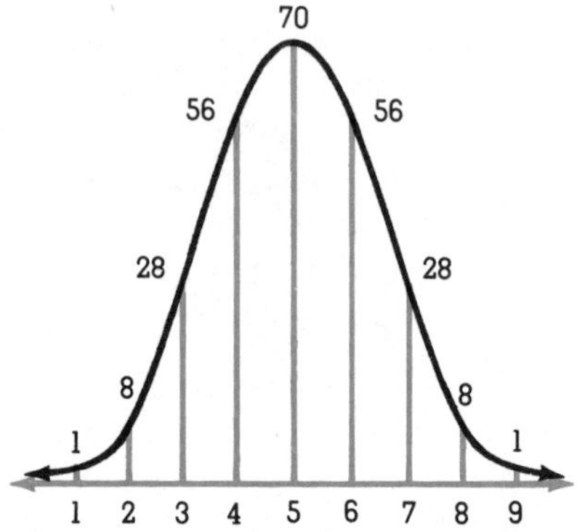

Exercises Solve each problem.

1. Draw a smooth curve connecting the tops of the ordinates whose lengths are proportional to the coefficients in the expansion of $(x + y)^{12}$.

2-7. A teacher decided to mark 64 tests with the grades A, B, C, D, E, and F (A highest) in proportion to the coefficients in the expansion of $(x + y)^5$. How many tests received each grade?

14-8 Sample Sets of Data

The population or universe in a statistical study is all of the items or individuals in the group being considered. It rarely happens that 100% of a population is accessible as a source of data. Therefore a random sample of the population must be selected. The sample should be representative of the population. The various characteristics of the population pertinent to the study should be found in the sample in about the same ratio as they exist in the population. Then, based upon this sample, certain inferences can be made about the population from which the sample was selected.

A random sample is a sample selected by chance.

Suppose, for example, that you need to know the mean height of 1031 high school senior boys in a certain city. It is impractical to measure all of them. However, 100 senior boys in the city are organized into an all-city boys' chorus in which all high schools are represented in proportion to their enrollment of boys. It is assumed that musical talent has no relationship to height. Hence, this sample of 100 boys is assumed to be random with respect to height.

At a practice session of the chorus you make actual measurements of the heights of the 100 boys correct to the nearest tenth of an inch. After tabulating the data, you compute the arithmetic mean and the standard deviation. $\overline{X}$ is 67.6 in. and σ is 2.7 in. Now you must estimate the mean of the heights of the entire population, that is, of all 1031 senior boys in the city.

You could say with nearly complete certainty that the true mean of all 1031 boys, represented by $\tilde{X}$, lies somewhere within a large range of the sample mean 67.6 (for example, 47.6 to 87.6). However, this range is so broad that it is of little value. On the other hand, if you give a narrow range around 67.6 (for example, 67.5 to 67.7), you cannot predict with any great degree of certainty or confidence that $\tilde{X}$ is in this range.

$\tilde{X}$ is read "X tilde."

Some level of confidence is needed. A statistic called the **standard error of the mean** is used to give a level of confidence about the sample mean.

The Standard Error of the Mean

If a sample set of data has N values and σ is the standard deviation, then the standard error of the mean, $\sigma_{\overline{x}}$, can be found as follows.

$$\sigma_{\overline{x}} = \frac{\sigma}{\sqrt{N}}$$

The symbol $\sigma_{\overline{x}}$ is read "sigma sub-x bar."

Sample means of various random samples of the same population are normally distributed about the true mean with the standard error of the mean as a measure of their variability. Thus the standard error of the mean behaves like the standard deviation. Probabilities of the occurrence of sample means and true means may be determined by referring to the table on page 415. For example, there is a 68.3% chance that the true mean, $\tilde{X}$, of a population lies within one standard error of the mean, or $\overline{X} \pm \sigma_{\overline{x}}$. Likewise, there is a 0.90 probability that the true mean lies in the range $\overline{X} \pm 1.65\,\sigma_{\overline{x}}$.

example 1 **The mean height of a random sample of 100 senior boys in a certain city is 67.6 in. and the standard deviation is 2.7 in. Find the range of heights such that the probability is 0.90 that the mean height of the entire population of senior boys lies within it.**

Find t when P = 0.90. $t = 1.65$

Find $\sigma_{\overline{x}}$. $\sigma_{\overline{x}} = \frac{2.7}{\sqrt{100}} = 0.27$

Find the range. $\overline{X} \pm t\sigma_{\overline{x}} = 67.6 \pm (1.65)(0.27)$
$= 67.6 \pm 0.4$

The probability is 0.90 that the true mean, $\tilde{X}$, is within the range 67.2 to 68.0.

If a higher level of confidence is desired for the same number of values, accuracy must be sacrificed by giving a wider range. However, if the number of values in the sample is larger, the range for a given probability or level of confidence is smaller.

The most commonly used levels of confidence are the 1% and the 5% levels. A 1% level of confidence means that there is less than a 1% chance that the true mean differs from the sample mean by a certain amount. That is, the probability that the true mean is within a certain range of the sample mean is 0.99. A 5% level of confidence means that the probability of the true mean being within a certain range of the sample mean is 0.95.

example 2 **The mean height of a random sample of 144 senior boys in a certain city is 68.5 in. and the standard deviation is 2.8 in. Find the range of the sample mean which has a 1% level of confidence.**

A 1% level of confidence is given when $P = 0.99$.

Find t when P = 0.99. $t = 2.58$

Find $\sigma_{\overline{x}}$. $\sigma_{\overline{x}} = \frac{2.8}{\sqrt{144}} = 0.23$

Find the range. $\overline{X} \pm t\sigma_{\overline{x}} = 68.5 \pm (2.58)(0.23)$
$= 68.5 \pm 0.6$

Thus the range which has a 1% level of confidence is 67.9 in. to 69.1 in.

exercises

Exploratory Find the probabilities of each of the following.

1. The true mean of a set of data is within 2 standard errors from the sample mean.
2. The true mean of a set of data is within 1.5 standard errors from the sample mean.

Find the standard error of the mean, $\sigma_{\bar{x}}$, for each of the following.

3. $\sigma = 40$, $N = 64$, $\overline{X} = 200$
4. $\sigma = 5$, $N = 36$, $\overline{X} = 45$
5. $\sigma = 2.4$, $N = 100$, $\overline{X} = 24$
6. $\sigma = 12$, $N = 200$, $\overline{X} = 80$

7-10. Find the range which has a 1% level of confidence for problems 3-6.

11-14. Find the range which has a 5% level of confidence for problems 3-6.

Written **In Middletown a random sample of 100 families showed that the mean number of hours the television set was turned on was 4.6 hours. The standard deviation was 1.4 hours.**

1. Find the standard error of the mean.
2. Find the range about the sample mean which has a 1% level of confidence.
3. Find the range about the sample mean that gives a 50% chance that the true mean lies within it.
4. Find the range about the sample mean such that the probability is 0.90 that the true mean lies within it.

A random sample of 50 acorns from an oak tree reveals a mean diameter of 16.2 mm and a standard deviation of 1.4 mm.

5. Find the standard error of the mean.
6. Find the range about the sample mean which has a 5% level of confidence.
7. Find the range about the sample mean that gives a 99% chance that the true mean lies within it.
8. Find the range about the sample mean such that the probability is 0.80 that the true mean lies within it.

The following is a frequency distribution of the time in minutes required for student registration at Bell College. The distribution is a random sample from a total population of 2361 students.

Class Marks	4	6	8	10	12	14	16	18	20
Frequency	1	3	5	12	17	13	7	4	2

9. Find the standard deviation of the data in the frequency distribution.
10. Find the standard error of the mean.
11. Find the range about the sample mean such that the probability is 0.95 that the true mean lies within it.
12. Find the probability that the mean of the population will be less than one point from the mean of the sample.

Solve each problem.

13. The standard deviation of the weights of 36 seven-year olds in the United States is 8 pounds. What is the probability that the mean weight of the random sample will differ by more than one pound from the mean weight of all seven year olds?
14. Eighty-one beef cattle were fed a special fattening diet for six weeks. The mean gain in weight was 40 lb with a standard deviation of 5 lb. With what level of confidence can it be said that the diet will cause an average gain in weight of between 30 to 50 lb in a similar group of cattle?

Chapter Summary

1. If a set of data has n values, given by X_i such that $1 \leq i \leq n$, then the arithmetic mean, $\overline{X}$, is $\frac{1}{n}\sum_{i=1}^{n} X_i$. (394)
2. The median, M_d, of a set of data is the mid-value. If there are two mid-values, it is the arithmetic mean of these values. (395)
3. The mode of a set of data is the most frequently occurring value. (395)
4. A set of data has n values, given by X_i such that $1 \leq i \leq n$, with arithmetic mean, $\overline{X}$.
   a. The harmonic mean, H, is $\frac{n}{\sum_{i=1}^{n} \frac{1}{X_i}}$. (397)
   b. The quadratic mean, Q, is $\sqrt{\frac{\sum_{i=1}^{n} X_i^2}{n}}$. (398)
   c. The mean deviation, $M.D.$, is $\frac{1}{n}\sum_{i=1}^{n} |X_i - \overline{X}|$. (400)
   d. The standard deviation, σ, is $\sqrt{\frac{1}{n}\sum_{i=1}^{n} (X_i - \overline{X})^2}$. (401)
5. If a set of data has first quartile point, Q_1, and third quartile point, Q_3, the semi-interquartile range, Q_R, is $\frac{Q_3 - Q_1}{2}$. (401)
6. A frequency distribution organizes a large number of data in classes. (403)
7. Graphs can be used to represent the data in a frequency distribution. Bar graphs and histograms are used to compare frequencies. Broken line graphs show trends. Circle graphs show the relationship between the parts and the whole. (407)
8. A frequency distribution has k classes where X_i are class marks, such that $1 \leq i \leq k$, and f_i are the corresponding frequencies of each class.
   a. The arithmetic mean, $\overline{X}$, of the data is approximated by $\frac{\sum_{i=1}^{k} f_i \cdot X_i}{\sum_{i=1}^{k} f_i}$. (411)
   b. The standard deviation, σ, of the data is approximated by $\sqrt{\frac{\sum_{i=1}^{k} (X_i - \overline{X})^2 f_i}{\sum_{i=1}^{k} f_i}}$. (412)
9. The median of the data in a frequency distribution is in the median class of the cumulative frequency distribution. (412)

10. The normal distribution often occurs when there is a large number of values in the frequency distribution. (414)
11. If a sample set of data has N values and σ is the standard deviation, then the standard error of the mean, $\sigma_{\bar{x}}$, is $\frac{\sigma}{\sqrt{N}}$. (419)
12. A 1% level of confidence means that the probability of the true mean being within a certain range of the sample mean is 0.99. A 5% level of confidence means that the probability of the true mean being within a certain range of the sample mean is 0.95. (420)

Chapter Review

14-1 **A die was tossed 10 times with the following results.**

5 1 5 4 2 3 6 2 5 1

1. Find the range of the data.
2. Find the arithmetic mean of the data.
3. Find the median of the data.
4. Find the mode of the data.

14-2
5. Find the harmonic mean of the data.
6. Find the quadratic mean of the data.

14-3
7. Find the mean deviation of the data.
8. Find the semi-interquartile range of the data.
9. Find the standard deviation of the data.

14-4 **At Founder's University the achievement of students is reported as a number from 0 to 5, where 5 is the highest rating. The point averages for a random sample of 500 freshmen are summarized in the following frequency distribution.**

Point Average	below 1.0	1.0 - 2.0	2.0 - 3.0	3.0 - 4.0	4.0 - 5.0
Frequency	54	92	124	145	85

10. What are the class marks?
11. Find the class interval.

14-5
12. Make a bar graph of the data.
13. Make a broken line graph of the data in the frequency distribution.

14-6
14. Find the arithmetic mean of the data in the frequency distribution.
15. Find the median of the data in the frequency distribution.
16. Find the standard deviation of the data in the frequency distribution.

14-7 **Assume the data in the frequency distribution given above is normally distributed.**

17. Find the range about the mean which includes 80% of the data.
18. Find the probability that a student selected at random will have a point average of 4.0 or higher.

14-8
19. Find the standard error of the mean.
20. Find the range about the sample mean which has a 1% level of confidence.

Chapter Test

A small metal object is weighed on a laboratory balance by each of 15 pupils in a class. The weight of the object in grams is reported as 2.341, 2.347, 2.338, 2.350, 2.344, 2.342, 2.345, 2.348, 2.340, 2.345, 2.343, 2.344, 2.347, 2.341, and 2.344.

1. Make an array of the data.
2. Find the range of the data.
3. Find the arithmetic mean of the data.
4. Find the median of the data.
5. Find the mode of the data.
6. Find the mean deviation of the data.
7. Find the semi-interquartile range of the data.
8. Find the standard deviation of the data.

A fruit stand owner mixed four different grades of apples into one pile for resale. His costs for the different grades are as follows.

Grades	Costs
A	20¢ per pound
B	24¢ per pound
C	16¢ per pound
D	30¢ per pound

9. Assume the owner purchased the same quantity of apples for each grade. Find the average cost per pound of the mixed grade.
10. Assume that the owner spent the same amount of money for each grade. Find the average cost per pound of the mixed grade.

The days missed for a random sample of 80 high school students at Main High School in a certain school year are given below.

6	16	12	7	7	9	13	12	7	7
4	11	13	10	16	20	10	17	11	12
3	8	8	12	13	8	8	11	12	1
16	13	5	10	1	10	8	15	10	13
9	15	11	18	12	14	10	16	8	10
10	12	17	14	6	9	12	10	14	8
19	4	9	6	9	10	11	5	11	9
20	5	2	11	19	9	7	9	6	14

11. Make a frequency distribution of the data using a class interval of three.
12. Draw a histogram for the data in the frequency distribution.
13. Draw a circle graph for the data in the frequency distribution.
14. Find the mean of the data in the frequency distribution.
15. Find the median of the data in the frequency distribution.
16. Find the standard deviation of the data in the frequency distribution.

Assume the data given above for problems 11-16 is normally distributed.

17. Find the lower and upper limits within which 90% of the data lie.
18. Find the probability that a value selected at random from the data will be between 8 and 12.
19. Find the standard error of the mean.
20. Find the range about the sample mean which has a 5% level of confidence.

Chapter

15

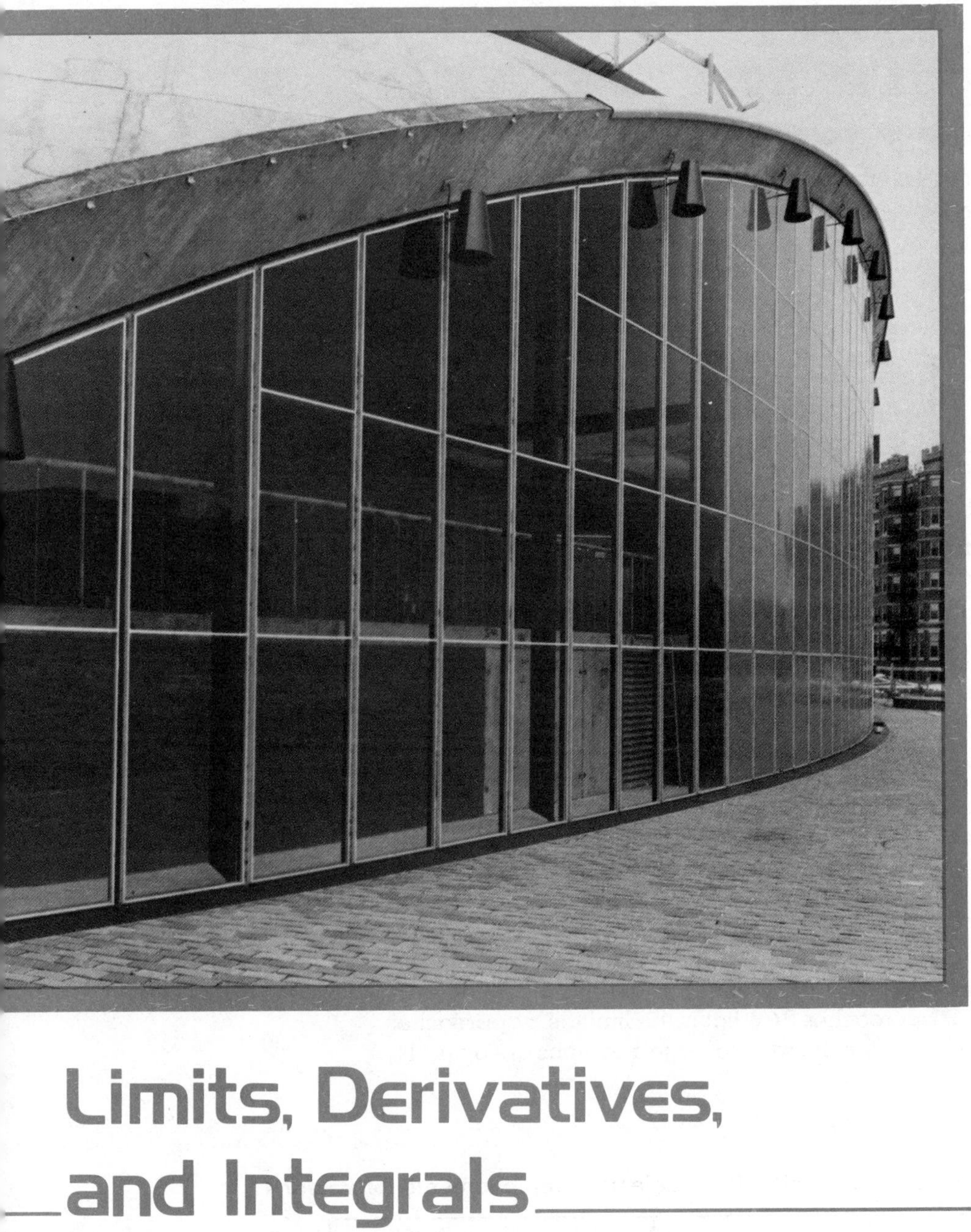

Limits, Derivatives, and Integrals

Rectangles can be used to approximate the area under a curve by a process called integration. If the width of each rectangle is decreased and the number of rectangles is increased, their total area approaches the actual area under the curve. The windows under the curving roof of this building architecturally illustrate how integration finds the area under a curve.

15-1 Concept of Limit

Consider the sequence, $\frac{1}{2}, \frac{1}{4}, \frac{1}{8}, \ldots, \frac{1}{2^n}$ as n increases without limit. The graph below suggests that the sequence converges to zero. As n increases, the denominator of $\frac{1}{2^n}$ increases, and the value of the fraction approaches zero. The limit of this sequence is represented as follows.

$$\lim_{n \to \infty} \frac{1}{2^n} = 0$$

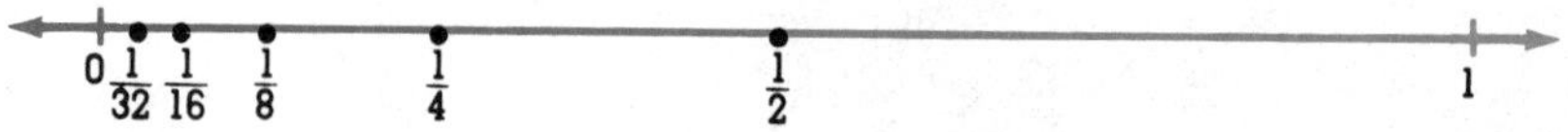

Consider the sum $\frac{1}{2} + \frac{1}{4} + \frac{1}{8} + \cdots + \frac{1}{2^n}$ as n increases without limit. This sum approaches a limit if it becomes and remains close to some constant for large values of n. The limit of the sum itself is the constant being approached as n increases indefinitely. The sum of n terms can be represented by the length of the line segment from zero to the nth point as shown below.

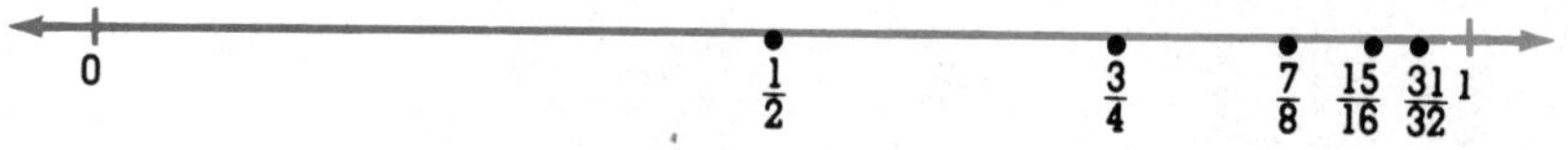

As n increases without limit, the points representing the sum cluster closer and closer to 1, but always remain less than 1. Thus, the limit of the sum $\frac{1}{2} + \frac{1}{4} + \frac{1}{8} + \cdots + \frac{1}{2^n}$ as n increases indefinitely is 1.

The concept of a limit may be extended to a function. What is the limit of $2x + 3$ as x approaches 0? What is the limit as x approaches 4? As you would expect, the answers to these questions are 3 and 11, respectively.

example

1 Show that $\lim_{x \to 4} (x^2 - 4) = 12$ by selecting replacements for x near 4.

x	3.8	3.9	3.99	3.999
$x^2 - 4$	10.44	11.21	11.9201	11.992001

x	4.1	4.01	4.001	4.0001
$x^2 - 4$	12.81	12.0801	12.008001	12.00080001

Thus, the limit of $x^2 - 4$ as x approaches 4 is 12.

Consider any polynomial function with real coefficients of the form $P(x) = a_0x^n + a_1x^{n-1} + a_2x^{n-2} + \cdots + a_{n-1}x + a_n$. Let the domain of P be the set of all real numbers. Then, for any real number r, there exists a real number $P(r)$. The limit of such a polynomial function as x approaches r is $P(r)$. For example, the limit of $x^2 - x + 3$ as x approaches 2 is $2^2 - 2 + 3$ or 5.

The limit of a polynomial function, $P(x)$, as x approaches r, is $P(r)$.

$$\lim_{x\to r} P(x) = P(r)$$

Limit of a Polynomial Function

Now consider the rational function $f(x) = \frac{x^3}{x}$. The graph of $f(x)$ is shown at the right. What value of x is *not* in the domain? Suppose you wish to find the limit of $\frac{x^3}{x}$ as x approaches 2. Let $r = 2$.

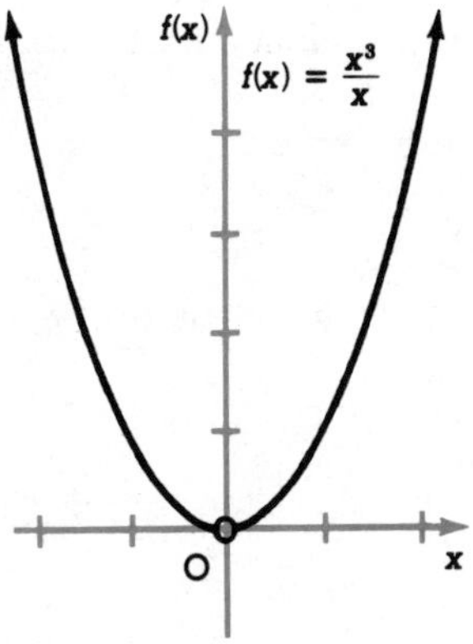

$$\lim_{x\to r} f(x) = f(r)$$

$$\lim_{x\to 2} \frac{x^3}{x} = f(2)$$

$$= \frac{8}{2} \text{ or } 4$$

What is $\lim_{x\to 0} \frac{x^3}{x}$? Let $r = 0$. In this case, $f(r)$ is undefined. Replace x by values close to zero to obtain values close to $\frac{x^3}{x}$ at zero.

x	1	0.1	0.01	0.001	0.0001
$\frac{x^3}{x}$	1	0.01	0.0001	0.000001	0.00000001

It appears that $\lim_{x\to 0} \frac{x^3}{x} = 0$. Although the function is undefined at zero, the limit of the function exists as x approaches zero. The limit is 0.

An alternate way of showing that $\lim_{x\to 0} \frac{x^3}{x} = 0$ is to transform $\frac{x^3}{x}$ into x^2 since the two functions are equal for all values of x except $x = 0$. Because x^2 is a polynomial, $\lim_{x\to 0} x^2 = 0$. This method succeeds whenever a transformation is possible, even if the given function is *not* defined at that point.

example 2 Find $\lim_{x \to 2} \frac{x^2 - 4}{x - 2}$.

$$\lim_{x \to 2} \frac{(x^2 - 4)}{x - 2} = \lim_{x \to 2} \frac{(x + 2)(x - 2)}{(x - 2)}$$ *Factor.*

$$= \lim_{x \to 2} (x + 2)$$ *Note that $\frac{x^2 - 4}{x - 2} = x + 2$ for all real values of x*

$$= 4$$ *except 2. However this fact does not affect the value of the limit as x approaches 2.*

The limit of $\frac{x^2 - 4}{x - 2}$ as x approaches 2 is 4.

Sometimes you may need to find the limit of a function which involves the function $f(x) = \frac{1}{x}$. The graph of $y = \frac{1}{x}$ is shown at the right. Notice that $\frac{1}{x}$ approaches zero as x increases in value. Thus, $\lim_{x \to \infty} \frac{1}{x} = 0$.

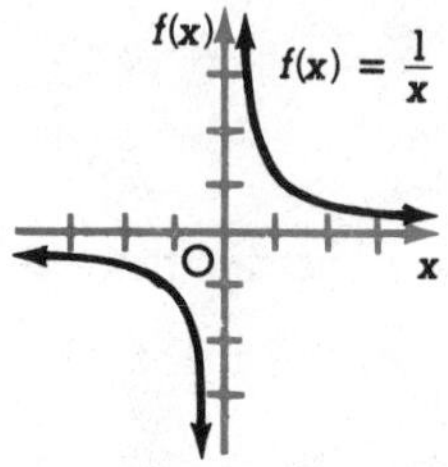

example 3 Find $\lim_{n \to \infty} \frac{7n^2}{n^2 + 3n + 1}$.

$$\lim_{n \to \infty} \frac{7n^2}{n^2 + 3n + 1} = \lim_{n \to \infty} \frac{7n^2 \cdot \frac{1}{n^2}}{(n^2 + 3n + 1)\frac{1}{n^2}}$$

$$= \lim_{n \to \infty} \frac{7}{1 + \frac{3}{n} + \frac{1}{n^2}}$$ *The values of $\frac{3}{n}$ and $\frac{1}{n^2}$ both approach zero as n increases.*

$$= 7$$

Thus, $\lim_{n \to \infty} \frac{7n^2}{n^2 + 3n + 1} = 7$.

exercises

Exploratory Show that the limit of each function, $F(x)$, as x approaches r, is $F(r)$ by selecting four successive replacements for x near r.

1. $\lim_{x \to 2} 5x$
2. $\lim_{x \to 2} (x^2 + 3x + 2)$
3. $\lim_{x \to 1} \frac{x - 2}{x + 2}$
4. $\lim_{x \to 3} x^2$
5. $\lim_{x \to -2} (x^2 - 4)$
6. $\lim_{x \to 5} \sqrt{25 - x^2}$
7. $\lim_{x \to 4} (3x + 2)$
8. $\lim_{x \to 0} (4x + 1)$
9. $\lim_{x \to -3} (2x - 5)$
10. $\lim_{x \to 2} (x^2 - 4x + 1)$
11. $\lim_{x \to 3} \frac{x - 2}{x + 2}$
12. $\lim_{x \to -2} \frac{x^2 - 4}{x^2 + 4}$

Written Find each limit.

1. $\lim_{x\to 2} x^2$
2. $\lim_{x\to 1} (x^2 + 4x + 3)$
3. $\lim_{x\to 1} \frac{x+1}{x+2}$
4. $\lim_{n\to 0} \left(5^n + \frac{1}{5^n}\right)$
5. $\lim_{x\to 5} (3x - 8)$
6. $\lim_{x\to 3} \frac{x^2-9}{x+3}$
7. $\lim_{x\to 3} \frac{x^2-9}{x-3}$
8. $\lim_{x\to {}^-3} \frac{x^2-9}{x+3}$
9. $\lim_{x\to 2} \frac{x^2-4}{x^3-8}$
10. $\lim_{x\to 3} \frac{x-3}{x^2-9}$
11. $\lim_{x\to {}^-2} (x^4 - x^2 + x - 2)$
12. $\lim_{x\to 2} \frac{x^3-8}{x-2}$
13. $\lim_{x\to {}^-1} \frac{x^3+1}{x+1}$
14. $\lim_{n\to {}^-2} \frac{n^3-8}{n-2}$
15. $\lim_{x\to 2} \frac{x^2-x-2}{x^2-4}$
16. $\lim_{x\to\infty} \frac{x+1}{x}$
17. $\lim_{x\to\infty} \frac{2x-5}{x}$
18. $\lim_{n\to\infty} \frac{n^2+n-6}{n^2}$
19. $\lim_{n\to 0} \frac{(1+n)^2-1}{n}$
20. $\lim_{x\to\infty} \frac{\sqrt{x+4}-2}{x}$
21. $\lim_{n\to\infty} \frac{(n-2)(n+1)}{n^2}$

15-2 Formal Definition of a Limit

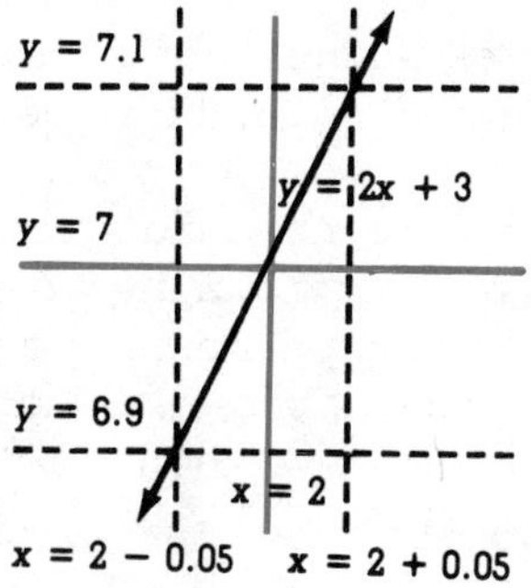

Consider the function $y = 2x + 3$. Suppose it is required that the value of $2x + 3$ be within 0.1 of 7. That is, $6.9 < 2x + 3 < 7.1$. Can you find an interval of values of x around 2 so that this condition is met? Will $1.9 < x < 2.1$ satisfy the requirement? Replacing x by 1.9 and 2.1 in $y = 2x + 3$ yields $6.8 < 2x + 3 < 7.2$. Thus, this interval of values of x around 2 is not close enough for $2x + 3$ to be within 0.1 of 7. Will $1.95 < x < 2.05$ satisfy the requirement that $6.9 < 2x + 3 < 7.1$? This gives $6.9 < 2x + 3 < 7.1$. Thus an interval of values of x around 2 such that the value of $2x + 3$ is within 0.1 of 7 has been found. This interval is $2 - 0.05 < x < 2 + 0.05$. *Will any range less than 0.05 around 2 also be acceptable?*

To generalize the preceding problem, substitute the symbol ϵ for the specified value 0.1. Thus, $7 - \epsilon < 2x + 3 < 7 + \epsilon$. This inequality can be solved for x.

The symbol ϵ, lower case Greek letter epsilon, is usually used when referring to closeness in the range. ϵ is a positive real number.

$$7 - \epsilon < 2x + 3 < 7 + \epsilon$$
$$(7 - \epsilon) - 3 < 2x < (7 + \epsilon) - 3$$
$$4 - \epsilon < 2x < 4 + \epsilon$$
$$\frac{4-\epsilon}{2} < x < \frac{4+\epsilon}{2}$$
$$2 - \frac{\epsilon}{2} < x < 2 + \frac{\epsilon}{2}$$

Thus, if $2 - \frac{\epsilon}{2} < x < 2 + \frac{\epsilon}{2}$, then $7 - \epsilon < 2x + 3 < 7 + \epsilon$.

So an interval of the domain around 2, $\left|\frac{\epsilon}{2}\right|$, can be found for any value of ϵ.

example

1 **How close to 2 must x be chosen so that 5x − 1 is within 0.01 of 9?**

$$9 - 0.01 < 5x - 1 < 9 + 0.01$$
$$^{-}0.01 < (5x - 1) - 9 < 0.01$$
$$^{-}0.01 < 5x - 10 < 0.01$$
$$^{-}0.002 < x - 2 < 0.002$$
$$2 - 0.002 < x < 2 + 0.002$$
$$1.998 < x < 2.002$$

Thus, if values of x are within 0.002 of 2, then $5x - 1$ is within 0.01 of 9.

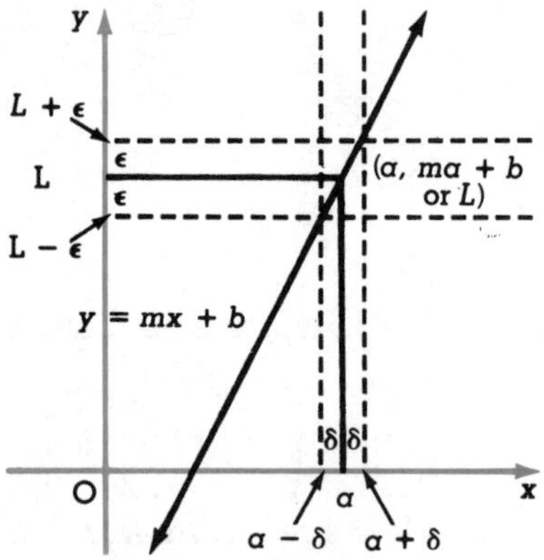

Consider the general function $y = mx + b$. The concept of finding values of x close to a such that $mx + b$ is within a certain interval of $ma + b$ is illustrated at the right. Let $L = ma + b$. Consider the neighborhood of L between $L - \epsilon$ and $L + \epsilon$ where ϵ is a positive real number. How close to a must the value of x be selected in order to insure that $L - \epsilon < mx + b < L + \epsilon$? Let the values of x be limited by the interval $a - \delta < x < a + \delta$ where δ is a positive real number. Can a value of δ be found that will insure that the value of $mx + b$ falls within the interval from $L - \epsilon$ to $L + \epsilon$ no matter how small ϵ is chosen. If such a value of δ can be found, regardless of the choice of ϵ, then the limit of $mx + b$ as x approaches a is L or $\lim_{x \to a} (mx + b) = L$.

The symbol δ, lower case Greek letter delta, is usually used when referring to closeness in the domain. δ is a positive real number.

To prove that $\lim_{x \to a} (mx + b) = ma + b$ it must be shown that for any choice of $\epsilon > 0$, there is a $\delta > 0$ such that whenever $a - \delta < x < a + \delta$, the following double inequality is satisfied.

$$(ma + b) - \epsilon < mx + b < (ma + b) + \epsilon$$
$$^{-}\epsilon < (mx + b) - (ma + b) < \epsilon$$
$$^{-}\epsilon < m(x - a) < \epsilon$$
$$\frac{^{-}\epsilon}{m} < x - a < \frac{\epsilon}{m}$$

If m is less then zero, the inequality is reversed.

$$a - \frac{\epsilon}{m} < x < a + \frac{\epsilon}{m}$$

Thus, if δ is equal to $\frac{\epsilon}{|m|}$ or any smaller positive number, the required inequality will be satisfied when $a - \delta < x < a + \delta$. Therefore, a value of δ can be found for any given value of ϵ which will insure that $(mx + b)$ is in the desired range whenever x is within δ units of a.

Absolute value notation can be used to represent a double inequality. Recall that $|x| = x$ if $x \geq 0$ or $|x| = {}^-x$ if $x < 0$. So $|x| < 5$ expresses the same relationship as ${}^-5 < x < 5$.

example 2 **Express ${}^-\delta < x - a < \delta$ as a single inequality using absolute value notation.**

The expression ${}^-\delta < x - a < \delta$ is equivalent to $|x - a| < \delta$. This is true because $|x - a| < \delta$ means that $x - a < \delta$ if $x \geq a$, but $x - a > {}^-\delta$ if $x < a$.

The absolute value notation is used in the formal definition of the limit of a function.

The limit of a function $f(x)$ as x approaches a is L, written $\lim\limits_{x \to a} f(x) = L$, if, for every real number $\epsilon > 0$, there exists a real number $\delta > 0$ such that $|f(x) - L| < \epsilon$ when $0 < |x - a| < \delta$.

Limit of a Function

For the limit of $f(x)$ to be L, when values of x are selected in the neighborhood of a for any $f(x)$, values of $f(x)$ must be in the neighborhood of L. If it is required that $f(x)$ be arbitrarily close to L, say within ϵ units of L, then it must be possible to meet this requirement by selecting values of x sufficiently close to a, that is, within δ units of a. If this is satisfied, it is said that $f(x)$ approaches the limit L as x approaches a. The inequality $0 < |x - a|$ in the last line of the definition means that $x \neq a$. Thus, it is *not* required that a be in the domain of $f(x)$. *Why?*

example 3 **Prove $\lim\limits_{x \to 2} (3x + 7) = 13$.**

You can guess that the limit $L = 13$. But to prove $\lim\limits_{x \to 2} (3x + 7) = 13$, for each $\epsilon > 0$ you must find a $\delta > 0$ such that $|f(x) - L|$ or $|(3x + 7) - 13| < \epsilon$ when $0 < |x - 2| < \delta$.

$$\begin{aligned} |f(x) - L| &= |(3x + 7) - 13| \\ &= |3x - 6| \\ &= 3|x - 2| \end{aligned}$$

Thus, $|(3x + 7) - 13|$ or $3|x - 2|$ will be less than ϵ when $|x - 2| < \frac{\epsilon}{3}$.

Therefore, if you choose $\delta \leq \frac{\epsilon}{3}$, the conditions of the definition are satisfied and $\lim\limits_{x \to 2} (3x + 7) = 13$.

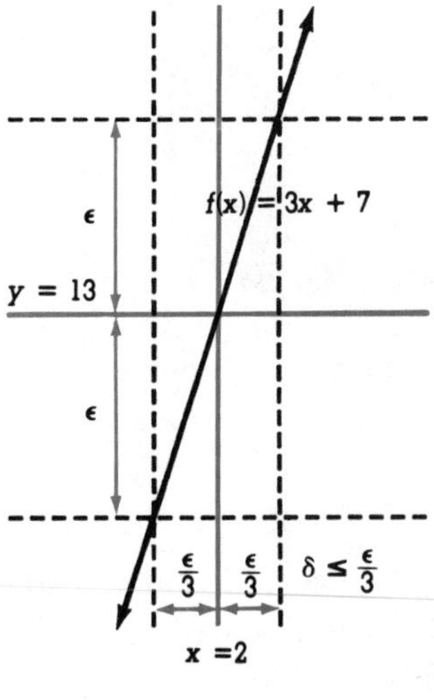

example

4 **Prove that $\lim_{x \to 2} x^2 = 4$.**

To prove $\lim_{x \to 2} x^2 = 4$, for each $\epsilon > 0$ you must find a $\delta > 0$ such that $|f(x) - L|$ or $|x^2 - 4| < \epsilon$ when $0 < |x - 2| < \delta$. But $|x^2 - 4|$ or $|x - 2| \cdot |x + 2| < \epsilon$ only if $|x - 2| < \frac{\epsilon}{|x + 2|}$. If you choose $\delta = 0.5$, then $0 < |x - 2| < 0.5$ and $1.5 < x < 2.5$. This means $|x + 2| < |2.5 + 2|$ or $|x + 2| < 4.5$. Therefore, to have $|x^2 - 4| < \epsilon$ and $1.5 < x < 2.5$, you must have $|x - 2| < \frac{\epsilon}{4.5}$. *Remember that* $|x - 2| < \frac{\epsilon}{|x + 2|}$.

So for each $\epsilon > 0$, choose δ to be smaller than either 0.5 or $\frac{\epsilon}{4.5}$.

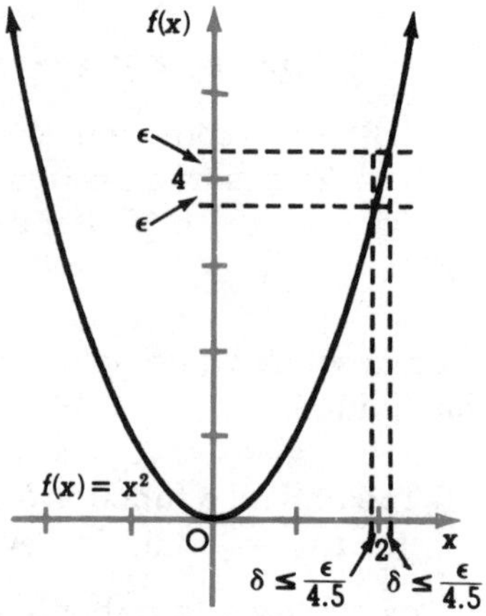

Thus, the $\lim_{x \to 2} x^2 = 4$ because for each $\epsilon > 0$ there corresponds a $\delta > 0$ such that $|x^2 - 4| < \epsilon$ when $0 < |x - 2| < \delta$.

There are many functions for which $\lim_{x \to a} f(x)$ does *not* exist. For example $\lim_{x \to 0} \frac{1}{x}$ and $\lim_{x \to 2} [x]$ do *not* exist, as indicated by their graphs.

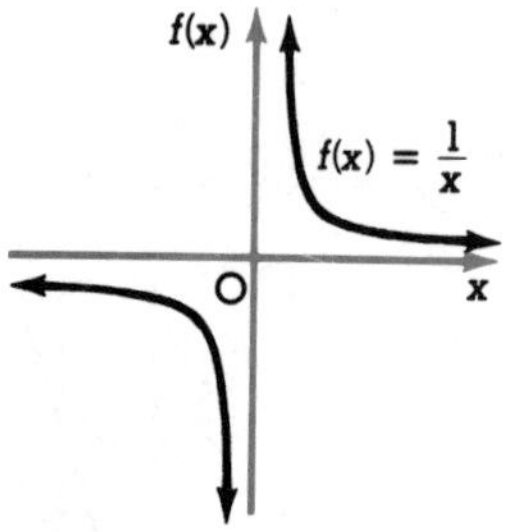

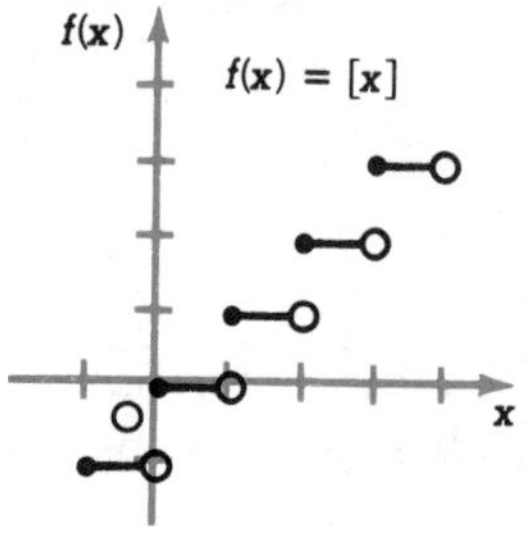

exercises

Exploratory Express each inequality as a single inequality using absolute value notation.

1. $^{-}0.1 < x - 2 < 0.1$
2. $^{-}0.002 < x - 5 < 0.002$
3. $^{-}\delta < x - 8 < \delta$
4. $^{-}\delta < x - 1 < \delta$
5. $^{-}0.001 < x - 8 < 0.001$
6. $^{-}\delta < x - 2 < \delta$

State each inequality without using absolute value notation.

7. $|x - 4| < 0.001$
8. $|x - 3| < 0.2$
9. $|x - 7| < \delta$
10. $|x - 2| < 0.1$
11. $|x - 8| < 0.00003$
12. $|x - 1| < \delta$

Describe each shaded area with double inequalities.

13. 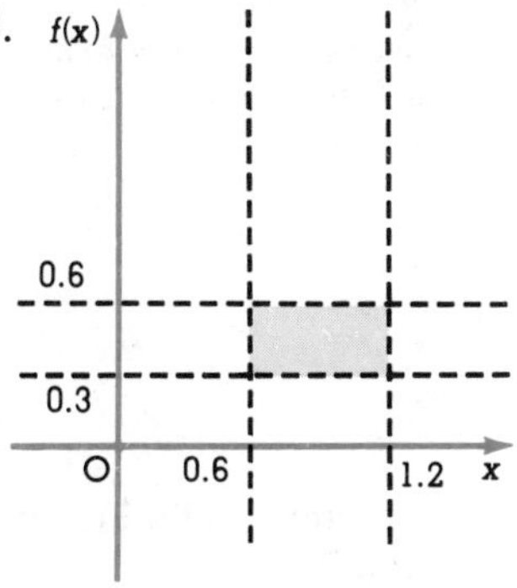

14. 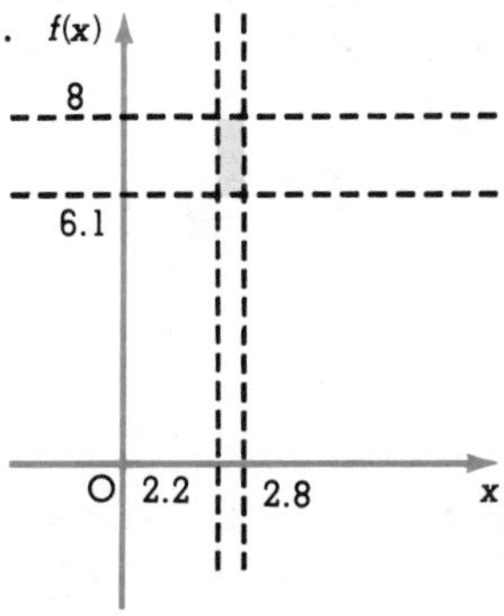

15. 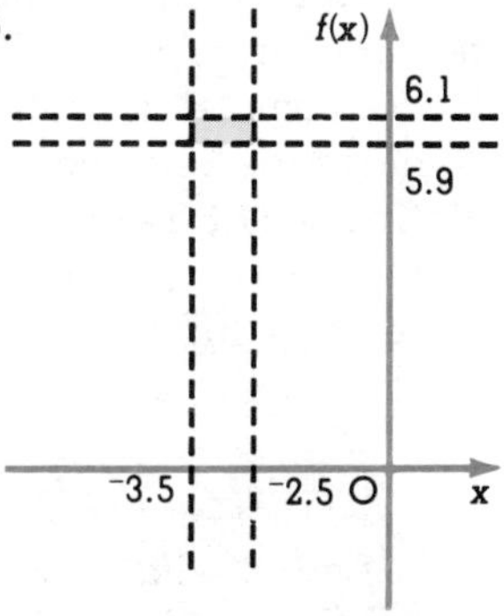

16-18. Describe each shaded area in problems 13-15 using absolute value notation.

Written **Find the interval which x must be within so that each inequality is satisfied.**

1. $^{-}0.01 < 4 - 2x < 0.01$
2. $7.8 < 5x + 3 < 8.2$
3. $2.9 < x - 2 < 3.1$
4. $6.8 < 2x + 3 < 7.2$
5. $|6 - 3x| < 0.01$
6. $15.99 < 15x + 1 < 16.01$
7. $3.7 < \frac{3x - 2}{4} < 4.3$
8. $\left|\frac{x + 1}{2}\right| < 0.01$

Find the smallest interval that $f(x)$ will be within if x is within each given interval.

9. $f(x) = 3x - 8;\ 3 < x < 5$
10. $f(x) = 2x - 1;\ 2.9 < x < 3.1$
11. $f(x) = x^2;\ 6.5 < x < 7.5$
12. $f(x) = 3x + 1;\ 1.6 < x < 1.7$
13. $f(x) = \frac{x}{2};\ ^{-}1.7 < x < {}^{-}1.3$
14. $f(x) = x^2 - 2x;\ ^{-}0.1 < x < 0.1$
15. $f(x) = 6 - x;\ a > 0;\ 2 - a < x < 2 + a$
16. $f(x) = 2x;\ a > 0;\ ^{-}a < x - 3 < a$

Solve each problem.

17. Show that the limit of $2x - 6$ as x approaches 4 is 2 by finding a value $\delta > 0$ for any $\epsilon > 0$ so that $2 - \epsilon < 2x - 6 < 2 + \epsilon$ whenever $4 - \delta < x < 4 + \delta$.
18. Graph the function $f(x) = 3x - 5$. Show the relationship between ϵ and δ on the graph by finding values of δ corresponding to ϵ values of 0.1 and 0.01 as x approaches 2.

Given that $\epsilon = 0.01$, find a δ such that the following limits are verified using the definition.

19. $\lim_{x \to {}^{-}1} (x + 3) = 2$
20. $\lim_{x \to 1} \frac{x - 1}{3} = 0$
21. $\lim_{x \to 3} \frac{2x - 5}{2} = \frac{1}{2}$
22. $\lim_{x \to 0} (4x + 5) = 5$
23. $\lim_{x \to 0} x = 0$
24. $\lim_{x \to \frac{1}{2}} (2x - 1) = 0$
25. $\lim_{x \to 2} \frac{x^2 - 4}{x - 2} = 4$
26. $\lim_{x \to 2} \frac{1}{x} = \frac{1}{2}$

15-3 Continuity

A function is **continuous** if there are no "breaks" in the graph of the function. That is, the graph of a continuous function may be drawn completely without lifting the pencil.

A function which is not continuous at a point is said to be discontinuous at that point.

There are three conditions that must be met for a function to be **continuous at a point.** The function must be defined at that point. It must have a limit for the x-value of the point in question. Also, the value of the function must be equal to the limit of the function at that point.

Continuity of a Function at a Point

> **A function f is continuous at $x = a$ if $f(a)$ exists and if $\lim_{x \to a} f(x) = f(a)$.**

examples

1 **Show that $f(x) = x^2 + 2x$ is continuous at $x = 2$.**

Show that $f(2)$ exists.

$$f(x) = x^2 + 2x$$
$$f(2) = 2^2 + 2 \cdot 2 \text{ or } 8$$

Show that $\lim_{x \to 2} f(x) = f(2)$.

Since $f(x)$ is a polynomial, the limit of $f(x)$ as x approaches 2 is $f(2)$.

Thus, the function is continuous at 2.

2 **Show that $\lim_{x \to 2} \frac{x^2 - 4}{x - 2} = 4$. Then state whether the function, $f(x) = \frac{x^2 - 4}{x - 2}$, is continuous or discontinuous at $x = 2$.**

Find a value of δ such that if $0 < |x - 2| < \delta$, then $\left|\frac{x^2 - 4}{x - 2} - 4\right| < \epsilon$ for any choice of ϵ.

$$\left|\frac{x^2 - 4}{x - 2} - 4\right| < \epsilon$$
$$^{-}\epsilon < \frac{x^2 - 4}{x - 2} - 4 < \epsilon$$
$$4 - \epsilon < \frac{x^2 - 4}{x - 2} < 4 + \epsilon$$
$$4 - \epsilon < \frac{(x - 2)(x + 2)}{(x - 2)} < 4 + \epsilon$$
$$4 - \epsilon < x + 2 < 4 + \epsilon$$
$$^{-}\epsilon < x - 2 < \epsilon$$
$$0 < |x - 2| < \epsilon$$

Thus, if $0 < |x - 2| < \delta$, you must choose $\delta \leq \epsilon$. Therefore, the conditions of the definition of a limit are satisfied and $\lim_{x \to 2} \frac{x^2 - 4}{x - 2} = 4$.

The function, $f(x) = \frac{x^2 - 4}{x - 2}$, is *not* continuous at $x = 2$ because $f(2)$ is undefined.

The concept of continuity may be extended from a point to an interval and then to the whole domain of a function.

A function f is continuous on an interval if it is continuous at each point of the interval.

Continuity of a Function on an Interval

A function f is continuous if it is continuous at each point of its domain.

Continuous Function

It is obvious that any polynomial function, $P(x)$, is continuous since for any value r, there exists $P(r)$ and $\lim_{x \to r} P(x) = P(r)$.

Several types of discontinuous functions are shown below.

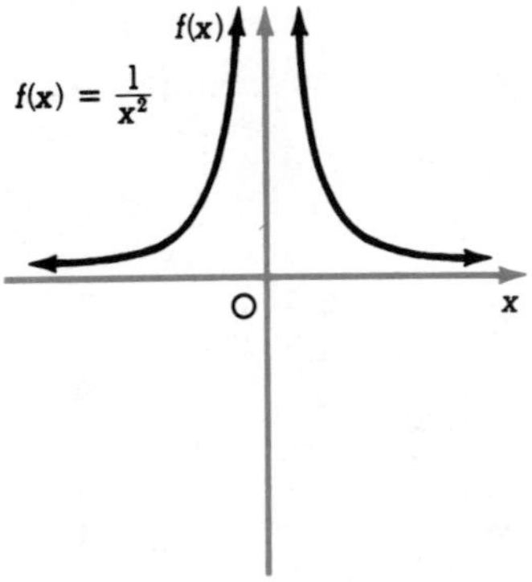

Infinite Discontinuity

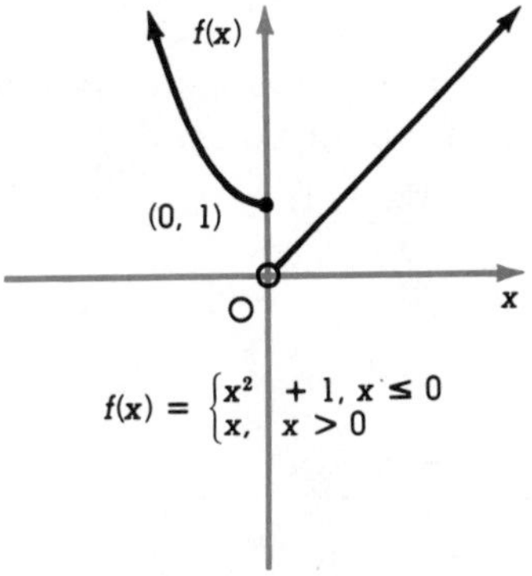

Jump Discontinuity

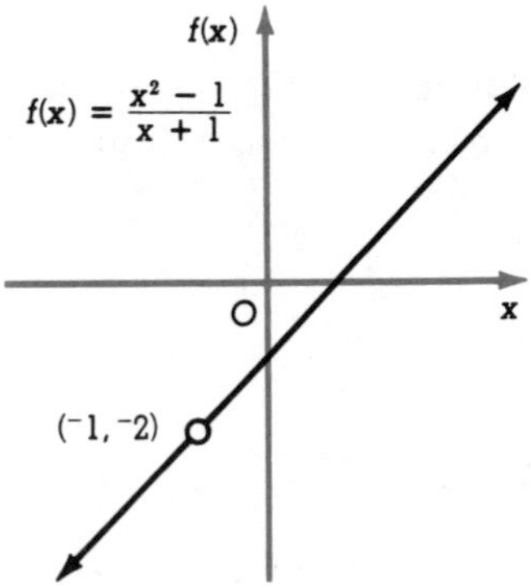

Point Discontinuity

The function, $f(x) = \begin{cases} 1, & x \text{ rational} \\ 0, & x \text{ irrational} \end{cases}$, is an example of a discontinuous function which is everywhere discontinuous.

It is impossible to graph this function.

example

3 **Determine if $f(x) = \dfrac{|x|}{x}$ is continuous or discontinuous.**

If it is discontinuous, state the type of discontinuity indicated by its graph.

Graph the function.

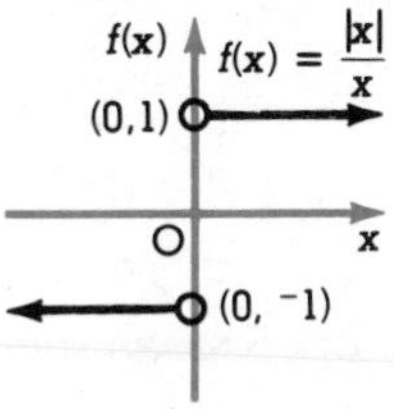

The graph indicates that $f(x)$ is discontinuous. The function $f(x) = \dfrac{|x|}{x}$ has jump discontinuity at $x = 0$.

exercises

Exploratory Identify a point(s) at which each function is discontinuous.

1. $f(x) = \frac{8}{x}$
2. $f(x) = 1 - \frac{1}{x}$
3. $f(x) = \frac{1}{(x-3)^2}$
4. $f(x) = \frac{x-2}{x^2 - 3x + 2}$
5. $f(x) = [x]$
6. $f(x) = \begin{cases} 1, & x > 0 \\ 0, & x = 0 \\ ^{-}1, & x < 0 \end{cases}$

Each of the following functions has point discontinuity. Assign values to $f(x)$ that remove the discontinuity.

7. $f(x) = \frac{x^2 - 1}{x - 1}$
8. $f(x) = \frac{x^2 - 5x + 6}{x - 2}$
9. $f(x) = \frac{x^2 - 5}{x + \sqrt{5}}$
10. $f(x) = \frac{x^3 + 8}{x + 2}$

Written State whether each function is continuous or discontinuous. If it is discontinuous, identify the discontinuity as infinite, jump, or point.

1. $f(x) = x^2 + 2$
2. $f(x) = \frac{x(x-1)}{x-1}$
3. $f(x) = \frac{1}{x}$
4. $f(x) = \begin{cases} x, & x \le 0 \\ x^2 + 1, & x > 0 \end{cases}$
5. $f(x) = \begin{cases} |x| + x + 1, & x < 0 \\ |x| - x + 1, & x \ge 0 \end{cases}$
6. $f(x) = \begin{cases} x, & x > 0 \\ ^{-}x, & x < 0 \end{cases}$
7. $f(x) = \frac{x^2 - 1}{x - 1}$
8. $f(x) = x + \frac{1}{x}$
9. $f(x) = \begin{cases} \frac{x^2 - 1}{x - 1}, & x \neq 1 \\ 2, & x = 1 \end{cases}$
10. $f(x) = x + [x]$
11. $f(x) = |x - 1|$
12. $x^2y = 1$

Write an example of a function that satisfies each condition.

13. everywhere continuous
14. discontinuous only at $x = 0$
15. discontinuous only at $x = 2$
16. discontinuous at odd multiples of π

Show that each of the following functions are either continuous or discontinuous at the given value of x.

17. $f(x) = x + 5$ at $x = 1$
18. $f(x) = x^2 + 2x - 1$ at $x = 0$
19. $f(x) = \frac{x^2 - 16}{x + 4}$ at $x = 4$
20. $f(x) = \frac{x^2 - 16}{x - 4}$ at $x = 4$

15-4 Theorems about Limits

It is useful to have principles which define operations involving limits when attempting to find the limits of some functions. These operations include addition, subtraction, multiplication, and division as well as using powers and roots. The principles are stated as theorems without proofs.

The following theorems are given for $\lim_{x \to a} f(x) = F$ and $\lim_{x \to a} g(x) = G$ and real numbers a and c, and n a positive integer.		
Limit of a Constant Function	If $f(x) = c$, then $\lim_{x \to a} f(x) = c$.	Theorem 1
Addition	$\lim_{x \to a} [f(x) + g(x)] = \lim_{x \to a} f(x) + \lim_{x \to a} g(x) = F + G$	Theorem 2
Subtraction	$\lim_{x \to a} [f(x) - g(x)] = \lim_{x \to a} f(x) - \lim_{x \to a} g(x) = F - G$	Theorem 3
Multiplication	$\lim_{x \to a} [f(x) \cdot g(x)] = \left[\lim_{x \to a} f(x)\right]\left[\lim_{x \to a} g(x)\right] = F \cdot G$	Theorem 4
Division	$\lim_{x \to a} \frac{f(x)}{g(x)} = \frac{\lim_{x \to a} f(x)}{\lim_{x \to a} g(x)} = \frac{F}{G} (G \neq 0)$	Theorem 5
Product of a Constant and a Limit	$\lim_{x \to a} [c \cdot g(x)] = c \lim_{x \to a} g(x) = cG$	Theorem 6
Powers	$\lim_{x \to a} [f(x)^n] = \left[\lim_{x \to a} f(x)\right]^n = F^n$	Theorem 7
Roots	$\lim_{x \to a} \sqrt[n]{f(x)} = \sqrt[n]{\lim_{x \to a} f(x)} = \sqrt[n]{F}$	Theorem 8

examples

1 Use the limit theorems to evaluate $\lim_{x \to 1} \frac{x^2 + x - 5}{3x^2 + 2}$.

$$\lim_{x \to 1} \frac{x^2 + x - 5}{3x^2 + 2} = \frac{\lim_{x \to 1} (x^2 + x - 5)}{\lim_{x \to 1} (3x^2 + 2)}$$

$$= \frac{1 + 1 - 5}{3 + 2} \text{ or } \frac{^-3}{5}$$

2 Find $\lim_{x \to 0} \frac{\sqrt{3x^2 + x + 1}}{\sqrt[3]{x^3 - x + 8}}$.

$$\lim_{x \to 0} \frac{\sqrt{3x^2 + x + 1}}{\sqrt[3]{x^3 - x + 8}} = \frac{\lim_{x \to 0} \sqrt{3x^2 + x + 1}}{\lim_{x \to 0} \sqrt[3]{x^3 - x + 8}}$$

$$= \frac{\sqrt{\lim_{x \to 0} (3x^2 + x + 1)}}{\sqrt[3]{\lim_{x \to 0} (x^3 - x + 8)}}$$

$$= \frac{1}{\sqrt[3]{8}} \text{ or } \frac{1}{2}$$

If $f(x)$ and $g(x)$ are two functions of x, the composite of f and g is defined to be $f[g(x)]$. For example, if $f(x) = x^2$ and $g(x) = x + 2$, $f[g(x)] = f(x + 2)$ or $(x + 2)^2$. In general, composition of functions is *not* a commutative operation. In other words, the value of $f[g(x)]$ is usually not the same as the value of $g[f(x)]$.

Given functions $f(x)$ and $g(x)$, $\lim_{x \to a} g(x) = G$, and any real number a, the limit of the composite of functions $f(x)$ and $g(x)$ is as follows.

$$\lim_{x \to a} f[g(x)] = f\left[\lim_{x \to a} g(x)\right] = f(G)$$

Theorem 9

example

3 Find $\lim_{x \to 2} f[g(x)]$ if $f(x) = x^2$ and $g(x) = x + 2$.

$$\begin{aligned} \lim_{x \to 2} f[g(x)] &= f\left[\lim_{x \to 2} g(x)\right] \\ &= f\left[\lim_{x \to 2} (x + 2)\right] \\ &= f(4) \\ &= 4^2 \text{ or } 16 \qquad\qquad f(x) = x^2 \end{aligned}$$

The following theorem is used to find the limits of trigonometric functions.

The limit of $\dfrac{\sin x}{x}$ is equal to 1 as x approaches 0 where x is the radian measure of an angle. $\lim_{x \to 0} \dfrac{\sin x}{x} = 1$

Theorem 10

This can be shown as follows. Suppose that $0 < x < \frac{\pi}{2}$. Arc AB is part of a circle with center O and radius 1 unit. As x approaches 0, the length of $\overline{AD}$ approaches the length of AB. Thus, $\dfrac{AD}{\text{measure of } AB}$ approaches 1 as x approaches 0. But $AD = \sin x$ and the measure of $AB = x$, so $\lim_{x \to 0} \dfrac{\sin x}{x} = 1$.

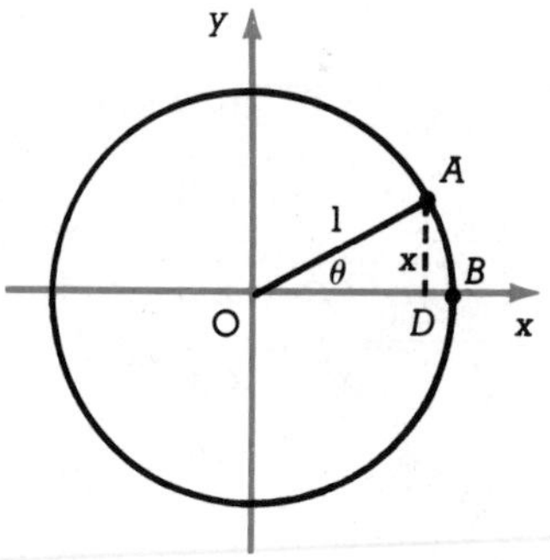

example

4 Find $\lim_{x \to 0} \frac{\sin 2x}{x}$.

$$\lim_{x \to 0} \frac{\sin 2x}{x} = \lim_{x \to 0} \frac{2 \cdot \sin 2x}{2x}$$ *Multiply numerator and denominator by 2.*

$$= 2 \cdot \lim_{x \to 0} \frac{\sin 2x}{2x}$$ *$\lim_{x \to 0} \frac{\sin nx}{nx} = \lim_{x \to 0} \frac{\sin x}{x}$*

$$= 2 \cdot 1 \text{ or } 2$$

exercises

Exploratory Evaluate each limit.

1. $\lim_{x \to 4} 6(x - 5)$
2. $\lim_{x \to 1} (x + 2)(x - 3)$
3. $\lim_{x \to 0} [(x^2 + 3x) - (2x + 5)]$
4. $\lim_{x \to 2} \frac{x + 1}{x}$
5. $\lim_{x \to 0} \frac{x^2 + 5x}{x + 4}$
6. $\lim_{x \to 3} (x + 2)^4$

Find $f[g(2)]$ given each $f(x)$ and $g(x)$.

7. $f(x) = x^2 + 2$, $g(x) = x - 3$
8. $f(x) = x^2 + 2x + 1$, $g(x) = x^2 - 1$
9. $f(x) = |x + 1|$, $g(x) = 2|x - 3|$

10-12. Find $g[f(2)]$ given each $f(x)$ and $g(x)$ in problems 7-9.

Written Solve each problem.

1. Show that $\lim_{x \to 2} (x^2 - 5x + 6) = \lim_{x \to 2} (x - 2) \cdot \lim_{x \to 2} (x - 3) = 0$.
2. Show that $\lim_{x \to 0} x^2 = 0$ by using the fact that $x \cdot x = x^2$.
3. Express $\lim_{x \to a} (px^2 + qx + r)$ as the product of the limits of two linear functions.
4. Find $\lim_{x \to 3} (x - 1)^3$ in two ways.

Use the limit theorems to evaluate each limit.

5. $\lim_{x \to 3} \frac{x^2 - 2x + 1}{x^3}$
6. $\lim_{x \to 1} \frac{x^2 + 2}{x}$
7. $\lim_{x \to 1} \frac{x - 3}{2x - 4}$
8. $\lim_{x \to 3} (2x^2 + 3x + 4)$
9. $\lim_{x \to {}^-1} \sqrt{x^2 - 1}$
10. $\lim_{x \to 3} (x^3 - 5x^2 + 2x - 1)$
11. $\lim_{x \to 2} \frac{x^2 - 4}{x - 2}$
12. $\lim_{x \to {}^-1} \frac{2x^2 + 3x - 5}{5x^3 - 2}$
13. $\lim_{x \to 1} \frac{x - 1}{x^3 - 1}$

Find the limit of $f[g(x)]$ as x approaches 1 for each $f(x)$ and $g(x)$.

14. $f(x) = 2x + 1$, $g(x) = x - 3$
15. $f(x) = 3x - 4$, $g(x) = 2x + 5$
16. $f(x) = x^2 + 3$, $g(x) = 2x - 1$

Use Theorem 10 to evaluate each limit.

17. $\lim_{x \to 0} \frac{\sin^2 x}{x}$
18. $\lim_{x \to 0} \frac{\sin 3x}{5x}$
19. $\lim_{x \to 0} \frac{1 - \cos x}{x^2}$

15-5 Derivatives

The concept of the limit is used in the definition of the **derivative** of a function f. Consider the function $f(x)$ at the values a and $(a + h)$. The slope of the secant line intersecting the graph of f at $(a, f(a))$ and $(a + h, f(a + h))$ is given by $\frac{f(a+h) - f(a)}{(a+h) - a}$ or $\frac{f(a+h) - f(a)}{h}$. This ratio is called the **difference quotient.** The limit of the difference quotient as h approaches zero is the **derivative** of f at $x = a$ and is denoted by $f'(a)$. Thus, $f'(a)$ is actually the slope of the tangent to the graph of f at $(a, f(a))$.

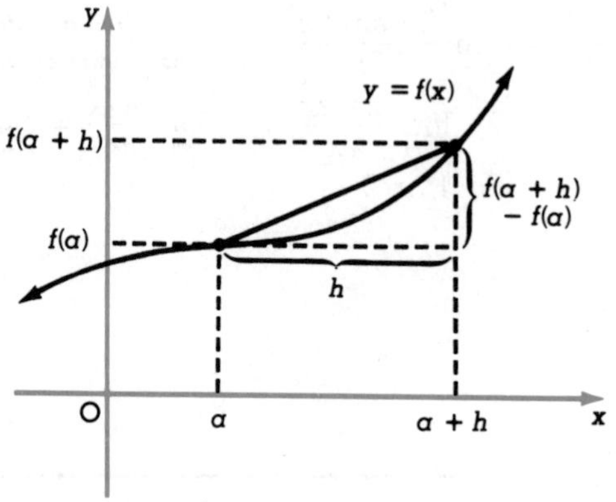

Derivative of a Function

For a function f, the derivative of f at $x = a$, $f'(a)$, is defined as follows.

$$f'(a) = \lim_{h \to 0} \frac{f(a+h) - f(a)}{h}$$

The process of finding derivatives, which are defined as limits of difference quotients, is called **differentiation.** A function is **differentiable** at a if the derivative of the function exists at a and is finite.

example

1 **Find the derivative of $f(x) = x^2$.**

Find the difference quotient and simplify.

$$\frac{f(x+h) - f(x)}{h} = \frac{(x+h)^2 - x^2}{h}$$
$$= \frac{x^2 + 2hx + h^2 - x^2}{h}$$
$$= \frac{2hx + h^2}{h}$$
$$= 2x + h$$

Find the limit of the difference quotient as h approaches 0.

$\lim_{h \to 0} (2x + h) = 2x$

Thus, $f'(x) = 2x$.

example

2 **Find the slope of the tangent and the equation of the tangent to the curve $y = 2x^2 + 3$ at the point (2, 11).**

Find the slope of the tangent using the definition of the derivative.

$$\begin{aligned}\lim_{h\to 0}\frac{f(x+h)-f(x)}{h} &= \lim_{h\to 0}\frac{[2(x+h)^2+3]-(2x^2+3)}{h}\\ &= \lim_{h\to 0}\frac{2(x^2+2hx+h^2)+3-2x^2-3}{h}\\ &= \lim_{h\to 0}\frac{2x^2+4hx+2h^2+3-2x^2-3}{h}\\ &= \lim_{h\to 0}\frac{4hx+2h^2}{h}\\ &= \lim_{h\to 0}(4x+2h)\\ &= 4x\end{aligned}$$

So the slope of the tangent is $4x$ at any point on the curve.

Next, find the slope of the tangent at the point (2, 11) by substituting 2 for x.

$$\text{Slope of tangent} = 4(2) \text{ or } 8$$

Use the point slope form to find the equation of the tangent.

$$\begin{aligned}y - y_1 &= m(x - x_1)\\ y - 11 &= 8(x - 2)\\ y &= 8x - 5\end{aligned}$$

Thus, the slope of the tangent at the point (2, 11) is 8 and the equation of the tangent at the point (2, 11) is $y = 8x - 5$.

The symbol h often is replaced by Δx to show the change in x. Then the difference quotient is $\frac{f(x+\Delta x)-f(x)}{\Delta x}$. But $f(x + \Delta x) - f(x)$ can be denoted as Δy since it is actually the change in y. Thus the derivative of $f(x)$ may be written with the delta notation as follows.

ΔX is read "delta X."

$$f'(x) = \lim_{\Delta x\to 0}\frac{f(x+\Delta x)-f(x)}{\Delta x} \text{ or } \lim_{\Delta x\to 0}\frac{\Delta y}{\Delta x}$$

When the function is written in the form $y = f(x)$, the derivative is sometimes written as $\frac{dy}{dx}$. Thus, $\frac{dy}{dx} = \lim_{\Delta x\to 0}\frac{f(x+\Delta x)-f(x)}{\Delta x}$ or $\lim_{\Delta x\to 0}\frac{\Delta y}{\Delta x}$. The notation, $\frac{dy}{dx}$, is called **derivative notation** and is read "the derivative of y with respect to x."

example

3 If $y = 2x^2 + 1$, find $\frac{dy}{dx}$ at $x = 2$.

Find $\frac{\Delta y}{\Delta x}$.

$$\frac{\Delta y}{\Delta x} = \frac{f(x + \Delta x) - f(x)}{\Delta x}$$
$$= \frac{[2(x + \Delta x)^2 + 1] - [2(x)^2 + 1]}{\Delta x}$$
$$= \frac{2(x^2 + 2x\,\Delta\,x + \Delta x^2) + 1 - 2x^2 - 1}{\Delta x}$$
$$= \frac{4x\Delta x + 2\Delta x^2}{\Delta x}$$
$$= 4x + 2\Delta x$$

Find $\frac{dy}{dx}$.

$$\frac{dy}{dx} = \lim_{\Delta x \to 0} \frac{\Delta y}{\Delta x}$$
$$= \lim_{\Delta x \to 0} (4x + 2\Delta x)$$
$$= 4x$$

Thus, $\frac{dy}{dx}$ at $x = 2$ is 8. *The slope of the tangent to $y = 2x^2 + 1$ at $x = 2$ is 8.*

exercises

Exploratory Find the difference quotient of each function and simplify.

1. $f(x) = x$
2. $f(x) = 3x + 2$
3. $f(x) = {}^-2x - 4$
4. $f(x) = {}^-x$
5. $f(x) = 2x^2$
6. $f(x) = {}^-2x^2$
7. $f(x) = x^3$
8. $f(x) = 2x^3$
9. $f(x) = 5x - 9$
10. $f(x) = 4x^2$
11. $f(x) = x^2 + 1$
12. $f(x) = x^2 + x$

Written Solve each problem.

1-12. Find the derivative of each function in problems **1-12** of the exploratory exercises.

Find the slope and the equation of the tangent to each of the following curves at the given point.

13. $y = x^2$ at $(0, 0)$
14. $y = 2x^2$ at $(3, 18)$
15. $y = x^2 + 2x + 1$ at $({}^-2, 1)$
16. $y = x^3$ at $({}^-1, {}^-1)$
17. $y = 3x^2 + 5$ at $(1, 8)$
18. $y = x^3 + x^2 + x + 1$ at $({}^-2, {}^-5)$
19. $y = \frac{1}{x}$ at $\left(3, \frac{1}{3}\right)$
20. $y = \frac{1}{x - 3}$ at $(4, 1)$
21. $y = \frac{x}{x - 1}$ at $(2, 2)$
22. $y = \frac{1}{x^2}$ at $\left({}^-2, \frac{1}{4}\right)$

23-32. Find the point(s) on each curve in problems **13-22** where the slope of the tangent to the curve is 2. If no such point exists, write *none*.

15-6 Differentiation Techniques

The process of finding a derivative by setting up a difference quotient and then finding its limit can become rather involved. To shorten this process, formulas can be used to find derivatives of functions.

Consider the function $f(x) = c$, where c is a constant.

$$f'(x) = \lim_{h \to o} \frac{f(x + h) - f(x)}{h}$$

$$= \lim_{h \to o} \frac{c - c}{h} \text{ or } 0$$

Thus, the derivative of a constant function, $f(x) = c$, is zero. For example, if $f(x) = 5$, then $f'(x) = 0$.

One of the most important differentiation formulas is the power formula.

If $f(x) = cx^n$ and n is a real number and c is a constant, then $f'(x) = cnx^{n-1}$.

Power Formula

examples

1 **Find $f'(x)$ if $f(x) = x^2$.**

Use the power formula.

$f(x) = x^2$

$f'(x) = 2x^{2-1}$ or $2x$

2 **Find $f'(x)$ if $f(x) = 5x^8$.**

$f(x) = 5x^8$

$f'(x) = 5 \cdot 8x^{8-1}$

$= 40x^7$

The notation $\frac{dy}{dx}$ is used in the statement of the following theorems. This notation can be used with other functions of x. For example, $\frac{du}{dx}$ is the derivative of the function u with respect to x.

If $u = f(x)$ and $v = g(x)$ are differentiable functions of x, then $\frac{d(u + v)}{dx} = \frac{du}{dx} + \frac{dv}{dx}$

Theorem 11

example

3 Find the derivative of $x^3 + (x^2 + 2)$.

Use $\frac{d(u + v)}{dx} = \frac{du}{dx} + \frac{dv}{dx}$.

$$\frac{d[x^3 + (x^2 + 2)]}{dx} = \frac{d(x^3)}{dx} + \frac{d(x^2 + 2)}{dx}$$

$u = x^3$ and $v = x^2 + 2$

$$= (3x^2) + (2x + 0)$$
$$= 3x^2 + 2x$$

If $u = f(x)$ is a differentiable function of x and c is a constant, then $\frac{d(cu)}{dx} = c\frac{du}{dx}$.

Theorem 12

example

4 Find the derivative of $3(x^2 + 2x + 1)$.

Use $\frac{d(cu)}{dx} = c\frac{du}{dx}$.

$$\frac{d[3(x^2 + 2x + 1)]}{dx} = 3\frac{d(x^2 + 2x + 1)}{dx}$$

$C = 3$ and $u = x^2 + 2x + 1$

$$= 3(2x + 2)$$
$$= 6x + 6$$

If $u = f(x)$ and $v = g(x)$ are differentiable functions of x, then $\frac{d(uv)}{dx} = u\frac{dv}{dx} + v\frac{du}{dx}$.

Theorem 13

example

5 Find the derivative of $(x^2 + 2x)(x^3)$.

Use $\frac{d(uv)}{dx} = u\frac{dv}{dx} + v\frac{du}{dx}$.

$$\frac{d(x^2 + 2x)(x^3)}{dx} = (x^2 + 2x)(3x^2) + (x^3)(2x + 2)$$

$u = x^2 + 2x$
$v = x^3$

$$= 3x^4 + 6x^3 + 2x^4 + 2x^3$$
$$= 5x^4 + 8x^3$$

If $u = f(x)$ is a differentiable function of x and n is a nonzero rational number, then $\frac{d(u^n)}{dx} = nu^{n-1}\frac{du}{dx}$.

Theorem 14

example

6 Find the derivative of $\sqrt{x^2 - 1}$.

Use $\dfrac{d(u^n)}{dx} = nu^{n-1}\dfrac{du}{dx}$.

$$\frac{d(\sqrt{x^2 - 1})}{dx} = \frac{1}{2}(x^2 - 1)^{-\frac{1}{2}}(2x) \qquad u = x^2 - 1; n = \frac{1}{2}; \sqrt{x^2 - 1} = (x^2 - 1)^{\frac{1}{2}}$$

$$= \frac{2x}{2\sqrt{x^2 - 1}}$$

$$= \frac{x}{\sqrt{x^2 - 1}}$$

If $u = f(x)$ and $v = g(x)$ are differentiable functions of x at a point where $v \neq 0$, then $\dfrac{d\left(\frac{u}{v}\right)}{dx} = \dfrac{v\frac{du}{dx} - u\frac{dv}{dx}}{v^2}$.

Theorem 15

example

7 Find the derivative of $\dfrac{x^2 - 2x + 1}{x + 1}$.

Use $\dfrac{d\left(\frac{u}{v}\right)}{dx} = \dfrac{v\frac{du}{dx} - u\frac{dv}{dx}}{v^2}$

$$\frac{d\left(\frac{x^2 - 2x + 1}{x + 1}\right)}{dx} = \frac{(x + 1)(2x - 2) - (x^2 - 2x + 1)(1)}{(x + 1)^2}$$

$$= \frac{(2x^2 - 2) - (x^2 - 2x + 1)}{x^2 + 2x + 1}$$

$$= \frac{x^2 + 2x - 3}{x^2 + 2x + 1}$$

exercises

Exploratory Name the theorem(s) that would be used to find the derivative of each function.

1. $f(x) = 8x^4 - 10x^3$
2. $f(x) = x^{\frac{1}{2}}$
3. $f(x) = \sqrt[3]{x}$
4. $f(x) = x^2(x^2 - 3)$
5. $f(x) = (x^3 - 2x)(3x^2)$
6. $f(x) = (x^2 + 4)^3$
7. $f(x) = (x^3 - 2x + 1)^4$
8. $f(x) = \sqrt{x^2 + 2x - 1}$
9. $f(x) = (x^2 - 4)^{-\frac{1}{2}}$
10. $f(x) = \dfrac{x + 1}{x^2 - 4}$
11. $f(x) = \left(\dfrac{x + 1}{x - 1}\right)^2$
12. $f(x) = \dfrac{1}{\sqrt{x + 1}}$
13. $f(x) = x^5 + 3x^3 - 4x^2 + 3$
14. $f(x) = \dfrac{1}{4}x^4 - \dfrac{1}{3}x^3 + \dfrac{1}{2}x^2 - x$

Written Solve each problem.

1-14. Find the derivative of each function in problems **1-14** of the exploratory exercises.

Find $f'(2)$ for each of the following functions.

15. $f(x) = \frac{x^2}{2}$
16. $f(x) = 6x$
17. $f(x) = x^2 + 2x + 5$
18. $f(x) = (x + 3)(2x - 1)$
19. $f(x) = (x^2 - 3x)^2$
20. $f(x) = 1 + 2x - 3x^2 + 4x^3$

Find the derivative of each function.

21. $f(x) = x^2(x + 1)^{-1}$
22. $f(x) = (x + x^{-1})^2$
23. $f(x) = (x^2 - x)^{-2}$
24. $f(x) = \frac{3x}{1 + x^3}$
25. $f(x) = x\sqrt{1 - x^3}$
26. $f(x) = 2x^3 + \frac{2}{x^3}$
27. $f(x) = x^4(x - 5)^6$
28. $f(x) = \sqrt{2x} - \sqrt{2x}$
29. $f(x) = \frac{x - 1}{x + 1}$

15-7 Applying the Derivative

The derivative of a function can be used in sketching the graph of the function in a certain interval. For example, the sign of the derivative indicates whether the function is increasing or decreasing at a point.

Remember that the derivative of the function at a point is the slope of the tangent line at that point.

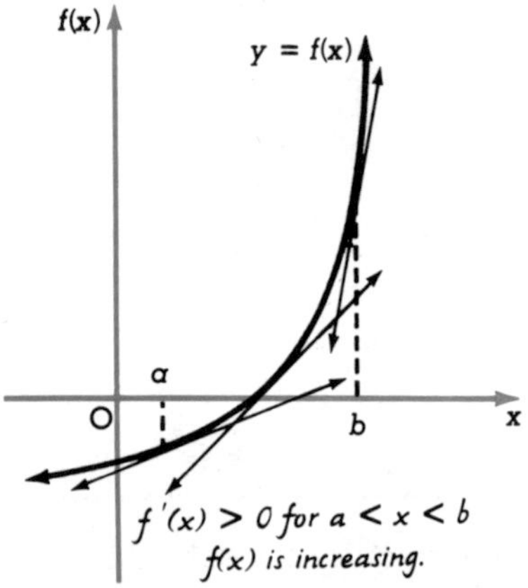

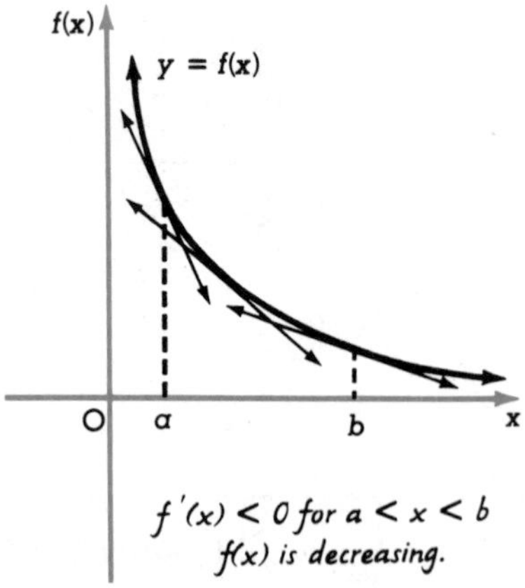

Increasing and Decreasing Functions

> If $f'(x) > 0$ for all values of x in the interval, $a < x < b$, then the function is increasing in the interval. If $f'(x) < 0$ for all values of x in the interval, $a < x < b$, then the function is decreasing in the interval.

example

1 **Find the values of x for which the function $f(x) = x^2 + 6x - 6$ is increasing.**

$f(x) = x^2 + 6x - 6$
$f'(x) = 2x + 6$

The function $f(x)$ is increasing when $f'(x) > 0$.

$2x + 6 > 0$
$2x > {}^{-}6$
$x > {}^{-}3$

Thus, the function is increasing when $x > {}^{-}3$.

If the derivative of a function at a certain point is zero, the point is a **critical point.** At these points the function is neither increasing or decreasing and is said to have **stationary values.** For example, the function $f(x) = 5x^3 - 3x^5$ shown at the right has stationary values at $x = {}^{-}1$, 0, and 1. Since $f'(x)$ changes sign from positive through zero to negative at $x = 1$, $f(1)$ or 2 is a **maximum value.** Since $f'(x)$ changes from negative through zero to positive at $x = {}^{-}1$, $f({}^{-}1)$ or ${}^{-}2$ is a **minimum value.** However, notice that at $x = 0$, $f'(x)$ does not change sign through zero and $f'(x) = 0$ at $x = 0$. The point $(0, f(0))$ or $(0, 0)$ is a **point of inflection** on the graph of $f(x) = 5x^3 - 3x^5$.

Suppose $f'(a) = 0$ and $f'(x)$ exists at every point near a. Then at $x = a$ there are four possibilities for the graph of f.

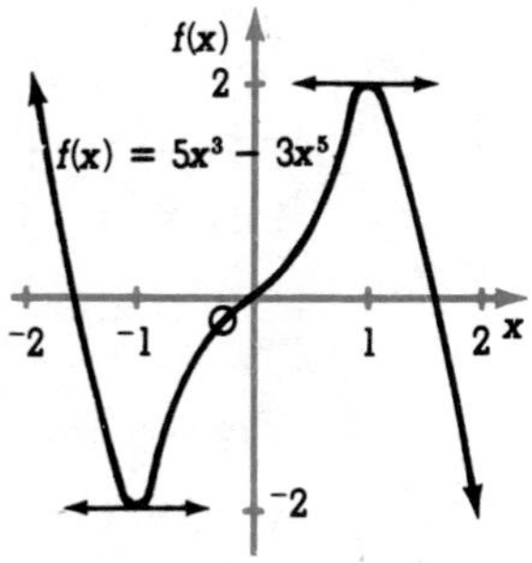

$f'(x) = 15x^2 - 15x^4$ or $15x^2(1 - x^2)$

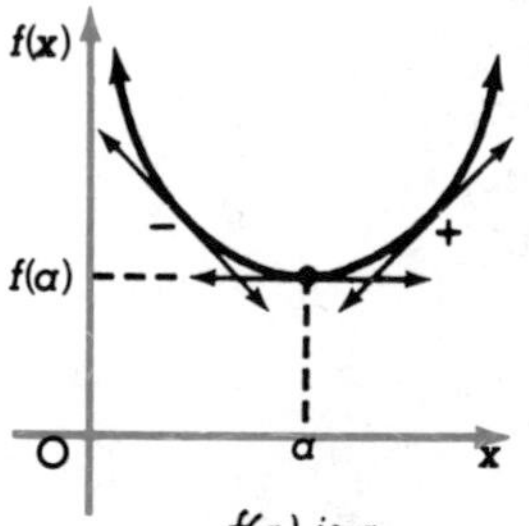

f(a) is a minimum value

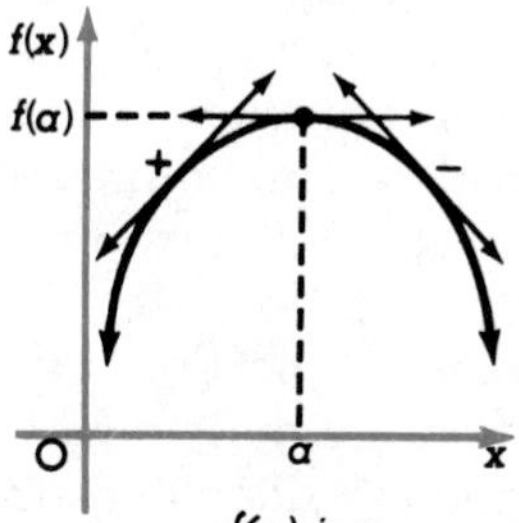

f(a) is a maximum value

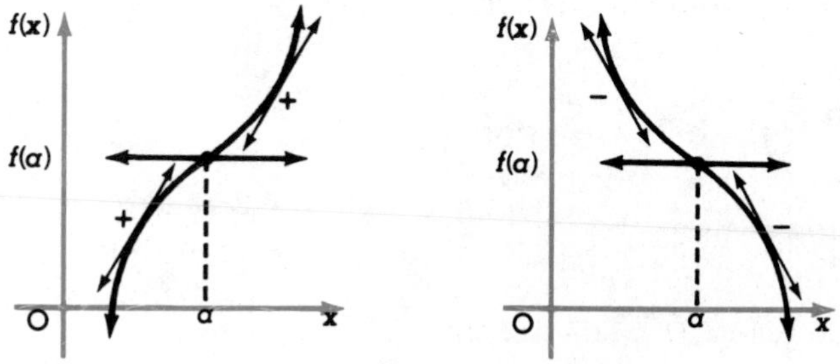

Point (a, f(a)) is a point of inflection.

example

2 **Find the stationary values of $f(x) = x^3(4 - x)$. Determine whether each is a maximum, minimum, or a point of inflection.**

$$f(x) = x^3(4 - x)$$
$$= 4x^3 - x^4$$
$$f'(x) = 12x^2 - 4x^3$$
$$= 4x^2(3 - x)$$

To find the stationary values, let $f'(x) = 0$.

$$4x^2(3 - x) = 0$$
$$x = 0 \text{ or } x = 3$$

Thus, f has stationary values at $x = 0$ and at $x = 3$.

Determine values of $f'(x)$ near 0.

$f'(^-0.1) = 4(^-0.1)^2(3 + 0.1)$ or 0.124 — *f(x) is increasing*
$f'(0.1) = 4(0.1)^2(3 - 0.1)$ or 0.116 — *f(x) is increasing*

Since $f'(0)$ does not change sign through zero, the point $(0, f(0))$ or $(0, 0)$ is a point of inflection.

Determine values of x near 3.

$f'(2.9) = 4(2.9)^2(3 - 2.9)$ or 3.364 — *f(x) is increasing*
$f'(3.1) = 4(3.1)^2(3 - 3.1)$ or $^-3.844$ — *f(x) is decreasing*

Since $f'(3)$ changes sign from positive through zero to negative, $f(3)$ is a maximum value.

Maximum or minimum values can be **relative maximum values** or **relative minimum values**. These are local properties of a function. They refer only to the behavior of a function in the neighborhood of a critical point. The terms **absolute maximum** and **absolute minimum** refer to the greatest or least value assumed by a function throughout its domain of definition.

Since the derivative of a polynomial function, $f(x)$, also is a polynomial function, $f'(x)$, you can find the derivative of $f'(x)$. It is called the **second derivative** of $f(x)$ and is written $f''(x)$. The value of the second derivative indicates whether the derivative, $f'(x)$, is increasing or decreasing at a point. A second derivative test can be used to find relative maximum and relative minimum values.

If $f'(x) = 0$ at x, then $f(x)$ is one of the following stationary values.

1. **If $f''(x) > 0$, then $f(x)$ is a relative minimum.**
2. **If $f''(x) < 0$, then $f(x)$ is a relative maximum.**
3. **If $f''(x) = 0$ or does not exist, then the test fails.**

Second Derivative Test

example

3 **Find the stationary values of $f(x) = x^3 - 3x$. Determine whether each is a relative maximum, relative minimum or neither. Then graph the function.**

$f(x) = x^3 - 3x$
$f'(x) = 3x^2 - 3$
$3x^2 - 3 = 0$ *Let $f'(x) = 0$ to find the stationary values.*
$3(x + 1)(x - 1) = 0$
$x = {}^-1$ or $x = 1$

Thus, the stationary values occur at $x = {}^-1$ and at $x = 1$.

Find $f''(x)$ and use the second derivative test.

$f''(x) = 6x$
$f''({}^-1) = {}^-6$ and $f''(1) = 6$

Since $f''({}^-1) < 0$, $f(x)$ has a relative maximum at $x = {}^-1$.
Since $f''(1) > 0$, $f(x)$ has a relative minimum at $x = 1$.

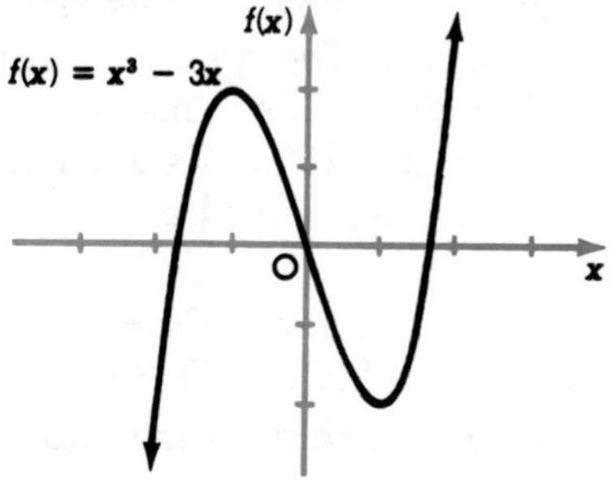

exercises

Exploratory Find $f'(x)$ for each of the following functions.

1. $f(x) = x^2 + 6x - 27$
2. $f(x) = {}^-x^2 - 8x - 15$
3. $f(x) = x^2 - 2x$
4. $f(x) = x^3$
5. $f(x) = x^3 - 3x$
6. $f(x) = 2x^3 - 9x^2 + 12x$
7. $f(x) = x^3(4 - x)$
8. $f(x) = x^3 - 12x + 3$
9. $f(x) = 2x^4 - 2x^2$
10. $f(x) = x(x - 2)^2$

11–20. Find $f''(x)$ for each function in problems 1–10.

Written **Find the values of x for which each of the following functions is increasing.**

1. $f(x) = x^2$
2. $f(x) = x^2 - 2x$
3. $f(x) = x^2 + 6x - 6$
4. $f(x) = x^3 - 3x$
5. $f(x) = 2x^3 - 9x^2 + 12x$
6. $f(x) = x(x - 2)^2$
7. $f(x) = \frac{1}{4}x^4 - \frac{9}{2}x^2$
8. $f(x) = x^3(4 - x)$
9. $f(x) = x + \frac{1}{x}$

10–18. Find the values of x for which each function in problems 1–9 is decreasing.

Find the stationary values of each of the following functions. State whether each is a maximum, minimum, or neither.

19. $f(x) = x - x^2$
20. $f(x) = x^3$
21. $f(x) = 2x^3 - 9x^2 + 12x$
22. $f(x) = \frac{1}{4}x^4 - \frac{9}{2}x^2$
23. $f(x) = x^3(4 - x)$
24. $f(x) = 2x^4 - 2x^2$

25–30. Graph each function in problems 19–24.

Using Mathematics

Differentiation techniques may be used to solve problems in which maximum or minimum solutions are necessary. Consider the following example.

Example Suppose a rectangular field along a straight river is to be fenced. There are 300 m of fencing available. What is the greatest area that can be enclosed?

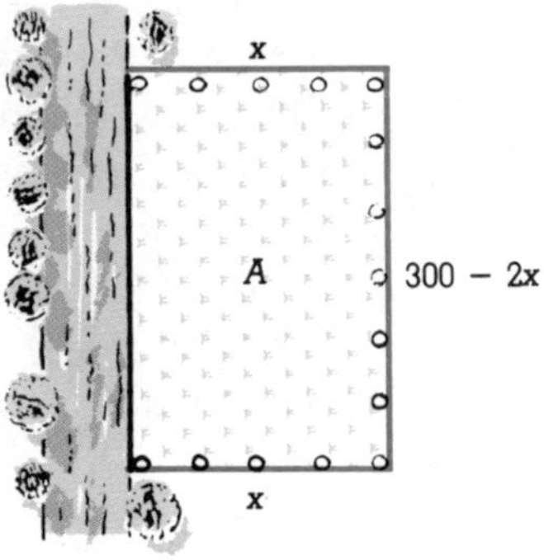

Let the width of the field be x meters. Then the length is $300 - 2x$ meters. The area in square meters is $A = x(300 - 2x)$ or $300x - 2x^2$. This defines a function f for which $f(x) = 300x - 2x^2$. Since $x \geq 0$ and $300 - 2x \geq 0$, the maximum value must be in the interval $0 \leq x \leq 150$.

$$f(x) = 300x - 2x^2$$
$$f'(x) = 300 - 4x$$

Let $f'(x) = 0$ to find relative minima or maxima.

$$300 - 4x = 0$$
$$x = 75$$

Find the second derivative of f to determine if 75 is a minimum or maximum.

$$f''(x) = {}^{-}4$$

Since $f''(x) < 0$, $f(0) = 0$, and $f(150) = 0$, $x = 75$ gives a maximum stationary value $f(75) = 11{,}250$. Thus, the required maximum area is 11,250 sq m. This occurs when the width is 75 m and the length is 150 m.

Exercises Solve each problem.

1. An area of farmland along a stone wall is to be fenced. There are 500 m of fencing available. What is the maximum rectangular area that can be fenced?
2. The perimeter of a field must be 600 m. Find the dimensions of the maximum rectangular area of the field.
3. The sum of two positive integers is 36. Find the maximum value of the product of the integers and also the integers.
4. The sum of two positive integers is 120. Find the maximum value of the product of one integer and the square of the other and also the integers.
5. An open pan is to be made from a 20 inch square piece of metal by cutting four equal square pieces from each corner and turning up the sides. What size pieces should be cut out so that the pan will have maximum volume?

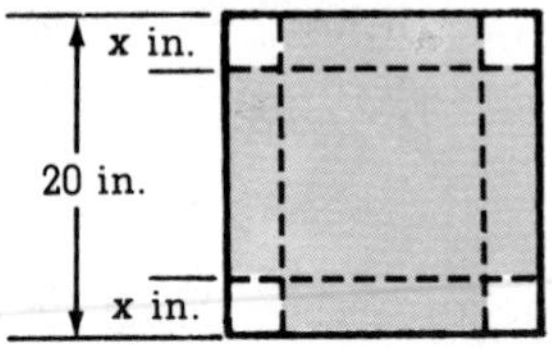

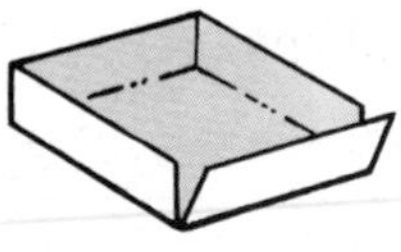

15-8 Area Under a Curve

Consider the area between a function $f(x)$ and the x-axis for an interval from $x = a$ to $x = b$. Suppose that the interval is separated into n subintervals of equal width and vertical lines are drawn at each interval to form rectangles.

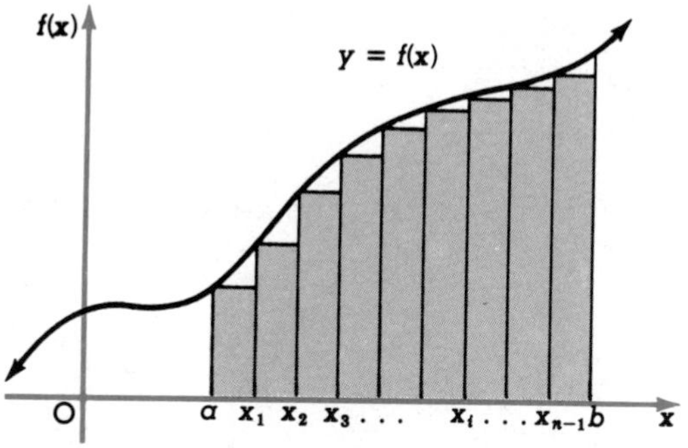

The area of the rectangles under the curve and above the x-axis is given by A_u.

The area of the first rectangle is $f(a)(x_1 - a)$.

The area of the second rectangle is $f(x_1)(x_2 - x_1)$.

The area of the third rectangle is $f(x_2)(x_3 - x_2)$.

⋮

The area of the $(i + 1)$th rectangle is $f(x_i)(x_{i+1} - x_i)$.

⋮

The area of the nth rectangle is $f(x_{n-1})(b - x_{n-1})$.

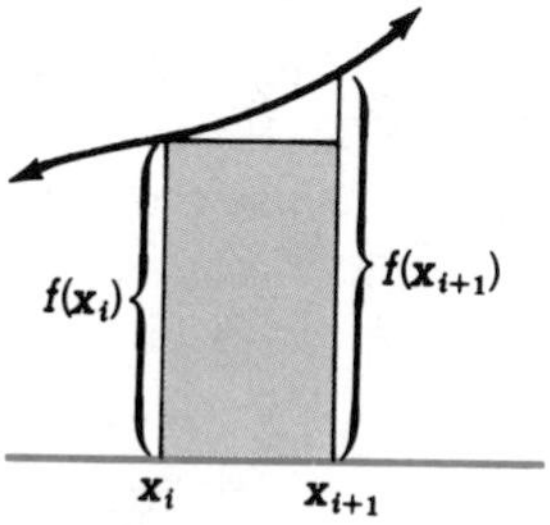

The total area, A_u, is the sum of the areas of these rectangles.

$$A_u = f(a)(x_1 - a) + f(x_1)(x_2 - x_1) + f(x_2)(x_3 - x_2) + \cdots + f(x_i)(x_{i+1} - x_i) + \cdots + f(x_{n-1})(b - x_{n-1})$$

The area of the rectangles above the curve and the x-axis is given by A_a. It is found in a similar manner as A_u.

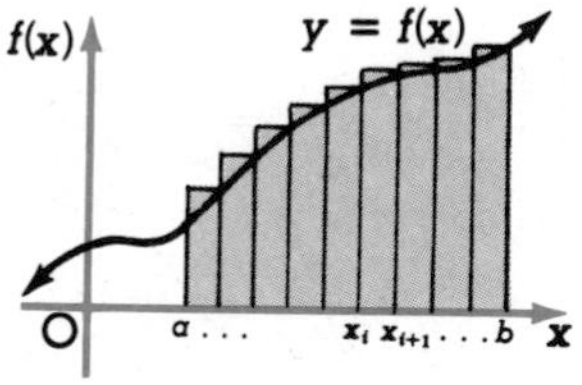

$$A_a = f(x_1)(x_1 - a) + f(x_2)(x_2 - x_1) + f(x_3)(x_3 - x_2) + \cdots + f(x_i + 1)(x_{i+1} - x_i) + \cdots + f(b)(b - x_{n-1})$$

Thus, the actual area, A, is between A_u and A_a. Therefore, $A_u \le A \le A_a$. As the number of subintervals, n, is increased, the areas A_u and A_a approach the actual area A. So A is the limit of A_u as n increases without limit. The area A_u may be written using summation notation.

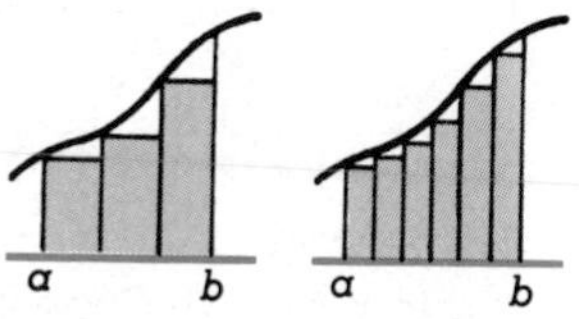

$$A_u = \sum_{i=1}^{n} f(x_i)(x_{i+1} - x_i)$$

The area A between the curve $y = f(x)$ and the x-axis from $x = a$ to $x = b$ is as follows.

$$A = \lim_{n \to \infty} \sum_{i=1}^{n} f(x_i)(x_{i+1} - x_i)$$

where the width of each rectangle, $x_{i+1} - x_i$, approaches zero.

Area Under a Curve

example

1 Find the area of the region between $y = x^3$ and the x-axis from $x = 0$ to $x = 1$.

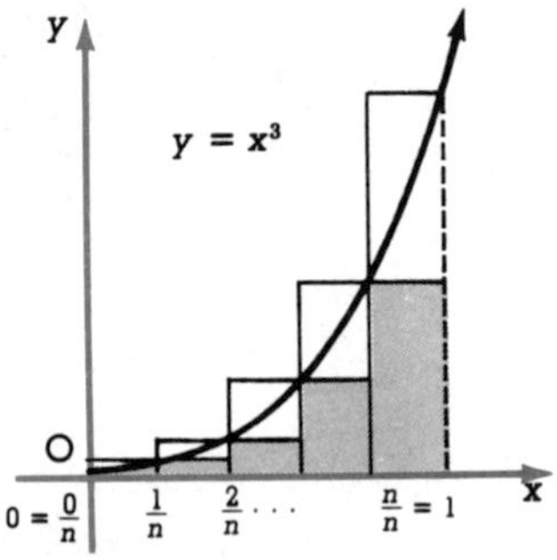

Form n equal intervals on the x-axis such that

$$0 < \frac{1}{n} < \frac{2}{n} < \frac{3}{n} < \cdots < \frac{i}{n} < \cdots < \frac{n-1}{n} < 1.$$

The area of each rectangle can be represented by $f\left(\frac{i}{n}\right)(x_{i+1} - x_i)$ or $\left(\frac{i}{n}\right)^3\left(\frac{1}{n}\right)$.

Why is $(x_{i+1} - x_i) = \frac{1}{n}$?

Use the definition of the area under a curve, $A = \lim_{n \to \infty} \sum_{i=1}^{n} f(x_i)(x_{i+1} - x_i)$.

$$\begin{aligned}
A &= \lim_{n \to \infty} \sum_{i=1}^{n} \left(\frac{i}{n}\right)^3\left(\frac{1}{n}\right) \\
&= \lim_{n \to \infty} \frac{1}{n^4}(1^3 + 2^3 + \cdots + n^3) \\
&= \lim_{n \to \infty} \frac{1}{n^4} \cdot \left(\frac{n^2(n+1)^2}{4}\right) \\
&= \lim_{n \to \infty} \frac{(n+1)^2}{4n^2} \\
&= \lim_{n \to \infty} \frac{1}{4}\left(\frac{n^2 + 2n + 1}{n^2}\right) \\
&= \lim_{n \to \infty} \frac{1}{4}\left(1 + \frac{2}{n} + \frac{1}{n^2}\right) \\
&= \frac{1}{4}
\end{aligned}$$

Recall that $1^3 + 2^3 + \cdots + n^3 = \frac{n^2(n+1)^2}{4}$.

Thus, the area is $\frac{1}{4}$ sq units.

Sometimes it is necessary to find the area under a curve from $x = a$ to $x = b$. This can be determined by finding the area from $x = 0$ to $x = b$ and then subtracting the area from $x = 0$ to $x = a$.

example

2 **Find the area of the region between $y = x^2$ and the x-axis from $x = 1$ to $x = 4$.**

First find the area under the curve from $x = 0$ to $x = 4$. Form n equal intervals on the x-axis such that

$$0 < \frac{4 \cdot 1}{n} < \frac{4 \cdot 2}{n} < \frac{4 \cdot 3}{n} < \cdots < \frac{4 \cdot i}{n} < \cdots < \frac{4(n-1)}{n} < \frac{4n}{n} \text{ or } 4.$$

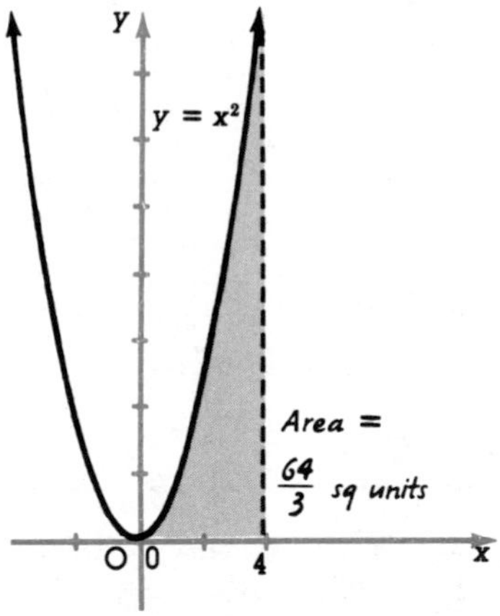

The area of each rectangle can be represented as follows.

$$f\left(\frac{4 \cdot i}{n}\right)(x_{i+1} - x_i) \text{ or } \left(\frac{4i}{n}\right)^2\left(\frac{4}{n}\right)$$

$$A = \lim_{n\to\infty} \sum_{i=1}^{n} \left(\frac{4i}{n}\right)^2\left(\frac{4}{n}\right)$$

$$= \lim_{n\to\infty} \frac{64}{n^3}(1^2 + 2^2 + 3^2 + \cdots + n^2)$$

$$= \lim_{n\to\infty} \frac{64}{n^3}\left(\frac{n(n+1)(2n+1)}{6}\right)$$

Recall that $1^2 + 2^2 + 3^2 + \cdots + n^2 = \frac{n(n+1)(2n+1)}{6}$.

$$= \lim_{n\to\infty} \frac{64}{6}\left(\frac{2n^3 + 3n^2 + n}{n^3}\right)$$

$$= \lim_{n\to\infty} \frac{64}{6}\left(2 + \frac{3}{n} + \frac{1}{n^2}\right)$$

$$= \frac{64}{6} \cdot 2 \text{ or } \frac{64}{3}$$

Then find the area under the curve from $x = 0$ to $x = 1$.

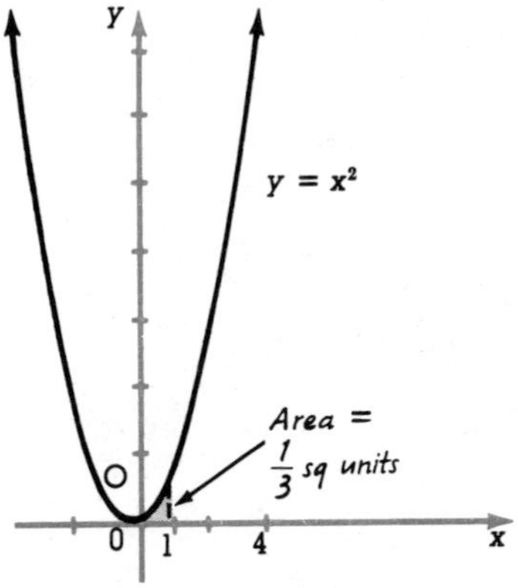

$$A = \lim_{n\to\infty} \sum_{i=1}^{n} \left(\frac{i}{n}\right)^2\left(\frac{1}{n}\right)$$

$$= \lim_{n\to\infty} \frac{1}{n^3}(1^2 + 2^2 + 3^2 + \cdots + n^2)$$

$$= \lim_{n\to\infty} \frac{1}{n^3}\left(\frac{n(n+1)(2n+1)}{6}\right)$$

$$= \lim_{n\to\infty} \frac{1}{6}\left(2 + \frac{3}{n} + \frac{1}{n^2}\right)$$

$$= \frac{1}{6} \cdot 2 \text{ or } \frac{1}{3}$$

Thus, the area of the region between $y = x^2$ and the x-axis from $x = 1$ to $x = 4$ is $\frac{64}{3} - \frac{1}{3}$ or 21 sq units.

The following list of formulas are the sums of series which may be needed to solve problems in this section.

$$1 + 2 + 3 + \cdots + n = \frac{n(n+1)}{2}$$

$$1^2 + 2^2 + 3^2 + \cdots + n^2 = \frac{n(n+1)(2n+1)}{6}$$

$$1^3 + 2^3 + 3^3 + \cdots + n^3 = \frac{n^2(n+1)^2}{4}$$

$$1^4 + 2^4 + 3^4 + \cdots + n^4 = \frac{6n^5 + 15n^4 + 10n^3 - n}{30}$$

$$1^5 + 2^5 + 3^5 + \cdots + n^5 = \frac{2n^6 + 6n^5 + 5n^4 - n^2}{12}$$

exercises

Exploratory Write a limit to find the area between each curve and the x-axis for the given interval. Do *not* find the area.

1. $y = x^2$ from $x = 0$ to $x = 1$
2. $y = x$ from $x = 0$ to $x = 1$
3. $y = x^5$ from $x = 0$ to $x = 1$
4. $y = x^2$ from $x = 0$ to $x = a$, $a > 0$
5. $y = x^3$ from $x = 0$ to $x = a$, $a > 0$
6. $y = x^2$ from $x = a$ to $x = b$, $0 < a < b$
7. $y = x$ from $x = 2$ to $x = 5$
8. $y = x^4$ from $x = 4$ to $x = 7$

9-12. Sketch a graph of the indicated regions in problems 1-4.

Written Solve each problem.

1-8. Find the area described by each function and interval in problems 1-8 of the exploratory exercises.

9. Find the area between $y = x^2$ and the x-axis from $x = {}^-3$ to $x = 2$.
10. Find the area between $y = |x|$ and the x-axis from $x = {}^-2$ to $x = 4$.

Write a formula for the areas between each curve and the x-axis for the given interval. Assume that $0 < a < b$.

11. $y = x$ from $x = a$ to $x = b$
12. $y = x^2$ from $x = a$ to $x = b$

15-9 Integration

The formal notation for the area, A, under a curve from $x = a$ to $x = b$ is as follows.

$$A = \int_a^b f(x)dx$$

It is read "the integral of f, with respect to x, from a to b." By definition $\int_a^b f(x)dx$ is equal to $\lim_{n\to\infty} \sum_{i=1}^{n} f(x_i)(x_{i+1} - x_i)$.

To understand the concept of an integral, consider the function $f(x)$ in the following equation.

$$\frac{dy}{dx} = f(x) \text{ with } a < x < b$$

Can you find a function $y = F(x)$ for which $f(x)$ is the derivative? This is the "anti" or "inverse" problem of finding the derivative. Thus, the function $F(x)$ is called an **antiderivative** of $f(x)$ if and only if $F'(x) = f(x)$.

F(x) and f(x) represent different functions.

Can you find an antiderivative of $f(x)$, represented by $F(x)$, if $f(x) = 3x^2$? Several possibilities are $y = x^3 + 3$, $y = x^3 + \pi$, and $y = x^3 - 5$. These are all valid answers and can be summarized as $y = x^3 + C$ where C is a constant.

The following theorem gives the connection between the antiderivative and the integral.

The function $F(x)$ is an integral of $f(x)$ with respect to x if and only if $F(x)$ is an antiderivative of $f(x)$. That is, $F(x) = \int f(x)dx$ if and only if $F'(x) = f(x)$.

Definition of an Integral

Thus, in the previous example, $\int 3x^2dx = x^3 + C$ since $F'(x^3 + C) = 3x^2$.

examples

1 **Find $\int 1\, dx$.**

Since $F'(x) = 1$ when $F(x) = x + C$, then $\int 1\, dx = x + C$.

2 **Find $\int x^2dx$.**

Since $F'(x) = x^2$ when $F(x) = \frac{x^3}{3} + C$, then $\int x^2dx = \frac{x^3}{3} + C$.

Several formulas which are useful in finding integrals are listed below.

1. If h is a constant, $\int hdx = hx + C$.
2. If $n \neq {}^-1$, $\int u^n du = \frac{u^{n+1}}{n+1} + C$ where u is a differentiable function.
3. The integral of a sum of functions is the sum of the integrals of the functions.

$$\int (f(x) + g(x))dx = \int f(x)dx + \int g(x)dx$$

4. The integral of the product of a constant, a, and a function, $f(x)$, is the product of the constant and the integral of the function.

$$\int af(x)dx = a\int f(x)dx$$

examples

3 **Find $\int(2x + 5)dx$.**

$$\int(2x + 5)dx = \int 2x\,dx + \int 5\,dx$$ *Use the third formula.*

$$= 2\int x\,dx + \int 5\,dx$$ *Use the fourth formula.*

$$= 2\left(\frac{x^2}{2}\right) + C_1 + 5x + C_2$$ *Use the second and first formulas, respectively.*

$$= x^2 + 5x + C$$ *Let $C = C_1 + C_2$.*

Thus, $\int(2x + 5)dx = x^2 + 5x + C$.

4 **Find $\int(3x^2 + 2x + 4)dx$.**

$$\int(3x^2 + 2x + 4)dx = \int 3x^2dx + \int 2x\,dx + \int 4dx$$

$$= 3\int x^2dx + 2\int x\,dx + \int 4dx$$

$$= 3\left(\frac{x^3}{3} + C_1\right) + 2\left(\frac{x^2}{2} + C_2\right) + (4x + C_3)$$

$$= x^3 + x^2 + 4x + C$$

Thus, $\int(3x^2 + 2x + 4)dx = x^3 + x^2 + 4x + C$.

5 **Find $\int(x^2 + 1)2x\,dx$.**

Use the formula $\int u^n du = \dfrac{u^{n+1}}{n + 1} + C$.

If you let $u = x^2 + 1$, then $\dfrac{du}{dx} = \dfrac{d(x^2 + 1)}{dx} = 2x$.

$$\int(x^2 + 1)2x\,dx = \int u \cdot \frac{du}{dx} \cdot dx$$ *Substitute.*

$$= \int udu$$ *Simplify.*

$$= \frac{u^2}{2} + C$$ *Use the second formula.*

$$= \frac{(x^2 + 1)^2}{2} + C$$ *Substitute.*

Thus, $\int(x^2 + 1)2x\,dx = \dfrac{(x^2 + 1)^2}{2} + C$.

exercises

Exploratory Find two functions, $F(x)$ and $G(x)$, such that $F'(x) = f(x)$ and $G'(x) = f(x)$ for each function.

1. $f(x) = 2x$
2. $f(x) = 3x^2$
3. $f(x) = 2x + 1$
4. $f(x) = 2x - 3$
5. $f(x) = 4x^3$
6. $f(x) = 8x^7 + 2x$

Written Find each integral.

1. $\int 2x\,dx$
2. $\int 3x^2dx$
3. $\int (8x^7 + 2x)dx$
4. $\int (\pi x + \sqrt{x})dx$
5. $\int (x + 5)^{20}dx$
6. $\int \sqrt{1 + x}\,dx$
7. $\int (^-2x + 3)dx$
8. $\int \frac{^-2x}{\sqrt{1 - x^2}}\,dx$
9. $\int \frac{(x + 1)dx}{\sqrt[3]{x^2 + 2x + 2}}$

Find the antiderivative of each function.

10. $f(x) = 5x^3$
11. $f(x) = 4\sqrt[3]{x}$
12. $f(x) = \sqrt{2x}$
13. $f(x) = \frac{2}{x^3}$
14. $f(x) = \frac{4}{x^2}$
15. $f(x) = \frac{2}{\sqrt{x}}$

15-10 The Fundamental Theorem of Calculus

The derivative has been defined as the limit of the difference quotients.

$$f'(x) = \lim_{h \to 0} \frac{f(x + h) - f(x)}{h}$$

The integral has been defined as the limit of the sum of areas.

$$A = \lim_{n \to \infty} \sum_{i=1}^{n} f(x_i)(x_{i+1} - x_i) \text{ where } (x_{i+1} - x_i) \text{ approaches zero}$$

The **Fundamental Theorem of Calculus** formally states that these limiting processes are inverse operations.

> If the function $f(x)$ is continuous and $F(x)$ is such that $F'(x) = f(x)$, then $\int_a^b f(x)dx = F(b) - F(a)$.

Fundamental Theorem of Calculus

The Fundamental Theorem of Calculus provides a way to evaluate the **definite integral** $\int_a^b f(x)dx$ if an antiderivative $F(x)$ can be found. A square bracket on the right side is used to abbreviate $F(b) - F(a)$. Thus, the principal statement of the theorem may be written as follows.

a and b are called the lower and upper limits or bounds of the integration.

$$\int_a^b f(x)dx = F(x)\Big]_a^b$$

examples

1 **Evaluate $\int_1^2 (1 - 2x)^2 dx$.**

$$\int_1^2 (1 - 2x)^2 dx = \int_1^2 (1 - 4x + 4x^2) dx$$

$$= x - 2x^2 + \frac{4}{3}x^3 \Big]_1^2 \qquad F(x)\Big]_a^b = F(b) - F(a)$$

$$= \left(2 - 2 \cdot 2^2 + \frac{4}{3} \cdot 2^3\right) - \left(1 - 2 \cdot 1^2 + \frac{4}{3} \cdot 1^3\right) \text{ or } 4\frac{1}{3}$$

Since F(x) is any antiderivative of f(x), the constant C is omitted when using the integration formulas to find a definite integral.

2 **Evaluate $\int_1^4 \left(\sqrt{x} + \frac{1}{\sqrt{x}}\right) dx$.**

$$\int_1^4 \left(\sqrt{x} + \frac{1}{\sqrt{x}}\right) dx = \int_1^4 (x^{\frac{1}{2}} + x^{-\frac{1}{2}}) dx$$

$$= \frac{x^{\frac{3}{2}}}{\frac{3}{2}} + \frac{x^{\frac{1}{2}}}{\frac{1}{2}} \Bigg]_1^4$$

$$= \left[\frac{(4)^{\frac{3}{2}}}{\frac{3}{2}} + \frac{(4)^{\frac{1}{2}}}{\frac{1}{2}}\right] - \left[\frac{(1)^{\frac{3}{2}}}{\frac{3}{2}} + \frac{(1)^{\frac{1}{2}}}{\frac{1}{2}}\right]$$

$$= \left(\frac{16}{3} + 4\right) - \left(\frac{2}{3} + 2\right) \text{ or } \frac{20}{3}$$

The definite integral will produce a negative value if $f(x) < 0$ in the interval from $x = a$ to $x = b$. It will produce a positive value if $f(x) > 0$ in the same interval. Therefore, if the integral is being used to find the area between a curve and the x-axis, the absolute value of the integral is used.

example

3 **Find the area between the x-axis and the function $f(x) = x^2 - 9$ from $x = {}^-3$ to $x = 3$.**

$$A = \left| \int_{-3}^3 (x^2 - 9) dx \right|$$

The absolute value is used since area is being found.

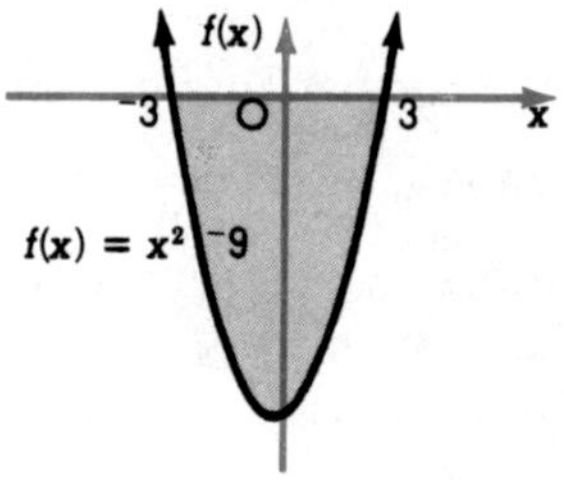

$$= \left| \frac{x^3}{3} - 9x \Big]_{-3}^3 \right|$$

$$= \left| \left[\frac{27}{3} - 9(3)\right] - \left[\frac{^-27}{3} - 9(^-3)\right] \right|$$

$$= |^-36| \text{ or } 36 \text{ sq units}$$

When a function $f(x)$ is both positive and negative in the interval from $x = a$ to $x = b$, and the area is to be found, the limits of integration must be split at the zeros of the function.

example

4 Find the total area between $f(x) = x^3 - x$ and the x-axis from $x = {}^-1$ to $x = 1$.

The graph of $f(x) = x^3 - x$ is shown at the right.

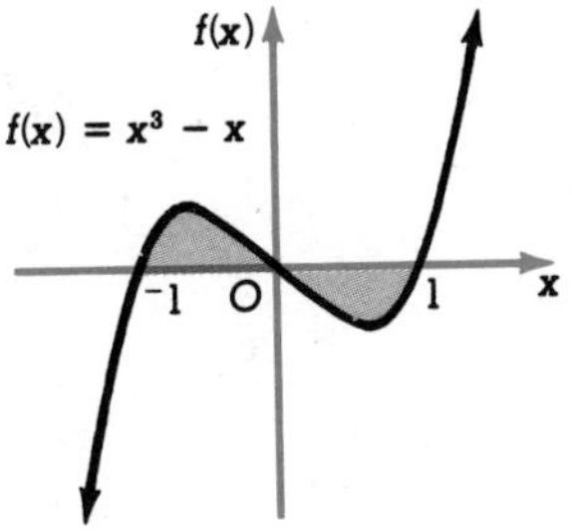

$$A = A_1 + A_2$$

$$A_1 = \left|\int_{-1}^{0} (x^3 - x)dx\right| \qquad A_2 = \left|\int_{0}^{1} (x^3 - x)dx\right|$$

$$= \left|\frac{x^4 - 2x^2}{4}\Bigg]_{-1}^{0}\right| \qquad = \left|\frac{x^4 - 2x^2}{4}\Bigg]_{0}^{1}\right|$$

$$= \left|\frac{(0)^4 - 2(0)^2}{4} - \frac{(^-1)^4 - 2(^-1)^2}{4}\right| \qquad = \left|\frac{(1)^4 - 2(1)^2}{4} - \frac{(0)^4 - 2(0)^2}{4}\right|$$

$$= \left|\frac{1}{4}\right| \qquad = \left|-\frac{1}{4}\right|$$

$$A = \left|\frac{1}{4}\right| + \left|-\frac{1}{4}\right| \text{ or } \frac{1}{2} \text{ sq units}$$

exercises

Exploratory Use integration to find the area of each shaded region. Verify your answers by finding the area geometrically.

1. 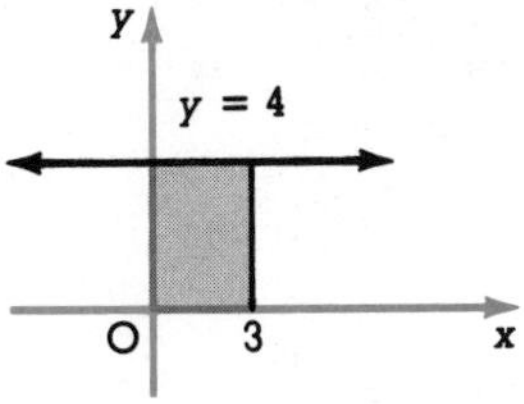

2. 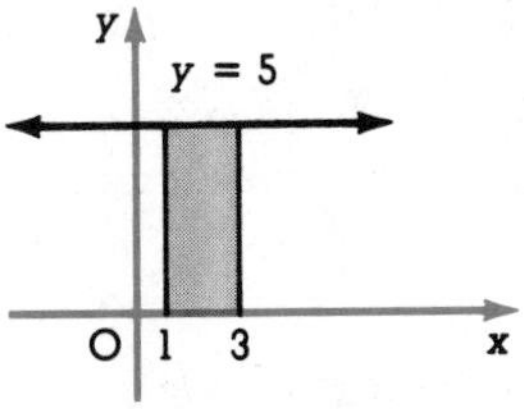

3. 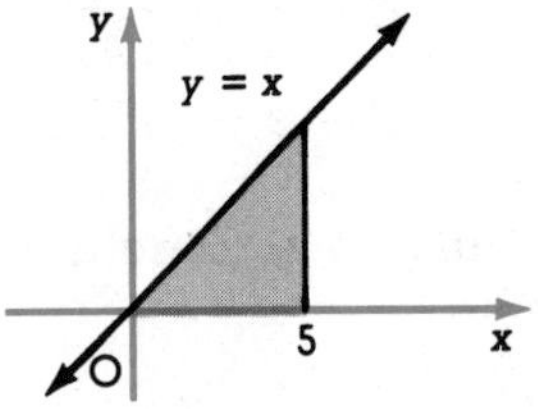

4. 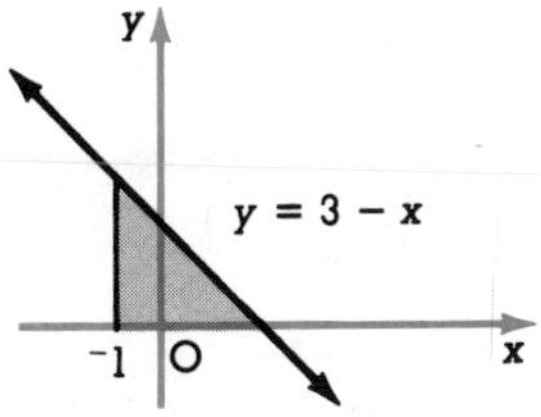

5. 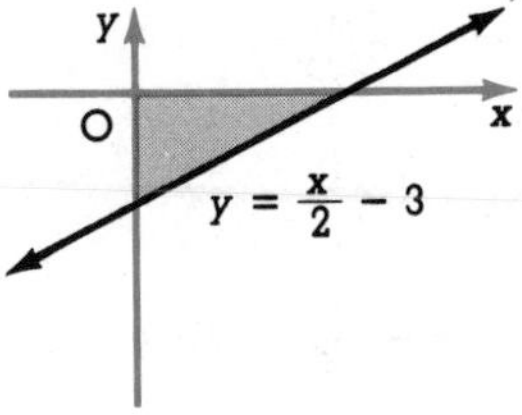

6. 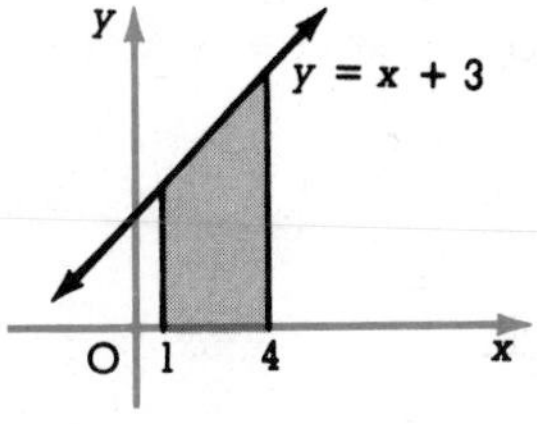

Written Use integration to find the area of each shaded region.

1.
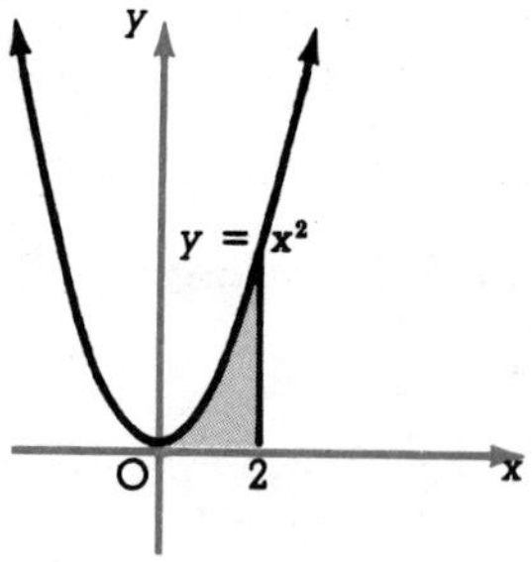

2.
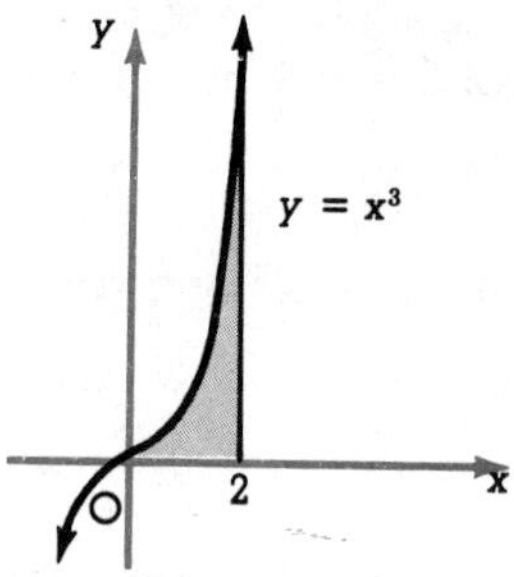

3.
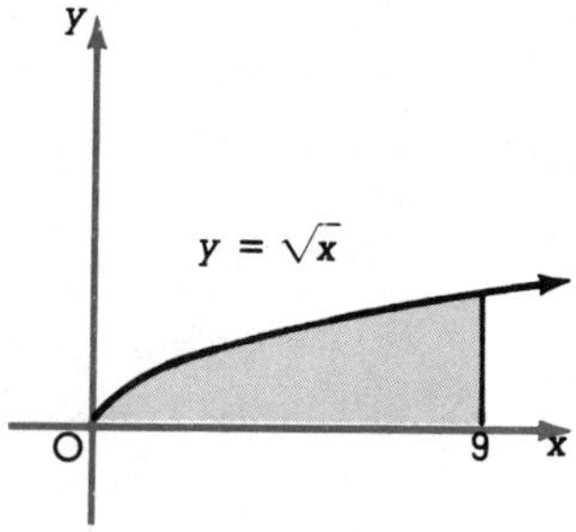

4.
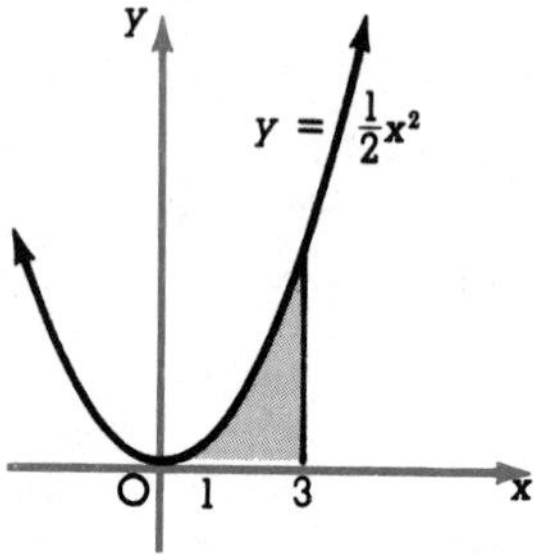

5.
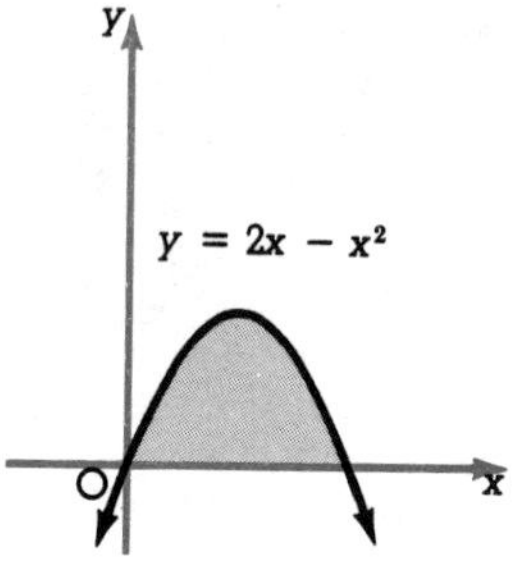

6.
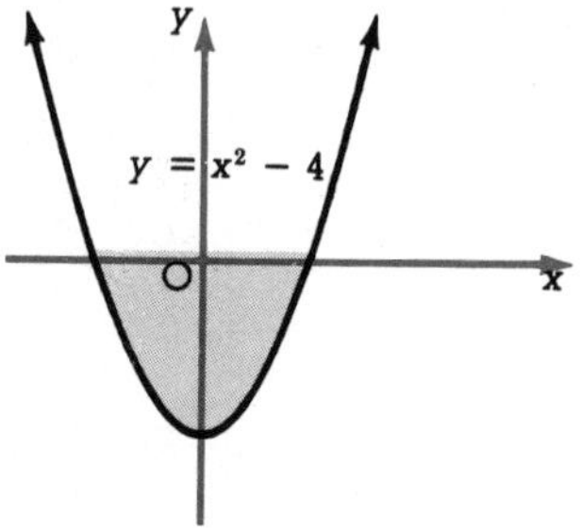

Graph each of the following functions. Then find the area between the function and the x-axis for the given interval using integration.

7. $f(x) = 2x + 3$ for $x = 1$ to $x = 4$
8. $f(x) = {}^-x$ for $x = 1$ to $x = 4$
9. $f(x) = x^2$ for $x = {}^-2$ to $x = 2$
10. $f(x) = x^3$ for $x = {}^-1$ to $x = 2$
11. $f(x) = {}^-x^2$ for $x = 0$ to $x = 5$
12. $f(x) = {}^-x^3$ for $x = {}^-4$ to $x = 0$
13. $f(x) = x^3 - 4x$ for $x = {}^-2$ to $x = 2$
14. $f(x) = x^3 - 4x$ for $x = {}^-3$ to $x = 3$
15. $f(x) = \dfrac{3x^2 - 18x + 15}{5}$ for $x = 0$ to $x = 6$
16. $f(x) = 9 - 3x^2$ for $x = 0$ to $x = 3$

Evaluate each definite integral.

17. $\int_0^1 (2x + 3)dx$
18. $\int_0^1 (3x^2 + 6x + 1)dx$
19. $\int_{-1}^1 (x + 1)^2 dx$
20. $\int_{-1}^1 (4x^3 + 3x^2)dx$
21. $\int_1^4 \left(x^2 + \dfrac{2}{x^2}\right)dx$
22. $\int_{-1}^1 12u(u + 1)(u - 1)du$
23. $\int_0^2 (x - 4x^2)dx$
24. $\int_4^5 (x^2 + 6x - 7)dx$
25. $\int_{-1}^0 (1 - x^2)dx$
26. $\int_1^4 (3x^2 - 6x)dx$
27. $\int_{-2}^{-1} (2x^2 - 3x + 4)dx$
28. $\int_{-2}^3 (x + 2)(x - 3)dx$

Chapter Summary

1. Limit of a Polynomial Function: The limit of a polynomial function, $P(x)$, as x approaches r, is $P(r)$.
$$\lim_{x \to r} P(x) = P(r) \qquad (427)$$
2. Limit of a Function: The limit of a function, $f(x)$, as x approaches a is L, written $\lim_{x \to a} f(x) = L$, if, for every real number $\epsilon > 0$, there exists a real number $\delta > 0$ such that $|f(x) - L| < \epsilon$ when $0 < |x - a| < \delta$. (431)
3. Continuity of a Function at a Point: A function f is continuous at $x = a$ if $f(a)$ exists and if $\lim_{x \to a} f(x) = f(a)$. (434)
4. Continuity of a Function on an Interval: A function f is continuous on an interval if it is continuous at each point of the interval. (435)
5. Continuous Function: A function f is continuous if it is continuous at each point of its domain. (435)
6. The following theorems are given for $\lim_{x \to a} f(x) = F$ and $\lim_{x \to a} g(x) = G$ and real numbers a and c, and n a positive integer. (437)

Theorem 1	Limit of a Constant Function	If $f(x) = c$, then $\lim_{x \to a} f(x) = c$.
Theorem 2	Addition	$\lim_{x \to a} [f(x) + g(x)] = \lim_{x \to a} f(x) + \lim_{x \to a} g(x) = F + G$
Theorem 3	Subtraction	$\lim_{x \to a} [f(x) - g(x)] = \lim_{x \to a} f(x) - \lim_{x \to a} g(x) = F - G$
Theorem 4	Multiplication	$\lim_{x \to a} [f(x) \cdot g(x)] = \left[\lim_{x \to a} f(x)\right]\left[\lim_{x \to a} g(x)\right] = F \cdot G$
Theorem 5	Division	$\lim_{x \to a} \frac{f(x)}{g(x)} = \frac{\lim_{x \to a} f(x)}{\lim_{x \to a} g(x)} = \frac{F}{G} \quad (G \neq 0)$
Theorem 6	Product of a Constant and a Limit	$\lim_{x \to a} [c \cdot g(x)] = c \lim_{x \to a} g(x) = cG$
Theorem 7	Powers	$\lim_{x \to a} [f(x)^n] = \left[\lim_{x \to a} f(x)\right]^n = F^n$
Theorem 8	Roots	$\lim_{x \to a} \sqrt[n]{f(x)} = \sqrt[n]{\lim_{x \to a} f(x)} = \sqrt[n]{F}$

7. Theorem 9: Given functions $f(x)$ and $g(x)$, $\lim_{x \to a} g(x) = G$, and any real number a, the limit of the composite of the functions $f(x)$ and $g(x)$ is as follows.
$$\lim_{x \to a} f[g(x)] = f\left[\lim_{x \to a} g(x)\right] = f(G) \qquad (438)$$
8. Theorem 10: The limit of $\frac{\sin x}{x}$ is equal to 1 as x approaches 0 where x is the radian measure of an angle. $\lim_{x \to 0} \frac{\sin x}{x} = 1$ (438)

9. Derivative of a Function: For a function f, the derivative of f at $x = a$, $f'(a)$, is defined as follows.

$$f'(a) = \lim_{h \to 0} \frac{f(a + h) - f(a)}{h} \qquad (440)$$

10. Power Formula: If $f(x) = cx^n$ and n is a real number and c is a constant, then $f'(x) = cnx^{n-1}$. (443)
11. Theorem 11: If $u = f(x)$ and $v = g(x)$ are differentiable functions of x, then $\frac{d(u + v)}{dx} = \frac{du}{dx} + \frac{dv}{dx}$. (443)
12. Theorem 12: If $u = f(x)$ is a differentiable function of x and c is a constant, then $\frac{d(cu)}{dx} = c\frac{du}{dx}$. (444)
13. Theorem 13: If $u = f(x)$ and $v = g(x)$ are differentiable functions of x, then $\frac{d(uv)}{dx} = u\frac{dv}{dx} + v\frac{du}{dx}$. (444)
14. Theorem: 14: If $u = f(x)$ is a differentiable function of x and n is a nonzero rational number, then $\frac{d(u^n)}{dx} = nu^{n-1}\frac{du}{dx}$. (444)
15. Theorem 15: If $u = f(x)$ and $v = g(x)$ are differentiable functions of x at a point where $v \neq 0$, then $\frac{d\frac{u}{v}}{dx} = \frac{v\frac{du}{dx} - u\frac{dv}{dx}}{v^2}$. (445)
16. Increasing and Decreasing Functions: If $f'(x) > 0$ for all values of x in the interval, $a < x < b$, then the function is increasing in the interval. If $f'(x) < 0$ for all values of x in the interval, $a < x < b$, then the function is decreasing in the interval. (446)
17. Second Derivative Test: If $f'(x) = 0$ at x, then $f(x)$ is one of the following stationary values.
    1. If $f''(x) > 0$, then $f(x)$ is a relative minimum.
    2. If $f''(x) < 0$, then $f(x)$ is a relative maximum.
    3. If $f''(x) = 0$ or does not exist, then $(x, f(x))$ is a point of inflection. (448)
18. Area Under a Curve: The area A between the curve $y = f(x)$ and the x-axis from $x = a$ to $x = b$ is as follows. (452)

$$A = \lim_{n \to \infty} \sum_{i=1}^{n} f(x_i)(x_{i+1} - x_i)$$

where the width of each rectangle, $x_{i+1} - x_i$, approaches zero.

19. Definition of an Integral: The function, $F(x)$, is an integral of $f(x)$ with respect to x if and only if $F(x)$ is an antiderivative of $f(x)$. That is, $F(x) = \int f(x)dx$ if and only if $F'(x) = f(x)$. (455)
20. Fundamental Theorem of Calculus: If the function $f(x)$ is continuous and $F(x)$ is such that $F'(x) = f(x)$, then $\int_a^b f(x)dx = F(b) - F(a)$. (457)

Chapter Review

15-1 Find each limit or state that the limit does not exist.

1. $\lim_{x\to 1} (x^2 + 3x + 2)$
2. $\lim_{x\to 0} \left(4^x + \frac{1}{4^x}\right)$
3. $\lim_{x\to 3} \frac{x^2 - 9}{x + 3}$

15-2 Find the interval which x must be within so that each inequality is satisfied.

4. $^-0.05 < x - 2 < 0.05$
5. $\left|\frac{x + 1}{2} - 3\right| < 0.01$

Given that $\epsilon = 0.01$, find a δ such that the following limits are verified using the formal definition of a limit.

6. $\lim_{x\to 2} \frac{x - 2}{3} = 0$
7. $\lim_{x\to 3} \frac{x^2 - 9}{x - 3} = 6$

15-3 State whether each function is continuous or discontinuous. If it is discontinuous, identify the discontinuity as infinite, jump, or point.

8. $f(x) = x^3 + 1$
9. $f(x) = \frac{x - 3}{x^2 + x - 6}$
10. $f(x) = \left|\frac{1}{x}\right|$

15-4 Use the limit theorems to evaluate each limit.

11. $\lim_{x\to ^-1} (x^2 - 1)$
12. $\lim_{x\to 0} \frac{3x^3 - 2x}{2x^2 - 3x}$
13. $\lim_{x\to 0} \frac{\sqrt{3x^2 + x + 1}}{\sqrt[3]{x^3 - x + 8}}$

15-5 Find the slope and equation of the tangent to each of the following curves at the given point.

14. $y = 1 - x^2$ at $(0, 1)$
15. $y = 2x^4$ at $(^-1, 2)$

15-6 Find the derivative of each function.

16. $f(x) = x^6$
17. $f(x) = 4x^3$
18. $f(x) = 3x + 4x^2$

15-7 Find the values of x for which each of the following functions is increasing.

19. $f(x) = x^2 - 2x$
20. $f(x) = \frac{1}{x} + x$

Find the stationary values of each function. State whether each is a maximum, minimum, or a point of inflection.

21. $f(x) = x^3 - 2x$
22. $f(x) = x + \frac{4}{x}$

15-8 Find the area between each curve and the x-axis for the given interval using the limit of the area of rectangles.

23. $y = 2x$ from $x = 0$ to $x = 2$
24. $y = x^3$ from $x = 0$ to $x = 1$

15-9 Find each integral.

25. $\int \frac{4}{x^2}\,dx$
26. $\int 5x^3\,dx$
27. $\int (1 - x)\,dx$

15-10 28. Find the area between $f(x) = 3x^2$ and the x-axis from $x = 1$ to $x = 3$.

Evaluate each integral.

29. $\int_2^4 6x\,dx$
30. $\int_{-3}^{2} 3x^2\,dx$
31. $\int_{-2}^{2} (3x^2 - x + 5)\,dx$

Chapter Test

Find each limit or state that the limit does not exist.

1. $\lim_{x\to 2} \frac{x^2 - 4}{x - 2}$

2. $\lim_{x\to 3} \frac{x^2 - 9}{x^3 - 27}$

Given that $\epsilon = 0.1$, find a δ such that the following limits are verified using the formal definition of a limit.

3. $\lim_{x\to 0} (3x + 4) = 4$

4. $\lim_{x\to -2} \frac{x^2 - 4}{x + 2} = -4$

5. Find the points at which the function $f(x) = \frac{x - 2}{x^2 + 2x - 8}$ is discontinuous.

Use the limit theorems to evaluate each limit.

6. $\lim_{x\to 2} \frac{x^2 - 1}{x^2 + 1}$

7. $\lim_{x\to 1} \frac{x^2 - 2x + 3}{3x^2 - 5}$

8. $\lim_{x\to -1} (x^2 - 3x + 4)$

Find the slope and the equation of the tangent to each of the following curves at the given point.

9. $y = x^2 - 3x + 2$ at $(1, 0)$

10. $y = 2x^2 - 3$ at $(2, 5)$

Find the derivative of each function.

11. $f(x) = 3x + 4x^2$

12. $f(x) = (x + 3)^2$

13. $f(x) = \frac{2x}{1 + x^2}$

Find the values of x for which each of the following functions is decreasing.

14. $f(x) = x^3 - 3x$

15. $f(x) = \frac{1}{4}x^4 - \frac{9}{2}x^2$

Find the stationary values of each function. State whether each is a maximum, minimum, or a point of inflection.

16. $f(x) = \frac{1}{3}x^2$

17. $f(x) = x^4 - 2x^2 + 2$

18. Find the area between $y = x^2$ and the x-axis from $x = 0$ to $x = 2$ using the limit of the area of rectangles.

Find each integral.

19. $\int (1 - x)\, dx$

20. $\int (3x^2 + 4x + 7)\, dx$

Evaluate each integral.

21. $\int_0^1 (2x + 3)\, dx$

22. $\int_1^4 \left(x^2 + \frac{2}{x^2}\right) dx$

Appendix

BASIC

The BASIC Language

BASIC, an abbreviation for Beginner's All-purpose Symbolic Instruction Code, is a frequently used computer language.

In BASIC a variable may be represented by either a single letter such as A, B, C, . . . , Z, or a letter followed by a single digit such as A0, A1, A2, . . . , B0, B1, B2, . . . ,Z9.

A list of operations and their corresponding notation in BASIC is given below.

Operation	BASIC Notation
Addition	+
Subtraction	−
Multiplication	*
Division	/
Raising to a power	↑

In BASIC an operation symbol *cannot* be omitted. For example, the product of A and B must be written A*B, *not* AB.

The order of operations in BASIC is the same as in algebra.

Order of Operations in BASIC

1. **Operations in parentheses are performed from the innermost parentheses outward.**
2. **Powers are evaluated from left to right.**
3. **Multiplications and/or divisions are performed from left to right.**
4. **Additions and/or subtractions are performed from left to right.**

The following examples illustrate the correct notation of some expressions and also the value of each expression.

Expression	BASIC notation	Value of Expression
$2(8 + 2)$	2*(8+2)	20
$(3 - 1.5)^2$	(3−1.5)↑2	2.25
$\frac{4 \times 9 + 4}{15 - 5^2}$	(4*9+4)/(15−5↑2)	$^-4$

example

1 Evaluate (4*(3+9))/6+2↑3*2.

(4*(3+9))/6+2↑3*2 = (4*12)/6+2↑3*2	*Do operations in innermost parentheses.*
= 48/6+2↑3*2	*Do operations in parentheses.*
= 48/6+8*2	*Evaluate the power*
= 8 + 16	*Do the division and multiplication.*
= 24	*Do the addition.*

The value of the expression is 24.

example

2 Write an expression in BASIC for $\left(\frac{(a+b)^2}{c}\right)^3 - \sqrt{x}$.

The expressions, $(a + b)^2$ and $\sqrt{x}$, are written (A+B)↑2 and X↑.5, respectively.

Thus, $\left(\frac{(a+b)^2}{c}\right)^3 - \sqrt{x}$ is written ((A+B)↑2/C)↑3−X↑.5.

A computer program consists of a series of instructions required to solve a specific problem on a computer. The purpose of a computer program is to put instructions and data into the computer (*input*), have the computer do the calculations (*execution*), and get results out of the computer (*output*).

The standard BASIC language consists of about twenty statement types, such as LET, GO TO, PRINT, READ, and END. Each statement in a BASIC program has a line number which identifies the line and also specifies the order in which the statements are to be executed by the computer. The program below shows how various statements are used.

The line number must be a positive integer less than 100,000.

```
10 READ X, Y
20 DATA 3, 2
30 PRINT X*Y, X↑Y
40 END
```

line numbers (pointing to 10, 20, 30, 40)

The computer assigns the numbers from the DATA statement in line 20 to the variables X and Y in order.

Computations may be included in the PRINT statement.

Every program must have an END statement.

These optional blanks make the program easier to read.

The output of this program is as follows.

6   9

Every READ statement *must* be accompanied by a DATA statement. Each item in both READ and DATA statements must be separated by a comma. Although variables appear in the READ statement, they must *not* appear in the DATA statement.

example

3 Write a program to find the average of the numbers 22, 24, 28, 31, and 34.

```
10 READ A,B,C,D,E
20 PRINT (A+B+C+D+E)/5
30 DATA 22,24,28,31,34
40 END
```

The DATA statement does not have to follow the READ statement.

A REM statement provides a means of identification for the program. It does *not* affect the execution of the program. The general form of the REM statement is as follows.

REM stands for remark.

<u>*line number*</u> REM <u>*comment*</u>

Consider the following program.

```
10 REM FIND AREA OF A SQUARE, GIVEN LENGTH OF SIDE
20 READ S
30 DATA 4,9,10
40 PRINT S↑2
50 GO TO 20
60 END
```

Line 50 introduces a GO TO statement. The computer will return to line 20 each time it comes to line 50 until all of the data have been used. The GO TO statement has a general form as follows.

<u>line number</u> GO TO <u>line number</u>

The output of this program is as follows.
16
81
100

exercises

Exploratory Determine whether each of the following is an acceptable BASIC variable. Write *yes* or *no*.

1. X
2. XY
3. A8
4. 3X
5. B74
6. DIF

Copy each of the following BASIC expressions. Put numerals under each operation sign to indicate the order in which the operations will be performed.

7. ((13+11)/4)/6
8. (2*(4+8))/6
9. (1−3↑3)/(5↑2+1)
10. (−3)↑2+(−4)↑2−2*(−3)*(−4)
11. (((1+2)↑2+4)↑3+4↑1)
12. 3*(−4)↑2−3*(−3)↑2+3*(−5)

Written Solve each problem.

1-6. Evaluate each expression in problems **7-12** of the exploratory exercises.

Write an expression in BASIC for each of the following.

7. $3.14r^2$
8. $x^2 + 2xy + y^2$
9. $(a + b)^2$
10. $\frac{a + b}{2}$
11. $\frac{a + b}{c + d}$
12. $3 - \frac{x^2}{3}$
13. $^-4y^2 - 2y + 3$
14. $\frac{x(x - 1)(x - 2)}{6}$
15. $\sqrt{\frac{x}{y} + w}$

Each of the following expressions is incorrectly written in BASIC. Rewrite each expression using the correct BASIC notation.

16. 5X
17. 184÷2
18. 2(X+Y)
19. $3\frac{1}{2}$*Y
20. 2+X↑2+3X
21. (2+7)/4)

Write programs in BASIC to compute and print each of the following. Use READ and DATA statements.

22. Find the sum and product of 13, 41, and 26.
23. Find the circumference and area of a circle with radius 3.67 cm. Use 3.1416 for π.
24. Find the product of A and the sum of B and C when $A = 5$, $B = 4$, and $C = 3$.
25. Find the value of $A^2 - B^2$, $(A - B)^2$, $A^2 + B^2$, and $(A + B)^2$ when $A = 4$ and $B = 3$.

LET and PRINT Statements

Specific values can be assigned to a variable by using a LET statement. Consider each of the following statements.

```
20 LET X=X+1          How does the use of the equals sign
20 LET X=Y↑A+M        differ from its use in algebra?
```

The equals sign tells the computer to assign the value of the expression on the right to the variable on the left. The left side of the equation must have only one variable. Variables may appear on the right side of the equation as above. However, these variables should be assigned a specific value prior to this statement.

```
10 READ X,Y           The data are assigned as follows.
20 DATA 4,2                X=4        Y=2.
30 LET A=5*Y+20/X     The value of 5*Y+20/X is then
40 PRINT A            computed and assigned to A in
50 END                line 30. This value is then
RUN                   printed.
15                    Output
```

The RUN command after the program above tells the computer to execute the program. Notice that it does *not* have a line number.

example

1 **Write a program in BASIC to find the squares of 10, 20, and 30.**

```
10 LET N=10           The value of N is 10.
20 PRINT N,N↑2        Output      10      100
30 LET N=N+10         The value of N is 20.
40 PRINT N, N↑2       Output      20      400
50 LET N=N+10         What value is assigned to N?
60 PRINT N,N↑2        What is the output?
70 END
```

The PRINT statement can be used to print words as well as the results of calculations. Examples of PRINT statements are given below.

```
30 PRINT "PROBLEM 8"     Anything placed between quotation marks
                         will be printed exactly as typed.

30 PRINT X,Y*Z           A comma tells the computer to print
                         the output in columns or zones.

30 PRINT A+B;C           A semicolon tells the computer to print
                         the output close together on one line.
```

30 PRINT	*A blank line will appear in the output.*
30 PRINT A,	*The next output will be printed in the next column or zone.*
30 PRINT A;	*The next output will be printed on the same line, close to this output, or on the next line if this line is full.*

example

2 Write a program in BASIC to find the average test score for each person given their scores on four tests. Then show the output of the program.

Marilyn—91, 78, 88, 94; Ted—79, 77, 84, 92; Bernie—70, 80, 91, 84

```
10 READ A,B,C,D
20 DATA 91,78,88,94,79,77,84,92,70,80,91,84
30 LET V=(A+B+C+D)/4
40 PRINT "TEST SCORES";A;B;C;D
50 PRINT "AVERAGE = ";V
60 PRINT
70 GO TO 10
80 END
RUN
TEST SCORES 91 78 88 94
AVERAGE = 87.75

TEST SCORES 79 77 84 92
AVERAGE = 83

TEST SCORES 70 80 91 84
AVERAGE = 81.25
```

Note the positions of the spaces between the quotes. (line 50)

exercises

Exploratory State whether each of the following is an acceptable LET statement. Write *yes* or *no*.

1. 20 LET A1=6
2. LET 8=X
3. 20 LET X=2*X
4. LET A+B=Z
5. 20 LET N=R−1
6. LET X/2=Z/2

Find the value assigned to X by each of the following LET statements if A = 2, B = 4, and C = 3.

7. 20 LET X=A+B/C
8. 20 LET X=(A+B)/C
9. 20 LET X=A/B*C
10. 20 LET X=A/(B*C)
11. 20 LET X=A+B/A+6
12. 20 LET X=(A+B)↑2/(B−C)↑2

Written Show the output of each of the following programs.

1.
```
10 PRINT "X";"Y"
20 READ X,Y
30 PRINT X,Y
40 DATA 7,100
50 END
```

2.
```
10 READ X
20 LET Y=2*X↑2-7*X
30 PRINT Y
40 GO TO 10
50 DATA 1,2,3
60 END
```

3.
```
10 PRINT "BASE","HEIGHT","AREA"
20 READ B,H
30 LET A=B*H
40 PRINT B,H,A
45 GO TO 20
50 DATA 10,4,14,3
60 END
```

4.
```
10 LET N=3
20 LET Y=5
30 LET Y=Y+7
40 LET X=Y+N
50 PRINT X
60 END
```

5.
```
10 LET T=4
20 PRINT T,T↑2
30 LET T=T+3
40 PRINT T,T↑2
50 LET T=T+1
60 PRINT 3*T
70 END
```

6.
```
10 READ B,H
20 LET A=B*H
30 LET C=B+H
40 LET C=C+1
50 PRINT A,C
60 DATA 10,12
70 END
```

7.
```
10 LET T=0
20 READ X,Y
30 LET T=T+1
40 PRINT X↑T,Y↑T
50 GO TO 20
60 DATA 1,2,3,4,5,6
70 END
```

8.
```
10 LET A=2
20 LET B=3
30 LET C=3
40 LET X=A+B+C
50 LET Y=X↑3
60 LET U=Y+A-7
70 PRINT U
80 END
```

Each of the following programs contains at least one error. Find each error and write a correct program.

9.
```
20 PRINT 6(5+4)
15 END
```

10.
```
10 PRINT 3↑2
20 END
30 RUN
```

11.
```
LET X=7
LET Y=X+6
PRINT X+Y
END
```

12.
```
20 LET X=Y+1
10 LET Y=2
30 PRINT XY
40 END
```

13.
```
10 LET A=6
20 LET A*3=Y
30 PRINT Y
40 END
```

14.
```
10 LET X=7
20 LET Y=A*X
30 PRINT Y
40 END
```

Two lines of a BASIC program are as follows.

```
10 READ A,B,C,D
20 DATA 6,7,8,9
```

Write a PRINT statement or statements that would produce each of the following outputs.

15.
```
6  7  8  9
```

16.
```
6    7
8    9
```

17.
```
6
7
8
9
```

18.
```
A is 6
B is 7
C is 8
D is 9
```

Write a program in BASIC to compute and print each of the following.

19. The Carefree Car Rental company rents cars for $28.95 per day plus $.18 per mile. Find the cost of driving 1263 miles in two days.

20. A certain telephone call costs $1.38 for the first three minutes and $.34 for each minute thereafter. Find the cost of a 15-minute telephone call.

21. Convert 1 yard, 2 yards, and 3 yards to meters.

22. Print a table showing each integer from 1 to 10 with its square and square root.

IF-THEN Statements

The IF-THEN statement makes a comparison of two numbers. It tells the computer what to do based on results of the comparison.

The general form of the IF-THEN statement is as follows.

IF <u>algebraic sentence</u> THEN <u>line number</u>

If the algebraic sentence is true, then the computer proceeds to the line whose number follows THEN. If the algebraic sentence is false, the computer simply goes in normal sequence to the next line.

The algebraic sentence in the IF-THEN statement uses one of the following symbols.

BASIC symbol	Meaning
=	is equal to
<	is less than
<=	is less than or equal to
>	is greater than
>=	is greater than or equal to
<>	is not equal to

example 1 Write a program which finds the square root of a number. If the number is negative, instruct the computer to print NO REAL SQUARE ROOT.

```
10 READ A
20 IF A<0 THEN 50                          Test line
30 PRINT A↑.5
40 GO TO 10                                Why is this GO TO statement necessary?
50 PRINT "NO REAL SQUARE ROOT"
60 GO TO 10
70 DATA 64,-5,34,15,0
80 END
```

An IF-THEN statement also can be used to count how many times an operation is performed. In the program of the following example, the count is kept in line 50.

example 2 A large sheet of paper is 0.5 mm thick. Write a program to determine how many times it should be folded to make it 1 kilometer thick. Then show the output of the program.

```
10 REM FOLDING PAPER PROBLEM
20 PRINT "TIMES FOLDED","HEIGHT IN METERS"
25 PRINT
30 LET K=1                    Assign a starting value for K.
40 LET S=2                    On the first fold (K=1), S, the
45 PRINT K,S*.0005            the number of sheets, will be 2.
50 LET K=K+1                  Increase counter K by 1.
60 LET S=S*2                  Each fold doubles the number of sheets.
70 PRINT K,S*.0005            0.5 mm = 0.0005 m, 1 km = 1000 m.
80 IF S*.0005 < 1000 THEN 50  The program will end when the
90 END                        thickness of the paper becomes
RUN                           equal to or greater than 1000 m.
TIMES FOLDED        HEIGHT IN METERS

1                   .001
2                   .002
3                   .004
.                   .
.                   .
.                   .
20                  524.288
21                  1048.576
```

exercises

Exploratory Suppose $X = 3$, $Y = 10$, and $Z = 15$. State what line number the computer will go to after it executes the IF-THEN statement.

1.
```
30 IF X > 2 THEN 50
40 PRINT X
```
2.
```
40 IF Y<>0 THEN 90
50 PRINT Y
```
3.
```
30 IF X+Y<Z THEN 70
40 PRINT X↑2+Y↑2
```
4.
```
50 IF Y↑2>Z↑2 THEN 70
60 PRINT Y
```
5.
```
20 IF Y>=12 THEN 40
30 PRINT X*Y
```
6.
```
20 IF X>Y THEN 50
30 IF Y<Z THEN 70
40 PRINT X+Z
```

Each of the following expressions is incorrectly written in BASIC. Rewrite each statement correctly.

7. `30 IF X<100 THEN GO TO 50`
8. `IF B<>400 THEN LET X=B↑2`

Written Use the partial program at the right to tell whether A, B, or both A and B will be printed. Give the value of any variables printed.

1. A = 13, B = 18
2. A = 8, B = 16
3. A = 19, B = 5
4. A = 8, B = 8
5. A = 4, B = 14
6. A = 13, B = 14

```
10 IF A>B THEN 50
20 LET A=A+10
30 LET B=B+2
40 IF A>=B THEN 60
50 PRINT A
60 PRINT B
70 END
```

Write the output of each of the following programs.

7.
```
10 LET A=1
20 PRINT A,A↑3
30 LET A=A+2
40 IF A<7 THEN 20
50 END
```
8.
```
10 LET X=5
20 PRINT X
30 LET X=X-2
40 IF X<>-1 THEN 20
50 END
```
9.
```
10 READ X
20 IF X>4 THEN 70
30 LET Y=X↑2
40 PRINT X,Y
50 GO TO 10
60 DATA 1,2,3,4,5,6
70 END
```
10.
```
10 LET S=0
20 LET N=1
30 LET S=S+N
40 IF N=4 THEN 70
50 LET N=N+1
60 GO TO 30
70 PRINT S
80 END
```

Write a program using BASIC to compute and print each of the following.

11. Given four numbers, no two of which are equal, find and print the greatest.
12. Given three numbers, no two of which are equal, print them from least to greatest.
13. Given two unequal numbers a and b, print either "A > B" or "B > A".
14. Count the powers of four less than 900,000. Print value of the greatest one in decimal notation and also as a power of four.

Flow Charts

Before writing a program, a programmer usually draws a diagram that shows a step-by-step procedure for solving the problem. Such diagrams are called **flow charts.**

The shapes which are used to draw flow charts have special meanings.

An oval is used to begin or end a program.

A parallelogram shows input or output. It is used with READ or PRINT statements.

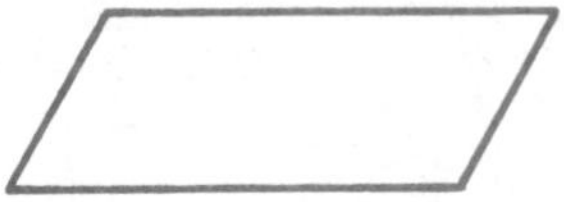

A rectangle shows processing operations. It is used with LET statements.

A diamond shows a decision. Arrows show how the flow continues. It is used with IF-THEN statements.

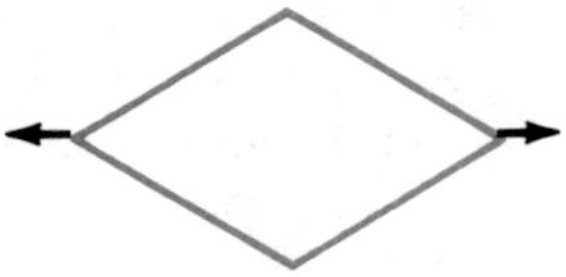

A circle is used to connect shapes when drawing an arrow is inconvenient.

Consider the following flow chart for the program on the right which reads two numbers and then prints the larger number.

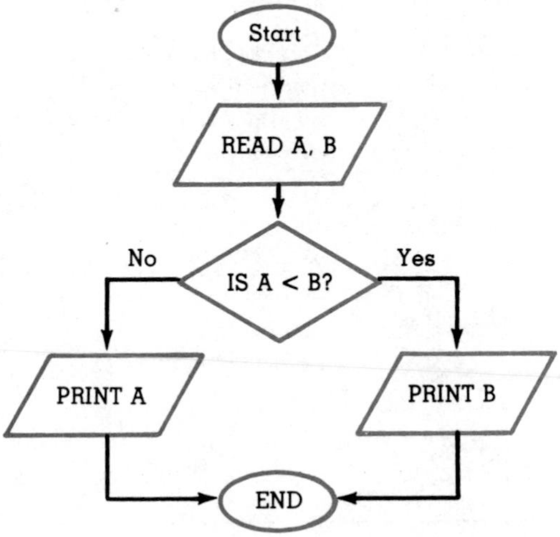


```
10 READ A,B
20 IF A<B THEN 50
30 PRINT A
40 GO TO 70
50 PRINT B
60 DATA . . .
70 END
```

examples

1 Make a flow chart and write a program to determine if the equations $3x^2 - 4x + 2 = 0$ and $5y^2 - 5y - 8 = 0$ have real solutions.

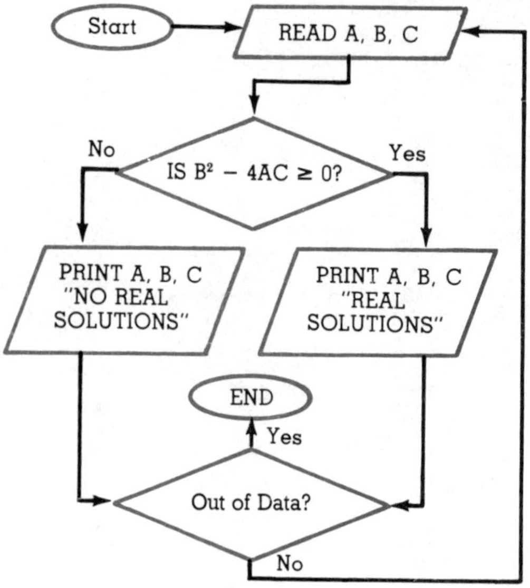

Recall the quadratic formula,

$$x = \frac{^-b \pm \sqrt{b^2 - 4ac}}{2a}.$$

When the discriminant, $b^2 - 4ac$, is negative, there are no real solutions.

Thus, the computer needs to determine if $b^2 - 4ac < 0$.

```
10 READ A,B,C
20 DATA 3,−4,2,5,−5,−8
30 IF B↑2−4*A*C>=0 THEN 60
40 PRINT A;B;C,"NO REAL SOLUTIONS"
50 GO TO 10
60 PRINT A;B;C,"REAL SOLUTIONS"
70 GO TO 10
80 END
```

Note the use of commas and semicolons in lines 40 and 60.

2 Suzanne earns \$5.72 an hour. She is paid double her regular rate for any hours worked over forty. Make a flow chart and write a program to find her weekly wages given the hours worked each week for 26 weeks.

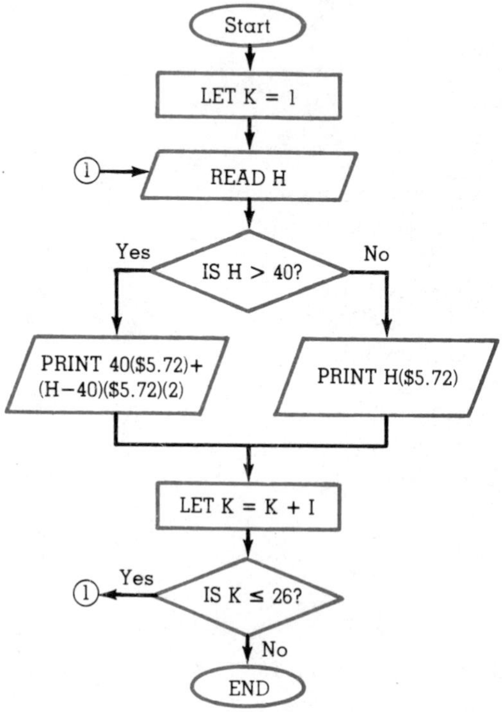


```
 10 PRINT "HOURS", "WAGES"
 20 LET K=1
 30 READ H
 40 IF H > 40 THEN 70
 50 PRINT H,"$";H*5.72
 60 GO TO 80
 70 PRINT H,"$";40*5.72+(H−40)*5.72*2
 80 LET K=K+1
 90 IF K < = 26 THEN 30
100 DATA . . .
110 END
```

To use the program, the number of hours for each of the 26 weeks must be listed in the data statement.

example

3 Write a program from the flow chart below and then show the output.

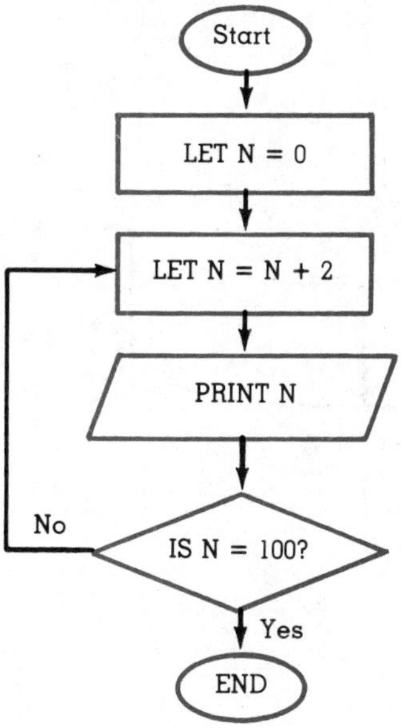


```
10 LET N=0
20 LET N=N+2
30 PRINT N
40 IF N=100 THEN 60
50 GO TO 20
60 END
RUN
2
4
.
.
.
100
```

The output consists of the even numbers from 2 to 100 inclusive.

exercises

Exploratory State whether each of the following is an acceptable flow chart box. Write *yes* or *no*.

1.
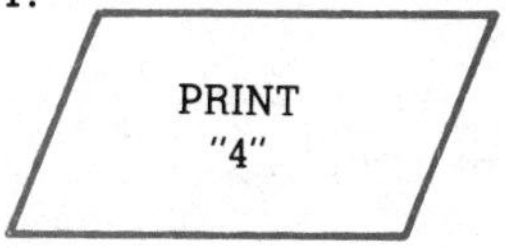

2.
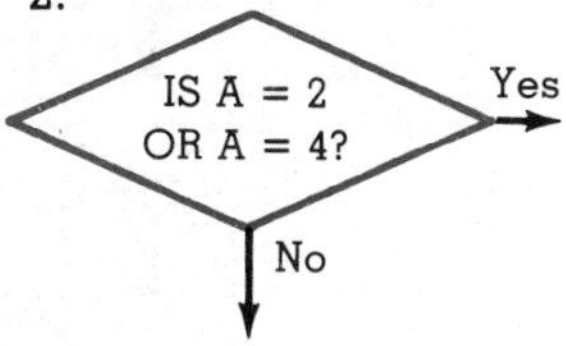

3.
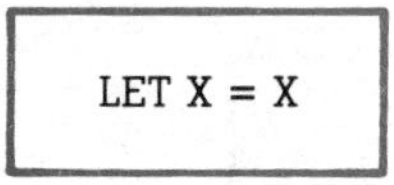

4.
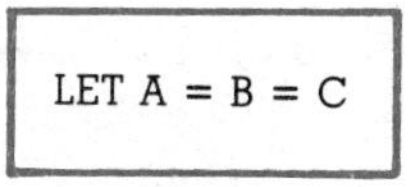

5.
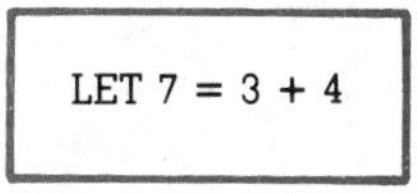

6.
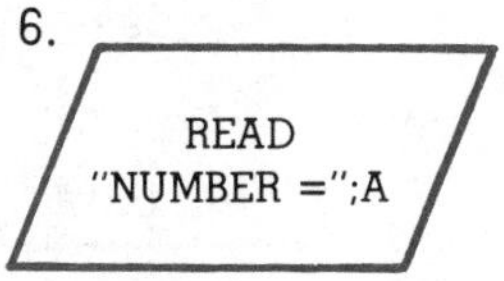

7.
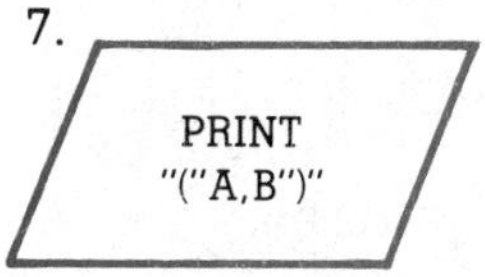

8.
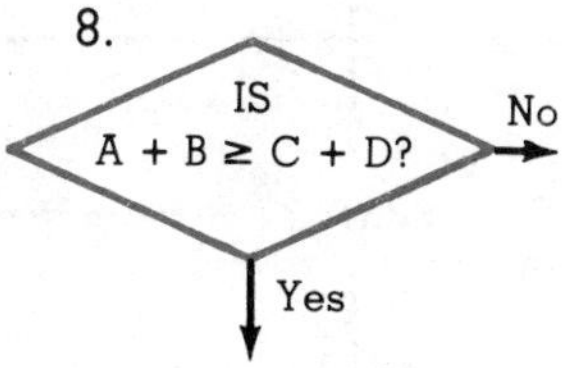

9.
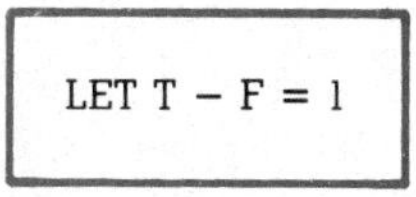

10.
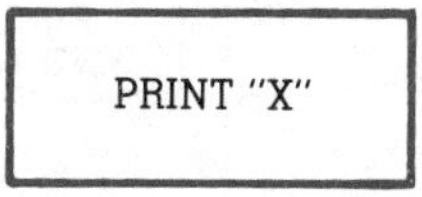

11.

12.
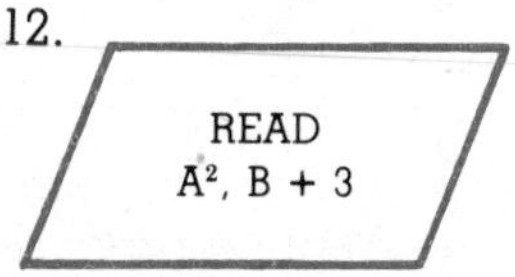

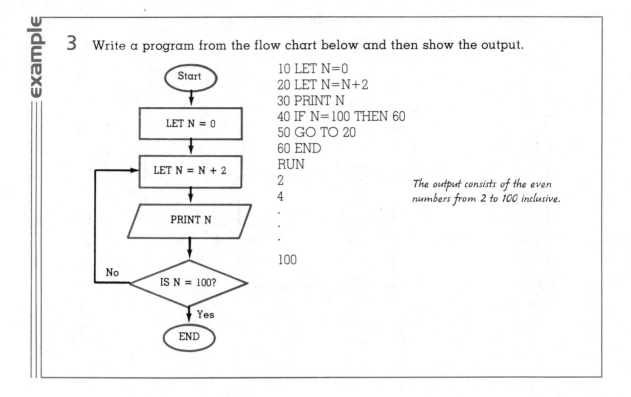

Written Explain what each of the following flow charts does.

1.

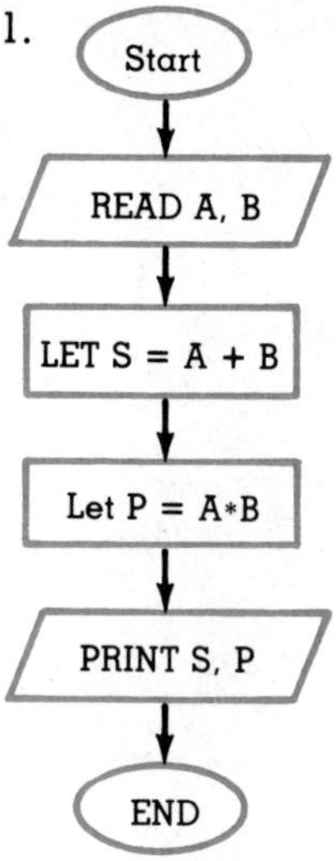
Start
READ A, B
LET S = A + B
Let P = A*B
PRINT S, P
END

2.

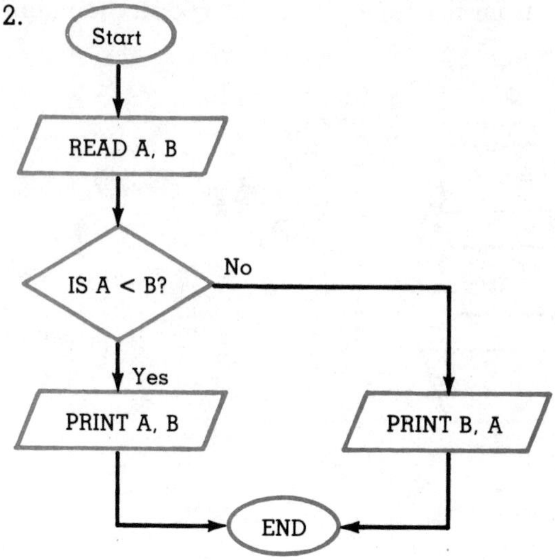
Start
READ A, B
IS A < B?
No
Yes
PRINT A, B
PRINT B, A
END

3.

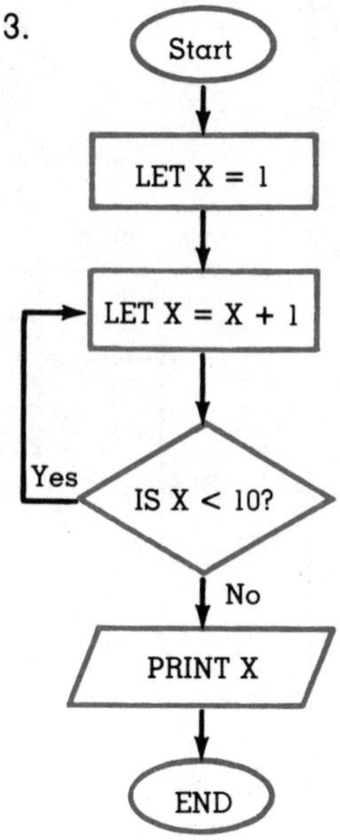
Start
LET X = 1
LET X = X + 1
Yes
IS X < 10?
No
PRINT X
END

4.

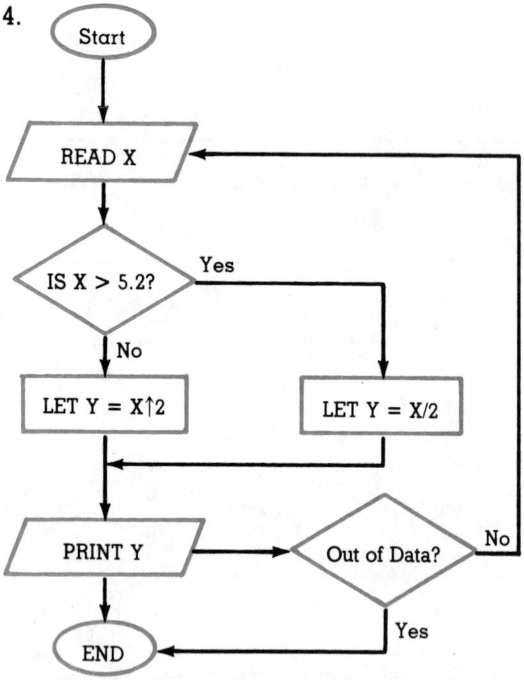
Start
READ X
IS X > 5.2?
Yes
No
LET Y = X↑2
LET Y = X/2
PRINT Y
Out of Data?
No
Yes
END

5.

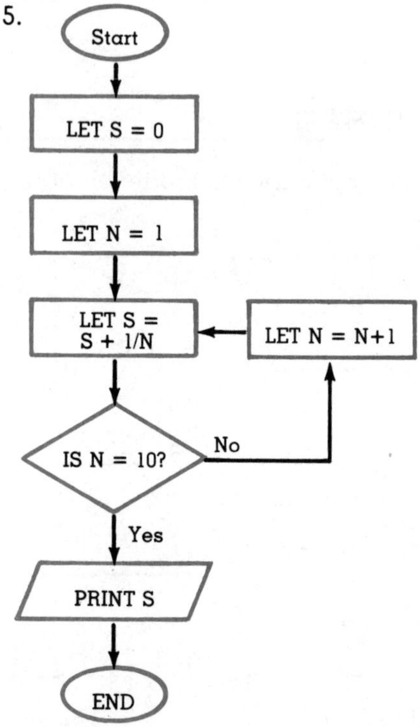
Start
LET S = 0
LET N = 1
LET S = S + 1/N
LET N = N+1
IS N = 10?
No
Yes
PRINT S
END

6-10. Write a program in BASIC for each flow chart in problems 1-5.

Make a flow chart for each of the following problems.

11. Given two numbers, find the square of the lesser number and the cube of the greater number.
12. Find the midpoint of the line segment with endpoints (a, b) and (c, d).
13. Determine if the ordered pair (a, b) lies on the line, $y = 3x - 5$.
14. Determine if three integers are Pythagorean triples.
15. Determine if three real numbers could be the measures of the sides of a triangle.
16. Classify a given angle as acute, right, or obtuse.
17. Find the supplement and complement of an angle.
18. Given three numbers, find the greatest number.

19-26. Write a program in BASIC for problems 11-18.

FOR-NEXT Loops

Loops are often written in a program to direct the computer to repeat a portion of the program a certain number of times. Consider the following flow chart and program.

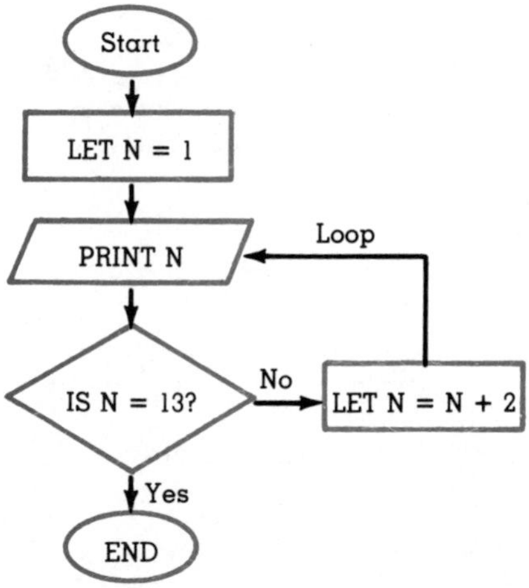


```
10 LET N=1
20 PRINT N;
30 IF N=13 THEN 60
40 LET N=N+2
50 GO TO 20
60 END
```

The same looping procedure can be accomplished by using FOR and NEXT statements.

```
10 FOR N=1 TO 13 STEP 2
20 PRINT N;
30 NEXT N
40 END
```

FOR-NEXT loop

A FOR-NEXT loop must begin with a FOR statement and end with a NEXT statement. The variable used in each statement must be the same. Any number of lines may appear between the FOR statement and the NEXT statement.

The general form of the FOR statement is as follows.

FOR <u>Variable</u> = <u>Number</u> TO <u>Number</u> STEP <u>Number</u>

If the step is not indicated, most computers will automatically use a step of one.

The second number must be greater than the first number unless the step number is negative. The three numbers may also be variables that have had values assigned to them previously.

When the computer executes a FOR-NEXT loop, the computer automatically tests the value of the variable each time it is incremented. If it is less than or equal to the second number listed in the FOR statement, the computer increases the value by the indicated step and continues in the loop. Otherwise the computer goes to the first statement following the NEXT statement that can be executed.

example

1 **Write a program that computes y values for the equation $y = 8x^2 - 30x + 25$ when $x = 1, 1.25, 1.50, 1.75, \ldots, 3$.**

```
10 PRINT "X","Y"
20 FOR X=1 TO 3 STEP .25
30 LET Y=8*X↑2-30*X+25
40 PRINT X,Y
50 NEXT X
60 END
```

What would be different about output if line 40 were given the line number 55?

When making flow charts for programs which will contain FOR-NEXT statements, an **iteration box** as shown at the right is used. It shows all parts of a loop. For example, the iteration box below represents the part of a program shown next to it.

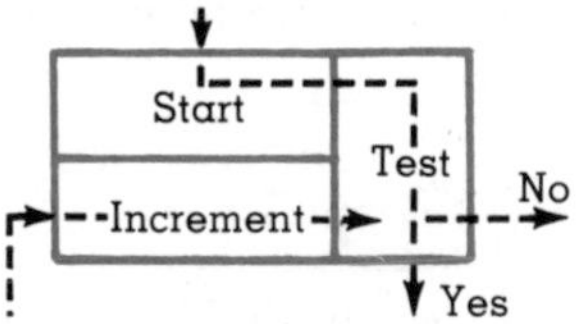


```
10 FOR A=1 TO 5 STEP 2
.
.
.
50 NEXT A
```

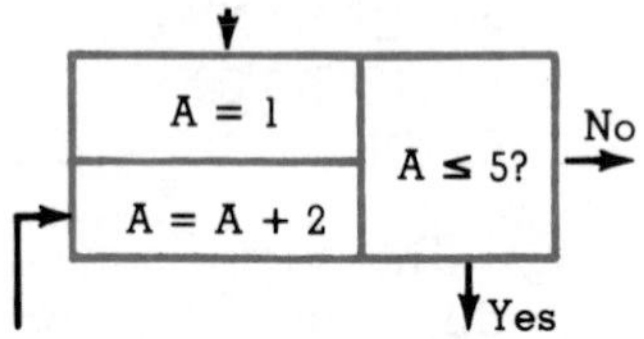

example

2 **Make a flow chart and write a program that prints the sum of the squares of the first 100 positive integers.**

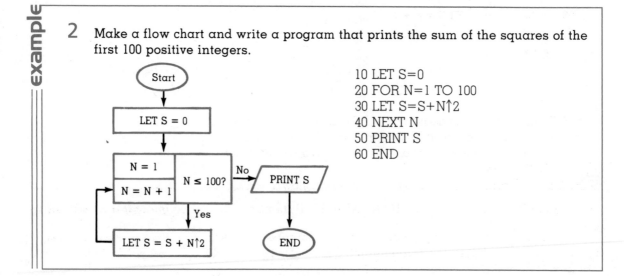

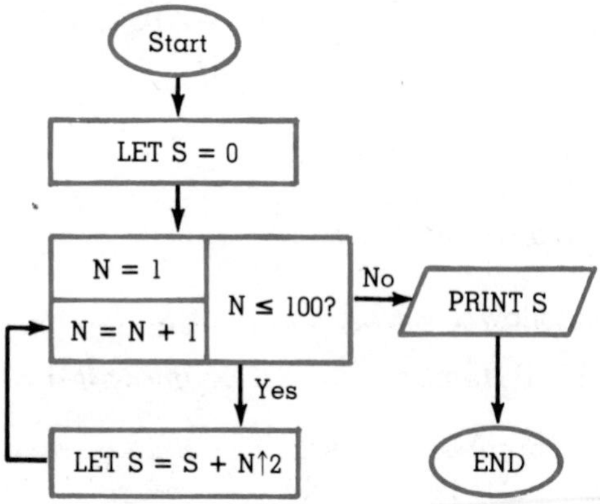


```
10 LET S=0
20 FOR N=1 TO 100
30 LET S=S+N↑2
40 NEXT N
50 PRINT S
60 END
```

An IF-THEN statement can be written in a FOR-NEXT loop. Consider the following example.

example

3 **Make a flow chart and write a program that will print a solution, if it exists, to the linear equation 9(x + 1) = 6(x − 2). The domain is all integers between ⁻10 and 10 inclusive.**

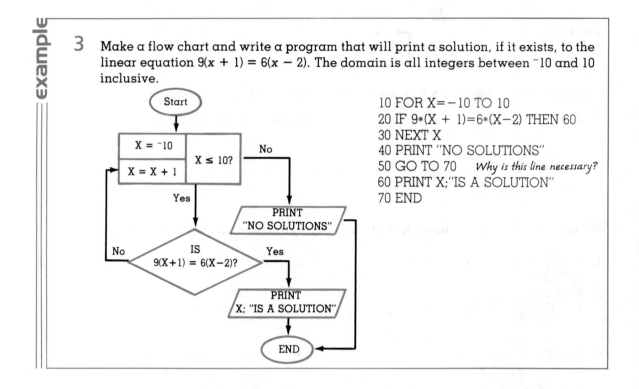

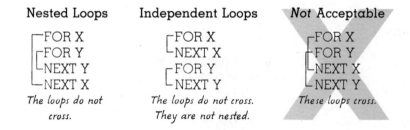

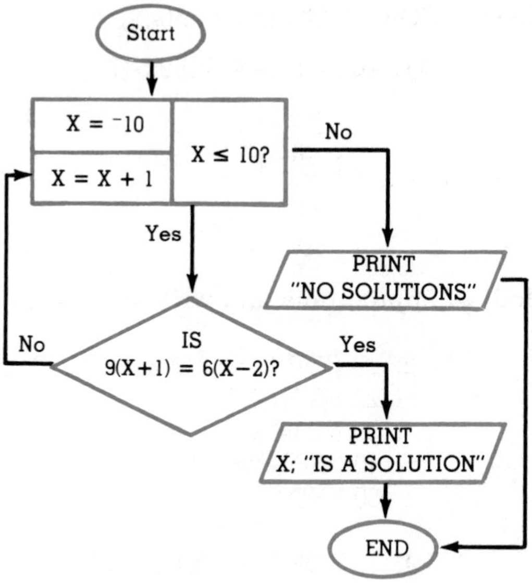


```
10 FOR X=−10 TO 10
20 IF 9*(X + 1)=6*(X−2) THEN 60
30 NEXT X
40 PRINT "NO SOLUTIONS"
50 GO TO 70
60 PRINT X;"IS A SOLUTION"
70 END
```

Why is this line necessary? (line 50)

More than one FOR-NEXT loop may occur in a program. There are only two ways that they can appear in a program.

Nested Loops	Independent Loops	Not Acceptable
FOR X FOR Y NEXT Y NEXT X	FOR X NEXT X FOR Y NEXT Y	FOR X FOR Y NEXT X NEXT Y
The loops do not cross.	*The loops do not cross. They are not nested.*	*These loops cross.*

exercises

Exploratory Write a FOR statement that assigns the numbers in each of the following lists to the variable X.

1. 1, 2, 3, 4, 5, 6, 7, 8
2. 0, 2, 4, 6, 8
3. ⁻12, ⁻10, ⁻8, . . . , 14
4. 0, 4, 8, 12, . . . , 48
5. 2.25, 2.5, 2.75, . . . , 18
6. ⁻5, ⁻3.5, ⁻2, . . . , 9

Write FOR-NEXT statements for each of the following iteration boxes.

7.

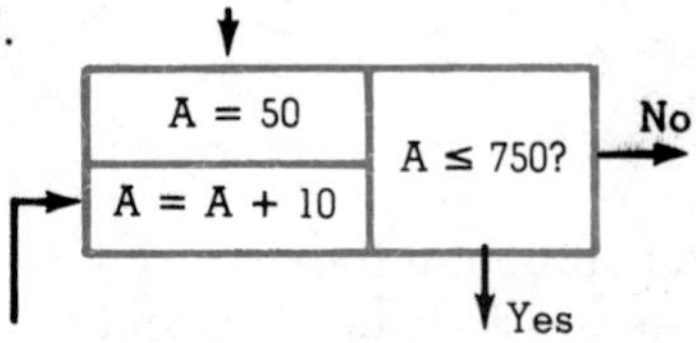

8.

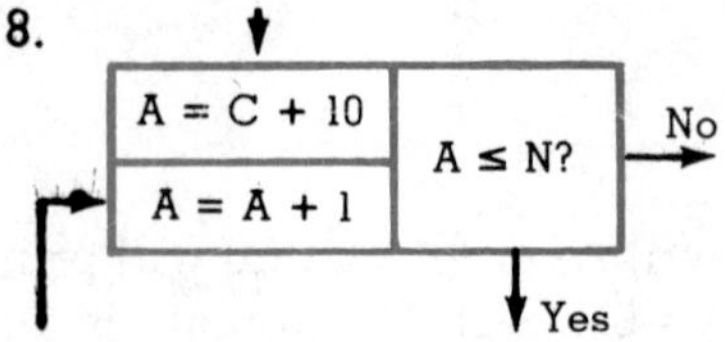

9.

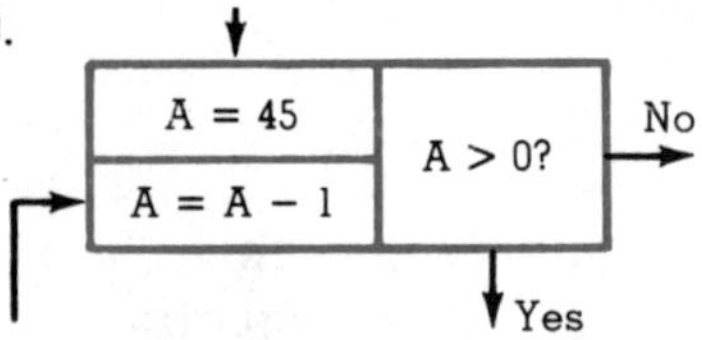

Make an iteration box for each of the following FOR-NEXT statements.

10.
```
10 FOR A=1 TO 75
   .
   .
   .
100 NEXT A
```

11.
```
40 FOR J=K TO 9 STEP 3
   .
   .
   .
80 NEXT J
```

Written Find the error(s) in each of the following programs and write a correct program.

1.
```
10 FOR X=1 TO -10
20 NEXT X
30 PRINT X
40 END
```

2.
```
10 FOR M=3 TO 25, STEP 2
20 PRINT M
30 NEXT M
40 PRINT M↑2;M↑.5
50 END
```

3.
```
10 LET X=3
20 FOR C=1 TO 5
30 PRINT C+X
40 NEXT X
50 END
```

4.
```
10 FOR X=1 TO 6 STEP 3
20 FOR Y=2 TO 4 STEP 2
30 PRINT X*Y
40 NEXT X
50 NEXT Y
60 END
```

Write the output of each program.

5.
```
10 LET S=0
20 FOR N=1 TO 4
30 LET S=S+N
40 PRINT S
50 NEXT N
60 END
```

6.
```
10 PRINT "X","Y"
20 FOR X=-2 TO 2
30 LET Y=X↑2+3*X-4
40 PRINT X,Y
50 NEXT X
60 END
```

7.
```
10 LET S=0
20 FOR X=1 TO 5 STEP 2
30 LET S=S+X
40 NEXT X
50 PRINT S
60 END
```

8.
```
10 READ A,B,C
20 FOR X=A TO B STEP C
30 LET Y=X↑2
40 PRINT "X=";X,"Y=";Y
50 NEXT X
60 DATA -2,2,1
70 END
```

Write a program in BASIC for each of the following flow charts.

9.

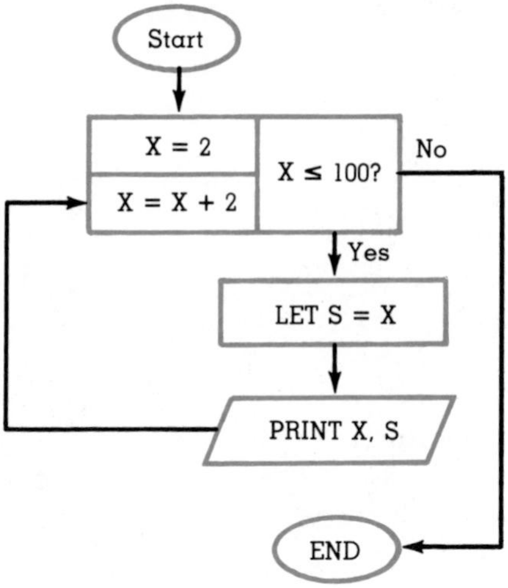

10.

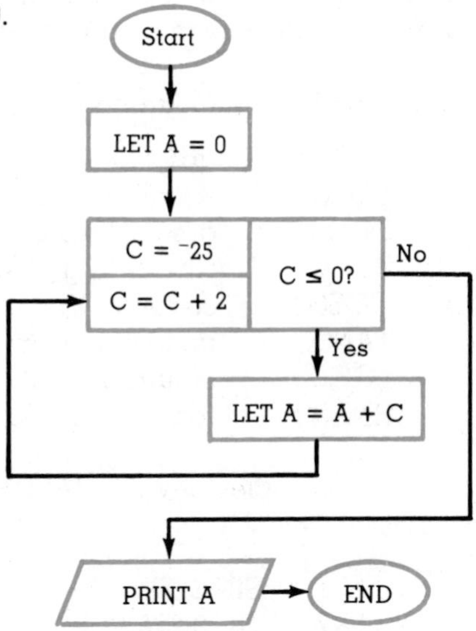

11.

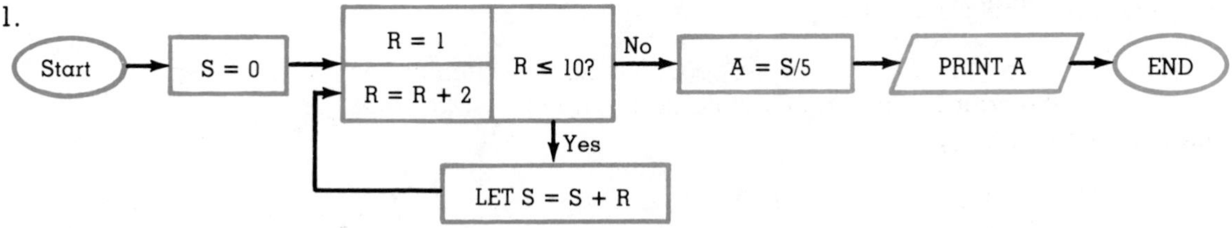

Make a flow chart for each of the following problems.

12. Find the squares and square roots of the first 100 positive integers.

13. Find the least integral value of x such that $3^x \geq 50{,}000$.

14. Find the value of y for $x = {}^-5$ to 5 if $y = x^2 + 5x + 6$.

15. Find all integers between $^-20$ and 20 that are solutions of $3x^2 + 20x \leq 3$.

16–19. Write a program in BASIC for problems **12–15**.

BASIC Functions and E Notation

BASIC functions are subprograms, stored in the computer, that may be used to simplify a program. For example, a programmer may need to find the absolute value of a number. Instead of writing a program to find the absolute value, a code can be used to have this done automatically by the computer.

Each BASIC function has an abbreviation and an argument. The argument is enclosed by parentheses and may be any BASIC expression. Some common functions are listed below.

Function	Meaning
ABS(X)	absolute value of X
SQR(X)	square root of X
INT(X)	greatest integer less than or equal to X
SIN(X)	sine of X, measured in radians
COS(X)	cosine of X, measured in radians
TAN(X)	tangent of X, measured in radians
LOG(X)	natural logarithm of X
RND(X)	random numbers between 0 and 1 are generated

Some examples of valid BASIC statements using these functions are listed below.

```
10 LET Y=SIN(2*X)
10 IF Z=SQR(X) THEN 90
10 FOR I=1 TO INT(A) STEP 4
10 PRINT ABS(Y)+LOG(3.2↑3)
```

Notice that the functions may be used in IF-THEN and FOR-NEXT statements.

However, these functions *cannot* appear in a READ statement or to the left of the equal sign in a LET statement. The following statements are invalid.

```
10 LET SIN(X)=SQR(1−COS(X)↑2)
10 READ TAN(P)
```

The INT(X) function is the greatest integer function. After reading or computing the value of X, it finds the greatest integer less than or equal to X. For example, INT(16.9) = 16 and INT(−7.6) = ⁻8.

example

1 **Write a program to find integers which are multiples of 4 from 1 to 100.**

```
10 FOR I=1 TO 100
20 IF INT(I/4)<>I/4 THEN 40
30 PRINT I
40 NEXT I
50 END
```

If INT(I/4)= I/4, then I/4 must be an integer. Therefore, 4 divides I evenly or I is a multiple of 4.

The RND(X) function generates six-digit decimal numbers greater than 0 and less than 1. The function can be used to simulate experiments such as tossing a coin or throwing dice.

The argument may be any number.

example

2 **Write a BASIC statement which will generate random integers from 1 to 6.**

Multiplying a decimal between 0 and 1 by six gives a number between 0.0 and 5.99999. If 1 is added, the number is between 1.0 and 6.99999. Taking the greatest integer gives a number between 1 and 6.

Thus, the statement PRINT INT(6*RND(X)+1) will give random integers from 1 to 6.

This could be used in a program that simulates the throw of a die.

In general, when random integers are to be chosen from a set containing A integers, with B the least one, the following statement can be used.

In some systems the RND(X) function generates random integers from 0 to X if X is a positive integer.

```
PRINT INT(A*RND(X)+B)
```

example

3 **Write a program to simulate the results of tossing a coin. Print the total number of heads and tails after one hundred tosses.**

Let heads occur when X has a value of 1 and tails when X has a value of 2.

```
10 LET H=0
20 LET T=0
30 FOR I=1 to 100
40 LET X=INT(2*RND(X)+1)        This statement generates the integers 1 or 2.
50 IF X=1 THEN 80
60 LET T=T+1                    This statement counts the tails.
70 GO TO 90
80 LET H=H+1                    This statement counts the heads
90 NEXT I
100 PRINT "NUMBER OF HEADS = ";H
110 PRINT "NUMBER OF TAILS = ";T
120 END
```

The output of a program in BASIC generally contains a maximum of six significant digits. When the output would be more than six significant digits, the computer will round off and shift to E notation. Several examples of E notation are given below.

E notation is the computer equivalent of scientific notation.

Number	Scientific Notation	E Notation
4,280,920,616	$4.280920616 \times 10^{9}$	4.28092E + 09
0.00000011945	1.1945×10^{-7}	1.1945E − 07
0.0000264280	2.64280×10^{-5}	2.64280E − 05

exercises

Exploratory Write each of the following using scientific notation.

1. 7,600,000
2. 0.001278123
3. 0.0000000005
4. 8,432,311,458,810
5. 0.0000001357
6. 300,527,201,864,088,600

7-12. Write each number in problems 1-6 in E notation.

Write the value of each expression without using scientific notation.

13. 6.20000E+10
14. 4.20315E−07
15. 7.28914E−05
16. 1.23150E+09
17. 9.15023E−06
18. 2.20222E+13

Written Write the output of each of the following PRINT statements.

1. PRINT INT(4.8)
2. PRINT INT(4.3-4.7)
3. PRINT ABS(−2)
4. PRINT SQR(49)
5. PRINT INT(10*RND(X)+2)
6. PRINT (12*RND(X)+28)

Write the output of each of the following PRINT statements if A = $^{-}3$, B = 16, C = 4.2, and D = 1.

7. PRINT ABS(B↑D)
8. PRINT INT(C)
9. PRINT SQR(B)−SQR(D)
10. PRINT INT(SQR(C))
11. PRINT 12*INT(C)
12. PRINT INT(ABS(A))

Find the error(s) in each expression or statement and write a correct expression or statement.

13. 20 LET X=SQR A
14. LOG(6*A)−ABS(TAN(B+C))
15. SQR(SINE(X)↑2+COS(X)↑2
16. 20 LET ABS(A)=−A
17. 20 LET X=INT(SQR(A+7)
18. 20 READ A,SQR(A)

Write each expression in BASIC. Use BASIC functions.

19. $|3x + 2|$
20. $\sqrt{4 + 9a}$
21. $\sqrt{|a + b|}$
22. $\sqrt{a^2 + b^2}$

Write an IF-THEN statement for each of the following.

23. If x is a multiple of 3, then go to 40.
24. If x is not an integer, then go to 30.
25. If a is even, then go to 60.
26. If a is a multiple of 5 and 6, then 45.
27. If a is not a multiple of 4, then 30.
28. If $x + y$ is not divisible by 5, then 90.

Write a program in BASIC for each of the following problems. Use BASIC functions.

29. Find the square root of a number if it exists. Print the number and its square root if it exists. If it does not exist, print the number and "NO REAL SQUARE ROOT."
30. Select five random integers from 1 to 100,000 as winning numbers for a local lottery.
31. Find the sum of the greatest integers of the square roots of integers from 1 to 10.
32. Find the greatest integer of the sum of the square roots of integers from 1 to 10.
33. Print an integer and state whether it is odd or even.
34. Print $\sin^2 x + \cos^2 x$ for values of x from 0 to 1 in increments of 0.05.

Subscripted Variables

Sometimes you may need to input and print a large amount of data. In this case, subscripted variables may be used. In BASIC, subscripted variables consist of a variable followed by a positive integer in parentheses. The integer may be represented by a variable or a BASIC expression.

Mathematical Notation	BASIC Notation
x_1	X(1)
a_{2k+1}	A(2*K+1)

example

1 **Write a program to print the scores 74, 78, 81, 85, 85, 90, 97, and 98 in reverse order.**

```
10 FOR I=1 to 8
20 READ S(I)
30 NEXT I
40 FOR I=8 to 1 STEP-1
50 PRINT S(I)
60 NEXT I
70 DATA 74,78,81,85,85,90,97,98
80 END
```

This loop stores the 8 scores. Thus, X(1)=74, X(2)=78, . . . , X(8)=98. (lines 10–30)

This loop prints the 8 scores in reverse order. (lines 40–60)

If the value of a subscript is greater than 10, the size of the list must be given. A dimension or DIM statement assigns storage space in the computer for the list. For example, the statement 10 DIM X(250) reserves 250 memory spaces in the computer for subscripted variables using X.

The number of values in a list may be less than the number shown in the DIM statement; however, it can never be greater.

example

2 **Determine the output of the following program.**

```
10 DIM X(13)
20 FOR I=1 TO 13
30 READ X(I)
40 NEXT I
50 LET S=1
60 FOR I=1 TO 13 STEP 3
70 LET S=S*X(I)
80 NEXT I
90 PRINT S
100 DATA 1,1,4,5,7,8,10,11,12,16,17,21,22
110 END
```

Values are assigned to the variables X(1),X(2),X(3), . . . ,X(13). (lines 20–40)

The product of certain variables is computed. (lines 60–80)

X(1) · X(4) · X(7) · X(10) · X(13) = 1 · 5 · 10 · 16 · 22 or 17,600

Thus, the output of the program is 17600.

example 3 Write a program which finds the average of 500 scores and then finds how far each score is from the average.

```
10 DIM N(500)
20 LET S=0
30 FOR I=1 to 500
40 READ N(I)
50 LET S=S+N(I)
60 NEXT I
70 LET A=S/500
80 PRINT "AVERAGE = ";A
90 FOR I=1 TO 500
100 IF N(I)<=A,THEN 130
110 PRINT "SCORE "; N(I);" IS";
115 PRINT N(I)-A; " POINTS ABOVE AVERAGE."
120 GO TO 140
130 PRINT "SCORE "; N(I);" IS";
135 PRINT A-N(I); " POINTS BELOW AVERAGE."
140 NEXT I
150 DATA . . .
160 DATA . . .
.
.
.
999 END
```

This loop assigns values to N(1), N(2), N(3), . . . , N(500). It also computes the sum of all the values. (lines 30–60)

This statement computes the average. (line 70)

This loop has the computer print each score and how far it is from the average. (lines 90–140)

The data would be listed in a series of DATA statements. (lines 150–160)

exercises

Exploratory State whether each of the following BASIC subscripted variables is acceptable. Write *yes* or *no*.

1. A 1)
2. 3(K)
3. X(1.7)
4. R3(29)
5. X(B)
6. A(INT(B/C))

Write a BASIC subscripted variable for each of the following.

7. X_4
8. a_x
9. X_{n+1}
10. K_{m+n}
11. q_{24}
12. Z_{i-1}

Find the error in each of the following DIM statements. Write a correct statement.

13. 10 DIM (40)
14. 10 DIM A1(50)
15. 10 DIM A,28

Write the necessary DIM statement.

16. $x_1, x_2, x_3, \ldots, x_{40}$
17. $a_{31}, a_{32}, a_{33}, \ldots, a_{60}$
18. x_n where $n = 1, 2, 3, \ldots, 28$

Written The first four lines of a program are given at the right. Use them to evaluate each of the following.

1. A(2)
2. A(5−1)
3. A(3)−1
4. 2*A(4)
5. A(1)/2
6. A(A(3))
7. 6+A(3)
8. A(6)−A(4)

```
10 DATA -4,16,2,8,-12,17
20 FOR R=1 TO 6
30 READ A(R)
40 NEXT R
```

Write a BASIC expression for each of the following.

9. $a_1 + (n - 1)d$
10. $\frac{n}{2}(a_1 + a_n)$
11. $a_1 r^{n-1}$
12. $\frac{a_1 - a_1 r^n}{1 - r}$
13. $f(x_1)(x_{i+1} - x_i)$
14. $\frac{Q_1 - Q_3}{2}$

Write the output of each of the following programs.

15.
```
10 FOR I=1 TO 7
20 READ X(I)
30 NEXT I
40 LET S=0
50 FOR I=1 TO 7 STEP 3
60 LET S=S+X(I)
70 NEXT I
80 PRINT S
90 DATA 20,61,36,62,97,12,45
100 END
```

16.
```
10 FOR I=1 TO 6
20 READ X(I)
30 NEXT I
40 FOR I=1 TO 6
50 LET D=7-I
60 PRINT X(D)
70 NEXT I
80 DATA 98,10,81,9,36,13
90 END
```

Write a program in BASIC for each flow chart.

17.

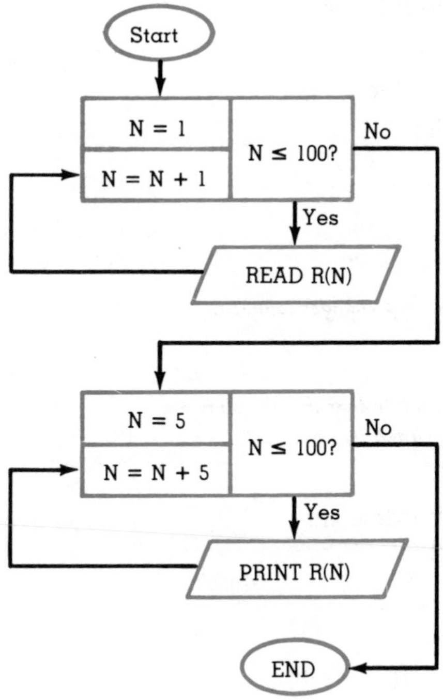

18.

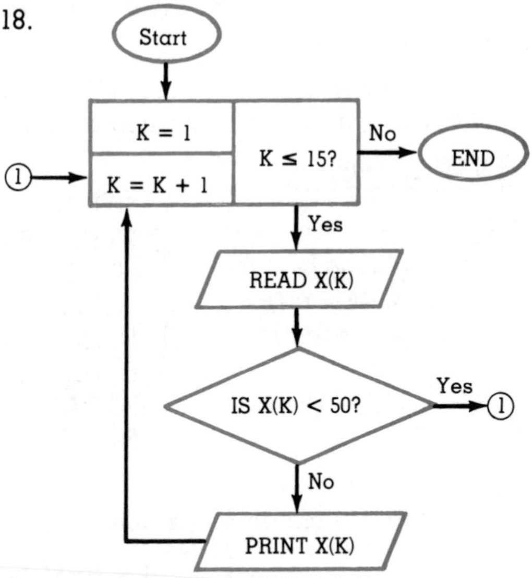

Write a program in BASIC for each of the following.

19. Rafael has grades of 76, 72, 74, 63, and 85 in history. Carlos has grades of 91, 78, 81, 83, and 98. Find the average of each boy's grades.

20. Stan's Used Cars is reducing the price of its cars by 25%. Find the average reduction in the prices of cars which originally cost \$6341, \$5578, \$4294, \$5677, \$4479, \$6002, \$5505, and \$7098.

21. Given a list of numbers in which an element may occur more than once, print a new list without duplications.

22. Determine if a ticket number is a winning ticket by checking a list of ten winning numbers.

Matrices

Subscripted variables can be used to identify elements of a matrix. Two subscripts separated by a comma are written inside the parentheses following the variable. The first subscript indicates the row and the second subscript indicates the column.

Consider the matrix, $A = \begin{bmatrix} 7 & 3 & 4 \\ 0 & 1 & 2 \end{bmatrix}$. In BASIC, the values of A(1, 2) and A(2, 1) would be 3 and 0, respectively.

The DIM statement for this matrix would be 10 DIM A(2, 3). As in arrays, the DIM statement is necessary only if either of the subscripts is greater than ten.

Suppose the above matrix is to be read and stored in the computer. This can be accomplished by using nested loops.

```
10 DIM A(2,3)
20 FOR R=1 TO 2
30 FOR C=1 TO 3
40 READ A(R,C)
50 NEXT C
60 NEXT R
70 DATA 7,3,4,0,1,2
80 END
```

This loop changes rows. In each row, the inner loop goes through a full cycle. (lines 20–60)

This loop changes columns. (lines 30–50)

Note that the elements are listed by rows.

Each square matrix has a determinant. The value of a determinant of a 2 × 2 matrix $\begin{bmatrix} a & b \\ c & d \end{bmatrix}$ is $ad - bc$.

$$\det \begin{bmatrix} a & b \\ c & d \end{bmatrix} \text{ or } \begin{vmatrix} a & b \\ c & d \end{vmatrix} = ad - bc$$

1 Write a program to find the value of the determinant of the matrix, $Z = \begin{bmatrix} 2 & 8 \\ 3 & 3 \end{bmatrix}$.

```
10 FOR R=1 TO 2
20 FOR C=1 TO 2
30 READ Z(R,C)
40 NEXT C
50 NEXT R
60 PRINT "DETERMINANT IS" Z(1,1)*Z(2,2)−Z(1,2)*Z(2,1)
65 DATA 2, 8, 3, 3
70 END
```

A BASIC program may be used to add matrices or multiply a matrix by a scalar. Consider the following examples.

2 Write a program to add A and B if $A = \begin{bmatrix} 7 & 2 & 1 & 3 \\ 9 & 1 & 4 & 5 \\ 0 & 8 & 1 & 9 \end{bmatrix}$ and $B = \begin{bmatrix} 1 & 8 & 3 & 5 \\ 2 & 1 & 4 & 6 \\ 1 & 0 & 9 & 7 \end{bmatrix}$.

Then show the output of the program.

```
10 DIM A(3,4),B(3,4)        This statement may be omitted in this case.
20 FOR R=1 TO 3
30 FOR C=1 TO 4
40 READ A(R,C)              These loops read and store the elements
50 NEXT C                   of matrix A.
60 NEXT R
70 FOR R=1 TO 3
80 FOR C=1 TO 4
90 READ B(R,C)              These loops read and store the elements
100 PRINT A(R,C)+B(R,C);    of matrix B. Then the sum of corresponding
110 NEXT C                  elements is computed and printed.
120 PRINT
130 NEXT R                  Line 120 causes the matrix to be printed row by row.
140 DATA 7,2,1,3,9,1,4,5,0,8,1,9
150 DATA 1,8,3,5,2,1,4,6,1,0,9,7
160 END
RUN
8    10    4    8

11    2    8    11

1    8    10    16
```

example

3 Make a flow chart and write a program to multiply an 18 × 32 matrix, X, by a scalar, M.

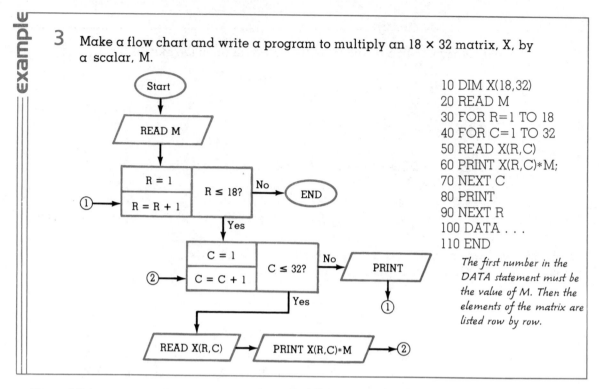

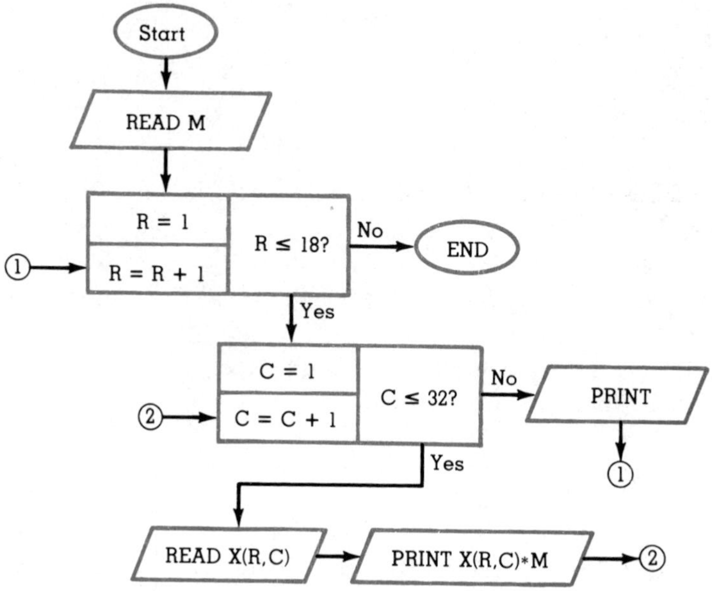


```
10 DIM X(18,32)
20 READ M
30 FOR R=1 TO 18
40 FOR C=1 TO 32
50 READ X(R,C)
60 PRINT X(R,C)*M;
70 NEXT C
80 PRINT
90 NEXT R
100 DATA . . .
110 END
```

The first number in the DATA statement must be the value of M. Then the elements of the matrix are listed row by row.

The additive inverse of a matrix is found by multiplying a matrix by the scalar ⁻1. The additive inverse is used when subtracting matrices.

example

4 Write a program to find A − B if $A = \begin{bmatrix} ^-3 & 6 & ^-9 \\ 4 & ^-3 & 0 \\ 8 & ^-2 & 7 \end{bmatrix}$ and $B = \begin{bmatrix} 1 & 5 & 7 \\ ^-11 & 13 & ^-8 \\ 0 & ^-2 & 4 \end{bmatrix}$.

```
10 FOR R=1 TO 3
20 FOR C=1 TO 3
30 READ A(R,C)
40 NEXT C
50 NEXT R
60 FOR R=1 TO 3
70 FOR C=1 TO 3
80 READ B(R,C)
90 PRINT A(R,C)+(⁻1)*B(R,C);
100 NEXT C
110 PRINT
120 NEXT R
130 DATA ⁻3,6,⁻9,4,⁻3,0,8,⁻2,7
140 DATA 1,5,7,⁻11,13,⁻8,0,⁻2,4
150 END
```

exercises

Exploratory   Write a BASIC subscripted variable for each of the following.

1. $x_{1,3}$
2. $y_{a,r}$
3. $x_{a-1,a+1}$
4. $m_{2x,2y}$
5. $c_{11,7}$
6. $x_{a+1,n}$

Write a BASIC subscripted variable to name each of the following elements in matrix A given on the right.

7. 7
8. ‾6
9. ‾3
10. 2
11. 6
12. ‾14

$$A = \begin{bmatrix} ^-3 & 6 & ^-6 \\ 8 & ^-14 & 7 \\ 0 & 9 & 2 \end{bmatrix}$$

Written   Write the output when the following statements are added to the program given at the right.

1. 40 PRINT X(R,C);
2. 40 PRINT X(R,C);
   55 PRINT
3. 40 PRINT X(R,C)

```
10 FOR R=1 TO 3
20 FOR C=1 TO 4
30 READ X(R,C)
50 NEXT C
60 NEXT R
70 DATA 3,0,5,2,7,2,0,1,8,6,4,8
80 END
```

4. Write the DATA statements for the program at the right so that matrix A will be stored correctly.

$$A = \begin{bmatrix} 4 & 6 & 4 & ^-7 \\ 11 & ^-4 & 6 & 0 \\ ^-2 & 2 & 8 & ^-3 \\ 16 & 5 & 0 & 1 \end{bmatrix}$$

```
10 DIM A(4,4)
20 READ M,N
30 FOR R=1 TO M
40 FOR C=1 TO N
50 READ A(R,C)
60 NEXT C
70 NEXT R
80 DATA . . .
90 END
```

Let $A = \begin{bmatrix} 1 & 3 \\ ^-2 & 2 \end{bmatrix}$, $B = \begin{bmatrix} ^-7 & 9 \\ 0 & 2 \end{bmatrix}$, and $C = \begin{bmatrix} 4 & 7 \\ 6 & ^-1 \end{bmatrix}$. Write a program in BASIC to find each of the following.

5. $3B$
6. $A + C$
7. $B - 3C$
8. A^2
9. $C + (^-C)$
10. $(A - C)^2$

Write a program in BASIC to solve each of the following.

11. Given two matrices, find their sum if possible. If not possible, print "CANNOT BE ADDED."

12. Reverse the rows and columns of a given matrix. The first row becomes the first column, the second row becomes the second column, and so on.

13. Print two given matrices side-by-side and then print their sum.

14. Find the largest element in a given matrix. Print the element and its row and column indices.

Computer Programming Exercises

The following section provides a variety of problems that are to be solved by computer programs. The BASIC programming techniques in the previous lessons are to be used when writing the computer programs. The problems are listed by chapter for easy reference.

Most of the problems do not have specific data. In these problems a blank DATA statement must be inserted in the program. Before the program is run, data must be inserted in the DATA statement(s). If specific data is given, the problem is to be solved using this data only.

All programs must label the output with appropriate headings.

Chapter 1 Linear Relations and Functions

1. Find the zero of the function, $f(x) = mx + b$, given values of m and b.
2. Find the values of x for which $ax + b < c$ given values of a, b, and c.
3. Given two points, P and Q, in the coordinate plane, find the slope of the line through the two points, if defined, or state that the slope is undefined.
4. Find the perimeter of a triangle that has vertices (a,b), (c,d), and (e,f).

A linear equation of the form $ax + by + c = 0$ is given. Assume that a and b are rational numbers that are *not* both zero.

5. Find the slope of the graph of the equation if it exists.
6. Determine whether a given point $P(r,s)$ lies on the graph of the equation.
7. Given the coordinates of a point (a,b) determine whether the point lies in the solution set of the following system of inequalities.
$$x + y \le 5$$
$$y - x \le 5$$
$$y \ge {}^-10$$
8. Find the minimum and maximum values of the function $f(x,y) = \frac{1}{2}x + 3y$ defined for the polygonal convex set having vertices (a,b), (c,d), (e,f), and (g,h).

Chapter 2 Theory of Equations

1. Evaluate $f(x) = x^4 - x^3 + x^2 - x + 1$ for integral values of x from $^-6$ to 6 inclusive.
2. Find the discriminant of $ax^2 + bx + c$ given a, b, and c.
3. Find the square roots, real or imaginary, of any real number R.
4. A quadratic equation of the form $ax^2 + bx + c = 0$ is given. Determine if r is a root by using substitution for integral values of r from $^-20$ to 20 inclusive.

5. Determine if an equation of the form $ax^2 + bx + c$ has real roots.

6. Use the Factor Theorem to find factors of the polynomial $P(x) = ax^3 + bx^2 + cx + d$.

7. Find the integers which are factors of x given that x is an integer.

8. Use the Rational Root Theorem to find all possible rational roots of the equation $ax^3 + bx^2 + cx + d = 0$ given that a, b, c, and d are integers.

9. Given the degree and coefficients of a polynomial, use Descarte's Rule of Signs to find the number of possible positive real zeros and negative real zeros.

10. Approximate to the nearest hundredth the positive real zero(s) of the function $f(x) = 2x^3 - 4x^2 - 3$.

Chapter 3 Matrices and Vectors

1. Evaluate the determinant of a third order matrix.

2. Given a third order matrix, find its additive inverse.

3. Use Cramer's rule to solve the following system of equations.

$$3x - y = 3$$
$$6x + 5y = {}^{-}1$$

4. Given a second order matrix, find its multiplicative inverse if it exists.

5. Find the ordered pair which represents $\overrightarrow{AB}$ given $A(p,q)$ and $B(r,s)$.

6. Find the magnitude of the vector from $A(p,q)$ to $B(r,s)$.

7. Find the inner product of $\vec{a}$ and $\vec{b}$ if $\vec{a} = (p,q)$ and $\vec{b} = (r,s)$.

8. Find the cross product of $\vec{a}$ and $\vec{b}$ if $\vec{a} = (l,m,n)$ and $\vec{b} = (r,s,t)$.

Chapter 4 The Circular Functions

1. A real number s is given. Determine in which quadrant or on which axis the arc measured by s on the unit circle terminates.

2. Given $\sin x$, find $\cos x$, $\tan x$, $\cot x$, $\sec x$, and $\csc x$. Assume that the arc measured by x on the unit circle terminates in the third quadrant.

Use the double and half number formulas to solve each of the following.

3. Given $\cos s = 0.6$ and the arc measured by s terminates in the first quadrant, find $\sin 2s$.

4. Given $\sin s = 0.8$ and the arc measured by s terminates in the second quadrant, find $\cos 2s$.

5. Given $\cos s = 0.2$ and the arc measured by s terminates in the fourth quadrant, find $\sin \frac{s}{2}$.

6. Given $\cos s = {}^{-}0.3333$ and the arc measured by s terminates in the third quadrant, find $\cos \frac{s}{2}$.

Chapter 5 The Trigonometric Functions

1. Given the lengths of the hypotenuse and one leg of a right triangle, find the values of the six trigonometric functions of each acute angle of the triangle.
2. Given the degree measure of an angle in standard position, determine the quadrant in which the terminal side of the angle lies or if the terminal side lies on an axis, which part of which axis.
3. Find the values of the six trigonometric functions of α if the point (x,y) lies on the terminal side of an angle with measure α.
4. If $\tan \theta = x$, find the values of the other trigonometric functions of θ. Assume θ is between 0° and 90°.
5. Make a table of the degree measures of angles given their radian measures in increments of 0.01 from 0 to 2.
6. Given the degree measure of an angle, find the measure of its reference angle.

Chapter 6 Graphs and Inverses of the Trigonometric Functions

1. Find the amplitude of the function $y = A \cos \theta$ for integer values of A from $^-4$ to 4 inclusive.
2. Find the period of the function $y = \sin k\theta$ for integer values of k from 1 to 5 inclusive.
3. Find the phase shift of the function $y = \tan(k\theta + c)$ given the values of k and c. Determine if the shift is to the left or right.
4. Find the amplitude, period, and phase shift of the function $y = A \sin(k\theta + c)$ given values of A, k, and c.

The Arctangent of an angle may be found in BASIC using the internal function, ATN(X). The answer is in radians. Use this function to evaluate each of the following.

5. $\sin[\arctan(^-\sqrt{3})]$
6. $\cos\left(2 \tan^{-1} \dfrac{3}{5}\right)$

Chapter 7 Applications of Trigonometry

Use the ATN function as described for problems 5-6 of Chapter 6 to solve each equation for principal values of x.

1. $\tan^2 x - 1 = 0$
2. $\tan^2 x - 3 \tan x + 2 = 0$

Suppose $\triangle ABC$ is a right triangle. Let A and B be the acute angles, and a and b be the measures of the sides opposite these angles. The measure of the hypotenuse is c. Solve the triangle given each of the following.

3. The measures of b and angle A
4. The measures of a and angle B
5. The measures of a and c
6. The measures of c and angle A

7. Given the measures of two sides of a triangle and an angle not included between them, determine the number of possible triangles.

8. If the information in problem 7 determines at least one triangle, solve the triangle(s).

Given each of the following parts of a nonright triangle, solve each triangle. Use the Law of Sines and/or Law of Cosines.

9. The measures of two angles and their included side.

10. The measures of two angles and a side not included between them.

11. The measures of the triangle(s) sides.

12. The measures of two sides and their included angle.

Find the area of a triangle given each of the following.

13. The measures of two sides and the included angle.

14. The measures of the sides. (Use Hero's formula.)

An airplane is heading due west at a given speed.

15. The wind blows from the north at a given speed. Find the ground speed and direction of the plane.

16. The wind blows from the southwest at a given speed. Find the ground speed and direction of the plane.

Chapter 8 Sequences and Series

Let a be the first term of an arithmetic sequence, d be the common difference, and n be a positive integer.

1. Find the nth term of the sequence.

2. Find the sum of the first n terms of the sequence.

3. Given two real numbers, a and b, find three arithmetic means between a and b.

4. Given two real numbers, a and b, find three geometric means between a and b.

Let a be the first term of a geometric sequence, r the common ratio, and n a positive integer.

5. Find the nth term of the sequence.

6. Find the sum of the first n terms of the sequence.

7. Find the least integral value of n such that $1 + \frac{1}{2} + \frac{1}{3} + \frac{1}{4} + \cdots \frac{1}{n} > 4$.

8. Find the sum of the series $1 + 2 + 4 + 8 + \cdots + 2^n$ for any positive integer, n.

9. Generate the numbers in Pascal's triangle up to row 10.

10. Find the sum of the first ten terms of $1 - \frac{1}{2!} + \frac{1}{4!} - \frac{1}{6!} + \cdots$.

11. Estimate $\sin x$ for 10 to 40 terms in steps of 2 using the following series.

$$\sin x = x - \frac{x^3}{3!} + \frac{x^5}{5!} - \frac{x^7}{7!} + \cdots + \frac{x^n}{n!}$$

(x is in radians)

12. Estimate $\cos x$ for 10 to 40 terms in steps of 2 using the following series.

$$\cos x = 1 - \frac{x^2}{2!} + \frac{x^4}{4!} - \frac{x^6}{6!} + \cdots + \frac{x^n}{n!}$$

(x is in radians)

Chapter 9 Polar Coordinates and Complex Numbers

1. Given the polar coordinates of a point, find its rectangular coordinates.
2. Given the rectangular coordinates of a point, find its polar coordinates. (Use the ATN function as described for problems 5-6 of Chapter 6.)
3. Change the polar equation $r = \sin\theta + \cos\theta$ to an equation in rectangular coordinates.
4. Change the equation $x^2 + y^2 = r^2$ into an equation in polar coordinates.
5. Given two complex numbers $a + bi$ and $c + di$, find their sum.
6. Given two complex numbers $a + bi$ and $c + di$, find their product.

Given a complex number $a + bi$ find each of the following.

7. conjugate of $a + bi$
8. amplitude of $a + bi$
9. modulus of $a + bi$
10. polar form of $a + bi$
11. Given two complex numbers in polar form, find their product.
12. Use DeMoivre's Theorem to find the nth roots of a complex number.

Chapter 10 Exponential and Logarithmic Functions

1. Find logarithms of n to the base eight for $n = 1, 2, 3, \ldots 50$.
2. Given a real number x such that $1 < x < 10^9$, print x and the characteristic of its common logarithm.
3. Estimate the value of e by evaluating $(1 + x)^{\frac{1}{x}}$ for values of x close to 0. Let $x = 1, 0.1, 0.01, 0.001, 0.0001$, and 0.00001.
4. Find which value is larger, e^{π} or π^{e}.
5. The formula for the amount of money accumulated, A, on an investment, P, deposited for t years at r% interest rate, and compounded n times annually is $A = P\left(1 + \frac{r}{n}\right)^{nt}$. Find the amount of interest earned on \$2500 for 5 years at interest rates of 5.5%, 5.75%, 6.00%, . . . , 12% compounded quarterly.
6. When the interest is compounded continuously, the formula in problem 5 becomes $A = Pe^{rt}$ where e is approximately 2.718. If \$1000 is deposited in a savings account at an interest rate of 6% compounded continuously, when will the money be double the original amount?
7. A radioactive substance decays according to the equation, $A = A_o \times 10^{-0.024t}$ where t is in hours. Find the half life of the substance (when $A = 0.5A_o$).
8. A piece of machinery valued at \$50,000 depreciates 10% per year. The value at the end of n years is $V(n) = 50{,}000 \times 0.9^n$. Make a table which shows the value of the machine after 1 to 20 years for each year.

Chapter 11 The Straight Line

A linear equation of the form $Ax + By + C = 0$ is given. Assume that A and B are rational numbers that are *not* both zero.

1. Find the slope of the graph of the equation.
2. Find the y-intercept of the graph of the equation.

Two linear equations, $ax + by = c$ and $dx + ey = f$, are given.

3. Determine if the graphs of the equations are parallel.
4. Determine if the graphs of the equations are perpendicular.
5. Find the angle from the first line to the second line.
6. Make a table of ordered pairs of $ax + by = c$ if a and b are constant and c varies from $^{-}20$ to 20.
7. Find the distance d from a point $P(r, s)$ to a line $Ax + By + C = 0$.

Chapter 12 Conics

1. Find the center and radius of a circle given by the equation $Ax^2 + Cy^2 + Dx + Ey + F = 0$.
2. Find the center and radius of a circle given by the equation $Ax^2 + Cy^2 + F = 0$.

The equation of a parabola with directrix parallel to the x-axis is $(x - h)^2 = 4p(y - k)$.

3. Find the coordinates of the vertex of the parabola.
4. Find the coordinates of the focus.

The standard form of the equation of a hyperbola with center (h, k) and transverse axis of length $2a$, parallel to the x-axis, is $\frac{(x - h)^2}{a^2} - \frac{(y - k)^2}{b^2} = 1$.

5. Find the coordinates of the foci.
6. Find the length of the latus rectum.

Find the point(s) of intersection of a conic section with each of the following equations and the circle $x^2 + y^2 = r^2$.

7. $ax^2 + bx + c = y$
8. $\frac{x^2}{a^2} - \frac{y^2}{b^2} = 1$
9. $(x - h)^2 + (y - k)^2 = s^2$

Chapter 13 Probability

1. How many different ways can n charms be put on a charm bracelet with no clasp?
2. How many different 13-card hands can be dealt from a standard deck of cards?
3. Simulate the tossing of six coins 1000 times and count the number of heads and tails for each coin.
4. Simulate the throwing of a die 1000 times. Count the number of times each number shows.

5. Simulate the throwing of 2 dice for 1000 times. Count the number of times that the sum is 7 or 11.

6. Find the probability of a number between 2 and 100 being a prime number.

7. Suppose n persons are chosen at random from a certain population. Find the probability that two of them have the same birthday if n varies from 10 to 30.

8. Simulate the dealing of four five-card hands from a standard deck of cards.

Chapter 14 **Statistics**

Andy bowls three games every Tuesday for 10 weeks. Given his scores of the three games each Tuesday, solve each problem.

1. Find the arithmetic mean of his scores each Tuesday.
2. Find the arithmetic mean of all thirty scores.
3. Make an array of the thirty scores from lowest to highest.
4. Find the mode(s) (if any) of the thirty scores.
5. Find the harmonic mean of the thirty scores.
6. Find the quadratic mean of the thirty scores.
7. Find the mean deviation of the thirty scores.
8. Find the median of the thirty scores.
9. Find the semi-interquartile range of the thirty scores.
10. Find the standard deviation of the thirty scores.
11. Print a frequency distribution of the thirty scores. Use an appropriate class width.

Chapter 15 **Limits, Derivatives, and Integrals**

1. Determine the limit of $\dfrac{x^2 - 4}{x - 2}$ as x approaches 2 by finding $\dfrac{x^2 - 4}{x - 2}$ for $x = 1$, 1.5, 1.75, 1.875, . . . until the difference between successive values is less than 0.0001.

2. Determine the limit of $\dfrac{\sin x}{x}$ as x approaches zero by finding $\dfrac{\sin x}{x}$ for $x = 1$, 0.5, 0.25, . . . until the difference between successive values is less than 0.0005.

3. Given a polynomial P, find the first derivative of the function determined by P.

4. Find the slope of the secant line intersecting the graph of $f(x) = x^2 + 2x + 1$ at $(a, f(a))$ and $(a + h, f(a + h))$ as h varies from 3 to 0 in steps of 0.1.

5. Given a polynomial of the form $ax^3 + bx^2 + cx + d$, find the critical point(s) (if any) and determine whether each is a maximum or minimum.

6. Find the area under the curve $y = x^2$ from $x = 0$ to $x = 1$ by finding the limit of the area of N rectangles under the curve.

SYMBOLS

$=$	is equal to
$\neq$	is not equal to
$<$	is less than
$\leq$	is less than or equal to
$>$	is greater than
$\geq$	is greater than or equal to
$\approx$	is approximately equal to
$\{\ \}$	set notation
$\pm$	plus or minus
$\mp$	minus or plus
$f(x)$	f of x or the value of function f at x
$f'(x)$	f prime of x or the derivative of f at x
$f''(x)$	the second derivative of $f(x)$
$f \circ g$ or $f(g(x))$	composite of functions f and g
$\lim\limits_{x \to a}$	the limit as x approaches a
$\triangle ABC$	triangle ABC
$\overset{\frown}{RTS}$	arc RTS
$\angle ABC$	angle ABC
$m\angle ABC$	measure of angle ABC
AB	measure of line segment AB
$\overline{AB}$	line segment AB
$\|n\|$	the absolute value of n
x^n	the nth power of x
$\sqrt{x}$	the square root of x
$\sqrt[n]{x}$ or $x^{\frac{1}{n}}$	the nth root of x
$[x]$	greatest integer not greater than x
A^{-1}	inverse of A
a_{ij}	the element in the ith row and the jth column
$\begin{vmatrix} a_1 & b_1 \\ a_2 & b_2 \end{vmatrix}$	the determinant $a_1b_2 - a_2b_1$

$\vec{v}$ or $\overrightarrow{AB}$	a vector or directed line segment
$\|\vec{v}\|$	magnitude of the vector v
$\vec{a} \cdot \vec{b}$	inner product or dot product of vectors a and b
$\vec{a} \times \vec{b}$	cross product of vectors a and b
$\sin^{-1}x$	arcsin x
∞	infinity
i	$\sqrt{-1}$
e	base of natural logarithms; ≈ 2.718
$n!$	n factorial
$\ln x$	logarithm of x to the base e; natural logarithm
$\log_a x$	logarithm of x to the base a
$\log x$	logarithm of x to the base 10
$P(n, r)$	permutation of n objects, taken r at a time
$C(n, r)$	combination of n objects, taken r at a time
$\overline{X}$	X bar or arithmetic mean
M_d	median
$\sigma_{\overline{X}}$	standard error of the mean
$\tilde{X}$	X tilde
$\frac{dy}{dx}$	the derivative of y with respect to x
$\int$	integral
α	alpha
β	beta
Δ or δ	delta
ϵ	epsilon
θ	theta
λ	lambda
π	pi
σ	sigma; standard deviation
Σ	sigma; summation symbol
ϕ	phi

Squares and Square Roots

n	n^2	$\sqrt{n}$	$\sqrt{10n}$
1.0	1.00	1.000	3.162
1.1	1.21	1.049	3.317
1.2	1.44	1.095	3.464
1.3	1.69	1.140	3.606
1.4	1.96	1.183	3.742
1.5	2.25	1.225	3.873
1.6	2.56	1.265	4.000
1.7	2.89	1.304	4.123
1.8	3.24	1.342	4.243
1.9	3.61	1.378	4.359
2.0	4.00	1.414	4.472
2.1	4.41	1.449	4.583
2.2	4.84	1.483	4.690
2.3	5.29	1.517	4.796
2.4	5.76	1.549	4.899
2.5	6.25	1.581	5.000
2.6	6.76	1.612	5.099
2.7	7.29	1.643	5.196
2.8	7.84	1.673	5.292
2.9	8.41	1.703	5.385
3.0	9.00	1.732	5.477
3.1	9.61	1.761	5.568
3.2	10.24	1.789	5.657
3.3	10.89	1.817	5.745
3.4	11.56	1.844	5.831
3.5	12.25	1.871	5.916
3.6	12.96	1.897	6.000
3.7	13.69	1.924	6.083
3.8	14.44	1.949	6.164
3.9	15.21	1.975	6.245
4.0	16.00	2.000	6.325
4.1	16.81	2.025	6.403
4.2	17.64	2.049	6.481
4.3	18.49	2.074	6.557
4.4	19.36	2.098	6.633
4.5	20.25	2.121	6.708
4.6	21.16	2.145	6.782
4.7	22.09	2.168	6.856
4.8	23.04	2.191	6.928
4.9	24.01	2.214	7.000
5.0	25.00	2.236	7.071
5.1	26.01	2.258	7.141
5.2	27.04	2.280	7.211
5.3	28.09	2.302	7.280
5.4	29.16	2.324	7.348

n	n^2	$\sqrt{n}$	$\sqrt{10n}$
5.5	30.25	2.345	7.416
5.6	31.36	2.366	7.483
5.7	32.49	2.387	7.550
5.8	33.64	2.408	7.616
5.9	34.81	2.429	7.681
6.0	36.00	2.449	7.746
6.1	37.21	2.470	7.810
6.2	38.44	2.490	7.874
6.3	39.69	2.510	7.937
6.4	40.96	2.530	8.000
6.5	42.25	2.550	8.062
6.6	43.56	2.569	8.124
6.7	44.89	2.588	8.185
6.8	46.24	2.608	8.246
6.9	47.61	2.627	8.307
7.0	49.00	2.646	8.367
7.1	50.41	2.665	8.426
7.2	51.84	2.683	8.485
7.3	53.29	2.702	8.544
7.4	54.76	2.720	8.602
7.5	56.25	2.739	8.660
7.6	57.76	2.757	8.718
7.7	59.29	2.775	8.775
7.8	60.84	2.793	8.832
7.9	62.41	2.811	8.888
8.0	64.00	2.828	8.944
8.1	65.61	2.846	9.000
8.2	67.24	2.864	9.055
8.3	68.89	2.881	9.110
8.4	70.56	2.898	9.165
8.5	72.25	2.915	9.220
8.6	73.96	2.933	9.274
8.7	75.69	2.950	9.327
8.8	77.44	2.966	9.381
8.9	79.21	2.983	9.434
9.0	81.00	3.000	9.487
9.1	82.81	3.017	9.539
9.2	84.64	3.033	9.592
9.3	86.49	3.050	9.644
9.4	88.36	3.066	9.695
9.5	90.25	3.082	9.747
9.6	92.16	3.098	9.798
9.7	94.09	3.114	9.849
9.8	96.04	3.130	9.899
9.9	98.01	3.146	9.950

Values of Trigonometric Functions

Angle	Radians	Sin	Cos	Tan	Cot	Sec	Csc		
0°00′	0.0000	0.0000	1.0000	0.0000	—	1.000	—	1.5708	90°00′
10′	0.0029	0.0029	1.0000	0.0029	343.8	1.000	343.8	1.5679	50′
20′	0.0058	0.0058	1.0000	0.0058	171.9	1.000	171.9	1.5650	40′
30′	0.0087	0.0087	1.0000	0.0087	114.6	1.000	114.6	1.5621	30′
40′	0.0116	0.0116	0.9999	0.0116	85.94	1.000	85.95	1.5592	20′
50′	0.0145	0.0145	0.9999	0.0145	68.75	1.000	68.76	1.5563	10′
1°00′	0.0175	0.0175	0.9998	0.0175	57.29	1.000	57.30	1.5533	89°00′
10′	0.0204	0.0204	0.9998	0.0204	49.10	1.000	49.11	1.5504	50′
20′	0.0233	0.0233	0.9997	0.0233	42.96	1.000	42.98	1.5475	40′
30′	0.0262	0.0262	0.9997	0.0262	38.19	1.000	38.20	1.5446	30′
40′	0.0291	0.0291	0.9996	0.0291	34.37	1.000	34.38	1.5417	20′
50′	0.0320	0.0320	0.9995	0.0320	31.24	1.001	31.26	1.5388	10′
2°00′	0.0349	0.0349	0.9994	0.0349	28.64	1.001	28.65	1.5359	88°00′
10′	0.0378	0.0378	0.9993	0.0378	26.43	1.001	26.45	1.5330	50′
20′	0.0407	0.0407	0.9992	0.0407	24.54	1.001	24.56	1.5301	40′
30′	0.0436	0.0436	0.9990	0.0437	22.90	1.001	22.93	1.5272	30′
40′	0.0465	0.0465	0.9989	0.0466	21.47	1.001	21.49	1.5243	20′
50′	0.0495	0.0494	0.9988	0.0495	20.21	1.001	20.23	1.5213	10′
3°00′	0.0524	0.0523	0.9986	0.0524	19.08	1.001	19.11	1.5184	87°00′
10′	0.0553	0.0552	0.9985	0.0553	18.07	1.002	18.10	1.5155	50′
20′	0.0582	0.0581	0.9983	0.0582	17.17	1.002	17.20	1.5126	40′
30′	0.0611	0.0610	0.9981	0.0612	16.35	1.002	16.38	1.5097	30′
40′	0.0640	0.0640	0.9980	0.0641	15.60	1.002	15.64	1.5068	20′
50′	0.0669	0.0669	0.9978	0.0670	14.92	1.002	14.96	1.5039	10′
4°00′	0.0698	0.0698	0.9976	0.0699	14.30	1.002	14.34	1.5010	86°00′
10′	0.0727	0.0727	0.9974	0.0729	13.73	1.003	13.76	1.4981	50′
20′	0.0756	0.0756	0.9971	0.0758	13.20	1.003	13.23	1.4952	40′
30′	0.0785	0.0785	0.9969	0.0787	12.71	1.003	12.75	1.4923	30′
40′	0.0814	0.0814	0.9967	0.0816	12.25	1.003	12.29	1.4893	20′
50′	0.0844	0.0843	0.9964	0.0846	11.83	1.004	11.87	1.4864	10′
5°00′	0.0873	0.0872	0.9962	0.0875	11.43	1.004	11.47	1.4835	85°00′
10′	0.0902	0.0901	0.9959	0.0904	11.06	1.004	11.10	1.4806	50′
20′	0.0931	0.0929	0.9957	0.0934	10.71	1.004	10.76	1.4777	40′
30′	0.0960	0.0958	0.9954	0.0963	10.39	1.005	10.43	1.4748	30′
40′	0.0989	0.0987	0.9951	0.0992	10.08	1.005	10.13	1.4719	20′
50′	0.1018	0.1016	0.9948	0.1022	9.788	1.005	9.839	1.4690	10′
6°00′	0.1047	0.1045	0.9945	0.1051	9.514	1.006	9.567	1.4661	84°00′
10′	0.1076	0.1074	0.9942	0.1080	9.255	1.006	9.309	1.4632	50′
20′	0.1105	0.1103	0.9939	0.1110	9.010	1.006	9.065	1.4603	40′
30′	0.1134	0.1132	0.9936	0.1139	8.777	1.006	8.834	1.4573	30′
40′	0.1164	0.1161	0.9932	0.1169	8.556	1.007	8.614	1.4544	20′
50′	0.1193	0.1190	0.9929	0.1198	8.345	1.007	8.405	1.4515	10′
7°00′	0.1222	0.1219	0.9925	0.1228	8.144	1.008	8.206	1.4486	83°00′
10′	0.1251	0.1248	0.9922	0.1257	7.953	1.008	8.016	1.4457	50′
20′	0.1280	0.1276	0.9918	0.1287	7.770	1.008	7.834	1.4428	40′
30′	0.1309	0.1305	0.9914	0.1317	7.596	1.009	7.661	1.4399	30′
40′	0.1338	0.1334	0.9911	0.1346	7.429	1.009	7.496	1.4370	20′
50′	0.1367	0.1363	0.9907	0.1376	7.269	1.009	7.337	1.4341	10′
8°00′	0.1396	0.1392	0.9903	0.1405	7.115	1.010	7.185	1.4312	82°00′
10′	0.1425	0.1421	0.9899	0.1435	6.968	1.010	7.040	1.4283	50′
20′	0.1454	0.1449	0.9894	0.1465	6.827	1.011	6.900	1.4254	40′
30′	0.1484	0.1478	0.9890	0.1495	6.691	1.011	6.765	1.4224	30′
40′	0.1513	0.1507	0.9886	0.1524	6.561	1.012	6.636	1.4195	20′
50′	0.1542	0.1536	0.9881	0.1554	6.435	1.012	6.512	1.4166	10′
9°00′	0.1571	0.1564	0.9877	0.1584	6.314	1.012	6.392	1.4137	81°00′
		Cos	Sin	Cot	Tan	Csc	Sec	Radians	Angle

Values of Trigonometric Functions

Angle	Radians	Sin	Cos	Tan	Cot	Sec	Csc		
9°00′	0.1571	0.1564	0.9877	0.1584	6.314	1.012	6.392	1.4137	81°00′
10′	0.1600	0.1593	0.9872	0.1614	6.197	1.013	6.277	1.4108	50′
20′	0.1629	0.1622	0.9868	0.1644	6.084	1.013	6.166	1.4079	40′
30′	0.1658	0.1650	0.9863	0.1673	5.976	1.014	6.059	1.4050	30′
40′	0.1687	0.1679	0.9858	0.1703	5.871	1.014	5.955	1.4021	20′
50′	0.1716	0.1708	0.9853	0.1733	5.769	1.015	5.855	1.3992	10′
10°00′	0.1745	0.1736	0.9848	0.1763	5.671	1.015	5.759	1.3963	80°00′
10′	0.1774	0.1765	0.9843	0.1793	5.576	1.016	5.665	1.3934	50′
20′	0.1804	0.1794	0.9838	0.1823	5.485	1.016	5.575	1.3904	40′
30′	0.1833	0.1822	0.9833	0.1853	5.396	1.017	5.487	1.3875	30′
40′	0.1862	0.1851	0.9827	0.1883	5.309	1.018	5.403	1.3846	20′
50′	0.1891	0.1880	0.9822	0.1914	5.226	1.018	5.320	1.3817	10′
11°00′	0.1920	0.1908	0.9816	0.1944	5.145	1.019	5.241	1.3788	79°00′
10′	0.1949	0.1937	0.9811	0.1974	5.066	1.019	5.164	1.3759	50′
20′	0.1978	0.1965	0.9805	0.2004	4.989	1.020	5.089	1.3730	40′
30′	0.2007	0.1994	0.9799	0.2035	4.915	1.020	5.016	1.3701	30′
40′	0.2036	0.2022	0.9793	0.2065	4.843	1.021	4.945	1.3672	20′
50′	0.2065	0.2051	0.9787	0.2095	4.773	1.022	4.876	1.3643	10′
12°00′	0.2094	0.2079	0.9781	0.2126	4.705	1.022	4.810	1.3614	78°00′
10′	0.2123	0.2108	0.9775	0.2156	4.638	1.023	4.745	1.3584	50′
20′	0.2153	0.2136	0.9769	0.2186	4.574	1.024	4.682	1.3555	40′
30′	0.2182	0.2164	0.9763	0.2217	4.511	1.024	4.620	1.3526	30′
40′	0.2211	0.2193	0.9757	0.2247	4.449	1.025	4.560	1.3497	20′
50′	0.2240	0.2221	0.9750	0.2278	4.390	1.026	4.502	1.3468	10′
13°00′	0.2269	0.2250	0.9744	0.2309	4.331	1.026	4.445	1.3439	77°00′
10′	0.2298	0.2278	0.9737	0.2339	4.275	1.027	4.390	1.3410	50′
20′	0.2327	0.2306	0.9730	0.2370	4.219	1.028	4.336	1.3381	40′
30′	0.2356	0.2334	0.9724	0.2401	4.165	1.028	4.284	1.3352	30′
40′	0.2385	0.2363	0.9717	0.2432	4.113	1.029	4.232	1.3323	20′
50′	0.2414	0.2391	0.9710	0.2462	4.061	1.030	4.182	1.3294	10′
14°00′	0.2443	0.2419	0.9703	0.2493	4.011	1.031	4.134	1.3265	76°00′
10′	0.2473	0.2447	0.9696	0.2524	3.962	1.031	4.086	1.3235	50′
20′	0.2502	0.2476	0.9689	0.2555	3.914	1.032	4.039	1.3206	40′
30′	0.2531	0.2504	0.9681	0.2586	3.867	1.033	3.994	1.3177	30′
40′	0.2560	0.2532	0.9674	0.2617	3.821	1.034	3.950	1.3148	20′
50′	0.2589	0.2560	0.9667	0.2648	3.776	1.034	3.906	1.3119	10′
15°00′	0.2618	0.2588	0.9659	0.2679	3.732	1.035	3.864	1.3090	75°00′
10′	0.2647	0.2616	0.9652	0.2711	3.689	1.036	3.822	1.3061	50′
20′	0.2676	0.2644	0.9644	0.2742	3.647	1.037	3.782	1.3032	40′
30′	0.2705	0.2672	0.9636	0.2773	3.606	1.038	3.742	1.3003	30′
40′	0.2734	0.2700	0.9628	0.2805	3.566	1.039	3.703	1.2974	20′
50′	0.2763	0.2728	0.9621	0.2836	3.526	1.039	3.665	1.2945	10′
16°00′	0.2793	0.2756	0.9613	0.2867	3.487	1.040	3.628	1.2915	74°00′
10′	0.2822	0.2784	0.9605	0.2899	3.450	1.041	3.592	1.2886	50′
20′	0.2851	0.2812	0.9596	0.2931	3.412	1.042	3.556	1.2857	40′
30′	0.2880	0.2840	0.9588	0.2962	3.376	1.043	3.521	1.2828	30′
40′	0.2909	0.2868	0.9580	0.2994	3.340	1.044	3.487	1.2799	20′
50′	0.2938	0.2896	0.9572	0.3026	3.305	1.045	3.453	1.2770	10′
17°00′	0.2967	0.2924	0.9563	0.3057	3.271	1.046	3.420	1.2741	73°00′
10′	0.2996	0.2952	0.9555	0.3089	3.237	1.047	3.388	1.2712	50′
20′	0.3025	0.2979	0.9546	0.3121	3.204	1.048	3.356	1.2683	40′
30′	0.3054	0.3007	0.9537	0.3153	3.172	1.049	3.326	1.2654	30′
40′	0.3083	0.3035	0.9528	0.3185	3.140	1.049	3.295	1.2625	20′
50′	0.3113	0.3062	0.9520	0.3217	3.108	1.050	3.265	1.2595	10′
18°00′	0.3142	0.3090	0.9511	0.3249	3.078	1.051	3.236	1.2566	72°00′
		Cos	Sin	Cot	Tan	Csc	Sec	Radians	Angle

Values of Trigonometric Functions

Angle	Radians	Sin	Cos	Tan	Cot	Sec	Csc		
18°00′	0.3142	0.3090	0.9511	0.3249	3.078	1.051	3.236	1.2566	72°00′
10′	0.3171	0.3118	0.9502	0.3281	3.047	1.052	3.207	1.2537	50′
20′	0.3200	0.3145	0.9492	0.3314	3.018	1.053	3.179	1.2508	40′
30′	0.3229	0.3173	0.9483	0.3346	2.989	1.054	3.152	1.2479	30′
40′	0.3258	0.3201	0.9474	0.3378	2.960	1.056	3.124	1.2450	20′
50′	0.3287	0.3228	0.9465	0.3411	2.932	1.057	3.098	1.2421	10′
19°00′	0.3316	0.3256	0.9455	0.3443	2.904	1.058	3.072	1.2392	71°00′
10′	0.3345	0.3283	0.9446	0.3476	2.877	1.059	3.046	1.2363	50′
20′	0.3374	0.3311	0.9436	0.3508	2.850	1.060	3.021	1.2334	40′
30′	0.3403	0.3338	0.9426	0.3541	2.824	1.061	2.996	1.2305	30′
40′	0.3432	0.3365	0.9417	0.3574	2.798	1.062	2.971	1.2275	20′
50′	0.3462	0.3393	0.9407	0.3607	2.773	1.063	2.947	1.2246	10′
20°00′	0.3491	0.3420	0.9397	0.3640	2.747	1.064	2.924	1.2217	70°00′
10′	0.3520	0.3448	0.9387	0.3673	2.723	1.065	2.901	1.2188	50′
20′	0.3549	0.3475	0.9377	0.3706	2.699	1.066	2.878	1.2159	40′
30′	0.3578	0.3502	0.9367	0.3739	2.675	1.068	2.855	1.2130	30′
40′	0.3607	0.3529	0.9356	0.3772	2.651	1.069	2.833	1.2101	20′
50′	0.3636	0.3557	0.9346	0.3805	2.628	1.070	2.812	1.2072	10′
21°00′	0.3665	0.3584	0.9336	0.3839	2.605	1.071	2.790	1.2043	69°00′
10′	0.3694	0.3611	0.9325	0.3872	2.583	1.072	2.769	1.2014	50′
20′	0.3723	0.3638	0.9315	0.3906	2.560	1.074	2.749	1.1985	40′
30′	0.3752	0.3665	0.9304	0.3939	2.539	1.075	2.729	1.1956	30′
40′	0.3782	0.3692	0.9293	0.3973	2.517	1.076	2.709	1.1926	20′
50′	0.3811	0.3719	0.9283	0.4006	2.496	1.077	2.689	1.1897	10′
22°00′	0.3840	0.3746	0.9272	0.4040	2.475	1.079	2.669	1.1868	68°00′
10′	0.3869	0.3773	0.9261	0.4074	2.455	1.080	2.650	1.1839	50′
20′	0.3898	0.3800	0.9250	0.4108	2.434	1.081	2.632	1.1810	40′
30′	0.3927	0.3827	0.9239	0.4142	2.414	1.082	2.613	1.1781	30′
40′	0.3956	0.3854	0.9228	0.4176	2.394	1.084	2.595	1.1752	20′
50′	0.3985	0.3881	0.9216	0.4210	2.375	1.085	2.577	1.1723	10′
23°00′	0.4014	0.3907	0.9205	0.4245	2.356	1.086	2.559	1.1694	67°00′
10′	0.4043	0.3934	0.9194	0.4279	2.337	1.088	2.542	1.1665	50′
20′	0.4072	0.3961	0.9182	0.4314	2.318	1.089	2.525	1.1636	40′
30′	0.4102	0.3987	0.9171	0.4348	2.300	1.090	2.508	1.1606	30′
40′	0.4131	0.4014	0.9159	0.4383	2.282	1.092	2.491	1.1577	20′
50′	0.4160	0.4041	0.9147	0.4417	2.264	1.093	2.475	1.1548	10′
24°00′	0.4189	0.4067	0.9135	0.4452	2.246	1.095	2.459	1.1519	66°00′
10′	0.4218	0.4094	0.9124	0.4487	2.229	1.096	2.443	1.1490	50′
20′	0.4247	0.4120	0.9112	0.4522	2.211	1.097	2.427	1.1461	40′
30′	0.4276	0.4147	0.9100	0.4557	2.194	1.099	2.411	1.1432	30′
40′	0.4305	0.4173	0.9088	0.4592	2.177	1.100	2.396	1.1403	20′
50′	0.4334	0.4200	0.9075	0.4628	2.161	1.102	2.381	1.1374	10′
25°00′	0.4363	0.4226	0.9063	0.4663	2.145	1.103	2.366	1.1345	65°00′
10′	0.4392	0.4253	0.9051	0.4699	2.128	1.105	2.352	1.1316	50′
20′	0.4422	0.4279	0.9038	0.4734	2.112	1.106	2.337	1.1286	40′
30′	0.4451	0.4305	0.9026	0.4770	2.097	1.108	2.323	1.1257	30′
40′	0.4480	0.4331	0.9013	0.4806	2.081	1.109	2.309	1.1228	20′
50′	0.4509	0.4358	0.9001	0.4841	2.066	1.111	2.295	1.1199	10′
26°00′	0.4538	0.4384	0.8988	0.4877	2.050	1.113	2.281	1.1170	64°00′
10′	0.4567	0.4410	0.8975	0.4913	2.035	1.114	2.268	1.1141	50′
20′	0.4596	0.4436	0.8962	0.4950	2.020	1.116	2.254	1.1112	40′
30′	0.4625	0.4462	0.8949	0.4986	2.006	1.117	2.241	1.1083	30′
40′	0.4654	0.4488	0.8936	0.5022	1.991	1.119	2.228	1.1054	20′
50′	0.4683	0.4514	0.8923	0.5059	1.977	1.121	2.215	1.1025	10′
27°00′	0.4712	0.4540	0.8910	0.5095	1.963	1.122	2.203	1.0996	63°00′
		Cos	Sin	Cot	Tan	Csc	Sec	Radians	Angle

Values of Trigonometric Functions

Angle	Radians	Sin	Cos	Tan	Cot	Sec	Csc		
27°00′	0.4712	0.4540	0.8910	0.5095	1.963	1.122	2.203	1.0996	63°00′
10′	0.4741	0.4566	0.8897	0.5132	1.949	1.124	2.190	1.0966	50′
20′	0.4771	0.4592	0.8884	0.5169	1.935	1.126	2.178	1.0937	40′
30′	0.4800	0.4617	0.8870	0.5206	1.921	1.127	2.166	1.0908	30′
40′	0.4829	0.4643	0.8857	0.5243	1.907	1.129	2.154	1.0879	20′
50′	0.4858	0.4669	0.8843	0.5280	1.894	1.131	2.142	1.0850	10′
28°00′	0.4887	0.4695	0.8829	0.5317	1.881	1.133	2.130	1.0821	62°00′
10′	0.4916	0.4720	0.8816	0.5354	1.868	1.134	2.118	1.0792	50′
20′	0.4945	0.4746	0.8802	0.5392	1.855	1.136	2.107	1.0763	40′
30′	0.4974	0.4772	0.8788	0.5430	1.842	1.138	2.096	1.0734	30′
40′	0.5003	0.4797	0.8774	0.5467	1.829	1.140	2.085	1.0705	20′
50′	0.5032	0.4823	0.8760	0.5505	1.816	1.142	2.074	1.0676	10′
29°00′	0.5061	0.4848	0.8746	0.5543	1.804	1.143	2.063	1.0647	61°00′
10′	0.5091	0.4874	0.8732	0.5581	1.792	1.145	2.052	1.0617	50′
20′	0.5120	0.4899	0.8718	0.5619	1.780	1.147	2.041	1.0588	40′
30′	0.5149	0.4924	0.8704	0.5658	1.767	1.149	2.031	1.0559	30′
40′	0.5178	0.4950	0.8689	0.5696	1.756	1.151	2.020	1.0530	20′
50′	0.5207	0.4975	0.8675	0.5735	1.744	1.153	2.010	1.0501	10′
30°00′	0.5236	0.5000	0.8660	0.5774	1.732	1.155	2.000	1.0472	60°00′
10′	0.5265	0.5025	0.8646	0.5812	1.720	1.157	1.990	1.0443	50′
20′	0.5294	0.5050	0.8631	0.5851	1.709	1.159	1.980	1.0414	40′
30′	0.5323	0.5075	0.8616	0.5890	1.698	1.161	1.970	1.0385	30′
40′	0.5352	0.5100	0.8601	0.5930	1.686	1.163	1.961	1.0356	20′
50′	0.5381	0.5125	0.8587	0.5969	1.675	1.165	1.951	1.0327	10′
31°00′	0.5411	0.5150	0.8572	0.6009	1.664	1.167	1.942	1.0297	59°00′
10′	0.5440	0.5175	0.8557	0.6048	1.653	1.169	1.932	1.0268	50′
20′	0.5469	0.5200	0.8542	0.6088	1.643	1.171	1.923	1.0239	40′
30′	0.5498	0.5225	0.8526	0.6128	1.632	1.173	1.914	1.0210	30′
40′	0.5527	0.5250	0.8511	0.6168	1.621	1.175	1.905	1.0181	20′
50′	0.5556	0.5275	0.8496	0.6208	1.611	1.177	1.896	1.0152	10′
32°00′	0.5585	0.5299	0.8480	0.6249	1.600	1.179	1.887	1.0123	58°00′
10′	0.5614	0.5324	0.8465	0.6289	1.590	1.181	1.878	1.0094	50′
20′	0.5643	0.5348	0.8450	0.6330	1.580	1.184	1.870	1.0065	40′
30′	0.5672	0.5373	0.8434	0.6371	1.570	1.186	1.861	1.0036	30′
40′	0.5701	0.5398	0.8418	0.6412	1.560	1.188	1.853	1.0007	20′
50′	0.5730	0.5422	0.8403	0.6453	1.550	1.190	1.844	0.9977	10′
33°00′	0.5760	0.5446	0.8387	0.6494	1.540	1.192	1.836	0.9948	57°00′
10′	0.5789	0.5471	0.8371	0.6536	1.530	1.195	1.828	0.9919	50′
20′	0.5818	0.5495	0.8355	0.6577	1.520	1.197	1.820	0.9890	40′
30′	0.5847	0.5519	0.8339	0.6619	1.511	1.199	1.812	0.9861	30′
40′	0.5876	0.5544	0.8323	0.6661	1.501	1.202	1.804	0.9832	20′
50′	0.5905	0.5568	0.8307	0.6703	1.492	1.204	1.796	0.9803	10′
34°00′	0.5934	0.5592	0.8290	0.6745	1.483	1.206	1.788	0.9774	56°00′
10′	0.5963	0.5616	0.8274	0.6787	1.473	1.209	1.781	0.9745	50′
20′	0.5992	0.5640	0.8258	0.6830	1.464	1.211	1.773	0.9716	40′
30′	0.6021	0.5664	0.8241	0.6873	1.455	1.213	1.766	0.9687	30′
40′	0.6050	0.5688	0.8225	0.6916	1.446	1.216	1.758	0.9657	20′
50′	0.6080	0.5712	0.8208	0.6959	1.437	1.218	1.751	0.9628	10′
35°00′	0.6109	0.5736	0.8192	0.7002	1.428	1.221	1.743	0.9599	55°00′
10′	0.6138	0.5760	0.8175	0.7046	1.419	1.223	1.736	0.9570	50′
20′	0.6167	0.5783	0.8158	0.7089	1.411	1.226	1.729	0.9541	40′
30′	0.6196	0.5807	0.8141	0.7133	1.402	1.228	1.722	0.9512	30′
40′	0.6225	0.5831	0.8124	0.7177	1.393	1.231	1.715	0.9483	20′
50′	0.6254	0.5854	0.8107	0.7221	1.385	1.233	1.708	0.9454	10′
36°00′	0.6283	0.5878	0.8090	0.7265	1.376	1.236	1.701	0.9425	54°00′
		Cos	Sin	Cot	Tan	Csc	Sec	Radians	Angle

Values of Trigonometric Functions

Angle	Radians	Sin	Cos	Tan	Cot	Sec	Csc		
36°00′	0.6283	0.5878	0.8090	0.7265	1.376	1.236	1.701	0.9425	54°00′
10′	0.6312	0.5901	0.8073	0.7310	1.368	1.239	1.695	0.9396	50′
20′	0.6341	0.5925	0.8056	0.7355	1.360	1.241	1.688	0.9367	40′
30′	0.6370	0.5948	0.8039	0.7400	1.351	1.244	1.681	0.9338	30′
40′	0.6400	0.5972	0.8021	0.7445	1.343	1.247	1.675	0.9308	20′
50′	0.6429	0.5995	0.8004	0.7490	1.335	1.249	1.668	0.9279	10′
37°00′	0.6458	0.6018	0.7986	0.7536	1.327	1.252	1.662	0.9250	53°00′
10′	0.6487	0.6041	0.7969	0.7581	1.319	1.255	1.655	0.9221	50′
20′	0.6516	0.6065	0.7951	0.7627	1.311	1.258	1.649	0.9192	40′
30′	0.6545	0.6088	0.7934	0.7673	1.303	1.260	1.643	0.9163	30′
40′	0.6574	0.6111	0.7916	0.7720	1.295	1.263	1.636	0.9134	20′
50′	0.6603	0.6134	0.7898	0.7766	1.288	1.266	1.630	0.9105	10′
38°00′	0.6632	0.6157	0.7880	0.7813	1.280	1.269	1.624	0.9076	52°00′
10′	0.6661	0.6180	0.7862	0.7860	1.272	1.272	1.618	0.9047	50′
20′	0.6690	0.6202	0.7844	0.7907	1.265	1.275	1.612	0.9018	40′
30′	0.6720	0.6225	0.7826	0.7954	1.257	1.278	1.606	0.8988	30′
40′	0.6749	0.6248	0.7808	0.8002	1.250	1.281	1.601	0.8959	20′
50′	0.6778	0.6271	0.7790	0.8050	1.242	1.284	1.595	0.8930	10′
39°00′	0.6807	0.6293	0.7771	0.8098	1.235	1.287	1.589	0.8901	51°00′
10′	0.6836	0.6316	0.7753	0.8146	1.228	1.290	1.583	0.8872	50′
20′	0.6865	0.6338	0.7735	0.8195	1.220	1.293	1.578	0.8843	40′
30′	0.6894	0.6361	0.7716	0.8243	1.213	1.296	1.572	0.8814	30′
40′	0.6923	0.6383	0.7698	0.8292	1.206	1.299	1.567	0.8785	20′
50′	0.6952	0.6406	0.7679	0.8342	1.199	1.302	1.561	0.8756	10′
40°00′	0.6981	0.6428	0.7660	0.8391	1.192	1.305	1.556	0.8727	50°00′
10′	0.7010	0.6450	0.7642	0.8441	1.185	1.309	1.550	0.8698	50′
20′	0.7039	0.6472	0.7623	0.8491	1.178	1.312	1.545	0.8668	40′
30′	0.7069	0.6494	0.7604	0.8541	1.171	1.315	1.540	0.8639	30′
40′	0.7098	0.6517	0.7585	0.8591	1.164	1.318	1.535	0.8610	20′
50′	0.7127	0.6539	0.7566	0.8642	1.157	1.322	1.529	0.8581	10′
41°00′	0.7156	0.6561	0.7547	0.8693	1.150	1.325	1.524	0.8552	49°00′
10′	0.7185	0.6583	0.7528	0.8744	1.144	1.328	1.519	0.8523	50′
20′	0.7214	0.6604	0.7509	0.8796	1.137	1.332	1.514	0.8494	40′
30′	0.7243	0.6626	0.7490	0.8847	1.130	1.335	1.509	0.8465	30′
40′	0.7272	0.6648	0.7470	0.8899	1.124	1.339	1.504	0.8436	20′
50′	0.7301	0.6670	0.7451	0.8952	1.117	1.342	1.499	0.8407	10′
42°00′	0.7330	0.6691	0.7431	0.9004	1.111	1.346	1.494	0.8378	48°00′
10′	0.7359	0.6713	0.7412	0.9057	1.104	1.349	1.490	0.8348	50′
20′	0.7389	0.6734	0.7392	0.9110	1.098	1.353	1.485	0.8319	40′
30′	0.7418	0.6756	0.7373	0.9163	1.091	1.356	1.480	0.8290	30′
40′	0.7447	0.6777	0.7353	0.9217	1.085	1.360	1.476	0.8261	20′
50′	0.7476	0.6799	0.7333	0.9271	1.079	1.364	1.471	0.8232	10′
43°00′	0.7505	0.6820	0.7314	0.9325	1.072	1.367	1.466	0.8203	47°00′
10′	0.7534	0.6841	0.7294	0.9380	1.066	1.371	1.462	0.8174	50′
20′	0.7563	0.6862	0.7274	0.9435	1.060	1.375	1.457	0.8145	40′
30′	0.7592	0.6884	0.7254	0.9490	1.054	1.379	1.453	0.8116	30′
40′	0.7621	0.6905	0.7234	0.9545	1.048	1.382	1.448	0.8087	20′
50′	0.7650	0.6926	0.7214	0.9601	1.042	1.386	1.444	0.8058	10′
44°00′	0.7679	0.6947	0.7193	0.9657	1.036	1.390	1.440	0.8029	46°00′
10′	0.7709	0.6967	0.7173	0.9713	1.030	1.394	1.435	0.7999	50′
20′	0.7738	0.6988	0.7153	0.9770	1.024	1.398	1.431	0.7970	40′
30′	0.7767	0.7009	0.7133	0.9827	1.018	1.402	1.427	0.7941	30′
40′	0.7796	0.7030	0.7112	0.9884	1.012	1.406	1.423	0.7912	20′
50′	0.7825	0.7050	0.7092	0.9942	1.006	1.410	1.418	0.7883	10′
45°00′	0.7854	0.7071	0.7071	1.000	1.000	1.414	1.414	0.7854	45°00′
		Cos	Sin	Cot	Tan	Csc	Sec	Radians	Angle

Common Logarithms of Numbers

n	0	1	2	3	4	5	6	7	8	9
10	0000	0043	0086	0128	0170	0212	0253	0294	0334	0374
11	0414	0453	0492	0531	0569	0607	0645	0682	0719	0755
12	0792	0828	0864	0899	0934	0969	1004	1038	1072	1106
13	1139	1173	1206	1239	1271	1303	1335	1367	1399	1430
14	1461	1492	1523	1553	1584	1614	1644	1673	1703	1732
15	1761	1790	1818	1847	1875	1903	1931	1959	1987	2014
16	2041	2068	2095	2122	2148	2175	2201	2227	2253	2279
17	2304	2330	2355	2380	2405	2430	2455	2480	2504	2529
18	2553	2577	2601	2625	2648	2672	2695	2718	2742	2765
19	2788	2810	2833	2856	2878	2900	2923	2945	2967	2989
20	3010	3032	3054	3075	3096	3118	3139	3160	3181	3201
21	3222	3243	3263	3284	3304	3324	3345	3365	3385	3404
22	3424	3444	3464	3483	3502	3522	3541	3560	3579	3598
23	3617	3636	3655	3674	3692	3711	3729	3747	3766	3784
24	3802	3820	3838	3856	3874	3892	3909	3927	3945	3962
25	3979	3997	4014	4031	4048	4065	4082	4099	4116	4133
26	4150	4166	4183	4200	4216	4232	4249	4265	4281	4298
27	4314	4330	4346	4362	4378	4393	4409	4425	4440	4456
28	4472	4487	4502	4518	4533	4548	4564	4579	4594	4609
29	4624	4639	4654	4669	4683	4698	4713	4728	4742	4757
30	4771	4786	4800	4814	4829	4843	4857	4871	4886	4900
31	4914	4928	4942	4955	4969	4983	4997	5011	5024	5038
32	5051	5065	5079	5092	5105	5119	5132	5145	5159	5172
33	5185	5198	5211	5224	5237	5250	5263	5276	5289	5302
34	5315	5328	5340	5353	5366	5378	5391	5403	5416	5428
35	5441	5453	5465	5478	5490	5502	5514	5527	5539	5551
36	5563	5575	5587	5599	5611	5623	5635	5647	5658	5670
37	5682	5694	5705	5717	5729	5740	5752	5763	5775	5786
38	5798	5809	5821	5832	5843	5855	5866	5877	5888	5899
39	5911	5922	5933	5944	5955	5966	5977	5988	5999	6010
40	6021	6031	6042	6053	6064	6075	6085	6096	6107	6117
41	6128	6138	6149	6160	6170	6180	6191	6201	6212	6222
42	6232	6243	6253	6263	6274	6284	6294	6304	6314	6325
43	6335	6345	6355	6365	6375	6385	6395	6405	6415	6425
44	6435	6444	6454	6464	6474	6484	6493	6503	6513	6522
45	6532	6542	6551	6561	6571	6580	6590	6599	6609	6618
46	6628	6637	6646	6656	6665	6675	6684	6693	6702	6712
47	6721	6730	6739	6749	6758	6767	6776	6785	6794	6803
48	6812	6821	6830	6839	6848	6857	6866	6875	6884	6893
49	6902	6911	6920	6928	6937	6946	6955	6964	6972	6981
50	6990	6998	7007	7016	7024	7033	7042	7050	7059	7067
51	7076	7084	7093	7101	7110	7118	7126	7135	7143	7152
52	7160	7168	7177	7185	7193	7202	7210	7218	7226	7235
53	7243	7251	7259	7267	7275	7284	7292	7300	7308	7316
54	7324	7332	7340	7348	7356	7364	7372	7380	7388	7396

Common Logarithms of Numbers

n	0	1	2	3	4	5	6	7	8	9
55	7404	7412	7419	7427	7435	7443	7451	7459	7466	7474
56	7482	7490	7497	7505	7513	7520	7528	7536	7543	7551
57	7559	7566	7574	7582	7589	7597	7604	7612	7619	7627
58	7634	7642	7649	7657	7664	7672	7679	7686	7694	7701
59	7709	7716	7723	7731	7738	7745	7752	7760	7767	7774
60	7782	7789	7796	7803	7810	7818	7825	7832	7839	7846
61	7853	7860	7868	7875	7882	7889	7896	7903	7910	7917
62	7924	7931	7938	7945	7952	7959	7966	7973	7980	7987
63	7993	8000	8007	8014	8021	8028	8035	8041	8048	8055
64	8062	8069	8075	8082	8089	8096	8102	8109	8116	8122
65	8129	8136	8142	8149	8156	8162	8169	8176	8182	8189
66	8195	8202	8209	8215	8222	8228	8235	8241	8248	8254
67	8261	8267	8274	8280	8287	8293	8299	8306	8312	8319
68	8325	8331	8338	8344	8351	8357	8363	8370	8376	8382
69	8388	8395	8401	8407	8414	8420	8426	8432	8439	8445
70	8451	8457	8463	8470	8476	8482	8488	8494	8500	8506
71	8513	8519	8525	8531	8537	8543	8549	8555	8561	8567
72	8573	8579	8585	8591	8597	8603	8609	8615	8621	8627
73	8633	8639	8645	8651	8657	8663	8669	8675	8681	8686
74	8692	8698	8704	8710	8716	8722	8727	8733	8739	8745
75	8751	8756	8762	8768	8774	8779	8785	8791	8797	8802
76	8808	8814	8820	8825	8831	8837	8842	8848	8854	8859
77	8865	8871	8876	8882	8887	8893	8899	8904	8910	8915
78	8921	8927	8932	8938	8943	8949	8954	8960	8965	8971
79	8976	8982	8987	8993	8998	9004	9009	9015	9020	9025
80	9031	9036	9042	9047	9053	9058	9063	9069	9074	9079
81	9085	9090	9096	9101	9106	9112	9117	9122	9128	9133
82	9138	9143	9149	9154	9159	9165	9170	9175	9180	9186
83	9191	9196	9201	9206	9212	9217	9222	9227	9232	9238
84	9243	9248	9253	9258	9263	9269	9274	9279	9284	9289
85	9294	9299	9304	9309	9315	9320	9325	9330	9335	9340
86	9345	9350	9355	9360	9365	9370	9375	9380	9385	9390
87	9395	9400	9405	9410	9415	9420	9425	9430	9435	9440
88	9445	9450	9455	9460	9465	9469	9474	9479	9484	9489
89	9494	9499	9504	9509	9513	9518	9523	9528	9533	9538
90	9542	9547	9552	9557	9562	9566	9571	9576	9581	9586
91	9590	9595	9600	9605	9609	9614	9619	9624	9628	9633
92	9638	9643	9647	9652	9657	9661	9666	9671	9675	9680
93	9685	9689	9694	9699	9703	9708	9713	9717	9722	9727
94	9731	9736	9741	9745	9750	9754	9759	9763	9768	9773
95	9777	9782	9786	9791	9795	9800	9805	9809	9814	9818
96	9823	9827	9832	9836	9841	9845	9850	9854	9859	9863
97	9868	9872	9877	9881	9886	9890	9894	9899	9903	9908
98	9912	9917	9921	9926	9930	9934	9939	9943	9948	9952
99	9956	9961	9965	9969	9974	9978	9983	9987	9991	9996

Natural Logarithms of Numbers

Use ln 10 = 2.3026 to find logarithms of numbers greater than 10 or less than 1.

n	0	1	2	3	4	5	6	7	8	9
1.0	0.0000	0.0100	0.0198	0.0296	0.0392	0.0488	0.0583	0.0677	0.0770	0.0862
1.1	0.0953	0.1044	0.1133	0.1222	0.1310	0.1398	0.1484	0.1570	0.1655	0.1740
1.2	0.1823	0.1906	0.1989	0.2070	0.2151	0.2231	0.2311	0.2390	0.2469	0.2546
1.3	0.2624	0.2700	0.2776	0.2852	0.2927	0.3001	0.3075	0.3148	0.3221	0.3293
1.4	0.3365	0.3436	0.3507	0.3577	0.3646	0.3716	0.3784	0.3853	0.3920	0.3988
1.5	0.4055	0.4121	0.4187	0.4253	0.4318	0.4383	0.4447	0.4511	0.4574	0.4637
1.6	0.4700	0.4762	0.4824	0.4886	0.4947	0.5008	0.5068	0.5128	0.5188	0.5247
1.7	0.5306	0.5365	0.5423	0.5481	0.5539	0.5596	0.5653	0.5710	0.5766	0.5822
1.8	0.5878	0.5933	0.5988	0.6043	0.6098	0.6152	0.6206	0.6259	0.6313	0.6366
1.9	0.6419	0.6471	0.6523	0.6575	0.6627	0.6678	0.6729	0.6780	0.6831	0.6881
2.0	0.6932	0.6981	0.7031	0.7080	0.7130	0.7178	0.7227	0.7276	0.7324	0.7372
2.1	0.7419	0.7467	0.7514	0.7561	0.7608	0.7655	0.7701	0.7747	0.7793	0.7839
2.2	0.7885	0.7930	0.7975	0.8020	0.8065	0.8109	0.8154	0.8198	0.8242	0.8286
2.3	0.8329	0.8373	0.8416	0.8459	0.8502	0.8544	0.8587	0.8629	0.8671	0.8713
2.4	0.8755	0.8796	0.8838	0.8879	0.8920	0.8961	0.9002	0.9042	0.9083	0.9123
2.5	0.9163	0.9203	0.9243	0.9282	0.9322	0.9361	0.9400	0.9439	0.9478	0.9517
2.6	0.9555	0.9594	0.9632	0.9670	0.9708	0.9746	0.9783	0.9821	0.9858	0.9895
2.7	0.9933	0.9970	1.0006	1.0043	1.0080	1.0116	1.0152	1.0189	1.0225	1.0260
2.8	1.0296	1.0332	1.0367	1.0403	1.0438	1.0473	1.0508	1.0543	1.0578	1.0613
2.9	1.0647	1.0682	1.0716	1.0750	1.0784	1.0818	1.0852	1.0886	1.0919	1.0953
3.0	1.0986	1.1019	1.1053	1.1086	1.1119	1.1151	1.1184	1.1217	1.1249	1.1282
3.1	1.1314	1.1346	1.1378	1.1410	1.1442	1.1474	1.1506	1.1537	1.1569	1.1600
3.2	1.1632	1.1663	1.1694	1.1725	1.1756	1.1787	1.1817	1.1848	1.1878	1.1909
3.3	1.1939	1.1970	1.2000	1.2030	1.2060	1.2090	1.2119	1.2149	1.2179	1.2208
3.4	1.2238	1.2267	1.2296	1.2326	1.2355	1.2384	1.2413	1.2442	1.2470	1.2499
3.5	1.2528	1.2556	1.2585	1.2613	1.2641	1.2670	1.2698	1.2726	1.2754	1.2782
3.6	1.2809	1.2837	1.2865	1.2892	1.2920	1.2947	1.2975	1.3002	1.3029	1.3056
3.7	1.3083	1.3110	1.3137	1.3164	1.3191	1.3218	1.3244	1.3271	1.3297	1.3324
3.8	1.3350	1.3376	1.3403	1.3429	1.3455	1.3481	1.3507	1.3533	1.3558	1.3584
3.9	1.3610	1.3635	1.3661	1.3686	1.3712	1.3737	1.3762	1.3788	1.3813	1.3838
4.0	1.3863	1.3883	1.3913	1.3938	1.3962	1.3987	1.4012	1.4036	1.4061	1.4085
4.1	1.4110	1.4134	1.4159	1.4183	1.4207	1.4231	1.4255	1.4279	1.4303	1.4327
4.2	1.4351	1.4375	1.4398	1.4422	1.4446	1.4469	1.4493	1.4516	1.4540	1.4563
4.3	1.4586	1.4609	1.4633	1.4656	1.4679	1.4702	1.4725	1.4748	1.4771	1.4793
4.4	1.4816	1.4839	1.4861	1.4884	1.4907	1.4929	1.4952	1.4974	1.4996	1.5019
4.5	1.5041	1.5063	1.5085	1.5107	1.5129	1.5151	1.5173	1.5195	1.5217	1.5239
4.6	1.5261	1.5282	1.5304	1.5326	1.5347	1.5369	1.5390	1.5412	1.5433	1.5454
4.7	1.5476	1.5497	1.5518	1.5539	1.5560	1.5581	1.5603	1.5624	1.5644	1.5665
4.8	1.5686	1.5707	1.5728	1.5749	1.5769	1.5790	1.5810	1.5831	1.5852	1.5872
4.9	1.5892	1.5913	1.5933	1.5953	1.5974	1.5994	1.6014	1.6034	1.6054	1.6074
5.0	1.6094	1.6114	1.6134	1.6154	1.6174	1.6194	1.6214	1.6233	1.6253	1.6273
5.1	1.6292	1.6312	1.6332	1.6351	1.6371	1.6390	1.6409	1.6429	1.6448	1.6467
5.2	1.6487	1.6506	1.6525	1.6544	1.6563	1.6582	1.6601	1.6620	1.6639	1.6658
5.3	1.6677	1.6696	1.6715	1.6734	1.6752	1.6771	1.6790	1.6808	1.6827	1.6846
5.4	1.6864	1.6883	1.6901	1.6919	1.6938	1.6956	1.6975	1.6993	1.7011	1.7029

Natural Logarithms of Numbers

n	0	1	2	3	4	5	6	7	8	9
5.5	1.7048	1.7066	1.7084	1.7102	1.7120	1.7138	1.7156	1.7174	1.7192	1.7210
5.6	1.7228	1.7246	1.7263	1.7281	1.7299	1.7317	1.7334	1.7352	1.7370	1.7387
5.7	1.7405	1.7422	1.7440	1.7457	1.7475	1.7492	1.7509	1.7527	1.7544	1.7561
5.8	1.7579	1.7596	1.7613	1.7630	1.7647	1.7664	1.7682	1.7699	1.7716	1.7733
5.9	1.7750	1.7767	1.7783	1.7800	1.7817	1.7834	1.7851	1.7868	1.7884	1.7901
6.0	1.7918	1.7934	1.7951	1.7968	1.7984	1.8001	1.8017	1.8034	1.8050	1.8067
6.1	1.8083	1.8099	1.8116	1.8132	1.8148	1.8165	1.8181	1.8197	1.8213	1.8229
6.2	1.8246	1.8262	1.8278	1.8294	1.8310	1.8326	1.8342	1.8358	1.8374	1.8390
6.3	1.8406	1.8421	1.8437	1.8453	1.8469	1.8485	1.8500	1.8516	1.8532	1.8547
6.4	1.8563	1.8579	1.8594	1.8610	1.8625	1.8641	1.8656	1.8672	1.8687	1.8703
6.5	1.8718	1.8733	1.8749	1.8764	1.8779	1.8795	1.8810	1.8825	1.8840	1.8856
6.6	1.8871	1.8886	1.8901	1.8916	1.8931	1.8946	1.8961	1.8976	1.8991	1.9006
6.7	1.9021	1.9036	1.9051	1.9066	1.9081	1.9095	1.9110	1.9125	1.9140	1.9155
6.8	1.9169	1.9184	1.9199	1.9213	1.9228	1.9243	1.9257	1.9272	1.9286	1.9301
6.9	1.9315	1.9330	1.9344	1.9359	1.9373	1.9387	1.9402	1.9416	1.9431	1.9445
7.0	1.9459	1.9473	1.9488	1.9502	1.9516	1.9530	1.9545	1.9559	1.9573	1.9587
7.1	1.9601	1.9615	1.9629	1.9643	1.9657	1.9671	1.9685	1.9699	1.9713	1.9727
7.2	1.9741	1.9755	1.9769	1.9782	1.9796	1.9810	1.9824	1.9838	1.9851	1.9865
7.3	1.9879	1.9892	1.9906	1.9920	1.9933	1.9947	1.9961	1.9974	1.9988	2.0001
7.4	2.0015	2.0028	2.0042	2.0055	2.0069	2.0082	2.0096	2.0109	2.0122	2.0136
7.5	2.0149	2.0162	2.0176	2.0189	2.0202	2.0216	2.0229	2.0242	2.0255	2.0268
7.6	2.0282	2.0295	2.0308	2.0321	2.0334	2.0347	2.0360	2.0373	2.0386	2.0399
7.7	2.0412	2.0425	2.0438	2.0451	2.0464	2.0477	2.0490	2.0503	2.0516	2.0528
7.8	2.0541	2.0554	2.0567	2.0580	2.0592	2.0605	2.0618	2.0631	2.0643	2.0656
7.9	2.0669	2.0681	2.0694	2.0707	2.0719	2.0732	2.0744	2.0757	2.0769	2.0782
8.0	2.0794	2.0807	2.0819	2.0832	2.0844	2.0857	2.0869	2.0882	2.0894	2.0906
8.1	2.0919	2.0931	2.0943	2.0956	2.0968	2.0980	2.0992	2.1005	2.1017	2.1029
8.2	2.1041	2.1054	2.1066	2.1078	2.1090	2.1102	2.1114	2.1126	2.1138	2.1151
8.3	2.1163	2.1175	2.1187	2.1199	2.1211	2.1223	2.1235	2.1247	2.1259	2.1270
8.4	2.1282	2.1294	2.1306	2.1318	2.1330	2.1342	2.1354	2.1365	2.1377	2.1389
8.5	2.1401	2.1412	2.1424	2.1436	2.1448	2.1459	2.1471	2.1483	2.1494	2.1506
8.6	2.1518	2.1529	2.1541	2.1552	2.1564	2.1576	2.1587	2.1599	2.1610	2.1622
8.7	2.1633	2.1645	2.1656	2.1668	2.1679	2.1691	2.1702	2.1713	2.1725	2.1736
8.8	2.1748	2.1759	2.1770	2.1782	2.1793	2.1804	2.1816	2.1827	2.1838	2.1849
8.9	2.1861	2.1872	2.1883	2.1894	2.1905	2.1917	2.1928	2.1939	2.1950	2.1961
9.0	2.1972	2.1983	2.1994	2.2006	2.2017	2.2028	2.2039	2.2050	2.2061	2.2072
9.1	2.2083	2.2094	2.2105	2.2116	2.2127	2.2138	2.2149	2.2159	2.2170	2.2181
9.2	2.2192	2.2203	2.2214	2.2225	2.2235	2.2246	2.2257	2.2268	2.2279	2.2289
9.3	2.2300	2.2311	2.2322	2.2332	2.2343	2.2354	2.2365	2.2375	2.2386	2.2397
9.4	2.2407	2.2418	2.2428	2.2439	2.2450	2.2460	2.2471	2.2481	2.2492	2.2502
9.5	2.2513	2.2523	2.2534	2.2544	2.2555	2.2565	2.2576	2.2586	2.2597	2.2607
9.6	2.2618	2.2628	2.2638	2.2649	2.2659	2.2670	2.2680	2.2690	2.2701	2.2711
9.7	2.2721	2.2732	2.2742	2.2752	2.2762	2.2773	2.2783	2.2793	2.2803	2.2814
9.8	2.2824	2.2834	2.2844	2.2854	2.2865	2.2875	2.2885	2.2895	2.2905	2.2915
9.9	2.2925	2.2935	2.2946	2.2956	2.2966	2.2976	2.2986	2.2996	2.3006	2.3016

Exponential Functions

x	e^x	e^{-x}
0.00	1.0000	1.0000
0.01	1.0101	0.9901
0.02	1.0202	0.9802
0.03	1.0305	0.9705
0.04	1.0408	0.9608
0.05	1.0513	0.9512
0.06	1.0618	0.9418
0.07	1.0725	0.9324
0.08	1.0833	0.9331
0.09	1.0942	0.9139
0.10	1.1052	0.9048
0.11	1.1163	0.8958
0.12	1.1275	0.8869
0.13	1.1388	0.8781
0.14	1.1503	0.8694
0.15	1.1618	0.8607
0.16	1.1735	0.8521
0.17	1.1853	0.8437
0.18	1.1972	0.8353
0.19	1.2092	0.8270
0.20	1.2214	0.8187
0.21	1.2337	0.8106
0.22	1.2461	0.8025
0.23	1.2586	0.7945
0.24	1.2712	0.7866
0.25	1.2840	0.7788
0.30	1.3499	0.7408
0.35	1.4191	0.7047
0.40	1.4918	0.6703
0.45	1.5683	0.6376
0.50	1.6487	0.6065
0.55	1.7333	0.5769
0.60	1.8221	0.5488
0.65	1.9155	0.5220
0.70	2.0138	0.4966
0.75	2.1170	0.4724
0.80	2.2255	0.4493
0.85	2.3396	0.4274
0.90	2.4596	0.4066
0.95	2.5857	0.3867
1.0	2.7183	0.3679
1.1	3.0042	0.3329
1.2	3.3201	0.3012
1.3	3.6693	0.2725
1.4	4.0552	0.2466

x	e^x	e^{-x}
1.5	4.4817	0.2231
1.6	4.9530	0.2019
1.7	5.4739	0.1827
1.8	6.0496	0.1653
1.9	6.6859	0.1496
2.0	7.3891	0.1353
2.1	8.1662	0.1225
2.2	9.0250	0.1108
2.3	9.9742	0.1003
2.4	11.023	0.0907
2.5	12.182	0.0821
2.6	13.464	0.0743
2.7	14.880	0.0672
2.8	16.445	0.0608
2.9	18.174	0.0550
3.0	20.086	0.0498
3.1	22.198	0.0450
3.2	24.533	0.0408
3.3	27.113	0.0369
3.4	29.964	0.0334
3.5	33.115	0.0302
3.6	36.598	0.0273
3.7	40.447	0.0247
3.8	44.701	0.0224
3.9	49.402	0.0202
4.0	54.598	0.0183
4.1	60.340	0.0166
4.2	66.686	0.0150
4.3	73.700	0.0136
4.4	81.451	0.0123
4.5	90.017	0.0111
4.6	99.484	0.0101
4.7	109.95	0.0091
4.8	121.51	0.0082
4.9	134.29	0.0074
5.0	148.41	0.0067
5.5	244.69	0.0041
6.0	403.43	0.0025
6.5	665.14	0.0015
7.0	1096.6	0.0009
7.5	1808.0	0.0006
8.0	2981.0	0.0003
8.5	4914.8	0.0002
9.0	8103.1	0.0001
10.0	22026	0.00005

GLOSSARY

absolute maximum or minimum values Absolute maximum or minimum values are the greatest or least values, respectively, assumed by a function throughout its domain of definition. (448)

absolute value If x is a nonzero real number, the absolute value of x, $|x|$, is x or ^-x, whichever is positive. $|0| = 0$. (3)

addition of matrices The sum of two $m \times n$ matrices is an $m \times n$ matrix in which the elements are the sum of the corresponding elements of the given matrices. (63)

amplitude 1. The amplitude of a sine or a cosine function of the form $y = A \sin k\theta$ or $y = A \cos k\theta$ is the absolute value of A, $|A|$. (151) 2. The amplitude of a vector is the directed angle between the positive x-axis and the vector. (72)

angle An angle is the union of two rays that have a common endpoint. (116)

angle of depression An angle of depression is the angle formed by a horizontal line and the line of sight to an object at a lower level. (179)

angle of elevation An angle of elevation is the angle formed by a horizontal line and the line of sight to an object at a higher level. (179)

antiderivative The antiderivative of $f(x)$ is $F(x)$ if and only if $F'(x) = f(x)$. (455)

antilogarithm If $\log x = a$, then x is called the antilogarithm of a, abbreviated antilog a. If $\ln x = a$, then $x = \text{antiln } a$. (284)

Arccosine function The Arccosine function is the inverse of the cosine function. (162)

Arcsine function The Arcsine function is the inverse of the sine function. (162)

Arctangent function The Arctangent function is the inverse of the tangent function. (162)

arithmetic mean (average) The arithmetic mean of a set of data, $\overline{X}$, is the sum of the values in the set divided by the number of values in the set.

$$\overline{X} = \frac{1}{n}\sum_{i=1}^{n} X_i \quad (394)$$

arithmetic means Arithmetic means are the terms between any two nonconsecutive terms of an arithmetic sequence. (205)

arithmetic sequence An arithmetic sequence is a sequence in which each term after the first is equal to the sum of the preceding term and the common difference. (204)

array An array is formed by arranging statistical data into an ordered sequence. (395)

asymptotes 1. Asymptotes are lines which a curve approaches. (339) 2. The equations of the asymptotes of a hyperbola with a horizontal transverse axis are $y - k = \pm\frac{b}{a}(x - h)$. If the transverse axis is vertical, the equations are $y - k = \pm\frac{a}{b}(x - h)$. (341)

augmented matrix An augmented matrix is an array of the coefficients and constants of a system of equations. (70)

axis of symmetry An axis of symmetry is a line around which a figure is symmetric. (325)

bar graph A bar graph consists of parallel bars, either vertical or horizontal, which represent the frequency, f, of the values in a class. (407)

BASIC BASIC, an abbreviation for Beginner's All-purpose Symbolic Instruction Code, is a computer language. (466)

BASIC function A BASIC function is a subprogram, stored in the computer. Some common BASIC functions are ABS(X), SQR(X), INT(X), SIN(X), COS(X), TAN(X), LOG(X), and RND(X). (484)

binomial experiment A binomial experiment is a problem which can be solved using a binomial expansion. (387)

bisector of an angle The bisector of an angle is the set of points equidistant from the sides of the angle. (312)

broken line graph The broken line graph, sometimes called a frequency polygon, is a statistical graph which shows changing conditions over a period of time. (407)

characteristic The characteristic of a logarithm is the numeral which precedes the decimal point. In 2.314, 2 is the characteristic. (283)

circle A circle is a set of points in a plane at a given distance from a fixed point. The given distance is the radius of the circle and the given point is the center of the circle. The standard form of the equation of a circle with radius r and center (h, k) is $(x - h)^2 + (y - k)^2 = r^2$. (322)

circle graph A circle graph is a statistical graph which shows the relationship between the parts and the whole. A circle is separated into proportional parts called sectors. (408)

circular permutations Suppose n objects are arranged in a circle. Then there are $\frac{n!}{n}$ or $(n - 1)!$ permutations of the n objects around the circle. (369)

class A class is a set of values grouped together in a frequency distribution. (403)

classical curves Classical curves are special graphs formed by graphing polar equations. Roses, lemniscates, limaçons, cardioids, and spirals of Archimedes are examples of classical curves. (241)

class interval The class interval is the width of each class in a frequency distribution. (403)

class limits Class limits are the boundaries of each class in a frequency distribution. (403)

class marks Class marks are the averages of the class limits in a frequency distribution. (403)

combination A combination is the arrangement of objects where the order is not a consideration. (372)

common difference The common difference of an arithmetic sequence is the constant that is the difference between successive terms. (204)

common logarithms Common logarithms are logarithms which use 10 as the base. (282)

common ratio The common ratio is the constant which is the ratio of successive terms in a geometric sequence. (207)

complement Two events are complements when the sum of their probabilities is one. (375)

complex number A complex number is any number that can be written in the form $a + bi$, where a and b are real numbers and i is the imaginary unit. (31)

composite of functions The composite of functions f and g is symbolized $f \circ g$, and maps x into $f(g(x))$. (276)

compound functions Compound functions consist of sums or products of trigonometric functions and/or other functions. (159)

conditional probability The conditional probability of event A, given event B, is found as follows.

$$P(A/B) = \frac{P(A \text{ and } B)}{P(B)}, \text{ where } P(B) \neq 0.$$

(384)

conic section 1. A conic section is a curve formed by the intersection of a plane with a conical surface. (347) 2. A conic section is a set of points in the plane such that for any point of the set the ratio of its distance from a fixed point to its distance from a fixed line is constant. The fixed point is called a focus. The fixed line is called a directrix. (347)

conjugate of a complex number The conjugate of the complex number $a + bi$ is $a - bi$. (31)

conjugate axis The conjugate axis of a hyperbola is the segment perpendicular to the transverse axis at its center. (339)

conjugate hyperbolas Conjugate hyperbolas are two hyperbolas such that the transverse axis of one is the conjugate axis of the other and conversely. Conjugate hyperbolas share the same asymptotes. (344)

constant function A constant function is a function of the form $f(x) = b$. The graph is a horizontal line. (7)

constraints Constraints are conditions given to variables. Constraints are often expressed as linear inequalities. (17)

continuous function A function f is continuous if it is continuous at each point of its domain. (435)

continuous on an interval A function f is continuous on an interval if it is continuous at each point of the interval. (435)

continuous at a point A function f is continuous at $x = a$ if $f(a)$ exists and if $\lim_{x \to a} f(x) = f(a)$. (434)

convergent An infinite series is convergent if it has a sum or limit. (217)

cosecant function 1. For any real number s, the cosecant function is defined as follows.

$$\csc s = \frac{1}{\sin s} \quad (\sin s \neq 0) \quad (94)$$

2. For any angle with measure α, point $P(x, y)$ on its terminal side, and $r = \sqrt{x^2 + y^2}$, the cosecant of α is as follows.

$$\csc \alpha = \frac{r}{y} \quad (y \neq 0) \quad (116)$$

cosine function 1. For any real number s, where $C(s) = (x, y)$ such that $x^2 + y^2 = 1$, the cosine of $s = x$ or $\cos s = x$. (93) 2. For any angle with measure α, point $P(x, y)$ on its terminal side, and $r = \sqrt{x^2 + y^2}$, the cosine of α is as follows.

$$\cos \alpha = \frac{x}{r} \quad (r \neq 0) \quad (116)$$

cotangent function 1. Let s represent any real number. The cotangent function is defined as follows.

$$\cot s = \frac{\cos s}{\sin s} \quad (\sin s \neq 0) \quad (94)$$

2. For any angle with measure α, point $P(x, y)$ on its terminal side, and $r = \sqrt{x^2 + y^2}$, the cotangent of α is as follows.

$$\cot \alpha = \frac{x}{y} \quad (y \neq 0) \quad (116)$$

Cramer's rule Cramer's rule states that the solution to $a_1x + b_1y = c_1$ and $a_2x + b_2y = c_2$ is (x, y) where

$$x = \frac{\begin{vmatrix} c_1 & b_1 \\ c_2 & b_2 \end{vmatrix}}{\begin{vmatrix} a_1 & b_1 \\ a_2 & b_2 \end{vmatrix}} \text{ and } y = \frac{\begin{vmatrix} a_1 & c_1 \\ a_2 & c_2 \end{vmatrix}}{\begin{vmatrix} a_1 & b_1 \\ a_2 & b_2 \end{vmatrix}}. \quad \begin{vmatrix} a_1 & b_1 \\ a_2 & b_2 \end{vmatrix} \neq 0$$

(61)

critical points Critical points are points for which the derivative of a function is zero. (52)

cross product The cross product of $\vec{a}$ and $\vec{b}$ for $\vec{a} = (a_1, a_2, a_3)$ and $\vec{b} = (b_1, b_2, b_3)$ is defined as follows. (83)

$$\vec{a} \times \vec{b} = \begin{vmatrix} a_2 & a_3 \\ b_2 & b_3 \end{vmatrix} \vec{i} - \begin{vmatrix} a_1 & a_3 \\ b_1 & b_3 \end{vmatrix} \vec{j} + \begin{vmatrix} a_1 & a_2 \\ b_1 & b_2 \end{vmatrix} \vec{k}$$

cubic polynomial A cubic polynomial is a polynomial of the third degree such as $7x^3 + 4x^2 + 2x - 1$. (28)

DATA statement A DATA statement is a BASIC statement which lists information to be used in a computer program. (467)

decreasing function If $f'(x) < 0$ for all values of x in the interval $a < x < b$ of function f, then the function is decreasing in that interval. (446)

definite integral A definite integral is an integral which has lower and upper limits defined. (457)

degree of a polynomial The degree of a polynomial in one variable is the greatest exponent of its variable. (28)

dependent events Two events, A and B, are dependent if the outcome of event A affects the outcome of event B. The probability of two dependent events occurring is found as follows.

$$P(A \text{ and } B) = P(A) \cdot P(B \text{ following } A). \quad (378)$$

derivative The derivative of $f(x)$ is the function $f'(x)$ which is defined as follows.

$$f'(x) = \lim_{h \to 0} \frac{f(x + h) - f(x)}{h} \quad (50)$$

Descartes Rule of Signs Suppose $P(x)$ is a polynomial whose terms are arranged in descending powers of the variable. The number of positive real zeros of $y = P(x)$ is the same as the number of changes in sign of the coefficients of the terms, or is less than this by an even number. The number of negative real zeros is the same as the number of changes in sign of $P(^-x)$, or is less than this by an even number. (44)

determinant The determinant is defined as follows for a 2×2 matrix.

$$\det \begin{bmatrix} a_1 & b_1 \\ a_2 & b_2 \end{bmatrix} = \begin{vmatrix} a_1 & b_1 \\ a_2 & b_2 \end{vmatrix} = a_1b_2 - a_2b_1 \quad (60)$$

difference quotient The difference quotient is the slope of the secant line intersecting the graph of function f at $(a, f(a))$ and $(a + h, f(a + h))$. It is given by the following ratio.

$$\frac{f(a + h) - f(a)}{h} \quad (440)$$

differentiable A function is differentiable at a if the derivative of the function exists at a and is finite. (440)

differential notation Differential notation is $\frac{dy}{dx}$ and is read "the derivative of y with respect to x." (441)

differentiation Differentiation is the process of finding derivatives. (440)

DIM statement A DIM statement is a BASIC statement which assigns storage space in the computer for subscripted variables. (487)

dimensions of a matrix The dimensions of a matrix are the number of rows and number of columns. (60)

directrix See conic section.

discontinuous A function is discontinuous if there is a "break" in the graph of the function. (434)

distance formula The distance, d, between two points (x_1, y_1) and (x_2, y_2) is given by the following formula.

$$d = \sqrt{(x_2 - x_1)^2 + (y_2 - y_1)^2} \quad (9)$$

distance from a point to a line The distance from a point (x_1, y_1) to a line $Ax + By + C = 0$ can be found by the following formula.

$$d = \frac{Ax_1 + By_1 + C}{\pm\sqrt{A^2 + B^2}} \quad (310)$$

divergent An infinite series is divergent if it has no sum or limit. (217)

domain **1.** The domain of a relation is the set of all abscissas of the ordered pairs of the relation. (2) **2.** The domain of a function is the set for which the function is defined. (4)

dot product See inner product.

double angle identities The double angle identities are as follows.

$$\sin 2\theta = 2 \sin\theta \cos\theta$$
$$\cos 2\theta = \cos^2\theta - \sin^2\theta$$
$$= 1 - 2\sin^2\theta$$
$$= 2\cos^2\theta - 1$$
$$\tan 2\theta = \frac{2\tan\theta}{1 - \tan^2\theta} \quad (139)$$

e The following limit defines the number e.
$$e = \lim_{k\to\infty}\left(1 + \frac{1}{k}\right)^k = 1 + 1 + \frac{1}{2!} + \frac{1}{3!} + \cdots$$
Thus, $e \approx 2.718$. (271)

eccentricity 1. The eccentricity, e, of an ellipse is defined as $e = \frac{c}{a}$. For an ellipse, $e < 1$. (334) 2. The eccentricity of a hyperbola is defined as $e = \frac{c}{a}$. For a hyperbola, $e > 1$. (343) 3. The eccentricity of a parabola is 1. (347)

ellipse An ellipse is the set of all points in the plane such that the sum of the distances from two given points, called the foci, is constant. The standard form of the equation of an ellipse which has center (h, k) and major axis of length $2a$ is as follows. The equation is $\frac{(x-h)^2}{a^2} + \frac{(y-k)^2}{b^2} = 1$ when the major axis is parallel to the x-axis. The equation is $\frac{(y-k)^2}{a^2} + \frac{(x-h)^2}{b^2} = 1$ when the major axis is parallel to the y-axis. For an ellipse, $b^2 = a^2 - c^2$. (332, 334)

END statement An END statement is the final statement in a BASIC computer program. (475)

equilateral hyperbola An equilateral hyperbola has perpendicular asymptotes. In the standard form of an equilateral hyperbola, $a = b$. (344)

Euler's formula Euler's formula is $e^{i\alpha} = \cos\alpha + i\sin\alpha$. (291)

even function An even function is a function f such that $f(^-x) = f(x)$. The cosine function is an even function. (133)

exponential function 1. An exponential function has the form $y = a^x$, where a is a positive real number. (269) 2. The function $y = e^x$ is often called *the exponential function.* (272)

exponential series The following series is called the exponential series.
$$e^x = 1 + x + \frac{x^2}{2!} + \frac{x^3}{3!} + \cdots \quad (272)$$

factorial The expression $n!$ (n factorial) is defined as follows if n is an integer greater than zero.
$$n! = n(n-1)(n-2)\cdots(1)$$
Also, $0! = 1$. (225)

failure A failure is when the desired outcome of an event does not occur. (374)

flow charts A flow chart is a diagram that shows a step-by-step procedure for solving a problem. (475)

focus See conic section.

FOR-NEXT loops FOR-NEXT loops are used in a BASIC computer program to repeat a portion of the program a certain number of times. (479)

frequency The frequency, f, is the number of values in a class of a frequency distribution. (403)

frequency distribution A frequency distribution is a system of organizing data by determining classes and the frequency of values in each class. (403)

function A function is a relation in which each element of the domain is paired with exactly one element of the range. (2)

function C Function C is defined such that for each real number s, there corresponds exactly one ordered pair of real numbers, $C(s) = (x, y)$ which are coordinates of a point on the unit circle. (90)

Fundamental Theorem of Calculus If the function $f(x)$ is continuous and F is such that $F'(x) = f(x)$, then $\int_a^b f(x)dx = F(b) - F(a)$ where $F(x)$ is the antiderivative of $f(x)$. (457)

general equation for conic sections The general equation for conic sections can be written in the form $Ax^2 + Bxy + Cy^2 + Dx + Ey + F = 0$ where A, B, and C are not all zeros. (348)

geometric means Geometric means are the terms between any two nonconsecutive terms of a geometric sequence. (208)

geometric sequence A geometric sequence is a sequence in which each term after the first is the product of the preceding term and the common ratio. (207)

GO TO statement A GO TO statement is a BASIC statement which returns the computer to a particular step in a program. (468)

half angle identities The half angle identities are as follows.

$$\sin\frac{\alpha}{2} = \pm\sqrt{\frac{1-\cos\alpha}{2}}$$
$$\cos\frac{\alpha}{2} = \pm\sqrt{\frac{1+\cos\alpha}{2}}$$
$$\tan\frac{\alpha}{2} = \pm\sqrt{\frac{1-\cos\alpha}{1+\cos\alpha}} \quad (140)$$

harmonic mean The harmonic mean, H, of a set of values is a measure of central tendency. It is found by the following formula.

$$H = \frac{n}{\frac{1}{X_1} + \frac{1}{X_2} + \cdots + \frac{1}{X_n}} = \frac{n}{\sum_{i=1}^{n} \frac{1}{X_i}} \quad (397)$$

Hero's formula Hero's formula for the area, K, of triangle ABC is

$$K = \sqrt{s(s-a)(s-b)(s-c)}$$

where $s = \frac{a+b+c}{2}$. (190)

histogram A histogram is a vertical bar graph whose bars are next to each other. (407)

horizontal line test The horizontal line test can be used to determine if a function will have an inverse function. If any horizontal line drawn on the graph of a function passes through no more than one point of the graph, then the function has an inverse which is also a function. (278)

hyperbola A hyperbola is the set of all points in the plane such that the absolute value of the difference of the distance from two given points, called the foci, is constant. The standard form of the equation of a hyperbola which has center (h, k) and transverse axis of length $2a$ is as follows. The equation is $\frac{(x-h)^2}{a^2} - \frac{(y-k)^2}{b^2} = 1$ when the transverse axis is parallel to the x-axis. The equation is $\frac{(y-k)^2}{a^2} - \frac{(x-h)^2}{b^2} = 1$ when the transverse axis is parallel to the y-axis. For the hyperbola, $b^2 = c^2 - a^2$. (338, 340)

identity An identity is any equation which is true for all values of the variables. (122)

identity matrix under addition The identity matrix under addition for any $m \times n$ matrix is an $m \times n$ zero matrix. (64)

identity matrix under multiplication The identity matrix of nth order, I_n, is the square matrix whose elements in the main diagonal, from upper left to lower right, are 1's, while all other elements are 0's. (68)

IF-THEN statements The IF-THEN statement is a BASIC statement which makes a comparison of two numbers and then tells the computer what to do based on this comparison. (472)

imaginary number An imaginary number is a complex number of the form $a + bi$ where $b \neq 0$. (31)

imaginary unit The imaginary unit i is defined by $i^2 = {}^-1$. (31)

inclusive events Two events, A and B, are inclusive if the outcomes of A and B may be the same. The probability of two inclusive events, A and B, occurring is found as follows.

$P(A \text{ or } B) = P(A) + P(B) - P(A \text{ and } B)$
(381)

increasing function If $f'(x) > 0$ for all values of x in the interval $a < x < b$ of function f, then the function is increasing in the interval. (446)

independent events Two events, A and B, are independent if the outcome of one event does not affect the outcome of the other event. The probability of two independent events, A and B, occurring is found as follows.

$$P(A \text{ and } B) = P(A) \cdot P(B) \quad (378)$$

index of summation The index of summation is the variable used with the summation symbol (Σ). (222)

infinite sequence An infinite sequence has an unlimited number of terms. (210)

infinite series An infinite series is the indicated sum of the terms of an infinite sequence. (213)

initial side The initial side of an angle is the starting position of a ray used to generate an angle by rotation. (116)

inner product of vectors If $\vec{a}$ and $\vec{b}$ are two vectors, (a_1, a_2) and (b_1, b_2), then the inner product (or dot product) of $\vec{a}$ and $\vec{b}$ is defined as follows.

$$\vec{a} \cdot \vec{b} = a_1b_1 + a_2b_2 \quad (82)$$

integral The function $F(x)$ is an integral of $f(x)$ with respect to x if and only if $F(x)$ is an antiderivative of $f(x)$. That is, $F(x) = \int f(x)dx$ if and only if $F'(x) = f(x)$. (455)

inverse functions Two functions f and g are inverse functions if and only if both their compositions are the identity function. That is, $f(g(x)) = g(f(x)) = x$. (277)

irrational exponents If x is an irrational number and $a > 0$, then a^x is the real number between a^{x_1} and a^{x_2} for all possible choices of rational numbers x_1 and x_2 and $x_1 < x < x_2$. (268)

irrational number An irrational number is a number which cannot be expressed as $\frac{a}{b}$ where a and b are integers and $b \neq 0$. (216)

inverse of a function The inverse of a function can be found by interchanging the elements of the ordered pairs of the function. The domain becomes the range and the range becomes the domain. (162)

latus rectum A latus rectum of a conic is a line segment through a focus perpendicular to the axis with endpoints on the conic. For a parabola, the length of this segment is $4p$, where p is the distance from the focus to the vertex. The length of the latus rectum of an ellipse or hyperbola is $\frac{2b^2}{a}$. (327, 337)

LET statement A LET statement is a BASIC statement which assigns specific values to indicated variables. (469)

limit of a function The limit of a function $f(x)$ as x approaches a is L, written $\lim_{x \to a} f(x) = L$, if, for every real number $\epsilon > 0$, there exists a real number $\delta > 0$ such that $|f(x) - L| < \epsilon$ and $0 < |x - a| < \delta$. (431)

limit of a polynomial function The limit of a polynomial function, $P(x)$, as x approaches r, is $P(r)$.

$$\lim_{x \to r} P(x) = P(r) \quad (427)$$

limit of a sequence The limit of a sequence, if it exists, is the value which the terms of the sequence approach as n approaches infinity. (211)

linear function A linear function has the form $f(x) = mx + b$ where m and b are real numbers. (6)

linear programming Linear programming is a procedure for finding the maximum or the minimum value of a function in two variables subject to given conditions, called constraints, on the variables. (17)

logarithmic function The logarithmic function $y = \log_a x$, $a > 0$ and $a \neq 1$, is the inverse of the exponential function $y = a^x$. Thus, $y = \log_a x$ if and only if $x = a^y$. (280)

magnitude The magnitude, $|\vec{v}|$, of $\vec{v}$ is the absolute value of the length of the directed line segment which represents $\vec{v}$. (72)

major axis The major axis of an ellipse is the segment with endpoints at the vertices of the ellipse. (332)

mantissa The mantissa of a common logarithm is a positive decimal less than 1. The mantissa of 3.6990, is 0.6990. The mantissa always represents the common logarithm of a number between 1 and 10. (283)

matrix A matrix is any rectangular array of terms called elements. An $m \times n$ matrix is a matrix with m rows and n columns. (60)

mean deviation The mean deviation, *M.D.*, is a measure of variability which can be found by the following formula.

$$M.D. = \frac{1}{n}\sum_{i=1}^{n} |X_1 - \overline{X}| \quad (400)$$

measure of central tendency A measure of central tendency is a number which represents a set of data. (394)

median The median, M_d, is the mid-value of a set of data. (395)

midpoint The midpoint of the segment with endpoints (x_1, y_1) and (x_2, y_2) is

$$\left(\frac{x_1 + x_2}{2}, \frac{y_1 + y_2}{2}\right) \quad (300)$$

minor axis The minor axis of an ellipse is the segment perpendicular to the major axis at the center, with endpoints on the ellipse. (332)

mode The mode of a set of data is the value which appears more frequently than any other in the set. (395)

modulus The modulus of a complex number $x + yi$ is the distance from the origin to the point (x, y) in the complex plane. That is, $r = \sqrt{x^2 + y^2}$. (249)

multiplication of matrices The product of an $m \times n$ matrix, A, and an $n \times r$ matrix, B, is an $m \times r$ matrix, AB. The ijth element of AB is the product of the ith row of A and the jth column of B. (66)

mutually exclusive events Two events, A and B, are mutually exclusive if the outcomes of A and B can never be the same. The probability of two mutually exclusive events, A and B, occurring is found as follows. $P(A \text{ or } B) = P(A) + P(B)$ (380)

natural logarithms Natural logarithms, symbolized $\ln x$, are logarithms to base e. (288)

normal 1. The normal to a curve at any point on it is the line perpendicular to the tangent at the point. (353) 2. The normal of a line is the line segment from the origin to the line, perpendicular to the line. (306)

normal distribution A normal distribution has a bell-shaped, symmetrical graph centered about the mean of the data. About 68% of the items are within one standard deviation of the mean. About 95% of the items are within two standard deviations. About 99% of the items are within three standard deviations. (415)

normal form Normal form of a linear equation is $x \cos \phi + y \sin \phi - p = 0$, where ϕ is the angle from the positive x-axis to the normal and p is the length of the normal. (306)

nth order matrix A matrix of the nth order is a square matrix with n rows and n columns. (60)

odd function An odd function is a function f such that $f(^-x) = {}^-f(x)$. The sine function is an odd function. (133)

odds The odds of the successful outcomes of an event is the ratio of the probability of its success to the probability of its failure. (376)

parabola A parabola is the set of all points which are the same distance from a given point, the focus, and a given line, the directrix. In the standard form of the equation of a parabola, the center is (h, k) and the distance from the vertex to the focus is p. The equation is $(y - k)^2 = 4p(x - h)$ when the directrix is parallel to the y-axis. The equation is $(x - h)^2 = 4p(y - k)$ when the directrix is parallel to the x-axis. (325)

parallel lines Two lines are parallel if and only if the slopes of the lines are equal. (298)

Pascal's triangle Pascal's triangle is a triangular array of numbers. The numbers in the array are the coefficients of the terms in the expansion of $(x + y)^n$ for $n = 0, 1, 2,$ etc. (226)

period of a function The period of a function is the least positive value of α for which $f(x) = f(x + \alpha)$. (91)

periodic function A function is periodic if, for some real number α, $f(x + \alpha) = f(x)$ for each x in the domain of f. (91)

permutation A permutation is the arrangement of objects in a certain order. (365)

permutations with repetitions The number of permutations of n objects of which p are alike and q are alike is found by evaluating the expression $\frac{n!}{p!q!}$. (368)

perpendicular lines Two lines are perpendicular if and only if the slope of one is the negative reciprocal of the slope of the other. (299)

perpendicular vectors Perpendicular vectors are two vectors whose inner product is zero. (82)

phase shift The phase shift of a function of the form $y = A \sin (k\theta + C)$, is $-\frac{c}{k}$. If $c > 0$, the shift is to the left and if $c < 0$ the shift is to the right. This definition applies to all trigonometric functions. (153)

point-slope form If the point (x_1, y_1) lies on a line having slope m, the point-slope form of the equation of the line can be written as follows.

$$y - y_1 = m(x - x_1) \quad (11)$$

polar axis The polar axis is a ray whose initial point is the pole. (236)

polar coordinates The polar coordinates of a point P are written in the form (r, θ), where r is the distance from the pole to the point P and θ is the measure of an angle which has the polar axis as its initial side and $\overrightarrow{OP}$ as its terminal side. (236)

polar equation A polar equation is an equation which uses polar coordinates. (238)

polar equation of a conic section The polar equation of any conic section where the pole is at a focus and the polar axis is perpendicular to the directrix can be written as follows, where e is the eccentricity and $2p$ is the distance from the focus to the directrix.

$$r = \frac{2ep}{1 + e \cos \theta} \quad (358)$$

polar graph A polar graph represents the set of all points (r, θ) which satisfy a given polar equation. (238)

pole The pole is a fixed point O in a plane. It is also called an origin. (236)

polygonal convex set A polygonal convex set is the region formed when a system of linear inequalities is graphed so that the intersection set is a convex polygon and its interior. (15)

polynomial A polynomial, in one variable, x, is an expression of the form $a_0x^n + a_1x^{n-1} + \cdots + a_{n-1}x + a_n$. The coefficients are real numbers and n is a nonnegative integer. (28)

polynomial equation A polynomial equation is a polynomial which is set equal to zero. (28)

principal values Principal values of trigonometric functions are the values in the domain of the functions sine, cosine, and tangent. (164)

PRINT statement A PRINT statement is a BASIC statement which instructs the computer to print out data or messages. (467)

quadrantal angle A quadrantal angle is an angle in standard position whose terminal side coincides with one of the coordinate axes. (134)

quadratic equation A quadratic equation is a second degree polynomial such as $5x^2 + 6x - 3 = 0$. (28)

quadratic formula The roots of a quadratic equation of the form $ax^2 + bx + c = 0$ are given by the following formula.

$$x = \frac{^-b \pm \sqrt{b^2 - 4ac}}{2a} \quad (30)$$

quadratic mean The quadratic mean, Q, is a measure of central tendency which can be found by using the following formula.

$$Q = \sqrt{\frac{X_1^2 + X_2^2 + X_3^2 + \cdots + X_n^2}{n}}$$

$$= \sqrt{\frac{\sum_{i=1}^{n} X_i^2}{n}} \quad (398)$$

quartic polynomial A quartic polynomial is a polynomial of the fourth degree. (28)

quartile A quartile is one of four parts of data formed when an array of a set of data is separated into four parts having an equal number of data. (400)

quintic polynomial A quintic polynomial is a polynomial of the fifth degree. (28)

radian A radian is the measure of a central angle whose sides intercept an arc which has length 1 unit. (128)

range 1. The range is the set of all ordinates of a relation. (2) 2. The range is the difference of the largest and smallest values in the array of a set of data. (395)

rational exponents For any nonzero number b, and any integers m and n, with $n > 1$, $b^{\frac{m}{n}} = \sqrt[n]{b^m} = (\sqrt[n]{b})^m$ except when $\sqrt[n]{b}$ is not a real number. (265)

rational number A rational number is a number which can be expressed as $\frac{a}{b}$, where a and b are integers and $b \neq 0$. (216)

READ statement A READ statement is a BASIC statement which instructs the computer to input the indicated data. (467)

reference angle A reference angle is an acute angle in the first quadrant with vertex at the origin which is used to find the trigonometric functions of angles in other quadrants. (132)

relation A relation is a set of ordered pairs. A relation can also be represented as a graph, a table of values, or by any rule in words or symbols which determines pairs of values. (2)

relative maximum or minimum A relative maximum or minimum is a point which represents the maximum or minimum respectively, for a certain interval. (52)

REM statement A REM statement is a BASIC statement which provides a means of identification for the program. It does *not* affect the execution of the program. (467)

resultant vector A resultant vector is the sum of two or more vectors. (73)

root A root of a polynomial equation $P(x) = 0$ is a value of x for which the value of the polynomial $P(x)$ is zero. (28)

RUN RUN is a BASIC command that instructs the computer to execute the program. (469)

scalar A scalar is a real-number constant. The term scalar is used to distinguish a vector or matrix from a real number. (65)

scalar product 1. The product of an $m \times n$ matrix, A, and a scalar, k, is an $m \times n$ matrix, kA. Each element of kA is equal to k times the corresponding element of A. (65) 2. The product of a vector, (a_1, a_2), and a scalar, k, is a vector, (ka_1, ka_2). (78)

secant function 1. For any real number s, the secant function is defined as follows.

$$\sec s = \frac{1}{\cos s} \quad (\cos s \neq 0) \quad (94)$$

2. For any angle with measure α, point $P(x, y)$ on its terminal side, and $r = \sqrt{x^2 + y^2}$, the secant of α is as follows.

$$\sec \alpha = \frac{r}{x} \quad (x \neq 0) \quad (116)$$

secant line A secant line to a curve is a line which intersects the curve at two or more points. (49)

second derivative The second derivative of function f, $f''(x)$, is the derivative of $f'(x)$. (448)

sector A sector of a circle is the region bounded by an arc of a circle and the radii drawn to its endpoints. (196)

segment A segment of a circle is the region of the circle bounded by an arc and its chord. (196)

semi-interquartile range The semi-interquartile range, Q_R is a measure of variability of a set of data. It is half of the difference between the first quartile point and the third quartile point.

$$Q_R = \frac{Q_3 - Q_1}{2} \quad (401)$$

sequence A sequence is a set of numbers in a specific order. (204)

series A series is the indicated sum of the terms of a sequence. (205, 209)

sine function 1. For any real number s, where $C(s) = (x, y)$ such that $x^2 + y^2 = 1$, the sine of $s = y$ or $\sin s = y$. (93) **2.** For any angle with measure α, point $P(x, y)$ on its terminal side, and $r = \sqrt{x^2 + y^2}$, the sine of α is as follows.

$$\sin \alpha = \frac{y}{r} \quad (r \neq 0) \quad (116)$$

slope 1. The slope of a line through (x_1, y_1) and (x_2, y_2) is given by the following equation, if $x_2 \neq x_1$.

$$\text{slope} = \frac{y_2 - y_1}{x_2 - x_1} \quad (9)$$

2. The slope of a line is equal to the tangent of the angle that the line makes with the positive x-axis. (303)

slope-intercept form The slope-intercept form of the equation of a line is $y = mx + b$. The slope is m and the y-intercept is b. (10)

slope of the tangent The slope of the tangent to the graph of $y = f(x)$ at the point (x, y) is $f'(x)$, defined as follows.

$$f'(x) = \lim_{h \to 0} \frac{f(x + h) - f(x)}{h} \quad (50)$$

square matrix A square matrix has the same number of rows as columns. (60)

standard deviation Standard deviation, σ, of a set of data is the quadratic mean of the individual deviations from the arithmetic mean. It can be found as follows.

$$\sigma = \sqrt{\frac{1}{n} \sum_{i=1}^{n} (X_i - \overline{X})^2} \quad (401)$$

standard error of the mean The standard error of the mean is used to give a level of confidence about the sample mean. It can be found as follows.

$$\sigma_{\overline{x}} = \frac{\sigma}{\sqrt{n}} \quad (419)$$

standard form The standard form of a linear equation is $Ax + By + C = 0$, where A, B, and C are real numbers and A and B are not both 0. (5)

standard position An angle with its vertex at the origin and its initial side along the positive x-axis is in standard position. (116)

stationary values Stationary values are points at which the function is neither increasing nor decreasing. (447)

success A success is when the desired outcome of an event occurs. (374)

sum of an infinite geometric series The sum, S, of an infinite geometric series for which $|r| < 1$ is given by the following formula.

$$S = \frac{a}{1 - r} \quad (214)$$

sum of an infinite series If S_n is the sum of n terms of a series, and S is a number such that $S > S_n$ for all n, and $S - S_n$ approaches zero as n increases without limit, then the sum of the infinite series is S.

$$\lim_{n \to \infty} S_n = S \quad (214)$$

tangent line A tangent line, or tangent, is a straight line which touches a curve at a point. If A is a fixed point on the curve and B is a variable point, then the tangent line is the limiting position of $\overleftrightarrow{AB}$ as B approaches A. (49)

tangent function 1. Let s represent any real number. The tangent function is defined as follows.

$$\tan s = \frac{\sin s}{\cos s} \quad (\cos s \neq 0) \quad (94)$$

2. For any angle with measure α, point $P(x, y)$ on its terminal side, and $r = \sqrt{x^2 + y^2}$, the tangent of α is as follows.

$$\tan \alpha = \frac{y}{x} \quad (x \neq 0) \quad (116)$$

terminal side The terminal side of an angle is the final position of a ray used to generate the angle by rotation. (116)

translation formulas The translation formulas are $x = x^1 + h$ and $y = y^1 + k$ where (h, k) represents the origin of the coordinate system (x^1, y^1). (330)

transverse axis The transverse axis of a hyperbola is the line segment of length $2a$ which has its endpoints at the vertices. (339)

trigonometric equation A trigonometric equation is an equation involving a trigonometric function which is true for some, but not all, values of the variable. (174)

trigonometric functions 1. For any angle with measure α, point $P(x, y)$ on its terminal side, and $r = \sqrt{x^2 + y^2}$, the trigonometric functions of α are as follows.

$$\sin \alpha = \frac{y}{r} \quad \cos \alpha = \frac{x}{r} \quad \tan \alpha = \frac{y}{x}$$

$$\csc \alpha = \frac{r}{y} \quad \sec \alpha = \frac{r}{x} \quad \cot \alpha = \frac{x}{y} \quad (116)$$

2. For an acute angle A in right triangle ABC, the trigonometric functions are as follows.

$$\sin A = \frac{\text{side opposite}}{\text{hypotenuse}} \quad \cos A = \frac{\text{side adjacent}}{\text{hypotenuse}}$$

$$\tan A = \frac{\text{side opposite}}{\text{side adjacent}} \quad \cot A = \frac{\text{side adjacent}}{\text{side opposite}}$$

$$\sec A = \frac{\text{hypotenuse}}{\text{side adjacent}} \quad \csc A = \frac{\text{hypotenuse}}{\text{side opposite}}$$

(117)

trigonometric series The trigonometric series for $\cos x$ and $\sin x$ are given as follows.

$$\cos x = 1 - \frac{x^2}{2!} + \frac{x^4}{4!} - \frac{x^6}{6!} + \cdots$$

$$\sin x = 1 - \frac{x^3}{3!} + \frac{x^5}{5!} - \frac{x^7}{7!} + \cdots (291)$$

two-point form The two-point form of the equation of a line is as follows.

$$y - y_1 = \frac{y_2 - y_1}{x_2 - x_1}(x - x_1) \quad (299)$$

unit circle A unit circle is a circle on the coordinate plane with its center at the origin and radius 1 unit. (90)

unit vectors Unit vectors are vectors of length one unit in the directions of the x, y, and z axes. They are denoted $\vec{\mathbf{i}}$, $\vec{\mathbf{j}}$, and $\mathbf{k}$, respectively. (78, 81)

vector A vector is a quantity which possesses both magnitude and direction. (72)

x-intercept The x-intercept is the x-coordinate of the point at which the graph of a function crosses the x-axis. (6)

y-intercept The y-intercept is the y-coordinate of the point at which the graph of a function crosses the y-axis. (6)

zero of a function A zero of a function is a value of x for which $f(x) = 0$. (44)

SELECTED ANSWERS

CHAPTER 1 RELATIONS AND FUNCTIONS

Exploratory Exercises Page 4 1. D-{0}, R-{0} 3. D-{5, 6}, R-{5, 6} 5. D-{$^-3$, 0, 1, 2}, R-{0, 2, 4, $^-6$} 7. D-{$^-2$}, R-{7, 8, 9} 9. D-{4, 9}, R-{$^-3$, $^-2$, 2, 3} 11. yes 13. yes 15. yes 17. no 19. no

Written Exercises Page 4 1. {(1, 0), (2, 3), (3, 6), (4, 9), (5, 12)} 3. {($^-3$, 9), ($^-2$, 4)} 5. {(4, 2), (4, $^-2$)} 7. D-{1, 2, 3, 4, 5}, R-{0, 3, 6, 9, 12} 9. D-{$^-3$, $^-2$}, R-{9, 4} 11. D-{4}, R-{2, $^-2$} 13. yes 15. yes 17. no 19. yes 21. yes 23. no 25. 7 27. $^-2$ 29. $6\frac{3}{4}$ 31. $7 - 4a^2$ 33. 4 35. $^-5$ 37. $^-671$ 39. $8 - 6a - 6a^2 - a^3$ 41. 0 43. $^-3$ 45. 2 47. $[t]$ 49. 13 51. 0 53. 10.04 55. $|n^2 + 8n + 3|$ 57. 1 59. 0 61. $\pm 4\frac{1}{2}$

Exploratory Exercises Page 7 1. $3x - y + 2 = 0$ 3. $x - 3 = 0$ 5. $y + 4 = 0$ 7. 2 9. none 11. yes 13. no 15. no 17. yes

Written Exercises Page 8

1.
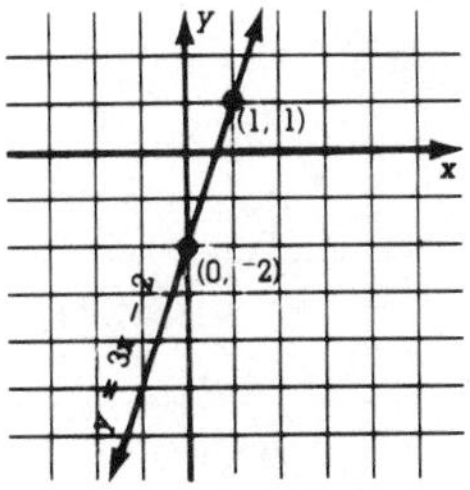

3.
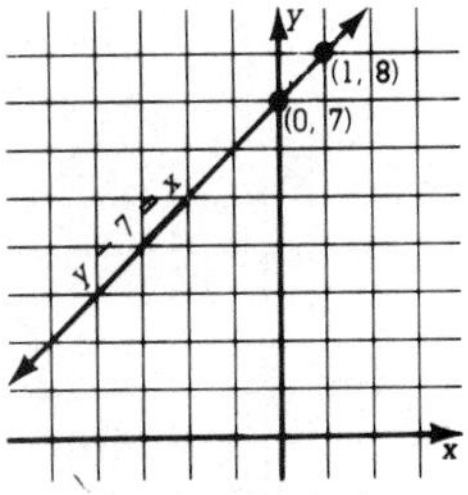

5.
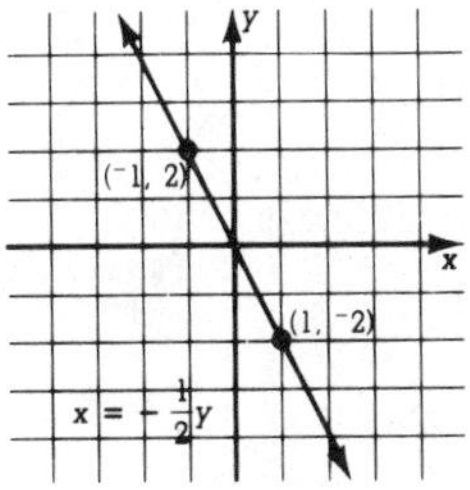

7.
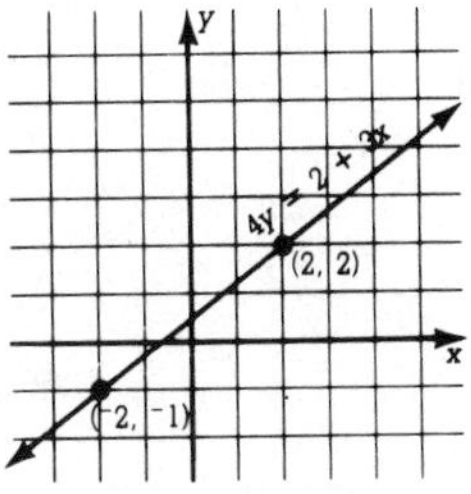

9. $^-12$ 11. $-\frac{5}{9}$ 13. none 15. (0, 1) 17. (0, 3) 19. (2, $^-4$)

Exploratory Exercises Page 10 1. 3 3. 6 5. 13 7. 0 9. undefined 11. $\frac{12}{5}$

Written Exercises Page 10 1. $3\sqrt{5}$ 3. $\sqrt{74}$ 5. 5 7. $5t$ 9. $\sqrt{1 + 9n^2}$ 11. $^-1$ 13. $^-2$ 15. undefined 17. $-\frac{1}{2}$ 19. 30 21. 12

Challenge Page 10 1. 4 3. 2 5. 4

Exploratory Exercises Page 12 1. $m = \frac{3}{2}$, y-intercept is $-\frac{7}{2}$, $y = \frac{3}{2}x - \frac{7}{2}$ 3. $m = -\frac{5}{11}$, y-intercept is $\frac{2}{11}$, $y = -\frac{5}{11}x + \frac{2}{11}$ 5. $m = \frac{1}{2}$, y-intercept is $^-2$, $y = \frac{1}{2}x - 2$ 7. $m = 4$, y-intercept is $\frac{1}{2}$, $y = 4x + \frac{1}{2}$ 9. $m = -\frac{4}{3}$, y-intercept is 0, $y = -\frac{4}{3}x$

Written Exercises Page 12 1. $y = 4x - 10$ 3. $y = {}^-6x - 22$ 5. $y = {}^-5x - 37$ 7. $y = \frac{3}{4}x + 11\frac{1}{2}$ 9. $y = \frac{2}{3}x + 5$ 11. $y = {}^-x - 2$ 13. $x = {}^-1$ 15. $y = \frac{7}{2}x - \frac{31}{2}$ 17. $y = -\frac{3}{5}x + \frac{14}{5}$

Exploratory Exercises Page 16 1. $x > 2$ 3. $y \le x + 2$ 5. $1 < y < 4$ 7. (3, 2) 9. (0, 0), (3, 2) 11. (0, 0), (3, 2), ($^-4$, 2), ($^-2$, 4) 13. (3, 2), ($^-4$, 2), ($^-2$, 4) 15. ($^-4$, 2), ($^-2$, 4)

Written Exercises Page 16

1.
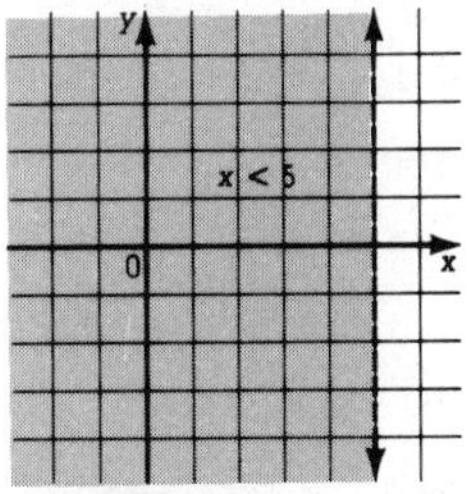

3.
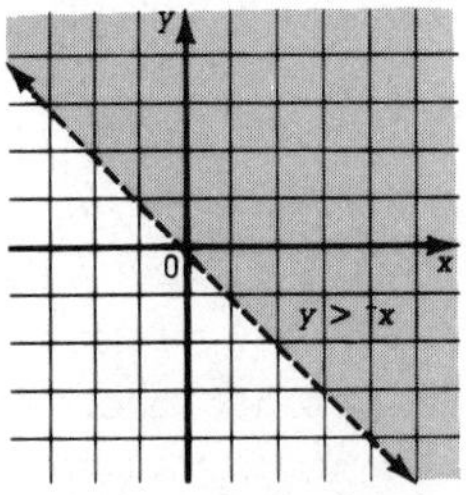

5.
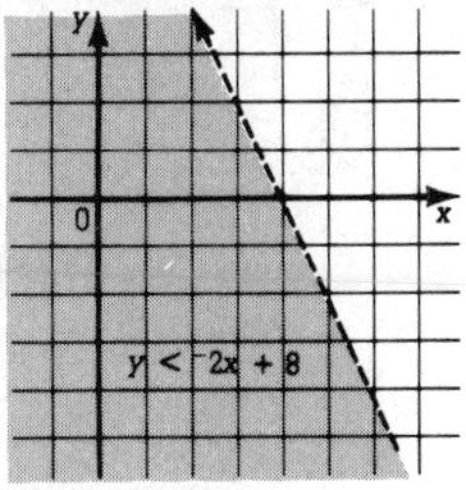

7.
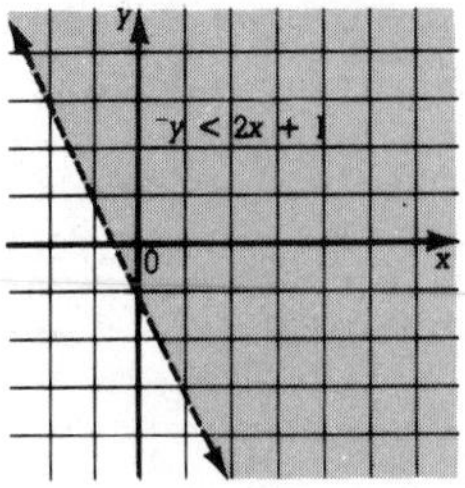

9. 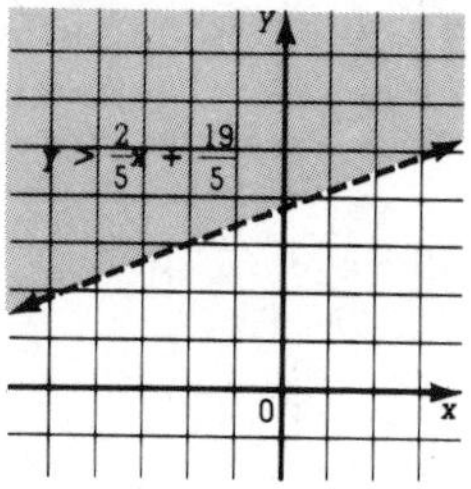

11. 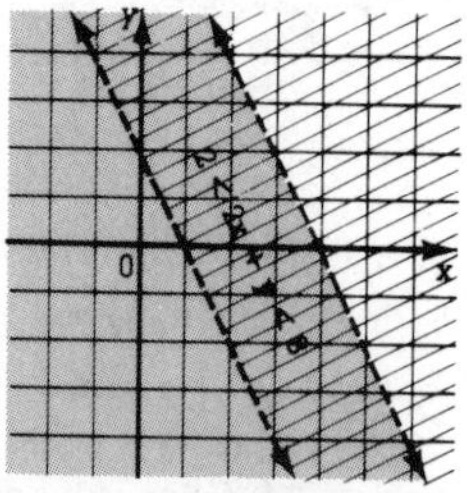

13. 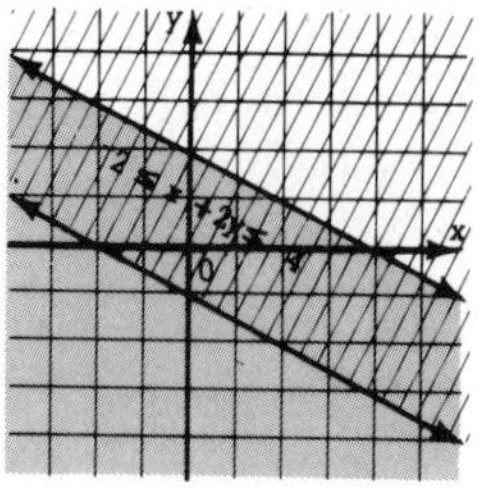

15. 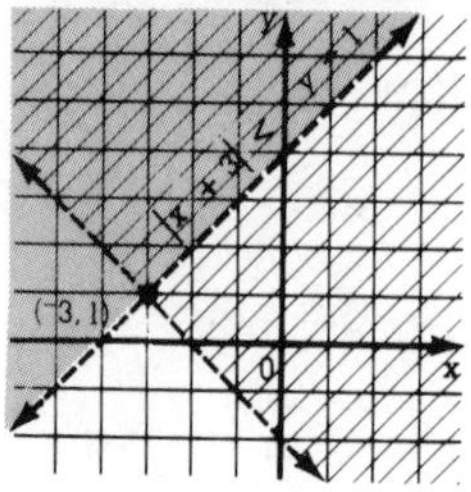

17. 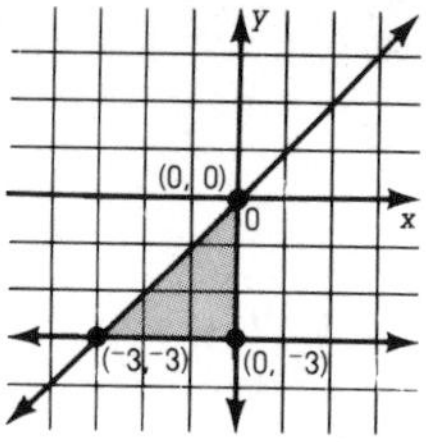

19. 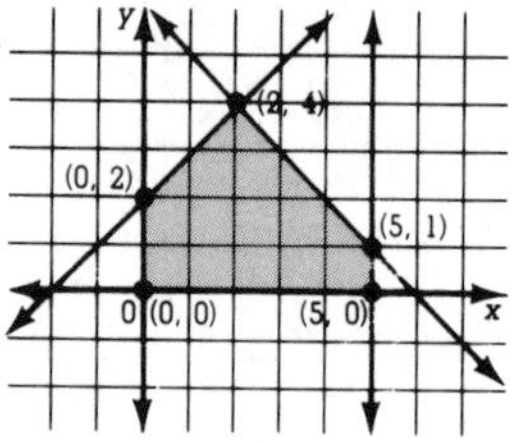

21. 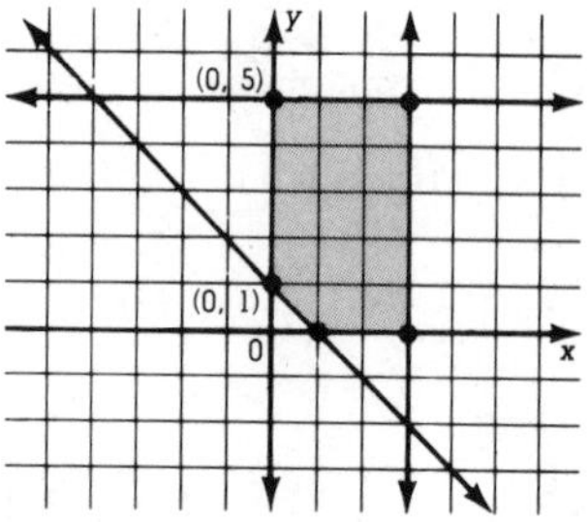

Exploratory Exercises Page 18 1. 14 3. 15 5. 1 7. 9 9. 1 11. $^-4$ 13. 17 15. $^-32$ 17. max 8, min 0 19. max 20, min $^-12$ 21. max 13, min 0

Written Exercises Page 18

1. 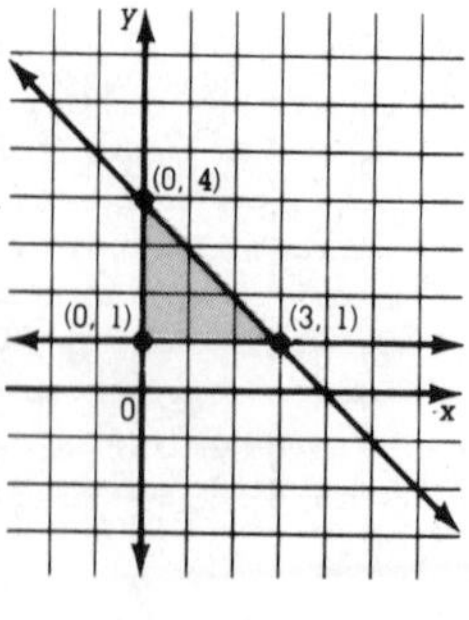

3. 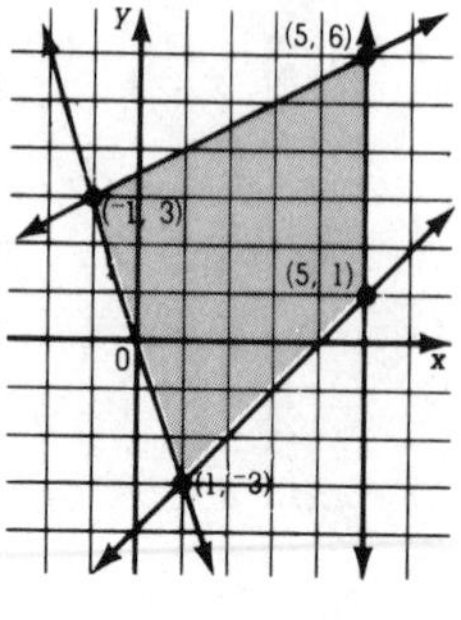

5. max 27, min $^-1$ 7. max 4, min $^-2$ 9. max 6, min $^-2$ 11. max 17, min 3 13. max 42, min 18 15. max 68, min $^-12$

Exploratory Exercises Page 20 1. $x + y \le 800$ 3. $y \ge 300$

5. 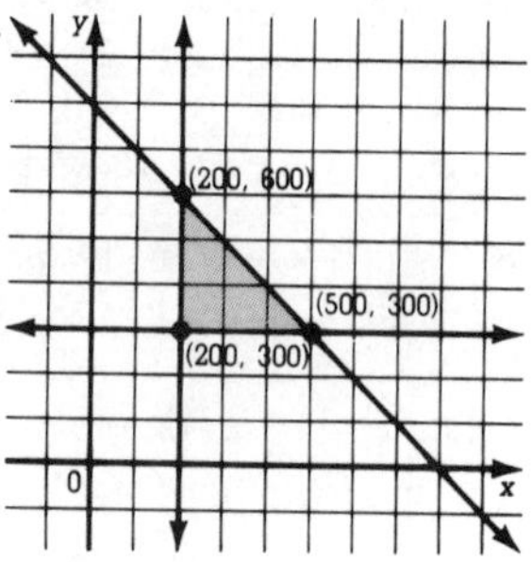

7. 200 units of lumber, 600 units of plywood

Written Exercises Page 21 1. 900 widgets, 1400 gadgets; $1060 3. 900 widgets, 1400 gadgets; $773 5. 1200 widgets, 1100 gadgets; $748 7. 30% beef, 20% pork, $76 9. 30% beef, 20% pork; $102

Chapter Review Page 24 1. D-{3, 4, 5}, R-{5} 3. D-{8, 10}, R-{$^-5$, $^-4$, 4, 5} 5. D-{7, 8, 9}, R-{49, 64, 81} 7. {(0, $^-7$), (1, $^-2$), (2, 3), (3, 8)} 9. {(5, 1), (6, 2), (5, $^-1$), (6, $^-2$)} 11. yes 13. no 15. yes 17. yes 19. no 21. 6 23. 126 25. 0 27. $^-3$ 29. $x - 3y + 5 = 0$ 31. $2x - 2y = 0$ or $x - y = 0$ 33. $y + 8 = 0$

35. 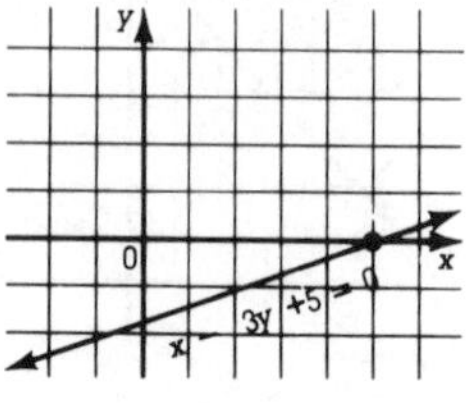

37. 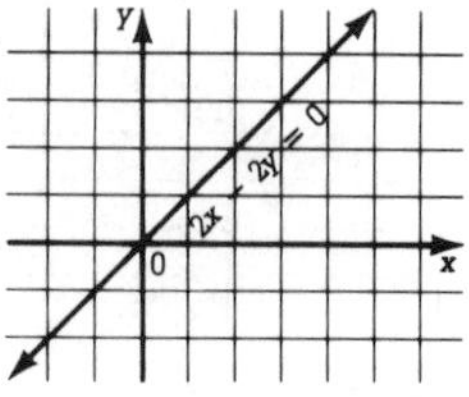

39. 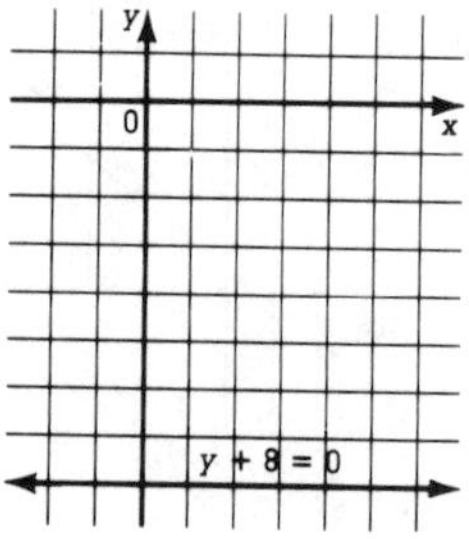

41. $\frac{8}{3}$ 43. 20

45. 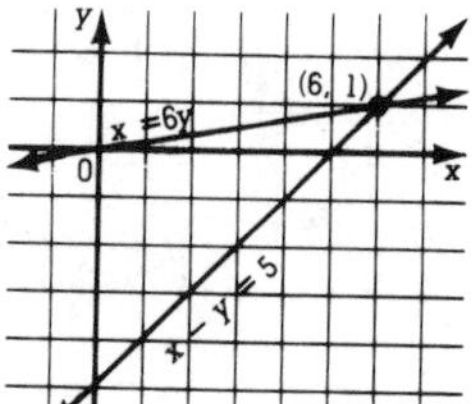

47. 13 49. 5 51. $\frac{12}{5}$ 53. $\frac{4}{3}$ 55. $y = 2x - 5$ 57. $y = \frac{3}{5}x$ 59. $y = x + 4$ 61. $y = \frac{1}{4}x + \frac{15}{4}$ 63. $y = \frac{7}{2}x - 10$

65.
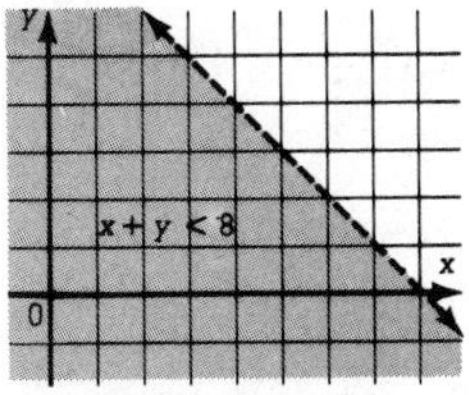

67.
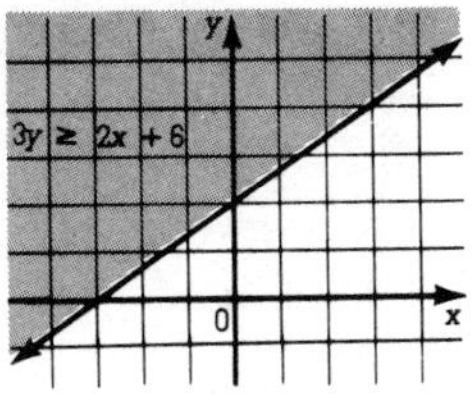

69.
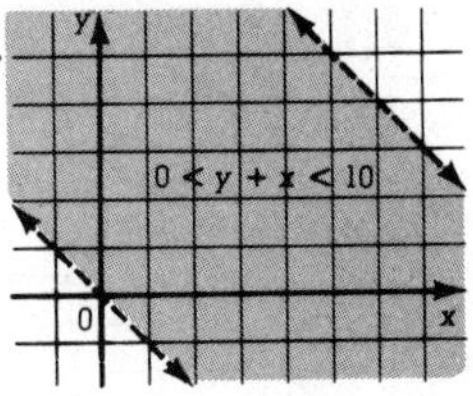

71.
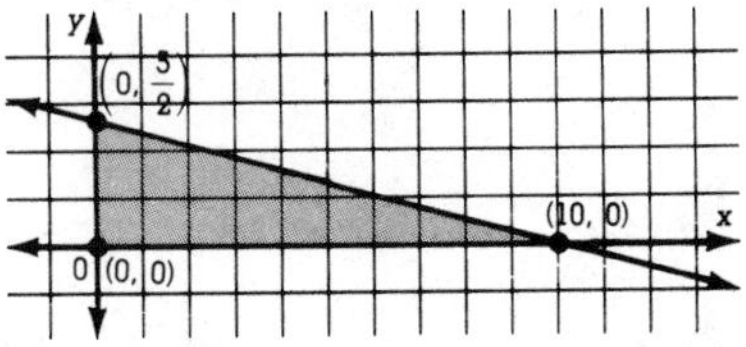

73.
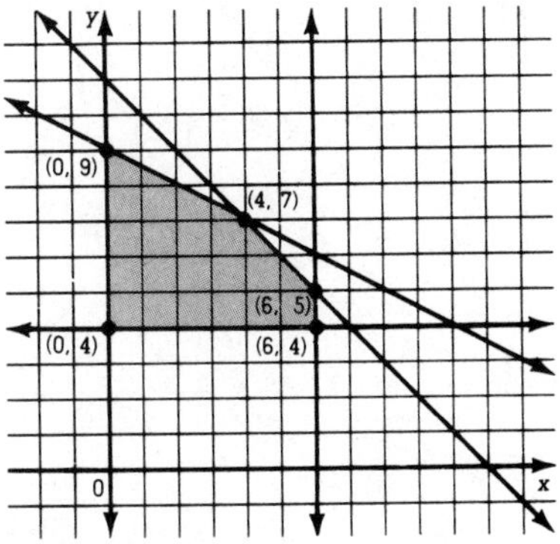

75. 49 77. $^-27$ 79. 31.1 81. 14 83. max 70, min 10 85. max 13, min $^-8$ 87. 2 large, 6 small; \$220

CHAPTER 2 THEORY OF EQUATIONS

Exploratory Exercises Page 29 1. no 3. no 5. yes 7. yes 9. no 11. yes 13. yes 15. no

Written Exercises Page 29 1. $x = 2$ 3. $x = \pm 2$ 5. $z = 2, ^-1$ 7. $u = \pm 2$ 9. $x = 1,2,3,4$ 11. $r = 9$ 13. $y = \pm 3$ 15. $y = \frac{1}{7}, \frac{-3}{2}$ 17. $x = \frac{9}{4}, \frac{7}{5}$ 19. $x = \frac{1}{6}, \frac{-1}{3}$ 21. $x = \frac{5}{6}, \frac{-3}{2}$ 23. $b = \pm \frac{11}{4}$

Exploratory Exercises Page 32 1. ^-i 3. $5 + 2i$ 5. $\frac{-1}{2} - \frac{1}{2}i$ 7. $5 + i\sqrt{2}$ 9. 4 11. $\frac{1}{4}$ 13. $\frac{4}{9}$ 15. 225 17. $\frac{1}{64}$ 19. $\frac{4}{49}$

Written Exercises Page 32 1. $y = 11, ^-8$ 3. $x = 2, ^-10$ 5. $x = \frac{1}{2}, \frac{1}{4}$ 7. $y = \frac{3}{2}, ^-7$ 9. $x = \frac{3 \pm \sqrt{37}}{2}$ 11. $x = 2 \pm \frac{2\sqrt{6}}{3}$ 13. $x = 4, \frac{-5}{3}$ 15. $x = \frac{5}{4}, 1$ 17. $n = \frac{8}{7}, ^-4$ 19. $y = \frac{3}{2}, \frac{-2}{3}$ 21. $x = \frac{^-3 \pm i\sqrt{15}}{4}$ 23. $y = \frac{^-4 \pm i\sqrt{14}}{6}$ 25. $x = ^-1, \frac{-4}{3}$ 27. $b = \frac{^-1 \pm \sqrt{97}}{8}$ 29. $x = \frac{1 \pm i\sqrt{39}}{5}$

Exploratory Exercises Page 35 1. Divisor, $x - 2$; Dividend, $3x^3 - 5x + 10$; Quotient, $3x^2 + 6x + 7$; Remainder, 24 3. Divisor, $x + 3$; Dividend, $x^3 - 11x + 10$; Quotient, $x^2 - 3x + 2$; Remainder, 16 5. Divisor, $x + 1$; Dividend, $2x^3 - 5x + 1$; Quotient, $2x^2 - 2x - 3$; Remainder, 4 7. Divisor, $x - \frac{1}{2}$; Dividend, $x^3 + \frac{3}{2}x^2 + 3x - 2$; Quotient, $x^2 + 2x + 4$; Remainder, 0

Written Exercises Page 35 1. $x + 6$ 3. $x^2 + 2x + 6, R = 15$ 5. $x^3 - 2x^2 - 4x + 8$ 7. $x^2 - 2x + 2$ 9. $x^2 + 4x + 4, R = 4$ 11. $2x^2 + 2x, R = ^-3$ 13. $8x - 44, R = 231$ 15. 4; no 17. 55; no 19. 0; yes 21. 0; yes 23. $^-3$; no

Challenge Page 35 1. $2y^3 + 3y^2 + 2y - 1$ 3. $b^2 - 2b - 3, R = 7$ 5. $x^2 - \frac{5}{2}x - \frac{1}{2}$

Exploratory Exercises Page 38 1. $P(3) = 0$ 3. $P(3) = 0$ 5. yes 7. yes

Written Exercises Page 38 1. $R = ^-1$ 3. $R = 11$ 5. $R = 0$ 7. $R = 12$ 9. $R = 92$ 11. no 13. no 15. yes 17. no 19. no 21. $k = ^-20$ 23. $k = ^-4$

Challenge Page 38 1. $x^2 - 6x + 25$

Exploratory Exercises Page 41 1. 2 3. 2 5. 2 7. 3 9. 3 11. 3 13. 3

Written Exercises Page 41 1. $0, \frac{1}{2}$ 3. $\frac{5}{2}, ^-4$ 5. $\frac{-3}{2}, \frac{1}{3}$ 7. $^-2, \frac{1}{2}, 3$ 9. $\frac{-3}{2}, ^-5, \frac{1}{3}$ 11. $2, ^-2, ^-1$ 13. $3, 3, \frac{-1}{2}$ 15. once 17. twice 19. twice

21. twice 23. 2, $^{-}2$, 1, $^{-}1$ 25. 2, 2, $^{-}2$, $^{-}2$
27. $^{-}1$, $^{-}1$, $^{-}3$, $^{-}3$ 29. $^{-}1$, $^{-}1$, 3
31. $x^3 - 4x^2 + 6x - 4 = 0$ 33. $x^3 - 1 = 0$
35. $x^4 - 6x^3 + 13x^2 - 24x + 36 = 0$

Exploratory Exercises Page 43 1. $\pm 2, \pm 1$
3. $\pm 6, \pm 1, \pm 3, \pm 2$ 5. $\pm 18, \pm 1, \pm 2, \pm 9, \pm 3, \pm 6$ 7. $\pm 3, \pm 1, \pm \frac{3}{2}, \pm \frac{1}{2}$
9. $\pm 6, \pm 1, \pm 2, \pm 3, \pm \frac{3}{2}, \pm \frac{1}{4}, \pm \frac{1}{2}, \pm \frac{3}{4}$
11. $\pm 12, \pm 1, \pm 4, \pm 3, \pm 2, \pm 6$

Written Exercises Page 44 1. 1 3. ± 1, $^{-}2$, $^{-}3$
5. none 7. 1, $^{-}3$, $\frac{1}{2}$ 9. $\frac{3}{4}$ 11. $^{-}6$ 13. ± 1
15. none 17. $\frac{1}{2}$ 19. $\frac{1}{2}, \frac{^{-}1}{3}$

Exploratory Exercises Page 47 1. 2 or 0 3. 1
5. 1 7. 0 9. 4, 2, or 0 11. 1 13. 3 or 1
15. 2 or 0 17. 3 or 1 19. 0

Written Exercises Page 47 1. between $^{-}3$ and $^{-}2$, between $^{-}1$ and 0 3. between $^{-}1$ and 0, between 4 and 5 5. between 1 and 2 7. $^{-}1$, 2
9. 2.8, $^{-}1.8$ 11. $^{-}1$, $^{-}2$ 13. $^{-}2.5$ 15. 1, $^{-}1$
17. 2 19. 1 21. $^{-}5$

Exploratory Exercises Page 51 1. $2x + h$
3. $4x + 2h$ 5. $^{-}4x - 2h + 3$ 7. $2x$ 9. $4x$
11. $^{-}4x + 3$

Written Exercises Page 51 1. 2 3. 4 5. 8
7. 2 9. 3 11. 0.6 13. $\frac{7}{6}$ 15. $^{-}11$
17. $y = 4x - 4$ 19. $y = {}^{-}7x - 2$ 21. $y = \frac{^{-}1}{4}$
23. $y = 12x + 17$

Exploratory Exercises Page 55 1. (1, $^{-}4$)
3. $\left(\frac{^{-}3}{2}, \frac{^{-}19}{2}\right)$ 5. (3, $^{-}19$), ($^{-}3$, 17)

Written Exercises Page 55 1. $\left(\frac{1}{2}, {}^{-}6\frac{1}{4}\right)$, min.
3. ($^{-}1$, $^{-}16$), min. 5. (0, 3), max; $\left(\frac{2}{3}, \frac{77}{27}\right)$, min.

7.
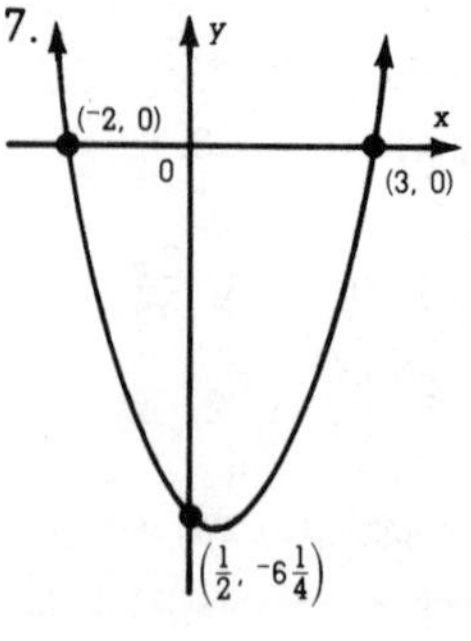

9.
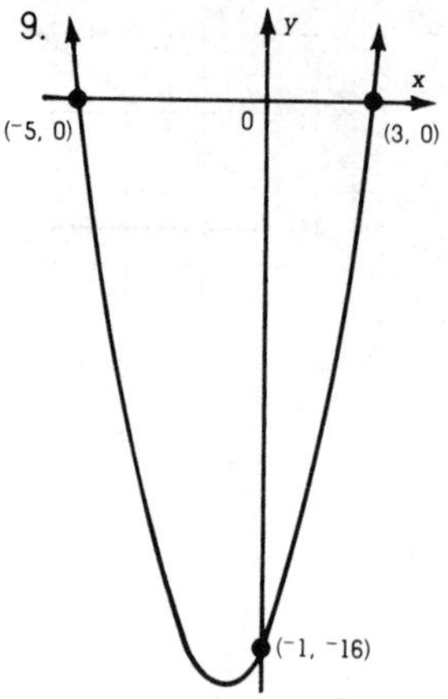

11.
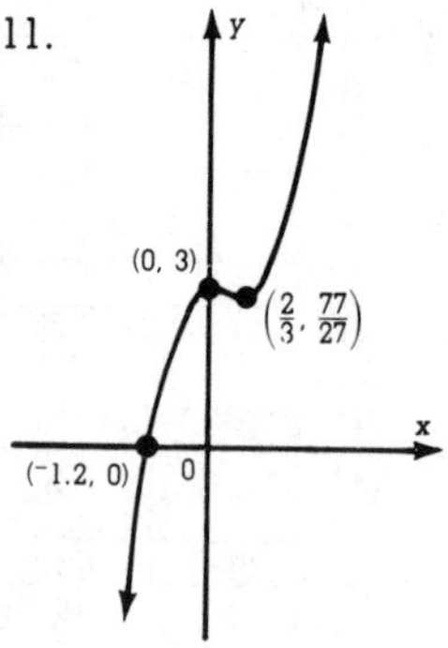

13.
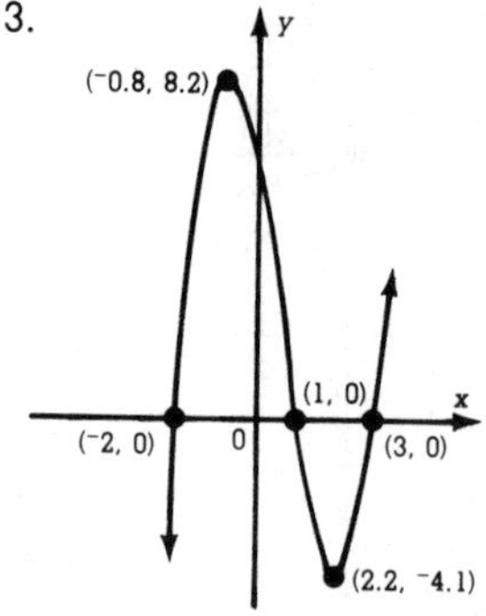

15.
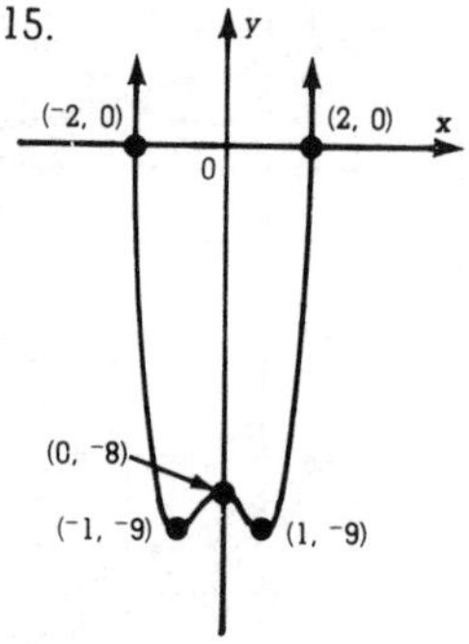

Chapter Review Page 57 1. $x = 4, 6, \frac{2}{3}$
3. $x = \frac{1}{2}, {}^{-}4$ 5. $x = \frac{^{-}5 \pm \sqrt{61}}{6}$
7. $5x^2 + 6x + 4$, $R = 10$ 9. $R = {}^{-}4$ 11. $^{-}3$, $^{-}3$, 2
13. $\frac{1}{2}, \frac{1}{4}$ 15. 2 or 0 17. 0 19. 2 21. $^{-}2$
23. ± 1.4 25. 10 27. $y = 10x - 5$
29. $\left(\frac{1}{2}, \frac{17}{4}\right)$ max. 31. $^{-}1.6$, 2.6

CHAPTER 3 MATRICES AND VECTORS

Exploratory Exercises Page 62 1. 62 3. $^{-}8$
5. 0 7. $x = \frac{\begin{vmatrix} 5 & 2 \\ 1 & ^{-}3 \end{vmatrix}}{\begin{vmatrix} 3 & 2 \\ 4 & ^{-}3 \end{vmatrix}}$, $y = \frac{\begin{vmatrix} 3 & 5 \\ 4 & 1 \end{vmatrix}}{\begin{vmatrix} 3 & 2 \\ 4 & ^{-}3 \end{vmatrix}}$ 9. $x = \frac{\begin{vmatrix} 6 & 1 \\ 2 & ^{-}1 \end{vmatrix}}{\begin{vmatrix} 2 & 1 \\ 6 & ^{-}1 \end{vmatrix}}$
$y = \frac{\begin{vmatrix} 2 & 6 \\ 6 & 2 \end{vmatrix}}{\begin{vmatrix} 2 & 1 \\ 6 & ^{-}1 \end{vmatrix}}$ 11. $x = \frac{\begin{vmatrix} 6 & 1 \\ ^{-}12 & ^{-}2 \end{vmatrix}}{\begin{vmatrix} 4 & 1 \\ 1 & ^{-}2 \end{vmatrix}}$, $y = \frac{\begin{vmatrix} 4 & 6 \\ 1 & ^{-}12 \end{vmatrix}}{\begin{vmatrix} 4 & 1 \\ 1 & ^{-}2 \end{vmatrix}}$

Written Exercises Page 62 1. $^-50$ 3. 1 5. $^-93$ 7. $x = 1, y = 1$ 9. $x = 1, y = 4$ 11. $x = 0, y = 6$ 13. $x = 3, y = {}^-1$ 15. $x = 4, y = 3$ 17. $x = 4, y = {}^-4$ 19. $x = 3, y = \frac{1}{2}$ 21. $x = -\frac{3}{5}, y = 3$

Challenge Page 62 1. $^-109$ 3. 3411 5. $x = {}^-4, y = 2, z = 1$

Exploratory Exercises Page 65 1. $\begin{bmatrix} a_{11} & a_{12} & a_{13} \\ a_{21} & a_{22} & a_{23} \\ a_{31} & a_{32} & a_{33} \end{bmatrix}$

3. $\begin{bmatrix} a_{11} & a_{12} & a_{13} & a_{14} \\ a_{21} & a_{22} & a_{23} & a_{24} \\ a_{31} & a_{32} & a_{33} & a_{34} \\ a_{41} & a_{42} & a_{43} & a_{44} \\ a_{51} & a_{52} & a_{53} & a_{54} \\ a_{61} & a_{62} & a_{63} & a_{64} \end{bmatrix}$ 5. $\begin{bmatrix} ^-6 & ^-5 \\ ^-8 & ^-4 \end{bmatrix}$ 7. $\begin{bmatrix} 2 & ^-1 \\ 0 & 3 \end{bmatrix}$

Written Exercises Page 65 1. $\begin{bmatrix} ^-2 & 11 & ^-2 \\ 9 & ^-1 & ^-6 \\ 11 & ^-2 & 1 \end{bmatrix}$

3. $\begin{bmatrix} 3 & 15 & ^-13 \\ ^-7 & 10 & ^-8 \\ 28 & 2 & 1 \end{bmatrix}$ 5. $\begin{bmatrix} ^-4 & 1 & ^-16 \\ ^-1 & ^-5 & 6 \\ 5 & ^-2 & 5 \end{bmatrix}$

7. $\begin{bmatrix} ^-9 & ^-3 & ^-5 \\ 15 & ^-16 & 8 \\ ^-12 & ^-6 & 5 \end{bmatrix}$ 9. $x = 7, y = 2$

11. $x = 4, y = 0$

Exploratory Exercises Page 67 1. $[18 \quad 30]$

3. $[6\sqrt{5} \quad ^-6 \quad 24]$ 5. $\begin{bmatrix} \frac{9}{2} & -\frac{3}{2} \\ -3 & 3 \end{bmatrix}$ 7. 2×6

9. 4×3 11. 3×1

Written Exercises Page 67 1. $\begin{bmatrix} 21 & 0 \\ 15 & 9 \end{bmatrix}$

3. $\begin{bmatrix} 6 & ^-6 & 12 \\ 10 & 8 & ^-4 \end{bmatrix}$ 5. $\begin{bmatrix} 34 & 12 \\ 36 & ^-12 \\ 16 & 18 \end{bmatrix}$ 7. $\begin{bmatrix} ^-30 & 60 \\ 46 & ^-8 \end{bmatrix}$

9. $\begin{bmatrix} 49 & 0 \\ 50 & 9 \end{bmatrix}$ 11. $\begin{bmatrix} 162 & ^-54 & 180 \\ 48 & ^-156 & 240 \\ 138 & 24 & 60 \end{bmatrix}$ 13. $\begin{bmatrix} 14 & ^-29 \\ 3 & 7 \end{bmatrix}$

15. $a_{11}x + a_{12}y + b_1 = 0$
$a_{21}x + a_{22}y + b_2 = 0$

Exploratory Exercises Page 70 1. $^-1$ 3. 0 5. $^-78$ 7. $^-15$ 9. yes 11. no 13. yes 15. yes

Written Exercises Page 70 1. $\begin{bmatrix} ^-5 & 3 \\ 2 & ^-1 \end{bmatrix}$

3. The inverse does not exist. 5. $\begin{bmatrix} \frac{1}{26} & \frac{3}{26} \\ \frac{7}{78} & -\frac{5}{78} \end{bmatrix}$

7. $\begin{bmatrix} \frac{1}{5} & \frac{1}{5} \\ \frac{14}{15} & \frac{3}{5} \end{bmatrix}$ 9. $x = \begin{bmatrix} \frac{21}{13} & 1 \\ -\frac{10}{13} & ^-1 \end{bmatrix}$ 11. $x = \begin{bmatrix} 0 & 0 \\ 0 & 0 \end{bmatrix}$

13. $x = \begin{bmatrix} \frac{60}{29} & -\frac{12}{29} \\ -\frac{5}{29} & \frac{59}{29} \end{bmatrix}$

Exploratory Exercises Page 72 Answers may vary. One possible answer is given. 1. Multiply row 2 by 5 and add to row 1. 3. Multiply row 2 by $^-3$ and add to row 1. 5. Multiply row 1 by 3 and row 2 by 2. Then add row 2 to row 1.
7. Multiply row 1 by $^-2$ and add to row 2.
9. Multiply row 1 by 2 and row 2 by 3. Then add row 1 to row 2. 11. Multiply row 1 by 2 and row 2 by 3. Then add row 1 to row 2.

Written Exercises Page 72 1. $x = {}^-1, y = 2$
3. $x = \frac{1}{3}, y = -\frac{10}{3}$ 5. $x = {}^-1, y = 2, z = {}^-3$
7. $x = -\frac{97}{19}, y = \frac{155}{19}$ 9. $x = 7, y = 1, z = {}^-2$
11. $w = {}^-2, x = 1, y = {}^-1, z = 2$

Written Exercises Page 75

1.

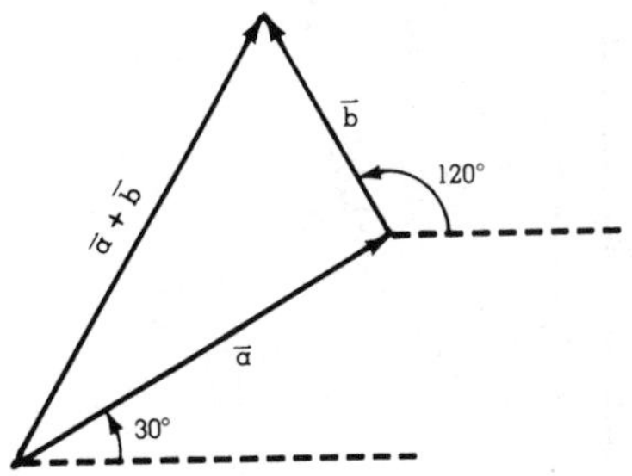

3.

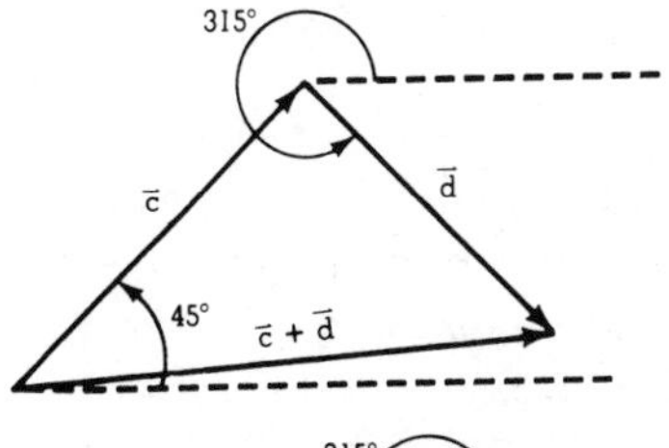

5.

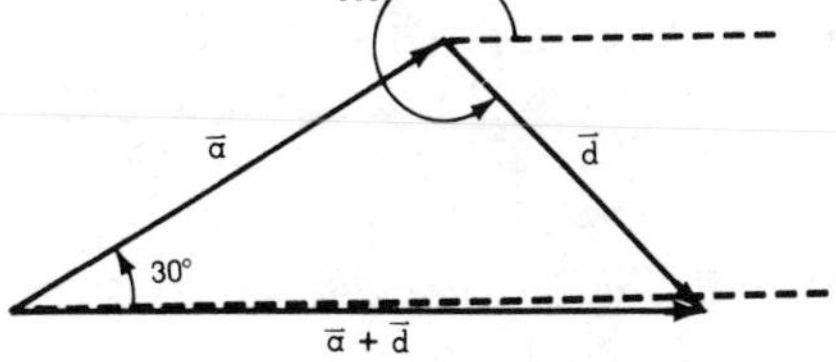

13. 4.0 cm; 60° 15. 3.9 cm; 5° 17. 4.8 cm; -2° or 358° 19. 7.0 cm; 53° 21. 10.3 cm; 16° 23. 3.1 cm; 187° 25. 3.0 cm; 1.8 cm 27. 2.1 cm; 2.1 cm

Exploratory Exercises Page 79 1. 5 3. $\sqrt{89}$ or 9.4 5. $\sqrt{106}$ or 10.3 7. $\sqrt{377}$ or 19.4 9. $4\vec{i} + 3\vec{j}$ 11. $5\vec{i} + 8\vec{j}$ 13. $5\vec{i} + {}^-9\vec{j}$ 15. $^-16\vec{i} + 11\vec{j}$ 17. (2,7) 19. (-9,1) 21. (1,1) 23. (3,4) 25. (-7,5) 27. no

Written Exercises Page 79 1. (-3,2) 3. (2,6) 5. (1,1) 7. $\sqrt{13}$ or 3.6 9. $2\sqrt{10}$ or 6.3 11. $\sqrt{2}$ or 1.4 13. (-1,-3) 15. (-20,10) 17. (-10,12) 19. (0,-14) 21. (-30,22) 23. (0,0)

Exploratory Exercises Page 81

1.

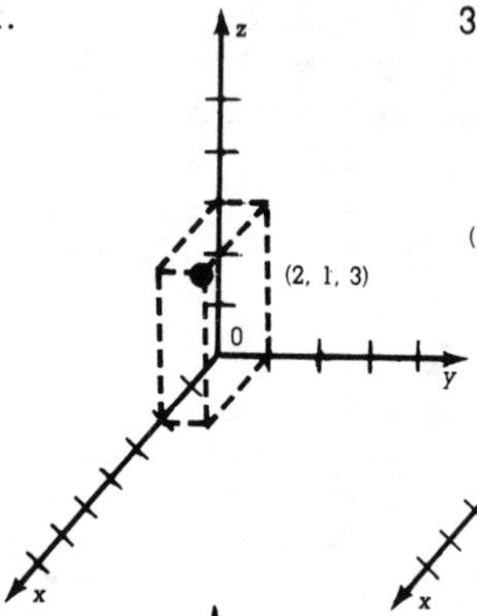

3.

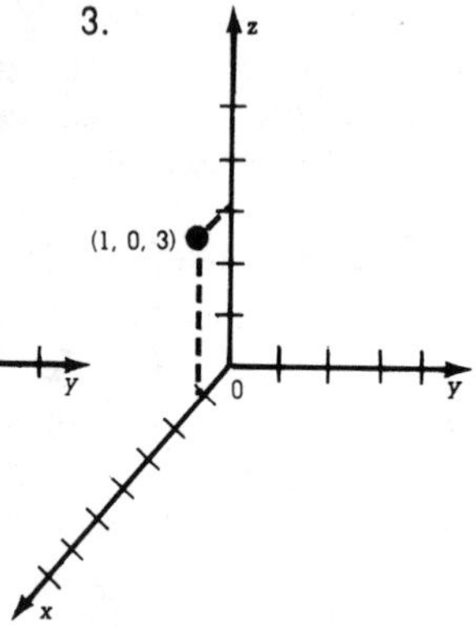

5.

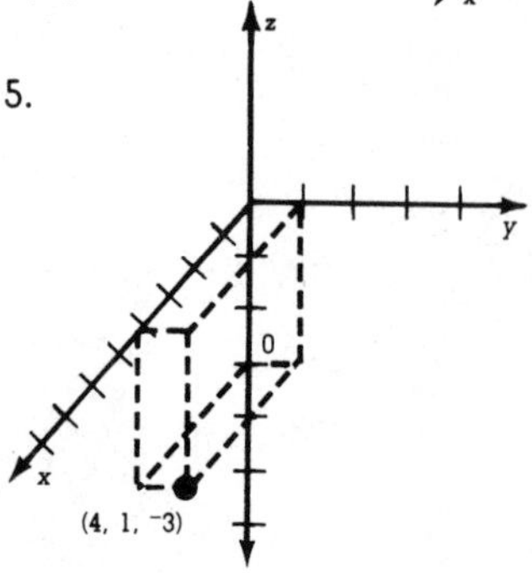

7. $\sqrt{14}$ or 3.7 9. $\sqrt{10}$ or 3.2 11. $\sqrt{26}$ or 5.1 13. $2\vec{i} + \vec{j} + 3\vec{k}$ 15. $\vec{i} + 3\vec{k}$ 17. $4\vec{i} + \vec{j} + {}^-3\vec{k}$

Written Exercises Pages 81-82 1. (2,0,3) 3. (5,4,-11) 5. (-12,5,1) 7. $\sqrt{13}$ or 3.6 9. $\sqrt{162}$ or 12.7 11. $\sqrt{170}$ or 13.0 13. $2\vec{i} + 3\vec{k}$ 15. $5\vec{i} + 4\vec{j} + {}^-11\vec{k}$ 17. $^-12\vec{i} + 5\vec{j} + \vec{k}$ 19. (-1,-1,-10) 21. (9,-19,-2) 23. (19,-37,6) 25. $^-\vec{i} + {}^-\vec{j} + {}^-10\vec{k}$ 27. $9\vec{i} + {}^-19\vec{j} + {}^-2\vec{k}$ 29. $19\vec{i} + {}^-37\vec{j} + 6\vec{k}$

Exploratory Exercises Page 84 1. 2 3. 32 5. 1 7. no 9. no 11. no

13. $\begin{vmatrix} \vec{i} & \vec{j} & \vec{k} \\ 2 & 3 & -4 \\ -2 & -3 & 1 \end{vmatrix} = \begin{vmatrix} 3 & -4 \\ -3 & 1 \end{vmatrix}\vec{i} - \begin{vmatrix} 2 & -4 \\ -2 & 1 \end{vmatrix}\vec{j} + \begin{vmatrix} 2 & 3 \\ -2 & -3 \end{vmatrix}\vec{k}$ 15. $\begin{vmatrix} \vec{i} & \vec{j} & \vec{k} \\ 7 & -2 & 4 \\ 3 & 8 & 1 \end{vmatrix} = \begin{vmatrix} -2 & 4 \\ 8 & 1 \end{vmatrix}\vec{i} - \begin{vmatrix} 7 & 4 \\ 3 & 1 \end{vmatrix}\vec{j} + \begin{vmatrix} 7 & -2 \\ 3 & 8 \end{vmatrix}\vec{k}$ 17. $\begin{vmatrix} \vec{i} & \vec{j} & \vec{k} \\ -6 & 2 & 10 \\ 4 & 1 & 9 \end{vmatrix} = \begin{vmatrix} 2 & 10 \\ 1 & 9 \end{vmatrix}\vec{i} - \begin{vmatrix} -6 & 10 \\ 4 & 9 \end{vmatrix}\vec{j} + \begin{vmatrix} -6 & 2 \\ 4 & 1 \end{vmatrix}\vec{k}$

Written Exercises Page 84 1. -17 3. 9 5. 68 7. no 9. no 11. no 13. (-9,6,0) 15. (-34,5,62) 17. (8,94,-14) 19. (-9,6,0) · (2,3,-4) = -18 + 18 + 0 = 0; (-9,6,0) · (-2,-3,1) = 18 + -18 + 0 = 0 21. (-34,5,62) (7,-2,4) = -238 + -10 + 248 = 0 (-34,5,62) (3,8,1) = -102 + 40 + 62 = 0 23. (8,94,-14) (-6,2,10) = -48 + 188 + -140 = 0 (8,94,-14) (4,1,9) = 32 + 94 + -126 = 0

Chapter Review Pages 86-87 1. -1 3. 0 5. $x = \frac{2}{3}, y = {}^-2$ 7. $\begin{bmatrix} 9 & -1 & 9 \\ 3 & 3 & 0 \\ -2 & -8 & 4 \end{bmatrix}$ 9. $\begin{bmatrix} 3 & -1 & 6 \\ 6 & -4 & 1 \\ -13 & 0 & 2 \end{bmatrix}$ 11. $\begin{bmatrix} 6 & 3 \\ -9 & 12 \end{bmatrix}$ 13. $[31 \quad {}^-23]$ 15. $\begin{bmatrix} \frac{5}{17} & \frac{2}{17} \\ \frac{1}{17} & -\frac{3}{17} \end{bmatrix}$ 17. $\begin{bmatrix} -3 & -4 \\ -4 & -5 \end{bmatrix}$ 19. $x = \begin{bmatrix} 6 & 11 \\ 7 & 12 \end{bmatrix}$ 21. $x = {}^-10, y = {}^-6, z = 0$ 27. 1.6 cm; 140° 29. 11.4 cm; 35° 31. 1.4 cm; 1.4 cm 33. 0.9 cm; 0.5 cm 35. (5,12) 37. 13 39. (5,-6) 41. (12,-17) 43. (4,-1,-3) 45. $\sqrt{26}$ or 5.1 47. (1,5,2) 49. (-2,9,6) 51. $\vec{i} + 5\vec{j} + 2\vec{k}$ 53. $^-2\vec{i} + 9\vec{j} + 6\vec{k}$ 55. -16 57. 0 59. (7,22,2)

CHAPTER 4 THE CIRCULAR FUNCTIONS

Exploratory Exercises Page 92 1. III 3. II 5. I 7. II 9. I 11. Answers may vary. 13. $4 - 2n\pi$ where n is any positive integer

Written Exercises Page 93 1. (-1, 0) 3. (1, 0) 5. $\left(-\frac{\sqrt{2}}{2}, \frac{\sqrt{2}}{2}\right)$ 7. (0, -1) 9. $\frac{\pi}{3}$ 11. π 13. $\frac{5\pi}{3}$ 15. $\left(\frac{1}{2}, \frac{\sqrt{3}}{2}\right)$ 17. (-1, 0) 19. $\left(\frac{1}{2}, -\frac{\sqrt{3}}{2}\right)$ 21. $\left(\frac{1}{2}, -\frac{\sqrt{3}}{2}\right)$ 23. $\left(\frac{1}{2}, \frac{\sqrt{3}}{2}\right)$ 25. $\left(\frac{5}{13}, -\frac{12}{13}\right)$ 27. $\left(-\frac{5}{13}, -\frac{12}{13}\right)$ 29. 1.57 31. 0.25 33. -4.71

35. $^-6.03$ **37.** $7.85 + 2\pi n$, where n is any positive integer. **39.** $6.53 + 2\pi n$ where n is any positive integer.

Exploratory Exercises Page 95 1. positive **3.** negative **5.** positive **7.** positive **9.** I **11.** III **13.** 0.6 **15.** 0.8 **17.** 1 **19.** 1

Written Exercises Page 96

1.

S	cos s	sin s	tan s	sec s	csc s	cot s
0	1	0	0	1	—	—
$\frac{\pi}{6}$	$\frac{\sqrt{3}}{2}$	$\frac{1}{2}$	$\frac{\sqrt{3}}{3}$	$\frac{2\sqrt{3}}{3}$	2	$\sqrt{3}$
$\frac{\pi}{4}$	$\frac{\sqrt{2}}{2}$	$\frac{\sqrt{2}}{2}$	1	$\sqrt{2}$	$\sqrt{2}$	1
$\frac{\pi}{3}$	$\frac{1}{2}$	$\frac{\sqrt{3}}{2}$	$\sqrt{3}$	2	$\frac{2\sqrt{3}}{3}$	$\frac{\sqrt{3}}{3}$
$\frac{\pi}{2}$	0	1	—	—	1	0

3. 1 **5.** $-\frac{\sqrt{2}}{2}$ **7.** $^-1$ **9.** $-\frac{\sqrt{3}}{3}$ **11.** $^-1$ **13.** $\frac{\sqrt{3}}{2}$ **15.** $\frac{\sqrt{7}}{3}$ **17.** $\frac{4\sqrt{7}}{7}$ **19.** $\frac{^-\sqrt{3}}{3}$ **21.** $-\frac{2\sqrt{3}}{3}$ **23.** $\frac{17}{8}$

25. $-\frac{17}{15}$ **27.** any multiple of 2π **29.** 2π

Exploratory Exercises Page 100 1. IV **3.** IV **5.** II **7.** III **9.** II

Written Exercises Page 100 1. 0.1736 **3.** 1.5597 **5.** $^-0.3249$ **7.** 1.211 **9.** $^-0.6361$ **11.** none **13.** $^-0.4173$ **15.** $^-0.4617$ **17.** 0.1454 **19.** 0.7330 **21.** 0.1367 **23.** 0.5061 **25.** 1.3235 **27.** 1.4108

Challenge Page 100

1.

x	0	0.2	0.4	0.6	0.8	1.0	1.2	1.4	1.6
sin x	0	0.20	0.39	0.56	0.72	0.84	0.93	0.99	1.0

1.8	2.0	2.2	2.4	2.6	2.8	3.0	3.2	3.4	3.6
0.97	0.91	0.81	0.68	0.52	0.34	0.14	$^-0.06$	$^-0.26$	$^-0.44$

3.8	4.0	4.2	4.4	4.6	4.8	5.0	5.2
$^-0.61$	$^-0.76$	$^-0.87$	$^-0.95$	$^-0.99$	$^-1.0$	$^-0.96$	$^-0.88$

5.4	5.6	5.8	6.0	6.2	6.4
$^-0.77$	$^-0.63$	$^-0.46$	$^-0.28$	$^-0.08$	0.12

3.

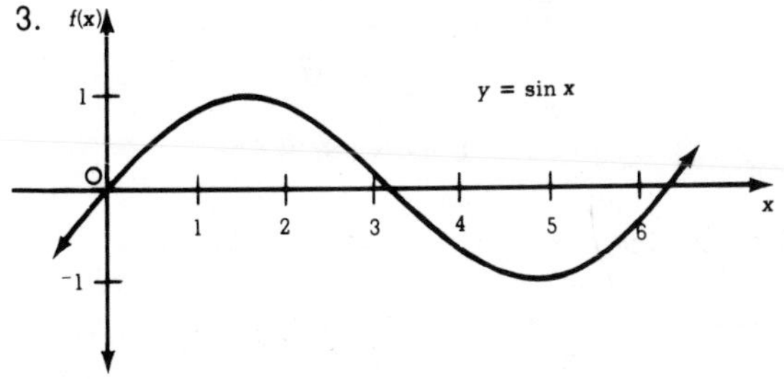

$y = \sin x$

Exploratory Exercises Page 104 1. decreasing **3.** increasing **5.** increasing **7.** decreasing **9.** increasing **11.** decreasing

Written Exercises Page 105 1. none **3.** $\frac{\pi}{2}, \frac{3\pi}{2}$

5. $\frac{\pi}{2}, \frac{3\pi}{2}$ **7-9.** Answers may vary.

11.-13.

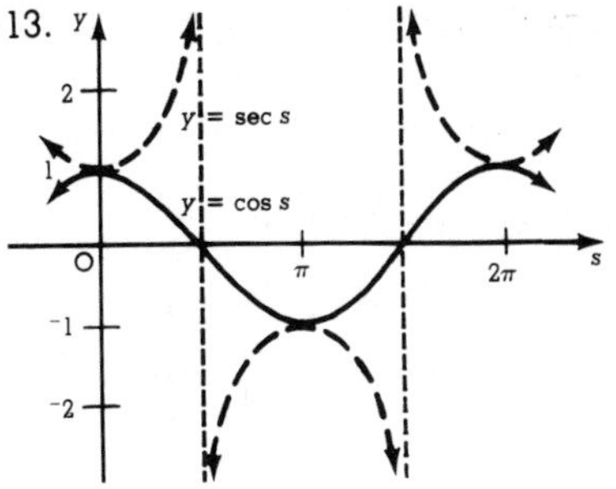

15. Graph on page 103 of text. **17.** $-\frac{\pi}{2}$ **19.** $-\frac{3\pi}{2}$

21. III **23.** IV **25.** $\frac{\pi}{4}, \frac{5\pi}{4}$ **27.** none **29.** $0, \frac{3\pi}{2}$

Exploratory Exercises Page 107 1. $\frac{\pi}{2} + \frac{\pi}{3}$

3. $\frac{\pi}{4} - \frac{7\pi}{6}$ **5.** $\frac{\pi}{4} + \frac{\pi}{6}$ **7.** $\frac{5\pi}{4} + \frac{\pi}{3}$

Written Exercises Page 108

1. $\cos\left(\frac{\pi}{2} + \frac{\pi}{2}\right) = \cos\frac{\pi}{2}\cos\frac{\pi}{2} - \sin\frac{\pi}{2}\sin\frac{\pi}{2}$

$\cos \pi = (0 \cdot 0) - (1 \cdot 1)$

$^-1 = ^-1$

3. $\sin\left(\frac{\pi}{2} + \frac{\pi}{2}\right) = \sin\frac{\pi}{2}\cos\frac{\pi}{2} - \cos\frac{\pi}{2}\sin\frac{\pi}{2}$

$\sin \pi = (1 \cdot 0) + (0 \cdot 1)$

$0 = 0$

5. $\cos\left(0 - \frac{\pi}{3}\right) = \cos 0\cos\frac{\pi}{3} + \sin 0\sin\frac{\pi}{3}$

$\cos\left(-\frac{\pi}{3}\right) = \left(1 \cdot \frac{1}{2}\right) + \left(0 \cdot \frac{\sqrt{3}}{2}\right)$

$\frac{1}{2} = \frac{1}{2}$

7. $\frac{\sqrt{6} + \sqrt{2}}{4}$ **9.** $\frac{\sqrt{2} + \sqrt{6}}{4}$ **11.** $\frac{^-\sqrt{2} - \sqrt{6}}{4}$

13. $\frac{\sqrt{2} + \sqrt{6}}{4}$ **15.** $\frac{^-\sqrt{2} - \sqrt{6}}{4}$ **17.** sin s

19. $^-\cos s$ **21.** $^-\sin s$ **23.** cos s

25. $\frac{\tan s_1 - \tan s_2}{1 + \tan s_1 \tan s_2}$ **27.** $\frac{\cot s_1 \cot s_2 + 1}{\cot s_2 - \cot s_1}$

Exploratory Exercises Page 110 1. $\frac{\sqrt{2 - \sqrt{3}}}{2}$

3. $\frac{\sqrt{2 - \sqrt{2 - \sqrt{2}}}}{2}$ **5.** $\frac{\sqrt{2 - \sqrt{2}}}{2}$

7. $\dfrac{\sqrt{2+\sqrt{2-\sqrt{2}}}}{2}$

Written Exercises Page 110 1. $\frac{\sqrt{3}}{2}$ 3. $\frac{4\sqrt{5}}{9}$ 5. $-\frac{120}{169}$ 7. $-\frac{3\sqrt{7}}{8}$ 9. $\frac{\sqrt{2+\sqrt{3}}}{2}$ 11. $-\frac{\sqrt{6}}{6}$ 13. $\frac{\sqrt{26}}{26}$ 15. $-\frac{1}{4}\sqrt{8+2\sqrt{7}}$ 17. $\frac{\sqrt{2-\sqrt{3}}}{2}$ 19. $\frac{\sqrt{30}}{6}$ 21. $\frac{5\sqrt{26}}{26}$ 23. $\frac{1}{4}\sqrt{8-2\sqrt{7}}$ 25. $\frac{1}{2}$ 27. $-\frac{1}{9}$ 29. $\frac{119}{169}$ 31. $-\frac{1}{8}$ 33. $\frac{2\tan s}{1-\tan^2 s}$ 35. $3\sin s - 4\sin^3 s$

Chapter Review Page 113 1. $\left(-\frac{\sqrt{2}}{2}, -\frac{\sqrt{2}}{2}\right)$ 3. $(^-1, 0)$ 5. $(1, 0)$ 7. $\left(\frac{1}{2}, -\frac{\sqrt{3}}{2}\right)$ 9. $\frac{4}{5}$ 11. $\frac{4}{3}$ 13. 1 15. $\sqrt{3}$ 17. $\frac{2\sqrt{3}}{3}$ 19. $^-1$ 21. $\frac{\sqrt{3}}{2}$ 23. 0 25. 0.3283 27. 0.9611 29. 1.022 31. $^-4.876$ 33. 1.4603 35. 1.2537 37. 0.7941

39.

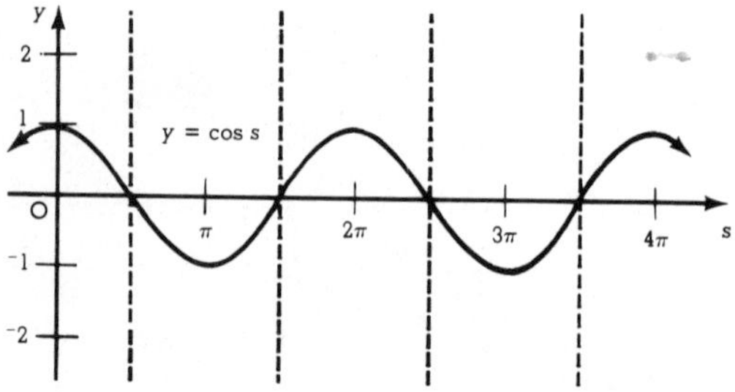

41.

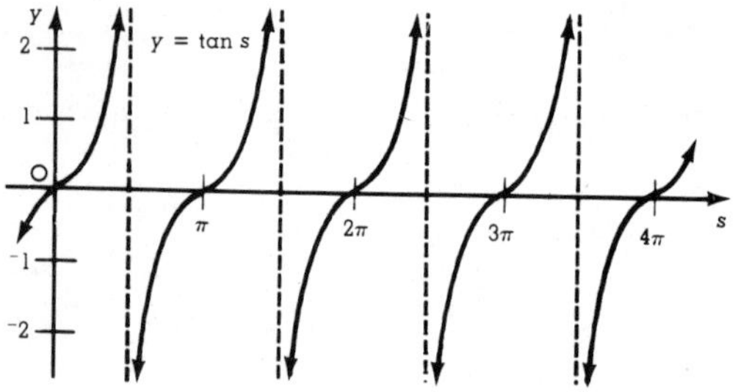

43. $\frac{\sqrt{6}-\sqrt{2}}{4}$ 45. $\frac{\sqrt{2}+\sqrt{6}}{4}$ 47. $\frac{7}{8}$

CHAPTER 5 THE TRIGONOMETRIC FUNCTIONS

Exploratory Exercises Page 118 1. $\frac{y}{a}$ 3. $\frac{h}{b}$ 5. $\frac{h}{a}$ 7. $\frac{h}{x}$ 9. $\frac{x}{b}$ 11. 0 13. $\frac{1}{2}$ 15. $\frac{2\sqrt{3}}{3}$ 17. $\sqrt{3}$ 19. 1

Written Exercises Page 119 1. $\sin\alpha = \frac{12}{13}$, $\csc\alpha = \frac{13}{12}$, $\tan\alpha = \frac{12}{5}$, $\cot\alpha = \frac{5}{12}$, $\cos\alpha = \frac{5}{13}$, $\sec\alpha = \frac{13}{5}$ 3. $\sin\alpha = \frac{4}{5}$, $\csc\alpha = \frac{5}{4}$, $\tan\alpha = \frac{4}{3}$, $\cot\alpha = \frac{3}{4}$, $\cos\alpha = \frac{3}{5}$, $\sec\alpha = \frac{5}{3}$
5. $\sin\alpha = 0$, $\csc\alpha$ undefined, $\tan\alpha = 0$, $\cot\alpha$ undefined, $\cos\alpha = {}^-1$, $\sec\alpha = {}^-1$
7. $\sin\alpha = -\frac{3}{\sqrt{34}}$, $\csc\alpha = -\frac{\sqrt{34}}{3}$, $\tan\alpha = -\frac{3}{5}$, $\cot\alpha = -\frac{5}{3}$, $\cos\alpha = \frac{5}{\sqrt{34}}$, $\sec\alpha = \frac{\sqrt{34}}{5}$
9. $\frac{1+\sqrt{3}}{2}$ 11. $\frac{\sqrt{2}+1}{2}$ 13. $\frac{\sqrt{2}-2}{2}$ 15. $\sqrt{3}-1$ 17. $\sqrt{3}$ 19. $\frac{\sqrt{3}}{2}$ 21. $2+\sqrt{3}$ 23. 0.6000 25. 0.7500 27. 0.8824 29. 0.3492 31. 0.9370 33. 1.3333 35. 2.8636 37. 2.1250
39. $1 - 2\sin^2 30° \stackrel{?}{=} \cos 60°$

$$1 - 2\left(\frac{1}{2}\right)^2 \stackrel{?}{=} \frac{1}{2}$$
$$1 - \frac{1}{2} \stackrel{?}{=} \frac{1}{2}$$
$$\frac{1}{2} = \frac{1}{2}$$

43. $\sec^2 30° - \cot^2 60° \stackrel{?}{=} 1$

$$\left(\frac{2\sqrt{3}}{3}\right)^2 - \left(\frac{\sqrt{3}}{3}\right)^2 \stackrel{?}{=} 1$$
$$\frac{12}{9} - \frac{3}{9} \stackrel{?}{=} 1$$
$$\frac{9}{9} = 1$$

47. $\sin A = 0.5547$, $\csc A = 1.8028$, $\cos A = 0.8321$, $\sec A = 1.2019$, $\tan A = 0.6667$, $\cot A = 1.5$, $\sin B = 0.8321$, $\csc B = 1.2019$, $\cos B = 0.5547$, $\sec B = 1.8028$, $\tan B = 1.5$, $\cot B = 0.6667$

Exploratory Exercises Page 122 1. 0.2784 3. 2.282 5. 1.150 7. 0.1074 9. 42°40′ 11. 32°30′ 13. 8°10′

Written Exercises Page 122 1. 0.4384 3. 1.471 5. 0.9981 7. 0.8098 9. 0.2717 11. 4.554 13. 0.8331 15. 0.0701 17. 5°00′ 19. 17°30′ 21. 30°40′ 23. 23°30′ 25. 67°12′ 27. 86°46′ 29. 38°33′ 31. 46°15′

Exploratory Exercises Page 125 1. $\frac{\sqrt{3}}{3}$ 3. 0.109 5. $\frac{\sqrt{3}}{3}$ 7. 0.9976 9. 9.514

Written Exercises Page 125 1. $\frac{4\sqrt{7}}{7}$ 3. $\frac{1}{3}$ 5. $\frac{\sqrt{7}}{3}$ 7. $\frac{3\sqrt{5}}{5}$ 9. $\frac{1}{1.3}$ 11. $\frac{3}{5}$ 13. $\frac{4}{3}$ 15. $\frac{1}{1.7}$

17. $\frac{4\sqrt{17}}{17}$ 19. 1 21. $\frac{\sqrt{3}}{2}$ 23. $\frac{3}{4}$ 25. 1 27. $2 \sin x$

29. 2 31. $\frac{\sin \theta}{\sin (90 - \theta)}$ 33. $\pm\sqrt{1 - \left(\frac{1}{\sec \theta}\right)^2}$

35. $\pm\sqrt{\csc^2 \theta - 1}$

Exploratory Exercises Page 127 1. Pythagorean Identity 3. Reciprocal Identity 5. Quotient Identity 7. Quotient Identity 9. Pythagorean Identity

11.
$$\csc^2 \alpha - \cot^2 \alpha \stackrel{?}{=} 1$$
$$(1 + \cot^2 \alpha) - \cot^2 \alpha \stackrel{?}{=}$$
$$1 = 1$$

15.
$$\sin \theta \cot \theta \stackrel{?}{=} \cos \theta$$
$$\sin \theta \cdot \frac{\cos \theta}{\sin \theta} \stackrel{?}{=}$$
$$\cos \theta = \cos \theta$$

19.
$$\sec^2 \theta - 1 \stackrel{?}{=} \tan^2 \theta$$
$$(\tan^2 \theta + 1) - 1 \stackrel{?}{=}$$
$$\tan^2 \theta = \tan^2 \theta$$

Written Exercises Page 127

1.
$$\sin^2 A \cot^2 A \stackrel{?}{=} (1 - \sin A)(1 + \sin A)$$
$$\stackrel{?}{=} 1 - \sin^2 A$$
$$\stackrel{?}{=} \cos^2 A$$
$$\stackrel{?}{=} (\sin A \cot A)^2$$
$$\sin^2 A \cot^2 A = \sin^2 A \cot^2 A$$

5.
$$\frac{1}{\sec^2 x} + \frac{1}{\csc^2 x} - 1 \stackrel{?}{=} 0$$
$$\cos^2 x + \sin^2 x - 1 \stackrel{?}{=}$$
$$1 - 1 \stackrel{?}{=} 0$$

9.
$$\frac{\sin (90° - w)}{\cos (90° - w)} \stackrel{?}{=} \cot w$$
$$\frac{\cos w}{\sin w} \stackrel{?}{=}$$
$$\frac{1}{\tan w} = \cot w$$

13.
$$\frac{\sec B}{\cos B} - \frac{\tan B}{\cot B} \stackrel{?}{=} 1$$
$$\left(\sec B \cdot \frac{1}{\cos B}\right) - \left(\tan B \cdot \frac{1}{\cot B}\right) \stackrel{?}{=}$$
$$\sec^2 B - \tan^2 B \stackrel{?}{=}$$
$$(\tan^2 B + 1) - \tan^2 B \stackrel{?}{=}$$
$$1 = 1$$

17.
$$\frac{1 + \tan^2 A}{\csc^2 A} \stackrel{?}{=} \tan^2 A$$
$$\frac{\sec^2 A}{\csc^2 A} \stackrel{?}{=}$$
$$\frac{\frac{1}{\cos^2 A}}{\frac{1}{\sin^2 A}} \stackrel{?}{=}$$
$$\frac{\sin^2 A}{\cos^2 A} = \tan^2 A$$

19. $\tan x = 1$
21. $\tan x = 2$

23. $\tan x = \pm\frac{\sqrt{6}}{2}$ 25. $\sec x = \sqrt{2}$ 27. $\frac{1}{9}$

Exploratory Exercises Page 130 1. 0.314 3. 4.187 5. 180° 7. 135°

Written Exercises Page 130 1. 4.71 3. 3.663 5. 1.308 7. 3.925 9. 225° 11. 330° 13. 720° 15. 43° 17. 7.8 19. 26.2 21. 7.85 23. 20.2 25. 35.8° 27. 172° 29. 8.28 cm

Exploratory Exercises Page 133 1. 26° 3. 16° 5. 53° 7. 2° 9. sin 45° 11. $^-$tan 40° 13. $^-$sin 20° 15. tan 24°

Written Exercises Page 133 1. $^-$sin 30° 3. $^-$cot 80° 5. $^-$cos 30° 7. $^-$sec 45° 9. $^-$tan 40° 11. tan 30° 13. $^-$cos 35° 15. $^-$cot 8° 17. $^-$sec 33° 19. $^-$sec 17° 21. 0.7071 23. $^-$0.8391 25. $^-$0.3420 27. 0.4452 29. $^-$0.5 31. $^-$0.1763 33. $^-$0.866 35. $^-$1.414 37. $^-$0.8391 39. 0.5774 41. $^-$0.8192 43. $^-$7.115 45. $^-$1.192 47. $^-$1.046 49. odd 51. odd

Exploratory Exercises Page 135

1.

x										
x	radians	0	$\frac{\pi}{2}$	π	$\frac{3\pi}{2}$	2π	$-\frac{\pi}{2}$	$^-\pi$	$-\frac{3\pi}{2}$	$^-2\pi$
x	degrees	0°	90°	180°	270°	360°	$^-$90°	$^-$180°	$^-$270°	$^-$360°
sin x		0	1	0	$^-$1	0	$^-$1	0	1	0
cos x		1	0	$^-$1	0	1	0	$^-$1	0	1

3. $\frac{\pi}{2}$ or 90°, $-\frac{3\pi}{2}$ or $^-$270° 5. π or 180°, $^-\pi$ or $^-$180°

Written Exercises Page 135 1. $^-$1 3. 0 5. $^-$1 7. undefined 9. undefined 11. undefined 13. k is an even integer 15. $k = 4n - 3$ for some integer n 17. $k = 2n - 1$ for some integer n.

Challenge Page 135 1. Let $k = 2n$, where n is any integer. Then $\sin (k \cdot 90°) = \sin (2n \cdot 90°) = \sin (180° \cdot n)$. But $\sin (180° \cdot n) = \sin 0°$ for all integers n. Since $\sin 0° = 0$, $\sin (k \cdot 90°) = 0$.

Exploratory Exercises Page 137 1. $\frac{\sqrt{6} + \sqrt{2}}{4}$ 3. $2 + \sqrt{3}$ 5. $\frac{\sqrt{6} + \sqrt{2}}{4}$ 7. $2 - \sqrt{3}$ 9. $-\frac{\sqrt{3}}{2}$ 11. cos x 13. $^-$tan x 15. 1

Written Exercises Page 138 1. $\frac{\sqrt{6} + \sqrt{2}}{4}$ 3. $\frac{\sqrt{2} - \sqrt{6}}{4}$ 5. $-\left(\frac{\sqrt{6} + \sqrt{2}}{4}\right)$ 7. $\sqrt{3} - 2$

9. $-\left(\frac{\sqrt{6}+\sqrt{2}}{4}\right)$ 11. $\frac{1}{2}$ 13. $\frac{33}{65}$ 15. $\frac{31}{481}$ 17. $-\frac{16}{65}$
19. $\frac{360}{481}$ 21. $\frac{56}{33}$ 23. $\frac{480}{31}$

27.
$$\cos\left(\frac{3\pi}{2}+\theta\right) \stackrel{?}{=} \sin\theta$$
$$\cos\frac{3\pi}{2}\cos\theta - \sin\frac{3\pi}{2}\sin\theta \stackrel{?}{=}$$
$$(0\cdot\cos\theta) - (^-1\cdot\sin\theta) \stackrel{?}{=}$$
$$0+\sin\theta \stackrel{?}{=}$$
$$\sin\theta = \sin\theta$$

31.
$$\tan(\pi-\theta) \stackrel{?}{=} {}^-\tan\theta$$
$$\frac{\tan\pi - \tan\theta}{1+\tan\pi\tan\theta} \stackrel{?}{=}$$
$$\frac{0-\tan\theta}{1+0} \stackrel{?}{=}$$
$${}^-\tan\theta = {}^-\tan\theta$$

35.
$$\cos(\pi+\theta) \stackrel{?}{=} {}^-\cos\theta$$
$$\cos\pi\cos\theta - \sin\pi\sin\theta \stackrel{?}{=}$$
$${}^-\cos\theta - 0\cdot\sin\theta \stackrel{?}{=}$$
$${}^-\cos\theta = {}^-\cos\theta$$

39. $\cos(\alpha+B)+\cos(\alpha-B) \stackrel{?}{=} 2\cos\alpha\cos B$
$\cos\alpha\cos B - \sin\alpha\sin B + \cos\alpha\cos B +$
$\sin\alpha\sin B \stackrel{?}{=}$ $2\cos\alpha\cos B = 2\cos\alpha\cos B$

Challenge Page 138 1. $\frac{\cot\alpha\cot B - 1}{\cot B + \cot\alpha}$

Exploratory Exercises Page 141 1. I or II 3. II 5. I or II 7. II 9. I, II, III, or IV 11. cos 20° 13. sin 70° 15. tan 100° 17. cos 31°

Written Exercises Page 142 1. $\frac{24}{25}$ 3. $\frac{24}{7}$
5. $\frac{3\sqrt{10}}{10}$ 7. $\frac{120}{169}$ 9. $\frac{120}{119}$ 11. $-\frac{\sqrt{26}}{26}$
13. $\frac{\sqrt{2-\sqrt{2}}}{2}$ 15. $\sqrt{2}-1$ 17. $\frac{\sqrt{2+\sqrt{2+\sqrt{3}}}}{2}$
19. $-\frac{4}{5}$ 21. $\frac{4}{3}$ 23. $-\frac{7}{25}$ 25. $\frac{2\sqrt{5}}{5}$ 27. -2

29.
$$1+\cos 2A \stackrel{?}{=} \frac{2}{1+\tan^2 A}$$
$$\stackrel{?}{=} \frac{2}{\frac{\cos^2 A}{\cos^2 A}+\frac{\sin^2 A}{\cos^2 A}}$$
$$\stackrel{?}{=} \frac{2}{\frac{1}{\cos^2 A}}$$
$$\stackrel{?}{=} 2\cos^2 A$$
$$1+\cos 2A = \cos 2A + 1$$

33.
$$\csc A\sec A \stackrel{?}{=} 2\csc 2A$$
$$\frac{1}{\sin A}\cdot\frac{1}{\cos A} \stackrel{?}{=}$$
$$\frac{1}{\sin A\cos A} \stackrel{?}{=}$$
$$\frac{1}{\frac{\sin 2A}{2}} \stackrel{?}{=}$$
$$2\cdot\frac{1}{\sin 2A} \stackrel{?}{=}$$
$$2\csc 2A = 2\csc 2A$$

37.
$$\cos^4 A \stackrel{?}{=} \frac{2\cos 2A + \cos^2 2A + 1}{4}$$
$$\stackrel{?}{=} \frac{(\cos 2A + 1)^2}{4}$$
$$\stackrel{?}{=} \frac{2(\cos^2 A - 1 + 1)^2}{4}$$
$$\stackrel{?}{=} \frac{4\cos^4 A}{4}$$
$$\cos^4 A = \cos^4 A$$

41.
$$\tan\frac{x}{2} \stackrel{?}{=} \frac{1-\cos x}{\sin x}$$
$$\sqrt{\frac{1-\cos x}{1+\cos x}} \stackrel{?}{=}$$
$$\frac{\sqrt{1-\cos^2 x}}{1+\cos x} \stackrel{?}{=}$$
$$\frac{\sqrt{\sin^2 x}}{1+\cos x} \stackrel{?}{=}$$
$$\frac{\sin x(1-\cos x)}{(1+\cos x)(1-\cos x)} \stackrel{?}{=}$$
$$\frac{\sin x(1-\cos x)}{1-\cos^2 x} \stackrel{?}{=}$$
$$\frac{\sin x(1-\cos x)}{\sin^2 x} = \frac{1-\cos x}{\sin x}$$

Challenge Page 142 1. $\sin 3\alpha = 3\sin\alpha - 4\sin^3\alpha$ 3. $\tan 3\alpha = \frac{3\tan\alpha - \tan^3\alpha}{1-3\tan^2\alpha}$

Chapter Review Page 145 1. $\sin\alpha = \frac{3\sqrt{34}}{34}$, $\csc\alpha = \frac{\sqrt{34}}{3}$, $\cos\alpha = \frac{5\sqrt{34}}{34}$, $\sec\alpha = \frac{\sqrt{34}}{5}$, $\tan\alpha = \frac{3}{5}$, $\cot\alpha = \frac{5}{3}$ 3. $\sin\alpha = \frac{4}{5}$, $\csc\alpha = \frac{5}{4}$, $\cos\alpha = -\frac{3}{5}$, $\sec\alpha = -\frac{5}{3}$, $\tan\alpha = -\frac{4}{3}$, $\cot\alpha = -\frac{3}{4}$

5. 0 7. $\frac{3}{4}$ 9. 1.8714 11. 0.9276 13. 6°24′

15. $\frac{\sqrt{5}}{3}$ 17. $\sqrt{17}$ 19. $\frac{\sin\theta}{\sec\theta} \stackrel{?}{=} \frac{1}{\tan\theta + \cot\theta}$

$$\stackrel{?}{=} \frac{1}{\frac{\sin\theta}{\cos\theta} + \frac{\cos\theta}{\sin\theta}}$$

$$\stackrel{?}{=} \frac{1}{\frac{\sin^2\theta + \cos^2\theta}{\cos\theta\sin\theta}}$$

$$\stackrel{?}{=} \cos\theta\sin\theta$$

$$\frac{\sin\theta}{\sec\theta} = \frac{\sin\theta}{\sec\theta}$$

23. $\frac{1-\cos\theta}{1+\cos\theta} \stackrel{?}{=} (\csc\theta - \cot\theta)^2$

$$\stackrel{?}{=} \csc^2\theta - 2\cot\theta\csc\theta + \cot^2\theta$$

$$\stackrel{?}{=} \frac{1}{\sin^2\theta} - 2\left(\frac{\cos\theta}{\sin\theta}\cdot\frac{1}{\sin\theta}\right) + \frac{\cos^2\theta}{\sin^2\theta}$$

$$\stackrel{?}{=} \frac{1}{\sin^2\theta} - \frac{2\cos\theta}{\sin^2\theta} + \frac{\cos^2\theta}{\sin^2\theta}$$

$$\stackrel{?}{=} \frac{(1-\cos\theta)^2}{\sin^2\theta}$$

$$\stackrel{?}{=} \frac{(1-\cos\theta)^2}{1-\cos^2\theta}$$

$$\stackrel{?}{=} \frac{(1-\cos\theta)^2}{(1-\cos\theta)(1+\cos\theta)}$$

$$\frac{1-\cos\theta}{1+\cos\theta} = \frac{1-\cos\theta}{1+\cos\theta}$$

25. 60° 27. 240° 29. 16.75 cm 31. 3.91 cm 33. $^-\cos 30°$ 35. $^-\csc 38°$ 37. $^-0.8660$ 39. $^-1.624$ 41. 1 43. 0 45. $\frac{\sqrt{2}+\sqrt{6}}{4}$ 47. $\frac{\sqrt{6}+\sqrt{2}}{4}$

49. $\frac{\sqrt{10}}{10}$ 51. $\frac{3\sqrt{10}}{10}$

CHAPTER 6 GRAPHS AND INVERSES OF THE TRIGONOMETRIC FUNCTIONS

Exploratory Exercises Page 150 1. 1 3. 0 5. 0 7. 0 9. positive 11. negative 13. negative 15. negative 17. cos 20° 19. sin 50°

Written Exercises Page 151 1. $n \cdot 360°$ where n is any integer 3. $45° + n \cdot 180°$ where n is any integer 5. $n \cdot 180°$ where n is any integer 7. real numbers 9. real numbers except $\theta = n \cdot 180°$ where n is any integer 11. real numbers except $\theta = 90° + n \cdot 180°$ where n is any integer 13. $^-1 \le y \le 1$ 15. real numbers 17. real numbers

19.

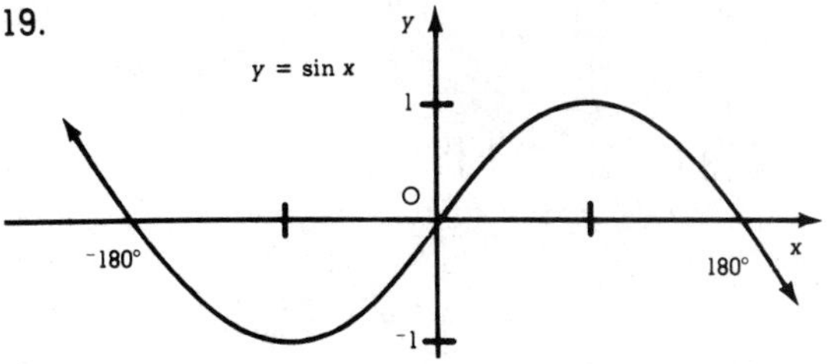

23.

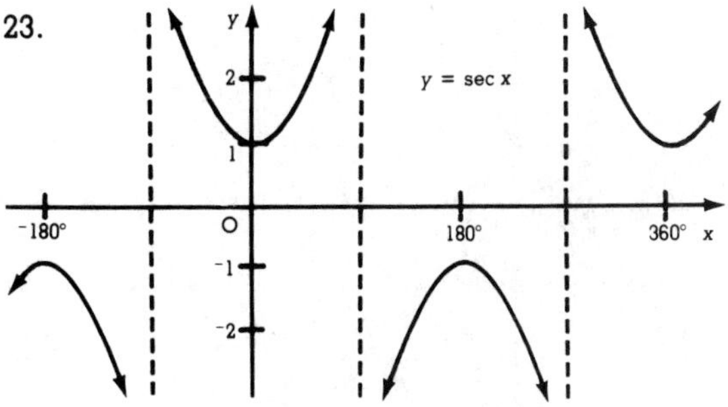

25. $x = 135°$ and $x = 315°$ 27. none 29. $x = 0°, 90°$ and $360°$

Exploratory Exercises Page 154 1. 2, 72°, none 3. 3, 360°, 90° 5. none, 90°, 90° 7. 110, 18°, none 9. 2, 360°, none 11. 7, 60°, none 13. $\frac{1}{4}$, 720°, none 15. 10, 1080°, 900°

Written Exercises Page 155

1. $y = 3\sin\left(\frac{1}{2}x - 30°\right)$ or $y = {}^-3\sin\left(\frac{1}{2}x - 30°\right)$

3. $y = \frac{2}{3}\sin(2x - 90°)$ or $y = -\frac{2}{3}\sin(2x - 90°)$

5. $y = \frac{1}{2}\sin\left(\frac{4}{3}x + \frac{\pi}{3}\right)$ or $y = -\frac{1}{2}\sin\left(\frac{4}{3}x + \frac{\pi}{3}\right)$

7. $y = \frac{1}{3}\cos 2x$ or $y = -\frac{1}{3}\cos 2x$

9. $y = 4\cos\left(\frac{1}{2}x - 45°\right)$ or $y = {}^-4\cos\left(\frac{1}{2}x - 45°\right)$

11. $y = \frac{7}{3}\cos(2.4x - 648°)$ or

$y = -\frac{7}{3}\cos(2.4x - 648°)$ 13. 3, 360°, none 15. 2, 360°, 180° 17. 4, 720°, none

19.

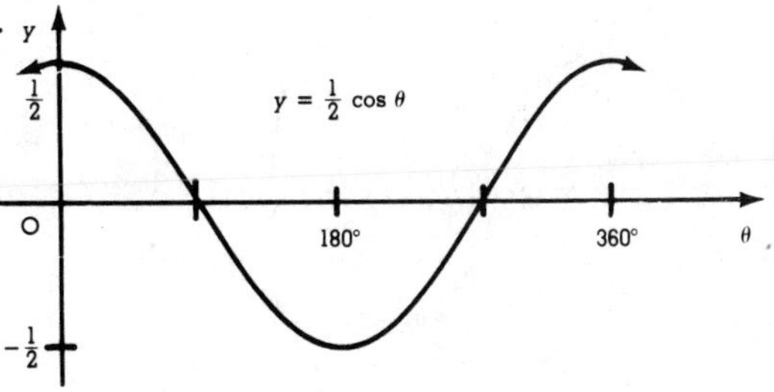

23.

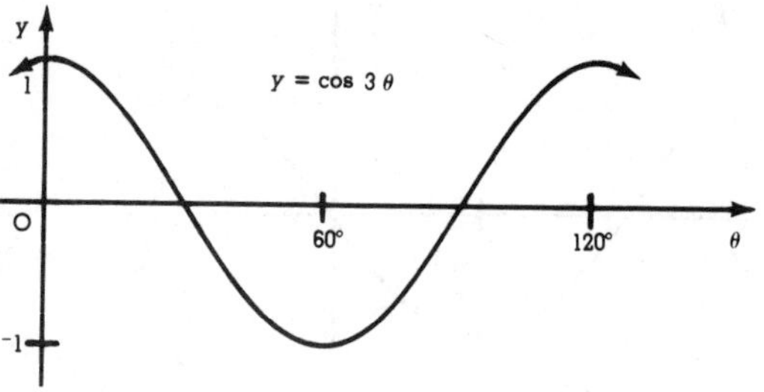

27.

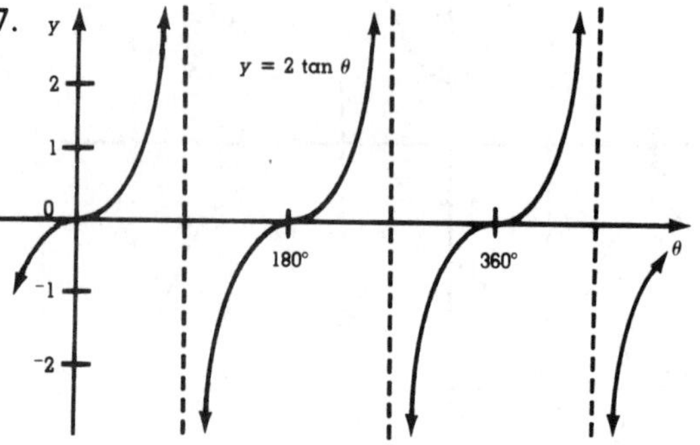

31.

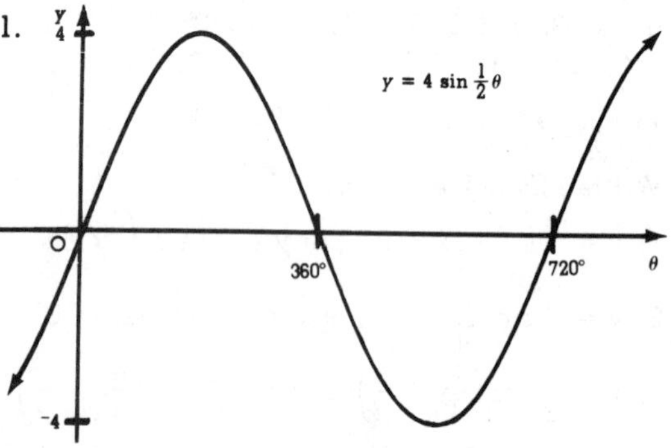

Exploratory Exercises Page 158 1. 1, 360°, ⁻90° 3. 3, 360°, 90° 5. 3, 60°, 30° 7. $\frac{1}{2}$, 720°, 360° 9. $\frac{1}{10}$, 3π, $\frac{\pi}{2}$ 11. 2, 60°, ⁻60°

Written Exercises Page 158

1.

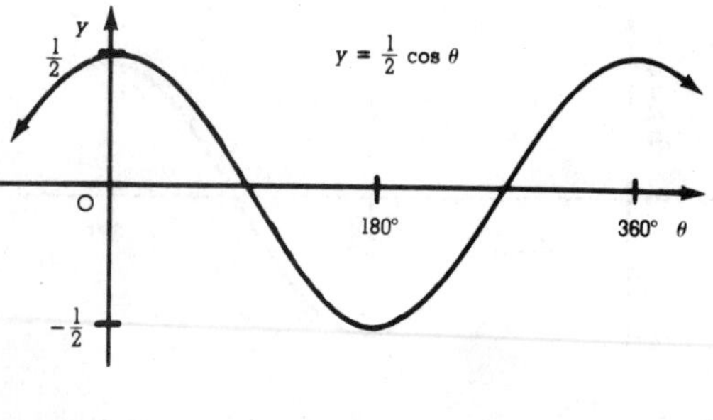

5.

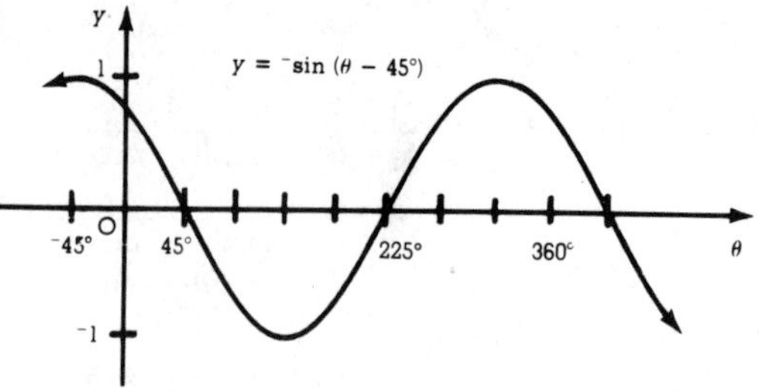

9.

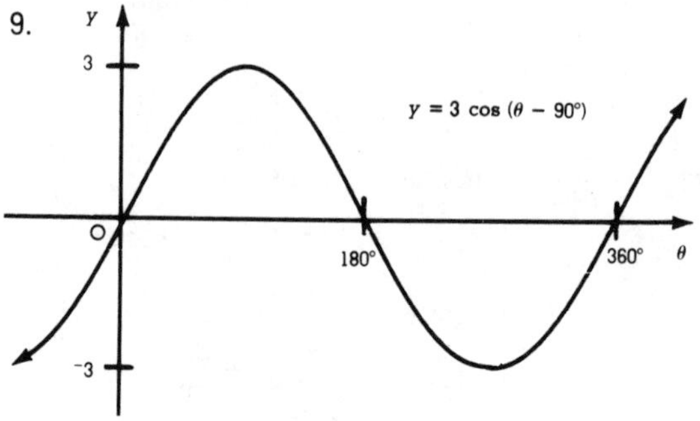

13.

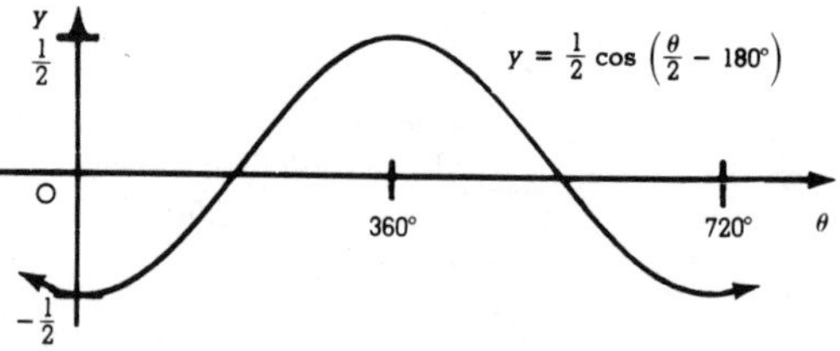

17.

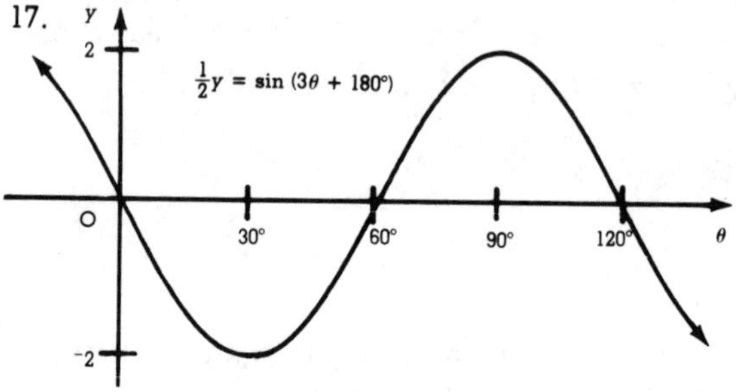

21.

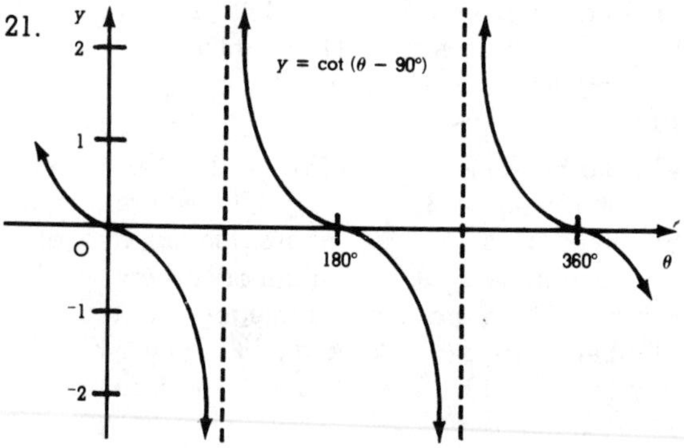

Exploratory Exercises Page 160 1. 1 3. $\frac{\pi}{2}$ 5. 3 7. $\frac{\pi}{2}$ 9. 0 11. 0 13. $\frac{\pi + 2\sqrt{2}}{4}$ 15. $\frac{2 + \sqrt{2}}{2}$ 17. $\frac{\pi\sqrt{2}}{8}$

Written Exercises Page 160

3.

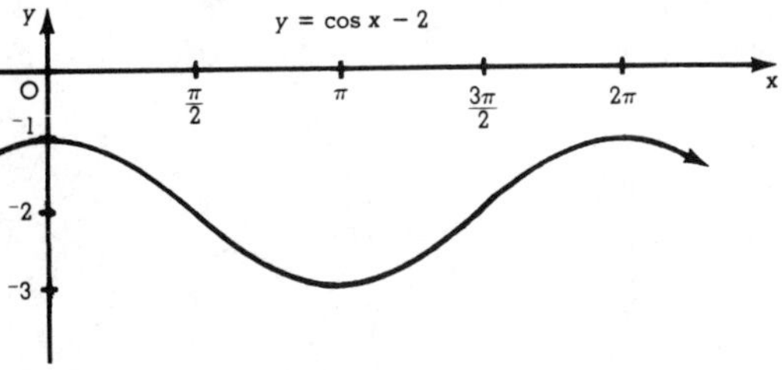

7.

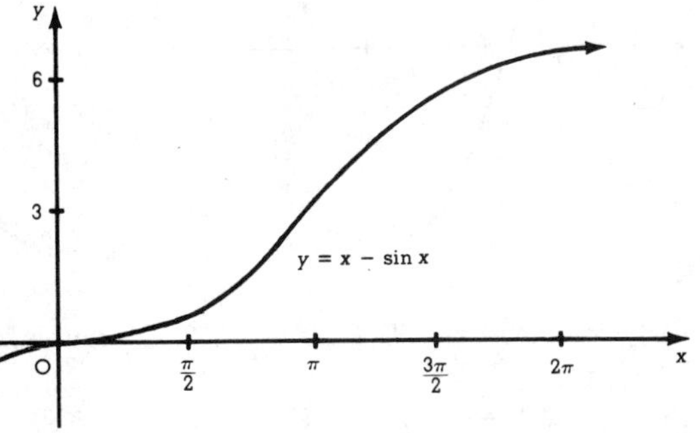

11.

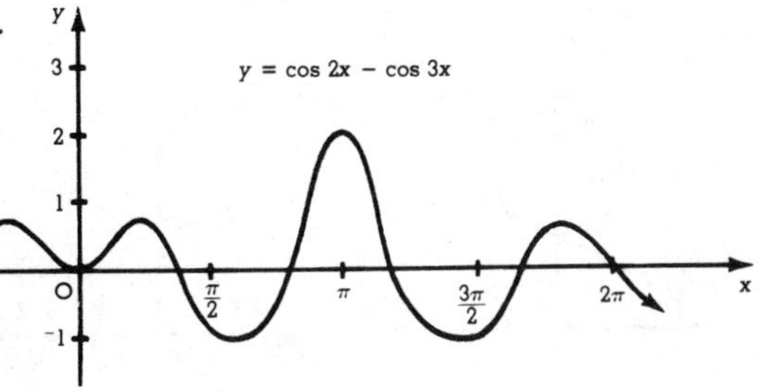

15.

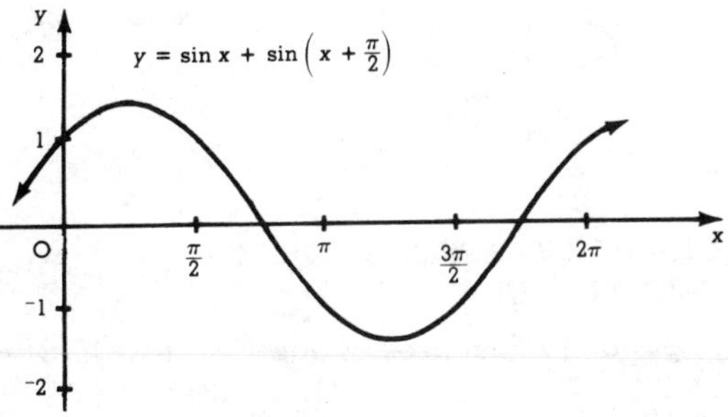

Exploratory Exercises Page 163 1. {(1,3), (4,2), (5,1)} 3. {(2,3), (2,4)} 5. {(⁻2,⁻1), (⁻2,⁻3), (⁻4,⁻1), (6,0)} 7. $\theta = \arcsin x$ 9. $y = \arctan(^-3)$ 11. $\theta = \arctan \frac{4}{3}$ 13. $\theta = \arcsin n$ 15. $\theta = \arccos y$

Written Exercises Page 164 1. $x = 0°, 180°, 360°$ 3. $x = 45°, 225°$ 5. $x = 30°, 210°$ 7. $x = 60°, 300°$ 9. $x = 210°, 330°$ 11. $\frac{5}{4}$ 13. $\frac{5}{12}$ 15. $\frac{4}{5}$ 17. 1 19. $\frac{\sqrt{3}}{3}$

21. $\arccos \frac{\sqrt{3}}{2} + \arcsin \frac{\sqrt{3}}{2} \stackrel{?}{=} \frac{\pi}{2}$

$$\frac{\pi}{6} + \frac{\pi}{3} \stackrel{?}{=}$$
$$\frac{\pi}{2} = \frac{\pi}{2}$$

23. $\tan^{-1} 1 + \cos^{-1} \frac{\sqrt{3}}{2} \stackrel{?}{=} \sin^{-1} \frac{1}{2} + \sec^{-1} \sqrt{2}$

$$45° + 30° \stackrel{?}{=} 30° + 45°$$
$$75° = 75°$$

Exploratory Exercises Page 166 1. 60° 3. 45° 5. 41° 7. 0° 9. 150° 11. ⁻45° 13. 60° 15. 90° 17. ⁻19° 19. 90°

Written Exercises Page 166 1. ⁻45° 3. $60° + n \cdot 360°$ and $120° + n \cdot 360°$ where n is any integer 5. $135° + n \cdot 180°$ where n is any integer 7. $45° + n \cdot 360°$ and $315° + n \cdot 360°$ where n is any integer 9. 0° 11. $48°35' + n \cdot 360°$ and $131°25' + n \cdot 360°$ where n is any integer. 13. $\frac{4}{5}$ 15. $78°41' + n \cdot 180°$ where n is any integer 17. $-\frac{4}{3}$ 19. $120° + n \cdot 360°$ and $240° + n \cdot 360°$ where n is any integer 21. $\frac{1}{2}$ 23. $26°34' + n \cdot 180°$ where n is any integer 25. $\frac{\sqrt{2}}{2}$ 27. $270° + n \cdot 360°$ where n is any integer 29. $\sqrt{\frac{1}{2}\left(1 - \frac{5}{\sqrt{34}}\right)} \approx 0.2669$ 31. $\frac{1}{2}$ 33. $\frac{\sqrt{3}}{2}$ 35. $-\frac{\sqrt{2}}{2}$ 37. $\frac{\sqrt{2}}{2}$ 39. $\frac{33}{56}$

Challenge Page 167 1. $uv - \sqrt{(1 - u^2)(1 - v^2)}$

Exploratory Exercises Page 169 1. real numbers 3. real numbers except $90° + n \cdot 180°$ where n is any integer 5. $0° \le x \le 180°$ 7. $^-1 \le x \le 1$ 9. real numbers 11. $^-1 \le x \le 1$ 13. $^-1 \le y \le 1$ 15. real numbers 17. $^-1 \le y \le 1$ 19. real numbers

21. real numbers except $90° + n \cdot 180°$
23. $0° \leq y \leq 180°$

Written Exercises Page 169 1. $y = x - 2$
3. $x = 3$ 5. $y = \text{Sin}\,x$ 7. $y = x$ 9. $y = \frac{x+1}{^-3}$
11. $y = \text{Sin}^{-1}x$

17.

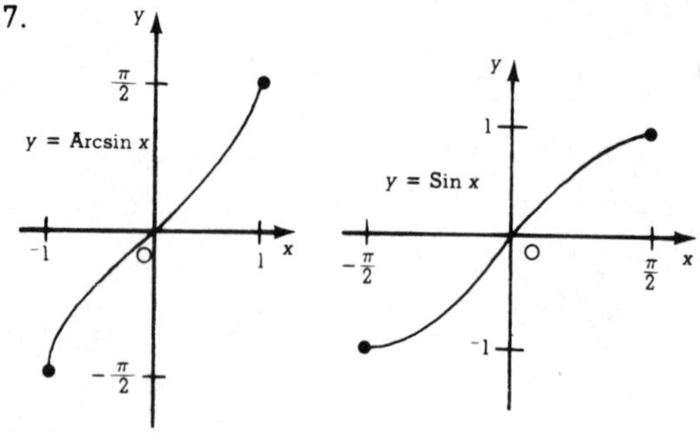

23.

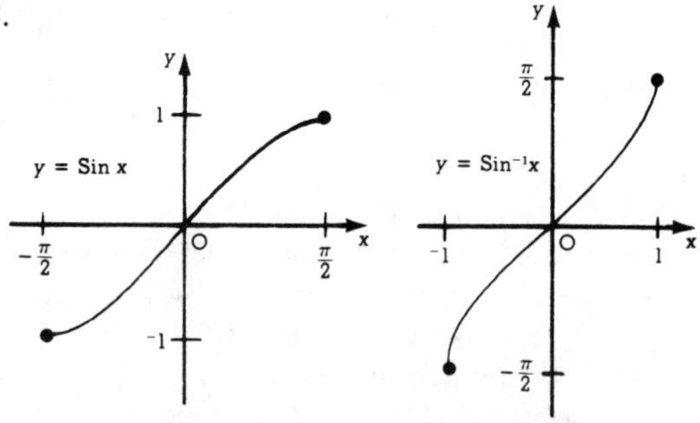

25. no 27. no 29. yes 31. true 33. False. There is no value for $\tan\frac{\pi}{2}$. 35. true 37. False. There is no value for $\cos^{-1}\pi$ while $\frac{1}{\cos\pi} = {}^-1$.

Chapter Review Page 171 1. sin 50° 3. cos 28°

5.

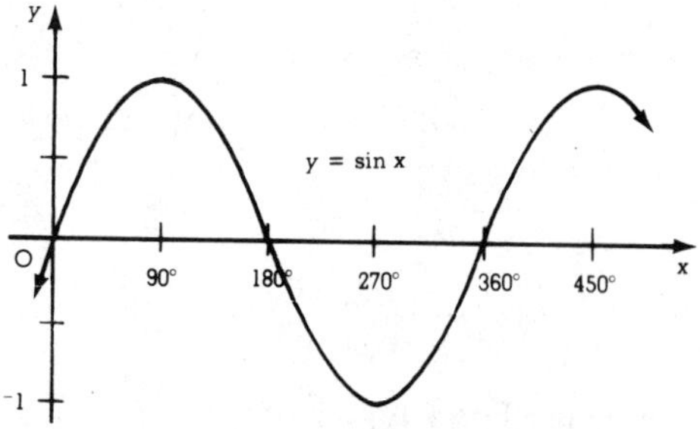

9. 4, 180°, none 11. none, 360°, 90° 13. none, 36°, none 15. $y = 3\sin(x - 45°)$ or $y = {}^-3\sin(x - 45°)$ 17. $y = \frac{1}{3}\sin(2x - 180°)$ or $y = -\frac{1}{3}\sin(2x - 180°)$

19.

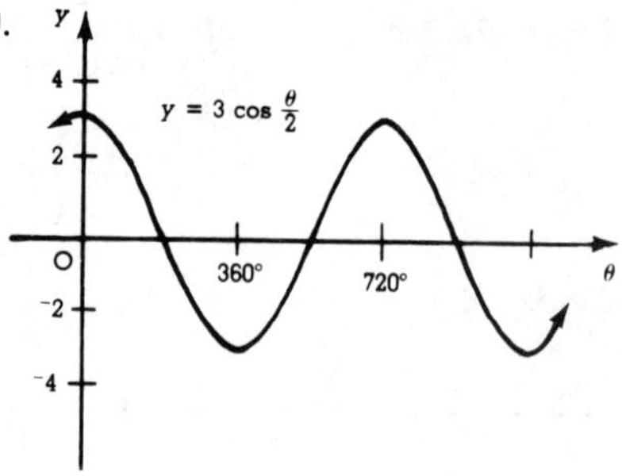

23.

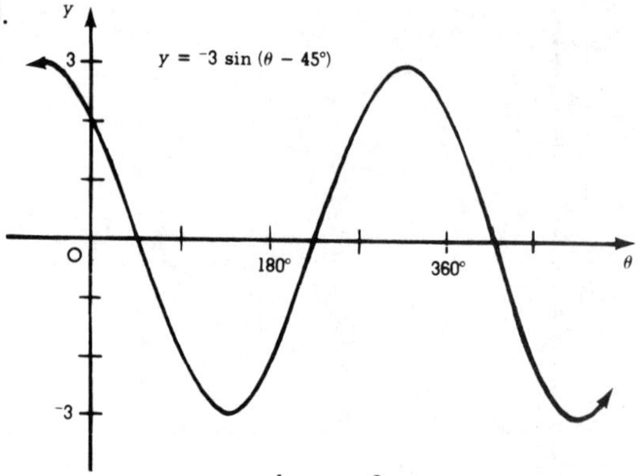

27. $y = \arctan x$ 29. $\frac{1}{2}$ 31. $\frac{3}{4}$ 33. undefined 35. $\frac{\sqrt{2}}{2}$ 37. $\frac{\sqrt{2}}{2}$ 39. 0 41. 0 43. $x = y^2 + 1$

45.

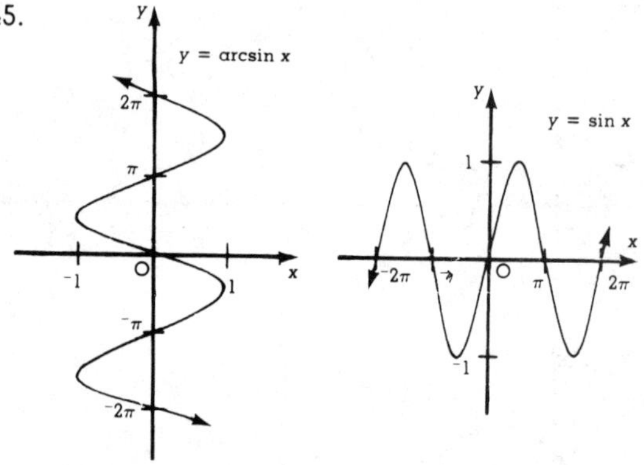

49. no

CHAPTER 7 APPLICATIONS OF TRIGONOMETRY

Exploratory Exercises Page 176 1. 60° 3. 45° 5. 120° 7. 45° 9. 30° 11. 2 13. 4 15. 0 17. 8

Written Exercises Page 176 1. $90° + n \cdot 360°$, $210° + n \cdot 360°$, $330° + n \cdot 360°$ where n is any integer 3. $45° + n \cdot 90°$ where n is any integer

5. $45° + n \cdot 90°$ where n is any integer 7. $60° + n \cdot 180°$, $120° + n \cdot 180°$ where n is any integer 9. $60° + n \cdot 360°$, $300° + n \cdot 360°$ where n is any integer 11. 0°, ⁻30° 13. 60°, ⁻60° 15. 30°, ⁻90° 17. 90° 19. 90°, 30° 21. 45° 23. 0°, 90° 25. ⁻90° 27. 90°, 150° 29. 0° 31. 0°, ≈ 71°30′ 33. 30°, ⁻30° 35. 0° 37. 18°, 90° 39. 0°

Exploratory Exercises Page 180 1. $\sin 20° = \frac{a}{35}$ 3. $\cos B = \frac{1}{2}$ 5. $\cos 16° = \frac{a}{13}$ 7. $7^2 + b^2 = 16^2$ 9. $5^2 + 6^2 = c^2$ 11. equal sides 6.98 cm; altitude 5.89 cm

Written Exercises Page 180 1. $B = 49°$, $c = 9.86$, $a = 6.47$ 3. $B = 67°38'$, $c = 23.8$, $a = 9.07$ 5. $B = 45°$, $a = 7$, $b = 7$ 7. $B = 52°45'$, $a = 8.4$, $c = 13.8$ 9. $B = 34°05'$, $a = 13.3$, $b = 9.0$ 11. 3.26 cm 13. 29°13′ 15. 131.7 ft 17. 10.57 cm 19. 31.71 cm² 21. 1167 ft 23. 42.1 meters

Exploratory Exercises Page 185 1. none 3. none 5. none 7. 1 9. 1 11. none 13. $\frac{20}{\sin 40°} = \frac{b}{\sin 60°}$ 15. $\frac{14}{\sin 50°} = \frac{10}{\sin B}$

Written Exercises Page 185 1. 1; $C = 74°$, $b = 8.9$, $c = 10.2$ 3. 1; $C = 91°10'$, $a = 75.8$, $b = 97.8$ 5. 1; $C = 80°$, $a = 13.1$, $b = 17.6$ 7. none 9. none 11. 2; $B = 30°28'$, $C = 124°32'$, $c = 243.7$; $B = 149°32'$, $C = 5°28'$, $c = 28.2$ 13. 536.2 ft 15. 109.7 ft

17. $$\begin{aligned} \frac{a-c}{c} &\stackrel{?}{=} \frac{\sin A - \sin C}{\sin C} \\ &\stackrel{?}{=} \frac{\sin A}{\sin C} - \frac{\sin C}{\sin C} \\ &\stackrel{?}{=} \frac{a}{c} - 1 \\ &\stackrel{?}{=} \frac{a-c}{c} \end{aligned}$$

19. $$\begin{aligned} \frac{a}{b} &\stackrel{?}{=} \frac{\sin A}{\sin B} \\ &\stackrel{?}{=} \frac{\frac{a \sin B}{b}}{\sin B} \\ &= \frac{a}{b} \end{aligned}$$

Exploratory Exercises Page 187 1. Law of cosines 3. Law of sines 5. Law of cosines 7. Law of cosines 9. Law of sines

Written Exercises Page 188 1. $a = 6.4$, $B = 47°46'$, $C = 80°4'$ 3. $a = 7.8$, $B = 44°12'$, $C = 84°48'$ 5. $A = 44°25'$, $B = 57°7'$, $C = 78°28'$ 7. $a = 202.6$, $B = 55°53'$, $C = 62°42'$ 9. $C = 14.1$, $A = 104°53'$, $B = 35°47'$ 11. $C = 81°$, $a = 9.1$, $b = 12.1$ 13. 35°41′ 15. 228.4 miles 17. 61.9 ft

Exploratory Exercises Page 190 1. $K = \frac{1}{2} \cdot 3 \cdot 4 \cdot \sin 120°$ 3. $K = \sqrt{9(9-4)(9-6)(9-8)}$ 5. $K = \frac{1}{2} \cdot 18.6^2 \cdot \frac{\sin 63°50' \sin 96°50'}{\sin 19°20'}$ 7. $K = \frac{1}{2} \cdot 6 \cdot 4 \cdot \sin 52°$

Written Exercises Page 191 1. 33.24 3. 6.4 5. 1.6 7. 97.87 9. 37.9 11. perimeter = 1434.3 ft, area = 86,804.3 sq ft 13. 24 sq cm 15. 70.7 sq cm

Exploratory Exercises Page 193

1.

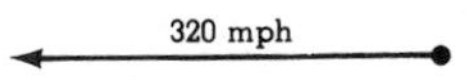

3.

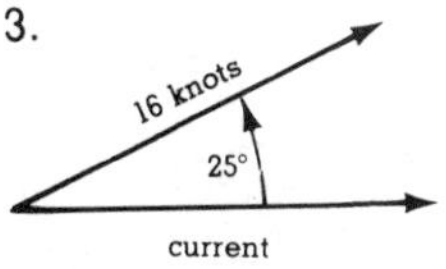

5. 60.2 kg, 48°22′ 7. 39.8 kg, 90°

Written Exercises Page 194 1. 19.3 lb 3. 10 lb 5. 111.8 kg, 26°34′ or 63°26′ 7. 260.5 mph, 3°32′ west of north 9. 171.5 kg, 28°7′ 11. 19°28′ 13. 3.7 kg, 10°4′ east of south 15. 8 seconds 17. 19 m

Exploratory Exercises Page 197 1. 3.93 3. 1.57 5. 1.08 7. 2.98 9. 3.14 11. 12.6

Written Exercises Page 198 1. 9.6 sq units 3. 202.7 sq units 5. 1.9 sq units 7. 238.5 sq units 9. 39.3 sq units 11. 18.71 sq units 13. radius = 5 cm, area = 78.5 sq cm 15. radius = 10 cm, area = 314.2 sq cm 17. 530.1 sq cm 19. 1680.7 ft

Chapter Review Page 200 1. $45° + n \cdot 90°$ where n is any integer 3. $0° + n \cdot 360°$ and $90° + n \cdot 180°$ where n is any integer 5. ⁻45°, 71°34′ 7. 0°, 30° 9. $B = 27°$, $c = 10.9$, $b = 4.9$ 11. $A = 7°$, $c = 5.6$, $a = 0.7$ 13. 24.35 ft 15. 7.42 ft 17. 2; $C = 47°33'$, $B = 93°45'$, $b = 274.5$; $C = 132°27'$, $B = 8°51'$, $b = 42.3$ 19. 2; $B = 37°18'$, $C = 113°42'$, $c = 22.7$; $B = 142°42'$, $C = 8°18'$, $c = 3.6$ 21. 28.8 cm 23. $a = 36.9$, $B = 57°28'$, $C = 71°36'$ 25. $b = 21.0$, $A = 52°15'$, $C = 108°45'$ 27. $A = 30°31'$, $B = 36°53'$, $C = 112°36'$ 29. $A = 36°1'$ 31. 9.7 sq units 33. 17.4 sq units 35. 2.8 sq units 37. 1039.2 sq cm 39. 215.1 km/h at 8°1′ west of south 41. 68°22′ 43. 159.3 sq units 45. 25.1 sq units 47. 118.5 sq units 49. 7.8 sq units

CHAPTER 8 SEQUENCES AND SERIES

Exploratory Exercises Page 206 1. 17, 21, 25, 29, 33 3. 37, 43, 49, 55, 61 5. 12, 19, 26, 33, 40

7. 6, 7.5, 9, 10.5, 12 9. $a + 9, a + 12, a + 15, a + 18, a + 21$ 11. $4x, 5x, 6x, 7x, 8x$ 13. $^-5b, ^-7b, ^-9b, ^-11b, ^-13b$ 15. $r + 1, r - 6, r - 13, r - 20, r - 27$

Written Exercises Pages 206-207 1. $^-25$ 3. 11 5. 15 7. 6 9. $3 - 4\sqrt{3}$ 11. 149 13. 12, 16.5, 21 15. $^-4, ^-1, 2, 5$ 17. $1, 1\frac{3}{4}, 2\frac{1}{2}, 3\frac{1}{4}, 4$ 19. 181.3 21. 77 23. 8 25. 231

Exploratory Exercises Page 209 1. $\frac{1}{2}, \frac{1}{4}, \frac{1}{8}, \frac{1}{16}$ 3. $\frac{4}{3}, \frac{8}{3}, \frac{16}{3}, \frac{32}{3}$ 5. 1.75, 0.875, 0.4375, 0.21875 7. 12.5, 31.25, 78.125, 195.3125 9. yes 11. yes 13. yes

Written Exercises Page 210 1. $^-2, ^-1\frac{1}{3}, -\frac{8}{9}, -\frac{16}{27}$ 3. $\frac{128}{6561}$ 5. $16\sqrt{2}$ 7. $8\sqrt{2}, ^-16, 16\sqrt{2}, ^-32$ 9. $\frac{1}{4}, 1, 4$, or $\frac{1}{4}, ^-1, 4$ 11. $^-2, 6, ^-18, 54$ 13. $\frac{127}{128}$ 15. $201\frac{2}{3}$ 17. 255.5

Exploratory Exercises Page 212 1. 2^{n-1} 3. $2n + 3$ 5. $3 \cdot \left(\frac{2}{3}\right)^{n-1}$ 7. $\frac{5n - 1}{2n}$

Written Exercises Page 213 1. 1 3. 3 5. 0 7. no limit exists 9. $\frac{2}{5}$ 11. 2 13. 3 15. 0 17. 0 19. no limit exists 21. no limit exists 23. 0 25. $\frac{5}{2}$

Exploratory Exercises Page 215 1. $\frac{4 - 4\left(\frac{1}{4}\right)^{10}}{1 - \frac{1}{4}}$ 3. $\frac{20 - 20(0.1)^{10}}{1 - 0.1}$ 5. $\frac{25 - 25(0.2)^{10}}{1 - 0.2}$ 7. $5\frac{1}{3}$ 9. $22\frac{2}{9}$ 11. $31\frac{1}{4}$

Written Exercises Page 215 1. $\frac{4}{3}$ 3. $\frac{3}{2}(\sqrt{3} + 1)$ 5. $\frac{1}{10}$ 7. $\frac{2}{9}$ 9. No sum exists since $r = 1.5$. 11. $\frac{5}{9}$ 13. $\frac{3}{11}$ 15. $\frac{41}{333}$ 17. $2\frac{205}{999}$ 19. $\frac{7}{22}$

Exploratory Exercises Page 220 1. divergent 3. convergent 5. convergent

Written Exercises Page 220 1. convergent 3. convergent 5. convergent 7. The ratio test fails. 9. convergent 11. divergent

Exploratory Exercises Page 223 1. $3 + 4 + 5 + 6$; 18 3. $8 + 10 + 12 + 14$; 44 5. $^-1 + 1 + 3 + 5 + 7 + 9$; 24 7. $17 + 20 + 23$; 60

Written Exercises Page 223 1. $5 + 7 + 9 + 11 + 13$; 45 3. $5 + 6 + 7 + 8$; 26 5. $10 + 11 + 12 + 13 + 14$; 60 7. $4 + 16 + 64 + 256$; 340 9. $6 + 12 + 20 + 30$; 68 11. $1.5 + 2.5 + 4.5 + 8.5 + 16.5$; 33.5 13. $2 + 1 + \frac{1}{2} + \cdots; s = \frac{2}{1 - \frac{1}{2}} = 4$ 15. $6 + 4 + \frac{8}{3} + \cdots$; 18 17. $\frac{81}{100} + \frac{729}{1000} + \frac{6561}{10{,}000} + \cdots; 8\frac{1}{10}$ 19. $\sum_{k=1}^{4} 3k$ 21. $\sum_{k=1}^{6} 2^k$ 23. $\sum_{k=2}^{10} \frac{1}{k}$ 25. $\sum_{k=1}^{4} (3 \cdot 10^k)$ 27. $\sum_{k=0}^{3} (11 - 2k)$ 29. $\sum_{k=0}^{3} (^-2)^{3-k}$ 31. $\sum_{k=1}^{\infty} 2k$ 33. $\sum_{k=2}^{\infty} \frac{k}{5}$ 35. $\sum_{k=1}^{\infty} 3^k$

Challenge Page 223 1. true 3. false 5. true 7. true

Exploratory Exercises Page 226 1. 6! 3. 8! 5. $\frac{8!}{4!}$ 7. $\frac{17!}{14!}$

Written Exercises Page 226-227 1. 120 3. 5040 5. 2160 7. 144 9. 5 11. 90 13. $(n + 2)^7 = n^7 + 14n^6 + 84n^5 + 280n^4 + 560n^3 + 672n^2 + 448n + 128$ 15. $(2 + d)^4 = 16 + 32d + 24d^2 + 8d^3 + d^4$ 17. $(2x - 3y)^3 = 8x^3 - 36x^2y + 54xy^2 - 27y^3$ 19. $(2x + y)^6 = 64x^6 + 192x^5y + 240x^4y^2 + 160x^3y^3 + 60x^2y^4 + 12xy^5 + y^6$ 21. $(2x + \sqrt{3})^4 = 16x^4 + 32\sqrt{3}x^3 + 72x^2 + 24\sqrt{3}x + 9$ 23. $\left(3v - \frac{1}{2}w\right)^5 = 243v^5 - \frac{405}{2}v^4w + \frac{135}{2}v^3w^2 - \frac{45}{4}v^2w^3 + \frac{15}{16}vw^4 - \frac{1}{32}w^5$ 25. $35a^4b^3$ 27. $90x^3y^2$ 29. $^-112\sqrt{2}a^5$ 31. $(x + y)^5 = x^5 + 5x^4y + 10x^3y^2 + 10x^2y^3 + 5xy^4 + y^5$ 33. $(r - s)^6 = r^6 - 6r^5s + 15r^4s^2 - 20r^3s^3 + 15r^2s^4 - 6rs^5 + s^6$ 35. $x^2 - x$ 37. $x^2 + x$ 39. $x - y$

Written Exercises Page 230-231 11. 600 13. 330 15. 3025 17. 2016

Chapter Review Pages 232-233 1. 6.9, 8.2, 9.5, 10.8, 12.1, 13.4 3. 6, 3.5, 1, $^-1.5$, $^-4$ 5. $1, \frac{1}{7}, \frac{1}{49}, \frac{1}{343}$ 7. 0.2, 1, 5, 25, 125 9. $\frac{2}{5}$ 11. no limit exists 13. no limit exists 15. $\frac{9}{2}$ 17. $\frac{8}{11}$ 19. convergent 21. divergent 23. $6 + 8 + 10 + 12 + 14 + 16 +$

18; 84 25. $\sum_{k=0}^{\infty}(2k-1)$ 27. 720 29. 210
31. $a^6 - 6a^5x + 15a^4x^2 - 20a^3x^3 + 15a^2x^4 - 6ax^5 + x^6$ 33. $128x^7 - 448x^6y + 672x^5y^2 - 560x^4y^3 + 280x^3y^4 - 84x^2y^5 + 14xy^6 - y^7$
35. $5005x^6$

CHAPTER 9 POLAR COORDINATES AND COMPLEX NUMBERS

Exploratory Exercises Page 238 1. 180° 3. $^-45°$ 5. $^-480°$ 7. 330° 9. 115° 11. $^-172°$
13. $\left(3, -\frac{11\pi}{6}\right), \left(^-3, \frac{7\pi}{6}\right), \left(^-3, -\frac{5\pi}{6}\right)$
15. $(^-2.4, {}^-305°), (2.4, {}^-125°), (2.4, 235°)$

Written Exercises Page 239

5.

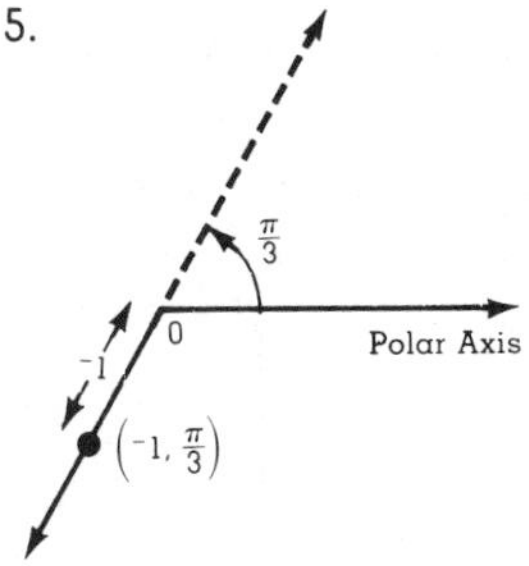

11.

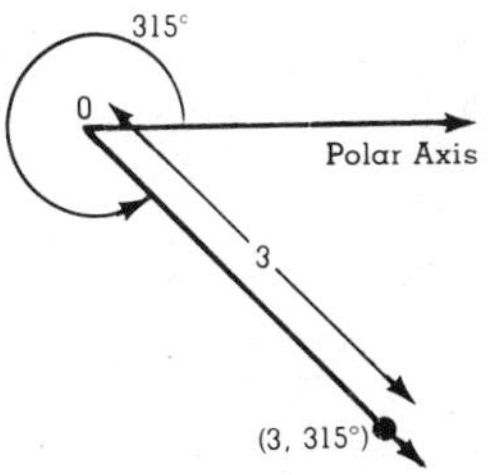

15.

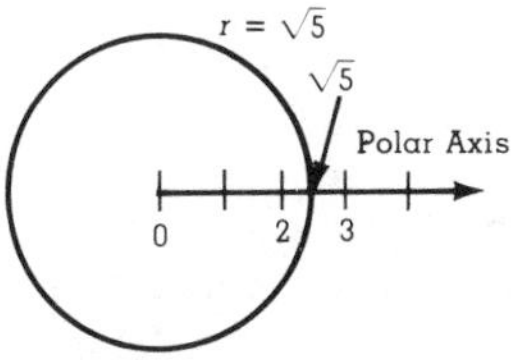

21.

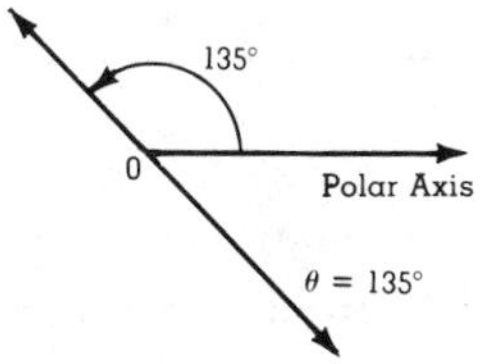

Exploratory Exercises Page 242 1. 1; 6; (6, 0°) 3. 0.5; 4.5; (4.5, 60°) 5. $^-0.5$; 1.5; (1.5, 120°) 7. $^-1$; 0; (0, 180°) 9. $^-0.5$; 1.5; (1.5, 240°) 11. 0.5; 4.5; (4.5, 300°)

Written Exercises Page 243

5.

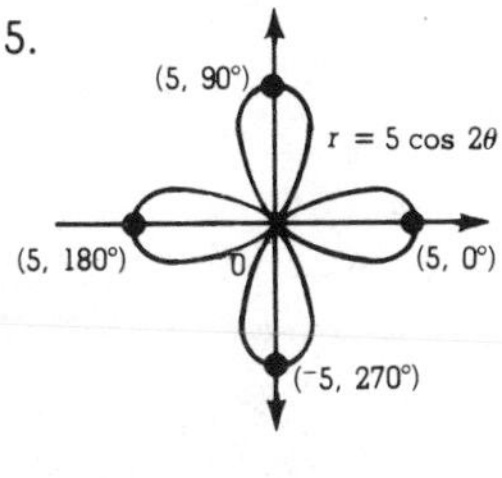

11.

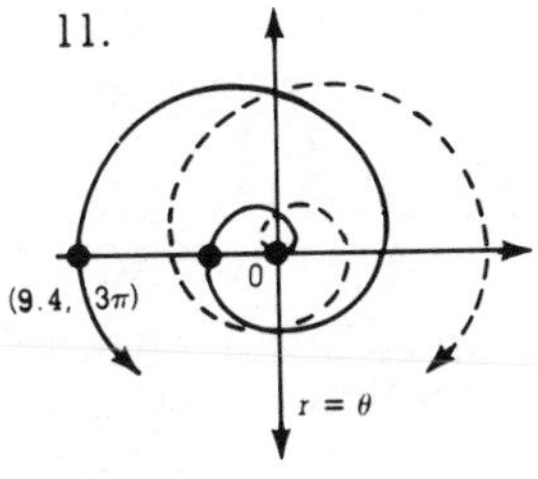

13. (6, 0°) 15. (1.7, 60°) or $(^-1.7, 240°)$

Exploratory Exercises Page 245 1. $\frac{\pi}{3}$ or 1.05 3. 1.29

Written Exercises Page 245 1. (5, 0.93) or (5, 53°) 3. $\left(\sqrt{2}, \frac{\pi}{4}\right)$ or $(\sqrt{2}, 45°)$ 5. $(\sqrt{29}, {}^-1.19)$ or $(\sqrt{29}, {}^-68°)$ 7. $(\sqrt{13}, {}^-0.59)$ or $(\sqrt{13}, {}^-34°)$
9. $\left(\frac{\sqrt{3}}{2}, \frac{1}{2}\right)$ or (0.87, 0.5) 11. (0, 3) 13. (2, 0)
15. $(^-1.04, 2.27)$ 17. $r\cos\theta = 5$ 19. $\tan\theta = 1$; $\theta = \frac{\pi}{4}$ or 45° 21. $r = \pm 5$ 23. $x^2 + y^2 = 49$
25. $x = y$ 27. $y = 2$ 29. $x = {}^-2$

Exploratory Exercises Page 248 1. ^-i
3. $^-6 + 4i$ 5. $4 + 5i$ 7. $2 + i$ 9. $^-10 + 10i$
11. $24 - 10i$ 13. 13 15. 49

Written Exercises Pages 248-249 1. 1
3. $^-2 - 7i$ 5. $^-2 - i$ 7. $2 + 2i\sqrt{2}$ 9. $1 + i$
11. $7 + 5i\sqrt{2}$ 13. 3 15. $20 + 15i$ 17. $^-9 - 46i$
19. $\frac{7 - 3i}{2}$ 21. $\frac{^-29 + 17i}{10}$ 23. $\frac{1 + 4i\sqrt{3}}{7}$
25. $\frac{7\sqrt{2} + 21i}{11}$ 27. $\frac{^-44 + 117i}{50}$

Exploratory Exercises Page 251
1. $\sqrt{2}\left(\cos\left(-\frac{\pi}{4}\right) + i\sin\left(-\frac{\pi}{4}\right)\right)$
3. $7\left(\cos\frac{\pi}{2} + i\sin\frac{\pi}{2}\right)$ 5. $5(\cos\pi + i\sin\pi)$
7. $2\sqrt{3}\left(\cos\left(-\frac{\pi}{6}\right) + i\sin\left(-\frac{\pi}{6}\right)\right)$ 9. 2 11. i
13. $-\frac{\sqrt{3}}{4} + \frac{1}{4}i$

Written Exercises Page 251 1. $\sqrt{2}\left(\cos\frac{\pi}{4} + i\sin\frac{\pi}{4}\right)$ 3. $3\left(\cos\frac{\pi}{2} + i\sin\frac{\pi}{2}\right)$ 5. $\sqrt{26}(\cos 3.34 + i\sin 3.34)$ 7. $\sqrt{29}(\cos 1.95 + i\sin 1.95)$ 9. $^-1 - i$
11. $6 - 6i\sqrt{3}$ 13. $^-1.98 + 0.28i$

Exploratory Exercises Page 253 1. $10(\cos 3\pi + i\sin 3\pi)$ 3. $2\left(\cos\left(-\frac{\pi}{6}\right) + i\sin\left(-\frac{\pi}{6}\right)\right)$ 5. $^-10$
7. $\sqrt{3} - i$

Written Exercises Page 253 1. $16(\cos 2\pi + i\sin 2\pi)$ 3. $3\left(\cos\frac{\pi}{12} + i\sin\frac{\pi}{12}\right)$ 5. $6.4(\cos 2.3 + i\sin 2.3)$ 7. ^-2i 9. $^-2\sqrt{3} + 2i$ 11. ^-4i 13. 16
15. $2.90 + 0.78i$ 17. $^-4.26 + 4.77i$

Exploratory Exercises Page 257 1. $^-27$
3. $-\frac{1}{2} + \frac{\sqrt{3}}{2}i$ or $^-0.5 + 0.87i$ 5. $^-16\sqrt{2} - 16\sqrt{2}i$ or $^-22.63 - 22.63i$ 7. $\sqrt{2} + \sqrt{2}i$ 9. $-\frac{1}{2} - \frac{\sqrt{3}}{2}i$ or $^-0.5 - 0.87i$

Written Exercises Page 257 1. $^-4 + 4i$ 3. $54 + 54i$ 5. $^-527 - 336i$ 7. $1.08 + 0.29i$ 9. $0.72 + 1.08i$ 11. $0.81 + 0.59i$ 13. $\frac{1}{2} + \frac{\sqrt{3}}{2}i$, $^-1$, $\frac{1}{2} - \frac{\sqrt{3}}{2}i$ 15. $0.31 + 0.95i$, $^-0.81 + 0.59i$, $^-0.81 - 0.59i$, $0.31 - 0.95i$ 17. $\frac{\sqrt{3}}{2} + \frac{1}{2}i$, i, $-\frac{\sqrt{3}}{2} + \frac{1}{2}i$, $-\frac{\sqrt{3}}{2} - \frac{1}{2}i$, ^-i, $\frac{\sqrt{3}}{2} - \frac{1}{2}i$

19.

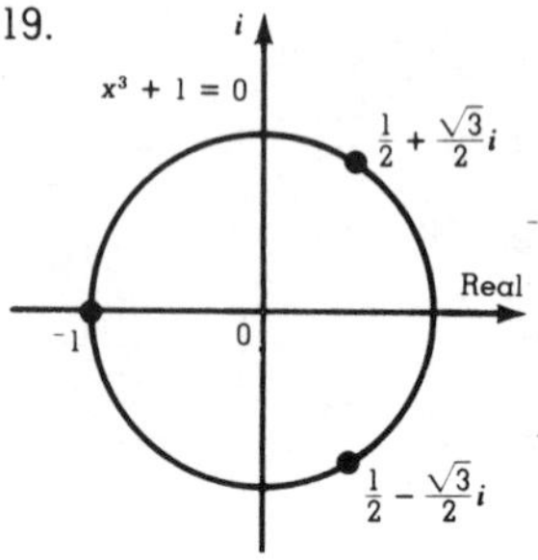

21.

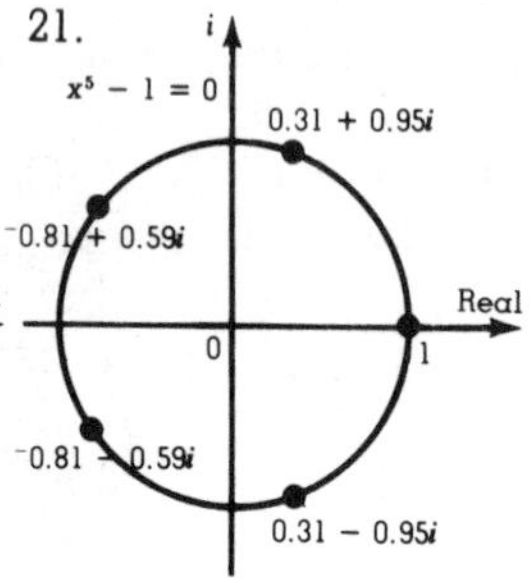

Chapter Review Pages 260-261

5. $(^-3, ^-310°)$, $(3, 230°)$, $(3, ^-130°)$ 7. $\left(2, -\frac{7\pi}{4}\right)$, $\left(^-2, -\frac{3\pi}{4}\right)$, $\left(^-2, \frac{5\pi}{4}\right)$

11.

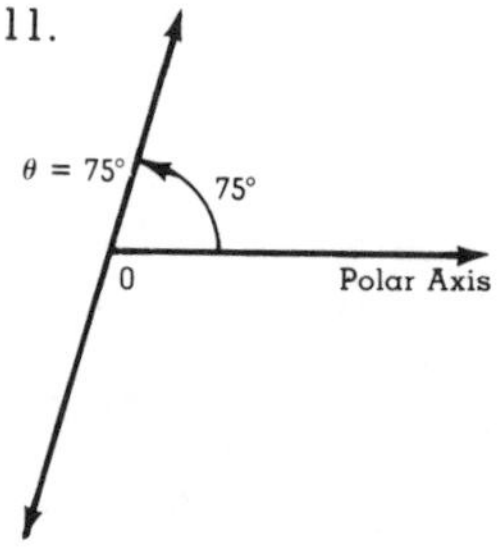

17.

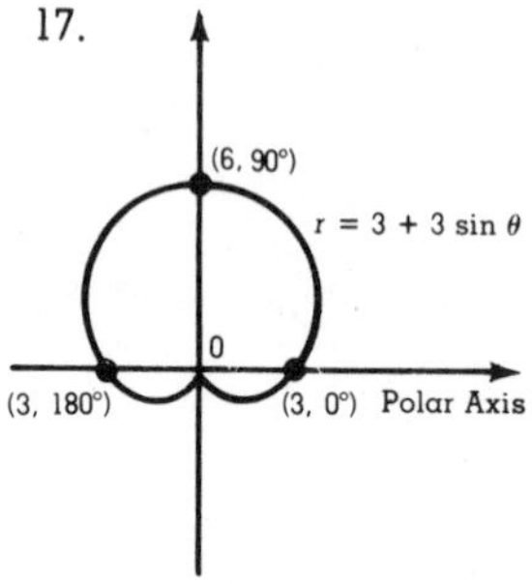

19. $\left(2\sqrt{3}, \frac{4\pi}{3}\right)$ 21. $(\sqrt{13}, ^-0.59)$ 23. $(3\sqrt{2}, 3\sqrt{2})$ or $(4.24, 4.24)$ 25. $(1.33, ^-1.49)$ 27. ^-i 29. $6 - i$ 31. $^-3 - 4i$ 33. $29 + 3i$ 35. $\frac{18 + 13i}{29}$ 37. $\frac{12 + 35i}{37}$ 39. $6\left(\cos\frac{\pi}{2} + i \sin\frac{\pi}{2}\right)$ 41. $4\left(\cos\frac{2\pi}{3} + i \sin\frac{2\pi}{3}\right)$ 43. $\sqrt{34}(\cos(^-0.54) + i \sin(^-0.54))$

45. $^-2\sqrt{3} + 2i$ 47. $^-i\sqrt{3}$ 49. $1.62 + 2.52i$

51. $^-4 + 4i\sqrt{3}$ 53. $^-5.53 + 1.36i$ 55. $\frac{3}{4} + \frac{3\sqrt{3}}{4}i$ 57. $^-12 - 4i\sqrt{3}$ 59. $\frac{5\sqrt{3}}{4} + \frac{5}{4}i$

61. 4096 63. $^-4$ 65. $0.92 + 0.38i$ 67. 2, $0.62 + 1.90i$, $^-1.62 + 1.18i$, $^-1.62 - 1.18i$, $0.62 - 1.90i$

CHAPTER 10 EXPONENTIAL AND LOGARITHMIC FUNCTIONS

Exploratory Exercises Page 266 1. 49 3. $\frac{1}{9}$ 5. 4 7. 81 9. 2 11. $\frac{1}{8}$ 13. $8\frac{8}{9}$ 15. $\frac{9}{4}$ 17. $\frac{1}{25}$ 19. 4

Written Exercises Pages 266-267 1. $r^3s^{\frac{3}{2}}$ 3. $a^{\frac{1}{4}}$ 5. x^4y^2 7. $5a^{\frac{2}{3}}b$ 9. $4x^3y^5$ 11. $2xy^{\frac{8}{5}}$ 13. $24^{\frac{1}{4}}a^3b^4$ 15. $4y^4c^{\frac{1}{2}}$ 17. $y^{\frac{3}{5}}$ 19. $20^{\frac{1}{2}}x^2y^6$ 21. $12^{\frac{1}{6}}a^{\frac{2}{3}}b^{\frac{1}{3}}c^{\frac{1}{2}}$ 23. $25^{\frac{1}{3}}a^{-1}b^{-2}$ or $\frac{25^{\frac{1}{3}}}{ab^2}$ 25. $\sqrt[6]{64}$ 27. $\sqrt[5]{15}$ 29. $\sqrt[4]{a^3y}$ 31. $\sqrt[7]{x^4y^3}$ 33. $r^2\sqrt[4]{r^2q^3}$ 35. $\sqrt[10]{a^2b}$ 37. $3x^2\sqrt[3]{9x}$ 39. $2a\sqrt[3]{4ay}$ 41. $\sqrt[5]{4m^2n^3}$ 43. $\sqrt{17}$ 45. x^5 47. $125x$ 49. 1 51. $x^{-2}y^8a^{-5}$ 53. $5^{\frac{1}{4}}ac^{\frac{1}{4}}$

Exploratory Exercises Page 270 1. 1.4 3. 0.4 5. 1.7 7. 0.9

Written Exercises Page 270 1. 22.6 3. 0.2 5. 2.0 7. 3.6 9. 5.6

11.

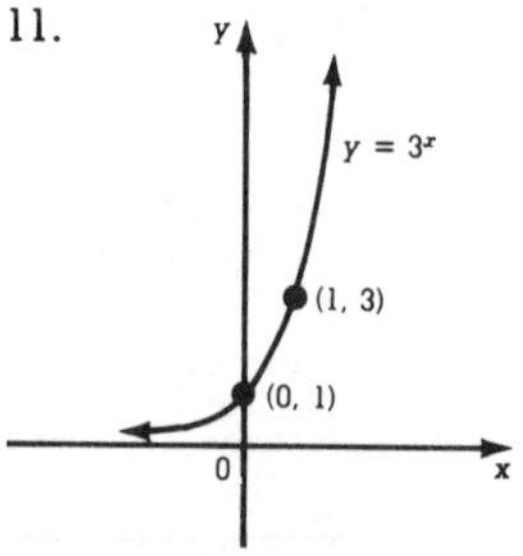

15.

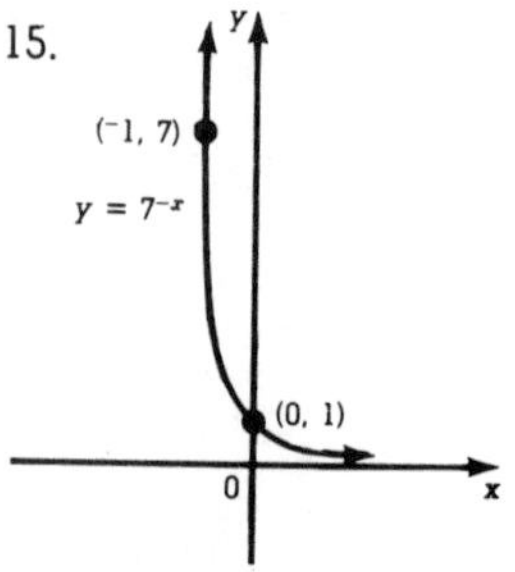

Challenge Page 270 1. 8 3. 1024

Exploratory Exercises Page 273 1. 3.0 3. 1.6 5. 1.9 7. 1.7

Written Exercises Page 273 1. 81.5 3. 49.4 5. 3.3 7. 1.8 9. 2.0 11. 601.8 13. 3.5 or 3.466 15. 64 17. 2.8 or 2.773

Challenge Page 273

1. $1 + 1.5 + \frac{(1.5)^2}{2} + \frac{(1.5)^3}{6} + \frac{(1.5)^4}{24} = 4.398$

Exploratory Exercises Page 279 1. $f \circ g(4) = 3$, $g \circ f(4) = 3$ 3. $f \circ g(4) = 24$, $g \circ f(4) = 16$ 5. $f \circ g(4) = 4^{10}$ or 1,048,576, $g \circ f(4) = 4^{10}$ or 1,048,576 7. $f \circ g(4) = 1319$, $g \circ f(4) = 221$ 9. $f \circ g(4) = 14$, $g \circ f(4) = 13.5$ 11. yes

Written Exercises Page 279 1. $f \circ g(x) = 2x + 8$, $g \circ f(x) = 2x + 11$ 3. $f \circ g(x) = \frac{1}{2}x - 4$, $g \circ f(x) = \frac{1}{2}x - 1$ 5. $f \circ g(x) = 3x^2 - 24x + 48$, $g \circ f(x) = 3x^2 - 4$ 7. $f \circ g(x) = 16x - 4$, $g \circ f(x) = 16x - 10$

9. $f \circ g(x) = 5x^4 - 10x^2 + 5$, $g \circ f(x) = 25x^4 - 1$
11. $f \circ g(x) = x^2 + 7x + 12$, $g \circ f(x) = x^2 + 5x + 7$
13. yes 15. no 17. no

21.

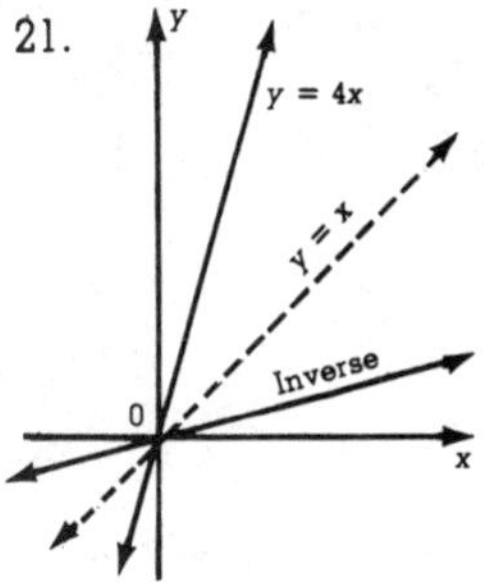

23.

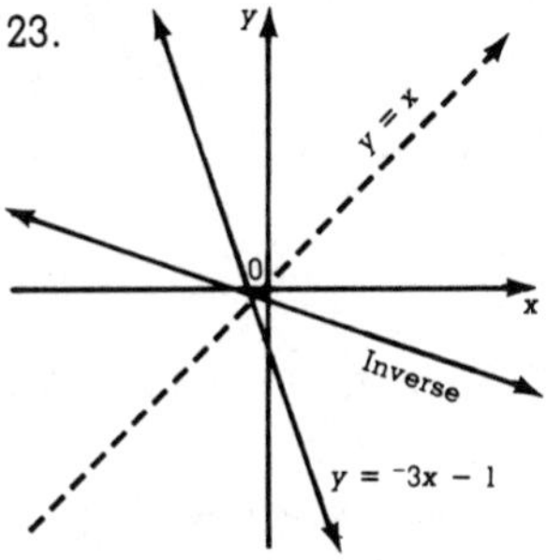

Exploratory Exercises Page 281 1. $\log_2 8 = 3$
3. $\log_{10} 10{,}000 = 4$ 5. $\log_3 \frac{1}{27} = {}^-3$ 7. $2^4 = 16$
9. $2^5 = 32$ 11. $16^{\frac{1}{2}} = 4$ 13. 3 15. ⁻3 17. ⁻4
19. 5 21. 3

Written Exercises Page 282 1. 5 3. ⁻2 5. 15
7. 81 9. $\frac{1}{2}$ 11. $\frac{1}{3}$ 13. 24 15. 4 17. 5184
19. $\frac{1}{2}$ 21. 2

Exploratory Exercises Page 285 1. 2 3. 3.5740
5. 0.375 7. 37,500 9. 0.00375

Written Exercises Page 285 1. 1.8116
3. 0.9499 5. 0.5527 − 3 7. 0.0899 − 2 9. 7760
11. 0.0543 13. 0.0822 15. 8.44 17. 236
19. 597 21. 10.8 23. 6.9 25. 0.0085

Exploratory Exercises Page 287 1. $x = \frac{\log 46}{\log 2}$
3. $x = \frac{\log 63}{2 \log 6}$ 5. $x = \frac{\log 121}{\log 5}$ 7. $x = \frac{\log 16}{\log 3}$
9. $x = -\frac{1}{\log 2}$ 11. $x = \frac{\log 14}{\log 2}$ 13. $\frac{\log 7}{\log 4}$
15. $\frac{\log_8 5}{\log_8 10}$ 17. $\frac{\log t}{\log a}$

Written Exercises Page 287 1. 5.524 3. 1.156
5. 2.980 7. 2.524 9. 3.322 11. 3.808
13. 3.092 15. 3.965 17. 4.894 19. 3.609
21. 145 23. 1.756 25. ⁻7.743 27. $\frac{1}{8}$ 29. $-\frac{1}{3}$
31. $t = 11.6$ days 33. $T = 7.48$ years 35. $T = 1.85$ hours or about 111 min.

Exploratory Exercises Page 290 1. 0.9478
3. 1.4540 5. 1.53 7. 4.81 9. 5.48

Written Exercises Page 290 1. 4.0413
3. 6.4770 5. 107.7 7. $t = 133$ 9. $t = 48.5$
11. $t = 51$ 13. $t = 4.28$ hours or about 4 hours, 17 min. 15. $k = {}^-0.0462$ 17. $t = 4.447$ days
19. \$2187 21. \$2383.60 23. 4.4%
25. $k = {}^-0.2299$

Exploratory Exercises Page 293 1. $i\pi + 1.3863$
3. $i\pi + 2.1972$ 5. $i\pi + 2.0605$ 7. $i\pi + 0.6981$
9. $2e^{\frac{i\pi}{3}}$ 11. $\sqrt{2}e^{\frac{5i\pi}{4}}$ 13. $e^{\frac{i\pi}{4}}$

Written Exercises Page 293 1. $i\pi + 3.8754$
3. $i\pi + 6.2916$ 5. $i\pi + 4.2298$ 7. $i\pi + 8.3710$
9. $\sqrt{2}e^{\frac{3i\pi}{4}}$ 11. $6e^{\frac{i\pi}{2}}$ 13. $2e^{\frac{2i\pi}{3}}$ 15. $4e^{\frac{7i\pi}{6}}$

Chapter Review Page 295 1. $a^{\frac{3}{8}}$ 3. $2ab^{\frac{3}{4}}c^2$
5. $\sqrt[5]{15}$ 7. $\sqrt[5]{(4x)^6}$ or $4x\sqrt[5]{4x}$ 9. $\frac{1}{3}$ 11. $\frac{1}{8}x^{12}$

13.

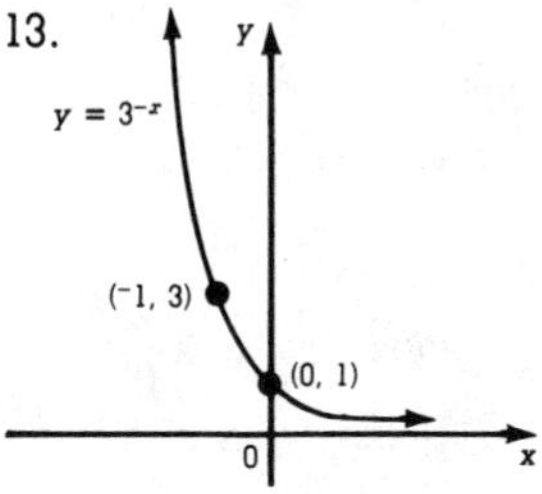

15.

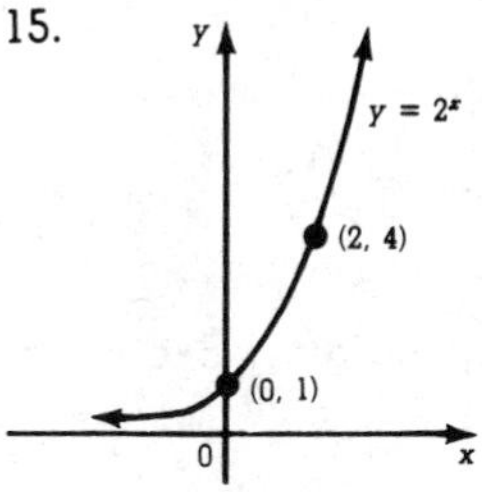

17. 2.25 19. $f \circ g(x) = 3x + 1$, $g \circ f(x) = 3x - 3$
21. $f \circ g(x) = x^2 + 4x + 6$, $g \circ f(x) = x^2 + 2x + 4$
23. $x = 15$ 25. 0.6618 − 2 27. 1.6314 29. $x = 1.990$ 31. 2.1552 33. 40.5 35. 7.7 years
37. $i\pi + 3.8330$ 39. $3e^{\frac{5i\pi}{4}}$

CHAPTER 11 THE STRAIGHT LINE

Exploratory Exercises Page 300 1. neither
3. perpendicular 5. parallel 7. $2x - y - 6 = 0$
9. $2x - y - 18 = 0$ 11. $x + 2y - 8 = 0$
13. $x + 2y - 4 = 0$

Written Exercises Page 300 1. $3x - y + 6 = 0$
3. $6x - y - 3 = 0$ 5. $2x + 3y - 16 = 0$
7. $x - 2y - 6 = 0$ 9. $5x + 4y + 43 = 0$
11. $2x + 3y - 40 = 0$

Exploratory Exercises Page 302 1. (1,0)
3. (8,9) 5. $\left(\frac{a}{2}, \frac{b}{2}\right)$

Written Exercises Page 302 1. 16 square units
3. 13, $\sqrt{61}$ or 7.8 5. Draw a figure and label the vertices $A({}^-3,1)$, $B(0,5)$, $C(12,0)$ and $D(9,{}^-4)$. The slope of $\overline{AB}$ is $\frac{1-5}{{}^-3}$ or $\frac{4}{3}$. The slope of $\overline{BC}$ is $\frac{{}^-5}{12}$. The slope of $\overline{DC}$ is $\frac{{}^-4}{9-12}$ or $\frac{4}{3}$. The slope of $\overline{AD}$ is $\frac{1+4}{{}^-3-9}$ or $\frac{{}^-5}{12}$. Thus $\overline{AB}$ is parallel to $\overline{DC}$, $\overline{BC}$ is parallel to $\overline{AD}$, and $ABCD$ is a parallelogram.

7. $AC = \sqrt{(a-0)^2 + (0-c)^2} = \sqrt{a^2 + c^2}$; $BD = \sqrt{(c-0)^2 + (a-0)^2} = \sqrt{a^2 + c^2}$; Therefore $\overline{AC} \cong \overline{BD}$.
11. Draw a figure and label the vertices $A(a,0)$, $B(0,b)$, and $C(0,0)$. The square of side $\overline{CA}$ is a^2. The square of side $\overline{CB}$ is b^2. The square of the hypotenuse $\overline{AB}$ is $(\sqrt{(a-0)^2 + (0-b)^2})^2$ or $a^2 + b^2$. Therefore the square of the hypotenuse is equal to the sum of the squares of the other sides.

Exploratory Exercises Page 304 1. 71°34′ 3. 116°34′ 5. 75°58′ 7. 68°12′ 9. 33°41′ 11. 5°54′ 13. 17°6′ 15. ⁻17°1′

Written Exercises Page 305 1. 26°34′ 3. 21°10′ 5. ⁻26°34′ 7. ⁻78°41′ 9. ⁻25°21′ 11. 4°24′ 15. 82°52′ 17. 25°21′ 19. ⁻15.5 21. $3x + y = 0$ or $x - 3y = 0$

Exploratory Exercises Page 308 1. $A = 2$, $B = 3$, $C = 4$, $\sqrt{A^2 + B^2} = \sqrt{13}$ 3. $A = 5$, $B = 1$, $C = {}^-7$, $\sqrt{A^2 + B^2} = \sqrt{26}$ 5. $A = 4$, $B = {}^-1$, $C = 9$, $\sqrt{A^2 + B^2} = \sqrt{17}$ 7. $\frac{-2x}{\sqrt{13}} - \frac{3y}{\sqrt{13}} - \frac{4}{\sqrt{13}} = 0$, $p = \frac{4}{\sqrt{13}}$, Quadrant III 9. $\frac{5x}{\sqrt{26}} + \frac{y}{\sqrt{26}} - \frac{7}{\sqrt{26}} = 0$, $p = \frac{7}{\sqrt{26}}$, Quadrant I 11. $\frac{-4x}{\sqrt{17}} + \frac{y}{\sqrt{17}} - \frac{9}{\sqrt{17}} = 0$, $p = \frac{9}{\sqrt{17}}$, Quadrant II 13. $\frac{1}{2}x + \frac{\sqrt{3}}{2}y - 7 = 0$ or $x + \sqrt{3}y - 14 = 0$ 15. $\frac{-\sqrt{2}}{2}x - \frac{\sqrt{2}}{2}y - 6 = 0$ or $x + y + 6\sqrt{2} = 0$

Written Exercises Page 308 1. $x + \sqrt{3}y - 6 = 0$ 3. $x + y + 25\sqrt{2} = 0$ 5. $-\sqrt{3}x + y - 4 = 0$ 7. $\frac{x}{\sqrt{2}} + \frac{y}{\sqrt{2}} - \frac{8}{\sqrt{2}} = 0$ 9. $\frac{2x}{\sqrt{13}} - \frac{3y}{\sqrt{13}} - \frac{1}{\sqrt{13}} = 0$ 11. $\frac{3}{5}x + \frac{4}{5}y - \frac{1}{5} = 0$ 13. $p = \frac{1}{\sqrt{13}}$ or 0.28, $\phi = 303°41'$ 15. $p = \frac{1}{5}$, $\phi = 53°8'$ 17. $x + y - 6 = 0$ 19. $x + \sqrt{3}y - 2 = 0$ or $x + \sqrt{3}y + 2 = 0$

Exploratory Exercises Page 312 1. positive 3. negative 5. positive 7. $|d| = \frac{3\sqrt{5}}{2}$ or 3.35 9. $|d| = \frac{18}{\sqrt{53}}$ or 2.47

Written Exercises Page 312 1. $|d| = \frac{1}{\sqrt{29}}$ or 0.19 3. $|d| = \frac{1}{\sqrt{10}}$ or 0.32 5. $|d| = \frac{8}{\sqrt{34}}$ or 1.37 7. $x - 5y + 10 + 3\sqrt{26} = 0$, $x - 5y + 10 - 3\sqrt{26} = 0$ 9. $|d_1| = \frac{11}{\sqrt{2}}$ or 7.78, $|d_2| = \frac{55}{\sqrt{65}}$ or 6.82, $|d_3| = \frac{55}{\sqrt{85}}$ or 5.97

Exploratory Exercises Page 314 1. $d_1 = d_2$ 3. $d_1 = d_2$

Written Exercises Page 314 1. $(\sqrt{5} + 2\sqrt{2})x + (\sqrt{2} - \sqrt{5})y + 3\sqrt{5} - \sqrt{2} = 0$ 3. $x + y = 0$ 5. $(2\sqrt{10} + 3\sqrt{29})x + (5\sqrt{10} + \sqrt{29})y + 3\sqrt{10} - 7\sqrt{29} = 0$ 7. $(\sqrt{10} - 3\sqrt{2})x + (\sqrt{10} + \sqrt{2})y + 2\sqrt{10} + \sqrt{2} = 0$ 9. $x - 1 = 0$, $y - 4 = 0$ 11. $x - 3y + 2 = 0$, $3x + y + 6 = 0$

Exploratory Exercises Page 317 1. $-\frac{x}{\sqrt{2}} + \frac{y}{\sqrt{2}} - \frac{4}{\sqrt{2}} = 0$ 3. $-\frac{2x}{\sqrt{5}} + \frac{y}{\sqrt{5}} - \frac{6}{\sqrt{5}} = 0$ 5. $22°37' + n \cdot 360°$ 7. $p = \frac{4}{\sqrt{13}}$ or 1.11, $\phi = 146°19'$ 9. $p = \frac{3}{\sqrt{82}}$ or 0.33, $\phi = 186°20'$ 11. 2.31, 2.83, 4, ⁻11.52 13. 3.46, 4.24, 6, 17.3

Written Exercises Page 317 7. $r \cos \theta = 10$ 9. $\frac{4}{\sqrt{10}} = r \cos (\theta - 161°34')$ 11. $\frac{1}{\sqrt{13}} = r \cos (\theta - 56°19'$ 13. $y = 0$ 15. $x = 1$ 17. $x + \sqrt{3}y - 8 = 0$ 19. $0 = r \cos (\theta - 116°34')$ or $0 = r \cos (\theta - 296°34')$ 21. $\frac{20}{\sqrt{34}} = r \cos (\theta - 120°58')$

Chapter Review Page 319 1. $4x - y + 11 = 0$ 3. $x + 3y - 12 = 0$ 7. ⁻8°8′ 9. 45° 11. 87°16′ 13. $\frac{3x}{\sqrt{13}} + \frac{2y}{\sqrt{13}} - \frac{6}{\sqrt{13}} = 0$; $p = \frac{6}{\sqrt{13}}$ or 1.66; $\phi = 33°41'$ 15. $-\frac{3x}{\sqrt{13}} + \frac{2y}{\sqrt{13}} - \frac{5}{2\sqrt{13}} = 0$, $p = \frac{5}{2\sqrt{13}}$ or 0.69, $\phi = 146°19'$ 17. $\frac{2x}{\sqrt{85}} + \frac{9y}{\sqrt{85}} - \frac{10}{\sqrt{85}} = 0$, $p = \frac{10}{\sqrt{85}}$ or 1.08, $\phi = 77°28'$ 19. $|d| = 1.66$ 21. $|d| = 6.37$ 23. $(\sqrt{10} + 3\sqrt{5})x + (2\sqrt{10} + \sqrt{5})y - 3\sqrt{10} - 2\sqrt{5} = 0$ 25. $x + \sqrt{3}y - 6 = 0$ 27. $\frac{3}{\sqrt{5}} = r \cos (\theta - 206°34')$

CHAPTER 12 CONICS

Exploratory Exercises Page 324 1. $x^2 + y^2 = 64$ 3. $(x - 2)^2 + (y + 7)^2 = 81$ 5. $(x + 3)^2 + (y + 5)^2 = 1$ 7. $(2, 3)$, $\sqrt{7}$ 9. $(2, 6)$, $\sqrt{10}$ 11. $(^-3, ^-2)$, $\frac{\sqrt{7}}{2}$

Written Exercises Page 324 1. $x^2 + y^2 = 18$ 3. $(x - 3)^2 + (y + 2)^2 = 16$ 5. $(x + 4)^2 + (y + 1)^2 = 25$ 7. $\left(x + \frac{1}{4}\right)^2 + (y - 1)^2 = 9$ 9. $(x - 1)^2 + (y + 3)^2 = 16$ 11. $\left(x - \frac{3}{2}\right)^2 + \left(y - \frac{7}{2}\right)^2 = \frac{29}{2}$ 13. $(x - 3)^2 + (y - 4)^2 = 5$ 15. $(x - 2)^2 + (y + 1)^2 = 25$ 17. $(y - 4)^2 + (y - 2)^2 = 18$ 19. $(x - 4)^2 + (y + 3)^2 = 25$ 21. $(x - 5)^2 + (y + 5)^2 = 25$ 23. $(x - 1)^2 + (y - 1)^2 = 25$

Challenge Page 324 1. $x^2 + y^2 = 1$ or $(x - \sqrt{2})^2 + y^2 = 1$ 3. $(x - k)^2 + (y - k)^2 = 49$ Each circle has its center on the line $x - y = 0$. 5. $3x - 4y - 4 = 0$

Exploratory Exercises Page 328 1. $y^2 = 8x$ 3. $(x - 2)^2 = 8(y - 4)$ 5. $(y + 1)^2 = 24(x - 4)$ 7. vertex $(0, 0)$, focus $\left(-\frac{1}{2}, 0\right)$, directrix $x = \frac{1}{2}$ 9. vertex $(0, 3)$, focus $(1, 3)$, directrix $x = {}^-1$ 11. vertex $(2, ^-1)$, focus $(2, 1)$, directrix $y = {}^-3$ 13. $x^2 = 11y$ 15. $(x - 3)^2 = 10(y + 1)$ 17. $(y + 1)^2 = 4(x - 1)$

Written Exercises Page 328 1. vertex $(0, 0)$, focus $(0, 2.75)$, directrix $y = {}^-2.75$, axis $x = 0$, latus rectum 11 3. vertex $(3, ^-1)$, focus $\left(3, 1\frac{1}{2}\right)$, directrix $y = {}^-3\frac{1}{2}$, axis $x = 3$, latus rectum 10 5. vertex $(1, ^-1)$, focus $(2, ^-1)$, directrix $x = 0$, axis $y = {}^-1$, latus rectum 4 7. $x^2 = {}^-12y$ 9. $(x - 3)^2 = 4(y - 4)$ 11. $(y - 1)^2 = 4(x + 2)$ 13. $(x - 4)^2 = {}^-1(y - 3)$ 15. $(x - 2)^2 = {}^-8(y + 4)$ 17. $y^2 = {}^-6\left(x - 1\frac{1}{2}\right)$

Challenge Page 328 1. $y^2 - 4x - 4y = 0$ 3. $(x - 4)^2 + (y - 3)^2 = 16$ 7. It represents the maximum height the object reaches under given conditions.

Exploratory Exercises Page 331 1. $(3, 1)$, $x = x' + 3$, $y = y' + 1$ 3. $(^-1, 0)$, $x = x' - 1$, $y = y'$ 5. $(3, 4)$, $x = x' + 3$, $y = y' + 4$ 7. $(^-2, 5)$, $x = x' - 2$, $y = y' + 5$

Written Exercises Page 332 1. $(x')^2 + (y')^2 = 4$ 3. $(x')^2 + (y')^2 = 1$ 5. $(y')^2 = 2x'$ 7. $(x')^2 = 6y'$ 9. $(x')^2 + (y')^2 = 25$ 11. $(x' + a)^2 + (y' - a)^2 = c^2$ 13. $(x')^2 = 4y'$ 15. $(x')^2 = 4p(y' + 4)$

Exploratory Exercises Page 335 1. $\frac{x^2}{36} + \frac{y^2}{16} = 1$ 3. $\frac{(y - 5)^2}{16} + \frac{(x - 3)^2}{4} = 1$ 5. $\frac{x^2}{49} + \frac{y^2}{45} = 1$

Written Exercises Page 335 1. center $(5, 0)$, foci $(5 + \sqrt{21}, 0)$ and $(5 - \sqrt{21}, 0)$, vertices $(10, 0)$ and $(0, 0)$ 3. center $(3, 4)$, foci $(6, 4)$ and $(0, 4)$, vertices $(8, 4)$ and $(^-2, 4)$ 5. center $(^-3, 1)$, foci $(^-3 + \sqrt{3}, 1)$ and $(^-3 - \sqrt{3}, 1)$, vertices $(^-1, 1)$ and $(^-5, 1)$ 7. center $(0, ^-5)$, foci $(\sqrt{21}, ^-5)$ and $(^-\sqrt{21}, ^-5)$, vertices $(5, ^-5)$ and $(^-5, ^-5)$ 9. center $(^-5, 4)$, foci $(^-5, 6)$ and $(^-5, 2)$, vertices $(^-5, 4 + \sqrt{6})$ and $(^-5, 4 - \sqrt{6})$ 11. center $\left(-\frac{1}{2}, \frac{1}{2}\right)$, foci $\left(-\frac{1}{2}, \frac{1}{2} + \sqrt{3}\right)$ and $\left(-\frac{1}{2}, \frac{1}{2} - \sqrt{3}\right)$, vertices $\left(-\frac{1}{2}, 2\frac{1}{2}\right)$ and $\left(-\frac{1}{2}, ^-1\frac{1}{2}\right)$

Exploratory Exercises Page 338 1. $(2\sqrt{5}, 0)$, $(^-2\sqrt{5}, 0)$ 3. $(3 + \sqrt{15}, 5)$, $(3 - \sqrt{15}, 5)$ 5. $\frac{\sqrt{5}}{3}$ 7. $\frac{\sqrt{15}}{4}$ 9. $\frac{16}{3}$ 11. $\frac{1}{2}$

Written Exercises Page 338 1. center $(0, 0)$, foci $(\sqrt{5}, 0)$ and $(^-\sqrt{5}, 0)$, $e = \frac{\sqrt{5}}{3}$, latus rectum $= \frac{8}{3}$ 3. center $(3, 1)$, foci $(3, 1 + \sqrt{5})$ and $(3, 1 - \sqrt{5})$, $e = \frac{\sqrt{5}}{3}$, latus rectum $= \frac{8}{3}$ 5. center $(2, ^-3)$, foci $(2, ^-3 + 2\sqrt{6})$ and $(2, ^-3 - 2\sqrt{6})$, $e = \frac{2\sqrt{6}}{5}$, latus rectum $= \frac{2}{5}$ 7. $\frac{y^2}{4} + \frac{3x^2}{4} = 1$ 9. $\frac{(x - 2)^2}{81} + \frac{(y + 2)^2}{45} = 1$ 11. $\frac{(x - 2)^2}{16} + \frac{(y - 5)^2}{15} = 1$ 13. $\frac{(y - 2)^2}{18} + \frac{(x - 1)^2}{9} = 1$

Challenge Page 338 1. $49x^2 + 9y^2 + 294x - 126y + 441 = 0$ 3. $x^2 + y^2 = 19.24$

Exploratory Exercises Page 342 1. $\frac{x^2}{64} - \frac{y^2}{25} = 1$ 3. $\frac{(y + 2)^2}{16} - \frac{(x - 6)^2}{25} = 1$ 5. $\frac{x^2}{64} - \frac{y^2}{36} = 1$ 7. $\frac{y^2}{4} - \frac{(x - 1)^2}{4} = 1$

Written Exercises Page 342 1. center (0, 0), foci (0, 10) and (0, $^-$10), vertices (0, 8) and (0, $^-$8), asymptotes $y = \pm\frac{4}{3}x$ 3. center (0, 0), foci ($\sqrt{117}$, 0) and ($^-\sqrt{117}$, 0), vertices (6, 0) and ($^-$6, 0), asymptotes $y = \pm\frac{3}{2}x$ 5. center ($^-$6, $^-$3), foci ($^-6 + 3\sqrt{5}$, $^-$3) and ($^-6 - 3\sqrt{5}$, $^-$3), vertices (0, $^-$3) and ($^-$12, $^-$3), asymptotes $y + 3 = \pm\frac{1}{2}(x + 6)$ 7. $\frac{(x-4)^2}{4} - \frac{(y+2)^2}{5} = 1$ 9. $\frac{(x-3)^2}{9} - \frac{(y+1)^2}{4} = 1$

Exploratory Exercises Page 345 1. $\frac{x^2}{9} - \frac{y^2}{5} = 1$ 3. $y^2 - \frac{(x-2)^2}{4} = 1$ 5. $e = \frac{\sqrt{14}}{3}$ 7. $e = \sqrt{5}$ 9. $\frac{10}{3}$ 11. 8 13. $\frac{y^2}{5} - \frac{x^2}{9} = 1$ 15. $\frac{(x-2)^2}{4} - y^2 = 1$

17.

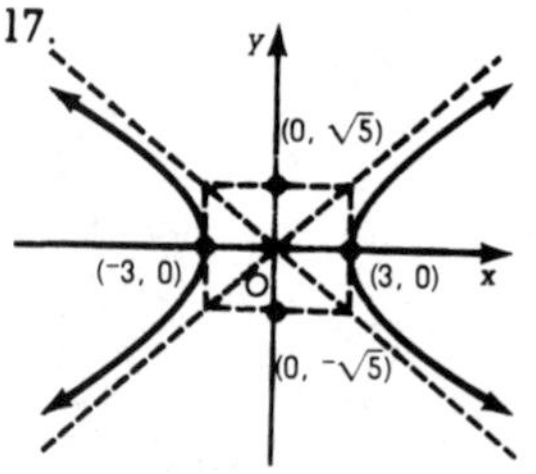

19.

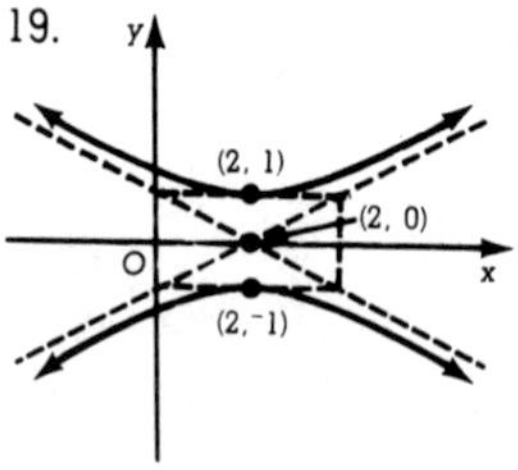

Written Exercises Page 345

3.

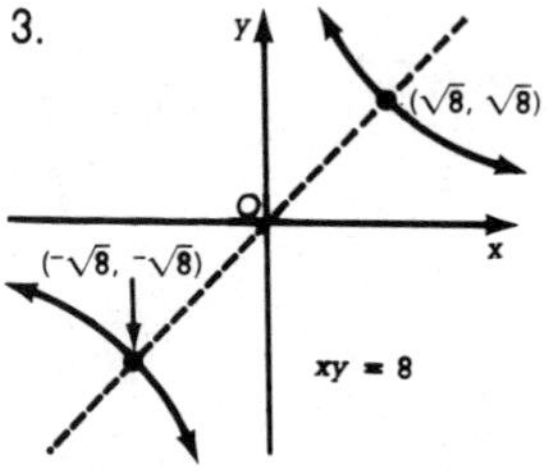

5.

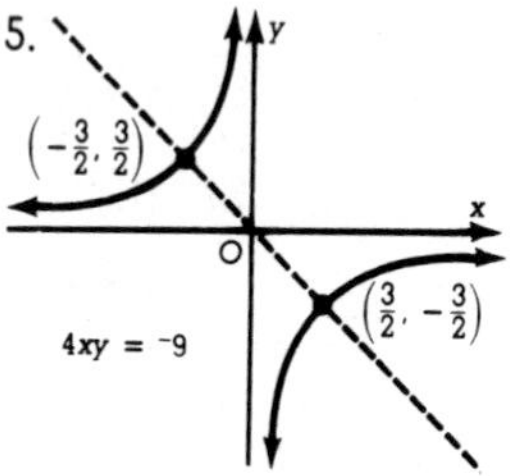

7. center (2,0), foci (2,6) and (2,$^-$6), vertices (2,$\sqrt{30}$) and (2,$^-\sqrt{30}$), asymptotes $y = \pm\sqrt{5}(x-2)$
9. center (5, $^-$3), foci ($5 + \sqrt{13}$, $^-$3) and ($5 - \sqrt{13}$, $^-$3), vertices (7, $^-$3) and (3, $^-$3), asymptotes $y + 3 = \pm\frac{3}{2}(x - 5)$

11. $\frac{(y+1)^2}{4} - \frac{(x-3)^2}{5} = 1$ 13. $\frac{x^2}{9} - \frac{y^2}{16} = 1$

15. $\frac{17(x-1)^2}{9} - \frac{17y^2}{144} = 1$

17. $\frac{(x+3)^2}{16} - \frac{(y-1)^2}{16} = 1$

19. $\frac{(y-3)^2}{16} - \frac{(x-5)^2}{48} = 1$ 21. $\frac{2y^2}{25} - \frac{2x^2}{25} = 1$

Challenge Page 345 1. $\frac{x^2}{4} - y^2 = 1$ 3. $\frac{5}{3}$

Exploratory Exercises Page 349

1. $(x-4)^2 + y^2 = 5$ 3. $\frac{(x-3)^2}{25} + \frac{(y-1)^2}{9} = 1$

5. $\left(y + \frac{1}{2}\right)^2 = {^-2}(x-2)$ 7. $\frac{(y+4)^2}{2} - \frac{(x+1)^2}{6} = 1$

9.

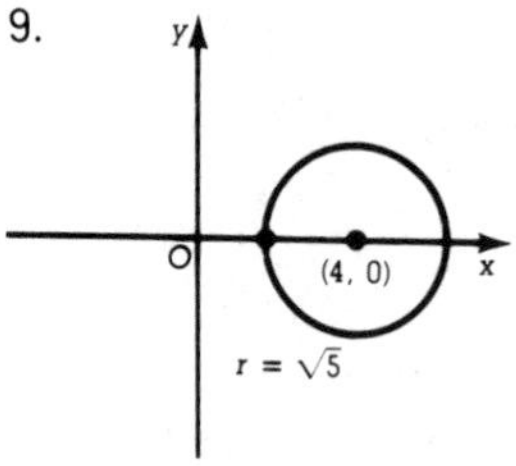

11.

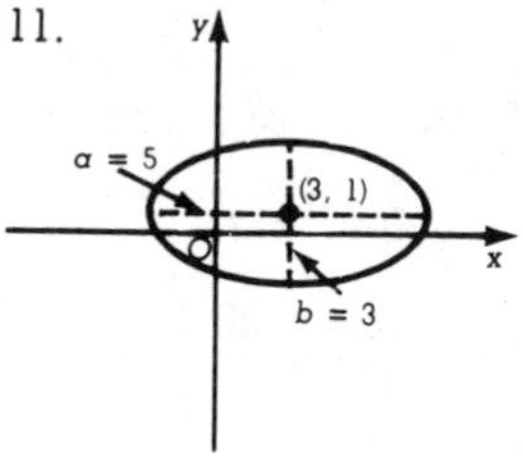

13.

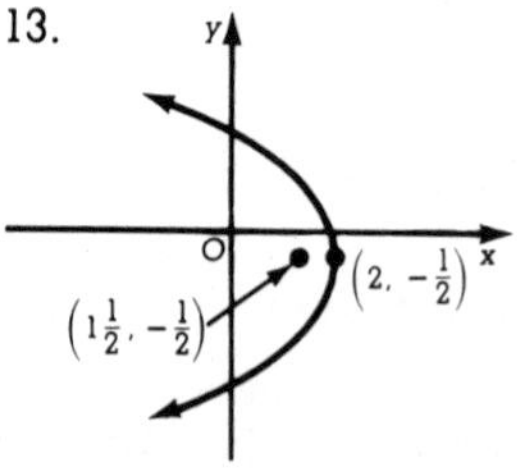

15.

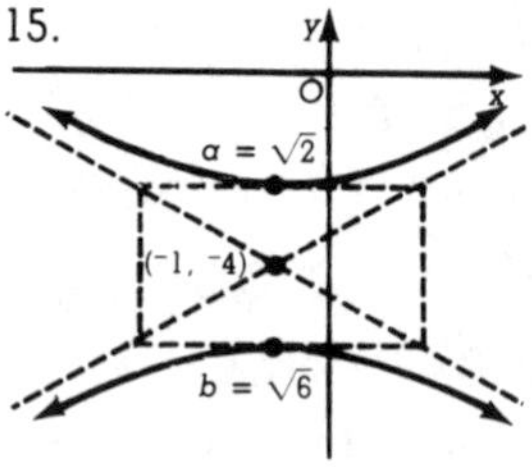

Written Exercises Page 349

1.

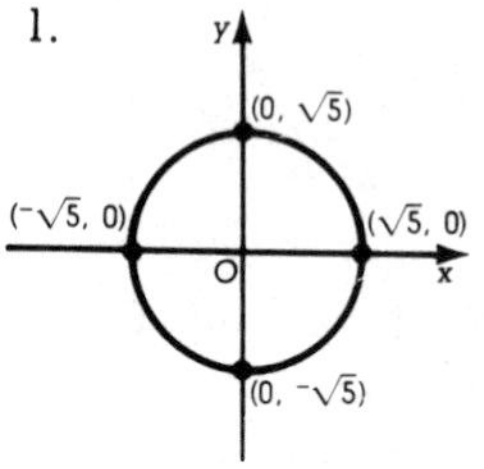

3.

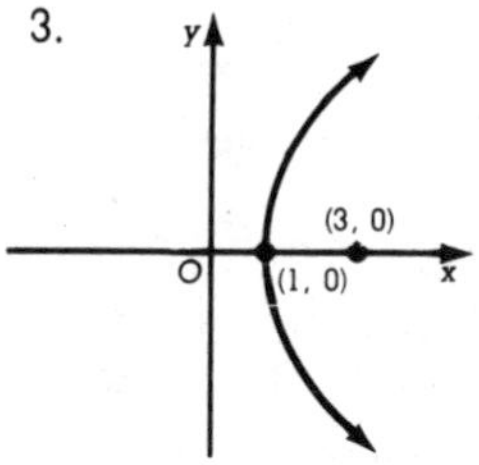

5.

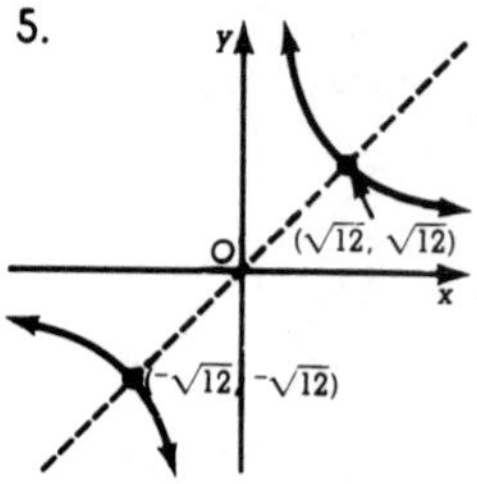

7.

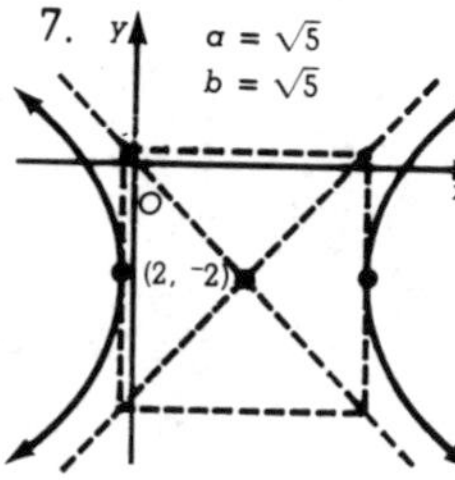

11.

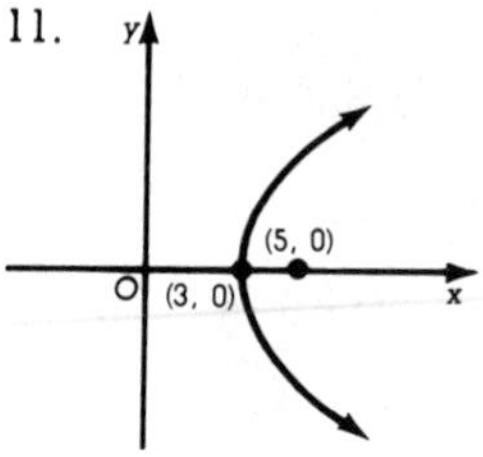

15.

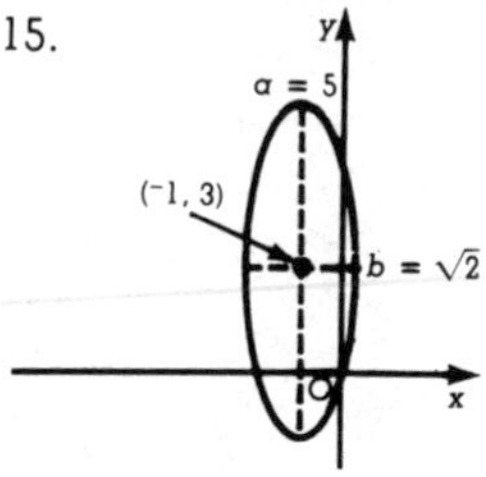

Written Exercises Pages 350-351

1.

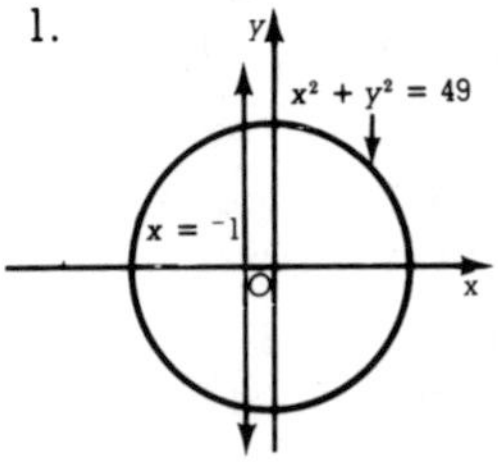

3.

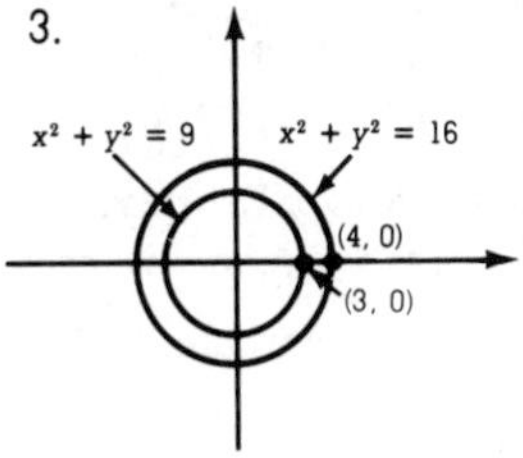

5.

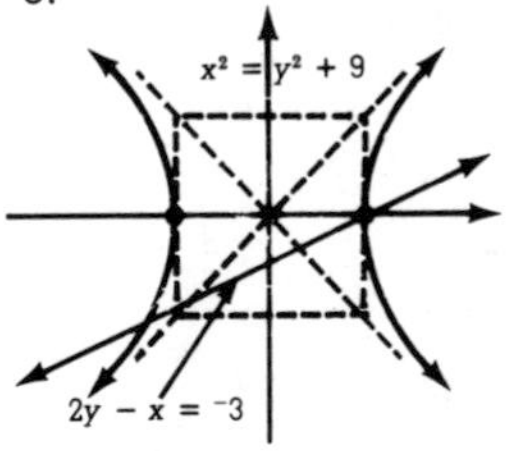

7.

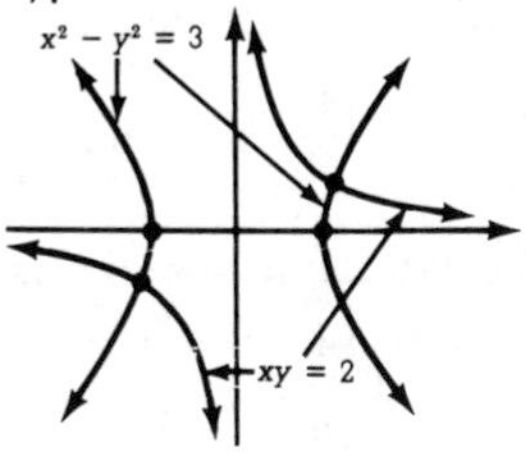

9.

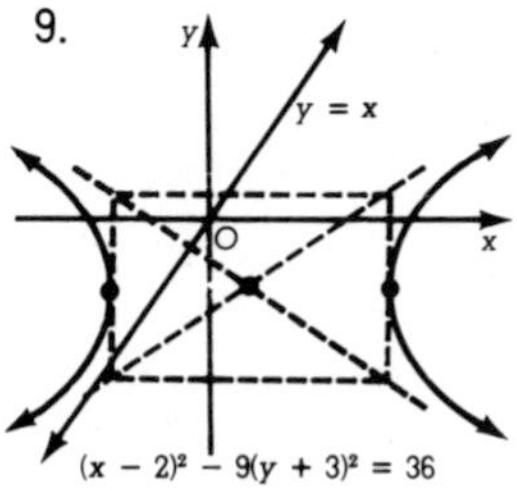

11.

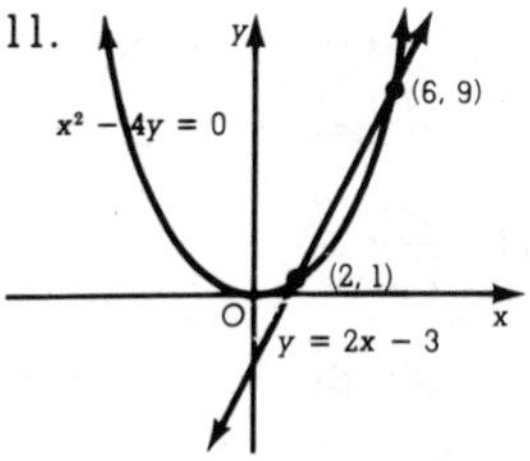

13.

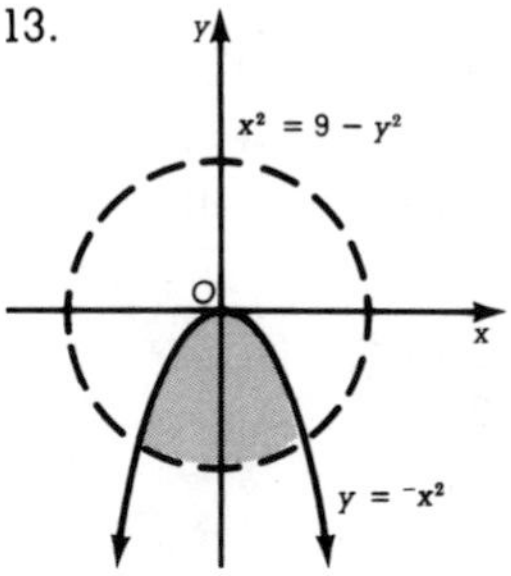

15.

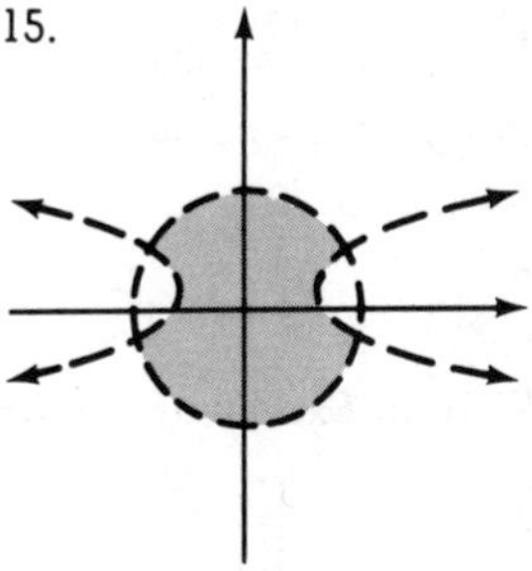

17.

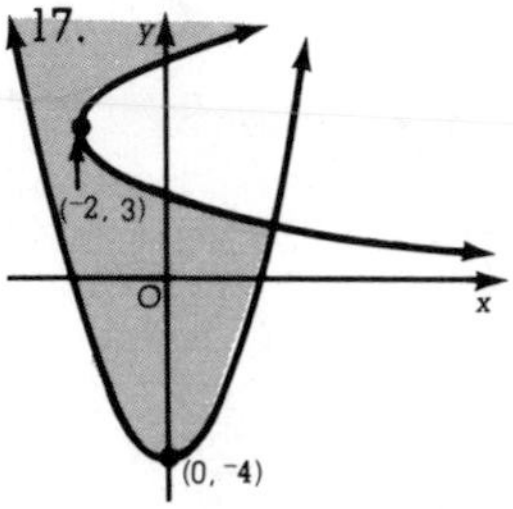

19.

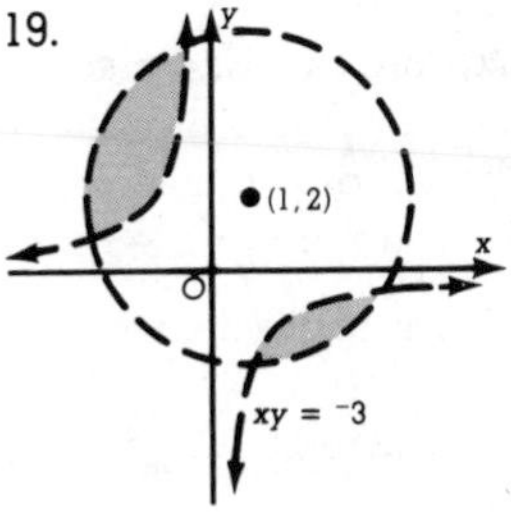

21.

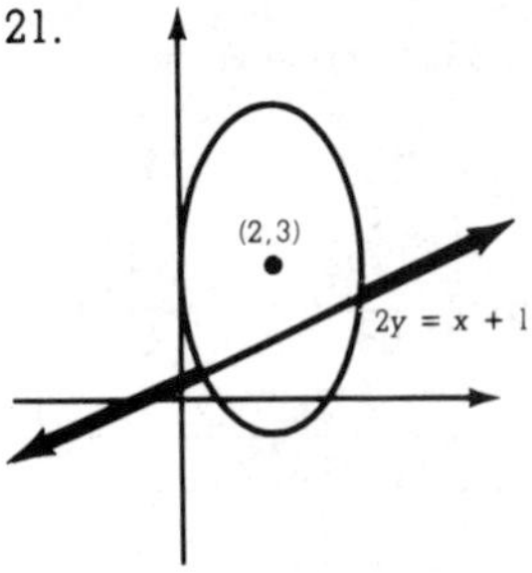

23.

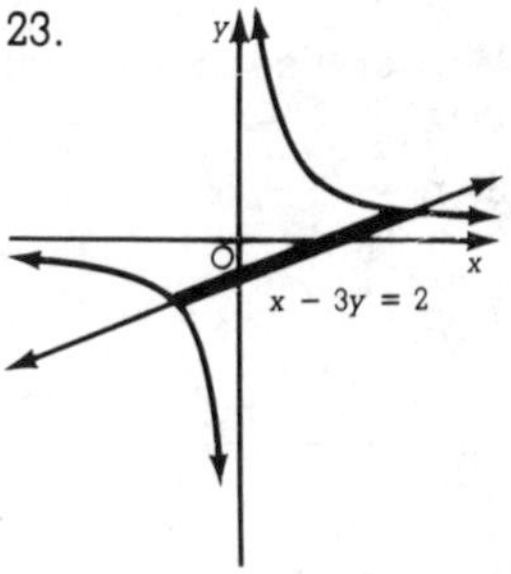

Exploratory Exercises Page 354 1. $-\frac{8}{3\sqrt{5}}$ 3. $\frac{16}{25}$ 5. $2x + \sqrt{21}\,y - 25 = 0$ 7. $9x - 8y - 145 = 0$ 9. $^-3$ 11. 0 13. 1

Written Exercises Page 354
1. $^-2x + \sqrt{15}\,y = 19$, $2y = {}^-\sqrt{15}\,x$ 3. $x = 8$, $y = 3$ 5. $y = 4x + 11$, $4y = {}^-x + 4$ 7. $5y = 11x + 13$, $11y = {}^-5x - \frac{3}{5}$ 9. $7y = {}^-8\sqrt{3} + 112$, $24y = 7\sqrt{3x} + \frac{45}{2}$ 11. $y = {}^-x + 8$, $y = x - 6$ 13. $6y = 5x - 16$, $5y = {}^-6x + 37\frac{1}{2}$ 15. $x = -4$, $y = {}^-3$ 17. $\sqrt{55}$ or 7.42 19. $\sqrt{3}$ or 1.73 21. $\sqrt{46}$ or 6.78 23. $y = 5$ and $y = {}^-5$ 25. $y = {}^-8$ and $y = 8$ 27. 1 and $^-1$, the tangents are perpendicular to each other

Exploratory Exercises Page 358 1. ellipse 3. circle 5. parabola 7. hyperbola

9.

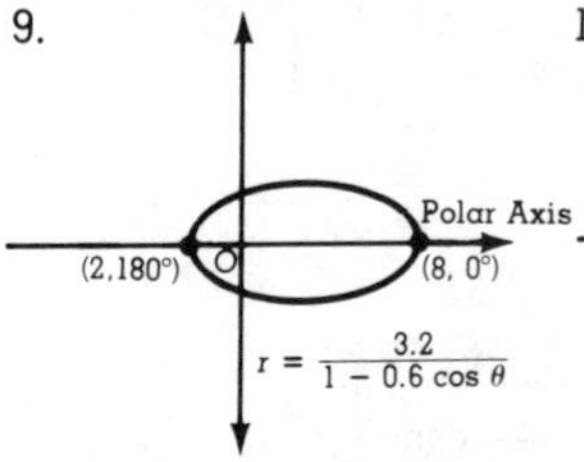

11.

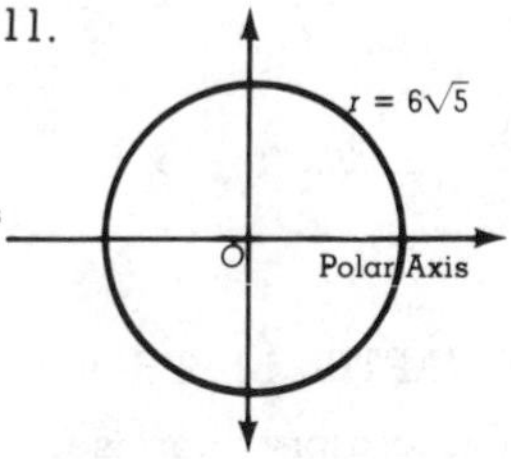

13.

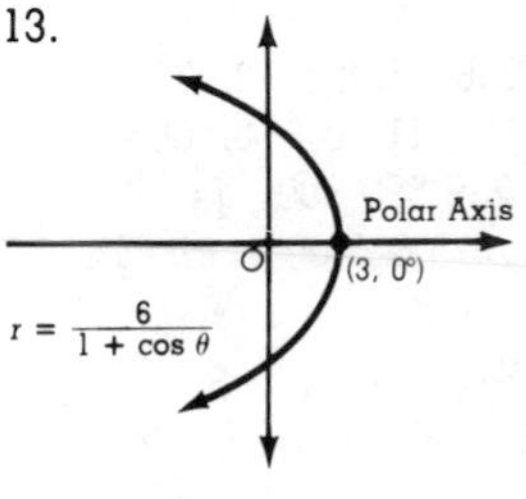

15.

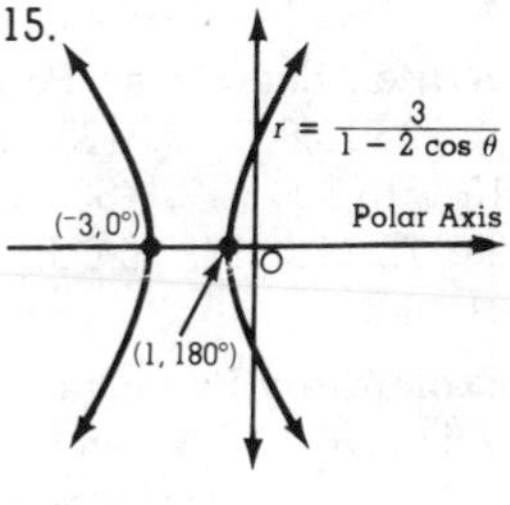

17. $r = 5$

Written Exercises Page 358 1. $p = \frac{9}{4}$, $e = 1$
3. $p = \frac{9\sqrt{7}}{14}$, $e = \frac{\sqrt{7}}{4}$ 5. $p = \frac{2\sqrt{5}}{5}$, $e = \sqrt{5}$
7. $p = \frac{4}{\sqrt{5}}$, $e = \frac{\sqrt{5}}{3}$ 9. $p = \frac{9\sqrt{34}}{68}$, $e = \frac{\sqrt{34}}{5}$,
11. $r = \frac{4.5}{1 - \cos\theta}$ 13. $r = \frac{2.25}{1 - 0.25\sqrt{7}\cos\theta}$
15. $r = \frac{4}{1 - \sqrt{5}\cos\theta}$ 17. $r = \frac{8}{3 - \sqrt{5}\cos\theta}$
19. $r = \frac{9}{5 - \sqrt{34}\cos\theta}$

Chapter Review Pages 360-361
1. $(x - 3)^2 + (y + 7)^2 = 9$ 3. focus (7,5), vertex (7,3), directrix $y = 1$, axis $x = 7$
5. $(x')^2 + (y')^2 = 4$ 7. center (4,6), foci $(4 + 3\sqrt{3}, 6)$ and $(4 - 3\sqrt{3}, 6)$, vertices (⁻2,6) and (10,6) 9. $\frac{(x - 2)^2}{25} + \frac{(y + 1)^2}{16} = 1$ 11. center (2,3), foci (2,8) and (2,⁻2), vertices (2,6) and (2,0), asymptotes $(y - 3) = \pm\frac{3}{4}(x - 2)$
13. $\frac{2y^2}{49} - \frac{2x^2}{49} = 1$ 15. $\frac{(y - 1)^2}{4} - \frac{(x - 1)^2}{5} = 1$

17.
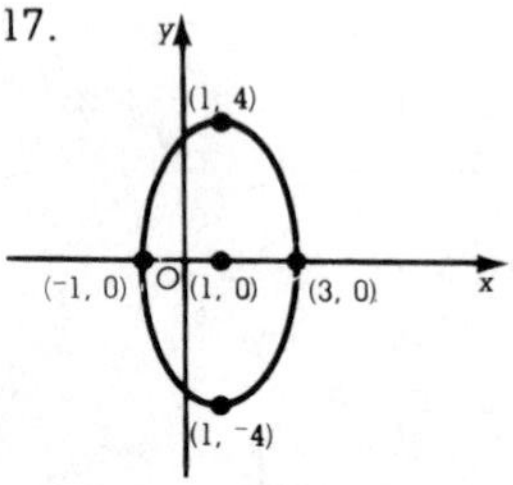

21.
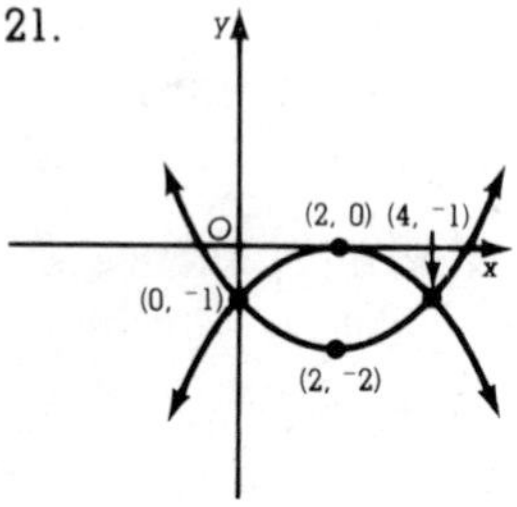

23. 8 25. $r = 3$

CHAPTER 13 PROBABILITY

Exploratory Exercises Page 366 1. independent 3. not independent 5. independent 7. false 9. false 11. true

Written Exercises Page 366 1. 24 3. 7 5. 39,916,800 7. 120 9. 72 11. 6 13. 60 15. 518,400 17. 480 19. 239,500,800 21. 24 23. 72 25. 17,576,000 27. 15,625,000 29. 14 31. 4

Exploratory Exercises Page 371 1. not reflective 3. reflective 5. not reflective 7. not reflective 9. circular 11. circular 13. circular 15. linear

Written Exercises Page 371 1. 720 3. 3360 5. 420 7. 181,440 9. 907,200 11. 180 13. 14,400 15. 120 17. 144 19. 120 21. 969 23. 144

Exploratory Exercises Page 373 1. permutation 3. combination 5. combination 7. combination

Written Exercises Page 373 1. 6 3. 1 5. 30 7. 12 9. 2002 11. 715 13. 56 15. 3570 17. 28,561 19. 126 21. 2808 23. 2520 25. 252 27. 64

Exploratory Exercises Page 376 1. $\frac{1}{1}$ 3. $\frac{7}{8}$ 5. $\frac{3}{7}$ 7. $\frac{4}{13}$ 9. $\frac{1}{7}$ 11. $\frac{1}{4}$ 13. $\frac{1}{52}$

Written Exercises Page 377 1. $\frac{1}{6}$ 3. $\frac{1}{51}$ 5. $\frac{1}{6}$ 7. $\frac{9}{11}$ 9. $\frac{1}{2}$ 11. $\frac{7}{50}$ 13. $\frac{3}{38}$ 15. $\frac{9}{38}$ 17. $\frac{2}{7}$ 19. $\frac{1}{7}$ 21. $\frac{11}{25}$ 23. $\frac{46}{125}$ 25. $\frac{14}{65}$ 27. $\frac{9}{50}$

Exploratory Exercises Page 379 1. dependent 3. independent 5. dependent 7. $\frac{1}{15}$ 9. $\frac{1}{36}$ 11. $\frac{8}{195}$

Written Exercises Page 379 1. $\frac{1}{36}$ 3. $\frac{1}{24}$ 5. $\frac{1}{16}$ 7. $\frac{1}{117{,}600}$ 9. $\frac{25}{36}$ 11. $\frac{5}{6}$ 13. $\frac{27}{1000}$ 15. $\frac{121}{204}$ 17. $\frac{1}{635{,}013{,}559{,}600}$ 19. $\frac{19}{1{,}160{,}054}$

Exploratory Exercises Page 382 1. mutually exclusive 3. mutually exclusive 5. inclusive 7. $\frac{4}{15}$ 9. $\frac{34}{39}$ 11. $\frac{2}{3}$

Written Exercises Page 382 1. $\frac{2}{3}$ 3. $\frac{39}{135}$ 5. $\frac{26}{33}$ 7. $\frac{12}{221}$ 9. $\frac{188}{663}$ 11. $\frac{35}{64}$ 13. $\frac{21}{64}$ 15. $\frac{2}{429}$ 17. $\frac{175}{429}$ 19. $\frac{3}{5}$ 21. $\frac{16}{25}$

Exploratory Exercises Page 385 1. *A* is a 4 on the die; *B* is a 6 on the die 3. *A* is one coin shows tails; *B* is at least one coin shows heads 5. *A* is the marble came from the first bag; *B* is a blue marble drawn 7. $\frac{1}{6}$ 9. $\frac{2}{3}$ 11. $\frac{4}{5}$

Written Exercises Page 386 1. $\frac{1}{6}$ 3. $\frac{1}{3}$ 5. $\frac{3}{11}$

7. $\frac{1}{4}$ 9. $\frac{1}{7}$ 11. $\frac{2}{15}$ 13. $\frac{1}{15}$ 15. $\frac{1}{4}$ 17. $\frac{2}{5}$ 19. $\frac{3}{10}$
21. $\frac{3}{7}$ 23. $\frac{19}{51}$

Exploratory Exercises Page 388 1. binomial, $\frac{3}{8}$
3. binomial, $\frac{1}{28,561}$ 5. binomial, $\frac{1}{9}$

Written Exercises Page 389 1. $\frac{1}{8}$ 3. $\frac{1}{2}$
5. $\frac{3125}{7776}$ 7. $\frac{625}{648}$ 9. $\frac{1}{81}$ 11. $\frac{16}{27}$ 13. $\frac{193}{512}$ 15. $\frac{319}{512}$
17. $\frac{32}{625}$ 19. $\frac{64}{15,625}$ 21. $\frac{576}{15,625}$ 23. $\frac{59,049}{100,000}$
25. $\frac{1}{100,000}$ 27. $\frac{1,959,552}{9,765,625}$ 29. $\frac{236,196}{1,953,125}$

Chapter Review Page 391 1. 120 3. $\frac{-9}{5}$
5. 240 7. 50,400 9. 60 11. 165 13. 2860
15. $\frac{4}{5}$ 17. $\frac{1}{11}$ 19. $\frac{125}{4096}$ 21. $\frac{5}{36}$ 23. $\frac{11}{14}$ 25. $\frac{1}{6}$
27. $\frac{1}{4}$ 29. $\frac{3}{8}$

CHAPTER 14 DESCRIPTIVE STATISTICS

Exploratory Exercises Page 396 1. 15.5
3. 27.5 5. no mode 7. 10 9. 15.5 11. 30.75
13-15. Answers may vary.

Written Exercises Page 396 1. 78.8 3. 1 lb.
5. 17.5 7. Answers may vary. 9. {$8700, $8700, $8700, $8700, $9600, $9600, $12,700, $12,700, $50,000, $50,000} 11. $9600
13. company - mean; union - mode 15. higher
17. More American families own cars than do not. More American women wear size 7 shoes than any other size. 19. 2.9 21. 204

Challenge Page 397 1. 68 cm

Exploratory Exercises Page 399 1. harmonic mean 3. arithmetic mean

Written Exercises Page 399 1. 4.21 3. 8.9
5. $\overline{X} = 4.8$, $M_d = 5$, $H = 3.8$, $Q = 5.3$
7. 48.6 mph 9. $3.10 11. 43.5 mph

Exploratory Exercises Page 402 1. 11.09
3. 0.084 5. 0.16 7. 0.0948 9. 0.75 11. 0.6

Written Exercises Page 402 1. 7.70 3. 3.05
5. 85 7. 403.5 9. 20.25 11. 16.75 13. 25.31
15. 23 17. 10.25 19. $M.D. = 8.53$, $\sigma = 10.45$. The standard deviation is greater.

Exploratory Exercises Page 404 1. $6000
3. $3000, $9000, $15,000, $21,000, $27,000 5. 39%
7. class interval, 0.2; class limits, 2.0, 2.2, 2.4, 2.6, 2.8, 3.0, 3.2, 3.4, 3.6; class marks, 2.1, 2.3, 2.5, 2.7, 2.9, 3.1, 3.3, 3.5 9. class interval, 10; class limits, 5, 15, 25, 35, 45, 55 11. class interval, 2.5; class limits, 1.25, 3.75, 6.25, 8.75, 11.25, 13.75

Written Exercises Page 405

1.

Class Limits	Class Marks	Tally	Frequency (f)
0–10	5	𝍷𝍷𝍷	3
10–20	15	𝍷𝍷𝍷	3
20–30	25	𝍸 𝍷𝍷	7
30–40	35	𝍸 𝍷𝍷𝍷𝍷	9
40–50	45	𝍸 𝍸 𝍷	11
50–60	55	𝍸 𝍷𝍷𝍷	8
60–70	65	𝍸 𝍷𝍷𝍷	8
70–80	75	𝍸 𝍷𝍷	7
80–90	85	𝍷𝍷𝍷	3
90–100	95	𝍷	1

5.

Class Limits	Class Marks (X)	Tally	Frequency (f)
65–75	70	𝍷𝍷𝍷𝍷	4
75–85	80	𝍸 𝍸	10
85–95	90	𝍸 𝍸 𝍸 𝍷	16
95–105	100	𝍸 𝍸 𝍸 𝍸 𝍸 𝍸 𝍸 𝍷𝍷𝍷	38
105–115	110	𝍸 𝍸 𝍸	15
115–125	120	𝍸 𝍸 𝍷𝍷	12
125–135	130	𝍷𝍷𝍷	3
135–145	140	𝍷𝍷	2

9. Answers may vary. 11. A measurement reported as 2112.7 m would usually be discarded. One could not rely on the error being in the second digit.

Exploratory Exercises Page 409 1. 0, 50, 100, 150, 200 3. 50 5. 360 7. 28%

9.

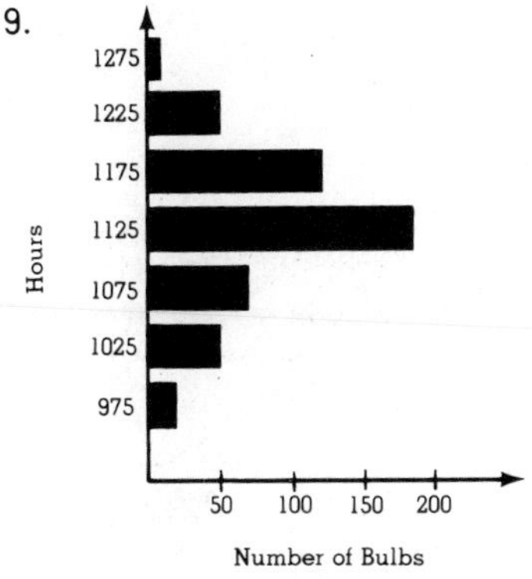

Written Exercises Page 410

1.

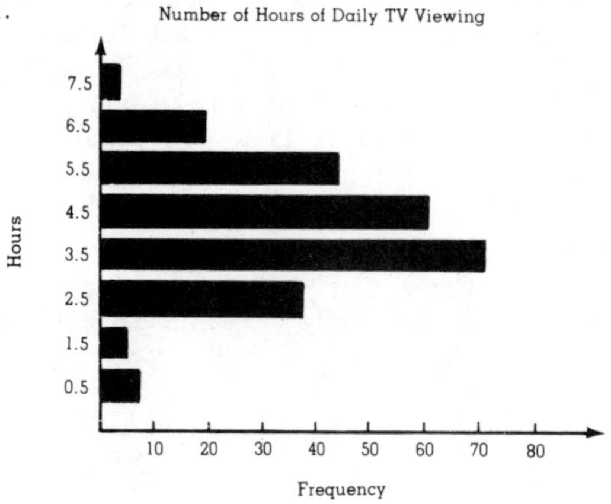

7.

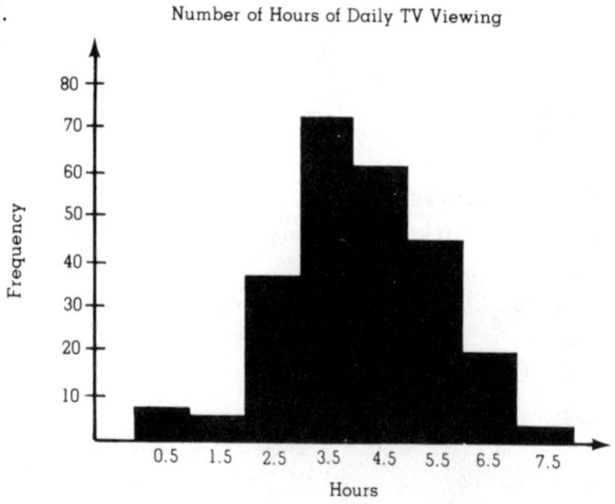

13.

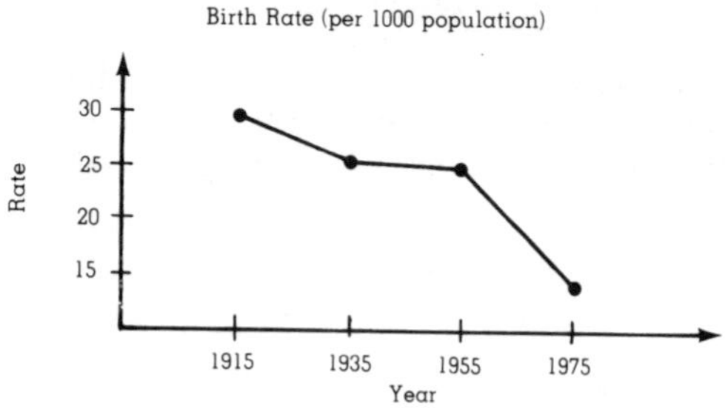

17.

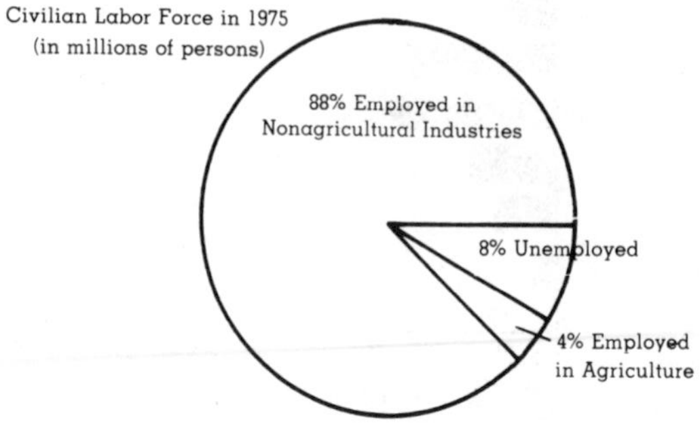

Exploratory Exercises Page 413 **1.** \$1485 **3.** \$4650 **5.** \$2275 **7.** \$780 **9.** 100 **11.** cumulative frequency 11, 35, 65, 75, 88, 96, 100 **13.** \$155

Written Exercises Page 413 **1.** 19.3 **3.** 20.1 **5.** No. There is no limit in the class "\$50,000 and over." **7.** \$30,000 - \$40,000

9.

Class Limits	Class Marks *(X)*	Tally	Frequency
0–\$8.00	\$4.00	|||	3
\$8.00–\$16.00	\$12.00	卌 卌 ||	12
\$16.00–\$24.00	\$20.00	卌 |||	8
\$24.00–\$32.00	\$28.00	卌 |	6
\$32.00–\$40.00	\$36.00	卌 |||	8
\$40.00–\$48.00	\$44.00	卌	5
\$48.00–\$56.00	\$52.00	||||	4
\$56.00–\$64.00	\$60.00	||	2

11. Cumulative frequency 3, 15, 23, 29, 37, 42, 46, 48 **13.** \$25.33

Exploratory Exercises Page 417 **1.** 136 **3.** 68 **5.** 3415 **7.** 1707.5 **9.** 68,300 **11.** 34,150 **13.** 6.7% **15.** 38.3% **17.** 6.7%

Written Exercises Page 417 **1.** 68.3% **3.** 20.1 to 27.9 **5.** 68.3% **7.** 0.866 **9.** 0.1585 **11.** 107 to 173 **13.** 45.82 to 55.18 **15.** 0.325 **17.** 0.500 **19.** 25.5%

Exploratory Exercises Page 421 **1.** 0.955 **3.** 5 **5.** 0.24 **7.** 187.1 to 212.9 **9.** 23.38 to 24.62 **11.** 190.2 to 209.8 **13.** 23.53 to 24.47

Written Exercises Page 421 **1.** 0.14 **3.** 4.506 to 4.694 **5.** 0.198 **7.** 15.684 to 16.716 **9.** 3.4 **11.** 11.542 to 13.208 **13.** 0.454

Chapter Review Page 423 **1.** 5 **3.** 3.5 **5.** 2.3 **7.** 1.6 **9.** 1.74 **11.** 1.0

13.

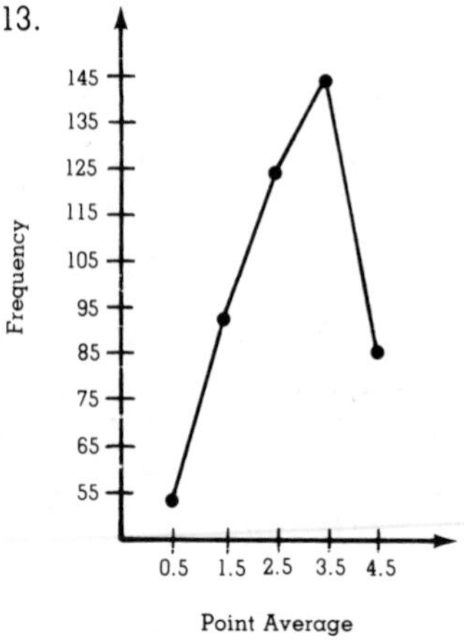

15. 2.84
17. 1.12 to 4.34
19. 0.06

CHAPTER 15 LIMITS, DERIVATIVES, AND INTEGRALS

Exploratory Exercises Page 428

1.

x	1.9	1.95	2.05	2.1
$5x$	9.5	9.75	10.25	10.5

; $\lim\limits_{x\to 2} 5x = 10$

3.

x	0.9	0.95	1.05	1.1
$\frac{x-2}{x+2}$	$^{-}0.38$	$^{-}0.36$	$^{-}0.31$	$^{-}0.29$

; $\lim\limits_{x\to 1} \frac{x-2}{x+2} = -\frac{1}{3}$

5.

x	$^{-}2.1$	$^{-}2.05$	$^{-}1.95$	$^{-}1.9$
$x^2 - 4$	0.41	0.2025	$^{-}0.1975$	$^{-}0.39$

; $\lim\limits_{x\to ^{-}2} (x^2 - 4) = 0$

7.

x	3.9	3.95	4.05	4.1
$3x + 2$	13.7	13.85	14.15	14.3

; $\lim\limits_{x\to 4} (3x + 2) = 14$

9.

x	$^{-}3.1$	$^{-}3.05$	$^{-}2.95$	$^{-}2.9$
$2x - 5$	$^{-}11.2$	$^{-}11.1$	$^{-}10.9$	$^{-}10.8$

; $\lim\limits_{x\to ^{-}3} (2x - 5) = {^{-}11}$

11.

x	2.9	2.95	3.05	3.1
$\frac{x-2}{x+2}$	0.18	0.19	0.21	0.22

; $\lim\limits_{x\to 3} \frac{x-2}{x+2} = \frac{1}{5}$

Written Exercises Page 429 1. 4 3. $\frac{2}{3}$ 5. 7 7. 6 9. $\frac{1}{3}$ 11. 8 13. 3 15. $\frac{3}{4}$ 17. 2 19. 2 21. 1

Exploratory Exercises Page 432 1. $|x - 2| < 0.1$ 3. $|x - 8| < \delta$ 5. $|x - 8| < 0.001$ 7. $^{-}0.001 < x - 4 < 0.001$ 9. $^{-}\delta < x - 7 < \delta$ 11. $^{-}0.00003 < x - 8 < 0.00003$ 13. $0.6 < x < 1.2$, $0.3 < f(x) < 0.6$ 15. $^{-}3.5 < x < {^{-}2.5}$, $5.9 < f(x) < 6.1$ 17. $|x - 2.5| < 0.3$; $|f(x) - 7.05| < 0.95$

Written Exercises Page 433 1. $1.995 < x < 2.005$ 3. $4.9 < x < 5.1$ 5. $1.997 < x < 2.0003$ 7. $5.6 < x < 6.4$ 9. $1 < f(x) < 7$ 11. $42.25 < f(x) < 56.25$ 13. $^{-}0.85 < f(x) < {^{-}0.65}$ 15. $4 - a < f(x) < 4 + a$ 17. $|f(x) - L|$ or
$|(2x - 6) - 2| < \epsilon$ when $0 < |x - 4| < \delta$

$$2|x - 4| < \epsilon$$
$$|x - 4| < \frac{\epsilon}{2}$$

Choose $\delta \le \frac{\epsilon}{2}$ and the conditions of the definition are satisfied. 19. $\delta \le 0.01$ 21. $\delta \le 0.01$ 23. $\delta \le 0.01$ 25. $\delta \le 0.01$

Exploratory Exercises Page 436 1. $x = 0$ 3. $x = 3$ 5. at every integer x 7. $f(1) = 2$ 9. $f(^{-}\sqrt{5}) = {^{-}2\sqrt{5}}$

Written Exercises Page 436 1. continuous 3. infinite discontinuity at $x = 0$ 5. continuous 7. point discontinuity at $x = 1$ 9. continuous 11. continuous 13. Answers may vary. A typical answer is $f(x) = x$. 15. Answers may vary. A typical answer is $f(x) = \frac{x^2 - 4}{x - 2}$ 17. $f(1) = 6$, $\lim\limits_{x\to 1} (x + 5) = f(1)$; continuous 19. $f(4) = 0$, $\lim\limits_{x\to 4} \frac{x^2 - 16}{x + 4} = f(4)$; continuous

Exploratory Exercises Page 439 1. $^{-}6$ 3. $^{-}5$ 5. 0 7. 3 9. 3 11. 80

Written Exercises Page 439 1. $\lim\limits_{x\to 2} (x^2 - 5x + 6)$
$= \lim\limits_{x\to 2} (x - 3)(x - 2)$
$= \left[\lim\limits_{x\to 2} (x - 3)\right]\left[\lim\limits_{x\to 2} (x - 2)\right] = (^{-}1)(0)$ or 0
3. $\lim\limits_{x\to a} \left(\sqrt{p} \cdot x + \frac{q - \sqrt{q^2 - 4pr}}{2\sqrt{p}}\right) \cdot \lim\limits_{x\to a} \left(\sqrt{p} \cdot x + \frac{q + \sqrt{q^2 - 4pr}}{2\sqrt{p}}\right)$ 5. $\frac{4}{27}$ 7. 1 9. 0 11. 4 13. $\frac{1}{3}$ 15. 17 17. 0 19. $\frac{1}{2}$

Exploratory Exercises Page 442 1. 1 3. $^{-}2$ 5. $4x + 2h$ 7. $3x^2 + 3xh + h^2$ 9. 5 11. $2x + h$

Written Exercises Page 442 1. 1 3. $^{-}2$ 5. $4x$ 7. $3x^2$ 9. 5 11. $2x$ 13. 0, $y = 0$ 15. $^{-}2$, $y = {^{-}2x} - 3$ 17. 6, $y = 6x + 2$ 19. $-\frac{1}{9}$, $y = \frac{^{-}x + 6}{9}$ 21. $^{-}1$, $y = {^{-}x} + 4$ 23. (1,1) 25. (0,1) 27. $\left(\frac{1}{3}, 5\frac{1}{3}\right)$ 29. none 31. none

Exploratory Exercises Page 445 1. Theorem 11 3. Power formula 5. Theorem 13 7. Theorems 11 and 14 9. Theorem 14 11. Theorems 14 and 15 13. Theorem 11

Written Exercises Page 445 1. $32x^3 - 30x^2$ 3. $\frac{1}{3\sqrt[3]{x^2}}$ 5. $15x^4 - 18x^2$ 7. $4(x^3 - 2x + 1)^3(3x^2 - 2)$ 9. $-\frac{x}{\sqrt{(x^2 - 4)^3}}$ 11. $\frac{^{-}4(x + 1)}{(x - 1)^3}$ 13. $5x^4 + 9x^2 - 8x$ 15. 2 17. 6 19. $^{-}4$ 21. $\frac{x^2 + 2x}{(x + 1)^2}$ 23. $\frac{^{-}2(2x - 1)}{(x^2 - x)^3}$ 25. $\frac{^{-}3x^3}{2\sqrt{1 - x^3}} + \sqrt{1 - x^3}$ 27. $10x^3(x - 5)^5(x - 2)$

29. $\frac{2}{(x+1)^2}$

Exploratory Exercises Page 449 1. $f'(x) = 2x + 6$ 3. $f'(x) = 2x - 2$ 5. $f'(x) = 3x^2 - 3$ 7. $f'(x) = 4x^2(3 - x)$ 9. $4x(2x^2 - 1)$ 11. 2 13. 2 15. $6x$ 17. $24x - 12x^2$ 19. $24x^2 - 4$

Written Exercises Page 449 1. $x > 0$ 3. $x > {}^-3$ 5. $x > 2$ or $x < 1$ 7. $x > 3$ or ${}^-3 < x < 0$ 9. $x < {}^-1$ or $x > 1$ 11. $x < 1$ 13. ${}^-1 < x < 1$ 15. $\frac{2}{3} < x < 2$ 17. $x > 3$ 19. $x = \frac{1}{2}$, maximum 21. $x = 2$, minimum; $x = 1$, maximum 23. (0,0), point of inflection; $x = 3$, maximum

27.

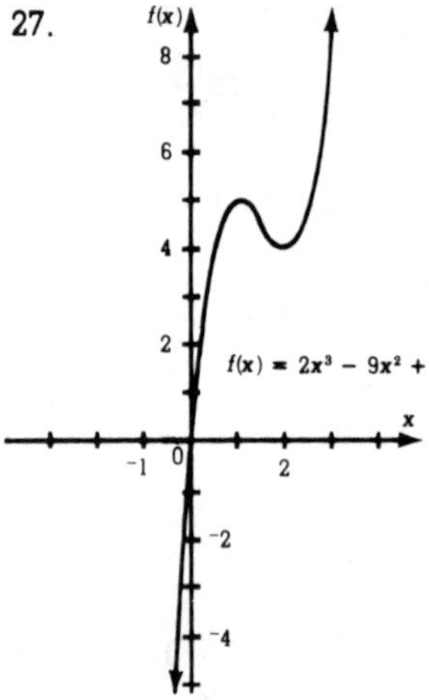

29.

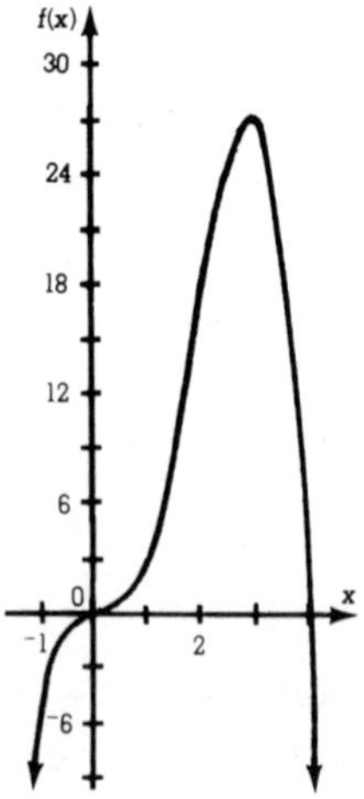

Exploratory Exercises Page 454

1. $\lim_{n\to\infty}\sum_{i=1}^{n}\left(\frac{i}{n}\right)^2\left(\frac{1}{n}\right)$ 3. $\lim_{n\to\infty}\sum_{i=1}^{n}\left(\frac{i}{n}\right)^5\left(\frac{1}{n}\right)$

5. $\lim_{n\to\infty}\sum_{i=1}^{n}\left(\frac{ai}{n}\right)^3\left(\frac{a}{n}\right)$ 7. $\lim_{n\to\infty}\sum_{i=1}^{n}\left(\frac{5i}{n}\right)\left(\frac{5}{n}\right) - \lim_{n\to\infty}\sum_{i=1}^{n}\left(\frac{2i}{n}\right)\left(\frac{2}{n}\right)$

9.

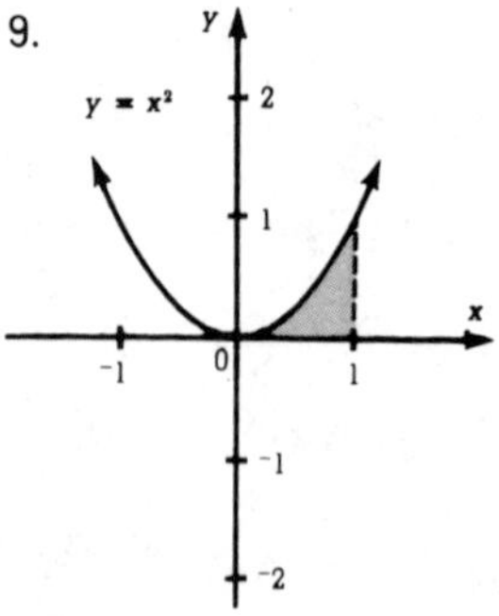

11.

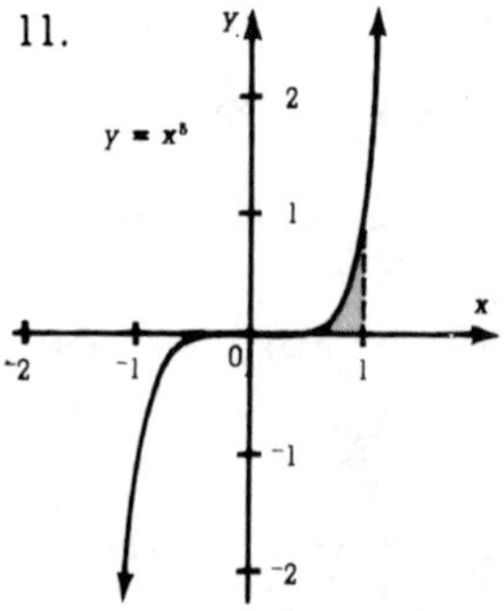

Written Exercises Page 454 1. $\frac{1}{3}$ 3. $\frac{1}{6}$ 5. $\frac{a^4}{4}$ 7. $\frac{21}{2}$ 9. $\frac{35}{3}$ 11. $\frac{b^2 - a^2}{2}$

Exploratory Exercises Page 457 Answers may vary. Typical answers are given.
1. $F(x) = x^2 + 7$ or $F(x) = x^2 - 9$
3. $F(x) = x^2 + x + 7$ or $F(x) = x^2 + x - 10$
5. $F(x) = x^4 + 7$ or $F(x) = x^4 - 11$

Written Exercises Page 457 1. $x^2 + C$ 3. $x^8 + x^2 + C$ 5. $\frac{1}{21}(x + 5)^{21} + C$ 7. ${}^-x^2 + 3x + C$ 9. $\frac{3}{4}\sqrt[3]{(x^2 + 2x + 2)^2} + C$ 11. $3\sqrt[3]{x^4} + C$ 13. $-\frac{1}{x^2} + C$ 15. $4\sqrt{x} + C$

Exploratory Exercises Page 459 1. 12 sq units 3. $\frac{25}{2}$ sq units 5. 9 sq units

Written Exercises Page 460

1. $\frac{8}{3}$ sq units 3. 18 sq units 5. $\frac{4}{3}$ sq units

7.

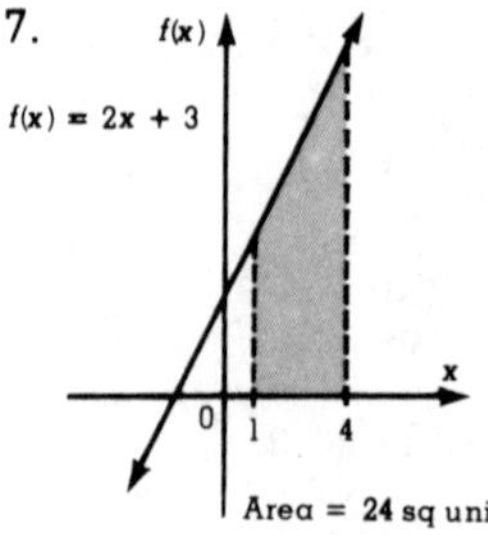

9.

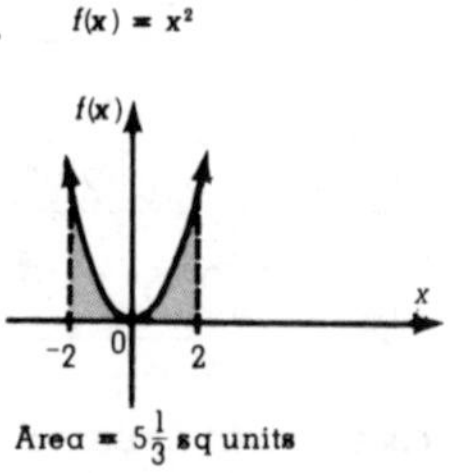

11.

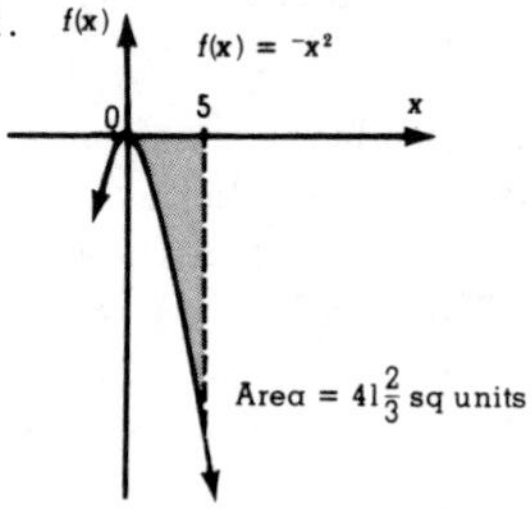

15.

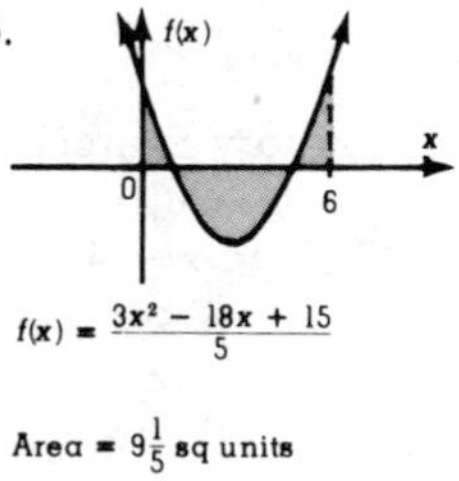

17. 4 19. $2\frac{2}{3}$ 21. $22\frac{1}{2}$ 23. ${}^-8\frac{2}{3}$ 25. $\frac{2}{3}$ 27. $13\frac{1}{6}$

Chapter Review Page 463 1. 6 3. 0 5. $4.98 < x < 5.02$ 7. $\delta \le 0.01$ 9. point discontinuity at $x = {}^-3$ and $x = 2$ 11. 0 13. $\frac{1}{2}$ 15. ${}^-8$, $y = {}^-8x - 6$ 17. $12x^2$ 19. $x > 1$ 21. $x = +\sqrt{\frac{2}{3}}$, minimum; $x = {}^-\sqrt{\frac{2}{3}}$, maximum 23. 4 sq units 25. $-\frac{4}{x} + C$ 27. $x - \frac{x^2}{2} + C$ 29. 36 31. 44

INDEX

A

B

C

D

E

H

I

L

M

N

O

P

Q

R

S

T

U

V

W

X

Y

Z